AMERICAN GOVERNMENT

AMERICAN
GOVERNMENT

CONTINUITY AND CHANGE

1997 EDITION

Karen O'Connor

Professor of Political Science
American University

Larry J. Sabato

Robert Kent Gooch Professor of Government and Foreign Affairs
University of Virginia

Allyn and Bacon

BOSTON ■ LONDON ■ TORONTO ■ SYDNEY ■ TOKYO ■ SINGAPORE

Vice-President, Editor-in-Chief, Social Sciences: *Sean W. Wakely*
Senior Editor: *Joseph P. Terry*
Developmental Editor: *Jane Tufts*
Senior Developmental Editor: *Sue Gleason*
Editorial Assistant: *Sue Hutchinson*
Marketing Manager: *Quinn Perkson*
Production Administrator: *Joe Sweeney*
Editorial-Production Service: *Thomas E. Dorsaneo*
Composition and Prepress Buyer: *Linda Cox*
Manufacturing Buyer: *Megan Cochran*
Cover Administrator: *Linda Knowles*
Photo Researcher: *Laurel Anderson/Photosynthesis*

Copyright © 1997, 1995, 1993 by Allyn & Bacon
A Viacom Company
160 Gould Street
Needham Heights, MA 02194

Internet: www.abacon.com
America Online: Keyword: College Online

Chapters 1–16 are also published under the title *American
Government: Continuity and Change, 1997 Alternate Edition,* by Karen
O'Connor and Larry Sabato, copyright © 1997 by Allyn and Bacon.

Library of Congress Cataloging-in-Publication Data

O'Connor, Karen
   American government : continuity and change / Karen O'Connor,
Larry J. Sabato—3rd ed.
     p.   cm.
   Includes bibliographical references and index.
   ISBN 0-205-19811-2
   1. United States—Politics and government.   I. Sabato, Larry.
II. Title.
JK274.O26 1997
320.473—dc20   96-16182
                                                 CIP

To Meghan, always the trouper

KAREN O'CONNOR

To my Government 101 students

over the years, who all know that

"politics is a good thing"

LARRY SABATO

BRIEF CONTENTS

CONTENTS

PART TWO

INSTITUTIONS OF GOVERNMENT

PART THREE

POLITICAL BEHAVIOR

CHAPTER 11

PUBLIC OPINION AND POLITICAL SOCIALIZATION — 408

PART FOUR

PUBLIC POLICY

CHAPTER 19

APPENDICES

PREFACE

*T*eaching introductory American government presents special challenges and rewards. It is a challenge to introduce a new discipline to beginning students. It is a challenge to jump from topic to topic each week. Above all, it is a challenge to motivate large and disparate groups of students to master new material and, one hopes, to enjoy it in the process. The rewards of success, however, are students who pay more attention to their government, who participate in its workings as more informed citizens, and who better understand the workings of democracy as practiced in the United States.

We have witnessed some of these rewards from the lecture podium. With this book, we hope to offer our experiences in written form. Students need perspective and motivation; they also need to be exposed to information that will withstand the test of time. Our goal with this text is to transmit just this sort of information while creating and fostering student interest in American politics despite growing national skepticism about government and government officials at all levels. In fact, we hope that this new edition of our text will explain and put the national mood about politics in better context for students to understand their role in a changing America.

WHAT'S CHANGED?

*I*n this 1997 Edition of *American Government,* there is change afoot. Our new subtitle—*Continuity and Change*—captures some of its flavor. Although there is continuity in our overall approach and organization, this edition reflects pervasive change in American government, change arising from widespread dissatisfaction and frustration with government. And yet this state of affairs is not so very different from the past. Our government has survived throughout its history by evolving, changing, and compromising.

To provide students with a fuller understanding of current issues in American politics and a better appreciation of their role in the American political system, we have rewritten each chapter to encourage students to reflect on the reasons for and consequences of the changes that the electorate appears to be demanding in light of the 1994 and 1996 elections. We have heavily revised certain chapters, such as Chapter 1, The Political Landscape; and introduced key features that retain our initial focus on history ("Roots of Government"). To highlight changes occurring in government and to make the study of American government more relevant to students, we have added a new feature (each beginning with the phrase "Changing . . .") at the end of each chapter.

Voter frustration with the federal government has led to a call for power to be returned to the states. Thus, our treatment of federalism has been revised to reflect that fact, and we have added a separate chapter (Chapter 4) devoted to state and local government, positioned on the heels of the federalism chapter.

You will also, of course, see major changes in our chapters reflecting 1994 and 1996 electoral upheavals: Chapters 7 (Congress), 8 (The Presidency), and 12 through 14 (Political Parties, Voting and Elections, and The Campaign Process).

APPROACH

$\mathcal{W}$e believe that one cannot fully understand the actions, issues, and policy decisions facing the U.S. government, its constituent states, or "the people" unless these issues are examined from the perspective of how they have evolved over time. Consequently, the title of this book is *American Government: Continuity and Change*. In its pages we try to examine how the United States is governed today by looking not just at present behavior but also at the Framers' intentions and how they have been implemented and adapted over the years. For example, we believe that it is critical to an understanding of the role of political parties in the United States to understand the Framers' fears of factionalism, how parties evolved, and when and why realignments in party identification occurred.

In addition to questions raised by the Framers, we explore issues that the Framers could never have envisioned, and how the basic institutions of government have changed in responding to these new demands. For instance, no one more than two centuries ago could have foreseen election campaigns in an age when nearly all American homes contain television sets, and the Internet and fax machines allow instant access to information. Moreover, increasing citizen demands and expectations have routinely forced government reforms, making an understanding of the dynamics of change essential for introductory students.

Our overriding concern is that students understand their government as it exists today. In order to do so, they must understand how it was designed in the Constitution. Each chapter, therefore, approaches its topic from a combination of perspectives which we believe will facilitate this approach. In writing this book, we chose to put the institutions of government (Part Two) before political behavior (Part Three). Both sections, however, were written independently, making them easy to switch for those who prefer to teach about the actors in government and elections before discussing its institutions. To test the book, each of us has taught from it in both orders, with no pedagogical problems.

FEATURES

Historical Perspective

Every chapter uses history to serve three purposes: first, to show how institutions and processes have evolved to their present states; second, to provide some of the color that makes information memorable; and third, to provide students with a more thorough appreciate that government was born amid burning issues of representation and power, issues that continue to smolder today. A richer historical texture helps to explain the present.

Comparative Perspective

Changes in Eastern Europe, the former Soviet Union, North America, and Asia all remind us of the preeminence of democracy, in theory if not always in fact. As new democratic experiments spring up around the globe, it becomes increasingly important for students to understand the rudiments of presidential versus parliamentary government, of multiparty versus two-party systems, and so on. In order to put American government in perspective, we continue to draw comparisons with Great Britain. We draw comparisons with our North American neighbors—Canada and Mexico—in new "North–South" features throughout the text.

Enhanced Pedagogy

We have revised and enhanced many pedagogical features to help students become stronger political thinkers and to echo the book's theme of evolving change.

Preview and Review.   To pique student interest and draw them into each chapter, we now begin each chapter with a contemporary vignette. Each vignette is followed by a bridge paragraph linking the vignette with the chapter's topics and a roadmap previewing the chapter's major headings. Chapter Summaries, too, have been more logically restructured to restate the major points made under each of these same major headings.

Key Terms.   Glossary definitions are now included in the margins of the text for all boldfaced key terms. Key terms are listed once more at the end of each chapter, with page references for review and study.

Special Features.   Four new boxed features have been added to this edition, in keeping with its theme:

- *Roots of Government* boxes highlight the role that a particular institution, process, or person has played in the course of American politics as it has evolved to the present.
- *North–South* boxes provide comparative insights on various institutions and processes in our closest neighbors—Canada and Mexico.
- *Politics Now* boxes act as a counterpoint to the text's traditional focus on "roots." Based on current clippings, editorials, and moments in time, these boxes are designed to encourage students to think about current issues in the context of the continuing evolution of the American political system.
- *Highlight* boxes provide additional tidbits of information outside the stream of the text discussion.
- A section entitled *Changing . . .* concludes each chapter, tying in with the book's theme of change in America and focusing on the possibilities of governmental, institutional, and citizen reform. In considering the role of the individual citizen, we hope to encourage students to reassess their roles in the political system and to explore ways to become more informed members of the electorate.

THE ANCILLARY PACKAGE

*T*he ancillary package for *American Government: Continuity and Change, 1997 Edition,* reflects the pedagogical goals of the text: to provide information in a useful context and with colorful examples. We have tried especially hard to provide materials that are useful for instructors and helpful to students.

FOR INSTRUCTORS

- *Instructor's Manual*   The Instructor's Manual includes lecture ideas, discussion questions, classroom activities, and a guide to video and other resources.
- *Test Bank*   Completely revised and expanded, the test bank provides more than 2,500 multiple-choice, true/false and essay questions. A *Computerized Test Bank* in IBM (DOS or Windows) or Macintosh formats is also available.
- *Transparencies*   A full set of over 50 color transparencies, including U.S. and world maps, is available for classroom use.
- *The Washington Post Just-In-Time ("JIT") Custom Reader*   By exclusive arrangement with the *Washington Post*, the Allyn & Bacon JIT reader in American government allows faculty to assemble their own collection of articles to suit individual course demands. Faculty can choose from a frequently updated database of over 300 articles on topics ranging across the spectrum of American government. Ask your Allyn & Bacon representative for details.

FOR STUDENTS

- *Study Guide*   A study guide for students is available that includes chapter synopses, outlines, key terms, and multiple-choice, true/false, and matching questions with answers.
- *American Government: Readings and Cases*   This separate, full-scale reader in American government by Karen O'Connor may be packaged along with the text at a reduced price to students. This reader combines classic articles, including extensive selections from *The Federalist*, with some of the best current political science articles and landmark cases. Thoughtful pedagogy includes chapter introductions and end-of-chapter critical thinking questions.

MULTIMEDIA SUPPLEMENTS

*T*o further extend the application of multimedia learning enhancements to the teaching of American government, the following supplements are available for use in conjunction with the text.

- *Video Library*   A full set of videos on every major course topic is available to adopters of the text. Again, your Allyn & Bacon representative has details.
- *CD-ROM*   A set of interactive learning modules are available for students to purchase on CD-ROM. Combining text, graphics, still photographs, and video, the CD-ROM contains study modules on Congress, the presidency, and the judiciary, as well as an extensive archive collection of historical and current resources. Ask your Allyn & Bacon representative for details.

- *Web site*   Visit the World Wide Web site for this textbook, www.abacon.com/ oconnor, to find a wealth of activities and links to other sites relevant to American government.

ACKNOWLEDGMENTS

Karen O'Connor thanks the thousand-plus students in her American Government courses at Emory and American who, over the years, have pushed her to learn more about American government and to have fun in the process. She especially thanks her American University colleagues who offered books and suggestions for this most recent revision—Gregg Ivers, Ron Schaiko, Christine DeGregorio, Neil Kerwin, and Jim Thurber. Her former professor and long-time friend and co-author Nancy E. McGlen has offered support for more than two decades. Her former students, too, have contributed in various ways to this project. John R. Hermann and Paul Fabrizio offered numerous suggestions.

While we were writing the first edition, Laura Van Assendelft provided the assistance and fresh perspective that only a graduate student studying for her Ph.D. comprehensive exam in American Government could offer. Laura worked tirelessly on the book and even brought homemade cookies as a reward for completed chapters. Now a professor at Mary Baldwin College, she is our most regular source of constructive comments and criticisms. Bernadette Nye, now teaching at Union College, helped tremendously in the preparation of the second edition. And, without Sue Davis's help, now at Grand Rapids State University, this edition would never have been complete. Larry Sabato wishes to thank his University of Virginia colleagues and staff, including graduate student Lawrence Schack and technical assistant Nancy Rae, both of whom were essential to the research and writing of this edition.

Particular thanks from both of us go to Charles S. Bullock of the University of Georgia, who revised Chapters 7 (Congress), 17 (Social Welfare Policy), and 18 (Economic Policy); to Richard Cupitt at the Center for East-West Trade at the University of Georgia, who coauthored Chapter 19 (Foreign and Military Policy); and to Dennis L. Dresang at the University of Wisconsin—Madison, who coauthored the new Chapter 4 (State and Local Government). We also thank Jeffrey Anderson of Brown University, who helped provide comparisons between the American and British systems of government, and Chip Hauss of the University of Reading (UK), who prepared the North—South features. Jessica Waters at American University provided invaluable assistance proofreading and fact checking.

In the now many years we have been writing and rewriting this book, we have been blessed to have been helped by many people at Macmillan and at Allyn and Bacon. Bruce Nichols signed the project and nurtured us through writing our first drafts. Now, we have been lucky to have the new insights and help of Sean Wakely, Joe Terry, and Sue Gleason at Allyn and Bacon. Many of the features new to this book are a result of the fresh insights they were able to offer as we worked to revise this edition. Production editor Joe Sweeney, with the help of Tom Dorsaneo, skillfully guided us through an unusually harrowing schedule; and marketing manager Quinn Perkson promoted our book with what can only be described as messianic zeal. We would also like to thank and acknowledge our development editor, Jane Tufts, who has been with us through all three editions. She has become a dear friend in spite of her constant suggestions which usually require far more work than we want to do. Finally, we would like to acknowledge the tireless efforts of the Allyn and Bacon sales force. In the end, we hope that all of these talented people see how much their work and support have helped us to write a better book.

Finally, many of our peers reviewed various stages of the manuscript and earned our gratitude in the process:

Danny Adkison
Oklahoma State University

Ruth Bamberger
Drury College

Jon Bond
Texas A&M University

Greg Caldeira
Ohio State University

David Cingranelli
SUNY, Binghamton

Cary Covington
University of Iowa

Evelyn Fink
University of Nebraska

Doris Graber
University of Illinois at Chicago

Charles Hadley
University of New Orleans

Chip Hauss
George Mason University/University of Reading

Marjorie Hershey
Indiana University

Kenneth Kennedy
College of San Mateo

Jonathan E. Kranz
John Jay College of Criminal Justice

Mark Landis
Hofstra University

Steve Mazurana
University of Northern Colorado

Bruce Oppenheimer
Vanderbilt University

Mark Silverstein
Boston University

Shirley Anne Warshaw
Gettysburg College

Martin Wiseman
Mississippi State University

The Second Edition greatly profited from the painstaking reviews and comments of the following people:

James Anderson
Texas A&M University

Judith Baer
Texas A&M University

Christine Barbour
Indiana University

Stephen A. Borrelli
University of Alabama

Ann Bowman
University of South Carolina

Steve Chan
University of Colorado

Clarke E. Cochran
Texas Tech University

Anne N. Costain
University of Colorado

John Domino
Sam Houston State University

Alan S. Engel
Miami University

Stacia L. Haynie
Louisiana State University

Marjorie Hershey
Indiana University

Cornell Hooton
Emory University

Dennis Judd
University of Missouri—St. Louis

Donald F. Kettl
University of Wisconsin

John Kincaid
University of North Texas

Jonathan E. Kranz
John Jay College

Nancy Kucinski
University of North Texas

Valerie Martinez
University of North Texas

Clifton McCleskey
University of Virginia

Joseph Nogee
University of Houston

Mary Alice Nye
University of North Texas

Richard Pacelle
University of Missouri—St. Louis

Marian Lief Palley
University of Delaware

Leroy N. Rieselbach
Indiana University

David Robertson
Public Policy Research Centers,
University of Missouri—St. Louis

Frank Rourke
Johns Hopkins University

Frank J. Sorauf
University of Minnesota

This latest, 1997 Edition was evaluated by the following reviewers and focus group participants:

Weston H. Agor
University of Texas at El Paso

Gary Brown
Montgomery College

John Francis Burke
University of Houston-Downtown

David E. Camacho
Northern Arizona University

Richard Christofferson, Sr.
University of Wisconsin-Stevens Point

Lane Crothers
Illinois State University

Abraham L. Davis
Morehouse College

Robert DiClerico
West Virginia University

Craig F. Emmert
Texas Tech University

Frank B. Feigert
University of North Texas

Evelyn C. Fink
University of Nebraska-Lincoln

Scott R. Furlong
University of Wisconsin-Green Bay

James D. Gleason
Victoria College

Sheldon Goldman
University of Massachusetts,
Amherst

Roger W. Green
University of North Dakota

William K. Hall
Bradley University

Robert L. Hardgrave, Jr.
The University of Texas at Austin

John R. Hermann
Trinity University

Marjorie Hershey
Indiana University

Jon Hurwitz
University of Pittsburgh

Joseph Ignagni
University of Texas-Arlington

Carol J. Kamper
Rochester Community College

Sue Lee
North Lake College

Brad Lockerbie
University of Georgia

Larry Martinez
California State University-Long Beach

Lynn Mather
Dartmouth College

Steve J. Mazurana
University of Northern Colorado

John O'Callaghan
Suffolk University

Richard M. Pious
Barnard College

David H. Provost
California State University-Fresno

Lawrence J. Redlinger
The University of Texas at Dallas

David Robinson
University of Houston-Downtown

David W. Rohde
Michigan State University

Ronald Rubin
City University of New York
Borough of Manhattan Community College

Daniel M. Shea
The University of Akron

James R. Simmons
University of Wisconsin-Oshkosh

Elliot E. Slotnick
The Ohio State University

Gerald Stanglin
Cedar Valley College

Richard J. Timpone
SUNY-Stony Brook

Shirley Anne Warshaw
Gettysburg College

AMERICAN GOVERNMENT

The Roots of American Government: Where Did the Ideas Come From?

Characteristics of American Democracy

Characteristics of the American People

The Frustrated Public

Changing America

THE POLITICAL LANDSCAPE

*W*e the People of the United States, in Order to form a more perfect Union, establish Justice, insure domestic Tranquility, provide for the common defence, promote the general Welfare, and secure the Blessings of Liberty to ourselves and our Posterity, do ordain and establish the Constitution for the United States of America.

So begins the Preamble to the United States Constitution. Written in 1787, this document has guided our nation, its government, its politics, its institutions, and its inhabitants for over 200 years.

Back when the Constitution was written, the phrases "We the People" and "ourselves" meant something very different than they do today. Although the Framers—the men who wrote the Constitution—probably intended to include nearly all white men and women, they still envisioned an electorate that was made up of less than half of those who lived in the thirteen original states. After all, voting was largely limited to property-owning white males. Indians, slaves, and women could not vote. Today, through the expansion of the right to vote, the phrase "the People" encompasses men and women of all races, ethnic origins, and social and economic status—a variety of peoples and interests the Framers could not have imagined.

In the goals it outlines, the Preamble describes what the people of the United States can expect from their government. But many Americans today are questioning how well the country and its government can deliver on these goals. Few Americans today would classify the Union as "perfect"; many feel excluded from "Justice" and the "Blessings of Liberty"; many more do not feel our domestic situation is particularly tranquil. Furthermore, judging from recent poll results and economic statistics, many Americans do not feel their general welfare is being very well promoted by their government.

The Framers intended the Constitution to last more than a few years or decades, as we can see from the phrase "our Posterity." Clearly, they envisioned a nation that would last throughout many generations. Despite a number of turbulent and disruptive episodes in our nation's history, our government *has* survived: by evolving, changing, accommodating, and compromising. Nevertheless, many Americans feel dissatisfied with how things are, and they want change.

Change. If there has been one constant in the life of the United States, it is change. The Framers would be astonished to see the forms and functions the institutions they so carefully outlined in the Constitution have taken on, and the number of additional political institutions that have arisen to support and fuel the functioning of the national government. The Framers would also be amazed at the array of services and programs the government—especially the national government—provides. They would be further surprised to see how the physical boundaries and the composition of the population have changed in 200 plus years. And they might well wonder, "How did we get here?"

It is virtually part of the American creed that each generation should hand down to the next not only a better America, but an improved economic, educational, and social status. And for most of our history, this has been the case. But, today, for the first time in decades, although most Americans report that their lives are better than their parents', nearly the same proportion believes things will be worse for the next generation. In fact, according to a recent poll, while 60 percent believe that they have a better life than their parents, 58 percent think that the future of the next generation will be worse. And 85 percent believe the American dream will be harder to achieve for future generations.[1]

Americans today are looking for a place to lay blame for their perceived failure to make progress. In past decades Americans relied heavily on governmental programs such as Veterans Administration housing loans to finance their homes and the G.I. Bill to pay for their college educations. Today, most Americans believe that government programs actually hinder their families' quest to achieve the American dream.[2]

The "American Dream"–a house, a dog, two kids, a picket fence, the chance to realize one's dreams–has been part of the American political landscape for nearly as long as there has been a United States. Today's Americans are increasingly beginning to wonder whether their children's lives will continue to be better than theirs or their parents'. (Photo courtesy: Sue Ann Miller/Tony Stone Images, Inc.)

This feeling reflects a general public dissatisfaction and distrust of government that is at its highest point since polling began. And while it is certainly true that levels of dissatisfaction are high (a fact the media and politicians have made much of over the last few years), one wonders what levels of dissatisfaction and distrust would have shown up if public opinion polls had been around during the Revolutionary War, the period during which the Constitution was ratified, the periods preceding, during, and after the Civil War, the economic contraction that lasted from 1873 to 1879, or the Great Depression of 1929 to 1933.

In this book we present you with the tools to understand the current state of our nation's government, institutions, and political system by examining their development and the events that changed them. Such an understanding helps us see where the nation is today, how it is changing, and how it might change in the future. We believe that a thorough understanding of the workings of government will allow you to question and think about the system—the good parts and the bad—and decide for yourself the advantages and disadvantages of possible changes and reforms. Equipped with such an understanding, we hope you will become better informed and more active participants in the political process.

Every long journey begins with a single step. In this chapter we'll examine the following topics:

- First, we'll look at *the roots of American government*. To understand how the U.S. government and our political system work today, it is critical to understand the philosophies that guided the American colonists as they created a system of governance different from those then in existence.

- Second, we'll explore the *characteristics of American democracy*. Several enduring characteristics have defined American democracy since its beginning and continue to influence our nation's government and politics today.

- Third, we'll explore the *characteristics of the American people*. Because government derives its power from the people it governs, an understanding of who the American people are and how they are changing is critical to an understanding of American politics.

- Fourth, we'll discuss why more and more *Americans are expressing frustration with their lives* and with the role government plays in their lives.

- Finally, we'll see that as *America changes*, its institutions are changed too. In the concluding section to this and all chapters in this book, we ask: What factors are at work to change America now? What issues most concern Americans and how might they affect the operation of our government and political system?

THE ROOTS OF AMERICAN GOVERNMENT: WHERE DID THE IDEAS COME FROM?

*T*he current American political system did not spring into being overnight. It is the result of philosophy, trial and error, and yes, even luck. To begin our examination of why we came to have the type of government we have today, we look at the theories of government that influenced the Framers: those men who gathered in Philadelphia and drafted a new Constitution, thereby creating the United States of America.

From Aristotle to the Enlightenment

natural law: A doctrine that society should be governed by certain ethical principles that are part of nature and, as such, can be understood by reason.

Aristotle (384–322 B.C.) and the Greeks were the first to articulate the notion of **natural law,** the doctrine that human affairs should be governed by certain ethical principles. Being nothing more nor less than the nature of things, these principles can be understood by reason. In the thirteenth century, the Italian priest and philosopher Thomas Aquinas (1225–74) gave the idea of natural law a new, Christian framework. He argued that natural law and Christianity were compatible because God created the natural law that established individual rights to life and liberty. In contradiction to this view, kings throughout Europe continued to rule as absolute monarchs, claiming this divine right came directly from God. Thus citizens were bound by the government under which they found themselves, regardless of whether they had a say in its workings: If government reflected God's will, who could argue with it?

In the early sixteenth century, a religious movement to reform the doctrine and institutions of Roman Catholicism began to sweep through Europe. In many cases these efforts at reform resulted in the founding of Protestant churches separate from their Catholic source. This Reformation and the resultant growth in the Protestant faith, which promoted the belief that people could talk directly to God without the intervention of a priest, altered the nature of government as people began to believe they could also have a say in their own governance.

During the seventeenth and eighteenth-century period called the Enlightenment, the ideas of philosophers and scientists such as Galileo and Isaac Newton worked further to affect peoples' views of government. Newton and others argued that the world could be improved through the use of human reason, science, and religious toleration. He and other theorists directly challenged earlier notions that fate alone controlled an individual's destiny and that kings ruled by divine right. Together the intellectual and religious developments of the Reformation and Enlightenment periods encouraged people to seek alternatives to absolute monarchy and to ponder new methods of governing.

A Growing Idea: Popular Consent

In England, when one faction called "separatists" split from the Anglican Church, they did so believing that the ability to speak directly to God gave them the power to participate directly in the governing of their own local congregations. In establishing self-governing congregations, the separatists were responsible for the first widespread appearance of self-government in the form of social compacts. The separatists who moved to the English colonies in America during the 1600s brought their beliefs about self-governance with them. The Mayflower Compact, deemed sufficiently important to be written while that ship was still at sea, reflects this tradition. Although it addressed itself to secular government, the Pilgrims called it a "covenant" and its form was akin to other common religious "covenants" adopted by Congregationalists, Presbyterians, and Baptists.[3]

social contract theory: The belief that people are free and equal by God-given right and that this in turn requires that all people give their consent to be governed; espoused by John Locke and influential in the writing of the Declaration of Independence.

Two English theorists of that period, Thomas Hobbes (1588–1679) and John Locke (1632–1704), built on conventional notions about the role of government and the relationship of the government to the people in proposing a **social contract theory** of government (see Roots of Government: The Philosophies of Thomas Hobbes and John Locke). They argued that, even before the creation of God-ordained governments theorized by Aquinas, all individuals were free and equal by natural right. This freedom, in turn, required that all men give their consent to be governed.

Hobbes and Locke. In his now-classic political treatise *Leviathan* (1651), in which he argued for King Charles's restoration to the throne (which finally occurred in 1661),

Roots of Government

The Philosophies of Thomas Hobbes and John Locke

In almost any newspaper or TV news report, on any given day, you can find stories that show Americans grappling with questions about the proper role of government in their lives. These questions are not new. Centuries ago, Thomas Hobbes and John Locke both wrote extensively on these issues. Their ideas, however, differed remarkably. For Hobbes, who viewed men as basically evil, a government that regulated all kinds of conduct was necessary. Locke, who was more optimistic, saw the need only for more limited government.

Hobbes

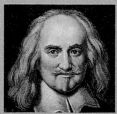

Thomas Hobbes was born in 1588 in Gloucestershire (Glouster), England, and began his formal education at the age of four. By the age of six he was learning Latin and Greek, and by the age of nineteen he had obtained his bachelor's degree from Oxford University. In 1608 Hobbes accepted a position as a family tutor with the earl of Devonshire, a post he retained for the rest of his life.

Hobbes was greatly influenced by the chaos of the English Civil War during the mid-seventeenth century. Its impact is evident in his most famous work, *Leviathan* (1651), a treatise on governmental theory that states his views on Man and Citizen. *Leviathan* is commonly described as a book about politics, but it also deals with religion and moral philosophy.

Hobbes characterized humans as selfishly individualistic and constantly at war with one another. Thus he believed that people must surrender themselves to rulers in exchange for protection from their neighbors.

Locke

John Locke, born in England in 1632, was admitted to an outstanding public school at the age of fifteen. It was there that he began to question his upbringing in the Puritan faith. At twenty he went on to study at Oxford, where he later became a lecturer in Aristotelian philosophy. Soon, however, he found a new interest in medicine and experimental science.

In 1666 Locke met Anthony Ashley Cooper, the first earl of Shaftesbury, and a politician who believed in individual rights and parliamentary reform. It was through Cooper that Locke discovered his own talent for philosophy. In 1689 Locke published his most famous work, *Second Treatise on Civil Government,* in which he set forth a theory of natural rights. He used natural rights to support his "social contract [theory]—the view that the consent of the people is the only true basis of any sovereign's right to rule." A government exists, he argued, because individuals agree, through a contract, to form a government to protect their rights under natural law. By agreeing to be governed, individuals agree to abide by decisions made by majority vote in the resolution of disputes.

Both men, as you can see, relied on wealthy royal patrons to allow them the time to work on their philosophies of government. While Hobbes and Locke agreed that government was a social contract between the people and their rulers, they differed significantly about the proper scope of government. Which man's views about government (and people) reflect your views?

(Photos courtesy: Stock Montage, Inc.)

Hobbes argued pessimistically that man's natural state was war. Government, Hobbes theorized, particularly a monarchy, was necessary to restrain man's bestial tendencies because life without government was a "state of nature." Without written, enforceable rules, people would live like animals—foraging for food, stealing, and killing when necessary. To escape the horrors of the natural state and to protect their lives, Hobbes argued, men must give up to government certain rights. Without government, Hobbes warned, life would basically be "solitary, poor, nasty, brutish, and short"—a constant struggle to survive against the evil of others. For this reason, governments had to intrude on people's rights and liberties in order to better control society and provide the necessary safeguards for property.[4]

The title page from Thomas Hobbes's *Leviathan*, 1651. (Photo courtesy: The Bettmann Archive)

Hobbes argued strongly for a single ruler, no matter how evil, to guarantee the rights of the weak against the strong. Leviathan, a biblical sea monster, was his characterization of an all-powerful government. Strict adherence to Leviathan's laws, however encompassing or intrusive on liberty, was but a small price to pay for living in a civilized society, or even for life itself.

In contrast, John Locke—like many other political philosophers of the era—took the basic survival of humanity for granted. He argued that government's major responsibility was the preservation of private property, an idea that ultimately found its way into the Constitution of the United States. In two of his works (*Essay Concerning Human Understanding* [1690] and *Second Treatise on Civil Government* [1689]), Locke responded to King James II's abuses of power, which were largely directed at the Anglican Church and Parliament. Locke not only denied the divine right of kings to govern, but argued that men were born equal and with equal rights in nature that no king had the power to void. Under what Locke termed social contract theory, the consent of the people is the only true basis of any sovereign's right to rule. According to Locke, men form governments largely to preserve life, liberty, and property, and to assure justice. If governments act improperly, they break their "contract" with the people and therefore no longer enjoy the consent of the governed. Because he believed that true justice comes from laws, Locke argued that the branch of government that makes laws—as opposed to the one that enforces or interprets laws—should be the most powerful.

Locke believed that having a chief executive to administer laws was important, but that he should necessarily be limited by law or by the social contract with the governed. Locke's writings influenced many American colonists, especially Thomas Jefferson, whose original draft of the Declaration of Independence noted the rights to "life, liberty, and property" as key reasons to split from England.[5] This document was "pure Locke" because it based the justification for the split with England on the English government's violation of the social contract implicit in its dealings with the American colonies.

Devising a National Government

Although social contract theorists agreed on the need for government, they did not necessarily agree on the form that a government should take. Thomas Hobbes argued for a single leader; John Locke and Jean-Jacques Rousseau, a French philosopher (1712–78), saw the need for less centralized power.

The colonists rejected a system with a strong ruler, like the British **monarchy,** as soon as they had declared their independence. Most European monarchical systems gave hereditary rulers absolute power over all forms of activity. Many of the colonists had fled Great Britain to avoid religious persecution and other harsh manifestations of power wielded by George II, whom they viewed as a malevolent despot. They naturally were reluctant to put themselves in the same position in their new nation.

While some colonies, such as Massachusetts, originally established theocracies in which religious leaders eventually ruled claiming divine guidance, they later looked to more secular forms of governance. Colonists also did not want to create an **oligarchy,** or "rule by the few or an elite," in which the right to participate is conditioned on the possession of wealth, property, social status, military position, or achievement. Aristotle defined this form of government as a perversion of an **aristocracy,** or "rule of the highest." Again, the colonists were fearful of replicating the landed and titled system of the British aristocracy, and viewed the formation of a representative form of government as far more in keeping with the ideas of social contract theorists. But the **democ-**

monarchy: A form of government in which power is vested in hereditary kings and queens.

oligarchy: A form of government in which the right to participate is always conditioned on the possession of wealth, social status, military position, or achievement.

aristocracy: A system of government in which control is based on rule of the highest.

democracy: A system of government that gives power to the people, whether directly or through their elected representatives.

racy in which we live, as settled on by the Framers, is difficult to define. Nowhere is the word mentioned in the Declaration of Independence or the U.S. Constitution. The term comes from two Greek words: *demos* (the people) and *kratia* (power or authority). Thus democracy can be interpreted as a form of government that gives power to the people. The question, then, is how and to which people is this power given?

The Theory of Democratic Government

As evidenced by the creation in 1619 of the Virginia House of Burgesses as the first representative assembly in North America, and its objections to "taxation without representation," the colonists were quick to create participatory forms of government in which most men were allowed to participate. The New England town meeting, where all citizens gather to discuss and decide issues facing the town, today stands as a surviving example of a **direct democracy,** such as was used in ancient Greece when all free, male citizens came together periodically to pass laws and "elect" leaders by lot (see Politics Now: The Electronic Democracy?).

Direct democracies, in which the people rather than their elected representatives make political decisions, soon proved unworkable in the colonies. But as more and more settlers came to the New World, many town meetings were replaced by a system called an **indirect democracy** (this is also called *representative democracy*). This system of government, in which representatives of the people are chosen by ballot, was considered undemocratic by ancient Greeks, who believed that all citizens must have a direct say in their governance.[6] Later, in the 1760s, the French political philosopher Jean-Jacques Rousseau would also argue that true democracy is impossible unless all citizens participate in governmental decision making. Nevertheless, indirect democracy was the form of government opted for throughout most of the colonies.

Representative or indirect democracies, which call for the election of representatives to a governmental decision-making body, were formed first in the colonies and then in the new Union. Many citizens were uncomfortable with the term "democracy" and used the term "republic" to avoid any confusion between the system adopted and direct democracy. Historically, the term **republic** implied a system of government in

direct democracy: A system of government in which members of the polity meet to discuss all policy decisions and then agree to abide by majority rule.

indirect (representative) democracy: A system of government that gives citizens the opportunity to vote for representatives who will work on their behalf.

republic: A government rooted in the consent of the governed; a representative or indirect democracy.

The traditional New England town meeting—where citizens meet, have their say, and vote on the town budget and other policy decisions—survives in certain communities as a modern-day embodiment of direct democracy. (Photo courtesy: Richard Sobol/Stock Boston)

Politics Now

The Electronic Democracy?

- In 1994 voters in Minnesota participated in the first electronic campaign debates as they logged on to interact with the candidates for governor and senator.
- Soon after President Bill Clinton took office in 1993, the White House switchboard was effectively shut down when it was unable to handle the thousands of telephone calls made to it after talk radio hosts urged their listeners to make the president aware of their views on allowing openly gay soldiers to serve in the military.

These are just two examples of what Lawrence K. Grossman, the former president of NBC News, called "the 'electronic democracy,' a democratic system that is vastly increasing the public's day-to-day influence on the decisions of state."[*] Ironically, at the same time that the American people feel distanced from government, says Grossman, they have more influence on policy makers than ever before—and certainly more than the Framers ever intended or even thought wise.

Populist measures—including the term-limits movement, state balanced-budget amendments, direct state primaries and caucuses, and the increasing use of the ballot initiative and referenda by concerned citizens—are drastically reducing the discretion of elected officials. Voters in many

states can even enact their own laws, as they did in the case of California's Proposition 187 to restrict benefits to illegal aliens.

These are just some of the obvious signs of the end of representative democracy we have known and the move toward a direct democracy. Constant public opinion polling by ever more sophisticated methods, and increasing use of interactive technology developments, make elected representatives immediately "aware of and responsive to popular will."[**]

Political philosophers as early as Plato warned that citizens are often bad judges of political matters, without the experience and facts to make wise decisions. Direct democracy, moreover, said Plato, encourages bad leadership as leaders bend and bow to the whims of the masses.

It was this control and sway of the masses that the Framers tried to avoid as they shaped the new government. The president and senators were not to be elected by the people directly. Only the House of Representatives was to be responsible to the people. And those "people" were all white male property owners, not the vastly expanded electorate of the late twentieth century, which includes almost all citizens over the age of eighteen.

Grossman says he can envision a nation of the future where the president and chiefs of staff explain an international conflict to the American people, who then can call in to 1-800-U-DECIDE to press 1 if you want to go to war; 2 if you want to stay

out. This kind of pressure to act quickly in response to the masses was just the kind of pure democracy that Plato advocated and the Framers tried to avoid.

Ted Koppel, journalist and host of ABC's *Nightline,* has had a career that might cause one to imagine that he would welcome more citizen involvement through electronic media. But Koppel also fears for the consequences of the coming electronic democracy.

The country may be moving in the direction of a purer democracy than anything the ancient Greeks envisioned. It promises to be a fiasco. Opinion polls and focus groups are Stone Age implements in the brave new world of interactivity just down the communications superhighway. Imagine an ongoing electronic plebiscite [consultation] in which millions of Americans will be able to express their views on any public issue at the press of a button. Surely nothing could be a purer expression of representational government. . . . Now imagine the paralysis that would be induced if constituencies could be polled instantly by an all-but-universal interactive system. No more guessing what the voters were thinking; Presidents and lawmakers would have access to [a] permanent electrocardiogram, hooked up to the body politic.[***]

Is this the way the government of the future will work? Should work? What are its implications for minority rights as majority rule prevails?

[*]Lawrence K. Grossman, *The Electronic Republic: Reshaping Democracy in the Information Age* (New York: Time Books, 1995), 3.

[**]Grossman, *The Electronic Republic,* 3.

[***]Ted Koppel, "The Perils of Info-Democracy." *The New York Times* (July 1, 1994): A25.

which the interests of the people were represented by more educated or wealthier citizens who were responsible to those who elected them. Today, representative democracies are more commonly called "republics," and the words "democracy" and "republic" often are used interchangeably.

Why a Capitalist System?

In addition to fashioning a democratic form of government, the colonists also were confronted with the dilemma of what kind of role the government should play in the economy. Concerns with liberty, both personal and economic, were always at the forefront of their actions and decisions in creating a new government. They were well aware of the need for a well-functioning economy and saw that government had a key role in maintaining one. What a malfunction in the economy is, however, and what steps the government should take to remedy it, were questions that dogged the Framers and continue to puzzle politicians and theorists today.

The American economy is characterized by the private ownership of property and a **free market economy**—two key tenets of **capitalism,** a form of economic system that favors private control of business and minimal governmental regulation of private industry. (For a description of other types of economic systems see Highlight 1.1: Other Economic Systems.)

Capitalism is a mode of economic production characterized by private ownership (by individuals or groups) of land, factories, raw materials, and other instruments of production. It is the economic system found in the United States, Great Britain, and most parts of Western Europe. In capitalist systems the laws of supply and demand, interacting freely in the marketplace, set prices of goods and drive production.

In 1776, at the same time as the signing of the Declaration of Independence, Adam Smith (1723–90) published *An Inquiry into the Nature and Causes of the Wealth of Nations* (generally known as *The Wealth of Nations*). Smith's book marked the beginning of the modern capitalist era. He argued that free trade would result in full production and economic health. These ideas were greeted with great enthusiasm in the colonies as independence was proclaimed. Colonists no longer wanted to participate in the **mercantile system** of Great Britain and other Western European nations. Mercantile systems bound trade and its administration to national governments. Smith and his supporters saw free trade as "the invisible hand" that produced the wealth of nations. This wealth, in turn, became the inspiration and justification for capitalism.

Under capitalism, sales occur for the profit of the individual. Capitalists believe that both national and individual production is greatest when individuals are free to do with their property or goods as they wish. The government, however, plays an indispensable role in creating and enforcing the rules of the game.

From the mid- to late eighteenth century, and through the mid-1930s in the United States and in much of the Western world, the idea of *laissez-faire* economics (from the French, "to leave alone") enjoyed considerable popularity. While most states regulated and intervened heavily in their economies well into the nineteenth century, the national government routinely followed a "hands-off" economic policy. By the late 1800s, however, the U.S. national government felt increasing pressure to regulate some aspects of the economy (often in part because of the difficulties states faced in regulating large, multistate industries such as the railroads, and from industry's desire to override the patchwork regulatory scheme produced by the states). Thereafter, the Great Depression of the 1930s forced the national government to take a much larger role in the economy (see chapters 9 and 17). Afterward, any pretense that the United States was a purely capitalist system was abandoned. The worldwide extent of this trend, however, varied

free market economy: The economic system in which the "invisible hand" of the market regulates prices, wages, product mix, and so on.

capitalism: The economic system that favors private control of business and minimal governmental regulation of private industry.

mercantile system: A system that binds trade and its administration to the national government.

by country and over time. In post-World War II Britain, for example, the extent of government economic regulation of industry and social welfare was much greater than that attempted by American policy makers in the same period.

Highlight 1.1

Other Economic Systems

Capitalism is just one type of economic system. Others include socialism, communism, and totalitarianism.

Socialism

Socialism is a philosophy that advocates collective ownership and control of the means of economic production. Socialists call for governmental—rather than private—ownership of all land, property, and industry and, in turn, an equitable distribution of the income from those holdings. In addition, socialism seeks to replace the profit motive and competition with cooperation and social responsibility.

Some Socialists actually tolerate capitalism as long as the government maintains some kind of control over the economy. Others reject capitalism outright and insist on the abolition of all private enterprise.

Some Socialists, especially in Western Europe, have argued that socialism can evolve through democratic processes. Thus, in nations like Great Britain, certain critical industries or services such as health care or the coal industry have been *nationalized*, or taken over by the state, to provide for more efficient supervision and to avoid the major concentrations of wealth that occur when individuals privately own key industries.

Communism

German philosopher Karl Marx argued that government was simply a manifestation of underlying economic forces and could be understood according to types of economic production. In *Das Kapital* (1867) Marx argued that capitalism would always be replaced by Socialist states in which the working class would own the means of production and distribution and be able to redistribute the wealth to meet its needs.

Marx believed that it was inevitable for each society to pass through the stages of history: feudalism, capitalism, socialism, and then communism. When society reached communism, Marx theorized, all class differences would be abolished and government would become unnecessary. A system of common ownership of the means of sustenance and production would lead to greater social justice. In practice, most notably under Vladimir Ilyich Ulyanov, under the pseudonym Lenin, and the Soviet dictator Josef Stalin (also a pseudonym, his real name was Josif Vissarionivich Dzhugashvili), many of the tenets of Marxism were changed or modified.

Marx saw the change coming first in highly industrialized countries such as Britain and Germany, where a fully mature capitalism would pave the way for a Socialist revolution. But Lenin and the Bolshevik Party wanted to have such a revolution in underdeveloped Russia. So, instead of relying on the historical inevitability of the Communist future (as Marx envisioned), they advocated forcing that change. Lenin argued that by establishing an elite vanguard party of permanent revolutionaries and a dictatorship of the proletariat (working class), they could achieve socialism and communism without waiting for the historical forces to work. In the 1940s China followed the Leninist path led by Mao Ze Dong (formerly transliterated as Mao Tse Tung).

In practice, the Communist states rejected free markets as a capitalist and exploitative way of organizing production and turned instead to planning and state regulation. In capitalist economies, the market sets prices, wages, product mix, and so on. Under a planned economy, government makes conscious choices to determine prices, wages, product mix, and so on.

Totalitarianism

A totalitarian system is basically a modern form of extreme authoritarian rule. In contrast to governments based on democratic beliefs, totalitarian governments have total authority over their people and their economic system. The tools of totalitarianism are secret police, terror, propaganda, and an almost total prohibition on civil rights and liberties. These systems also tend to be ruled in the name of an ideology or a personality cult organized around a supreme leader. The reign of Saddam Hussein in Iraq comes close to the "total" control of forms of production, the airwaves, education, the arts, and even sports implied by totalitarianism. Some Communist systems also approached totalitarianism.

CHARACTERISTICS OF AMERICAN DEMOCRACY

*T*he United States, as created by the Framers, is an indirect democracy with several underlying concepts and distinguishing characteristics. Many of these characteristics are often in conflict, a factor that has led to some of the political discontent present in the population and, more specifically, the electorate. The political system, for example, is based on an underlying notion of the importance of balance among the legislative, executive, and judicial branches, between the state and federal governments, between the wants of the majority and the minority, between the rights of the individual and the best interests of the nation as a whole. The Framers built the system on the idea that there would be statesmen who would act for the good of the system. Without such statesmen, the system necessitates constant vigilance to keep a balance as the pendulum swings back and forth between various desires, demands, and responsibilities. To some, government may be a necessary evil; but a good government is less evil if it can keep things in balance as it operates in various spheres. The ideas of balance permeate many of the concepts and characteristics of American democracy presented below.

Popular Consent

popular consent: The idea that governments must draw their powers from the consent of the governed.

Popular consent, the idea that governments must draw their powers from the consent of the governed, is one distinguishing characteristic of American democracy. Derived from Locke's social contract theory, the notion of popular consent was central to the Declaration of Independence. A citizen's willingness to vote represents his or her consent to be governed and is thus an essential premise of democracy.

Popular Sovereignty

popular sovereignty: The right of the majority to govern themselves.

The notion of **popular sovereignty** has its basis in natural law: Ultimately, political authority rests with the people, who can create, abolish, or alter their governments. The idea that all governments derive their power from the people is found in the Declaration of Independence and the U.S. Constitution, but the term itself did not come into wide usage until pre-Civil War debates over slavery. At that time supporters of popular sovereignty argued that the citizens of new states seeking admission to the Union should be able to decide whether or not their states would allow slavery within their borders. (See Highlight 1.2: Who Makes Decisions in America? for some theories about who makes decisions about governing.)

Majority Rule

majority rule: The central premise of direct democracy in which only policies that collectively garner the support of a majority of voters will be made into law.

Majority rule, another basic democratic principle, means that the majority (normally) of citizens in any political unit should elect officials and determine policies. This principle holds for both voters and their elected representatives (50 percent of the total votes cast plus 1). Yet the American system also stresses the need to preserve minority rights as evidenced by the myriad protections of individual rights and liberties found in the Bill of Rights.

The concept of the preservation of minority rights has changed dramatically in the United States. It wasn't until after the Civil War that slaves were freed and African

Highlight 1.2

Who Makes Decisions in America?

How conflicts are resolved is often determined by how the government is operated and by whom. Over the years several theorists have posited widely different points of view in their attempts to explain who runs government. (Most political scientists probably subscribe to the pluralist view.) All of these theories provide interesting ways to think about how policy decisions are made, whether we are looking at local, state, or national policies.

Elite Theory
Elite theory posits that all important decisions in society are made by the few, called the elite, so that government is increasingly alienated from the people and rarely responsive to their wishes. There are a number of different interpretations of elite theory. For example, in *The Power Elite* (1956), American sociologist C. Wright Mills argued that important policies were set by a loose coalition of three groups with some overlap among each.[*] According to his elite theory, these three major influencers of policy—cor-

porate leaders, military leaders, and a small group of key governmental leaders—are the true "power elite" in America. Other elite theorists have argued that the news media should be included as a fourth source of political power in the United States.

Another proponent of elite theory, political scientist Thomas R. Dye, contends that all societies are divided into elites and masses. The elite are the few who have power, and the masses are the many who don't.[**] This distribution of functions and powers in society is inevitable. Elites, however, are not immune from public opinion, nor do they by definition oppress the masses. Dye argues that in a complex society, such as ours, only a "tiny minority" actually make policy.

Bureaucratic Theory
Max Weber (1864–1920), the founder of modern sociology, argued that all institutions, governmental and nongovernmental, have fallen under the control of a large and ever-growing bureaucracy—that is, the set of hierarchical departments, agencies, commissions, and their staffs that carry on policy on a day-to-day basis using standardized proce-

dures. This view is called *bureaucratic theory*. Because all institutions have grown more complex, Weber concluded that the expertise and competence of bureaucrats allows them to wrest power from others, especially elected officials.

Interest Group Theory
Political scientist David B. Truman postulated what is termed the *interest group theory* of democracy in *The Governmental Process* (1951). According to Truman, interest groups—not elites, sets of elites, or bureaucrats—control the governmental process.[***]

Truman believes there are so many potential pressure points in the executive, legislative, and judicial branches of the federal government—as well as at the state level—that groups can step in on any number of competing sides. According to Truman the government then becomes the equilibrium point in the system as it mediates between competing interests.

Pluralist Theory
Another, more widely accepted theory about the nature of power is held by those in the *pluralist* school of thought. According to political scientists like Robert A. Dahl, the structure of our democratic gov-

ernment allows only for a pluralistic model of democracy.[****] Borrowing from Truman's work, Dahl argues that resources are scattered so widely in our diverse democracy that no single elite group can ever have a monopoly over any substantial area of policy. In *Who Governs?* (1961), for example, Dahl found that political competition and elections coupled with the growing ethnic and socioeconomic diversity of New Haven, Connecticut, led to a situation in which a single elite could never take and hold power legally.

Adding to this debate, political scientist Theodore J. Lowi has described how political decision making takes place today in an era of what he terms "interest group liberalism." According to Lowi, participants in every political controversy get something; thus each has some impact on how political decisions are made. Lowi also states that governments rarely say no to any well-organized interests. Thus all interests ultimately receive some benefits or rewards. Lowi bemoans the fact that the public interest, that is, what is good for the public at large, often tends to lose in this system.[*****]

[*]C. Wright Mills, *The Power Elite* (New York: Oxford University Press, 1956).
[**]Thomas R. Dye, *Who's Running America?* (New York: Prentice Hall, 1976).
[***]David B. Truman, *The Governmental Process* (New York: Knopf, 1951).
[****]Robert A. Dahl, *Preface to Democratic Theory* (Chicago: University of Chicago Press, 1956).
[*****]Theodore J. Lowi, *The End of Liberalism* (New York: Norton, 1979).

Americans began to enjoy minimal citizenship rights. By the 1960s, however, rage at America's failure to guarantee minority rights in all sections of the nation fueled the civil rights movement, which ultimately led to congressional passage of the Civil Rights Act of 1964 and the Voting Rights Act of 1965, both designed to further minority rights.

Individualism

Tremendous value is placed on the individual in American democracy and culture. All individuals are deemed rational and fair, and endowed, as Thomas Jefferson proclaimed in the Declaration of Independence, "with certain unalienable rights." Individualism, which holds that the primary function of government is to enable the individual to achieve his or her highest level of development, makes the interests of the individual more important than those of the state and at the heart of our capitalistic system. It is also a concept whose meaning also has changed over time. The rugged individualism of the western frontier, for example, was altered as more citizens moved westward, cities developed, and demands for government services increased.

Equality

Another key characteristic of our democracy is the American emphasis on political equality, the definition of which has varied considerably over time (as discussed in chapter 6). The importance of political equality is another reflection of American stress on the importance of the individual. Although some individuals clearly wield more political clout than others, the adage "One man, one vote" implies a sense of political equality for all.

Personal Liberty

personal liberty: A key characteristic of U.S. democracy. Initially meaning freedom from governmental interference, today it includes demands for freedom to engage in a variety of practices free from governmental discrimination.

Personal liberty is perhaps the single most important characteristic of American democracy. The Constitution itself was written to assure "life" and "liberty." Over the years, however, our concepts of liberty have changed and evolved from "freedom *from*" to "freedom *to.*" The Framers intended Americans to be free from governmental infringements on freedom of religion and speech, from unreasonable search and seizure, and so on (see chapter 5). The addition of the Fourteenth Amendment to the Constitution and its emphasis on equal protection of the laws and subsequent passage of laws guaranteeing civil rights, however, expanded Americans' concept of liberty to include demands for "freedom to" be free from discrimination. Debates over how much the government should do to guarantee these rights or liberties illustrate the conflicts that continue to occur in our democratic system.

CHARACTERISTICS OF THE AMERICAN PEOPLE

*I*n the 1996 elections, many politicians—especially many of those on the right—tried to underscore how quickly and dramatically America is changing. But while America and its population are undergoing rapid change, this is not necessarily a new phenomenon. It is simply new to most of us.

In the pages that follow, we take a look at some of the characteristics of the American population. Because the people of the United States are the basis of political power and authority, these characteristics have important implications for how America is governed and how and what policies are made.

Size and Population

One year after the Constitution was ratified, less than 4 million Americans lived in the thirteen states. They were united by a single language and opposition to the king. Most shared a similar Protestant–Christian heritage, and those who voted were white, male property owners. The Constitution mandated that each of the 65 members of the original House of Representatives should represent 30,000 citizens. However, due to rapid growth, that number often was much higher. Anti-Federalists, who opposed a strong national government during the founding period, at least took solace in the fact that members of the House of Representatives, who generally represented far fewer people than senators, would be more in touch with "the people."

As revealed in Figure 1.1, as the nation grew westward, the population also grew. Although the physical size of the United States has remained stable since the addition of Alaska and Hawaii in 1959, there are now more than 263 million Americans. A single member of the House of Representatives now represents as many as 870,000 people.

As a result of this growth, most citizens today feel far removed from the national government and their elected representatives. Members of Congress, too, feel this change. Often they represent diverse constituencies with a variety of needs, concerns, and expectations, and they can meet only a relative few of these people in face-to-face electioneering.

FIGURE 1.1

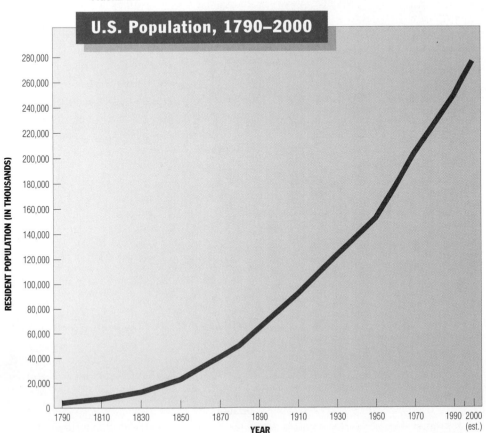

SOURCE: U.S. Bureau of the Census, *U.S. Census of Population: 1920–1990, vol. 1; Current Population Reports*, P25–P311, P25–1045, and P25–1097, and U.S. Bureau of the Census, *Statistical Abstracts of the U.S. 1995*, 115th ed., (Washington, D.C., 1995), P8 and 9.

"Micky M'Carty is Rising in the World, slowly, but surely—"

As for us, we are living on Fifth Avenue, near the Cinthral Park—

The immigrant has not often found American streets to be paved with gold, although letters back to the old country may have implied otherwise. (Photo courtesy: Culver Pictures)

Changing Demographics of the U.S. Population

As the physical size and population of the United States has changed, so have many of the bases and assumptions on which it was founded. Some of the dynamism of the American system actually stems from the racial and ethnic changes that have taken place throughout our history, a notion that often gets lost in debates about immigration policy. Moreover, for the first time, the U.S. population is getting much older. This "graying" of America also will assuredly lead to changes in our expectations of government and in our public policy demands. First we'll look at some demographic facts (that is, information on characteristics of America's population), and then we'll discuss some implications of these changes for how our nation is governed and what policy issues might arise.

Racial and Ethnic Change. From the start, the population of America has been constantly changed by the arrival of various kinds of immigrants to its shores—first those from Western Europe fleeing religious persecution in the 1600s to early 1700s, then Irish Catholics escaping the potato famine in the 1850s, then Chinese laborers to work on the railroads, and then later, from the 1880s to 1910s, Northern and Eastern Europeans, and most recently, Vietnamese, Cubans, Mexicans, and others.

FIGURE 1.2

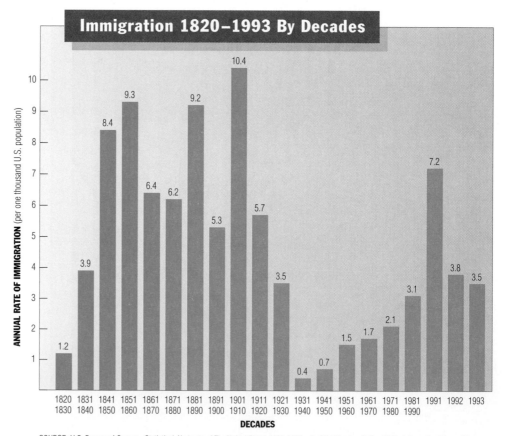

SOURCE: U.S. Bureau of Census, *Statistical Abstracts of The United States 1995*, 115th ed., (Washington, D.C., 1995); *Information Please Almanac*, 49th ed. (Boston: Houghton Mifflin, 1996).

As revealed in Figure 1.2, immigration to the United States peaked in the first decade of the 1900s, when nearly 9 million people, many of them from Eastern Europe, entered the country. The United States did not see another major wave of immigration until the 1980s, when over 7 million immigrants were admitted. Unlike the arrivals in other periods of high immigration, however, these "new" Americans were often nonwhite; many were Asians from Southeast Asia or Hispanics from Latin America.

While immigration has been a continual source of changing demographics in America, race, too, has played a major role in the development and course of politics in the United States. As revealed in Figure 1.3, the racial balance in America is changing dramatically. In 1996, for example, whites made up 73.6 percent of the U.S. population, blacks 12.0 percent, and Hispanics 10.2 percent. By 2050, it is estimated that Hispanics will account for 24.5 percent of the population, thus becoming the largest

FIGURE 1.3

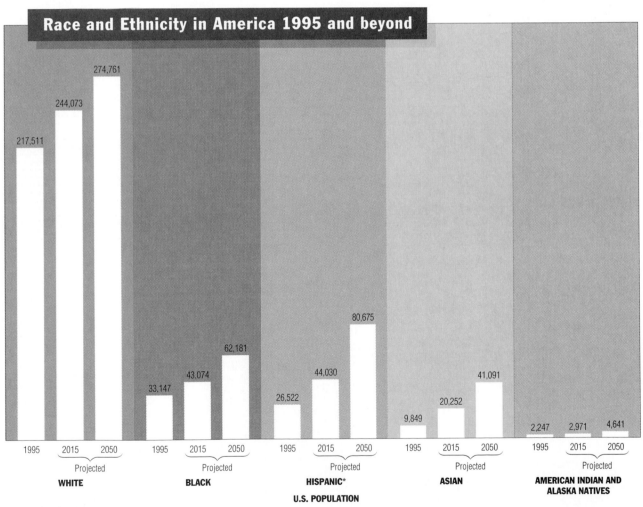

Projected U.S. Population, 2015
Projected U.S. Population, 2050

* Persons of Hispanic origin can be of any race.

SOURCE: U.S. Census Bureau, Resident Population—Selected Characteristics, 1970 to 1991, and Projections, 1995 to 2050.

minority group (African Americans will account for 13.6 percent). The Asian population, too, is growing as a proportion of the total U.S. population, and is expected to reach 8.2 percent in 2050.

Age.   Just as the racial and ethnic composition of the American population is changing, so too is the average age of the population. "For decades, the U.S. was described as a nation of the young because the number of persons under the age of twenty greatly outnumber(ed) those sixty-five and older,"[7] but this is no longer the case, as Figure 1.4 shows. Due to changes in patterns of fertility, life expectancy, and immigration, the nation's age profile has changed drastically.[8] As the age profile of the U.S. population has changed, political scientists and others have found it useful to assign labels to various generations (see Table 1.1). Such labels can be useful in understanding the various pressures put on our nation and its government, because when people were born and the kinds of events they experienced can have important consequences on how they view other political, economic, and social events.

FIGURE 1.4

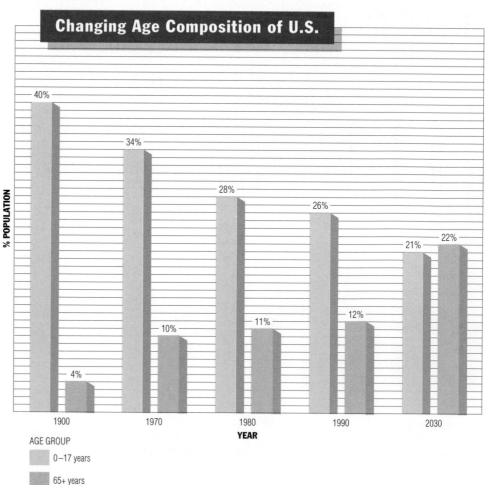

SOURCE: Susan A. McManus. *Young* v. *Old* (Boulder, CO: Westview Press, 1995), p.4.

TABLE 1.1

Three Classifications of Generations Born in the Twentieth Century

	GENERATION LABEL	BIRTH YEARS
Strauss and Howe, Generations[a]	G.I.	1901–1924
	Silent	1925–1942
	Boom	1943–1960
	Thirteenth	1961–1981
	Millennial	1982–2003
Torres–Gil, The New Aging[a]	Swing	1900–1926
	Silent	1927–1945
	Baby Boomers	1946–1964
	Baby Bust (Boomerang)	1965–1979
	Baby Boomlet (Echo)	1980–
MacManus, Young v. Old[b]	World War I	1899–1910
	Depression/World War II	1911–1926
	Cold War/Sputnik	1927–1942
	Civil Rights/Vietnam/Watergate	1943–1958
	Reagan	1959–1973

[a]The Strauss and Howe and Torres–Gil classifications include the nation's youngest generation (the under-eighteen nonvoters).

[b]The MacManus classification focuses exclusively on those of voting age (eighteen and over) as of 1991.

Sources: William Strauss and Neil Howe, *Generations: The History of America's Future, 1584–2069* (New York: Quill, William Morrow, 1991); Fernando Torres–Gil, *The New Aging: Politics and Change in America* (New York: Auburn House, 1992); Susan A. MacManus, *Young v. Old: Generational Combat in the 21st Century* (Boulder, CO: Westview Press, 1995).

Implications of Racial, Ethnic, and Generational Change

The varied races, ethnic origins, and sizes of the various age cohorts of the American people have important implications for government and politics. Today, many believe that immigrants (legal and illegal) are flooding onto our shores with disastrous consequences. Such anti-immigration sentiments are hardly new—in fact, American history is replete with examples of "Americans" set against any new immigration. In the 1840s, for example, the Know Nothing Party arose in part to oppose immigration from Roman Catholic nations, charging that the pope was going to organize the slaughter of all Protestants in the United States. In the 1920s the Ku Klux Klan, which had over 5 million members, called for barring immigration to stem the tide of Roman Catholics and Jews into the nation.

Today, in spite of the fact that almost all Americans have ancestors who emigrated to the United States, most Americans oppose unrestricted access to the United States and react negatively to reports that the foreign-born population is increasing. In the presidential campaign of 1996, immigration (legal and illegal) was a big issue. Many Americans felt (erroneously, for the most part) that floods of immigrants were putting Americans out of work and putting a strain on our already overburdened state and federal resources, especially school systems and welfare programs. During the presidential primary, Republican presidential hopeful Pat Buchanan tapped into the American public's frustration by reaching out to those who feared their jobs were being lost because of immigrants and international trade policies such as the General Agreement on Tariffs and Trade (GATT) and the North American Free Trade Agreement (NAFTA). He advocated banning *all* immigration to the United States for five years. He also suggested building a fence along the U.S./Mexico border to prevent illegal aliens from entering the United States. Another Republican challenger, Lamar Alexander, suggested building a new branch of the military to patrol our borders and enforce immigration laws.

Another indication of anti-immigrant sentiment was the most publicized initiative on the 1994 ballot, California's Proposition 187. This proposition was designed to stem the influx of illegal aliens to California, where 24.1 percent of state residents are foreign born. Proposition 187's purpose was to bar *illegal* aliens (who are thought to account for approximately 48 percent of California's population) from using already strained taxpayer-subsidized services.[9] In a 59 to 41 percent vote, Californians voted to ban the use of state funds for education, health, and social services for illegal aliens. A federal court immediately stayed the implementation of the law, however, and many lawyers and legal scholars alleged it was unconstitutional.

Hostility to immigrants manifests itself in a variety of ways in addition to those noted above. Some bemoan the fact that the nation is becoming less white, or criticize those who refuse to adopt "American" ways as they cling to the customs, language, and traditions of their old country. Immigrants, too, often face blame from the citizenry or elected officials, who blame them for lost jobs or depressed wages (because they are often willing to take low-wage jobs).

Changing racial and ethnic demographics also seem to intensify—at least for some—an "us" *versus* "them" attitude. Government affirmative action programs, for example, which were created in the 1960s to redress decades of overt racial discrimination, are now being attacked as unfair because they give African Americans and women an advantage in an increasingly competitive job market.

Sociologist James Davison Hunter defines the culture conflict that is the result of changing demographics as "political and social hostility rooted in very different systems of moral understanding."[10] These different worldviews—worker *versus* CEO; educated *versus* uneducated, young *versus* old, white *versus* black, native-born *versus* immigrant—create deep cleavages in society, as exemplified by the "polarizing impulses or tendencies" in American society.[11] Just as the two parties at times seem to be pushed to take extreme positions on many issues, so are many of those who speak out on those issues.

Demographics also affect politics and government because an individual's perspective often influences how he or she *hears* the debate on various issues. Thus many African Americans viewed O.J. Simpson's acquittal as vindication for decades of unjust treatment experienced by blacks in the criminal justice system; the wealthy view proposals for a flat tax with much more enthusiasm than do many of the poor; and those who saw their jobs jeopardized by NAFTA were more likely to decry it than their employers.

These cleavages and the emphasis many politicians put on our demographic differences play out in many ways in American politics. Baby boomers and the elderly object to any changes in Social Security or Medicare, while those in Generation X vote for politicians who support change. Many policies are targeted at one group or the other, further exacerbating differences—real or imagined—and lawmakers often find themselves the target of factions. All of this makes it difficult to devise coherent policies to "promote the general welfare," as promised in the Constitution.

Ideology of the American Public

Political ideology is a term used by political scientists to refer to the more or less consistent set of values that historically have been reflected in the political system, economic order, social goals, and moral values of any given society. "It is the means by which the basic values held by a party, class, group or individual are articulated."[12] A small percentage of Americans are libertarians. They have long believed in the evils of big government and stress that government should not involve itself in the plight of the people or attempt to remedy any social ills. Most who talk about political ideology, however, frame it on a continuum of liberal to conservative. As revealed in Figure 1.5, most Americans are able to place themselves somewhere on this continuum, with more Americans identifying themselves as conservative or moderate than liberal.

The definitions of liberal and conservative have changed over the years. During the nineteenth century, for example, conservatives supported governmental power and favored a role for religion in public life; in contrast, liberals supported freedom from undue governmental control. Today, these terms have very different meanings to the general public.

political ideology: An individual's coherent set of values and beliefs about the purpose and scope of government.

FIGURE 1.5

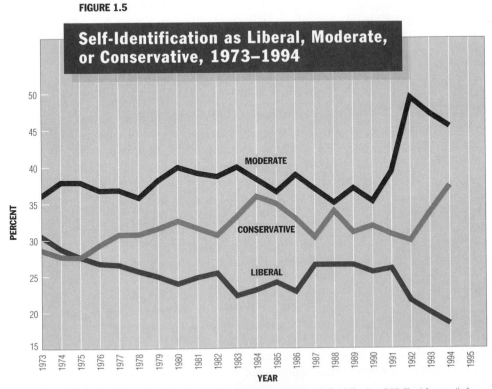

Self-Identification as Liberal, Moderate, or Conservative, 1973–1994

NOTE: "Liberal" equals the combined percentages of those identifying themselves as extremely liberal, liberal, or slightly liberal; "conservative" equals the combined percentages of those identifying themselves as extremely conservative, conservative, or slightly conservative.

SOURCE: General Social Survey, National Opinion Research Center, © Data from 1992 and 1994 from Everett Carl Ladd, *America at the Polls* (Storrs: Conn.: The Roper Center, 1995), p. 16.

Two senators who have come to be known for their political ideologies are conservative Strom Thurmond (R-S.C.) and liberal Edward M. Kennedy (D-Mass.). (Photos courtesy: top, Rob Crandall/Stock Boston, bottom, Mark Reinstein/The Image Works)

conservative: One thought to believe that a government is best that governs least and that big government can only infringe on individual, personal, and economic rights.

liberal: One considered to favor extensive governmental involvement in the economy and the provision of social services and to take an activist role in protecting the rights of women, the elderly, minorities, and the environment.

Conservatives.   According to William Safire's *New Political Dictionary*, a **conservative** "is a defender of the status quo who, when change becomes necessary in tested institutions or practices, prefers that it come slowly, and in moderation."[13] Conservatives are thought to believe that a government is best that governs least, and that big government can only infringe on individual, personal, and economic rights. They want less government, especially in terms of regulation of the economy. Conservatives favor local and state action over federal action, and emphasize fiscal responsibility, most notably in the form of balanced budgets.

Conservatives are likely to support smaller, less activist governments and believe that domestic problems like homelessness, poverty, and discrimination are better dealt with by the private sector than by the government. Less rigid conservatives see the need for governmental action in some fields and for steady change in many areas. They seek to achieve such change within the framework of existing institutions, occasionally changing the institutions when they show a need for it.

Liberals.   Safire defines a **liberal** as "currently one who believes in more government action to meet individual needs, originally one who resisted government encroachments on individual liberties."[14] Liberals now are considered to favor big governments that play active roles in the economy. They also stress the need for the government to provide for the poor and homeless, to provide a wide array of other social services, and to take an activist role in protecting the rights of women, the elderly, minorities, and the environment.

When considering what it means when someone identifies himself or herself as a conservative or liberal, it is important to remember that the labels "conservative" and "liberal" can be quite misleading and do not necessarily allow us to predict political opinions. In a perfect world, liberals would be liberal and conservatives would be conservative.

Studies reveal, however, that many people who call themselves conservative actually take fairly liberal positions on many policy issues. In fact, anywhere from 20 percent to 68 percent will take a traditionally "conservative" position on one issue and a traditionally "liberal" position on another.[15] People who take conservative stances against "big government," for example, often support increases in spending for the elderly, education, or health care. It is also not unusual to encounter a person who could be considered liberal on social issues such as abortion and civil rights but conservative on economic or "pocketbook" issues.

Today, Americans' positions on specific issues cut across these two ideological boundaries to such a degree that new, more varied ideological categories may soon be needed to capture division within American political thought.

To add to the confusion, these labels—and the public's perception of them—are constantly changing. When Michael Dukakis ran for president in 1988 against then Vice President George Bush, he was haunted by the label "liberal." The "L" word was deemed to be the kiss of death for him—and for any politician—because, to many, liberal implied being "soft on crime." But just four years later, in 1992, America elected a Democratic president considered liberal by many (although Bill Clinton did his best to stress his moderate positions). In 1993 most Americans believed Washington was more liberal under Clinton and they claimed not to be bothered by this phenomenon. But just one year later, in the 1994 congressional elections, several liberal Democrats lost their seats in Congress and the conservative Christian Coalition took credit for those defeats. Extremists in both of the major parties have tried to force the Republican and Democratic parties to take increasingly polar positions on issues including welfare reform, affirmative action, race relations, abortion, foreign aid, and health care. Thus these perceived rapid shifts in the ideological mood of the nation, and the tendency of the parties and interest groups to go to the extremes, make it difficult for policy makers to obtain consensus about policy and probably exacerbate some citizen dissatisfaction with government.

Today it seems that there are more extremists than ever. But this perception may be due to the fact that those on the far right or left are often more vocal and vehement about their views than are moderates. Thus because of television (which is always in search of a quick "sound bite" for the 6 o'clock news) and talk radio shows (which survive on controversy), these views may be the ones voiced and heard most often.

The perception that there are more extreme conservatives than ever may not be correct. In fact, since the 1970s, when ideological tracking began to be measured regularly, there has been little change in how the American public views itself. Former General Colin Powell has called this frustrated, moderate electorate "the sensible center."[16] His "sensible center" has remained firm at about 35 percent to 40 percent of the adult population, while those on either end of the spectrum have remained around 12 percent to 15 percent for liberals and 12 percent to 19 percent for conservatives.

THE FRUSTRATED PUBLIC

Frustration with politics, the economy, and the inability to achieve the American dream has been building steadily over the last two or three decades. In the 1990s it appears to have reached critical mass.

How Americans view politics, the economy, political institutions, and their ability to achieve the American dream is also influenced by their political ideology as well as by their social, economic, educational, and personal circumstances. One Republican pollster noted that angry, frustrated, and frightened voters have "the potential to blow through the roof."[17] This was underscored in a recent report in *Newsweek:*

> Frank Luntz is staring at a dozen average Americans. Half of them are in their 20s. Half are nearing retirement age. They are the sort of people you see in the mall and never give a second glance—pleasant, unexceptional, profoundly middle class. Which is just what Luntz, a Republican pollster, is looking for. He—and his client, the Coalition for Change (an unholy alliance of the Business Roundtable, Ross Perot's United We Stand and other groups)—wants to see if average Americans, young and old, can come to any agreement on how to balance the federal budget. And so he asks them, "Can you describe your feelings about the federal budget deficit in one or two words?" You bet they can. Suddenly they morph from mild-mannered suburbanites to a half crazed citizen rabble looking for the nearest available Bastille. They spit out their answers: "disgusting," *"pathetic,"* "outrageous," "a *joke,"* "revolting," and—an older man, laid off by a chemical company after 23 years: "It won't change."
>
> "Why won't it change?" Luntz asks.
>
> Hoots and tirades. Hoots about the nature of the political beast—the special interests, the pork barrel projects; someone mentions the scuzzy, corrupt Washington revealed in the Packwood diaries. Tirades about the way money is spent—on foreign aid, on welfare, on the folks who buy T-bones with food stamps.[18]

Many sectors of the American public are frustrated over downsizing, shutdowns, and possible job loss from any source. These Austin, Texas, workers protest the North American Free Trade Agreement (NAFTA) as a threat to their own livelihoods. (Photo courtesy: Bob Daemmrich/The Image Works)

News stories like this one abound in the popular press, where instantaneous communication often highlights the negative, the sensational, the sound bite, and usually the extremes. It's hard to remain upbeat about America or politics amidst the gloom and doom reported on the nightly news. It's hard to remain positive about the fate of Americans and their families if you listen to talk radio or watch daytime talk shows like *Jenny Jones* or *Ricki Lake*. Revelations and a litany of public scandals from Watergate (see Chapter 8) to Whitewater to Travelgate have fed public cynicism about government. It is far easier for the press to focus on Senator Bob Packwood's (R–Ore.) diaries, which painted a tawdry picture of how one lawmaker sold his votes to lobbyists and influence peddlers, than to devote time and space to a story of a teenage mother who, aided by government programs, went to college, got a job, and became an involved parent and citizen. Those people are generally showcased only in State of the Union addresses or presidential nominating conventions. Waste in government, bickering and posturing politicians, the deficit, affirmative action, immigration, job insecurity, and the shutdown of the federal government, all contribute to popular dissatisfaction with politicians and government, as do inflated expectations, inflated campaign promises, and lack of appreciation about the positive benefits of governmental programs.

This reported discontent with government and its institutions is a relatively new phenomenon in the United States. In the nineteenth and early twentieth centuries, immigrants who came to America lived in small, ethnic urban enclaves, but they made learning English and adopting American ways their first priority. At school their children were taught pride in the United States and its symbols. Compulsory civics classes taught them about the Framers and how to be good citizens. The public schools, in essence, were engaged in state building, and there was general agreement about America and what it stood for.[19]

Today, many people seem confused or unhappy about what America stands for. Turn on your TV or radio, open a newspaper or magazine, and you'll find Americans criticizing social programs, crime, the educational system, their elected representatives . . . you name it, and there's someone criticizing it.

Why Are Americans Frustrated?

Americans are frustrated with their government and their politicians for many reasons. We'll look at three of the most prominent ones: discontent with the economy, high expectations for government performance, and a lack of awareness as to just how much good the government has done for most citizens.

The Economy.   For most of U.S. history, the American dream has been alive and well: Hard work has been rewarded with a steady job and increased earning power and wages, and Americans have expected to hand down improved economic, social, and educational status to their children. In many ways World War II ushered in the era of the American dream: Men returned from the war and went to college, their tuition paid for by the G.I. Bill. Prior to the war, a college education was mainly the preserve of the rich; the G.I. Bill made it available to men from all walks of life. Many men got the education they needed to succeed and do much better than their parents before them. In addition, low-interest-rate mortgages were also made available through the Veteran's Administration, and the American dream of owning a home became a reality for millions.

FIGURE 1.6

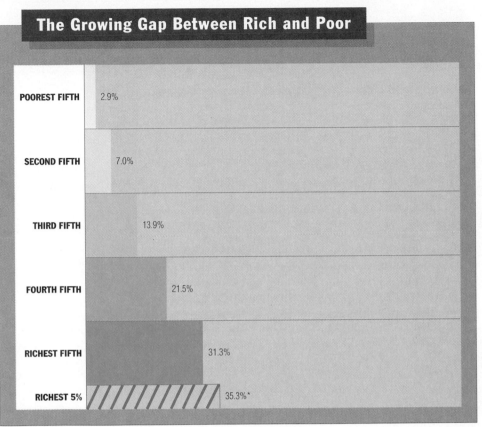

The Growing Gap Between Rich and Poor

POOREST FIFTH	2.9%
SECOND FIFTH	7.0%
THIRD FIFTH	13.9%
FOURTH FIFTH	21.5%
RICHEST FIFTH	31.3%
RICHEST 5%	35.3%*

*Also included in the richest fifth.

Data derived from Income Branch of the U.S. Census Bureau.

But today the trend toward downsizing and restructuring in American corporations has left workers of all ages, genders, and races, and at all economic levels, fearing for their jobs and "losing faith in their ability to prosper."[20] This fear is compounded by the fact that real weekly earnings and median family incomes have been just about stagnant for the past twenty-five years, while the rich have gotten richer (see Figure 1.6). The gap between rich and poor is widening. For example, in 1975, the average chief executive officer (CEO) made 41 times more than the average worker. In sharp contrast, in 1994, the average CEO made 225 times more than the average worker. Most workers are working harder than ever. In many families both spouses need to work in order to make ends meet. As a result of low incomes and job insecurity, most Americans sense that they can't get ahead. They feel frustrated economically, despite low levels of inflation and unemployment.

High Expectations.   In roughly the first 150 years of our nation's history, the federal government had few responsibilities, and its citizens had few expectations of it beyond national defense, printing money, collecting tariffs and taxes, and so on. The state governments were generally far more powerful than the federal government in matters affecting the everyday lives of Americans (see chapter 3).

North—South

POLITICS AROUND THE WORLD

American government is usually taught on its own. Although there are good reasons for doing so, one also can learn a great deal about the United States by considering our political system alongside that of other countries. There are two good reasons for this.

First, the United States is a most unusual country. It is, after all, the most powerful country in the world. More importantly for a political scientist, however, its political system is dramatically different from all the others, including those of the other wealthy, industrialized democracies. One of the most important things one needs to take away from this course is a sense of just how far the United States is from the global political mainstream—something academics call "American exceptionalism."

Second, by considering it in the light of other countries' political experiences, one can actually understand the United States better. Even the brief comparisons we will be able to make in this book will reinforce many of the central elements in American political life.

So, each chapter will have a box like this one that contrasts the United States with its neighbors to the north and south. We could have chosen any number of countries, but we settled on Mexico and Canada—and not simply because the three share over 11,000 kilometers (6,000 miles) of common borders.

The example of Canada will demonstrate just how much the United States differs from the other democracies. Despite the many cultural and other similarities between the two countries, they have quite different political systems. First and foremost, Canada uses a parliamentary, rather than a presidential, version of democracy. That allows a Canadian prime minister and the rest of his or her government to get their policy proposals passed more or less intact—unlike an American president, who has to engage in constant negotiations and make dozens of compromises before any bill becomes law.

As would be the case with most third world countries, comparisons with Mexico will drive home just how important the American Constitution and the rule of law are. Though loosely modeled on that of the United States, Mexico's political system has been dominated by a single party, the PRI (Institutional Revolutionary Party), for nearly three-quarters of a century. In that time the PRI has won (sometimes, it is alleged, by less than honest means) every election that matters and has created what one scholar recently called a "nonrepressive authoritarian regime." Furthermore, because the Mexican Constitution bars any official from running for reelection and because the PRI's presidential candidate controls who gets the all-important party nominations for other offices, the PRI is able to put its stamp on the government from the cabinet all the way down to city hall in ways no American president or party could ever imagine.

Before closing, we should note an embarrassing problem with the English language. For good or ill, people use the word *American* to describe the citizens, politics, and products of the United States. In fact, the term properly applies to all the countries in both North and South America. However, because there is no alternative adjective in common use, we have decided to stick with this misleading and biased usage.

As the nation and its economy grew in size and complexity, the federal government took on more responsibilities (such as regulating some businesses, providing poverty relief, and inspecting food). Then, in the 1930s, in response to the Great Depression, President Franklin D. Roosevelt's New Deal government programs proliferated in almost every area of American life (job creation, income security, aid to the poor, and so on). Since then, Americans have looked to the government for solutions to all kinds of problems.

Although we all complain about the government, we may lose sight of its invisible positive influence on almost every aspect of our lives. The tomato juice you drink for lunch, for example, is inspected by health department technicians for bacterial contamination. (Photo courtesy: Robert Daemmrich/Tony Stone Worldwide)

Politicians, too, at least until recently, have contributed to public frustration by promising far more than they could deliver. Although President Clinton's vow to end "welfare as we know it" was not realized until nearly the end of his first term, his ambitious promises to overhaul the health care system went nowhere. Similarly, few key provisions of the Republicans' Contract with America were passed by November 1996. Term limits, for example, a battle cry of Republicans running for the 104th Congress in 1994, were not really so attractive to them once they took over control of Congress. These rising expectations about government's ability to reform itself, as well as to cure all social and economic ills in the wake of downsizing and *perceived* economic and lifestyle stagnation, have led to cynicism and apathy, as evidenced in low voter turnout and high dissatisfaction with government. It may be that Americans have come to expect too much from the national government and must simply readjust their expectations.

A Missing Appreciation of the Good.   During the Revolutionary period, average citizens were passionate about politics because stakes—the very survival of the new nation—were so high. Today the stakes aren't readily apparent to many, and the government is a target for their blame and frustrations. If you don't have faith in America, its institutions, or symbols (and Table 1.2 shows that many of us don't), it becomes even easier to blame the government for all kinds of woes—personal as well as societal—in spite of the fact that on many objective measures of progress, Americans are doing better than ever before (as revealed in Table 1.3). Furthermore, while people complain about government, many of us take what government does for us for granted and don't realize all the things governments do well.

Even in the short time between when you get up in the morning and when you leave for classes or work, the government—or its rulings or regulations—pervades your life. The national or state governments, for example, set the standards for whether you wake up on Eastern, Central, or Western Standard Time. The national government regulates the airwaves and licenses the radio or television broadcasts you might listen to or glance at as you eat and get dressed. States, too, also regulate and tax telecommu-

TABLE 1.2

Trashing Our Leaders

	PERCENT OF AMERICANS DECLARING THEY HAD A "GREAT DEAL" OF CONFIDENCE IN THE INSTITUTION			
	1966	**1975**	**1985**	**1994**
Congress	42%	13%	16%	8%
Executive branch	41	13	15	12
The press	29	26	16	13
Major companies	55	19	17	19
Colleges/universities	61	36	35	25
Medicine	73	43	35	23

Source: Newsweek (January 8, 1996): 32.

TABLE 1.3

How Americans Are Really Doing

	1945	**1970**	**1995**
Population	132 million	203 million	263 million
Life expectancy	65.9	70.8	75.7**
Per capita income (1987 constant dollars)	$6,367	$9,875	$14,696**
Adults who are high-school grads	25%*	55%	81%**
Adults who are college grads	5%*	11%	22%**
Households with phones	46%	87%	94%**
Households with televisions	0%	95%	98%**
Households with cable TV	0%	4%	59%
Women in labor force	29%	38%	46%**
Annual airline passengers	7 million	170 million	538 million‡
Poverty rate	39.7%†	12.6%	14.5%**
Divorce rate (per 1,000 people)	3.5	3.5	4.6
Children born out of wedlock	3.9%	16.7%	31%***

*1940 figure.   †1949 figure.   **1994 figure.   ‡Estimate.   ***1993 figure.

Sources: U.S. Census Bureau, Dept. of Economic Analysis, Center for Health Statistics, Dept. of Education, Statistical Abstract, Bureau of Labor Statistics, The Air Transport Association.

nications. Whether or not the water you use as you brush your teeth contains fluoride is a state or local governmental issue. The federal Food and Drug Administration inspects your breakfast meat and sets standards for the advertising on your cereal box, orange juice carton, and other food packaging. And states also set standards for food labeling. Are they really "lite," "high in fiber," or "fresh squeezed"? Usually, one or more levels of government is authorized to decide these matters (see Highlight 1.3: How Does Government Affect Your Life?).

Highlight 1.3

How Does Government Affect Your Life?

Most of us take government, at all levels, for granted. But as federal government shutdowns and downsizing at all levels continues, and pet programs or projects are cut out or reduced, it's a good time to think about the diverse things government does. Is "less government" really better government?

Government sets the standard weights and measures that allow us to trade goods easily. Would you be assured of receiving three pounds of ground round if each farm and state computed "pound" differently? And what about a keg of beer? In colonial times the size of a "keg" varied by brewer and state. Now it is standardized by the government.

From cradle to grave, the government works to provide each of us with safety and security—from child-safety standards on cribs, infant car seats, bassinets, and toys to standards of care in nursing homes. The national government provides air traffic control and regulates the use of the skies as well as the public airwaves for radio and TV. The government licenses certain categories of workers who affect the "public health"—from beauticians and doctors to lawyers, teachers, and sheriffs protecting us from charlatans and fakers (at least to some extent!). Local governments issue zoning ordinances, which can prevent someone from putting a junk yard next to your home or an X-rated club next to an elementary school. They fund sidewalks, stop lights, crosswalks, and school crossing guards.

Local governments fluoridate water to prevent tooth decay. Governments inspect our food supplies and require safe handling of food from farms to restaurants. The federal government regulates food additives and standards, and periodically bans some considered harmful, like saccharin and red dye number 2. Federal regulators require food labeling so we can intelligently comparison shop to avoid fat grams and maximize nutritional value in our foods.

The government makes and enforces rules on compulsory education and provides funding and facilities for all levels of education. Government gets you to and from school on a bus. Colleges and universities, even private ones, receive huge amounts of federal funding through student aid programs, subsidies, research and development funding, and grants in aid. State universities would cost substantially more (as would private institutions) without large infusions of government monies.

One or more levels of government ensures job safety and maximum hours, and minimum wages, regulates benefits, provides income security and medical care in old age, and prevents child labor. The government sets and regulates the value of money and monitors commodities and stock exchanges.

Government provides water, sewer systems, garbage collections, recycling programs, highways and interstate roads. It provides mass transit to help you get to work and sets standards on car safety and emissions to make commuting safer and cleaner.

Government provides for the national defense by regulating customs and immigration, establishing borders and protecting them with military force. The Army, Navy, Air Force, and Marines, as well as the Coast Guard, are government agencies. Each of the branches of service has a college of its own, all funded by the government. ROTC is funded by the government. The GI Bill helps veterans go to college after military service. VA loans help them buy houses. Nonmilitary personnel also have government help in buying houses. The mortgage tax deduction is a large middle-class subsidy.

The federal government issues passports and provides embassies and consulates to aid you if you have trouble in a foreign country. It provides information on necessary inoculations and health hazards while traveling, as well as travel advisories regarding safety hazards such as wars, riots, and dangerous levels of pollutants in air and water.

Without government and its research and development funding, we would not have cellular telephones, satellite communications, the Internet, silicon chips (and thus computers), cable TV, fax machines, Velcro, freeze-dried foods, or four-wheel drive, to name just a few modern inventions we encounter in our daily lives.

In short, government affects our lives much more than we often think and in more ways than we often know. Are you so sure you want less?

Although all governments have problems, it is important to stress the good they can do. In the aftermath of the Great Depression in the United States, for example, the government created the Social Security program, which dramatically decreased poverty among the elderly. Our contract laws and judicial system provide an efficient framework for business, assuring people that they have a recourse in the courts should someone fail to deliver as promised. Government-guaranteed student loan programs make it possible for many students to attend college. And even something as seemingly mundane as our uniform bankruptcy laws help protect both a business enterprise and its creditors when the enterprise collapses.

In addition to having a better understanding and appreciation for what does go well, Americans often need to have a more accurate view of what is actually going on. As revealed in Highlight 1.4: Myths and Realities About America and Its Government, some of Americans' frustration and anger is based on misconceptions or just plain incorrect facts and figures. These misperceptions (and others) are problematic because decisions are driven by public perceptions in a democracy. If those perceptions turn out to be skewed, or even flat-out wrong, we can find ourselves squabbling over things that don't matter while ignoring things that do. Even worse, in trying to solve false problems, we may end up creating real ones.

The Effects of Frustration

Frustration with government has led to several strong trends in government and politics, many of which have been around since the nation's beginnings.

Returning Power to the States.   One outcome of this concern about government is a call to shift power away from the federal government back to the states. In 1964, just before President Lyndon B. Johnson's Great Society programs were launched, 35 percent of the American public believed that the federal government had the right amount of power; 31 percent thought it should use its powers more.[21] In 1995, 66 percent responded that local governments "should be more responsible for people's well being" and 75 percent favored the states taking over "more responsibilities now performed by the federal government." But this preference for more state power is not new—it's only billed as such by the media. Since poll taking began in 1936, with the exception of the New Deal and Great Society years, Americans have generally endorsed a broad state and local role.[22]

Electoral Changes.   Frustrations and disenchantment with politics have also led to electoral change. Americans are now more likely *not* to vote for an incumbent than ever before although incumbents still enjoy phenomenally high reelection rates. It's a "throw the bums out" mentality.

The idea of term limits is also symptomatic of voter frustration. The term-limits movement, which seeks to replace "professional politicians" with "citizen legislators" more closely in tune to their constituents, has gathered support over the past decade. In 1996, polls showed that 75 percent of Americans supported term limits.[23] Before that time many members of Congress, for example, were career legislators. Over one-half of the lawmakers in the 104th Congress were there two terms or less. Thus seniority rules that have operated in Congress no longer have as much sway, and freshmen Republicans in the 104th Congress were able to shut down the government. The effectiveness

Highlight 1.4

Myths and Realities About America and Its Government

Misperceptions drive policy decisions in almost every area of debate. It seems amazing that such fundamental misperceptions could thrive in this information age. But this is a media age as well, and the truth is that images and anecdotes often make a stronger impression than facts and figures. It's one thing to point out that the murder rate is roughly unchanged from twenty years ago; the nightly serving of blood and gore across the nation on the 6 o'clock news offers a more powerful, if less accurate, counterargument.

Our political leaders only compound the problem. They have concluded that the path to power lies in reinforcing our misperceptions rather than correcting them. That failure of leadership cannot help but have consequences. To borrow a central tenet of the information age, good data produces good deci-

sions, bad data produces bad decisions. Garbage in, garbage out! For example:

The perception: The federal government has spread like a cancer in the past twenty-five years, adding layers to its bureaucracy and uncounted thousands of employees to its payroll. It is sucking so much money out of the economy that it threatens to shut down productive economic growth.

The reality: In 1970 the federal government employed 2.99 million civilian workers; this year, the federal government employs 2.95 million civilian workers, 40,000 fewer than it did twenty-five years ago.

In 1970 the federal government employed 3.8 percent of all working Americans. Today it employs 2.4 percent of working Americans.

In 1980 the federal government spent 22.3 cents of every dollar generated by the economy. Fourteen years later, in 1994, the federal government was still spending 22.3 cents of every dollar generated by the economy.

The perception: The crime rate and murder rate are both soaring. This nation is no longer a safe place to raise children. Stern steps may be required to change that, including giving up some of the protections guaranteed by the Bill of Rights.

The reality: Crime is rising, but far more slowly than most people believe. In 1974, according to the FBI, 4.9 reported crimes were committed for every one hundred people. In 1993 that figure had risen to 5.5 crimes per hundred people. Over that same period, the chance of being murdered actually fell. In 1974, 9.95 murders were recorded for every 100,000 Americans. In 1993 the murder rate was 9.8 per 100,000, a small decrease.

The perception: Because of affirmative action, thousands of black Americans are being moved quickly into managerial and professional jobs, putting thousands of white employees on the streets.

The reality: Black Americans make up 12 percent of the population, but they

hold only 7.1 percent of managerial or professional jobs, up from 6.1 percent in 1989. That increase of one percentage point over a six-year period reflects slow, painful progress, and it does not begin to explain the economic insecurity of white Americans.

The perception: The federal deficit is largely the result of welfare. If we eliminated welfare fraud, we could eliminate most of the deficit. According to a poll taken earlier this year, Americans on average think welfare programs consume at least 20 percent to 30 percent of the federal budget. A substantial minority put the number even higher.

The reality: If you add up everything the federal government spends on housing assistance programs, food and nutrition programs such as food stamps, and income maintenance programs such as welfare and earned income tax credits for the working poor, it's less than 8 percent of the budget.

Source: "Bet You Didn't Know . . ." *The Atlanta Constitution* (October 22, 1995): B-6.

of the freshman Republicans in the 104th Congress may be viewed as a bad thing by some, but it may be just part of the political system's attempt to redefine itself as the United States undergoes many changes.

CHANGING AMERICA

politics: The process by which
policy decisions are made.

*J*ust as it is important to recognize that governments serve many important purposes, it is also important to recognize that government and **politics**—the process by which policy decisions are made—are not static. Politics, moreover, involves conflicts over different and sometimes opposing ideologies, and these ideologies are very much influenced by one's racial, economic, sexual, or historical experiences. These divisions are real and affect the political process at all levels. It is clear to most Americans today that politics and government no longer can be counted on to cure all of America's ills. Government, however, will always play a major role. True political leaders will need to help Americans come to terms with America as it is today—not as it was in the past—real or imaginary. Perhaps a discussion on how "community" is necessary for everybody to get along (and necessary for democracy) is in order. Some democratic theorists suggest that the citizen–activist must be ultimately responsible for the resolution of these divisions, and resolution of these divisions will require "leadership" from citizen–activists.

The current frustration and dissatisfaction about politics and government may be just another phase, as the changing American body politic seeks to redefine its ideas about government. This process is one that is likely to define politics into the millennium, but the individualistic nature of the American system will have long-lasting consequences on how it can be accomplished. Americans want less government; but as they get older, they don't want less Social Security. They want lower taxes and better roads, but they don't want to pay for toll roads. They want better education for their children but lower expenditures on schools. Some clearly want less for others but not themselves, which puts politicians in the position of nearly always disappointing voters. This inability to please voters and find a middle ground undoubtedly led to the unprecedented retirements in the House and Senate in 1994 and 1996.

Politicians, as well as their constituents, are looking for ways to redefine the role of government, much in the same way that the Framers did when they met in Philadelphia to forge a solution between Americans' quest for liberty and freedom tempered by order and governmental authority. While citizens charge that it is still government as usual, a change is taking place in Washington, D.C. The federal government, like most American organizations, is downsizing. Sacrosanct programs like Social Security and welfare are being reexamined, and power is slowly being returned to the states. Thus the times may be different, but the questions about government and its role in our lives remain the same.

Although the Civil War and other national crises, such as the Great Depression and even the Watergate scandal (see Chapter 8) created major turmoil, they demonstrated that our system can survive and even change in the face of enormous political, societal, and even institutional pressures. Often, these crises have produced considerable reforms. The Civil War led to the dismantling of the slavery system and to the passage of the Thirteenth, Fourteenth, and Fifteenth Amendments (see chapter 6), which led to the seeds of recognition of African Americans as American citizens. The Great Depression led to the New Deal and the creation of a government more actively involved in economic and social regulation. In the 1970s the Watergate scandal and resignation of President Richard M. Nixon resulted in stricter ethics laws that have led to the resignation or removal of many unethical elected officials.

Elections themselves, which often seem chaotic, help generation after generation remake the political landscape as new representatives seek to shake up the established order. Thus, while elections can seem like chaos, from this chaos comes order and often the explosive productivity of a democratic society.

As you make your way through the chapters in this book, remember that the ultimate force of all change in the United States, just as Alexander Hamilton and James Madison predicted, is the individual who goes to the polls and casts a ballot. We hope what you learn in this course will help you see the importance of your involvement (your *vote*) in the government. While you may think government is for the other person (the white person, the black person, the Hispanic person, the person on welfare, the person who wins big government contracts, the person whose wealth can buy influence and power . . .), the truth is that the government is for *you*. It can only represent you, however, if you take part in it by learning about the government and its policies, the issues facing you and the nation at large, and by voting.

Today governments at all levels are struggling to come to grips with the role they should play as the drama of the American political system continues to unfold. Just how the American political system has come to this point and where it is likely to go as it seeks to continue to be a partner with its citizenry in their pursuit of the American dream is the focus of this chapter and the remainder of this book. The study of American government is critical not only to its healthy functioning, but to your role in its functioning. As Americans seek to redefine their ideas about government, it is important for you to understand why Americans are dissatisfied today. To help you do this, we'll explore how some of our expectations about the role of government came about and how this crisis of confidence may play out as America continues to change in response to new challenges and opportunities.

In this text we present you with the tools you need to understand how our political system has evolved, and to prepare you to understand the changes that are yet to come. If you approach the study of American government and politics with an open mind, your study should help you become a better citizen. We hope that you learn to ask questions, to understand how various issues have come to be important, and to understand why a particular law was enacted and how it was implemented. With such understanding, we further hope you will learn not to accept at face value everything you see on the television news, hear on the radio, or read in the newspaper. Work to understand your government, and use your vote and other forms of participation to help ensure that your government works for you.

To understand our current system of government, it is important to understand choices that were made many years ago. It is also important to understand why so many Americans appear to be disgruntled about politics. Despite many of the problems discussed in this chapter and throughout the book, we think that politics remains "a good thing."

SUMMARY

In this chapter we have made the following points:

1. The Roots of American Government: Where Did the Ideas Come From?

The American political system was based on several notions that have their roots in classical Greek ideas, including natural law, the doctrine that human affairs should be governed by certain ethical principles that can be understood by reason. The ideas of social contract theorists John Locke and Thomas Hobbes, who held the belief that people are free and equal by God-given right, have continuing implications for our ideas of the proper role of government in our indirect democracy.

2. Characteristics of American Democracy.

Key characteristics of this democracy established by the Framers are popular consent, popular sovereignty, majority rule and the preservation of minority rights, equality, individualism, and personal liberty, as is the Framers' option for a capitalistic system.

3. Characteristics of the American People.

Several characteristics of the American electorate can help us understand how the system continues to evolve and change. Chief among these are changes in size and population, ideological beliefs, and composition of the political parties.

4. The Frustrated Public.

Americans are a frustrated lot due primarily to dissatisfaction with the economy and unrealistic expectations of government. In the past, each generation has turned over a better America to its children; but many today believe this is no longer the case. While there are many legitimate concerns about the economy, job security, and the role of government, it is important to remember that there are many things governments do well and many ways in which Americans are better off today than they were a few decades ago.

5. Changing America.

The political, economic, and social climate of the United States is constantly changing. The current negativity about politics is probably just another phase in the evolution of the political process. An understanding of the processes, institutions, and issues of the American government and political system will help us to meet the challenges that currently face the system.

KEY TERMS

aristocracy, p. 9
capitalism, p. 12
conservative, p. 24
democracy, p. 9
direct democracy, p. 10
free market economy, p. 12
indirect (representative) democracy, p. 10
liberal, p. 24
majority rule, p. 14
mercantile system, p. 12

monarchy, p. 9
natural law, p. 6
oligarchy, p. 9
personal liberty, p.16
political ideology, p. 23
politics, p. 34
popular consent, p. 14
popular sovereignty, p. 14
republic, p. 10
social contract theory, p. 6

SELECTED READINGS

Bentley, Arthur. *The Process of Government.* Chicago: University of Chicago Press, 1908.

Dahl, Robert A. *Polyarchy: Participation and Opposition.* New Haven, CT: Yale University Press, 1971.

Elshstain, Jean Bethke. *Democracy on Trial*. New York: Basic Books, 1995.

Glendon, Mary Ann. *Rights Talk: The Impoverishment of Political Discourse*. New York: Free Press, 1991.

Grossman, Lawrence K. *The Electronic Republic: Reshaping Democracy in the Information Age*. New York: Viking, 1995.

Higgs, Robert. *Crisis and Leviathan: Critical Episodes in the Growth of American Government*. New York: Oxford University Press, 1987.

Hobbes, Thomas. *Leviathan*. New York: Everyman (Library Edition), 1914.

Hunter, James Davison. *Culture Wars: The Struggle to Define America*. New York: Basic Books, 1991.

Jamieson, Kathleen Hall. *Dirty Politics: Deception, Distraction, and Democracy*. New York: Oxford University Press, 1992.

Locke, John. *Two Treatises of Government*, ed. Peter Lasleti. New York: Mentor, 1960.

Lynde, Robert S., and Helen Merrell Lynde. *Middletown: A Study in Contemporary American Culture*. New York: Harcourt, Brace, 1929.

Samuelson, Robert J. *The Good Life and Its Discontents: The American Dream in the Age of Entitlement 1945–1995*. New York: Times Books, 1995.

Skocpol, Theda. *Protecting Soldiers and Mothers: The Political Origins of Social Policy in the United States*. Cambridge: Harvard University Press, 1992.

Truman, David B. *The Governmental Process*. New York: Knopf, 1951.

(Photo courtesy: Leif Skoogfors/Woodfin Camp & Associates)

THE CONSTITUTION

$\mathcal{A}$sking Congress to vote for term limits, as Representative Bob Inglis (R–S.C.) once said, is a bit like asking the chicken to vote for Colonel Sanders.[1] And, in the aftermath of a 1995 U.S. Supreme Court decision, a vote from Congress for a constitutional amendment to limit congressional terms of office is in all likelihood the only way that formal term limits will ever be imposed on members of Congress.

The term-limits debate is as old as the U.S. Constitution. During that steamy summer in Philadelphia, the issue was hotly debated in the Constitutional Convention. Soon thereafter, when the Constitution was sent to the states for their ratification, Federalists and Anti-Federalists squared off as they debated the term limits issue in public. In *Federalist No. 72*, for example, Federalist Alexander Hamilton argued strenuously against term limits for the president, claiming that those not subject to reelection would have much "less zeal" in fulfilling the duties of their office. Similarly, in *Federalist Nos. 54* and *63*, James Madison stressed the need for some long-term members in both the House and the Senate, contending that too many new members would be bad and more likely "to fall into the snares" of misinformation or special interests.

On the other side of the term-limits debate were the anti-Federalists, who believed that government representatives needed to be close to the people and to mirror the citizenry as closely as possible. Thus, in arguing against even six-year terms for senators, "Brutus" (a pen name adopted by anti-Federalists) maintained that long terms would have a "tendency to wean (members) from their constituents," thus making them less likely to act in their best interests.

Over 200 years later, the term-limits movement exploded onto the public agenda. By the early 1990s, many voters were fed up with years of Democratic control of Congress; others were simply dissatisfied with gridlock and the special interest politics that appeared to permeate Capitol Hill. People wanted more from their elected representatives, and term limits appeared to be a way to get around the problem. The Republican Party tapped into this dissatisfaction, and during the 1994 congressional elections they made term limits one of the key elements in their Contract with America. By 1995, term-limits advocates had succeeded in placing the term-limits question on the public agenda and term-limits laws had been enacted in twenty-three states.[2] Said then-Representative and Speaker of the House for the 104th Congress Newt Gingrich—himself a ten-term member of the House—in explaining the Contract with America, "Isn't it time we sent the professional politicians a message—that politics shouldn't be a lifetime job?"[3]

Meanwhile, in Arkansas, site of a successful term-limits initiative, foes of term limits challenged their constitutionality in court. The Arkansas law, known as Amendment 23, banned incumbents from serving in the House of Representatives more than three terms (six years) or two terms (twelve years) in the Senate. Opponents of term limits argued that the most effective term limit was to vote someone out of office; good legislators should not be penalized for the misdeeds or misrepresentations of others. Furthermore, they argued, the Constitution itself did not allow states to change the qualifications of office for national legislators.

Toward the end of its 1994–95 term, the Supreme Court weighed in on the issue, agreeing with term-limits opponents in its decision in *U.S. Term Limits, Inc.* v. *Thornton*.[4] Writing for a slim five-member majority, Justice John Paul Stevens grounded the Court's decision on the belief in a distinct relationship between the federal government and its citizens—a relationship that cannot, according to the Court, be regulated by the states. But four justices strongly disputed the majority's interpretation of the Constitution and the Founders' intentions. They stated their belief that the qualifications clauses in the Constitution (which set basic age, citizenship, and residency requirements for members of Congress) were but a floor and not a ceiling concerning candidate requirements.

In ruling that term limits for members of Congress are unconstitutional, the Court sent the debate back to Congress, which (prior to the Court's decision) long had been unable to muster sufficient support to enact term-limits legislation or a constitutional amendment. Many critics charged that term limits looked much less desirable to Republicans now that they controlled Congress.

Undaunted by the Court's devastating decision, term-limits supporters are hoping that the cynicism of the American public will help their efforts. The head of a Massachusetts term-limits group called LIMITS, for example, said that she believes that the American public will quickly become dissatisfied with the GOP-controlled Congress if it fails to act on this issue. "Nothing has changed the frustration. I don't think people are totally convinced that there has been a permanent change. They are convinced, as I am, that those [newly elected] people will also get corrupted by the system."[5]

Is this activist right in her opinion about what "the people" believe? Most public opinion polls reveal that Americans generally support the notion of term limits. But as one political scientist notes, "For most Americans, it's way down on the list of our nation's problems."[6] "It may very well be that this issue has reached its peak and declined," predicted one Washington senator from a state where term limits had been invalidated by a federal judge.[7] In the wake of recent major turnovers in Congress, however, this question remains: Do Americans care enough about term limits to undertake the huge political effort of amending the Constitution? The Constitution was intentionally written to forestall the need for amendment, and the process by which it could be changed or amended was made intentionally time consuming and difficult. Over the years, thousands of amendments—including those to prohibit child labor, provide equal rights for women, grant statehood to the District of Columbia, and balance the budget—have been debated or sent to the states for their approval, only to die slow deaths. What the Framers came up with in Philadelphia has continued to work, in spite of continually increasing demands and dissatisfaction with our national government. Perhaps Americans are happier with the system of government created by the Framers than they realize.

The ideas that went into the making of the Constitution and how the Constitution has evolved to address the problems of a growing and ever-changing nation are at the core of our discussion in this chapter.

- First, we examine the *origins of the new nation* and the circumstances surrounding the break with Great Britain.
- Second, we discuss the *Declaration of Independence* and the ideas that lay at its core.
- Third, we discuss *the first American government* created by the *Articles of Confederation*.
- Fourth, we examine the circumstances surrounding the drafting of a *new Constitution* in Philadelphia.
- Fifth, we review the results of the Framer's efforts—The *U.S. Constitution*.
- Sixth, we present the *drive for ratification* of the new government.
- Seventh, we address the *process for amending the Constitution*.
- Finally, we explore the role of *judicial interpretation and cultural and technological change* in constitutional change.

THE ORIGINS OF A NEW NATION

Starting in the early seventeenth century, colonists came to the New World for a variety of reasons. Often it was to escape religious persecution. Others came seeking a new start on a continent where land was plentiful. The independence and diversity of the settlers in the New World made the question of how best to rule the new colonies a tricky one. More than merely an ocean separated England from the colonies; the colonists were independent people, and it soon became clear that the Crown could not govern the colonies with the same close rein used at home. King James I thus allowed some local participation in decision making through arrangements such as the first elected colonial assembly, the Virginia House of Burgesses, and the elected General Court that governed the Massachusetts Bay Company and that colony after 1629. Almost all the colonists agreed that the king ruled by divine right; but English monarchs allowed the colonists significant liberties in terms of self-government, religious practices, and economic organization. For 140 years, this system worked fairly well.[8]

By the early 1760s, however, a century and a half of physical separation, colonial development, and the relative self-governance of the colonies had led to weakening ties with—and loyalties to—the Crown. By this time, each of the thirteen colonies had drafted its own written constitution, which provided the fundamental rules or laws for each colony. Moreover, many of the most oppressive British traditions—feudalism, a rigid class system, and the absolute authority of church and king—were absent in the New World. Land was abundant. The restrictive guild and craft systems that severely limited entry into many skilled professions in England did not exist in the colonies. Although the role of religion was central to the lives of most colonists, there was no single state church, and the British practice of compulsory tithing (giving a fixed percentage of one's earnings to the state-sanctioned and -supported church) was nonexistent.

Trade and Taxation

Mercantilism, an economic theory based on the belief that a nation's wealth is measured by the amount of gold and silver in its treasury, justified Britain's maintenance of strict import/export controls on the colonies. After 1650, for example, Parliament passed a series of navigation acts to prevent its chief rival, Holland, from trading with the English colonies. From 1650 until well into the 1700s, England tried to regulate colonial imports and exports, believing that it was critical to export more goods than it imported as a way of increasing the gold and silver in its treasury. These policies, however, were difficult to enforce, and were widely ignored by the colonists, who saw little benefit for themselves in them. Thus, for years, an unwritten agreement existed. The colonists relinquished to the Crown and the British Parliament the authority to regulate trade and conduct international affairs, but they retained the right to levy their own taxes.

This fragile agreement was soon put to the test. The French and Indian War, fought from 1755 to 1760 on the "western frontier" of the colonies and in Canada, was part of a global war initiated by the British. The American phase of the Seven Years' War was fought between England and France with its Indian allies. In North America its immediate cause was the rival claims of those two European nations for the lands between the Allegheny Mountains and the Mississippi River. The Treaty of Paris (signed in 1763) signaled the end of the war. The colonists expected that with the "Indian problem" on the western frontier now "under control," westward migration and settlement could begin in earnest. They were shocked when the Crown decreed in 1763 that there was to be no further westward movement by British subjects. Parliament believed that expansion into Indian territory would lead to new expenditures for the defense of the settlers, draining the British treasury, which had yet to recover from the high cost of waging the war.

To raise money to pay for the war as well as the expenses of administering the colonies, Parliament enacted the Sugar Act in 1764, which placed taxes on sugar, wine, coffee, and other products commonly exported to the colonies. A postwar colonial depression heightened resentment of the tax. Around the colonies the political cry "No taxation without representation" was heard. Major protest, however, failed to materialize until imposition of the Stamp Act by the British Parliament in 1765. This law required the colonists to purchase stamps for all documents, including newspapers, magazines, and commercial papers. To add insult to injury, in 1765 Parliament passed the Mutiny or Quartering Act, which required the colonists to furnish barracks or provide living quarters within their own homes for British troops.

Most colonists, especially those in New England, where these acts hit hardest, were outraged. Men throughout the colonies organized the Sons of Liberty, under the leadership of Samuel Adams (see Roots of Government: Samuel Adams) and Patrick Henry. Whereas the Sugar Act was a tax on trade—still viewed as being within the legitimate authority of the Crown—the Stamp Act was a direct tax on many items not traditionally under the control of the king, and protests against it were violent and loud. Riots, often led by the Sons of Liberty, broke out. They were especially violent in Boston, where the colonial governor's home was burned by an angry mob, and British stamp agents charged with collecting the tax were threatened. A boycott of goods needing the stamps as well as British imports was also organized.

First Steps Toward Independence

In 1765 the colonists called for the **Stamp Act Congress,** the first official meeting of the colonies and the first step toward a unified nation. Nine of the thirteen colonies

Stamp Act Congress: Meeting of representatives of nine of the thirteen colonies held in New York City in 1765, during which representatives drafted a document to send to the king listing how their rights had been violated.

Roots of Government

Samuel Adams

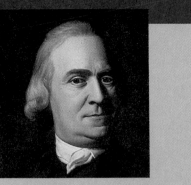

(Painting by John Singleton Copely. Deposited by the City of Boston. Courtesy: Museum of Fine Arts, Boston.)

Although Samuel Adams (1722–1803) today perhaps is known best for the beer that bears his name, his original claim to fame was as a leader against British and loyalist oppressors (although he did bankrupt his family's brewery business). A second cousin of President John Adams, Samuel Adams was a signer of the Declaration of Independence and a member of Massachusetts's constitutional convention that ratified the U.S. Constitution. He served as governor of Massachusetts from 1794 to 1797.

Adams was heavily influenced by John Locke's belief in man's natural right to be self-governing and free from taxation without representation. As a member of the Massachusetts legislature, he advocated defiance of the Stamp Act. With the passage of the Townshend Acts in 1767, he organized a letter-writing campaign urging other colonies to join in resistance. Later, in 1772, he founded the Committees of Correspondence to unite the colonies.

sent representatives to a meeting in New York City, where a detailed list of Crown violations of their fundamental rights was drawn up. Attendees defined what they thought to be the proper relationship between the various colonial governments and the British Parliament; they ardently believed that Parliament had no authority to tax them without colonial representation in the British Parliament. In contrast, the British believed that direct representation of the colonists was impractical and that members of Parliament represented the best interests of all the English, including the colonists.

The Stamp Act Congress and its petitions to the Crown did little to stop the onslaught of taxing measures. Parliament did, however, repeal the Stamp Act and revise the Sugar Act in 1766, largely because of the uproar made by British merchants who were losing large sums of money as a result of the boycotts. Rather than appeasing the colonists, however, these actions emboldened them to increase their resistance. In 1767 Parliament enacted the Townshend Acts, which imposed duties on all kinds of colonial imports, including tea. Response from the Sons of Liberty was immediate. Another boycott was announced, and almost all colonists gave up their favorite drink in a united show of resistance to the tax and British authority.[9] Tensions continued to run high, especially after the British sent 4,000 troops to Boston. On March 5, 1770, English troops opened fire on a mob that included disgruntled dock workers, whose jobs had been taken by British soldiers, and members of the Sons of Liberty who were taunting the soldiers in front of the Boston Customs House. Five colonists were killed in what became known as the "Boston Massacre." Following this confrontation, all duties except those on tea were lifted. The tea tax, however, continued to be a symbolic irritant. In

Committees of Correspondence: Organizations in each of the American colonies created to keep colonists abreast of developments with the British; served as powerful molders of public opinion against the British.

1772, at the suggestion of Samuel Adams, Boston and other towns around Massachusetts set up **Committees of Correspondence** to articulate ideas and keep communications open around the colony. By 1774 twelve colonies had formed committees to maintain a flow of information among like-minded colonists.

Meanwhile, despite dissent in England over the treatment of the colonies, Parliament passed another tea tax designed to shore up the sagging sales of the East India Company. The colonists' boycott had left that British trading house with more than 18 million pounds of tea in its warehouses. To rescue British merchants from disaster, in 1773 Parliament passed the Tea Act, granting a monopoly to the financially strapped East India Company to sell the tea imported from Britain. The company was allowed to funnel business to American merchants loyal to the Crown, thereby undercutting colonial merchants, who could sell only tea imported from other nations. The effect was to drive down the price of tea and to hurt colonial merchants, who were forced to buy tea at the higher prices from other sources.

When the next shipment of tea arrived in Boston from Great Britain, the colonists responded by throwing the Boston Tea Party. Similar "tea parties" were held in other colonies. When the news of these actions reached King George, he flew into a rage against the actions of his disloyal subjects. "The die is now cast," the king told his prime minister. "The colonies must either submit or triumph."

His first act was to persuade Parliament to pass the Coercive Acts in 1774. Known in the colonies as the Intolerable Acts, they contained a key provision calling for a total blockade of Boston Harbor until restitution was made for the tea. Another

Paul Revere's engraving of the Boston Massacre was a potent piece of political propaganda. Five men were killed, not seven, as the legend states, and the rioters in front of the State House (left) were scarcely as docile as Revere portrayed them. (Photo courtesy: The New York Historical Society)

provision reinforced the Quartering Act, giving royal governors the authority to quarter in the homes of private citizens the additional 4,000 British soldiers sent to patrol Boston.

The First Continental Congress

The British could never have guessed how the cumulative impact of these actions would unite the colonists. Samuel Adams's Committees of Correspondence spread the word, and food and money were sent to the people of Boston from all over the thirteen colonies. The tax itself was no longer the key issue; now the extent of British authority over the colonies was the far more important question. At the request of the colonial assemblies of Massachusetts and Virginia, all but one colonial assembly agreed to select a group of delegates to attend a continental congress authorized to communicate with the king on behalf of the now-united colonies.

The **First Continental Congress** met in Philadelphia from September 5 to October 26, 1774. It was made up of fifty-six delegates from every colony except Georgia. The colonists had yet to think of breaking with Great Britain; at this point they simply wanted to iron out their differences with the king. By October they had agreed on a series of resolutions to oppose the Coercive Acts and to establish a formal organization to boycott British goods. The Congress also drafted a Declaration of Rights and Resolves, which called for colonial rights of petition and assembly, trial by peers, freedom from a standing army, and the selection of representative councils to levy taxes. The Congress further agreed that if the king did not capitulate to their demands, they would meet again in Philadelphia in May 1775.

First Continental Congress: Meeting held in Philadelphia from September 5 to October 26, 1774, in which fifty-six delegates (from every colony except Georgia) adopted a resolution that opposed the Coercive Acts.

Second Continental Congress: Meeting that convened in Philadelphia on May 10, 1775, at which it was decided that an army should be raised and George Washington of Virginia was named commander-in-chief.

The Second Continental Congress

King George refused to yield, tensions continued to rise, and a **Second Continental Congress** was called. Before it could meet, fighting broke out early in the morning of April 19, 1775, at Lexington and Concord, Massachusetts, with what Ralph Waldo Emerson called "the shot heard round the world." Eight colonial soldiers, called Minutemen, were killed, and 16,000 British troops besieged Boston.

When the Second Continental Congress convened in Philadelphia on May 10, 1775, delegates were united by their increased hostility to Great Britain. The bloodshed at Lexington left no other course but war. To solidify colonial support, a Southerner was selected as the commander of the new Continental Army, since up to that date, British oppression had been felt most keenly in the Northeast. That task complete, the Congress then sent envoys to France to ask its assistance against France's perennial enemy. In a final attempt to avert conflict, the Second Continental Congress adopted the Olive Branch Petition on July 5, 1775, asking the king to end hostilities. King George rejected the petition and sent an additional 20,000 troops to quell the rebellion. The stage was set for war.

In January 1776, Thomas Paine, with the support and encouragement of Benjamin Franklin, issued (at first anonymously) *Common Sense,* a pamphlet forcefully arguing for independence from Great Britain. In frank, easy-to-understand language, Paine denounced the corrupt British monarchy and offered reasons for breaking with Great Britain. "The blood of the slain, the weeping voice of nature cries "'Tis Time to Part,'" wrote Paine. *Common Sense,* widely read throughout the colonies, was instrumental in changing minds in a very short time. In its first three months of publication, the forty-

After the success of *Common Sense,* Thomas Paine wrote a series of essays collectively entitled *The Crisis* to arouse colonists' support for the Revolutionary War. The first *Crisis* papers contain the famous words "These are the times that try men's souls." (Photo courtesy: Stock Montage, Inc.)

seven-page *Common Sense* sold 120,000 copies, the equivalent of approximately 18.75 million books today (given the U.S. population in 1995). One copy of *Common Sense* was in distribution for every thirteen people in the colonies—a truly astonishing number, given the low literacy rate.

THE DECLARATION OF INDEPENDENCE

*C*ommon Sense galvanized the American public against reconciliation with England. As the mood in the colonies changed, so did that of the Second Continental Congress. On May 15, 1776, Virginia became the first colony to call for independence, instructing one of its delegates to the Second Continental Congress to introduce a resolution to that effect. On June 7, 1776, Richard Henry Lee of Virginia rose to move "that these United Colonies are, and of right ought to be, free and independent States, and that all connection between them and the State of Great Britain is, and ought to be, dissolved." His three-part resolution—which called for independence, the formation of foreign alliances, and preparation of a plan of **confederation**—triggered hot debate among the delegates. A proclamation of independence from Great Britain was treason, a crime punishable by death. Although six of the thirteen colonies had already instructed their delegates to vote for independence, the Second Continental Congress was suspended to allow its delegates to return home to their respective colonial legislatures for final instructions. Independence was not a move to be taken lightly.

At the same time, committees were set up to consider each point of Lee's proposal. A committee of five was selected to begin work on a **Declaration of Independence.** The Congress selected Benjamin Franklin, John Adams, Robert Livingston, and Roger Sherman as members. Adams lobbied hard for a Southerner to add balance. Thus, owing to his Southern origin as well as his "peculiar felicity of expression," Thomas Jefferson was selected as chair.

On July 2 twelve of the thirteen colonies (with New York abstaining) voted for independence. Two days later the Second Continental Congress voted to adopt the Declaration of Independence penned by Thomas Jefferson. On July 9 the Declaration, now with the approval of New York, was read aloud in Philadelphia.[10]

confederation: Type of government in which the national government derives its powers from the states; a league of independent states.

Declaration of Independence: Document drafted by Thomas Jefferson in 1776 that proclaimed the right of the American colonies to separate from Great Britain.

A Theoretical Basis for a New Government

In simple but eloquent language, Jefferson set out the reasons for the colonies' separation from Great Britain. Most of his stirring rhetoric drew heavily on the works of seventeenth- and eighteenth-century political philosophers, particularly the English John Locke (see Roots of Government: Locke and Hobbes in Chapter 1), who had written South Carolina's first Constitution, a colonial charter drawn up in 1663 when South Carolina was formed by King Charles II and mercantile houses in England. In fact, many of the words in the opening words of the Declaration of Independence closely resemble passages from Locke's *Two Treatises of Government.*

Locke was a proponent of *social contract theory,* a philosophy of government that held that governments exist based on the consent of the governed. According to Locke, people leave the state of nature and agree to set up a government largely for the protection of property. In colonial times "property" did not mean just land. Locke's notion of property rights included life, liberty, and material possessions. Furthermore, argued Locke, individuals who give their consent to be governed have the right to resist or remove rulers who deviate from those purposes. Such a government exists for the good of its subjects and not for the benefit of those who govern. Thus rebellion was the ultimate sanction against a government that violated the rights of its citizens.

It is easy to see the colonists' debt to John Locke. In ringing language the Declaration of Independence proclaims:

> We hold these truths to be self-evident, that all men are created equal, that they are endowed by their Creator with certain unalienable Rights, that among these are Life, Liberty and the pursuit of Happiness.

Jefferson and others in attendance at the Second Continental Congress wanted to have a document that would stand for all time, justifying their break with the Crown and clarifying their notions of the proper form of government. So, Jefferson continued:

> That to secure these rights, Governments are instituted among Men, deriving their just powers from the consent of the governed. That whenever any Form of Government becomes destructive of these ends, it is the Right of the People to alter or abolish it, and to institute new Government, laying its foundation on such Principles and organizing its Powers in such form, as to them shall seem most likely to effect their Safety and Happiness.

After this stirring preamble, the Declaration went on to enumerate the wrongs that the colonists had suffered under British rule. All pertained to the denial of personal rights and liberties, many of which would later be guaranteed by the U.S. Constitution through the Bill of Rights.

After the Declaration was signed and transmitted to the king, the Revolutionary War was fought with a greater vengeance. At a September 1776 peace conference on Staten Island (New York), British General William Howe demanded revocation of the Declaration of Independence. The Americans refused, and the war raged on while the Congress attempted to fashion a new united government.

American Renaissance man Thomas Jefferson (1743-1826)–author of the Declaration of Independence and the third president of the United States–voiced the aspirations of a new America as no other individual of his era. As public official, historian, philosopher, and plantation owner, he served his country for over five decades and died at his home at Monticello on the Fourth of July. (Photo courtesy: The Bettmann Archive)

THE FIRST ATTEMPT AT GOVERNMENT: THE ARTICLES OF CONFEDERATION

*A*s noted earlier, the British had no written constitution. The colonists in the Second Continental Congress were attempting to codify arrangements that had never before been put into legal terminology. To make things more complicated, the delegates had to arrive at these decisions in a wartime atmosphere. Nevertheless, in late 1779 the **Articles of Confederation,** creating a loose "league of friendship" between the sovereign or independent states, were passed by the Congress and presented to the states for their ratification.

The Articles created a type of government called a confederation or confederacy. Unlike the unitary system of government in England, wherein all of the powers of the government reside in the national government, the national government in a confederation derives all of its powers directly from the states. Thus the national government in a confederacy is weaker than the sum of its parts, and the states often consider themselves independent states linked together only for limited purposes

Articles of Confederation: The compact among the thirteen original states that was the basis of their government. Written in 1776, the Articles were not ratified by all the states until 1781.

such as national defense. Key provisions in the Articles that created the confederacy included:

- A national government with a Congress empowered to make peace, coin money, appoint officers for an army, control the post office, and negotiate with Indian tribes.

- Each state's retention of its independence and sovereignty, or ultimate authority to govern within its territories.

- One vote in the Continental Congress for each state, regardless of size.

- The vote of nine states to pass any measure (a unanimous vote for any amendment).

- The selection and payment of delegates to the Congress by their respective state legislatures.

Thus the Articles—finally ratified by all thirteen states in 1781—fashioned a government well reflective of the political philosophy of the times.[11] Although it had its flaws, the government under the Articles of Confederation saw the nation through the Revolutionary War. However, once the British surrendered in 1782 and the new nation found itself no longer united by the war effort, the government quickly fell into chaos.

Problems Under the Articles of Confederation

In today's America we ship goods, travel by car and airplane across state lines, make interstate phone calls, and more. Nearly 255 years ago, Americans had great loyalties to their states and often did not even think of themselves as Americans. This lack of national sentiment or loyalty in the absence of a war to unite the citizenry fostered a reluctance to give any power to the national government. Thus, by 1784, just one year after the Revolutionary army was disbanded, governing the new nation under the Articles of Confederation proved unworkable.[12] Congress could rarely assemble the required quorum of nine states to conduct business. Even when it could, there was little agreement among the states. To raise revenue to pay off war debts and run the government, various land, poll, and liquor taxes were proposed. But since Congress had no specific power to tax, all these proposals were rejected. At one point Congress was even driven out of Philadelphia (then the capital) by its own unpaid army.

Although the national government could coin money, it had no resources to back up the value of its currency. Continental dollars were worth little, and trade between states became chaotic as some states began to coin their own money. Another weakness of the Articles was their failure to allow Congress to regulate commerce among the states and with foreign nations. As a result individual states attempted to enter into agreements with other countries, and foreign nations were suspicious of trade agreements made with the United States. In 1785, for example, Massachusetts banned the export of goods in British ships, and Pennsylvania levied heavy duties on ships of nations that did not have a treaty with the U.S. government.

Fearful of a chief executive who would rule tyrannically, moreover, the draftees of the Articles had made no provision for an executive branch of government that would be responsible for executing, or implementing, laws passed by the legislative branch. Instead, the "president" was merely the presiding officer at meetings. John Hanson, a former member of the Maryland House of Delegates and of the First Continental Congress, was the first person to preside over the Congress of the Confederation, as the new government under the Articles was called. Therefore he is often referred to as the first President of the United States.

In addition, the Articles of Confederation had no provision for a judicial system to handle the growing number of economic conflicts and boundary disputes among the individual states. Several states claimed the same lands to the west; Pennsylvania and Virginia went to war with each other; Vermont threatened to annex itself to Canada.

The Articles' greatest weakness, however, was their lack of creation of a strong central government. While states had operated independently before the war, during the war they acceded to the national government's authority to wage armed conflict. Once the war was over, however, each state resumed its sovereign status, and was unwilling to give up rights, such as the power to tax, to an untested national government. Consequently, the government was unable to force the states to abide by the provisions of the Treaty of Paris, signed in 1783, which had officially ended the war. For example, states passed laws to stay the bills of debtors who owed money to Great Britain. They also failed to restore property to many who had remained loyal to Britain during the war. Both actions were in violation of the treaty.

The crumbling economy and a series of bad harvests that failed to produce cash crops, making it difficult for farmers to get out of debt quickly, took their toll on the new nation. George Washington and Alexander Hamilton, both interested in the questions of trade and frontier expansion, soon saw the need for a stronger national government with the authority to act to solve some of these problems. They were not alone. In 1785 and 1786, some state governments began to discuss ways to strengthen the national government. Finally, several states joined together to call for a convention in Philadelphia in 1787.

With Daniel Shays in the lead, a group of farmers and Revolutionary War veterans marched on the courthouse in Springfield, Massachusetts, to prevent foreclosure on their mortgages. (Photo courtesy: The Bettmann Archive)

Before that meeting could take place, however, new unrest broke out in America. In 1780 Massachusetts adopted a state constitution that appeared to favor the interests of the wealthy. Property-owning requirements barred the lower and middle classes from voting and office holding. And, as the economy of Massachusetts worsened, banks foreclosed on farms to pay off debts to Massachusetts Continental Army veterans who were waiting for promised bonuses. The last straw came in 1786, when the Massachusetts legislature enacted a new law requiring the payment of all debts in cash. Frustration and outrage at the new law caused Daniel Shays, a former Revolutionary War army captain, and 1,500 armed, disgruntled, and angry farmers to march to Springfield. This group forcibly restrained the state court from foreclosing on mortgages on their farms.

The Congress immediately authorized the Secretary of War to call for a new national militia. A $530,000 appropriation was made for this purpose, but every state except Virginia refused the Congress's request for money. The governor of Massachusetts then tried to raise a state militia, but because of the poor economy, funds were unavailable in the state treasury. Frantic attempts at private support were made, and a militia was finally assembled. By February 4, 1787, this privately paid force put a stop to what was called **Shays's Rebellion.** The failure of the Congress to muster an army to put down the rebellion was yet another example of the weaknesses inherent in the Articles of Confederation.

Shays's Rebellion: A 1786 rebellion in which an army of 1,500 disgruntled and angry farmers led by Daniel Shays marched to Springfield, Massachusetts, and forcibly restrained the state court from foreclosing on their farms.

THE MIRACLE AT PHILADELPHIA: WRITING A CONSTITUTION

On February 21, 1787—in the throes of economic turmoil and with domestic tranquility gone haywire—the Congress passed an official resolution. It called for a Constitutional Convention in Philadelphia for "the sole and express purpose of revising the Articles of Confederation." All states but Rhode Island sent delegates.

Twenty-nine individuals met in sweltering Philadelphia on May 14. Many at that initial meeting were intellectuals, others were shrewd farmers or businessmen, and still others were astute politicians. All recognized that what they were doing could be considered treasonous. Revising the Articles of Confederation was one thing; to call for an entirely new government, as suggested by the Virginia delegation, was another. So they took their work quite seriously, even to the point of adopting a pledge of secrecy. George Washington, who was unanimously elected the convention's presiding officer, warned:

> Nothing spoken or written can be revealed to anyone—not even your family—until we have adjourned permanently. Gossip or misunderstanding can easily ruin all the hard work we shall have to do this summer.[13]

So concerned about leaks were those in attendance that the delegates agreed to accompany Benjamin Franklin to all of his meals. They feared that the normally gregarious gentleman might get carried away with the mood or by liquor and inadvertently let news of the proceedings slip from his tongue.

The Framers

Fifty-five out of the seventy-four delegates ultimately chosen by their state legislatures to attend the Constitutional Convention labored long and hard that hot summer behind closed doors in Philadelphia. All of them were men; hence they are often referred to as the "Founding Fathers." Most of them, however, were quite young; many were in their twenties and thirties, and only one—Benjamin Franklin, at eighty-one—was very old. Here we generally refer to those delegates as Framers because their work provided the framework for our new government. The Framers brought with them a vast amount of political, educational, legal, and business experience. Eight had signed the Declaration of Independence, thirty-nine had attended at least one Continental Congress, and seven were former governors. One-third were college graduates, and thirty-four were lawyers. Notably absent were individuals like Patrick Henry, who had proclaimed in the Virginia House of Burgesses before the Revolutionary War, "Give me liberty or give me death!" Now he stayed away because he "smelt a rat," fearing that the states could lose their powers. Also missing were Thomas Jefferson, author of the Declaration of Independence, and John Adams. Both were on ambassadorial stays in Europe. Although some scholarly debate continues concerning the motives of the Framers for shaping the new national government (see Highlight 2.1: The Motives of the Framers), it is clear that they were an exceptional lot who ultimately produced a brilliant document reflecting the best efforts of all present.

The Virginia and New Jersey Plans

The less populous states were concerned with being lost in any new system of government where states were not treated as equals regardless of population. Thus it is not surprising that a large state and then a small one, Virginia and New Jersey, respectively weighed in with ideas about how the new government should operate.

Virginia Plan: The first general plan for the Constitution, proposed by James Madison. Its key points were a bicameral legislature, an executive chosen by the legislature, and a judiciary also named by the legislature.

The Virginia Plan.   The **Virginia Plan** called for a national system with a powerful central government. It was based heavily on the European nation–state model, wherein the national government derives its powers from the people and not from the member states. The preamble of what is commonly referred to as the Virginia Plan proposed that "a national government ought to be established, consisting of a supreme Legisla-

Highlight 2.1

The Motives of the Framers

Debate about the Framers' motives filled the air during the ratification struggle and has provided grist for the mill of historians and political scientists over the years. Anti-Federalists, who opposed the new Constitution, charged that Federalist supporters of the Constitution were a self-serving, landed, and propertied elite with a vested interest in the capitalistic system that had evolved in the colonies. Federalists countered that they were simply trying to preserve the nation.

In his *Economic Interpretation of the Constitution of* *the United States* (1913), the highly respected political scientist and historian Charles A. Beard argued that the 1780s were a "critical period" (as the time under governance by the Articles of Confederation had come to be known) not for the nation as a whole, but rather for businessmen. These men feared that a weak, decentralized government could harm their economic interests. Beard argued that the merchants wanted a strong national government to promote industry and trade, protect private property, and most importantly, ensure payment of the public debt— much of which was owed to them. Therefore, according to Beard, the Constitution represents "an economic document drawn with superb skill by men whose property interests were immediately at stake."*

By the 1950s this view had fallen into disfavor when other historians were unable to find direct links between wealth and the Framers' motives for establishing the Constitution. In the 1960s, however, another group of historians began to argue that social and economic factors were, in fact, important motives for supporting the Constitution. In *The Anti-Federalists* (1961), Jackson Turner Main posited that while the Constitution's supporters might not have been the united group of creditors suggested by Beard, they were wealthier, came from high social strata, and had greater concern for maintaining the prevailing social order than the general public.

In 1969, Gordon S. Wood's *The Creation of the American Republic* resurrected this debate. Wood deemphasized economics to argue that major social divisions explained different groups' support for (or opposition to) the new Constitution. He concluded that the Framers were representatives of a class that favored order and stability over some of the more radical ideas that had inspired the Revolution.

*Quoted in Richard N. Current, *et al.*, *American History: A Survey*, 6th ed. (New York: Knopf, 1983), 170.

---

tive, Executive and Judiciary." The Virginia Plan contained several key elements that shaped the new government and its final structure including a national government with separate legislative, executive, and judicial branches of government and a national legislature with two parts, or houses—one house elected directly by the people; the other house chosen from among persons nominated by the state legislatures.

The Virginia Plan, the first structural aspect of the new government that the Framers agreed on, included a bicameral legislature, that is, one with two distinct bodies. When Thomas Jefferson returned from Paris, he asked Washington why the delegates had agreed to a two-house legislature. "Why do you pour coffee into your saucer?" asked Washington. "To cool it," responded Jefferson. "So," continued Washington, "we pour legislation into the senatorial saucer to cool it."[14]

Delegates initially appeared far from agreement over how members of each house of Congress were to be selected. Many of them appeared set against direct election of members of one house. Many who held to that view feared the idea of democracy. Their elitist views led them to believe that not "all the people" were fit to make decisions concerning the government. They feared the kinds of uprisings that Daniel Shays's actions had typified. On the other side, Madison and other supporters of a strong central government, while still fearful of a "mobocracy," continued to insist on direct election of some representatives. They reasoned that without the confidence of the people, government could not long exist.

The New Jersey Plan.   In contrast to those favoring a strong national government, several smaller states felt comfortable with the arrangements under the Articles of Confederation. They favored a looser confederation of states, in which powers could be shared between the national and state governments. These states offered another model of government, the **New Jersey Plan.**

The New Jersey Plan suggested that the Articles, instead of being replaced, only be strengthened. It called for a one-house legislature with one vote for each state with representatives chosen by state legislatures. The Congress would have the power to raise revenue from duties and a post office. All other funds had to be requested from the states.

New Jersey Plan: A framework for the Constitution proposed by a group of small states; its key points were a one-house legislature with one vote for each state, a multiperson "executive," the establishment of the acts of Congress as the "supreme law" of the land, and a supreme judiciary with limited power.

The Great Compromise

The most serious disagreement between the Virginia and New Jersey plans concerned representation in Congress. When a deadlock on this point loomed, Connecticut offered its own compromise. Each state would have an equal vote in the Senate. Again, there was a stalemate. As Benjamin Franklin put it,

> The diversity of opinions turns on two points. If a proportional representation takes place, the small states contend that their liberties will be in danger. If an equality of votes is to be put in its place, large states say that their money will be in danger.

He continued:

> When a broad table is to be made and the edges of a plank do not fit, the artist takes a little from both sides and makes a good joint. In like manner, both sides must part with some of their demands, in order that they both join in some accommodating position.[15]

A committee to work out an agreement soon reported back what became known as the **Great Compromise.** Taking ideas from both the Virginia and New Jersey plans, it recommended:

Great Compromise: A decision made during the Philadelphia Convention to give each state the same number of representatives in the Senate regardless of size; representation in the House was determined by population.

1. In one house of the legislature (later called the House of Representatives), there should be fifty-six representatives—one representative for every 40,000 inhabitants.

2. That house should have the power to originate all bills for raising and spending money.

3. In the second house of the legislature (later called the Senate), each state should have an equal vote, and representatives would be selected by the state legislatures.[16]

Still, a sticking point remained about how to determine state population. Slaves could not vote, but the Southern states wanted them included for purposes of determining population.

After considerable dissension, it was decided that population would be calculated by adding the "whole Number of Free Persons" to "three fifths of all other Persons."

"All other Persons" was the delegates' "tactful" way of referring to slaves. Known as the **Three-Fifths Compromise,** this formula was based on the prevailing assumption that slaves were only three-fifths as productive as white men.[17]

The Great Compromise ultimately met with the approval of all states in attendance. The smaller states were pleased because they got equal representation in the Senate; the larger states were satisfied with the proportional representation in the House of Representatives. The small states then would dominate the Senate while the large states, such as Virginia and New York, would control the House. But because both houses had to pass any legislation, neither body could dominate the other.

Compromise on the Presidency

With passage of the Great Compromise, agreement was reached on most of the new Constitution's basic principles. Still to be included, however, were provisions for an executive branch and a president. By August, the Framers had agreed on the idea of a one-person executive, but they could not settle on the length of the term of office, nor on how the chief executive should be selected. With Shays's Rebellion still fresh in their minds, the delegates feared putting too much power, including selection of a president, into the hands of the lower classes. At the same time, representatives from the smaller states feared that the selection of the chief executive by the legislature would put additional power into the hands of the large states.

Amid these fears the Committee on Unfinished Portions, whose sole responsibility was to iron out problems and disagreements concerning the office of chief executive, conducted its work. The committee recommended that the presidential term of office be fixed at four years instead of seven, as had earlier been proposed. By choosing not to mention a period of time within which the chief executive would be eligible for reelection, they made it possible for a president to serve more than one term. The president was to be chosen by electors. And, for the first time, the post of vice president was mentioned.

Rules for Electing and Removing the President

Two matters concerning the presidency remained to be resolved: selection and removal. The response was guidelines for the electoral college, and impeachment.

The Electoral College. In setting up a system for electing the president, the Framers put in place an electoral college (see chapter 13). The electoral college system gave individual states a key role, because each state would select electors equal to the number of representatives it had in the House and Senate. It was a vague compromise that removed election of the president and vice president from both the Congress and the people and put it in the hands of electors whose method of selection would be left to the states.

The delegates were quite happy with this compromise and believed that it would be acceptable to all sides. The smaller states thought they would have an equal voice should the election be forced into the House of Representatives, and the larger states believed they had a good opportunity to elect a president before this contingency would occur.

Removing a President. One more matter concerning the president remained, however. Still fearful of a leader who might turn out to resemble a British monarch, the

Three-Fifths Compromise: Agreement reached at the Constitutional Convention stipulating that each slave was to be counted as three-fifths of a person for purposes of determining population for representation in the U.S. House of Representatives.

Framers were careful to include a provision for removal of the chief executive. They proposed that both the legislative and the judicial branches be involved in the impeachment process. The House of Representatives was given the sole responsibility of investigating and charging a president or vice president with "Treason, Bribery, or other high Crimes and Misdemeanors." A majority vote would then result in issuing Articles of Impeachment against the president. In turn, the Senate was given sole responsibility to try the chief executive on the charges issued by the House. A two-thirds vote of the Senate was required to convict and remove the president from office. The Chief Justice of the United States was to preside over the Senate proceedings in place of the vice president (that body's usual leader) in order to prevent any appearance of impropriety on the vice president's part.

THE U.S. CONSTITUTION

After the compromise on the presidency, work proceeded quickly on the remaining resolutions of the Constitution. The Preamble to the Constitution, the last section to be drafted, contains exceptionally powerful language that forms the bedrock of American political tradition. Its opening line, "We the People of the United States," boldly proclaimed that a loose confederation of independent states no longer existed. Instead, there was but one American people and nation. The original version of the Preamble opened with:

> We the people of the States of New Hampshire, Massachusetts, Rhode Island and the Providence Plantations, Connecticut, New Jersey, New York, Pennsylvania, Delaware, Maryland, Virginia, North Carolina, South Carolina and Georgia, do ordain, declare and establish the following Constitution for the government of ourselves and our Posterity.

The simple phrase "We the people" ended, at least for the time being, the question of whence the government derived its power: It came directly from the people, not from the states. The next phrase of the Constitution explained the need for the new outline of government. "[I]n Order to form a more perfect Union" indirectly acknowledged the weaknesses of the Articles of Confederation in governing a growing nation. Next, the optimistic goals of the Framers for the new nation were set out: to "establish Justice, insure domestic Tranquility, provide for the common defense, promote the general Welfare, and secure the Blessings of Liberty to ourselves and our Posterity"; followed by the formal creation of a new government: "do ordain and establish this Constitution for the United States of America."

On September 17, 1787, the Constitution was approved by the delegates from all twelve states in attendance. While the completed document did not satisfy all the delegates, of the forty-one in attendance, thirty-nine ultimately signed it. The sentiments uttered by Benjamin Franklin probably well reflected those of many others: "Thus, I consent, Sir, to this Constitution because I expect no better, and because I am not sure that it is not the best."[18]

The Basic Principles of the Constitution

The ideas of political philosophers, especially the French Baron de la Brède et de Montesquieu (1689–1755) and the English John Locke (see Roots of Government:

The shootout at Ruby Ridge, the bombing of the federal building in Oklahoma City, and groups like the Freemen in Montana or "We the People" in Colorado, who believe that all forms of government, taxes, and licensing are illegal, provide an extreme example of the debate over the role of the federal government in the lives of American citizens, as well as in its control over the states. Here, a makeshift roadblock set up by the Freemen forewarns those who would trespass on "Justus township." (Photo courtesy: A. Lichtenstein/The Image Works)

Locke and Hobbes in Chapter 1), heavily influenced the shape and nature of the government proposed by the Framers. Montesquieu, who actually drew many of his ideas about government from the works of Greek political philosopher Aristotle, was heavily quoted during the Constitutional Convention.

The proposed structure of the new national government owed much to the writings of Montesquieu, who advocated distinct functions for each branch of government, called **separation of powers,** with a system of **checks and balances** between each branch. The Constitution's concern with the distribution of power between states and the national government also reveals the heavy influence of political philosophers, as well as the colonists' experience under the Articles of Confederation.[19]

Federalism.   Today, in spite of current calls for the national government to return power to the states, the question before and during the Convention was how much power states would give up to the national government. Given the nation's experiences under the Articles of Confederation, the Framers believed that a strong national government was necessary for the new nation's survival. However, they were reluctant to create a powerful government after the model of Britain, the country from which they had just won their independence. Its unitary system was not even considered by the colonists. Instead, they fashioned a system now known as the **federal system,** which divides the power of government between a strong national government and the individual states. This system, as the Court reaffirmed in 1995 in considering term limits, was based on the principle that the federal, or national, government derived its power from the citizens, not the states, as the national government had done under the Articles of Confederation.

Opponents of this system feared that a strong national government would infringe on their liberty. But James Madison argued that a strong national government with distinct state governments could, if properly directed by constitutional arrangements, actually be a source of expanded liberties and national unity. The Framers viewed the

separation of powers: A way of dividing power among three branches of government in which members of the House of Representatives, members of the Senate, the president, and the federal courts are selected by and responsible to different constituencies.

checks and balances: A governmental structure that gives each of the three branches of government some degree of oversight and control over the actions of the others.

federal system: Plan of government created in the U.S. Constitution in which power is divided between the national government and the state governments and in which independent states are bound together under one national government.

division of governmental authority between the national government and the states as a means of checking power with power, and providing the people with "double security" against governmental tyranny. Later, the passage of the Tenth Amendment, which stated that powers not given to the national government were reserved by the states or the people, further clarified the federal structure (see chapter 3).

Separation of Powers. Madison and many of the Framers clearly feared putting too much power into the hands of any one individual or branch of government. His famous words, "Ambition must be made to counteract ambition," were widely believed at the Philadelphia convention.

Separation of powers is simply a way of parceling out power among the three branches of government. It has three key features:

1. Three distinct branches of government: the legislative, the executive, and the judicial.
2. Three separately staffed branches of government to exercise these functions.
3. Constitutional equality and independence of each branch.

As illustrated in Figure 2.1, the Framers were careful to create a system in which lawmaking, law-enforcing, and law-interpreting functions were assigned to independent branches of government. On the national level (and in most states), only the legislature has the authority to make laws; the chief executive enforces laws, and the judiciary interprets them. Moreover, members of the House of Representatives, members of the Senate, the president, and members of the federal courts are selected by and are therefore responsible to different constituencies. Madison believed that the scheme devised by the Framers would divide the offices of the new government and their methods of selection among many individuals, providing each office holder with the "necessary means and personal motives to resist encroachment" on his or her power.

The Framers could not have foreseen the intermingling of governmental functions that has since evolved. Locke, in fact, cautioned against giving a legislature the ability to delegate its powers. In Article I of the Constitution, the legislative power is vested in the Congress. But the president is also given legislative powers via his ability to veto legislation, although his veto can be overridden by a two-thirds vote in Congress. Judicial interpretation then helps to clarify the implementation of legislation enacted through this process.

So instead of a pure system of separation of powers, a symbiotic, or interdependent, relationship among the three branches of government has existed from the beginning. Or, as one scholar has explained, there are "separated institutions sharing powers."[20] While Congress is still entrusted with making the laws, most proposals for legislation originate with the president. And although the Supreme Court's major function is to interpret the law, its involvement in areas such as criminal procedure, abortion, and other fields has led many to charge that it has surpassed its constitutional authority and become a law-making body.

Separation of Power and Checks and Balances. The separation of powers among the three branches of the national government is not complete. According to Montesquieu and the Framers, the powers of each branch (as well as the two houses of the national legislature and between the states and the national government) could be used to check the powers of the other two branches of government. This principle, called checks and balances,[21] is illustrated in Figure 2.1. The power of each branch of government is checked, or limited, and balanced because the legislative, executive, and judicial

FIGURE 2.1

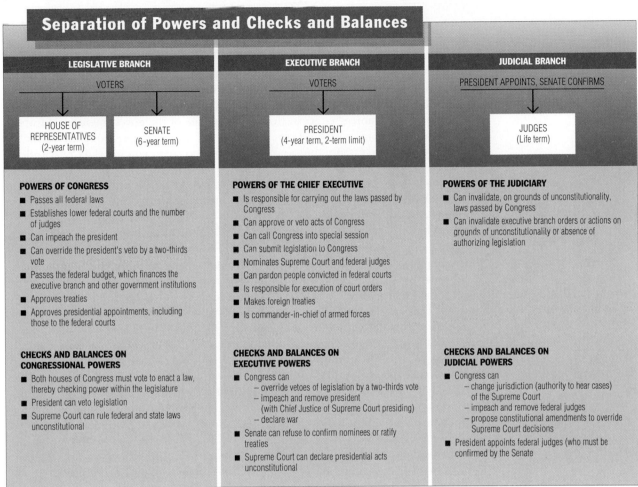

Separation of Powers and Checks and Balances

LEGISLATIVE BRANCH	EXECUTIVE BRANCH	JUDICIAL BRANCH
VOTERS	VOTERS	PRESIDENT APPOINTS, SENATE CONFIRMS
HOUSE OF REPRESENTATIVES (2-year term) — SENATE (6-year term)	PRESIDENT (4-year term, 2-term limit)	JUDGES (Life term)

POWERS OF CONGRESS

- Passes all federal laws
- Establishes lower federal courts and the number of judges
- Can impeach the president
- Can override the president's veto by a two-thirds vote
- Passes the federal budget, which finances the executive branch and other government institutions
- Approves treaties
- Approves presidential appointments, including those to the federal courts

POWERS OF THE CHIEF EXECUTIVE

- Is responsible for carrying out the laws passed by Congress
- Can approve or veto acts of Congress
- Can call Congress into special session
- Can submit legislation to Congress
- Nominates Supreme Court and federal judges
- Can pardon people convicted in federal courts
- Is responsible for execution of court orders
- Makes foreign treaties
- Is commander-in-chief of armed forces

POWERS OF THE JUDICIARY

- Can invalidate, on grounds of unconstitutionality, laws passed by Congress
- Can invalidate executive branch orders or actions on grounds of unconstitutionality or absence of authorizing legislation

CHECKS AND BALANCES ON CONGRESSIONAL POWERS

- Both houses of Congress must vote to enact a law, thereby checking power within the legislature
- President can veto legislation
- Supreme Court can rule federal and state laws unconstitutional

CHECKS AND BALANCES ON EXECUTIVE POWERS

- Congress can
  - override vetoes of legislation by a two-thirds vote
  - impeach and remove president (with Chief Justice of Supreme Court presiding)
  - declare war
- Senate can refuse to confirm nominees or ratify treaties
- Supreme Court can declare presidential acts unconstitutional

CHECKS AND BALANCES ON JUDICIAL POWERS

- Congress can
  - change jurisdiction (authority to hear cases) of the Supreme Court
  - impeach and remove federal judges
  - propose constitutional amendments to override Supreme Court decisions
- President appoints federal judges (who must be confirmed by the Senate)

branches share some authority and no branch has exclusive domain over any activity. The creation of this system allowed the Framers to minimize the threat of tyranny from any one branch. Thus, for almost every power granted to one branch, an equal control was established in the other two branches. The Congress could "check" the power of the president, the Supreme Court, and so on, carefully creating "balance" among the three branches.

The Supremacy Clause.   Another key constitutional principle that some argue is the linchpin of the entire federal system is the notion of national supremacy. The supremacy clause contained in Article VI of the Constitution provides that the "Constitution, and the laws of the United States" as well as all treaties are to be the supreme law of the land. All national and state officers and officials are bound by oath to support the national Constitution above any state law or state constitution. As a result, any legitimate exercise of national power supersedes or preempts any conflicting state action. It is up to the federal courts to determine if such conflict exists. Where it does, national law is always to take precedence.

The Articles of the Constitution

The document finally signed by the Framers condensed numerous resolutions into a Preamble and seven separate articles. The first three articles established the three branches of government, defined their internal operations, and clarified their relationships with one another. All branches of government were technically considered equal, yet some initially appeared more "equal" than others. It is likely that the order in which the articles appear, and especially the relative amount of detail in the first three articles, reflects the Framers' concern that the branches of the government might abuse their powers. The four remaining articles define the relationships among the states, declare national law to be supreme, and set out methods of amending the Constitution.

Article I: The Legislative Branch.   Article I vests all legislative powers in the Congress and establishes a bicameral legislature, consisting of the Senate and the House of Representatives. It also sets out the qualifications for holding office in each house, the terms of office, methods of selection of representatives and senators, and the system of apportionment among the states to determine membership in the House of Representatives. Operating procedures and the officers for each house are also outlined and described.

enumerated powers: Seventeen specific powers granted to Congress under Article I, section 8, of the U.S. Constitution; these powers include taxation, coinage of money, regulation of commerce, and the authority to provide for a national defense.

Perhaps the most important section of Article I is section 8. It carefully lists the powers the Framers wished the new Congress to possess. These specified or **enumerated powers** contain many key provisions that had been denied to the Continental Congress under the Articles of Confederation. For example, one of the major weaknesses of the Articles was Congress's lack of authority to deal with trade wars. The Constitution remedied this problem by authorizing Congress to "regulate Commerce with foreign Nations, and among the several States."

Today, Congress often enacts legislation that no specific clause of Article 1, section 8, appears to authorize. Laws dealing with the environment, welfare, education, and communications, among others, are often justified by reference to a particular power plus the necessary and proper clause. After careful enumeration of seventeen powers of Congress in Article 1, section 8, a final, general clause authorizing Congress to "make all Laws which shall be necessary and proper for carrying into Execution the foregoing Powers" was added to Article I. Often referred to as the **elastic clause,** the necessary and proper clause has been a source of tremendous congressional activity never anticipated by the Framers, as definitions of "necessary" and "proper" have been stretched to accommodate changing needs and times. The Supreme Court, for example, has coupled Congress's authority to regulate commerce with the necessary and proper clause to allow Congress to ban prostitution (where travel across state lines is involved), regulate trains and planes, establish uniform federal minimum-wage and maximum-hour laws, and mandate drug testing for certain workers (see chapter 7).

elastic clause: A name given to the "necessary and proper clause" found in the final paragraph of Article I, section 8, of the U.S. Constitution. It gives Congress the authority to pass all laws "necessary and proper" to carry out the enumerated powers specified in the Constitution.

Article II: The Executive Branch.   Article II vests the executive power, that is, the authority to execute the laws of the nation, in a president of the United States. Section 1 sets the president's term of office at four years and explains the electoral college. It also states qualifications for office and describes a mechanism to replace the president in case of death, disability, or removal.

The powers and duties of the president are set out in section 3. Among the most important of these are the president's role as commander-in-chief of the armed forces, the authority to make treaties with the consent of the Senate, and the authority to "appoint Ambassadors, other public Ministers and Consuls, the Judges of the supreme Court, and all other Officers of the United States." Other sections of Article II instruct the president to report directly to Congress "from time to time," in what has come to be known as the "State of the Union Address," and to "take Care that the Laws be faithfully executed." Section 4 provides the mechanism for removal of the president, vice president, and other officers of the United States for "Treason, Bribery, or other high Crimes and Misdemeanors" (see chapter 8).

Article III: The Judicial Branch.   Article III establishes a Supreme Court and defines its jurisdiction. During the Philadelphia meeting, the small and large states differed significantly as to the desirability of an independent judiciary and on the role of state courts in the national court system. The smaller states feared that a strong unelected judiciary would trample on their liberties. In compromise, Congress was permitted, but not required, to establish lower national courts. Thus state courts and the national court system would exist side by side with distinct areas of authority. Federal courts were given authority to decide cases arising under federal law. The Supreme Court was also given the power to settle disputes between states, or between a state and the national government.

Although some delegates to the convention had urged that the president be allowed to remove federal judges, ultimately judges were given appointments for life, presuming "good behavior." And, like the president's, their salaries cannot be lowered while they hold office. This provision was adopted to ensure that the legislature did not attempt to punish the Supreme Court or any other judges for unpopular decisions.

Judicial Review.   Perhaps the most important power of the Supreme Court, although it is not mentioned in the Constitution, is that of **judicial review,** the authority of a court to determine the constitutional validity of acts of the legislature. During the Constitutional Convention, the Framers debated and rejected the idea of a judicial veto of legislation or executive acts, and they rejected the Virginia Plan's proposal to give the judiciary explicit authority over Congress. They did, however, approve Article VI, which contains the supremacy clause discussed below.

In *Federalist No. 78,* Alexander Hamilton first publicly endorsed the idea of judicial review, noting, "whenever a particular statute contravenes the Constitution, it will be the duty of the judicial tribunals to adhere to the latter and disregard the former." Nonetheless, the actual authority of the Supreme Court to review acts of Congress to determine their constitutionality was an unsettled question. During its first decade, the Supreme Court (or justices riding circuit) had often reviewed acts of Congress, but it had not found any unconstitutional. But in *Marbury* **v.** *Madison* (1803), Chief Justice John Marshall claimed this sweeping authority for the Court by asserting the right of judicial review was a power that could be implied from the Constitution's supremacy clause.

Marbury v. *Madison* arose amidst a sea of political controversy. In the final hours of the Adams administration, William Marbury was appointed a justice of the peace for the District of Columbia. But in the confusion of winding up matters, John Marshall, Adams's Secretary of State, failed to deliver Marbury's commission. Marbury then asked James Madison, Thomas Jefferson's Secretary of State, for the commission. Under direct orders from Jefferson, who was irate over the Adams administration's last-minute appointment of several federal judges (quickly confirmed by the Federalist Senate), Madison refused to turn over the commission. Marbury and three other Adams appointees who were in the same situation then filed a writ of *mandamus* (a legal motion) asking the Supreme Court to order Madison to deliver their commissions.

Political tensions ran high as the Court met to hear the case. Jefferson threatened to ignore any order of the Court. Marshall realized that he and the prestige of the Court could be devastated by any refusal of the executive branch to comply with the decision.

judicial review: The authority of a court to review the acts of the legislature, the executive, or states to determine their constitutionality; enunciated by Chief Justice John Marshall in *Marbury* v. *Madison* (1803).

Marbury* v. *Madison: Supreme Court case in which the Court first asserted the power of judicial review in finding that a congressional statute extending the Court's original jurisdiction was unconstitutional.

Responding to this challenge, in a brilliant opinion that in many sections reads more like a lecture to Jefferson than a discussion of the merits of Marbury's claim, Marshall concluded that although Marbury and the others were entitled to their commissions, the Court lacked the power to issue the writ sought by Marbury. In *Marbury* v. *Madison,* Marshall further ruled that the parts of the Judiciary Act of 1789, in which Congress had established the structure and operation of the federal court system and had extended the jurisdiction of the Court to allow it to issue writs, was inconsistent with the Constitution and therefore unconstitutional.

Although the immediate effect of the decision was to deny power to the Court, its long-term effect was to establish the rule articulated by Marshall in *Marbury* that "it is emphatically the province and duty of the judicial department to say what the law is." Through judicial review, a power that Marshall concluded could be implied from the Constitution, the Supreme Court can dramatically exert its authority to determine what the Constitution means. And since *Marbury,* the Court has routinely exercised the power of judicial review, an implied power, to determine the constitutionality of acts of Congress, the executive branch, and the states. It was under its power of judicial review that the Court held the Arkansas statute designating term limits for members of Congress to be unconstitutional.

Articles IV through VII.   Article IV deals with relations between the state and national governments, and includes the mechanisms for admitting new states to the Union. Article V specifies how amendments can be added to the Constitution. Article VI contains the supremacy clause. Mindful of the potential problems that could occur if church and state were too enmeshed, Article VI specifies that no religious test shall be required for holding any office. The seventh and final article of the Constitution concerns the procedures for ratification of the new Constitution: Nine of the thirteen states would have to agree to, or ratify, its new provisions before it would become the supreme law of the land.

THE DRIVE FOR RATIFICATION

While delegates to the Constitutional Convention labored in Philadelphia, the Second Continental Congress continued to govern the former colonies under the Articles of Confederation. The day after the Constitution was signed, William Jackson, the secretary of the Constitutional Convention, left for New York City, then the nation's capital, to deliver the official copy of the document to the Congress. He also took with him a resolution of the delegates calling upon each of the states to vote on the new Constitution. Anticipating resistance from the representatives in the state legislatures, however, the Framers required the states to call special ratifying conventions to consider the proposed Constitution.

Jackson carried a letter from General George Washington with the proposed Constitution. In a few eloquent words, Washington summed up the sentiments of the Framers and the spirit of compromise that had permeated the long weeks in Philadelphia:

> That it will meet the full and entire approbation of every state is not perhaps to be expected, but each [state] will doubtless consider, that had her interest alone been consulted, the consequences might have been particularly disagreeable or injurious to others; that it is liable to as few exceptions as could

reasonably have been expected, we hope and believe; that it may promote lasting welfare of that country so dear to us all, and secure her freedom and happiness is our ardent wish.[22]

The Second Continental Congress immediately accepted the work of the convention and forwarded the proposed Constitution to the states for their vote. It was by no means certain, however, that the new Constitution would be adopted. From the fall of 1787 to the summer of 1788, the proposed Constitution was debated hotly around the nation. State politicians understandably feared a strong central government. Farmers and other working-class people were fearful of a distant national government. And those who had accrued substantial debts during the economic chaos following the Revolutionary War feared that a new government with a new financial policy would plunge them into even greater debt. The public in general was very leery of taxes—these were the same people who had revolted against the king's taxes. At the heart of many of their concerns was an underlying fear of the massive changes that would be brought about by a new system. Favoring the Constitution were wealthy merchants, lawyers, bankers, and those who believed that the new nation could not continue to exist under the Articles of Confederation. For them, it all boiled down to one simple question offered by Madison: "Whether or not the Union shall or shall not be continued."

Federalists Versus Anti-Federalists

Almost as soon as the ink was dry on the last signature to the Constitution, those who favored the new strong national government chose to call themselves **Federalists.** They were well aware that many still generally opposed the notion of a strong national government. Thus they did not want to risk being labeled "nationalists," so they tried to get the upper hand in the debate by nicknaming their opponents **Anti-Federalists.** Those put in the latter category insisted that they were instead "Federal Republicans" who believed in a federal system. As noted in Table 2.1, Anti-Federalists argued that they simply wanted to protect state governments from the tyranny of a too-powerful national government.[23]

Federalists: Those who favored a stronger national government and supported the proposed U.S. Constitution; later became the first U.S. political party.

Anti-Federalists: Those who favored strong state governments and a weak national government; opposed the ratification of the U.S. Constitution.

TABLE 2.1

Federalists and Anti-Federalists Compared

	FEDERALISTS	ANTI-FEDERALISTS
Who were they?	Property owners, landed rich, merchants of Northeast and Middle Atlantic states	Small farmers, shopkeepers, laborers
Political philosophy	Elitist: saw themselves and those of their class as most fit to govern (others were to *be* governed)	Believed in the decency of the common man and in participatory democracy; viewed elites as corrupt; sought greater protection of individual rights
Type of government favored	Powerful central government; two-house legislature; upper house (six-year term) further removed from the people, whom they distrusted	Wanted stronger state governments (closer to the people) at the expense of the powers of the national government. Sought smaller electoral districts, frequent elections, referendum and recall, and a large unicameral legislature to provide for greater class and occupational representation
Alliances	Pro-British Anti-French	Anti-British Pro-French

James Madison (left), Alexander Hamilton (center), and John Jay (right) were important early Federalist leaders. Jay wrote five of The Federalist Papers, and Madison and Hamilton wrote the rest. Madison served in the House of Representatives (1789-1797) and as *secretary of state* in the Jefferson administration (1801-1808). In 1808 he was elected fourth president of the United States and served two terms (1809-1817). Hamilton became the first *secretary of the treasury* (1789-1795) at the age of thirty-four. He was killed in 1804 in a duel with Vice President Aaron Burr, who was angered by Hamilton's negative comments about his character. Jay became the first *Chief Justice of the United States* (1789-1795) and negotiated the Jay Treaty with Great Britain in 1794. He then served as governor of New York from 1795 to 1801. (Photos courtesy: left, Colonial Williamsburg Foundation; center, The Metropolitan Museum of Art, Gift of Henry G. Marquand, 1881 (81.11) copyright (c) 1987 by The Metropolitan Museum of Art; right, The Bettman Archive)

Federalists and Anti-Federalists participated in the mass meetings that were held in state legislatures to discuss the pros and cons of the new plan. Tempers ran high at public meetings, where differences between the opposing groups were highlighted. Fervent debates were published in newspapers. Indeed, newspapers played a powerful role in the adoption process. The entire Constitution, in fact, was printed in the *Pennsylvania Packet* just two days after the convention's end. Other major papers quickly followed suit. Soon articles on both sides of the adoption issue began to appear around the nation, often written under pseudonyms such as "Caesar" or "Constant Reader," as was the custom of the day.

One name stood out from all the rest: "Publius" (Latin for "the people"). Between October 1787 and May 1788, eighty-five articles written under that pen name routinely appeared in newspapers in New York, a state where ratification was in doubt. Most were written by Alexander Hamilton and James Madison. Hamilton, a young, fiery New Yorker born in the British West Indies, wrote fifty-one, Madison wrote twenty-six, and jointly they penned another three. John Jay, also of New York, and later the first Chief Justice of the United States, wrote five of the pieces. These eighty-five essays became known as ***The Federalist Papers***.[24]

The Federalist Papers:
A series of eighty-five political papers written by John Jay, Alexander Hamilton, and James Madison in support of ratification of the U.S. Constitution.

Today *The Federalist Papers* are considered masterful explanations of the Framers' intentions as they drafted the new Constitution. At the time, although they were reprinted widely, they were far too theoretical to have much impact on those who would ultimately vote on the proposed Constitution. Dry and scholarly, they lacked the fervor of much of the political rhetoric that was then in use. *The Federalist Papers* did, however, highlight the reasons for the structure of the new government and its benefits. According to *Federalist No. 10*, for example, the new Constitution was called "a republican remedy for the disease incident to republican government." Moreover, these musings of Madison, Hamilton, and Jay continue to be the best single source of the political theories and philosophies at the heart of our Constitution.

Forced on the defensive, the Anti-Federalists responded with their own series of "letters" written by Anti-Federalists adopting the pen names of "Brutus" and "Cato," two ancient Romans famous for their intolerance of tyranny. These "letters" (actually essays) undertook a line-by-line critique of the Constitution and were designed to counteract *The Federalist Papers*.

Anti-Federalists argued that a strong central government would render the states powerless.[25] They stressed the strengths the government had been granted under the Articles of Confederation, and argued that these Articles, not the proposed Constitution, created a true federal system. Moreover, they argued that the strong national government would tax heavily, that the Supreme Court would overwhelm the states by invalidating state laws, and that the president eventually would have too much power, as commander-in-chief of a large and powerful army.

In particular, the Anti-Federalists feared the power of the national government to run roughshod over the liberties of the people. They proposed that the taxing power of Congress be limited, that the executive be curbed by a council, that the military consist of state militias rather than a national force, and that the jurisdiction of the Supreme Court be limited to prevent it from reviewing and potentially overturning the decisions of state courts. But their most effective argument concerned the absence of a bill of rights in the Constitution. James Madison answered these criticisms in *Federalists Nos. 10* and *51*. (The texts of these two essays are printed in the Appendix.) *In Federalist No. 10*, he pointed out that the voters would not always succeed in electing "enlightened statesmen" as their representatives. The greatest threat to individual liberties would therefore come from factions within the government, who might place narrow interests above broader national interests and the rights of citizens. While recognizing that no form of government could protect the country from unscrupulous politicians, Madison argued that the organization of the new government would minimize the effects of political factions. The great advantage of a federal system, Madison maintained, was that it created the "happy combination" of a national government too large to be controlled by any single faction, and several state governments that would be smaller and more responsive to local needs. Moreover, he argued in *Federalist No. 51* that the proposed federal government's separation of powers would prohibit any one branch from either dominating the national government or violating the rights of citizens.

Debate continued in the thirteen states as votes were taken from December 1787 to June 1788, in accordance with the ratifying process laid out in Article VII of the proposed Constitution. Three states acted quickly to ratify the new Constitution. Two small states, Delaware and New Jersey, voted to ratify before the large states could rethink the notion of equal representation of the states in the Senate. Pennsylvania, where Federalists were well organized, was one of the first three states to ratify. Massachusetts assented to the new government but tempered its support by calling for an immediate addition of amendments including one protecting personal rights. New Hampshire became the crucial ninth state to ratify on June 21, 1788. This action completed the ratification process outlined in Article VII of the Constitution and marked the beginning of a new nation. But because New York and Virginia (which between them accounted for more than 40 percent of the new nation's population) had not yet ratified the Constitution, the practical future of the new nation remained in doubt.

Hamilton in New York and Madison in Virginia worked feverishly to convince delegates to their state conventions to vote for the new government. In New York sentiment against it was high. In Albany, fighting broke out over the proposed Constitution, resulting in injuries and death. When news of Virginia's acceptance of the Constitution

FIGURE 2.2

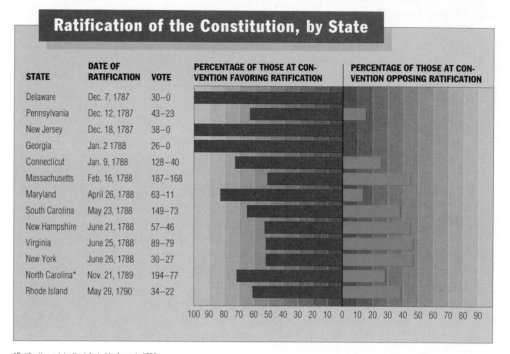

Ratification of the Constitution, by State

STATE	DATE OF RATIFICATION	VOTE	PERCENTAGE OF THOSE AT CONVENTION FAVORING RATIFICATION	PERCENTAGE OF THOSE AT CONVENTION OPPOSING RATIFICATION
Delaware	Dec. 7, 1787	30–0		
Pennsylvania	Dec. 12, 1787	43–23		
New Jersey	Dec. 18, 1787	38–0		
Georgia	Jan. 2 1788	26–0		
Connecticut	Jan. 9, 1788	128–40		
Massachusetts	Feb. 16, 1788	187–168		
Maryland	April 26, 1788	63–11		
South Carolina	May 23, 1788	149–73		
New Hampshire	June 21, 1788	57–46		
Virginia	June 25, 1788	89–79		
New York	June 26, 1788	30–27		
North Carolina*	Nov. 21, 1789	194–77		
Rhode Island	May 29, 1790	34–22		

100 90 80 70 60 50 40 30 20 10 0 10 20 30 40 50 60 70 80 90

*Ratification originally defeated in August, 1788.

reached the New York convention, Hamilton was finally able to convince a majority of those present to follow suit by a narrow margin of three votes. Both states also recommended the addition of a series of structural amendments, and a bill of rights.

Two of the original states—North Carolina and Rhode Island—continued to hold out against ratification. Both had recently printed new currencies and feared that values would plummet in a federal system where the Congress was authorized to coin money. On August 2, 1788, North Carolina became the first state to reject the Constitution on the grounds that no Anti-Federalist amendments were included. Soon after Congress submitted a **Bill of Rights** in September 1789, North Carolina ratified the Constitution by a vote of 194 to 77. Rhode Island, the only state that had not sent representatives to Philadelphia, remained out of the Union until 1790. Finally, under threats from its largest cities to secede from the state, the legislature called a convention that ratified the Constitution by only two votes (34 to 32)—one year after George Washington became the first president of the United States (see Figure 2.2).

Bill of Rights: The first ten amendments to the U.S. Constitution.

CHANGING THE CONSTITUTION

*O*nce the Constitution was ratified, elections were held. When Congress convened it immediately sent a set of amendments to the states for their ratification. An amendment authorizing the enlargement of the House of Representatives and another to prevent members of the House from raising their own salaries failed to garner favorable votes in the necessary three-fourths of the states (this Twenty-Seventh [Madison] Amendment, was ultimately ratified more than 200 years

Highlight 2.2

The Twenty-Seventh (Madison) Amendment

On June 8, 1789, in a speech before the House of Representatives, James Madison stated,

[T]here is seeming impropriety in leaving any set of men without controul [sic] to put their hand into the public coffers, to take out money to put into their pockets. . . . I have gone therefore so far as to fix it, that no law, varying the compensation, shall operate until there is a change in the legislation.

When Madison spoke these words about his proposal, now known as the Twenty-Seventh Amendment, he had no way of knowing that more than two centuries would pass before it would become an official part of the Constitution. In fact, Madison deemed it worthy of addi-

Gregory Watson with a document that contains the first ten amendments to the Constitution, as well as the compensation amendment ("Article the second: No law varying the compensation for the services of the Senators and Representatives shall take effect until an election of Representatives shall have intervened"), which was finally ratified as the Twenty-Seventh Amendment in 1992. (Photo courtesy: Zigy Kaluzny/PEOPLE Weekly (c) 1993)

tion only because the conventions of three states (Virginia, New York, and North Carolina) had demanded that it be included.

By 1791, when the Bill of Rights was added to the Constitution, only six states had ratified Madison's amendment, and it seemed destined to fade into obscurity. In 1982, however, Gregory Watson, a sophomore majoring in economics at the University of

Texas–Austin, discovered the unratified compensation amendment while looking for a paper topic for an American government class. Intrigued, Watson wrote a paper arguing that the proposed amendment was still viable because it had no internal time limit and, therefore, should still be ratified. Watson received a "C" on the paper.

Despite his grade, Watson began a ten-year,

$6,000 self-financed crusade to renew interest in the compensation amendment. Watson and his allies reasoned that the amendment should be revived because of the public's growing anger with the fact that members of Congress had sought to raise their salaries without going on the record as having done so. Watson's perseverance paid off, and on May 7, 1992, the amendment was ratified by the requisite thirty-eight states. On May 18, the United States Archivist certified that the amendment was part of the Constitution, a decision that was overwhelmingly confirmed by the House of Representatives on May 19 and by the Senate on May 20.

At the same time that the Senate approved the Twenty-Seventh Amendment, it also took action to ensure that a similar situation would never occur by declaring "dead" four other amendments that did not have internal deadlines.

Source: Fordham Law Review (December 1992): 497–539, and Anne Marie Kilday, "Amendment Expert Agrees with Congressional Pay Ruling." The Dallas Morning News (February 14, 1993): 13A.

after it was sent to the states). The remaining ten amendments, known as the Bill of Rights, were ratified by 1791 in accordance with the procedures set out in the Constitution (see Table 2.2). Sought by Anti-Federalists as a protection for individual liberties, they offered numerous specific limitations on the national government's ability to interfere with a wide variety of personal liberties, some of which were already guaranteed by many state constitutions (see chapters 5 and 6).

The Bill of Rights includes numerous specific protections of personal rights. Freedom of expression, speech, press, religion, and assembly are guaranteed by the First Amendment. The Bill of Rights also contains numerous safeguards for those accused of crimes.

TABLE 2.2

The Bill of Rights*

First Amendment	Freedom of religion, speech, press, and assembly
Second Amendment	The right to bear arms
Third Amendment	Prohibition against quartering of troops in private homes
Fourth Amendment	Prohibition against unreasonable searches and seizures
Fifth Amendment	Rights guaranteed to the accused: requirement for grand jury indictment; protections against double jeopardy, self-incrimination; due process guaranteed
Sixth Amendment	Right to a speedy and public trial before an impartial jury, to cross-examine witnesses, and to have counsel
Seventh Amendment	Right to a trial by jury in civil suits
Eighth Amendment	Prohibition against excessive bail and fines, and cruel and unusual punishment
Ninth Amendment	Rights not listed in the Constitution retained by the people
Tenth Amendment	States or people reserve those powers not denied to them by the Constitution or delegated to the national government

*For the full text of the Bill of Rights, see the Appendix.

In addition to guaranteeing these important rights, two of the amendments of the Bill of Rights were reactions to British rule—the right to bear arms (Second Amendment) and the right not to have soldiers quartered in private homes (Third Amendment). More general rights are also included in the Bill of Rights. The Ninth Amendment notes that these enumerated rights are not inclusive, meaning they are not the only rights to be enjoyed by the people, and the Tenth Amendment states that powers not given to the national government are reserved by the states or the people.

The Formal Amendment Process

Article V of the Constitution creates a two-stage amendment process: proposal and ratification.[26] The Constitution specifies two ways to accomplish each stage. As illustrated in Figure 2.3, amendments to the Constitution can be proposed by:

1. A vote of two-thirds of the members in both houses of Congress; or
2. A vote of two-thirds of the state legislatures specifically requesting Congress to call a national convention to propose amendments.

The second method has never been used. Historically, it has served as a fairly effective threat, forcing Congress to consider amendments that might otherwise never have been debated. In the 1980s, for example, several states called on Congress to enact a balanced-budget amendment. To forestall the need for a special constitutional convention, Congress enacted the Gramm–Rudman–Hollings Act, which called for a balanced budget. When that act proved ineffective, the 104th Congress took up the issue of passage of a Balanced Budget Amendment as one of its planks in what Republicans term their "Contract with America."

Of the more than 10,000 amendments that have been introduced on one or both floors of the Congress, only thirty-three mustered the two-thirds vote required for them to be sent to the states for debate and ratification through 1994. Only six proposed amendments sent to the states failed to be ratified.

FIGURE 2.3

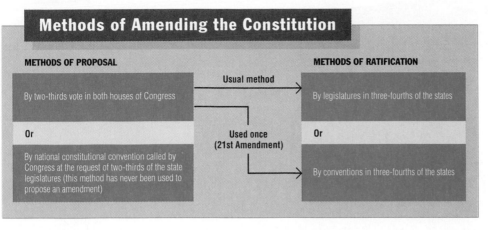

Methods of Amending the Constitution

METHODS OF PROPOSAL

By two-thirds vote in both houses of Congress

Or

By national constitutional convention called by Congress at the request of two-thirds of the state legislatures (this method has never been used to propose an amendment)

Usual method

Used once (21st Amendment)

METHODS OF RATIFICATION

By legislatures in three-fourths of the states

Or

By conventions in three-fourths of the states

The ratification process is fairly straightforward. When Congress votes to propose an amendment, the Constitution specifies that the ratification process must occur in one of two ways:

1. A favorable vote in three-fourths of the state legislatures; or
2. A favorable vote in specially called ratifying conventions in three-fourths of the states.

The Constitution itself, however, was to be ratified by specifically called ratifying conventions. The Framers feared that the power of special interests in state legislatures would prevent a positive vote on the new Constitution. Since ratification of the Constitution, however, only one ratifying convention has been called. The Eighteenth Amendment, which caused the Prohibition Era by outlawing the sale of alcoholic beverages, was ratified by the first method—a vote in state legislatures. Millions broke the law, others died from drinking homemade liquor, and still others made their fortunes selling bootleg or illegal liquor. After a decade of these problems, Congress decided to act. An additional amendment—the Twenty-First—was proposed to repeal the Eighteenth Amendment. It was sent to the states for ratification, but with a call for ratifying conventions, not a vote in the state legislatures.[27] Members of Congress correctly predicted that the move to repeal the Eighteenth Amendment would encounter opposition in the statehouses, which were largely controlled by conservative rural interests. Thus Congress's decision to use the convention method led to quick approval of the Twenty-First Amendment.

The intensity of efforts to amend the Constitution has varied considerably, depending on the nature of the change proposed. Whereas the Twenty-First Amendment took only ten months to ratify, an equal rights amendment (ERA) was introduced in every session of Congress from 1923 until 1972, when Congress finally voted favorably on it.

Even then, years of lobbying by women's groups were insufficient to garner necessary state support. By 1982, the congressionally mandated date for ratification, only thirty-five states—three short of the number required—had voted favorably on the amendment.[28]

Amendments passed after the Bill of Rights can be organized into four categories: (1) those effecting a structural change in government, (2) those affecting public policy, (3) those expanding rights, and (4) those overruling a U.S. Supreme Court decision. Most amendments that change the structure or mechanics of government have been

Politics Now

Amending the Constitution

In May 1987, in the aftermath of major national efforts to amend the Constitution to include an equal rights amendment and amidst calls for a constitutional amendment to prohibit abortion, a *CBS News/New York Times* poll asked respondents, "Do you think it is too easy or too hard to amend the Constitution, or is the process about right?" Of those polled, 11 percent responded, "Too easy"; 20 percent responded, "Too hard"; and 60 percent responded, "About right." A Gallup poll conducted the same year found that 72 percent of those questioned believed that a modern constitutional convention might make things worse, but 44 percent expressed their belief that the "Constitution needs basic changes." (Some of these respondents may have been ardent supporters of the ERA or a Right to Life Amendment, who continue to believe that the Constitution should be amended.)

The Republicans' 1994 Contract with America, as well as the Christian Coalition's own version, called the Contract with the American Family, and the 1996 Republican platform proposed several changes to the U.S. Constitution that would bring unprecedented changes in constitutional law and truly change the nature of several existing provisions in the U.S. Constitution. At no other time since the founding period, when the Bill of Rights was added to the Constitution, have as many alterations in the Constitution been suggested. This fact disturbs many scholars who believe that so much change in a short period of time could rock the very foundations of the American political system. Among key planks in the Contract with America calling for (or potentially necessitating) a constitutional amendment are a balanced budget amendment and congressional term limits, a change that the Supreme Court already ruled must be made by amendment, not state legislation. The Christian Coalition, likewise, has proposed several amendments, including ones to allow prayer in school as well as one to ban abortion. Similarly, the 1996 Republican platform called for amendments, including ones to protect victims' rights and prohibit flag burning.

Even if the U.S. Congress could muster enough votes to send any of these proposals to the states, their ability to win ratification remains very much in doubt. In spite of high public support, for example, the ERA failed. Most Americans, when push comes to shove, are reluctant to change what appears to work most of the time.

How do you feel about all of these efforts to change a document that has survived with so little change to this point in time?

ratified quite easily in response to some sort of "emergency." In the wake of President John F. Kennedy's assassination in 1963, which left the nation without a vice president when Lyndon B. Johnson became president, the Twenty-Fifth Amendment was added to the Constitution to allow the president to fill, subject to the approval of Congress, a vacancy in the office of vice president. For the most part, the public has accepted the structural changes as a natural working out of the kinks in the Constitution.

Amendments expanding rights, especially those concerned with enlarging the electorate, make up the next significant group of amendments. Generally, once these amendments secure congressional favor, state ratification follows quickly. For example, women tried for decades to secure a constitutional amendment guaranteeing their right to vote, yet once Congress voted favorably on the Nineteenth Amendment, ratification by the states took less than two years.[29]

Amendments designed to affect existing public policies form a third category of constitutional amendments. Many constitutional scholars regard these amendments as troublesome. They argue that the Constitution should be a basic outline of principles, and not a list of desired outcomes. Critics today, for example, fear that efforts to amend

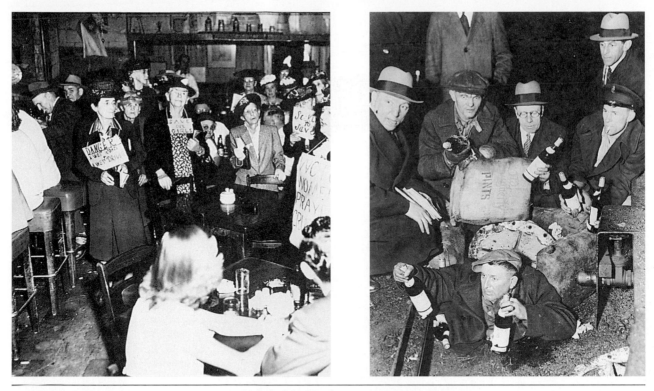

For all its moral foundation in groups like the Women's Christian Temperance Union (WCTU) (left), whose members invaded bars in support of it, the Eighteenth Amendment was a disaster. Among its side effects were the rise of powerful crime organizations responsible for (among other things) the cache of over 3,000 bags of bottled beverages uncovered by federal agents (right). Once proposed, it took only ten months to ratify the Twenty-First Amendment, which repealed the Prohibition amendment. (Photos courtesy: left, Archive Photos/American Stock; right, AP/Worldwide Studios)

the Constitution to prohibit flag burning, allow prayer in schools, or ban abortions would be foolhardy and unnecessary interference with the basic nature of the Constitution. The first two are regarded as particularly risky because they would alter the First Amendment, which to this day has never been modified.

A final category of amendments consists of those enacted to overrule specific Supreme Court decisions. As discussed in greater detail in chapter 10, the Supreme Court is the final authority on the Constitution. Once the Court construes a provision of the Constitution, only the Court itself or a constitutional amendment can change that interpretation. Through 1995, only two of the Supreme Court's decisions have been overruled by constitutional amendments.

THE CONSTITUTION IN A CHANGING AMERICA

*M*any Americans today are unhappy with government, especially the federal government, often decrying how slowly it moves. But, this deliberateness was built into the constitutional structure by the Framers. They did not want to fashion a government that could respond to the whims of the people, which often change quickly. Separation of powers and the checks and balances system are just two indications of the Framers' recognition of the importance of deliberation and thought as a check against both government tyranny and the rash judgments of intemperate majorities. James Madison, in particular, wanted to draft a system of government that would pit faction against faction, and ambition against am-

North—South

POLITICS AROUND THE WORLD

There is no better way to see the unique nature of the United States than through its Constitution.

Americans are justifiably proud that they have used the same Constitution since it was written in 1787.

Depending on how one counts such things, this is a record for political longevity matched by only one or two other countries.

By global standards, Canada and Mexico also have durable constitutions. The basics of Canada's system were set up when the English Parliament passed the British North American Act in 1867 and gave Canada what amounted to total control over its domestic affairs. Mexico's most recent Constitution was adopted in 1917 after the end of a century of violence and instability. Nevertheless, in important ways, these two constitutions and the practices laid out in them are not as effective as the U.S. Constitution.

In Mexico, as in many other countries, the Constitution does not tell us much about how political power is actually exercised. Although its Constitution was loosely patterned on the American model, political life from the beginning has been dominated by a single political party—the PRI—which is not mentioned in the Constitution but will be at the heart of these boxes in all subsequent chapters.

Canada's Constitution does come closer to describing what happens politically. Unlike the United States, however, there is considerable opposition to many of its provisions regarding federal–provincial relations, especially the status of French-speaking Quebec and the role of the upper house of the national parliament, the Senate. Since the Constitution was "patriated" from Great Britain in 1982, there have been two major attempts to revise it and a referendum on what the Quebecois call "sovereignty-association," all of which failed. Many observers feel that Canada has reached a "constitutional impasse." They find it hard to see how the country can hold together, though it is even harder to imagine it falling apart in anything like the bloody conflict of the former Yugoslavia.

In short, one of the most important and unusual aspects of politics in the United States is something virtually all of its citizens take for granted—the support for and impact of its constitutional order.

bition, in order to design a system of representation and policy making that would strengthen minority factions against possible encroachments by majority factions. Although it took a long time, the Constitution was eventually amended to protect the rights of African Americans through the addition of the Thirteenth, Fourteenth, and Fifteenth Amendments.

The Framers also made the formal amendment process a slow one to ensure that amendments were not added lightly to the Constitution. But the formal amendment process is not the only way that the Constitution has been changed over time. Judicial interpretation and cultural and social change also have had a major impact on the way the Constitution has evolved.

Judicial Interpretation

As early as 1803, under the brilliant leadership of Chief Justice John Marshall, the Supreme Court declared that the federal courts had the power to nullify acts of the nation's government when they were found to be in conflict with the Constitution. Over the years this check on the other branches of government and on the states has increased the authority of the Court and has significantly altered the meaning of various provisions of the Constitution, a fact that prompted Woodrow Wilson to call the

Supreme Court "a constitutional convention in continuous session." (More detail on the Supreme Court's role in interpreting the Constitution is found in chapters 5, 6, and 10 especially, as well as in other chapters in the book.)

Today some argue that the original intent of the Framers, as evidenced in *The Federalist Papers* as well as in private notes taken by James Madison at the Constitutional Convention, should govern judicial interpretation of the Constitution.[30] Others argue that the Framers knew that a changing society needed an elastic, flexible document that could conform to the ages.[31] In all likelihood, the vagueness of the document was purposeful. Those in attendance in Philadelphia recognized that they could not agree on everything and that it was wiser to leave interpretation to those who would follow them. What do you think?

Social and Cultural Change

Even the most far-sighted of those in attendance at the Constitutional Convention could not have anticipated the vast changes that have occurred in the United States. For example, although many were uncomfortable with the Three-Fifths Compromise and others hoped for the abolition of slavery, none could have imagined the status of African Americans today, or that Colin Powell could serve as Chairman of the Joint Chiefs of Staff and have been frequently mentioned as a viable candidate for president or vice president in 1996. Likewise, few of the Framers could have anticipated the diverse roles that women would come to play in American society. The Constitution has often been bent to accommodate such social and cultural changes. Thus, although there is no specific amendment guaranteeing women equal protection of the law, the federal courts have interpreted the Constitution to prohibit many forms of gender discrimination, thereby recognizing cultural and societal change.

Social change has also caused changes in the way institutions of government act. Thus, as problems such as the Great Depression appeared national in scope, Congress took on more and more power at the expense of the states to solve the economic and social crisis. Today, however, Congress is moving to return much of that power to the states. The actions of the 104th Congress to return powers to the states, for example, may be viewed as an *informal* attempt not necessarily to amend the Constitution but to return the balance of power between the national and state government to that which the Framers intended. Again, within the parameters of its constitutional powers, the Congress acted as the Framers intended without a changing the document itself.

Technological innovations have also contributed to a changing Constitution. The Framers could not have envisioned the need for a federally run air traffic control system or for federal regulation of the airwaves or the Internet.

Advances in technology have also required new interpretations of the Bill of Rights. Wiretapping and other forms of electronic surveillance, for example, are now regulated by the First and Fourth Amendments. Similarly, HIV testing must be balanced against constitutional protections. And all kinds of new constitutional questions are posed in the wake of congressional efforts to regulate what kinds of information can be disseminated on the Internet. Still, in spite of these massive changes, the Constitution still survives, changed and ever changing after more than 200 years.

SUMMARY

The U.S. Constitution has proven to be a remarkably enduring document. In explaining how and why the Constitution came into being, this chapter has covered the following points:

1. The Origins of a New Nation.

While settlers came to the New World for a variety of reasons, most remained loyal to Great Britain and considered themselves subjects of the king. Over the years, as new generations of Americans were born on colonial soil, those ties weakened. A series of taxes levied by the Crown ultimately led the colonists to convene a Continental Congress and to declare their independence.

2. The Declaration of Independence.

The Declaration of Independence (1776), which drew heavily on the writings of John Locke, carefully enumerated the wrongs of the Crown and galvanized public resentment and willingness to take up arms against Great Britain in the Revolutionary War (1775–82).

3. The First Attempt at Government: The Articles of Confederation.

The Articles of Confederation (1781) created a loose league of friendship between the new national government and the states. Numerous weaknesses in the new government became apparent by 1784. Among the major flaws were Congress's inability to tax or regulate commerce, the absence of an executive to administer the government, and a weak central government.

4. The Miracle at Philadelphia: Writing a Constitution.

When the weaknesses under the Articles of Confederation became apparent, the states called for a meeting to reform them. The Constitutional Convention (1787) quickly threw out the Articles of Confederation and fashioned a new, more workable form of government. The Constitution was the result of a series of compromises, including those over representation, questions involving large and small states, and over how to determine population. Compromises were also made about how members of each branch of government were to be selected. The electoral college was created to give states a key role in the selection of the president.

5. The U.S. Constitution.

The proposed U.S. Constitution created a federal system that drew heavily on Montesquieu's ideas about separation of powers. These ideas concerned a way of parcelling out power among the three branches of government, and checks and balances to prevent any one branch from having too much power.

6. The Drive for Ratification.

The drive for ratification became a fierce fight between Federalists and Anti-Federalists. Federalists lobbied for the strong national government created by the Constitution; Anti-Federalists favored greater state power.

7. Changing the Constitution.

The Framers created a formal two-stage amendment process to include the Congress and the states. Amendments could be proposed by a two-thirds vote in Congress or of state legislatures requesting that Congress call a national convention to propose amendments. Amendments could be ratified by a positive vote of three-fourths of the state legislatures or specially called state ratifying conventions.

8. The Constitution in a Changing America.

The formal amendment process is not the only way that the Constitution can be changed. Judicial interpretation and cultural and technological changes have also caused constitutional change.

KEY TERMS

Anti-Federalists, p. 61
Articles of Confederation, p. 47
Bill of Rights, p. 64
checks and balances, p. 55
Committees of Correspondence, p. 44
confederation, p. 46
Declaration of Independence, p. 46
elastic clause, p. 58

enumerated powers, p. 58
federal system, p. 55
The Federalist Papers, p. 62
Federalists, p. 61
First Continental Congress, p. 45
Great Compromise, p. 52
judicial review, p. 59
Marbury v. *Madison*, p. 59

New Jersey Plan, p. 52
Second Continental Congress, p. 45
separation of powers, p. 55
Shays's Rebellion, p. 49
Stamp Act Congress, p. 42
Three-Fifths Compromise, p. 53
Virginia Plan, p. 50

SELECTED READINGS

Bailyn Bernard. *The Ideological Origins of the American Revolution.* Cambridge, MA: Harvard University Press, 1967.

Beard, Charles. *An Economic Interpretation of the Constitution of the United States.* New York: Macmillan, 1913.

Bernstein, Richard B., and Jerome Agel. *Amending America.* New York: Random House, 1992.

Bowen, Catherine Drinker. *Miracle at Philadelphia.* Boston: Little, Brown, 1966.

Hamilton, Alexander, James Madison, and John Jay. *The Federalist Papers*, ed. Isaac Kramnick. New York: Penguin, 1987 (first published in 1788).

Ketchman, Ralph., ed. *The Anti-Federalist Papers and the Constitutional Convention Debated.* New York: New American Library, 1986.

Levy, Leonard W., ed. *Essays on the Making of the Constitution.* New York: Oxford University Press, 1969.

Main, Jackson Turner. *The Social Structure of Revolutionary America.* Princeton, NJ: Princeton University Press, 1965.

McDonald, Forest. *The Formation of the American Republic.* New York: Penguin, 1967.

Rossiter, Clinton. *1787: Grand Convention.* New York: Macmillan, 1966.

Vile, John R. *Encyclopedia of Constitutional Amendments, and Amending Issues, 1789–1995.* Santa Barbara, CA: ABC-CLIO, 1996.

Wood, Gordon S. *The Creation of the American Republic.* Chapel Hill: University of North Carolina Press, 1969.

Photo courtesy: Bonnie Kamin

FEDERALISM

This land is your land, this land is my land," sang Woody Guthrie in his ballad about America. Although his song conjures up "the image of like-minded people working together, . . . the ugly debate over the Utah wilderness reveals a dark side to this optimistic view of group ownership."[1] Writing in 1996, political scientist Daniel J. Elazar noted that certain regions of the country had certain, identifiable, "political cultures."[2] The American West today is one such area, particularly low-population states like Utah, Idaho, and Montana. As flocks of new residents (some ranchers, some survivalists) have moved there to escape what they view as the undesirable sides of urban life, open spaces have decreased in areas that once were "shunned even by Utah's hardy Mormon pioneers."[3]

From ranchers to those who depend on the tourist trade, many who live in the West depend on public lands—which constitute 85 percent of Western territory—for their livelihoods. Today, however, there is a heated debate over how much more federal land should be designated as wilderness (with restrictions against mining, logging, roads, vehicles, and development), as well as about how far the federal government can regulate the use of private resources to protect the environment. This debate is often one of old timers *versus* newcomers. The old timers are the ranchers, miners, and loggers. Their opponents are relative newcomers to the region who argue that recreation, tourism, and environmentally friendly alternatives are preferable to traditional Western land practices.

One of the biggest battlefields is southern Utah, which has 22 million acres of public lands (including wilderness, national parks, and government-owned range, timber, and mining lands). On August 2, 1995, a House committee approved a bill to add 1.8 million acres to the existing 801,000 acres of federal wilderness in Utah. Conservatives had argued for an additional 5.7 million acres, but the Utah congressional delegation sponsored the bill for fewer protected acres (see Figure 3.1). They wanted to weaken the 1964 Wilderness Act by allowing dams, roads, power lines, pipeline, off-road vehicles, and motor boats in the protected area.

The federal government's control of so much state land is just more fuel for the fire of many in the West who fear the national government, believe that it is unresponsive to their needs, and believe that it is trying to take over the states. The Western States Coalition, for example, was formed in 1994 by Western legislative and local governmental leaders to advocate a stronger role for the states, especially in environmental affairs. Its members, like many citizens in Utah, are

FIGURE 3.1

Wilderness Wars: The First Battle

Ogden

Salt Lake City

Provo

Cedar City

Moab

0 _____ 100 mi

0 _____ 100 km

Existing wilderness
(801,000 acres)

1.7 million acres of
southern Utah wilderness
that President Clinton set
aside for federal protection
in September, 1996.

Alternative wilderness plan
(5.7 million acres)

National parks

USN&WR–Basic data: Utah Wilderness Coalition

angry that the national government has such a great say in what happens in the West. "I do not appreciate decisions coming from another part of the country," said one Utah County Commissioner as he recounted a lobbying trip to Washington, D.C., to lobby for the public lands bill drafted by the Republicans in Utah's congressional delegation. Bemoaning the limited knowledge of the West in Washington, D.C., he noted, "A good 35 to 40 percent of the aides we talked to had never even heard of the Bureau of Land Management (BLM), and this is a (federal) BLM wilderness bill."[4] Thus Westerners routinely bridle at the idea of their lands being controlled by bureaucrats thousands of miles away.

So much nationally owned land under the control of the U.S. Department of the Interior and the BLM pits the states against the federal government as large portions of the state are taken off the tax roles, depriving the states of their right to exploit their natural resources for the good or profit of their citizens. In Utah, for example, federal agencies control 63.4 percent of the state's land, while the state legislatures, governor, and local elected officials control less than one third of the state's land.

Until recently, much of this debate over who had the right to control and regulate the natural resources within a state—the state or the national government—had taken place out of the national limelight. But the Republicans in the

Among issues behind the move to return power to the states are government regulations affecting the environment. These Austin, Texas, farmers are protesting restrictions imposed on them by the Endangered Species Act. (Photo courtesy: Kolvoord/The Image Works)

104th Congress made the rolling back of federal regulations, especially those dealing with the environment, a top priority. While Democrats in the 104th Congress didn't have the votes to stop some of the rollbacks, they were able to kill some of those moves. The Utah lands bill, however, was stopped by a successful filibuster led by Senator Bill Bradley (D.–N.J.). He, many other easterners, and many environmentalists see any move to open up new lands to mining, grazing, and other forms of commercial development in the West as disastrous. Said Bradley, "Our public lands belong to all Americans, whether they live in Utah or New Jersey."[5] And, to ensure that these lands will not be misused, in late 1996 President Clinton bypassed the divided Congress unilaterally by setting aside 1.7 million acres of southern Utah for protection as a national monument. Clinton used the obscure Antiquities Act of 1906, which empowers the president to protect public lands for their outstanding cultural, scientific, and natural values. While many environmentalists were happy, many in Utah claim this is a land grab by the federal government at the expense of Utah.

While much of the American public is angry and frustrated over the national government's handling of such issues as public welfare, crime, and health care, the hot-button issues for Westerners are land use and government regulation of the environment. Many, like some in Utah, are angry at federal takeovers of their land.

According to a poll conducted in 1995 for *Time*/CNN, 75 percent of Americans support having the "states take over more responsibilities now performed by the federal government."[6] Many, however, have probably not considered all of the ramifications of such a devolution. What happens if one state allows companies to pollute waterways that flow into adjoining states? Are state governments and state bureaucracies better equipped to handle welfare, medical care, job training, or other problems associated with poverty? And with more responsibilities comes the need for more funds. Will states begin to raise taxes? It's unlikely. With states taking on more responsibilities but having less money to execute them, everyone may have to make do with fewer governmental programs, no matter how beneficial or laudatory their goals.

From its very beginning, the challenge for the United States of America was to preserve the traditional independence and rights of the states while establishing an effective national government. In *Federalist No. 51,* James Madison highlighted the unique structure of governmental powers created by the Framers:

> The power surrendered by the people is first divided between two distinct governments, and then . . . subdivided among distinct and separate departments. Hence, a double security arises to the rights of the people.

The Framers, fearing tyranny, divided powers between the state and the national governments. At each level, moreover, powers were divided among executive, legislative, and judicial branches.

Although most of the delegates to the Constitutional Convention favored a strong federal government, they knew that some compromise about the distribution of powers would be necessary. Some of the Framers wanted to continue with the confederate form of government defined in the Articles of Confederation; others wanted a more centralized system, like that of Great Britain. Their solution was to create the world's first federal system, in which the thirteen sovereign or independent states were bound together under one national government. The result was a system of government that was "neither wholly national nor wholly federal," as Madison explained in *The Federalist Papers.*

The nature of the federal relationship between the national government and the states, including their respective duties, obligations, and powers, is outlined in the U.S. Constitution, although the word "federal" does not appear in that document. Throughout history, however, this system and the rules that guide it have been continually stretched, reshaped, and reinterpreted by crises, historical evolution, public expectations, and judicial interpretation. All these forces have had tremendous influence on who makes policy decisions and how these decisions get made.

Issues involving the distribution of power between the national government and the states affect you on a daily basis. You do not, for example, need a passport to go from Texas to Oklahoma. There is one national currency and a national minimum wage. But many differences exist among the laws of the various states: The age at which you may marry is a state issue, as are laws governing divorce, child custody, and the purchase of guns.

Although some policies or programs are under the authority of the state or local government, others, such as air traffic regulation, are solely within the province of the national government.[7] In many areas, however, the national and state governments work together cooperatively. For example, you may receive national as well as state loans, grants, or other forms of assistance to finance your education. Similarly, many of the poor receive help from the national, state, and local governments. At times the national government cooperates with or supports programs only if the states meet certain conditions. In order to receive federal funds for the construction and maintenance of highways, for example, states must follow federal rules about the kinds of roads they build.

To understand the current relationship between the states and the federal government and to better grasp some of the issues that arise from this constantly changing relationship, in this chapter, we

- Look at *the roots of the federal system* created by the Framers, and at their attempt to divide the power and the functions of government between one national and several state governments.

- Analyze the allocation of *the powers of government* between the national and state governments.

- Examine *the evolution and development of federalism* and the roles that crises, expectations, political ideologies, and decisions of the Supreme Court have played in the development of federalism.

- Explore the rapidly *changing nature of federalism.*

THE ROOTS OF THE FEDERAL SYSTEM

*T*he Framers worked to create a particular form of government: One that would be familiar to Americans yet unlike the unitary system found in Great Britain, and one that would remedy many of the problems experienced by the confederated government established by the Articles of Confederation (see chapter 2). (Figure 3.2 illustrates these different forms of government.) The relationship between the national and state governments, and their intertwined powers, are the heart of **federalism** (from the Latin *foedus*, or "covenant"), the philosophy that defines the allocation of power between the national government and the states. Ironically, as discussed in chapter 2, those who supported the government under the Articles of Confederation argued for what they called a federal system. But the fear of being labeled "nationalists" prompted supporters of the new Constitution to call themselves "Federalists," thus co-opting this popular term of the day. Federalist supporters of the new Constitution articulated three major arguments for federalism: (1) the prevention of tyranny; (2) the provision for increased participation in politics; and (3) the use of the states as testing grounds or "laboratories" for new policies and programs.

The national government created by the Framers draws its powers directly from the people, so that both national and state governments are ultimately directly accountable to the public. While each government has certain powers in common with the other (such as the ability to tax) and has its own set of public officials, the Framers also envisioned each government to be supreme in some spheres, as depicted in Figure 3.3. In *Federalist No. 51,* James Madison explained what he perceived to be the beauty of this system: The shifting support of the electorate between the two governments would serve to keep each in balance. In fashioning the new federal system of government, the Framers recognized that they could not define precisely how all the relations between the national government and the individual states would work. But the Constitution makes it clear that separate spheres of government were to be at the very core of the federal system, with some allowances made for concurrent powers. The addition of Article IV, section 2 of the Constitution underscored the notion that the national government was always to be supreme in situations of conflict between state and national law. It declares that the U.S. Constitution, the laws of the United States, and its treaties are to be "the supreme Law of the Land; and the Judges in every State shall be bound thereby. . . . "

In spite of this explicit language, the meaning of what is called the **supremacy clause** has been subject to continuous judicial interpretation and reinterpretation. In 1920,[8] for example, Missouri sought to prevent a U.S. game warden from enforcing the Migratory Bird Treaty Act of 1918, which prohibited the killing or capturing of many species of birds as they made their annual migration across the international border from Canada to parts of the United States. Missouri argued that the Tenth Amendment, which reserved a state's powers to legislate for the general welfare of its citizens, allowed Missouri to regulate hunting. But the Court ruled that since the treaty was legal, it must be considered the supreme law of the land. Thus, when national law and state

federalism: The philosophy that describes the governmental system created by the Framers; see also federal system.

supremacy clause: Portion of Article IV of the U.S. Constitution that mandates that national law is supreme to (that is, supersedes) all other laws passed by the states or by any other subdivision of government.

FIGURE 3.2

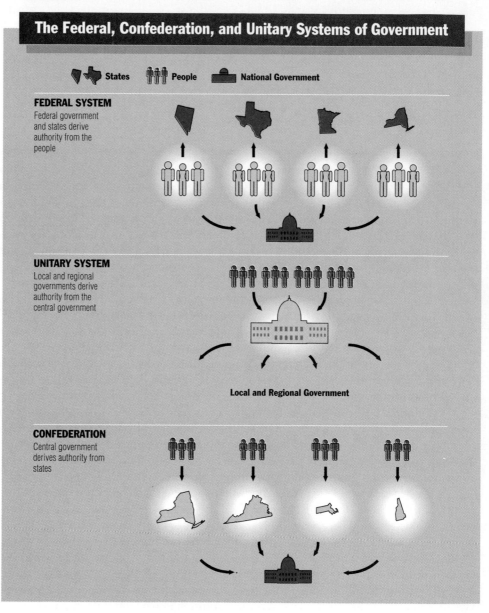

The Federal, Confederation, and Unitary Systems of Government

States · People · National Government

FEDERAL SYSTEM
Federal government and states derive authority from the people

UNITARY SYSTEM
Local and regional governments derive authority from the central government

Local and Regional Government

CONFEDERATION
Central government derives authority from states

law come into conflict, national law (including treaties) is supreme. (See also *McCulloch v. Maryland* [1819].)

The federal government's right to tax was also clearly set out in the new Constitution. The Framers wanted to avoid the financial problems that the national government had experienced under the Articles of Confederation. To survive as a strong national government, the power of the national government to raise revenue had to be unquestionable.

The new Constitution left the qualifications of suffrage to the individual states, as noted in Roots of Government: U.S. Citizenship Rights and the Franchise. Thus, over time, the right to vote even in national elections has varied.

Roots of Government

U.S. Citizenship Rights and the Franchise

On March 21, 1776, Abigail Adams wrote to her husband, John, who was in attendance at the Continental Congress. She urged him to "Remember the Ladies" in any "new Code of Laws" that was to be written, and to "be more generous . . . to them than [their] ancestors, . . ." She warned that ultimately, women would not consider themselves "bound by any Laws in which [they had] no voice, or Representation."* In spite of, or more likely simply ignoring, Abigail Adams's admonitions, neither the Articles of Confederation nor the Constitution even mentioned women. Article I, section 4, moreover, gave the states the authority to establish the "Time, Places, and Manner of holding Elections." Congress thus allowed the states to determine who would be eligible to cast their votes for their own representatives.

The Constitution begins with the ringing words "We the People," but it was silent on qualifications for citizenship and voting, noting only that the "Citizens of each State shall be entitled to all Privileges and Immunities of the Citizens of the several States." At the time the Constitution was ratified, while white women were considered citizens, *no* state allowed women to vote in their state election. Nor could they hold state or national elective office.

It was not only women who were denied full participation in government. Most states had stringent land-owning or property requirements. Thus few poor men could vote either. And in the Southern states, where slaves were not considered by the states to be citizens, they too could not vote.

Over the years states eliminated most of the restrictions on white male voting. Passage of the Fourteenth Amendment in 1868 defined U.S. citizenship—thereby making all former slaves citizens—noting that "All persons born or naturalized in the United States, and subject to the jurisdiction thereof, are citizens of the United States, and of the state wherein they reside." Passage of the Fifteenth Amendment specifically guaranteed the right to vote to newly freed male slaves—the first national statement of voter eligibility. This was soon followed without a provision to guarantee women the right to vote. Women did not secure the right to vote nationally until 1920, with passage of the Nineteenth Amendment, although several states allowed women to vote before then.

Over time, the national government was forced to step in when some states tried to deny the right to vote to portions of their citizenry. First, the U.S. Supreme Court ruled that many state practices that acted to disenfranchise African Americans were unconstitutional. Later, the U.S. Congress stepped in to pass the Voting Rights Act of 1965 to guarantee that Southern states would end their efforts to disenfranchise potential black voters.

It was not until 1971, fifty-one years after passage of the Nineteenth Amendment, that the Constitution was again altered specifically to expand the electorate. Prior to that time, some states had expanded the ranks of eligible voters by allowing those eighteen and older to vote. The states thus became laboratories of experiment. Soon the rest of the nation fell into synch with ratification of the Twenty-Sixth Amendment, guaranteeing the right to vote to all U.S. citizens "eighteen years of age or older."

*Quoted in H. L. Butterfield, *et al.*, eds., *The Book of Abigail and John* (Cambridge, MA: Harvard University Press, 1975), 21.

THE POWERS OF GOVERNMENT IN THE FEDERAL SYSTEM

*T*he distribution of powers in the federal system is often described as two overlapping systems, as illustrated in Figure 3.3. On the left are powers that specifically granted to Congress in Article I. Chief among the exclusive powers delegated to the national government are the authorities to coin money, conduct foreign relations, provide for an army and navy, declare war, and establish a national court system. All of these powers set out in Article I, section 8 of the Constitution, are called enumerated powers. Article I, section 8 also contains the **necessary and proper clause,** giving Congress the authority to enact any laws "necessary and proper" for carrying out any of its enumerated powers. Thus, for example, Congress's power to charter a national bank has been held to be an **implied power** derived from its enumerated power to tax and spend.[9]

The Constitution does not specifically delegate or enumerate many specific powers to the states. Because states had all the power at the time the Constitution was written, the Framers felt no need, as they did for the new national government, to list and restate the powers of the states. Article I, however, allows states to set the "Times, Places and Manner, for holding elections for senators and representatives," and Article II requires that each state appoint electors to vote for president. States were also given the power to ratify amendments to the U.S. Constitution. Nevertheless, the enumeration of so many specific powers to the national government and so few to the states is a clear indication of the Federalist leanings of the Framers. It was not until the addition of the Bill of Rights and the Tenth Amendment that the states' powers were better described: "The powers not delegated to the United States by the Constitution, nor prohibited by it to the States, are reserved to the States respectively, or to the people." These powers, often called the states' **reserve** or **police powers,** include the ability to legislate for the public health, safety, and morals of their citizens. The states' rights to

necessary and proper clause:
A name given to the clause found in the final paragraph of Article I, section 8 of the U.S. Constitution giving Congress the authority to pass all laws "necessary and proper" to carry out the enumerated powers specified in the Constitution; the "elastic" clause.

implied power: A power derived from an enumerated power and the necessary and proper clause. These powers are not stated specifically but are considered to be reasonably implied through the exercise of delegated powers.

reserve (or police) powers:
Powers reserved to the states by the Tenth Amendment that lie at the foundation of a state's right to legislate for the public health and welfare of its citizens.

FIGURE 3.3

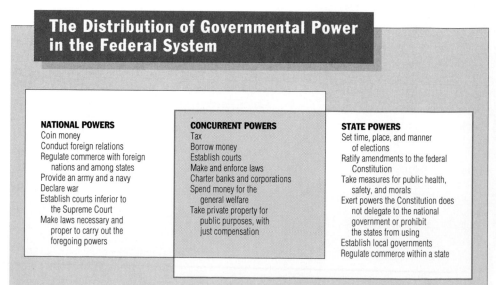

The Distribution of Governmental Power in the Federal System

NATIONAL POWERS
Coin money
Conduct foreign relations
Regulate commerce with foreign
    nations and among states
Provide an army and a navy
Declare war
Establish courts inferior to
    the Supreme Court
Make laws necessary and
    proper to carry out the
    foregoing powers

CONCURRENT POWERS
Tax
Borrow money
Establish courts
Make and enforce laws
Charter banks and corporations
Spend money for the
    general welfare
Take private property for
    public purposes, with
    just compensation

STATE POWERS
Set time, place, and manner
    of elections
Ratify amendments to the federal
    Constitution
Take measures for public health,
    safety, and morals
Exert powers the Constitution does
    not delegate to the national
    government or prohibit
    the states from using
Establish local governments
Regulate commerce within a state

legislate under their police powers today are used as the rationale for many states' restrictions on abortion, including twenty-four-hour waiting requirements and provisions requiring minors to obtain parental consent. Police powers are also the basis for state criminal laws. That is why some states have the death penalty and others do not. So long as the U.S. Supreme Court continues to find that the death penalty does not violate the U.S. Constitution, the states may impose it, be it by lethal injection, gas chamber, or the electric chair.

As revealed in Figure 3.3, national and state powers also overlap. The area where the systems overlap represents **concurrent powers**—powers shared by the national and state governments. States already had the power to tax; the Constitution extended this power to the national government as well. Other important concurrent powers include the right to borrow money, establish courts, and make and enforce laws necessary to carry out these powers.

concurrent powers: Powers shared by the national and state governments.

Denied Powers

Article I also denies certain powers to the national and state governments. In keeping with the Framers' desire to forge a national economy, states are prohibited from entering treaties, coining money, or impairing obligation of contracts. States are also prohibited from entering into "compacts" with other states without express congressional approval. In a similar vein, Congress is barred from favoring one state over another in regulating commerce, and it cannot lay duties on items exported from any state.

Both the national and state governments are denied the authority to take arbitrary actions affecting constitutional rights and liberties. Neither national nor state governments may pass a **bill of attainder,** a law declaring an act illegal without a judicial trial. The Constitution also bars either from passing *ex post facto* **laws,** laws that make an act punishable as a crime even if the action was legal at the time it was committed.

bill of attainder: A law declaring an act illegal without a judicial trial.

***ex post facto* law:** Law passed after the fact, thereby making previously legal activity illegal and subject to current penalty; prohibited by the U.S. Constitution.

Guarantees to the States

In return for giving up some of their powers, the states received several guarantees in the Constitution. Among them:

- Article I guarantees each state two members in the U.S. Senate and guarantees that Congress would not limit slavery before 1808.
- Article IV guarantees the citizens of each state the privileges and immunities of citizens of all other states; guarantees each state a "Republican Form of Government," meaning one that represents the citizens of the state; and guarantees that the national government will protect the states against foreign attacks and domestic rebellion.

Relations Among the States

The Constitution was designed to improve relations among the squabbling states. To that end it provides that disputes between states are to be settled directly by the U.S. Supreme Court under its original jurisdiction to avoid any sense of favoritism (see chapter 10). Moreover, Article IV requires that each state give "Full Faith and Credit . . . to the public Acts, Records and judicial Proceedings of every other State." This clause ensures that judicial decrees and contracts made in one state will be binding and enforceable in another, thereby facilitating trade and other commercial relationships. As Politics Now: Gay Marriages: Does "Full Faith and Credit" Apply?

The Port Authority jointly operated by New York and New Jersey is just one example of cooperative ventures by the states approved by Congress. States are encouraged to enter into these kinds of compacts by the nature of our federal system. Before adoption of the U.S. Constitution, the states were not encouraged to share their powers, and commerce often suffered. (Photo courtesy: Kunio Owaki/The Stock Market) illustrates, the scope of this provision may soon be tested should Hawaii recognize same-sex marriages. Historically, marriages conducted in one state are valid in another state. The prospect of gay marriages, however, already has prompted some states to enact laws specifying that same-sex marriages performed in other states will not be recognized and for the U.S. Congress to weigh in against same-sex marriages, too.

In a similar vein, the Constitution requires states to extradite, or return, criminals to states where they have been convicted or are to stand trial. In 1987, for example, when the governor of Iowa refused to honor Puerto Rico's request to extradite a man charged with first-degree murder, the Court ruled that the extradition clause is binding on the states and is not discretionary. Iowa's governor had argued that the charges against the accused were unreasonable, and that because the defendant was white, he would be unlikely to receive a fair trial in Puerto Rico.[10] Nevertheless, because the federal government today has the authority to enforce the extradition law, the Court found that Iowa was bound by the Constitution.

THE EVOLUTION AND DEVELOPMENT OF FEDERALISM

The victory of the Federalists—those who supported a strong national government—had long-lasting consequences on the future of the nation. Over the course of our nation's history, the nature of federalism and its allocation of power between the national government and the states have changed dramatically, as revealed in Table 3.1. The debate continues today, too, as many Americans, frustrated with the national government's performance on a number of issues, look for a return of more power to the states. Because the distribution of power between the national and state governments is not clearly delineated in the Constitution, over the years the U.S. Supreme Court has played a major role in defining the nature of the federal system.

TABLE 3.1

Periods in the Evolution of the Federal System

1789–1834	**Nationalization:** The Marshall Court broadly interprets the Constitution to expand and consolidate national power.
1835–1860	**Dual Federalism: Phase 1**—Power of national government limited to enumerated powers; states consider themselves sovereign; governments in state of tension over scope of their respective authorities.
1861–1933	**Dual Federalism: Phase 2**—Dual characteristics continue, but national government gains power; land-grant era
1934–1960	**Cooperative Federalism:** Dramatic increase in grants-in-aid; federal, state, and local sharing of responsibilities; increased regulation by national government.
1960–1968	**Creative Federalism:** Hallmark of Johnson era; increased grants to state and local governments and direct aid to individuals.
1968–1992	**New Federalism:** Emphasis on the return of power to the states; later characterized by the significant reduction in federal aid to the states.
1993–	**Newtonian Federalism:** Possible major restructuring of the federal system.

Politics Now

Gay Marriages: Does "Full Faith and Credit" Apply?

The Tenth Amendment to the Constitution specifies that the states were to retain all powers not specifically given to the federal government by the new Constitution. Historically, the Tenth Amendment has thus been used to justify state regulation of marriage and family law. Grounds for divorce, guidelines for child support, and minimum age at marriage are all items that vary considerably across states. But at this writing, no state law recognizes same-sex marriages, although some cities sanction what are termed domestic partnership arrangements that allow same-sex couples to take advantage of family health insurance and benefits.

In 1993 a decision of the Hawaiian Supreme Court called that state's ban on homosexual marriages into constitutional question. After three homosexual couples were denied marriage licenses by the State Department of Health in 1990, they filed suit in 1991 alleging that the state violated their rights to equal protection under the Hawaii Constitution, which prohibits discrimination based on sex. In 1993 the state Supreme Court ruled that the homosexual couples' rights appeared to have been violated, and sent the case back to the lower court

with instructions that the state must show a "compelling state interest" to continue to deny marriage licenses to same-sex couples. In June 1994 the governor signed a law stating that marriage licenses could only be for male–female couples and stipulating that state policy can be changed only by the legislature, not the courts. The bill also called for the creation of a Commission on Sexual Orientation and the Law. On December 9, 1995, the Commission recommended that Hawaii legalize marriage between same-sex couples or set up comprehensive domestic partnership laws.[*]

In early 1995 a Washington, D.C., Court of Appeals ruled that a D.C. opposite-sex-only marriage ordinance did not violate any constitutional rights, and other cases are moving through other state court systems. At this writing, the Hawaiian Supreme Court had yet to render its final decision. Once it does, however, since this case was litigated under the Hawaiian Constitution, no appeal to the U.S. Supreme Court is possible.

The U.S. Constitution requires that all states give "Full Faith and Credit" to the laws of and contracts made in the other states. Thus, if a couple gets married in Texas, they are still recognized as being married in California if they move or vacation there. Hawaii's potential legalization of same-sex marriages has therefore thrown many state legislatures into a tizzy. Conservative legislators in at least twenty

states are now at work to pass legislation that specifically would ban same-sex marriages. Others have enacted legislation stating that no matter what Hawaii does, they will not recognize such marriages performed there. If Hawaii legalizes same-sex marriages, travel agents speculate that huge numbers of gay couples would travel to Hawaii to legalize their union.

In essence, by acting preemptively to state that they will not recognize same-sex marriages, states are attempting to assert their police powers to ban what they believe are unnatural acts. However, all states are bound by the U.S. Constitution. Thus, should Hawaii ultimately allow homosexuals to marry, years of litigation are likely to lie ahead in states that refuse to recognize those unions. The picture is even muddier given recent congressional action. In 1996 it passed, and President Clinton signed, the Defense of Marriage Act designed to undercut the pending Hawaiian court action. This federal law permits states to disregard gay marriages even if they are legal in other states. The U.S. Constitution, however, doesn't give Congress the authority to create exceptions to the full faith and credit clause of the Constitution. Thus, more litigation is likely should Hawaii become the first state to recognize same-sex unions. Where do you stand on same-sex marriages? Regardless of your opinion, should they be a state or federal matter?

[*]Cheryl Wetzstein, "Hawaii on Threshold to OK Gay Marriages," *The Washington Times* (February 5, 1996): A3.

Nationalization

From the beginning, the federal courts, especially the Supreme Court, were involved in developing the structure and mechanics of the federal system. John Marshall (1801–35), an ardent Federalist, sat at the head of the federal judiciary. In a series of important decisions, Chief Justice Marshall and the Supreme Court reaffirmed the Federalists' beliefs in a strong national government. Federalist sentiments could be seen especially clearly in the Court's broad interpretations of the Constitution's supremacy clause and the commerce clause, both of which were used to expand and consolidate the power of the national government.

It is important to remember how different government was in those days. During the period the Marshall Court was nationalizing the federal system, the national government was small, with limited activities and minimal spending, and the role of state government in everyday life was far more pervasive than it is today. States exercised tremendous powers over the electoral process (including who voted and how congressional districts were drawn) and were the center of party organizations. States also controlled labor conditions, race relations, education, property rights, criminal and family law, and, in the South, slavery.

McCulloch v. *Maryland* (1819).

McCulloch was the first major decision of the Marshall Court to define the relationship between the national and state governments. In 1816 Congress chartered the Second Bank of the United States. (The charter of the First Bank had been allowed to expire.) The Second Bank was never popular and had detractors on several fronts. Farmers and the poor had a strong suspicion and hatred of banks (as was true since the time of Daniel Shays's march on the courthouse in Massachusetts). So did many Jeffersonian Democratic-Republicans (see chapter 12) who felt that the national government lacked the authority to establish a bank. They believed that because the power to issue corporate charters was not granted to Congress by the Constitution, the Bank of the United States was unconstitutional. States also disliked the national bank; it was the largest corporation in the United States and provided stiff competition for state-chartered banks.

In 1818 the Democratic-Republican-controlled Maryland assembly tried to do something about it. Maryland levied a tax requiring all banks not chartered by Maryland (that is, the Second Bank of the United States) to (1) buy stamped paper from the state on which the Second Bank's notes were to be issued; (2) pay the state $15,000 a year; or (3) go out of business. Maryland was not the only state to attempt to tax the U.S. bank out of business. Tennessee, Georgia, Ohio, and North Carolina, for example, enacted laws requiring each branch of the national bank to pay $50,000 to their respective state treasuries to stay in business. Illinois and Indiana, which had no branches of the national bank, passed laws prohibiting their establishment.

James McCulloch, the head cashier of the Baltimore branch of the Bank of the United States, refused to pay the tax, and Maryland brought suit against him. After losing in a Maryland court, McCulloch appealed his conviction to the U.S. Supreme Court by order of the U.S. Secretary of the Treasury. Daniel Webster, a former Federalist member of Congress and one of the best lawyers in the nation, argued on behalf of the federal government and for the constitutionality of the Bank. Maryland was represented by Luther Martin, who had been an active opponent of the new Constitution at the Philadelphia Convention. There he had railed against the chains being forged for "his country"—Maryland—and its subjugation to new national power. Although Chief Justice John Marshall still presided over the Court, only he and one other Federalist justice remained. The other five justices were Democratic-Republicans appointed by Presidents Jefferson and Madison. Nevertheless, in a unanimous opinion, the Court answered the two central questions that had been put to it: First, did Congress have the authority to charter a bank? And, second, if it did, could a state tax it?

Chief Justice Marshall's answer to the first question—whether Congress had the right to establish a bank or another type of corporation, given that the Constitution does not explicitly mention such a power—continues to stand as the classic exposition of the doctrine of implied powers, and as a reaffirmation of the propriety of a strong national government. Although the word "bank" cannot be found in the Constitution, the Constitution enumerates powers that give Congress the authority to levy and collect taxes, issue a currency, and borrow funds. From these enumerated powers, Marshall found, it was reasonable to imply that Congress had the power to charter a bank, which could be considered "necessary and proper" to the exercise of its enumerated powers.

In some of the most famous language from the case, Marshall carefully set out an expansive interpretation of the necessary and proper clause of Article I, section 8, and the possible scope of implied powers, proclaiming:

> Let the end be legitimate, let it be within the scope of the Constitution, and all means which are appropriate, which are plainly adapted to that end, which are not prohibited, but consistent with the letter and spirit of the Constitution, are constitutional.[11]

Marshall next addressed the question of whether a federal bank could be taxed by any state government. To Marshall, this was not a difficult question. The national government was dependent on the people, not the states, for its powers. In addition, Marshall noted, the Constitution specifically calls for the national law to be supreme. Thus the national government and its "instrumentalities," such as the Bank, had to be immune from state interference. "The power to tax involves the power to destroy," wrote Marshall. Thus the state tax violated the supremacy clause, since states cannot interfere with the operations of the national government, whose laws are supreme.

Gibbons v. Ogden (1824).　　Shortly after *McCulloch*, the Marshall Court had another opportunity to rule in favor of a broad interpretation of the scope of national power. *Gibbons* involved a dispute that arose after the New York State legislature granted to Robert Fulton the exclusive right to operate steamboats on the Hudson River. Simultaneously, Congress licensed a ship to sail on the same waters. By the time the case reached the Supreme Court, it was complicated both factually and procedurally. Suffice it to say that both New York and New Jersey wanted to control shipping on the lower Hudson River. But *Gibbons* actually addressed one simple, very important question: What was the scope of Congress's authority under the commerce clause? The

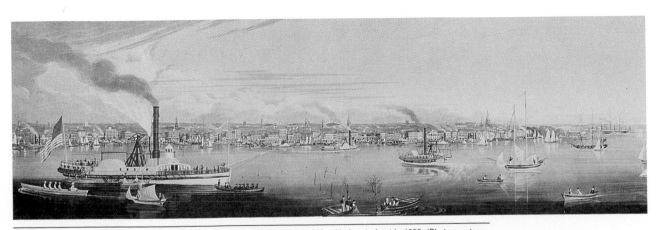

The *Gibbons* v. *Ogden* decision opened the waters to free competition; this is the New York waterfront in 1839. (Photo courtesy: I. N. Phelps Stokes Collection, Miriam and Ira D. Wallach Division of Art, Prints, and Photographs, The New York Public Library Astor, Lenox and Tilden Foundations)

states argued that "commerce," as mentioned in Article I, should be interpreted narrowly to include only direct dealings in products. Thus regulation of shipping on inland waterways would be beyond the scope of Congress's authority to regulate. In *Gibbons*, however, Chief Justice Marshall ruled that Congress's power to regulate interstate commerce included the power to regulate commercial activity as well, and that the commerce power had no limits except those specifically found in the Constitution. Thus New York had no constitutional authority to grant a monopoly to a single steamboat operator, thereby interfering with interstate commerce.[12]

Dual Federalism: Phase I

In spite of the nationalist Marshall Court decisions, strong debate continued in the United States over national versus state power. It was under the leadership of Chief Justice Marshall's successor, Roger B. Taney (1835–63), that the Supreme Court articulated the notions of concurrent power, the belief that separate and equally powerful levels of government is the best arrangement; and **dual federalism,** which holds that the national government should not exceed its enumerated powers expressly set out in the Constitution.

dual federalism: The belief that having separate and equally powerful levels of government is the best arrangement.

In a series of cases involving the scope of Congress's power under the commerce clause, the Taney Court further developed doctrines first enunciated by Marshall, but put greater stress on a concurrent national/state relationship that allowed state involvement in commerce, so long as it did not interfere with federal law. The Taney Court attempted to allow new businesses to flourish, broadened the sphere of *laissez-faire*, and allowed the states greater involvement in corporate affairs. In spite of Taney's major contributions defining the economic and commercial roles of the national and state governments in the federal system, his Court is best remembered for its unfortunate handling of the slavery issue, which threatened the federal system itself.

Federalism and Slavery. During the Taney era, the comfortable role of the Court as the arbiter of competing national and state interests became troublesome when the Court found itself called upon to deal with the highly political issue of slavery. In cases such as *Dred Scott* v. *Sandford* (1857) and others, the Court tried to manage the slavery issue by resolving questions of ownership, the status of fugitive slaves, and slavery in the new territories. These cases generally were settled in favor of slavery and states' rights within the framework of dual federalism. In its treatment of slavery (see Highlight 3.1: Dred Scott) the Taney Court erred grievously and thereby contributed to the coming of the Civil War, since its decision seemed to rule out any political (legislative) solution to slavery by the national government.

nullification doctrine: The claimed right of a state to nullify, or reject, a federal law.

While the Court was carving out the appropriate role of each level of government in the federal system, the political debate over states' rights (especially where slavery was concerned) continued to swirl, in large part over what was called the **nullification doctrine,** the purported right of a state to nullify a federal law. As early as 1798, Congress approved the very unpopular Alien and Sedition Acts to prevent criticism of the national government (see chapter 5). Men like Thomas Jefferson and James Madison, who opposed the acts, suggested that the states had the right to nullify any federal law that in the opinion of the states violated the Constitution.

The question of nullification of federal law came up again in 1828, when the national government enacted a tariff act that raised duties on raw materials (iron, hemp, and flax) and reduced protections against imported woolen goods. John C. Calhoun, who served as vice president from 1825 to 1832 under President Andrew Jackson, broke

Highlight 3.1

Dred Scott

Dred Scott, born into slavery around 1795, became the named plaintiff in a case that was to have major ramifications on the nature of the federal system. In 1833 Scott was sold by his original owners, the Blow family, to Dr. Emerson, an army surgeon in St. Louis, Missouri. The next year he was taken to Illinois and later to the Wisconsin Territory, returning to St. Louis in 1838.*

When Dr. Emerson died in 1843, Scott tried to buy his freedom. Before he

(Photo courtesy: Missouri Historical Society)

could, however, he was transferred to Emerson's widow, who moved to New York leaving Scott in the custody of his first owners, the Blows. Some of the Blows (Henry Blow later

founded the antislavery Free Soil Party) and other abolitionists gave money to support a test case seeking Scott's freedom: They believed that his residence in Illinois and later in the Wisconsin Territory, both of which prohibited slavery, in essence made him a free man.

In 1857, after many delays, the U.S. Supreme Court ruled seven to two that Scott was not a citizen and that slaves "were never thought of or spoken of except as property." At the urging of President James Buchanan, Justice Roger B. Taney tried to fashion a

broad ruling that would settle the slavery question. He ruled that the Congress of the United States lacked the constitutional authority to bar slavery in the territories, thus narrowing the scope of national power while enhancing that of the states. Moreover, for the first time since *Marbury v. Madison* (1803), the Court found an act of Congress—the Missouri Compromise—unconstitutional. And, by limiting what the national government could do concerning slavery, it in all likelihood quickened the march toward the Civil War.

*Don E. Ferenbacher, "The Dred Scott Case," in *Quarrels That Have Shaped the Constitution*, John A. Garraty, ed (New York: Harper & Row, 1964), chapter 6.

with Jackson over the tariff act because it badly affected his home state of South Carolina. Not only did South Carolinians have to pay more for raw materials because of the new tariff law; it was also becoming more and more difficult for them to sell their dwindling crops abroad for a profit. Calhoun thus resorted to the nullification doctrine to justify South Carolina's refusal to abide by the federal law. Later, he used the same doctrine to justify the Southern states' resistance to national actions to limit slavery.

Calhoun theorized that the federal government was but the agent of the states (the people and the individual state governments) and that the Constitution was simply a compact that provided instructions about how the agent was to act. Calhoun thus reasoned that the U.S. Supreme Court was not competent to pass on the constitutional validity of acts of Congress. Like Congress, the Court was only a branch of a government created by and answerable to the states. Calhoun posited that if the people of any individual state did not like an act of Congress, they could hold a convention to declare that act null and void. In the state contesting the act, the law would have no force until three-fourths of all of the states ratified an amendment expressly giving Congress that power. If the nullifying state still did not wish to be bound by the new provision, it could secede (withdraw) from the Union. In their fight (begun in the 1850s) to keep slavery, the Southern states relied heavily on Calhoun's theories to justify their secession from the Union, ultimately leading to the Civil War.

Dual Federalism: Phase 2

The Civil War forever changed the nature of federalism, but the Supreme Court continued to adhere to its belief in the concept of dual federalism. Thus the importance and powers of the states were not diminished in spite of the addition of the Thirteenth, Fourteenth, and Fifteenth Amendments to the Constitution (see chapter 6), or by Abraham Lincoln's appointment of the first Republican Chief Justice, Salmon Chase (1864–73). In *The Slaughterhouse Cases* (1873), for example, the Court interpreted the Civil War Amendments very narrowly, signaling the Court's reluctance to allow Congress to expand its authority further, whether by amendment or by statute.[13]

Between 1865 (the end of the Civil War) and 1933 (when the next major change in the federal system occurred), the Court generally continued to support dual federalism along several lines. State courts, for example, were considered to have the final say on the construction of laws affecting local affairs.[14] Generally, the Court upheld any laws passed under the states' police powers, which allow states to pass laws to protect the general welfare of their citizens. These laws included those affecting commerce, labor relations, and manufacturing. After the Court's decision in *Plessy* v. *Ferguson* (1896),[15] in which the Court ruled that state maintenance of "separate but equal" facilities for blacks and whites was constitutional, most civil rights and voting cases also became state matters, in spite of the Civil War amendments.

The Court also developed legal doctrine in a series of cases that reinforced the national government's ability to regulate commerce. By the 1930s these two somewhat contradictory approaches led to confusion: States, for example, could not tax gasoline used by federal vehicles,[16] and the national government could not tax the sale of motorcycles to the city police department.[17] In this period the Court did recognize the need for national control over new technological developments, such as the telegraph.[18] And beginning in the 1880s, the Court allowed Congress to regulate many aspects of economic relationships such as outlawing monopolies, a type of regulation or power formerly thought to be in the exclusive realm of the states. Passage of laws such as the Interstate Commerce Act in 1887 and the Sherman Anti-Trust Act in 1890 allowed Congress to establish itself as an important player in the growing national economy.

Despite finding that most of these federal laws were constitutional, the Supreme Court did not consistently enlarge the scope of national power. In 1895, for example, the United States filed suit against four sugar refiners, alleging that their sale would give their buyer control of 98 percent of the U.S. sugar-refining business. The Supreme Court ruled that congressional efforts to control monopolies (through passage of the Sherman Anti-Trust Act) did not give Congress the authority to prevent the sale of these sugar-refining businesses, because manufacturing was not commerce. Therefore the companies and their actions were beyond the scope of Congress's authority to regulate.[19]

Cooperative Federalism

The era of dual federalism came to an abrupt end in the 1930s. Its demise began in a series of economic events that ended in the cataclysm of the Great Depression:

- In 1921 the nation experienced a severe slump in agricultural prices.
- In 1926 the construction industry went into decline.
- In the summer of 1929, inventories of consumer goods and automobiles were at an all-time high.

This famous cartoon by noted political cartoonist Thomas Nast pokes fun at the myriad trusts that led to congressional passage of the Sherman Anti-Trust Act. (Photo courtesy: The Bettmann Archive)

- Throughout the 1920s bank failures had become common.

- On October 29, 1929, stock prices, which had risen steadily since 1926, crashed, taking with them the entire national economy.

The New Deal.   Rampant unemployment (historians estimate it was as high as 40 percent to 50 percent) was the hallmark of the Great Depression. To combat this unemployment and a host of other problems facing the nation, newly elected President Franklin D. Roosevelt, (FDR) proposed in 1933 a variety of innovative programs under the rubric "the New Deal" and ushered in a new era in American politics. FDR used the full power of the office of president as well as his highly effective communication skills to sell the American public and Congress on a whole new ideology of government. Not only were the scope and role of national government remarkably altered, but so was the relationship between each state and the national government. It is, in fact, the growth in the federal government that began with the New Deal that many who urge less federal power bemoan today.

The New Deal period (1933–39) was characterized by intense government activity on the national level. It was clear to most politicians that to find national solutions to the Depression, which was affecting the citizens of every state in the Union, the national government would have to exercise tremendous authority.

In the first few weeks of the legislative session after FDR's inauguration, Congress and the president acted quickly to bolster confidence in the national government. Soon after, Congress passed a series of acts creating programs proposed by the president. These new agencies, often known by their initials, created what many termed an "alphabetocracy." Among the more significant programs were the Federal Housing Administration (FHA), which provided federal financing for new home construction; the Civilian Conservation Corps (CCC), a work relief program for farmers and homeowners; and the Agricultural Adjustment Administration (AAA) and the National Recovery Administration (NRA), both of which imposed restrictions on production in agriculture and many industries.

These programs tremendously enlarged the scope of the national government. Those who feared this unprecedented use of national power quickly challenged the constitutionality of New Deal programs in court. And, at least initially, the Supreme Court often agreed with them.

Through the mid-1930s, the Supreme Court continued to rule that certain aspects of the New Deal went beyond the authority of Congress to regulate commerce. In fact, many believe that the Court considered the Depression to be no more than the sum of the economic woes of the individual states and that it was a problem most appropriately handled by the states. The Court's *laissez-faire* or "hands-off" attitude toward the economy was reflected in a series of decisions ruling various aspects of New Deal programs unconstitutional.

FDR and the Congress were outraged. FDR's frustration with the *laissez-faire* attitude of the Court prompted him to suggest what was ultimately nicknamed his "Court-packing plan." Knowing that he could do little to change the minds of those already on the Court, FDR suggested enlarging its size from nine to thirteen justices. This would have given him the opportunity to "pack" the Court with a majority of justices predisposed to the constitutional validity of the New Deal.

Even though Roosevelt was popular, the Court-packing plan was not. Congress and the public were outraged that he even suggested tampering with an institution of government. Nevertheless, the Court appeared to respond to this threat. In 1937 it reversed its series of anti-New Deal decisions, concluding that Congress (and therefore the na-

One of the hallmarks of the New Deal and FDR's presidency was the national government's new involvement of cities in the federal system. Here, New York City Mayor Fiorello La Guardia is commissioned as Director of Civil Defense by FDR. (Photo courtesy: AP/Worldwide Photos)

tional government) had the authority to legislate in areas that only affected commerce. Congress then used this newly recognized power to legislate in a wide array of areas, including maximum hour and minimum wage laws, and regulation of child labor. Moreover, the Court also upheld the constitutionality of the bulk of the massive New Deal relief programs, such as the National Labor Relations Act of 1935, which authorized collective bargaining between unions and employees in *NLRB* v. *Jones and Laughlin Steel Co.* (1937);[20] and the Fair Labor Standards Act of 1938, which prohibited the interstate shipment of goods made by employees earning less than the federally mandated minimum wage;[21] and the Agriculture Adjustment Act of 1938, which provided crop subsidies to farmers.[22]

The New Deal programs forced all levels of government to work cooperatively with one another. Indeed, local governments—mainly in big cities—became a third partner in the federal system, as FDR relied on big-city Democratic political machines to turn out voters to support his programs. For the first time in U.S. history, in essence, cities were embraced as equal partners in an intergovernmental system and became players in the national political arena because many in the national legislature wanted to bypass state legislatures, where urban interests were usually significantly underrepresented.

The Changing Nature of Federalism: From Layer Cake to Marble Cake.   Before the Depression and the New Deal, most political scientists likened the federal system to a layer cake: Each level or layer of government—national, state, and local—had clearly defined powers and responsibilities. After the New Deal, however, the nature of the federal system changed. Government now looked something like a marble cake:

> Wherever you slice through it you reveal an inseparable mixture of differently colored ingredients. . . . Vertical and diagonal lines almost obliterate the hori

zontal ones, and in some places there are unexpected whirls and an imperceptible merging of colors, so that it is difficult to tell where one ends and the other begins.[23]

This kind of "marble cake" federalism is often called **cooperative federalism,** a term that describes the relationship between the national, state, and local governments that began with the New Deal as a stronger, more influential national government was created in response to economic and social crises. States began to take a secondary, albeit important, "cooperative" role in the scheme of governance, as did many cities. Nowhere is this shift in power from the states *to* the national government more clear than in the growth of federal grant programs that began in earnest during the New Deal. The tremendous growth in these programs and in federal government spending in general, as illustrated in Table 3.2, changed the nature and discussion of federalism from that time to 1997: from "How much power should the national government have?" to "How much say in the policies of the states can the national government buy?"

Federal Grants. As early as 1790, Congress appropriated funds for the states to pay debts incurred during the Revolutionary War. But it wasn't until the Civil War that Congress enacted its first true federal grant program, which allocated federal funds to the states for a specific purpose.

Most view the start of this redistribution of funds with the Morrill Land Grant Act of 1862, which gave each state 30,000 acres of public land for each representative in Congress. Income from the sale of these lands was to be earmarked for the establishment and support of agricultural and mechanical arts colleges. Sixty-nine land-grant

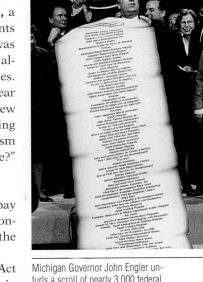

Michigan Governor John Engler unfurls a scroll of nearly 3,000 federal antipoverty programs that several Republican governors wanted dismantled in favor of lump-sum block grants that would allow the states to decide where federal dollars in the states are best spent. (Photo courtesy: Jym Wilson/Gannett News Service)

cooperative federalism: A term used to characterize the relationship between the national and state governments that began with the New Deal.

TABLE 3.2

Federal Grants-in-Aid, 1950–97

YEAR	TOTAL (IN BILLIONS OF DOLLARS)	Grants-in-Aid as a Percentage of	
		FEDERAL OUTLAYS	STATE AND LOCAL OUTLAYS
1950	$ 2.3	5.3	—
1955	3.2	4.7	—
1960	7.0	8.0	15.0
1965	10.9	9.0	16.0
1970	24.1	12.0	20.0
1975	49.8	15.0	24.0
1980	91.4	15.0	28.0
1985	105.9	11.0	23.0
1990	135.3	11.0	20.0
1995	225.0	15.0	23.0
1997 *est.*	249.3	15.0	NA

Source: 1950–91: Office of Management and Budget, *Budget Baselines, Historical Data, and Alternatives for the Future* (Washington, DC: U.S. Government Printing Office, 1993), 428; *Budget of the United States Government, Fiscal Year 1997* (Washington, DC: U.S. Government Printing Office, 1996), 170.

colleges—including Texas A&M University, the University of Georgia, and Michigan State University—were founded, making this grant program the single most important piece of education legislation passed in the United States up to that time.

Franklin D. Roosevelt's New Deal program increased the flow of federal dollars to the states with the infusion of massive federal dollars for a variety of public works programs, including building and road construction. These grants made the imposition of national goals on the states easier. No state wanted to decline funds, so states often secured funds for any programs for which money was available—whether they needed it for that specific purpose or not.

In the boom times of World War II, even more new federal programs were introduced; and by the 1950s and 1960s, federal grant-in-aid programs were well entrenched. They often defined federal/state relationships and made the national government a major player in domestic policy. Until the 1960s, however, most federal grants programs were constructed in cooperation with the states and were designed to assist the states in furthering their traditional responsibilities to protect the health, welfare, and safety of their citizens. Most of these programs were **categorical grants,** ones for which Congress appropriates funds for specific purposes. Funds are allocated by a precise formula and are subject to detailed conditions imposed by the national government, often on a matching basis; that is, states must contribute money to match federal funds, although the national government may pay as much as 90 percent of the total.

categorical grant: Grant for which Congress appropriates funds for a specific purpose.

Creative Federalism

By the early 1960s, as concern about the poor and minorities rose, and as states (especially in the South) were blamed for perpetuating discrimination,[24] those in power in the national government saw grants as a way to force states to behave in ways desired by the national government. If the states would not cooperate with the national government to further its goals, it would withhold funds.

In 1964 the Democratic administration of President Lyndon B. Johnson (LBJ) (1963–69) launched its renowned "Great Society" program, which included what LBJ called a "War on Poverty." The Great Society program was a broad attempt to combat poverty and discrimination. In a frenzy of activity in Washington not seen since the New Deal, federal funds were channeled to states, to local governments, and even directly to citizen action groups in an effort to alleviate social ills that the states had been unable or unwilling to remedy. There was money for urban renewal, education, and poverty programs, including Head Start and job training. The move to fund local groups directly was made by the most liberal members of Congress in order to bypass not only conservative state legislatures, but also conservative mayors and councils in cities like Chicago, who were not frequently moved to help their poor, often African-American, constituencies. Thus these programs often pitted governors and mayors against community activists, who became key players in the distribution of federal dollars.

These new grants altered the fragile federal/state balance of power that had been at the core of most older federal grant programs. During the Johnson administration, the national government began to use federal grants as a way to further what federal (and not state) officials perceived to be national needs. Thus grants based on what states wanted or believed they needed began to decline, while grants based on what the national government wanted states to do in order to foster national goals increased dramatically. Soon states routinely asked Washington for help: "Pollution, transportation, recreation, economic development, law enforcement and even rat control evoked the same response from politicians: create a federal grant."[25] As shown in Table 3.2, by 1970

In New Jersey, Christine Todd Whitman defeated incumbent Democratic Governor James Florio in 1993, promising to reduce taxes and government spending. Today, after reducing taxes by 30 percent, she is considered a rising star in the Republican Party. (Photo courtesy: Allan Tannenbaum/Sygma)

federal aid accounted for 20 percent of all state and local government spending; this amount of money made the states ever more dependent on the national government.

New Federalism, 1968–92

As Congress increased the number of great programs for which cities were eligible, many critics argued that the federal grants system was out of hand. In 1964 only fifty-one types of federal grants were available; by 1971 there were more than 500.[26] Each program had its own complicated set of rules and formulas for matching and distributing the money, and each had entrenched bureaucracies and recipients with vested interests in enlarging "their" program.

Between 1965 and 1980, federal aid to cities and states tripled. One political scientist ventured that—in the world of bake-shop metaphors—a "new special" was in the offing: "fruitcake federalism." Not only was it formless, but it also offered (political) plums to all.[27] Negative reaction to this far-reaching federalism was not long in coming. States simply wanted more control. Many believed that the grant situation had produced ridiculous consequences as states and local governments found themselves applying for federal money they did not particularly need. These "federal-aid junkies," as one commentator called them, could not resist the lure of federal funds, no matter what the nature of the grant.[28] As states and localities tailored their budgets to maximize their share of federal dollars, they often neglected basic services. Said New York City Mayor Edward I. Koch,

> Left unnoticed in the cities' rush to reallocate their budgets so as to draw down maximum . . . aid were the basic service-delivery programs. . . . New roads, bridges, and subway routes were an exciting commitment to the future, but they were launched at the expense of routine maintenance to the unglamorous, but essential, infrastructure of the existing systems.[29]

Money wasn't there for those kinds of programs, so cities kept going after programs for which there were funds.

Revenue Sharing.   In 1964 the Chair of President Johnson's Council of Economic Advisers proposed a new program, called **revenue sharing,** to channel federal dollars back to the states without the strings that went with categorical grants. Johnson, a federalist at heart, rejected the proposal and favored continued national control of grant programs. But President Richard M. Nixon, who ran in 1968 on the Republican Party platform pledged to return power to the states, found the idea attractive. He believed that states and local governments needed federal assistance but should have greater freedom to spend it. Under his revenue-sharing program, money was given to state and local governments to spend where they believed the money was most needed, with no strings attached.

revenue sharing: Method of redistributing federal monies back to the states with "no strings attached"; favored by President Richard M. Nixon.

The revenue-sharing idea was popular with the states, which in 1972 were in fiscal crisis. But during the second Reagan administration, when the budget deficit soared, there were few funds to share. Congress terminated the program, over which it had little control, and by 1987 it had been phased out completely. Many Republicans in the 104th Congress, however, suggested a return to revenue-sharing programs as a way to give power back to the states.

New Federalism.   In 1976 Jimmy Carter, a former governor of Georgia, successfully ran for president as an "outsider" opposed to big government and federal grants that mandated state spending for a variety of programs, including education and pollution-reduction programs. The unfunded mandates discussed later in the chapter were programs passed by Congress requiring state compliance but that came with no funds for the states to meet federal standards. Although Carter was the first president to reduce intergovernmental grant expenditures, the reforms in federal grant programs Carter introduced were insufficient to override the rest of his political woes, and in 1980 former California Governor Ronald Reagan was elected president. Reagan pledged what he called a "New Federalism" and a return of power back to the states.

President Reagan's New Federalism had many facets. The Republican "Reagan Revolution" had at its heart strong views about the role of states in the federal system. Shortly after taking office, he proposed massive cuts in federal domestic programs (which had not become federal functions until the New Deal) and drastic income tax cuts.

The Reagan administration's budget and its policies dramatically altered the relationships among federal, state, and local governments. For the first time in thirty years, federal aid to state and local governments declined.[30] Picking up on Nixon's revenue-sharing plan, Reagan persuaded Congress to consolidate many categorical grants (for specific programs that often require matching funds) into far fewer, less restrictive **block grants**—broad grants to states for specified activities such as secondary education or health services, with few strings attached. Eventually, in 1981, Congress consolidated fifty-seven categorical grants covering a broad range of programs—including health care, child welfare, and crime prevention—into seven block grants. The states were happy with this action—until they learned that the administration also proposed to cut back on the financing of these programs by 25 percent. These cuts fell heaviest on cities. In 1980 federal funds made up 26 percent of state expenditures and 17.7 percent of city and county budgets. By 1990, however, federal dollars were 18 percent of state and 6.4 percent of city and county budgets, respectively. Moreover, the proportion of federal income security aid to individuals in the forms of assistance programs such as Medicaid, Social Security, and Aid to Families with Dependent Children (AFDC) rose significantly at the same time that the proportion of money to the state and local governments for general purposes fell by half.

The New Federalism changed the nature of state politics. Many state governments—as well as cities within a single state—found themselves competing for funds. States were faced with revenue shortfalls caused by the recession of the early 1990s, legal requirements mandating balanced budgets, and growing demands for new social services and the replacement of some formerly provided by the federal government. Many governors around the nation found themselves in political trouble as they had to slash services and ask for tax increases. "A governor with over a 50 percent approval is more the exception than the rule now, and that just wasn't true three or four years ago," noted one pollster in 1991.[31]

Rightly or wrongly, the public blamed governors for the effects of New Federalism. This first became evident in the fall of 1990, when an unprecedented ten incumbent governors chose not to seek reelection and an additional six were defeated. In contrast, only one incumbent senator was ousted. The mood continued, and in 1993 New Jersey Governor James Florio was ousted by voters who were angered by tax increases. Similarly, incumbent mayors and county executives were turned out of office by voters angered by property tax increases, which were often required to fund federally mandated programs.

Ironically, the fiscal policies of Reagan–Bush New Federalism left many states weakened. In 1991 legislators in forty-six states narrowly missed deadlines for their new budget authorizations because of rising costs. Nevertheless, in the 1994 Republi-

block grant: Broad grant with few strings given to states by the federal government for specified activities, such as secondary education or health services.

Republican governors (from left) John Engler (Mich.), Christine Todd Whitman (N.J.), Mike Leavitt (Utah), George Pataki (N.Y.), and Steve Merrill (N.H.) sharing stories prior to a news conference on welfare reform legislation, in which they formed a united front criticizing President Clinton for continuing to insist on keeping the status quo.(Photo courtesy: Kathy Willens/AP Photo)

can sweep of Congress, no Republican governor who sought reelection was defeated, while some popular Democratic governors such as Ann Richards of Texas lost. By 1996 thirty-one statehouses were controlled by Republican governors, including Christine Todd Whitman of New Jersey and William Weld of Massachusetts, fiscal conservatives with relatively liberal social positions.

Many programs cut by the Reagan and then Bush administrations involved those that aided the "have nots" of society, and the poor and working poor were hard hit. Though even more people were poorer and technically qualified for benefits, the rate of spending growth for programs declined. By 1993 most block grants fell into one of four categories—health, income security, education, or transportation; yet many politicians, including most state governors, urged the consolidation of even more programs into block grants. Calls to reform the welfare system—particularly to allow more latitude to the states in an effort to get back to the Hamiltonian notion of states as laboratories of experiment—seem especially popular with citizens and governments alike.

Clinton's New Federalism. President Clinton, another former governor, came to office keenly aware of the impact of the national government's actions on the states. Many of his initial ideas about the federal/state relationship built on those of former President Reagan. In his 1995 State of the Union Message, for example, he proposed a "New Covenant" that reminded some of Reagan's new federalism—with a twist. Clinton argued for the redirection of responsibilities to the states to avoid costly duplication of programs. But he also saw the need for more funding from the national government to accompany those shifts. Those proposals, however, did not go far enough or quickly enough for many American voters who were frustrated by the power of the national government.

Newtonian Federalism

In *Federalist No. 17*, Alexander Hamilton noted that "it will always be far more easy for the State government to encroach upon the national authorities than for the national government to encroach upon the State authorities." He was wrong. Today, some argue, the federal/state relationship has moved from "cooperation to coercion,"[32] a fact that in 1994 led many state governors and the Republican Party (remember, both increases in federal power—the New Deal and Great Society Program—were launched during Democratic administrations) to rebel openly against this growth of national power.

preemption: A concept derived from the Constitution's supremacy clause that allows the national government to override or preempt state or local actions in certain areas.

Preemption.[33]   One method the federal government has used to cut into the authority of the states to set their own policy preferences derives from the Constitution's supremacy clause. This practice, known as **preemption,** allows the national government to override, or preempt, state or local actions in certain areas. As discussed earlier, the Tenth Amendment expressly reserves to the states and the people all powers not delegated to the national government. The phenomenal growth of preemption statutes, laws that Congress has passed to allow the federal government to assume partial and/or full responsibility for traditional state and local governmental functions, began in 1965 during the Johnson administration. Since then, Congress has routinely used its authority under the commerce clause to preempt state laws. The Clean Air Act Amendments of 1990, the Hazardous and Solid Waste Amendments of 1984, the Safe Drinking Water Act Amendments of 1986, and the Water Quality Act of 1987 are examples of federal preemption at work. These statutes not only take authority away from states, they often impose significant costs on them in the form of unfunded mandates. In fact, the cost to the states—along with the perceived federal interference with local matters—is one reason that the electorate so willingly embraced the campaign message of the Republican Party in 1994.

The **Contract with America,** proposed by then House Minority Whip Newt Gingrich, was a campaign document signed by all Republican candidates (and incumbents) for the House of Representatives. Republican candidates pledged themselves to force a national debate on the role of the national government in regard to the states. Republicans lambasted the growth of federal power over the states and were particularly critical of several features of the federal–state relationship that they believed robbed the states of their power to set policy for the health and welfare of their citizens (see Highlight 3.2: Forcing a National Policy: The Twenty-One-Year-Old Drinking Age). Thus the Contract pledged Republicans to vote on, although not necessarily pass, a variety of pieces of legislation, many of them aimed at altering the nature of federalism by returning power to the states from the federal government. A key component of the Contract was a commitment to end unfunded mandates.

mandate: National law that directs states or local governments to comply with federal rules or regulations (such as clean air or water standards) under threat of civil or criminal penalties or as a condition of receipt of any federal grants.

Unfunded Mandates.   From the beginning, most categorical grants were matching grants that came with a variety of strings attached. As categorical grants declined, the national government continued to exercise a significant role in state policy priorities through **mandates**—laws that direct states or local governments to comply with federal rules or regulations (such as clean air or water standards) under threat of civil or criminal penalties or as a condition of receipt of any federal grants (a city might not get federal transportation funds, for example, unless the disabled have access to particular means of transportation).

Until passage in 1995 of what is called the unfunded mandates bill, the federal government required the states to shoulder the financial programs it did not fund. Through 1994, unfunded mandates often made up as much as 30 percent of a local government's annual operating budget. Between 1983 and 1990, it is estimated that the cumulative cost of unfunded mandates to state and local governments was between 8.9 and 12.7 billion dollars.[34]

As shown in Figure 3.4, the enactment of federal regulations requiring state and local spending increased tremendously through 1990. During the 1980s Congress added twenty-seven new programs requiring state spending, and many expensive unfunded provisions were attached to existing grant-in-aid programs. For example, costly new requirements were tacked on to the Medicaid program, workfare conditions were added to the AFDC program as a welfare reform measure, and local contributions to mandated federal water projects were added.[35] Columbus, Ohio, for example, with

Highlight 3.2

Forcing a National Policy: The Twenty-One-Year-Old Drinking Age

In 1984 only sixteen U.S. senators voted against an amendment to the Surface Transportation Act of 1982, a provision designed to withhold 5 percent of federal highway funds from states that did not prohibit those under the age of twenty-one from drinking alcoholic beverages. Because the national government did not have the power to regulate the drinking age, it resorted to the carrot-and-stick nature of federalism, whereby the national government dangles money in front of the states but places conditions on its use. To force states to raise their drinking age to twenty-one by 1988, Congress initially decided to withhold 5 percent of all federal highway grants to the recalcitrant states. (This was later raised to 10 percent.) In other words, no raised drinking age, no federal dollars. Even most conservative Republican senators—those most attached to the notion of states' rights—supported the provision, in spite of the fact that it imposed a national ideal on the states. After congressional action, the bill was signed into law by Ronald Reagan, another conservative long concerned with how the national government had trampled on state power. States still retain the power to decide who is legally drunk, however. And the blood alcohol content required for determining legal intoxication varies dramatically, from a low of .05 in Colorado to a high of .1 in several states.

633,000 residents, faced a $1 billion bill to comply with the federal Clean Water Act and the Safe Drinking Water Act at an estimated cost of $685 a year per household. Likewise, New York City faced a $1.3 billion bill with no federal financial support to refit elevators in subways to accommodate the disabled.[36]

FIGURE 3.4

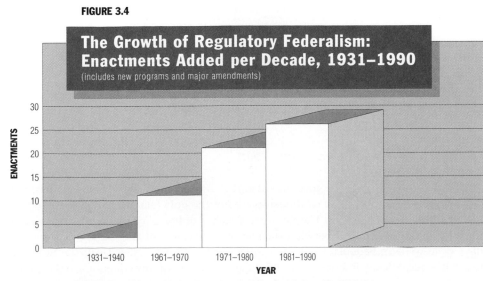

The Growth of Regulatory Federalism: Enactments Added per Decade, 1931–1990
(includes new programs and major amendments)

SOURCE: ACIR, *Regulatory Federalism,* Appendix Table 1. Reprinted in Timothy J. Conlan and David R. Beam, "Federal Mandates: The Record of Reform and Future Prospects," *Intergovernmental Perspective* (Fall 1992): 9.

Unlike the national government, most states are required to have balanced budgets. Thus mandates increasingly meant more taxes and more trouble for state and local legislators. In 1993 the high cost of mandates led Alabama and South Dakota to pass laws summoning their senators and representatives home to explain to their state legislatures why laws are passed imposing costly regulations on states without providing funds to implement them.[37] It is not surprising, then, to understand why Republicans were able to enact the unfunded mandates bill. Moreover, as Speaker of the House for the 104th Congress, Newt Gingrich tried to set aside a day each month called "Corrections Day" to "correct" existing laws and regulations to ease the financial burdens on states.

THE CHANGING NATURE OF FEDERALISM

Federal grants-in-aid and unfunded mandates clearly have forced the states to rethink their position in the federal system, and most are unhappy with it, especially since in 1996 Republicans controlled thirty-one of the fifty state houses. Most Republicans, who generally favor a more limited role for the national government, attack many grants-in-aid programs as a way for the national government to exercise powers reserved to the states under the Tenth Amendment.

Some argue that one of the original reasons for federal grants—perceived overrepresentation of rural interests in state legislatures, for example—has been removed, as the Supreme Court has ordered redistricting to ensure better representation of urban and suburban interests. Moreover, state legislatures have become more professional, state and local bureaucracies more responsive, and the delivery of services better. In fact, the greatest growth in government hiring has been in the state and local sectors. Poll after poll, moreover, reveals that Americans believe that the national government has too much power (48 percent) and that they favor their states assuming many of the powers and functions now exercised by the federal government (59 percent).[38]

While many argue that grants-in-aid are an effective way to raise the level of services provided to the poor, others attack them as imposing national priorities on the states. Policy decisions are largely made at the national level; and the states, always in search of funds, are forced to follow the priorities of the national government. States find it very hard to resist the lure of grants, even though many are contingent on some sort of state investment of matching or proportional funds.

Federalism and the Supreme Court

Funds from the national government and changing presidential and congressional views about the federal–state relationship are not the only factors that have altered the nature of the federal system. The Supreme Court also has played an important role in the configuration of power between the national government and the states. From the days of Marshall's Federalist opinions to *laissez-faire* to the New Deal, the Supreme Court has periodically interjected itself into areas (most notably education and the electoral process) that the Framers intended to leave within the authority of the states.

North—South

POLITICS AROUND THE WORLD

In some ways the United States and its neighbors aren't all that different—at least in comparison with most of the other countries in the world.

Many are what political scientists call "unitary states," in which the equivalents of state and local governments have no real power. In Great Britain, for example, the central government determines almost all education, welfare, and health policy and can restructure local governing authorities at will.

Like the United States, however, Canada and Mexico have federal systems in which the ten provinces and two territories (Canada) and thirty-one states and the federal district (Mexico) have powers and responsibilities guaranteed them in their constitutions.

Although political scientists have not done the research that would allow us to reach such a conclusion with any degree of certainty, it does seem that the aspects of federalism that leave subnational units with real power are stronger in the United States. American state and local governments retain the lion's share of decision making in many of the policy areas that matter most to average citizens.

The same cannot be said for either Canada or Mexico. For instance, Canada's Constitution lacks the flexibility of the U.S. Constitution's Articles 9 and 10, which allow power to flow back and forth between federal and local units over time, and instead gives the national government control over all policy areas not explicitly granted to the provinces. Even though political power has gravitated substantially back to the provincial level, that has happened after a century of nearly total federal domination of political life. Similarly, in Mexico, the Senate (which is to say, the PRI) can remove elected governors, and most policy of any importance is determined nationally.

In both countries, federalism is certainly more controversial than it is today in the United States. In Canada, the debate over the status of Quebec and the growth of anti-Ottawa parties in the western part of the country in many ways reflect disagreements over how much autonomy the provinces should have (see chapters 6 and 12 for more details). In Mexico, the growing ability of the opposition parties to win state and municipal elections (see North–South features in chapters 12 and 13) suggests that conflict between them and the federal government (that is to say, the PRI) may be an important part of the political landscape in the next few years.

Education. Through grants-in-aid programs like the Morrill Land Grant Act of 1862, and into the 1950s, Congress has long tried to encourage the states to develop their university and educational systems. Still, education was usually considered a function of the states under their police powers, which allow them to provide for public health and welfare. That tradition was shattered when the Supreme Court ruled in *Brown* v. *Board of Education of Topeka, Kansas* (1954) that state-mandated segregation has no place in the public schools (see chapter 6). *Brown* forced states to dismantle their segregated school systems and ultimately led the federal courts to play an important role in monitoring the efforts of state and local governments to tear down the vestiges of segregation.

FIGURE 3.5

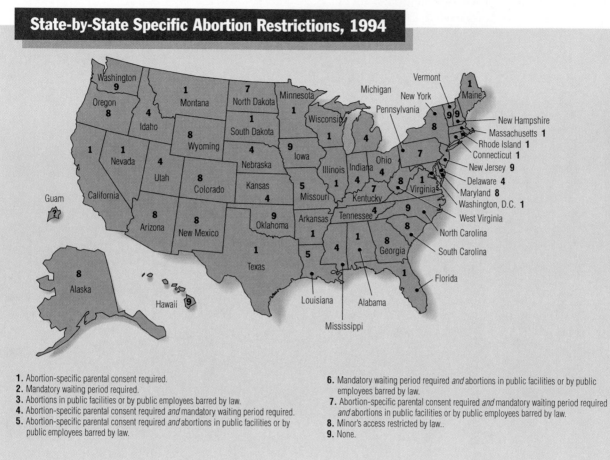

State-by-State Specific Abortion Restrictions, 1994

1. Abortion-specific parental consent required.
2. Mandatory waiting period required.
3. Abortions in public facilities or by public employees barred by law.
4. Abortion-specific parental consent required *and* mandatory waiting period required.
5. Abortion-specific parental consent required *and* abortions in public facilities or by public employees barred by law.
6. Mandatory waiting period required *and* abortions in public facilities or by public employees barred by law.
7. Abortion-specific parental consent required *and* mandatory waiting period required *and* abortions in public facilities or by public employees barred by law.
8. Minor's access restricted by law..
9. None.

SOURCE: Data provided by NARAL.

The Electoral Process.   A decade after *Brown,* the Supreme Court again involved itself in one of the most sacred areas of state regulation in the federal system—the conduct of elections. As a trade-off for giving the national government more powers, the Constitutional Convention allowed the states control over voter qualifications in national elections as well as over how elections were to be conducted. But in 1964 the Court began to limit the states' ability to control the process of congressional redistricting. In 1966, for example, the Supreme Court invalidated the poll tax, a state-imposed tax ranging from one to five dollars levied on those who wished to vote. The poll tax was widely used in the Southern states to curtail voting by the poor, who often were black.[39] Most Southern legislators assailed the Court's decision, viewing it as illegal interference with their powers to regulate elections under the Constitution, and as a violation of state sovereignty.

In 1995 the Supreme Court again reined in state power. In *U.S. Term Limits* v. *Thornton,* by a five to four margin, the Court struck down as unconstitutional state-imposed term limits on members of Congress.[40]

The Commerce Clause and the Performance of State Functions.   After the constitutional revolution of 1937, the Supreme Court "upheld every New Deal statute that came before it," often basing its decision on an elastic reading of the commerce clause, which gives Congress the authority to regulate interstate commerce.[41] Since that time, the commerce clause has been the rationale for virtually any federal intervention in state and local governmental affairs. In *Garcia* v. *San Antonio Metropolitan Transit Authority* (1985), for example, which involved the constitutionality of applying federally imposed minimum wage and maximum hour provisions to state governments, the Court ruled that Congress has broad power to impose its will on state and local governments, even in areas that traditionally have been left to their discretion. The Court ruled that the "political process ensures that laws that unduly burden the states will not be promulgated" and that it should not be up to an "unelected" judiciary to preserve state powers.[42] Furthermore, the majority of the Court concluded that the Tenth Amendment, which ensures that any powers not given to the national government be reserved for the states, was—at least for the time being—essentially meaningless!

Of late, however, the U.S. Supreme Court has "begun to rein in the commerce clause" as there were indications that the Court believes that Congress has gone too far in interfering with functions best left to the states.[43] In *U.S.* v. *Lopez,* which involved the conviction of a student charged with carrying a concealed handgun onto school property, a five-person majority of the Court ruled that Congress lacked constitutional authority under the commerce clause to regulate guns within 1,000 feet of a school.[44] The majority concluded that local gun control in the schools was a state, not a federal, matter.

Reproductive Rights.   Mario M. Cuomo, the former liberal Democratic New York governor, has referred to the decisions of the Reagan–Bush Court as creating "a kind of new judicial federalism." According to Cuomo, this new federalism can be characterized by the Court's withdrawal of "rights and emphases previously thought to be national."[45] Perhaps most illustrative of this trend are the Supreme Court's decisions in *Webster* v. *Reproductive Health Services* (1989)[46] and *Casey* v. *Planned Parenthood of Southeastern Pennsylvania* (1992).[47] In *Webster* the Court first gave new latitude—and even encouragement—to the states to fashion more restrictive abortion laws. Since *Webster,* as illustrated in Figure 3.5, numerous states have enacted or are considering new restrictions. In 1991 alone more than 200 bills restricting abortion were introduced in forty-five state legislatures.[48] Moreover, the Court has consistently upheld the authority of the individual states to limit a minor's access to abortion through imposition of parental consent or notification laws. And it has consistently declined to review other restrictions, including twenty-four-hour waiting period requirements.

More Changes to Come?

As the power of the national government has risen at the expense of the states, politicians and political scientists have made a variety of calls for devolution of the federal system. For example, inconsistent Court decisions—on the one hand returning costly national programs to the states, while on the other hand continuing to order expensive educational and penal programs—prompted fifteen state legislatures to approve resolutions calling for an amendment to the Constitution giving the states more authority in relation to the federal government. With the strong support of the Bush administration, those states proposed two avenues of change, largely in response to recent Court decisions. One sought to allow the states to initiate amendments without calling a constitutional convention. The other would change the Tenth Amendment to direct the state courts to determine whether the Supreme Court had overstepped its boundaries with respect to the states.

Highlight 3.3

The Intergovernmental Lobby

In January 1996 the nation's governors met in Washington, D.C., to come up with a solution to Congress's inability to reach a consensus with the president on Medicaid and welfare reform. The governors were wined and dined by the Clintons at the White House but they also met in serious policy sessions. This is just one example of how the states and the national government are working together. This kind of work is not new although it is going on in earnest at a far greater rate than ever before.

Increasing federal regulations, mandates, and conditions of aid have all contributed to the need for state and local governments (of which there are thousands; see Table 3.3) to lobby Congress as well as to hire lobbyists to advance their interests in Washington. School districts, school systems, cities, states, police chiefs, hospital administrators, and many more groups form part of what is called the **intergovernmental lobby.** Many of these groups have either banded with others or set up individual offices in Washington to lobby for funds. Others hire full-time or part-time lobbyists to work solely on their behalf to keep abreast of funding opportunities, or to lobby for programs. Today, searches for scarcer federal dollars can be nearly as futile as Ponce de Leon's search for the Fountain of Youth.

Some scholars cite the "Big Seven" as the premier intergovernmental lobbies (see Table 3.4). These groups, primarily founded from the turn of the century to the New Deal during a period of rapid growth in the tasks of national government, are well organized and well established.

Several of the Big Seven focus on state issues. The National Governors' Association (NGA) is composed of incumbent governors from each state. The governors meet twice a year but have a staff and standing committees that meet more regularly. Adoption of policy positions requires a quorum and vote of three-quarters of the governors. Small states tend to be more active within the group than larger states. The Council of State Governments (CSG), located in Washington, D.C., is an umbrella organization designed to gather information and provide assistance to the states. The National Conference of State Legislatures (NCSL), headquartered in Denver, publishes a monthly magazine, *State Legislatures,* and uses its Washington office to monitor and publish information about the federal government that is useful to the states. It provides a variety of legislative services to all fifty state legislatures plus Puerto Rico.

Three other groups are often called the "urban lobby." The National League of Cities (NLC) represents medium and small cities, the U.S. Conference of Mayors (USCM) represents large cities, and the National Association of Counties (NAC) represents rural, suburban, and urban counties. The remaining member of the Big Seven is the International City/ County Management Association (ICMA), which represents the country's appointed local chief executives.

Not all of these groups actively lobby, but they do compete with each other and other organizations for funding, access, and resources. Especially now, in this time of lean budgets and calls to fiscal responsibility, as the federal pie gets smaller, competition gets keener. The National Governors' Association, for example, has been a major player in coming up with a compromise with the national government on how the Medicaid and welfare programs are to be overhauled.

intergovernmental lobby The pressure group or groups that are created when state and local governments hire lobbyists to lobby the national government.

In the wake of the resolve of the 104th Congress, however, more changes may be coming in the federal system and in the relationship of the national government to the states than in any period since the New Deal. Political scientist David B. Walker argues that this is an especially auspicious time for reform, given the rampant distrust of government that permeates all levels of government.[49]

Speaker of the House for the 104th Congress Newt Gingrich and his fellow Republicans, along with Republican governors who control the majority of the state houses, committed themselves to dramatic overhaul of the federal system and a return

TABLE 3.3

Number of Governments in the U.S. in 1994

U.S. government	1
State governments	50
Local governments	84,955
County	3,043
Municipal (city)	19,279
Township and town	16,691
Sub-county	35,935
TOTAL	85,006

Source: U.S. Bureau of the Census, "Number of Elected Officials Exceeds Half Million—Almost All Are With Local Governments." Press Release, January 30, 1995.

of substantial power to the states. Some of these changes require state ratification of constitutional amendments; others require acts of Congress. And others, such as the major overhaul of the welfare system passed by Congress in 1996, require cooperative action and reform by both the national governments and the states. The nation's governors have even formed a Conference of the States where the fifty governors and bipartisan delegates from each state meet biannually to suggest proposals for structural

TABLE 3.4

The "Big Seven" Intergovernmental Associations

ASSOCIATION (CURRENT TITLE)	DATE FOUNDED	MEMBERSHIP
National Governors' Association (NGA)	1908	Incumbent governors
Council of State Governments (CSG)	1933	Direct membership by states and territories; serves all branches of government; has dozens of affiliate organizations of specialists
National Conference of State Legislatures (NCSL)	1948	State legislators and staff
National League of Cities (NLC)	1924	Direct, by cities and state leagues of cities
National Association of Counties (NACo)	1935	Direct by counties; loosely linked state associations; affiliate membership for county professional specialists
United States Conference of Mayors (USCM)	1933	Direct membership by cities with population over 30,000
International City/County Management Association (ICMA)	1914	Direct membership by appointed city and county managers, and other professionals

Source: Allan J. Cigler and Burdett A. Loomis, *Interest Group Politics* 4th ed. (Washington D.C.: CQ Press, 1995), 135.

constitutional changes in the federal system aimed at "redressing the balance" between the national government and the states.[50] But, as discussed in chapter 16, public concern over what the governors might do at such a conference prompted the governors to abandon their most ambitious plans concerning restructuring the federal system constitutionally. (But see Highlight 3.3: The Intergovernmental Lobby.)

SUMMARY

The inadequacies of the confederate form of government created by the Articles of Confederation led the Framers to create an entirely new, federal system of government. From the summer of 1776 until today, the tension between the national and state governments has been at the core of our federal system. In describing the origins of that tension and the renewed debate about the role of the national government in the federal system, we have made the following points:

1. The Roots of the Federal System.

The Framers created a federal system to replace the confederate form of government that had existed under the Articles of Confederation.

2. The Powers of Government in the Federal System.

The national government has both enumerated and implied powers, and also exercises concurrent powers with the states. Certain powers are denied to both the state and national governments. Certain guarantees concerning representation in Congress and protection against foreign attacks and domestic rebellion were made to the states in return for giving up some of their powers in the new federal system. Despite limitations, the national government is ultimately supreme.

3. The Evolution and Development of Federalism.

Over the years, the powers of the national government have increased tremendously at the expense of the states. The Supreme Court, in particular, has played a key role in defining the relationship and powers of the national government through its broad interpretations of the supremacy and commerce clauses. For many years, however, it adhered to the notion of dual federalism, which tended to limit the national government's authority in areas such as slavery and, after the Civil War, civil rights. This notion of a limited role for the national government in some spheres ultimately fell by the wayside after the Great Depression.

The rapid creation of New Deal programs to alleviate many problems caused by the Depression led to a tremendous expansion of the federal government through the growth of federal services and grant-in-aid programs. This growth escalated during the Johnson administration and in the mid- to late 1970s. After his election in 1980, Ronald Reagan, upset by the growth of federal services, tried to reverse the tide through what he termed New Federalism. He built on earlier efforts by Richard M. Nixon to consolidate categorical grants into fewer block grant programs, and to give state and local governments greater control over programs. Since 1993 the national government and the states have been in a constant dialogue to reframe the structure of the federal–state relationship.

4. The Changing Nature of Federalism.

Over the years, the Supreme Court has been a major player in recent trends in the federal–state relationship. Its decisions in the areas of education, civil rights, voting rights, and the performance of state functions have given the federal government a wider role in the day-to-day functioning of the states, and have limited the scope of the states' police powers. During the Reagan–Bush era, however, the Supreme Court, especially in the area of abortion, was willing to return some powers to the states, but recent cases cast doubt on the Court's willingness to expand congressional powers at the expense of the states.

KEY TERMS

bill of attainder, p. 83
block grant, p. 96
categorical grant, p. 94
concurrent powers, p. 83
cooperative federalism, p. 93
dual federalism, p. 88
ex post facto law, p. 83
federalism, p. 79
implied power, p. 82

intergovernmental lobby, p. 104
mandates, p. 98
necessary and proper clause, p. 82
nullification doctrine, p. 88
preemption, p. 98
reserve (or police) powers, p. 82
revenue sharing, p. 95
supremacy clause, p. 79

SELECTED READINGS

Bowman, Ann O'M., and Richard Kearney. *The Resurgence of the States.* Englewood Cliffs, NJ: Prentice Hall, 1986.

Derthick, Martha. *The Influence of Federal Grants.* Cambridge, MA: Harvard University Press, 1970.

Elazar, Daniel J. *American Federalism: A View from the States.* New York: Harper & Row, 1984.

Gillespie, Ed, and Bob Schellhas, eds. *Contract with America.* New York: Times Books, 1994.

Grodzins, Morton. *The American System.* Chicago: Rand McNally, 1966.

Hamilton, Christopher, and Donald T. Wells. *Federalism, Power, and Political Economy: A New Theory of Federalism's Impact on American Life.* Englewood Cliffs, NJ: Prentice Hall, 1990.

Kenyon, Daphne A., and John Kincaid, eds. *Competition among States and Local Govern-* *ments.* Washington, D.C.: The Urban Institute Press, 1991.

Phillips, Kevin. *The Politics of Rich and Poor: Wealth and the American Electorate in the Reagan Aftermath.* New York: HarperCollins, 1990.

Riker, William H. *Federalism: Origin, Operation, Significance.* Boston: Little, Brown, 1964.

Rivlin, Alice M. *Reviving the American Dream: The Economy, the States, and the Federal Government.* Washington, D.C.: The Brookings Institution, 1993.

Walker, David B. *The Rebirth of Federalism.* Chatham, NJ: Chatham House, 1994.

Zimmerman, Joseph F. *Contemporary American Federalism: The Growth of National Power.* New York: Praeger, 1992.

Photo courtesy: Bob Daemmrich/The Image Works

Grassroots Power and Politics

State Governments

Local Governments

Finances

Changing State and Local Governments

N o blacktop in the marsh! Protect the wildlife, join our march!"

The chant went on all morning. Students from the local college paraded up and down the shopping mall, protesting plans to expand the parking lot into a marsh located between the mall and their campus. The marsh served as a natural silt basin filtering water that ran into a lake. The environmental issue was a classic example of the challenges faced as communities grow in areas with prized natural resources.

For the manager of the shopping mall, there was another, more immediate issue: The students were on private property, and they were disrupting business. Several shopkeepers had already complained to the manager. She called the city police.

The police dispatcher informed the manager, who was new to her position, that the shopping mall was actually just outside the city's boundaries, even though for all practical purposes it was an integral part of the urban community. The dispatcher told her that since the mall was outside the jurisdiction of the city police, she might want to call the county sheriff. The sheriff, in turn, said that the mall was actually part of a nearby village. The village's police force should respond first and call the county if they needed any backup support.

Understandably, the mall manager was now educated, but also very frustrated. The village police officer confronted the protesters and warned them that if they did not leave immediately, he would arrest them for trespassing on private property and disturbing the peace. The protesters refused to leave and continued to march and chant. The police arrested the students and transported them to the village hall for booking.

In the litigation that followed, the attorney for the protesters argued that the arrests violated constitutional protections of the right to assemble and express views on public policy issues. The district attorney countered that the students can exercise their free speech rights in a public park or a similar facility, but they need not and cannot do so in a place and manner that disturbs shopkeepers and customers. A central question in court became whether free speech rights exist when exercised on private property. The case went through both the federal courts and the state courts.

In the federal courts, the justices ruled that the First Amendment of the U.S. Constitution constrains *government* from restricting political expression. Owners and managers of a private shopping mall, however, are not restricted by the Constitution and do not have an obligation to uphold free speech rights. The police acted appropriately to recognize the rights of property owners and to maintain peace and order.

Judges in the state courts, applying the provisions of the *state* constitution, differed from their federal counterparts. State jurists considered facilities that were open generally to the public, even if privately owned, to be covered by the state constitution. Thus shopping malls are public, and individuals who go to shopping malls have the same legal rights as if they were in publicly owned parks or buildings.

When state constitutions and state courts provide more protections of individual liberties than does the federal government, the state rulings prevail. The charges against the students were dropped.[1]

Governance in the United States federal system is by multiple authorities, sometimes in conflict with one another and sometimes in harmony. A shopping mall may be subject to land use regulation by a county, receive police and fire protection from a village, have water and sewerage service from one special district, and be part of yet another district that provides mass transit. Students expressing their concerns about a community problem are protected by a state constitution as well as by the U.S. Constitution.

The relationships between the various governments in our country are dynamic. The legal authority, the financial resources, and the political will of the federal government, state governments, municipal governments, school districts, water districts, and all the other public bodies are constantly changing. On the one hand, this provides groups and individuals with many points of access to government. On the other hand, the multiple, changing jurisdictions that govern our society can be a challenging puzzle, so complex that in effect citizens will have very little governmental access and influence.

As the twentieth century comes to a close, some trends in federalism have enhanced the importance of state and local governments. The antigovernment theme that has run throughout U.S. history manifested itself in conscious efforts since the Nixon presidency to reverse the aggregation of power and authority in Washington, D.C. Related to this philosophical stance, the federal government found itself unable to expand or even to maintain its presence in domestic policy areas. During the Reagan administration, the debt of the federal government more than tripled and there was no choice but to curtail spending.

In 1995 the U.S. Supreme Court contributed to the limitations on the federal government vis-à-vis state and local governments. In *U.S.* v. *Lopez,* the Court ruled that Congress and the president did not have authority to require the establishment of gun-free zones around local schools: That was a matter for state and local governments. The Court left open, however, the option of the federal government attaching strings—such as a local law prohibiting the possession of guns in zones around schools—as a condition of receiving federal funds. Congress and the president nonetheless seemed inclined to eliminate strings and to give state and local governments more discretion. For example, they removed the requirement that states have certain speed limits in order to receive federal transportation funds and gave local governments more leeway in determining how they would meet clean water standards. The twentieth century is closing with many changes and uncertainties, but with a clear message that state and local governments will have roles and responsibilities of increasing importance.

This chapter will present the basic patterns and principles of state and local governance so that you might readily understand how public policies in your community are made and applied.

■ First, we identify the nature of *power and politics in communities.*

■ Second, we describe the *development of state constitutions* and the major institutions of *state governments,* including trends in state elections.

■ Third, we examine the different types of *local governments* and explain the bases for their authority as well as the special traits of their institutions.

■ Fourth, we explain the budgeting process for state and local *finances.*

■ Finally, we highlight key issues that will affect the future of *changing state and local governments.*

GRASSROOTS POWER AND POLITICS

*T*he most powerful and influential people in a state or community are not necessarily the ones who hold government office. While there is always a distinction between formal and informal power, the face-to-face character of governance at the grassroots level provides increased visibility to this dimension of politics. Most of the positions in local governments and some in state governments are only part-time. Mayors, school board presidents, and state legislators are also teachers, business owners, accountants, and farmers. They have a more ambiguous identity than full-time government officials do.

In small to medium-size communities, in particular, it is common for a single family or a traditional elite to be the major decision maker, whether or not they have one of their members in a formal governmental position.[2] If you want to advocate for some

State and local politics focus more closely on personal issues of concern to specific communities. Lousiana gubernatorial candidate Cleo Fields (center) and Tipper Gore (right), wife of Vice President Al Gore, Jr., field questions on health care in a town meeting in New Orleans. (Photo courtesy: David Rae Morris/AP Photo)

improvements in a local park, a curriculum change in the schools, or a different set of priorities for the police department, it may be more important to get the support of a few key community leaders (the "hidden" decision makers) than the sympathy of the village president or the school board president. A newcomer interested in starting a business in a town likewise would be well advised to identify and court the informal elite and not just focus on those who hold a formal office.

Political participation in state and especially local politics is both more personal and more issue oriented than at the national level. Much of what happens is outside the framework of political parties. Elections for some state and local government offices, in fact, are **nonpartisan elections,** which means parties do not nominate candidates and ballots do not include any party identification of those running for office. Access and approaches are usually direct. School board members receive phone calls at their homes. Members of the city council and county board bump into constituents while shopping for groceries or cheering their children in youth sports. The concerns that are communicated tend to be specific and neither partisan nor ideological: A particular grade school teacher is unfair and ineffective. Playground equipment is unsafe. It seems to be taking forever for the city to issue a building permit so that you can get started on a remodeling project.

Local news media invariably play a key role in this setting. The major newspaper in the state and what might be the only newspaper in a community can shape the agendas of government bodies and the images of government officials. The mere fact that a newsperson covers a problem makes it an issue. If the protest in the shopping mall is not a story on the evening television newscast or in the morning newspaper, public officials might ignore it. Coverage, on the other hand, virtually assures attention. Then the question is how the media define the issue—as a test of free speech on private property, or as a threat to the quality of water in the lake?

Ad hoc, issue-specific organizations are prevalent in state and local governments.[3] Individuals opposed to the plans of a state department of transportation to expand a stretch of highway from two to four lanes will organize, raise funds, and lobby hard to

nonpartisan election: A contest in which candidates run without formal identification or association with a political party.

Specific issues arise from the grassroots to try to make their way onto the state and national political agendas. Sentiment among residents of the Mojave Desert town of Needles, California, obviously runs strongly against development of a nuclear waste dump in the Ward Valley, some twenty miles west of town. (Photo courtesy: Reed Saxon/AP Photo)

stop the project. Once the project is stopped or completed, that organization will go out of existence. Likewise, neighbors will organize to support or oppose specific development projects or to press for revitalization assistance and then disband once the decision is made. The sporadic but intense activity focused on specific local or regional concerns is an important supplement to the ongoing work of parties and interest groups in state and local governments. A full understanding of what happens at the grassroots level requires an appreciation of ad hoc, issue-specific politics as well as the institutions and processes through which state and local governments make and implement public policies.

STATE GOVERNMENTS

State governments have traditionally had primary responsibility for education (see Politics Now: School Choice), public health, transportation, economic development, and criminal justice. States have also been the unit of government that licenses and regulates various professions, such as doctors, lawyers, barbers, and architects. More recently, state governments have been active in welfare and the environment, in part as agents administering federal policies and programs and in part on their own.

State officials, in other words, have been and continue to be in charge of fundamental components of our society. They have also been challenged with problems that seem to defy solutions. For example, it seems to be beyond our ability to do anything more about crime than try to minimize it. Poverty is another such challenge. Likewise, we have not been fully satisfied with our efforts to educate every citizen.

Despite these awesome responsibilities, Americans have had a historic reluctance to make state governments capable. This reluctance continues, although efforts have been made since the 1960s to enhance the capacity of state government institutions to make and implement policies.

State Constitutions

A major goal of the writers of the U.S. Constitution in 1787 was to *empower* the national government. But the intent of the authors of the original state constitutions was to *limit* government. The Constitutional Convention in Philadelphia was convened, as you recall from chapter 2, because of the perception that the national government under the Articles of Confederation was not strong enough. The debates were primarily over how strong the national, or federal, government should be.

In contrast, the assumption of the authors of the first thirteen state constitutions, based on their backgrounds in the philosophy and experiences of monarchical rule, was that government was all powerful and should be limited. The state constitutions were written and adopted *before* the Philadelphia convention, and included provisions that government may not interfere with basic individual liberties. These provisions, which were integral parts of each of the state constitutions, were added to the federal constitution as the first ten amendments, often called the Bill of Rights.

The first state constitutions provided for the institutions of government, such as governors, legislatures, and courts, with an emphasis on the limits of the authority of each institution.[4] These constitutions did not fully embrace the principle of checks and balances that is found in the U.S. Constitution. The office of governor was particularly

Politics Now

School Choice

Few countries match the United States in its historic commitment to providing a quality public education to every child. The fulfillment of that commitment is a fundamental responsibility of state and local governments. Parents, regardless of their income or location, can count on being able to send their children to school through the twelfth grade for little or no cost, other than the general taxes that they and everyone else pay. Parents who want to send their children to a private school, of course, may do so but must pay whatever extra costs are involved.

State and local officials now face controversial proposals for government sponsorship of parental choice in schools. Advocates contend that parents should be able to choose the school that best meets the needs of their children and that competition among schools will inevitably lead to higher quality. Those opposed argue that competitive market analogies don't apply when some parents cannot afford the time or money to transport children away from their neighborhood schools and that attention and resources should be focused on providing good education for everyone.

The controversy is fueled by more than differences in philosophies. There is perennial conflict over whether schools should include subjects like sex education or creationism. The real agendas of some political activists in this arena, moreover, have little to do with education. Goals range from being able to recruit superior athletic teams to seeking a government subsidy for private schools that are religious or are without racial minorities.

Education politics is typically intense and emotional. The issues of values and taxes are of fundamental importance, and the consequences are often immediate and personal. Do you have personal experience with education politics in your home town?

weak. Not surprisingly, the most powerful institution was the legislature. In fact, initially, only South Carolina, New York, and Massachusetts gave their governors the authority to veto legislation. (After over 200 years, the state of North Carolina still does not let its governor use a veto.)

The first state constitutions set the pattern for what was to come. In one of its last actions, the national Congress under the Articles of Confederation passed the Northwest Ordinance of 1787 (see Roots of Government: The Northwest Ordinance of 1787), which addressed how new states might join the Union. Lawmakers were responding primarily to settlers in what is now Ohio, but extended coverage to the territory that includes Minnesota, Wisconsin, Iowa, Illinois, Michigan, and Indiana—which to the people in the original states was considered the "Northwest." The basic blueprint included in the Ordinance was that a territory might successfully petition for statehood if it had at least 60,000 free inhabitants (slaves and Native Americans did not count) and a constitution that was both similar to the documents of existing states and compatible with the national Constitution. The first white settlers in the territory covered by the Northwest Ordinance were primarily from New York and Massachusetts, with some individ-

Roots of Government

The Northwest Ordinance of 1787

The Northwest Ordinance was the first national effort to create a system of governance for the territories, which ultimately became the basis for several state and local governments. It specifically set out some duties now reserved to the states, including the role of states in education and legislating for the morality of their citizens. More specifically it specified that:

1. Congress shall appoint a governor, a secretary, and three judges for the Northwest Territory. These officials shall adopt suitable laws from the original states. When the territory has five thousand free male inhabitants of full age, they shall be allowed to elect representatives. These, together with the governor and a legislative council of five, shall form a general assembly to make laws for the territory.

2. The inhabitants shall be entitled to the benefits of trial by jury and other judicial proceedings according to the common law.

3. Religion, morality, and knowledge being necessary to good government and the happiness of mankind, schools and the means of education shall forever be encouraged.

4. There shall be formed in the said territory not less than three nor more than five States. . . . And, whenever any of the said States shall have sixty thousand free inhabitants therein, such State shall be admitted, by its delegates, into the Congress of the United States, on an equal footing with the original States.

5. There shall be neither slavery nor involuntary servitude in the said territory, otherwise than in the punishment of crimes whereof the party shall have been duly convicted.

uals and families directly from Europe. Not surprisingly, the initial constitutions of these states were almost identical to those of New York and Massachusetts.[5]

The traumas of slavery and the Civil War had a profound impact on the constitutions of Southern states. Events that led to the secession of Southern states included the Missouri Compromise of 1820–21, which simultaneously admitted Missouri and Maine, the former with a constitution that legalized slavery and the latter as a "free state." The Missouri Compromise also included an agreement that no more states that had constitutions allowing slavery would be admitted to the Union. When, in 1854, that provision was violated by the admission of Kansas as a slave state and Nebraska as a free state, the confrontation between the two sides escalated.[6]

Slavery was a specific and very emotional issue. It raised the general question of the extent to which the national Congress could insist on specific clauses in state constitutions. The Civil War, of course, answered that question. That war also precipitated an era in which the states in the Confederacy wrote and discarded constitutions at a rapid pace and ended the process with documents that established state governments that were even weaker than those of the first thirteen states.

Southern states adopted new constitutions when they seceded and formed the Confederacy. After the Civil War, they had to adopt new constitutions, acceptable to the Congress in Washington, D.C. These constitutions typically provided former slaves with considerable power and disenfranchised those people who had been active in the Confederacy. These were not realistic constitutions. They divorced political power from economic wealth and social status. White communities simply ignored government and ruled themselves informally as much as possible. After less than ten years of this, whites reasserted political control and rewrote state constitutions.

The new documents reflected white distrust and provided for a narrow scope of authority for state governments and for weak, fragmented institutions. Governors could serve for only two years. Legislatures could only meet for short periods of time and in some cases only once every other year. Law enforcement authority, both police and justices of the peace, rested squarely in local community power structures.

Western states entered the Union with constitutions that also envisioned weak governments. Here the central concerns were not slavery or national government interference, but rather political machines. Particularly in large cities in the Northeast and Midwest, machines based on bloc voting by new, non-English-speaking immigrants wrested political control and began amassing economic wealth, sometimes in corrupt ways.

In response, the Progressive movement, led by such figures as Woodrow Wilson, Theodore Roosevelt, Robert M. La Follette, and Hiram Johnson, advocated changes that involved direct voter participation and bypassed traditional institutions.[7] These reforms included the use of *primaries* for nominating candidates instead of closed party processes, the *initiative* for allowing voters to enact laws directly and avoid legislatures and governors, and the *recall* for constituents to remove officials from office in the middle of their term. Progressives succeeded in getting their proposals adopted as statutes in existing states and in the constitutions of new states emerging from Western territories.

While weak state government institutions may have been a reasonable response to earlier concerns, they are inappropriate for current issues. The trend since the 1960s, throughout the United States, has been to amend state constitutions in order to enhance the capacity of governors, legislatures, and courts to address problems (see Highlight 4.1: The Hawaiian Constitution—A Special Case). Over 300 amendments to state constitutions were adopted in the 1970s alone. Most were to lengthen the terms of governors and provide chief executives with more authority over spending and administration, to streamline courts, and to make legislatures professional and full-time.[8]

Constitutional changes have also reflected some ambivalence. While there is widespread recognition that state governments must be more capable, there is also concern about what that might mean in taxes and in the entrenchment of power. Thus reforms have included severe restrictions on the ability of state and local governments to raise taxes and limits on how long legislators in some states might serve. Historic distrust of government continues.

State constitutions are relatively easy to amend, especially when compared to the U.S. Constitution. Every state allows for the convening of a constitutional convention, and over 200 have been held. Every state also has a process by which the legislature can pass an amendment, usually by a two-thirds or three-fourths vote, and then submit the change to the voters for their approval in a referendum. Seventeen states, mostly in the West, allow for amendments simply by getting the proposal on a statewide ballot, without involvement of the legislature or governor.

The relatively simple amendment processes lead to frequent changes. All but nineteen states have adopted wholly new constitutions since they were first admitted, and

Highlight 4.1

The Hawaiian Constitution— A Special Case

Hawaii was a kingdom ruled by an absolute monarch through the reign of Kamehameha the Great (1782–1819). Out of deference to the traditions of this monarchy, when the federal government ruled Hawaii as a territory (1900–59), it established an executive that was more powerful than is common in states. Also, the government did not foster local governments, but instead relied on the sugar and pineapple plantations to provide their own police and fire protection and other basic services.

As a result of this legacy, Hawaii's constitution provides for a more centralized governance than any of the other states. Public education, police and fire protection, library services, and health and welfare programs commonly run by local governments are operated directly by the state government in Hawaii.

Another unique feature of Hawaii's constitution is the special attention to the welfare of native Hawaiians. Anyone who is at least 50 percent descended from the islands' indigenous inhabitants has land rights that are specially protected, as are the benefits from income from certain lands originally designated by the federal government and now by state government. By contrast, other states may be affected by treaties agreed to by the federal government and Native American tribes. Hawaiians relate directly to the state for governance, whereas Native Americans continue to have their primary relationship with the federal government.

almost 6,000 specific amendments have been adopted. Another effect of the process is that state constitutions tend to be longer than the U.S. Constitution and include provisions that more appropriately should be statutes or administrative rules. The California constitution, for example, not only establishes state government institutions and protects individual rights, but also defines how long a wrestling match may be. Arkansas includes in its constitution what colors should be used for copies of registration documents. Clearly these are violations of the expectation that constitutions are where the authority of government and its institutions is established and where policy-making processes are described.

Governors

Governors have always been the most visible elected official in state governments. Initially, that visibility supported the ceremonial role of governors as their primary function. Now that visibility serves governors as they set the agenda and provide leadership for others in state governments.

The most important role current governors play is in identifying the most pressing problems facing their respective states and proposing solutions to those problems. Governors first establish agendas when they campaign for office. After inauguration, the most effective way for the chief executive to initiate policy changes is when submitting the budget for legislative approval.

Budgets are critical to the business of state governments. The ways in which money is raised and spent say a lot about the priorities of decision makers. Until the 1920s, state legislatures commonly compiled and passed budgets and then submitted

governor: Chief elected executive in state government.

New Jersey Governor Christine Todd Whitman won her race largely on the basis of her predecessor's budget-balancing woes. In a highly unusual move meant to underscore the Republicans' commitment to transferring power back to the states, Whitman was chosen to deliver the Republican Party's rebuttal to President Clinton's 1995 State of the Union Address. (Photo courtesy: Charles Rex Arbogast/AP Photo)

line-item veto: The authority of a chief executive to delete part of a bill passed by the legislature that involves taxing and/or spending. The legislature may override a veto, usually with a two-thirds majority of each chamber.

package or general veto: The authority of a chief executive to void an entire bill that has been passed by the legislature. This veto applies to all bills, whether or not they have taxing or spending components, and the legislature may override this veto, usually with a two-thirds majority of each chamber.

them for gubernatorial approval or veto. As part of the efforts to strengthen the capacities of state governments to deliberate and take action, governors were, like presidents, given the major responsibility for starting the budget process. Now all but four states have their governors propose budgets.

The role of governor as budget initiator is especially important when coupled with the governor's veto authority and executive responsibilities. Governors in all but seven states may exercise a **line-item veto** on bills that involve spending or taxing. A line-item veto strikes only part of a bill that has been passed by the legislature. (Like presidents, governors in all states except North Carolina also have **package** or **general veto** authority, which rejects a bill in its entirety.) A line-item veto allows a chief executive to delete a particular program or expenditure from a budget bill and let remaining provisions become law. The intent of this authority is to enable governors to revise the work of legislators in order to produce a balanced budget.

Governor Tommy Thompson of Wisconsin has been the most extensive and creative user of the line-item veto. He has reversed the intent of legislation by vetoing the word "not" in a sentence and created entirely new law by eliminating specific letters and numerals to make new words and numbers. Voters in Wisconsin were so upset with this free use of the veto pen that in 1993 they passed the "Vanna White amendment" to the state constitution, prohibiting the governor from striking letters within words and numerals within numbers. Not to be outmaneuvered, Governor Thompson then used his veto authority to actually insert new words and numbers in bills that had passed the legislature. The state supreme court, in 1995, upheld this interpretation of veto, as long as the net effect of the vetoes was not to increase spending.

While the Wisconsin case is extreme, it illustrates the significant power that veto authority can provide. Legislators can override vetoes, usually with a two-thirds vote in each of the chambers. But this rarely happens. Only 6 percent of gubernatorial vetoes are overturned,[9] and Governor Thompson has had enough support from his party to sustain all of his.

The executive responsibilities of governors provide an opportunity to affect public policies after laws have been passed. Agencies are then responsible for implementing the laws. That may mean improving a road, enforcing a regulation, or providing a service. The speed and care with which implementation occurs are often under the influence of the governor.[10] Likewise, governors can affect the many details and interpretations that must be decided. State statutes require drivers of vehicles to have a license, but they typically let an agency decide exactly what one must do to get a license, where one can take the tests, and what happens if someone fails a test. Governors can influence these decisions primarily through appointing the heads of state administrative agencies.

One of the methods of limiting gubernatorial power was to curtail appointment authority.[11] Unlike the federal government, for example, states have some major agencies headed by individuals who are elected rather than by people appointed by the chief executive. Forty-three states, for example, elect their attorney general, a position that is part of the president's cabinet. The positions of secretary of state, treasurer, and auditor are also usually filled by elected rather than appointed officials. Some states elect their head of education or agriculture or labor. The movement throughout states to strengthen the institutions of their governments has included increasing the number of senior positions that are filled by gubernatorial appointments so that governors, like heads of major corporations, can assemble their own policy and management teams.

Another position that is filled by presidential appointment in the federal government but, in most cases, by election in state governments is judge. The structure of state courts and how judges are selected will be discussed in detail later. Here it should be noted that this is one more example of approaches that have been taken to restrict the authority of governors.

Nonetheless, governors are major actors in the judicial system. With the legislature, they define what is a crime within a state and attach penalties that should be meted out to those convicted of committing crimes. A person who has been convicted will be institutionalized or supervised by an agency that is, in every state, headed by a gubernatorial appointee. Moreover, governors have authority to pardon someone who has been convicted, thereby eliminating all penalties and wiping the court action from an individual's record. Governors may also commute all or part of a sentence, which leaves the conviction on record even though the penalty is affected.

In addition, governors grant parole to prisoners who have served part of their terms. Typically governors are advised by a parole board on whether or not to grant a parole. Paroles usually have conditions that must be met, like staying in a certain area, avoiding contact with certain people or organizations, and participating in therapy or a work program. Violation of these conditions could mean a return to prison.

Finally, under the U.S. Constitution, governors have the discretion to extradite individuals. This means that a governor may decide to send someone, against his or her will, to another state to face criminal charges. When Mario Cuomo, who opposed the death penalty, was governor of New York, he refused to extradite someone to a state that used capital punishment. That refusal became an issue in Governor Cuomo's unsuccessful bid for reelection in 1994. Shortly after George Pataki was inaugurated, he ordered the extradition.

Gubernatorial participation in the judicial process has led to some of the most colorful controversies in state politics. James E. Ferguson, as Governor of Texas, granted 2,253 pardons between 1915 and 1917. His successor, William P. Hobby, granted 1,518 during the next two years, and Governor Miriam "Ma" Ferguson outdid her husband by issuing almost 3,800 during her term. Texans were used to shady wheeling and dealing in politics, but this volume of pardons seemed a bit excessive. The Texas constitution was amended to remove authority to grant pardons and paroles from the governor and place it in the hands of a board. Governors of the Lone Star state now have the lowest amount of authority among the fifty state chief executives to check actions of the judiciary.[12]

The general trend since the 1960s, as has been noted, has been to increase rather than decrease the power and authority of governors.[13] This is particularly the case with veto authority and the role in the budgetary process. Capacity, however, has both absolute and relative dimensions. Legislatures and courts have also developed into more capable institutions since the 1960s.

State Legislatures

The principles of representative democracy are embodied primarily in the legislature. Legislatures, as mentioned above, were initially established to be the most powerful of the institutions of state government. In over half of the original states, legislatures began without the check of a gubernatorial veto. Until the twentieth century, most state legislatures were responsible for executive chores such as formulating a budget and making administrative appointments.

These tasks were to be done by "citizen legislators" as a part-time responsibility. The image was that individuals would convene in the state capitol for short periods of time to conduct the state's business. State constitutions and statutes specified the part-time operation of the legislature and provided only limited compensation for those who served.

To some extent, this vision worked too well. State legislatures were dominated by rural America and therefore neglected urban interests and problems. Rural domination was a result primarily of how legislative district boundaries were drawn. States did not always revise the districts from which state legislators were elected in response to urban growth.[14] Increasingly, as Chief Justice of the United States Earl Warren once noted, legislators seemed to be representing trees and acres rather than voters.

In 1962, beginning with a challenge to the district boundaries used in Tennessee in *Baker* v. *Carr*, the Court issued a series of rulings that required the adherence to the one-person, one-vote principle. This meant that each legislative district within a state had to have approximately the same number of people. Alabama tried unsuccessfully to argue that states could be like the federal government and have one legislative chamber with equal representation and the other based on some other grounds. The U.S. Supreme Court rejected this view. The justices reasoned that while states enjoy a special sovereignty that may be recognized in the way the U.S. Senate is constructed, no such concept applies to areas within a state.[15]

All states except Nebraska have two legislative houses. One, the senate, typically has fewer members than the other, usually called the "house" or the "assembly." The most common ratio between the two chambers is 1:3. In fourteen states the ratio is 1:2, and in New Hampshire it is 1:16. The other difference between the two bodies in thirty-four of the states is that senators serve four-year terms, whereas representatives in the larger house serve two-year terms. In eleven states everyone in both houses serves two-year terms and in the remaining, including Nebraska, everyone serves for four years.

term limit: Restriction that exists in some states concerning how long an individual may serve in state and/or local elected offices.

Although it has been common to have limits on how many terms someone may serve as governor, **term limits** for legislators are a development of the 1980s and 1990s (see Table 4.1). By 1996, twenty-one states passed measures limiting the number of years one might be a state legislator. In thirteen states the limit is eight consecutive years per house. In three states the limit is twelve years, and in the others the number varies with each house and ranges from six to twelve.

Proponents of term limits, frankly, included minority party leaders who calculated—sometimes in error—that they stood a better chance of gaining seats if incumbents had to leave after a certain period of time. Others saw term limits as a way of making the ideal of citizen legislator more probable. They saw intuitive appeal in the concept of having people being legislators in addition to whatever else they did in life, as opposed to pursuing a career as an elected official.[16]

The movement to limit legislative service is a contrast to the pattern that evolved especially since the *Baker* v. *Carr* ruling. With an end to rural overrepresentation, state legislatures became relevant. Urban and economic development issues got serious attention, and state budgets included a wider array of programs. The wider scope of state issues, enhanced when the federal government shed some of its responsibilities to the states, attracted individuals who were seriously interested in public service and required increased staff to help with analysis and evaluation.

State legislatures not only became more representative, they became more professional. Legislators worked more days—some of them full-time. In 1960 only eighteen state legislatures met annually. By 1995 forty-three met every year and only seven every other year. Moreover, the floor sessions were longer, and legislators and their staff increasingly did committee work and conducted special studies between sessions.[17]

Ideally, bills are drafted and votes are cast based on evaluations. An important role of legislatures besides passing laws is to monitor and assess the activities of adminis-

TABLE 4.1

Term Limits for Elected Offices in State Government in Years

STATE	SENATE	HOUSE
Arizona	8	8
Arkansas	8	6
California	8	6
Colorado	8	8
Florida	8	8
Idaho	8	8
Maine	8	8
Massachusetts	8	8
Michigan	8	6
Missouri	8	8
Montana	8	6
Nebraska	8	(unicameral)
North Dakota	12	12
Ohio	8	8
Oklahoma	12	12
Oregon	8	6
South Dakota	8	8
Utah	12	12
Washington	8	6
Wyoming	12	6

Note: Arizona and Florida limit individuals to eight and Oklahoma to twelve consecutive years, regardless of whether they serve in one or more chambers of the legislature. Missouri and Ohio allow eight years in each house and a maximum of sixteen years in both houses. Other states do not address this issue explicitly.

Source: U.S. Term Limits, 1511 K Street, NW, Washington, D.C. 20005.

trative agencies. Legislatures need to consider the many initiatives for policy change that come from agencies. To develop the capacity to provide oversight, conduct analyses, and serve constituents, state legislatures increased their staff by almost 130 percent between 1968 and 1974.[18] Growth since then has been at a rather steady 4 percent rate. Staff resources have been supplemented by the services of the National Conference of State Legislatures, established in 1973, and, increasingly, by computer technology and information-sharing on the Internet. Like Congress, state legislatures have established library reference services and audit agencies to help serve their needs.

State legislatures, although much more capable and serious institutions than they were prior to the early 1960s, are still primarily part-time, citizen bodies.[19] Every election puts new members in about one-fourth of the seats. Only a handful of legislators in each state envision careers as lawmakers. Those with long-term political aspirations tend to view service in a state chamber as a step on a journey to some other office, in the state capitol or in Washington, D.C. For some, their goal is to don a black robe and preside in a courtroom.

State Courts

Virtually everyone is in a courtroom at some point. It may be as a judge, a juror, an attorney, a court officer, or a litigant. It may also be for some administrative function like an adoption, a name change, or the implementation of a will. Few of us will ever be in a federal court. Almost all of us will be in a state court.

The primary function of courts is to settle disputes, and most disputes are matters of state, not federal, laws. For the most part, criminal behavior is defined by state legislatures. Family law, dealing with marriage, divorce, adoption, child custody, and the like, is found in state statutes. Contracts, land use, and much that is fundamental to everyday business activity and economic development also are part of state governance.

A common misunderstanding is that the courts in the United States are all part of a single system, with the U.S. Supreme Court at the head. In fact, state and federal courts are separate, with their own rules, procedures, and routes for appeal. The only time state and federal courts converge is when a case involves both federal and state laws or issues.

A famous example of overlap between state and federal courts was in 1991, when Rodney King was arrested by Los Angeles police for a traffic violation. An amateur photographer taped the arrest and captured shots of the police officers severely beating Rodney King. The officers were first tried in California state court for using excessive force. They convinced the jury that King was resisting arrest and thus force was justified. Federal prosecutors nonetheless proceeded to try the officers for violating Rodney King's civil rights, a federal crime. In federal court, the jury came to a different conclusion and convicted the officers.

Although the state and federal courts had essentially the same facts, the laws that applied here were somewhat different. The central question posed by state law was whether the police officers used more force than was professionally accepted. The issue focused on professional standards. The federal law centered on racial discrimination and Rodney King's civil rights. Here the racial slurs and jokes made by police officers weighed more heavily and were more relevant than for the state issue of whether excessive force was used.

Sometimes federal and state laws are directly related. If there is a contradiction between the two, then federal law prevails. A state statute that allowed or encouraged racial hiring, for example, would directly conflict with the federal Civil Rights Act of 1964. And because federal law is always supreme, state courts would be obliged to enforce the federal version.

The issue may be "more or less" rather than "either-or." Since the 1970s the U.S. Supreme Court has generally taken the position that, especially with regard to individual rights protected in the Constitution, state courts should be encouraged to regard the federal government as setting minimums.[20] If, as in the opening vignette, state constitutions and laws provide additional protections or benefits, then state courts should enforce those standards.

common law: Traditions of society that are for the most part unwritten but based on the aggregation of rulings and interpretations of judges beginning in thirteenth-century England.

State judges must incorporate **common law** as well as federal law into their analyses. Common law began with the decisions made by judges in England in the thirteenth century and has evolved as the interpretation and application of those rulings over the years. While some states and communities have made parts of common law into written laws, most of the rulings and rationale remain unwritten. Courts nonetheless are expected to apply traditional common law as they rule on family disputes, disorderly conduct, charges of indecency, and social conflicts in a community. Louisiana used to follow the Napoleonic Code of French tradition, but like other states now subscribes to fundamental edicts of Anglo–American common law and culture.

Like other state government institutions, courts have modernized in the past few decades. The Justice of the Peace, a judicial position that became part of American lore, humor, and dismay, is now virtually extinct. These were part-time judges. (Some of the ridicule aimed at justices of the peace identified their "other" jobs as the sheriffs!) One might count on a Justice of the Peace for a quick wedding (or divorce) but rarely for consistent, impartial, well-reasoned rulings.

Many states reorganized their court systems in the 1970s to follow a model that relied on full-time, qualified judges and simplified appeal routes, and enabled state supreme courts to have a manageable workload. Figure 4.1 illustrates the court structure that is now common among the states.

Most court cases in urban areas begin in a court that specializes in issues like family disputes, traffic, small claims (less than $500 or $1,000), or probate (wills) or in a general jurisdiction municipal court. Small towns and rural areas usually do not have specialized courts. Cases there start in county-level courts that deal with the full array of disputes.

The specialized courts do not use juries. A single judge hears the case and decides. Other courts at this level do have juries if requested by the litigants. A major responsibility of the judges and juries that deliberate on cases when they are originated is to evaluate the credibility of the witnesses and evidence. Although mistakes can be made, judges and jurors have the opportunity to see and consider the demeanor and apparent competence of witnesses. When cases are heard on appeal, the only individuals making oral presentations are attorneys.

Appellate courts have panels of judges. There are no juries in these courtrooms. An important feature of the court reorganizations of the 1970s is that a court of appeals exists between the circuit or county courts and the state supreme court. This court is

FIGURE 4.1

State Court Structure

	JURY OR BENCH TRIALS	JURISDICTION	JUDGES
STATE SUPREME COURT	Bench only	Appeal (limited)	Panel of judges, elected/appointed for fixed term
APPEALS COURTS	Bench only	Appeal (readily granted)	Panel of judges, elected/appointed for fixed term
CIRCUIT OR COUNTY COURTS	Jury and Bench	Original and appeal	One judge per court, elected/appointed for fixed term
MUNICIPAL AND SPECIAL COURTS	Bench only	Original	One judge per court, elected/appointed for fixed term

to cover part of the state and is supposed to accept all appeals. In part, this appellate level is to allow supreme courts to decide whether or not they will hear a case. The basic principle is that all litigants should be able to have at least one opportunity to appeal a decision. If the state supreme court is the only place where an appeal can be lodged, that court is almost inevitably going to have too heavy a caseload, and unreasonable backlogs will develop.

Most state judges are elected to the bench for a specific term. The first states had their legislatures elect judges, and that is still the case in Connecticut, Rhode Island, South Carolina, Vermont, and Virginia. As Table 4.2 shows, in sixteen states voters elect judges and use party identification. Another sixteen use nonpartisan elections. Only six states use gubernatorial appointments. The remaining states follow what is referred to as the Missouri Plan, also called the "Merit Plan," in which judges are initially ap-

TABLE 4.2

Judicial Selection Patterns

PARTISAN ELECTION	NONPARTISAN ELECTION
Alabama	Arizona
Arkansas	California
Georgia	Florida
Indiana	Idaho
Illinois	Kentucky
Kansas	Michigan
Louisiana	Minnesota
Mississippi	Montana
Missouri	Nevada
New Mexico	North Dakota
New York	Ohio
North Carolina	Oregon
Pennsylvania	Oklahoma
Tennessee	South Dakota
Texas	Washington
West Virginia	Wisconsin

ELECTION BY LEGISLATURE	APPOINTMENT BY GOVERNOR
Connecticut	Delaware
Rhode Island	Hawaii
South Carolina	Maryland
Vermont	Massachusetts
Virginia	New Hampshire
	New Jersey

MERIT PLAN

Alaska	Iowa	Oklahoma
California	Kansas	Tennessee
Colorado	Missouri	Utah
Indiana	Nebraska	Wyoming

Source: The Book of the States, 1992–1993 (Lexington, KY: Council of State Governments, 1993), 132–34. © 1992, Council of State Governments. Reprinted by permission.

pointed for a specific term of years by the governor, who must select someone from a list prepared by an independent panel. A judge who wishes to serve for an additional term must receive approval from the voters, who express themselves on a "yes–no" ballot. If a majority of voters cast a "no" ballot, the process starts all over. Five states (California, Kansas, Missouri, Oklahoma, and Tennessee) use the Missouri Plan for some judicial positions and elections for the others.

Different selection processes can be expected to yield different results. Partisan elections and gubernatorial appointments would seem to emphasize patronage and politics, whereas the Missouri Plan and nonpartisan elections seem to suggest more independence. Studies, however, have found that selection processes do not seem to have any noticeable impact. The education, experience, and social backgrounds of judges are all similar, regardless of how they got to the bench. Likewise, there are no links between how judges were selected and whether their decisions favored criminal defendants, corporations, government agencies, or poor people.[21] In short, selection processes seem to be more important for how voters feel than for how courts behave.

Elections

Elections are the vehicle for determining who will fill major state government positions and who will direct the institutions of state government. Almost all contests for state government posts are partisan. The major exceptions are judicial elections in many states, as noted above, and the senate elections in Nebraska's unicameral legislature. Although party labels are not visible and political parties are not formally participants in nonpartisan races, party identity of some candidates may be known and may have some influence.

Political parties have different histories and roles in the various states. The map in Figure 4.2 presents the states according to the level of competition between the two major national political parties. Most states have experienced significant competition between Republicans and Democrats since the Civil War. These states usually have party control split between the two houses of the legislature and the governor's office or have frequent changes in party control of state government.

The Democratic Party has been dominant in Arkansas, Louisiana, Mississippi, Alabama, and Georgia since 1865. This means Democrats have elected the governor and majorities in both houses of the legislature over 60 percent of the time. The Republican Party has occasionally won the governor's race in some of these states, and there have been small blocs of Republicans in state legislatures. No state has experienced long-term dominance by Republicans similar to the Democratic control of these five states.

States are classified as having "majority party rule" if a single party wins the governorship at least 40 percent of the time and both houses of the legislature over 50 percent of the time. Both parties in these states typically win at least 40 percent of the votes cast. There has been Republican majority rule in only two states, New Hampshire and South Dakota. The states of Hawaii, New Mexico, Texas, Oklahoma, Florida, South Carolina, North Carolina, Kentucky, Rhode Island, and Maryland have had Democratic Party majority rule.

The elections in the fall of 1994 may have initiated some long-term changes in state electoral politics. The Republican Party scored impressive gains. Besides securing majorities in the U.S. Senate and House of Representatives, Republican candidates won gubernatorial contests in populous states like New York, Texas, California, Illinois, and Pennsylvania. Democrats lost control of fifteen chambers in state legisla-

FIGURE 4.2

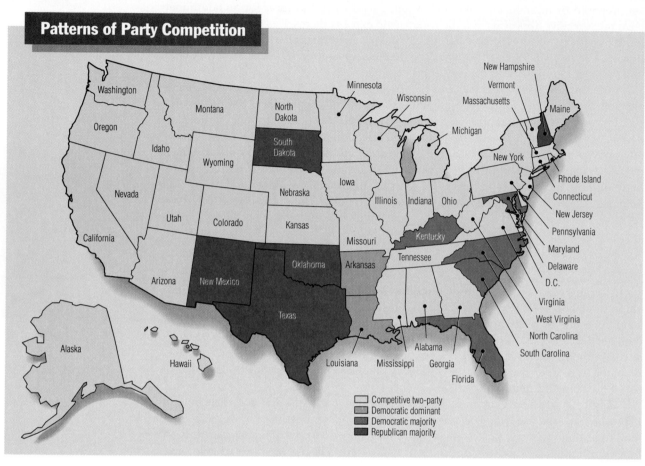

Patterns of Party Competition

Legend:
- ☐ Competitive two-party
- ☐ Democratic dominant
- ☐ Democratic majority
- ☐ Republican majority

tures. In state senate races across the country, Republicans won 110 seats that had been held by Democrats, whereas Democrats took only three seats away from Republicans. The pattern was similar in contests for state houses or assemblies, where Republicans took 362 seats from Democrats and Democrats won only eight seats that had been held by Republicans.

While impressive, it is not clear that Republican successes in 1994 will lead to major long-term changes in party competition for state positions. Changes are most likely to be long-lasting in the South, where voters and officials who had identified themselves as a conservative minority within the Democratic Party seem increasingly and understandably to prefer being part of the conservative majority in the Republican Party. Southern Democrats tended to support Republican candidates for president after national Democratic leaders affirmed for civil rights after World War II. Local Democratic politicians in the South reflected the views of their constituents and continued to garner support. Conservative Republicans in the South have, however, continued to win converts; after votes were counted in the 1994 election, seven of the eleven Southern states had Republican governors. Democrats continued to control all state legislative chambers except for the senate in Florida and the house in North Carolina.

Democrats in the South made a modest comeback in 1995 contests, although Republicans made important gains in Louisiana. They won the governor's race and, due in part to a scandal and FBI investigation involving payments from video gambling interests to Democratic legislators, secured an additional seven seats in the Senate and ten in the House. Republicans are still distinctly in the minority in both chambers in the Louisiana legislature, but their victories at the polls suggest the party will be in a more competitive position than they have been in the past. Even if Democrats regroup and revitalize, it seems clear that in the foreseeable future the Republicans will be viable and competitive in Southern states.

It is easy to exaggerate the importance of partisanship in state politics. Whether at the state or the national level, the differences between Republicans and Democrats are important but not drastic. While party labels and organizations matter, campaigns are primarily centered on individual candidates. Voters usually have an opportunity to meet face-to-face with those contending for state government offices. A common strategy of candidates is to downplay their party identification, both to emphasize their strengths as individuals and to appeal to independent voters. After the election, party labels are important in determining who is in the majority and therefore who will control committees and who will preside in the legislature. That affects the agenda and the dynamics of policy making, but even here parties typically lack the homogeneity and the discipline to determine outcomes.

Direct Democracy

Ballots almost always include referenda and initiative questions, as well as the names of candidates. These questions are part of governance in states and communities. As mentioned above, a Progressive reform meant to weaken parties was to provide opportunities for voters to legislate directly, and not have to go through state legislatures and governors.[22] That process, known as the **direct initiative,** is available in nineteen states, most of them in the West (see Table 4.3). A disadvantage of the direct initiative is the possibility that a law may be passed solely because of a public opinion, which might be shaped largely by thirty-second television commercials and short slogans. An issue is placed on the ballot by securing enough signatures on a petition. There is no guarantee that those who sign the petition or those who cast votes have considered the issue thoroughly or secured all the evidence or arguments that are relevant.

direct initiative: A process in which voters can place a proposal on a ballot and enact it into law without involving the legislature or the governor.

Sometimes initiatives are passed and then set aside by courts because they violate the state and/or federal constitution or because the state is preempted by the federal government. For example, when California passed Proposition 187 in 1994 denying most public services to unregistered immigrants, federal courts kept the state from implementing the law because it trespassed on federal immigration policy and violated the U.S. Constitution. Likewise, the courts thwarted an Oregon initiative passed in 1994 that would have allowed doctors under certain conditions to prescribe lethal drugs to terminally ill individuals.

The **indirect initiative** responds to the concern for debate and deliberation. In this process, legislatures first consider the issue and then pass a bill that will become law if approved by the voters. The governor plays no role. Of the eight states that have the indirect initiative, five also have the direct.

Voters in twenty-four states have the opportunity to veto some bills. In these states, voters may circulate a petition objecting to a particular law passed in a recent session

indirect initiative: A process in which the legislature places a proposal on a ballot and allows voters to enact it into law, without involving the governor or further action by the legislature.

TABLE 4.3

Authority for the Initiative and Popular Referendum

STATE	DIRECT INITIATIVE	INDIRECT INITIATIVE	POPULAR REFERENDUM
Alabama			X
Alaska	X		X
Arizona	X		X
Arkansas	X		X
California	X		X
Colorado	X		
Florida	X		
Idaho			X
Illinois	X		
Kentucky			X
Maine		X	X
Maryland			X
Massachusetts		X	X
Michigan	X	X	X
Missouri	X		X
Montana	X		X
Nebraska	X		X
Nevada	X	X	X
New Mexico			X
North Dakota	X		X
Ohio	X	X	X
Oklahoma	X		X
Oregon	X		X
South Dakota	X		X
Utah	X	X	X
Washington	X	X	X
Wyoming		X	X

Source: The Book of the States, 1992–1993 (Lexington, KY: Council of State Governments, 1992), 329. © 1992, Council of State Governments. Reprinted with permission.

direct (popular) referendum: A process in which voters can veto a bill recently passed in the legislature by placing the issue on a ballot and expressing disapproval.

advisory referendum: A process in which voters cast nonbinding ballots on an issue or proposal.

of the legislature. If enough signatures are collected, then an item appears on the next statewide ballot, giving the electorate the chance to object and therefore veto the legislation. This is known as a **direct (popular) referendum.**

All state and local legislative bodies may place an **advisory referendum** on a ballot. As the name implies, this is a device to take the pulse of the voters on a particular issue and has no binding effect. In addition, voter approval is required in a referendum to amend constitutions and, in some cases, to allow a governmental unit to borrow money through issuing bonds.

LOCAL GOVERNMENTS

*T*he institutions and politics of local governance are even more personalized than one finds in state governments. In part this is because officials are friends, neighbors, and acquaintances living in the communities they serve. Except in large cities, most elected officials fulfill their responsibilities on a part-time basis. In part the personal nature of local governance is due to the immediacy of the issues. The responsibilities of local governments include public health and safety in their communities, education of children in the area, jobs and economic vitality, zoning land for particular uses, and assistance to those in need. Local government policies and activities are the stuff of everyday living.

Charters

Romantic notions of democracy in America regard local governments as the building blocks of governance by the people. Alexis de Tocqueville, who is often cited as the critic who captured the essence of early America, described government in the new country as a series of social contracts starting at the grassroots. He said, "The township was organized before the county, the county before the state, the state before the union."[23] It sounds good, but it's wrong.

A more accurate description was included in a ruling issued by Judge John F. Dillon in 1868, and known as *Dillon's Rule:*

> The true view is this: Municipal corporations owe their origins to and derive their power and rights wholly from the (state) legislature. It breathes into them the breath without which they cannot exist. As it creates, so it may destroy. If it may destroy, it may abridge and control.[24]

There are a variety of types of local governments. Some of these are created in a somewhat arbitrary way by state governments. Counties and school districts are good

Responsibilities of local governments are wide ranging—from collecting the garbage in Minneapolis and filling potholes in Buffalo to patrolling the beach at Corpus Christi on spring break. (Photo courtesy: Bob Daemmrich/Stock Boston)

examples. State statutes establish the authority for these jurisdictions, set the boundaries, and determine what these governments may and may not do and how they can generate funds.

charter: A document that, like a constitution, specifies the basic policies, procedures, and institutions of a municipality.

Some local governments emerge as people and industries locate together and form a community. These governments must have a **charter** that is acceptable to the state legislature, much as states must have a constitution acceptable to Congress. Charters describe the institutions of government, the processes used to make legally binding decisions, and the scope of issues and services that fall within the jurisdiction of the governmental bodies. There are five basic types of charters:

1. *Special Charters.* Historically, as urban areas emerged, each one developed and sought approval for its own charter. In order to avoid inconsistencies, most state constitutions now prohibit granting special charters for a particular community.

2. *General Charters.* Some states use a standard charter for all jurisdictions, regardless of size or circumstance.

3. *Classified Charters.* This approach classifies cities according to population and then has a standard charter for each classification.

4. *Optional Charters.* A more recent development is for the state to provide several acceptable charters and then let voters in a community choose from among them.

5. *Home Rule Charters.* Increasingly, states are specifying the major requirements that a charter must meet and then allowing communities to draft and amend their own charters. State government must still approve the final product. Every state allows this process except Alabama, Indiana, Illinois, Kentucky, North Carolina, and Virginia.

An important feature of home rule is that the local government is authorized to legislate on any issue that does not conflict with existing state or federal laws. Other approaches list the subjects that a town or city may address.

In the early 1990s Minnesota, California, and Colorado extended the concept of charters to public schools. They allowed teachers, parents, and community leaders to operate a school according to a charter instead of the standard rules and regulations of the state and the school district. In order to establish a charter school, a document would have to be approved that described the administration of the school, its curricula, admission policies, facilities, and general philosophy.

Types of Local Governments

There are about 90,000 local governments in the United States. Table 3.3 on p. 105 presents the major categories and shows some of the changes between 1962 and 1994.

county: A geographic district created within a state with a government that has general responsibilities for land, welfare, environment, and, where appropriate, rural service policies.

1. *Counties.* Every state except Connecticut and Rhode Island have **counties,** although in Louisiana they are called parishes and in Alaska boroughs. With few exceptions, counties have very broad responsibilities and are used by state governments as basic administrative units for welfare and environmental programs, courts, and the registration of land, births, and deaths. County and city boundaries may and do overlap, although state actions have merged city and county in New York, San Francisco, Denver, St. Louis, Nashville, Jacksonville, Miami, and Honolulu.

2. *Towns.* In the first states and in the Midwest, "town" refers to a form of government in which everyone in a community is invited to an annual meeting to elect officers, adopt ordinances, and pass a budget. Another use of this term is simply to refer to a medium-sized city.

3. *Municipalities.* Villages, towns, and cities are established and authorized by state governments as individuals congregate and form communities. Some of the most intense struggles among governments within the United States are over the boundaries, scope of authority, and sources of revenue for **municipalities.**

4. *Special Districts.* As shown in Table 3.3, **special districts** are the most numerous form of government. A special district is restricted to a particular policy or service area. School districts are the most common form of special districts. Others exist for library service, sewerage, water, and parks. Special districts are governed through a variety of structures. Some have elected heads and others appointed. Some of these jurisdictions levy a fee to generate their revenues, while others depend on appropriations from a state or city or county. A reason for the recent proliferation of special districts is to avoid restrictions on funds faced by municipalities, schools, or other jurisdictions. The creation of a special park district, for example, may enable the park to have its own budget and sources of funding and relieve a city or county treasury.

The reasons why an individual local government was established and given the authority it has are generally sound, but the multiple governments serving the same community and controlling the same area create incredible complexity and confusion. The puzzlement faced by the mall manager in the opening vignette pales when compared to what a developer confronts. He or she may have to deal with a separate governing body for each of the following tasks: getting vacant land zoned appropriately; securing the necessary building permits; assuring prospective new residents of the adequacy of schools and parks for their children; knowing who provides police and fire protection; and arranging for streets, sewerage, refuse collection, and water. In short, the access that one might expect because of the proximity of local officials may be compromised by the complexity of knowing which local officials should be contacted.

There are examples of formal and informal arrangements among local governments to cooperate and coordinate their work in a single community. Miami and Dade

municipality: A government with general responsibilities that is created in response to the emergence of relatively densely populated areas.

special district: A local government that is responsible for a particular function, such as K–12 education, water, sewerage, or parks.

One type of informal local governmental body is the neighborhood association, such as this association holding a meeting to debate zoning problems. Whether or not such associations succeed in communicating clearly and resolving their problems is an open question. (Photo courtesy: Bob Daemmrich/The Image Works)

County have been an early and visible example. St. Paul and Minneapolis have also pioneered cooperative arrangements. The establishment of the 911 emergency service can be a catalyst for cooperation by various police, fire, and paramedical agencies in a metropolitan area. The norm, however, continues to be conflict and often a failure to even communicate. Local officials and citizens alike find the legacies of past actions creating local governments a serious challenge.

Executives and Legislatures

Except for the traditional New England town meeting, where anyone who attends has the authority to vote on policy and management issues, local governments have some or all of the following decision-making offices:

1. Elected executive, such as a mayor, village president, or county executive

2. Elected council or commission, such as a city council, school board, or county board

3. Appointed manager, such as a city manager or school superintendent

Local government institutions are not necessarily bound to the principles of separation of powers or checks and balances that the U.S. Constitution requires of the federal government and most state constitutions require of their governments. School boards, for example, commonly have both legislative and executive authority. They make policies regarding instruction and facilities and they do the hiring and contracting to implement those policies. With few exceptions, school board members are part-time officials, so they hire superintendents and rely heavily on them for day-to-day management and for ideas for new policies. The legislative and executive authority and responsibility, nonetheless, remains with the school board.

The patterns of executive and legislative institutions in local government have their roots in some of the most profound events in our history. The influx of non-English-

Political machines like Chicago's were built on the reciprocal relationships of city officials and leaders of ethnic communities. Chicago's Milwaukee Avenue runs through just such a Polish community. (Photo courtesy: Zbigniew Bzdak/The Image Works)

speaking immigrants into urban areas in the North after the Civil War prompted the growth of political machines.[25] New immigrants needed help getting settled. They naturally got much of that help from ethnic neighborhoods, where, for example, a family from Poland would find people who spoke Polish, restaurants that served Polish food, and stores and churches with links to the old country. Politicians dealt with these ethnic neighborhoods. If the neighborhood voted to help provide victory for particular candidates for **mayor** and **city council,** then city jobs and services would be provided. Political machines were built on these quid pro quo arrangements. The bosses of those machines were either the elected officials or people who controlled the elected officials.

As part of their efforts to destroy the political machines, Progressives sought reforms that would minimize the politics in local government institutions.[26] Progressives favored local governments headed by professional **managers** instead of elected executives. Managers would be appointed by councils, the members of which were elected on a nonpartisan ballot, thus removing the role of parties.

As another way of making the ethnic bloc voting of the machines irrelevant, Progressive reformers advocated that council members be elected from the city at large rather than from neighborhood districts. The choice between **district-based** and **at-large elections** later raised concerns about discrimination against Hispanics and African Americans. A strategy for excluding these communities from influence and power would be to use at-large elections and keep them a minority, rather than to divide the city into districts that might have an ethnic group constitute a majority within a district. The at-large elections, in short, would have the same minimizing effect on these ethnic groups that was intended by Progressives on white ethnic groups.

Progressives argued that the **commission** form of government was an acceptable alternative to mayors and boss politics. The commission evolved as a response to a tidal wave in 1900 that killed over 5,000 people in Galveston, Texas. After the disaster, a group of prominent business leaders in Galveston formed a task force, with each member of the force assuming responsibility for a specific area, such as housing, public safety, and finance. Task force members essentially assumed the roles of both legislators making policy and managers implementing policy. The citizens of Galveston were so impressed with how well this worked that they amended their charter to replace the mayor and city council with a commission, elected at-large and on a nonpartisan basis.

As Table 4.4 indicates, half of all U.S. cities have an elected mayor and a council. Mayors differ in how much authority they have. Some are strong and have the power to veto city council action, to appoint agency heads, and to initiate as well as execute budgets. The charters of other cities do not provide mayors with these formal powers. Except for the largest cities, mayors serve on a part-time basis.

Slightly more than 40 percent of the municipalities have the Progressive model of government, with an appointed, professional manager and an elected city council. This is the most common pattern among medium-size cities, whereas the very large and the very small have mayors and councils. Some jurisdictions have both mayors and managers, as in Highlight 4.2: Pete Wilson, Mayor of San Diego.

Only 2 percent of U.S. cities still have the commission form of government. Tulsa, Oklahoma, and Portland, Oregon, are the largest cities run by commissions. Galveston is one of the cities that has abandoned this structure.

Over 1,800 of the almost 3,000 county governments are run by boards or councils that are elected from geographic districts and without any executive. Committees of the county board manage personnel, finance, roads, parks, social services, and the like. Almost 400 counties elect an executive as well as a board, and thus follow the mayor–council model. Almost 800 hire a professional manager.

mayor: Chief elected executive of a city.

city council: The legislature in a city government.

manager: A professional executive hired by a city council or county board to manage daily operations and to recommend policy changes.

district-based election: Election in which candidates run for an office that represents only the voters of a specific district within the jurisdiction.

at-large election: Election in which candidates for office must compete throughout the jurisdiction as a whole.

commission: Form of local government in which several officials are elected to top positions which have both legislative and executive responsibilities.

In the aftermath of the devastating 1900 flood in Galveston, Texas, the commission form of city government came into being. Although Galveston has abandoned the commission form, the model spread quickly, and by 1917 almost 500 cities had adopted the commission form of government. (Photo courtesy: Corbis-Bettmann)

TABLE 4.4

Major Forms of Municipal Government

POPULATION GROUP	All Cities	FORM OF GOVERNMENT (NUMBER AND PERCENT) Mayor–council	Council–manager	Commission	Town meeting[a]
Over 1,000,000	8	6 (75%)	2 (25%)	0 (0%)	0(0%)
500,000 to 1,000,000	16	13 (81%)	3 (19%)	0 (0%)	0 (0%)
250,000 to 499,999	39	16 (41%)	22 (56%)	1 (3%)	0 (0%)
25,000 to 249,999	1137	407 (36%)	681 (60%)	22 (2%)	27 (2%)
10,000 to 24,999	1602	676 (42%)	751 (47%)	52 (3%)	123 (8%)
2,500 to 9,999	3792	2192 (58%)	1240 (33%)	73 (2%)	287 (8%)
Total (all cities over 2,500)	6594	3310 (50%)	2699 (41%)	148 (2%)	437 (7%)

[a]Includes representative town meeting

Note: The mayor–council form of government is most popular in very large and very small cities. The council–manager form is most popular in medium-size cities. The commission form continues to lose popularity.

Source: Calculated from International City/County Management Association, *The Municipal Year Book 1993* (Washington, D.C.: International City/County Management Association, 1993), Table 2, xi. Reprinted by permission.

School districts, with very few exceptions, follow the council–manager model. Other special districts have boards (sometimes called corporations or authorities) that are elected or appointed by elected officials. If the district is responsible for services like water or sewerage or mass transit, the board is likely to hire and then supervise a manager.

FINANCES

tate and local governments must, of course, have money. Getting that money is one of the most challenging and thankless tasks of public officials. The requirement to achieve a rather precisely balanced budget is unique to state and local governments. Unlike the federal government, state and local units may not, on a continual basis, spend more money than they have. Unlike private businesses, state and local governments may not spend less money than they have. Whereas the goal of a private business is to have significantly more income than expenses, a governor or mayor or other local public executive would be criticized for taxing too heavily if something akin to profits appeared on the books.

The budgeting process involves making projections of expenses and revenues. State and local officials face some special uncertainties when they make these guesses. One important factor is the health of the economy. If one is taxing sales or income, those will vary with levels of employment and economic growth. Moreover, the public sector faces double jeopardy when the economy declines. Revenues will go down as

Highlight 4.2

Pete Wilson, Mayor of San Diego

(Photo courtesy: Bob Daemmrich/The Image Works)

Before Pete Wilson was elected as either Governor of California or U.S. Senator from California, he served as Mayor of San Diego. The city of San Diego has both a city manager and a mayor. The city manager, according to the city's charter, is the full-time, chief administrator and the mayor has limited formal authority beyond presiding at city council meetings.

In the 1970s, thanks primarily to the city manager, San Diego was completing almost two decades of rapid, but smooth, growth. Once the population reached about 700,000, the community debated whether further growth should be encouraged. Pete Wilson ignored the restrictions on his authority and asserted effective leadership in slowing San Diego's expansion. The city manager left for a job that better fit his philosophies of urban growth.

sales and incomes decline, and at the same time expenses go up as more families and individuals need assistance during harsh times.

Another important factor affecting state and local government budgets is the level of funding that governments give to one another. States have been getting about one-fourth of their funds from Washington, D.C. That level has varied over time and, especially with the pattern of deficit spending begun in the early 1980s, is likely to decline. The amount of the decline will depend as much on political dynamics as it will on the health of the national economy. Local governments do not receive as much, but water and sewerage districts have been getting about 15 percent of their funds from the federal government. Local governments depend heavily on aid from state governments. The pattern varies from one state to another, but on the average school districts get slightly over half of their funds from state governments, counties get almost one-third, and cities about one-fifth.[27]

Different governments depend on different types of taxes and fees. Figure 4.3 presents the pattern of funding for state and local governments. Unlike the federal government, which relies primarily on the income tax, state governments rely almost equally on income taxes and sales taxes. States differ among themselves, of course. Alaska, Delaware, Montana, New Hampshire, and Oregon have no sales tax at all, whereas some of the Southern states have a double-digit sales tax. Likewise, Alaska, Florida, Nevada, South Dakota, Texas, Washington, and Wyoming do not tax personal incomes. Tax rates differ among those states that do have an income tax, but the levels are generally less than 10 percent.

Local governments rely primarily on property taxes, have little from levies on sales, and virtually nothing from income. Schools, in particular, depend on property taxes. Both local and state governments levy user fees, such as admission to parks, licenses for hunting and fishing, tuition for public universities, and charges based on the amount of water used. States, more than local governments, administer retirement systems and insurance programs for public employees. Income from the investment of retirement funds is listed but is not generally available for any use other than paying

FIGURE 4.3

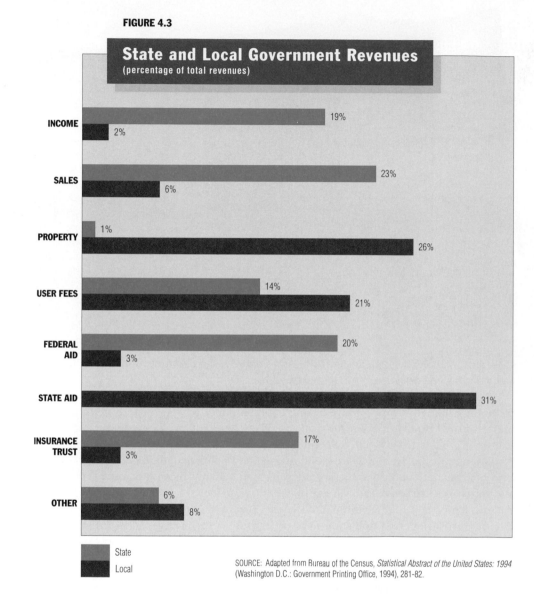

State and Local Government Revenues
(percentage of total revenues)

	State	Local
INCOME	19%	2%
SALES	23%	6%
PROPERTY	1%	26%
USER FEES	14%	21%
FEDERAL AID	20%	3%
STATE AID		31%
INSURANCE TRUST	17%	3%
OTHER	6%	8%

State
Local

SOURCE: Adapted from Bureau of the Census, *Statistical Abstract of the United States: 1994* (Washington D.C.: Government Printing Office, 1994), 281-82.

retirement benefits. Similarly, user fees are typically placed in segregated funds, which means they can only be used to provide the service for which the fee was charged. Tuition must, in other words, be used by the university and cannot pay for prison costs or maintaining highways.

Most people accept user fees as the fairest type of taxation. The problem is that the income is both limited and segregated. Taxes generally can be evaluated according to how much money they can raise, whether the revenue is certain, and who bears the burden. Income taxes generate large sums of money, although there will be variations with how well the economy is doing, how many people are employed, and the like. Of all the taxes, those based on income are the most progressive, which means that they are based on the ability to pay.

North—South

POLITICS AROUND THE WORLD

People who live in the United States have to pay a lot of attention to state and local government. Much of what happens with their schools, neighborhoods, roads, police, and social service are determined by them, rather than by the national government.

To an outsider, what happens in state and local government looks quite different from what goes on in Washington. To be sure, most states have bicameral legislatures, separately elected governors, and other institutions that mirror those at the federal level. And nonnational governments are frequent recruiting grounds for national politicians—Presidents Clinton, Reagan, and Carter had all served as governors but had never held national office before moving into the White House. Nonetheless, elections at the state and local level are largely fought over state and local issues. In many cases, especially at the local level, they are nonpartisan, which means that national concerns rarely enter into those contests.

In Canada and Mexico—as in most other countries—historically there has been a much closer link between national and local politics, and their equivalents of state and local politics have mattered less. In both countries, however, the balance of political power is shifting "downward."

In Canada, the weakness of local government was a by-product of the 1867 Constitution, which granted far more power to the federal government than the provinces and to a string of powerful, long-serving prime ministers who reinforced those centralizing tendencies. Over the last thirty to forty years, the provinces have asserted themselves far more, and all the constitutional reforms being discussed these days envision a far more decentralized country. Most provinces already have their own economic development offices, and many have taken the lead in vital policy areas including welfare reform and deficit reduction.

In Mexico, the dominance of the national government has little to do with constitutional provisions. As with almost everything else in Mexican politics, it has been an outgrowth of the PRI's control over all aspects of political life, including who gets elected to state and local office.

On those rare occasions when state or communal governments acted in ways the national government (in other words, the PRI's national leadership) did not like, it was more than willing to use its power to intervene and even appoint a new state government. Since the early 1980s, however, that has not been as easy, especially since opposition parties have begun winning elections in a substantial number of states and large cities.

The role of subnational government is also a lot more controversial in these two countries. As we have already seen, it is a major source of Canada's constitutional impasse. In Mexico, it is one of the reasons why we are seeing more political protest, such as the uprising in the poor southern state of Chiapas that has been going on since 1994.

Sales taxes are also good at generating money and they also vary with how well the economy is doing. These are not based on earnings but on purchases. Since those with a low income must spend virtually all that they earn in order to live, sales taxes are regressive. To counter the regressive nature of sales taxes, some states exempt food, medicine, and other necessities.

The property tax varies with the value of one's property, not one's current income or spending. Thus, farmers and those with a fixed income, like retired persons, might bear more of a burden than their current wealth suggests they should carry. The property tax can be a good revenue earner and is the most stable, since a jurisdiction can set a tax rate that virtually guarantees a certain level of revenue, regardless of economic trends. The local officials who set these rates invariably hear complaints about the regressive, arbitrary nature of property taxes.

CHANGING STATE AND LOCAL GOVERNMENTS

The good news is that state and local governments have become increasingly more competent since the 1960s. The governments that provide the services that affect us most directly and regularly have more capable people and more efficient processes than they have ever had before. Governments run by our neighbors and friends and co-workers are not only more accessible, but they are more able.

The uncertainty is whether state and local governments are able enough. Both by design and of necessity, the federal government is shedding some of its responsibilities in social and environmental policy and asking state and local governments to do more. At times, in fact, the federal government is *requiring* states and cities and schools to do more. There must be measures to ensure that children under eighteen cannot buy tobacco products. New pollutants must be removed from drinking water. Convicted criminals must serve longer sentences in already crowded state prisons and county jails. And all this must happen with fewer federal dollars being sent to state and local governments.

Simultaneously, a more complex society and a more demanding population are challenging subnational governments to do more with less. Advances in telecommunications and computer technology make some existing government policies obsolete. Economic uncertainties and job demands threaten traditional family support systems and sometimes almost invite the development of gangs and other dysfunctional surrogates. Existing transportation systems, education programs, and housing patterns struggle to meet the needs of changing communities. The pressure to respond to these challenges is more than matched by the pressures to avoid paying more taxes.

Concern over the future of Medicaid and welfare illustrates the issues that affect state and local governments. Federal legislation established programs in which families and individuals below a given income level were eligible for medical care, food, and cash assistance. These programs were funded by the federal government and state governments, and states had some flexibility in determining eligibility and benefits for their citizens. In order to cut annual deficit spending, presidents and Congress have been considering ways of limiting the federal share of welfare costs. The National Governors' Association in 1966 suggested a scheme in which the federal government gave state governments money based on a general formula rather than on how many individuals were eligible for benefits and then let each state decide how it wanted to address the needs of its poor.

The initial welcome of the governors' plan soon turned to discord. The key stumbling blocks were the severity of the cuts in federal spending that Congress wanted to make and the concern that some states might be considerably less responsive than others to the needs of the poor.

In a sense, health and welfare reform efforts are still grappling with an ambiguity contained in the Preface to the Constitution, which was cited at the very beginning of this book. "We the people of the United States . . ." can be interpreted to emphasize *people* or to emphasize *states*. Should our national government in Washington, D.C., assume the role of ensuring that individuals have certain basic rights and benefits, no matter where they live? If so, the abandonment of health and welfare programs based on individual needs contradicts a fundamental principle of our government. Or was the intent of the Founders that states be allowed to offer families and individuals substantially different opportunities and guarantees?

In fact, the issue was not resolved by the authors of the Constitution. It is still unresolved. Like our political system generally, the role of state and local governments is constantly changing. The most important factors shaping that role in the near future are the ability and willingness of the federal government to distribute funds to state and local governments and whether the natural competition between states will be confined to economic growth and the quality of life at the upper end or will extend to basic standards at the lower end of income levels.

SUMMARY

The expectations are that state and local governments are readily accessible to citizens and that they are likely to be responsive to the needs and wishes of a particular community. In this chapter we have examined the changing character of governance at the state and local levels in order to appreciate both the variation and the common patterns in subnational governments, and have made the following points:

1.   Grassroots Power and Politics.

Those who wield the most influence over the making and implementation of public policy in a community are not always the ones elected to formal offices. Sometimes power is in the hands of a family or a small number of individuals or the local media. Whether or not those who are most powerful are the ones in government offices, governance at the grassroots is face-to-face, between neighbors, friends, and former high school classmates.

2.   State Governments.

State governments have traditionally had primary responsibility for criminal justice, education, public health, and economic development. Recently, state officials have assumed a larger role in welfare and environmental policy. State constitutions, which reflect major historical developments in American society, provide the basic framework of institutions and values in which state governments fulfill their roles. Since the 1960s these governments have dramatically become increasingly competent, professional, and accessible to the general public.

3. Local Governments.

Local governance in the United States is conducted by a myriad of almost 80,000 units, most of which are run by part-time officials. These governments range from general jurisdictions covering densely urbanized areas to special districts functioning for a very specific and narrow purpose. The forms of local governments also differ. There are town meetings in which all eligible voters in a community gather to conduct business, elected and appointed boards that have both executive and legislative powers, and governments with distinct legislative councils, elected executives, and professional managers. Local politics is frequently nonpartisan, thanks in part to conscious efforts to avoid control by political party machines.

4. Finances.

State and local governments may not legally spend more than they earn, except in unusual, emergency situations. Politically, state and local officials cannot generate more revenue than they spend, lest they be accused of taxing too heavily. It is difficult to achieve a balance between revenue and expenditures. When the economy is bad and tax revenues go down, the demand for government spending tends to go up. Also, officials can never be sure how much aid they will get from the federal and state governments.

5. Changing State and Local Governments.

The trends of increasing competence and expanding responsibilities for state and local governments is undoubtedly going to continue. The antigovernment, antitax mood presents a major challenge at the state and, especially, local levels as the demands and expectations for more services and functions is not matched by a willingness to provide more funding. This challenge is likely to become more complicated as the federal government no longer defines its role as ensuring minimal rights and standards of living for all Americans and states and communities are left to determine how they will respond to individuals and families with short-term and long-term needs.

KEY TERMS

advisory referendum, p. 128

at-large election, p. 133

charter, p. 130

city council, p. 133

commission, p. 133

common law, p. 122

county, p. 130

direct initiative, p. 127

direct (popular) referendum, p. 128

district-based election, p. 133

governor, p. 117

indirect initiative, p. 127

line-item veto, p. 118

manager, p. 133

mayor, p. 133

municipality, p. 131

nonpartisan election, p. 112

package or general veto, p. 118

special district, p. 131

term limit, p. 120

SUGGESTED READINGS

Banfield, Edward C. *The Unheavenly City*. Boston: Little, Brown, 1970.

Benjamin, Gerald and Michael J. Malbin, eds. *Limiting Legislative Terms*. Washington, D.C.: Congressional Quarterly Press, 1992.

Burns, Nancy E. *The Formation of American Local Governments: Private Values in Public Institutions*. New York: Oxford University Press, 1994.

Crenson, Matthew A. *Neighborhood Politics*. Cambridge: Harvard University Press, 1983.

Dahl, Robert A. *Who Governs? Democracy and Power in an American City*. New Haven: Yale University Press).

Erie, Steven P. *Rainbow's End: Irish American and the Dilemmas of Urban Machine Politics, 1840–1985*. Berkeley: University of California Press, 1988.

Erikson. Robert S., Gerald C. Wright, and John P. McIver, *Statehouse Democracy: Public Opinion and Policy in the American States*. Cambridge: Cambridge University Press, 1993.

Jewell, Malcolm E., and Marcia Lynn Whicker. *Legislative Leadership in the American States*. Ann Arbor: University of Michigan Press, 1994.

Stone, Clarence N. *Regime Politics: Governing Atlanta, 1946–1988*. Lawrence: University of Kansas Press.

Woliver, Laura R. *From Outrage to Action: The Politics of Grass-Roots Dissent*. Urbana: University of Illinois Press, 1993.

Photo courtesy: Bonnie Kamin

CIVIL LIBERTIES

On March 3, 1993, James McNally was arrested while driving the car of a man who was murdered in a Santa Monica, California, apartment. A transcript of McNally's interrogation by the police reveals that, although McNally repeatedly invoked his constitutional rights to remain silent and to consult with an attorney, the detectives continued to question him, pressing him for information. They even promised to advise the district attorney of McNally's cooperation and suggested to him that the district attorney would go easier on him if he cooperated with them.

At one point during the interrogation, McNally asked the detectives to turn off their tape recorder. In response, one detective responded, "Okay, and [expletive] your attorney. It's just—I don't care about him anymore. . . . As far as I'm concerned, you know, they really mess up the system. I want to know now what you're gonna tell me later. It can't be used against you."[1]

Under this kind of pressure and misinformation, McNally ended up giving a statement. Although the statement was not used at trial because it was illegally obtained, McNally's attorneys contended that his defense was hampered: They could not put him on the witness stand because they were afraid that his statement could then be used to impeach his credibility. McNally was convicted of manslaughter and is serving an eleven-year term.

Like McNally, James Bey also ran into trouble with the Santa Monica police department. Parts of a statement he made to the police were introduced as evidence at trial, even though Bey had been told that what he said could not be used against him. The detective who questioned Bey even testified at a pretrial hearing that he had been trained to conduct interrogations "outside *Miranda*."[2] Bey was convicted of murder. An appeals judge ruled that although the use of Bey's statement at trial had been wrong, it did not affect the validity of his conviction.

In late December 1995, four California civil liberties groups announced that they would file suit in federal court accusing the Santa Monica police department of "routinely subjecting criminal suspects to coercive questioning after they have invoked their right to remain silent and to have counsel . . . exacting a heavy toll on individual liberty and trading on the weakness of the individual."[3] The lawsuit seeks to stop police from questioning suspects after they have invoked their *Miranda* rights. Attorneys are using McNally and Bey as the clients upon which to challenge police practices, but a favorable ruling from the courts could have far wider applications, as did the case of Ernesto Miranda.

As you probably know from watching television, in the Supreme Court's landmark ruling in *Miranda* v. *Arizona* (1966),[4] the Court declared that criminal suspects must be informed that any statements they make can be used against them at trial and that they have the right to remain silent and to be represented by an attorney. The Court furthermore ruled that if a suspect invokes those rights, all police questioning must stop. In 1971, however, the Court also ruled that when *Miranda* procedures are not followed, statements made by suspects can be used to undermine their credibility if they later take the witness stand, which most defendants do not. Thus many police officers are now trained to question "outside of *Miranda*." "You don't have to be Sherlock Holmes to figure out why they're doing it," said the legal director of the southern California American Civil Liberties Union. "They have plenty of incentive to continue the interrogation."[5]

While civil liberties groups bemoan actions such as those taken by the Santa Monica police, public opinion supports such practices. Many Americans, including several Supreme Court justices, are reluctant to bar the use of illegally obtained or coerced confessions or statements because such statements often indicate guilt.

Civil liberties issues often bring up such dilemmas. Frequently, courts or policy makers are called on to balance competing interests and rights. As a society, for example, do we want to protect all citizens from illegal searches or are we willing to allow some if it means that the guilty will not go free? Similarly, as we discuss later in this chapter, Congress has recently grappled with the scope of the right to free speech on the Internet. Should citizens have unfettered discretion to write and print what they want, or should government impose limits? In most of the cases discussed in the chapter, there is a conflict between an individual or group of individuals seeking to exercise what they believe to be a right and the government—local, state, or national—seeking to control the exercise of that right in an attempt to keep order and preserve the rights of others. It generally falls to the judiciary to balance those interests. And, depending on the times and the composition of the Supreme Court, the balance may be tilted toward civil liberties or toward the right of the government to limit those liberties.

civil liberties: The personal rights and freedoms that the federal government cannot abridge by law, constitution, or judicial interpretation.

Civil liberties are the personal rights and freedoms that the federal government cannot abridge, either by law, constitution, or judicial interpretation, unless there is a compelling state interest or need to do so. Civil liberties place limitations on the power of the government to restrain or dictate how individuals act. Thus, when we discuss civil liberties such as those found in the Bill of Rights, we are concerned with limits on what governments can and cannot do. In this chapter we explore the various dimensions of civil liberties guarantees contained in the U.S. Constitution and the Bill of Rights as we

- discuss the *Bill of Rights*, the reasons for its addition to the Constitution, and its eventual application to the states via the incorporation doctrine.

- survey the meaning of *the First Amendment's freedom of religion clauses.*

- discuss the meanings of *the free speech and press guarantees found in the First Amendment.*

- analyze the reasons for many of *the criminal defendants' rights* found in the Bill of Rights and how those rights have been expanded and contracted by the U.S. Supreme Court.

- discuss the meaning of *the right to privacy* and how that concept has been interpreted by the Court.

- explore some of the proposals that have been made to *change existing definitions of civil liberties* guarantees.

THE FIRST CONSTITUTIONAL AMENDMENTS: THE BILL OF RIGHTS

In 1787, most state constitutions explicitly protected a variety of personal liberties: speech, religion, freedom from unreasonable searches and seizures, trial by jury, and more. It was clear that the new Constitution would redistribute power in the new federal system between the national government and the states. Without an explicit guarantee of specific civil liberties, could the national government be trusted to uphold the freedoms already granted to citizens by their states?

Recognition of the increased power that would be held by the new national government led Anti-Federalists to stress the need for a bill of rights. Anti-Federalists and many others were confident that they could control the actions of their own state legislators, but didn't trust the national government to be so protective of their civil liberties.

The notion of adding a bill of rights to the Constitution was not a popular one at the Constitutional Convention. When George Mason of Virginia proposed that such a bill be added to the preface of the proposed Constitution, for example, his resolution was defeated unanimously.[6] In the subsequent ratification debates, Federalists argued that a bill of rights was unnecessary. Not only did most state constitutions already contain those protections, Federalists believed it was foolhardy to list things that the national government had no power to do since the proposed Constitution didn't give the national government the power to regulate speech, religion, and the like.

Some Federalists, however, supported the idea. After the Philadelphia convention, for example, James Madison conducted a lively correspondence about the need for a national bill of rights with Thomas Jefferson. Jefferson was far quicker to support such guarantees than was Madison, who continued to doubt their utility because he believed that a list of "protected" rights might suggest that those not enumerated were not protected. Politics soon intervened, however, when Madison found himself in a close race against James Monroe for a seat in the House of Representatives in the First Congress. The district was largely Anti-Federalist. So to garner support, Madison, in an act of political expediency, issued a new series of public letters similar to the earlier *Federalist Papers*, vowing support for a bill of rights.

Once elected to the House, Madison made good on his support. He became the prime mover and author of the Bill of Rights, although he considered the Congress to have far more important matters to handle and viewed his labors on the Bill of Rights "a nauseous project."[7]

The insistence of Anti-Federalists on a bill of rights, the fact that some states conditioned their ratification of the Constitution on the addition of these guarantees, and the disagreement among Federalists about writing specific liberty guarantees into the Constitution led to prompt congressional action to put an end to further controversy. This was a time when national stability and support for the new government were particularly needed. Thus in 1789 the proposed Bill of Rights was sent to the states by Congress for ratification, which was finally achieved in 1791.

The **Bill of Rights,** the first ten amendments to the Constitution, contains numerous specific guarantees, including those of free speech, press, and religion (see

Bill of Rights: The first ten amendments to the U.S. Constitution guaranteeing specific rights and liberties.

Appendix II for the full text). The Ninth and Tenth Amendments in particular highlight Anti-Federalist fears of a too-powerful national government. The Ninth Amendment, strongly favored by Madison, makes it clear that this special listing of rights does not mean that others don't exist; and the Tenth Amendment simply reiterates that powers not delegated to the national government are reserved to the states or the people.

The Incorporation Doctrine: The Bill of Rights Made Applicable to the States

due process clause: Clause contained in the Fifth and Fourteenth Amendments. Over the years, it has been construed to guarantee to individuals a variety of rights ranging from economic liberty to criminal procedural rights to protection from arbitrary governmental action.

incorporation doctrine: Principle in which the Supreme Court has held that most, but not all, of the specific guarantees in the Bill of Rights limit state and local governments by making those guarantees applicable to the states through the due process clause of the Fourteenth Amendment.

The Bill of Rights was intended to limit the powers of the *national* government to infringe on the rights and liberties of the citizenry. And in *Barron* v. *Baltimore* (1833),[8] the Supreme Court ruled that the federal Bill of Rights limited only the U.S. government and not the states. In 1868, however, the Fourteenth Amendment was added to the U.S. Constitution. Its language suggested the possibility that some or even all of the protections guaranteed in the Bill of Rights might be interpreted to prevent state infringement of those rights. Section 1 of the Fourteenth Amendment reads: "No State shall . . . deprive any person of life, liberty, or property, without due process of law."

Until nearly the turn of the century, the Supreme Court steadfastly rejected numerous arguments urging it to interpret the **due process clause** in the Fourteenth Amendment as making various provisions contained in the Bill of Rights applicable to the states. In 1897, however, the Court began to increase its jurisdiction over the states.[9] It began to hold states to a substantive due process standard whereby state laws had to be shown to be a valid exercise of the state's power to regulate the health, welfare, or public morals of its citizens. Interferences with state power, however, were rare. As a consequence, states continued to pass sedition laws (laws that made it illegal to speak or write any political criticism that threatened to diminish respect for the government, its laws, or public officials), expecting that the Supreme Court would uphold their constitutional validity. Then, in 1925 all of this changed dramatically. Benjamin Gitlow, a member of the Left Wing Section of the Socialist Party, was convicted of violating a New York law that—in language very similar to that of the federal Espionage Act—prohibited the advocacy of the violent overthrow of the government. Gitlow had printed 16,000 copies of a manifesto in which he urged workers to rise up to overthrow the U.S. government. Although Gitlow's conviction was upheld, in *Gitlow* v. *New York* (1925) the Supreme Court noted that the states were not completely free to limit forms of political expression:

> For present purposes we may and do assume that freedom of speech and of the press—which are protected by the First Amendment from abridgement by Congress—are among the *fundamental personal rights and "liberties"* protected by the due process clause of the Fourteenth Amendment from impairment by the states [emphasis added].[10]

Until *Gitlow* v. *New York* (1925), involving Benjamin Gitlow, the executive secretary of the Socialist Party, it was generally thought that the Fourteenth Amendment did not apply the protections of the Bill of Rights to the states. Here Gitlow is shown testifying before the Dees Committee, which was investigating un-American activities. (Photo courtesy: AP/Worldwide Photos)

Gitlow, with its finding that states could not abridge free speech protections, was the first step in the slow development of the **incorporation doctrine.** After *Gitlow,* it took the Court six more years to "incorporate" another First Amendment freedom—that of the press. *Near* v. *Minnesota* (1931) was the first case in which the Supreme Court found that a state law violated freedom of the press as protected by the First Amendment. Jay Near, the publisher of a weekly Minneapolis newspaper, regularly attacked a variety of groups—African Americans, Catholics, Jews, and labor union leaders. Few escaped his hatred. Near's paper was closed under the authority of a state criminal libel law banning "malicious, scandalous, or defamatory" publications. Near appealed the closing of his paper, and the Supreme Court ruled that "The fact that the liberty of the press may be abused by miscreant purveyors of scandal does not make any the less necessary the immunity of the press from previous restraint."[11]

As revealed in Table 5.1, not all the specific guarantees in the Bill of Rights have been made applicable to the states through the due process clause of the Fourteenth Amendment. Instead, the Court has selectively chosen to limit the rights of states by protecting the rights it considers most fundamental, and thus subject to the Court's most rigorous strict scrutiny review. This process is referred to as *selective incorporation*.

TABLE 5.1

The Selective Incorporation of the Bill of Rights

DATE	AMENDMENT	RIGHT	CASE
1925	I.	Speech	*Gitlow* v. *New York*
1931		Press	*Near* v. *Minnesota*
1937		Assembly	*DeJonge* v. *Oregon*
1940		Religion	*Cantwell* v. *Connecticut*
	II.	Right to bear arms	*not incorporated* (Generally, the Supreme Court has upheld reasonable regulations of the right of private citizens to bear arms. Should a tough gun-control law be adopted by a state or local government and a challenge to it be made, a test of incorporation might be presented to the Court in the future.)
	III.	No quartering of soldiers	*not incorporated* (The quartering problem has not recurred since colonial times.)
1949	IV.	Unreasonable searches and seizures	*Wolf* v. *Colorado*
1961		The exclusionary rule	*Mapp* v. *Ohio*
1897	V.	Just compensation	*Chicago, B&O RR. Co.* v. *Chicago*
1964		Self-incrimination	*Malloy* v. *Hogan*
1969		Double jeopardy	*Benton* v. *Maryland*
		Grand jury indictment	*not incorporated* (The trend in state criminal cases is away from grand juries and toward reliance upon the sworn written accusation of the prosecuting attorney.)
1948	VI.	Public trial	*In re Oliver*
1963		Right to counsel	*Gideon* v. *Wainwright*
1965		Confrontation of witnesses	*Pointer* v. *Texas*
1966		Impartial trial	*Parker* v. *Gladden*
1967		Speedy trial	*Klopfer* v. *North Carolina*
1967		Compulsory trial	*Washington* v. *Texas*
1968		Jury trial	*Duncan* v. *Louisiana*
	VII.	Right to jury trial in civil cases	*not incorporated* (While Warren Burger was Chief Justice he conducted a campaign to abolish jury trials in civil cases to save time and money, among other reasons.)
1962	VIII.	Freedom from cruel and unusual punishment	*Robinson* v. *California*
		Freedom from excessive fines or bail	*not incorporated*

Selective incorporation requires the states to respect freedoms of press, speech, and assembly among other rights. Other guarantees contained in the Second, Third, and Seventh amendments, such as the right to bear arms, have not been incorporated because the Court has yet to consider them sufficiently fundamental to national notions of liberty and justice.

Selective Incorporation and Fundamental Freedoms

selective incorporation: A judicial doctrine whereby most but not all of the protections found in the Bill of Rights are made applicable to the states via the Fourteenth Amendment.

The rationale for **selective incorporation,** the judicial application to the states of only some of the rights enumerated by the Bill of Rights, was set out by the Court in 1937 in its decision in *Palko* v. *Connecticut.*[12] Frank Palko was charged with first-degree murder for killing two Connecticut police officers, found guilty of a lesser charge of second-degree murder, and sentenced to life imprisonment. Connecticut appealed. Palko was retried, found guilty of first-degree murder, and resentenced to death. Palko then appealed his second conviction on the grounds that it violated the Fifth Amendment's prohibition against double jeopardy because the Fifth Amendment had been made applicable to the states by the due process clause of the Fourteenth Amendment.

The Supreme Court upheld Palko's second conviction and the death sentence, thereby choosing not to bind states to the Fifth Amendment's double jeopardy clause. This decision set forth principles that were to guide the Court's interpretation of the incorporation doctrine for the next several decades. Some protections found in the Bill of Rights were absorbed into the concept of due process only because they are so fundamental to our notions of liberty and justice that they cannot be denied by the states unless the state can show what is called a compelling reason for the liberties' curtailment. This is a very high burden of proof for the state. Thus abridgment of a fundamental right is not often sustained by the Court. Because the Court concluded that the protection against double jeopardy was *not* a fundamental right, Palko's appeal was rejected and he died in Connecticut's gas chamber one year later. Those rights deemed fundamental are only those selectively drawn from the Bill of Rights and incorporated into the due process clause of the Fourteenth Amendment to apply to the states. Fundamental rights include not only less than the whole of the Bill of Rights, but more—that is, other unenumerated rights, such as the right to privacy. The term *selective incorporation plus* suggests the reality of those rights recognized as fundamental and thus within the meaning of liberty protected by the due process clause of the Fourteen Amendment.

FIRST AMENDMENT GUARANTEES: FREEDOM OF RELIGION

Today, many lawmakers bemoan the absence of religion in the public schools and voice their concerns that America is becoming a godless nation. Many of the Framers were religious men, but they knew what evils could arise if the new nation was not founded with religious freedom as one of its core ideals. Despite the fact that many colonists had fled Europe primarily to escape religious persecution, most colonies actively persecuted those who did not belong to their predominant religious groups. Pennsylvania, for example, was a "Quaker" colony. The Congregationalist Church of Massachusetts, a "Puritan" colony, taxed and harassed those who held other religious beliefs. Nevertheless, the colonists were uniformly outraged in 1774 when the British Parliament passed a law establishing Anglicanism and Roman Catholicism as official religions in the colonies. The First Continental Congress immediately sent a letter of protest announcing its "astonishment that a British Parliament should ever consent to establish . . . a religion [Catholicism] that has deluged [England] in blood and dispersed bigotry, persecution, murder and rebellion through every part of the world."[13]

This distaste for a national church or religion was reflected in the Constitution. Article VI, for example, provides that "no religious Test shall ever be required as a Qualification to any Office or Public Trust under the United States." This simple statement, however, did not reassure those who feared the new Constitution would curtail individual liberty. Thus the First Amendment to the Constitution was ultimately ratified to lay those fears to rest.

The First Amendment to the Constitution begins, "Congress shall make no law respecting an establishment of religion, or prohibiting the free exercise thereof." This statement sets the boundaries of governmental action. The **establishment clause** ("Congress shall make no law respecting an establishment of religion") directs the national government not to involve itself in religion. It creates, in Thomas Jefferson's words, a "wall of separation" between church and state. The **free exercise clause** ("or prohibiting the free exercise thereof") guarantees citizens that the national government will not interfere with their practice of religion. These guarantees, however, are not absolute. In the mid-1800s, Mormons traditionally practiced and preached polygamy, the taking of multiple wives. In 1879, when it was first called on to interpret the free exercise clause, the Supreme Court upheld the conviction of a Mormon under a federal law barring polygamy. The Court reasoned that to do otherwise would provide constitutional protections to a full range of religious beliefs, including those as extreme as human sacrifice. "Laws are made for the government of actions," noted the Court, "and while they cannot interfere with mere religious belief and opinions, they may with practices."[14] Later, in 1940, the Supreme Court observed that the First Amendment "embraces two concepts—freedom to believe and freedom to act. The first is absolute,

establishment clause: The first clause in the First Amendment. It prohibits the national government from establishing a national religion.

free exercise clause: The second clause of the First Amendment. It prohibits the U.S. government from interfering with a citizen's right to practice his or her religion.

In spite of the First Amendment's general ban on state entanglement with religion, prayer is still common at many public ceremonies. Here the president of the United States is shown praying at the 1993 graduation at West Point, a public institution. (Photo courtesy: Lisa Quinones/Black Star)

but in the nature of things, the second cannot be. Conduct remains subject to regulation of society."[15]

The Establishment Clause

Over the years, the Court has been divided over how to interpret the establishment clause. Does this clause erect a total wall between church and state, or is some governmental accommodation of religion allowed? While the Supreme Court has upheld the constitutionality of many kinds of church/state entanglements such as public funding to provide sign language interpreters for deaf students in religious schools,[16] the Court has held fast to the rule of strict separation between church and state when issues of prayer in school are involved. In *Engel* v. *Vitale* (1962),[17] the Court first ruled that the recitation in public school classrooms of a twenty-two-word nondenominational prayer drafted by the New Hyde Park, New York, school board was unconstitutional. In 1992 the Court continued its unwillingness to allow prayer in public schools by finding unconstitutional the saying of prayer at a middle school graduation.[18]

The Court has gone back and forth in its effort to come up with a workable way to deal with church/state questions. In *Lemon* v. *Kurtzman* (1971),[19] the Court heard a case that challenged direct state aid to parochial schools, including the use of state funds to pay salaries of teachers at these schools. In its decision, the Court tried—as it often does—to carve out a new "test" by which to measure the constitutionality of these types of laws. Under the **Lemon test,** to be constitutional a challenged law or practice must:

Lemon test: The Court devised tests designed to measure the constitutionality of state laws that appear to further a religion.

1.   Have a secular purpose;
2.   Have a primary effect that neither advances nor inhibits religion; and
3.   Not foster an excessive government entanglement with religion.

State funding of parochial school teachers' salaries was found to fail this test and was therefore prohibited by the Constitution, said the Court in *Lemon.*[20] In 1980 the *Lemon* test was interpreted to invalidate a Kentucky law that required the posting of the Ten Commandments in public school classrooms. The Court ruled the posting had no secular purpose.[21]

Since 1980, however, the Supreme Court has appeared more willing to ignore the *Lemon* test and lower the wall between church and state as long as school prayer is not involved. In 1981, for example, the Court ruled unconstitutional a Missouri law prohibiting the use of state university buildings and grounds for "purposes of religious worship," which had been used to ban religious groups from using school facilities.[22]

This decision was taken by many members of Congress as a sign that this principle could be extended to secondary and even primary schools. In 1984 Congress passed the Equal Access Act, which bars public schools from discriminating against groups of students on the basis of "religious, political, philosophical or other content of the speech at such meetings." The constitutionality of this law was upheld in 1990 when the Court ruled that a school board's refusal to allow a Christian Bible club to meet in a public high school classroom during a twice-weekly "activity period" violated the act. According to the decision, the primary effect of the act was neither to advance religion nor to excessively entangle government and religion—in spite of the fact that religious meetings would be held on school grounds with a faculty sponsor. The important factor seemed to be that the students had complete choice in their selection of activities with numerous nonreligious options.[23] In 1993 the Court also ruled that religious groups must be allowed to use public schools after hours if that access is also given to other community groups.[24]

Highlight 5.1

The American Civil Liberties Union: Protector of First Amendment Rights

The American Civil Liberties Union (ACLU) was created in 1920 by a group that had tried to defend the civil liberties of those who were conscientious objectors to World War I. As the nation's oldest, largest, and premier nonpartisan civil liberties organization, the ACLU works in three major areas of the law: freedom of speech and religion, due process, and equality before the law. The ACLU lobbies for legislation affecting these areas and conducts extensive public education campaigns to familiarize Americans with the guarantees in the Bill of Rights. Its main energies historically have been devoted to litigating to maintain these rights and liberties.

The ACLU has been involved in most speech and religion cases heard by the U.S. Supreme Court. In its own words, it "has been a zealous advocate of the First Amendment and has steadfastly opposed government efforts to regulate either free speech or free thought, no matter how well-intentioned those efforts might be."* It also has

specialized projects. The National Prison Project, for example, monitors prison conditions to ensure that prisoner rights are not violated. Its Women's Rights Project, originally headed by Ruth Bader Ginsburg (now a Supreme Court justice), has been at the fore of advancing women's rights through litigation. Similarly, its Reproductive Freedom Project is one of the most active litigators on behalf of pro-choice activists. It regularly sponsors challenges to restrictive state abortion laws and files *amicus curiae,* or friend of the court's briefs in cases in which it is not lead counsel. *Amicus* briefs are a vehicle by which interested parties, usually interest groups or professional associations, can inform the Court of the policy and legal implications of its decision—from, of course, the filing group's perspective. Among the major cases it has participated in are:

First Amendment rights:
- The *Scopes Case* (1945): Challenged a Tennessee law that made it a crime to teach evolution.
- *Tinker* v. *Des Moines Independent School Board* (1969): Upheld the right of students to wear black armbands in protest of the Vietnam War.
- *Lynch* v. *Donnelly* (1984): In a defeat for the ACLU,

the Court held that a city's inclusion of a crèche in its annual Christmas display in a private park did not violate the establishment clause.

Criminal defendants' rights:
- *Mapp* v. *Ohio* (1961): Established that illegally obtained evidence can't be used at trial.
- *Gideon* v. *Wainwright* (1963): Granted indigents the right to counsel.
- *Miranda* v. *Arizona* (1966): Guaranteed all suspects a right to counsel.

Privacy rights:
- *Roe* v. *Wade* and *Doe* v. *Bolton* (1973): Established a woman's right to an abortion.
- *Bowers* v. *Hardwick* (1986): An unsuccessful challenge to Georgia's sodomy law.
- *Planned Parenthood* v. *Casey* (1992): An unsuccessful challenge to Pennsylvania's restrictive abortion regulations.

Although the positions taken by the ACLU on these cases generally have been extremely popular with its members, an outcry arose in 1977 when it decided to represent members of the National Socialist Party who had been denied a parade permit to march in Nazi uniforms through Skokie, Illinois,

home to many Jewish concentration camp survivors. The ACLU lost more than 60,000 members who protested its involvement in the case, but it stayed true to its purpose—upholding the First Amendment, no matter how offensive the speech or actions in question. Its membership in 1996 was approximately 275,000.

Recognition of the conservative nature of the Supreme Court during the Reagan/Bush era caused the ACLU to rethink its litigation strategies. In fact, from 1987 to 1993, the ACLU's policy was to stay as far away from the Supreme Court as possible, a major shift in strategy. Formerly, the ACLU had appeared before the Court more than any organization except the Justice Department. "We're going to be looking for appropriate ways to bring cases in state courts and to insulate them from Supreme Court review,"** said one ACLU official in 1987. Recognizing also that "Civil liberties are not something people intuitively grasp,"*** the ACLU undertook a campaign to gain more attention for its cause. But, with its former legal counsel, Ruth Bader Ginsburg, on the Court and a Democrat in the White House, it may rethink its strategies.

---

*Brief *Amicus Curiae, Wisconsin* v. *Mitchell,* October Term, 1992, LEXIS.

**Quoted in Tony Mauro, "Supreme Court v. Civil Liberties: The ACLU's New Strategy of Avoidance," *Legal Times* (June 1, 1987): 13.

***Mauro, "Supreme Court v. Civil Liberties."

Many believed that the 1993 replacement of Justice White by Ruth Bader Ginsburg, a former attorney for the ACLU (see Highlight 5.1: The American Civil Liberties Union: Protector of First Amendment Rights) would halt the trend toward lowering the wall between church and state. But in 1995 the Court signalled that it was willing to lower the wall even further. Ironically, it did so in a case involving Thomas Jefferson's own University of Virginia. In a five to four decision, the majority held that the university violated the First Amendment's establishment of religion clause by failing to fund a religious student magazine written by a fundamentalist Christian student group even though it funded similar magazines published by 118 other student groups, some of which were religiously based.[25] In dissent, the importance of this decision was highlighted by Justice David Souter, who noted: "The Court today, for the first time, approves direct funding of core religious activities by an arm of the state."[26]

The Free Exercise Clause

The free exercise clause of the First Amendment proclaims that "Congress shall make no law . . . prohibiting the free exercise [of religion]." As in the case of the establishment clause, the Supreme Court has been continually forced to interpret this clause, often trying to balance the sometimes conflicting implications of the two clauses. Is it, for example, permissible for a state to ban the use of poisonous snakes during religious services even though some fundamentalist Christians view snake handling as an important part of their religious services? Is it reasonable to force some men into combat if their religious beliefs ban them from participating? And if such exemptions (called "conscientious objector deferments") are given to some men and not to others, is the government favoring one religion over another?

Although the free exercise clause of the First Amendment guarantees individuals the right to be free from governmental interference in the exercise of their religion, this guarantee, like other First Amendment freedoms, is not absolute. When secular law comes into conflict with religious law, the right to exercise one's religious beliefs is often denied—especially if the religious beliefs in question are held by a minority or by an unpopular or "suspicious" religious group. State statutes barring the use of certain illegal drugs, snake handling, and polygamy—all practices of particular religious sects—have been upheld as constitutional when states have shown compelling reasons to regulate these practices. Nonetheless, the Court has made it clear that the free exercise clause requires that a state or the national government remain neutral toward religion.

Many critics of rigid enforcement of such neutrality argue that the government should do what it can to accommodate the religious diversity in our nation. In the early 1960s, for example, a South Carolina textile mill shifted to a six-day work week, requiring that all employees work on Saturday. When one employee—a Seventh-Day Adventist whose Sabbath was Saturday—said she could not work on Saturdays, she was fired. She sought to receive unemployment compensation and her claim was denied. She then sued to obtain her benefits.

The Supreme Court ordered South Carolina to extend benefits to the woman in spite of its law that required an employee to be available for work on all days but Sundays. The Court ruled that the state law was an unconstitutional violation of the free exercise clause because it failed to accommodate the worker's religious beliefs.[27]

In the same vein, the Court has interpreted the Constitution to mean that governmental interests can outweigh free exercise rights. In 1990, for example, the Supreme

Snake handling, once more common as part of certain Christian religious services, is banned by law in many parts of the South. (Photo courtesy: UPI/Corbis-Bettman)

Court ruled that the free exercise clause allowed Oregon to ban the use of sacramental peyote (an illegal hallucinogenic drug) in some American Indian tribes' traditional religious services. The focus of the case turned on what standard of review the Court should use. Should the Court use the compelling state interest test? In upholding the state's right to deny unemployment compensation to two workers who had been fired by a private drug rehabilitation clinic because they had ingested an illegal substance,[28] a majority of the Court held that the state did not need to show a compelling interest to limit the free exercise of religion. This decision prompted a dramatic outcry. Congressional response was passage of the Religious Freedom Restoration Act in 1993, which reinstated strict scrutiny as the required judicial standard of review. In contrast, in 1993 the Supreme Court ruled that members of the Santería Church, an Afro–Cuban religion, had the right to sacrifice animals during religious services. In upholding that practice, the Court ruled that a city ordinance banning such practices was unconstitutionally aimed at the group, thereby denying its members the right to free exercise of their religion.[29]

Although conflicts between religious beliefs and the government are often difficult to settle, the Court has attempted to walk the fine line between the free exercise and establishment clauses. In the area of free exercise, the Court often has had to confront questions of "What is a god?" and "What is a religious faith?"—questions that theologians have grappled with for centuries. In 1965, for example, in a case involving three men who had been denied conscientious objector deferments during the Vietnam War because they did not subscribe to "traditional" organized religions, the Court ruled unanimously that belief in a supreme being was not essential for recognition as a conscientious objector. Thus the men were entitled to the deferments because their views paralleled those who objected to war and who belonged to traditional religions. In contrast, despite the Court's having ruled that Catholic, Protestant, Jewish, and Buddhist prison inmates must be allowed to hold religious services,[30] in 1987 it ruled that Islamic prisoners could be denied the same right for security reasons.[31]

FIRST AMENDMENT GUARANTEES: FREEDOM OF SPEECH AND PRESS

Today some members of Congress criticize television talk shows, including *Ricki Lake* and *Geraldo*, for pandering to the least common denominator of society. Other groups criticize popular performers, especially rap groups, for lyrics that promote violence in general and against women in particular. Despite the distastefulness of talk show topics or rap lyrics, many civil libertarians have resisted even the suggestion that these things be regulated.

A democracy depends on a free exchange of ideas, and the First Amendment shows that the Framers were well aware of this fact. Historically, one of the most volatile areas of constitutional interpretation has been in the interpretation of the First Amendment's mandate that "Congress shall make no law . . . abridging the freedom of speech, or of the press." Like the establishment and free exercise clauses of the First Amendment, the speech and press clauses have not been interpreted as absolute bans against government regulation. In fact, over the years the Court has used a hierarchical approach, with some items getting greater protection than others. Generally, thoughts have received the greatest protection, and actions or deeds the least. Words have come somewhere in the middle, depending on their content and purpose.

In the United States, with few exceptions, thoughts are considered beyond the scope of governmental regulation. Although people may experience a negative reaction for revealing their thoughts, the government has no legal right to punish or sanction Americans for what they think. Words, or speech, which stand between thoughts and deeds, are subject to some forms of restraint. Speech that is obscene, libelous (false, or causing someone disrepute), or seditious (advocating violent overthrow of the government), or that could incite or cause injury to those to whom they are addressed, has been interpreted as not protected by the First Amendment. Often, however, these exceptions to constitutional protection have troubled the Court. What is considered obscene in rural Mississippi, for example, may not offend someone in another part of the nation.

Actions, or deeds, are given the least constitutional protection. Thus actions are subject to the greatest governmental restrictions. For example, you may have a right to shoot a pistol in your back yard, but it is illegal to do so on most city streets. Over the years these competing rights have been balanced by the now classic observation that your "right to swing your arm ends at the tip of my nose."[32]

prior restraint: Judicial doctrine stating that the government cannot prohibit speech or publication before the fact.

When the First Amendment was ratified in 1791, it was considered to protect only against **prior restraint** of speech or expression, that is, to guard against the prohibition of speech or publication before the fact. As was the case in Great Britain concerning free speech, the First Amendment was not considered to provide absolute immunity from governmental sanction for what speakers or publishers might say or print. Thus, over the years, the meaning of this amendment's mandate has been subject to thousands of cases seeking judicial interpretation of its meaning.

The Alien and Sedition Acts

In 1798, soon after passage of the Bill of Rights, a constitutional crisis arose when the Federalist Congress enacted the Alien and Sedition Acts. Designed to ban any political criticism by the growing numbers of Jeffersonian Democratic-Republicans, these acts made publication of "any false, scandalous writing against the government of the United States" a criminal offense. Overtly partisan Federalist judges imposed fines and even jail terms on at least ten Democratic-Republican newspaper editors for allegedly violating the acts. The acts became a major issue in the 1800 presidential election campaign, which led to the election of Thomas Jefferson, a vocal opponent of the acts. He quickly pardoned all who had been convicted under their provisions, and the new Democratic-Republican Congress allowed the acts to expire before the Supreme Court had an opportunity to rule on the constitutionality of these serious infringements of the First Amendment.

Slavery, the Civil War, and Rights Curtailments

After the public outcry over the Alien and Sedition Acts, the national government largely got out of the business of regulating speech, but in its place the states began to prosecute those who published articles critical of governmental policies. In the 1830s, at the urgings of abolitionists, the publication or dissemination of any positive information about slavery became a punishable offense in the North. In the opposite vein, in the South, supporters of the "peculiar institution" of slavery enacted laws to prohibit publication of any antislavery sentiments. Southern postmasters refused to deliver Northern abolitionist papers throughout the South, which amounted to censorship of the mails.

North—South

POLITICS AROUND THE WORLD

Every definition of democracy stresses respect for civil liberties. Through a combination of constitutional provisions, other laws, and political practice, the United States, Canada, and the rest of the industrialized democracies have largely lived up to those expectations. Indeed, the respect for the right of free expression and the rule of law is one of the characteristics that set them apart from other countries, where four-fifths of the world's people live. Again, a quick look at Canada and Mexico should illustrate that point.

Canada's Constitution guarantees basic civil liberties and in some respects goes even further than the U.S. Constitution. The 1982 act that brought the Constitution home from Great Britain, for instance, assures native peoples certain rights, and there is widespread agreement that any settlement to the Quebec problem will have to include some such guarantees about French language and culture.

Some critics claim that Canada's record regarding civil liberties is not perfect. They note, for example, the government clampdown following a series of terrorist attacks by Quebec separatists in the 1960s and 1970s. However, even Canada's severest critics have to acknowledge that such instances are few and far between and are ambiguous enough that a reasonable person could conclude that no permanently damaging breach of civil liberties occurred.

Mexico provides a rather different story, but not because of its Constitution, which guarantees civil liberties and rights much like those in the United States or Canada. The problems arise in the way those provisions are carried out—or are not, as the case may be.

We do not have complete information about the violation of human rights and civil liberties in Mexico. Nonetheless, organizations like Amnesty International have made convincing claims about the torture of political prisoners, unfair arrests, and other arbitrary behavior by the national police force and the chilling impact of the PRI's commitment to hold onto power, which has certainly included the widespread corruption of the electoral process (see North–South features in chapters 13 and 14). There are also concerns about the freedom of the press, as the PRI's political tentacles extend into the media as well as the government.

Mexico does not have a particularly bad record by third world standards. Members of the elite are not routinely executed for disagreeing with the president, as is the case in Iraq, and it has not seen anything like El Salvador's notorious death squads of the 1980s. Nonetheless, the fact that there are so many violations of these globally accepted norms and of its own constitutional and other legal provisions is one of the main reasons why few political scientists are willing to consider it a "real" democracy.

During the Civil War, President Abraham Lincoln effectively suspended the free press provision of the First Amendment (as well as many other sections of the Constitution) and even went so far as to order the arrest of the editors of two New York papers that were critical of him. Far from protesting against these blatant violations of the First Amendment, Congress acceded to them. Right after the war, for example, Congress actually prevented the Supreme Court from issuing a judgment on a case because members feared its decision would be critical of the powers Lincoln had taken on during the war.[33] William McCardle, a Mississippi newspaper editor, had sought to arouse sentiment against Lincoln and the Union occupation. Even though he was a civilian, McCardle was jailed by a military court without having any charges brought against him. He appealed his detainment to the U.S. Supreme Court, arguing that he was being held unlawfully. Congress, fearing that a victory for McCardle would prompt other Confederate newspaper editors to follow his lead, enacted a law barring the Supreme Court from hearing appeals of cases involving convictions for publishing statements critical of the Union. Because Article III of the Constitution gives Congress the power to determine the jurisdiction of the Court, the Court was forced to conclude that it had no authority to rule in the matter.

After the Civil War, states also began to prosecute individuals for seditious speech if they uttered or printed statements critical of the government. Between 1890 and 1900, for example, there were more than one hundred state prosecutions for sedition in state courts.[34] Moreover, by the dawn of the twentieth century, public opinion in the United States had become exceedingly hostile to the preachings of groups such as socialists and communists who attempted to appeal to the thousands of new and disheartened immigrants. Groups espousing socialism and communism became the targets of state laws curtailing speech and the written word. By the end of World War I, over thirty states had passed laws to punish seditious speech, and more than 1,900 individuals and over one hundred newspapers had been prosecuted for violations.[35]

New Restrictions/New Tests

The first major federal law restricting freedom of speech and the press since the Alien and Sedition Acts was the Espionage Act of 1917. Nearly 2,000 Americans were convicted of violating its various provisions, especially those making it illegal to urge resistance to the draft and prohibiting the distribution of anti-war leaflets.

In 1919 the Supreme Court decided several important cases calling for interpretation of the First Amendment. Charles T. Schenck, a secretary of the Socialist Party, was tried and convicted for printing, distributing, and mailing antiwar leaflets to men eligible for the draft. In 1919 his conviction for urging others to resist military induction was upheld in an opinion written by Justice Oliver Wendell Holmes.[36] The Court interpreted the First Amendment to allow Congress to restrict speech that was "of such a nature as to create a clear and present danger that will bring about the substantive evils that Congress has a right to prevent." Holmes relied on the bad tendency test, which had been used in earlier cases. He reasoned that in times of war, Schenck's leaflets could obstruct recruitment into the military because their "tendency" and "intent" were the same. During the same term, in another case involving the bad tendencies of antiwar speech, Holmes concluded for a unanimous Court that the leaflets in question constituted a danger. He explained that even the U.S. Constitution does not protect an individual from "falsely shouting fire in a theater and causing a panic."[37]

clear and present danger test: Used by the Supreme Court to draw the line between protected and unprotected speech; the Court looks to see if there is an imminent danger that illegal action would occur in response to the contested speech.

Under the **clear and present danger test,** which allowed Congress to ban speech that could cause a clear and present danger to society, the circumstances surrounding the incident count, according to the Court. The leaflets might have been permissible in peacetime, but they posed too much of a danger in wartime to be allowed. The clear and present danger test used by the Court attempted to draw a line between protected and unprotected speech in this new area of constitutional interpretation.

Division among the members of the Court concerning the clear and present danger test soon became apparent. In *Abrams* v. *United States* (1919),[38] a majority of the

Court upheld Abrams's conviction for distributing leaflets critical of President Wilson's decision to send American soldiers to Russia. In dissent, however, Holmes sought to give substance to the majority's reliance on the clear and present danger test. He concluded that the activities of six anarchists who had been convicted for writing a "silly leaflet by an unknown man" protesting the U.S. government's attempts to overthrow Russia's newly formed Bolshevik government posed no imminent danger to the United States. Words, concluded Holmes, must be "triggers of action." There must be an element of immediacy, and a "bad tendency" should not be enough to limit speech. The majority, however, remained unconvinced by Holmes's arguments. From 1919 to 1927, the convictions of defendants in five other cases brought under the Espionage Act were upheld by the Court.

For decades, the Supreme Court continued to wrestle with what constituted a "danger." Finally, fifty years after the *Abrams* decision, in *Brandenburg* v. *Ohio* (1969),[39] the Court fashioned a new test for deciding whether certain kinds of speech could be regulated: the **direct incitement test.** Now the government could punish the advocacy of illegal action only if "such advocacy is directed to inciting or producing imminent lawless action and is likely to incite or produce such action." Brandenburg was convicted under an Ohio law after he advocated racial strife during a televised KKK hearing. A trial court concluded that his speech, in context, produced no imminent danger. Thus the statute, in its interpretation, and his conviction were unconstitutional. The requirement of "imminent harm" makes it more difficult for the government to punish speech and is consistent with the Framers' notion of the special role played by speech in a democratic society.

> **direct incitement test:** The advocacy of illegal action is protected by the First Amendment unless imminent action is intended and likely to occur.

Symbolic Speech

In addition to the general protection accorded pure speech, the Supreme Court has extended the reach of the First Amendment to other means of expression often called **symbolic speech**—symbols, signs, and the like—as well as to activities like picketing, sit-ins, and demonstrations. In the words of Justice John Marshall Harlan, these kinds of "speech" are part of the "free trade in ideas."[40]

The Supreme Court first acknowledged that symbolic speech was entitled to First Amendment protection in *Stromberg* v. *California* (1931).[41] There the Court overturned

> **symbolic speech:** Symbols, signs, and other methods of expression generally also considered to be protected by the First Amendment.

(By Dana Summers © 1990, Washington Post Writers Group. Reprinted with permission.)

the conviction of the director of a Communist youth camp under a state statute prohibiting the display of a red flag, a symbol of opposition to the U.S. government. In a similar vein, the right of high school students to wear black armbands to protest the Vietnam War was upheld in *Tinker* v. *Des Moines Independent Community School District* (1969).[42]

Burning the American flag has also been held to be a form of protected symbolic speech. In 1989 a sharply divided Supreme Court (five to four) reversed the conviction of Gregory Johnson, who had been found guilty of setting fire to an American flag during the 1984 Republican national convention in Dallas.[43] As a result, there was a major public outcry against the Court. President George Bush and numerous members of Congress called for a constitutional amendment to ban flag burning to overturn *Texas* v. *Johnson.* Others, including Justice William J. Brennan, Jr., noted that if it had not been for acts like that of Johnson, the United States would never have been created nor would a First Amendment guaranteeing a right to political protest exist.

Instead of a constitutional amendment, Congress passed the Federal Flag Protection Act of 1989, which authorized federal prosecution of anyone who intentionally desecrated a national flag. Those who originally had been arrested burned another flag and were convicted. Their conviction was again overturned by the Supreme Court. As they had in *Johnson,* the justices divided five to four in holding that this federal law "suffered from the same fundamental flaw" as had the earlier state law that was declared in violation of the First Amendment.[44] After that decision by the Court, additional efforts were made to pass a constitutional amendment so that congressional attempts to ban flag burning would not be subject to "interpretation." Those efforts, however, initially fell short of passage in both houses of Congress, but many legislators continue to press for a flag desecration amendment as detailed in Politics Now: Motherhood, Apple Pie, and the Flag.

Prior Restraint

With only a few exceptions, the Court has made it clear that it will not tolerate prior restraint of speech. In 1971, for example, in *New York Times Co.* v. *United States* (1971)[45] (also called the "Pentagon Papers" case), the Supreme Court ruled that the U.S. government could not block the publication of secret Defense Department documents illegally furnished to the *Times* by antiwar activists. In 1976 the Supreme Court went even further, noting that any attempt by the government to prevent expression carried "a 'heavy presumption' against its constitutionality."[46] In a Nebraska case, a trial court issued a "gag order" barring the press from reporting the lurid details of a crime. In balancing the defendant's constitutional right to a fair trial against the press's right to cover a story, the trial judge concluded that the defendant's right carried greater weight. The Supreme Court disagreed, holding the press's right to cover the trial paramount.

"Politically Correct" Speech

A particularly thorny First Amendment issue involving not only prior restraint but an outright prohibition of some forms of speech has emerged as universities have attempted to ban what they view as offensive speech. Since 1989 more than 200 colleges and universities have banned racial slurs directed at minority groups. The University of Connecticut, for example, banned "inappropriately directed laughter" and "conspicuous exclusion of students from conversations."

Politics Now

Motherhood, Apple Pie, and the Flag

When Senate Majority Leader Bob Dole (R–Kan.) opened his bid to be the Republican Party's candidate for president in September 1994, he appeared before the American Legion to vow he would bring a constitutional amendment banning flag burning to the floor of the Senate for a vote before the 1996 elections.

Dole, an injured World War II veteran, hoped that the symbolism would be apparent. He had suffered for his country and now wanted to protect the stars and stripes, the symbol of the United States to the world. In contrast, his Democratic opponent, Bill Clinton, had avoided the draft during the Vietnam War and was against the proposed amendment.

Flag burning does not present an immediate threat to the military readiness of the United States. Only about eight flag burnings have been reported annually since the Supreme Court's decision in *Texas* v. *Johnson* (1989). Yet the more conservative House of Representatives took time out from the budget strife that

plagued the latter months of 1995 to vote for the proposed amendment by a vote of 312 to 120, well above the two-thirds majority needed.

The Senate was another story, however. In spite of at least fifty-six cosponsors, including eleven Democrats—among them the liberal Dianne Feinstein (D.–Cal.), supporters didn't press to bring the amendment to the floor because they knew they were several votes shy of the two-thirds necessary to send an amendment to the states for their ratification.

Why all the hullabaloo about an amendment? Critics, including the Clinton administration, argue that an amendment would only give those who burn flags undue importance. In contrast, Senators Orrin Hatch (R–Utah) and Howell Heflin (D–Ala.), the sponsors of the 1996 measure, called the flag "a unique symbol in our country."

To many supporters of the amendment, flag burning is not a free speech issue, but an issue of national pride. Allowing flag burning, to them, is tantamount to treason and simply another example of the decaying respect for God, country, and family in the United States. What do you think?

While easy to poke fun at, the "PC movement," as it is known, has a serious side. At one university, a student was expelled for shouting anti-Semitic, anti-African American, and antihomosexual obscenities at students in their dorm rooms at 2:00 A.M. At the University of Michigan in 1990, a student was accused of violating the university's regulation banning speech that stigmatizes individuals for their sexual orientation, when he said during a classroom discussion that he considered homosexuality to be a disease treatable with therapy. The university's code was challenged by the American Civil Liberties Union and found unconstitutional by a federal district court.

In 1993 some began to question if the PC movement had gone too far. In 1993 Eden Jacobowitz, an Israeli student at the University of Pennsylvania, was charged with violating the school's speech policy and threatened with expulsion when he called five African American women "water buffaloes." The women were noisily participating in

(From THATCH by Jeff Shesol. Copyright © 1991 by Jeff Shesol. Reprinted by permission of Random House, Inc.)

a sorority rite below the Israeli student's dorm room late at night. Frustrated by his inability to study, Jacobowitz yelled, "Shut up, you water buffaloes. If you're looking for a party there's a zoo a mile from here."[47] A national debate ensued, and much was made of the fact that the Israeli student maintained that "water buffalo" was a loose translation of a mild Hebrew epithet referring to a rude person. The African American students ultimately dropped their racial harassment charge, but the ACLU, which had represented Jacobowitz, vowed to continue seeking the repeal of the university's speech code, which it argues violates the First Amendment.

Libel and Slander

Today national tabloid newspapers such as the *National Enquirer* and the *Star* boast headlines that cause many just to shake their heads in disbelief. How can they get away with it, some may wonder. The Framers were very concerned that the press not be suppressed. The First Amendment works to allow all forms of speech, no matter how libelous. False or libelous statements are not restrained by the courts, yet the Supreme Court has consistently ruled that individuals or the press can be sued *after the fact* for untrue or libelous statements. **Libel** is a written statement that defames the character of a person. If the statement is spoken, it is **slander.** In many nations—such as Great Britain, for example—it is relatively easy to sue someone for libel. In the United States, however, the standards of proof are much more difficult. A person who

libel: False statements or statements tending to call someone's reputation into disrepute.

slander: Untrue spoken statements that defame the character of a person.

believes that he or she has been a victim of libel, for example, must show that the statements made were untrue. Truth is an absolute defense against the charge of libel, no matter how painful or embarrassing the revelations.

It is often more difficult for individuals the Supreme Court considers to be "public persons or public officials" to sue for libel or slander. ***New York Times Co. v. Sullivan*** (1964)[48] was the first major libel case considered by the Supreme Court. An Alabama state court had found the *Times* guilty of libel for printing a full-page advertisement accusing Alabama officials of physically abusing African Americans during various civil rights protests (the ad was paid for by civil rights activists, including former First Lady Eleanor Roosevelt). The Supreme Court overturned the conviction, ruling that a finding of libel against a public official could stand only if there were a showing of "actual malice." Proof that the statements were false or negligent was not sufficient to prove "actual malice." The concept of actual malice (a burden of proof imposed on public officials and public figures suing for defamation and falsity requiring them to prove with clear and convincing evidence that an offending story was published with knowing falsehood or reckless disregard for the truth) can be difficult and confusing. In 1991 the Court directed lower courts to use the phrases "knowledge of falsity" and "reckless disregard of the truth" when giving instructions to juries in libel cases. Given the high degree of proof required, few public officials or public persons have been able to win libel cases.

New York Times Co. v. Sullivan: "Actual malice" must be proved to support a finding of libel against a public figure.

Obscenity and Pornography*

Although the Supreme Court has allowed few governmental bans on most types of speech, some forms of expression are not protected. In *Chaplinsky* v. *New Hampshire* (1942), the Supreme Court set out the rationale by which it would distinguish between protected and unprotected speech. According to the Court, obscenity, lewdness, libel, and fighting words are not protected by the First Amendment because "such expressions are no essential part of any exposition of ideas, and are of such slight social value as a step to truth that any benefit that may be derived from them is clearly outweighed by the social interest in order and morality."[49]

Through 1957, U.S. courts often based their decisions of what was obscene on an English common-law test that had been set out in 1868: "whether the tendency of the matter charged as obscenity is to deprive and corrupt those whose minds are open to such immoral influences and into whose hands a publication of this sort might fall."[50]

In *Roth* v. *United States* (1957), the Court abandoned that approach and held that to be considered obscene, the material in question must be "utterly without redeeming social importance," and articulated a new test for obscenity: "whether to the average person, applying contemporary community standards, the dominant theme of the material taken as a whole appeals to the prurient interests."[51] In many ways the *Roth* test brought with it as many problems as it attempted to solve. Throughout the 1950s and 1960s, "prurient" remained hard to define, as the Court struggled to find a standard by which to judge actions or words. Moreover, it was very difficult to prove that a book or movie was "*utterly* without redeeming social value." In general, even some "hardcore" pornography passed muster under the *Roth* test, prompting some to argue that the

*Technically, obscenity refers to those things considered "disgusting, foul or morally unhealthy." Pornography, in contrast, is often broader in meaning and generally refers to "depictions of sexual lewdness or erotic behavior." While distasteful to many, pornography is not necessarily obscene. See Donald Downs, "Obscenity and Pornography," in Kermit Hall, ed., *The Oxford Companion to the Supreme Court of the United States* (New York: Oxford University Press, 1992), p. 602.

Highlight 5.2

The Porn Police

In 1996 Congress overwhelmingly passed the Telecommunications Reform Act of 1996. It was then signed by President Clinton, even though he expressed some reservations about the constitutionality of some sections of the act. He wasn't alone. Civil libertarians and some computer communications experts were shocked by the scope of the Communications Decency Act provisions included in the final omnibus legislation.*

What does the act do? It maintains the same ban on obscene material that already applies to the media and criminalizes the transmission of "indecent" speech or images to people younger than eighteen years of age. Indecency is defined as any communication that depicts or describes in patently offensive terms any sexual or excretory activities or organs as measured by contemporary community standards. This definition makes no exceptions for materials that have serious literary, artistic, scientific, or other redeeming social value as spelled out in *Miller v. California* (1973). The act also bans any discussion of abortion on the Internet.

Supporters of the act believed that barring the distribution of certain materials to those under eighteen years of age would protect the act from constitutional challenge. Nevertheless, the act was immediately challenged by the American Civil Liberties Union (ACLU). A federal judge issued a temporary injunction against enforcement of parts of the act, but not the section that makes it a crime to deliver patently offensive materials to minors over the Internet. Nonetheless, under a unique agreement worked out between the ACLU and the Justice Department, the government has decided not to enforce the act, pending the decision of a three-judge federal panel on its constitutionality.

Conservatives and the Christian Coalition say that the law does not go far enough because it penalizes only those who post the materials, not the servers, such as America Online and Prodigy. The American Family Association, for example, refused to support the act, saying it's not tough enough.**

Clearly, the Internet and the World Wide Web make it easier to distribute pornography quickly and extensively. But do you think that these kind of restrictions will actually work or are politically motivated at a time when many agree that national moral standards are on the decline? How can federal legislation like this be reconciled with appeals for less big government?

*Harvey A. Silvergate, "Cyber Speech at Risk," *The National Law Journal* (March 4, 1996): A19.
**Hiawatha Bray, "Stalled at the Gate: Confusion over New Law," *The Boston Globe* (February 24, 1996): 19.

Court fostered the increase in the number of sexually oriented publications designed to appeal to those living amidst what many called the "sexual revolution."

Richard M. Nixon made the growth in pornography a major issue when he ran for president in 1968, and he pledged to appoint to federal judgeships only those who would uphold "law and order" and stop coddling criminals and purveyors of porn. Once elected president, Nixon made four appointments to the Court, including Chief Justice Warren Burger. In *Miller v. California* (1973),[52] the Supreme Court began to formulate rules designed to make it easier for states to regulate obscene materials and to return to communities a greater role in determining what is obscene.

In *Miller* the Court set out a test that redefined obscenity. To determine whether or not material in question was obscene, the justices concluded that a lower court must ask "whether the work depicts or describes, in a patently offensive way, sexual conduct specifically defined by state law." Moreover, courts were to determine "whether the work, taken as a whole, lacks serious literary, artistic, political or scientific value." And in place of the contemporary community standards gauge used in earlier cases, the Court defined community standards to mean local, and not national, standards under the rationale that what is acceptable in Times Square in New York City might not be tolerated in Peoria, Illinois.

Local community standards still may not be the sole criterion of obscenity. In 1974, however, the Court overturned a decision of a Georgia state court that found *Carnal Knowledge* (a movie starring Jack Nicholson, Ann-Margret, and Art Garfunkel that included scenes of a partially nude woman) obscene. The Court concluded that the scenes were neither "patently offensive" nor designed to appeal to "prurient interest."[53] As Justice Potter Stewart had once announced, he couldn't define obscenity, but "I know it when I see it."[54] He did not see it in *Carnal Knowledge*.

Time and contexts clearly have altered the Court's and indeed, much of America's perceptions of what is obscene. *Carnal Knowledge* is now often shown on television on Saturday afternoons with only minor editing. But through the early 1990s, the Court allowed communities greater leeway in drafting statutes to deal with obscenity and, even more important, forms of non-obscene expression. In 1991, for example, the Supreme Court voted five to four to allow Indiana to ban totally nude erotic dancing, concluding that its statute did not violate the First Amendment's guarantee of freedom of expression and that it furthered an important or substantial governmental interest (thereby adopting the intermediate standard of review).[55]

While lawmakers have been fairly effective in restricting the sale and distribution of obscene materials, Congress recently turned to a more difficult task: monitoring the Internet, which some charge has become a vehicle for easy distribution of obscenity and pornography as well as a means for young children to be exposed to these kinds of materials. See Highlight 5.2: The Porn Police.

THE RIGHTS OF CRIMINAL DEFENDANTS AND THE CRIMINAL JUSTICE SYSTEM

*T*he O. J. Simpson trial not only riveted many Americans to their televisions, it also brought with it tremendous attention to the criminal justice system. The trial made Americans question some of the rights now guaranteed to defendants, the jury system, and many of the rules by which police, prosecutors, and the judicial system now work.

The O. J. Simpson case was not the only phenomenon that focused attention on the criminal justice system. Today more and more Americans cite crime as a major problem confronting the nation. And, as noted in Roots of Government: The Second Amendment and the Right to Bear Arms, concern with crime led to passage in 1994 of a $30.2 billion comprehensive crime bill to try to stem the wave of violence in the United States.

The Fourth, Fifth, Sixth, and Eighth amendments provide a variety of procedural guarantees (often called **due process rights**) for those accused of crimes. Particular amendments, as well as other portions of the Constitution, specifically provide procedural guarantees to protect individuals accused of crimes at all stages of the criminal justice process. And as is the case with the First Amendment, many of these rights have been interpreted by the Supreme Court to apply to the states.

In interpreting the amendments dealing with what are frequently termed "criminal rights," the courts have to grapple not only with the meaning of the amendments,

due process rights: Procedural guarantees provided by the Fourth, Fifth, Sixth, and Eighth Amendments for those accused of crimes.

Roots of Government

The Second Amendment and the Right to Bear Arms

James and Sarah Brady being applauded for their efforts to win congressional approval of the Brady Bill after it was signed into law by President Clinton. (Photo courtesy: John Ficara/Sygma)

During colonial times, the English tradition of distrust of standing armies was evident: Most colonies required all white men to keep and bear arms, and all white men in whole sections of the colonies were deputized to defend their settlements against Indians and other European powers. These local militias were viewed as the best way to keep order and liberty.

The Second Amendment was added to the Constitution to ensure that Congress could not pass laws to disarm state militias. This amendment appeased Anti-Federalists, who feared that the new Constitution would cause them to lose the right to "keep and bear arms" as well as an unstated right—the right to revolt against governmental tyranny.

Through the early 1920s, few state statutes were passed to regulate firearms (and generally these laws dealt with the possession of firearms by slaves). And, the Supreme Court's decision in *Barron v. Baltimore* (1833), which limited the application of the Bill of Rights to actions of Congress alone, prevented federal review of those state laws. Moreover, in *Dred Scott v. Sandford* (1857) (see chapter 3), Chief Justice Taney listed the right to own and carry arms as a basic right of citizenship.

In 1934 Congress passed the National Firearms Act in response to the increase in organized crime that occurred in the 1920s and 1930s as a result of Prohibition (see chapter 2). The act imposed taxes on automatic weapons (such as machine guns) and sawed-off shotguns. In *United States v. Miller* (1939), a unanimous Court upheld the constitutionality of the Act by voting that the Second Amendment was intended to protect a citizen's right to own ordinary militia weapons and *not* unregistered sawed-off shotguns, which were at issue in the *Miller* case. *Miller* was the last time the Supreme Court directly addressed the Second Amendment. In *Quilici v. Village of Morton Grove* (1983), the Supreme Court refused to review a lower court's ruling upholding the constitutionality of a local ordinance banning handguns against a Second Amendment challenge.

In the 1980s through 1990s, as crime and violence increased, the issue of gun control became and has remained a particularly hot topic in American politics. In the aftermath of the assassination attempt on President Ronald Reagan in 1981, many lawmakers called for passage of gun control legislation. At the forefront of that effort was Sarah Brady, the wife of James Brady, the presidential press secretary who was badly wounded and left partially disabled by John Hinkley, Jr., President Reagan's assailant. In 1993 her efforts helped to win passage of the so-called Brady Bill, which imposed a federal mandatory five-day waiting period on the purchase of handguns.

In 1994, in spite of extensive lobbying by the powerful National Rifle Association, Congress passed and President Clinton signed the Violent Crime Control and Law Enforcement Act. In addition to providing money to states for new prisons and law enforcement officers, the act banned the manufacture, sale, transport, or possession of nineteen different kinds of semi-automatic assault weapons.

The NRA immediately targeted some of the act's sponsors for defeat in the 1994 congressional elections. They successfully beat several Democratic members of Congress, including Jack Brooks (D–Tex.), who had chaired the House Judiciary Committee that had authored many portions of the bill.

In 1995 the new Republican Congress revamped the law by calling for convicts to compensate their victims. Debate concerning repeal of the assault weapons provisions continues.

but also with how their protections are to be implemented. The Eighth Amendment, for example, prohibits "cruel and unusual punishments." The question of what is cruel and unusual, however, has vexed the Supreme Court for years. In 1972, for example, the Supreme Court—by a vote of five to four—for the first time struck down the death penalty under the cruel and unusual punishments clause of the Eighth Amendment.[56] Three justices for the majority concluded that the death penalty was imposed in an arbitrary and random pattern, and that this randomness was cruel and unusual. Two justices said it was always a violation. This decision sent the states back to the drawing boards to draft new, nonarbitrary death penalty laws. In 1976 the Court upheld Georgia's new, more specific standards.[57]

Today a more conservative Court routinely allows executions to be carried out. Perhaps even more than in the area of First Amendment guarantees, prevailing thoughts about the rights of criminal defendants are changing quickly and dramatically not only as the public becomes more intolerant of crime but as more conservative and moderate justices have been appointed to the Supreme Court, causing it to move away from what some view as the "excesses" of the Warren Court (1953–69).

Over the years, many individuals have criticized the liberal Warren Court's rulings, arguing that its ruling gave criminals more "rights" than their victims. The Warren Court made several provisions of the Bill of Rights dealing with the rights of criminal defendants applicable to the states through the Fourteenth Amendment. It is important to remember that most procedural guarantees apply to individuals *charged* with crimes, that is, before they have been tried. These rights were designed to protect those wrongfully accused, although, of course, they often have helped the guilty. But as Justice William O. Douglas once noted, "Respecting the dignity even of the least worthy citizen . . . raises the stature of all of us."[58]

Many continue to argue, however, that only the guilty are helped by the American system and that criminals should not go unpunished because of simple police error. The dilemma of balancing the rights of the individual against those of society permeates the entire debate, and often even judicial interpretations of the rights of criminal defendants.

The Fourth Amendment and Searches and Seizures

The Fourth Amendment to the Constitution declares:

> The right of the people to be secure in their persons, houses, papers, and effects, against unreasonable searches and seizures, shall not be violated, and no Warrants shall issue, but upon probable cause, supported by Oath or affirmation, and particularly describing the place to be searched, and the persons or things to be seized.

This amendment's purpose was to deny the national government the authority to make general searches. The English Parliament had often issued general "writs of assistance" that allowed such searches. These general warrants were often used against religious and political dissenters, a practice the Framers wanted banned in the new nation. But still, the language that they chose left numerous questions to be answered, including, what is an "unreasonable" search?

Over the years, in a number of decisions, the Supreme Court has interpreted the Fourth Amendment to allow the police to search:

1. The person arrested;
2. Things in plain view of the accused person; and
3. Places or things that the arrested person could touch or reach or are otherwise in the arrestee's "immediate control."

In 1995 the Court also resolved a decades-old constitutional dispute by ruling unanimously that police must knock and announce their presence before entering a house or apartment to execute a search. But, said the Court, there may be "reasonable" exceptions to the rule to account for the likelihood of violence or the imminent destruction of evidence.[59]

Warrantless searches often occur if police suspect that someone is committing or is about to commit a crime. In these situations, police may "stop and frisk" the individual under suspicion. In 1989 the Court ruled that there need be only a "reasonable suspicion" for stopping a suspect—a much lower standard than "probable cause."[60] Thus a suspected drug courier may be stopped for brief questioning but only a frisk search (for weapons) is permitted. The answers to these questions may shift "reasonable suspicion" to "probable cause," thus permitting the officer to search. But except at international borders (or international airports), a *search* requires probable cause.

Searches can also be made without a warrant if consent is obtained, and the Court has ruled that consent can be given by a variety of persons. It has ruled, for example, that police can search a bedroom occupied by two persons as long as they have the consent of one of them.[61]

In situations where no arrest occurs, police must obtain search warrants from a "neutral and detached magistrate" prior to conducting more extensive searches of houses, cars, offices, or any other place where an individual would reasonably have some expectation of privacy.[62] Police can't get search warrants, for example, to require you to undergo surgery to remove a bullet that might be used to incriminate you, since your expectation of bodily privacy outweighs the need for evidence.[63] But courts don't require search warrants in possible drunk driving situations. Thus the police can require you to take a Breathalyzer test to determine whether you have been drinking in excess of legal limits.[64]

Homes, too, are presumed to be private. Firefighters can enter your home to fight a fire without a warrant. But if they decide to investigate the cause of the fire, they must obtain a warrant before their reentry.[65] In contrast, under the "open fields doctrine" first articulated by the Supreme Court in 1924,[66] if you own a field, and even if you post "No Trespassing" signs, the police can search your field without a warrant to see if you are illegally growing marijuana, because you cannot reasonably expect privacy in an open field.

Cars have proven problematic for police and the courts because of their mobile nature. As noted by Chief Justice William Howard Taft as early as 1925, "the vehicle can quickly be moved out of the locality or jurisdiction in which the warrant must be sought."[67] Over the years the Court has become increasingly lenient about the scope of automobile searches. In 1991, for example, the Court upheld a warrantless search of a container found in a car, even though the police lacked probable cause to search the car itself.[68]

Testing for Drugs and HIV. Testing for drugs and HIV has become an especially thorny search-and-seizure issue. If the government can require you to take a Breathalyzer test, can it require you to be tested for drugs? For HIV? In the wake of growing public concern over drug use, in 1986 President Ronald Reagan signed an executive order requiring many federal employees to undergo drug tests.

While many private employers and professional athletic organizations routinely require drug tests upon application or as a condition of employment, governmental requirements present constitutional questions about the scope of permissible searches and seizures. Initially, the federal courts adopted the view that mandatory testing of those in certain occupations such as the police and firefighting forces was unconstitutional unless there was suspicion that the employee had been using drugs. In 1989, however, the Supreme Court ruled that mandatory drug and alcohol testing of employees involved in accidents was constitutional.[69] And in 1995 the Court upheld the constitutionality of random drug testing of public high school athletes.[70]

Testing for the human immunodeficiency virus (HIV), which causes AIDS, has also produced questions of unreasonable searches and seizures, especially since those with the virus generally experience discrimination. In July 1991 the Centers for Disease Prevention and Control (CDC) recommended that all health-care professionals who perform surgery undergo voluntary testing to determine if they are infected with HIV. If they are, the CDC suggested that they disclose the condition to patients and refrain from practicing unless they are cleared to do so by a local medical review panel. In the absence of federal legislation, however, many medical organizations have refused to comply with the CDC's recommendations.

The Fifth Amendment and Self-Incrimination

The Fifth Amendment provides that "No person shall be . . . compelled in any criminal case to be a witness against himself." "Taking the Fifth" is shorthand for exercising one's constitutional right not to self-incriminate. The Supreme Court has interpreted this guarantee to be "as broad as the mischief against which it seeks to guard,"[71] finding that criminal defendants do not have to take the stand at trial to answer questions, nor can a judge make mention of their failure to do so as evidence of guilt. Moreover, lawyers cannot imply that a defendant who refuses to take the stand must be guilty or have something to hide.

Use of "Voluntary" Confessions. This right not to incriminate oneself also means that prosecutors cannot use as evidence in a trial any of a defendant's statements or confessions that were not "voluntary." As is the case in many areas of the law, however, judicial interpretation of the term voluntary has changed over time, as our opening vignette about Mr. McNally and Mr. Bey indicate.

Police often used to beat defendants to obtain their confessions. In 1936, however, the Supreme Court ruled convictions for murder based solely on confessions given after physical beatings unconstitutional.[72] Police then began to resort to other measures to force confessions. Defendants, for example, were "given the third degree"—questioned for hours on end with no sleep or food, or threatened with physical violence until they were mentally "beaten" into a confession. In other situations family members were threatened. In one case a young mother was told that her welfare benefits would be terminated and her children taken away from her if she failed to talk.[73]

Miranda* v. *Arizona (1966) was the Supreme Court's response to these creative efforts to obtain confessions that were not truly voluntary. On March 3, 1963, an eighteen-year-old girl was kidnapped and raped on the outskirts of Phoenix, Arizona. Ten days later police arrested Ernesto Miranda, a poor, mentally disturbed man with a ninth-grade education. In a police-station lineup, the victim identified Miranda as her attacker. Police then took Miranda to a separate room and questioned him for two hours. At first he denied guilt. Eventually, however, he confessed to the crime and wrote and signed a brief statement describing the crime and admitting his guilt. At no time was he told that he did not have to answer any questions or that he could be represented by an attorney.

Miranda **v.** *Arizona:*   The Fifth Amendment requires that individuals arrested for a crime must be advised of their right to remain silent and to have counsel present.

Even though Ernesto Miranda's confession was not admitted as evidence at his retrial, his ex-girlfriend's testimony and that of the victim were enough to convince the jury of his guilt. He served nine years in prison before he was released on parole. After his release, he routinely sold autographed cards inscribed with the Miranda rights now read to all suspects. In 1976, four years after his release, Miranda was stabbed to death in Phoenix in a bar fight during a card game. Two Miranda cards were found on his body, and the person who killed him was read his Miranda rights upon his arrest. (Photo courtesy: AP/Worldwide Photos)

After Miranda's conviction, his case was appealed on the grounds that his Fifth Amendment right not to incriminate himself had been violated because his confession had been coerced. Writing for the Court, Chief Justice Earl Warren, himself a former district attorney and California State Attorney General, noted that because police have a tremendous advantage in any interrogation situation, criminal suspects must be given greater protection. A confession obtained in the manner of Miranda's was not truly voluntary; thus it was inadmissible at trial.

To provide guidelines for police to implement *Miranda,* the Court mandated that:

> Prior to any questioning, the person must be warned that he has a right to remain silent, that any statements he does make may be used as evidence against him, and that he has a right to the presence of an attorney, either retained or appointed.

Miranda rights: Statements that must be made by the police informing a suspect of his or her constitutional rights protected by the Fifth Amendment, including the right to an attorney provided by the court if the suspect cannot afford one.

In response to this mandate from the Court, police routinely began to read suspects their *Miranda* **rights,** a practice you undoubtedly have seen repeated over and over in movies and TV police dramas.

Although the Burger Court did not enforce the reading of *Miranda* rights as vehemently as had the Warren Court, Chief Justice Warren Burger, Warren's successor, acknowledged that they had become an integral part of established police procedures.[74] The Rehnquist Court, however, has been more tolerant of the use of coerced confessions and has employed a much more flexible standard to allow their admissibility. In 1991, for example, it ruled that the use of a coerced confession in a criminal trial does not automatically invalidate a conviction if its admission is deemed a "harmless error," that is, if the other evidence is sufficient to convict.[75]

The Exclusionary Rule

exclusionary rule: Judicially created rule that prohibits police from using illegally seized evidence at trial.

In *Weeks* v. *United States* (1914),[76] the U.S. Supreme Court adopted the **exclusionary rule,** which bars the use of illegally seized evidence at trial. Thus, although the Fourth and Fifth Amendments do not prohibit the use of evidence obtained in violation of their provisions, the exclusionary rule is a judicially created remedy to deter constitutional violations. In *Weeks,* for example, the Court reasoned that allowing police and prosecutors to use the "fruits of a poisonous tree" (a tainted search) would only encourage that activity.

The Warren Court resolved the dilemma of balancing the goal of deterring police misconduct against the likelihood that a guilty individual would go free in favor of deterrence. In contrast, the Burger and Rehnquist Courts and, more recently, Congress have gradually chipped away at the exclusionary rule. In 1976 the Burger Court dramatically reduced the opportunities for defendants to appeal their convictions based on tainted evidence in violation of the Fourth Amendment.[77] The Court noted that the exclusionary rule "deflects the truth-finding process and often frees the guilty." Since then, the Court has carved out a variety of limited "good faith exceptions" to the exclusionary rule, allowing the use of "tainted" evidence in a variety of situations, especially when police have a search warrant, and "in good faith" conduct the search on the assumption that the warrant is valid—though it is subsequently found invalid. Since the purpose of the exclusionary rule is to deter police misconduct, and in this situation there is no police misconduct, the courts have permitted the introduction at trial of the seized evidence. Another exception to the exclusionary rule is "inevitable discovery." Evidence illegally seized may be introduced if it would have been discovered anyway in the course of continuing investigation.

DIVISION OF CORRECTIONS
CORRESPONDENCE REGULATIONS

MAIL WILL NOT BE DELIVERED WHICH DOES NOT CONFORM WITH THESE RULES

No. 1 -- Only 2 letters each week, not to exceed 2 sheets letter-size 8 1/2 x 11" and written on one side only, and if ruled paper, do not write between lines. Your complete name must be signed at the close of your letter. Clippings, stamps, letters from other people, stationery or cash must not be enclosed in your letters.

No. 2 -- All letters must be addressed in the complete prison name of the inmate. Cell number, where applicable, and prison number must be placed in lower left corner of envelope, with your complete name and address in the upper left corner.

No. 3 -- Do not send any packages without a Package Permit. Unauthorized packages will be destroyed.

No. 4 -- Letters must be written in English only.

No. 5 -- Books, magazines, pamphlets, and newspapers of reputable character will be delivered only if mailed direct from the publisher.

No. 6 -- Money must be sent in the form of Postal Money Orders only, in the inmate's complete prison name and prison number.

INSTITUTION _____ CELL NUMBER _____

NAME _____ NUMBER _____

In The Supreme Court of The United States
Washington D.C.
clarence Earl Gideon
Petitioner | *Petition for a writ*
vs. | *of Certiorari Directed*
H. G. Cochran, Jr, as | *to The Supreme Court*
director, Divisions | *State of Florida.*
of corrections State |
of Florida | No. 890 Misc.

OCT. TERM 1961
U. S. Supreme Court

To The Honorable Earl Warren, Chief
Justice of the United States
Comes now The petitioner, Clarence
Earl Gideon, a citizen of The United states
of America, in proper person, and appearing
as his own counsel. Who petitions this
Honorable Court for a Writ of Certiorari
directed to The Supreme Court of The State
of Florida. To review the order and Judge-
ment of the court below denying The
petitioner a writ of Habeus Corpus.
Petitioner submits That The Supreme
Court of The United States has The authority
and jurisdiction to review The final Judge-
ment of The Supreme Court of The State
of Florida the highest court of The State
Under sec. 344 (B) Title 28 U.S.C.A. and
Because The "Due process clause" of the

When Clarence Earl Gideon wrote out his petition for a writ of certiorari to the Supreme Court (asking the Court, in its discretion, to hear his case), he had no way of knowing that his case would lead to the landmark ruling on the right to counsel, *Gideon* v. *Wainwright.* Nor did he know that Chief Justice Earl Warren had actually instructed his law clerks to be on the lookout for a habeas corpus petition (literally, "you have the body," which argues that the person in jail is there in violation of some statutory or constitutional right) that could be used to guarantee the assistance of counsel for defendants in criminal cases. (Photo courtesy: The Supreme Court Historical Society)

The Sixth Amendment and the Right to Counsel

The Sixth Amendment guarantees to an accused person "the Assistance of Counsel in his defense." In the past this provision meant only that an individual could hire an attorney to represent him or her in court. Since most criminal defendants are impoverished, this provision was of little assistance to many who found themselves on trial. Recognizing this, Congress required federal courts to provide an attorney for defendants too poor to afford one. This was first required in capital cases (where the death penalty is a possibility); eventually, attorneys were provided to the poor in all federal criminal cases.[78] In 1932 the Supreme Court directed states to furnish lawyers to defendants in capital cases.[79] It also began to expand the right to counsel to other state offenses, but did so in a piecemeal fashion that gave the states little direction. Given the high cost of providing legal counsel, this ambiguity often made it cost-effective for the states not to provide counsel at all.

These ambiguities came to an end with the Court's decision in *Gideon* v. *Wainwright* (1963).[80] As depicted in Anthony Lewis's book *Gideon's Trumpet* and in the made-for-television movie of the same name, Clarence Earl Gideon, a fifty-one-year-old drifter, was charged with breaking into a Panama City, Florida, pool hall and stealing beer, wine, and some change from a vending machine. At his trial he asked the judge to appoint a lawyer for him because he was too poor to hire one himself. The judge refused, and Gideon was convicted and given a five-year prison term for petty larceny. The case against Gideon had not been strong, but as a layperson unfamiliar with the law and with trial practice and procedure, he was unable to point out its weaknesses.

The apparent inequities in the system that had resulted in Gideon's conviction continued to bother him. Eventually, he borrowed some paper from a prison guard, consulted books in the prison library, and then drafted and mailed to the U.S. Supreme Court a petition asking it to overrule his conviction.

In a unanimous decision, the U.S. Supreme Court agreed with Gideon and his court-appointed lawyer, Abe Fortas, a future associate justice of the Supreme Court. Writing for the Court, Justice Hugo Black explained that "lawyers in criminal courts are necessities, not luxuries." Therefore, the Court concluded, the state must provide an attorney to poor defendants in felony cases. Underscoring the Court's point, Gideon was acquitted when he was retried with a lawyer to argue his case.

In 1972 the Burger Court expanded the *Gideon* rule, holding that "even in prosecutions for offenses less serious than felonies, a fair trial may require the presence of a lawyer."[81] Seven years later, the Court clarified its decision by holding that defendants charged with offenses where imprisonment is authorized but not actually imposed do not have a Sixth Amendment right to counsel.[82] But the right to counsel *is* constitutionally required where any prison or jail term is imposed.

The Sixth Amendment and Jury Trials

The Sixth Amendment (and, to a lesser extent, Article III of the Constitution) provides that a person accused of a crime shall enjoy the right to a speedy and public trial by an impartial jury—that is, a trial in which a group of the accused's peers act as a fact-finding, deliberative body to determine guilt or innocence. The Supreme Court has held that jury trials must be available if a prison sentence of six or more months is possible.

"Impartiality" is a requirement of jury trials that has undergone significant change, with the method of selecting jurors being the most frequently challenged part of the process. For example, whereas potential individual jurors who have prejudged a case are not eligible to serve, no groups can be systematically excluded from serving. In 1880, for example, the Supreme Court ruled that African Americans could not be excluded from state jury pools (lists of those eligible to serve).[83] And in 1975 the Court ruled that to bar women from jury service violated the mandate that juries be a "fair cross section" of the community.[84]

In the 1980s the Court expanded the requirement that juries reflect the community by invalidating various indirect means of excluding African Americans. For example, when James Batson, a black man, was tried for second-degree burglary, the state prosecutor used all his peremptory challenges to the jury to eliminate all four potential black jurors, leaving an all-white jury.[85] The state court judge overruled the contention of Batson's lawyer that the exclusion of African Americans violated Batson's constitutional rights, and Batson was found guilty. The Supreme Court, however, overturned his conviction. While noting that lawyers historically used peremptory challenges to select juries they believed most favorable to the outcome they desired, the Court held that the use of peremptory challenges specifically to exclude African-American jurors violated the equal protection clause of the Fourteenth Amendment.[86]

In 1994 the Supreme Court answered the major remaining unanswered question about jury selection: Can lawyers exclude women from juries through their use of peremptory challenges? This question came up frequently because in rape trials and sex discrimination cases, one side or another often finds it advantageous to select jurors on the basis of their sex. At issue in *J. E. B.* v. *Alabama ex rel T. B.* (1994)[87] was Alabama's use of peremptory challenge to exclude nine men from a group of potential jurors in a case brought by the state to establish that James Bowman, Sr., had fathered a child and was responsible for child-support payments. Bowman was declared to be the father by a jury of twelve women. The Supreme Court ruled that the equal protection clause prohibits discrimination in jury selection on the basis of gender. Thus lawyers cannot strike all potential male jurors based on the belief that males might be more sympathetic to the arguments of a man charged in a paternity suit.

The Eighth Amendment and Cruel and Unusual Punishment

The Eighth Amendment prohibits "cruel and unusual punishments," a concept rooted in the English common-law tradition. In the 1500s religious heretics and those critical of the Crown were subjected to torture to extract confessions, and then were condemned to an equally hideous death by the rack, disembowelment, or other barbarous means. The English Bill of Rights and its safeguard against "cruel and unusual punishments" was a result of public outrage against those practices. The same language found its way into the U.S. Bill of Rights. Prior to the 1960s, however, little judicial attention was paid to the meaning of that phrase, especially in the context of the death penalty.

"Cruel and unusual punishment" has meant different things to different societies. In colonial America, the dunking stool was a common form of punishment that few would advocate today. (Photo courtesy: The Bettmann Archive)

The death penalty was in use in all the colonies at the time the Constitution was adopted, and its constitutionality went unquestioned. In fact, in two separate cases in the late 1800s, the Supreme Court ruled that deaths by public shooting[88] and electrocution were not "cruel and unusual" forms of punishment in the same category as "punishments which inflict torture, such as the rack, the thumbscrew, the iron boot, the stretching of limbs and the like. . . ."[89]

In the 1960s the National Association for the Advancement of Colored People (NAACP) Legal Defense Fund, believing that the death penalty was applied more frequently to African Americans than to members of other groups, orchestrated a carefully designed legal attack on its constitutionality.[90] Public opinion polls revealed that in 1971, on the eve of the NAACP's first major death sentence case to reach the Supreme Court, support for the death penalty had fallen to below 50 percent of the American public. With the timing just right, in *Furman* v. *Georgia* (1972), the Supreme Court effectively put an end to capital punishment, at least in the short run.[91] The Court ruled that because the death penalty was often imposed in an arbitrary manner, it constituted cruel and unusual punishment in violation of the Eighth and Fourteenth Amendments.

Following *Furman*, several state legislatures enacted new laws designed to meet the Court's objections to the arbitrary nature of the sentence. In 1976 in *Gregg* v. *Georgia*, Georgia's rewritten death penalty statute was ruled constitutional by the Supreme Court in a seven-to-two decision.[92] Troy Gregg had murdered two hitchhikers and was awaiting execution on Georgia's death row. Although his lawyers argued that to put him to death would constitute cruel and unusual punishment, the Court concluded that the death penalty "is an expression of society's outrage at particularly offensive conduct. . . . [I]t is an extreme action, suitable to the most extreme of crimes." Before he could be executed, however, Gregg escaped from death row using a hand-crafted hacksaw and a homemade prison guard uniform. He and three other inmates escaped to North Carolina, where Gregg was beaten to death before he could be recaptured by authorities.

Unless the perpetrator of a crime was fifteen years old or younger at the time of the crime, the Supreme Court is currently unwilling to intervene to overrule state courts' imposition of the death penalty. In *McCleskey* v. *Kemp* (1987),[93] a five-to-four Court ruled that imposition of the death penalty—even when it appeared to discriminate against African Americans—did not violate the equal protection clause. Despite the testimony of social scientists and evidence that Georgia was eleven times more likely to seek the death penalty against a black defendant, the Court upheld Warren McCleskey's death sentence. It noted that even if statistics show clear discrimination, there must be a showing of racial discrimination in the specific case. Five justices concluded that there was no evidence of specific discrimination against McCleskey proved at his trial. Within hours of that defeat, McCleskey's lawyers filed a new appeal, arguing that the informant who gave the only testimony against McCleskey at trial had been placed in McCleskey's cell illegally.

Four years later McCleskey's death sentence challenge again produced an equally, if not more important, ruling on the death penalty and criminal procedure from the U.S. Supreme Court. In the second McCleskey case, *McCleskey* v. *Zant* (1991), the Court found that the issue of the informant should have been raised during the first appeal, in spite of the fact that McCleskey's lawyers were initially told by the state that the witness was not an informer. *McCleskey* v. *Zant* produced new standards designed to make it much more difficult for death-row inmates to file repeated appeals, a practice frequently decried by many of the justices.[94] Ironically, the informant against McCleskey was freed the night before McCleskey was electrocuted. Justice Powell, one of those in the majority, later said (after his retirement) that he regretted his vote and should have voted the other way.

THE RIGHT TO PRIVACY

*T*o this point, the rights and freedoms we have discussed have been derived fairly directly from specific guaranties contained in the Bill of Rights. In contrast, the Supreme Court has also given protection to the rights not specifically enumerated in the Constitution or Bill of Rights.

There is no mention of a right to **privacy** in either the main body of the Constitution or the Bill of Rights. Nevertheless, as Justice William O. Douglas noted in 1965, the notion of privacy is "older than the Bill of Rights." It is questionable, however, whether the Framers would ever have considered birth control, surrogate motherhood, in vitro fertilization, or euthanasia, all defended under "right to privacy" claims, proper subjects of constitutional protection.

Although the Constitution is silent about the right to privacy, the Bill of Rights contains many indications that the Framers expected that some areas of life were "off limits" to governmental regulation. The right to freedom of religion guaranteed in the First Amendment implies the right to exercise private, personal beliefs. The guarantee against unreasonable searches and seizures contained in the Fourth Amendment similarly implies that persons are to be secure in their homes and should not fear that police will show up at their doorsteps without cause. As early as 1928, Justice Louis Brandeis hailed privacy as "the right to be left alone—the most comprehensive of rights and the right most valued by civilized men."[95] It was not until 1965, however, that the Court attempted to explain the origins of this right.

privacy: The right to be let alone; a judicially created doctrine encompassing an individual's decision to use birth control or secure an abortion.

Birth Control

Today most Americans take access to many forms of birth control as a matter of course. Condoms are sold in the grocery store, and some television stations even air ads for them. Easy access to birth control, however, wasn't always the case. Many states often barred the sale of contraceptives to minors, prohibited the display of contraceptives, or even banned their sale altogether. One of the last states to do away with these kinds of laws was Connecticut. It outlawed the sale of all forms of birth control and even prohibited physicians from discussing it with their patients until the Supreme Court ruled its restrictive laws unconstitutional.

Griswold v. *Connecticut* (1965)[96] involved a challenge to the constitutionality of an 1879 Connecticut law prohibiting the dissemination of information about and/or the sale of contraceptives. In 1943 and again in 1961, groups seeking legislative repeal of the law had challenged its constitutionality. The Supreme Court refused to decide on the merits of the 1961 case, concluding that a doctor who had not been charged with violating the statute had no standing (legal right) to bring the lawsuit.[97] But because the Court's 1961 opinion had stressed the fact that the law had long gone unenforced, Planned Parenthood officials decided that they would need to create a test case. So Estelle Griswold, the executive director of Planned Parenthood League of Connecticut, and Dr. C. Lee Buxton opened a birth-control clinic and were arrested ten days later. With their arrest Planned Parenthood had parties actually charged with violating the law. After Griswold and Buxton's conviction in the state courts, they appealed to the U.S. Supreme Court. In *Griswold,* seven justices decided that various portions of the Bill of Rights, including the First, Third, Fourth, Fifth, and Fourteenth Amendments, cast "penumbras" (unstated liberties on the fringes or in the shadow of more explicitly stated rights), thereby creating zones of privacy, including a married couple's right to plan a family. Thus the Connecticut statute was ruled unconstitutional as a violation of marital privacy, a right the Court concluded could be read into the U.S. Constitution.

Later, the Court expanded the right of privacy to include the right of unmarried individuals to have access to contraceptives. "If the right of privacy means anything," wrote Justice William J. Brennan, "it is the right of the individual, married or single, to be free from unwarranted governmental intrusion into matters so fundamentally affecting a person as the decision to bear or beget a child."[98]

Abortion

In the early 1960s, two birth-related tragedies occurred: Severely deformed babies were born to women who had been given the drug thalidomide while pregnant, and a nationwide measles epidemic resulted in the birth of more babies with severe problems. The increasing medical safety of abortions and the growing women's rights movement combined with these tragedies to put pressure on the legal and medical establishments to enact laws that would guarantee a woman's access to a safe and legal abortion.

By the late 1960s, fourteen states had voted to liberalize their abortion policies, and four states decriminalized abortion in the early stages of pregnancy. But many women's rights activists wanted more. They argued that the decision to carry a pregnancy to term was a woman's fundamental constitutional right. In 1973, in one of the most controversial decisions ever handed down, seven members of the Court agreed with this position.

The woman whose case became the catalyst for pro-choice and anti-abortion groups was Norma McCorvey, an itinerant circus worker. The mother of one toddler she was unable to care for, McCorvey could not leave another child in her mother's care. So she decided to terminate her second pregnancy. Unable to secure a legal abortion and frightened by the conditions she found when she sought an illegal, back-alley abortion, McCorvey turned to two young Texas lawyers who were looking for a plaintiff to bring a lawsuit to challenge Texas's restrictive statute, which allowed abortions only when they were necessary to save the life of the mother. McCorvey, who was unable to obtain a legal abortion, later gave birth and put the baby up for adoption. Nevertheless, she allowed her lawyers to proceed with the case using her as their plaintiff, under the pseudonym Jane Roe, to challenge the Texas law as enforced by Henry Wade, the district attorney for Dallas County, Texas.

When the case finally came before the Supreme Court, Justice Harry A. Blackmun, a former lawyer at the Mayo Clinic, relied heavily on medical evidence to rule that the Texas law violated a woman's constitutionally guaranteed right to privacy, which he argued included her decision to terminate a pregnancy. Writing for the majority in **Roe v. Wade,** Blackmun divided pregnancy into three stages. In the first trimester, a woman's right to privacy gave her an absolute right (in consultation with her physician), free from state interference, to terminate her pregnancy. In the second trimester, the state's interest in the health of the mother gave it the right to regulate abortions—but only to protect the woman's health. Only in the third trimester—when the fetus becomes potentially viable—did the Court find that the state's interest in potential life

Roe v. Wade: The Supreme Court found that a woman's right to an abortion was protected by the right to privacy that could be implied from specific guarantees found in the Bill of Rights and the Fourteenth Amendment.

outweighed the woman's privacy interests. Even in the third trimester, however, abortions to save the life or health of the mother were to be legal.[99]

Roe v. *Wade* unleashed a torrent of political controversy. Anti-abortion groups, caught off guard, scrambled to recoup their losses in Congress. Representative Henry Hyde (R–Ill.) persuaded Congress to ban the use of Medicaid funds for abortions for poor women, and the constitutionality of the Hyde Amendment was upheld by the Supreme Court in 1977 and again in 1980.[100]

From the 1970s through the present, the right to an abortion and its constitutional underpinnings in the right to privacy have been under attack by well-organized anti-abortion groups. The Reagan and Bush administrations were strong advocates of the anti-abortion position, regularly urging the Court to overrule *Roe*. They came close to victory in *Webster* v. *Reproductive Health Services* (1989).[101] In *Webster* the Court upheld state-required fetal viability tests in the second trimester, even though these tests would increase the cost of an abortion considerably. The Court also upheld Missouri's refusal to allow abortions to be performed in state-supported hospitals or by state-funded doctors or nurses. Perhaps most noteworthy, however, were the facts that four justices seemed willing to overrule *Roe* v. *Wade,* and that Justice Antonin Scalia publicly rebuked his colleague Sandra Day O'Connor, then the only woman on the Court, for failing to provide the critical fifth vote to overrule *Roe*.

After *Webster,* states began to enact more restrictive legislation (see map on p. 102). In the most important abortion case since *Roe, Planned Parenthood of Southeastern Pennsylvania* v. *Casey* (1992), Justices O'Connor, Anthony Kennedy, and David Souter, in a jointly authored opinion, wrote that Pennsylvania could limit abortions as long as its regulations did not pose "an undue burden" on pregnant women.[102]

The narrowly supported decision, which upheld a twenty-four-hour waiting period and parental consent requirements, did not overrule *Roe,* but clearly limited its scope by abolishing its trimester approach and substituting the "undue burden" standard. Since *Casey,* the Court has, for example, refused to find unconstitutional Mississippi's mandatory twenty-four-hour waiting period before an abortion. Mississippi has only three abortion clinics—all in Jackson. With this required waiting period, many women have to take time off work to drive over 100 miles, and then pay for a hotel. The number of abortions dropped 40 percent, and the clinics unsuccessfully argued that the waiting period posed an "undue burden." The U.S. Supreme Court refused to hear the appeal.[103] Moreover, in 1993, the Court ruled that judges cannot use federal civil rights laws to stop those who block access to abortion clinics, narrowing federal protections for women seeking abortions.[104]

Given these decisions, pro-choice activists concluded that the Supreme Court was not the place to seek protection of what they see as basic privacy rights. In the wake of the 1992 elections, they decided to press Congress to pass a Freedom of Choice Act and looked to President Clinton, who ran on a pro-choice platform, for support. While Congress failed to pass that act, on the twentieth anniversary of *Roe,* Clinton ended bans on fetal tissue research, abortions at military hospitals, and federal financing for overseas population control programs, and lifted the "gag" rule, a federal regulation enacted in 1987 which barred public health clinics receiving federal dollars from discussing abortion.[105] He also lifted the ban on testing of RU–486, the so-called French abortion pill.

President Clinton used the occasion of his first appointment to the U.S. Supreme Court to select a longtime supporter of abortion rights, Ruth Bader Ginsburg, to replace Justice Byron White, one of the original dissenters in *Roe*. Most commentators believe that this was an important first step in shifting the Court away from any further curtailment of abortion rights, as was the later appointment of Justice Stephen Breyer in 1994.

Anti-abortion group Operation Rescue has staged large-scale protests in front of abortion clinics across the nation. It now has a surprising new member–Norma McCorvey, the "Jane Roe" of *Roe* v. *Wade,* who announced in a 1995 press conference that she had become pro-life. (Photo courtesy: Tim Sharp/AP Photo)

While President Clinton was attempting to shore up abortion rights through judicial appointment, the newly elected Republican 104th Congress became the most active ever as it attempted to restrict abortion rights. There were nearly forty votes on reproductive choice taken in 1995, nearly double the next-highest year of anti-abortion legislative activity in Congress, 1977.[106] In fact, in March 1996 Congress passed and sent to President Clinton a bill that for the first time would ban a specific procedure used in late-term abortions.[107] The president vetoed the Partial Birth Abortion Act over the comments and pressure of the National Right to Life Committee, which had lobbied hard for the act.

At this writing the right to an abortion is a constitutionally guaranteed right, although one no longer accorded the highest level of constitutional scrutiny. Its uncertain status underscores the role of politics in the civil liberties process. Change in composition of the Court, the partisan makeup of the Congress, and the political beliefs of the president all play an important role in the changing nature of civil liberties, including access to safe and legal abortions.

Homosexuality

Although the Supreme Court has ruled that the right to privacy includes the right to decide whether "to bear or beget a child," it has declined to interpret the right of privacy to include the right to engage in homosexual acts. In 1985 the Court, in a four-to-four decision (Justice Powell was ill), upheld a lower-court decision that found unconstitutional an Oklahoma law allowing the dismissal of teachers who advocate homosexual relations.[108] So the next year, when another case involving homosexual rights, *Bowers* v. *Hardwick* (1986),[109] was argued before the Court, Lawrence Tribe, the lawyer representing Michael Hardwick, pitched his arguments toward Justice Powell, who he believed would be the crucial swing vote in this controversial area. Tribe, a professor at the Harvard Law School, argued against the constitutionality of a Georgia law prohibiting consensual heterosexual and homosexual oral or anal sex.

In August 1982, in Atlanta, Georgia, Michael Hardwick was arrested in his bedroom by a police officer who was there to serve an arrest warrant on Hardwick for his failure to appear in court on another charge. One of his roommates let the officer in and directed him to Hardwick's room. After Hardwick's arrest on a sodomy charge, the local prosecutor decided not to prosecute. Nonetheless, Hardwick, a local gay activist,

In a key First Amendment rights ruling, the Supreme Court held in 1995 that parade organizers had a free-speech right to ban gay marchers from Boston's annual St. Patrick's Day parade. The Court said that the organizers' free-speech rights took precedence over a state law barring discrimination in public places based on sexual orientation. (Photo courtesy: Lisa Quinones/Black Star)

joined forces with the American Civil Liberties Union to challenge the constitutionality of the law under which he had been arrested. In a five-to-four decision, the Supreme Court upheld the law. At conference, Justice Powell reportedly seemed torn by the case. He believed that the twenty-year sentence that came with conviction was excessive, but he was troubled by the fact that Hardwick hadn't actually been (and never was) tried and convicted. Although he originally voted with the majority to overturn the law, Powell was bothered by the broadness of Justice Blackmun's original draft of the majority opinion. Thus he changed his mind and voted with the minority view to uphold the law, making it the new majority.[110] And, like his change of heart in the *McCleskey* case, after his retirement Justice Powell confessed that he was wrong in *Bowers* and should have voted to overturn the Georgia law.

While the Court has refused to expand the right to privacy to invalidate state laws that criminalize some aspects of homosexual behavior, in 1996 it ruled that a state could not deny rights to homosexuals simply because they are homosexuals. Thus, as discussed in chapter 6, the Court ruled that the equal protection clause bars unreasonable state discrimination against homosexuals.[111]

The Right to Die

While the current Supreme Court is unlikely to expand the scope of the privacy doctrine to include greater protections for homosexuals in the near future, it is likely to continue to get more cases involving claims for personal autonomy. In 1990, for example, in *Cruzan by Cruzan* v. *Director, Missouri Department of Health,* the Supreme Court sided with the state against the privacy claims of the parents of Nancy Cruzan, a brain-injured woman living in a comatose state who, according to her doctors, could live like that for many more years. Her parents sued to remove her feeding tube, and the Bush administration and numerous anti-abortion groups filed briefs supporting the state against the Cruzans.

Writing for a five-person majority, Chief Justice Rehnquist rejected any attempts to expand the right of privacy into this thorny area of social policy. The Court did, however, note that individuals could terminate medical treatment if they were able to express, or had done so in writing via a living will, their desire to have medical treatment terminated in the event they became incompetent.[112]

States, too, have entered into this arena. Even before the *Cruzan* case, the New Jersey Supreme Court allowed the parents of a comatose woman to withdraw her feeding tube.[113] More recently, in a different but related vein, states have legislated to prevent what is often called "assisted suicide." Jurors, however, often appear unwilling to find loved ones or even Dr. Kervorkian guilty of helping the terminally ill carry out the decision to take their own lives. Nevertheless, the Supreme Court is expected to address this issue in 1997, when it will hear challenges to two state laws that ban assisted suicide.

CHANGING NOTIONS OF CIVIL LIBERTIES

*T*he addition of the Bill of Rights to the Constitution was one of the first acts of the First Congress. Since that time, no amendments have been added to the Constitution to alter the basic liberties guaranteed by the Bill of Rights. In the aftermath of the flag-burning controversy in the 1980s, many called for the enactment of an amendment to ban flag burning to overturn *Texas* v. *Johnson.*

But in the short run, reluctance to alter the First Amendment's far-reaching protections in any way ultimately led to the defeat of such proposals. Opponents argued fervently that this nation was built upon political protest and that free expression should be constitutionally protected at all costs, no matter how repugnant to the majority.

But the drive to make flag burning illegal continues. A proposed constitutional amendment to ban flag burning, for example, sailed through the Republican-controlled 104th House of Representatives in 1995, only to falter in the Senate over questions about what an amendment prohibiting "physical desecration" of the flag means. The 1996 Republican Party platform reiterated support for a flag-burning amendment.

When amendments aren't viable options because they are so difficult and time consuming to pass, Congress has occasionally acted to change or restrict various guarantees contained in the Bill of Rights, but the Supreme Court has often ruled those acts unconstitutional, as was the case with the flag desecration statute. In 1993, in the wake of stepped-up violence against abortion clinics and providers, a new drive was launched to make it a federal crime to threaten, commit violence, or to blockade clinics, and to give the U.S. Justice Department the power to obtain court orders to break up the blockaders. The need for this kind of law was lessened, however, after the U.S. Supreme Court ruled that the Pro-Life Action Network and groups such as Operation Rescue could be prosecuted under a federal criminal law for engaging in a national conspiracy to shut down abortion clinics "through threatened or actual force, violence or fear." Pro-life activists claimed that the ruling violated their First Amendment rights, arguing that it interfered with their rights to freedom of speech and assembly.[114] In spite of that ruling, however, in 1994 Congress passed legislation making it a crime to block access to women's reproductive health clinics or to threaten patients or employees of those clinics, and violence at clinics has declined appreciably.

Congress has also concerned itself with civil liberties and criminal rights of late. Shortly after his election in 1994, Speaker of the House Newt Gingrich called for the passage of a constitutional amendment to restore school prayer. He also has been a major leader of the move to pass laws to limit the protections offered by the search-and-seizure clause of the Fourth Amendment to make it easier for police to search for evidence of illegal activity. Gingrich and many other conservatives believe that liberal interpretations of that amendment only straightjacket the police while protecting criminals.

The Christian Coalition and Civil Liberties

The Christian Coalition's Contract with the American Family sets out an ambitious agenda for civil liberties changes. Announced on May 17, 1995 in a room in the U.S. Capitol with House Speaker Gingrich in attendance, the Contract contains ten points and is modeled after the Republicans' Contract with America. It seeks "to hold government accountable for the cultural crisis" that the Christian Coalition believes "has afflicted our nation over the past three decades."[115] Many of the key items in the contract deal directly with civil liberties issues and many would take an amendment to the Constitution to be legal or might not be considered constitutional by the Supreme Court if enacted. Among those provisions are:

- passage of the Religious Equality Amendment to allow prayer in public places, including public schools
- passage of legislation to "restore respect for human life," including placing severe limits on second trimester pregnancies
- passage of legislation to restrict pornography, especially on the Internet

- end government support for the arts, especially public funding for "obscene art"
- require convicts to pay restitution to their victims upon their release, and require drug and HIV testing of all inmates

At this writing some of these proposals, including banning pornography on the Internet, have been passed by Congress and more are likely to follow, showing the political force of the Christian Coalition and public concern with declining morals. As we discussed in chapter 1, the American public is not happy with things as they are today. Some voters and politicians see the kinds of changes advocated by the Christian Coalition as a promising step toward going back to America as it once was; others see that America as being far less idyllic and are ready to challenge the constitutionality of any of these proposals for change. Is it the role of government to set national moral and ethical standards? And if so, *whose* morals and ethics will serve as standards for *all* Americans?

SUMMARY

In this chapter, we have made the following points:

1. The First Constitutional Amendments: The Bill of Rights.

Most of the Framers originally opposed the Bill of Rights. Anti-Federalists, however, continued to stress the need for a Bill of Rights during the drive for ratification of the Constitution, and some states tried to make their ratification contingent on the addition of a Bill of Rights. Thus, during its first session, Congress sent the first ten amendments to the Constitution, the Bill of Rights, to the states for their ratification. Later, the addition of the Fourteenth Amendment allowed the Supreme Court to apply some of the amendments to the states through a process called selective incorporation.

2. First Amendment Guarantees: Freedom of Religion.

The First Amendment guarantees freedom of religion. The establishment clause, which prohibits the national government from establishing a religion, does not, according to Supreme Court interpretation, create an absolute wall between church and state. While the national and state governments may generally not give direct aid to religious groups, many forms of aid, especially many that benefit children, have been held to be constitutionally permissible. In contrast, the Court has generally barred prayer in public schools. The Court generally has adopted an accommodationist approach when interpreting the free exercise clause by allowing some governmental regulation of religious practices.

3. First Amendment Guarantees: Freedom of Speech and Press.

The First Amendment also guarantees freedom of speech and of the press. The Alien and Sedition Acts in 1798 were the first national efforts to curtail free speech, but they were never reviewed by the U.S. Supreme Court.

Some forms of speech were punished during the Civil War, and the Supreme Court refused to address their constitutionality directly. By the twentieth century, several states, and later the national government, passed laws restricting freedoms of speech and of the press. These curtailments were upheld by the Court, using the clear and present danger test. Later, the Court used the more liberal direct incitement test, which required a stronger showing of imminent danger before speech could be restricted.

Symbolic speech has been afforded the same protection as other forms of speech. Historically, the Supreme Court has disfavored any attempts at prior restraint of speech or press; thus so-called politically correct speech requirements have come under constitutional challenge.

Libel, slander, and obscenity (as well as some forms of pornography) are not protected by the First Amendment.

4. The Rights of Criminal Defendants and the Criminal Justice System.

The Fourth, Fifth, Sixth, and Eighth Amendments provide a variety of procedural guarantees to individuals accused of crimes. In particular, the Fourth Amendment prohibits unreasonable searches and seizures, and the Court has generally refused to allow evidence seized in violation of this safeguard to be used at trial.

Among other rights, the Fifth Amendment guarantees that "no person shall be compelled to be a witness against himself." The Supreme Court has interpreted this provision to require that the government inform the accused of his or her right to remain silent. This provision has also been interpreted to require that illegally obtained confessions must be excluded at trial.

The Sixth Amendment's guarantee of "assistance of counsel" has been interpreted by the Supreme Court to require that the government provide counsel to defendants unable to pay for it in cases where prison sentences may be imposed. The Sixth Amendment also requires an impartial jury, although the meaning of impartial continues to evolve through judicial interpretation.

The Eighth Amendment's ban against "cruel and unusual punishments" has been held not to bar imposition of the death penalty.

5. The Right to Privacy.

The right to privacy is a judicially created right carved from the implications of several amendments, including the First, Third, Fourth, Fifth, and Fourteenth Amendments. Statutes limiting access to birth control and abortion rights have been ruled unconstitutional violations of the right to privacy. In contrast, the Supreme Court has not expanded the right to privacy to invalidate state statutes criminalizing homosexual acts.

6. Changing Notions of Civil Liberties.

Few efforts have been made to alter the basic guarantees contained in the Bill of Rights. But, there is a serious move today, led by the Christian Coalition, to make major changes in civil liberties guarantees.

KEY TERMS

Bill of Rights, p. 145
civil liberties, p. 144
clear and present danger test, p. 156
direct incitement test, p. 157
due process clause, p. 146
due process rights, p. 163
establishment clause, p. 149
exclusionary rule, p. 168
free exercise clause, p. 149
incorporation doctrine, p. 146
Lemon test, p. 150

libel, p. 160
Miranda rights, p. 168
Miranda v. *Arizona*, p. 167
New York Times Co. v. *Sullivan*, p. 161
prior restraint, p. 154
privacy, p. 173
Roe v. *Wade*, p. 174
selective incorporation, p. 148
slander, p. 160
symbolic speech, p. 157

SELECTED READINGS

Clor, Harry M. *Obscenity and Public Morality.* Chicago: University of Chicago Press, 1967.

Craig, Barbara Hinkson, and David M. O'Brien. *Abortion and American Politics.* Chatham, NJ: Chatham House Publishers, 1993.

Friendly, Fred W. *Minnesota Rag: The Dramatic Story of the Landmark Case That Gave New Meaning to Freedom of the Press.* New York: Random House, 1981.

Ivers, Gregg. *Redefining the First Freedom: The Supreme Court and the Consolidation of State Power.* New Brunswick, NJ: Transaction Press, 1993.

Leonard, Levy, et al. *The First Amendment.* New York: Macmillan, 1986.

Lewis, Anthony. *Make No Law: The Sullivan Case and the First Amendment.* New York: Random House, 1991.

Manwaring, David R. *Render unto Caesar: The Flag Salute Controversy.* Chicago: University of Chicago Press, 1962.

O'Brien, David M. *Constitutional Law and Politics, Vol. 2: Civil Rights and Civil Liberties.* New York: Norton and Co., 1991.

O'Connor, Karen. *No Neutral Ground: Abortion Politics in an Age of Absolutes.* Boulder, CO: Westview Press, 1996.

Weddington, Sarah. *A Question of Choice.* New York: Grosset/Putnam, 1993.

CIVIL RIGHTS

On November 15, 1995, Hooters of America, Inc., operators of 172 restaurants in thirty-seven states, launched an unprecedented media blitz to try to dissuade the federal Equal Employment Opportunity Commission (EEOC) from forcing it to hire "Hooters guys" to work with its "Hooters girls" in its restaurant chain. To publicize its case, the restaurant chain took out full-page ads in newspapers. The ads attempted to capitalize on the country's anti-Washington, anti-big government, anti-unnecessary governmental intervention feelings by making fun of Washington and the EEOC, charging that the EEOC's investigation of its hiring practices was a waste of the taxpayer's money. It also held a rally a few blocks from the U.S. Capitol—complete with two dozen of its trademark scantily clad waitresses.

The EEOC, the federal agency charged with enforcing laws against workplace discrimination based on age, race, color, religion, sex, or national origin, was created by Congress to implement the Civil Rights Act of 1964. Individuals who believe that they have been discriminated against can file a complaint with an EEOC field office, which then investigates the complaint. If the investigation establishes that there is reasonable cause to believe the complaint is true, the agency first tries to mediate between the employee and employer. If that fails, the EEOC has the authority to file a lawsuit in federal court seeking to remedy the discriminatory treatment.

What happened with Hooters? After several men in different parts of the country were denied jobs and filed complaints, the EEOC investigated Hooters for four years. In September 1994 the EEOC then ruled that Hooters violated the Civil Rights Act of 1964 by failing to hire any men to act as servers in its restaurants. Hooters rejected the EEOC's settlement offer, which called for the chain to hire men and to put $22 million dollars into a fund to pay males who had been victims of its hiring policy. The agency also wanted Hooters to conduct sensitivity training to combat sex discrimination in its restaurants.

Hooters contended that federal law allows some gender-based hiring and that its customers wanted young, attractive female servers. Hooters, which spent more than $2 million in legal fees and for its media blitz, said it was prepared to spend up to $10 million to keep its all-female staff. "There's a time when governmental intervention goes too far, and this is a perfect illustration of good intentions that have gone haywire," said Mike McNeil, Hooters's vice president of marketing.[1] In response, Marcia Greenberger, co-president of the National

WHAT'S WRONG WITH THIS PICTURE?
The Government.

The infamous Hooters ad, which read in part: "The Equal Employment Opportunity Commission is wasting taxpayer dollars, ignoring its mission, and setting aside the interest of individuals with real discrimination claims in an effort to force Hooters Restaurants to hire men to be Hooters Girls. This excessive government interference in Hooters business is jeopardizing the interest of Hooters owners and their over 13,000 employees. Taking away good jobs from Hooters Girls and giving them to men is unfair. It is a waste of taxpayer money, and it is ridiculous." (Photo courtsy: John Basemore/AP Photo)

civil rights: Refers to the positive acts governments take to protect individuals against arbitrary or discriminatory treatment by governments or individuals based on categories such as race, sex, national origin, age, or sexual orientation.

Women's Law Center, characterized the Hooters publicity campaign as a "serious mischaracterization" of the facts and a "trivialization" of equal employment laws. "From our perspective," she said, "it's illegal for a restaurant to say it's only going to hire young, slim women that fit a particular stereotype." She compared the Hooters policy to that of the airlines, which failed for years to hire male flight attendants, citing customer preference.[2] The Hooters unprecedented media blitz triumphed in the end. In May 1996 the EEOC quietly dropped the case and said it won't intervene in the class action sex discrimination law suit filed by several men.

The Declaration of Independence, written in 1776, boldly proclaims: "We hold these truths to be self-evident, that all men are created equal, that they are endowed by their Creator with certain inalienable rights." The Constitution, written eleven years later, is silent on the concept of equality. Only through constitutional amendment and Supreme Court definition and redefinition of the rights contained in that document have Americans come close to attaining equal rights. No one at the Continental Congress or the Constitutional Convention ever envisioned that the national government would be involved in a lawsuit involving the hiring practices of a restaurant, let alone one that allowed men to be served by women wearing shorts and a tight T-shirt.

The term **civil rights** refers to the positive acts governments take to protect individuals against arbitrary or discriminatory treatment by governments or individuals. The Framers considered some civil rights issues. But, as James Madison reflected in *Federalist No. 42*, one entire class of citizens—slaves—were treated in the new Constitution more like property than like people. Without the Three-Fifths Compromise, "No union could possibly have been formed" because the Southern states would not have agreed to join the union if slavery was prohibited by the national government.[3] In stipulating that slaves could be counted for purposes of fixing state population to determine congressional apportionment, slaves were counted as three-fifths of a person. The Constitution also stipulated that the importation of slaves could not be prohibited for twenty years. Delegates to the Constitutional Convention put political expediency before the immorality of slavery, and basic civil rights. Moreover, the Constitution considered white women full citizens for purposes of determining state population, but voting qualifications were left to the states and none allowed women to vote at the time the Constitution was ratified.

In general, the idea of voting rights or any other civil rights did not concern the Framers; they were more concerned with creating a new, workable, and enduring form of government than with civil rights—then at best a nebulous term. Since the Constitution was written, however, concepts of civil rights have changed dramatically. The addition of the Fourteenth Amendment, one of three amendments ratified after the Civil War, introduced the notion of equality into the Constitution by specifying that states could not deny "any person within its jurisdiction equal protection of the laws."

Since its addition to the Constitution, the Fourteenth Amendment has generated more litigation to determine and specify its meaning than any other provision of the Constitution. Within a few years of its ratification, women—and later, African Americans and other minorities and disadvantaged groups—took to the courts to seek expanded civil rights in all walks of life. But the struggle to augment rights was not limited to the courts. Public protest, civil disobedience, legislative lobbying, and appeals to public opinion have all been part of the arsenal of those seeking equality. The Hooters case incorporates all of those actions as the company seeks to maintain hiring practices that many allege are discriminatory. And, while its campaign pokes fun at civil rights laws and their enforcement, it is important to remember that it wasn't all that long ago that employers believed they had the right not to hire African Americans, women, or people with disabilities. Homosexuals, moreover, continue to fight efforts by states and local governments to prohibit them from being protected *from* discrimination.

Since passage of the Civil War amendments (1865–70), there has been a fairly consistent pattern of the expansion of civil rights to more and more groups. In this chapter we will explore how notions of equality and civil rights have changed in this country. To do so we'll discuss slavery, its abolition, and the achievement of voting rights for African Americans and women by examining the evolution of African-American rights and women's rights in tandem. To appreciate how each group has drawn ideas, support, and success from the other, we discuss their parallel developments throughout this chapter as well as those of other historically disadvantaged political groups:

- We discuss *slavery, abolition, and the efforts of abolitionists, African Americans, and women to gain the vote* and expand civil rights.

- We examine these two groups' next *push for equality from 1885 to 1954,* using two of the Supreme Court's most famous decisions, *Plessy* v. *Ferguson* and *Brown* v. *Board of Education of Topeka, Kansas* as bookends for our discussion.

- We analyze *the civil rights movement* and the Civil Rights Act of 1964 and its effects, *including its facilitation of the development of a new women's rights movement* and its push for an equal rights amendment to the U.S. Constitution.

- We present *the efforts of other groups,* including Native Americans, Hispanic Americans, homosexuals, and disabled Americans, to secure constitutional and statutory rights using methods often modeled after the actions of African Americans and women.

- We discuss *affirmative action* as a remedy for vestiges of discrimination and analyze its continued relevance in a time of *changing notions of civil rights guarantees.*

SLAVERY, ABOLITION, AND WINNING THE RIGHT TO VOTE, 1800–85

Today we take the rights of women and blacks to vote for granted. Since 1980, in fact, women have outvoted men at the polls; and in the 1990s, African Americans and women have become the core of the Democratic Party. But it wasn't always this way. The period from 1800 to 1890 was one of tremendous change and upheaval in America. Despite the Civil War and the freeing of the slaves, the promise of equality guaranteed to African Americans by the Civil War amendments failed to become a reality. And while women's rights activists also began to make claims for equality, often using the arguments enunciated for the abolition of slavery, they too fell far short of their goals.

Slavery and Congress

Congress banned slave trade in 1808, after the expiration of the twenty-year period specified by the Constitution. In 1820 blacks made up 25 percent of the U.S. population and were in the majority in some Southern states. By 1840 that figure had fallen to 20 percent. After the invention of the cotton gin (a machine invented in 1793 that separated seeds from cotton very quickly), the South became even more dependent on agriculture and cheap slave labor as its economic base. At the same time, technological advances were turning the Northern states into an increasingly industrialized region, which intensified the cultural and political differences and animosity between North and South.

Ever since the first Africans had been brought to the New World in 1619, slavery had been a divisive issue. But as the nation grew westward in the early 1800s, conflicts between Northern and Southern states intensified over the admission of new states to the Union with "free" or "slave" status. The first major crisis occurred in 1820, when the territory of Missouri applied for admission to the Union as a "slave state"—that is, one in which slavery would be legal. Missouri's admission would have weighted the Senate in favor of slavery and was therefore opposed by Northern senators. The resultant Missouri Compromise of 1820 allowed the admission of Missouri as a slave state, along with the admission of Maine (formed out of the territory of Massachusetts with the permission of Congress and Massachusetts) as a free state. Other compromises concerning slavery were eventually necessitated as the nation continued to grow and new states were added to the Union.

The Abolitionist Movement: The First Civil Rights Movement

The Compromise of 1820 solidified the South in its determination to keep slavery legal, but it also fueled the fervor of those who opposed slavery. In the early 1800s, some private charities purchased slaves and transported them to the west coast of Africa, where, in the 1820s, eighty-eight former slaves formed the independent nation of Liberia. But this solution to the slavery problem was not all that practical. Few owners were willing to free their slaves, and the trip to Africa and conditions there were dangerous. The abolitionist movement might have fizzled had it not been for William Lloyd Garrison, a white New Englander who became active in the movement in the early 1830s. Garrison, a newspaper editor, founded the American Anti-Slavery Society in 1833; by 1838 it had more than 250,000 members—a number equivalent to the 3.8 million members of the National Association for the Advancement of Colored People (NAACP) today. (In 1996, it reported 500,000 members.)

The Women's Rights Tie-in. Slavery was not the only practice that people began to question in the decades following adoption of the Constitution. In 1840, for example, Garrison and even Frederick Douglass, a well-known black abolitionist writer (see Roots of Government: Frederick Douglass), parted from the Anti-Slavery Society when it refused to accept their demand that women be allowed to participate equally in all its activities. At that time, custom dictated that women not speak out in public, and most laws made women second-class citizens. In most states, for example, women could not divorce their husbands or keep their own wages and inheritances. And, of course, they could not vote.

Elizabeth Cady Stanton and Lucretia Mott, two women who were to found the women's movement, attended the 1840 meeting of the World's Anti-Slavery Society in London with their husbands. They were not allowed to participate because they were women. As they sat in the balcony apart from the male delegates, they paused to compare their status to that of the slaves they sought to free. They believed that women were not much better off than slaves, and resolved to address these issues. In 1848 they

Roots of Government

Frederick Douglass

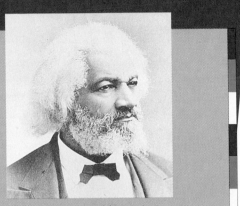

(Photo courtesy: Library of Congress)

Frederick Douglass (1817–95), a leading advocate of civil rights for both blacks and women, was the son of a slave and an unidentified white man. Although born into slavery, Douglass learned how to read and write. Once he escaped to the North (where 250,000 free blacks lived), he became a well-known orator and journalist. He spoke to abolitionist groups about his experiences as a slave and included these experiences in his autobiography, *Narrative of the Life of Frederick Douglass.* His life was also romanticized in song.

In 1847 he started a newspaper, *The North Star,* in Rochester, New York, and it quickly became a powerful voice against slavery. Douglass was a strong abolitionist, who urged President Abraham Lincoln to emancipate the slaves and helped recruit black soldiers for the Union forces in the Civil War. His home in Rochester, New York, was a station along the Underground Railroad. Douglass was also a firm believer in women's suffrage, and he attended the Seneca Falls Convention in 1848. He was a close friend of John Brown, whose raid at Harpers Ferry was a pivotal moment in the antislavery movement. Douglass was appointed to several minor federal posts, including that of minister to Haiti from 1889 to 1891. He was considered the greatest black leader of his time. When he died in 1895, five states adopted resolutions of regret, and two U.S. senators and one Supreme Court justice were among honorary pallbearers.

sent out a call for the first women's rights convention. Three hundred women and men, including Frederick Douglass, traveled to the sleepy little town of Seneca Falls, New York, to attend the first meeting for women's rights (see Table 6.1).

The Seneca Falls Convention (1848).   The Seneca Falls Convention attracted people from all over New York State who believed that all men and women should be able to enjoy all rights of citizenship equally. It passed resolutions calling for the abolition of legal, economic, and social discrimination against women. All of the resolutions reflected the attendees' dissatisfaction with contemporary moral codes, divorce and criminal laws, and the limited opportunities for women in education, the church, and in medicine, law, and politics. Only the call to extend the **franchise**—the legal right to vote—to women failed to win unanimous approval. Most who attended the Seneca Falls meeting continued to press for women's rights along with the abolition of slavery.

franchise: The right to vote.

TABLE 6.1

Landmark Events in the Quest for Civil Rights— From the Nineteenth Century to *Brown* v. *Board of Education of Topeka, Kansas*

1833	American Anti-Slavery Society founded by William Lloyd Garrison
1840	World's Anti-Slavery Convention held in London
1848	Seneca Falls Convention
1851	*Uncle Tom's Cabin* published
1857	*Dred Scott* v. *Sandford*
1861–65	Civil War
1863	Emancipation Proclamation
1865	Thirteen Amendment ratified
	Lincoln assassinated
1865–76	Reconstruction
1868	Fourteenth Amendment ratified
1869	American Woman Suffrage Association created
	National Woman Suffrage Association created
1870	Fifteenth Amendment ratified
1873	Women's Christian Temperance Union founded
1875	*Minor* v. *Happersett*
1889–1920	Dawn of the Progressive era
1890	National American Woman Suffrage Association founded
1896	*Plessy* v. *Ferguson*
1908	*Muller* v. *Oregon*
1909	NAACP founded
1914–18	World War I
1920	Nineteenth Amendment ratified
1939	NAACP creates the Legal Defense and Educational Fund, which begins to prepare test cases for litigation
1941–45	World War II
1947	Commission on Civil Rights created by Harry S Truman
1954	*Brown* v. *Board of Education of Topeka, Kansas*

The 1850s: The Calm Before the Storm. By 1850 much was changing in America— the Gold Rush had spurred westward migration, cities grew as people were lured from their farms, railroads and the telegraph increased mobility and communication, and immigrants flooded into the United States. Reformers called for change, the women's movement gained momentum, and slavery continued to tear the nation apart. Harriet Beecher Stowe's *Uncle Tom's Cabin,* a novel that showed the evils of slavery by depicting a slave family torn apart, further inflamed the country. *Uncle Tom's Cabin* sold more than 300,000 copies in a single year, 1852.

The tremendous national reaction to Stowe's work, which later prompted Abraham Lincoln to call Stowe "the little woman who started the big war," had not yet faded when a new controversy over the 1820 Missouri Compromise became the lightning rod for the first major civil rights case to be addressed by the U.S. Supreme Court. As discussed in chapter 3, in *Dred Scott* v. *Sandford* (1857), the Supreme Court bluntly ruled unconstitutional the 1820 Missouri Compromise, which prohibited slavery north of the geographical boundary at 360 degrees latitude on a map of the United States. It is also known as the Mason–Dixon Line for the surveyors who made maps of the region. Furthermore, in that case the Court found that slaves were not U.S. citizens and therefore could not bring suits in federal court, and concluded that "the Negro might justly and lawfully be reduced to slavery for his benefit." Ironically, after the case was decided, Scott's owner freed him.

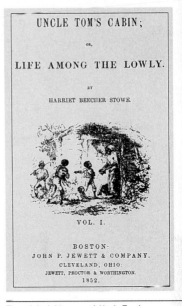

The original title page of *Uncle Tom's Cabin, or Life Among the Lowly,* by Harriet BeecherStowe. (Photo courtesy: Library of Congress)

The Civil War and Its Aftermath: Civil Rights Laws and Constitutional Amendments

The Civil War had many causes, including (1) the political conflict between the North and the South over nullification, a doctrine allowing states to declare federal laws null and void, and secession, which involved the right of states to leave the Union; (2) the Northern states' increasing political strength in Congress, especially in the House of Representatives; (3) Southern agriculture versus Northern industry; and (4) the clash of conservative Southern culture with more progressive Northern ideas. Slavery, however, was clearly the key issue.

During the war (1861–65), abolitionists kept their antislavery pressure on. They were rewarded when President Abraham Lincoln issued the Emancipation Proclamation, which provided that all slaves in states still in active rebellion against the United States would automatically be freed on January 1, 1863. Designed as a measure to gain favor for the war in the North, the Emancipation Proclamation did not free all slaves— it freed only those who lived in the Confederacy. Complete abolition of slavery did not occur until congressional passage and ultimate ratification of the Thirteenth Amendment in 1865.

The Civil War Amendments. The **Thirteenth Amendment** was the first of the three so-called Civil War amendments. It banned all forms of "slavery [and] involuntary servitude." Although Southern states were required to ratify the Thirteenth Amendment as a condition of their readmission to the Union after the war, most of the former Confederate states quickly passed laws that were designed to restrict opportunities for newly freed slaves dramatically. These **Black Codes** prohibited African Americans from voting, sitting on juries, or even appearing in public places. Although Black Codes differed from state to state, all empowered local law-enforcement officials to arrest unemployed blacks, fine them for vagrancy, and hire them out to employers to satisfy their fines. Some state codes went so far as to require African Americans to work on plantations or to be domestics. The Black Codes laid the groundwork for Jim Crow laws, which would later institute segregation in all walks of life (see Politics Now: The Thirteenth Amendment Revisited).

The outraged Reconstructionist Congress enacted the Civil Rights Act of 1866 to invalidate some state Black Codes. President Andrew Johnson vetoed the legislation, but—for the first time in history—Congress overrode a presidential veto. The Civil Rights Act formally made African Americans citizens of the United States and gave the Congress and the federal courts the power to intervene when states attempted to restrict male African-American citizenship rights in matters such as voting. Congress reasoned that African Americans were unlikely to fare well if they had to file

Thirteenth Amendment: One of the three Civil War amendments; specifically bans slavery in the United States.

Black Codes: Laws denying most legal rights to newly freed slaves; passed by Southern states following the Civil War.

Politics Now

The Thirteenth Amendment Revisited

You probably don't think of the Thirteenth Amendment as having continued vitality today, but you may be wrong. Were you ever forced to participate in some form of community service before being allowed to graduate from high school? Community service requirements are now quite popular in many school districts. But in the early 1990s, some students in Bethlehem, Pennsylvania, after studying the Constitution, decided that this state-ordered unpaid labor was slavery and as such it violated the Thirteenth Amendment. The students brought suit in federal court against the school district to challenge the constitutionality of the community service requirements.

"People should volunteer because they want to, not because of a government threat," said Lynn Steirer, one of the 175 seniors whose graduation was threatened because they failed to perform the sixty hours of public service required by their high school for graduation. They were helped in their challenge by attorneys from the Washington, D.C.-based libertarian Institute for Justice. The federal district court ruled against them, as did the Court of Appeals. In 1993 the U.S. Supreme Court refused to hear their appeal, thus letting the decision of the lower courts stand.* In spite of the federal courts' refusal to find in their favor, were the students on to something?

*987 F. 2d (3rd Cir.) 1993, cert. denied, 510 U.S. 824 (1995).

---

discrimination complaints in state courts, where judges were elected. Passage of a federal law allowed African Americans to challenge discriminatory state practices in the federal courts, where judges were appointed by the president.

Because controversy remained over the constitutionality of the act (since the Constitution gives states the right to determine qualifications of voters), the **Fourteenth Amendment** was proposed simultaneously with the Civil Rights Act to guarantee, among other things, citizenship to all freed slaves. Other key provisions of the Fourteenth Amendment barred states from abridging "the privileges or immunities of citizenship" or depriving "any person of life, liberty, or property without due process of law."

Unlike the Thirteenth Amendment, which had near-unanimous support in the North, the Fourteenth Amendment was opposed by many women. During the Civil War, women's rights activists, including Elizabeth Cady Stanton and Susan B. Anthony, put aside their claims for expanded rights for women, most notably the right to vote, and threw their energies into the war effort. They were convinced that once slaves were freed and given the right to vote, women similarly would be rewarded with the franchise. They were wrong.

In early 1869, after ratification of the Fourteenth Amendment (which specifically added the word "male" to the Constitution for the first time), women's rights activists met in Washington, D.C., to argue against passage of any new amendment that would extend suffrage to black males and not to women. The convention resolved that "a man's government is worse than a white man's government, because, in proportion as

Fourteenth Amendment: One of the three Civil War amendments; guarantees equal protection and due process of laws to all U.S. citizens.

you increase the tyrants, you make the condition of the disenfranchised class more hopeless and degraded."

In spite of these arguments, the **Fifteenth Amendment** was passed by Congress in February 1869. It guaranteed the "right of citizens" to vote regardless of their "race, color or previous condition of servitude." Again, sex was not mentioned.

Women's rights activists were shocked. Abolitionists' continued support of the Fifteenth Amendment, which was ratified by the states in 1870, prompted many women's rights supporters to leave the abolition movement to work solely for the cause of women's rights. Twice burned, Anthony and Stanton decided to form their own National Woman Suffrage Association (NWSA) to achieve that goal. In spite of the NWSA's opposition, however, the Fifteenth Amendment was ratified by the states in 1870.

Fifteenth Amendment: One of the three Civil War amendments; specifically enfranchises blacks.

Civil Rights and the Supreme Court

While the Congress was clear in its wishes that the rights of African Americans be expanded and that the Black Codes be rendered illegal, the Supreme Court was not nearly so protective of those rights under the Civil War amendments. In the first two tests of the scope of the Fourteenth Amendment, the Supreme Court ruled that the citizenship rights guaranteed by the amendment applied only to rights of national citizenship and not to state citizenship. Ironically, neither case involved African Americans. In *The Slaughterhouse Cases* (1873),[4] the Court upheld Louisiana's right to create a monopoly in the operation of slaughterhouses, despite the Butcher's Benevolent Association's claim that this action deprived its members of their livelihood and thus the privileges and immunities of citizenship guaranteed by the amendment.

Similarly, in *Bradwell* v. *Illinois* (1873), when Myra Bradwell asked the U.S. Supreme Court to find that Illinois's refusal to allow her to practice law (although she had passed the bar examination) violated her citizenship rights guaranteed by the privileges and immunities clause of the Fourteenth Amendment, her arguments fell on deaf ears. In *Bradwell* one justice went so far as to declare that it was reasonable for the state

Throughout the South, examples of Jim Crow laws abounded. One such law required separate public drinking fountains, shown here. Notice the obvious difference in quality. (Photo courtesy: The Bettmann Archive)

to bar women from the practice of law because "the natural and proper timidity and delicacy which belongs to the female sex evidently unfits it for many of the occupations of civil life."[5]

The combined message of these two cases was that state and national citizenship were separate and distinct. In essence, the Supreme Court ruled that neither African Americans nor any others could be protected from discriminatory state action, because the Fourteenth Amendment did not enlarge the limited rights guaranteed by U.S. citizenship.

Claims for expanded rights and requests for a clear definition of U.S. citizenship rights continued to fall on deaf ears in the halls of the Supreme Court. In 1875, for example, the Court heard *Minor* v. *Happersett,* the culmination of a series of test cases launched by women's rights activists.[6] Virginia Minor, after planning with Anthony and other NWSA members, attempted to register to vote in her hometown of St. Louis, Missouri. When the registrar refused to record her name on the list of eligible voters, Minor sued, arguing that the state's refusal to let her vote violated the privileges and immunities clause of the Fourteenth Amendment. Rejecting her claim, the justices ruled unanimously that voting was not a privilege of citizenship.

In the same year, Southern resistance to African-American equality led Congress to pass the Civil Rights Act of 1875, designed to grant equal access to public accommodations such as theaters, restaurants, and transportation. The act also prohibited the exclusion of African Americans from jury service. After 1877, however, as Reconstruction was dismantled, national interest in the legal condition of African Americans waned. Most white Southerners had never believed in equality for "freedmen," as former slaves were called. Any rights freedmen received had been contingent on federal enforcement. Once federal troops were no longer available to guard polls and prevent whites from excluding black voters, Southern states moved to limit African Americans' access to the ballot. Other forms of discrimination were also allowed by judicial decisions upholding **Jim Crow laws,** which required segregation in public schools and facilities including railroads, restaurants, and theaters (see Highlight 6.1: Who Was Jim Crow?). Many Jim Crow laws also barred interracial marriage. All these laws, at first glance, appeared to conflict with the Civil Rights Act of 1875. In 1883, however, a series of cases decided by the Supreme Court severely damaged the vitality of the 1875 Act. The ***Civil Rights Cases*** (1883)[7] were five separate cases involving the convictions of private individuals found to have violated the Civil Rights Act by refusing to extend accommodations to African Americans in theaters, a hotel, and a railroad. In deciding these cases, the Supreme Court ruled that Congress could prohibit only state or governmental action and not private acts of discrimination. The Court thus seriously limited the scope of the Fourteenth Amendment by concluding that Congress had no authority to prohibit private discrimination in public accommodations.

The Court's opinion in the *Civil Rights Cases* provided a moral reinforcement for the Jim Crow system. Southern states viewed the Court's ruling as an invitation to gut the Thirteenth, Fourteenth, and Fifteenth Amendments.

In devising ways to make certain that African Americans did not vote, Southerners had to avoid the *intent* of the Fifteenth Amendment. This amendment did not guarantee suffrage; it simply said that states could not deny anyone the right to vote on account of race or color. So to exclude African Americans in a seemingly racially neutral way, Southern states used two devices before the 1890s: (1) poll taxes (small taxes on the right to vote that often came due when poor African-American sharecroppers had the least amount of money on hand) or some form of property-owning qualifications; and (2) "literacy" or "understanding" tests, which allowed local registrars to administer difficult reading-comprehension tests to potential voters whom they did not know.

Jim Crow laws: Laws enacted by Southern states that discriminated against blacks by creating "whites only" schools, theaters, hotels, and other public accommodations.

Civil Rights Cases: Name attached to five cases brought under the Civil Rights Act of 1875. In 1883 the Supreme Court decided that discrimination in a variety of public accommodations, including theaters, hotels, and railroads, could not be prohibited by the act because it was private and not state discrimination.

Highlight 6.1

Who Was Jim Crow?

The term "Jim Crow" symbolized the continued discrimination against blacks in the South through state-enacted "separate-but-equal" laws following *Plessy v. Ferguson* (1896). The name Jim Crow came from a song-and-dance routine first performed in the 1830s, in which whites made fun of black songs and speech. Jim Crow was "a comic, jumping, stupid rag doll of a man." The term "Jim Crow" quickly became a synonym for "Negro."*

Jim Crow laws created separate facilities for blacks in such places as railroad cars, restaurants, and schools. The last was perhaps the most damaging to blacks, because the schools for black children were not given the same funding or quality of teachers as the schools for white children. It was not until 1954, in *Brown v. Board of Education of Topeka Kansas*, that racial segregation was ruled unconstitutional.

*Kenneth C. Davis, *Don't Know Much About History* (New York: Crown, 1990), 215.

These voting restrictions had an immediate impact. By the late 1890s, black voting fell by 62 percent from the Reconstruction period, while white voting fell by only 26 percent. To make certain that these laws didn't further reduce the numbers of poor or uneducated white voters, many Southern states added a **grandfather clause** to their voting qualification provisions, granting voting privileges to those who failed to pass a wealth or literacy test only if their grandfathers had voted before Reconstruction. Grandfather clauses effectively denied the descendants of slaves the right to vote.

While African Americans continued to face wide-ranging racism on all fronts, women also confronted discrimination. During this period married women, by law, could not be recognized as legal entities. Women often were treated in the same category as juveniles and "imbeciles," and in many states were not entitled to wages, inheritances, or custody of their children.

grandfather clause: Statute that allowed only those whose grandfathers had voted before Reconstruction to vote unless they passed a wealth or literacy test.

THE PUSH FOR EQUALITY, 1885–1954

The Progressive era (1889–1920) was characterized by a concerted effort to reform political, economic, and social affairs. Evils like child labor, the concentration of economic power in the hands of a few industrialists, limited suffrage, political corruption, business monopolies, and prejudice against African Americans were all targets of progressive reform efforts. Distress over the legal inferiority of African Americans was aggravated by the U.S. Supreme Court's decision in ***Plessy v. Ferguson*** (1896), a case that some commentators point to as the Court's darkest hour.

Plessy v. Ferguson: "Separate But Equal." In 1892 a group of African Americans in Louisiana decided to test the constitutionality of a Louisiana law mandating racial seg-

Plessy v. Ferguson: *Plessy* challenged a Louisiana statute requiring that railroads provide separate accommodations for blacks and whites. The Court found that separate but equal accommodations did not violate the equal protection clause of the Fourteenth Amendment.

regation on all public trains. They found an "ideal" individual to test the law. The blond-haired, blue-eyed Homer Adolph Plessy was widely known in the community to have had an African-American great-grandmother. His coloring made him an excellent subject for a potential test case of the Louisiana law. Plessy boarded a train in New Orleans and proceeded to the "whites only" car. He was arrested when he refused to leave his seat and take one in the car reserved for African Americans. Plessy sued the railroad company, arguing that racial segregation was illegal under the provisions of the Fourteenth Amendment.[8]

The Supreme Court disagreed. After analyzing the history of African Americans in the United States, the majority concluded that the Louisiana law was constitutional. The justices based the decision on their belief that separate facilities for blacks and whites provided equal protection of the laws. After all, they reasoned, African Americans were not prevented from riding the train; the Louisiana statute required only that the races travel separately. Justice John Marshall Harlan (1877–1911) was the lone dissenter on the Court. He argued that "the Constitution is colorblind" and that it was senseless to hold constitutional a law "which, practically, puts the badge of servitude and degradation upon a large class of our fellow citizens."

Not surprisingly, the separate-but equal doctrine enunciated in *Plessy* v. *Ferguson* soon came to mean only "separate," as new legal avenues to discriminate against African Americans were enacted into law throughout the South. The Jim Crow system soon became a way of life in the American South. In 1898 the Supreme Court upheld the constitutionality of literacy tests that were administered to African Americans and indicated its apparent willingness to allow the Southern states to define their own suffrage standards, whether or not they disproportionately affected blacks.[9] One year later, the Supreme Court upheld a school district's decision to maintain a whites-only high school but close a blacks-only high school to free up funds for a black elementary school.[10] The Supreme Court unanimously upheld the constitutionality of this disparate treatment.

By 1900, then, equality for African Americans was far from the promise first offered by the Civil War amendments. Again and again, the Supreme Court nullified the intent of the amendments and sanctioned racial segregation while the states avidly followed its lead. While discrimination was widely practiced in many parts of the North, Southern states passed laws legally imposing segregation in education, housing, public accommodations, employment, and most other spheres of life. Miscegenation laws, for example, prohibited blacks and whites from marrying.

Jim Crow laws were not the only practices designed to keep African Americans in a secondary position. Indeed, these laws established a way of life with strong social codes as well. Journalist Juan Williams notes in *Eyes on the Prize:*

> There were Jim Crow schools, Jim Crow restaurants, Jim Crow water fountains, and Jim Crow customs—blacks were expected to tip their hats when they walked past whites, but whites did not have to remove their hats even when they entered a black family's home. Whites were to be called "sir" and "ma'am" by blacks, who in turn were called by their first names by whites. People with white skin were to be given a wide berth on the sidewalk; blacks were expected to step aside meekly.[11]

Notwithstanding these degrading practices, by the early 1900s a small group of African Americans (largely from the North) had been able to attain some formal education and were ready to push for additional rights. They found some progressive white citizens and politicians amenable to their cause.

The Founding of the National Association for the Advancement of Colored People

In 1909 a handful of individuals active in a variety of progressive causes—including women's suffrage and the fight for better working conditions for women and children—met to discuss the idea of a group devoted to the problems of "the Negro." Major race riots had recently occurred in several American cities, and progressive reformers who sought change in political, economic, and social relations were concerned about these outbreaks of violence and the possibility of others. Oswald Garrison Villard, the influential publisher of the New York *Evening Post*—and grandson of William Lloyd Garrison—called a conference to discuss the problem. This group soon evolved into the National Association for the Advancement of Colored People (NAACP). Along with Villard, its first leaders included Jane Addams of Hull House, vice president of the National American Woman Suffrage Association; Moorfield Storey, a past president of the American Bar Association; and W. E. B. DuBois, a founder of the Niagara Movement, a group of educated African Americans who took their name from their first meeting place in Niagara Falls, Ontario, Canada. (The Niagara reformers met in Canada because no hotel on the U.S. side of the falls would accommodate them.)

William E. DuBois (second from right in the second row, facing left) is pictured with the original leaders of the Niagara Movement in this 1905 photo taken on the Canadian side of Niagara Falls. (Photo courtesy: Schomburg Center for Research in Black Culture/The New York Public Library)

Key Women's Groups

The NAACP was not the only group getting off the ground. The struggle for women's rights was revitalized by the formation of the National American Woman Suffrage Association (NAWSA) in 1890, when the National and American Woman Suffrage Associations merged, with Susan B. Anthony as its president. Unlike the National Woman Suffrage Association, which had sought a wide variety of expanded rights for women, this new association was devoted largely to securing women's suffrage. Its task was greatly facilitated by the proliferation of women's groups that emerged during the Progressive era. In addition to the rapidly growing temperance movement—the move to ban the sale of alcohol, which many women blamed for a variety of social ills—women's groups were created to seek protective legislation in the form of maximum hour or minimum wage laws for women and to work for improved sanitation, public morals, education, and the like. Other organizations that were part of what was called the "club movement" were created to provide increased cultural and literary experiences for middle-class women. With increased industrialization, some women found for the first time that they had the opportunity to pursue activities other than those centered on the home.

One of the most active groups lobbying on behalf of women during this period was the National Consumers' League (NCL), which successfully lobbied for Oregon legislation limiting women to ten hours of work a day. When Curt Muller was then convicted of employing women more than ten hours a day in his small laundry and brought his appeal to the U.S. Supreme Court, the NCL sought permission from the state to conduct the defense of the statute.

At the urging of NCL attorney and future U.S. Supreme Court Justice Louis Brandeis, NCL members amassed an impressive array of sociological and medical data that were incorporated into what became known as the "Brandeis brief." This contained only three pages of legal argument, while more than a hundred pages were devoted to nonlegal, sociological data that were used to convince the Court that Oregon's statute was constitutional. In finding the law constitutional in *Muller* v. *Oregon* (1908), the

Suffragettes demonstrating for the franchise. Parades like this one took place in cities all over the United States. (Photo courtesy: Library of Congress)

suffrage movement: Term used to refer to the drive for votes for women that took place in the United States from 1890 to 1920.

Court relied heavily on these data to document women's unique status as mothers to justify their differential treatment.[12]

Women seeking the vote used reasoning reflecting the Court's opinion in *Muller*. Discarding earlier notions of full equality, NAWSA based its claim to the right to vote largely on the fact that women, as mothers, should be enfranchised. Furthermore, although many members of the **suffrage movement** were NAACP members, the new women's movement—called the suffrage movement because of its focus on the vote alone and not on broader issues of women's rights—took on racist overtones as women argued that if undereducated African Americans could vote, why couldn't women? Some NAWSA members even argued that "the enfranchisement of women would ensure immediate and durable white supremacy."

Diverse attitudes were clearly present in the growing suffrage movement, which often tried to be all things to all people. Its roots in the Progressive movement gave it an exceptionally broad base that transformed NAWSA from a small organization of just over 10,000 members in the early 1890s to a true social movement of more than 2 million members in 1917. By 1920 a coalition of women's group led by NAWSA was able to secure ratification of the Nineteenth, or Susan B. Anthony, Amendment to the Constitution. It guaranteed *all* women the right to vote—fifty-five years after African-American males had been enfranchised by the Fifteenth Amendment.

After passage of the suffrage amendment in 1920, the fragile alliance of diverse women's groups that had come together to fight for the vote quickly disintegrated. Women returned to their "home" groups, such as the NCL or the Women's Christian Temperance Union, to pursue their individualized goals. In fact, after the tumult of the suffrage movement, widespread, organized activity on behalf of women's rights did not reemerge until the 1960s. In the meantime, however, the NAACP continued to fight racism and racial segregation. In fact, its activities and those of others in the civil rights movement would later give impetus to a new women's movement.

In 1908, the U.S. Supreme Court ruled that Oregon's law barring women from working more than ten hours a day in laundries was constitutional. Thus, the conviction of Curt Muller (with arms folded) for violating the statute was upheld. (Photo courtesy: The Supreme Court Historical Society/Courtesy Mrs. Neill Whisnant and Portland, Oregon Chamber of Commerce)

Litigating for Equality

During the 1930s leaders of the NAACP began to sense that the time was right to launch a full-scale challenge in the federal courts to the constitutionality of *Plessy*'s separate-but equal doctrine. The NAACP mapped out a long-range strategy that would first target segregation in professional and graduate education. Clearly, the separate-but equal doctrine and the proliferation of Jim Crow laws were a bar to any hope of full equality for African Americans. Traditional legislative channels were unlikely to work, given blacks' limited or nonexistent political power. Thus the federal courts and a long-range litigation strategy were the NAACP's only hope. The NAACP often relied on Brandeis-type briefs, so-called because they relied heavily on sociological data to support their legal arguments. In fact, the NAACP eventually hired a statistician to help its lawyers amass data to help present evidence of discrimination to the courts.

Test Cases.   The NAACP opted first to challenge the constitutionality of Jim Crow law schools. In 1935 all Southern states maintained fully segregated elementary and secondary schools. Colleges and universities were also segregated, but most states did not provide for postgraduate education for African Americans. NAACP lawyers chose to target law schools because they were institutions that judges could well understand, and integration there could prove less threatening to most whites.

Lloyd Gaines, a graduate of Missouri's all-black Lincoln University, sought admission to the all-white University of Missouri Law School in 1936. He was immediately rejected. In the separate-but equal spirit, the state offered to build a law school at Lincoln (although no funds were allocated for the project) or, if he didn't want to wait, to pay his tuition at an out-of-state law school. Gaines lost his appeal of this rejection in the lower court, and the case was appealed to the U.S. Supreme Court.[13]

Gaines's case was filed at an auspicious time. As you may recall from chapter 3, a "constitutional revolution" occurred in Supreme Court decision making in 1937. Before this time the Court was most receptive to and interested in the protection of economic liberties. In 1937, however, the Court reversed itself in a series of cases and began to place individual freedoms and personal liberties on a more protected footing. Thus, in 1938, Gaines's lawyers pleaded his appeal to a far more sympathetic Supreme

Lloyd Gaines was the subject of the major test case, *Missouri* ex rel. *Gaines* v. *Canada,* which contested the principle of segregated schools. Gaines chose to attend the University of Michigan, from which he strangely disappeared, never to be heard from again. (Photo courtesy: AP/Wide World Photos)

Court. NAACP attorneys argued that the creation of a separate law school of any less caliber than that of the University of Missouri would not and could not afford Gaines an *equal* education. The justices agreed with the NAACP's contention and ruled that Missouri had failed to meet the separate-but equal requirements of *Plessy*. The Court ordered Missouri either to admit Gaines to the school or to set up a law school for him.

Recognizing the importance of the Court's ruling, in 1939 the NAACP created a separate, tax-exempt legal defense fund to devise a strategy to build on the Missouri case to bring about equal educational opportunities for all African-American children. The first head of the NAACP Legal Defense and Educational Fund (LDF), as it was called, was Thurgood Marshall, who later became the first African American to serve on the U.S. Supreme Court (1967–91). Sensing that the Court would be more amenable to the NAACP's broader goals if it was first forced to address a variety of less threatening claims to educational opportunity, Marshall and the LDF brought a series of carefully crafted test cases to the Court.

The first case involved H. M. Sweatt, a forty-six-year-old African-American mail carrier, who in 1946 applied for admission to the all-white University of Texas Law School. Rejected on racial grounds, Sweatt sued. The judge gave the state six months to establish a law school or to admit Sweatt to the University of Texas. The university then rented a few rooms in downtown Houston and hired two local African-American attorneys to be part-time faculty members. (At that time there was only one full-time African-American law school professor in the United States.) The state legislature saw the handwriting on the wall and authorized $3 million for the creation of the Texas State University for Negroes. One hundred thousand dollars of that money was to be for a new law school in Austin across the street from the state capitol. It consisted of three small basement rooms, a library of more than 10,000 books, access to the state law library, and three part-time first-year instructors as the "faculty." Sweatt declined the opportunity to obtain an education there and instead chose to continue his legal challenge.

While working on the Texas case, the NAACP LDF and Marshall also decided to pursue another case. Thurgood Marshall chose to use the case of George W. McLaurin, a retired university professor who had been denied admission to the doctoral education program at the University of Oklahoma. Marshall reasoned that McLaurin, at sixty-eight years of age, would be immune from the charges that African Americans wanted integration in order to intermarry. After a lower court ordered McLaurin's admission, the university reserved a dingy alcove in the cafeteria for him to eat in during off hours, and he was given his own table in the library behind a shelf of newspapers. And, in what surely "was Oklahoma's most inventive contribution to legalized bigotry since the adoption of the 'grandfather clause,'"[14] McLaurin was forced to sit outside classrooms while lectures were given and seminars were held.

The Supreme Court handled these two cases together.[15] The eleven Southern states filed an *amicus curiae* (friend of the court) brief, in which they argued that *Plessy* should govern both cases. The NAACP LDF received assistance, however, from an unexpected source—the U.S. government. In a dramatic departure from the past, the administration of Harry S Truman filed a friend of the court brief urging the Court to overrule *Plessy*. Since the late 1870s, the U.S. government had never sided against the Southern states in a civil rights matter and had never submitted an *amicus* brief supporting the rights of African-American citizens. President Truman believed that because many African Americans had fought and died for their country in World War II, this kind of executive action was proper. The Court traditionally gives great weight to briefs from the U.S. government. The Court, however, again did not overrule *Plessy*, but the justices found that the measures taken by the states in each case failed to live up to the strictures of the separate-but equal doctrine. The Court unanimously ruled that the "remedies" to each situation were inadequate to afford a sound education. In the *Sweatt* case, for example, the Court declared that the "qualities which are incapable of objective measurement but which make for greatness in a law school . . . includ(ing) the reputation of the faculty, experience of the administration, position and influence of the alumni, standing in the community, traditions and prestige" made it impossible for the state to provide an equal education in a segregated setting.

In 1950, after these decisions were handed down, the NAACP LDF concluded that the time had come to launch a full-scale attack on the separate-but equal doctrine. The decisions of the Court were encouraging, and the position of the U.S. government and the population in general appeared to be more receptive to an outright overruling of *Plessy*.

Brown* v. *Board of Education of Topeka, Kansas* (1954).**[16] As discussed in Highlight 6.2: Why It's Called ***Brown* v. *Board of Education of Topeka, Kansas *Brown* was actually four cases brought from different areas of the South, the border states, and others involving public elementary or high school systems that mandated separate schools for blacks and whites.

In *Brown*, NAACP lawyers, again headed by Thurgood Marshall, argued that *Plessy*'s separate-but equal doctrine was unconstitutional under the **equal protection clause** of the Fourteenth Amendment, and that if the Court was still reluctant to overrule *Plessy*, the only way to equalize the schools was to integrate them. A major component of the NAACP's strategy was to prove that the intellectual, psychological, and financial damage that befell African Americans as a result of segregation precluded any court from finding that equality was served by the separate-but equal policy.

In *Brown*, the NAACP LDF presented the Supreme Court with evidence of the harmful consequences of state-imposed racial discrimination. To buttress its claims, the NAACP introduced the now-famous "doll study," conducted by Kenneth Clark, a prominent African-American sociologist who had long studied the negative effects of segregation on African-American children. His research revealed that black children not only preferred white dolls when shown black dolls and white dolls, but that most liked the white doll better, many adding that the black doll looked "bad." This information was used to illustrate the negative impact of racial segregation and bias on an African-American child's self-image.

The NAACP's legal briefs were supported by important *amicus curiae* briefs submitted by the U.S. government, major civil rights groups, labor unions, and religious groups decrying racial segregation. On May 17, 1954, Chief Justice Earl Warren delivered the fourth opinion of the day, *Brown v. Board of Education of Topeka, Kansas*. Writing for the Court, Warren stated:

> To separate [some school children] from others . . . solely because of their race generates a feeling of inferiority as to their status in the community that may affect their hearts and minds in a way very unlikely ever to be undone. We con-

Brown v. Board of Education of Topeka, Kansas: U.S. Supreme Court decision holding that school segregation is inherently unconstitutional because it violates the Fourteenth Amendment's guarantee of equal protection; marked the end of legal segregation in the United States.

equal protection clause: Section of the Fourteenth Amendment that guarantees that all citizens receive "equal protection of the laws"; has been used to bar discrimination against blacks and women.

Highlight 6.2

Why It's Called Brown v. Board of Education of Topeka, Kansas

Ten years after the Court's decision in *Brown* v. *Board of Education of Topeka*, Linda Brown Smith stood in front of the school whose refusal to admit her ultimately led to the Court's 1954 ruling named after her. The decision came too late for her, but her two younger sisters were able to attend integrated schools. (Photo courtesy: AP/Wide World Photos)

Seven-year-old Linda Brown of Topeka, Kansas, lived close to a good public school, but it was reserved for whites. So every day she had to cross railroad tracks in a nearby switching yard on her way to catch a run-down school bus that would take her across town to a school reserved for black students. Her father, Oliver Brown, concerned for her safety and the quality of her education, be-came increasingly frustrated with his youngster's having to travel far from home to get an education.

"The issue came up, and it was decided that Rev-erend Brown's daughter would be the goat, so to speak," recalled a member of the Topeka NAACP. "He put forth his daughter to test the validity of the [law], and we had to raise the money."*

The NAACP continued to gather plaintiffs and test cases from around the na-tion. The Supreme Court first agreed to hear *Brown* and *Briggs* v. *Elliott* (South Carolina) in 1952. Two days before they were to be heard, the Court issued a postponement and added *Davis* v. *Prince Edward County* (Virginia) to its docket. Just a few weeks later, the Court added *Bolling* v. *Sharpe* from the District of Columbia and *Gebhart* v. *Belton* (Delaware). According to U.S. Supreme Court Justice Tom Clark of Texas, the Court "consolidated them and made *Brown* the first so that the whole question would not smack of being purely a Southern one."** Thus, the case became known as *Brown* v. *Board of Education of Topeka, Kansas.*

*Quoted in Juan Williams, *Eyes on the Prize: America's Civil Rights Years, 1954–1965* (New York: Penguin, 1987), 21.
**Williams, *Eye on the Prize*, 31.

clude, unanimously, that in the field of public education the doctrine of "sepa-rate but equal" has no place.

There can be no doubt that *Brown* was the most important civil rights case decided in the twentieth century.[17] It immediately evoked an uproar that shook the nation. Some called the day the decision was handed down "Black Monday." The governor of South Carolina decried the decision, saying, "Ending segregation would mark the beginning of the end of civilization in the South as we know it."[18] The NAACP LDF lawyers who had argued these cases and those cases leading to *Brown*, however, were jubilant.

Remarkable changes had occurred in the civil rights of Americans since 1890. Women had won the right to vote, and after a long and arduous trail of litigation in the federal courts, the Supreme Court had finally overturned its most racist decision of the era, *Plessy* v. *Ferguson*. The Court boldly proclaimed that separate but equal (at least in education) would no longer pass constitutional muster. The question then became how *Brown* would be interpreted and implemented. Could it be used to invalidate other Jim Crow laws and practices? Would African Americans be truly equal under the law?

THE CIVIL RIGHTS MOVEMENT

*O*ur notion of civil rights has changed profoundly since 1954. First African Americans and then women have built upon existing organizations to forge successful movements for increased rights. *Brown* served as a catalyst for change, sparking the development of the modern civil rights movement. Women's work in that movement and the student protest movement that arose in reaction to the U.S. government's involvement in Vietnam gave women the experience needed to form their own organizations to press for full equality. As African Americans and women became more and more successful, they served as models for others who sought equality—Native Americans, Hispanic Americans, homosexuals, the disabled, and others.

School Desegregation After *Brown*

One year after *Brown*, in a case referred to as *Brown II*,[19] the Court ruled that racially segregated systems must be dismantled "with all deliberate speed." To facilitate implementation, the Court placed enforcement of *Brown* in the hands of appointed federal district court judges, who were considered more immune to local political pressures than were regularly elected state court judges.

The NAACP and its Legal Defense Fund continued to resort to the courts to see that *Brown* was implemented, while the South entered into a near-conspiracy to avoid the mandates of *Brown II*. In Arkansas, for example, Governor Orval Faubus, facing a reelection bid, announced that he would not "be a party to any attempt to force acceptance of change to which people are overwhelmingly opposed."[20] The day before school was to begin, Faubus announced that he would surround Little Rock's Central High School with National Guardsmen to prevent African-American students from entering. While the federal courts in Arkansas continued to order the admission of African-American children, the governor remained adamant. Finally, President Dwight D. Eisenhower sent federal troops to Little Rock to protect the rights of the nine students who had attempted to attend Central High.

In reaction to the governor's outrageous conduct, the Court broke with tradition and issued a unanimous decision in *Cooper v. Aaron* (1958), which was filed by the Little Rock School Board asking the federal district court for a two-and-one-half-year delay in implementation of its desegregation plans. Each justice signed the opinion individually, underscoring his individual support for the notion that "no state legislator or executive or judicial officer can war against the Constitution without violating his undertaking to support it."[21] The state's actions were thus ruled unconstitutional and its "evasive schemes" illegal.

The saga of Little Rock is telling and illustrative of the massive resistance to *Brown* and the NAACP throughout the South. It is hard to imagine these kinds of confrontations occurring today—a governor calling a press conference to announce that he would defy a federal order, a president sending in federal troops to protect the rights of African-American citizens against the state militia, and legislation requiring the NAACP to identify its members. All of this, including the violence that greeted the new students, was duly recorded in the press and on television in vivid detail. And it added fuel to the fire of opponents of racism throughout the South and elsewhere.

A New Move for African-American Rights

In 1955, soon after *Brown II*, the civil rights movement took another step forward—this time in Montgomery, Alabama. Rosa Parks, the local NAACP's Youth Council advisor, decided to challenge the constitutionality of the segregated bus system. First, Parks and other NAACP officials began to raise money for litigation and made speeches around town to garner public support. Then, on December 1, 1955, Rosa Parks made history when she refused to leave her seat on a bus to move to the back to make room for a white male passenger. She was arrested for violating an Alabama law banning integration of public facilities, including buses. After she was freed on bond, Parks and the NAACP decided to enlist city clergy to help her cause. At the same time, they distributed 35,000 handbills calling for African Americans to boycott the Montgomery bus system on the day of Parks's trial. Black ministers used Sunday services to urge their members to support the boycott. On Monday morning, African Americans walked, carpooled, or used black-owned taxicabs. That night, local ministers decided that the boycott should be continued. A twenty-six-year-old minister, Martin Luther King, Jr., was selected to lead the newly formed Montgomery Improvement Association. King was new to town, and church leaders had been looking for a way to get him more involved in civil rights work.

As the boycott dragged on, Montgomery officials and local business owners began to harass the city's African-American citizens. But King urged Montgomery's African-American citizens to continue their protest. The residents held out, despite suffering personal hardship for their actions, ranging from harassment to bankruptcy to job loss. In 1956 a federal court ruled that the segregated bus system violated the equal protection clause of the Fourteenth Amendment. After a year of walking, African Americans ended their protest as the buses were ordered to integrate. The first effort at nonviolent protest had been successful. Organized boycotts and other forms of nonviolent protest, including sit-ins at segregated restaurants and bus stations, were to follow.

Formation of New Groups

The recognition and respect that King earned within the African-American community helped him to launch the Southern Christian Leadership Conference (SCLC) in 1957, soon after the end of the Montgomery bus boycott. Unlike the NAACP, which had Northern origins and had come to rely largely on litigation as a means of achieving expanded equality, the SCLC had a Southern base and was rooted more closely in black religious culture. The SCLC's philosophy reflected King's growing belief in the importance of nonviolent protest.

On February 1, 1960, students at the all-black North Carolina Agricultural and Technical College participated in the first sit-in. Angered by their inability to be served at local lunch counters and heartened by the success of the Montgomery bus boycott, black students marched to the local Woolworth's and ordered cups of coffee. They were refused service. So they sat at the counter until police came and carted them off to jail. Soon thereafter, African-American college students around the South joined together to challenge Jim Crow laws. These mass actions immediately brought extensive attention from the national news media.

Over spring break 1960, with the assistance of an $800 grant from the SCLC, 200 student delegates—black *and* white—met at Shaw University in North Carolina to consider recent sit-in actions and to plan for the future. Later that year, two more meetings were held in Atlanta, Georgia, and the Student Nonviolent Coordinating Committee (SNCC) was formed.

A prime objective of the protesters in Birmingham was to focus national attention on their cause. For the first time in American history, a majority of the public owned television sets and could see the horrors of police brutality. But the print media continued to be a powerful tool. This picture was reprinted over and over again and even frequently mentioned on the floor of Congress during debates on the Civil Rights Act of 1964. (Photo courtesy: Charles Moore/Black Star)

Among the SNCC's first leaders were Marion Barry, who would later serve as mayor of Washington, D.C. (1978–90, 1995–); John Lewis, a six term Democratic member of the House of Representatives and Deputy House Minority Whip in the 104th Congress; and Marian Wright Edelman, who became first an NAACP lawyer and later the founder and head of the Children's Defense Fund. While the SCLC generally worked with church leaders in a community, the SNCC was much more of a grassroots organization. Always perceived as more radical than the SCLC, the SNCC tended to focus its organizing activities on the young, both black and white.

In addition to joining the sit-in bandwagon, the SNCC also came to lead what were called "freedom rides," designed to focus attention on segregated public accommodations. Bands of college students and other civil rights activists traveled by bus throughout the South in an effort to force bus stations to desegregate. Often these protesters were met by angry mobs of segregationists and brutal violence, as local police chose not to defend protesters' basic constitutional rights to free speech and peaceful assembly. African Americans were not the only ones to participate in freedom rides; increasingly, white college students from the North began to play an important role in the SNCC.

While the SNCC continued to sponsor sit-ins and freedom rides, in 1963 the Reverend Martin Luther King, Jr., launched a series of massive nonviolent demonstrations in Birmingham, Alabama, long considered a major stronghold of segregation. Thousands of blacks and whites marched to Birmingham in a show of solidarity. Peaceful marchers were met there by the Birmingham Police Commissioner, who ordered his officers to use dogs, clubs, and fire hoses on the marchers. Americans across the nation watched in horror as they witnessed the brutality and abuse heaped on the protesters. As the marchers hoped, these shocking scenes helped convince President John F. Kennedy to propose important civil rights legislation.

The Civil Rights Act of 1964

The older faction of the civil rights movement, as represented by the SCLC, and the younger branch, represented by the SNCC, both sought a similar goal: full implementation of Supreme Court decisions and an end to racial segregation and discrimination.

At this historic gathering in March 1963, on the Mall in Washington, D.C., Rev. Martin Luther King, Jr., delivered his famous "I Have a Dream" speech. (Photo courtesy: Flip Schulke/Black Star)

Civil Rights Act of 1964: Legislation passed by Congress to outlaw segregation in public facilities and racial discrimination in employment, education, and voting; created the Equal Employment Opportunity Commission.

The cumulative effect of collective actions including sit-ins, boycotts, marches, and freedom rides—as well as the tragic bombings and deaths inflicted in retaliation—led Congress to pass the first major piece of civil rights legislation since the post-Civil War era.

In 1963 President Kennedy requested that Congress pass a law banning discrimination in public accommodations. Seizing the moment and recognizing the potency of a show of massive support, the Reverend Martin Luther King, Jr., called for a monumental march on Washington, D.C., to demonstrate widespread support for legislation to ban discrimination in *all* aspects of life, not just public accommodations. The March on Washington for Jobs and Freedom was held in August 1963 only a few months after the Birmingham demonstrations. More than 250,000 people heard King deliver his famous "I Have a Dream" speech from the Lincoln Memorial. Before Congress had the opportunity to vote on any legislation, however, John F. Kennedy was assassinated on November 22, 1963, in Dallas, Texas.

It was clear that national laws outlawing discrimination were the only answer: Southern legislators would never vote to repeal Jim Crow laws. It was much more feasible for African Americans to first seek national laws and then their implementation from the federal judiciary. But through the 1960s, African Americans lacked sufficient political power or the force of public opinion to sway enough congressional leaders. Their task was further stymied by loud and strong opposition from Southern members of Congress. Many of these legislators, because of the Democratic Party's total control of the South, had been in office far longer than most, and therefore held powerful committee chairmanships that were awarded on seniority. The Senate Judiciary Committee was controlled by a coalition of Southern Democrats and conservative Republicans. The House Rules Committee was chaired by a Virginian opposed to any civil rights legislation, who by virtue of his position could block such legislation in committee.

When Vice President Lyndon B. Johnson, a Southern-born former Senate majority leader, succeeded Kennedy as president, he put civil rights reform at the top of his legislative priority list and civil rights activists gained a critical ally. Thus, through the 1960s, the movement subtly changed in focus from peaceful protest and litigation to legislative lobbying. Its focus broadened from integration of school and public facilities and voting rights to issues of housing, jobs, and equal opportunity.

The push for civil rights legislation in the halls of Congress was helped by changes in public opinion. Between 1959 and 1965, Southern attitudes toward integrated schools changed enormously. The proportion of Southerners who responded that they would not mind their child's attendance at a half-black school doubled.

In spite of strong presidential support and the sway of public opinion, the Civil Rights Act of 1964 did not sail through Congress. Southern senators, led by South Carolina's Strom Thurmond, a Democrat who later switched to the Republican Party, conducted the longest filibuster in the history of the Senate. For eight weeks they held up voting on the civil rights bill until cloture (see chapter 7) was invoked and the filibuster ended. Once passed, the **Civil Rights Act of 1964:**

1. Outlawed arbitrary discrimination in voter registration and expedited voting rights lawsuits.

2. Barred discrimination in public accommodations engaged in interstate commerce.

3. Authorized the U.S. Justice Department to initiate lawsuits to desegregate public facilities and schools.

4. Provided for the withholding of federal funds from discriminatory state and local programs.

5. Prohibited discrimination in employment on grounds of race, color, religion, national origin, or sex.
6. Created the Equal Employment Opportunity Commission (EEOC) to monitor and enforce the bans on employment discrimination.

Other changes were sweeping the United States. Violence rocked the nation as ghetto riots broke out in the Northeast. Although Northern African Americans were not subject to Jim Crow laws, many lived in poverty and faced pervasive daily discrimination and its resultant frustration. Some, including Black Muslim leader Malcolm X, even argued that to survive, African Americans must separate themselves from white culture in every way. Given this growing "black power" movement and increased racial tension, it is not surprising that from 1964 to 1968, many Northern African Americans took to the streets, burning and looting to vent their rage.

Violence also marred the continued activities of civil rights workers in the South. During the summer of 1964 three civil rights workers—one black, two white—were killed in Neshoba County, Mississippi. In 1965 Martin Luther King, Jr., again led his supporters on a massive march, this time from Selma, Alabama, to the state capital in Montgomery, in support of a pending voting rights bill. Again, Southern officials unleashed a reign of terror in Selma as they used whips, dogs, cattle prods, clubs, and tear gas on the protesters. Again, Americans watched in horror as they witnessed this brutality on their television screens. This march and the public's reaction to it led to quick passage of the Voting Rights Act of 1965, which suspended the use of literacy tests and authorized the federal government to monitor all elections in areas where discrimination was found to be practiced or where less than 50 percent of the voting-age public was registered to vote in the 1964 election (see Highlight 13.3: Voting Rights).

The Effect of the Civil Rights Act of 1964

Many Southerners were adamant in their belief that the Civil Rights Act of 1964 was unconstitutional because it went beyond the scope of Congress's authority to legislate under the Constitution, and lawsuits were quickly brought to challenge the act. The first challenge to the act was heard by the Supreme Court on an expedited review (which bypasses the intermediate courts). The Court upheld its constitutionality when it found that Congress was within the legitimate scope of its commerce power as outlined in Article I.[22]

Education. One the key provisions of the Civil Rights Act of 1964 authorized the U.S. Justice Department to bring actions against school districts that failed to comply with *Brown* v. *Board of Education*. In 1964, a full decade after *Brown*, fewer than 1 percent of African-American children in the South attended integrated schools.

After *Brown*, the Charlotte–Mecklenburg School District had assigned students to the school closest to their homes without regard to race, leaving over half of African-American students attending schools that were at least 99 percent black. In *Swann* v. *Charlotte–Mecklenburg School District* (1971), the Supreme Court ruled that all vestiges of state-imposed segregation, called **de jure discrimination**, or discrimination by law, must be eliminated at once and that lower federal courts had the authority to fashion a wide variety of remedies including busing, racial quotas, and the pairing of schools to end dual, segregated school systems.[23]

In *Swann* the Court was careful to distinguish *de jure* from **de facto discrimination**, unintentional discrimination often attributable to housing patterns and/or private

de jure discrimination: Racial segregation that is a direct result of law or official policy.

de facto discrimination: Racial discrimination that results from practice (such as housing patterns or other social factors) rather than the law.

acts. The Court noted that its approval of busing was a remedy for intentional, government-imposed or -sanctioned discrimination only.

Over the years, forced, judicially imposed busing has found less and less favor with the Supreme Court, even in situations where *de jure* discrimination had earlier been proven. In 1992 the U.S. Supreme Court even ruled that in situations where all-black schools still existed in spite of a 1969 court order to dismantle the *de jure* system, a showing that the persistent segregation was not a result of the school board's actions was sufficient to remove the district from court supervision. In 1995 the Court ruled five to four that school boards can use plans to attract white suburban students to mostly minority urban schools only if both city and suburban schools still show the effects of segregation, thus overruling a lower court desegregation order.[24]

Employment. Title VII of the Civil Rights Act of 1964 prohibits employers from discriminating against employees for a variety of reasons, including race, sex, age, and national origin. (In 1978 the act was amended to prohibit discrimination based on pregnancy.)

In 1971, in one of the first major cases decided under the act, the Supreme Court found that employers could be found liable for discrimination if the *effect* of their employment practices was to exclude African Americans from certain positions.[25] African-American employees were allowed to use statistical evidence to show that they had been excluded from all but one department of the Duke Power Company, because it required employees to have a high school education or pass a special test to be eligible for promotion.

The Supreme Court ruled that although the tests did not *appear* to discriminate against African Americans, their effects—that there were no African-American employees in any other departments—were sufficient to shift the burden of proving lack of discrimination on the employer. Thus the Duke Power Company would have to prove that the tests were "a business necessity" that had a "demonstrable relationship to successful performance" (of a particular job).

The notion of "business necessity," as set out in the Civil Rights Act of 1964 and interpreted by the federal courts, was especially important for women. Women had long been kept out of many occupations on the strength of the belief that customers preferred to deal with male personnel. Conversely, males were barred from flight-attendant positions because the airlines believed that passengers preferred to be served by young, attractive women—a position not unlike the one taken by Hooters. Similarly, many large factories, manufacturing establishments, and police and fire departments refused outright to hire women by subjecting them to arbitrary height and weight requirements, which also disproportionately affected Hispanics. Like the tests declared illegal by the Court, these requirements often could not be shown to be related to job performance and were eventually ruled illegal by the federal courts.

The Women's Rights Movement. Just as in the abolition movement in the 1800s, women from all walks of life also participated in the civil rights movement. Women were important members of both the SNCC and more traditional groups like the NAACP and the SCLC, yet they often found themselves treated as second-class citizens. At one point Stokely Carmichael, chair of the SNCC, openly proclaimed: "The only position for women in the SNCC is prone."[26] Statements and attitudes like these led some women to found early women's liberation groups that were generally quite radical, small in membership, and not intended to use more conventional political tactics.

As discussed earlier, initial efforts to convince the Supreme Court to declare women enfranchised under the Fourteenth Amendment were uniformly unsuccessful.

The paternalistic attitude of the Supreme Court, and perhaps society as well, continued well into the 1970s. As late as 1961, Florida required women who wished to serve on juries to travel to the county courthouse and register for that duty. In contrast, all men who were registered voters were automatically eligible to serve. When Gwendolyn Hoyt was convicted of bludgeoning her adulterous husband to death with a baseball bat, she appealed her conviction, claiming that the exclusion of women from juries prejudiced her case. She believed that female jurors—her peers—would have been more sympathetic to her and the emotional turmoil that led to her attack on her husband and her claim of "temporary insanity." She therefore argued that her trial by an all-male jury violated her rights as guaranteed by the Fourteenth Amendment. In rejecting her contention, Justice John Harlan (the grandson of the lone dissenting justice in *Plessy*) wrote in *Hoyt* v. *Florida* (1961):

> Despite the enlightened emancipation of women from the restrictions and protections of bygone years, and their entry into many parts of community life formerly considered to be reserved to men, a woman is still regarded as the center of home and family life.[27]

These kinds of attitudes and decisions (*Hoyt* was later unanimously reversed in 1975) were not sufficient to forge a new movement for women's rights. Shortly after *Hoyt*, however, three events occurred to move women to action. In 1961, soon after his election, President John F. Kennedy created the President's Commission on the Status of Women. The Commission's report, *American Women*, released in 1963, documented pervasive discrimination against women in all walks of life. In addition, the civil rights movement and publication of Betty Friedan's *The Feminine Mystique* (1963),[28] which led some women to question their lives and status in society, added to their dawning recognition that something was wrong. Soon after, the Civil Rights Act of 1964 prohibited discrimination based not only on race, but also on sex. Ironically, that provision had been added to Title VII of the Civil Rights Act by Southern Democrats. These senators saw a prohibition against sex discrimination in employment as a joke, and viewed its addition as a means to discredit the entire act and ensure its defeat. Thus it was added at the last minute and female members of Congress seized the opportunity to garner support for the measure.

In 1966, after the **Equal Employment Opportunity Commission** failed to enforce the law as it applied to sex discrimination, women activists formed the National Organization for Women (NOW). From its inception, NOW was closely modeled on the NAACP. Women in NOW were quite similar to the founders of the NAACP; they wanted to work within the system to prevent discrimination. Initially, most of this activity was geared toward two goals: achievement of equality through passage of an equal rights amendment to the Constitution, or by judicial decision. But because the Supreme Court failed to extend constitutional protections to women, the only recourse that remained was an amendment.

The Equal Rights Amendment (ERA).   Not all women agreed with the notion of full equality for women. Members of the National Consumers' League, for example, feared that an equal rights amendment would invalidate protective legislation of the kind specifically ruled constitutional in *Muller* v. *Oregon* (1908). Nevertheless, from 1923 to 1972, a proposal for an equal rights amendment was made in every session of every Congress. Every president since Harry S Truman backed it, and by 1972 public opinion favored its ratification.

Finally, in 1972, in response to pressure from NOW, the National Women's Political Caucus, and a wide variety of other feminist groups, Congress passed the Equal

Equal Employment Opportunity Commission: Federal agency created to enforce the Civil Rights Act of 1964, which forbids discrimination on the basis of race, creed, national origin, religion, or sex in hiring, promotion, or firing.

Rights Amendment (ERA) by overwhelming majorities (84 to 8 in the Senate; 354 to 24 in the House). The amendment provided that:

- Equality of rights under the law shall not be denied or abridged by the United States or by any state on account of sex.
- The Congress shall have the power to enforce, by appropriate legislation, the provisions of this article.

Within a year twenty-two states had ratified the amendment, most by overwhelming margins. But the tide soon turned. In *Roe* v. *Wade* (1973), the Supreme Court decided that women had a constitutionally protected right to privacy that included the right to terminate a pregnancy. Almost overnight *Roe* gave the ERA's opponents political fuel. Although privacy rights and the ERA have nothing to do with each other, opponents effectively persuaded many people in states that had yet to ratify the amendment that the two were linked. If abortion was legal, why not marriages between and adoptions by homosexuals? They also claimed that the ERA and feminists were antifamily and that the ERA would force women out of their homes and into the workforce because husbands would no longer be responsible for their wives' support.

These arguments and the amendment's potential to make women eligible for the military draft brought the ratification effort to a near standstill. In 1974 and 1975, the amendment only squeaked through the Montana and North Dakota legislatures, and two states—Nebraska and Tennessee—voted to rescind their earlier ratifications.

By 1978, one year before the deadline for ratification was to expire, thirty-five states had voted for the amendment—three short of the three-fourths necessary for ratification. Efforts in key states such as Illinois and Florida failed as opposition to the ERA intensified.

Faced with the prospect of defeat, ERA supporters heavily lobbied Congress to extend the deadline. Congress extended the time period for ratification by three years, but to no avail. No additional states ratified the amendment and three more rescinded their votes.

What began as a simple correction to the Constitution turned into a highly controversial proposed change. In spite of the fact that large numbers of the public favored the ERA, opponents needed to stall ratification in only thirteen states while supporters had to convince legislators in thirty-eight. The success that women's rights activists were having in the courts was hurting the effort. When women first sought the ERA in the late 1960s, the Supreme Court had yet to rule that women were protected by the Fourteenth Amendment's equal protection clause from any kind of discrimination, thus clearly showing the need for an amendment. But as the Court widened its interpretation of the Constitution to protect women from some sorts of discrimination, in the eyes of many the need for a new amendment became less urgent.

Litigation for Equal Rights.   While several women's groups worked toward passage of the ERA, NOW and several other groups, including the Women's Rights Project of the American Civil Liberties Union (ACLU), formed litigating arms to pressure the courts. But women faced an immediate roadblock in the Supreme Court's interpretation of the equal protection clause of the Fourteenth Amendment.

The Equal Protection Clause and Constitutional Standards of Review

The Fourteenth Amendment protects all U.S. citizens from state action that violates equal protection of the laws. Most laws, however, are subject to what is called the rational basis or minimum rationality test. This lowest level of scrutiny means that governments must allege a rational foundation for any distinctions they make. Early on, however, the Supreme Court decided that certain rights were entitled to a heightened standard of review. As early as 1937, the Supreme Court recognized that certain rights were so fundamental that a very heavy burden would be placed on any government that sought to restrict those rights. As discussed in chapter 5, when fundamental rights such as First Amendment freedoms or **suspect classifications** such as race are involved, the Court uses a heightened standard of review called **strict scrutiny** to determine the constitutional validity of the challenged practices, as detailed in Table 6.2. Beginning with *Korematsu* v. *United States* (1994), which involved a constitutional challenge to the internment of Japanese Americans, Justice Hugo Black noted that "all legal restrictions which curtail the civic rights of a single racial group are immediately suspect," and should be given "the most rigid scrutiny."[29] In *Brown* v. *Board of Education of Topeka, Kansas* (1954), the Supreme Court again used the strict scrutiny standard to evaluate the constitutionality of race-based distinctions. In legal terms this means that if a statute or governmental practice makes a classification based on race, the statute is presumed to be unconstitutional unless the state can provide "compelling affirmative justifications"—that is, unless the state can prove the law in question is necessary to accomplish a permissible goal and that it is the least restrictive means through which that goal can be accomplished.

During the 1960s and into the 1970s, the Court routinely struck down as unconstitutional practices and statutes that discriminated on the basis of race. "Whites-only" public parks and recreational facilities, tax-exempt status for private schools that dis-

suspect classification: Category or class, such as race, that triggers the highest standard of scrutiny from the Supreme Court.

strict scrutiny: A heightened standard of review used by the Supreme Court to determine the constitutional validity of a challenged practice.

TABLE 6.2

The Equal Protection Clause and Standards of Review Used by the Supreme Court to Determine Whether It Has Been Violated

TYPES OF CLASSIFICATION (What kind of statutory classification is an issue?)	STANDARD OF REVIEW (What standard of review will be used?)	TEST (What does the court ask?)	EXAMPLE (How does the court apply the test?)
Fundamental freedoms: Religion, assembly, press, privacy, "suspect" classifications (including race)	Strict scrutiny or heightened standard	Is classification *necessary* to the accomplishment of a permissible state goal? Is it the least restrictive way to reach that goal?	*Brown* v. *Board of Education of Topeka, Kansas* (1954) Racial segregation not necessary to accomplish the state goal of educating its students
Gender	Intermediate standard	Does the classification serve an important governmental objective, and is it substantially related to those ends?	*Craig* v. *Boren* (1976) Keeping drunk drivers off the roads may be an important governmental objective, but allowing eighteen- to twenty-one-year-old women to drink alcoholic beverages while prohibiting men of the same age from drinking is not substantially related to that goal.
Others (including age, wealth, and sexual preference)	Minimum rationality standard	Is there any rational foundation for the discrimination?	*Romer* v. *Evans* (1996) Colorado constitutional amendment precluding any legislative, executive, or judicial action at any state or local level designed to bar discrimination based on sexual preference is not rational or reasonable.

criminated, and statutes prohibiting racial intermarriage were declared unconstitutional. In contrast, the Court refused even to consider the fact that the equal protection clause might apply to discrimination against women. Finally, in a case brought in 1971 by Ruth Bader Ginsburg as Director of the Women's Rights Project of the ACLU (see Highlight 5.1: The American Civil Liberties Union), the Supreme Court ruled that an Idaho law granting male parents automatic preference over female parents as the administrator of their deceased children's estates violated the equal protection clause of the Fourteenth Amendment.

Reed v. *Reed* (1971),[30] the Idaho case, turned the tide in terms of constitutional litigation. While the Court did not rule that sex was a suspect classification, it concluded that the equal protection clause of the Fourteenth Amendment prohibited unreasonable classifications based on sex. And in 1976 the Court ruled that sex-discrimination complaints would be judged by a new, judicially created intermediate standard of review a step below strict scrutiny. In *Craig* v. *Boren* (1976),[31] the owner of the Honk 'n' Holler Restaurant in Stillwater, Oklahoma, and Craig, a male under twenty-one, challenged the constitutionality of a state law prohibiting the sale of 3.2 percent beer to males under the age of twenty-one and to females under the age of eighteen. The state introduced a considerable amount of evidence in support of the statute, including:

- Eighteen- to twenty-year-old males were more likely to be arrested for driving under the influence than were females of the same age.

- Youths aged seventeen to twenty-one were the group most likely to be injured or to die in alcohol-related traffic accidents, with males exceeding females.

- Young men were more inclined to drink and drive than females.

The Supreme Court found that this information was "too tenuous" to support the legislation. In coming to this conclusion, the Court carved out a new "test" to be used in examining claims of sex discrimination, "[T]o withstand constitutional challenge, . . . classifications by gender must serve important governmental objectives and must be substantially related to achievement of those objectives." According to the Court an intermediate standard of review was created within what previously was a two-tier distinction—strict scrutiny/rational basis.

As *Craig* demonstrates, men, too, can use the Fourteenth Amendment to fight gender-based discrimination. Since 1976, the Court has applied the intermediate standard of constitutional review to most claims that it has heard involving gender. Thus the following kinds of practices have been found to violate the Fourteenth Amendment:

- Single-sex public nursing schools.

- Laws that consider males adults at twenty-one years but females at eighteen years.

- Laws that allow women but not men to receive alimony.

- State prosecutors' use of preemptory challenges to reject men or women to create more sympathetic juries.

- Virginia's maintenance of an all-male military college, the Virginia Military Institute.

In contrast, the Court has upheld the following governmental practices and laws:

- Draft registration provisions for males only.

- Statutory rape laws that apply only to female victims.

The level of review used by the Court is crucial. Clearly, a statute excluding African Americans from draft registration would be unconstitutional. But because gender is

North—South

POLITICS AROUND THE WORLD

Although political scientists largely agree about what the relevant civil liberties are, there is much less agreement about the complicated issues of civil rights. As we saw in the United States, it is one thing to legislate equality along racial, gender, linguistic, or other lines. It is quite another to ensure that there is real equality in people's daily lives or their access to political power. In particular, people everywhere have found that steps to do so through programs such as affirmative action in the United States are both controversial and difficult to carry out.

Problems growing out of civil rights have an even more explosive potential in Canada and Mexico. Like the United States (and almost every other country in the world), they have quite diverse populations.

Canada now faces serious problems with both its aboriginal peoples and the growing number of nonwhites who have immigrated, mostly since the 1960s. Its most serious civil rights problem, however, is linguistic rather than racial.

Slightly more than a quarter of the people in Canada are of French origin, most of whom reside in or near the province of Quebec. For nearly 200 years after the British took Quebec from the French, the province and French speakers in general lived what everyone today acknowledges to be second-class lives. Until the 1960s, however, most Quebeckers (or Québecois) were conservative and passive, thereby allowing that most inegalitarian status quo to continue.

Since then, all that has changed. Now, most Quebeckers want some sort of autonomy, if not outright independence from Canada. The Parti Québecois, which supports that viewpoint, has controlled the provincial government much of the time since then, and its related party, the Bloc Québecois, now holds the lion's share of seats in the National Assembly. So far, Quebec voters have twice turned down referenda that would have started negotiations for sovereignty-association, but federal constitutional reforms that would have given the province a kind of special status have also been rejected. At this point, it is hard to see how the Quebec problem can be solved in a way that would both satisfy Quebeckers and keep the country intact.

In Mexico, the relevant differences arise over how well an individual or group is integrated into mainstream Mexican (that is, Spanish-speaking) culture. Perhaps as much as 10 percent of the total population still only speaks one of the Indian languages and is not at all well integrated into what is a predominantly Spanish culture. They are also the poorest people, clustered in the poorest regions. Like the Québecois before the 1960s, they have not been an active force in postrevolutionary Mexican politics, but there are signs that they are becoming more so—for instance, in the recent uprisings in Chiapas and Guerrero, two of the poorest states.

not subject to the same higher standard of review that is used in racial discrimination cases, the exclusion of women from the requirements of the Military Selective Service Act was ruled permissible because the government policy was considered to serve "important governmental objectives."[32]

This history has perhaps clarified why women's rights activists continue to argue that until the passage of an equal rights amendment, women will never enjoy the same rights as men. An amendment would automatically raise the level of scrutiny that the Court applies to gender-based claims.

Statutory Remedies for Sex Discrimination.   In part because of the limits of the intermediate standard of review and the fact that the equal protection clause applies only to *governmental* discrimination, women's rights activists began to bombard the courts with sex-discrimination cases. These cases have been filed under Title VII of the Civil Rights Act, which prohibits discrimination by private (and, after 1972, public) employers, or Title IX of the Education Amendments of 1972, which bars educational institutions receiving federal funds from discriminating against female students. Key victories under Title VII include:

- Consideration of sexual harassment as sex discrimination.
- Inclusion of law firms, which many argued were *private* partnerships, in the coverage of the act.
- A broad definition of what can be considered sexual harassment.
- Allowance of voluntary affirmative action programs to redress historical discrimination against women.

Title IX, which parallels Title VII, has also greatly expanded the opportunities for women in elementary, secondary, and postsecondary institutions. Since women's groups, like the NAACP before them, saw eradication of educational discrimination as key to improving other facets of women's lives, they lobbied for it heavily. Most of today's college students did not go through school being excluded from home economics or shop classes because of their sex. Nor, probably, did many attend schools that had no team sports for females. Yet this was commonly the case in the United States prior to passage of Title IX.[33] The 1996 Olympics showed the impact of the law on women's participation in sport. There, record numbers of women competed and won.

OTHER GROUPS MOBILIZE FOR RIGHTS

*A*frican Americans and women are not the only groups that have suffered unequal treatment under the law. Denial of civil rights has led many other disadvantaged groups to mobilize to achieve greater civil rights. And their efforts to achieve those rights have many parallels to the efforts made by African Americans and women. In the wake of the successes of those two groups in achieving enhanced rights, and sometimes even before, other traditionally disenfranchised groups have organized to gain fuller equality. Many of them have also recognized that litigation and the use of test-case strategies would be key to further civil rights gains. The Ford Foundation, which had heavily funded the NAACP LDF and some women's rights litigation, also helped interested Mexican Americans to found the Mexican American Legal Defense and Education Fund (MALDEF). Established in 1968, and modeled after the NAACP LDF, MALDEF has played and continues to play a major role in expanding civil rights for Hispanics. The Ford Foundation also facilitated the 1970 creation of the Native American Rights Fund to litigate for Indian rights.

Native Americans

Native Americans are the first "true" Americans, and their status under U.S. law is unique. Under the U.S. Constitution, "Indian tribes" are considered distinct governments, a situation that has affected Native Americans' treatment by the Supreme Court in contrast to other groups of ethnic minorities. And "minority" is a term that accurately describes American Indians. It is estimated that there were as many as 10 million Indians in the New World at the time it was discovered by Europeans in the 1400s, with 3 to 4 million living in what is today the United States. By 1900 the number of Indians in the continental United States had plummeted to less than 2 million.

Many commentators would agree that for years Congress and the courts manipulated Indian law to promote the westward expansion of the United States. The Northwest Ordinance of 1787, passed by the Continental Congress, specified that "the good faith should always be observed toward the Indians; their lands and property shall never be taken from them without their consent, and their property rights, and liberty, they shall never be invaded or disturbed, unless in just and lawful wars authorized by Congress." This is not what happened. Instead, over the years, "American Indian policy has been described as 'genocide-at-law' promoting both land acquisition and cultural extermination."[34] At first, during the eighteenth and nineteenth centuries, the U.S. government isolated Indians on reservations as it confiscated their lands and denied them basic political rights. Indian reservations were administered by the federal government and Native Americans often lived in squalid conditions.

With passage of the Dawes Act in 1887, however, the government switched policies to promote assimilation over separation. Each Indian family was given land within the reservation; the rest was sold to whites, thus reducing Indian lands from about 140 million acres to about 47 million. Moreover, to encourage Native Americans to assimilate, Indian children were sent to boarding schools off the reservation and native languages and rituals were banned. In 1924 Native Americans were made U.S. citizens and given the right to vote.

Native Americans in Washington, D.C., protesting the name of the Washington Redskins football team. Similar demonstrations took place in other cities with team names offensive to Native Americans, and at least one newspaper refused to refer to offending teams by any name other than their city's. (Photo courtesy: Bill Burke/Impact Visuals)

At least in part because tribes were small and scattered (and the number of Indians declining), they formed no protest movement in reaction to these drastic policy changes. It was not until the 1960s, at the same time that women were beginning to mobilize for greater civil rights, that Indians too began to mobilize to act. Like the civil rights and women's rights movements, it had a radical as well as a more traditional branch. In 1973, for example, national attention was drawn to the plight of Indians when members of the radical American Indian Movement took over Wounded Knee, South Dakota, the site of the massacre of 150 Indians by the U.S. Army in 1890. Just two years before the protest, the treatment of Indians had been highlighted in the best-selling *Bury My Heart at Wounded Knee,*[35] which in many ways served to mobilize public opinion against the oppression of Native Americans in the same way *Uncle Tom's Cabin* had against slavery.

At the same time, just as the growing number of women in the legal profession contributed to the push to secure greater rights for women through litigation, Indians, many attracted by the American Indian Law Center at the University of New Mexico, began to file hundreds of test cases in the federal courts involving tribal fishing rights, tribal land claims, and the taxation of tribal profits. Soon the Native American Rights Fund (NARF), founded in 1970, became the NAACP LDF of the Indian rights movement when the "courts became the forum of choice for Indian tribes and their members."[36]

Native Americans have won some very important victories concerning hunting, fishing, and land rights. Native American tribes all over America have begun to sue to reclaim lands they say were stolen from them by the United States, often more than 200 years ago. One of the largest Indian land claims was filed in 1972 on behalf of the Passamaquoddie and the Penobscot tribes, who were seeking return of 12.5 million acres in Maine—about two-thirds of the entire state—and $25 billion in damages. The suit was filed by the Native American Rights Fund and the Indian Service Unit of a legal services office that was funded by the U.S. Office of Economic Opportunity. It took intervention from the White House before a settlement was reached in 1980, giving each tribe over $40 million.

Native Americans are also litigating to gain access to their sacred places. All over the nation they have filed lawsuits to stop the building of roads and new construction on ancient burial grounds or other sacred spots. "We are in a battle for the survival of our very way of life," said one tribal leader. "The land is gone. All we've got left is our religion."[37]

But Native Americans have not fared nearly so well in areas such as religious freedom, especially where tribal practices come into conflict with state law. As noted in chapter 5, the Supreme Court used the rational basis test to rule that a state could infringe religious exercise (use of peyote as a sacrament in religious ceremonies) by a neutral law, and limited their access to religious sites during timber harvesting. Congress, however, quickly acted to restore some of those rights through passage of the Religious Freedom Restoration Act.

Given the uncertain and uneven treatment of Indians by the U.S Supreme Court, in the 1990s Congress has replaced the courts as the preferred forum of Native Americans.[38] The 1992 election of Ben Nighthorse Campbell (R–Colo.) as the only Native American in the U.S. Senate also has heightened legislative sensitivity to these issues. Campbell, for example, introduced a bill to prevent the U.S. government from transferring property to facilitate building a new football stadium for the Washington Redskins unless the team's owner changes the name, which Campbell considers derogatory to Native Americans.

Hispanic Americans

Like women's efforts to garner expanded political rights, Hispanic Americans, too, can date their first real push for equal rights to 1965–75. This civil rights movement included many tactics drawn from the African-American civil rights movement, including sit-ins, boycotts, marches, and other activities designed to attract publicity to their cause.[39] Like blacks, women, and Native Americans, Hispanic Americans have some radical militant groups, but have been dominated by more conventional organizations. The more conventional groups have pressed for Chicano and Latino studies programs and have built up ties with existing, powerful mainstream associations, including unions and the Roman Catholic church.

They have also relied heavily on litigation to secure greater rights. Key groups are the Mexican American Legal Defense and Educational Fund (MALDEF) and the Puerto Rican Legal Defense and Educational Fund.

MALDEF was founded in 1968 after members of the League of United Latin American Citizens (LULAC), the nation's largest and oldest Hispanic organization, met with NAACP LDF leaders and, with their assistance, secured a $2.2 million start-up grant from the Ford Foundation. It was created to bring test cases to force school districts to allocate more funds to schools with predominantly low-income minority populations, to implement bilingual education programs, to force employers to hire Chicanos, and to challenge election rules and apportionment plans that undercount or dilute Hispanic voting power. Just as Native American and women's rights groups had depended on the legal expertise of their own constituents, MALDEF quickly drew on the talent of Hispanic attorneys to staff offices in San Antonio and Los Angeles. It also started a scholarship fund to train more Hispanic attorneys, and established a New Mexico branch office in conjunction with the New Mexico Law School.

MALDEF lawyers quickly moved to bring major test cases to the U.S. Supreme Court, both to enhance the visibility of their cause and to win cases. MALDEF has been quite successful in its efforts to expand voting rights and opportunities to Hispanic Americans. In 1973, for example, it won a major victory when the Supreme Court ruled that multimember electoral districts (in which more than one person represents a single district) in Texas discriminated against African Americans and Hispanic Americans.[40] In multimember systems, legislatures generally add members to larger districts instead of drawing smaller districts in which a minority candidate could get a majority of the votes necessary to win.

While enjoying greater access to elective office, Hispanics still suffer discrimination. Language barriers and substandard educational opportunities continue to plague their progress. In 1973 the U.S. Supreme Court refused to find that a Texas law under which the state appropriated a set dollar amount to each school district per pupil, while allowing wealthier districts to enrich educational programs from other funds, violated the equal protection clause of the Fourteenth Amendment.[41] The lower courts had found that wealth was a suspect classification (see Table 6.1) entitled to strict scrutiny. Using that test, the lower courts had found the Texas plan discriminatory. In contrast, a divided Supreme Court concluded that education was not a fundamental right (see chapter 5), and that a charge of discrimination based on wealth would be examined only under a minimal standard of review (the rational basis test).

Throughout the 1970s and 1980s, inter-school-district inequalities continued, and frequently had their greatest impact on poor Hispanic children, who often had inferior educational opportunities. Recognizing that the increasingly conservative federal courts (see chapter 10) offered no recourse, in 1984 MALDEF filed suit in state court alleging that the Texas school finance policy violated the Texas constitution. In 1989 it won a case in which a state district judge elected by the voters of only a single county declared the state's entire method of financing public schools to be unconstitutional under the state constitution.

Homosexuals

Homosexuals have had an even harder time than African Americans, women, Native Americans, or Hispanics in achieving fuller rights. Gays do, however, have on average far higher household incomes and educational levels than do these other groups. And they are beginning to convert these advantages into political clout at the ballot box. As discussed in chapter 5, the cause of gay and lesbian rights, like that of African Americans and women early in their quest for greater civil rights, did not fare well in the Supreme Court initially. In the late 1970s, the Lambda Legal Defense and Education Fund, the Lesbian Rights Project, and Gay and Lesbian Advocates and Defenders were founded by gay and lesbian activists dedicated to ending legal restrictions on the civil rights of homosexuals. Although these groups have won important legal victories concerning HIV/AIDS discrimination, insurance policy survivor benefits, and even some employment issues, they generally have not been as successful as other historically legally disadvantaged groups.

In *Bowers* v. *Hardwick* (1986), for example, the Supreme Court ruled that a Georgia law that made private acts of consensual sodomy illegal (whether practiced by homosexuals or by heterosexual married adults) was constitutional. Gay and lesbian rights groups had argued that a constitutional right to privacy included the right to engage in consensual sex within one's home, but the Court disagreed. Although privacy rights may attach to relations of "family, marriage, or procreation," those rights did not extend to homosexuals, wrote Justice Byron White for the Court. In a concurring opinion—his last written on the Court—Chief Justice Warren Burger called sodomy "the infamous crime against nature."[42]

The public's and Congress's discomfort with gay and lesbian rights can be seen most clearly in the controversy that occurred after President Clinton attempted to lift the ban on gays in the armed services. Clinton tried to get an absolute ban on discrimination against homosexuals, who were subject to immediate discharge if their sexual orientation was discovered. Military leaders and Senator Sam Nunn (D–Ga.), as head of the Senate Armed Services Committee, led the effort against Clinton's proposal. Eventually, Clinton and the Senate leaders compromised on what was called the "Don't ask, don't tell" policy. It stipulated that gays and lesbians would no longer be asked if they were homosexual, but barred them from revealing their sexual orientation (under threat of discharge from the service). But when the Senate finally voted on the "compromise," its version of the new policy labeled homosexuality "an unacceptable risk" to morale. In spite of gay and lesbian groups' labeling the new policy "lie and hide," the Clinton administration chose to back off on the issue, correctly sensing only minimal support in Congress.

The Supreme Court's unwillingness to expand privacy rights or special constitutional protections to homosexuals, and Congress's failure to end discrimination in the military, has led many gay and lesbian rights groups to other, potentially more responsive, political forums: state and local governments. Around the nation, such groups have lobbied for antidiscrimination legislation with mixed success. In 1992, for example, Colorado voters passed a state constitutional amendment that *rescinded* several local gay and lesbian rights ordinances and also prevented the adoption of any such measures. The U.S. Supreme Court, however, ruled that the amendment was unconstitutional. Although the Court used the rational basis test to invalidate the amendment, it was the first time ever that a majority of the justices applied the equal protection clause of the Fourteenth Amendment to prevent discrimination against homosexuals.[43]

Disabled Americans

Disabled Americans also have lobbied hard for antidiscrimination legislation. In the aftermath of World War II, many veterans returned to a nation unequipped to handle their disabilities. The Korean and Vietnam wars made the problems of disabled veterans all the more clear. These disabled veterans saw the successes of African Americans, women, and other minorities, and they too began to lobby for greater protection against discrimination. In 1990, in coalition with other disabled people, veterans were finally able to convince Congress to pass the Americans with Disabilities Act. The statute defines a disabled person as someone with a physical or mental impairment that limits one or more "life activities," or who has a record of such impairment. It thus extends the protections of the Civil Rights Act of 1964 to all of those with physical or mental disabilities, including people with AIDS. It guarantees access to public facilities, employment, and communication services. It also requires employers to acquire or modify work equipment, adjust work schedules, and make existing facilities accessible. This means, for example, that buildings must be accessible to those in wheelchairs, and telecommunications devices be provided for deaf employees.

Simply changing the law, while often an important first step in achieving civil rights, is not the end of the process. Attitudes must also change. And, as history has shown, that can be a very long process.

In May 1993, members of ADAPT (Americans Disabled for Access to Public Transportation) protested and marched in Washington, D.C., to draw attention to the need for full implementation of the Americans with Disabilities Act. (Photo courtesy: Rick Reinhard/Impact Visuals)

CHANGING CIVIL RIGHTS

*T*he Civil Rights Act of 1964 was passed by a Democratic Congress at the urgings of a Democratic president, Lyndon B. Johnson. Discrimination was rampant and majorities of the public supported legislation to end overt forms of discrimination. Over the years, public attitudes about race and race discrimination also changed, as revealed in Figure 6.1. While most Americans agree that discrimination is wrong, most whites—57 percent—today believe that affirmative action programs are no longer needed although 86 percent thought that those programs were needed thirty years ago, as revealed in Figure 6.1. White men—in particular, 82 percent of them—believe that *qualified* minorities should not receive preference over equally qualified whites.

A 1994 *Times Mirror* poll revealed that Americans were less concerned about race and racial issues than in any poll since 1987. Fifty-one percent of all whites surveyed believed that the United States had gone "too far" in pushing equal rights, as opposed to only 26 percent of black respondents. Moreover, only 25 percent of white respondents agreed that "every possible effort" should be made to help minorities. And since 59 percent responded that blacks can't get ahead because it's "their own fault," it becomes easier to understand the hostility of many Americans toward affirmative action programs.[44]

Affirmative Action

How did affirmative action come to be such a controversial issue and one where attitudes, especially white attitudes, appear to be changing at the same time the federal courts and the national legislature is debating—and often siding against the continuance of—affirmative action programs? The civil rights debate has often centered on the question of equality of opportunity versus equality of results. Most civil rights and women's rights organizations argue that the lingering and pervasive burdens of racism and sexism can be overcome only by taking race or gender into account in fashioning remedies for discrimination. They argue that the Constitution is not and should not be blind to color or sex. Therefore busing should be used to integrate schools, and women should be given child-care assistance to allow them to compete equally in the marketplace.

The counter-argument holds that if it was once wrong to use labels to discriminate against a group, it should be wrong to use those same labels to help a group. Laws should be neutral or color-blind. According to this view, quotas and other forms of **affirmative action,** policies designed to give special attention or compensatory treatment to members of a previously disadvantaged group, should be illegal. As early as 1871, Frederick Douglass ridiculed the idea of racial quotas, arguing that they would promote "an image of blacks as privileged wards of the state." They were "absurd as a matter of practice" because some could use them to argue that blacks "should constitute one-eighth of the poets, statesmen, scholars, authors and philosophers."

The debate over affirmative action and equality of opportunity became particularly intense during the Reagan years in the wake of two court cases that were generally decided in favor of affirmative action shortly before Reagan's election. In 1978 the Supreme

affirmative action: A policy or program designed to redress prior discrimination.

FIGURE 6.1

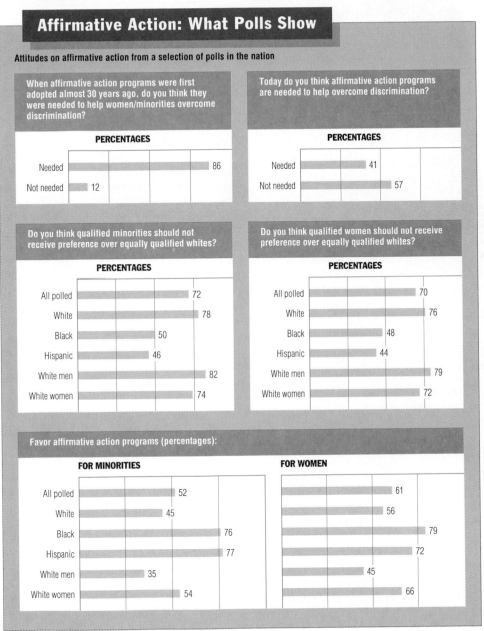

Affirmative Action: What Polls Show

Attitudes on affirmative action from a selection of polls in the nation

When affirmative action programs were first adopted almost 30 years ago, do you think they were needed to help women/minorities overcome discrimination?

PERCENTAGES

Needed	86
Not needed	12

Today do you think affirmative action programs are needed to help overcome discrimination?

PERCENTAGES

Needed	41
Not needed	57

Do you think qualified minorities should not receive preference over equally qualified whites?

PERCENTAGES

All polled	72
White	78
Black	50
Hispanic	46
White men	82
White women	74

Do you think qualified women should not receive preference over equally qualified whites?

PERCENTAGES

All polled	70
White	76
Black	48
Hispanic	44
White men	79
White women	72

Favor affirmative action programs (percentages):

FOR MINORITIES

All polled	52
White	45
Black	76
Hispanic	77
White men	35
White women	54

FOR WOMEN

All polled	61
White	56
Black	79
Hispanic	72
White men	45
White women	66

SOURCE: *Los Angeles Times* poll of 1,007 voters, March 15–19, 1995; Gallup Poll for CNN, *USA Today* Feb. 24–26, 1995; Field Poll of 725 California voters, Feb. 23–March 1, 1995; *Atlanta Journal/Constitution*, June 13, 1995.

Court for the first time fully addressed the issue of affirmative action. Alan Bakke, a thirty-one-year-old paramedic, sought admission to several medical schools and was rejected because of his age. The next year, he applied to the University of California at Davis and was placed on its waiting list. The Davis Medical School maintained two separate admissions committees—one for white students and another for minority students.

Politics Now

Affirmative Action as a Campaign Issue in the 1996 Presidential Race

In the aftermath of the Supreme Court's action in 1995, which could make most federal affirmative action programs extinct, the Clinton administration ordered a complete review of all existing federal affirmative action programs. Aides were faced with the task of searching for ways to acknowledge the legitimacy of some affirmative action programs to appease blacks—who are at the core of Clinton's Democratic support—and at the same time acknowledge the brewing public dislike and resentment of affirmative action programs.

Democratic political strategists said the task for Clinton was to "get affirmative action off his political plate. For Democrats to have a national debate over affirmative action can only hurt us."* Republicans in Congress, however, were not nearly so reticent. Sensing that affirmative action was a hot point for many of their target voters, they seized the opportunity to hold congressional hearings attacking affirmative action programs.

In response to the question: Do you favor or oppose rewriting existing laws and regulations that require affirmative action in hiring, promotion, college admission and housing? Why do you feel this way? What changes, if any, would you make in this area? Republican presidential candidate Bob Dole responded: "Bob Dole opposes quotas, set-asides, and other preferences that favor individuals simply because they belong to a particular group. He supports steps to remedy proven past discrimination against individuals and supports efforts to recruit qualified women and minorities so long as these efforts do not resort to preferences. Bob Dole introduced legislation that ends the federal government's practice of giving preference to individuals because they happen to belong to a particular group."** The Republican Party platform also came out squarely against affirmative action.

In contrast, Bill Clinton imposed a three year moratorium on new affirmative action programs while they are reviewed. Unlike Dole, however, he promised not to end affirmative action programs favoring modest tinkering over elimination. The 1996 Democratic platform, in fact, stipulated, "When it comes to affirmative action, we should mend it, not end it."*** Which party's platform comes closer to your view?

*Judy Keen, "Affirmative Action Takes a New Turn for '96 Race," *USA Today* (June 13, 1995): 5A.

**Politics USA, Issues '96 (www).

***Democratic National Convention. www.

Bakke was not admitted to the school, although his grades and standardized test scores were higher than those of all of the African-American students admitted to the school. In *Regents of the University of California* v. *Bakke* (1978),[45] a sharply divided Court concluded that Bakke's rejection had been illegal because the use of strict quotas was inappropriate. The medical school, however, was free to "take race into account."

Bakke was quickly followed in 1979 by another case in which the Court ruled that a factory and a union could voluntarily adopt a quota system in selecting black workers over more senior white workers for a training program. These kinds of programs outraged blue-collar Americans who had traditionally voted for the Democratic Party. In 1980 they abandoned the party in droves as they supported Ronald Reagan, an ardent foe of affirmative action.

For a while, in spite of the addition of Justice Sandra Day O'Connor to the Court, the Court continued to uphold affirmative action plans, especially when there was clear-cut evidence of prior discrimination, although it was by five-to-four votes. In 1987, for example, the Court for the first time ruled that a public employer could use a voluntary plan to promote women even if there was no judicial finding of prior discrimination.[46]

Alan Bakke, whose initial rejection from medical school led to an important Supreme Court ruling on affirmative action, was ultimately admitted to the medical school he sued. Here, he is shown at his 1982 medical school graduation. He did well enough in medical school to be selected to intern at the prestigious Mayo Clinic. (Photo courtesy: UPI/Bettmann Newsphotos)

In all these affirmative action cases, the Reagan administration strongly urged the Court to invalidate the plans in question, but to no avail. With changes on the Court, however, including the 1986 elevation of William Rehnquist to Chief Justice, a strong opponent of affirmative action, the continued efforts of the Reagan administration finally began to pay off as the Court heard a new series of cases signaling an end to the advances in civil rights law. In a three-month period in 1989, the Supreme Court handed down five civil rights decisions limiting affirmative action programs and making it harder to prove employment discrimination.

The Legislative Response. In February 1990 congressional and civil rights leaders unveiled legislation designed to overrule the Court's rulings, which, according to the bill's sponsor, "were an abrupt and unfortunate departure from its historic vigilance in protecting" the rights of minorities."[47] The bill passed both houses of Congress but was vetoed by President Reagan's successor, George Bush, and Congress failed to override the veto. In late 1991, however, Congress and the White House reached a compromise on a weaker version of the civil rights bill, which was passed by overwhelming majorities in both the House (381 to 31) and Senate (93 to 5). The Civil Rights Act of 1991 overruled the Supreme Court rulings noted above, but specifically prohibited the use of quotas.

The Supreme Court, however, has not stayed silent on the issue. In 1995 the U.S. Supreme Court ruled that Congress, like the states, must show that affirmative action programs meet the strict scrutiny test noted on page 209.[48] Today, in a decided retreat from its decisions in the late 1970s, the Court appears to allow race-based preferences only if they are narrowly tailored to meet unique circumstances.

In 1996, the 5th U.S. Circuit Court of Appeals ruled that the University of Texas Law School's affirmative action admissions program was unconstitutional, throwing college and university admissions programs in Texas, Oklahoma, and Mississippi (the three states in the 5th Circuit) into turmoil. Later that year, the U.S. Supreme Court refused to hear the case, thereby allowing the Court of Appeals decision to stand.[49] *Hopwood* v. *Texas* was filed on behalf of rejected white applicants who would automatically

have been admitted (based on grades and LSAT scores) had they been African American or Mexican American. While Justices Ginsburg and Souter noted that "whether it is constitutional for a public college or graduate school to use race or national origin as a factor in its admission process is an issue of great national importance," all nine justices decided to wait for a better case to address the issue.

Nevertheless, affirmative action *is* an issue of concern to many, including political candidates, as highlighted in Politics Now: Affirmative Action as a Campaign Issue in the 1996 Presidential Race.

Race- and gender-based remedies, initially designed by governments to allow them to redress the effects of decades of state-imposed discrimination, are now quickly going out of political favor—at least among whites, who still constitute a majority of legislators on all levels of government. If the Constitution is based on the premise of majority rule with protection of minority rights, is a governmental retreat on affirmative action a betrayal of minority interests or a validation that earlier programs designed to eliminate the vestiges of discrimination have worked?

Ideas about race, sex, and affirmative action aren't the only notions changing about civil rights. As the national government and the federal government back away from rights protection, some civil rights activists see state courts as possible bright lights. What is called the new judicial federalism generally refers to the authority of a state court to interpret its state constitution so as to provide broader rights protections than those recognized by U.S. Supreme Court interpretation of the federal Constitution. Such state decisions are immune from Supreme Court review when they are based on "independent and adequate" state constitutional grounds.

In a 1970 decision, for instance, the Alaska Supreme Court wrote:

> While we must enforce the minimum constitutional standards imposed upon us by the United States Supreme Court's interpretation of the Fourteenth Amendment, we are free, and we are under a duty to develop additional constitutional rights and privileges under our Alaska Constitution. . . . We need not stand by

idly and passively, waiting for constitutional direction from the highest court of the land.

The new judicial federalism revives some basic questions about rights. If rights are universal, should they not apply equally everywhere? If not, what rights are universal, and what rights can vary among states? Just as women once crossed state lines to obtain abortions, will ambulances carry people across borders to states with more liberal right-to-die laws? Will some ambulances go in the opposite direction, carrying patients away from relatives eager to "pull the plug" under liberal state rules?

Although universal rights may seem to be the natural order, independent state constitutions offer opportunities to entrench certain rights, at least in some places, when the nation or its highest court cannot agree on applying these rights. We have already seen signs of this with regard to privacy, victims' rights, women's rights, and environmental rights provisions in some state constitutions.[50]

SUMMARY

While the Framers and other Americans basked in the glory of the newly adopted Constitution and Bill of Rights, their protections did not extend to all Americans. In this chapter we have shown how rights have been expanded to ever-increasing segments of the population. To that end, we have made the following points:

1. Slavery, Abolition, and Winning the Right to Vote, 1800–85.

When the Framers tried to "compromise" on the issue of slavery, they only postponed dealing with a volatile question that was later to rip the nation apart. Ultimately, the Civil War was fought to end slavery. Among its results were the triumph of the abolitionist position and adoption of the Thirteenth, Fourteenth, and Fifteenth amendments. During this period women also sought expanded rights, especially the right to vote, but to no avail.

2. The Push for Equality, 1885–1954.

Although the Civil War amendments were added to the Constitution, the Supreme Court limited their application. As Jim Crow laws were passed throughout the South, the NAACP was founded in the early 1900s to press for equal rights for African Americans. Women's groups were also active during this period, successfully lobbying for passage of the Nineteenth Amendment, which assured them the right to vote.

First women's groups such as the National Consumers' League, and then others, including the NAACP, began to view litigation as a means to their ends. The NCL was forced to court to argue for the constitutionality of legislation protecting women workers; in contrast, the NAACP sought the Court's help in securing equality under the Constitution.

3. The Civil Rights Movement.

In 1954 the U.S. Supreme Court ruled in *Brown* v. *Board of Education of Topeka, Kansas* that state-segregated school systems were unconstitutional. This victory empowered African Americans as they sought an end to other forms of pervasive discrimination. Bus boycotts and sit-ins were common tactics. As new groups were formed, freedom rides, pressure for voting rights, and massive nonviolent demonstrations became common "lobbying" tactics. This activity culminated in the passage of the

Civil Rights Act of 1964 and the Voting Rights Act of 1965. These acts gave African-American and women's rights groups two potential weapons in their legal arsenals: They could attack private discrimination under the Civil Rights Act, or state-sanctioned discrimination under the equal protection clause of the Fourteenth Amendment. Over the years the Supreme Court developed different tests to determine the constitutionality of various forms of discrimination. In general, strict scrutiny, the most stringent standard, was applied to race-based claims. An intermediate standard of review was developed to assess the constitutionality of sex discrimination claims.

4. Other Groups Mobilize for Rights.

Building on the successes of African Americans and women, other groups, including Native Americans, Hispanic Americans, homosexuals, and the disabled, organized to litigate for expanded civil rights as well as to lobby for antidiscrimination laws.

5. Changing Civil Rights.

Although 1960s civil rights legislation was at first widely acclaimed in most sections of the country, lax enforcement soon plagued many of its provisions. Affirmative action programs came under particular attack as Americans' views of acceptable remedial action changed.

KEY TERMS

affirmative action, p. 218
Black Codes, p. 189
Brown v. *Board of Education of Topeka,
    Kansas* p. 199
civil rights, p. 184
Civil Rights Act of 1964, p. 204
Civil Rights Cases, p. 192
de facto discrimination, p. 205
de jure discrimination, p. 205
Equal Employment Opportunity Commission,
    p. 207

equal protection clause, p. 199
Fifteenth Amendment, p. 191
Fourteenth Amendment, p. 190
franchise, p. 187
grandfather clause, p. 193
Jim Crow laws, p. 192
Plessy v. *Ferguson,* p. 193
strict scrutiny, p. 209
suffrage movement, p. 196
suspect classification, p. 209
Thirteenth Amendment, p. 189

SELECTED READINGS

Bullock, Charles III, and Charles Lamb, eds. *Implementation of Civil Rights Policy.* Maunder, CA: Brooks/Cole, 1984.

Freeman, Jo. *The Politics of Women's Liberation.* New York: Longman, 1975.

Hacker, Andrew. *Two Nations: Black and White, Separate, Hostile, Unequal.* New York: Ballantine Books, 1992.

Kluger, Richard. *Simple Justice.* New York: Vintage, 1975.

Mansbridge, Jane J. *Why We Lost the ERA.* Chicago: University of Chicago Press, 1986.

McClain, Paula D., and Joseph Stewart, Jr. "Can We All Get Along?" *Racial and Ethnic Minorities in American Politics.* Boulder, CO: Westview Press, 1995.

McGlen, Nancy E., and Karen O'Connor. *Women, Politics and American Society.* Englewood Cliffs, NJ: Prentice Hall, 1995.

Verba, Sidney, and Gary R. Orren. *Equality in America: The View from the Top*. Cambridge, MA: Harvard University Press, 1985.

Vose, Clement E. *Constitutional Change: Amendment Politics and Supreme Court Litigation Since 1900*. Lexington, MA: Heath, 1972.

Williams, Juan. *Eyes on the Prize: America's Civil Rights Years, 1954–1965*. New York: Penguin, 1987.

Woodward, C. Vann. *The Strange Career of Jim Crow*. New York: Oxford University Press, 1957.

(Photo courtesy: John Duricka/AP Photo)

CONGRESS

*I*n November 1994 the frustration of the American public came through loud and clear at the ballot box. The 1994 elections gave Republicans control of both chambers of Congress for the first time in forty years. Being the minority party in the House for so long had given the Republicans plenty of time to think about how they would change things if they were in charge, and the new leadership sprang into action. A new session of Congress often gets off to a slow start, but Speaker Newt Gingrich (R–Ga.) was determined to demonstrate that dramatic change was under way. After taking the oath of office on January 4, 1995, the House went into an extended session. By the time it adjourned at 2:24 A.M. on January 5, a number of changes in the operation of the House had been adopted. The changes pushed through in the marathon session included:

- elimination of three standing committees—District of Columbia, Merchant Marine and Fisheries, and Post Office and Civil Service
- elimination of 600 committee staff positions
- restriction on the time a Speaker can serve in that position to eight years
- imposition of limits on how long a representative can chair a committee or subcommittee
- ban on the simultaneous referral of legislation to more than one committee
- elimination of proxy voting in committees and subcommittees
- requirement of a roll-call vote on all bills and conference reports that appropriate funds and raise taxes

On the second day of the session, appropriate congressional committees began hearings on the Republican agenda. The new majority had campaigned on what Gingrich dubbed a Contract with America. (Critics who felt that the proposed legislation threatened needed social programs labeled the package of bills the "Contract *on* America.") To show his party's commitment to change, Gingrich had promised that the ten reforms in the Contract would be voted on by the House during the first 100 days of the 104th Congress.

On April 5, House Republicans voted on the last item of their Contract with more than a week to spare. In three months of furious activity, the House voted to make antidiscrimination laws applicable to itself, to give the president a line-item veto, and to require the federal government to help pay the costs when new standards were imposed on state and local governments. Its last action was a

$189 billion tax cut. The one item on the agenda that was *not* adopted in the House was a constitutional amendment to limit the amount of time a person could serve in Congress. As a constitutional amendment, this proposal needed the support of two-thirds of the members of both chambers, a goal that could not be achieved without support from Democrats.

The House clearly worked overtime in early 1995, drafting legislation and passing it. During January and February of 1995, the House cast 175 roll calls, six times the number for the comparable period in recent years.[1] The Senate, which was not rejuvenated by an influx of new blood comparable to the seventy-three GOP House freshmen, moved at a more stately pace. By the end of 1995, it had not taken up all of the legislation that flew through the House in the first quarter of the year.

The more deliberate approach of the Senate reflects differences between the two chambers, which the Founding Fathers anticipated. The House, generally thought to be closer to the public, with its entire membership having to seek re-election every two years, acted on what it perceived to be widespread frustration with politics as usual. In the Senate, where two-thirds of the members did not face voters in 1994, the need for change was not seen as all that urgent. Not until Senator Robert Dole (R–Kan.), had wrapped up enough delegates to win his party's presidential nomination did the Senate get around to acting on some of the items that had passed the House more than a year earlier.

The relationship between Americans and these very different chambers of Congress is as schizophrenic as the relationship between the House and Senate itself. As each congressional representative pursues what appears to be his or her *individually* rational incentives to act on behalf of constituents, it can create centrifugal pressures that undermine Congress' *collective* capacity to get things done. Over the past three decades, changes both inside and outside Congress have enhanced the ability of congressional representatives to be somewhat more individualistic than in the past; this arguably has weakened the institution's collective capacities even more. Is it any wonder that, before the 1994 midterm elections, public confidence in Congress was at only 8 percent? This general disapproval of Congress as a whole stands in sharp contrast to the public's generally high level of support for individual representatives. One 1994 poll, for example, found that 59 percent of those polled believed that their own representatives deserved another term.[2] Even more significant, the rate at which incumbents are reelected to the House continues to exceed 90 percent, despite the chamber's poor standing with the public. Part of the public's strange split on these issues may stem from the dual roles that Congress plays—its members must combine and balance their roles as law and policy makers with their role as representatives selected to look after and serve the best interests of their constituents. Not surprisingly, this balancing act often results in role conflict.

In this chapter we analyze the powers of Congress and the competing roles members of Congress play as they represent the interests of their constituents, make laws, and oversee the actions of the other two branches of government. We also see that, as these functions have changed throughout U.S. history, so has Congress itself. We will:

- Look at *the roots of the legislative branch* to better understand its place today.

- Examine what *the Constitution* has to say about Congress—the legislative branch of government. We also examine the *consequences of redistricting* on the House of Representatives and then look at the *constitutional powers* of Congress.

- Look at *the membership of Congress,* how members get elected, and how they spend their days.
- Describe *how Congress is organized.* We compare the two chambers and how their differences affect the course of legislation.
- Outline *how Congress makes laws.*
- Examine the various factors that influence *how members of Congress make decisions.*
- Discuss the ever-changing *relationship between Congress and the president.*
- Review the *changes and reforms* working their way through Congress today.

THE ROOTS OF THE LEGISLATIVE BRANCH

*A*s discussed in chapter 2, Congress's powers evolved from Americans' experiences in the colonies and under the Articles of Confederation. When the colonists came to the New World, their general approval of Britain's parliamentary system led them to adopt similar two-house legislative bodies in the individual colonies. One house was directly elected by the people; the other was a Crown-appointed council that worked under the authority of the colonial government.

The colonial assemblies were originally established as advisory bodies to the royal governors appointed by the king. Gradually, however, they assumed more power and authority in each colony, particularly over taxation and spending. The assemblies also legislated on religious issues and established quality standards for such colonial goods as flour, rice, tobacco, and rum. Before the American Revolution, colonists turned to their colonial legislatures (the only bodies elected directly by the "people") to represent and defend their interests against British infringement.

The first truly national legislature in the colonies, the First Continental Congress, met in Philadelphia in 1774 to develop a common colonial response to the Coercive Acts. All the colonies except Georgia sent a representative. Even though this Congress had no power to force compliance, it advised each colony to establish a militia and organized an economic boycott of British goods, among other things (see chapter 2).

By the time the Second Continental Congress met in Philadelphia in May 1775, fighting had broken out at Lexington and Concord. The Congress quickly helped the now-united colonies gear up for war, raise an army, and officially adopt the Declaration of Independence. During the next five years, the Congress directed the war effort and administered a central government. But it did so with little money or stability—because of the war, it had to move from city to city.

Although the Articles of Confederation were drafted and adopted by the Second Continental Congress in 1777, the states did not ratify them until 1781. Still, throughout the Revolutionary War, the Congress exercised the powers the Articles granted it: to declare war, raise an army, make treaties with foreign nations, and coin money. As described in chapter 2, however, the Congress had no independent sources of income; it had to depend on the states for money and supplies.

After the war the states began acting once again as if they were separate nations rather than parts of one nation, despite the national government that was created under the Articles of Confederation. The "national" government, moreover, was insufficient to establish the new nation securely and to serve its needs. Discontent with the Articles grew, and led eventually to the Constitutional Convention in Philadelphia in 1787.

THE CONSTITUTION AND THE LEGISLATIVE BRANCH OF GOVERNMENT

bicameral legislature: A legislature divided into two houses; the U.S. Congress and every U.S. state legislature are bicameral (except Nebraska, which is unicameral).

Article I of the Constitution created the legislative branch of government we know today. Any two-house legislature, such as the one created by the Framers, is called a **bicameral legislature.** All states except Nebraska, which has a one-house or *unicameral legislature,* follow this model. As discussed in chapter 2, the Great Compromise resulted in the creation of an upper house, the Senate, and a lower house, the House of Representatives. Each state is represented in the Senate by two senators, regardless of the state's population. The number of representatives each state sends to the House of Representatives, in contrast, is determined by that state's population.

The U.S. Constitution sets out the formal, or legal, requirements for membership in the House and Senate. House members must be at least twenty-five years of age; Senators, thirty. Members of the House must have resided in the United States for at least seven years; those elected to the Senate, nine. And representatives and senators must be legal residents of the states from which they are elected.

Members of each body were to be elected differently and would thus represent different interests and constituencies. Senators were to be elected to six-year terms by state legislatures, and one-third of them would be up for reelection every two years. Senators were to be tied to their state legislatures closely and were expected to represent those interests in the Senate. State legislators lost this influence with ratification of the Seventeenth Amendment in 1913, which provides for the direct election of senators by the voters.

In contrast to senators' six-year terms, members of the House of Representatives were to be elected to two-year terms by a vote of the eligible voters in each congressional district. It was expected that the House would be the more "democratic" branch of government because its members would be more responsible to the people (because they were directly elected by them) and more responsive to them (because they were up for reelection every two years).

Apportionment and Redistricting

The U.S. Constitution requires that a census, which entails the counting of all Americans, be conducted every ten years. Until the first census could be taken, the Constitution fixed the number of representatives in the House at sixty-five. In 1790, then, one member represented 37,000 people. As the population of the new nation grew and states were added to the Union, the House became larger and larger. In 1910 it expanded to 435 members, and in 1929 its size was fixed at that number by statute.

redistricting: The redrawing of congressional districts to reflect increases or decreases in seats allotted to the states, as well as population shifts within a state.

Because the Constitution requires that representation in the House be based on state population, congressional districts must be redrawn by state legislatures to reflect population shifts, so that each member in Congress will represent approximately the same number of residents. This process of redrawing congressional districts to reflect increases or decreases in seats allotted to the states, as well as population shifts within a state, is called **redistricting.** When shifts occur in the national population, states gain or lose congressional seats. For example, in the 1990 census (as in most censuses since 1960), many Northeastern states showed a population decline and lost congressional seats, whereas states in the South, Southwest, and West (the sunbelt) showed great population growth and gained seats. For example, California picked up seven seats in 1990 for a total of fifty-two seats. In contrast, Alaska, Delaware, Montana, North Dakota, South Dakota, Vermont, and Wyoming, the least populous states, have only one representative each (but two senators).

Through redistricting, the political party in each statehouse with the greatest number of members tries to assure that the maximum number of its party members can be elected to Congress. This redistricting process, which has gone on since the first census in 1790, often involves what is called **gerrymandering.** The term was first coined in 1812, when the powerful Republican governor of Massachusetts, Elbridge Gerry, persuaded the state legislature to create the oddly shaped district reproduced in Figure 7.1 to favor the election of a fellow Republican. On seeing how the district was drawn, one critic is said to have observed, "Why, that looks like a salamander!" to which another retorted, "That's not a salamander, that's a gerrymander."

Creative redistricting and the actions of state legislators have often created problems that have ended up in litigation. The Supreme Court faced the question of **apportionment**—the determination and assignment of representation in a legislature—in *Baker* v. *Carr* (1962).[3] The Court found that the Tennessee legislature's apportionment plan, which failed to alter district lines despite large shifts in population, was unconstitutional because it violated the constitutional principle of equal protection of the law. Furthermore, the Court ruled that the equitable apportionment of voters among districts was a legal question of constitutional rights and not a political question, thereby allowing the courts to direct states to correct malapportionment. Two years later the Supreme Court ruled that congressional as well as state legislative districts must have "substantially equal" populations and enunciated the principle of "one man, one vote."[4]

In 1986 the Supreme Court ruled that any gerrymandering of a congressional district that purposely dilutes minority strength—a common reason for gerrymandering in the past—was illegal under the Voting Rights Act of 1965.[5] Most observers interpreted the ruling to mean that the drawing of districts to enhance party strength was permissible, but redistricting to dilute African-American or Hispanic political clout was not.

Just how far a state could go to "create" congressional districts to facilitate the election of minority representatives was the next question that vexed lawmakers and judges. After the 1990 census, for example, North Carolina proposed to create one African-American majority congressional district; the Bush administration Justice Department demanded two districts to reflect the racial composition of the state more accurately. (African Americans made up 22 percent of North Carolina's population; the state had twelve congressional districts.) To create the second district, the Democratic majority in the statehouse created the serpentine district shown in Figure 7.1. It basically connected small black population centers by winding down Highway I-85 like a 160-mile-long ribbon. White residents in North Carolina and in several other states filed suit arguing that their voting strength was diluted by the strangely redrawn districts designed to enhance minority voting strength. In finding this kind of gerrymander in violation of the Voting Rights Act of 1965, Justice Sandra Day O'Connor called the North Carolina district "bizarre" and even quoted one legislator's joke about the district: "If you drove down the interstate with both car doors open, you'd kill most of the people in the district." A majority of the Court concluded that this kind of redrawing of districts for obvious racial purposes was unconstitutional because it denies the constitutional rights of white citizens.[6]

In the aftermath of that decision, state legislators and the U.S. Justice Department were left in a quandary about how future congressional districts were to be drawn. Their quandary was increased in 1995 when the Supreme Court threw out Georgia's oddly drawn 11th district, which was created to encompass as many black voters as

gerrymandering: The legislative process through which the majority party in each statehouse tries to assure that the maximum number of representatives from its political party can be elected to Congress through the redrawing of legislative districts.

apportionment: The determination and assignment of representation in a legislature based on population.

FIGURE 7.1

Gerrymandering

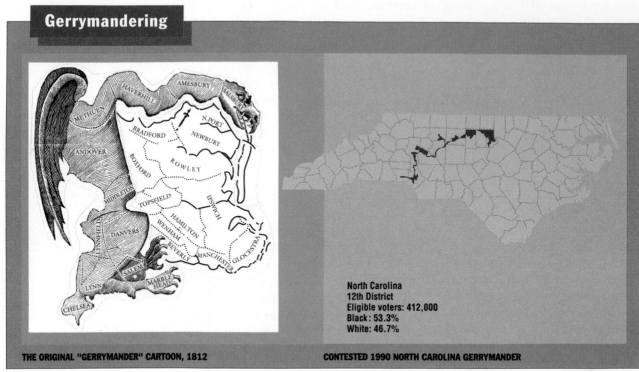

North Carolina
12th District
Eligible voters: 412,000
Black: 53.3%
White: 46.7%

THE ORIGINAL "GERRYMANDER" CARTOON, 1812   CONTESTED 1990 NORTH CAROLINA GERRYMANDER

SOURCE: From David Van Biema, "Snakes or Ladders?" *Time* (July 12, 1993): 30. Copyright 1993 Time, Inc. Reprinted by permission.

possible. The Court concluded that ignoring traditional districting principles such as compactness and county or city boundaries to draw a minority district violated the equal protection clause of the Fourteenth Amendment.[7] That decision and two others in 1996 make it clear that states can no longer overtly fashion districts to ensure minority representation in Congress.[8]

Constitutional Powers of Congress

bill: A proposed law.

The Constitution specifically gives to Congress its most important power—the authority to make laws. (See Highlight 7.1: The Powers of Congress.) This law-making power is shared by both houses. No **bill** (proposed law) can become law, for example, without the consent of both houses. Examples of other constitutionally shared powers include the power to declare war, raise an army and navy, coin money, regulate commerce, establish the federal courts and their jurisdiction, establish rules of immigration and naturalization, and "make all Laws which shall be necessary and proper for carrying into Execution the foregoing Powers." As interpreted by the Supreme Court, the *necessary and proper clause,* when coupled with one or more of the specific powers enumerated in Article I, section 8, has allowed Congress to increase the scope of its authority, often at the expense of the states and into areas not necessarily envisioned by the Framers. (See the discussion of Congress's *implied powers* in chapter 3).

Congress alone is given formal lawmaking powers in the Constitution, but it is important to remember that presidents issue proclamations and executive orders with the force of law (see chapter 8), bureaucrats issue quasi-legislative rules (see chapter 9),

Highlight 7.1

The Powers of Congress

The powers of Congress, found in Article I, section 8 of the Constitution, are to:

- Lay and collect taxes and duties
- Borrow money
- Regulate commerce with foreign nations and among the states
- Establish rules for naturalization (that is, the process of becoming a citizen) and bankruptcy

- Coin money, set its value, and fix the standard of weights and measures
- Punish counterfeiting
- Establish a post office and post roads
- Issue patents and copyrights
- Define and punish piracies, felonies on the high seas, and crimes against the law of nations
- Create courts inferior to (that is, below) the Supreme Court
- Declare war

- Raise and support an army and navy and make rules for their governance
- Provide for a militia (reserving to the states the right to appoint militia officers and to train the militia under congressional rules)
- Exercise legislative powers over the seat of government (the District of Columbia) and over places purchased to be federal facilities (forts, arsenals, dockyards,

and "other needful buildings")
- "Make all laws which shall be necessary and proper for carrying into execution the foregoing powers, and all other powers vested by this Constitution in the government of the United States" (Note: This "necessary and proper," or "elastic," clause has been expansively interpreted by the Supreme Court, as explained in chapter 2.)

---

and the Supreme Court renders opinions, as was the case with its redistricting decisions, which generate principles that also have the force of law (see chapter 10).

Reflecting the different constituencies and size of each house of Congress (as well as the Framers' intentions), Article I gives special, exclusive powers to each house in addition to their shared role in lawmaking. For example, as noted in Table 7.1, the Constitution specifies that all revenue bills must originate in the House of Representatives. Over the years, however, this mandate has been blurred, and it is not unusual to see budget bills being considered simultaneously in both houses, especially since each must approve all bills in the end, whether or not they involve revenues. In 1995, for example, when President Clinton submitted his budget deficit-reduction plan, both houses deliberated similar proposals simultaneously.

The House also has the power of **impeachment,** the authority to charge the president, vice president, or other "civil officers," including federal judges, with *"Treason, Bribery or other high Crimes and Misdemeanors."* Only the Senate is authorized to conduct trials of impeachment, with a two-thirds vote being necessary before a federal official can be removed from office.

Only one president, Andrew Johnson, has been impeached by the House, but he was acquitted by the full Senate by a one-vote margin. More recently, as we will discuss in greater detail in chapter 7, President Richard M. Nixon resigned from office in 1974 after the House Judiciary Committee voted to impeach him for his role in the Watergate scandal. In 1988, for only the second time in fifty years, the House voted to impeach a federal judge. Florida's first African-American federal judge, Alcee Hastings,

impeachment: The power delegated to the House of Representatives in the Constitution to charge the president, vice president, or other "civil officers," including federal judges, with "Treason, Bribery, or other high Crimes and Misdemeanors." This is the first step in the constitutional process of removing such government officials from office.

TABLE 7.1

Key Differences Between the House and Senate

CONSTITUTIONAL DIFFERENCES

House	Senate
Initiates all revenue bills	Offers "advice and consent" on many major presidential appointments.
Initiates impeachment procedures and passes articles of impeachment	Tries impeached officials.
Two-year terms	Six-year terms (One-third up for reelection every two years)
435 members (apportioned by population)	100 members (two from each state)
	Approves treaties

DIFFERENCES IN OPERATION

House	Senate
More centralized, more formal; stronger leadership	Less centralized, less formal; weaker leadership
Rules Committee fairly powerful in controlling time and rules of debate (in conjunction with the Speaker)	No Rules Committee; limits on debate come through unanimous consent or cloture of filibuster
More impersonal	More personal
Power less evenly distributed	Power more evenly distributed
Members are highly specialized	Members are generalists
Emphasizes tax and revenue policy	Emphasizes foreign policy

CHANGES IN THE INSTITUTION

House	Senate
Power centralized in the Speaker's inner circle of advisors	Senate workload increasing and informality breaking down; filibusters more frequent
House procedures are becoming more efficient	Becoming more difficult to pass legislation
Turnover is relatively high	Turnover is moderate

Representative Alcee Hastings (D-Fla.) is shown here before his impeachment from the federal bench, which inspired him to run for Congress. (Photo courtesy: Susan Greenwood/Gamma-Liaison)

was subsequently removed from the bench after Senate action even though he was acquitted of bribery charges in a U.S. federal district court. In 1992, twelve years after the original charges were filed, Hastings was elected to the House of Representatives, the body that first initiated the impeachment proceedings against him.

The House and Senate share in the impeachment process, but the Senate has the sole authority to approve major presidential appointments, including federal judges, ambassadors, and Cabinet- and sub-Cabinet-level positions. The Senate, too, must approve by a two-thirds vote all treaties entered into by the president. Failure by the president to court the Senate can be costly. At the end of World War I, for example, President Woodrow Wilson worked long and hard to get other nations to accept the Treaty of Versailles, which contained the charter of the proposed League of Nations. He overestimated his support in the Senate, however, and that body refused to ratify the treaty, thereby dealing Wilson and his international stature a severe setback.

THE MEMBERS OF CONGRESS

*T*oday, many members of Congress find the job exciting in spite of public criticism of the institution. But it wasn't always so. Until D.C. got air-conditioning and drained the swamps, Washington was a miserable town. Most representatives spent as little time as possible there, viewing the Congress, especially the House, as a stepping stone to other political positions. Thus, after spending a brief tour of duty in D.C., most representatives went home to run for local or state political office or were rewarded for their service by party bosses with a federal judgeship. It is only a post-World War I phenomenon that House members, in particular, have become what are termed "congressional careerists" and have seen their work in Washington as rewarding and long term.[9] So while Representative Newt Gingrich (R.–Ga.) once gleefully remarked, "There are very few games as fun as being a congressman," it is only a sentiment likely to be shared by those who have served more recently.[10]

Gingrich and many other members of Congress clearly relish their work, although there are indications that the high cost of living in Washington and maintaining two homes, political scandals, intense media scrutiny, the need to tackle hard issues, and a growth of partisan dissention is taking a toll on many members. Retiring after twenty-two years, Senator Paul Simon (D–Ill.) lamented this phenomenon, noting that "[partisanship] has not served the country well."[11] Those no longer in the majority, in particular, often don't see Congress as satisfying. Being a member of Congress is hard work, often made even harder by the amount of criticism many members routinely encounter at home, in the press, and even in the Capitol.

Members, moreover, actually live in two worlds. They must attempt to appease two constituencies—party leaders, colleagues, and lobbyists in Washington, D.C., and their constituents at home. As revealed in Table 7.2, members spend full days at home as well as in D.C. According to one study of House members in nonelection years, average representatives made thirty-five trips back home to their districts, and spent an average 138 days a year there.[12] Hedrick Smith, a Pulitzer Prize–winning reporter for *The New York Times,* has aptly described a member's days as a "kaleidoscopic jumble: breakfast with reporters, morning staff meetings, simultaneous committee hearings to juggle, back-to-back sessions with lobbyists and constituents, phone calls, briefings, constant buzzers interrupting office work to make quorum calls and votes on the run, afternoon speeches, evening meetings, receptions, fund-raisers, all crammed into four days so they can race home for a weekend gauntlet of campaigning. It's a rat race."[13]

Members are often criticized for being out of touch with their constituents. As Table 7.2 underscores, most members of Congress try almost frantically to keep in touch with their constituents. And, even if they come under charges of losing touch, members can try to step up their at-home activities.

How do senators and representatives accomplish all that they must and also satisfy their constituents? They send newsletters to stay in touch, hold town meetings throughout their districts, and get important help from their staffs. **Casework** is the term applied to tasks designed to help constituents frustrated by the faceless, form-filled federal bureaucracy. Although rarely indulged in by legislators themselves, casework is a major responsibility for selected staff members called caseworkers. Veterans who believe that they are getting the runaround at the V.A. hospitals, retirees who experience delays in receiving Social Security checks, or entrepreneurs eager to start new businesses who needs assistance from the Small Business Administration may contact their member of Congress. Other contacts ask the legislator to intercede to overturn an

casework: The process of solving constituents' problems dealing with the bureaucracy.

TABLE 7.2

A Day in the Life of a Member of Congress

TYPICAL MEMBER'S AT-HOME SCHEDULE*

Monday, March 20

7:30 A.M.	Business group breakfast, 20 members of the business community leaders	(1 hour)
8:45 A.M.	Hoover Elementary School, 6th grade class assembly	(45 min)
9:45 A.M.	National Agriculture Day, speech, Holiday Inn South	(45 min)
10:45 A.M.	Supplemental Food Shelf, pass foodstuffs to needy families	(1 hour)
12:00 noon	Community College, student/faculty lunch, speech and Q & A	(45 min)
1:00 P.M.	Sunset Terrace Elementary School, assembly 4,5,6 graders, remarks/ Q & A	(45 min)

(Travel Time: 1:45 P.M.–2:45 P.M.)

2:45 P.M.	Plainview Day Care Facility, owner wishes to discuss changes in federal law	(1 hour)
4:00 P.M.	Town Hall Meeting, American Legion	(1 hour)

(Travel Time: 5:00 P.M.–5:45 P.M.)

5:45 P.M.	PTA Meeting, speech, education issues before Congress (also citizen involve- ment with national associations)	(45 min)
6:30 P.M.	Annual Dinner, St. John's Lutheran Church Developmental Activity Center	(30 min)
7:15 P.M.	Association for Children for Enforcement of Support meeting, discuss problems of enforcing child support payments	(45 min)

(Travel Time: 8:00 P.M.–8:30 P.M.)

8:30 P.M.	Students Against Drunk Driving (SADD) meeting, speech, address: drinking age, drunk driving, uniform federal penalties	(45 min)
9:30 P.M.	State University class, discuss business issues before Congress	(1 hour)

TYPICAL MEMBER'S WASHINGTON SCHEDULE**

Wednesday, April 10

8:00 A.M.	Budget Study Group—Chairman Leon Panetta, Budget Committee, room 340 Cannon Building
8:45 A.M.	Mainstream Forum Meeting, room 2344 Rayburn Building
9:15 A.M.	Meeting with Consulting Engineers Council of N.C. from Raleigh about various issues of concern
9:45 A.M.	Meet with N.C. Soybean Assn. representatives re: agriculture appropriations projects
10:15 A.M.	WCHL radio interview (by phone)
10:30 A.M.	Tape weekly radio show—budget
11:00 A.M.	Meet with former student, now an author, about intellectual property issue
1:00 P.M.	Agriculture Subcommittee Hearing—Budget Overview and General Agriculture Outlook, room 2362 Rayburn Building
2:30 P.M.	Meeting with Chairman Bill Ford and southern Democrats re: HR-5, Striker Replacement Bill, possible amendments
3:15 P.M.	Meet with Close-Up students from district on steps on Capitol for photo and discussions
3:45 P.M.	Meet with Duke professor re: energy research programs
4:30 P.M.	Meet with constituent of Kurdish background re: situation in Iraq
5:30–7:00 P.M.	Reception—Sponsored by National Assn. of Home Builders, honoring new president Mark Tipton from Raleigh, H-328 Capitol
6:00–8:00 P.M.	Reception—Honoring retiring Rep. Bill Gray, Washington Court Hotel
6:00–8:00 P.M.	Reception—Sponsored by Firefighters Assn., room B-339 Rayburn Building
6:00–8:00 P.M.	Reception—American Financial Services Assn., Gold Room

*Craig Shultz, ed., *Setting Course: A Congressional Management Guide* (Washington, DC: The American University, 1994), 335.

**David E. Price, *The Congressional Experience: A View from the Hill* (Boulder, CO: Westview Press, 1992), 38

administrative decision such as one on eligibility for participation in a program or the receipt of benefits.

Increasingly, senators and representatives are placing most of their caseworkers back in the home district, where they are more accessible to constituents, who can drop by and talk to a friendly face about their problems. In larger districts caseworkers may "ride the circuit," taking the helping hand of the congressional office to county seats, crossroads, post offices, and mobile offices.

incumbency: The fact that being in office helps a person stay in office because of a variety of ben- efits which go with the position.

The caseworker gets the needed information from constituents and then contacts the appropriate agency, taking care not to appear to be putting pressure on the agency to resolve the problem in the favor of the constituent. Although contact from a congressional office ensures that the agency will review the file, if the constituent's claim is not meritorious, the constituent may still be disappointed. If the constituent's concerns are favorably resolved, the legislator may have won life-long support from a voter. Even if the agency rejects the request, the constituent may think more positively of the legislator for having expended the effort. Each House member can hire as many as eighteen full-time and four part-time staff members; the maximum size of a senator's office varies with the population of his or her state.

Vermont Representative Bernie Sanders (I—Vt.) in a way falls into the third-party category; he is actually a socialist. Said Sanders of his election, "What Vermonters wanted is somebody to go down there and stand up and fight for ordinary people, rather than as the vast majority of members of Congress do—protect the interests of the wealthy and the powerful." (Photo courtesy: Bernie Sanders)

Running for Office and Staying in Office

Despite the long hours and hard work senators and representatives put in, thousands aspire to these jobs every year. Yet only 535 men and women actually serve in the U.S. Congress. Membership in one of the two major political parties is almost always a prerequisite for election because election laws in various states often discriminate against independents (those without party affiliation) and minor-party candidates. And, as discussed in chapter 14, money is the mother's milk of politics—the ability to raise money is often key to any member's victory.

Incumbency is an informal factor that helps members to stay in office once they are elected. Simply put, being in office helps you stay in office. It's often very difficult for outsiders to win because they don't have the advantages (enumerated in Highlight 7.2) enjoyed by incumbents, including name recognition, access to media, and

Highlight 7.2

The Advantages of Incumbency

Incumbents enjoy the following advantages:

- Name recognition gained through previous campaigns and repeated visits to the district to make appearances at various public events.
- Credit claiming for bringing federal money into the district in the form of grants and contracts.
- Positive evaluations from constituents earned by doing favors (casework) such as helping cut red tape and tracking down federal aid, tasks handled by publicly supported professional staff members.
- Distribution of newsletters and other noncampaign materials free through the mails by using the "frank" (an envelope that contains the legislator's signature in place of a stamp).
- Access to media— after all, incumbents are news makers who provide reporters with tips and quotes.
- Greater ease in fund raising—their high reelection rates make them a good bet for people or groups willing to give campaign contributions in hopes of having access to powerful decision makers.
- Experience in running a campaign, putting together a campaign staff, making speeches, understanding constituent concerns, and connecting with people.
- Superior knowledge about a wide range of issues gained through work on committees, review of legislation, and previous campaigns.
- A record for supporting locally popular policy positions.

FIGURE 7.2

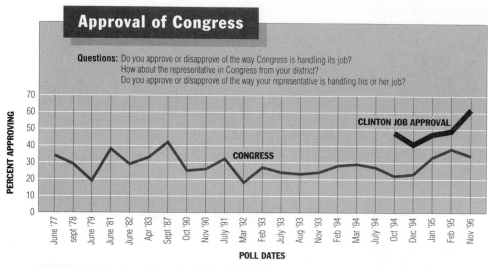

Approval of Congress

Questions: Do you approve or disapprove of the way Congress is handling its job?
How about the representative in Congress from your district?
Do you approve or disapprove of the way your representative is handling his or her job?

CLINTON JOB APPROVAL

CONGRESS

PERCENT APPROVING

POLL DATES

SOURCE: Marjorie Randon Hershey, "Congressional Elections," in *The Election of 1992* by Gerald M. Pomper, et al. (1993). Reprinted by permission of Chatham House Publishers.

fund raising. As illustrated in Figure 7.2, which compares the way poll respondents feel about their own representatives to how they feel about the Congress as an institution, most Americans approve of their *own* members of Congress.

It is not surprising, then, that from 1980 to 1990, an average of 95 percent of the incumbents who sought reelection actually won their primary and general election races.[14] One study basically concluded that unless a member of Congress was involved in a serious scandal, his or her chances of defeat were minimal.[15] In 1994, about 90 percent of the incumbents who ran for reelection succeeded, even though that election produced a freshman class of more than seventy Republicans and a handful of Democrats. In 1996, only one senator seeking reelection was defeated. Only twenty house members were defeated giving incumbents a 94 percent reelection rate. Voluntary retirements, regular district changes, and some defeats continue to make turnover in Congress substantial in spite of the benefits reaped by incumbents.

Term Limits

term limits: Legislation designating that state or federal elected legislators can serve only a specified number of years.

The presence of so many new members has made the idea of **term limits** less pressing to many who viewed the incumbency advantage enjoyed by members of Congress as a roadblock to significant change in the institution and the way it did business. A term-limits movement began sweeping the nation in the late 1980s because of voter frustration with gridlock and ethics problems in Congress and in state legislatures. Citizens and citizens groups approved referenda limiting the elected terms not only of their state representatives, but also of members of Congress. Given the power of incumbency, proponents of term limits argued that election to Congress, in essence, equaled life tenure. The concept of term limits is a simple one that appeals to many who oppose the notion of career politicians. As it generally applies to Congress, term limits allow members of the House to serve three two-year terms; senators can serve two six-year terms. By 1995 twenty-five states had enacted some form of term-limits laws and action was pending in eight more.

Term limits aren't a new idea. In 1787 the Framers considered, but rejected, a section of the Virginia Plan, which called for members of the House to be restricted to one term. Still, many of the Framers believed in the regular rotation of offices among worthy citizens, and this was generally the practice in the early years of the republic. There is also a precedent for term limitation in the office of governor. From the very first, Americans were suspicious of executive power and have preferred to restrict their governors to a fixed number of terms in the statehouse; even today the two-term limit (with each term four years in length) is the gubernatorial norm. And, of course, the president of the United States has been limited to two full four-year terms since ratification of the Twenty-second Amendment after the death of the only four-term president, Franklin D. Roosevelt.

The Contract with America promised that a Republican House would bring a term-limits amendment to a vote. Gaining control of Congress from the Democrats, however, appeared to have changed some Republicans' perspective on the desirability of term limits. Before the 1994 elections, many Republicans argued that incumbents had too many advantages in running for office and that term limits would build in competition and ensure turnover. They argued that many good people, hesitant to start a lengthy second career in politics, would be willing to serve for a short time, as the Founders, especially the Anti-Federalists, envisioned. They also saw term limits as a way of increasing Republican representation in Congress; many career Democrats would be forced out of office, making it easier for Republicans to win in open seats.

Term-limits opponents have a very different view of this reform. They note that the people already have the ultimate power to limit terms—they don't have to reelect their representatives. In theory, if the electorate so desired, it could replace the entire U.S. House of Representatives every two years. This does not happen, however, because many voters are pleased with the job being done by their legislators. Yet term limits would deny voters the right to retain good members of Congress; under term limitation, good and bad legislators are ousted equally and without distinction.

STILL THE BEST CONGRESSIONAL TERM-LIMITING DEVICE.

Term-limits opponents also note that the loss of senior, experienced legislators would diminish an important check on other actors in the legislative process *not* subject to term limits, such as lobbyists, legislative staff, and executive department bureaucrats. Few Americans are any more fond of these groups than they are of legislators. This last problem with term limits is an example of the *unintended consequences* of reform. The American system of government is so complex that each new action can produce somewhat unpredictable reactions, and wise reformers must be alert to the "ripple effects" of their proposals. It seems clear, for example, that the American public does not want *more* special interest influence in Congress.

In 1994 the U.S. Supreme Court upheld the constitutionality of an Arkansas term-limits provision that set term limits for state legislators. But the Court ruled that state-imposed limitations on the terms of members of Congress was unconstitutional.[16] Thus any efforts to enact congressional term limits would necessitate a constitutional amendment—not an easy feat. To honor the Contract with America in the 104th Congress, Speaker Gingrich and House leaders nevertheless brought a term-limits amendment to the floor for a vote, knowing that it would be harder to pass than other Contract items that required only a simple majority. The proposal fell sixty votes short of the two-thirds vote needed to propose a constitutional amendment. The measure also failed in the Senate, where Republicans failed to muster enough votes to cut off a Democratic filibuster.

What Does Congress Look Like?

Term limits might have the unintended consequence of electing many of traditionally underrepresented groups to Congress. When Bill Clinton was elected president in 1992, for example, he said that he wanted to appoint an administration that "looked like America"—meaning one that reflected the racial, ethnic, and gender characteristics of the nation. Historically, Congress has never looked like America—it is older, better educated, white, and male. Congress is not only more white and more male than the rest of the United States, it is also richer. Most members of Congress are well off, if not wealthy. The Senate, moreover, has often been called the "Millionaires' Club," and its members sport names like Rockefeller and DuPont. In the 105th Congress (1997–98), the average age of Senators is fifty eight, and their average length of service is ten years. House members, on average, are younger—fifty-two—and have served eight years. Ninety-four percent of the Senators have a college degree, eighty-eight percent are married, and ninety-five percent have children. Ninety-three percent of House members graduated from college, eighty-four percent are married, and eighty-six percent have children.

The 1992 elections saw a record number of women, African Americans, and other minorities elected to Congress (see Figure 7.3). Twenty-nine new women were elected, bringing the total number of women to fifty-five. The number of women in the Senate rose from two to seven—a 350 percent increase! For the first time ever, both senators elected from a single state—California—were women. By the 105th Congress, elected in 1996, the total number of women increased only by five, to fifty-one in the House and nine in the Senate. And Maine became the second state to send two women to the U.S. Senate with the election of Republican Sue Collins.

Similarly, the number of Hispanic Americans rose from thirteen in 1990 to twenty-two in 1992, as revealed in Figure 7.3. Moreover, in 1992 the first Korean American was elected to the House of Representatives (Jay Kim, R–Cal.), and Ben Nighthorse Campbell, who originally ran as a Democrat in Colorado and later switched to the Republican Party (perhaps in response to the growing pro-Republican tide in the mountain West),

became the first Native American to serve in the U.S. Senate in more than sixty years. In the 105th Congress, there were nineteen Hispanics and three Asian/Pacific Islanders.

The 103rd Congress elected in 1992 also saw the election of the largest class of new African-American legislators since Reconstruction (see Figure 7.3) and the election of the first and only African-American woman in the Senate, Carol Moseley-Braun. In the 105th Congress, in spite of the redistricting changes ordered by the U.S. Supreme Court, the number of African-American legislators only declined by one, going from thirty-eight to thirty-seven. Only a Republican African-American representative from Connecticut was defeated in his bid for reelection. In Georgia, in fact, where two African-American representatives were forced out of their majority black district and into majority white districts, both won. At a time when representation is often viewed in descriptive terms, however, even small declines in the number of African-American legislators in Congress is not likely to do much to buttress African-Americans' trust in the national government or the political system.

The Representational Role of Members of Congress

Questions of who should be represented and how that should happen are critical in a republic. Over the years, political theorists have enunciated various ideas about how constituents' interests are best represented in any legislative body. Does it make a difference if the members of Congress come from or are members of a particular group? Are they bound to vote the way their constituents expect them to vote even if they personally favor another policy ? Your answer to these questions may depend on your view of the representative function of legislators.

British political philosopher Edmund Burke (1729–87), who also served in the British Parliament, believed that although he was elected from Bristol, it was his duty to represent the interests of the *entire* nation. He reasoned that elected officials were

FIGURE 7.3

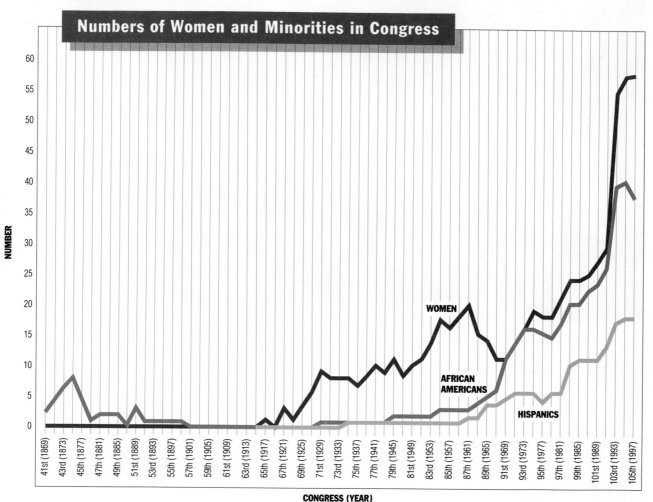

SOURCE: Harold W. Stanley and Richard G. Niemi, eds., *Vital Statistics on American Politics,* 4th ed. (Washington D.C.: CQ Press, 1994), 203. Data updated by authors.

trustee: Role played by elected representatives who listen to constituents' opinions and then use their best judgment to make final decisions.

delegate: Role played by elected representatives who vote the way their constituents would want them to, regardless of their own opinions.

obliged to vote as they personally thought best. According to Burke, representatives should be **trustees** who listen to the opinions of their constituents and then can be trusted to use their own best judgment to make final decisions.

A second theory of representation holds that representatives are **delegates.** True delegates are representatives who vote the way their constituents would want them to, whether or not those opinions are the representative's. Delegates, therefore, must be ready and willing to vote against their conscience or policy preferences if they know how the folks back home feel about a particular issue. Consider the case of Representative Sue Kelly (R–N.Y.). In 1994 she ran as an environmentalist, which set her apart in a crowded Republican primary. She then went on to win in the 1994 general election. When she voted against nine of the first ten environmental bills considered in the 104th Congress, many of her constituents were outraged. "Sue Kelly went down there to Washington and got caught up in all the excitement and forgot what her district wanted," said Robert F. Kennedy, Jr., a resident of her district and a lawyer for the Natural Resources Defense Council.[17] "But, she came home to a surprise—a lot of angry constituents who were saying they didn't send her there to gut our environmental laws."[18] Despite her campaign promises, as a freshman Republican Kelly felt obliged to vote for items in the Contract with America, including bills to sharply reduce protected wetlands and reduce the enforcement of several other environmental protection laws. In 1996, Kelly fended off a strong challenge and won her three person race with 46 percent of the vote.

Members of Congress often find themselves pulled in two directions that parallel the two worlds in which they often find themselves: the home district and the District of Columbia. Doing what's best for the district or what those back at home think is best for the district (or the nation, or the party leadership) pulls members in the direction of the delegate role; concern with national issues or looking at the bigger picture (or through the lens of party loyalty) moves the representative in the direction of the trustee role.

Not surprisingly, then, members of Congress and other legislative bodies generally don't fall neatly into either category. It is often unclear how constituents feel about a particular issue, or there may be conflicting opinions within a single constituency. With these difficulties in mind, a third theory of representation holds that **politicos** alternately don the hats of trustee or delegate, depending on the issue. On an issue of great concern to their constituents, representatives will most likely vote as delegates; on other issues, perhaps those that are less visible, representatives will act as trustees and use their own best judgment. Research by political scientists buttresses this view.[19]

politico: Role played by elected representatives who act as trustees or as delegates, depending on the issue.

How a representative views his or her role—as a trustee, delegate, or politico—may still not answer the question of whether or not it makes a difference if a representative or senator is male or female, African American or Hispanic or Caucasian, young or old, gay or straight. Burke's ideas about representation don't even begin to address more practical issues of representation. Can a man, for example, represent the interests of women as well as a woman? Can a rich woman represent the interests of the poor? The combinations are endless.

Senator Edward M. Kennedy (D–Mass.), for example, is one of the wealthiest members of the Senate, yet he has been an effective champion of the poor, women, and other minorities throughout his six terms in the Senate. During the Clarence Thomas hearings, however, many commentators noted that Kennedy's well-chronicled personal problems precluded him from effectively questioning Thomas. Kennedy was criticized for his uncharacteristic silence during those hearings. In addition, women representatives in the House were outraged by the glaring absence of any women on the Senate Judiciary Committee that grilled Anita Hill concerning her charges that Thomas had sexually harassed her while he was her supervisor at the Equal Employment Opportunity Commission. (Two women—Diane Feinstein [D–Cal.] and Carol Moseley-Braun [D–Ill.] were added to the committee in 1993.)

Female representatives historically have played prominent roles in efforts to expand women's rights. Studies reveal that female legislators are more likely than their male counterparts to sponsor legislation of concern to women.[20] One such study by the Center for the American Woman and Politics, for example, found that most women in the 103rd Congress "felt a special responsibility to represent women, particularly to represent the life experiences. . . . They undertook this additional responsibility while first, and foremost, like all members of Congress, representing their own districts."[21] Said Representative Nancy Johnson (R–N.J.), "We need to integrate the perspective of women into the policy-making process, just as we have now successfully integrated the perspective of environmental preservation, [and] the perspective of worker safety."[22] As Table 7.3 reveals, men and women voted quite differently in Congress regardless of party affiliation, with the greatest differences in voting patterns occurring between Republican male and female representatives.

TABLE 7.3

Selected Votes of Male and Female House Members in the 103rd Congress

	VOTES			
ISSUES/BILLS	**Republican Men**	**Republican Women**	**Democratic Men**	**Democratic Women**
For the Crime Bill	30%	83%	93%	100%
For the Assault Weapons Ban	23	67	93	89
For the Conference Report on the Freedom of Access to (Abortion) Clinics Act	20	75	80	91
For the Brady Bill (gun control)	30	67	70	89
For the Family & Medical Leave Act	21	50	87	100

Source: Adapted from Center for the American Woman and Politics, *Voices, Views, Votes: The Impact of Women in the 103rd Congress,* (New Brunswick, NJ: Eagleton Institute of Politics, Rutgers, 1995), 9.

Ben Nighthorse Campbell (R—Col.). Campbell was elected as a Democrat in 1992 but changed political parties in 1995. (Photo courtesy: AP/Wide World Photos)

Actions of the one Native American and one African American in the Senate underscore the representative function that can be played in Congress. Ben Nighthorse Campbell (R–Col.), for example, is the only Native American who sits on the Senate Committee on Indian Affairs. Earlier, as a member of the House, he led the fight to change the name of Custer Battlefield Monument in Montana to Little Bighorn Battlefield National Monument to honor the Indians who died in battle. He also fought successfully for legislation to establish the National Museum of the American Indian within the Smithsonian Institution. But, his biggest fight on behalf on Native Americans was his effort to block congressional approval of a $200 million stadium for the Washington Redskins unless the football team changed its name. Campbell told a House panel that the word "redskin" is a racial slur. Nonvoting Delegate Eni Feleomevaega (D–American Samoa) concurred, calling the team name offensive.[23]

The only African American in the Senate also has tried to sensitize her colleagues about issues of race. In 1993 Senator Jesse Helms (R–N.C.) sought to amend the national service bill in such a way to preserve the design patent held by the United Daughters of the Confederacy that included the Confederate flag. Most senators had no idea what they were voting on, and the amendment to the bill passed by a vote of 52 to 48. Then Senator Moseley-Braun took to the floor to express her outrage at Helms's support of a symbol of slavery: "On this issue there can be no consensus. It is an outrage. It is an insult."[24] Although Helms angrily insisted that slavery or race were not in issue, the Senate killed the Helms amendment by a vote of 75 to 25, as twenty-seven senators changed their votes. Said Senator Barbara Boxer (D–Cal.), "If there ever was proof of the value of diversity, we have it here today."[25]

Members even see committee assignments as a way to facilitate representation of their districts or states. Some committee assignments, for example, allow members to act on behalf of the specific interests of their constituents. Western representatives favor an assignment to the Resources Committee because of its jurisdiction over all Western lands. Rural Midwestern and Southern representatives, on the other hand, often favor an assignment to the Agriculture (Agriculture, Nutrition and Forestry in the Senate) Committee because of its jurisdiction over farm matters.

HOW CONGRESS IS ORGANIZED

*E*very two years, a new Congress is seated. After ascertaining the formal qualifications of new members, the Congress organizes itself as it prepares for the business of the coming session. Among the first items on its agenda are the election of new leaders and the adoption of rules for conducting its business. As illustrated in Figure 7.4, each house has a hierarchical leadership structure.

The House of Representatives

Even in the first Congress in 1789, the House of Representatives was almost three times larger than the Senate. It is not surprising then, that from the beginning the House has been more tightly organized, more elaborately structured, and governed by stricter rules. Traditionally, loyalty to the party leadership and voting along party lines have been more common in the House than in the Senate. House leaders also play a key role in moving the business of the House along. Historically, the Speaker of the House, the majority and minority leaders, and the majority and minority House whips have made up the party leadership that runs Congress. This has now been expanded to include deputy minority whips of both parties.

The Speaker of the House.   The **Speaker of the House** is the only officer of the House of Representatives specifically mentioned in the Constitution. The office, the chamber's most powerful position, is modeled after a similar office in the British Parliament—the Speaker was the one who spoke to the king and conveyed the wishes of the House of Commons to the monarch.[26]

The Speaker is elected at the beginning of each new Congress by the entire House. Traditionally, the Speaker is a member of the **majority party,** the party in each house with the greatest number of members, as are all committee chairs. (The **minority party** is the major party with the second most members in either House.) While typically not the member with the longest service, the Speaker generally has served in the House for a long time and in other House leadership positions as sort of an apprenticeship. Newt Gingrich spent sixteen years in the House, while his predecessor Thomas Foley (D–Wash.) took twenty-five years to work his way to the gavel and dais. Generally, a Speaker is reelected until he chooses to retire or his party ceases to be in the majority.

The Speaker presides over the House, oversees House business, is the official spokesperson for the House of Representatives, and is second in the line of presidential succession. Moreover, he is the House liaison with the president and generally has great political influence within the chamber. Through his parliamentary and political skills, he is expected to smooth the passage of party-backed legislation through the House.

The first "powerful" Speaker was Henry Clay. (See Roots of Government: Life on the Floor and in the Halls of Congress.) Serving in Congress at a time when turnover was high, he was elected to the position in 1810, his first term in office. He was Speaker of the House of Representatives for a total of six terms—longer than anyone else in the nineteenth century.

By the late 1800s, the House ceased to have a revolving door and average stays of members increased. With this professionalization of the House came professionalization in the Speakership. Between 1896 and 1910, a series of Speakers initiated changes

Speaker of the House: The only officer of the House of Representatives specifically mentioned in the Constitution; elected at the beginning of each new Congress by the entire House; traditionally a member of the majority party.

majority party: The political party in each house of Congress with the most members.

minority party: Party with the second most members in either house of Congress.

FIGURE 7.4

Organizational Structure of the House of Representatives and the Senate during the 104th Congress (1995–96)

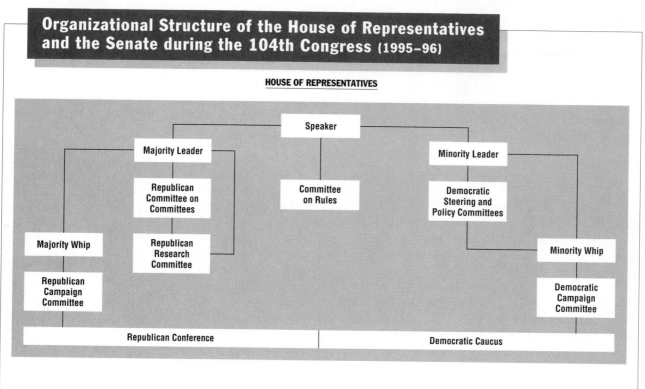

HOUSE OF REPRESENTATIVES

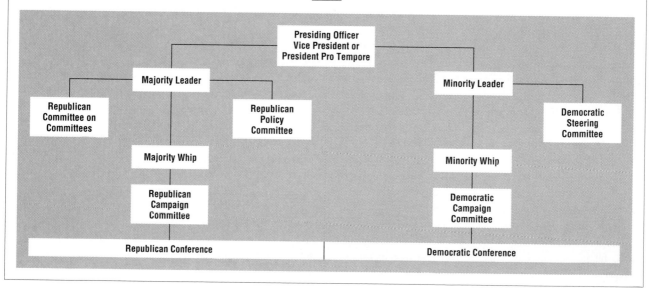

SENATE

that brought more power to the Speaker's office. Filibusters could be broken (see Roots of Government), and Speakers largely took control of committee assignments and appointing committee chairs. Institutional and personal rule reached its height during the tenure of Speaker Joseph Cannon (1903–10).

Roots of Government

Life on the Floor and in the Halls of Congress

Throughout Congress's first several decades, partisan, sectional, and state tensions of the day often found their way onto the floors of the U.S. House and Senate. Many members were armed, and during one House debate thirty members showed their weapons. In 1826, for example, Senator John Randolph of Virginia insulted Secretary of State Henry Clay from the floor of the Senate, referring to Clay as "this being, so brilliant yet so corrupt, which, like a rotten mackerel by moonlight, shined and stunk." Clay immediately challenged Randolph to a duel on the Virginia side of the Potomac River. Both missed, although Randolph's coat fell victim to a bullet hole. Reacting to public opinion, however, in 1839 Congress passed a law prohibiting dueling in the District of Columbia.

Nevertheless, dueling continued. A debate in 1851 between representatives from Alabama and North Carolina ended in a duel, but no one was hurt. In 1856 Representative Preston Brooks of South Carolina, defending the honor of his region and family, assaulted Senator Charles Sumner of Massachusetts on the floor of the Senate. Sumner was disabled and unable to resume his seat in Congress for several years. Guns and knives were abundantly evident on the floor of both House and Senate, along with a wide variety of alcoholic beverages.

Today the House and the Senate are usually much more quiet. In 1984, however, a group of newly elected Republican representatives began taking over the House floor every day after the end of normal hours to berate their Democratic colleagues. The chamber was usually empty but, like all other action on the floor, these speeches were broadcast live on C-SPAN and often used by the members for distribution to local television stations back home. During a particularly strong attack on several Democrats' views on Central America, Representative Newt Gingrich paused suggestively mid-speech, as though waiting for an objection or daring the Democrats to respond. No other House member was on the floor at the time, but since C-SPAN cameras at that time focused only on the speaker, viewers were unaware of that fact.

Democratic House Speaker Thomas P. O'Neill angrily reacted by ordering C-SPAN cameras to span the empty chamber to expose Gingrich's and other Republicans' tactics, but what Republicans labeled "CAM-SCAM" ignited a firestorm on the floor. Incensed by remarks made by Gingrich, O'Neill dropped his gavel, left his spot on the dais, and took to the floor, roaring at Gingrich, "You challenged their [House Democrats'] patriotism, and it is the lowest thing that I have ever seen in my thirty-two years in Congress!" Trent Lott (R–Miss.) then demanded that the Speaker be "taken down," the House term to call someone to order for violating House rules prohibiting personal attacks. The House Parliamentarian looked in the dictionary to see if the word "lowest" was a slur. As a hush fell on the House, the presiding officer told O'Neill that he had violated House rules. Bristled O'Neill, "I was expressing my views very mildly because I think much worse than I said."

O'Neill's penalty? The rarely invoked enforced silence for the remainder of the day's debate. So uncomfortable with that action was the House minority leader that he asked Lott to make a motion exempting O'Neill from the penalty, to which Lott agreed. No other House Speaker has ever been so reprimanded.[*]

In the much more media savvy House of today, Gingrich, himself, has been the object of numerous attacks. After he signed a lucrative book contract, for example, several Democrats took to the floor to criticize the deal. When Carrie Meek (D–Fla.) asked, "Who does the Speaker really work for? Is it the American people or his New York publishing house?" Speaker Gingrich's best friend, Robert Walker (R–Penn.) demanded her words be stricken from the record. A two-hour fracas ensued, and her words were stricken as "innuendo" against the Speaker by a highly partisan 217 to 178 vote.[**]

[*]Alexander Stanley, "Tip Topped: O'Neill Tangles with Some Republican Turks over Camera Angles," *Nation* (May 28, 1984): 36.

[**]Tim Curran, "Book Deal Sparks Nasty Floor Brawl," *Roll Call* (January 19, 1995).

Representative Barney Frank (D-Mass.) has been in the rare position of having fun while being in the minority party. Says Frank, "I'm a counterpuncher, happiest fighting on the defensive. Besides, I really dislike what the Republicans are doing. I think they are bad for the country and for vulnerable people. I feel, 'Boy, this is a moral opportunity—you've got to fight this.' Also, I'm used to being in a minority. Hey, I'm a left-handed gay Jew. I've never felt, automatically, a member of any majority. So, I started swinging from the opening bell of this Congress." (Photo courtesy: AP/Wide World Photos)

Negative reaction to those strong speakers eventually led to a revolt in 1910 and 1911 in the House and to a reduction of the formal powers of the Speaker. Thus many Speakers between Cannon and Gingrich often relied on more informal powers that came from their personal ability to persuade.

Newt Gingrich, the first Republican Speaker in forty years, immediately tried to restore a strong Speaker system with increased formal powers. As fiftieth Speaker, Gingrich served as minority whip before being elected in 1994 to preside over the House when it convened in 1995. Gingrich, a former college professor, had long aspired to become House Speaker. As minority whip he took every opportunity to bolster other Republicans' electoral successes, thereby gaining the loyalty of new members. His well-publicized Contract with America solidified Republicans behind a common ideal, and also gave him a blueprint for action when the 104th Congress met.

During the early organizational meetings of the 104th Congress, Speaker Gingrich convinced fellow Republicans to return important formal powers to the Speaker in order to facilitate quick action on the Contract with America. In return for a rule preventing Speakers from serving for more than four consecutive sessions, the Speaker was given unprecedented authority, including the power to refer bills to committee, ending the practice of joint referral of bills to more than one committee, where they might fare better.

More importantly, he began a system of bypassing committee chairs on important issues and many Contract with America items. For example, he called the chairs of the Commerce and Ways and Means committees into his office and proposed that he lead an ad hoc design team on Medicare. This group then worked out of the Speaker's conference room for over four months, often meeting daily, and eventually unveiled its own Medicare proposals in September 1995.[27] (See Politics Now: A Season of Discontent?).

These formal changes, along with his personal leadership skills, allowed Gingrich to exercise greater control over the House and its agenda than any other Speaker since the days of Joe Cannon. Gingrich participated in the selection of committee members and ensured that freshmen that he could count on as loyalists were assigned to the chamber's three most coveted committees—Appropriations, Rules, and Ways and

Politics Now

A Season of Discontent?

It didn't take a rocket scientist to figure out that Republicans kept Speaker Newt Gingrich under wraps during the Republican National Convention. Where was the architect of the 1994 Republican congressional victories who has led the party to new heights? While individual members of the House were still lining up to have Gingrich visit their districts for fund raisers, most agreed that Gingrich's negatives made it better not to spotlight the Speaker and the Contract with America at the convention in San Diego.

What happened? While Americans seem, at least at first, enthusiastic about the message that Republicans delivered in a unified voice in 1994, they soon again became disillusioned with Congress and the Speaker. Members of the Republican Caucus, too, began to complain that the "GOP message is muddled, if it gets out at all, and the people at the top seem to lack direction and focus."* Much of the unrest among House Republicans can be traced to the two winter 1995–1996 government shutdowns, which many blamed—rightly or wrongly—on Republicans. And, when Republicans lost the budget battle with President Clinton, they lost much of the momentum they had going from the Contract with America and the headiness that went with taking over both houses of Congress.

This, in turn, made it more difficult for the House leadership to govern in 1996, especially as election day 1996 drew closer. Gingrich, too, became concerned when Republicans began to vote against him on procedural motions, which he saw as a threat to his authority. Gingrich, a student of history, even privately "lectur(ed) his troops about (Speaker Joe) Cannon's eventual fall from power at the hands of his own troops."**

Exit polls conducted on election day 1996 revealed that 60 percent had an unfavorable opinion of the Speaker although that dislike did not appear to translate into votes against incumbent House Republicans.

*Koszcuk, Jackie, "For GOP Leadership, A Season of Discontent," American Voter '96. CQ Alert, www.
**Ibid.

Means—assignments that formerly were almost exclusively given to members with more seniority. He also hand-picked committee chairs, ignoring the seniority norm, which (with rare exception under Democratic rule) always made the most senior member of a committee its chair. He also initially took a more visible role as a policy spokesperson on issues including the budget, health, and welfare reform, usurping the traditional role of committee chairs. In the 104th Congress, Gingrich also kept a tight control of the schedule, putting pressure on committee chairs to move legislation.

Outside of these formal and informal legislative powers, Gingrich's long-term efforts on behalf of House Republicans and the party in general helped him personally. He virtually singlehandedly masterminded the short-lived Republican revolution in Congress and helped finance it through GOPAC, a political action committee he created. Thus, "(T)here's a personal loyalty to him that is without precedent in recent history," said one former House member.[28]

In time, Gingrich's highly visible role as a revolutionary transformed him into a negative symbol outside the Beltway as his public popularity plunged. The announcement that he got a $4.5 million book contract advance was met with so much criticism that he was forced to return it to the publisher. He was belittled by Democrats and many members of the press for suggesting orphanages as a partial solution to the wel-

fare problem. Gingrich's popularity also suffered when he made an off-the-cuff comment suggesting that he had allowed the government to be closed down during the budget impasse with the White House to pay back President Clinton for forcing him to exit
Air Force One from the rear when he accompanied the president to the funeral of Prime
Minister Yitzhak Rabin in Israel. A striking 70 percent of the public blamed Gingrich
for the government shutdown.[29]

These incidents did little to add to public confidence in, or approval of, the
Speaker. Claims of a "revolution" in Washington scared some who began to question
how far the Speaker was willing to go to balance the budget. While the public liked the
idea of a balanced budget, when they realized it could mean Medicare cuts and a roll-
back in environmental protection, they got nervous. Gingrich's personal style and harsh
language didn't help his image either. Sixty-four percent of voters in a March 1996
Today/CNN/Gallup Poll, for example, rated him as "too extreme",[30] and more (46 percent) disapproved of what he stands for politically than approved (40 percent).[31] The
Speaker, moreover, was largely kept out of the public eye during the 1996 Republican
National Convention. Still, Republican House members remained loyal to him. By the
end of the 104th Congress, there appeared to be little of the resentment that ultimately
brought about the 1910–11 Revolution that stripped autocratic Speaker Joe Cannon
(R–Ill.) and his successors of many powers.

majority leader: The elected
leader of the party controlling the
most seats in the U.S. House of
Representatives or the Senate;
is second in authority to the
Speaker of the House and in the
Senate is regarded as its most
powerful member.

minority leader: The elected
leader of the party with the second
highest number of elected representatives in either the House or
the Senate.

Other House Leaders.   After the Speaker, the next most powerful people in the
House are the majority and minority leaders, who are elected in their individual party
caucuses. The **majority leader** is the second most important person in the House; his
counterpart on the other side of the aisle (the House is organized so that if you are
standing on the podium, Democrats sit on the right side and Republicans on the left
side of the center aisle) is the **minority leader.** Both work closely with the Speaker, and
the majority leader helps the Speaker schedule proposed legislation for debate on the
House floor.

The Speaker and majority and minority leaders are assisted in their leadership efforts by the majority and minority **whips,** who are elected by party members in caucuses. The concept of whips originated in the British House of Commons, where they were named after the "whipper in," the rider who keeps the hounds together in a fox hunt. Party whips—who were first designated in the House in 1899 and in the Senate in 1913—do, as their name suggests, try to "whip" fellow Democrats or Republicans into line on partisan issues. They try to maintain close contact with all members on important votes, prepare summaries of content and implications of bills, get "nose counts" during debates and votes, and in general get members to toe the party line. Whips also serve as communications links, distributing word of the party line from leaders to rank-in-file members and alerting leaders to concerns in the ranks. For example, when John Conyers, Jr. (D–Mich.) became upset that no one consulted him in drafting the crime bill in 1993, he voted against the budget package out of irritation. "House Democratic whips swarmed over him like bees to honey," and he soon fell in line after being told he would become a major player.[32]

whip: One of several representatives who keep close contact with all members and take "nose counts" on key votes, prepare summaries of bills, and in general act as communications links within the party.

The Senate

The Constitution specifies that the presiding officer of the Senate is the Vice President of the United States. Because he is not a member of the Senate, he votes only in the case of a tie. Vice President Al Gore, Jr., for example, cast the tie-breaking vote in the Senate on the Budget Deficit Reduction bill in 1993.

The official chair of the Senate is the president pro tempore, who is selected by the majority party and presides over the Senate in the absence of the vice president. The position of president pro tempore is today primarily an honorific office that generally goes to the most senior senator of the majority party. Once elected, the pro tem, as he is called, stays in that office until there is a change in the majority party in the Senate. Since presiding over the Senate can be a rather perfunctory duty, neither the vice president nor the president pro tempore performs the task often. Instead, the duty of actually presiding over the Senate rotates among junior members of the chamber, allowing more senior members to attend more important meetings unless a key vote is being debated.

The true leader of the Senate is the majority leader, elected to the position by the majority party. Because the Senate is a smaller and more collegial body, operating without many of the more formal House rules concerning debate, the majority leader is not nearly as powerful as the Speaker of the House, a more overtly partisan body that requires more control by the speaker. The majority and minority whips round out the leadership positions in the Senate and perform functions similar to those of their House counterparts. But leading and whipping in the Senate can be quite a challenge. Senate rules have always given tremendous power to individual senators; in most cases senators can offer any kind of amendments to legislation on the floor, and an individual senator can bring all work on the floor to a halt indefinitely through a filibuster unless sixty senators vote to cut him or her off.[33]

Because of the Senate's smaller size (see Figure 7.5), organization and formal rules have never played the same role in the Senate as they do in the House. Until recently, it was a "Gentlemen's Club" whose folkways—unwritten rules of behavior—governed its operation. One such folkway, for example, stipulated that political disagreements not become personal criticisms. A senator who disliked another referred to that senator as "the able, learned, and distinguished senator." A member who really couldn't stand another called that senator "my very able, learned, and distinguished colleague." In refer-

FIGURE 7.5

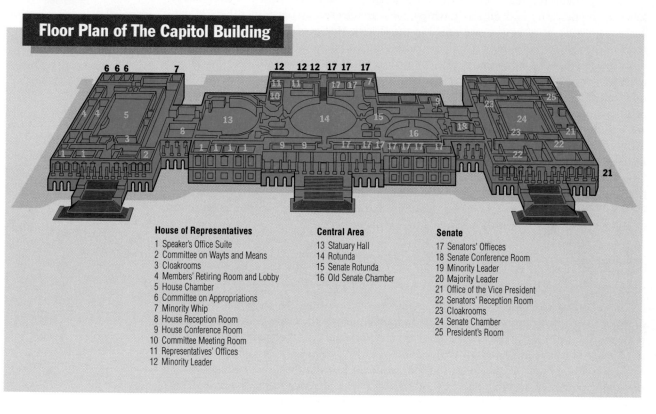

Floor Plan of The Capitol Building

House of Representatives
1 Speaker's Office Suite
2 Committee on Ways and Means
3 Cloakrooms
4 Members' Retiring Room and Lobby
5 House Chamber
6 Committee on Appropriations
7 Minority Whip
8 House Reception Room
9 House Conference Room
10 Committee Meeting Room
11 Representatives' Offices
12 Minority Leader

Central Area
13 Statuary Hall
14 Rotunda
15 Senate Rotunda
16 Old Senate Chamber

Senate
17 Senators' Offices
18 Senate Conference Room
19 Minority Leader
20 Majority Leader
21 Office of the Vice President
22 Senators' Reception Room
23 Cloakrooms
24 Senate Chamber
25 President's Room

ring to members of their body by title and not by their name, senators would sometimes go out of their way not to offend one another on the floor. For example, the following took place on the Senate floor while Lyndon B. Johnson served in the Senate:

> *Mr. [Lyndon B.] Johnson of Texas:* The Senator from Texas does not have any objection, and the Senator from Texas wishes the Senator from California to know that the Senator from Texas knew the Senator from California did not criticize him.[34]

In the 1960s and 1970s, senators became more and more active on and off the Senate floor in a variety of issues and extended debates that often occurred on the floor—without the rigid rules of courtesy that had once been the hallmark of the body. These changes weren't accompanied by giving additional powers to the Senate majority leader, who now often has difficulty controlling "the more active, assertive, and consequently less predictable membership" of the Senate.[35] Thus, while the majority leader sets the agenda, there's often not much he can formally do to control the other members of the Senate. Holds, filibusters, and the threat of filibusters have tied up the Senate, which partly explains why many of the House's Contract with America items took so long to see the light of day in the Senate.

The Role of Political Parties

The organization of both houses of Congress is closely tied to political parties, which play a key role in the committee system, an organizational feature of Congress that facilitates its law-making and oversight functions. When the first Congress met in 1789 in the nation's temporary capital in New York City, it consisted of only twenty-six senators and sixty-five representatives. Those men faced the enormous task of creating much of the machinery of government as well as that of drafting a bill of rights, for which the Anti-Federalists had argued so vehemently. During their debates, the political differences that divided Americans during the early years of the Union were renewed. When Alexander Hamilton, the first Secretary of the Treasury and a staunch Federalist, proposed to fund the national debt and create a national bank, for example, he aroused the ire of those who feared vesting the national government with too much power. This conflict led Hamilton's opponents to create the Democratic-Republican Party to counter the Federalists, creating a two-party system in Congress. Control of the political parties quickly gave Congress far more powers. The Democratic-Republican **party caucus** (the name for a formal gathering of all party members in the House) nominated Thomas Jefferson (1804), James Madison (1808 and 1812), and James Monroe (1816) for president, all of whom were elected.

party caucus: A formal gathering of all party members.

At the beginning of each new Congress—the 105th Congress sits in two sessions, one in 1997 and one in 1998—the members of each party gather in caucus or conference. Historically, these caucuses have enjoyed varied powers, but today the party caucuses—called "caucus" by House Democrats and "conference" by House and Senate Republicans and Senate Democrats—have several roles, including nominating or electing party officers, reviewing committee assignments, discussing party policy, imposing party discipline, and setting party themes and coordinating media, including talk radio.[36]

Each caucus or conference has specialized committees that fulfill certain tasks. House Republicans, for example, have a Committee on Committees that makes committee assignments. The Democrats' Steering Committee performs this function. Each party also has a Congressional Campaign Committee to assist members in their re-election bids.

Loyalty to party is an important concept in both houses. Senate and House leaders and whips try to keep members of their respective party in line, although this is often a very difficult task. During the vote on NAFTA, for example, the House majority leader and a deputy whip opposed NAFTA, while the Speaker of the House and the House majority whip supported it. In general, however, party loyalty is more common in the House, whose members rely more on the party for reelection help. Because of the House's larger size, its members also rely on the party for rewards of committee assignments. In contrast, members of the Senate are often wealthier and rely more on media than the party in their reelection bids, making it more difficult for party leaders to enforce discipline there. Senate rules don't make it any easier either.

The Committee System

The saying "Congress in session is Congress on exhibition, whilst Congress in its committee rooms is Congress at work" may not be as true today as it was when Woodrow Wilson wrote it in 1883.[37] Still, "The work that takes place in the committee and subcommittee rooms of Capitol Hill is critical to the productivity and effectiveness of Congress."[38] **Standing committees** are the first and last places that most bills go. (When different versions of a bill are passed in the House and Senate, a **conference committee** with members of both houses meets to iron out the differences.) It is usually committee members who play key roles in floor debate in the full House or Senate about the merits of the proposed bill.

standing committee: Committee to which proposed bills are referred.

conference committee: Joint committee created to iron out differences between Senate and House versions of a specific piece of legislation.

Committees are especially important in the House of Representatives because its size makes organization and specialization key, as noted in Table 7.1. The establishment of subcommittees allows for even greater specialization.

An institutionalized committee system was created in 1816, and more and more committees have been added over time. So many committees resulted in duplication and jurisdictional battles that the legislative process suffered. Changes were made to the committee system in the 103rd Congress and then again in the 104th. Still, the growth of committees over the years greatly concerned House Republicans. Thus, when Republicans took control in 1995, they immediately targeted several committees and subcommittees (and the staffs of each of those committees) for cutting.

The plethora of committees and subcommittees, for example, allowed so many House members to become subcommittee chairs and have their own base of power that former Representative Morris K. Udall (D–Ariz.) once joked that if he passed a young colleague in the hall and didn't remember his name, he'd simply greet him with "Good morning, Mr. Chairman," knowing he'd be right about half the time.[39] In the 103rd Congress, for example, before recent reductions, nearly half of all Democrats in the House chaired some committee or subcommittee.

Types of Committees.   There are four types of congressional committees: (1) standing; (2) ad hoc, special, or select; (3) joint; and (4) conference.

1. *Standing committees,* so called because they continue from one Congress to the next, are the committees to which proposed bills are referred for consideration. Fewer than 10 percent of the more than 8,000 measures sent to committees are ever reported out. Standing committees also conduct investigations, such as the Senate Banking Committee's investigation of Whitewater or the Senate Committee on Commerce, Science and Transportation's investigation of the Valujet crash. These are part of a committee's oversight function, discussed later in the chapter.

2. *Ad hoc, special,* or *select committees* are temporary committees appointed for specific purposes, generally to conduct special investigations or studies and to report back to the chamber that established them. Unlike standing committees, select committees do not ordinarily draft legislation but study issues such as the assassinations of John F. Kennedy and Reverend Martin Luther King, Jr.

3. *Joint committees* include members from both houses of Congress who conduct investigations or special studies. They are set up to expedite business between the houses and to help focus public attention on major matters, such as the economy, taxation, or scandals. A joint committee, for example, investigated the Iran–Contra scandal.

4. *Conference committees* are a special kind of joint committee that reconciles differences in bills passed by the House and Senate. The conference committee is made up of members from the House and Senate committees that originally considered the bill. Because the Constitution mandates that all bills pass both houses in the same form, compromises are often needed between the versions that pass each house of Congress. Once the committee comes up with a satisfactory compromise, the reformulated bill is returned to both houses of Congress for their approval. At this point they can only accept or decline the compromise legislation; they cannot change or amend it in any way.

The House and Senate standing committees listed in Table 7.4 were created by statute. In the 104th Congress, the House had twenty-two standing committees, each with an average of about thirty-one members. Together, they had a total of eighty-six subcommittees that collectively acted as the eyes, ears, and hands of the House. They considered issues roughly parallel to those of the departments represented in the president's Cabinet. For example, there were committees on agriculture, national security, the judiciary, veterans affairs, transportation, and commerce.

Although most committees in one house parallel those in the other, the House Rules Committee, for which there is no counterpart in the Senate, plays a key role in the law-making process. Indicative of the importance of Rules, majority party members are appointed directly by the Speaker. This committee reviews most bills after they come from a committee and before they go to the full chamber for consideration. Performing a "traffic cop" function, the House Rules Committee gives each bill what is called a *rule*, which contains the date the bill will come up for debate and the time that will be allotted for discussion, and often specifies what kinds of amendments can be offered. Bills considered under a closed rule cannot be amended.

Standing committees have considerable power. They can kill bills, amend them radically, or hurry them through the process. In the words of Woodrow Wilson, once a bill is referred to a committee, it "crosses a parliamentary bridge of sighs to dim dungeons of silence from whence it never will return." Thus a committee reports out to the full House or Senate only a small fraction of the bills assigned to it. Bills can be "forced" out of a House committee by a **discharge petition** signed by a majority (218) of the House membership, but legislators are reluctant to take this drastic measure.

Until the 104th Congress, a House rule kept the names of those signing discharge petitions secret. In late 1993 the system was targeted by House Republicans who charged that the secrecy surrounding discharge petitions allowed members to claim that they supported legislation, yet it assured that there was no way for constituents to learn if a member indeed had tried to force a stalled bill out of committee. Under a new House rule, adopted in 1995, the clerk is required to publish the names of those who sign a discharge petition each week in the *Congressional Record* as well as to make that information available to the public electronically.

In the 104th Congress, the Senate had fifteen standing committees that ranged in size from twelve to twenty-eight members. It also had sixty-eight subcommittees, which allowed all majority party senators to chair one. For example, the Senate Judiciary Committee had six subcommittees, as illustrated in Table 7.4.

In contrast to the House, whose members hold few committee assignments (an average of 1.8 standing and three subcommittees), senators are spread more thinly, with each serving on an average of three to four committees and seven subcommittees. Whereas the committee system allows House members to become policy or issue specialists, Senate members are often generalists. In the 104th Congress, Senator Connie Mack (R–Fla.), grandson of the long-time owner and manager of the Philadelphia Athletics (before they moved to Kansas City on their way to Oakland) and descendent of three Texans who served in Congress, chaired the Joint Economic Committee. He also served on the Appropriations Committee, the Banking Committee, the Housing and Urban Affairs Committee, and the Select Intelligence Committee. Mack chaired a subcommittee of each of these standing committees and sat on six other subcommittees. (House rules prohibit a committee chair from chairing a subcommittee). In addition to his committee work, the Florida senator was also the chair of the Senate Republican Conference.

Senate committees enjoy the same power over framing legislation as do House committees, but the Senate, being an institution more open to individual input than the House, gives less deference to the work done in committees. In the Senate, legislation is more likely to be rewritten on the floor, where all senators can participate and add amendments at any time.

discharge petition: Petition that gives a majority of the House of Representatives the authority to bring an issue to the floor in the fact of committee inaction.

TABLE 7.4

Committees of the 104th Congress (with a Subcommittee Example)

STANDING COMMITTEES

House

Agriculture
Appropriations
Banking and Financial Services
Budget
Commerce
Economic and Educational Opportunities
Government Reform and Oversight
House Oversight
International Relations
Judiciary
National Security
Resources
Rules
Science
Small Business
Standards of Official Conduct (Ethics)
Transportation and Infrastructure
Veterans' Affairs
Ways and Means

Senate

Agriculture, Nutrition, and Forestry
Appropriations
Armed Services
Banking, Housing, and Urban Affairs
Budget
Commerce, Science and Transportation
Energy and Natural Resources
Environment and Public Works
Finance
Foreign Relations
Governmental Affairs
Indian Affairs
Judiciary   *Judiciary Subcommittees:*
　　　　　　　Administrative Oversight and the Courts
　　　　　　　Antitrust, Business Rights and Competition
　　　　　　　Constitution, Federalism, and Property Rights
　　　　　　　Immigration
　　　　　　　Terrorism, Technology, and Government
　　　　　　　　Information
　　　　　　　Youth Violence
Labor and Human Resources
Rules and Administration
Small Business
Veterans' Affairs

SELECT AND SPECIAL COMMITTEES

House	**Senate**
Select Intelligence	Special Aging
	Select Ethics
	Select Intelligence

JOINT COMMITTEES

Joint Committee on the Library
Joint Committee on Printing
Joint Committee on Taxation
Joint Economic Committee

Committee Membership.   Many newly elected members of Congress come into the body with their sights set on certain committee assignments. Others are more flexible. Many legislators seeking committee assignments inform their party's selection committee of their preferences. They often request assignments based on their own interests or expertise or on a particular committee's ability to help their prospects for reelection. Political scientist Kenneth Shepsle has noted that committee assignments are to members what stocks are to investors—they seek to acquire those that will add to the value of their portfolios.[40]

Representatives often seek committee assignments that have access to what is known as the **pork barrel.** Pork barrel legislation allows representatives to "bring home the bacon" to their districts in the form of public works programs, military bases, or other programs designed to benefit districts directly (see Highlight 7.3: Concrete for America?). A seat on the National Security Committee, for example, allows members to bring lucrative defense contracts back to their districts, or discourage base closings within their districts or states.

Legislators who bring this kind of pork barrel back to their districts are hard to beat at the polls. But, ironically, these programs are the ones that attract much of the public criticism directed at the federal government in general and Congress in particular. Thus it is somewhat paradoxical that pork barrel improves a member's chances for reelection or for election to higher office. In 1984 Jesse Helms (R–N.C.), for example, turned down the chairmanship of the Senate Committee on Foreign Relations to stay on the less prestigious Committee on Agriculture, Nutrition, and Forestry, where he could better ensure continued support for the tobacco industry so vital to his home state's economy.

Pork isn't the only motivator for those seeking lush committee assignments. Some committees, such as Commerce, facilitate reelection by giving members influence over decisions that affect large campaign contributors. Other committees, such as Eco-

> **pork barrel:** Legislation that allows representatives to "bring home the bacon" to their districts in the form of public works programs, military bases, or other programs designed to benefit their districts directly.

Highlight 7.3

Concrete for America?

One young Republican representative from rural California, John Doolittle, embodied the conflict between the Contract with America's commitment to shrinking the costs of government and old-fashioned pork barrel politics. Much of California's $20 billion farm industry depends heavily on federally sponsored dams and irrigation programs—including the farmland and suburbs served by Doolittle. Thus he has become an avid proponent of a dam within his district. Auburn Dam would cost at least $2.2 billion, yielding water and power for the American River flood plain in Doolittle's district.

The dam's construction was halted in the 1970s, when geologists found that simply filling the reservoir could trigger an earthquake in the fault zone where the dam sat. Nevertheless, in the 104th Congress, Doolittle staunchly advocated the Auburn Dam, arguing for flood control measures that would protect the region against hypothetical floods from the dam's reservoir. Why the enthusiasm for a project of questionable value and enormous cost? Much of the huge construction budget (including $700 million out of taxpayers' pockets) would be spent in his district, and, as Doolittle says, the dam would offer "badly needed recreation to our area."

This is the same John Doolittle who received an award from the National Taxpayers Union for federal budget cutting. When, in February of 1995, that same organization singled out Auburn Dam from among other federal projects as a perfect combination of wasteful spending and environmental damage, Doolittle responded, "These people don't know the first thing about economics."

Members of Congress can indeed be zealous about saving taxpayers' money—except, of course, when the needs of their constituencies come first.*

*Marc Reisner, "Concrete for America? Count Him In!" *The New York Times* (August 20, 1995), OpEd.

nomic and Educational Opportunities or Judiciary, attract members eager to work on the policy responsibilities assigned to the committee even if the appointment does them little good at the ballot box. A third motivator for certain committee assignments is the desire to have power and influence within the chamber. The Appropriations and Budget Committees provide that kind of reward for some members.

Inevitably, some members end up with "bad" committee assignments. After her 1968 election, Representative Shirley Chisholm (D–N.Y.), the first African-American woman elected to Congress, was assigned to the House Agriculture Committee. "Apparently, all they know here in Washington about Brooklyn is that a tree grows there," complained Chisholm. "I think it would be hard to imagine an assignment that is less relevant to my background or to the needs of the predominantly black and Puerto Rican people who elected me," she protested. Although some urban Democrats welcome serving on the committee that oversees the food stamp program, Chisholm fought for a different assignment and ultimately landed one on the Veterans Affairs Committee. "There are a lot more veterans in my district than there are trees," she later explained.[41]

In both the House and the Senate, committee membership generally reflects the party distribution within that chamber. For example, at the outset of the 104th Congress, Republicans held 53 percent of the House seats and claimed about that same share of the seats on several committees, including International Relations, Commerce, and House Oversight. On committees more critical to the operation of the House or to setting national policy, the majority often takes a disproportionate share of the slots. Since the Rules Committee regulates access to the floor for legislation approved by other standing committees, control by the majority party is essential for it to manage the flow of legislation. For this reason, no matter how narrow the majority party's margin in the chamber, it makes up at least two-thirds of Rules's membership.

Due to the smaller size of Senate committees, the majority party has a narrow margin on its committees. For example, in the 104th Congress, if one Republican joined a united Democratic contingent, then the Republicans would be unable to report legislation out of all but three committees. And, unlike the House, no Senate committees have a disproportionate number of majority party members.

The Declining Power of Committee Chairs?   Before recent changes giving the Speaker more power, committee chairs long enjoyed tremendous power and prestige. Even today's chairs may choose not to schedule hearings on a bill to kill it. They may convene meetings when opponents are absent, or they may adjourn meetings when things are going badly. Personal skill, influence, and expertise are a chair's best allies. After the 1910–11 Revolt, against Speaker Cannon, the member of the majority party with the most continuous service on a committee was automatically made its chair. In the 1970s moderate and liberal Democrats pushed through changes in the House designed to break the hold that conservative committee chairs from the South had long enjoyed. In 1971, House Democrats voted to elect committee chairs by secret ballot in the party caucus at the beginning of the session, and seniority was no longer the sole criterion for becoming a House chair. Democrats occasionally ousted a chair for being too conservative, or too senile. (In the Senate there was little change, because seniority is not nearly so important there; however, if one-fifth of the party caucus requests it, a secret ballot may be used to elect committee chairs.)

In 1995 Speaker Gingrich ignored the seniority system and selected several committee chairs whom he trusted to move his reforms through the House. The "amiable" and moderate seventy-two-year-old Carlos Moorhead (R–Cal.), for example, was in line to chair either the Commerce or Judiciary Committees, but Gingrich selected others to head those key committees. Moorhead was viewed as not being tough enough to shepherd key Contract items through committee. To Appropriations, Gingrich appointed Robert Livingston (R–La.), who stood fifth in seniority.

Republicans also dramatically limited the long-term power of committee chairs. New rules prevent chairs from serving more than six years—three consecutive Congresses—or heading their own subcommittees.

The power of committee chairs was somewhat diminished by the actions of Speaker Gingrich, who often bypassed chairs by creating dozens of task forces to help perfect legislation. Another blow to the power of committee chairs, and committees in general, came with the frequent use of amendments to appropriations bills to bar expenditures for programs opposed by Republican leaders.

Allies of Gingrich were, however, given some important powers. As committee chairs, they were given the authority to select all subcommittee chairs. Chairs also call meetings, strategize, recommend majority members to sit on conference committees, and are in charge of the committee staff.

Political scientist Roger Davidson suggests that it was necessary for Republicans to restructure the committee system in order to achieve the reforms they sought. Democrats, Davidson argues, promoted a proliferation of semiautonomous committees and subcommittees as a way to allow multiple points for interest groups to influence the lawmaking process. So, in situations where the relationship between a committee and an interest group that benefited from existing policies appeared too cozy, Gingrich shifted responsibility for finalizing substantive legislation to the Rules or Budget Committees, where he and other House leaders had more influence.[42]

THE LAWMAKING FUNCTION OF CONGRESS

$\mathcal{T}$he organization of Congress allows it to fulfill its constitutional responsibilities, chief among which is its lawmaking function. It is through this power that Congress affects the day-to-day lives of all Americans as well as sets policy for the future. Proposals for legislation—be they about education, v-chips, crime, or foreign aid—can come from the president, executive agencies, committee staffs, interest groups, or even private individuals. Only members of the House or Senate, however, can formally submit a bill for congressional consideration. Once a bill is proposed, it usually reaches a dead end. Of the approximately 9,000 bills introduced during each session of Congress, fewer than 5 percent to 10 percent are enacted, or made into law.

It is probably useful to think of Congress as a system of multiple vetoes, which was what the Framers desired. They wanted to disperse power; and as Congress has evolved, it has come closer and closer to the Framers' intentions. As a bill goes through Congress, a dispersion of power occurs as roadblocks to passage must be surmounted at numerous steps in the process. In addition to realistic roadblocks, caution signs and other opportunities for delay abound. A member who sponsors a bill must get through *every* obstacle; in contrast, successful opposition means "winning" at only one of many stages, including: (1) the subcommittee, (2) the House full committee, (3) the House Rules Committee, (4) the House, (5) the Senate subcommittee, (6) the full Senate committee, (7) the Senate, (8) floor leaders in both Houses, (9) the House–Senate Conference Committee, and (10) the president.

The story of how a bill becomes a law in the United States can be told in two different ways. The first is the "textbook" method, which provides a greatly simplified road map of the process to make it easier to understand. We'll review this method first. But real life, of course, rarely goes according to plan. So we will next look at an actual example of how a particular bill became a law, and explore the true complexities of the process.

How a Bill Becomes a Law: The Textbook Version

A bill must survive three stages before it becomes a law. It must be approved by one or more standing committees and both chambers, and, if House and Senate versions differ, a conference report resolving those differences must be accepted by each house. A bill may be killed during any of these stages, so it is much easier to defeat a bill than it is to get one passed. The House and Senate have parallel processes, and often the same bill is introduced in each chamber at the same time.

A bill must be introduced by a member of Congress, but it is often sponsored by a whole list of other members in an early effort to show support for it. Once introduced, the bill is sent to the clerk of the chamber, who gives it a number (for example, HR 1 or S 1—indicating House or Senate bill number one for the session). The bill is then printed, distributed, and sent to the appropriate committee or committees for consideration.

The first action takes place within the committee, after it is referred there by the Speaker. The committee usually refers the bill to one of its subcommittees, which researches the bill and decides whether to hold hearings on it. The subcommittee hearings provide the opportunity for those on both sides of the issue to voice their opinions. Most of these hearings are now open to the public because of 1970s sunshine laws, which require open sessions. After the hearings, the bill is revised, and the subcommittee votes to approve or defeat the bill. If the subcommittee votes in favor of the bill, it is returned to the full committee, which then either rejects the bill or sends it to the House or Senate floor with a favorable recommendation (see Figure 7.6).

The second stage of action takes place on the House or Senate floor. In the House, before a bill may be debated on the floor, it must be approved by the Rules Committee and given a rule and a place on the calendar, or schedule. (House budget bills don't go to the Rules Committee.) In the House, the rule given to a bill determines the limits on the floor debate and specifies what types of amendments, if any, may be attached to the bill. Once the Rules Committee considers the bill, it is put on the calendar.

When the day arrives for floor debate, the House may choose to form a Committee of the Whole. This allows the House to deliberate with only 100 members present to expedite consideration of the bill. On the House floor, the bill is debated, amendments are offered, and a vote ultimately is taken by the full House. If the bill survives, it is sent to the Senate for consideration if it was not considered there simultaneously.

Unlike the House, where debate is necessarily limited given the size of the body, bills may be held up by a hold or a filibuster in the Senate. A **hold** is a tactic by which a senator asks to be informed before a particular bill is brought to the floor. This request signals the Senate leadership and the sponsors of the bill that a colleague may have objections to the bill and should be consulted before further action is taken. Because any single member can filibuster a bill or other action to death, the Senate leadership is very reluctant to bring actions with a hold on them to the floor. Explained one Senate staffer, "Four or five years ago it started to mean that if you put a hold on something, it would never come up. It became, in fact, a veto."[43]

The hold system has been under attack by observers and Senate members for some time. The ability of a senator to place a hold on a bill exposes senators to demands from

hold: A tactic by which a senator asks to be informed before a particular bill is brought to the floor.

FIGURE 7.6

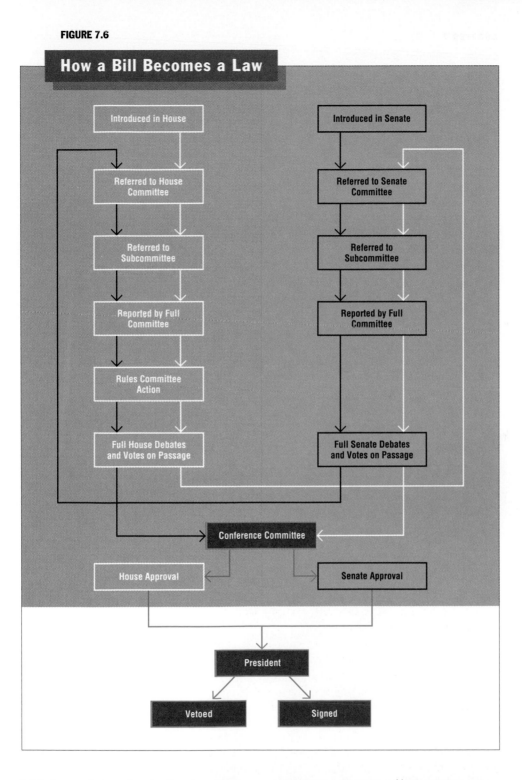

How a Bill Becomes a Law

Introduced in House

Introduced in Senate

Referred to House Committee

Referred to Senate Committee

Referred to Subcommittee

Referred to Subcommittee

Reported by Full Committee

Reported by Full Committee

Rules Committee Action

Full House Debates and Votes on Passage

Full Senate Debates and Votes on Passage

Conference Committee

House Approval

Senate Approval

President

Vetoed

Signed

lobbyists and constituents to stop action on any bill they don't like.[44] The hold system simply has "gotten out of control," says former Senator Bennett Johnston (D–La.).[45] In the first sessions of the 103rd and 104th Congresses, for example, holds were placed on more than two-thirds of the 250 bills reported out of committee in the Senate. (Since holds are not made public, it is difficult to know how many are actually placed and who exercises the privilege.) In the 103rd Congress, holds were used to delay several presidential appointments, including that of political scientist Robert Pastor of Emory University to be ambassador to Panama. After months of Senate inaction, Pastor removed his name from consideration.

filibuster: A formal way of halting action on a bill by means of long speeches or unlimited debate in the Senate.

Filibusters, which allow for unlimited debate on a bill, grew out of the absence of rules to limit speech in the Senate and are often used to "talk a bill to death." In contrast to a hold, a filibuster is a more formal and public way of halting action on a bill by means of long speeches or unlimited debate in the Senate. The filibuster became an increasingly common feature of Senate life during the slavery debates. In 1917, eleven senators waged a filibuster against an important foreign policy matter supported by President Woodrow Wilson. The Senate then adopted a rule to avoid the potential disaster of tying the president's hands during World War I.

To end a filibuster, *cloture* must be invoked. To cut off debate, sixteen senators must first sign a motion for cloture, then sixty senators must vote to end debate. If cloture is invoked, no more than thirty additional hours can be devoted to debate before the legislation at issue is brought to a vote (see Highlight 7.4: Filibusters: Then and Now).

The third stage of action takes place when the two chambers of Congress approve different versions of the same bill. When this happens, a conference committee is established to iron out the differences between the two versions of a bill. The president is not given a multiple choice and allowed to select which version he prefers. The conference committee, whose members are from the original House and Senate committees, hammers out a compromise, which is returned to each chamber for a final vote.

Highlight 7.4

Filibusters: Then and Now

The term "filibuster" is derived from a Dutch word that means "continuous talking." Today the filibuster is a tactic senators may use in an effort to talk a bill to death. In 1854, for example, senators attempted to talk to death the Kansas–Nebraska Act in an effort to forestall deciding the issue of slavery.

There are no rules on the content of a filibuster as long as the senator keeps on talking. A senator may read from a phone book, recite poetry, or read cookbooks in order to delay a vote. Often, a team of senators will take turns speaking to keep the filibuster going in the hope that a bill will be tabled or killed. In 1964, for example, a group of Northern liberal senators continued a filibuster for eighty-two days in an effort to prevent amendments that would weaken a civil rights bill. Historically Southern senators made the most use of the filibuster in their efforts to circumvent or at least delay civil rights legislation. Senator Strom Thurmond (D–S.C.)* holds the record for the longest one-man filibuster: In 1957 he opposed civil rights legislation in a personal filibuster that lasted more than twenty-four hours.

As the number of filibusters has increased dramatically, it has become harder and harder for the Senate to get its work done.

As revealed below, the average number of filibusters shows no sign of slowing down, and it is easy to understand why calls for reform include changing Senate rules regarding this opportunity for a single member to hold up the work of the rest.

YEAR	AVERAGE NUMBER OF FILIBUSTERS
1951–60	1 (per Congress)
1961–70	4.6
1971–80	11.2
1981–86	16.7
1987–92	26.7

*Thurmond changed his party affiliation from Democrat to Republican on September 16, 1964, shortly after passage of the Civil Rights Act of 1964, which he vehemently opposed.

No changes or amendments are allowed at this stage. If the bill is passed it is sent to the president, who either signs it or vetoes it. If the bill is not passed, it dies.

The president has ten days to consider a bill. He has five options: (1) He can sign the bill, at which point it becomes law. (2) He can veto the bill, which is more likely to occur when the president is of a different party than the majority in Congress. In the 103rd Congress, President Clinton became the first president in 140 years not to veto a single bill during a two-year Congress. Congress may override the president's veto with a two-thirds vote in each chamber, a very difficult task. (3) He can wait the full ten days, at the end of which time the bill becomes law without his signature if Congress is still in session. (4) If the Congress adjourns before the ten days are up, the president can choose not to sign the bill, and it is considered "pocket vetoed." A **pocket veto** figuratively allows bills stashed in the president's pocket to die. The only way for a bill then to become law is for it to be reintroduced in the next session and go through the process all over again. Because Congress sets its own date of adjournment, technically the session could be continued the few extra days necessary to prevent a pocket veto. Extensions are unlikely, however, as sessions are scheduled to adjourn close to the November elections or the December holidays. (5) The last action that the president can take is to exercise a **line-item veto.**

pocket veto: If Congress adjourns during the ten days the president has to consider a bill passed by both houses of Congress, without the president's signature, the bill is considered vetoed.

Presidents since Ulysses S. Grant urged Congress to give them a line-item veto as a way to curb wasteful spending, particularly in pork barrel projects added to bills to assure member support. The line-item veto allows the president to strike or reduce any discretionary budget authority or eliminate any targeted tax provision (the line item) in any bill sent to him by the Congress. The president must then prepare a separate rescisions package for each piece of legislation he wishes to veto and then submit his proposal to Congress within twenty working days. The president's proposed recisions take effect if Congress does nothing unless both houses of Congress pass a disapproval bill by a two-thirds vote within twenty days of receiving the rescisions.[46]

line-item veto: The power to veto specific provisions of a bill without vetoing the bill in its entirety.

The line-item veto was an item in the Contract with America, and some wondered if a Republican-controlled Congress would be hesitant to give such potentially expansive authority to a Democratic president. On Ronald Reagan's eighty-fourth birthday, however, the House honored the former president, a long-time proponent of the line-item veto, by passing it on a vote of 294 to 134. This vote was followed by quick, positive action in the Senate. In enthusiastically signing the bill, President Clinton pledged to give unprecedented scrutiny to the "darkest corners of the federal budget."

How a Bill *Really* Becomes a Law: The Clean Air Act Amendments of 1990

The textbook version of a bill's life gives you an idea of the hurdles a bill must pass to become a law. But there is more to it than meets the eye. Republicans in the 104th Congress made several efforts to repeal sections of the Clean Air Act Amendments passed in 1990, and state and local legislators often were behind or in support of those efforts. While in theory everyone wants clean air, large corporations and localities are upset when costs of compliance with federal legislation reduce their profits or eat into their already strained budgets.

As controversy over the Clean Air Act amendments continues, it is useful to examine how they came to pass. The story is a good illustration of how the actual passage of laws deviates in complex and interesting ways from the textbook way described above. It also underscores the fact that even when these hard-fought battles appear to be complete, the real legislative process is never over—bills may be reconsidered, or appropriations to implement them fully may be reduced or eliminated altogether (see Figure 7.7).

FIGURE 7.7

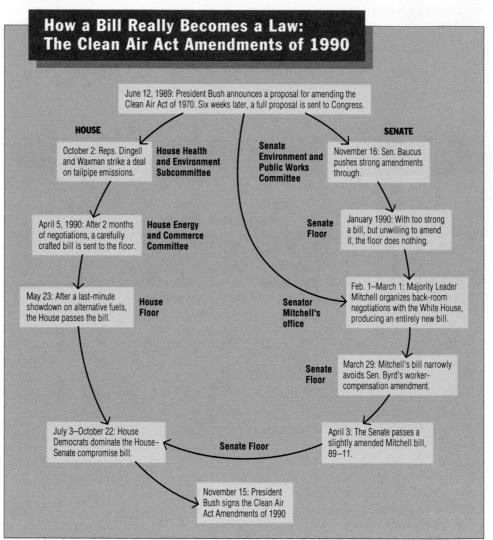

How a Bill Really Becomes a Law: The Clean Air Act Amendments of 1990

June 12, 1989: President Bush announces a proposal for amending the Clean Air Act of 1970. Six weeks later, a full proposal is sent to Congress.

HOUSE

SENATE

October 2: Reps. Dingell and Waxman strike a deal on tailpipe emissions. — **House Health and Environment Subcommittee**

Senate Environment and Public Works Committee

November 16: Sen. Baucus pushes strong amendments through.

April 5, 1990: After 2 months of negotiations, a carefully crafted bill is sent to the floor. — **House Energy and Commerce Committee**

Senate Floor

January 1990: With too strong a bill, but unwilling to amend it, the floor does nothing.

May 23: After a last-minute showdown on alternative fuels, the House passes the bill. — **House Floor**

Senator Mitchell's office

Feb. 1–March 1: Majority Leader Mitchell organizes back-room negotiations with the White House, producing an entirely new bill.

Senate Floor

March 29: Mitchell's bill narrowly avoids Sen. Byrd's worker-compensation amendment.

July 3–October 22: House Democrats dominate the House-Senate compromise bill. — **Senate Floor** — April 3: The Senate passes a slightly amended Mitchell bill, 89–11.

November 15: President Bush signs the Clean Air Act Amendments of 1990

As with most major modern legislation, passage of the Clean Air Act Amendments of 1990 officially began at the White House. After campaigning for president in 1988 as an environmentalist, George Bush promised in his inaugural address to send Congress a major clean air legislative package. Over the next several months, he assembled an executive team: Robert Grady of the Office of Management and Budget (OMB); William Reilly, the head of the Environmental Protection Agency (EPA), and several aides; Roger Porter, the president's domestic policy adviser; and, in an unusual move, C. Boyden Gray, the White House chief counsel. Gray was a close adviser to the president and was considered by many to be the "real clean air nut" in the administration. Notably excluded were members of the Department of Energy.

After considerable discussion, study, and interviewing of academics and others, this team hammered together a vast proposal in Bush's name. Fully 140 representatives and twenty-five senators, led by Representative John Dingell (D–Mich.) and Senator John Chafee (R–R.I.), introduced it as a bill in each house.

In the Senate the bill was assigned to the Environment and Public Works Committee, which was considered extremely pro-environmentalist and out of sync with the rest of the Senate. When its version of the bill was reported back to the floor, the committee had stretched the proposed bill's provisions so much that the package was unacceptable to the full Senate. Automobile tailpipe emission standards, for example, were far too strict to win passage in the Senate. Instead of igniting a flurry of amendments and arguments, individual senators ignored the extreme bill entirely because they didn't want to touch it. Supporters knew that calling a vote would bring defeat.

George Mitchell (D–Me.), the Senate majority leader, then took over in a typical modern party leadership maneuver. He called a series of closed-door negotiations that included representatives of the administration; Bob Dole (R–Kan.), the minority leader; and other key senators who were called in on those points in which they had a vested interest. After six long weeks of hard negotiating, this process produced an agreement among Democrats, Republicans, and the administration on every single point in the package, including tailpipe emissions and air-quality standards. As a group, the participants agreed to fight off every amendment that might be proposed from the floor, with the stipulation that any amendment successfully passed would free up any party to walk away from the deal.

This process, though extraordinary by historical standards, has become quite common on major bills as political parties have strengthened and the committees have proven unsuccessful at managing a more unruly Senate or House floor. Speaker Gingrich's formation of special task forces to formulate important legislation was thus the continuation of a trend. When the act was brought to the floor of the Senate, the powerful team led by Mitchell, Dole, and the White House succeeded in fending off all major amendments—only a few minor adjustments were allowed to pass—and the Senate proceeded to pass the resultant package by an overwhelming margin.

In the House, meanwhile, the Energy and Commerce Committees had much more say, partly because until recently, members of the House generally deferred to the typically greater expertise of the specialized committees, particularly when technical issues were involved. First a rule was assigned to the bill so that no amendments could be offered without the approval of key committee members. Like representatives from tobacco-growing states, who for years have tried to prevent any legislation adverse to the tobacco industry, the powerful chair of the committee, John Dingell (D–Mich.), had long been trying to scuttle clean air legislation to protect his constituents, Detroit auto workers. The Environment and Health subcommittee of his panel, however, was chaired by Henry Waxman (D–Cal.), who for just as many years had championed clean air for his smog-ridden constituents in Los Angeles. Once Bush broke the legislative deadlock with a proposal, Dingell knew he would have to deal with Waxman and have the committee report out some kind of bill.

Taking a cue from the Senate, these two pulled back behind closed doors in informal negotiations that only indirectly involved other members of the committee. When they reached a deal on tailpipe emissions, their biggest sticking point, the official committee proceedings got back on track. Unlike what had transpired in the Senate, however, none of these behind-the-scenes or committee negotiations involved the White House. This was because House Republicans had become so ineffectual after so many years of Democratic control that the Democrats, in effect, could ignore them and their party leader in the White House. (It was this kind of arrogance that was to come back to haunt the Democrats when they lost power.) Dingell, Waxman, Speaker Thomas Foley, and their colleagues were much more willing to slam the door on those on the other side of the aisle than were their counterparts in the Senate.

Once both houses passed versions of the bill, the conference committee phase commenced. Because of House members' greater knowledge and expertise (they sit on fewer committees), they controlled the course of deliberations, making the bill stronger than the one originally proposed by the White House. President Bush was in no position to veto the stronger bill, however, because he had taken part (through his teammates) in the Senate's side of the deal making and had campaigned so loudly as a friend of the environment. In the end, therefore, the House crafters like Waxman who wanted a strong bill were able to carry the day.

Divided Government

Any kind of legislation is, of course, more difficult to pass when the president and Congress are of different political parties. For years Republican presidents blamed the Democrats who controlled the Congress for legislative gridlock—increasingly, the two parties could agree on fewer and fewer important pieces of legislation. If Presidents Reagan or Bush wanted a particular bill passed into law, the Democratic Congress often rejected it. When Congress passed bills opposed by President Bush, however, Democrats repeatedly failed to muster enough votes to override his vetoes. Then in 1993, for the first time since 1980, both Houses of Congress and the presidency were controlled by the same political party. Several major presidential programs were passed, including bills previously passed by Congress but vetoed by George Bush. "Gridlock is gone," declared House Majority Leader Richard Gephardt (D–Mo.) after the end of the first session of the 103rd Congress, which was one of the most productive sessions in recent years. In 1993 Bill Clinton enjoyed an exceptionally high success rate as Congress supported 86.4 percent of legislation he supported, including the budget bill, The North American Free Trade Agreement (NAFTA) the Family and Medical Leave Act, and the Brady Bill.

Gephardt's boasting, however, was premature. The 103rd Congress totally rejected Clinton's efforts to reform health care and the President was forced to withdrawal his plan. Nor did the president make any progress on his campaign promise to "end welfare as we know it."

In 1995 Republicans gained control of both houses, and the partisan division that characterized most of the 1970s and 1980s returned. Efforts by congressional Republicans to slice deficits and eliminate social programs while spreading around tax cuts were impaled on President Clinton's veto pen. As a result of these basic disagreements over the role of the federal government, late in 1995 and again in early 1996, large portions of the U.S. government were forced to shut down when President Clinton vetoed budget and appropriations bills that he believed cut social programs too deeply.

Although our Constitution provides for separation of powers, the American public has come to expect Congress to be the junior partner. When Congress fails to go along with presidential initiatives, many people become frustrated and the legislature's reputation suffers. When the government shutdown occurred after Republicans in Congress stood their ground in the face of presidential vetoes of budget and appropriations bills, public disapproval of the job being done by Congress rose from 56 percent in October 1995 to 68 percent one month later.[47] During the course of 1995, voters changed their views of which branch they wanted to have greater influence over public policy. In February 1995, 52 percent wanted Congress to dominate as opposed to 37 percent favoring the president. Nine months later 42 percent opted for Congress while 48 percent preferred the president.[48]

The multitude of ever newer surveys that surround us makes it seem that many Americans are fickle—or perhaps they pay so little attention to politics that their attitudes are easily swayed. Immediately after the 1994 election that gave Republicans control of Congress, Americans told pollster Louis Harris that they liked *divided government* by a 48 percent to 36 percent margin.[49] Perhaps it is because many do not understand that the president can veto congressional initiatives, or because they do not appreciate the significance of partisan differences, that most Americans believed that the 104th Congress would be able to accomplish more than most congresses do.[50] The positive attitudes toward Republicans registered in the 1994 election had already begun to dissipate before the newly elected had an opportunity to enact legislation. From November 1994 to January 1995, the share of the public who thought that Republicans had better policy ideas than President Clinton dropped from 55 percent to 37 percent.[51] Still, in November 1996, Republicans were returned to power in Congress and many Americans seem quite comfortable with divided government.

HOW MEMBERS MAKE DECISIONS

As a bill makes its way through the labyrinth of the lawmaking process described above, members are confronted with the question: How should I vote? Trustees worry that they will "miss" something in a bill and vote the "wrong" way, alienating voters at home. Delegates worry that they don't know which way their constituents actually want them to vote. Although most legislation pertains to fairly mundane matters, members nonetheless fear that they will cast that one wrong vote that will become a major issue in their next campaign for reelection.

Members often listen to their own personal beliefs on many matters, but those views can often be moderated by other considerations. To avoid making any voting mistakes, members look to a variety of sources for cues. Major cue givers, of course, include constituents as well as colleagues, political parties, caucuses, interest groups, staff members, and the president. And, frequently, how a member ultimately decides or votes on any particular measure will vary according to the issues involved and the context in which they are presented.[52]

Constituents

If an issue affects their constituency, a representative often will try to determine how the people back home feel. Staff members often keep running tallies of the letters and phone calls for and against a policy that will be voted on soon. Only if a legislator has strong personal preferences will he or she vote against a clearly expressed desire of their constituents. Studies by political scientists show that members vote in conformity with prevailing opinion in their districts about two-thirds of the time.[53] And, on average, Congress passes laws that reflect national public opinion at about the same rate.[54] Legislators tend to act on their own preferences as trustees when dealing with topics that have come through the committees on which they serve or issues that they know about as a result of experience in other contexts, such as their vocation. On items of little concern to people back in the district or for which the legislator has little firsthand knowledge, the tendency is to turn to other sources for voting cues. The opinions of one's colleagues, especially those who belong to his or her party, often weigh heavily when casting a roll-call vote.

Constituents—the people who live and vote in the home district or state—are always in the member's mind when casting a vote. It is rare for a legislator to vote against the wishes of his or her constituency regularly, particularly on issues of welfare rights, domestic policy, or other highly salient issues such as affirmative action, abortion, or war. Most constituents often have strong convictions on one or more of these issues. For example, during the 1960s, representatives from Southern states could not hope to keep their seats for long if they voted in favor of proposed civil rights legislation. But gauging how voters feel about any particular issue often is not easy. Because it is virtually impossible to know how the folks back home feel on all issues, a representative's *perception* of their preferences is important. Even when voters have opinions, legislators may get little guidance if their district is narrowly divided. Abortion is an issue about which many voters feel passionately; but a legislator whose district has roughly equal numbers of pro-choice and pro-life advocates can satisfy only a portion of his or her constituents.

Political scientist Richard F. Fenno, Jr., observed a linkage between the two spheres —Washington and back in the home district—in which a member of Congress operates.[55] Efforts back home can buy legislators freedom in Washington. By frequently returning to the district (many House members east of the Mississippi go home almost every weekend) and making presentations to all kinds of groups, from Little League breakfasts to the Chamber of Commerce, the legislator can demonstrate competence to promote the district's well-being and to handle complex foreign and domestic policy issues. By repeatedly demonstrating competence, a legislator earns the constituents' trust. Once trusted, the majority of the electorate will grant its member of Congress some latitude in voting on issues that come before Congress. Thus, as another incumbency advantage, senior members may have greater freedom to follow their own judgment when casting roll-call votes than junior members, who may feel more constrained to determine their constituents' preferences about issues and then to follow the position of the majority back home.

Fenno concludes that members perceive their constituencies to consist of four groups, as illustrated in Figure 7.8. Members initially describe their "geographical con-

FIGURE 7.8

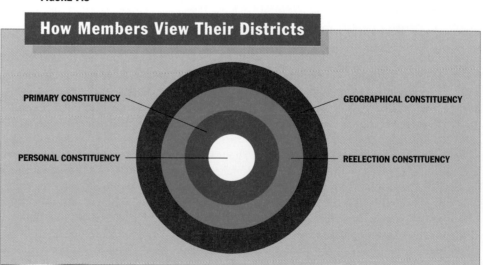

How Members View Their Districts

PRIMARY CONSTITUENCY

GEOGRAPHICAL CONSTITUENCY

PERSONAL CONSTITUENCY

REELECTION CONSTITUENCY

SOURCE: From Richard F. Fenno, Jr., *Homestyle: House Members in Their Districts.* Reprinted by permission of Harper Collins College Publishers.

stituency"—the location and size of the district—and its internal makeup, or socioeconomic and political characteristics and the proportion of people who are "blue collar," Jewish, Democratic, or elderly, for example. Within the geographical constituency, members define a "reelection constituency," consisting of the people who the member thinks vote for him or her. This is the member's perceived political base; to disagree with the reelection constituency could cost the member his or her seat. Within the reelection constituency is a smaller group consisting of the member's strongest supporters, the "primary constituency." These loyalists vote for the member and provide campaign assistance and financial support. The fourth and final constituency is made up of the people closest to the member—his or her "personal constituency"—including friends and advisers. Thus a member of Congress perceives his or her district in a variety of ways, and sometimes the four constituencies may be in conflict. The typical voter in the district may have quite different views from those of the member's strongest supporters. Although few of the member's constituents will usually be actually aware of the member's voting decisions, it would be foolish for a representative or senator to ignore an overwhelming majority of his or her constituents' views on highly visible issues, such as abortion, international trade in a blue-collar district, the defense budget in a district with a large military installation, or crop supports in a rural district.

Colleagues, Class, and Political Parties

Members of Congress tend to make their closest friends among colleagues who share their partisan tie. Having been elected to Congress on the same party label rarely produces lock-step conformity, but it indicates agreement on at least some important issues. Legislators have been socialized to see the members of the other party as opponents—sometimes as dishonest, misguided opponents—while they have cooperated with members of their own party to achieve common goals. Members of a party are also drawn together because they often share similar fates. When Democrats are in the majority, they have better prospects for passing legislation and they chair all committees and subcommittees and Republican desires are ignored. When Republicans are in the majority, these roles and fates are reversed.

Colleagues. The range and complexity of issues confronting Congress means that no one can be up to speed on more than a few topics. When members must vote on bills about which they know very little, they often turn for advice to colleagues who have served on the committee that handled the legislation. On issues that are of little interest to a legislator, *logrolling*, or vote trading, often occurs. Logrolling often takes place on specialized bills targeting money or projects to selected congressional districts. A yea vote by an unaffected member often is given to a member in exchange for the promise of a future yea vote on a similar piece of specialized legislation.

Other appeals are of a more personal nature. During the Democrats' last-minute efforts to secure passage of the Omnibus Budget Reconciliation Act in 1993, President Clinton and many of his aides did all they could to convince Senator Robert Kerrey (D–Neb.) to cast his critical vote for the act. At the request of the majority leader, Daniel Patrick Moynihan (D–N.Y.), Chair of the Senate Finance Committee, talked to Kerrey and even brought him home to talk to his wife. The next day, after Kerrey had again been courted by the president at a White House breakfast, Moynihan went to Kerrey's office and told him: "I need you on this one. If you give me this one, I promise I'll never ask you for anything else."[56] Sometimes a personal plea from a close colleague is what can ultimately win a vote. (In this case, without Kerrey's vote, Clinton's budget plan would have failed.)

Class. Members are also strongly influenced by their class—that is, the year in which they were elected. For example, until 1993, the largest "new" class in years was the class elected in 1974, when the Watergate scandal and the resignation of President Richard M. Nixon resulted in a Democratic landslide that produced seventy-five new House Democrats. In 1979 thirty-six new Republicans arrived in the House, followed by fifty-two more in 1981. Members of the same class share information with one another and form networks that often solidify as the members' tenure in the House increases.

The seventy-three new House freshmen Republicans elected to the 104th Congress have been a particularly close group and a potent political force. In that Congress they were a pivotal voting bloc in the Republican Conference and consistently promoted conservative causes. The freshman were even far more revolutionary than the Speaker and were ready to vote against him to advance their more conservative agenda.

Party. Political parties are another important source of influence. The cohesion of the political parties in congressional floor votes has varied greatly over time. At the turn of the century, most roll calls found a majority of the Democrats lined up against a majority of the Republicans, and often the parties divided, with 90 percent of the Democrats facing off against an equally cohesive set of Republicans.[57] The issues along which Democratic President Franklin D. Roosevelt's New Deal were fought, such as the passage of social welfare policies and government regulation of the economy, typically found united parties squared off against each other.[58]

During much of the period after World War II, congressional parties, and particularly the Democrats, often divided so that a conservative coalition consisting of Southern Democrats and Republicans frequently formed majorities on issues such as civil rights and social welfare issues. The growth of the role of a black electorate in the South's Democratic Party began in the early 1970s, after passage of the Voting Rights Act of 1965, and resulted in a gradual healing of the rift within the Democratic Party. After 1980 the frequency with which the conservative Southern Democrat/Republican coalition declined and clear cut party voting became more common. From 1970 to the mid-1990s, the incidence of party votes in which majorities of the two parties took opposing sides roughly doubled to more than 60 percent of all roll-call votes. In 1993 about two-thirds of the votes taken in each chamber broke along party lines. When the Republicans took control of Congress in 1995 with the Contract with America as its agenda, the parties divided on 73 percent of the House and 69 percent of the Senate roll call votes, making 1995 the most partisan year in generations. Legislators are loyal to their parties about 80 percent of the time when issues divide the parties.[59]

Today, many members of Congress elected on a partisan ticket feel a degree of obligation to their party and to the president if he is of the same party. The national political parties have little say in who gets a party's nomination for the U.S. Senate or the House. But once a candidate has emerged successfully from a primary contest (see chapter 13), both houses have committees that provide campaign assistance. It is to each party's advantage to win as many seats as possible in each house. If a member is elected with the financial support or campaign visits from popular members and party leaders, they're much more inclined to toe the party line. Newt Gingrich, for example, personally campaigned in the districts of 65 members of the 104th Congress and raised $6 million for their campaigns.[60] By May 1996, in spite of mixed public sentiment about the Speaker, 140 House members had asked the Speaker to appear in their districts.[61]

Each party in Congress also has a whip system that is used to disseminate information, keep track of who is voting with the party and who is not, and influence and pressure the undecided. Generally, this pressure is subtle; however, in some instances, party leaders turn on the heat. For example, when Senate Democratic leaders wanted to override a veto by President Ronald Reagan in 1987, they adopted a "baby-sitting" strategy in which wavering Democrats were accompanied at all times by two other Democrats with the "right" views. Clearly, the party cue can be strong at times, and going along on legislation of importance to the party leadership can have its rewards.

Caucuses

Special interest caucuses were created to facilitate member communication—often across party lines—over issues of common concern. By 1994 there were at least 140 special interest caucuses, including many formed to promote certain industries, such as textiles, tourism, wine, coal, steel, mushrooms, and cranberries, or to advance particular views or interests. Traditionally, most of these caucuses were not particularly active unless their interests were threatened. In the 1970s, for example, when an influx of mushrooms from China and Taiwan threatened the sale of U.S. mushrooms, the sixty-member Mushroom Caucus sprang into action to defend the mushroom growers in their districts.

Before 1995 twenty-seven caucuses enjoyed special status as legislative service organizations (LSOs). Included among these were the liberal Black Caucus, the Congressional Caucus for Women's Issues, and the Democratic Study Group. The Congressional Black Caucus (CBC) was formed by African-American legislators in 1971 in an effort to counter perceived hostility for their agenda from President Nixon. In 1996 all black House members except Republican J. C. Watts of Oklahoma belonged to the CBC. The Congresswoman's Caucus was formed in 1977, with fifteen of the eighteen women in the House joining. In 1981 it changed its name to the Congressional Caucus for Women's Issues, and opened its doors to men. In 1993 the caucus, bolstered by the addition of twenty-four new women, had its most successful year ever. "Issues of concern to women and families truly came of age . . . and, largely, it was the congresswomen who set the agenda," said now-retired Representative Patricia Schroeder (D–Col.), then co-chair of the caucus.[62]

As LSOs, these caucuses could pool contributions from members' office allowances and were given office space in congressional buildings. In 1995, the Republican majority voted to end the advantages given to LSOs, eliminating ninety-six staff positions and making sixteen offices available.[63] The Speaker also claimed that elimination of these perks would save taxpayers $4 billion annually, although many questioned this claim since the funds simply reverted to the members who had contributed them to particular LSOs. Some members were forced to hire additional staff to work on policy issues previously handled by the caucuses. It seems far more likely that the LSOs were hit because they generally existed to advance liberal interests not favored by the new Republican majority in the House.

About one-third of the caucuses have died or just faded away without institutional support. Said Representative Charles Rangle (D–N.Y.) of the bipartisan Narcotics Abuse and Control Caucus, "We just couldn't keep it together."[64] Others have lost influence and members. Some, however, like the women's caucus, have sought outside sources of support to help them continue their mission.

State and regional caucuses are another important source of information exchange among members and across party lines. Large state delegations, such as those of California, New York, and Texas, often work together, regardless of party lines, to bring the bacon home to their states. Some state caucuses hold weekly meetings to assure that their interests are adequately represented on important committees and to keep abreast of pending legislation that might affect their states.

Regional caucuses cut across not only state lines but both houses of Congress as well. In the early years of the nation, members of Congress even roomed in boarding houses organized around regions. These "boarding house networks"[65] enforced discipline through the threat of social ostracism. While these kinds of strictures no longer exist, informal frostbelt and sunbelt caucuses exist to advance sectional interests. The frostbelt, or Northeast–Midwest Coalition, for example, was formed in the 1970s when the energy crisis prompted many firms and factories to move to lower-cost locations in the South. In 1990 its members called for California and Texas to pay larger shares of the bailout costs of the savings and loan industry. "The leading culprit in this Texas-sized problem is none other than the Lone Star State itself— a veritable bailout blackhole," charged Representative (now Senator) Olympia V. Snowe (R–Me.), a frostbelt spokesperson. Reaction from the sunbelt caucus was quick. Representative Steve Bartlett (R–Tex.) retorted: "This is merely Texas-bashing for home consumption."[66]

Interest Groups

The primary function of most interest group lobbyists is to provide information to supportive or potentially supportive legislators and their staffs. It's likely, for example, that a representative knows the National Rifle Association's (NRA) position on gun control legislation. What the legislator needs to get from the NRA is information and substantial research on the feasibility and impact of such legislation. How could the states implement such legislation? Is it constitutional? Will it really have an impact on violent crime or crime in schools? Interest groups can win over undecided legislators or confirm the support of their friends by providing information that legislators use to justify the position they have embraced.

Pressure groups also use grassroots appeals to pressure legislators by urging their members in a particular state or district to call or write to their senators or representatives. Lobbyists can't vote, but voters back home can and do.

As technology has improved, so has the force of interest groups. In 1993, when Congress proposed to cut the deductabilty of business meals from 80 percent to 50 percent, the National Restaurant Association fought back. It launched a well-done television ad featuring a middle-age waitress discussing how she might lose her job and her ability to support her three sons. The punch line? "Call 1-800-999-8945 now, and you'll be connected to your Senator."[67] Banks of operators were on hand to patch irate constituents through to their representatives' offices. (Ultimately, however, the 50 percent deduction was passed.) Today, constituents are urged by interest groups to e-mail or fax concerns to their representatives. These techniques are thought to be more effective than deluging congressional offices with hundreds of identical letters that show little thought.

While a link to a legislator's constituency may be the most effective way to influence behavior, that is not the only path of interest group influence on member decision-making. The high cost of campaigning had made members of Congress— especially those without huge personal fortunes—attentive to those who help pay the tab for tens of thousands of dollars worth of television commercials that have become staples in contested elections. The 4,000 or so political action committees (PACs) organized by interest groups are a major source of most members' campaign funding. When an issue comes up on which the legislator has no strong opinion and which is of little consequence to constituents, there is, not surprisingly, a tendency to support the stand taken by those nice folks who helped pay for the last campaign. After all, who wants to bite the hand that feeds him? (Interest groups and PACs are discussed in detail in chapter 16).

Staff

Members of Congress rely heavily on members of their staffs for information on pending legislation. Staff members prepare summaries of bills and brief the representative or senator based on their research. If the bill is nonideological or one on which the member has no real position, staff members can be very influential. Staff members also do research on and even draft bills that a member wishes to introduce.

Staff aides are especially crucial in the Senate. Because senators have so many committee assignments and are often spread so thin, they frequently rely heavily on aides. Every legislator has personal staff and other staff who work for each committee and subcommittee. The support personnel at the Congressional Budget Office and the Congressional Research Service at the Library of Congress are also considered to be staff working for Congress. Even with the reduction in House committee staffers enacted by Republicans in 1995, the ranks of the staffed total more than 15,000 (see Figure 7.9).

The next time you see a televised Senate hearing, notice how each senator has at least one aide sitting behind him or her, ready with information and often even with questions for the senator to ask. Some believe that staff members have become too important, too powerful, and that their bosses are too dependent on them. As Majority Leader, Bob Dole, for example, came under intense criticism by many conservative members of Congress for the alleged influence of his chief aide, Sheila Burke, a moderate Republican, who ultimately was the subject of a Sunday *New York Times Magazine* cover story about the woman behind the man.

FIGURE 7.9

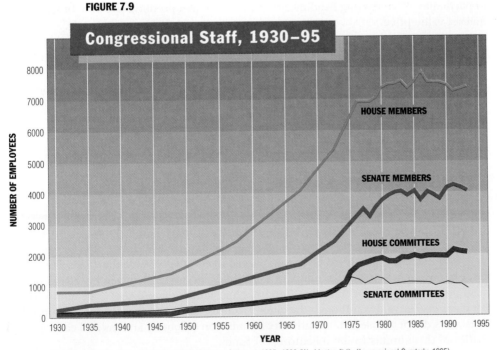

Congressional Staff, 1930–95

SOURCE: Norman Ornstein, *et al.*, eds., *Vital Statistics on Congress, 1995–1996* (Washington D.C.: Congressional Quarterly, 1995), tables 5-2 and 5-5.

Support Agencies

Congress has developed three support agencies—the Congressional Research Service, the General Accounting Office, and the Congressional Budget Office—to provide the specialized knowledge necessary for members of Congress to make informed decisions on complex issues.

Congressional Research Service (CRS).   Created in 1914 as the Legislative Research Service (LRS), the CRS is administered by the Library of Congress and responds to more than a quarter of a million congressional requests for information each year. The CRS is staffed with almost 900 employees, many of whom have advanced academic training. The service provides nonpartisan studies of public issues, compiling facts on both sides of issues, and it conducts major research projects for committees at the request of members. The CRS also prepares summaries of all bills introduced and tracks the progress of major bills. All of this information is available via computer terminals in the Senate and House Offices.

General Accounting Office (GAO).   The GAO was established in 1921 as an independent regulatory agency for the purpose of auditing the financial expenditures of the executive branch and federal agencies. The original intent was to better help Congress perform its oversight function of the bureaucracy. This entails the GAO's reviewing of agency, department, or office activities to see if they are carrying out its responsibilities the way Congress intended. Today, staffed with more than 5,000 employees, the GAO performs four additional functions: It sets government standards for accounting, it provides a variety of legal opinions, it settles claims against the government, and it conducts studies upon congressional request. Through its investigation of the efficiency and effectiveness of agencies, the GAO has acted as a watchdog of military funds in particular, often making headlines by reporting when products are bought far above market value price.

Congressional Budget Office (CBO).   The CBO was created in 1974 in order to evaluate the economic effect of different spending programs and to provide information on the cost of proposed policies. The CBO employs more than 200 people and is responsible for analyzing the president's budget and economic projections. It provides Congress and individual members with a valuable second opinion to use in budget debates.

CONGRESS AND THE PRESIDENT

*T*he Constitution envisioned that the Congress and the president would have discreet powers and that one branch would be able to hold the other in check. Over the years, and especially since the 1930s, the president has often held the upper hand. In times of crisis or simply when it was unable to meet public demands for solutions, Congress has willingly handed over its authority to the chief executive. Even though the chief executive has been granted greater latitude, legislators do, of course, retain authority to question executive actions and can halt activities of the administration by cutting off funds.

The Shifting Balance of Power

Over the years, especially since the presidency of Franklin D. Roosevelt, Congress has ceded to the president a major role in the legislative process. Today, for example, Congress often finds itself responding to executive branch proposals, as it did in the case of the Clean Air Act Amendments of 1990, discussed earlier in this chapter. Critics of Congress point to its slow, unwieldy process and the complexity of national problems as reasons why Congress often doesn't seem to act on its own. Moreover, the line-item veto is destined to give the president even more power in the lawmaking process.

Individual members, especially if the president is popular with voters, often support White House initiatives. Legislators who are "on the fence" often find themselves targeted by the White House or inundated with invitations to state dinners. Lyndon B. Johnson was a master of this strategy. One widely recounted story tells how Johnson called Senator Harry Byrd (D–Va.) over to the White House because he was resisting passage of the civil rights bill in 1964. According to Senator Dale Bumpers (D–Ark.), Johnson said, 'You know, Harry, [Defense Secretary Robert] McNamara says we got to close that Norfolk naval base down there, and I don't much want to do it.' And Harry Byrd couldn't wait to get back over to the Senate to vote for the civil rights bill."[68]

Bill Clinton's efforts at "persuasion" have been hailed by some. During his efforts to convince Congress to pass his budget deficit reduction plan and then NAFTA, he courted and cajoled numerous legislators and punished those who didn't go along. After Richard Shelby (D–Ala.) immediately criticized Clinton's tax plan, the White House retaliated by moving ninety federal jobs out of the Marshall Space Flight Center in Alabama and even denied Shelby an extra ticket to a White House South Lawn ceremony honoring his alma mater's champion football team.[69] It doesn't take many episodes like these to convince some legislators how to vote, although some may say that Shelby got in the last laugh when he switched to the Republican Party.

Over the years the balance of power between Congress and the executive branch has seesawed. The post-Civil War Congress attempted to regain control of the vast executive powers that President Abraham Lincoln, recently slain, had taken from it. Angered at the refusal of Lincoln's successor, Andrew Johnson, to go along with its radical "reforms" of the South, Congress passed the Tenure of Office Act, which prevented the president, under the threat of civil penalty, from removing any Cabinet-level appointments of the previous administration. Johnson accepted the challenge and fired Lincoln's secretary of war, who many believed was guilty of heinous war crimes. The House voted to impeach Johnson, but only the desertion of a handful of Republican senators prevented him from being removed from office. (The effort fell short by one vote.) Nonetheless, the president's power had been greatly weakened, and the Congress again became the center of power and authority in the federal government.

Beginning in the early 1900s, however, a series of strong presidents acted at the expense of congressional power. Theodore Roosevelt, Franklin D. Roosevelt, and Lyndon B. Johnson, especially, all viewed the presidency as carrying with it enormous powers. Although these presidents facilitated an expansion of the role of the federal government, over time the perception grew that presidents were abusing their power, particularly after the events of the Vietnam War and Watergate. By the 1970s, then, scholars were discussing the "imperial presidency,"[70] and Congress made efforts to reassert itself through exercising its oversight function zealously. Still, the line-item veto gives presidents a greater opportunity to involve themselves in the lawmaking process.

Congressional Oversight of the Executive Branch

oversight: Congressional review of the activities of an agency, department, or office.

According to political scientist Joel Aberbach, since 1961 there has been a substantial increase in the **oversight** activity by Congress.[71] Congressional oversight of the executive branch involves a committee or subcommittee reviewing activities of an agency, department, or office to see if it has carried out its responsibilities the way Congress intended. It also includes checking on possible abuses of power by governmental officials, including the president.

Key to Congress's performance of its oversight function is its ability to question members of the administration and the bureaucracy to see if they are enforcing and interpreting the laws passed by Congress as the members intended. These committee hearings, now routinely televised, are among Congress's most visible and dramatic actions. Millions, for example, tuned in to watch the House's investigation of President Nixon and the Senate's investigation of the Iran–Contra affair. Scandals such as Watergate, the failure of the savings and loan industry, Whitewater, and problems with the White House travel office (Travelgate) often trigger highly publicized and often highly partisan oversight hearings.

Hearings are not simply used to gather information. Rather, hearings that focus on the Bureau of Alcohol, Tobacco and Firearms handling of the Branch Davidians in Waco, Texas, or the shootings of the Weavers in Ruby Ridge, Idaho, are clear signals that changes need to be made before the agency next comes before the committee to justify its budget. Thus it is easier to understand the go-slower approach the FBI took in 1996 when it chose to wait out the Freemen as opposed to taking more potentially violent action.

Randy Weaver sits pensively in the midst of a conference between lawyers Gary Gillman and Gerry Spence. Congressional oversight hearings were held after Weaver's wife and son were shot at Ruby Ridge, Idaho, by federal law enforcement officials serving an arrest warrant on Weaver. (Photo courtesy: Colburn/Photoreporters)

Hearings are also used to improve the administration of programs. Since most members of House and Senate committees and subcommittees are interested in the issues under their jurisdiction, they often *want* to help bureaucrats and not hinder them.

Congress, in fact, has been criticized for trying to oversee the executive branch's implementation of programs too much. The challenge for Congress is clearly to reach a balance.

The **legislative veto,** a procedure by which one or both houses of Congress can disallow an act of an executive agency by a simple majority vote, also helps Congress perform its oversight function. Provisions for so-called legislative vetoes were first added to statutes in 1932 but were not used frequently until the 1970s. They were usually included in laws that delegated congressional powers to the executive branch while retaining the power of Congress to restrict their use. By 1981 more than 200 statutes contained legislative veto provisions.

In *Immigration and Naturalization Service* v. *Chadha* (1983), however, the U.S. Supreme Court ruled that the legislative veto as it was used in many circumstances was unconstitutional because it violated separation of powers principles.[72] The Court concluded that although the Constitution gave Congress the power to make laws, the Framers were clear in their intent that Congress should separate itself from executing or enforcing the laws. It is the president's responsibility to sign or veto legislation, not the Congress's. This case offered a classic example of the separations of powers doctrine underlying the Constitution. In spite of *Chadha*, however, the legislative veto continues to play an important role in executive–legislative relations. In signing the Omnibus Consolidation Recision and Appropriation Act in April 1996, for example, President Clinton noted that Congress had included a legislative veto that the Supreme Court would in all likelihood find unconstitutional under *Chadha*. Nevertheless, he signed the bill. The continued use by Congress, and the acceptance by the president, of the legislative veto, moreover, underscores the limits of judicial intervention without the cooperation of the other branches of government.

legislative veto: A procedure by which one or both houses of Congress can disallow an act of the president or executive agency by a simple majority vote; ruled unconstitutional by the Supreme Court.

Foreign Affairs Oversight. The Constitution divides foreign policy powers between the executive and the legislative branches. The president has the power to wage war and negotiate treaties, whereas the Congress has the power to declare war and the Senate alone has the power to ratify treaties. Throughout the twentieth century, the executive branch has become preeminent in foreign affairs despite the constitutional division of powers. This is partly due to the series of crises and the development of nuclear weapons in this century; both have necessitated quick decision-making and secrecy, which is far easier to manage in the executive branch.

Confirmation of Presidential Appointments. The Senate plays a special oversight function through its ability to confirm key members of the executive branch, as well as presidential appointments to the federal courts. As discussed in chapters 9 and 10, although the Senate generally confirms most presidential nominees, it does not always do so. A wise president considers senatorial reaction before nominating potentially controversial individuals to his administration or to the federal courts. In the case of federal district court appointments, senators often have a considerable say in the nomination of judges from their states through what is called senatorial courtesy, a process by which presidents generally defer selection of district court judges to the choice of senators of their own party who represent the state in which a vacancy occurs (see chapter 10).

CHANGING CONGRESS

As House whip, Newt Gingrich was quick to realize that American voters were angry with Congress. This tremendous electoral discontent had first manifested itself in 1992. In 1994 he expected it to be more of the same. But, for the first time in American history, Republican candidates for the House ran as Republicans pledged to make major changes in the way Congress does business.

People were simply fed up with congressional pay raises, check overdraft privileges, and freebies from special interests. The House, in particular, was intended to be responsive to the people, but how could members be in tune given their six-figure salaries, full medical insurance, and ability to skirt basic employment laws?

Gingrich tested out themes with focus groups and seasoned pollsters to tap the seeds of Americans' discontent. For Generation Xers, the Contract with America promised to protect social security and bring the cost of Medicare under control. For businesspersons who found themselves struggling under excessive regulations, the Contract promised to make Congress subject to the same laws as employers. The voters responded, and pundits and politicians alike were shocked by the magnitude of the Republicans' victory.

From day one the new Speaker moved to bring every item in the Contract up for a vote within the first 100 days as promised. But Congress is a two-chamber institution; and the Senate, a much slower and more deliberative body, had not acted on many agenda items by the November 1996 elections. It took the Senate much longer to get around to considering items in the Contract.

Change was made more difficult once many Americans realized what passage of some Contract items really meant. While most people favor budget cuts and reducing the deficit in the abstract, they don't want to cut programs that affect *them*. Thus House and Senate members soon began to hear from their constituents that Congress was going too far and making too many changes.

In November 1996, the American public failed to give the Republican Revolution in Congress a ringing endorsement, although most House Republicans who sought reelection won. The brashness of their 1995 takeover of Congress, however, was gone. There were no promises of quick change or to bring X number of proposals to the floor quickly for a vote. Speaker Gingrich, in fact, held out a conciliatory hand to the White House remarking that we "don't have to live in a world of confrontation." But, at the same time, he and other House and Senate Republicans made it clear that they would be taking their oversight function to heart; there would be no let up in their diligent oversight of the executive branch. Broader and deeper probes into Democrat Party finances, allegations of foreign influence peddling during the 1996 presidential campaign, Whitewater, and Travelgate were promised. And, at the same time, several members of the Clinton Cabinet made it known that they would be retiring forcing new presidential nominees to withstand Senate confirmation hearings in a body that saw the number of Republicans actually grow.

Thus, the next few years will continue to be ones of divided government. The Republican Revolution has yet to be fully realized, and still more changes in the institution are undoubtedly to come. The American public still has yet to figure out what it wants from Congress exactly, which often causes Congress and its leaders to seek band aid remedies for problems that are perhaps much larger in scope.

North—South

POLITICS AROUND THE WORLD

In a book about almost any other country that political scientists normally consider democratic, the material in this chapter and the next would be combined into a few short pages. That's the case because, unlike the United States, most use a version of the parliamentary system in which the roles of the executive and legislature are pretty much one and the same.

Canada has a typical parliamentary system. This means that, although Parliament has two houses, the upper house—the Senate—is virtually powerless. More importantly for our purposes, the prime minister (the closest equivalent to the U.S. president) is also the leader of the majority party in the lower house, the House of Commons, and can stay in office only if the government wins the support of the Commons on all critical pieces of legislation in what are informally known as "votes of confidence." If the prime minister loses such a vote, he or she must resign, which usually means that new elections are held within a matter of a few weeks. Because the very existence of their party's government is at stake on each and every piece of major legislation, the members of the majority party respect party discipline and vote as a bloc. In other words, unlike U.S. presidents, Canadian prime ministers can assume that the legislation they propose will be passed virtually intact. Parliament, in short, does little more than ratify decisions made by the cabinet (see North–South feature in chapter 8).

This has two important, if somewhat contradictory, implications. On the one hand, under situations like the one in late 1996, when Liberal Prime Minister Jean Chrétien had a clear majority in the House of Commons, the government can expect to see its platform passed into law relatively easily—something no American president can even dream of. As a result, it is far easier for the Canadian government to pass coherent legislation and act quickly than it is in the United States (see the discussion of budget cuts in chapter 18), even when the president and congressional majority come from the same party. On the other hand, because the individual members of Parliament (MPs) have to toe the party line, they cannot represent the interests of their constituents or vote their own consciences to anywhere near the degree their counterparts do in the United States.

Mexico does not have a parliamentary system in this classic sense of the term. There is no prime minister, and the president cannot be forced to resign through a vote of confidence. But, because the president in his role as head of the PRI controls the party's choice of candidates for all offices, both the Chamber of Deputies (which mostly represents single-member districts, as in the U.S. House of Representatives) and the Senate (which represents the states) are little more than rubber stamps for presidential initiatives. Over the last few decades, the government has changed the electoral system so that minority parties are guaranteed a share of seats in both houses. However, the PRI still has solid control over both so that it can pass legislation more or less at will. In short, as in so many areas covered in this book, the key to understanding Mexican politics lies not in what its Constitution calls for, but in how the PRI has adapted its provisions over the course of this century.

(continued)

North—South, cont'd

As noted in chapter 1's North–South feature, one of the two reasons for including these features is to highlight just how unusual the American political system is. There is no better example of this than the material in this chapter, because the United States is the only major democracy in which the legislature has a major role in making the laws. Parliaments are wonderful debating chambers, especially during question time (the British version of which is telecast on C-SPAN), when the prime minister comes to the House of Commons to defend his actions against the criticisms in the form of questions from the opposition. But the sharpness of those debates should not obscure the fact that the Parliament in Canada, Great Britain or Mexico does not really make laws.

The 104th Congress did implement a wide variety of institutional changes, but the Joint Committee on the Organization of Congress recommended far more. Congress is a large, complex organization, which makes change very difficult. It must respond to external demands for laws, investigations, or reform amidst a setting of demographic shifts, economic cycles, and international and domestic crises. Demand for government services continues to increase—witness the calls for new laws of better oversight of the FAA after a major plane crash; but, at the same time, large portions of the American electorate say they want less federal government.

These calls often clash with a member of Congress's prime goal—reelection. Members make demands on Congress, often shaping and changing "its structures and procedures to serve their own needs as well as external demands."[73] The size of Congress and conflicting demands on members and institutions thus make major change, at least in so far as could be recognized as such by the American public, unlikely.

SUMMARY

The size and scope of Congress, and demands put on it, have increased tremendously over the years. In presenting the important role that Congress plays in American politics, we have made the following points:

1. The Roots of the Legislative Branch.

Congress was molded after the bicameral British Parliament, but with an important difference. The U.S. Senate is probably the most powerful upper house in any national legislature. The Senate has unique powers to ratify treaties and to approve presidential nominees.

2. The Constitution and the Legislative Branch of Government.

The Constitution created a bicameral legislature with members of each body to be elected differently, and thus to represent different constituencies. Article 1 of the Constitution sets forth qualifications for office, specifies age minimums and specifies how legislators are to be distributed among the states. The Constitution also requires seats in the House of Representatives to be apportioned by population. Thus, after every census, district lines must be redrawn to reflect population shifts. The Constitution also provides a vast array of enumerated and implied powers to Congress. Some, such as lawmaking and oversight, are shared by each house of Congress; others are not.

3. The Members of Congress.

Members of Congress live in two worlds—in their home districts and in the District of Columbia. Casework is one way to keep in touch with the district, since members, especially those in the House, never stop running for office. Incumbency is an important factor in winning reelection. Thus many have called for limits on congressional terms of office. Several theories exist concerning how members represent their constituents.

4. How Congress is Organized.

Political parties play a major role in the way Congress is organized. The Speaker of the House is always a member of the majority party, and members of the majority party chair all committees. In 1995 Speaker Newt Gingrich became the most powerful Speaker of the House since the first decade of this century. Because the House of Representatives is large, the Speaker enforces more rigid rules on the House than exist in the Senate.

In addition to the party leaders, Congress has a labyrinth of committees and subcommittees that cover the entire range of government policies, often with a confusing tangle of shared responsibilities. Each legislator serves on one or more committees and multiple subcommittees. It is in these environments that many policies are shaped and that members make their primary contributions to solving public problems.

5. The Lawmaking Function of Congress.

The road to enacting a bill into law is long and strewn with obstacles, and only a small share of the proposals introduced become law. Legislation must be approved by committees in each house and on the floor of each chamber. In addition, most House legislation is initially considered by a subcommittee and must be approved by the Rules Committee before getting to the floor. Legislation that is passed in different forms by the two chambers must be resolved in a conference before going back to each chamber for a vote and then to the president, who can sign the proposal into law, veto it, or allow it to become law without his signature. If Congress adjourns within ten days of passing legislation, that bill will die if the president does not sign it. A president can also use a line-item veto to eliminate specific spending provisions.

6. How Members Make Decisions.

A multitude of factors impinge on legislators as they decide policy issues. The most important of the many considerations are constituents' preferred options and the advice given by better informed colleagues. When clear and consistent cues are given by voters back home, legislators usually heed their demands. In the absence of strong constituency preferences, legislators may turn for advice to colleagues who are experts on the topic or to interest group lobbyists, especially those who have donated to their campaign.

7. Congress and the President.

The president can successfully twist arms or appeal to party loyalty when dealing with legislators who belong to his party. A president's influence both with fellow partisans and opponents is related to the chief executive's popularity with the public. Ronald Reagan, a popular president, succeeded in getting an economic package adopted by a House controlled by Democrats. In contrast, Jimmy Carter and Bill Clinton had trouble getting their proposals through Congress, even though their fellow Democrats had majorities in both houses.

8. Changing Congress.

Although the 104th Congress ushered in substantial changes in the institution, the American public continues to clamor for change in Congress. Most Americans have little appreciation for the deliberative function of Congress and even less tolerance for partisan disagreements. While some members of Congress want to see the institution strengthened, many in the public want an institution that will quickly and quietly accede to presidential initiatives.

KEY TERMS

apportionment, 231
bicameral legislature, 230
bill, 232
casework, 235
conference committee, 253
delegate, 242
discharge petition, 255
filibuster, 262
gerrymandering, 231
hold, 260
impeachment, 233
incumbency, 236
legislative veto, 277
line-item veto, 263
majority party, 245

minority party, 245
majority leader, 250
minority leader, 250
oversight, 276
party caucus, 253
pocket veto, 263
politico, 243
pork barrel, 257
redistricting, 230
Speaker of the House, 245
standing committee, 253
term limits, 238
trustee, 242
whip, 251

SELECTED READINGS

Aberbach, Joel D. *Keeping a Watchful Eye.* Washington, D.C.: Brookings Institution, 1990.

Cain, Bruce, John Ferejohn, and Morris Fiorina. *The Personal Vote.* Cambridge: Harvard University Press, 1987.

Davidson, Roger H., ed. *The Postreform Congress.* New York: St. Martin's, 1992.

Davidson, Roger H. and Walter J. Oleszek. *Congress and Its Members,* 5th ed. Washington, D.C.: Congressional Quarterly Press, 1996.

Dodd, Lawrence C., and Bruce I. Oppenheimer, eds. *Congress Reconsidered,* 4th ed. Washington, D.C.: CQ Press, 1985.

Fenno, Richard F., Jr., *Congressmen in Committees.* Boston: Little, Brown, 1973.

———. *Home Style: House Members in Their Districts.* Boston: Little, Brown, 1978.

Fox, Harrison W., and Susan Webb Hammond. *Congressional Staffs: The Invisible Force in American Lawmaking.* New York: Free Press. 1977.

Hibbing, John R. *Congressional Careers: Contours of Life in the U.S. House of Representatives.* Chapel Hill: University of North Carolina, 1991.

Hinckley, Barbara. *Coalitions and Politics.* San Diego: Harcourt Brace Jovanovich, 1981.

Kaptur, Marcy. *Women of Congress.* Washington, D.C.: CQ Press, 1996.

Mayhew, David R. *Congress: The Electoral Connection*. New Haven: Yale University Press, 1974.

Price, David E. *The Congressional Experience: A View from the Hill*. Boulder, CO: Westview Press, 1992.

Sabato, Larry J. *PAC Power*. New York: Norton, 1984.

Smith, Hedrick. *The Power Game*. New York: Ballantine, 1988.

Thurber, James A., and Roger Davidson, eds. *Remaking Congress: Change and Stability in the 1990s*. Washington, D.C.: Congressional Quarterly Press, 1995.

THE PRESIDENCY

 don't give a . . . what happens, I want you to stonewall it, let them plead the Fifth Amendment, cover up or anything else, if it'll save the plan."

—*Richard M. Nixon, in a recorded conversation from the Oval Office, March 22, 1973*

In the end, no amount of stonewalling, pleading, or covering up could save Nixon's plan, or his presidency. Richard M. Nixon began his first term of office in 1969 during one of the most divisive periods in American history. Although he began the strategic withdrawal of U.S. forces from Vietnam and opened diplomatic relations with China for the first time since 1949, the country remained sharply divided during his first three years in office. By the summer of 1972, all of Nixon's energies were devoted to winning Republican Party primaries and his eventual reelection that fall. His strategic and fund-raising group, the Committee to Re-elect the President (CREEP), was staffed with White House advisers and headed by John Mitchell, who had resigned as Attorney General to direct Nixon's campaign.

On June 17, 1972, five men broke into the Democratic National Committee's (DNC) headquarters at the Watergate office complex in Washington, D.C. They were to have installed listening devices in DNC phones, which would have transmitted Democratic campaign strategy and information back to CREEP. Instead, they were caught with their burglary tools, bugging devices, and a stack of $100 bills. From that moment on, Americans have never perceived the office of the president in quite the same way. The spreading crisis known as **Watergate** played itself out in the national spotlight over a period of twenty-six months. During that time Americans were riveted by newspaper reports of coverups and misappropriations and by televised coverage of Senate hearings, in a way approached only recently by the O. J. Simpson trial. Despite the best efforts of Nixon and his staff to cover up or minimize the scandal, over the course of the two-year investigation evidence steadily mounted, directly implicating the president himself. Among the evidence:

- Immediately following the arrest, the White House and CREEP shredded all documents in their possession that might link the burglars to the White House.

- One of the Watergate burglars was James W. McCord, security director at CREEP. After pleading guilty in 1973, McCord wrote to Judge John J. Sirica

Watergate: Term used to describe the events and scandal resulting from a break-in at the Democratic National Committee headquarters in 1972 and the subsequent coverup of White House involvement.

285

John Dean testifies before the Senate Watergate Committee, under the searching gaze of Senator Sam Ervin (D—N.C.). Dean's testimony as White House lawyer was pivotal in confirming Richard M. Nixon's participation in a coverup of the Watergate break-in. (Photo courtesy: UPI/Corbis-Bettmann)

explaining that he and other defendants had been pressured to remain silent, and that other highly placed officials were involved.

- Soon after McCord's letter, FBI Director Patrick Gray resigned after admitting he had destroyed evidence. Ten days later Attorney General Richard Kleindienst and two top presidential aides also resigned, as did counselor and White House lawyer John Dean.

- In June 1973 Dean testified before the specially impaneled Senate Watergate Committee that despite assurances to the contrary, Nixon had participated in a coverup of Watergate, and that the break-in was part of a larger program of political espionage.

- In July 1973 another former aide disclosed that Nixon had secretly tape recorded all conversations that took place in the oval office.

The committee immediately demanded the tapes and obtained a subpoena for several of them. The president refused to turn them over, citing "executive privilege" while he continued to maintain his innocence. White House Special Prosecutor Archibald Cox, appointed by Nixon to investigate the break-in, also requested the tapes and refused to accept a compromise plan to provide a synopsis of their content. When Cox refused to back down, the president ordered Attorney General Elliott Richardson to fire Cox. Richardson resigned after he said he would not fire Cox. His deputy also refused to fire Cox and was immediately fired by Nixon. It then fell to Solicitor General Robert H. Bork to fire the Nixon-appointed Special Prosecutor, Cox in what was called the Saturday Night Massacre.

Only after the House Judiciary Committee announced it would begin hearing impeachment charges against the president did Nixon reluctantly turn over the requested tapes on October 30. It turned out that two tapes were "missing" and one had a mysterious eighteen-and-a-half-minute gap that the White House claimed was an accidental erasure by Nixon's secretary, Rose Mary Woods. (Later analysis of the tape revealed that the erasure had been deliberate.) Nixon refused to turn over an additional 500 tapes and documents subpoenaed by the committee. The U.S. Supreme Court, acknowledging the gravity of the matter, agreed to hear the case on expedited review. On July 24, 1974, in ***United States v. Nixon,*** it ruled unanimously that there was no overriding "executive privilege" that sanctioned the president's refusal to comply with a court order to produce information. Nixon was ordered to turn over the tapes. One of them revealed that the president had ordered a halt to the FBI's investigation of the Watergate break-in and a coverup to disguise CREEP's involvement. This was the "smoking gun" congressional investigators had been looking for. On July 27, 1974, the House Judiciary Committee approved the first of three articles of impeachment against the president. On August 9, 1974, Nixon resigned and Vice President Gerald R. Ford automatically became the thirty-eighth president of the United States. One month later President Ford pardoned Nixon, arguing that the pardon was necessary to prevent the spectacle of having a former president on trial, and that it was time for the nation to turn its attentions to more pressing policy problems.

United States* v. *Nixon: There is no constitutional absolute executive privilege that would allow a president to refuse to comply with a court order to produce information needed in a criminal trial.

Watergate forever changed the nature of the presidency. Because the president long had been held up as a symbol of the nation, the knowledge that corruption could exist at the highest levels of government changed how Americans viewed all institutions of government, and mistrust of government ran rampant. Watergate demystified the office and its occupant. As Richard M. Nixon toppled from office, so did the prestige of the office itself. Except for the affable Ronald Reagan, only two presidents to serve since Nixon's resignation have served more than one term. Presidents Gerald R. Ford, Jimmy Carter, George Bush, and Bill Clinton all sought reelection, yet only Clinton was successful. No longer was the president to be considered above the law or the scrutiny of the public or of the press. President Ford, too, became tarnished when the public was outraged by his pardon of Nixon and suspicious that a deal had been struck. For all the turmoil it created, however, Watergate proved that the system created by the Framers worked: Under threat of certain impeachment and conviction, a president left office and was succeeded in an orderly, nonviolent fashion.

Watergate not only forever changed the public's relationship to the president, it also spurred many reforms in how government and politics were run: Ethics and campaign finance laws were tightened up, and a special prosecutor law, which allowed for independent investigation of the executive branch, was enacted. Perhaps even more than these changes, Watergate bruised Americans' optimism about what was good about America. Furthermore, intensive media attention to the president and the presidency brought him closer to the people (*and* to their intense public criticism) at the same time that the public expectations about the presidency itself increased. People began to look to the president rather than Congress to solve pressing and increasingly complex national problems even as their respect for the office—and often its occupant—declined.

Writing in the 1940s, decades before Watergate, the great author John Steinbeck said, "We give the president more work than a man can do, more responsibility than a man should take, more pressure than a man can bear. We abuse him often, and rarely praise him. We wear him out, use him up, eat him up. And with all this, Americans have a love for the president that goes beyond party loyalty or nationality; he is ours, and we exercise the right to destroy him."[1]

The constitutional authority, statutory powers, and burdens of the presidency make it a powerful position and an awesome responsibility. Most of the men who have been president in the past two decades have done their best; yet, in the heightened expectations of the American electorate, most have come up short. Not only did the Framers not envision such a powerful role for the president, they could not have foreseen the skepticism with which many presidential actions are now greeted in the press, on talk radio, and on the Internet. These expectations have also led presidents into policy areas never dreamed of by the Framers. Imagine, for example, what the Framers might have thought about President Clinton's war on teenage smoking. (See Politics Now: Clinton and Teenage Smoking.)

At the same time the modern media has brought us "closer" to our presidents, it has also made them seem more human, a mixed blessing for those trying to lead. Only two photographs exist of Franklin D. Roosevelt, in a wheelchair—his paralysis was a closely guarded secret. Five decades later, Bill Clinton was asked on national TV what kind of underwear he preferred (briefs). This demystifying of the president, along with simultaneous increases in our general mistrust of government and in our expectations of it, have made governing a difficult job. A president does not rely only on the formal powers of office to lead the nation: Public opinion and public confidence are key components of his ability to get his programs adopted and his vision of the nation implemented. As political scientist Richard E. Neustadt has noted, the president's power often rests on his power to persuade.[2] And to persuade, he must not only be able to forge links with members of Congress, he must also have the support of the American people and the respect of foreign leaders.

The tension between public expectations and the formal powers of the president permeates our discussion of how the presidency has evolved from its humble origins in Article II of the Constitution to its current stature.

- First, we examine *the roots of the office of president of the United States* and discuss how the Framers created a chief executive officer for the new nation.

- Second, we discuss Article II and *the constitutional powers of the president.*

- Third, we examine *the development of presidential power* and a more personalized presidency: how well a president is able to execute the laws often depends strongly on his personality, popularity, and leadership style.

- Fourth, to help you understand more fully the development of the office of the president as a central focus of power and action in the American political system, we also discuss the development of what is called *the presidential establishment.* Myriad departments, special assistants, and a staff of advisers help the president, but also make it easier for a president to lose touch with the common citizen.

- Fifth, we focus on *the role of the president in the legislative process.* Since the days of Franklin D. Roosevelt, most presidents have played major roles in setting the national policy agenda—a power that Congress is now trying to reclaim.

- Finally, we focus on *the president's changing role* in the building of a better America by looking at some formal proposals for reforming the presidency and at how citizen expectations about the office and its occupants have made governance more difficult for whoever holds the nation's highest office.

THE ROOTS OF THE OFFICE OF PRESIDENT OF THE UNITED STATES

The earliest example of executive power in the colonies was the position of royal governor. The king of England appointed a royal governor to govern a colony. He was normally entrusted with the "powers of appointment, military command, expenditure, and—within limitations—pardon, as well as with large powers in connection with the powers of law making."[3] Royal governors often found themselves at odds with the colonists and especially with the elected colonial legislatures. As representatives of the Crown, the governors were distrusted and disdained by the people, many of whom had fled from Great Britain to escape royal domination. Others, generations removed from England, no longer felt strong ties to the king.

When the colonists declared their independence from England in 1776, their distrust of a strong chief executive remained. Most state constitutions reduced the office of governor to a symbolic post elected annually by the legislature. Governors were stripped of most rights we assume an executive must have today, including the right to call the legislature into session or to veto its acts. The constitution adopted by Virginia in 1776 illustrates prevailing colonial sentiment. It cautioned that "the executive powers of government" were to be exercised "according to the laws" of the state, and that no powers could be claimed by the governor on the basis of "any law, statute, or custom of England."[4]

Although most of the states opted for a more "symbolic" governor, some states did entrust wider powers to their chief executives. The governor of New York, for example, was elected directly by the people. And, perhaps *because* he was directly accountable to the people, he was given the power to pardon, the duty to execute the law faithfully to the best of his ability, and to act as "commander-in-chief" of the state militia.

The Constitutional Convention

As we saw in chapter 2, the delegates to the Philadelphia Convention quickly decided to dispense with the Articles of Confederation and fashion a new government composed of three branches—the legislative (to make the laws), the executive (to execute, or implement, the laws), and the judicial (to interpret the laws). The Framers had little difficulty in agreeing that executive authority should be vested in one person, although some delegates suggested multiple executives to diffuse the power of the executive branch. Under the Articles of Confederation, there had been no executive branch of government; and the eighteen different men who served as the president of the Continental Congress of the United States of America were president in name only—they had no actual authority or power in the new nation. Yet, because the Framers were so sure that George Washington—whom they had trusted with their lives during the Revolutionary War—would become the first president of the new nation, many of their deepest fears were calmed. They agreed on the necessity of having one individual speak on behalf of the new nation, and they all agreed that one individual should be George Washington.

The Framers also had no problem in agreeing on a title for the new office. Borrowing from the constitutions of Pennsylvania, Delaware, New Jersey, and New Hampshire, the Framers called the new chief executive the president. How the president was to be chosen and by whom was a major stumbling block. James Wilson of Philadelphia suggested a single, more powerful president, who would be elected by the people and "independent of the legislature." Wilson also suggested giving the executive an absolute veto over the acts of Congress. "Without such a defense," he wrote, "the legislature can at any moment sink it [the executive] into non-existence."[5]

The manner of the president's election haunted the Framers for a while, and their solution to the dilemma is described in detail in chapter 13. We leave the resolution of that issue—the creation of the electoral college—aside for now and turn instead to details of the issues the Framers resolved quickly.

Qualifications for Office.   The Constitution requires that the president (and the vice president, whose major function was to succeed the president in the event of his death or disability) be a natural-born citizen of the United States, at least thirty-five years old, and a resident of the United States for at least fourteen years. In the 1700s it was not uncommon for those engaged in international diplomacy to be out of the country for substantial periods of time, and the Framers wanted to make sure that prospective presidents spent some time on this country's shores before running for its highest elective office.

Terms of Office.   While many recent presidents seem to have had considerable difficulty being reelected to a second term, at one time, the length of a president's term was controversial. Four-, seven-, and eleven-year terms with no eligibility for reelection were suggested by various delegates to the Constitutional Convention. Alexander Hamilton suggested that a president serve during "good behavior." The Framers of the Constitution reached agreement on a four-year term with eligibility for reelection.

The first president, George Washington (1789–97), sought reelection only once, and a two-term limit for presidents became traditional. Although Ulysses S. Grant unsuccessfully sought a third term, the two terms established by Washington remained the standard for 150 years, avoiding the Framers' much-feared "constitutional monarch," a perpetually reelected tyrant. In the 1930s and 1940s, however, Franklin D. Roosevelt, ran successfully in four elections as Americans fought first the Great Depression and then World War II. Despite Roosevelt's popularity, negative reaction to his long tenure in office ultimately led to passage (and ratification in 1951) of the Twenty-Second Amendment, which limited presidents to two four-year terms or a total of ten years in office, should a vice president assume a portion of a president's remaining term.

impeachment: Actual bringing of charges against a public official; not the hearings or trial on those charges.

Removal.   During the Constitutional Convention, Benjamin Franklin was a staunch supporter of **impeachment,** a process for removing an official from office. He noted that "historically, the lack of power to impeach had necessitated recourse to assassination."[6] Not surprisingly, then, he urged the rest of the delegates to formulate a legal mechanism to remove the president and vice president.

Just as the veto power was a check on Congress, the impeachment provision ultimately included in Article II was adopted as a check on the power of the president. Each house of Congress was given a role to play in the impeachment process to assure that the chief executive could be removed only for "Treason, Bribery, or other high Crimes and Misdemeanors."

The Constitution gives the House of Representatives the power to conduct a thorough investigation in a manner similar to a grand jury proceeding to determine whether or not the president has engaged in any of those offenses (see chapter 5). If the finding is positive, the House is empowered to vote to impeach the president by a simple majority vote. The Senate then acts as a court of law and tries the president for the charged offenses, which are called **articles of impeachment.** (The Chief Justice of the United States presides over the vote on the articles and the Senate hearing.) A two-thirds majority vote in the Senate on any count contained in the articles of impeachment is necessary to remove the president from office. As noted in chapter 7, only one president, Andrew Johnson, has ever been impeached by the House of Representatives. But the Senate vote fell one vote short of forcing his removal in 1868.

articles of impeachment: The specific charges brought against a president or a federal judge by the House of Representatives.

Succession.   Through 1996 eight presidents have died in office from illness or assassination. William Henry Harrison was the first president to die in office—he caught a cold at his inauguration in 1841 and died one month later. (John Tyler thus became the first vice president to succeed to the presidency.) In 1865 Abraham Lincoln became the first president to be assassinated. And in 1974, Richard M. Nixon, facing impeachment and likely conviction, became the first president to resign from office. The Framers were aware that a system of orderly transfer of power was necessary, so they created the office of the vice president. Moreover, the Constitution directs Congress to select a successor if the office of vice president is vacant. To clarify this provision, Congress passed the Presidential Succession Act of 1947, which lists—in order—those in line (after the vice president) to succeed the president:

1. Speaker of the House of Representatives
2. President *pro tempore* of the Senate
3. Secretaries of State, Treasury, and Defense, and other Cabinet heads in order of the creation of their department

The Succession Act has never been used because there has always been a vice president to take over when a president died in office. The Twenty-Fifth Amendment, in fact, was added to the Constitution in 1967 to assure that this will continue to be the case. Should a vacancy occur in the office of the vice president, the Twenty-Fifth Amendment directs the president to appoint a new vice president, subject to the approval (by a simple majority) of both houses of Congress. (See also Highlight 8.1: What Happens If a President Can't Do His Job?).

In keeping with and even expanding upon the "Mondale model," President Clinton has involved Vice President Al Gore, Jr. in all aspects of decision making. Gore plays a key role in policy making, especially concerning the environment and bureaucratic waste. (Photo courtesy: Les Stone/Sygma)

Highlight 8.1

What Happens If a President Can't Do His Job?

Woodrow Wilson with his wife, Edith. (Photo courtesy: Stock Montage, Inc.)

When the twentieth president, James A. Garfield, was wounded by an assassin's bullet in July 1881, he lingered until mid-September. In 1919 President Woodrow Wilson had what many believed to be a nervous collapse in the summer and a debilitating stroke in the fall that incapacitated him for several months. His wife, Edith Bolling Galt Wilson, refused to admit his advisers to his sickroom, and rumors flew about the "First Lady President," as many suspected it was his wife and not Wilson who was issuing written orders.

Mindful of the possible crises that could have occurred in the Wilson years, a section of the Twenty-Fifth Amendment allows the vice president and a majority of the Cabinet (or some other body determined by Congress) to deem a president unable to fulfill his duties. It sets up a procedure to allow the vice president to become "acting president" if the president is incapacitated. The president can also voluntarily relinquish his power. In 1985, following the spirit of the amendment, President Ronald Reagan sent George Bush a letter that made Bush the acting president for the eight hours that Reagan was incapacitated as he underwent surgery for colon cancer.

The Twenty-Fifth Amendment has been used twice in its relatively short history. In 1973 President Richard M. Nixon selected the House Minority Leader, Gerald R. Ford, to replace Vice President Spiro T. Agnew after Agnew resigned in the wake of charges of bribe taking, corruption, and income tax evasion. Less than a year later, when Vice President Ford became the thirty-eighth president after Nixon's resignation, he appointed (and the Senate approved) former New York Governor Nelson A. Rockefeller to vice president. This chain of events set up for the first time in U.S. history a situation in which neither the president nor the vice president had been elected to those positions.

The Vice President

The Framers paid little attention to the office of vice president beyond the need to have an immediate official "stand-in" for the president. Initially, for example, the vice president's one and only function was to assume the office of president in the case of the death of the president or some other emergency. After further debate the delegates made the vice president the presiding officer of the Senate (except in cases of presidential impeachment). They feared that if the Senate's presiding officer was chosen from the Senate itself, one state would be short a representative. The vice president was given the authority to vote only in the event of a tie, however.

With so little authority, until recently, the office of vice president was considered a sure place for a public official to disappear into obscurity. When John Adams wrote to his wife, Abigail, about his position as America's first vice president, he said it was "the most insignificant office that was the invention of man . . . or his imagination conceived."[7]

Power and fame generally come only to those vice presidents who become president. Just "one heartbeat away" from the presidency, the vice president serves as a constant reminder of the president's mortality. In part, this situation has given rise to a trend of uneasy relationships between presidents and vice presidents that began as early as Adams and Thomas Jefferson. As historian Arthur M. Schlesinger, Jr., once noted, "The Vice President has only one serious thing to do: that is, to wait around for the President to die. This is hardly the basis for a cordial and enduring friendship."[8]

In the past, presidents chose their vice presidents largely to "balance"—politically, geographically, or otherwise—the presidential ticket, with little thought given to the possibility of the vice president becoming president. Franklin D. Roosevelt, for example, a liberal New Yorker, selected John Nance Garner, a conservative Texan, to be his running mate in 1932. After serving two terms, Garner—who openly disagreed with Roosevelt over many policies, including Roosevelt's Court-packing plan (see chapter 10) and his decision to seek a third term—unsuccessfully sought the 1940 presidential nomination himself.

In general, presidential candidates since Eisenhower have selected running mates of the caliber that would allow them to take over the reins of the nation's highest office. Bob Dole's selection of Jack Kemp, a former professional quarterback, member of Congress, and Housing and Urban Development secretary, surprised many, although he clearly had the experience to be president. Kemp and Dole disagreed on important issues and had campaigned vigorously against each other for the Republican presidential nomination in 1988.

Since Jimmy Carter's presidency, presidents have given their vice presidents more and more responsibility as well as access to information vital to the country's national security. Thus the office of vice president has begun to come into its own after years of ridicule and insignificance. Today it is more often viewed as a jumping off point for higher office than as a dead-end position.

How much power a vice president has, however, depends on how much the president is willing to give him. Although Jimmy Carter, a Southerner, chose Walter F. Mondale, a Northerner, as his running mate in 1976 to balance the ticket, he was also the first president to give his vice president more than ceremonial duties. In fact, Mondale was the first vice president to have an office in the White House. (It wasn't until 1961 that a vice president even had an office in the Executive Office Building next door to the White House!) Mondale—a former senator from Minnesota with Washington connections—became an important adviser to President Carter, a former governor who had run for office as a Washington "outsider."

The "Mondale model" of an active vice president set the expectations for what the influence, powers, and limitations of modern vice presidents should be. President Ronald Reagan's vice president, George Bush, a former director of the Central Intelligence Agency (CIA), was given the unprecedented responsibility of heading the National Security Crisis Management team. Following the assassination attempt on President Reagan in March 1981, Vice President Bush worked closely with the recuperating president to keep the government in order.

President Clinton expanded tremendously on the Mondale model. Al Gore, Jr., and Clinton forged a close working (and apparently personal) relationship when they traveled the country campaigning by bus in 1992. With more personal characteristics in common than many president/vice president teams (they're both Southerners, young, religious, fathers of teenage girls, and married to strong independent women, for example), Clinton made sure Gore was at his side in Arkansas when key early appointments were announced, and the two claim to consult on a daily basis. Moreover, Clinton placed Gore in charge of his effort to reform the bureaucracy (see chapter 9) and, because of Gore's long-standing interest in the environment, made him his front-man on those issues. Unlike past vice presidents, Gore is often at Clinton's side when major policy initiatives are announced. In 1996, in what ABC News correspondent Cokie Roberts called a "remarkable laying on of hands," President Clinton allowed his vice president to speak in prime time, a day before Clinton accepted his party's nomination, at the Democratic National Convention. Never before had a sitting president so clearly indicated his support of his vice president as his sucessor.

THE CONSTITUTIONAL POWERS OF THE PRESIDENT

*T*hough the Framers nearly unanimously agreed about the need for a strong central government and a greatly empowered Congress, they did not agree about the proper role of the president or the sweep of his authority. In contrast to Article I's laundry list of provisions for authority of the legislative branch, Article II details few presidential powers. Distrust of a powerful chief executive led to the Constitution's intentionally vague prescriptions for the presidency. Nevertheless, it is these constitutional powers, when coupled with a president's own personal style and abilities, that allow him to lead the nation. As you read Politics Now: President Clinton and Teenage Smoking, think how the Framers might have reacted to this kind of presidential exercise of power. Which constitutional powers do you think allow a president to take this kind of action?

President Clinton and Teenage Smoking

According to the Centers for Disease Control and Prevention (CDC) in Atlanta, Georgia, the health-care costs to the United States of smoking-related problems in 1993 were over $50 billion. Moreover, the social costs of smoking (such as lost productivity from disabilities and premature deaths) were estimated by the Office of Technology Assessment at $68 billion in 1990. In spite of extensive scientific evidence about the disastrous consequences of smoking, more and more teenagers are lighting up: Each day 3,000 more children and teenagers are added to the ranks of U.S. smokers. In 1995 the White House estimated that 7.3 million children and teens are regular smokers and that from 1991 to 1994, the percentage of eighth graders who smoked had increased 30 percent. In August 1995, in a move to reduce teen smoking, save the federal government millions in future health-care costs attributable to smoking, and shore up his public image, President Clinton authorized the federal Food and Drug Administration (FDA) to regulate nicotine as a drug. In August 1996, in noting that teens are particularly susceptible to the "deadly temptation" of tobacco, Clinton announced new FDA regulations to curb teen smoking:

- require merchants to verify that all buyers of tobacco are over age eighteen by requiring photo ID
- bar cigarette vending machines from all places that teens can enter as well as end the distribution of

Joe Camel, shown here lighting up in a building-sized ad at 42nd Street and 8th Avenue in New York City, helped provide the impetus for President Clinton's move to limit cigarette advertising in an effort to curb teen-age smoking. (Photo courtesy: Lee Snider/The Image Works)

free samples of cigarettes and other tobacco products

- end brand-name sponsorship by tobacco companies of sporting or entertainment events
- require that all outdoor, newspaper, and direct mail advertising for tobacco products be in black and white
- ban products such as hats and T-shirts that advertise particular brands of cigarettes or tobacco

"I would prefer it if we could have done this in some other way," said Clinton, noting that "if Congress were to write these restrictions into law . . . this rule could become unnecessary."

The goal of these rules, said the FDA, was to cut in half the number of minors who smoke.

Critics of Clinton's proposals included the tobacco industry, which took out full-page advertisements in scores of leading newspapers explaining their opposition to the president's involvement in the issue, which, of course, could ultimately negatively affect their sales. Conservative legislators, too, chimed in that there was no need for the federal chief executive to be weighing in on an issue that was a family matter or a state matter, not one for the president.

At a time when many Americans appear to oppose the intrusion of the national government into their lives, the president's antismoking campaign did not seem to hurt him. In fact, it probably helped. In an age when more and more adults are opting not to light up, they understand the future costs of a nation of smokers. Moreover, by involving himself in this issue, the president appeared to take on the mantle of a national father, an image that past presidents have been able to exploit to their political advantage in other spheres. (Until his antismoking campaign Clinton's young age and baby-boomer lifestyle had made it difficult for him to exploit this politically effective image.) Thus, although Clinton's actions were criticized by some, they probably helped in many other areas with little political capital lost. In fact, one study conducted in Virginia—a tobacco-growing state—showed that 55 percent of those surveyed favored federal regulation of tobacco as a drug.* What's your view?

*"Virginia Survey," *The Atlanta Journal*, August 24, 1996, A8.

Despite the Framers' faith in George Washington as their intended first president, it took considerable compromise to overcome their continued fear of a too-powerful president. The specific powers of the executive branch that the Framers agreed on are enumerated in Article II of the Constitution. Perhaps the most important section of Article II is its first sentence: "The executive Power shall be vested in a President of the United States of America." Just what the Framers meant by "executive power" was left intentionally vague.

Over the years, the expected limits of these specific constitutional powers have changed as individual presidents asserted themselves in the political process. Some presidents are powerful and effective; others just limp along in office. Much of the president's authority stems from his position as the symbolic leader of the nation and his ability to wield power, whether those powers are specifically enumerated in the Constitution or not. When the president speaks—especially in the area of foreign affairs—he speaks for the whole nation. *But* the base of all presidential authority is Article II, which outlines only a limited policy-making role for the president. Thus, as administrative head of the executive branch, the president is charged with taking "Care that the Laws be faithfully executed," but he has no actual power to make Congress enact legislation he supports. Nonetheless, the sum total of his powers, enumerated below, allow him to become a major player in the policy process, as the discussion of his efforts to curtail teenage smoking reveal.

The Appointment Power

To help the president enforce the laws passed by Congress, the Constitution authorizes him to appoint, with the advice and consent of the Senate, "Ambassadors, other public Ministers and Consuls, judges of the supreme Court, and all other Officers of the United States, whose Appointments are not herein otherwise provided for, and which shall be established by Law. . . ." Although this section of the Constitution deals only with appointments, behind that language is a powerful policy-making tool. Not only does the president have the authority to make more than 3,000 appointments to his administration (technically more than 75,000, if military officers are included), many of those appointees are in positions to wield substantial authority over the course and direction of public policy. Although Congress has the authority "to make all laws," through the president's enforcement power—and his chosen assistants—he often can set the policy agenda for the nation. And, especially in the context of his ability to make appointments to the federal courts, his influence can be felt far past his term of office.

It is not surprising, then, that selecting the "right" people is often one of a president's most important tasks. Presidents look for a blend of loyalty, competence, and integrity. Identifying these qualities in people is a major challenge that every new president faces. Recent presidents, especially Bill Clinton, have also tried to appoint more women and minorities to top positions (see Table 8.1, for example). "Bad" appointments, moreover, can endanger an administration's ability to make policy.

When a president forwards a nomination to the Senate for its approval, his selections are traditionally given great respect—especially those for the **Cabinet,** an advisory group selected by the president to help him make decisions and execute the laws. In fact, the vast majority (97 percent) of all presidential nominations are confirmed.[9] But even a few rejections can have a major impact on the course of an administration. Rejections leave a president without first choices, have a chilling effect on other potential nominees, affect a president's relationship with the Senate, and affect how the president is perceived by the public. President Bill Clinton, for example, lost valuable

Cabinet: The formal body of presidential advisers who head the fourteen departments. Presidents often add others to this body of formal advisers.

Chief law enforcer: National Guard troops sent by President Eisenhower enforce federal court decisions ordering the integration of public schools in Little Rock, Arkansas. (Photo courtesy: UPI/The Bettmann Archive)

Commander-in-chief: President Bush and his wife, Barbara, with troops in the Persian Gulf. (Photo courtesy: Wally McNamee/Folio, Inc.)

Leader of the party: Bill Clinton accepts his party's nomination for president at the 1992 Democratic National Convention. (Photo courtesy: Brooks Kraft/Sygma)

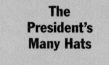

The President's Many Hats

Key player in the legislative process: Clinton confers with Republican leaders to promote bipartisanship. (Photo courtesy: Sygma)

Shaper of domestic policy: President Lyndon B. Johnson confers with the Reverend Martin Luther King, Jr., and other black leaders about Johnson's War on Poverty. (Photo courtesy: UPI/The Bettmann Archive)

Chief of State: President John F. Kennedy and his wife, Jacqueline, are greeted by the president of France and his wife during the Kennedys' widely publicized 1961 trip to that nation. (Photo courtesy: UPI/The Bettmann Archive)

TABLE 8.1

Presidential Teams (Senior Administrative Positions Requiring Senate Confirmation)

	TOTAL APPOINTMENTS	TOTAL WOMEN	PERCENTAGE WOMEN
Jimmy Carter	1,087	191	17.6%
Ronald Reagan	2,349	277	11.8%
George Bush	1,079	215	19.9%
Bill Clinton	1,257	364	29%

Source: "Insiders Say White House Has Its Own Glass Ceiling," *Atlanta Journal Constitution* (April 10, 1995): A-4.

policy-making time when key positions were unfilled; time after time he announced prospective nominees whose confirmation ran into trouble after press or other public revelations. Zöe Baird, for example, withdrew her name from Senate consideration for Attorney General after it became known that she had not paid Social Security taxes for her nanny and other household help. Lani Guinier's nomination to head the Civil Rights Division of the Justice Department was withdrawn by Clinton after he decided he could not support her views on race-based remedies. Other nominations, such as physician Henry Foster's for U.S. Surgeon General, were rejected by the Senate. In the case of Foster, Senate Republicans launched a full-court press against the physician, who had performed legal abortions early in his career.

Although nominees are defeated (or their nominations withdrawn) on occasion, it is actually rare for presidential appointees to Cabinet-level positions to be rejected by the Senate. Most presidents withdraw their nominees before they can be defeated to avoid the blow to their prestige. In fact, the Senate's rejection of President Bush's nominee for secretary of defense, former U.S. Senator John Tower, marked only the eighth time in history that a president's choice for a Cabinet post was rejected.

Certain kinds of nominees receive more congressional scrutiny than others. Regulatory commission members, discussed in detail in chapter 9, are located in the world of politics somewhere between the legislative and executive branches, yet they are appointed by the president and are often the subject of intense Senate scrutiny. Supreme Court appointees also lie outside the executive branch of government and are increasingly subject to greater senatorial review and public, televised grilling.

The Power to Convene Congress

The Constitution requires the president to inform the Congress periodically of "the State of the Union," and authorizes the president to convene either or both houses of Congress on "extraordinary Occasions." In *Federalist No. 77* Hamilton justified the latter by noting that because the Senate and the chief executive enjoy concurrent powers to make treaties, "it might often be necessary to call it together with a view to this object, when it would be unnecessary and improper to convene the House of Representatives." The power to convene Congress was important when Congress did not sit in nearly year-round sessions. Today this power has little more than symbolic significance.

The Power to Make Treaties

The president's power to make treaties with foreign nations is checked by the Constitution's stipulation that all treaties must be approved by at least two-thirds of the members of the Senate. The chief executive can also "receive ambassadors," wording that has been interpreted to allow the president to recognize the very existence of other nations.

Historically, the Senate ratifies about 70 percent of the treaties submitted to it by the president.[10] Only sixteen treaties that have been put to a vote have been rejected, often under highly partisan circumstances. Perhaps the most notable example of the Senate's refusal to ratify a treaty was its defeat of the Treaty of Versailles submitted by President Woodrow Wilson. The treaty was an agreement among the major nations to end World War I. At Wilson's insistence, it also called for the creation of the League of Nations—a precursor of the United Nations—to foster continued peace and international disarmament. In struggling to gain international acceptance for the league, Wilson had taken American support for granted. This was a dramatic miscalculation. Isolationists, led by Senator William Jennings Bryan (D–Neb.), opposed U.S. participation in the league on the grounds that the league would place the United States in the center of every major international conflict. Proponents countered that, league or no league, the United States had emerged from World War I as a world power and that membership in the League of Nations would enhance its new role. The vote in the Senate for ratification was very close, but the isolationists prevailed—the United States stayed out of the league, and Wilson was devastated.

The Senate also may require substantial amendment of a treaty prior to its consent. When President Carter proposed the controversial Panama Canal Treaties in 1977, for example, the Senate required several conditions to be ironed out between the Carter and Torrijos administrations before its approval was forthcoming.

When trade agreements are at issue, presidents are often also forced to be mindful of the wishes of Congress. The North American Free Trade Agreement (NAFTA) and the General Agreement on Tariffs and Trade (GATT) came to Congress after the president and his aides had negotiated these trade agreements under special rules referred to as "fast-track" procedures. These special rules are designed to protect a president's ability to negotiate with confidence that his accords will not be altered by Congress. The rules bar amendment and require an up or down vote in Congress within ninety days of introduction.

Presidents often try to get around the "advise and consent" requirement for ratification of treaties and the congressional approval required for trade agreements by entering into an **executive agreement,** which allows the president to enter into secret and highly sensitive arrangements with foreign nations without Senate approval. Presidents have used these agreements since the days of George Washington, and their use has been upheld by the courts. Although executive agreements are not binding on subsequent administrations, since 1900 they have been used far more frequently than treaties (see chapter 19), further cementing the role of the president in foreign affairs.

Veto Power

Presidents can also affect the policy process through the **veto power,** the authority to reject any congressional legislation. The threat of a presidential veto often

executive agreement: secret and highly sensitive arrangements with foreign nations entered into by the president that do not require the "advise and consent" of the Senate.

veto power: The formal, constitutional authority of the president to reject bills passed by both houses of Congress thus preventing their becoming law without further congressional action.

prompts members of Congress to fashion legislation that they know will receive presidential acquiescence, if not support. Thus just threatening to veto legislation often gives a president another way to influence law making.

Proponents of a strong executive at the Constitutional Convention argued that the president should have an absolute and final veto over acts of Congress. Opponents of this idea, including Benjamin Franklin, countered that in their home states the executive veto "was constantly made use of to extort money" from the legislatures. James Madison made the most compelling argument for a compromise on the issue:

> Experience has proven a tendency in our governments to throw all power into the legislative vortex. The Executives of the States are in general little more than Ciphers, the legislatures omnipotent. If no effectual check be devised for restraining the instability and encroachments of the latter, a revolution of some kind or other would be inevitable.[11]

In keeping with the system of checks and balances, then, the president was given the veto power, but only as a "qualified negative." Although the president was given the authority to veto any act of Congress (with the exception of joint resolutions that propose constitutional amendments), Congress was given the authority to override an executive veto by a two-thirds vote in each House. The veto is a powerful policy tool because Congress cannot usually muster enough votes to override a veto. Thus, in over 200 years, there have been approximately 2,500 presidential vetoes and only about a hundred have been overridden.

President Bush was never reluctant to use his veto power: He often vetoed bills that were considered to enjoy wide popular support and had only one of his vetoes overridden. During Bill Clinton's first two years in office, he became the first president since James A. Garfield (1881) not to veto any act of Congress. But, beginning in August 1995, when he exercised his first veto involving Congress's passage of legislation to require the United States to lift its embargo of arms sales to Bosnian Muslims, Clinton found himself at odds with the Republican-controlled Congress and was forced to veto sixteen pieces of legislation through November 1996.

The Line-Item Veto.   As early as 1873, in his State of the Union message, President Ulysses S. Grant proposed a constitutional amendment to give the president a **line-item veto,** a power enjoyed by many governors to disapprove of individual items within a spending bill and not just the bill in its entirety. Since then, over 150 resolutions calling for a line-item veto have been introduced in Congress. FDR, Eisenhower, Ford, Carter, Reagan, Bush, and Clinton supported the concept. In 1994 congressional passage of a line-item veto was a key item in the Contract with America and was finally passed by Congress in 1996.

George Bush was a particularly vocal proponent of the line-item veto, although only one of his vetoes was overridden. Said Bush during his 1992 State of the Union message, "The press has a field day making fun of outrageous examples [of pork barrel appropriations]: A Lawrence Welk museum, research grants for Belgian endive. . . . Maybe you need someone to help you say no. I know how to say it, and I know what I need to make it stick. Give me the same thing forty-three governors have: the line-item veto."[12] Many, including a majority in the 104th Congress, agreed with Bush that the line-item veto could result in considerable savings, since it would allow a president to do away with more outrageous examples of "pork" (legislators' pet projects, which often find their way into a budget) and to eliminate what a president might see as needless fat in the budget. The line-item veto will undoubtedly allow presidents to project their policy priorities into the budget by vetoing any programs inconsistent with their policy goals.

line-item veto: The power to veto specific provisions of a bill without vetoing the bill in its entirety.

The Power of the President to Preside over the Military as Commander-in-Chief

One of the most important constitutional executive powers is the president's authority over the military. Article II states that the president is "Commander-in-Chief of the Army and Navy of the United States." The Framers saw this power as consistent with state practices, and since the eighteenth century, it has proved to be wide-ranging. While the Constitution specifically grants Congress the authority to declare war, presidents since Abraham Lincoln have used the commander-in-chief clause in conjunction with the chief executive's duty to "take Care that the Laws be faithfully executed" to wage war (and to broaden various powers).

Modern presidents continually clash with Congress over the ability to commence hostilities. The Vietnam War, in which 58,000 American soldiers were killed and 300,000 were wounded, was conducted (at a cost of $150 billion) without a congressional declaration of war. In fact, acknowledging President Johnson's claim to war-making authority, in 1964 Congress passed—with only two dissenting votes—the Gulf of Tonkin Resolution, which authorized a massive commitment of U.S. forces in South Vietnam.

During that highly controversial war, presidents Johnson and then Nixon routinely assured members of Congress that victory was near. In 1971, however, publication of what were called *The Pentagon Papers* revealed what many had suspected all along—Lyndon B. Johnson had systematically altered casualty figures and distorted key facts to place the conduct of the war in a more positive light. In 1973 Congress passed the **War Powers Act** to limit the president's authority to introduce American troops into hostile foreign lands without congressional approval. President Nixon's veto of the act was overridden by a two-thirds majority in both houses of Congress.

War Powers Act: Law requiring presidents to obtain congressional approval before introducing U.S. troops into a combat situation; passed in 1973 over President Nixon's veto.

Presidents since Nixon have continued to insist that the War Powers Act is an unconstitutional infringement of their executive power. Thus, over and over again, presidents—Democratic and Republican—have ignored one or more provisions of the act. In 1980 Jimmy Carter failed to inform members of Congress before he initiated the unsuccessful effort to rescue American hostages at the U.S. Embassy in Iran. In 1983 President Reagan ordered the invasion of Grenada. In 1990 President Bush ordered 13,000 troops to invade Panama. And in 1993 President Clinton sent U.S. troops to Haiti to restore its president to power. On each of these occasions, members of Congress have criticized the president. Yet the president's actions in each case have been judged in terms of his success and not on his possible abuse of power.

The Pardoning Power

pardon: The restoration of all rights and privileges of citizenship to a specific individual charged or convicted of a crime.

Presidents can exercise a check on judicial power through their constitutional authority to grant reprieves or pardons. A **pardon** is an executive grant releasing an individual from the punishment or legal consequences of a crime before or after conviction, and restores all rights and privileges of citizenship. Presidents exercise complete pardoning power for federal offenses except in cases of impeachment, which cannot be pardoned. President Gerald R. Ford granted the most famous presidential pardon when he pardoned former President Richard M. Nixon—who had not been formally charged with any crime—"for any offenses against the United States, which he, Richard Nixon, has committed or may have committed while in office." This unilateral, absolute pardon, which prevented the former president from ever being tried for any crimes he may have committed, unleashed a torrent of public criticism against

Ford and questions about whether or not Nixon had discussed the pardon with Ford before Nixon's resignation. Many attribute Ford's ultimate defeat in his 1976 bid for the presidency on that pardon.

In the waning days of his term, George Bush was showered with a torrent of criticism when he pardoned former Secretary of Defense Caspar Weinberger and five other administration officials on Christmas Eve 1993 for their conduct related to the Iran–Contra affair. Bush tried to place his pardons in the context of the historic use of the pardoning power to "put bitterness behind us and to look to the future."

Even though pardons are generally directed toward a specific individual, presidents have also used them to offer general amnesties. Presidents Washington, John Adams, Madison, Lincoln, Andrew Johnson, Theodore Roosevelt, Harry S Truman, and Jimmy Carter all used general pardons to grant amnesty to large classes of individuals for illegal acts. Carter, for example, incurred the wrath of many veterans' groups when he made an offer of unconditional amnesty to approximately 10,000 men who had fled the United States or gone into hiding to avoid being drafted to serve in the Vietnam War.

While the pardoning power is not normally considered a key presidential power, its use by a president can get him in severe trouble with the electorate. Three presidents defeated in their reelection bids—Ford, Carter, and Bush—all incurred the wrath of the electorate for unpopular pardons. Thus, just as members of Congress are always on the lookout for potentially disastrous votes, it may be that presidents should be equally as wary of using their pardoning power.

THE DEVELOPMENT OF PRESIDENTIAL POWER

*E*ach one of the men who has served as president of the United States has brought with him some expectation about the use of presidential authority and some vision (often outlined by campaign promises) of how the country could be improved through his guidance and leadership. Through 1997, the forty-one men who have held the nation's highest office have been a diverse lot. (While there have been forty-two presidents, only forty-one men have held the office—Grover Cleveland served as the twenty-second and twenty-fourth presidents because he was elected to nonconsecutive terms in 1884 and 1892.) Yet most presidents have found accomplishing their goals much more difficult than they envisioned, even if they were elected with a sizable majority. After John F. Kennedy had been in office two years, for example, he noted publicly that there were "greater limitations upon our ability to bring about a favorable result than I had imagined."[13] Similarly, as he was leaving office, Harry S Truman mused about what surprises awaited his successor, Dwight D. Eisenhower, a former general: "He'll sit here and he'll say, 'Do this! Do that!' *And nothing will happen.* Poor Ike—it won't be a bit like the army. He'll find it very frustrating."[14]

A president's personal expectation of authority (and the public's expectations of him) are limited by the formal powers bestowed on the president by the Constitution and by the Supreme Court's interpretation of those constitutional provisions. These formal checks on presidential power are also affected by the times in which the president serves, by his selection of confidantes and advisers, and by the president's personality and leadership abilities. The postwar era of good feelings and economic prosperity presided over by the grandfatherly former war hero Dwight D. Eisenhower in the 1950s, for instance, called for a very different kind of leader from that needed by the

Highlight 8.2

The Best and the Worst Presidents

Who was the best president and who was the worst? Many surveys of scholars have been taken over the years to answer this question, and virtually all have ranked Abraham Lincoln the best and Warren G. Harding the worst. A 1995 *Chicago Sun-Times* poll, for example, came up with these results:

Ten Best Presidents	Ten Worst Presidents
1. Lincoln (best)	1. Harding (worst)
2. Washington	2. Nixon
3. F. Roosevelt	3. Buchanan
4. Jefferson	4. Pierce
5. T. Roosevelt	5. Grant
6. Wilson	6. Fillmore
7. Truman	7. A. Johnson
8. Jackson	8. Coolidge
9. Eisenhower	9. Tyler
10. Polk (10th best)	10. Carter (10th worst)

Source: Steve Neal, "Putting Presidents in Their Place; Longtime Favorites Top the List," *Chicago Sun-Times* (November 19, 1995): 30–1.

Civil War-torn nation governed by Abraham Lincoln. Furthermore, not only do different times call for different kinds of leaders, they also often provide limits, or conversely, wide opportunities, for whoever serves as president at the time.

A president's authority can also be limited or expanded by the demands of the times in which he governs. Crises in particular have triggered expansions of presidential power. The danger to the Union posed by the Civil War in the 1860s required strong leaders to take up the reins of government. Because of his leadership during this crisis, Lincoln is generally ranked as the "best" president. (See Highlight 8.2: The Best and the Worst Presidents.)

The First Three Presidents

The first three presidents, and their conception of the presidency, continue to have a profound impact on both the office and the public's expectations about the office and its inhabitants. When George Washington was sworn in as the first president of the United States on a cold, blustery day in New York City in April 1789, he took over an office and government that were really yet to be created. Eventually, a few hundred postal workers were hired and Washington appointed a small group of Cabinet advisers and clerks. During Washington's two terms, the entire federal budget was only about $40 million, or approximately $10 for every citizen in America. In contrast, in 1995 the federal budget was $1.5 trillion, or $5,883 for every man, woman, and child.

Like Washington (see Roots of Government: George Washington's Impact on the Presidency), the next two presidents, John Adams and Thomas Jefferson, also acted in ways that were critical to the development of the office of the chief executive and the

Roots of Government

George Washington's Impact on the Presidency

In furtherance of his belief in the importance of the executive office to the development of the new nation, George Washington set several important precedents for future presidents:

■ He took every opportunity to establish the primacy of the national government. In 1794, for example, Washington used the militia of four states to put down the Whiskey Rebellion, an uprising of 3,000 western Pennsylvania farmers opposed to the payment of federal excise tax on liquor. Leading those 1,500 troops was Secretary of the Treasury Alexander Hamilton, whose duty it was to collect federal taxes. Washington's action helped establish the idea of federal supremacy and the authority of the executive branch to collect the taxes levied by Congress.

■ Washington began the practice of regular meetings with his advisers (called the Cabinet), thus establishing the Cabinet system.

■ He asserted the prominence of the role of the chief executive in the conduct of foreign affairs. He sent envoys to negotiate the Jay Treaty with Great Britain. Then, over senatorial objection, he continued to assert his authority to negotiate treaties first and then simply submit them to the Senate for its approval. Washington made it clear that the Senate's function was limited to approval of treaties and did *not* include negotiation with foreign powers.

■ He claimed the inherent power of the presidency as the basis for proclaiming a policy of strict neutrality when the British and French were at war. Although the Constitution is silent about a president's authority to declare neutrality, Washington's supporters argued that the Constitution granted the president **inherent powers,** that is, powers that can be derived or inferred from what is formally described in the Constitution. Thus they argued that the president's power to conduct diplomatic relations could be inferred from the Constitution. Since neither Congress nor the Supreme Court later disagreed, this power was presumed added to the list of specific, enumerated presidential powers found in Article II.

president's role in the political system. Adams's poor leadership skills, for example, heightened the divisions between Federalists and Anti-Federalists and probably quickened the development of political parties (see chapter 12). Soon thereafter, Jefferson used the party system to cement strong ties with the Congress and thereby expand the role of the president in the legislative process. He also expanded on the concept of **inherent powers** by taking the opportunity to expand the size of the nation dramatically through the **Louisiana Purchase** in 1803.

Congressional Triumph: 1804–1933

The first three presidents made enormous contributions to the office of the chief executive and established important precedents to guide the conduct of those who came after them. But the very nature of the way government had to function in its formative years caused the balance of power to be heavily weighted in favor of a strong Congress. Americans routinely had intimate contacts with their representatives in Congress, while to most, the president seemed a remote figure. Members of Congress were frequently at home, where they could be seen by the voters; few ever even gazed on a president.

inherent powers: Powers of the president that can be derived or inferred from specific powers in the Constitution.

Louisiana Purchase: The 1803 land purchase authorized by Thomas Jefferson, which expanded the size of the United States dramatically and expanded the concept of inherent powers.

By the end of Jefferson's first term, it was clear that the Framers' initial fear of an all-powerful, monarchical president was unfounded. The strength of Congress and the relatively weak presidents who came after Jefferson allowed Congress quickly to assert itself as the most powerful branch of government. In fact, with but few exceptions, most presidents from Jefferson to Franklin Roosevelt failed to exercise the powers of the presidency in any significant manner.

Andrew Jackson was the first president to act as a strong *national* leader, representing more than just a landed, propertied elite. By the time Jackson ran for president in 1828, eleven new states had been added to the Union, and the number of white males eligible to vote had increased dramatically as property requirements for voting were removed by nearly all states. When Jackson, a Tennessean, was elected the seventh president, it signaled the end of an era: He was the first president not to be either a Virginian or an Adams. His election launched the beginning of "Jacksonian democracy," a label that embodied the Western, frontier, egalitarian spirit personified by Jackson, the first "common man" to be elected president. The masses loved him, and legends were built around his down-to-earth image. Jackson, for example, once was asked to give a postmastership to a soldier who had lost his leg on the battlefield and needed the job to support his family. When told that the man hadn't voted for him, Jackson responded: "If he lost his leg fighting for his country, that is vote enough for me."[15]

Jackson used his image and personal power to buttress the developing party system by rewarding loyal followers of his Democratic Party with presidential appointments. He frequently found himself at odds with Congress, and made extensive use of the veto power. His veto of twelve bills surpassed the combined total of nine vetoes used by his six predecessors. Jackson also reasserted the supremacy of the national government (and the presidency) by facing down South Carolina's nullification of a federal tariff law.

Abraham Lincoln's approach to the presidency was similar to Jackson's. Moreover, the unprecedented emergency of the Civil War allowed Lincoln to assume powers that no president before him had claimed. Because Lincoln believed he needed to act quickly for the very survival of the Union, he frequently took action without first obtaining the approval of Congress. Among many of Lincoln's "questionable" acts:

- He suspended the writ of *habeas corpus*, which allows those in prison to petition to be released, citing the need to jail persons even suspected of disloyal practices.
- He expanded the size of the U.S. army above congressionally mandated ceilings.
- He ordered a blockade of Southern ports, in effect initiating a war without the approval of Congress.
- He closed the U.S. mails to treasonable correspondence.

Lincoln argued that the inherent powers of his office allowed him to circumvent the Constitution in a time of war or national crisis. Since the Constitution conferred on the president the duty to make sure that the laws of the United States are faithfully executed, reasoned Lincoln, the acts enumerated above were constitutional. He simply refused to allow the nation to crumble because of what he viewed as technical requirements of the Constitution. Noting the secession of the Southern states and their threat to the sanctity of the Union, Lincoln queried, "Are all of the laws *but one* to go unexecuted, and the Government itself go to pieces lest that one be violated?"[16]

Later, both Theodore Roosevelt (1901–9) and Woodrow Wilson (1913–21) expanded the powers of the presidency. Roosevelt worked closely with Congress, sending it several messages defining his legislative program. Roosevelt also followed the **stewardship theory** of executive power, believing that Article II conferred on the president not only the power, but the duty to take whatever actions are deemed necessary in the national

stewardship theory: The theory that holds that Article II confers on the president the power *and* the duty to take whatever actions are deemed necessary in the national interest, unless prohibited by the Constitution or by law.

interest, unless prohibited by the Constitution or by law. Wilson helped formulate bills and reinstated the practice of personally delivering the State of the Union message to Congress. World War I also forced him to take a pivotal role in international affairs.

Few presidents other than Jackson, Lincoln, Theodore Roosevelt, and Wilson subscribed to a broad and expansive interpretation of executive power prior to the administration of Franklin D. Roosevelt (1933–45), possibly because the nation was not ready to submit to a series of strong presidents and because the times and national events did not seem to call for strong, charismatic leaders. Instead, most other presidents adopted what is known as the **Taftian theory** of presidential power, which holds that the president is limited by the specific grants of executive power found in the Constitution. President Taft argued explicitly for this literalist view of presidential power, a view shared by Presidents Harding and Coolidge, among others.

Taftian theory: The theory that holds that the president is limited by the specific grants of executive power found in the Constitution.

The Growth of the Modern Presidency

Before the days of instantaneous communication, the nation could afford to allow Congress, with its relatively slow deliberative processes, to make most decisions. Furthermore, decision making might have been left to Congress because its members, and not the president, were closest to the people. As times and technology have changed, however, so have the public's expectations of anyone who becomes president. For example, the breakneck speed with which the electronic media such as the Cable News Network (CNN) report national and international events have intensified the public's expectation that in a crisis the president will be the individual to act quickly and decisively on behalf of the entire nation. Congress is often just too slow to respond to fast-changing events—especially in foreign affairs.

President Franklin Delano Roosevelt delivering one of his famous "fireside chats" to the American people. Roosevelt projected the voice and image of such a vigorous and active president that no one listening to him or seeing him in the newsreels would have guessed that he was confined to a wheelchair as a result of polio. (Photo courtesy: AP/Wide World Photos)

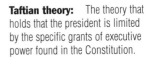

In the twentieth century, the general trend has been for presidential—as opposed to congressional—decision making to be more and more important. The start of this trend can be traced to the four-term presidency of Franklin D. Roosevelt (FDR), who led the nation through several crises, including the Great Depression and World War II. This growth of presidential power and the growth of the federal government and its programs in general are now criticized by many. To understand the basis for many of the calls for reform of the political system being made today, it is critical to understand how the growth of government and the role of the president occurred.

FDR took office in 1933 in the midst of a major crisis—the Great Depression—during which as many as 25 percent of the U.S. workforce was unemployed. Noting the sorry state of the national economy in his inaugural address, FDR concluded, "This nation asks for action and action now." To jump-start the American economy, FDR asked Congress for *and was given* "broad executive powers to wage a war against the emergency, as great as the power that would be given to me if we were in fact invaded by a foreign foe."[17]

Just as Lincoln had taken bold steps on his inauguration, Roosevelt also acted quickly. He immediately fashioned a plan for national recovery called the **New Deal,** a package of bold and controversial programs designed to invigorate the failing American economy. As part of that plan, Roosevelt:

- Declared a bank holiday to end public runs on the depleted resources of many banks
- Persuaded Congress to pass legislation to provide for emergency relief, public works jobs, regulation of farm production, and improved terms and conditions of work for thousands of workers in a variety of industries
- Made standard the executive branch practice of sending legislative programs to Congress for its approval; before, the executive branch had generally just reacted to congressional proposals
- Increased the size of the federal bureaucracy from fewer than 600,000 to more than 1 million workers

Throughout Roosevelt's unprecedented twelve years in office (he was elected to four terms but died shortly after beginning the last one), which saw the nation go from the economic "war" of the Great Depression to the real international conflict of World War II, the institution of the presidency changed profoundly and permanently. All kinds of new federal agencies were created to implement New Deal programs, and the executive branch became more and more involved in implementing the wide variety of programs overseen by these agencies.

Not only did FDR create a new bureaucracy to implement his pet programs, he also personalized the presidency by establishing a new relationship between the presidency and the people. In his radio addresses—or "fireside chats," as he liked to call them—he spoke directly to the public in a relaxed and informal manner about serious issues. He opened his radio addresses with the words, "My friends . . . ," which made it seem as though he were speaking directly to each listener. In response to these chats, Roosevelt began to receive about 4,000 letters per day, in contrast to the forty letters per day received by his predecessor, Herbert Hoover. The head of the White House correspondence section remembered that "the mail started coming in by the truckload. They couldn't even get the envelopes open."[18] One letter that found its way to the White House was simply addressed "My Friend, Washington, D.C."

To his successors FDR left the "modern presidency," including a burgeoning (many would say bloated) federal bureaucracy (see chapter 9), an active and usually leading role in both domestic and foreign policy and legislation, and a nationalized executive

New Deal: The name given to the program of "Relief, Recovery, Reform" begun by President Franklin D. Roosevelt, in 1933 designed to bring the United States out of the Great Depression.

Politics Now

Going Public

Direct, presidential appeals to the electorate like those often made by Bill Clinton are referred to as "going public."[*] Going public means that a president goes over the heads of members of Congress to gain support from the people, who can then place pressure on their elected officials in Washington. Ronald Reagan, for example, went directly to the American public to get control of his war on drugs. Similarly, President Gerald R. Ford went directly to the public to try to get support for his anti-inflation policies. Sporting a "WIN" button, Ford addressed the nation calling on them to rally Congress to "Whip Inflation Now."

Like most presidents, Clinton is keenly aware of the importance of maintaining his connection with the public. Beginning with his 1992 campaign, Clinton often appeared on Larry King's TV talk show. Even after becoming president, Clinton continued to take his case directly to the people. He launched his health-care reform proposals, for example, on a prime-time edition of *Nightline* hosted by Ted Koppel. For an hour and a half, the president took audience questions about his health plan, impressing even those who doubted the plan with his impressive grasp of details. Moreover, at a black-tie dinner honoring radio and television correspondents, Clinton responded to criticisms levied against him for not holding traditional press conferences by pointing out how clever he was to ignore the traditional press. "You know why I can stiff you on the press conferences? Because Larry King liberated me from you by giving me to the American people directly," quipped Clinton.[**] In 1996, for example, President Clinton used the "bully pulpit" to convince television networks to get behind the idea of a rating system for television programs.

But some personal, direct appeals by a president appear to make no difference. In the case of health care, which the American public *seemed* to think was important in the 1992 presidential campaign, Clinton's personal approach had little apparent positive impact. The "people" didn't *really* rank health-care reform as a priority, so his direct appeal was a complete failure and a media disaster, which ultimately made it more difficult for the president to get other programs passed by Congress. Clearly, going public—unless the public favors a policy not favored by Congress—is not a useful strategy. If the public does favor a policy or program caught up in congressional politics, however, it makes sense for a president to go directly to "the people," who in turn can place pressure on their elected representatives. What issues do you think might be good targets for personalized presidential appeals?

[*]Samuel Kernell, *Going Public: New Strategies of Presidential Leadership* 3rd ed. (Washington, D.C.: CQ Press, 1996).
[**]Dan Balz, "Strange Bedfellows: How Television and Presidential Candidates Changed American Politics," *Washington Monthly* (July 1993).

office which used technology—first radio and then television—to bring the president closer to the public than ever before.

The communication and leadership styles of post-FDR presidents are very different from those of eighteenth- and nineteenth-century presidents. George Washington believed that the purpose of public appearances was to "see and be seen," and not to discuss policy issues. Abraham Lincoln was applauded for refusing to speak about the impending Civil War. Today presidents use every opportunity to sell their economic, domestic, and foreign programs. In addition, the modes of communication have changed greatly. The rhetoric of early presidents was written, formal, and addressed principally to Congress. Today press conferences and speeches addressed directly to the public are the norm (see Politics Now: Going Public).

THE PRESIDENTIAL ESTABLISHMENT

*A*s the responsibilities and scope of presidential authority have grown over the years, especially since FDR's time, so has the executive branch of government and the number of people working directly for the president in the White House itself. While the U.S. Constitution makes no special mention of a Cabinet, it does imply that a president will be assisted by advisers. It is unlikely, however, that anyone at the Constitutional Convention envisioned the growth in the presidency that has occurred. It is highly unlikely that the Framers—even Alexander Hamilton, who was probably the greatest supporter of a strong chief executive—ever envisioned the growth in executive power that has occurred over the years. Just think of the differences in governance faced by two Georges—Washington and Bush. George Washington supervised the nation from a temporary headquarters with a staff of but one aide—his nephew, paid out of Washington's own funds—and only four Cabinet members. In contrast, when George Bush left office in 1993, he had presided over a White House staff of 461, a Cabinet of fourteen members, and an executive branch of government that employed more than 3 million people. Today a president is surrounded by policy advisers of all types—from the attorney general, who advises him on legal issues, to the surgeon general, who advises him on health matters. The White House staff, the First Lady (see Highlight 8.3) and vice president and their staffs, the Cabinet, and the Executive Office of the President all help the president fulfill his duties as chief executive.

The Cabinet

The Cabinet, which has no basis in the Constitution, is an informal institution based on practice and precedent whose membership is determined by tradition and presidential discretion. By custom, this advisory group selected by the president includes the heads of major departments. Most presidents also include their vice presidents in Cabinet meetings, as well as any other agency heads or officials to whom he would like to accord Cabinet status.

As a body, the Cabinet's major function is to help the president execute the laws and assist him in making decisions. Although the Framers had discussed the idea of some form of national executive council, they did not include a provision for one in the Constitution. They did, however, recognize the need for departments of government and departmental heads.

As revealed in Table 8.2, over the years the Cabinet has grown as departments have been added to accommodate new pressures on the president to act in areas that were not initially considered within the scope of concern of the national government. As interest groups, in particular, pressured Congress and the president to recognize their demands for services and governmental action, they often were rewarded by the creation of an executive department. Since each was headed by a secretary who automatically became a member of the president's Cabinet, powerful groups including farmers (Agriculture), businesspeople (Commerce), workers (Labor), and teachers (Education) saw the creation of a department as increasing their access to the president.

The size of the president's Cabinet has increased over the years at the same time that most presidents' reliance on their Cabinet secretaries has decreased, although some individual members of a president's Cabinet may be very influential. Because the

TABLE 8.2

The U.S. Cabinet

DEPARTMENT	DATE OF CREATION	RESPONSIBILITIES
Department of State	1789	Responsible for the making of foreign policy, including treaty negotiation
Department of the Treasury	1789	Responsible for government funds and regulation of alcohol, firearms, and tobacco
Department of Defense	1789; 1947	Created by consolidating the former Departments of War, the Army, the Navy, and the Air Force; responsible for national defense
Department of Justice	1870	Represents U.S. government in all federal courts, investigates and prosecutes violations of federal law
Department of the Interior	1849	Manages the nation's natural resources, including wildlife and public lands
Department of Agriculture	Created in 1862; Elevated to Cabinet status in 1889	Assists the nation's farmers, oversees food-quality programs, administers food stamp and school lunch programs
Department of Commerce	1903	Aids businesses and conducts the U.S. census (originally the Department of Commerce and Labor)
Department of Labor	1913	Runs manpower programs, keeps labor statistics, aids labor through enforcement of laws
Department of Health and Human Services	1953	Runs health, welfare, and Social Security programs; created as the Department of Health, Education, and Welfare (lost its education function in 1979)
Department of Housing and Urban Development	1965	Responsible for urban and housing programs
Department of Transportation	1966	Responsible for mass transportation and highway programs
Department of Energy	1977	Responsible for energy policy and research, including atomic energy
Department of Education	1979	Responsible for the federal government's education programs
Department of Veterans' Affairs	1989	Responsible for programs aiding veterans

cabinet secretaries and high-ranking members of their departments are routinely subjected to congressional oversight and interest group pressures, they often have divided loyalties. In fact, Congress, through the necessary and proper clause, even has the authority to reorganize executive departments, create new ones, or abolish existing ones altogether. For this reason most presidents now rely most heavily on members of their inner circle of advisers (the Executive Office of the President and the White House Office) for advice and information. (Chapter 9 provides a more detailed discussion of the Cabinet's role in executing U.S. policy.)

The Executive Office of the President (EOP)

The **Executive Office of the President (EOP)** was established by FDR in 1939 to oversee his New Deal programs. It was created to provide the president with a "general staff" to help him direct the diverse activities of the executive branch. In fact, it is a mini-bureaucracy of several advisers and offices located in the ornate Executive Office Building next to the White House on Pennsylvania Avenue, as well as in the White House itself, where his closest advisers often are located.

The EOP has expanded over time to include several advisory and policy-making agencies and task forces, each of which is responsible to the executive branch. Over

Executive Office of the President (EOP): Establishment created in 1939 to help the president oversee the bureaucracy.

President Clinton meeting with his national security team to discuss the situation in Bosnia. (Photo courtesy: The White House/Sipa Press)

President Clinton meeting with his national security team to discuss the situation in Bosnia. (Photo courtesy: The White House/Sipa Press)

time, the units of the EOP have become more responsive to individual presidents rather than to the executive branch as an institution. They are often now the prime policy makers in their fields of expertise as they play key roles in advancing the president's policy preferences. Two of the most important agencies are the National Security Council, the Council of Economic Advisers, and the Office of Management and Budget.

The National Security Council (NSC) was established in 1947 to advise the president on American military affairs and foreign policy. The NSC is composed of the president, the vice president, and the Secretaries of State and Defense. The president's national security adviser runs the staff of the NSC, coordinates information and options, and advises the president (see chapter 19).

Although the president appoints the members of each of these bodies, they must still perform their tasks in accordance with congressional legislation. Thus, like the Cabinet, depending on who serves in key positions, these mini-agencies may not be truly responsible to the president.

White House Staff

Often more directly responsible to the president are the members of the White House staff: the personal assistants to the president, including senior aides, their deputies, assistants with professional duties, and clerical and administrative aides. As personal assistants, these advisers are not subject to Senate confirmation, nor do they have divided loyalties. Their power is derived from their personal relationship to the president and they have no independent legal authority.

George Washington's closest confidantes were Alexander Hamilton and Thomas Jefferson—both Cabinet secretaries—but that has often not been the case with modern presidents. As the size and complexity of the government grew, Cabinet secretaries had to preside over their own ever-burgeoning staffs, and presidents increasingly looked to a different inner circle of loyal informal advisers. By the 1830s Andrew Jackson had chosen to rely on his own inner circle, nicknamed his "Kitchen Cabinet," instead of his

Highlight 8.3

First Ladies

From Martha Washington to Hillary Rodham Clinton, First Ladies (a term coined during the Civil War) have made significant contributions to American society. Until recently, the only formal national recognition given to First Ladies was an exhibit of inaugural ball gowns at the Smithsonian Institution. Not any more. Heightened interest—undoubtedly at least partially attributable to the highly visible role Hillary Rodham Clinton plays in the Clinton administration—led the Smithsonian to launch an exhibit that highlights the personal accomplishments of First Ladies since Martha Washington. The new exhibit is built around three themes: the political role of the First Ladies, including how they were portrayed in the media and perceived by the public; their contributions to society, especially their personal causes; and, still, of course, their inaugural gowns.

Although every action and even every haircut of Hillary Rodham Clinton is chronicled by the media, she is not the first First Lady to work for or with her husband.

- Martha Washington followed George to all the winter camps. At Valley Forge she helped feed the troops and nursed the wounded.

- Abigail Adams was a constant sounding board for her husband. An early feminist, as early as 1776 she cautioned him "To Remember the Ladies" in any new code of laws.

- Edith Bolling Galt Wilson was probably the most powerful First Lady. When Woodrow Wilson collapsed and was left partly paralyzed in 1919, Mrs. Wilson became his surrogate and decided who and what the stricken president saw. Her detractors dubbed her "Acting First Man."

- Eleanor Roosevelt also played a powerful and much criticized role in national affairs. Not only did she write a nationally syndicated daily newspaper column, she traveled and lectured widely, worked tirelessly on thankless Democratic Party matters, and raised six children. After FDR's death she shone in her own right as U.S. delegate to the United Nations, where she headed the commission that drafted the covenant on human rights. Later she headed John F. Kennedy's Commission on the Status of Women.

- Rosalyn Carter also took an activist role by attending Cabinet meetings and traveling to Latin America as her husband's policy representative.

When Hillary Clinton is viewed in the light of some strong First Ladies who came before her, her prominent role in the administration is not that surprising. Her role is not so much a radical breach with tradition as a logical evolution in a society where women's role is no longer simply that of homemaker. Yet public disapproval of her prominent policy-making role in the White House caused her to retreat to a much more traditional role. Breaking her vow not to put her daughter in the public spotlight, in 1995 she traveled to India with Chelsea in an effort to highlight her roles as a mother and a First Lady interested in the plight of children and women in developing countries. Both were fairly safe issues to support.

But, even her new focus on children and families brought more targeted barbs from her detractors. During the 1996 Republican National Convention, for example, nominee Bob Dole pointedly noted it took "a family" and not "a village" to raise a child. Hillary Rodham Clinton's best-seller *It Takes A Village* makes the case for community involvement in child rearing.

department heads to advise him. FDR surrounded himself with New York political operatives and an intellectual "brain trust"; Jimmy Carter brought several Georgians to the White House with him; and Ronald Reagan initially surrounded himself with fellow Californians.

Although each president organizes his staff in different ways, presidents typically have a chief of staff whose job is to facilitate the smooth running of the staff and the executive branch of government. Successful chiefs of staff have also protected the president from mistakes and helped implement their policies to obtain the maximum political advantage for the president. Other key White House aides include those who help plan domestic policy, maintain relations with Congress and interest groups, deal with the media, provide economic expertise, and execute political strategies.

As presidents have tried to consolidate power in the White House, and as public demands on the president have grown, so has the size of the White House staff—from fifty-one in 1943, to 247 in 1953, to a high of 583 in 1972. Since that time, staffs have been trimmed, generally running around 400. During his 1992 presidential campaign, Bill Clinton promised to cut the size of the White House staff and that of the Executive Office of the President, and eventually he reduced the size of his staff by approximately 15 percent.

While White House staffers prefer to be located in the White House, in spite of its small offices, many staffers are relegated to the old Executive Office Building next door because White House office space is limited. In Washington, the size of the office is not the measure of power it often is in corporations. Instead, power in the White House goes to those who have the president's ear and the offices closest to the Oval Office. Figure 8.1 shows the offices of key presidential advisers.

FIGURE 8.1

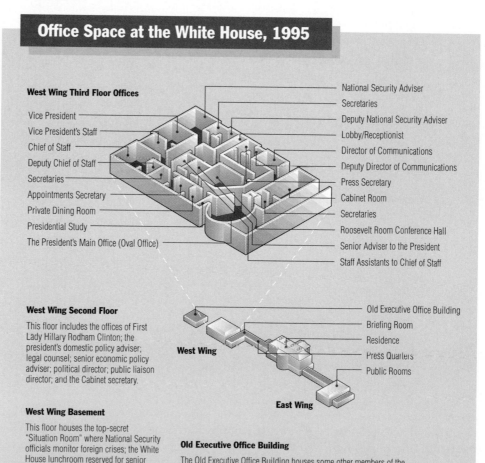

Office Space at the White House, 1995

West Wing Third Floor Offices

Vice President
Vice President's Staff
Chief of Staff
Deputy Chief of Staff
Secretaries
Appointments Secretary
Private Dining Room
Presidential Study
The President's Main Office (Oval Office)

National Security Adviser
Secretaries
Deputy National Security Adviser
Lobby/Receptionist
Director of Communications
Deputy Director of Communications
Press Secretary
Cabinet Room
Secretaries
Roosevelt Room Conference Hall
Senior Adviser to the President
Staff Assistants to Chief of Staff

Old Executive Office Building
Briefing Room
Residence
Press Quarters
Public Rooms

West Wing

East Wing

West Wing Second Floor

This floor includes the offices of First Lady Hillary Rodham Clinton; the president's domestic policy adviser; legal counsel; senior economic policy adviser; political director; public liaison director; and the Cabinet secretary.

West Wing Basement

This floor houses the top-secret "Situation Room" where National Security officials monitor foreign crises; the White House lunchroom reserved for senior officials; administrative offices; official photographiers; and the copying room.

Old Executive Office Building

The Old Executive Office Building houses some other members of the president's staff, which totals more than 1,800. Among those next door at the Old EOB are the budget director; chairman of the Council of Economic Advisers; director of the Office of National Service; many of Hillary Rodham Clinton's aides, the staff of the health care task force, and Vice President Gore's second office suite.

President Nixon showing piled-up telegrams and letters from supporters to HEW Secretary George Romney, as his omnipresent and overly powerful chief of staff, H. R. ("Bob") Haldeman, looks on. (Photo courtesy: UPI/Corbis-Bettmann)

THE ROLE OF THE PRESIDENT IN THE LEGISLATIVE PROCESS: THE PRESIDENT AS POLICY MAKER

*W*hen FDR sent his first legislative package to Congress, he broke the traditional model of law making. As envisioned by the Framers, it was to be the *Congress* that made the laws. Now FDR was claiming a leadership role for the president in the legislative process. Said the president of this new relationship, "It is the duty of the President to propose and it is the privilege of the Congress to dispose."[19] With those words and the actions that followed, FDR shifted the presidency into a law- and policy-maker role. Now not only did the president and the executive branch *execute* the laws, he and his aides generally suggested them, too.

FDR's view of the role of the president in the law-making process of government is often called a **presidentialist** view. Thus a president such as FDR could claim that his power to oversee and direct the vast and various executive departments and their policies is based on the simple grant of executive power found in Article II that includes the duty to take care that the laws be faithfully executed. Presidentialists take an expansive view of their powers and believe that presidents should take a key role in policy making. For whatever reason, Democratic presidents since FDR have tended to embrace this view of the president's role in law and policy making. In contrast, Republicans in the White House and in Congress have generally subscribed to what is called the **congressionalist** view, which holds that Article II's provision that the president should ensure "faithful execution of the laws" should be read as an injunction against substituting presidential authority for legislative intent.[20] These conflicting views of the proper role of the president in the law-making process should help you understand why presidents, especially Democratic presidents who have faced Republican majorities in the Congress or Republican presidents who have faced Democratic majorities, have experienced difficulties in governing in spite of public expectations.

From FDR's presidency to the Republican-controlled 104th Congress, the public routinely looked to the president to formulate concrete legislative plans to propose to Congress, which then adopted, modified, or rejected his plans for the nation. Although the public continues to look to the president to set the legislative and policy agenda for

presidentialist: One who believes that Article II's grant of executive power is a broad grant of authority and power allowing a president wide discretionary powers.

congressionalist: A view of the president's role in the law-making process that holds Article II's provision that the president should ensure "faithful execution of the laws" should be read as an injunction against substituting presidential authority for legislative intent.

the nation, "merely placing a program before Congress is not enough," as President Lyndon B. Johnson (LBJ) once explained. "Without constant attention from the administration, most legislation moves through the congressional process at the speed of a glacier."[21] The president's most important power (and often the source of his greatest frustration), then, in addition to support of the public, is his ability to construct coalitions within Congress that will work for passage of his legislation. FDR and LBJ were among the best presidents at "working" Congress, but they were helped by Democratic majorities in both houses of Congress.[22]

On the whole, presidents have a hard time getting Congress to pass their programs. Passage is especially difficult if the president presides over what is called a "divided government," which occurs when the presidency and Congress are controlled by different political parties (see chapter 7). And presidents generally experience declining support for policies they advocate throughout their terms. That's why it is so important for a president to propose key plans early in his administration during the honeymoon period, a time when the good will toward the president often allows a president to secure passage of legislation that he would not be able to do at a later period. Even LBJ, who was able to get about 57 percent of his programs through Congress, noted: "You've got to give it all you can, that first year . . . before they start worrying about themselves. . . . You can't put anything through when half the Congress is thinking how to beat you."[23] For example, during his honeymoon period, Bill Clinton saw several of his pet programs enacted into law with the support of a Democrat-controlled Congress. These included the National Service Education Plan, which revitalized national service and helped students pay for their education, and a crime bill, which included a federal waiting period for the purchase of guns, a ban on assault weapons, and more money to the states for police.

Presidential Involvement in the Budgetary Process

In addition to proposing new legislation or new programs, a president can also set national policy and priorities through his budget proposal. The budget proposal not only outlines the programs he proposes but indicates the importance of each program by the amount of funding requested for each program and its associated agency or department. Because the Framers gave Congress the power of the purse, Congress had primary responsibility for the budget process until 1930. The economic disaster set off by the stock market crash of 1929, however, gave FDR the opportunity to assert himself in the congressional budgetary process, just as he inserted himself into the legislative process. In 1939 the Bureau of the Budget, which had been created in 1921 to help the president tell Congress how much money it would take to run the executive branch of government, was made part of the newly created Executive Office of the President. In 1970, President Nixon changed its name to the Office of Management and Budget (OMB) to clarify its function in the executive branch.

OMB works exclusively for the president and employs hundreds of budget and policy experts. Key OMB responsibilities include preparing the president's annual budget proposal, designing the president's program, and reviewing the progress, budget, and program proposals of the executive department agencies. It also supplies economic forecasts to the president and conducts detailed analyses of proposed bills and agency rules. OMB reports allow the president to attach price tags to his legislative proposals and defend the presidential budget. The OMB budget is a huge document, and even those who prepare it have a hard time deciphering all of its provisions. Even so, the expertise of the OMB directors often gives them an advantage over members of Congress.

The importance of the executive branch in the budget process has increased in the wake of the Balanced Budget and Emergency Deficit Reduction Act of 1985 (often called Gramm–Rudman, for two of the three senators who sponsored it). This act outlined debt ceilings and targeted a balanced budget for 1993. To meet that goal, the act required that the president bring the budget in line by reducing or even eliminating cost-of-living and similar automatic spending programs found in programs such as Social Security. It also gave tremendous power to the president's Director of the Office of Management and Budget who was made responsible for keeping all appropriations in line with congressional understanding and presidential goals.

In 1990 Congress, recognizing that its goal of a balanced budget would not be met, gave OMB the authority to access each appropriations bill. Although this action gutted Gramm–Rudman, it "had the effect of involving [OMB] even more directly than it already is in congressional law-making."[24] Growing public (and even congressional) concern over the deficit thus has contributed to the president's and executive branch's increasing role in the budget process. As a single actor, the president may be able to do more to harness the deficit and impose order on the federal budget and its myriad programs than the 535 members of Congress, who are torn by several different loyalties. Thus, as a president facing the specter of a reelection campaign in 1996, it is not hard to see why President Clinton embraced the balanced budget mantra, an idea embraced by the general public.

Winning Support for Programs Through Politics and Personal Charm

As we have seen, the job of the president is ever expanding, a trend that makes it more and more difficult for any one individual to govern well enough to meet the rising expectations of the American public. Yet ability to govern often comes down to a president's ability to get his programs through Congress.

According to political scientist Thomas Cronin, a president has three ways to improve his role as a legislative lobbyist to get his favored programs passed.[25] The first two involve what you may think of as traditional political avenues. For example, he can use **patronage** (jobs, grants, or other special favors that are given as rewards to friends and political allies for their support) and personal rewards to win support. Invitations to the White House and campaign visits to members of Congress running for office are two ways to curry favor with legislators, and inattention to key members can prove deadly to a president's legislative program. House Speaker Thomas P. O'Neill reportedly was quite irritated when the Carter team refused O'Neill's request for extra tickets to Carter's inaugural. This did not exactly get the president off to a good start with the powerful Speaker.

A second political way a president can bolster support for his legislative package is to call on his political party. As the informal leader of his party, he should be able to use that position to his advantage in Congress, where party loyalty is very important. This strategy works best when the president has carried members of his party into office on his coattails, as was the case in the Johnson and Reagan landslides of 1964 and 1984, respectively. In fact, many scholars regard LBJ as the most effective legislative leader. Not only had he served in the House and as Senate majority leader, he also enjoyed a comfortable Democratic Party majority in Congress.[26]

Presidential Style.   The third way a president can influence Congress is a less "political" and far more personalized strategy. A president's ability to lead and to get his programs adopted or implemented depends on many factors, including his personal-

patronage: Jobs, grants, or other special favors that are given as rewards to friends and political allies for their support.

ity, his approach to the office, others' perceptions of his ability to lead, and his ability to mobilize public opinion to support his actions.

Some presidents have been modest in their approach to the office. Jimmy Carter, for example, adopted an unassuming approach to the presidency. During the energy crunch of the 1970s, he ordered White House thermostats set to a chilly 65 degrees and suggested that his advisers wear sweaters to work. Carter often appeared before the nation in cardigan sweaters instead of suits. He tried to build his "common man" image by carrying his own luggage and prohibiting the Marine band from playing the traditional fanfare, "Hail to the Chief," to signal his arrival on official occasions. In contrast, other presidents have been much more attuned to the trappings of office. Many believe that the Kennedys did it best.

Frequently, the difference between great and mediocre presidents centers on their ability to grasp the importance of leadership style. Truly great presidents, such as Lincoln and Franklin D. Roosevelt, understood that the White House was a seat of power from which decisions could flow to shape the national destiny. They recognized that their day-to-day activities and how they went about them should be designed to bolster support for their policies and to secure congressional and popular backing that could translate their intuitive judgment into meaningful action. Mediocre presidents, on the other hand, have tended to regard the White House as "a stage for the presentation of performances to the public" or a fitting honor to cap a career.[27]

Presidential Leadership.   Leadership is not an easy thing to exercise, and it remains an illusive concept for scholars to identify and measure. Yet Americans demand that their presidents be great leaders, and ideas about the importance of effective leaders have deep roots in our political culture. The leadership abilities of the "great presidents"—Washington, Jefferson, Lincoln, and FDR—have been extolled over and over again, leading us to fault modern presidents who fail to cloak themselves in the armor of leadership. Americans have thus come to believe that "If presidential leadership works some of the time, why not all of the time?"[28] This attitude, in turn, directly influences what we expect presidents to do and how we evaluate them (see Highlight 8.4: The Character Issue). Anything less than strong executive–congressional relations and a string of popular legislative successes, then, can be blamed on the president.

The Power to Persuade.   In trying to lead against long odds, a president must not only exercise the constitutional powers of the chief executive, but also persuade enough of the country that his actions are the right ones so that he can carry them out without national strife.[29] A president's personality and ability to persuade others are key to amassing greater power and authority.

Presidential personality and political skills often determine how effectively a president can exercise the broad powers of the modern president. To be a successful president, says political scientist Richard E. Neustadt, a president must not only have a will for power, he must use that will to set the agenda for the nation. In setting that agenda, in effect, he can become a true leader. According to Neustadt, "Presidential power is the *power to persuade,*" which comes largely from an individual's ability to bargain. And, according to Neustadt, persuasion is key because constitutional powers alone don't provide modern presidents with the authority to meet rising public expectations.[30]

Public Opinion.   The recognition of and ability to persuade not only Congress but the public are also necessary to a successful presidency. Even before the days of FDR's personal presidency, others reached out to gain public support for their programs.

During the thousand days the Kennedys lived in the White House, it became a trend-setting center of culture and style, a royal palace, a "Camelot." John F. Kennedy and his family had looks, youth, and wealth, and JFK was a witty and gifted speaker. (Photo courtesy: The Bettmann Archive)

Highlight 8.4

The Character Issue

Not all discussions of presidential character center around lying, as was the case with Richard M. Nixon, or womanizing and draft evasion, as was the case with Bill Clinton. In an approach to analyzing and predicting presidential behavior criticized or rejected by many political scientists, political scientist James David Barber has suggested that patterns of behavior, many that may be ingrained during childhood, exist and can help explain presidential behavior.[*] Barber believes that there are four presidential character types, based on (1) energy level (whether the president is active or passive) and (2) the degree of enjoyment a president finds in his job (whether the president has a positive or negative attitude about his job). Barber believes that active and positive presidents are more successful than passive and negative presidents. Active–positive presidents generally enjoyed warm and supportive childhood environments and are basically happy individuals open to new life experiences. They approach the presidency with a characteristic zest for life and have a drive to lead and succeed. In contrast, passive presidents find themselves reacting to circumstances, are likely to take direction from others, and fail to make full use of the enormous resources of the executive office. Table 8.3 classifies presidents from Taft through Bush according to Barber's categories. Where would you place Bill Clinton?

[*]James David Barber, *The Presidential Character: Predicting Performance in the White House*, 3d ed. (Englewood Cliffs, NJ: Prentice Hall, 1985).

TABLE 8.3

Barber's Presidential Personalities

	ACTIVE	PASSIVE
POSITIVE	F. D. Roosevelt Truman Kennedy Ford Carter[a] Bush	Taft Harding Reagan
NEGATIVE	Wilson Hoover L. B. Johnson Nixon	Coolidge Eisenhower

[a]Some scholars think that Carter better fits the active–negative typology.

[*]James David Barber, *The Presidential Character: Predicting Performance in the White House*, 3d ed. (Englewood Cliffs, NJ: Prentice Hall, 1985).

Theodore Roosevelt (1901–9) referred to the presidency as a "bully pulpit" that he used to try to garner support for progressive programs.

In this century, the development of commercial air travel and radio, news reels, television, and communication satellites have made direct communication to larger numbers easier. Presidents no longer stay at home but instead travel all over the world to expand their views, as underscored in Highlight 8.5: On the Go: Clinton's Hectic Schedule.

Most presidents do all that they can to woo public opinion because of its impact on their ability to govern: historically, a president has the best chances of convincing Congress to follow his policy lead when his public opinion ratings are up. Presidential popularity, however, generally follows a cyclical pattern. These "cycles" have occurred since 1938, when pollsters first began to track presidential popularity.

Highlight 8.5

On the Go: Clinton's Hectic Schedule

On October 11, 1994, President Clinton went to Michigan to begin a month of campaigning for Democratic candidates in the midterm congressional elections. From October 15 to 16, he swung through nine states, including Connecticut, Florida, and New Mexico. On October 23 he attended a fund raiser in California. He then spent three days working on the peace process, visiting six countries in the Middle East from October 25 to 28. From October 31 to November 7, he did another round of multistate campaigning, visiting California, New York, Michigan, Iowa, Washington, and Pennsylvania. On November 14 he began a three-day state visit to the Philippines and Indonesia. On November 17 he was in Hawaii. By December 3 President Clinton was back in California for a fund raiser hosted by Hollywood director Steven Spielberg. On December 4 he attended a gala at the Kennedy Center and the next day he flew to Budapest, Hungary, for a one-day meeting of the Council on Security and Cooperation in Europe (CSCE) and a meeting with Russian President Boris Yeltsin. By that evening he was back in Washington, D.C., to host the annual congressional Christmas party at the White House. From December 8 to 10, Clinton went to Miami for the Summit of the Americas with leaders of all countries in the Western hemisphere except Fidel Castro from Cuba. And finally, on December 11, Bill Clinton went to Haiti to visit U.S. troops there and congratulate the new Haitian president, Jean-Bertrand Aristide.

Here we have only highlighted two months of President Clinton's hectic schedule. In that time he visited over fifteen states (some more than once) and ten foreign countries, and met with numerous foreign leaders. These activities are in addition to the normal day-to-day activities of the president, ranging from a weekly radio address to press conferences to meetings with visiting foreign dignitaries and ambassadors, as well as the daily requirements of running the executive branch.

Typically, presidents enjoy their highest level of popularity at the beginning of their terms and try to take advantage of this honeymoon period to get their programs passed by Congress as soon as possible. Each action a president takes, however, is divisive—some people will approve, and others will disapprove. And disapproval tends to have a cumulative effect. Inevitably, as a general rule, a president's popularity wanes. As revealed in Figure 8.2, until the presidency of George Bush, the general trend has been increasingly lower rates of support for presidents. Many credit this trend to events such as Vietnam, Watergate, the Iran hostage crisis, and the Iran–Contra scandal, which have made the public increasingly skeptical of presidential performance. Both presidents Bush and Clinton, however, experienced increases in their presidential performance scores during the course of their presidencies. Bush's rapid rise in popularity occurred after the major and, perhaps more important, quick victory in the 1991 Persian Gulf war. His popularity, however, plummeted as the good feelings faded and Americans began to feel the pinch of recession. In contrast, Bill Clinton's highest approval scores came after the 1996 Democratic National Convention on the eve of the 1996 election.

Although surges in popularity caused by major international events do occur to bolster a president's popularity, they generally don't last long. As revealed in Table 8.4, each of the last ten presidents before Bill Clinton experienced at least one "rallying" point based on a foreign event. Rallies lasted an average of ten weeks, with the longest being seven months.[31] These popularity surges have allowed presidents to make some

FIGURE 8.2

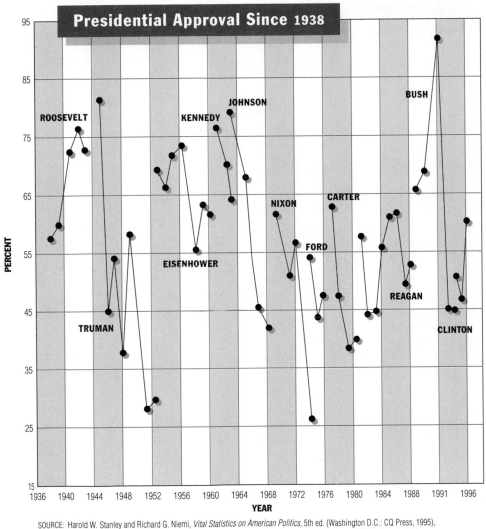

Presidential Approval Since 1938

SOURCE: Harold W. Stanley and Richard G. Niemi, *Vital Statistics on American Politics*, 5th ed. (Washington D.C.: CQ Press, 1995), Figure 8-1, p. 261, from Gallup Poll data, 1938–1991. 1991–September 1996 data based on USA Today/CNN/Gallup Poll data

policy decisions that they believe are for the good of the nation, even though the policies are unpopular with the public.

CHANGING THE PRESIDENCY

The presidency is a peculiar institution. The men who have held the position have differed greatly in style and temperament. Each has wielded power quite differently and with greater or lesser success, depending on the national and international political environment in which they sought to govern. Some have been smart, some not too intelligent; some have appeared to thrive in office; others have labored under the strain. Several broke laws but for different reasons

TABLE 8.4

Temporary Rise in Presidential Popularity

Gallup poll measurements of the size and duration of the largest increase in each president's approval rating before and after dramatic international events.

PRESIDENT	EVENT	PERCENTAGE POINT INCREASE IN PUBLIC APPROVAL	DURATION OF THE INCREASE IN WEEKS
Franklin D. Roosevelt Jr.	Pearl Harbor	12	30
Harry S Truman	Truman Doctrine;	12	N.A.[a]
	Korea invaded	9	10
Dwight D. Eisenhower	Bermuda Conf./Atoms for Peace speech	10	20
John F. Kennedy	Cuban Missile Crisis	13	31
Lyndon B. Johnson	Speech halting bombing of North Vietnam and withdrawing from 1968 campaign	14	19
Richard M. Nixon	Vietnam peace agreement	16	15
Gerald R. Ford	*Mayaguez* incident	11	25
Jimmy Carter	Hostages seized in Iran	19	30
Ronald Reagan	Beirut bombing/Grenada invasion;	8	N.A.[b]
	1st summit with Gorbachev	7	4
George Bush	Iraq invasion of Kuwait	14	9
		18	30

[a]No polls conducted

[b]Overlapping events

Source: The New York Times (May 22, 1991): A10. Information from the Gallup Organization.

and to very different fates. Lincoln's "lawlessness" earned him a place in history as one of the greats; Richard M. Nixon's dirty tricks forced him to resign to avoid impeachment. Still, some big questions about the presidency and the president cause some to wonder if the presidency is simply too large a job for one person.

Over the years various structural reforms have been proposed to "improve" the presidency. Most serious calls for reform have not been concerned with the Framers' chief fear—a too-powerful president. Instead they have centered on relieving presidents of their ceremonial duties or giving the president greater formal power, especially in the legislative process. The recent passage of the line-item veto, for example, could significantly increase the role of the president in the legislative process and allow him better control of the budget and the deficit. But is such increased power in one office in keeping with the system of checks and balances created by the Framers? Will it concentrate too much power in the hands of a single individual? It may be that the federal courts will eventually rule that a constitutional amendment, and not a simple law, may be necessary to alter this allocation of power between Congress and the president.

The president—whether you voted for him, like him, or agree with him on any particular issue or philosophical debate—is the elected leader of the nation and a key player in the policy process. A president is many things to many people: a symbol of the nation, a political organizer, a moral teacher. As we discussed in chapter 1, until the 1960s most Americans looked up to their president. Watergate heightened cynicism

North—South

POLITICS AROUND THE WORLD

This chapter largely revolves around a single, vital paradox. Because the United States is by far the most powerful country in the world, its president is typically seen as the most powerful politician in the world. Yet, if we turn our attention to American domestic politics, we find a relatively weak president who, in the words of Richard E. Neustadt, only has the "power to persuade" because of the checks and balances built into the American system at its very beginning, which were designed to dilute the power of the presidency. The situation is quite different for Mexican presidents and most Canadian prime ministers.

As we have noted in a number of other chapters, Canada, like all other industrial democracies, uses a version of the parliamentary system in which legislative and executive functions are largely fused. The governor–general is the official head of state but, much like the Queen of England, has no real political power. This is the province of the prime minister (or premier, in French).

On paper, the prime minister doesn't seem all that influential, because he or she (Canada has had one woman prime minister) is simply a member of Parliament representing a single "riding" as its constituencies are known. However, because the system of cabinet responsibility discussed in chapter 7's North–South feature, the prime minister has quite a bit of power. The prime minister, currently the Liberal, Jean Chrétien, is the leader of the majority party in the House of Commons. He then names a cabinet much like the one in the United States, all of whose members are also members of Parliament (MPs), positions they keep while they hold government office. Thus the prime minister is able to assemble an experienced team of politicians who are used to working with each other. They can then use the levers given them by the parliamentary system to see their policy proposals put into practice.

In Mexico, the power of the president revolves around the PRI's longstanding hold on power and the even longer-standing principle of nonreelection. Thus an incoming president cleans house and brings in an entirely new team, not only in his cabinet, but in the legislature, bureaucracy, judiciary, and local government as well. He does not have the leverage or the need to win votes of confidence given a Canadian prime minister. But his control of the PRI and its vast patronage network gives him roughly as much power until he turns into a political lame duck in the last third of his six-year term.

about the president and government in general. Nevertheless, until the 1990s it was highly unusual to see a sitting president vilified in the press or on radio or television talk shows. Never before have Americans known so much about the activities of their presidents, their background, who they dated in high school and college, what affairs they've had, and what they eat. Unlike the U.S. Supreme Court, whose members deliberate in secret and wear long, black judicial robes, Bill Clinton's legs, his running shorts (and even his undershorts) are the frequent objects of public attention and comment. Americans may need to step back and ask themselves if this is a good or a bad thing. While some feel this demystification has brought the president closer to the people, some argue that it has made it more difficult for the president to govern. Think about your mental images of some presidents. The tendency of Americans to lionize former presidents—especially those in the distant past—makes it even more difficult for modern-day presidents to govern by comparison as the past looks better to many than the future.

Growing expectations about the presidency repeatedly leave the American public disappointed with their chief executive. How do presidents Washington, Lincoln, and even FDR compare to a Nixon, Carter, Bush, or Clinton? How has the public's demand for information and a candidate's or president's willingness to be out in front of the American public on a daily basis made a difference in the presidency and your evaluation of a president? In the end, what is important in determining a person's ability to lead this complex nation? A person's moral fiber? Gender? Preference in underwear or religion? Or a person's ability to address the problems facing the nation and to get something done? In an era in which the media rushes to report everything personal and political about a president, his family, his advisers, and even his friends, the likelihood that the media will stop personalizing the president seems unlikely. Thus it may be up to presidents to put limits on their accessibility and candor with the American public to increase or maintain their personal prestige and ability to lead.

SUMMARY

Because the Framers feared a tyrannical monarch, they gave considerable thought to the office of the chief executive. Since ratification of the Constitution, the office has changed considerably—more through practice and need than from changes in the Constitution. In chronicling these changes, we have made the following points:

1.   The Roots of the Office of President of the United States.

Distrust of a too-powerful leader led the Framers to create an executive office with limited powers. They mandated that a president be thirty-five years old and opted not to limit the president's term of office. To further guard against tyranny, they also made provisions for the removal of the president and created an office of vice president to provide for an orderly transfer of power.

2.   The Constitutional Powers of the President.

The Framers gave the president a variety of specific constitutional powers in Article II, including the appointment power, the power to convene Congress, the power to make treaties, and the power to veto. The president also derives considerable power from being commander-in-chief of the military. The Constitution also gives the president the power to grant pardons.

3.   The Development of Presidential Power.

The development of presidential power has depended on the personal force of those who have held the office. George Washington, in particular, took several actions to establish the primacy of the president in national affairs and as true chief executive of a strong national government. But, with only a few exceptions, subsequent presidents often let Congress dominate in national affairs. The election of FDR, however, forever changed all that, as a new era of the modern presidency began. A hallmark of the modern presidency is the close relationship between the American people and their chief executive.

4.   The Presidential Establishment.

As the responsibilities of and expectations about the president have grown, so has the executive branch of government. The Cabinet has grown, and FDR established the

Executive Office of the President to help him govern. Perhaps the most key policy advisers are those closest to the president—the White House staff and some members of the Executive Office of the President.

5. The Role of the President in the Legislative Process: The President as Policy Maker.

Since FDR, the public has looked to the president to propose legislation to Congress. The modern president also plays a major role in the budgetary process. To gain support for his programs or proposed budget, the president can use patronage, personal rewards, his party connections, and can go directly to the public. How the president goes about winning support is determined by his leadership and personal style, affected by his character and his ability to persuade, and, in general, his ability to maintain high ratings in public opinion polls.

6. Changing the Presidency.

Over the years, several suggestions concerning formal reform of the presidency have been made. One, the line-item veto, was signed into law in 1996 and could increase the power of the president in the legislative process. This change may help to increase the role of the president in the legislative process. Personalization of the president and increased expectations about what he can do has led to a situation where it appears difficult for presidents to lead the nation to the satisfaction of a majority of the public.

KEY TERMS

articles of impeachment, p. 290

Cabinet, p. 295

congressionalist, p. 313

executive agreement, p. 298

Executive Office of the President (EOP), p. 309

impeachment, p. 290

inherent powers, p. 303

line-item veto, p. 299

Louisiana Purchase, p. 303

New Deal, p. 306

pardon, p. 300

patronage, p. 315

presidentialist, p. 313

stewardship theory, p. 304

Taftian theory, p. 305

United States v. *Nixon*, p. 287

veto power, p. 298

War Powers Act, p. 300

Watergate, p. 285

SELECTED READINGS

Campbell, Colin, S. J., and Bert Rockman, eds. *The Clinton Presidency: First Appraisals.* Chatham, NJ: Chatham House, 1995.

Corwin, Edwin S. *The Presidential Office and Powers,* 4th ed. New York: New York University Press, 1957.

Cronin, Thomas. *The State of the Presidency.* Boston: Little, Brown, 1975.

Edwards, George C., III. *At the Margins.* New Haven, CT: Yale University Press, 1989.

Edwards, George, C. III., and Stephen J. Wayne. *Presidential Leadership: Politics and Policy Making.* New York: St. Martins, 1997.

Kellerman, Barbara. *The Political Presidency.* New York: Oxford University Press, 1984.

Kernell, Samuel. *Going Public: New Strategies for Presidential Leadership,* 3rd ed. Washington, D.C.: CQ Press, 1997.

Neustadt, Richard E. *Presidential Power,* rev. ed. New York: Wiley, 1980.

Pious, Richard M. *The American Presidency.* New York: Basic Books, 1979.

Ragsdale, Lyn. *Vital Statistics on the Presidency: Washington to Clinton.* Washington, D.C.: CQ Press, 1995.

Reedy, George E. *The Twilight of the Presidency.* New York: New American Library, 1970.

Thomas, Norman, and Joseph A. Pika. *The Politics of the Presidency,* 4th ed. Washington, D.C.: CQ Press, 1996.

DUE TO THE FEDERAL GOVERNMENT SHUTDOWN, THE NATIONAL PARK SITES ARE TEMPORARILY CLOSED TO VISITOR SERVICES. WE APOLOGIZE FOR ANY INCONVENIENCES.

THE BUREAUCRACY

*O*n November 14, 1995, after learning that his brother in Italy was desperately ill, Sudjai Patturna flew from St. Louis to Chicago, the only place in the Midwest that processes same-day passports. When he breathlessly arrived at the doors of the federal office building, he was told by guards on duty that the passport office was closed. Without the passport, he could not visit his brother.

The same day, Michelle Castillon went to her local Internal Revenue Service office to obtain forms that she needed in order to be able to close the sale of her house, which was scheduled for the next day. The IRS office was closed.

In the Rocky Mountains, families who had dreamed of and saved for their vacation were turned away. The Rocky Mountain National Park was closed.

Karen O'Connor's American University American Politics class had a long-awaited tour of the Supreme Court canceled.

People calling the Social Security Administration were greeted with a recording: "Due to the shutdown of the government, our 800 number is temporarily closed."

People surfing the Internet could not reach Thomas, the computer service of the Library of Congress that allows the public to read legislation including the budget bill that was at the core of the 1996 budget impasse between Congress and the president.

In Atlanta, Georgia, as the flu season began in earnest, 75 percent of the workers at the Centers for Disease Control and Prevention (CDC) were sent home. While flu rates weren't monitored, CDC Director David Satcher tried to reassure the public by telling a *New York Times* reporter, "I guess what we're trying to say is that we have tried to maintain employees who are in the front line and who have to respond most urgently to disease outbreaks."[1]

Life-threatening problems? Probably not. Yet many Americans, some for the first time, were made painfully aware of the role that the federal government plays in their lives as many government agencies were closed as a result of the budget impasse in late 1995. While Americans in general rail against bureaucrats, the bureaucracy, and big government—especially the federal government—many were quick to learn that the national government provides services that they often take for granted. Not only do Americans take many programs for granted, they often don't agree on the kinds of programs the government should fund. Thus the battle rages on over federal funding of the arts, National Public Radio, and other other programs that survive only with federal dollars.

Newspaper columnists, television commentators, and radio talk show programs were abuzz with comments on the shutdown. They noted that congressional aides were still on the payroll, but that National Park Service rangers were closing the Statue of Liberty, D.C. tourist attractions, and national parks. They noted that gravediggers at Arlington National Cemetery continued to work, but federal health inspectors—who kept people alive—were not. Even *The New York Times* weighed in on the "essential" debate, reminding readers that what's essential today may not be tomorrow.[2]

The government shutdown made many citizens aware of the range of activities the U.S. government affects. The breadth of governmental involvement in our daily lives is one of the reasons that some Americans distrust government in general, and the bureaucracy in particular.

Often called the "fourth branch of government," because of the power agencies and bureaus can exercise, conservatives charge that the bureaucracy—the thousands of government agencies and institutions that implement and administer laws and programs established by Congress and the executive branch—is too liberal and that its functions constitute unnecessary government meddling in our lives. They argue that the bureaucracy is too large, too powerful, and too unaccountable to the people or to elected officials. In contrast, liberals view it as too slow, too unimaginative to solve America's problems, and too zealous a guardian of the status quo. Whether conservative, liberal, or moderate, most Americans think that the bureaucracy works poorly and is wasteful. Tales of bureaucratic agency payments for $640 toilet seats and $7,622 coffee makers (no matter how these costs are justified) do not help the public's image of the bureaucracy.

Candidates for public office, presidents, and Congress constantly criticize the bureaucracy and speak about it as though it were a foreign power to be conquered. Members of Congress joke that there is a game called "Bureaucracy" in which "There is only one rule. The first one to move loses." Even *Roget's Thesaurus* equates the term "bureaucracy" with officialism and red tape.[3] In fact, the **bureaucracy** consists of a set of complex hierarchical departments, agencies, commissions, and their staffs that exist to help the president carry out his constitutionally mandated charge to enforce the laws of the nation. As such, the bureaucracy is part of the executive branch of the federal government (the states and even local governments also have bureaucracies).

Harold D. Lasswell once defined political science as the "study of who gets what, when, and how."[4] It is by studying the bureaucracy that those questions can perhaps best be answered. To allow you to understand the role of the bureaucracy in the policy and governmental processes, this chapter:

- traces *the roots and development of the federal bureaucracy*
- examines *the modern bureaucracy* by discussing bureaucrats and the formal organization of the bureaucracy
- discusses *policy making*, including the role of rule making and adjudication
- analyzes *how agencies are held accountable*
- discusses problems that continue to plague *bureaucratic politics* and *reforms* aimed at addressing them

bureaucracy: A set of complex hierarchical departments, agencies, commissions, and their staffs that exist to help the president carry out his constitutionally mandated charge to enforce the laws of the nation.

THE ROOTS AND DEVELOPMENT OF THE FEDERAL BUREAUCRACY

*J*n the American system, the bureaucracy can be thought of as the part of the government that makes policy as it links together the three branches of the national government and the federal system. Although Congress makes the laws, it must rely on the executive branch and the bureaucracy to enforce them. Commissions such as the Equal Employment Opportunity Commission (EEOC) have the power not only to make rules, but also to settle disputes between parties concerning the enforcement and implementation of those rules. Often agency determinations are challenged in the courts. And because most administrative agencies that make up part of the bureaucracy enjoy reputations for special expertise in clearly defined policy areas, the federal judiciary routinely defers to bureaucratic administrative decision makers.

German sociologist Max Weber believed bureaucracies were a rational way for complex societies to organize themselves. Model bureaucracies, said Weber, are characterized by certain features, including:

1. A chain of command in which authority flows from top to bottom

2. A division of labor whereby work is apportioned among specialized workers to increase productivity

3. A specification of authority where there are clear lines of authority among workers and their superiors

4. A goal orientation that determines structure, authority, and rules

5. Impersonality, whereby all employees are treated fairly based on merit and all clients are served equally, without discrimination, according to established rules

6. Productivity, whereby all work and actions are evaluated according to established rules.[5]

This characterization more or less aptly describes the development of the federal bureaucracy since George Washington's time.

While in 1996 the executive branch had nearly three million employees employed directly by the president or his advisers or in independent agencies or commissions, in 1789 conditions were quite different. George Washington's bureaucracy consisted of only three departments, which had existed under the Articles of Confederation: State (called Foreign Affairs under the Articles of Confederation), War, and Treasury. Soon, the head of each department was called its *secretary*. To help the president with legal advice, Congress created the office of attorney general. The original status of the attorney general, however, was unclear—was he a member of the judicial or executive branch? That confusion was remedied in 1870 with the creation of the Justice Department as part of the executive branch, with the attorney general as its head. From the beginning, individuals appointed as Cabinet secretaries (as well as the attorney general) were subject to approval by the U.S. Senate, but were "removable by the president" alone. Even the first Congress realized how important it was for a president to be surrounded by those in whom he had complete confidence and trust.

From 1816 to 1861, the size of the federal bureaucracy grew as increased demands were made on existing departments and new departments were created. The Post Office, for example, which Congress was constitutionally authorized to create in Article I, was forced to expand to meet the needs of a growing and westward-expanding population. In 1829 the Post Office was removed from the jurisdiction of the Treasury Department by Andrew Jackson, and the Postmaster General was promoted to Cabinet rank, thereby giving him greater control over the separate office and its immense number of employees.

The Civil War

The Civil War (1861–65) permanently changed the nature of the federal bureaucracy. As the nation geared up for war, thousands of additional employees were added to existing departments. The Civil War also spawned the need for new government agencies. A series of poor harvests and marketing problems led President Abraham Lincoln (who understood that one needs food in order to conduct a war) to create the Department of Agriculture in 1862, although it was not given full Cabinet-level status until 1889.

After the Civil War, the need for big government continued unabated. The Pension Office was established in 1866 to pay benefits to the thousands of northern veterans who had fought in the war (more than 127,000 veterans were initially eligible for benefits). Justice was made a department in 1870, and other departments were added

FIGURE 9.1

Number of Federal Employees in the Executive Branch, 1792–1995

SOURCE: U.S. Department of Commerce, Bureau of the Census, *Historical State of U.S.. Colonial through 1970* (Washington: U.S. Government Printing Office, 1975): U.S. Bureau of Labor Statistics, *Monthly Labor Review*, November 1988.
Note: The rapid increase in 1940 and subsequent decrease in 1945 was due to World War II.

through 1900. Agriculture became a full-fledged department and began to play an important role in informing farmers about the latest developments in soil conservation, livestock breeding, and planting techniques. The increase in the types and nature of government services resulted in a parallel rise in the number of federal jobs, as illustrated in Figure 9.1. Many of the new jobs were used by the president or leaders of the president's political party for **patronage,** that is, jobs, grants, or other special favors given as rewards to friends and political allies for their support. Political patronage is often defended as an essential element of the party system because it provides rewards and inducements for party workers.

patronage: Jobs, grants, or other special favors that are given as rewards to friends and political allies for their support.

From Spoils to Merit

In 1831, describing a "rotation in office" policy for bureaucrats supported by President Andrew Jackson, Senator William Learned Marcy of New York commented, "To the victor belong the spoils." From his statement derives the phrase **spoils system** to describe the firing of public-office holders of the defeated political party and their replacement with loyalists of the new administration. Jackson, in particular, faced severe criticism for populating the federal government with his political cronies. But many presidents, including Jackson, argued that in order to implement their policies, they had to be able to appoint those who subscribed to their political views.

spoils system: The firing of public-office holders of a defeated political party and their replacement with loyalists of the newly elected party.

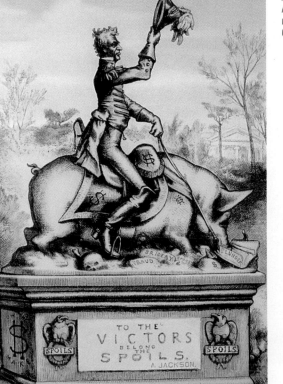

A political cartoonist's view of how President Andrew Jackson would be immortalized for his use of the spoils system. (Photo courtesy: Corbis-Bettmann)

The spoils system reached a high-water mark during Abraham Lincoln's presidency. By the time James A. Garfield, a former distinguished Civil War officer, was elected president in 1880, many reformers were calling publicly for changes in the patronage system. On his election to office, Garfield, like many presidents before him, was besieged by office seekers. Washington, D.C., had not seen such a demand for political jobs since Abraham Lincoln became the first president elected as a Republican. Garfield's immediate predecessor, Rutherford B. Hayes, had favored the idea of the replacement of the spoils system with a merit system based on test scores and ability. Congress, however, failed to pass the legislation he proposed. Possibly because potential job seekers wanted to secure positions before Congress had the opportunity to act on an overhauled civil service system, thousands pressed Garfield for positions. This siege prompted Garfield to record in his diary: "My day is frittered away with the personal seeking of people when it ought to be given to the great problems which concern the whole country."[6] Garfield resolved to reform the civil service, but his life was cut short by the bullets of an assassin who, ironically, was a frustrated job seeker.

Public reaction to Garfield's death and increasing criticism of the spoils system prompted Congress to pass the Civil Service Reform Act in 1883, more commonly known as the **Pendleton Act,** named in honor of its sponsor, George H. Pendleton (D–Ohio), to reduce patronage. It established the principle of federal employment on the basis of open, competitive exams and created a bipartisan three-member Civil Service Commission, which operated until 1978. Initially, only about 10 percent of the positions in the federal **civil service system** were covered, but later laws and executive orders have extended coverage of the act to over 90 percent of all federal employees. This new system was called the **merit system.**

The civil service system as it has evolved today provides a powerful base for federal agencies and bureaucrats. Federal workers have tenure and the leverage of politicians is reduced. The good part is that the spoils system was reduced (but not eliminated). The bad part, however, is that federal agencies can and often do take on a life of their own making administrative law, passing judgments, and so on. With 90 per-

Pendleton Act: Reform measure that created the Civil Service Commission to administer a partial merit system. It classified the federal service by grades to which appointments were made based on the results of a competitive examination. It made it illegal for political appointees to be required to contribute to a particular political party.

civil service system: The system created by civil service laws by which many appointments to the federal bureaucracy are made.

merit system: The system by which federal civil service jobs are classified into grades or levels to which appointments are made on the basis of performance on competitive examinations.

An artist's interpretation of President Garfield's assassination at the hands of an unhappy office seeker. (Photo courtesy: The Bettmann Archive)

cent of the federal workforce secure in their positions, some bureaucrats have been able to thwart reforms passed by legislators and wanted by the people. This often makes the bureaucracy the target of public criticism and citizen frustration.

National Efforts to Regulate the Economy

As the nation grew, so did the bureaucracy. In the wake of the tremendous growth of big business (especially railroads), widespread price fixing, and other unfair business practices that occurred after the Civil War, Congress created the Interstate Commerce Commission (ICC). It became the first **independent regulatory commission,** an agency outside of the major executive departments, generally concerned with particular aspects of the economy. Independent regulatory commissions such as the ICC are created by Congress to be independent of direct presidential authority. Commission members, although appointed by the president, hold their jobs for fixed terms and are not removable by the president unless they fail to uphold their oaths of office. In 1887 the creation of the ICC also marked a shift in the focus of the bureaucracy from service to regulation. Its creation gave the government—in the shape of the bureaucracy—vast powers over individual and property rights. In creating the ICC, Congress was reacting to public outcries over the exorbitant rates charged by railroad companies for hauling freight.

independent regulatory commission: An agency created by Congress that is generally concerned with a specific aspect of the economy.

The 1900 election of Theodore Roosevelt, a progressive Republican, strengthened the movement toward governmental regulation of the economic sphere and further increased the size of the bureaucracy when, in 1903, Roosevelt asked Congress to establish a Department of Commerce and Labor to oversee employer–employee relations. Roosevelt was motivated by the existence of intolerable labor practices, including low wages, long hours, substandard working conditions, the refusal of employers to recognize the rights of workers to join a union, and the fact that many businesses had grown so large and powerful that they could force workers to accept substandard conditions.

In 1913 President Woodrow Wilson divided the Department of Commerce and Labor and created a separate Department of Labor when it became clear that one agency could not well represent the interests of both employers and employees, factions with greatly differing perspectives. The creation of this department reflected the economic and societal changes that occurred as immigration increased and the economy became increasingly industrialized. One year later, in 1914, Congress created the Federal Trade Commission (FTC). Its function was to protect small businesses and the public from unfair competition, especially from big business.

The ratification of the Sixteenth Amendment to the Constitution in 1913 also affected the size of government and the possibilities for growth. It gave Congress the authority to implement a federal income tax to supplement the national treasury and provided an infusion of funds to support new federal agencies, services, and governmental programs.

What Should Government Do?

During the early 1900s, while Progressives raised the public cry for governmental regulation of business, many Americans, especially members of the business community, continued to resist such moves. They believed that any federal government regulation was wrong. Instead they favored governmental facilitation of the national economy through a commitment to *laissez-faire,* a French term that means to leave alone. In America the term was used to describe a governmental hands-off policy concerning the economy. This philosophical debate about the role of government in regulating the economy had major ramifications on the size of government and the bureaucracy. A *laissez-faire* attitude, for example, implied little need for the creation of new independent regulatory commissions or executive departments. In many ways this philosophy guided the current Republican Congress's efforts to downsize and deregulate the economy.

The New Deal and Bigger Government.   In the wake of the high unemployment and weak financial markets of the Great Depression, Franklin D. Roosevelt, planned to revitalize the economy by creating hundreds of new government agencies to regulate business practices and various aspects of the economy. Roosevelt proposed and the Congress enacted far-ranging economic legislation. The desperate mood of the nation supported these moves, as most Americans began to change their ideas about the proper role of government and the provision of governmental services. Formerly, Americans had believed in a hands-off approach; now they considered it the government's job to get the economy going and get Americans back to work.

Within the first hundred days of Roosevelt's administration, Congress approved every new regulatory measure proposed by the president. Other measures that Congress approved were the National Industrial Recovery Act (NIRA), an unprecedented attempt to regulate industry, and the Agricultural Adjustment Act (AAA), to provide government support for farm prices and to regulate farm production to ensure market-competitive prices. Congress also created the Federal Deposit Insurance Corporation (FDIC) to insure bank deposits, and it passed the Federal Securities Act, which gave the Federal Trade Commission the authority to supervise and regulate the issuance, buying, and selling of stocks and bonds.

Until 1937 the Supreme Court refused to allow Congress or the president to delegate to the executive branch or the bureaucracy such far-ranging authority to regulate the economy. *Laissez-faire* was alive and well at the Court, and attempts to end the economic slump through greater governmental involvement were repeatedly stymied by the justices. In a series of key decisions made through 1937, the Supreme Court repeatedly invalidated key provisions in congressional legislation designed to regulate various aspects of the economy. The Court and others who subscribed to *laissez-faire* principles of a free enterprise system argued that natural economic laws at work in the marketplace control the buying and selling of goods. Thus advocates of *laissez-faire* believed that the government had no right to regulate business in any way.

In response, FDR, frustrated by the decisions of the Court, proposed his famous Court-packing plan (see chapter 10), which would have allowed him to add appointees to the Court. In the wake of that institution-threatening proposal, the Court quickly fell into sync with public opinion. In a series of cases, the Supreme Court reversed a number of its earlier decisions and upheld what some have termed the "alphabetocracy." For example, the Court upheld the constitutionality of the National Labor Relations Act of 1935 (NLRA), which allowed recognition of unions and established formal arbitration procedures for employers and employees.[7] Subsequent decisions upheld the validity of the Fair Labor Standards Act (FLSA) and the Agricultural Adjustment Act (AAA).[8]

Once these new programs were declared constitutional, the proverbial floodgates were open to the creation of more governmental agencies. And with the growth in the bureaucracy came more calls for reform of the system. (See Roots of Government: World War II and Its Aftermath.)

President Franklin D. Roosevelt, urges the Supreme Court to work with the executive and legislative branches in a cooperative effort to end the Great Depression. (Photo courtesy: *Richmont-Times Dispatch*)

Roots of Government

World War II and Its Aftermath

During World War II, as revealed in Figure 9.1 (page 328), the federal government grew tremendously to meet the needs of a nation at war. Tax rates were increased to support the war, and they never again fell to prewar levels. After the war, this infusion of new monies and veterans' demands for services led to a variety of new programs and a much bigger government. The G.I. Bill, for example, provided college loans for returning veterans and reduced mortgage rates to allow them to buy homes. The national government's involvement in these programs not only affected more people, but also led to its greater involvement in more regulation. Homes bought with Veterans' Housing Authority loans, for example, had to meet certain specifications. With these programs Americans became increasingly accustomed to the national government's

role in entirely new areas, such as middle-class housing.

After World War II, the civil rights movement and President Lyndon B. Johnson's War on Poverty (see chapter 6) produced additional growth in the bureaucracy. The Equal Employment Opportunity Commission (EEOC) was created in 1964, and the departments of Housing and Urban Development (HUD) and Transportation were created in 1966. These expansions of the bureaucracy corresponded to increases in the president's power and his ability to persuade Congress that new agencies would be an effective way to solve pressing social problems. Remember from Chapter 8 that most major expansions in the power of the presidency have occurred during times of war or economic emergency. Similarly most of the important changes that have occurred in the size of the bureaucracy through the 1970s occurred in response to war, economic, or social crises.

The Hatch Act. As an increasing proportion of the American workforce came to work for the U.S. government as a result of the New Deal recovery programs, many began to fear that the members of the civil service would play major roles not only in implementing public policy but also in electing members of Congress and even the president. Consequently, Congress enacted the Political Activities Act of 1939, commonly known as the **Hatch Act,** which was designed to prohibit the use of federal employees to become directly involved in working for political candidates. In effect, the Hatch Act was intended to neutralize the civil service politically by prohibiting civil servants from taking activist roles in partisan campaigns. Under its provisions, federal employees could not run for public office, campaign for or against candidates, make speeches, raise funds for candidates, organize political rallies, circulate petitions, or participate in partisan registration drives.

Although presidents as far back as Thomas Jefferson had advocated efforts to limit the opportunities for federal civil servants to influence the votes of others, many criticized the Hatch Act as too extreme. Critics argued that it denied millions of federal em-

Hatch Act: Laws enacted in 1939 to prohibit civil servants from taking activist roles in partisan campaigns. This act prohibited federal employees from making political contributions, working for a particular party, or campaigning for a particular candidate.

ployees the First Amendment guarantees of freedom of speech and association, and discouraged political participation among a group of people who might otherwise be strong political activists. Critics also argued that civil servants *should* become more involved in campaigns, particularly at the state and local level, in order to understand better the needs of the citizens they serve.

Federal Employees Political Activities Act: 1993 liberalization of Hatch Act. Federal employees are now allowed to run for office in nonpartisan elections and to contribute money to campaigns in partisan elections.

The Federal Employees Political Activities Act. In response to criticisms of the Hatch Act and at the urgings of President Bill Clinton, Congress enacted the **Federal Employees Political Activities Act.** This liberalization of the Hatch Act allows employees to run for public office in nonpartisan elections, contribute money to political organizations, and campaign for or against candidates in partisan elections. During the signing ceremony, Clinton said the law will "mean more responsive, more satisfied, happier, and more productive federal employees."[9] (See Highlight 9.1: The Liberalized Hatch Act.)

Highlight 9.1

The Liberalized Hatch Act

Here are some examples of permissible and prohibited activities for federal employees under the Hatch Act, as modified by the Federal Employees Political Activities Act of 1993. Federal employees

- **May** be candidates for public office in nonpartisan elections
- **May** assist in voter registration drives
- **May** express opinions about candidates and issues

- **May** contribute money to political organizations
- **May** attend political fund-raising functions
- **May** attend and be active at political rallies and meetings
- **May** join and be active members of a political party or club
- **May** sign nominating petitions
- **May** campaign for or against referendum questions, constitutional amendments, and municipal ordinances
- **May** campaign for or against candidates in partisan elections

- **May** make campaign speeches for candidates in partisan elections
- **May** distribute campaign literature in partisan elections
- **May** hold office in political clubs or parties
- **May not** use their official authority or influence to interfere with an election
- **May not** collect political contributions unless both individuals are members of the same federal labor organization or employee organization and the one solicited is not a subordinate employee
- **May not** knowingly solicit or discourage the po-

litical activity of any person who has business before the agency
- **May not** engage in political activity while on duty
- **May not** engage in political activity in any government office
- **May not** engage in political activity while wearing an official uniform
- **May not** engage in political activity while using a government vehicle
- **May not** solicit political contributions from the general public
- **May not** be candidates for public office in partisan elections

Source: U.S. Special Counsel's Office.

THE MODERN BUREAUCRACY

*W*hen H. Ross Perot ran for president in 1992 and 1996, he repeatedly lamented that the national government was not run like a business. But the national government differs from private business in ways too numerous to cover here adequately. Governments exist for the public good, not to make money. Businesses are driven by a profit motive; government leaders, but not bureaucrats, are driven by reelection. Businesses get their money from customers; the national government gets its money from taxpayers. Another difference between a bureaucracy and a business is that it is difficult to determine to whom bureaucracies are responsible. Is it the president? Congress? The citizenry?

These kinds of differences have a tremendous consequence on the way the bureaucracy operates.[10] Because all of the incentive in government "is in the direction of not making mistakes,"[11] public employees view risks and rewards very differently than their private sector counterparts. The key to the modern bureaucracy is to understand not only who bureaucrats are, how the bureaucracy is organized, and how it works, but also to see that it cannot be run like a business. An understanding of these facts and factors can help in the search for ways to motivate positive change in the bureaucracy.

Who Are Bureaucrats?

Federal bureaucrats are career government employees who work in the executive branch, in the fourteen Cabinet-level departments and the more than sixty independent agencies that comprise more than 2,000 bureaus, divisions, branches, offices, services, and other subunits of the federal government. There are approximately 2.8 million

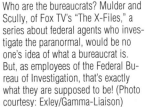

Who are the bureaucrats? Mulder and Scully, of Fox TV's "The X-Files," a series about federal agents who investigate the paranormal, would be no one's idea of what a bureaucrat is. But, as employees of the Federal Bureau of Investigation, that's exactly what they are supposed to be! (Photo courtesy: Exley/Gamma-Liaison)

FIGURE 9.2

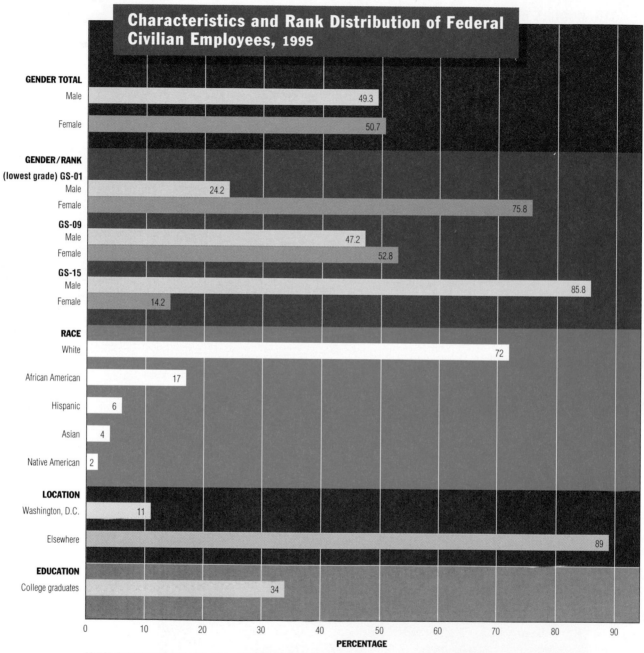

Characteristics and Rank Distribution of Federal Civilian Employees, 1995

GENDER TOTAL
- Male — 49.3
- Female — 50.7

GENDER/RANK
(lowest grade) GS-01
- Male — 24.2
- Female — 75.8

GS-09
- Male — 47.2
- Female — 52.8

GS-15
- Male — 85.8
- Female — 14.2

RACE
- White — 72
- African American — 17
- Hispanic — 6
- Asian — 4
- Native American — 2

LOCATION
- Washington, D.C. — 11
- Elsewhere — 89

EDUCATION
- College graduates — 34

PERCENTAGE (0 10 20 30 40 50 60 70 80 90)

SOURCE: *Statistical Abstract of the United States, 1990* (Washington: U.S. Government Printing Office, 1990), 323–326. Office of Personnel Management, *Federal Civilian Workforce Statistics, Employment and Trends as of November 1988* (Washington: U.S. Government Printing Office, 1989), 70. Harold W. Stanley and Richard G. Niemi, *Vital Statistics on American Politics*, 4th ed. (Washington, D.C.: CQ Press, 1994), 406.

federal workers in the executive branch who come from all walks of life—they vary in race, religion, ethnicity, level of education, and income, as revealed in Figure 9.2, Congress has ordered federal agencies to make special efforts to recruit minority and other disadvantaged workers.

As a result of reforms made during the Truman administration that built on the Pendleton Act, most civilian federal governmental employees today are selected by

Highlight 9.2

How to Fire a Federal Bureaucrat

Firing a bureaucrat can be very difficult. In fiscal year 1994, 2,719 federal employees were fired for misconduct, and 314 were fired for poor performance. That's only .0015 percent of the federal civilian workforce. Civil service rules make it easier to fire someone for misconduct than poor performance. Incompetent employees must be given notice by their supervisors and given an opportunity for remedial training.

To fire a member of the competitive civil service, explicit procedures must be followed:

1. At least thirty days' written notice must be given to an employee in advance of firing or demotion for incompetence or misconduct.

2. The written notification must contain a statement of reasons for the action and specific examples of unacceptable performance.

3. The employee has the right to reply both orally and in written form to the charges, and has the right to an attorney.

4. Appeals from any adverse action against the employee can be made to the three-person Merit Systems Protection Board (MSPB), a bipartisan body appointed by the president and confirmed by the Senate.

5. All employees have the right to a hearing and to an attorney in front of the MSPB.

6. All decisions of the MSPB may be appealed by the employee to the U.S. Court of Appeals.

---

merit standards, which include tests (such as civil service or foreign service exams) and educational criteria. Merit systems protect federal employees from being fired for political reasons. (For a description of how a federal employee can be fired, see Highlight 9.2: How to Fire a Federal Bureaucrat.)

Federal employees are stereotyped as "paper pushers," but more than 15,000 job skills are represented in the federal government and its workers are perhaps the best trained and most skilled and efficient in the world (although not all are deemed "essential" to the functioning of government, as shown in Highlight 9.3: Who's Essential?) Government employees include forest rangers, FBI agents, foreign service officers, computer programmers, security guards, librarians, administrators, engineers, plumbers, lawyers, doctors, postal carriers, and zoologists, among others. The diversity of government jobs mirrors the diversity of jobs in the private sector.

Another myth is the perception that most bureaucrats work in Washington. In reality only about 11 percent of all federal bureaucrats work in the nation's capital; the rest are located in regional, state, and local offices scattered throughout the country. The decentralization of the bureaucracy facilitates accessibility to the public. The Social Security Administration, for example, has numerous offices so that its clients may have a place nearby to take their paperwork, questions, and problems. Decentralization also helps distribute jobs and incomes across the country.

Many Americans also believe that the federal bureaucracy is growing bigger each year, but they are wrong. Efforts to reduce the federal workforce have worked. Although it is true that the number of total government employees has been increasing until lately, most growth has taken place at the state and local levels, as revealed in Figure 9.3. And, as more federal programs are shifted back to the states, the size of state payrolls is likely to rise to reflect these new responsibilities.

FIGURE 9.3

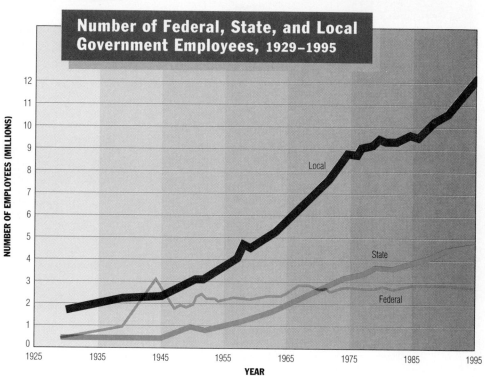

Number of Federal, State, and Local Government Employees, 1929–1995

SOURCE: Harold W. Stanley and Richard G. Niemi, *Vital Statistics on American Politics*, 4th ed. (Washington: CQ Press, 1994), 315. U.S. Advisory Commission on Intergovernmental Relations, *Significant Features of Fiscal Federalism, 1990*, vol. 2 (Washington: U.S. Advisory Commission on Intergovernmental Relations, 1990), 177; Bureau of the Census, *Historical Statistics of the United States*, Series Y189–198 (Washington: U.S. Government Printing Office, 1975), 1100, U.S. Bureau of Labor Statistics: *Employment and Earnings*, December 1995, 82.

Formal Organization

While even experts can't agree on the exact number of separate governmental agencies, commissions, and departments that make up the federal bureaucracy,[12] there are probably more than 2,000. A distinctive feature of the executive bureaucracy is its traditional division into areas of specialization. For example, one agency, the Occupational, Safety and Health Administration, handles occupational safety, the Department of Education specializes in education, the State Department in foreign affairs, the Environmental Protection Agency in the environment, and so on. It is not unusual, however, for more than one agency to be involved in a particular issue or for one agency to be involved in myriad issues. In fact, numerous agencies often have authority in the same issue areas, making administration even more difficult. Agencies fall into four general types: (1) departments, (2) government corporations, (3) independent agencies, and (4) regulatory commissions.

The Cabinet Departments. The fourteen Cabinet **departments** are major administrative units that have responsibility for conducting a broad area of government operations. Cabinet departments account for about 60 percent of the federal workforce.

As depicted in Figure 9.4, executive branch departments are headed by Cabinet members called secretaries (except the Justice Department, which is headed by the at-

department: A major administrative unit with responsibility for a broad area of government operations. Departmental status usually indicates a permanent national interest in that particular governmental function, such as Defense, Health, or Agriculture.

FIGURE 9.4

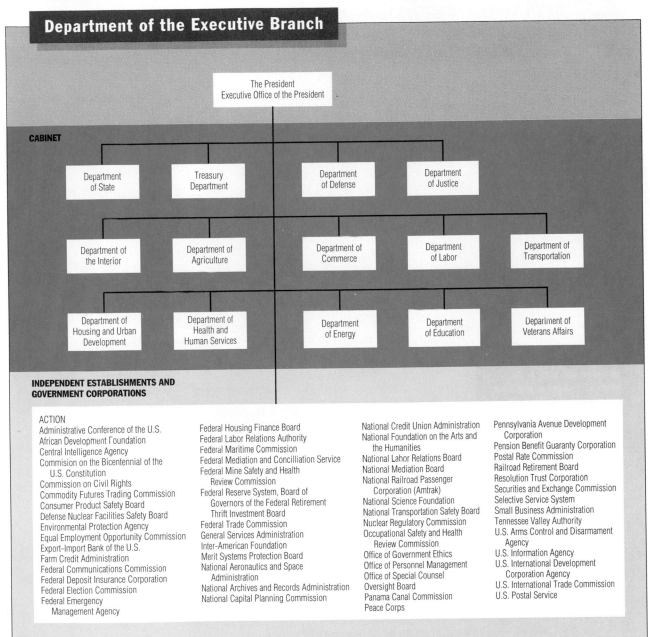

Department of the Executive Branch

SOURCE: *United States Government Manual 1990–91* (Washington: Government Printing Office).

torney general) The secretaries are responsible for establishing their department's general policy and overseeing its operations. As discussed in chapter 8, Cabinet secretaries are directly responsible to the president, but are often viewed as having two masters—the president and those affected by their department. Cabinet secretaries are also tied to Congress, from which they get their appropriations and the discretion to implement legislation and make rules and policy.

Highlight 9.3

Who's Essential?

When the U.S. government first shut down in the fall of 1995, many employees quickly found out that no matter how impressive their titles sounded, they were not automatically considered essential. When the government ran out of money to pay its employees when the Congress and the president refused to agree on a budget, nonessential workers were sent home. The nonessential workers included the staff at the Library of Congress and food service workers in the Congress and the White House (causing a run on pizza delivery services). Washington D.C.'s Department of Public Works was closed, and all seventy-eight employees who write tickets were furloughed. The essential workers included the per-

Dr. Emily McClure, an epidemiological investigative officer for the Center for Disease Control and Prevention (CDC) in Atlanta, records information for an investigation of a hemorrhagic fever epidemic in Nicaragua. Few would argue that the work of the CDC is not essential. (Photo courtesy: Anita Baca/AP Wide World Photos)

sonnel needed to feed and care for animals at the National Zoo and the National Institutes of Health. Two cooks were deemed essential at the White House, two others were furloughed. The Pentagon kept all 1.5 million active duty military personnel on the job but recalled military bands from their tours.

Although departments vary considerably in size, prestige, and power, they share certain features. Each department covers a broad area of responsibility generally reflected by its name. Each secretary is assisted by a deputy or undersecretary to take part of the administrative burden off the secretary's shoulders, as well as by several assistant secretaries, who direct major programs within the department. In addition, each secretary, like the president, has numerous assistants who help with planning, budgeting, personnel, legal services, public relations, and other key staff functions. Most departments are subdivided into bureaus, divisions, sections, or other smaller units, and it is at this level that the real work of each agency is done. Most departments are subdivided along function lines, but the basis for division may be geography, work processes (for example, the Economic Research Service in the Department of Agricul-

ture), or clientele (such as the Bureau of Indian Affairs in the Department of the Interior). In addition to national offices in Washington, D.C., or its immediate suburbs, each executive department has regional offices to serve all parts of the United States.

Departmental status generally signifies a strong permanent national interest to promote a particular function. Moreover, departments are organized to foster and promote the interests of a given clientele—that is, a specific social or economic group. Such departments are called **clientele agencies.** The Departments of Agriculture, Education, Energy, Labor, and Veterans Affairs and the Bureau of Indian Affairs in the Department of the Interior are examples of clientele agencies/bureaus.

Because many of these agencies were created at the urging of well-organized interests to advance their particular objectives, it is not surprising that clientele groups are powerful lobbies with their respective agencies in Washington. The clientele agencies and groups are also active at the regional level, where the agencies devote a substantial part of their resources to program implementation. One of the most obvious examples of regional "outreach" is the Extension Service of the Department of Agriculture. Agricultural extension agents are scattered throughout the farm belt and routinely work with farmers on farm productivity and other problems. Career bureaucrats in the Agriculture Department know that farm interests will be dependable allies year in and year out. Congress and the president are not nearly so reliable because they must balance the interests of farmers with those of other segments of society.

clientele agency: Executive department directed by law to foster and promote the interests of a specific segment or group in the U.S. population (such as the Department of Education).

Government Corporations. **Government corporations** are businesses set up and created by Congress to perform functions that could be provided by private businesses. The corporations are formed when the government chooses to engage in activities that are primarily commercial in nature, produce revenue, and require greater flexibility than Congress generally allows regular departments. Some of the better-known government corporations include Amtrak and the Federal Deposit Insurance Corporation. Unlike other governmental agencies, government corporations charge for their services. For example, the largest government corporation, the U.S. Postal Service—whose functions could be handled by a private corporation, such as Federal Express

government corporation: Business set up and created by Congress that performs functions that could be provided by private businesses (such as the U.S. Postal Service).

or the United Parcel Service (UPS)—exists today to ensure delivery of mail throughout the United States at cheaper rates than those a private business might charge. Similarly, the Tennessee Valley Authority (TVA) provides electricity at reduced rates to millions of Americans in the Appalachian region of the Southeast, generally a low-income area that had failed to attract private utility companies to provide service there.

In cases like that of the TVA, where the financial incentives for private industry to provide services are minimal, Congress often believes that it must act. In other cases it steps in to salvage valuable public assets. For example, when passenger rail service in the United States no longer remained profitable, Congress stepped in to create Amtrak and thus nationalized the passenger-train industry to keep passenger trains running.

independent agency: Governmental unit that closely resembles Cabinet departments, these have narrower areas of responsibility (such as the Central Intelligence Agency), and are not part of any Cabinet departments.

Independent Agencies. **Independent agencies** closely resemble Cabinet departments, but have narrower areas of responsibility. Generally speaking, independent agencies perform service rather than regulatory functions. Many of these agencies are tied to the president and Congress as closely as executive departments because the heads of these agencies are appointed by the president and serve, like Cabinet secretaries, at his pleasure.

Independent agencies exist apart from executive departments for practical or symbolic reasons. The National Aeronautics and Space Administration (NASA), for example, could have been placed within the Department of Defense. That kind of placement, however, could have conjured up thoughts of a space program dedicated solely to military purposes, rather than for civilian satellite communication or scientific exploration. Similarly, the Environmental Protection Agency (EPA) was created in 1970 to administer federal programs aimed at controlling pollution and protecting the nation's environment. It administers all congressional laws concerning the environment and pollution. Along with the Council on Environmental Quality, a staff agency in the Executive Office of the President, the EPA advises the president on environmental concerns. It also administers programs transferred to it along with personnel from the Departments of Agriculture, Energy, Interior, and Health and Human Services, as well as the Nuclear Regulatory Commission, among others. The expanding national focus on the environment, in fact, has brought about numerous calls to elevate the EPA to Cabinet-level status to reinforce a long-term national commitment to improved air and water and other environmental issues.

Independent Regulatory Commissions. Independent regulatory commissions are agencies that exist outside of the major departments and often regulate important aspects of the economy. Examples include the National Labor Relations Board, the Federal Reserve Board, the Federal Communications Commission, and the Securities and Exchange Commission (SEC).[13] Congress started setting up regulatory commissions as early as 1887, recognizing the need for close and continuous guardianship of particular economic activities. Because of the complexity of modern economic problems, Congress sought to create agencies that could develop expertise and provide continuity of policy with respect to economic issues because neither Congress nor the courts have the time or talent to do so. Older boards and commissions, such as the Securities and Exchange Commission and the Federal Reserve Board, are generally charged with overseeing a certain industry. Regulatory agencies created since the 1960s are more concerned with how the business sector relates to public health and safety. The Occupational Safety and Health Administration (OSHA) promotes job safety.

Most of the older independent agencies were specifically created to be relatively free from immediate (partisan) political pressure. They are headed by a board composed of several members (always an odd number, to avoid ties) who are selected by the president and confirmed by Congress. (Commissioners are appointed for fixed, staggered terms to increase the chances of a bipartisan board.) Unlike executive department heads, they cannot be easily removed by the president. In 1935 the U.S. Supreme Court ruled that in creating independent commissions, the Congress had intended that they be independent panels of experts as far removed as possible from immediate political pressures.[14]

Newer regulatory boards lack this kind of autonomy and freedom from political pressures; they are generally headed by a single administrator who can be removed by the president. These boards and commissions, such as the EEOC, are therefore far more susceptible to political pressure and the political wishes of the president who appoints them.

POLICY MAKING

One of the major functions of the bureaucracy is policy making—and bureaucrats can be, and often are, major policy makers. When Congress creates any kind of department, agency, or commission, it is actually delegating some of its powers listed in Article I, section 8, of the U.S. Constitution. Therefore the laws creating departments, agencies, corporations, or commissions carefully describe their purpose and give them the authority to make numerous policy decisions, which have the effect of law. Congress recognizes that it does not have the time, expertise, or ability to involve itself in every detail of every program; therefore it sets general guidelines for agency action and leaves it to the agency to work out the details. How agencies execute congressional wishes is called **implementation,** the process by which a law or policy is put into operation.(See chapter 17 for more detail on the policy-making process.) Much of the policy-making process occurs in the form of what some call iron triangles or issue networks.

> **implementation:** The process by which a law or policy is put into operation by the bureaucracy.

Iron Triangles and Issue Networks

Iron Triangles. The relatively stable relationships and patterns of interaction that occur among an agency, interest groups, and congressional committees or subcommittees as policy is made are often referred to as **iron triangles,** or subgovernments (see Figure 9.5).

Policy-making subgovernments are "iron" because they are virtually impenetrable to outsiders and are largely autonomous. Even presidents have difficulty piercing the workings of these subgovernments, which have endured over time. Examples of iron triangles abound. Senior citizens' groups (especially the American Association of Retired Persons), the Social Security Administration, and the House Subcommittee on Aging all are likely to agree on the need for increased Social Security benefits. Similarly, the Department of Veterans Affairs, the House Committee on Veterans Affairs, and the American Legion and Veterans of Foreign Wars—the two largest organizations representing veterans—usually agree on the need for expanded programs for veterans.

The policy decisions made within these iron triangles often foster the interests of a clientele group and have little to do with the advancement of national policy goals. In part, subgovernmental decisions often conflict with other governmental policies and

> **iron triangle:** The relatively stable relationship and pattern of interaction that occur among an agency, interest groups, and congressional committees or subcommittees.

FIGURE 9.5

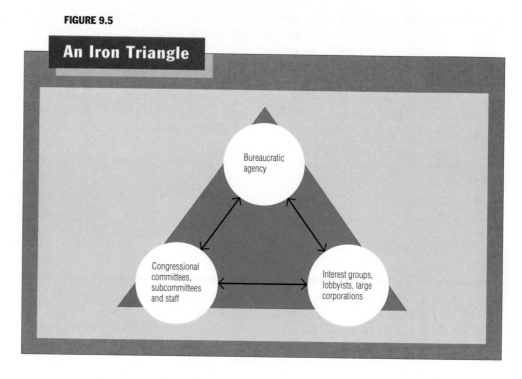

An Iron Triangle

tend to tie the hands of larger institutions such as Congress and the president. The White House is often too busy dealing with international affairs or crises to deal with smaller issues like veterans' benefits. Likewise, Congress defers to its committees and subcommittees. Thus these subgovernments decentralize policy making and make policy making difficult to control.[15]

The Department of Veterans' Affairs helps veterans' groups, such as the Veterans of Foreign Wars, work with the House and Senate Veterans' Affairs Committees to lobby for increased funds for veterans' hospitals. (Photo courtesy: Loren Santow/Impact Visuals)

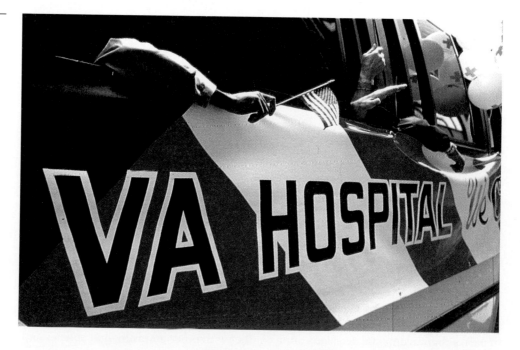

Issue Networks.   Today, iron triangles no longer dominate most policy processes for three main reasons: an increasingly complex society, issues that cut across several policy areas, and the phenomenal increase in number of Washington, D.C.-based interest groups. As these three changes have occurred, many iron triangles have become rusty, and new terms have been coined to describe the policy-making process and the bureaucracy's role in it. Hugh Heclo argues that this system of separate subgovernments is overlaid with an amorphous system of **issue networks,**[16] that is, the fuzzy set of relationships among a large number of actors in broad policy areas. In general, like iron triangles, issue networks are made up of agency officials, members of Congress (and committee staffers), and interest-group lobbyists. But they also often include lawyers, consultants, academics, public relations specialists, and sometimes even the courts.[17] Unlike iron triangles, issue networks are constantly changing as members with technical expertise become involved in various issues.

Issue networks reflect the complexity of the issues that lawmakers and policy makers face. As an example, let's look at the plight of many American children. Lawmakers routinely call for new programs to make children's lives better, and the Clinton administration is sympathetic. First Lady Hillary Rodham Clinton, in fact, at one time chaired the board of the Children's Defense Fund, a national child advocacy group. But the plight of children isn't an easy problem to solve. All kinds of complex and interrelated issues are involved. It is, for example, a health issue, because many children don't have access to medical care; an education issue because many can't read, go to poor schools, or are dropouts; a labor issue because many have no job skills; and a drug and crime issue because many of these children live in drug-infested neighborhoods and often ultimately turn to crime, ending up in jail as a result. But given the segmented nature of policy making, how can the nation expect one coherent and encompassing policy to better the lives of American children to come from the Departments of Health and Human Services, Education, Labor, and Justice—plus all their associated House and Senate subcommittees, interest groups, and experts? And most of these agencies have to make do in the face of growing budget cutbacks.

Policy making and implementation of the kind characterized by iron triangles or issue networks often take place on informal and formal levels. Practically, many decisions are left to individual government employees on a day-to-day basis. Justice Department lawyers, for example, make daily decisions about whether or not to prosecute someone. Similarly, street-level Internal Revenue Service agents make many decisions during personal audits.[18] These street-level bureaucrats make policy on two levels. First, they exercise wide discretion in decisions concerning citizens with whom they interact. Second, taken together, their individual actions add up to agency behavior.[19] Thus how bureaucrats interpret or apply (or choose not to apply) various policies are equally important parts of the policy-making process. Administrative discretion allows decision makers (whether they are in a Cabinet-level position or at the lowest GS levels) a tremendous amount of leeway.

issue network: A term used to describe the loose and informal set of relationships that exist among a large number of actors who work in broad policy areas.

Administrative Discretion

Essentially, bureaucrats make as well as implement policy. They take the laws and policies made by Congress, the president, and the courts, and develop rules and procedures for making sure they are carried out. Most implementation involves what is called **administrative discretion,** the ability to make choices concerning the best way to implement congressional intentions. Administrative discretion is also exercised through two formal administrative procedures: rule making and administrative adjudication.

administrative discretion: The ability of bureaucrats to make choices concerning the best way to implement congressional intentions.

At times, the wisdom of administrative discretion by government agencies, such as the Bureau of Alcohol, Tobacco, and Firearms, has been hotly debated—especially in the assault on the Branch Davidian compound at Waco, Texas. Here FBI special agent Bob Ricks holds a press briefing to explain the actions of federal agents at the compound. (Photo courtesy: Reuters/Bettmann)

rule making: A quasi-legislative administrative process that has the characteristics of a legislative act.

regulation: Rule that governs the operation of a particular government program and has the force of law.

Rule making.   **Rule making** is a quasi-legislative administrative process that results in regulations and has the characteristics of a legislative act. **Regulations** are the rules that govern the operation of all government programs and have the force of law. In essence, then, bureaucratic rule makers often act as lawmakers as well as law enforcers when they make rules or draft regulations to implement various congressional statutes. Thus rule making is called a quasi-legislative process (see Figure 9.6). Some political scientists say that "(R)ulemaking is the single most important function performed by agencies of government."[20]

Because regulations often involve political conflict, the 1946 Administrative Procedure Act established rule-making procedures to give everyone the chance to participate in the process. The act requires that (1) public notice of the time, place, and nature of the rule-making proceedings be provided in the *Federal Register;* (2) interested parties be given the opportunity to submit written arguments and facts relevant to the rule; and (3) the statutory purpose and basis of the rule be stated. Once rules have been written, thirty days must generally elapse before they take effect.

Sometimes an agency is required by law to conduct a formal hearing before issuing rules. Evidence is gathered, and witnesses testify and are cross-examined by opposing interests. The process can take weeks, months, or even years, at the end of which agency administrators must review the entire record and then justify the new rules. Although cumbersome, the process has reduced criticism of some rules and bolstered the deference given by the courts to agency decisions.

administrative adjudication: A quasi-judicial process in which a bureaucratic agency settles disputes between two parties in a manner similar to the way courts resolve disputes.

Administrative Adjudication.   **Administrative adjudication** is a quasi-judicial process in which a bureaucratic agency settles disputes between two parties in a manner similar to the way courts resolve disputes. Administrative adjudication, like rule making, is referred to as "quasi" (Latin for "seemingly") judicial, because law making by any body other than Congress or adjudication by any body other than the judiciary would be a violation of the constitutional principle of separation of powers.

Agencies regularly find that persons or businesses are not in compliance with the federal laws the agencies are charged with enforcing, or that they are in violation of an

FIGURE 9.6

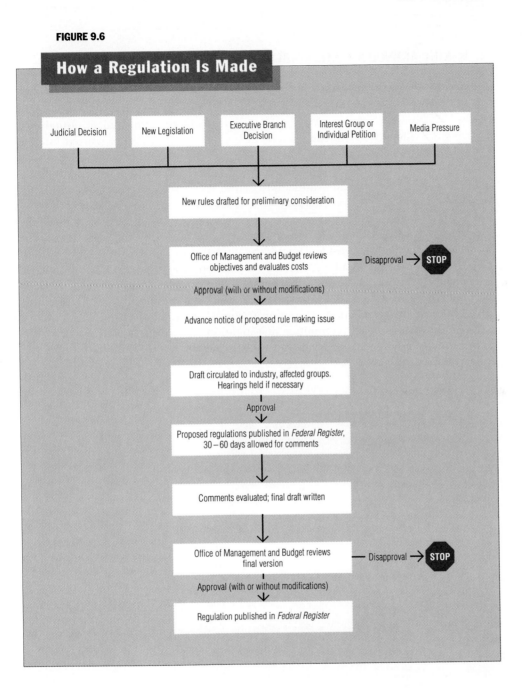

How a Regulation Is Made

Judicial Decision	New Legislation	Executive Branch Decision	Interest Group or Individual Petition	Media Pressure

New rules drafted for preliminary consideration

Office of Management and Budget reviews objectives and evaluates costs — Disapproval → **STOP**

Approval (with or without modifications)

Advance notice of proposed rule making issue

Draft circulated to industry, affected groups. Hearings held if necessary

Approval

Proposed regulations published in *Federal Register*, 30–60 days allowed for comments

Comments evaluated; final draft written

Office of Management and Budget reviews final version — Disapproval → **STOP**

Approval (with or without modifications)

Regulation published in *Federal Register*

agency rule or regulation. To force compliance, some agencies resort to administrative adjudication, which is generally less formal than a trial. Several agencies and boards employ administrative law judges to conduct the hearings. Although these judges are employed by the agency, they are strictly independent and cannot be removed except for gross misconduct. Congress, for example, empowers the Federal Trade Commission (FTC) to determine what constitutes an unfair trade practice.[21] Its actions, however, are reviewable in the federal courts.

MAKING AGENCIES ACCOUNTABLE

*T*he question of to whom bureaucrats should be responsible is one that continually comes up in any debate about governmental accountability. Should the bureaucracy be answerable to itself? to organized interest groups? to its clientele? to the president? to Congress? or to some combination of all of these? While many would argue that bureaucrats should be responsive to the public interest, the public interest is difficult to define. As it turns out, several factors work to control the power of the bureaucracy, and, to some degree, the same kinds of checks and balances that operate among the three branches of government serve to check the bureaucracy (Table 9.1).

Many argue that the president should be in charge of the bureaucracy because it is up to him to see that popular ideas and expectations are translated into administrative action. But under our constitutional system, the president is not the only actor in the policy process. Congress creates the agencies, funds them, and establishes the broad rules of their operation. Moreover, Congress continually reviews the various agencies through oversight committee investigations, hearings, and its power of the purse. And the federal judiciary, as in most other matters, has the ultimate authority to review administrative actions.

TABLE 9.1

Making Agencies Accountable

The president has the authority to:	• Appoint and remove agency heads and a few additional top bureaucrats. • Reorganize the bureaucracy (with congressional approval). • Make changes in an agency's annual budget proposals. • Ignore legislative initiatives originating within the bureaucracy. • Initiate or adjust policies that would, if enacted by Congress, alter the bureaucracy's activities. • Issue executive orders. • Reduce an agency's annual budget.
Congress has the authority to:	• Pass legislation that alters the bureaucracy's activities. • Abolish existing programs. • Investigate bureaucratic activities and force bureaucrats to testify about them. • Influence presidential appointments of agency heads and other top bureaucratic officials. • Write legislation to limit the bureaucracy's discretion.
The judiciary has the authority to:	• Rule on whether bureaucrats have acted within the law and require policy changes to comply with the law. • Force the bureaucracy to respect the rights of individuals through hearings and other proceedings. • Rule on the constitutionality of all rules and regulations.

Executive Control

As the size and scope of the American national government in general, and of the executive branch and the bureaucracy in particular, have grown, presidents have delegated more and more power to bureaucrats. But most presidents have continued to try to exercise some control over the bureaucracy, although they have often found that task more difficult than they first envisioned. John F. Kennedy, for example, once lamented that to give anyone at the State Department an instruction was comparable to putting it in a dead-letter box.[22]

Recognizing these potential problems, each president tries to appoint the best possible persons to carry out his wishes and policy preferences. Presidents may make thousands of appointments to the executive branch; in doing so, they have the opportunity to appoint individuals who share their views on a range of policies. And although presidential appointments make up less than 1 percent of all federal jobs, presidents usually fill most top policy-making positions.

Presidents can also, with the approval of Congress, reorganize the bureaucracy. They can also make changes in an agency's annual budget requests and ignore legislative initiatives originating within the bureaucracy.

Presidents also issue **executive orders** to provide direction to bureaucrats. Executive orders are presidential directives to an agency that provide the basis for carrying out laws or for establishing new policies. Even before Congress acted to protect women from discrimination by the federal government, for example, the National Organization for Women convinced President Lyndon B. Johnson to sign Executive Order 11375 in 1967. This amended an earlier order prohibiting the federal government from discriminating on the basis of race, color, religion, or national origin in the awarding of federal contracts, by adding to it the category of "gender." Nevertheless, although the president signed the Order, the Office of Federal Contract Compliance (the executive agency charged with implementing the order) failed to draft appropriate guidelines for implementation of the order until several years later.[23] A president can direct an agency to act, but it may take some time for his orders to be carried out. Given the many "jobs" of any president, few can ensure that all their orders will be carried out or that they will like all the rules that are made. In 1981 Executive Order 12291 was issued by President Reagan with detailed rules "to reduce the burdens of existing and future regulations, increase agency accountability for regulatory actions, provide for presidential oversight of the regulatory process, and to minimize duplication and conflict of regulations."

executive order: Presidential directive to an agency that provides the basis for carrying out laws or for establishing new policies.

Congressional Control

Congress, too, plays an important role in checking the power of the bureaucracy. Constitutionally, it possesses the authority to create or abolish departments and agencies as well as to transfer agency functions. It can also expand or contract bureaucratic discretion. And the Senate's authority to confirm (or reject) presidential appointments also gives Congress a "check" on the bureaucracy. Congress also exercises considerable oversight over the bureaucracy in several ways, as detailed in Table 9.2.

Political scientists distinguish between two different forms of oversight: *police patrol* and *fire alarm* oversight.[24] As their names might imply, police patrol oversight is proactive and allows Congress to set its own agenda for programs or agencies to review. In contrast, fire alarm oversight is reactive and generally involves a congressional response to a complaint filed by a constituent or politically significant actor.

TABLE 9.2

Frequency and Effectiveness of Oversight Techniques in a Single Congress

OVERSIGHT TECHNIQUE	NUMBER OF CASES IN WHICH TECHNIQUE WAS USED	EFFECTIVENESS RANKING
Staff communication with agency personnel	91	1
Member communication with agency personnel	86	2
Program reauthorization hearings	73	3
Oversight hearings	89	4
Hearings on bills to amend ongoing programs	70	5
Staff investigations	90	6
Program evaluations done by committee staff	89	7
Program evaluations done by congressional support agencies	89	8
Legislative veto	82	9
Analysis of proposed agency rules and regulations	90	10
Program evaluations done by outsiders	88	11
Agency reports required by Congress	91	12
Program evaluations done by the agencies	87	13
Review of casework	87	14

Source: Joel Aberbach, *Keeping a Watchful Fye* (Washington, D.C.: Brookings Institution, 1990), 132, 135.

The range of congressional responses can vary from simple inquiries about an issue to full-blown hearings.

Given the prevalence of iron triangles and issue networks, it is not surprising that the most frequently used form of oversight and the most effective is communication between house staffers and agency personnel. Various forms of program evaluations make up the next most commonly used forms of congressional control. Congress and its staff routinely conduct evaluations of programs and conduct oversight hearings.

Congress also uses many of its constitutional powers to exercise control over the bureaucracy. These include its:

1. Investigatory powers. It is not at all unusual for a congressional committee or subcommittee to hold hearings on a particular problem, and then to direct the relevant agency to study the problem or find ways to remedy it. Representatives of the agencies also appear before these committees on a regular basis to inform members about agency activities, ongoing investigations, and so on.

2. Power of the purse. To control the bureaucracy, Congress dangles its ability to fund or not fund an agency's activities like the sword of Damocles over the heads of various agency officials.[25] The House Appropriations Committee routinely holds hearings to allow agency heads to justify their budget requests. Authorization legislation originates in the various legislative committees that oversee particular agencies (such as Agriculture, Veterans Affairs, Education, and Labor) and sets the maximum amounts that agencies can spend on particular programs. While some authorizations, such as Social Security, are permanent, others, including the State Department and Defense Department procurements, are watched closely and are subject to annual authorizations.

Once funds are authorized, they must be appropriated before they can be spent. Appropriations originate with the House Appropriations Committee, not the specialized legislative committees. Often, the Appropriations Committee allocates sums smaller than those authorized by the legislative committee. Thus the Appropriations Committee, a budget cutter, has an additional oversight function.

To help Congress's oversight of the bureaucracy's financial affairs, in 1921 Congress created the General Accounting Office (GAO; see chapter 8) at the same time that the Office of the Budget was created in the executive branch. With the establishment of the GAO, the Congressional Research Service, and later, the Congressional Budget Office (CBO), Congress essentially created its own bureaucracy to keep an eye on what the executive branch and *its* bureaucracy were doing. Today the GAO not only tracks how money is spent in the bureaucracy, but also monitors how policies are implemented. The CBO also conducts oversight studies. If it or the GAO uncovers problems with an agency's work, Congress is notified immediately.

3. *Law Making and the Legislative Veto.*   Congress can also pass new legislation to clarify policies or overturn regulations or rules. If Congress, for example, does not approve of agency regulations written to enforce existing statutes, it can redraft legislation to make its wishes clearer. Although it has been declared unconstitutional by the U.S. Supreme Court, the "**legislative veto** was the most aggressive, intrusive, and potentially effective means of holding rule makers accountable."[26]

> **legislative veto:** A procedure by which one or both houses of Congress can disallow an act of an executive agency by a simple majority vote.

Legislative vetoes, which allow Congress to reject the action of an administrative agency without the consent of the president, first began to appear in the 1930s, and they often required government agencies to submit proposed rules to Congress for its approval.[27] The legislative veto combined elements of police patrol and fire alarm models of oversight: police patrol because they were directed at whole programs and fire alarm because interest groups or constituents could call programs to a member of Congress's attention for quick action. During the 1970s congressional use of the legislative veto skyrocketed by 507 percent over the preceding decade, with 423 provisions passed with some form of legislative veto.[28] It peaked between 1970 and 1975 as Congress reacted to Richard M. Nixon's imperial presidency by adding veto provisions to all kinds of legislation it enacted. But in 1983 the U.S. Supreme Court ruled in *Immigration and Naturalization Service* v. *Chadha* that the legislative veto was an unconstitutional violation of separation of powers principles because, in effect, it bypassed the role of the president in the law-making process.[29]

> ***Immigration and Naturalization Service* v. *Chadha:*** Legislative veto ruled unconstitutional.

Judicial Control

While the president's and Congress's control over the actions of the bureaucracy is very direct, the judiciary's oversight function is less so. The federal judiciary, for example, can directly issue injunctions or orders to an executive agency even before a rule is formally promulgated. The courts have also ruled that agencies must give all affected individuals their due process rights guaranteed by the U.S. Constitution. A Social Security recipient's checks cannot be stopped, for example, unless that individual is provided with reasonable notice and an opportunity for a hearing. On a more informal, indirect level, litigation, or even the threat of litigation, often exerts a strong influence on bureaucrats. Injured parties can bring suit against agencies for their failure to enforce the law, and can challenge agency interpretations of the law. In general, however, the courts give great weight to the opinions of bureaucrats and usually defer to their expertise.[30]

CHANGING AMERICA: BUREAUCRATIC POLITICS

The kinds of oversight engaged in by the president, Congress, and the courts do not always work to control the bureaucracy, as evidenced by the repeated calls by lawmakers and the public for reform of the bureaucracy. Calls for bureaucratic reform usually center on one main issue: accountability. Accountability—that is, holding members of the bureaucracy responsible for how they implement laws and presidential directives—is one major issue facing Congress and the president. Because the way bureaucracies are designed affects the way they operate, most presidents have tried with little success to change the structure and design of many agencies to make them function better and to facilitate oversight. This would make bureaucrats more accountable to both the president and Congress for their decisions. Attempts to achieve greater accountability for the bureaucracy have included efforts to curb waste, reduce spending, decrease redundancy, and ultimately reduce the size of the bureaucracy itself.

Thomas Jefferson was the first president to address the issue of accountability. He attempted to cut waste and bring about a "wise and frugal government." But it wasn't until the Progressive era (1890–1920) that calls for reform began to be taken seriously. Later, Calvin Coolidge urged spending cuts and other reforms. His Two Percent Club

President Clinton and Vice President Gore stand in front of a forklift loaded with tons of government regulations to dramatize their plan to cut and re-shape government in an effort to trim over $100 billion from the national budget. (Photo courtesy: J. Scott Applewhite/AP Wide World Photos)

was created to cut staff, as its name implies, by 2 percent each year; his Correspondence Club was designed to reduce bureaucratic letter writing by thirty percent.[31]

As underscored in Highlight 9.4: Re-Re-Re-Re-Re-Reinventing Government, all recent presidents have tried to streamline the bureaucracy, a persistent goal of government reform, to make it smaller and thus more accountable. President Nixon, for example, proposed a plan to combine fifty domestic agencies and seven different departments into four large "super departments." But according to his former aide John Erlichman, this plan to "disrupt iron triangles" was dead on arrival. "Why? Because such a reorganization would have broken up the hoary congressional committee organization that corresponded to the existing departments and agencies." Said Erlichman, "A subcommittee chairman with oversight of the Agriculture Department would lose power, perks and status if we were authorized to fold Agriculture into a new Department of Natural Resources. The powerful farm lobbies were equally hostile to the idea."[32]

President Bill Clinton also offered a reform plan to increase the accountability of the bureaucracy. The President's Task Force on Reinventing Government, headed by Vice President Gore, issued a 200-page task force report in 1993 making over 800

Highlight 9.4

Re-Re-Re-Re-Re-Reinventing Government

U.S. leaders before Bill Clinton and Al Gore, Jr., have had high hopes for domestic *perestroika*.

PRESIDENT	NAME OF PLAN	COMMENT
Johnson	Programming, Planning, and Budgeting Systems	"[This is] a very revolutionary system . . . so that through the tools of modern management the full promise of a finer life can be brought to every American at the lowest possible cost."
Nixon	Management By Objectives	"The time has come . . . to organize the government by conscious, comprehensive design to meet the new needs of a new era."
Carter	Zero-Based Budgeting	"It's simple and it works . . . It will make sure that the money that is allocated . . . goes further."
Reagan	President's Private Sector Survey On Cost Control (Grace Commission)	"[The commission] will work like tireless bloodhounds, leaving no stone unturned in their search to root out inefficiency and waste of taxpayer dollars."
Bush	Right-Sizing Government	"I honestly believe that this is the only way to get the size and spending of government under control."
Clinton/Gore	Reinventing Government (National Performance Review)	"It's about whether we can restore the trust of the American people in their government."

Source: From "Re-Re-Re-Re-Re-Reinventing Government," *Time* (September 13, 1993). Copyright © 1993 Time, Inc. Reprinted by permission. Clinton/Gore information provided by authors.

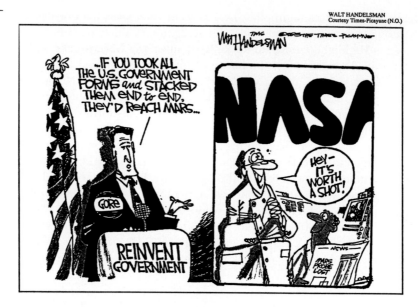

recommendations to cut waste and paperwork and to streamline the government.[33]
Moreover, in early 1993, Clinton signed executive orders to

- cut the size of the federal workforce by 252,000 people within five years.

- cut in half the growing number of federal regulations within three years.

- set customer service standards to direct agencies to put the people they serve
  first.

In 1995 both President Clinton and the Republican-controlled Congress began to
call for dramatic reforms not seen in American politics since the New Deal. During the
New Deal era, however, the president and the Congress were from the same political
party. The differences in the Democrats' and Republicans' basic views of the role of government as well as of bureaucracy quickly got in the way of major change. Nevertheless, calls for downsizing government continue to come from both sides of the aisle in
Congress and from the president. More specifically, in Congress, Republicans have
called for eliminating the Department of Education, downsizing the Department of
Housing and Urban Development and the Environmental Protection Agency, slashing
funds to or eliminating the Corporation for Public Broadcasting, the National Endowment for the Arts, the Federal Trade Commission, and the Consumer Product Safety
Commission, and also for privatizing the U.S. Postal Service. (See Politics Now: Downsizing the Bureaucracy.)

In spite of these calls for change, some basic problems continue to exist within the
bureaucratic system that will make any reform, no matter how broad in terms of agencies dismantled, difficult to attain. These include:

1. Red Tape.   As rules and regulations established by the huge bureaucracy become increasingly complex, policy goals are often lost in a series of complex rules and
procedures that must be followed before anything can get done. The paperwork and
the maze of regulations that one must get through to obtain, say, Social Security disability benefits or veteran's benefits are so overwhelming that many people are discouraged from ever applying for what is rightfully theirs.

Downsizing the Bureaucracy

When Republicans took over control of both houses of Congress in 1995, they took it as a mandate from the public to cut wasteful spending and the duplication of government functions. The membership of the House Commerce Committee took this mandate to heart. Charging that the Commerce Department had become an agency full of miscellaneous and unrelated functions, many of which duplicated programs in other departments and agencies, the committee chair noted, "It is Fibber McGee's closet, filled with agencies and functions that few people even know about, but put there because nobody could figure out where else they should go, and left there, because until now, Congress lacked the will or the leadership to clean out the file."*

What kinds of functions was he talking about? Housed in Commerce are the Office of the U.S. Trade Representatives, the National Weather Service, the Census Bureau, the Bureau of Economic Analysis (which calculates the gross domestic product), the Coast Guard, the Patent and Trademark Office, the National Oceanic and Atmospheric Administration, and the U.S. Geological Survey.

The Clinton administration reacted angrily to the congressional hearings on legislation to disband the depart-

ment, calling them a "trophy hunt." Commerce Secretary Ronald Brown claimed that the dismantling of the department and the transfer of important functions to other departments would actually cost more money and not realize the $7.7 billion savings over the next five years that the Republicans claimed.

It's hard to figure out who is right because there are no precedents for closing a Cabinet-level department. In 1981 the Community Services Administration, a Cabinet-size agency, was replaced by a block grant program, but no departments have ever gotten the axe. Freshman Republicans wanted to be able to go back home and point to concrete actions, and Commerce appeared to be an agency that no longer enjoyed much support.

Although originally begun as a clientele agency to meet the needs of American business interests, the Commerce Department also now appears to enjoy little support in the business community save for concern about export and import programs, the responsibility for which could be moved to another department. Furthermore, the diversity of its programs has left it without a strong natural constituency such as those still enjoyed by other departments unpopular with the Republicans, including Education and Energy.

Dismantling the agency must be done in the eleven authorizing committees with jurisdiction over the Commerce Department,** and the un-

timely death of Secretary Brown caused some House members to lay low on this issue. And, while trying to stall the dismantling of the Commerce Department, the Clinton administration has been on a downsizing campaign of its own. Not to be outdone by the Republicans in the 104th Congress—and needing to be able to show specific cuts in the federal government—the Clinton Administration submitted a bill to Congress calling for the elimination of the Interstate Commerce Commission (ICC), the nation's oldest regulatory agency, and to transfer its remaining few functions to the Department of Transportation (DOT), including safety. Although the ICC was originally created to regulate the railroads, over the years it was given authority over truck and bus companies. But, since Congress has largely deregulated those industries, there wasn't much left for the ICC and its 400 employees to do. "The ICC was created to solve problems in the last century," said Transportation Secretary Federico Peña. "Modernizing our government means weeding out programs that are no longer useful."*** Congress quickly agreed with him and agreed to abolish the ICC. Thus about half of ICC staffers lost their jobs and others were transferred to DOT. The savings to taxpayers, according to Peña, was about $25 million. Which agencies do you see as likely targets for the axe? Why?

*Quoted in "House Panel to Consider Bill Dismantling Commerce Department," *BNA International Trade Daily* (September 15, 1995) Nexis.

**Donna Cassata, "Freshmen 'Have to Get' Commerce," *Congressional Quarterly* (July 29, 1995): 2273.

***Quoted in Jerry Kronsberg, United Press International, (April 7, 1995) Nexis.

Title IX of the Education Amendments of 1972 mandated nondiscrimination in women's sports. Since its passage, there has been a dramatic increase in the number of high school and college women competing in school sports—from 72,000 college women in 1972 to well over 170,000 today. And, according to the Soccer Industry Council of America, the number of girls playing soccer in the United States grew from 85,173 in 1986 to 191,358 in 1995. (Photo courtesy: Karen O'Connor)

2. Waste and Inefficiency. Duplication of services and faulty coordination are also problems in most bureaucracies. Within the executive branch, for example, economic policy is split among the Office of Management and Budget, the Departments of Treasury and Commerce, the Council of Economic Advisors, and the Federal Reserve Board. Lack of coordination among these bodies helps explain the problems inherent in economic policy and highlights some of the efficiency problems in the bureaucracy.

3. Inadequate Mechanisms for Evaluation. Often, the success of a program may be difficult to gauge because there are no precise standards for evaluation. EPA air cleanup targets in the 1970s, for example, were not based on scientific analysis. And if information concerning success is not available or cannot be measured with any precision, it becomes difficult for policy makers to know what to do with a program. Should it be continued, changed, or eliminated? Evaluation is also often difficult because of competing problems. If money is cut for teen sex education programs, for example, the budget deficit might be reduced in the short run, but added teen pregnancies could result in an increase on the welfare rolls.

4. Decentralized Authority. The basic structure of a central agency in Washington, D.C., and regional offices makes coordination difficult, as does the structure of the federal system itself. While an agency in Washington, D.C., may have clear ideas concerning how a particular program should work, state and local officials may have very different ideas and different ways of implementing them.

5. Vague Objectives. Vague instructions are yet another problem that haunts bureaucrats. Congress often states only broad policy goals in its legislation and leaves the specifics of how to achieve these goals up to bureaucrats. In this way Congress cannot be blamed for any particularly unpopular interpretations.

One particularly controversial policy was at the heart of Title IX of the Education Amendments of 1972, which mandated that "No person in the United States shall, on the basis of sex, be excluded from participation in, be denied the benefits of, or be subjected to discrimination under any education program or activity receiving federal financial assistance."

The law further instructed the secretary of Health, Education, and Welfare (HEW; it now applies to the secretary of Education) to "prepare and publish proposed regulations . . . which shall include with respect to intercollegiate athletic activities reasonable provisions considering the nature of particular sports" to implement the amendments. Supporters of women's athletics in colleges and universities went around and around with HEW officials over the intent of Congress. Supporters of women's sports argued that discrimination against women in all sports was prohibited. Others said that revenue-producing sports such as basketball and football were exempt.

Finally, in December 1978—six years after passage of the Education Amendments—the Office for Civil Rights in HEW released a "policy interpretation" of the law, dealing largely with the section that concerned intercollegiate athletics.[34] More than thirty pages of text were devoted to dealing with a hundred or so words from the statute. Football was recognized as unique, because of the huge revenues it produces, so it could be inferred that male-dominated football programs could continue to outspend women's athletic programs. The more than sixty women's groups that had lobbied for equality of spending were outraged, and turned their efforts toward seeking more favorable rulings on the construction of the statute from the courts.

6. Insufficient Funding. Congress often fails to fund some programs fully, making their success unlikely. Head Start and the Food Stamps program, for example, are never sufficiently funded to allow all who are eligible to receive the benefits of those programs. Domestic social welfare programs are perennially the target of presidential and congressional budget cutters who seek political gains from attacking the "bloated bureaucracy" while seriously attempting to get the national deficit in check.

North—South

POLITICS AROUND THE WORLD

It will come as a surprise to most American readers that bureaucrats and bureaucracies are often held in high regard in other countries, where they often attract the best and brightest young people at least at the beginnings of their careers. In countries like France and Japan, high-level civil servants who are experts in management or substantive fields often play a vital role not only in how policy is carried out, but also in how it is made in the first place.

Canada does not go quite that far. Nonetheless, the fact that the prime minister names only about a hundred colleagues to political positions compared to the thousands of appointments of an American president means that civil servants there are more involved in determining what bills, decrees, rules, and other government documents look like.

The Canadian bureaucracy is not quite as prestigious as some of the others because it was entirely based on patronage until 1908. A long period of Liberal Party domination until the election of John Diefenbaker left the widespread belief that only his supporters could rise to the top of the civil service. Today, the federal and most provincial services are purely nonpartisan, but it is taking time for their reputations to catch up with reality.

Mexico's bureaucracy, on the other hand, has problems that far overshadow any criticisms of the American bureaucracy and as such are all-too-typical of what one finds in the third world. Although its civil servants, too, are supposedly chosen and promoted on the basis of merit, the bureaucracy is under the PRI's thumb, just like everything else in the country's political life. No matter what the law says, bureaucratic staffs change following each election. In other words, the supposedly apolitical civil servants hold office at the president's whim; because they are typically moved from ministry to ministry every six years (or less), it is far harder for them to develop the expertise that comes from years of working on a narrow range of subjects. And, of course, the leverage exercised by the president and the PRI machine as a whole lends the bureaucracy its share of corrupt officials. One observer put it pithily when he recently reported that he was able to find only "pockets of professionalism" in the Mexican bureaucracy.

There is one exception to this all-too-typical picture of a third-world bureaucracy. Despite the spread of the PRI throughout Mexican society, most national politicians are chosen from the bureaucracy. During the first fifty years of PRI rule, presidential candidates tended to come from the military and, later, from the ministry in charge of civil administration and the police. The last three, however, have come from the economic ministries, which is not all that surprising given the new-found importance of economic reform in Mexican political life (see chapter 18's North–South feature).

SUMMARY

The bureaucracy plays a major role in America as a shaper of public policy, earning it the nickname the "fourth branch" of government. To explain the evolution and scope of bureaucratic power, in this chapter we have made the following points:

1. The Roots and Development of the Federal Bureaucracy.

According to Max Weber, all bureaucracies have similar characteristics. These characteristics can be seen in the federal bureaucracy as it developed from George Washington's time, when the executive branch that had only three departments—State, War, and Treasury—through the Civil War. Significant gains occurred in the size of the federal bureaucracy as the government geared up to conduct a war. As employment opportunities within the federal government increased, concurrent reforms in the civil service system assured that more and more jobs were filled according to merit and not by patronage. By the late 1800s, reform efforts led to further increases in the size of the bureaucracy, as independent regulatory commissions were created. And in the wake of the Depression, many new agencies were created to get the national economy back on course as part of FDR's New Deal.

2. The Modern Bureaucracy.

The modern bureaucracy is composed of nearly 3 million civilian workers from all walks of life. In general, bureaucratic agencies fall into four general types: departments, government corporations, independent agencies, and independent regulatory commissions.

3. Policy Making.

Bureaucrats not only make but implement public policy. Iron triangles or issue networks often can be used to describe how this policy making occurs. Much policy making occurs at the lowest levels of the bureaucracy, where administrative discretion can be exercised on an informal basis. More formal policy is often made through rule making and administrative adjudication.

4. Making Agencies Accountable.

Agencies enjoy considerable discretion, but they are also subjected to many formal controls. The president, Congress, and the judiciary all exercise various degrees of control over the bureaucracy.

5. Changing America: Bureaucratic Politics.

Accountability and size are two of the greatest issues in bureaucratic politics. To improve accountability, to reduce waste and duplication, and to save money, most presidents have suggested bureaucratic reforms but to little avail because systems problems make reform difficult. These include red tape, waste and inefficiency, inadequate mechanisms for evaluation, and decentralized authority. Reforms are made almost impossible by the vast size of the bureaucracy and several systems problems, including inadequate mechanisms for evaluation, decentralized authority, vague objectives, and insufficient funding.

KEY TERMS

administrative adjudication, p. 346

administrative discretion, p. 345

bureaucracy, p. 326

civil service system, p. 330

clientele agency, p. 341

department, p. 338

executive order, p. 349

Federal Employees Political Activities Act, p. 334

government corporation, p. 341

Hatch Act, p. 333

Immigration and Naturalization Service v. *Chadha*, p. 351

implementation, p. 343

independent agency, p. 342

independent regulatory commission, p. 331

iron triangle, p. 343

issue network, p. 345

legislative veto, p. 351

merit system, p. 330

patronage, p. 329

Pendleton Act (Civil Services Reform Act of 1883), p. 330

regulation, p. 346

rule making, p. 346

spoils system, p. 329

SUGGESTED READINGS

Bennett, Linda M., and Stephen E. Bennett. *Living with Leviathan*. Lawrence, KS: University of Kansas Press, 1990.

Derthick, Martha, and Paul J. Quirk. *The Politics of Deregulation*. Washington: Brookings Institution, 1985.

Dodd, Lawrence, and Richard Schott. *Congress and the Administrative State*. New York: Wiley, 1979.

Gormley, William T., Jr. *Taming the Bureaucracy: Muscles, Prayers and Other Strategies*. Princeton, NJ: Princeton University Press, 1989.

Kerwin, Cornelius M. *Rulemaking: How Government Agencies Write Law and Make Policy*. Washington, D.C.: CQ Press, 1994.

Knott, Jack H., and Gary J. Miller. *Reforming Bureaucracy: The Politics of Institutional Choice*. Englewood Cliffs, NJ: Prentice Hall, 1987.

Osborne, David, and Ted Gaebler. *Reinventing Government: How the Entrepreneurial Spirit is Transforming the Public Sector*. Reading, MA: Addison-Wesley, 1992.

Rourke, Francis E. *Bureaucracy, Politics and Public Policy*. Boston: Little, Brown, 1988.

Seidman, Harold, and Robert Gilmour. *Politics, Position, and Power*, 4th ed. New York: Oxford University Press, 1986.

Wilson, James Q. *Bureaucracy: What Government Agencies Do and Why They Do It*. New York: Basic Books, 1989.

(Photo courtesy: Mark Reinstein/The Image Works)

THE JUDICIARY

Sharon Taxman and Debra Williams were hired on the same day by the same school district to teach the same course. Their qualifications were also identical. Over the years they both received excellent teaching evaluations, and they were granted tenure at the same time. The single difference between the two women? Sharon Taxman is white; Debra Williams is black. When the Piscataway, New Jersey, school board was forced by budget constraints to cut its teaching staff, Sharon Taxman lost her job. Why? Because the school board decided to base its decision on a desire to enhance the diversity of its teaching staff.

Piscataway is a suburban community that houses two campuses of Rutgers, the state university. Its residents are a study in racial diversity. At the time Taxman was laid off, 51 percent of the high school students where Taxman taught were white, 25 percent were black, 17 percent were Asian, and 7 percent were Hispanic. No court had ordered the board to implement an affirmative action plan to increase the number of black teachers; there was no judicially determined history of discriminatory treatment, and, in fact, the percentage of black teachers at the high school was higher than the percentage of black teachers available in the community.

"Does the board not have the authority to hire a diverse teaching staff to be more representative of its population?" asked the board president.[1] No, claimed Taxman, who filed suit in federal district court in 1992, represented by lawyers from then President Bush's U.S. Department of Justice. She alleged that the school board had violated the Civil Rights Act of 1964, which outlaws discrimination in employment and specifically makes it illegal "to discharge any individual . . . because of such individual's race. . . . " Maryanne Trump Barry, a federal district court judge appointed by President Ronald Reagan, agreed with Waxman and Justice Department lawyers, concluding that while diversity is "a laudable goal," it is not a justifiable legal basis for discrimination.[2]

Taxman was rehired the next year and awarded nearly $150,000 in damages. But that was not the end of the story. When the school board appealed the verdict in February 1994, the Justice Department was controlled by Clinton Democrats. By the summer the Justice Department had repudiated its previous position and urged the U.S. Court of Appeals in Philadelphia to reverse its own victory. The department said that the district court decision would make it too difficult for school districts and any employers to adopt affirmative action plans on a voluntary basis. Taxman and her lawyer were outraged and charged that the Justice Department had not even informed them that they were thinking of changing sides.

The U.S. Court of Appeals originally heard oral argument in January 1995. In November 1995 it announced that it would rehear the case because one of the original three judges who heard the case had died. It also announced the Department of Justice would not be allowed to take part in the case as an *amicus curiae,* or friend of the court, on behalf of the school board. Third Circuit Chief Judge Dolores Sloviter, a Jimmy Carter appointee, named herself to the three-judge panel that had been considering the case for the last ten months. Later, in May 1996, the Third Circuit issued an unusual order setting the *Taxman* case down for oral argument before all thirteen judges of the circuit.

No matter what the Court of Appeals does, an appeal to the U.S. Supreme Court, the highest court in the land, is likely. Every day issues of great policy import are decided by federal courts of appeals; some of these decisions are then appealed to the highest court for the nine appointed Supreme Court justices to resolve. Cases concerning such issues as racial segregation, abortion, the rights of criminal defendants and victims, issues of free speech and press, and affirmative action are routinely contested in state and federal courts throughout the nation. Sometimes a definitive proclamation from the Supreme Court can resolve the issue. More often than not, however, the Court's decision resolves the *immediate* issue between the two parties in a specific case but creates even greater controversy among elected officials, policy makers, and the citizenry.

In 1787, when Alexander Hamilton wrote to urge support of the U.S. Constitution, he firmly believed that the judiciary was the weakest of the three departments of government. And in its formative years, the judiciary was, in Hamilton's words, "the least dangerous" branch. The judicial branch seemed so inconsequential that when the young national government made its move to the District of Columbia in 1800, Congress actually forgot to include any space to house the justices of the Supreme Court! Last-minute conferences with the Capitol architects led to the allocation of a small area in the basement of the Senate wing of the Capitol Building for a courtroom. No other space was allowed for the justices, however. Noted one commentator, "A stranger might traverse the darkest avenues of the Capitol for a week, without finding the remote corner in which justice is served in the American Republic."[3]

Today the role of the courts, particularly the U.S. Supreme Court, is significantly different from that envisioned in 1788, the year the national government came into being. The "least dangerous branch" is now perceived by many as having too much power. The Framers could never have envisioned that the authority of the Supreme Court and other federal courts would grow to include issues as diverse as the right of married couples to use birth control, the right of parents to withdraw life-support systems from their children, and the question of whether a pregnant woman can be forced to undergo a caesarean section prior to going into natural labor. Nor could the Framers have envisioned the separation of powers problems that would become routine. The halls of the 104th Congress, for example, rang with Republicans' criticism of the *Taxman* case and the Clinton administration's reversal of the Bush Administration's anti-affirmative action stand. Senator Orrin Hatch (R–Utah), chair of the Judiciary Committee, even threatened to hold hearings on the Justice Department switch and to pin down the administration on its affirmative action position. Clearly, the Framers never forsaw the

Pro-life protesters march before the Supreme Court. The Court has often been the target of interest group protests on account of its decisions on such controversial issues as abortion, affirmative action, and gay rights. (Photo courtesy: Larry Downing/ Woodfin Camp & Associates)

extent of the federal judiciary's involvement (or, in later periods, the Justice Department) in educational policy, let alone in hiring decisions or affirmative action.

During different periods of the judiciary's history, the role and power of the federal courts have varied tremendously. They have often played a key role in creating a strong national government and have boldly led the nation in social reform. Yet, at other times, the federal courts, especially the U.S. Supreme Court, have stubbornly stood as major obstacles to social and economic change.

In addition to being unaware of the expanded role of the federal judiciary, many Americans are also unaware of the political nature of the courts. They have been raised to think of the federal courts, especially the Supreme Court, as far above the fray of politics. That, however, is simply not the case. Elected presidents nominate judges to the federal courts and justices to the Supreme Court, often to advance their personal politics, and elected Senators ultimately confirm (or decline to confirm) presidential nominees. Not only is the selection process political, but the process by which cases ultimately get heard—if they are heard at all—by the Supreme Court is often political as well. Interest groups routinely seek out good test cases to advance their policy positions. Even the U.S. government, generally through the Justice Department and the U.S. solicitor general (another political appointee), seeks to advance its version of the public interest in court. Interest groups then often line up on opposing sides to advance their positions, much in the same way lobbyists do in Congress.

In this chapter we explore these issues and the scope and development of judicial power:

- First, we look at *the creation of the national judiciary.* Article III of the Constitution created a Supreme Court but left it to Congress to create any other federal courts, a task it quickly took up, which resulted in passage of the *Judiciary Act of 1789.*

- Second, we explore the structure and some rules of *the American legal system.* The American legal system contains parallel courts systems for the fifty states and the national government. Each court system has courts of original and appellate jurisdiction.

- Third, we discuss *the federal court system*. The federal court system is composed of specialized courts, district courts, courts of appeals, and the Supreme Court, which is the ultimate authority on all federal law.

- Fourth, we see *how federal court judges are selected*. All appointments to the federal district courts, courts of appeals, and the Supreme Court are made by the president and are subject to Senate confirmation.

- Fifth, we take a look at *the Supreme Court today*. Only a few of the millions of cases filed in courts around the United States every year eventually make their way to the Supreme Court through the lengthy appellate process, as cases are filtered out at a variety of stages.

- Sixth, we learn *how justices make decisions* and discuss how judicial decision making is based on a variety of legal and extra-legal factors.

- Seventh, we discuss *how judicial policies are made and implemented*.

- Finally, we examine some suggestions that have been offered to *change the judicial system* and the *judicial selection process*.

A note on terminology: When we refer to the "Supreme Court," the "Court," or the "high Court" here, we always mean the U.S. Supreme Court, which sits at the pinnacle of the federal and state court systems. The Supreme Court is referred to by the name of the chief justice who presided over it during a particular period (for example, the Marshall Court is the Court presided over by John Marshall from 1801 to 1835). When we use the term "courts," we refer to all federal or state courts unless otherwise noted.

THE CREATION OF THE NATIONAL JUDICIARY

*T*he detailed notes James Madison took at the Philadelphia Convention make it clear that the Framers devoted little time to the writing of or the content of Article III, which created the judicial branch of government. The Framers believed that a federal judiciary posed little of the threat of tyranny that they feared from the other two branches. One scholar has even suggested that, for at least some delegates to the Constitutional Convention,

> provision for a national judiciary was a matter of theoretical necessity . . . more in deference to the maxim of separation [of powers] than in response to clearly formulated ideas about the role of a national judicial system and its indispensability.[4]

Alexander Hamilton argued in *Federalist No. 78* that the judiciary would be the "least dangerous branch of government." Anti-Federalists, however, did not agree with Hamilton. They particularly objected to a judiciary whose members had life tenure and the ability to interpret what was to be "the supreme law of the land," a phrase that Anti-Federalists feared would give the Supreme Court too much power.

The Framers also debated the need for any federal courts below the level of the Supreme Court. Some argued in favor of deciding all cases in state courts, with only appeals going before the Supreme Court. Others argued for a system of federal courts. A compromise left the final choice to Congress, and Article III began simply by vesting "The judicial Power of the United States . . . in one supreme Court, and in such inferior Courts as the Congress may from time to time ordain and establish." Although there was some debate over whether the Court should have the power of **judicial review** (which allows the judiciary to review acts of the other branches of government and the states), the question was left unsettled in Article III (and not finally resolved until *Marbury* v. *Madison* [1803], regarding acts of the national government, and *Martin* v. *Hunter's Lessee* [1816],[5] regarding state law. This vagueness was not all that unusual, given the numerous compromises that took place in Philadelphia.

Had the Supreme Court been viewed as the potential policy maker it is today, it is highly unlikely that the Framers would have provided for life tenure with "good behavior" for federal judges in Article III. This feature was agreed on because the Framers did not want the justices (or any federal judges) subject to the whims of politics, the public, or politicians. Moreover, Alexander Hamilton argued in *Federalist No. 78* that the "independence of judges" was needed "to guard the Constitution and the rights of individuals." Because the Framers viewed the Court as quite powerless, Hamilton stressed the need to place federal judges above the fray of politics. Yet although there is no denying that judges are political animals and carry the same prejudices and preferences to the bench that others do to the statehouse, Congress, or the White House, the provision of life tenure for "good behavior" has generally functioned well.

Some checks on the power of the judiciary were nonetheless included in the Constitution. Congress can alter the Court's jurisdiction (its ability to hear certain kinds of cases). Congress can also propose constitutional amendments that, if ratified, can effectively reverse judicial decisions, and it can impeach and remove federal judges. In one further check, it is the president who (with the "advice and consent" of the Senate) appoints all federal judges.

judicial review: Power of the courts to review acts of other branches of government and the states.

The Judiciary Act of 1789 and the Creation of the Federal Judicial System

In spite of the Framers' intentions, the pervasive role of politics in the judicial branch quickly became evident with the passage of the **Judiciary Act of 1789.** Congress spent nearly the entire second half of its first session deliberating the various provisions of the act to give form and substance to the federal judiciary. As one early observer noted, "The convention has only crayoned in the outlines. It left it to Congress to fill up and colour the canvas."[6]

The Judiciary Act of 1789 established the basic three-tiered structure of the federal court system. At the bottom are the federal district courts—one in each state (except Massachusetts and Virginia, with two apiece)—each staffed by a federal judge. If the people participating in a lawsuit (called litigants) are unhappy with the district court's verdict, they could appeal their case to one of three circuit courts. Each circuit court, initially created to function as a trial court for important cases, was composed of one district court judge and two itinerant Supreme Court justices who met as a circuit court twice a year. Thus Supreme Court Justice Samuel Chase, in his capacity as a circuit court judge, presided over a Sedition Act trial resulting in the conviction of a Jeffersonian newspaper editor who was critical of the Federalist government. It wasn't until 1891 that circuit courts as we know them today took on their exclusively appellate function.

The third tier of the federal judicial system fleshed out by the Judiciary Act of 1789 was the Supreme Court of the United States. Although the Constitution mentions "the supreme Court," it was silent on its size. In the Judiciary Act Congress set the size of the Supreme Court at six—the chief justice plus five associate justices.

Judiciary Act of 1789: Established the basic three-tiered structure of the federal court system.

The Supreme Court building held its first two sessions in this building, called the Exchange. (Photo courtesy: The Bettmann Archive)

The minutes from the first session of the Supreme Court of the United States, held on February 1, 1790. Not much went on—the session had to be adjourned when too few justices showed up. (Photo courtesy: The Supreme Court Historical Society)

When the justices met in their first public session in New York City in 1790, they were magnificently garbed in black and scarlet robes in the English fashion, but they had discarded what Thomas Jefferson termed "the monstrous wig which makes English judges look like rats peeping through bunches of oakum!"[7] The elegance of their attire, however, could not make up for the relatively ineffective status of the Court. Its first session even had to be adjourned when a quorum of the justices failed to show up. That first session of the Court was presided over by John Jay, who was appointed Chief Justice of the United States by George Washington. It decided one really important case—*Chisholm* v. *Georgia* (1793) (discussed on page 367). Moreover, in an indication of its lowly status, one associate justice left the Court to become Chief Justice of the South Carolina Supreme Court. (Although such a move would be considered a step down today, keep in mind that in the early years of the United States, many viewed the states as more important than the new national government.)

Hampered by frequent changes in personnel, limited space for its operations, no clerical support, and no system of reporting its decisions, the Court and its meager activities did not impress many people. From the beginning, the circuit court duties of the Supreme Court justices presented problems for the prestige of the Court. Few good lawyers were willing to accept nominations to the high Court because its circuit court duties entailed a substantial amount of travel—most of it on horseback over poorly maintained roads in frequently inclement weather. Southern justices often tallied up as much as 10,000 miles a year on horseback. George Washington tried to prevail on several friends and supporters to fill vacancies on the Court as they appeared, but most refused the "honor." John Adams, the second president of the United States, ran into similar problems. When he asked John Jay, the first chief justice, to resume the position after he resigned to become governor of New York, Jay declined the offer. Jay had once remarked of the Court that it had lacked "energy, weight, and dignity" as well as "public confidence and respect." Given Jay's view of the Court and its performance statistics, his refusal was not surprising.

In spite of all its problems, in its first decade the Court took several actions to help mold the new nation. First, by declining to give George Washington advice on the legality of some of his actions, the justices attempted to establish the Supreme Court as an independent, nonpolitical branch of government. Although John Jay, as an individual, frequently gave the president advice in private, the Court refused to answer questions Washington posed to it concerning the construction of international laws and treaties. The justices wanted to avoid the appearance of prejudging an issue that could later arise before them.

The early Court also tried to advance principles of nationalism and to maintain the national government's supremacy over the states. As circuit court jurists, the justices rendered numerous decisions on such matters as national suppression of the Whiskey Rebellion and the constitutionality of the Alien and Sedition Acts, which made it a crime to criticize national governmental officials or their actions (see chapter 5).

During the ratification debates, Anti-Federalists had warned that Article III extended federal judicial power to controversies "between a State and Citizens of another State"—meaning that a citizen of one state could sue any other state in federal court, a prospect unthinkable to defenders of state sovereignty. Although Federalists, including Hamilton and Madison, had scoffed at the idea, the nationalist Supreme Court quickly proved them wrong in *Chisholm* v. *Georgia* (1793).[8] In *Chisholm* the justices interpreted the Court's jurisdiction under Article III, section 2, to include the right to hear suits brought by a citizen of one state against another state. For example, writing in *Chisholm,* Justice James Wilson denounced the "haughty notions of state independence, state sovereignty, and state supremacy." The states' reaction to this perceived attack on their authority led to passage and ratification (in 1798) of the Eleventh Amendment, which specifically limited judicial power by stipulating that the federal courts' authority could not "extend to any suit . . . commenced or prosecuted against one of the United States by citizens of another State."

Finally, in a series of circuit and Supreme Court decisions, the justices paved the way for announcement of the doctrine of judicial review by the third chief justice, John Marshall. (Oliver Ellsworth served from 1796 to 1800.) Justices "riding circuit" occasionally held state laws unconstitutional because they violated the U.S. Constitution. And in *Hylton* v. *United States* (1796),[9] the Court evaluated for the first time the constitutionality of an act of Congress. In *Hylton* the Court ruled that a congressional tax on horse-drawn carriages was an excise tax and not a direct tax and therefore it need not be apportioned evenly among the states (as direct taxes must be, according to the Constitution).

The Marshall Court (1801–1835)

John Marshall was appointed chief justice by President John Adams in 1801, three years after he declined to accept a nomination as associate justice (see Roots of Government: John Marshall). An ardent Federalist who also earlier had declined Washington's offer to become attorney general, Marshall later came to be considered the most important justice ever to serve on the high Court. Part of his reputation is the result of the duration of his service and the historical significance of this period in our nation's history. Marshall also, however, brought much-needed respect and prestige to the Court through his leadership in a progression of cases and a series of innovations.

One of Marshall's first innovations on the Court was to discontinue the practice of *seriatim* (Latin for "in a series") opinions, which was the custom of the King's Bench in Great Britain. Prior to the Marshall Court, the justices delivered their individual opinions in order. There was no single "opinion of the Court," as we are accustomed to today. For the Court to take its place as an equal branch of government, Marshall

Roots of Government

John Marshall

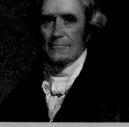

Photo courtesy: Boston Athenaeum

A single person can make a major difference in the development of an institution. Such was the case with John Marshall, who dominated the Court during his thirty-four years as chief justice. As one commentator noted, "Marshall found the Constitution paper, and he made it power. He found a skeleton, and he clothed it with flesh and blood." In essence, Marshall transformed the Court into a co-equal branch of government through a series of key decisions that established:

- The practice by which the view of the Court is expressed in a single opinion instead of individual opinions, as had previously been the case. Marshall encouraged unanimity and discouraged dissenting and concurring opinions, thereby winning for the Court the prestige it needed to resolve many of the conflicts and controversies that came before it.

- The Court as the final arbiter of constitutional questions, with the right to declare congressional acts void (*Marbury v. Madison* [1803]).

- The authority of the Supreme Court over the judiciaries of the various states, including the Court's power to declare state laws invalid (*Fletcher v. Peck* [1810]; *Martin v. Hunter's Lessee* [1816]; *Cohens v. Virginia* [1821]).

- The supremacy of the federal government and Congress over state governments through a broad interpretation of the "necessary and proper" clause (*McCulloch v. Maryland* [1819]).

Who was this man still so revered today? John Marshall (1755–1835) was born in a log cabin in Virginia, the first of fifteen children of Welsh immigrants. Although tutored at home by two clergymen, Marshall's inspiration was his father, who introduced him to English literature and Sir William Blackstone's influential work *Commentaries on the Laws of England*. After serving in the Continental Army and acquiring the rank of captain, Marshall taught himself the law. He attended only one formal course at the College of William and Mary before being admitted to the bar. Marshall practiced law in Virginia, where he and his wife lived and raised a family. Of their ten children, only six survived childhood.

More of a politician than a lawyer, Marshall served as a delegate to the Virginia legislature from 1782 to 1785, 1787 to 1790, and 1795 to 1796, and played an instrumental role in Virginia's ratification of the U.S. Constitution in 1787. As the leading Federalist in Virginia, Marshall was offered several positions in the Federalist administrations of George Washington and John Adams—including attorney general and associate justice to the Supreme Court—but he refused them all. Finally, in 1799, Washington persuaded him to run for the House of Representatives. Marshall was elected, but his career in the House was brief, for he became Secretary of State in 1800 under John Adams. When Oliver Ellsworth resigned as Chief Justice of the United States in 1800, Adams nominated Marshall. Marshall was an ardent Federalist and a third cousin of Democratic-Republican President Thomas Jefferson, whom he faced head on in *Marbury v. Madison*.

Marshall came to head the Court with little legal experience and *no* judicial experience, unlike the situation on the current Supreme Court, where all of the justices *except* Chief Justice Rehnquist had prior judicial experience. Still, it is unlikely that any contemporary justice will have anywhere near the impact that Marshall had on the Court and the course of U.S. politics.

strongly believed, the justices needed to speak as a *Court* and not as six individuals. In fact, during Marshall's first four years in office, the Court routinely spoke as one, and the chief justice wrote twenty-four of its twenty-six opinions. He also claimed for the Court the right of judicial review, from which the Supreme Court derives much of its day-to-day power and impact on the policy process.

Judicial Review

During the Philadelphia Convention, the Framers debated and rejected the idea of judicial veto of legislation or executive acts, and they rejected the Virginia Plan's proposal to give the judiciary explicit authority over Congress. They did, however, approve Article VI, which contains the supremacy clause (see chapter 3).

In *Federalist No. 78*, Alexander Hamilton first publicly endorsed the idea of judicial review, noting, "Whenever a particular statute contravenes the Constitution, it will be the duty of the judicial tribunals to adhere to the latter and disregard the former." Nonetheless, because the power of judicial review is not mentioned in the U.S. Constitution, the actual authority of the Supreme Court to review the constitutionality of acts of Congress was an unsettled question. During its first decade, the Supreme Court (or justices riding circuit) had reviewed acts of Congress, but it had not found any unconstitutional. But in ***Marbury v. Madison*** (1803),[10] John Marshall claimed this sweeping authority for the Court. *Marbury*'s long-term effect was to establish the rule that "it is emphatically the province and duty of the judicial department to say what the law is." Through judicial review, the Supreme Court most dramatically exerts its authority to determine what the Constitution means. And since *Marbury*, the Court has routinely exercised the power of judicial review to determine the constitutionality of acts of Congress, the executive branch, and the states.

***Marbury v. Madison* (1803):** Court first asserted the power of judicial review in finding that the congressional statute extending the Court's original jurisdiction was unconstitutional.

THE AMERICAN LEGAL SYSTEM

*T*he judicial system in the United States can best be described as a dual system consisting of the federal court system and the judicial systems of the fifty states. Cases may arise in either system. Both systems are basically three-tiered. At the bottom of the system are **trial courts,** where litigation begins. In the middle are appellate courts in the state systems and the courts of appeals in the federal system. At the top of each pyramid sits a high court. (Some states call these Supreme Courts; New York calls it the Court of Appeals; Oklahoma and Texas call the highest state court for criminal cases the Court of Criminal Appeals.) The federal courts of appeals and Supreme Court as well as states courts of appeals and supreme courts are **appellate courts** that, with few exceptions, review on appeal only cases that already have been decided in lower courts. These courts generally hear matters of both civil and criminal law (see Highlight 10.1: Criminal and Civil Law).

trial court: Court of original jurisdiction where cases begin.

appellate court: Courts that generally review only findings of law made by lower courts.

Jurisdiction

Before a state or federal court can hear a case, it must have **jurisdiction.** The term jurisdiction refers to the authority vested in a particular court to hear and decide the issues in any particular case. The jurisdiction of the federal courts is controlled by the U.S. Constitution and by statute. Jurisdiction is conferred based on issues, money involved in a dispute, or the type of offense. Procedurally, we speak of two types of jurisdiction: original and appellate. **Original jurisdiction** refers to a court's authority to hear disputes as a trial court. (The Menendez brothers' and O. J. Simpson's cases, for example, were heard in Los Angeles County, California, state trial courts of original ju-

jurisdiction: Authority vested in a particular court to hear and decide the issues in any particular case.

original jurisdiction: The jurisdiction of courts that hear a case first, usually in trial. Courts determine the facts of a case under their original jurisdiction.

TABLE 10.1

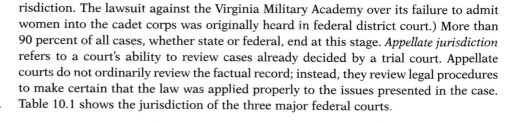

Federal Court Jurisdiction

	ORIGINAL JURISDICTION (APPROXIMATELY 6% OF CASES HEARD)	APPELLATE JURISDICTION (APPROXIMATELY 94% OF CASES HEARD)
The Supreme Court	Cases are heard in Supreme Court first when they involve: • Two or more states • The United States and a state • Foreign ambassadors and other diplomats • A state and a citizen of another state (if the action is begun by the state)	The Supreme Court can agree to hear cases first heard or decided on in lower courts or the state courts (generally the highest state court) involving appeals from: • U.S. Courts of Appeals • State highest courts (only in cases involving federal questions) • Court of Military Appeals
U.S. Courts of Appeals	none	Hears appeals of cases • from lower federal courts • U.S. regulatory commissions • legislative courts, including the U.S. Court of Federal Claims and the U.S. Court of Veterans' Appeals
U.S. District Courts	Cases are heard in U.S. District Courts when they involve: • the federal government • civil suits under federal law • civil suits between citizens of different states if the amount in issue is more than $50,000 • admiralty or maritime disputes • bankruptcy • other matters assigned to them by Congress	none

risdiction. The lawsuit against the Virginia Military Academy over its failure to admit women into the cadet corps was originally heard in federal district court.) More than 90 percent of all cases, whether state or federal, end at this stage. *Appellate jurisdiction* refers to a court's ability to review cases already decided by a trial court. Appellate courts do not ordinarily review the factual record; instead, they review legal procedures to make certain that the law was applied properly to the issues presented in the case. Table 10.1 shows the jurisdiction of the three major federal courts.

constitutional court: Federal courts specifically created by the U.S. Constitution or by Congress pursuant to its authority in Article III.

THE FEDERAL COURT SYSTEM

he federal district courts, circuit courts of appeals, and the Supreme Court are called **constitutional** (or Article III) **courts** because Article III of the Constitution either established them (as is the case with the

Highlight 10.1

Criminal and Civil Law

Criminal law is the body of law that regulates individual conduct and is enforced by the government.* Crimes are graded as felonies, misdemeanors, or offenses, according to their severity. Some acts—for example, murder, rape, and robbery—are considered crimes in all states. Although all states outlaw murder, their penal, or criminal, codes treat the crime quite differently; the penalty for murder differs considerably from state to state. Other crimes—such as sodomy and some forms of gambling, such as lotteries or bingo—are illegal only in some states.

Criminal law assumes that society itself is the victim of the illegal act; therefore, the government prosecutes, or brings an action, on behalf of an injured party (acting as a plaintiff) in criminal but not civil cases. Thus the murder charges against O. J. Simpson were styled as *The State of California v. Orenthal James Simpson.*

Civil law is the body of law that regulates the conduct and relationships between private individuals or companies. Because the actions at issue in civil law do not constitute a threat to society at large, people who believe they have been injured by another party must take action on their own to seek judicial relief. Civil cases, then, involve lawsuits filed to recover something of value, whether it is the right to vote, fair treatment, or monetary compensation for an item or service that cannot be recovered. Most cases seen on the television program *The People's Court* are civil cases.

Before a criminal or civil case gets to court, much has to happen. In fact, most legal disputes that arise in the United States never get to court. Individuals and companies involved in civil disputes routinely settle their disagreements out of court. Often these settlements are not reached until minutes before the case is to be tried. And many civil cases that go to trial are settled during the course of the trial—before the case can be handed over to the jury or submitted to a judge for a decision or determination of guilt.

Each civil or criminal case has a plaintiff, who brings charges against a defendant. Sometimes the government is the plaintiff. The government may bring criminal or civil charges on behalf of the citizens of the state or the national government against a person or corporation for violating the law, but it is always the government that brings a criminal case. Cases are known by the name of the plaintiff first and the defendant second. So in *Marbury v. Madison*, William Marbury was the plaintiff, suing the defendants, the U.S. government and James Madison as its secretary of state, for not delivering his judicial commission.

During trials, judges must often interpret the intent of laws enacted by Congress and state legislatures as they bear on the issues at hand. To do so, they read reports, testimony, and debates on the relevant legislation and study the results of other similar legal cases. They also rely on the presentations made by lawyers in their briefs and at trial. If it is a jury trial, the jury ultimately is the finder of fact, while the judge is the interpreter of the law.

*Jack C. Plano and Milton Greenberg, *The American Political Dictionary,* 6th ed. (New York: Holt, Rinehart and Winston, 1982), 252.

Supreme Court) or authorizes Congress to establish them. Judges who preside over these courts are nominated by the president (with the advice and consent of the Senate), and they serve lifetime terms, as long as they engage in "good behavior."

In addition to constitutional courts, **legislative courts** are set up by Congress, under its implied powers, generally for special purposes. The U.S. Territorial Courts (which hear federal cases in the territories) and the U.S. Court of Veterans' Appeals are examples of legislative courts, or what some call Article I courts. The judges who preside over these federal courts are appointed by the president (subject to Senate confirmation) and serve fixed, limited terms.

legislative courts: Courts established by Congress for specialized purposes, such as the Court of Military Appeals.

FIGURE 10.1

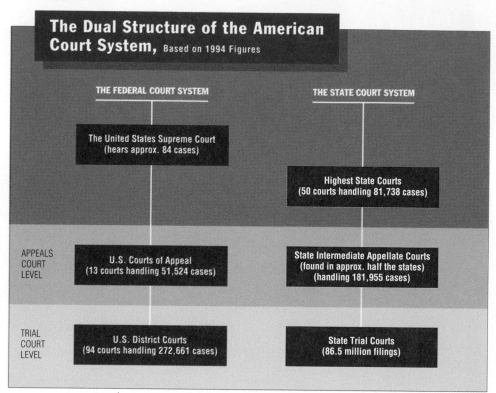

The Dual Structure of the American Court System, Based on 1994 Figures

THE FEDERAL COURT SYSTEM

THE STATE COURT SYSTEM

The United States Supreme Court
(hears approx. 84 cases)

Highest State Courts
(50 courts handling 81,738 cases)

APPEALS COURT LEVEL

U.S. Courts of Appeal
(13 courts handling 51,524 cases)

State Intermediate Appellate Courts
(found in approx. half the states)
(handling 181,955 cases)

TRIAL COURT LEVEL

U.S. District Courts
(94 courts handling 272,661 cases)

State Trial Courts
(86.5 million filings)

District Courts

Congress recognized the need for federal trial courts of original jurisdiction soon after ratification of the Constitution. The district courts were created by the Judiciary Act of 1789. By 1996 there were ninety-four federal district courts staffed by a total of 632 judges. (See Figure 10.1.) No district court cuts across state lines. Every state has at least one federal district court, and the largest states—California, New York, and Texas—each have four (see Figure 10.2).[11]

Federal district courts, where the bulk of the judicial work takes place in the federal system, have original jurisdiction over only specific types of cases, as indicated in Table 10.1. (Cases involving other kinds of issues generally must be heard in state courts.) Although the rules governing district court jurisdiction can be complex, cases heard in federal district courts by a single judge (with or without a jury) generally fall into one of three categories:

1. They involve the federal government as a party.

2. They present a federal question based on a claim under the U.S. Constitution, a treaty with another nation, or a federal statute. This is called federal question jurisdiction and it can involve criminal or civil law.

3. They involve civil suits in which citizens are from different states, and the amount of money at issue is more than $50,000.[12]

FIGURE 10.2

The Federal Court System

This map shows the locations of the U.S. Circuit Courts of Appeal and the boundaries of the federal district courts in states with more than one district.

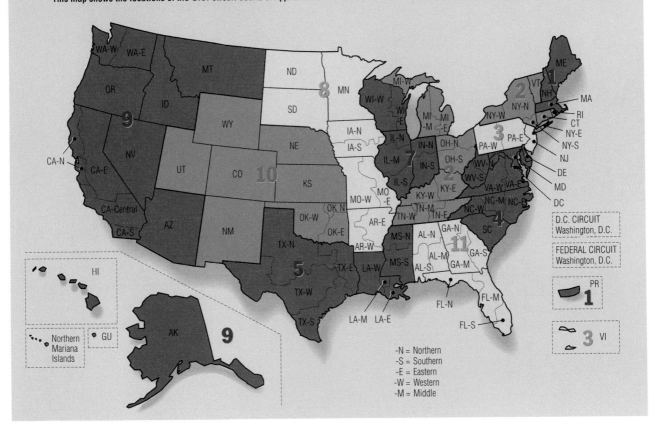

-N = Northern
-S = Southern
-E = Eastern
-W = Western
-M = Middle

Since 1789 the federal court system and the number of federal court judges who preside within it have grown tremendously. As illustrated in Figure 10.3, there were only thirteen federal judges and six Supreme Court justices nominated and confirmed in 1789. By 1994 that number had grown to 632. Although John Adams and the lame duck Federalist Congress created eighteen Courts of Appeals judgeships in 1801, those positions were quickly abolished by the Democratic-Republican Congress. It wasn't until 1869, then, that judges were selected specifically for the Court of Appeals. By 1994 there were 179 Court of Appeals judges and 632 district court judges.

Each federal judicial district has a U.S. attorney, who is nominated by the president and confirmed by the Senate. The U.S. attorney in each district is that district's chief law enforcement officer. The size of the staff and the number of assistant U.S. attorneys who work in each district depend on the amount of litigation in each district. U.S. attorneys, like district attorneys within the states, have a considerable amount of discretion as to whether they pursue criminal or civil investigations or file charges against individuals or corporations.

FIGURE 10.3

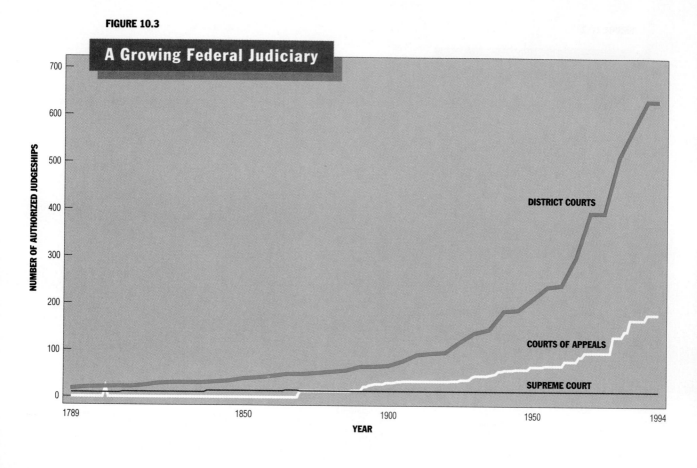

A Growing Federal Judiciary

NUMBER OF AUTHORIZED JUDGESHIPS

700

600

500

400

300

200

100

0

DISTRICT COURTS

COURTS OF APPEALS

SUPREME COURT

1789   1850   1900   1950   1994

YEAR

The Courts of Appeals

The losing party in a case heard and decided in a federal district court can appeal the decision to the appropriate court of appeals. The United States Courts of Appeals (known as the Circuit Courts of Appeals prior to 1948) are the intermediate appellate courts in the federal system and were established in 1789 to hear appeals from federal district courts. The present structure of the appeals courts, however, dates from the Judiciary Act of 1891. There are eleven numbered circuit courts (see Figure 10.2). A twelfth, the D.C. Court of Appeals, handles most appeals involving federal regulatory commissions and agencies, including, for example, the National Labor Relations Board and the Securities and Exchange Commission. The thirteenth federal appeals court is the U.S. Court of Appeals for the Federal Circuit, which deals with patents and contract and financial claims against the federal government.

In 1996 the courts of appeals were staffed by 179 judges, who were appointed by the president, subject to Senate confirmation. The number of judges within each circuit varies—depending on the workload and the complexity of the cases—and ranges from fewer than ten to nearly thirty. Each circuit is supervised by a chief judge, the most senior judge in terms of service below the age of seventy. In deciding cases, judges are divided into rotating three-judge panels, made up of the active judges within the circuit, visiting judges (primarily district judges from the same circuit), and retired judges. In rare cases, all the judges in a circuit may choose to sit together (*en banc*) to decide a case by majority vote.

The courts of appeals have no original jurisdiction. Rather, Congress has granted these courts appellate jurisdiction over two general categories of cases: appeals from criminal and civil cases from the district courts, and appeals from administrative agencies. Criminal and civil case appeals constitute about 90 percent of the workload of the courts of appeals. In contrast, appeals from administrative agencies make up only about 10 percent of their workload. And because so many agencies are located in Washington, D.C., the D.C. Circuit Court of Appeals hears an inordinate number of such cases. The D.C. Circuit Court of Appeals, then, is considered the second most important court in the nation because its decisions govern the regulatory agencies.

Once a decision is made by a federal court of appeals, a litigant no longer has an automatic right to an appeal. The losing party may submit a petition to the U.S. Supreme Court to hear the case, but the Court grants few of these requests, as illustrated in Figure 10.4. The courts of appeals, then, are the courts of last resort for almost all federal litigation. Keep in mind, however, that most cases, if they actually go to trial, go no further than the district court level.

In general, courts of appeals try to correct errors of law and procedure that have occurred in lower courts or administrative agencies. Courts of appeals hear no new testimony; instead, lawyers submit written arguments, in what is called a **brief** (also submitted in trial courts), and then appear to orally present and argue the case to the court.

brief: A document containing the collected legal written arguments in a case filed with a court by a party prior to a hearing or trial.

FIGURE 10.4

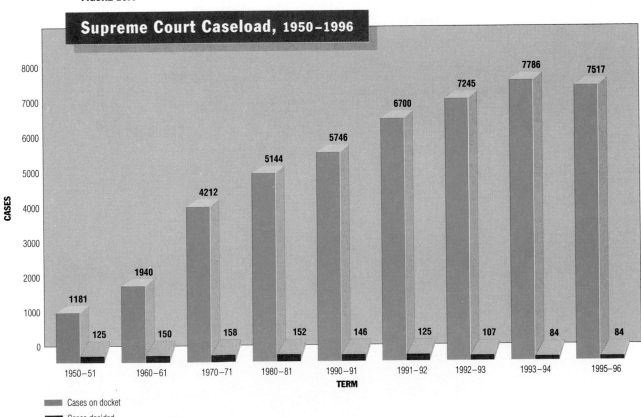

Supreme Court Caseload, 1950–1996

CASES

- Cases on docket
- Cases decided

SOURCE: Administrative Office of the Courts; Supreme Court Public Information Office.

precedent: Prior judicial decision that serves as a rule for settling subsequent cases of a similar nature.

stare decisis: In court rulings, a reliance on past decisions or precedents to formulate decisions in new cases.

Although decisions of any court of appeals are binding on only the district courts within the geographic confines of the circuit, decisions of the U.S. Supreme Court are binding throughout the nation and establish national **precedents.** This reliance on past decisions or precedents to formulate decisions in new cases is called *stare decisis* (a Latin phrase meaning "let the decision stand"). The principle of *stare decisis* allows for continuity and predictability in our judicial system. Although *stare decisis* can be helpful in predicting decisions, at times judges carve out new ground and ignore, decline to follow, or even overrule precedents in order to reach a different conclusion in a case involving similar circumstances. In one sense, that is why there is so much litigation in America today. Parties know that one cannot always predict the outcome of a case; if such prediction were possible, there would be little reason to go to court.

The Supreme Court

The U.S. Supreme Court is often at the center of the storm of highly controversial issues that have yet to be resolved successfully in the political process. As the court of last resort at the top of the judicial pyramid, it reviews cases from the U.S. courts of appeals and state supreme courts and acts as the final interpreter of the U.S. Constitution. It not only decides many major cases with tremendous policy significance each year, but it also ensures uniformity in the interpretation of national laws and the Constitution, resolves conflicts among the states, and maintains the supremacy of national law in the federal system.

TABLE 10.2

Chief Justices of the Supreme Court

CHIEF JUSTICE	NOMINATING PRESIDENT	YEARS OF SERVICE
John Jay	Washington	1789–1795
John Rutledge*	Washington	1795
Oliver Ellsworth	Washington	1796–1800
John Marshall	Adams	1801–1835
Roger B. Taney	Jackson	1836–1864
Salmon P. Chase	Lincoln	1864–1873
Morrison R. Waite	Grant	1874–1888
Melville W. White	Cleveland	1888–1910
Edward D. White	Taft	1910–1921
William Howard Taft	Harding	1921–1930
Charles Evans Hughes	Hoover	1930–1941
Harlan Fiske Stone	F. Roosevelt	1941–1946
Fred M. Vinson	Truman	1946–1953
Earl Warren	Eisenhower	1953–1969
Warren E. Burger	Nixon	1969–1986
William H. Rehnquist	Reagan	1986–present

*Not confirmed by the Senate

Highlight 10.2

Law Clerks

As early as 1850, the justices of the Supreme Court had beseeched Congress to approve the hiring of an "investigating clerk" to assist each justice, particularly in copying opinions. Congress denied the request, so when Justice Horace Gray hired the first law clerk in 1882, he paid the clerk himself. Justice Gray's clerk was a top graduate of Harvard Law School whose duties included cutting Justice Gray's hair and running personal errands. Finally, in 1886, Congress authorized each justice to hire a "stenographer clerk" for $1,600 a year.

Today, clerks generally serve for periods of one to two years. In the past, however, some justices employed their clerks for longer periods. Pierce Butler's clerk, for example, served sixteen years, from 1923 to 1939.

Over time, the number of clerks employed by the justices has increased. Through the 1946 to 1969 terms, most justices employed two clerks. By 1970 most had three; and by 1980 all but three had four. In 1996 there were thirty-four clerks serving the nine justices, whereas twenty years ago there were about half as many. This growth in clerks has had many interesting ramifications for the Court. As noted by Richard A. Posner, "between 1969 and 1972—the period during which the justices each became entitled to a third law clerk— . . . the number of opinions increased by about 50 percent and the number of words tripled."* After the justices were authorized to hire a fourth clerk in 1980, a substantial growth in the number of citations and footnotes in each case occurred again.** And until recently, the number of cases decided annually increased as more

help was available to the justices.

The justices have complete discretion over whom they hire and the nature and amount of the work they assign. Clerks are typically selected from candidates at the top of the graduating classes of prestigious law schools. They perform a variety of tasks, ranging from searching every page of *United States Reports* for some particular information to playing tennis or taking walks with the justices. Clerks spend most of their time researching material relevant to particular cases, reading and summarizing cases, and helping justices write opinions. Just how much help they provide in the writing of opinions is not known. Although it is occasionally alleged that a particular clerk wrote a particular opinion delivered by a justice, no such allegation has ever been proven. The relationship between clerks and the justices for whom they work is close and con-

fidential, and many aspects of the relationship are kept secret. Clerks may sometimes talk among themselves about the views and personalities of their justices, but rarely has a clerk leaked such information to the press.

Some former clerks try to exploit their connection to their justice, but at times this tactic can backfire. When North Dakota Attorney General Nicholas Spaeth, a former clerk to Justice Byron White, appeared before the Court, he did so sporting a necktie covered with buffaloes that White had given him years earlier. He jokingly referred to the tie, saying he had worn it because he particularly needed the vote of White, the only justice in the majority of an earlier, similar case decided by the Court. White looked annoyed, the other justices did not laugh, and Justice Kennedy's later questioning revealed his obvious displeasure with Spaeth's theatrics.†

*Richard A. Posner, *The Federal Courts: Crisis and Reform* (Cambridge, MA: Harvard University Press, 1985), 114.
**Ibid., 114.
†Tony Mauro, "The Highs and Lows of the 1992 Court," *Legal Times* (December 28, 1992): 12.
Source: Karen O'Connor and John R. Hermann, "The Clerk Connection: A History and Analysis of Clerk Participation Before the U.S. Supreme Court," paper delivered at the 1993 annual meeting of the Midwest Political Science Association.

Since 1869 the U.S. Supreme Court has consisted of eight associate justices and one chief justice, who is nominated by the president specifically for that position. There is no special significance about the number nine, and the Constitution is silent about the size of the Court. Between 1789 and 1869, Congress periodically altered the size of the Court. The lowest number of justices on the Court was six; the most, ten. Since 1869, the number has remained at nine. Through 1996, only 108 justices had served on the Court, and there had been fifteen chief justices (see Table 10.2).

The chief justice presides over public sessions of the Court, conducts the Court's conferences, and assigns the writing of opinions (if he is in the majority; otherwise, the most senior justice in the majority makes the assignment). By custom, he administers the oath of office to the president and the vice president on Inauguration Day (any federal judge can administer the oath, as has happened when presidents have died in office).

Unlike the president or even members of Congress, the Supreme Court operates with very few support staff. Along with the clerks, there are only 300 staff members at the Supreme Court.

HOW FEDERAL COURT JUDGES ARE SELECTED

Although specific, detailed provisions in Articles I and II specify the qualifications for president, senator, and member of the House of Representatives, the Constitution is curiously silent on the qualifications for federal judges. This may have been because of an assumption that all federal judges would be lawyers, but to make such a requirement explicit might have marked the judicial branch as too elite for the tastes of common men and women. Also, it would have been impractical to require formal legal training, given that there were so few law schools in the nation, and the fact that most lawyers became licensed after clerking or apprenticing with another attorney.[13]

The selection of federal judges is often a very political process with important political ramifications because judges are nominated by the president and must be confirmed by the U.S. Senate. During the Reagan–Bush years, for example, 553 basically conservative Republican judges were appointed to the lower federal bench (see Figure 10.5). The cumulative impact of this conservative block of judges led many liberal groups to abandon their efforts to expand rights through the federal courts (see Highlight 5.1: The American Civil Liberties Union). The politicization of the bench also has made the selection and confirmation process a hotbed of interest group activity as groups lobby for or against particular nominees based on their politics and apparent ideological bent.

Typically, federal district court judges have held other political offices, such as those of state court judge or prosecutor, as illustrated in Table 10.3. Most have been involved in politics, which is what usually brings them into consideration for a position on the federal bench. Griffin Bell, a former federal circuit court judge, once remarked, "For me, becoming a federal judge wasn't very difficult. I managed John F. Kennedy's presidential campaign in Georgia."[14]

Presidents generally defer selection of district court judges to senators of their own party who represent the state in which a vacancy occurs on the federal bench, a practice called **senatorial courtesy**. By tradition, the Senate Judiciary Committee will not confirm a presidential nominee who has not been agreed to by the senator(s) of the nominee's home state. This tradition is an important source of political patronage for senators.

senatorial courtesy: A practice by which senators can have near veto power over appointments to the federal judiciary if the opening is in a district in their state.

Senatorial courtesy does not operate to the same degree in the selection of the more prestigious courts of appeals judgeships, largely because the jurisdiction of each circuit includes at least three states. When vacancies on the courts of appeals occur, presidents frequently consult senators of the various states in the circuit. Ultimately, however, the Justice Department plays the key role in the selection process.

FIGURE 10.5

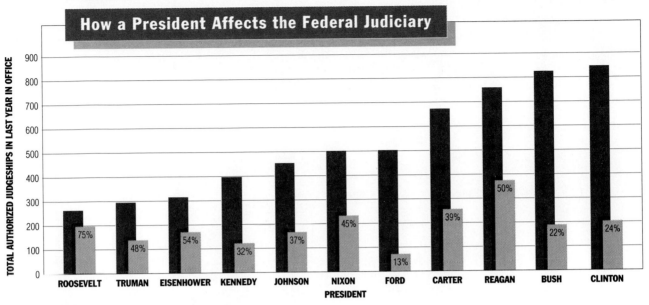

How a President Affects the Federal Judiciary

Sitting judges not appointed by president by end of term in office

Sitting judges appointed by president by end of term in office

PRESIDENT	APPOINTED TO SUPREME COURT	APPOINTED TO COURT OF APPEALS [a]	APPOINTED TO DISTRICT COURTS [b]	TOTAL APPOINTED	TOTAL NUMBER OF JUDGESHIPS [c]	PERCENTAGE OF JUDGESHIPS FILLED BY PRESIDENT
Roosevelt (1933–45)	9	52	136	197	262	75%
Truman (1945–53)	4	26	115	141	292	48
Eisenhower (1953–61)	5	45	125	175	322	54
Kennedy (1961–63)	2	21	103	126	395	32
Johnson (1963–69)	2	40	122	164	449	37
Nixon (1969–74)	4	45	179	228	504	45
Ford (1974–77)	1	12	52	65	504	13
Carter (1977–81)	0	56	202	258	657	39
Reagan (1981–89)	3	78	290	368	740	50
Bush (1989–93)	2	37	148	185	825	22
Clinton [d] (1993–94)	2	13	71	100	846	24

(a) Does not include the appeals court for the Federal Circuit
(b) Includes district courts in the territories
(c) Total judgeships authorized in president's last year in office
(d) Data for Clinton is through August 1996.

SOURCE: "Imprints on the Bench," *CQ Weekly Report* (January 19, 1991): 173. Reprinted by permission. Data on Clinton and Bush provided by the Senate Judiciary Committee.

TABLE 10.3

Characteristics of Appointees to the Lower Federal Courts from Carter to Clinton

	CARTER APPOINTEES	REAGAN APPOINTEES	BUSH APPOINTEES	CLINTON NOMINEES*
Occupation (percent)				
Politics/gov't	4.7%	11.4%	10.8%	11.2%
Judiciary	45.0	41.0	45.4	43.9
Lawyer	47.2	46.8	42.7	44.0
Other	0.8	0.8	0.1	0.9
Experience (percent)				
Judicial	54.3%	49.5%	49.7%	48.6%
Prosecutorial	37.2	40.8	37.3	35.5
Neither	30.2	29.6	31.9	32.7
Political Affiliation (percent)				
Democrat	90.3%	3.8%	5.4%	88.8%
Republican	5.0	94.0	88.6	2.8
Independent	4.7	1.9	5.9	7.5
ABA Rating				
Extremely/well qualified	56.2%	55.2%	58.9%	60.7%
Qualified	42.6	44.8	41.1	36.4
Not Qualified	1.2	—	—	2.8
Race/ethnicity (percent)				
White	78.7%	93.5%	89.2%	64.5%
Black	14.3	1.9	6.5	25.2
Asian-American	0.8	0.5	—	0.9
Hispanic	6.2	4.5	4.3	8.4
Native American	—	—	—	0.9
Gender				
Female	15.5%	7.6%	19.5%	31.8%
Male	84.5	92.4	80.5	68.2
White male (percent)	66.3	86.4	72.4	39.2
Net Worth (percent)				
Under $200,000	33.3%**	17.1%	9.2%	15.9%
200,000-499,999	38.4**	36.4	30.8	27.1
500,000-999,999	17.7**	24.2	25.4	28.0
1,000,000+	5.1**	22.0	34.6	29.0
Total number of appointees	258	368	185	125
Average age at nomination (years)	50.1	49.0	48.2	48.7

*Appointees through 1994.

**These figures are for appointees confirmed by the 96th Congress. Professor Elliot Slotnick of Ohio State University provided the net worth figures for all but six Carter district court appointees, for whom no data were available.

Source: Sheldon Goldman and Matthew D. Saranson, "Clinton's Nontraditional Judges: Creating a More Representative Bench," *Judicature* 77 (September–October 1994): 72; and Sheldon Goldman, "Judicial Selection under Clinton: A Midterm Examination," *Judicature* 78 (May–June 1995): 281. Reprinted by permission.

[1]Clinton data, except for total, based only on district court appointees.

Since the 1970s, most presidents have pledged (with varying degrees of success) to do their best to appoint more African Americans, women, and other groups traditionally underrepresented on the federal bench (see Table 10.3). Each president, moreover, has created a special group to help him identify and nominate candidates for the bench. Jimmy Carter, for example, created judicial nominating commissions,[15] but these commissions were abandoned by President Reagan, whose Justice Department (and increasingly, the White House counsel) played a key role in selecting court of appeals judges. George Bush's administration followed in this tradition as it searched for ideological conservatives who could further his administrations' political agendas through rulings from the bench.

While getting off to a slow start in filling the 100 vacancies left by President Bush on the federal courts (from January to June 1993, no vacancies were filled), President Clinton assigned the initial task of judicial selection to the Office of Policy Development in the Justice Department. Until the head of that office, Eleanor D. Acheson, was confirmed by the Senate, judicial selection was centered in the Office of the White House Counsel, called Judicial Appointments Central by some staffers. Today judicial appointments are a shared process between the Justice Department and the White House. At the Justice Department as many as fifteen people work full time on judicial selection, gathering and analyzing candidate records including judicial decisions. Interviews with prospective candidates are also conducted at the Justice Department. Although, "on occasion, discussion with candidates touch(es) upon issues such as abortion and the death penalty . . . care (is) taken not to discuss with candidates how they w(ill) rule in specific cases."[16] By June 1996, using this process, the Clinton administration was able to fill 24 percent of the total 846 federal judgeships.[17] All but three of his nominees were supported by then Senate Majority Leader Bob Dole. Studies by political scientists reveal that Clinton appointees have been more moderate than earlier Republican or Democratic appointees.[18]

Appointments to the U.S. Supreme Court

The Constitution is silent on the qualifications for appointment to the Supreme Court (as well as to other constitutional courts), although Justice Oliver Wendell Holmes once remarked that a justice should be a "combination of Justinian, Jesus Christ and John Marshall."[19]

Like other federal court judges, the justices of the Supreme Court are nominated by the president and must be confirmed by the Senate. Few appointments, however, have been subject to the kind of lobbying that occurred when Ruth Bader Ginsburg was nominated to the U.S. Supreme Court in 1993 (see Politics Now: Lobbying for a Top Spot).

Historically, because of the special place the Supreme Court enjoys in our constitutional system, its nominees have encountered more opposition than district or court of appeals judges. As the role of the Court has increased over time, so too has the amount of attention given to nominees. And with this increased attention has come greater opposition, especially to nominees with controversial views.

Nomination Criteria

Justice Sandra Day O'Connor once remarked that "You have to be lucky" to be appointed to the Court.[20] Although luck is certainly important, over the years nominations to the bench have been made for a variety of reasons. Depending on the timing of a vacancy, a president may or may not have a list of possible candidates or even a specific individual in mind. Until recently, presidents often have looked within their circle of friends or their administration to fill a vacancy. Nevertheless, whether the nominee is a friend or someone known to the president only by reputation, at least six criteria are especially important: competence, ideology or policy preferences, rewards, pursuit of political support, religion, and race and gender.

Competence.   Most prospective nominees are expected to have had at least some judicial or governmental experience. John Jay, the first chief justice, was one of the authors of *The Federalist Papers* and was active in New York politics. Most have had some prior judicial experience. In 1996 eight sitting Supreme Court justices had prior judicial experience (see Table 10.4).

Ideological or Policy Preferences.   Most presidents seek to appoint to the Court individuals who share their policy preferences, and almost all have political goals in mind when they appoint a justice. Presidents Franklin D. Roosevelt, Richard M. Nixon, and Ronald Reagan were very successful in molding the Court to their own political beliefs. Roosevelt was quickly able to appoint eight justices from 1937 to his death in 1945, solidifying support for his liberal New Deal programs. In contrast, Nixon and Reagan publicly proclaimed that they would nominate only conservatives who favored a **strict constructionist** approach to constitutional decision making—that is, an approach emphasizing the initial intentions of the Framers.

strict constructionist: An approach to constitutional interpretation that emphasizes the Framers' initial intentions.

Rewards.   Historically, although not so often more recently, many of those appointed to the Supreme Court have been personal friends of presidents. Abraham Lin-

TABLE 10.4

The Supreme Court, 1996

NAME	YEAR OF BIRTH	YEAR OF APPOINTMENT	POLITICAL PARTY	LAW SCHOOL	APPOINTING PRESIDENT	RELIGION	PRIOR JUDICIAL EXPERIENCE	PRIOR GOVERNMENT EXPERIENCE
William H. Rehnquist	1924	1971 1986*	R	Stanford	Nixon	Lutheran	Associate Justice U.S. Supreme Court	Assistant U.S. Attorney General
John Paul Stevens	1920	1975	R	Chicago	Ford	Non-denominational Protestant	U.S. Court of Appeals	—
Sandra Day O'Connor	1930	1981	R	Stanford	Reagan	Episcopalian	Arizona Court of Appeals	State Legislator
Antonin Scalia	1936	1986	R	Harvard	Reagan	Catholic	U.S. Court of Appeals	—
Anthony Kennedy	1936	1988	R	Harvard	Reagan	Catholic	U.S. Court of Appeals	—
David Souter	1939	1990	R	Harvard	Bush	Episcopalian	U.S. Court of Appeals	New Hampshire Assistant Attorney General
Clarence Thomas	1948	1991	R	Yale	Bush	Catholic	U.S. Court of Appeals	Chair, Equal Employment Opportunity Commission
Ruth Bader Ginsburg	1933	1993	D	Columbia	Clinton	Jewish	U.S. Court of Appeals	—
Stephen Breyer	1938	1994	D	Harvard	Clinton	Jewish	U.S. Court of Appeals	Chief Counsel, Senate Judiciary Committee

*Promoted to Chief Justice by Reagan in 1986.

coln, for example, appointed one of his key political advisers to the Court. More recently, Lyndon B. Johnson appointed his longtime friend Abe Fortas to the bench. In addition, most presidents select justices of their own party affiliation. Chief Justice Rehnquist was long active in Arizona Republican Party politics, as was Justice O'Connor before her appointment to the bench; both were appointed by Republican presidents. Party activism can also be used by presidents as an indication of a nominee's commitment to certain ideological principles.

Pursuit of Political Support.   During Ronald Reagan's successful campaign for the presidency in 1980, some of his advisers feared that the "gender gap" would hurt him. Polls repeatedly showed that he was far less popular with female voters than with men. To gain support from women, Reagan announced during his campaign that should he win, he would appoint a woman to fill the first vacancy on the Court. When Justice Potter Stewart, a moderate, announced his early retirement from the bench, President Reagan nominated Sandra Day O'Connor of the Arizona State Court of Appeals to fill the vacancy. It probably did not hurt President Clinton that his first appointment (Ruth Bader Ginsburg) was a woman and Jewish (at a time when no Jews served on the Court).

Religion.   Ironically, religion, which historically has been an important issue, was hardly mentioned during the most recent Supreme Court vacancies. Some, however, hailed Clinton's appointment of Ginsburg, noting that the traditionally "Jewish" seat on the Court had been vacant for over two decades.

Through 1996, of the 108 justices who have served on the Court, almost all have been members of traditional Protestant faiths.[21] Only nine have been Catholic and only seven have been Jewish.[22] Twice during the Rehnquist Court, more Catholics—Brennan, Scalia, and Kennedy, and then Scalia, Kennedy, and Thomas—served on the Court at one time than at any other period in history. Today, however, it is clear that religion cannot be taken as a sign of a justice's conservative or liberal ideology: When William Brennan was on the Court, he and fellow Catholic Antonin Scalia were at ideological extremes.

Race and Gender.   Only two African Americans and two women have served on the Court. Race was undoubtedly a critical issue in the appointment of Clarence Thomas to replace Thurgood Marshall, the first African-American justice. But President Bush refused to acknowledge his wish to retain a "black seat" on the Court. Instead, he announced that he was "picking the best man for the job on the merits," a claim that was met with considerable skepticism by many observers.

In contrast, O'Connor was pointedly picked because of her gender. Ginsburg's appointment was more matter-of-fact, and her selection surprised many because the Clinton administration appeared to be considering seriously several men for the appointment first (see Politics Now: Lobbying for a Top Spot).

The Supreme Court Confirmation Process

The Constitution gives the Senate the authority to approve all nominees to the federal bench. Before 1900 about one-fourth of all presidential nominees to the Supreme Court were rejected by the Senate. In 1844, for example, President John Tyler sent six nominations to the Senate, and all but one were defeated. In 1866 Andrew Johnson nominated his brilliant attorney general, Henry Stanberry, but the Senate's hostility to Johnson led it to *abolish* the seat to prevent Johnson's filling it. Ordinarily, nominations are referred to the Senate Committee on the Judiciary. As detailed later, this commit-

Politics Now

Lobbying for a Top Spot

The Supreme Court is not now, nor has it ever been, above politics. Politics permeates the selection process of federal court judges, including those on the Supreme Court. And, on occasion, some individuals or their friends have actively lobbied for the spot on the bench.

In their classic insider's view on the Supreme Court, *The Brethren*, Bob Woodward and Scott Armstrong wrote critically of court of appeals Judge Warren Burger's somewhat clumsy efforts to lobby Richard M. Nixon for the position of chief justice.* Burger's lobbying for the position was portrayed as unseemly.

Once Justice Byron White announced that he would retire from the high court in March 1993, the Clinton administration went to work on possible nominees. A long list of more than fifty names was first put together. Later that list was culled down to fewer than twenty serious nominees. As the time since White's announcement dragged on, however, the names

Lobbying on Ginsburg's behalf paid off when she became the second woman on the nation's highest court, joining Sandra Day O'Connor. (Photo courtesy: Ken Heinen)

of Secretary of Interior Bruce Babbit and court of appeals judge Stephen Breyer seemed to emerge as front runners.

On a trip to New York with Senator Daniel Patrick Moynihan (D–N.Y.), the President asked Moynihan who was his top nominee. "There's only one name: Ruth Bader Ginsburg,"** responded the senator. Yet Ginsburg's name never seemed to reach the top.

To draw more attention to his wife's qualifications, sixteen years after Burger lobbied for a seat on the Court, Martin Ginsburg, husband of court of appeals judge Ruth Bader Ginsburg, unabashedly orchestrated a letter-writing campaign on behalf of his wife's nomination to the Supreme

Court. Martin Ginsburg, a prominent tax attorney and Georgetown University law professor, contacted his wife's former students, the presidents of Stanford and Columbia universities, academics, legal scholars, and even Texas Governor Ann W. Richards, urging them to call or write the White House on behalf of his wife's nomination. Said Ginsburg of his campaign on his wife's behalf after her nomination, "If there was something I could have done to be helpful, I would have done it, because I think my wife is super, and the president couldn't have made a better appointment than the one he just made."***

Unconventional? Yes. Effective? Maybe. Appropriate? You decide.

*Bob Woodward and Scott Armstrong, *The Brethren* (New York: Simon and Schuster, 1979).
**Richard L. Berke, "The Supreme Court: An Overview," *The New York Times* (June 15, 1993): A1.
***Eleanor Randolph, "Ginsburg's Spouse Says He Arranged Letter Campaign," *The Washington Post* (June 17, 1993): A17.

tee investigates the nominees, holds hearings, and votes on its recommendation for Senate action. The full Senate then deliberates on the nominee before voting. A simple majority vote is required for confirmation.

Investigation.   As a president begins to narrow his list of possible nominees to the Supreme Court, those names are sent to the Federal Bureau of Investigation before a nomination is formally made. At the same time, the president also forwards names of prospective nominees to the American Bar Association (ABA), the politically powerful organization that represents the interests of the legal profession. After its own investigation, the ABA rates each nominee, based on his or her qualifications, as Highly Qualified (now called "Well-Qualified"), Qualified, or Not Qualified. (The same system is used for lower federal court nominees; over the years, however, the exact labels have varied.)

David Souter, Bush's first nominee to the Court, received a unanimous rating of Highly Qualified from the ABA, as did both of Clinton's nominees, Ruth Bader Ginsburg and Stephen Breyer. In contrast, another Bush nominee, Clarence Thomas, was given only a Qualified rating (well before the charges of sexual harassment became public), with two members voting Not Qualified. Of the twenty-two previous successful nominees rated by the ABA, he was the first to receive less than at least a unanimous Qualified rating.

The key role of the ABA, a voice for the traditional, established bar with 370,000 members, is not without its critics. Some argue that a professional organization should not carry so much clout in the process. Republican presidential candidate Bob Dole went so far as to pledge, if elected, he would remove the ABA from the selection process, viewing it as "another blatantly partisan liberal advocacy group."[23] The ABA counters that it is "completely nonpartisan" and that its fifteen-person selection committee members are chosen for their "credibility and contacts in their communities, so lawyers and judges will speak frankly to them" about a prospective nominee's fitness for the federal bench.[24] Other supporters of the current system argue that it is an independent check on the quality of judicial appointees who, once confirmed, serve for life.[25]

Anita Hill testifies before the then all-male Senate Judiciary Committee as it considered the appointment of Clarence Thomas to the Supreme Court. (Photo courtesy: Rick Wilking/Reuters-The Bettmann Archive)

After a formal nomination is made and sent to the Senate, the Senate Judiciary Committee also begins its own investigation. (The same process is used for nominees to the lower federal courts, although such investigations generally are not nearly as extensive as for Supreme Court nominees.) To begin its task, the Senate Judiciary Committee asks each nominee to complete a lengthy questionnaire detailing previous work (dating as far back as high school summer jobs), judicial opinions written, judicial philosophy, speeches, and even all interviews ever given to members of the press. Committee staffers also contact potential witnesses who might offer testimony concerning the nominee's fitness for office.

Lobbying by Interest Groups.   While the ABA is the only organization that is asked formally to rate nominees, other groups are also keenly interested in the nomination process. Until recently, interest groups played a minor and backstage role in most appointments to the Supreme Court. Although interest groups generally have not lobbied *on behalf* of any one individual, in 1981 women's rights groups successfully urged President Reagan to honor his campaign commitment to appoint a woman to the high court.

It is more common for interest groups to lobby *against* a prospective nominee. Even this, however, is a relatively recent phenomenon. In 1987 the nomination of Robert H. Bork to the Supreme Court produced an unprecedented amount of interest group lobbying on both sides of the nomination. The Democratic-controlled Judiciary Committee delayed the hearings, thus allowing liberal interest groups time to mobilize the most extensive radio, television, and print media campaign ever launched against a nominee to the U.S. Supreme Court. This opposition was in spite of the fact that Bork sat with distinction on the D.C. Court of Appeals, and was a former U.S. solicitor general, a top-ranked law school graduate, and a Yale Law School professor. (His actions as solicitor general, especially his firing of the Watergate special prosecutor, made him a special target for traditional liberals.)

The scrutiny by the public and press of President Reagan's Supreme Court nominee Robert H. Bork set a new standard of inquiry into the values—both political and personal—of future nominees. Bork's nomination was rejected by the Senate in 1987. (Photo courtesy: Frank Fournier/Contact Press Images)

The Senate Committee Hearings and Senate Vote.   As the uneventful 1994 hearings of Stephen Breyer attest (he was confirmed by a Senate vote of ninety-seven to three), not all nominees inspire the kind of intense reaction that kept Bork from the Court and, more recently, almost blocked the confirmation of Clarence Thomas. Until 1929 all but one Senate Judiciary Committee hearing on a Supreme Court nominee was conducted in executive session—that is, closed to the public. The 1916 hearings on Louis Brandeis, the first Jewish justice, were conducted in public and lasted nineteen days, although Brandeis himself was never called to testify. In 1939 Felix Frankfurter became the first nominee to testify in any detail before the committee. Subsequent revelations about Brandeis's secret financial payments to Frankfurter to allow him to handle cases of social interest to Brandeis (while Brandeis was on the Court and couldn't handle them himself) raise questions about the fitness of both Frankfurter and Brandeis for the bench. Still, no information about Frankfurter's legal arrangements with Brandeis was unearthed during the committee's investigations or Frankfurter's testimony.[26]

Until recently, modern nomination hearings were no more thorough in terms of the attention given to nominees' backgrounds. In 1969, for example, Chief Justice Warren E. Burger was confirmed by the Senate on a vote of ninety-four to three, just nineteen days after he was nominated!

Since the 1980s it has become standard for senators to ask the nominees probing questions; but most nominees (with the notable exception of Robert H. Bork) have declined to answer most of them on the grounds that these issues might ultimately come before the Court. After hearings are concluded, the Senate Judiciary Committee usually makes a recommendation to the full Senate. Any rejections of presidential nominees to the Supreme Court generally occur only after the Senate Judiciary Committee has recommended against a nominee's appointment. Few recent confirmations have been close; prior to Clarence Thomas's fifty-two to forty-eight vote in 1991, Rehnquist's nomination in 1971 as associate justice (sixty-eight to twenty-six) and in 1986 as chief justice (sixty-nine to thirty-three) were the closest in recent history.

THE SUPREME COURT TODAY

*G*iven the judicial system's vast size and substantial power (although often indirect power) over so many aspects of our lives, it is surprising that so many Americans know next to nothing about the judicial system in general and the Supreme Court in particular. Even today, at a time when all other institutions of government and government officials receive unprecedented media attention, the work of the Court proceeds in relative anonymity. Few Americans can correctly name the current chief justice, let alone the other eight justices. A *Washington Post* poll found that while more than 50 percent of Americans knew of Judge Joseph Wapner of the TV show *The People's Court*, fewer than 10 percent knew of Chief Justice Rehnquist.[27] Another poll conducted in 1990 for the Court's 200th anniversary revealed that only 23 percent of Americans queried knew how many justices sit on the Court, and nearly two-thirds could not name a single member of the Court.[28] To fill in any gaps in your knowledge of the current Supreme Court, see Table 10.4.

Much of this ignorance can be blamed on the American public's lack of interest. But the Court itself has taken great pains to insure its privacy and sense of decorum. Its rites and rituals contribute to the Court's mystique and encourage a "cult of the robe."[29] Consider, for example, the way Supreme Court proceedings are conducted. Oral arguments are not televised, and deliberations concerning the outcome of cases are conducted in utmost secrecy. In contrast, C-SPAN brings us daily coverage of various congressional hearings and floor debate on bills and important national issues, and Court TV (and sometimes other networks) provides gavel-to-gavel coverage of many important state court trials. The Supreme Court, however, remains adamant in its refusal to televise its proceedings—including public oral arguments.

The justices of the Court gather before the 1994-1995 term, on the occasion of the investiture of its newest member, Justice Stephen Breyer, the sixth new justice since 1986. Left to right are Justices Clarence Thomas, Antonin Scalia, Sandra Day O'Connor, Anthony Kennedy, David Souter, Stephen Breyer, John Paul Stevens, Chief Justice William H. Rehnquist, and Ruth Bader Ginsburg. (Photo courtesy: Ken Heinen/AP Wide World Photos)

Deciding to Hear a Case

Although as many as 8,000 cases a year have been filed at the Supreme Court, this was not always the case. From 1790 to 1801, the Court heard only eighty-seven cases under its appellate jurisdiction.[30] In the Court's early years, the bulk of the justices' workload involved their circuit-riding duties. From 1862 to 1866, only 240 cases were decided. Creation of the courts of appeals in 1891 resulted in an immediate reduction in Supreme Court filings—from 600 in 1890 to 275 in 1892.[31] As recently as the 1940s, fewer than 1,000 cases were filed annually. Since that time, filings have increased at a dramatic rate until the 1995–1996 term, as revealed earlier in Figure 10.4, although that does not mean the Court is actually deciding more cases. In fact, of the 7,517 petitions it received during the 1995–1996 term, it handed down opinions in only eighty-four. The process by which cases get to the Supreme Court is outlined in Figure 10.6.

Just as it is up to the justices to "say what the law is," they can also exercise a significant role in policy making and politics by opting *not* to hear a case. The content of the Court's docket is, of course, every bit as significant as its size. Prior to the 1930s, the Court generally heard cases of interest only to the immediate parties. During the 1930s, however, cases requiring the interpretation of constitutional law began to take a grow-

FIGURE 10.6

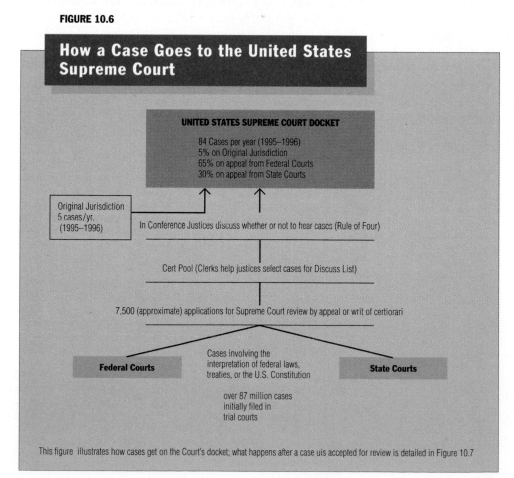

How a Case Goes to the United States Supreme Court

UNITED STATES SUPREME COURT DOCKET

84 Cases per year (1995–1996)
5% on Original Jurisdiction
65% on appeal from Federal Courts
30% on appeal from State Courts

Original Jurisdiction
5 cases/yr.
(1995–1996)

In Conference Justices discuss whether or not to hear cases (Rule of Four)

Cert Pool (Clerks help justices select cases for Discuss List)

7,500 (approximate) applications for Supreme Court review by appeal or writ of certiorari

Federal Courts

Cases involving the interpretation of federal laws, treaties, or the U.S. Constitution

State Courts

over 87 million cases initially filed in trial courts

This figure illustrates how cases get on the Court's docket; what happens after a case uis accepted for review is detailed in Figure 10.7

ing portion of its workload, leading the Court to take a more important role in the policy-making process. At that time only 5 percent of the Court's cases involved questions concerning the Bill of Rights. By the late 1950s, one-third of filed cases involved such questions; and by the 1960s, half did.[32] In 1990, however, only 30 percent of the Court's caseload dealt with constitutional questions.

The Supreme Court's Jurisdiction

The Court has two types of jurisdiction, as indicated in Table 10.1. Its original jurisdiction is specifically set out in the Constitution. The Court has original jurisdiction in "all Cases affecting Ambassadors, other public Ministers and Consuls, and those in which a State shall be a party." Most cases arising under the Court's original jurisdiction involve disputes between two states, usually over issues such as ownership of offshore oil deposits, territorial disputes caused by shifting river boundaries, or controversies caused by conflicting claims over water rights, such as when a river flows through two or more states.[33] In earlier days, the Court would actually sit as a trial court and hear evidence and argument. Today, the Court usually appoints a Special Master—often a retired judge or an expert on the matter at hand—to hear the case in a district court on behalf of the Supreme Court and then report his or her findings and recommendations to the Court. It is rare for more than two or three of these cases to come to the Court in a year.

A second kind of jurisdiction enjoyed by the Court is appellate jurisdiction (see Table 10.1). The appellate jurisdiction of the Court can be changed by the Congress at any time, a power that has been a potent threat to the authority of the Court. The Judiciary Act of 1925 gave the Court discretion over its own jurisdiction, meaning that it does not have to accept all appeals that come to it. The idea behind the act was that the intermediate courts of appeals should be the final word for almost all federal litigants, thus freeing the Supreme Court to concentrate on constitutional issues, unless the Court decided that it wanted to address other matters. The Court, then, is not expected to exercise its appellate jurisdiction simply to correct errors of other courts. Instead, appeal to the Supreme Court should be taken only if the case presents important issues of law, or what is termed "a substantial federal question." Since 1988, nearly all appellate cases that had gone to the Supreme Court arrived there on a petition for a **writ of *certiorari*** (from the Latin "to be informed"), which is a request for the Supreme Court—at its discretion—to order up the records of the lower courts for purposes of review.

About one-third of all Supreme Court filings involve criminal law issues.[34] Many of these, in fact more than half of all petitions to the Court, are filed ***in forma pauperis*** (IFP) (literally from the Latin, "as a pauper"). About 80 percent of these are filed by indigent prison inmates seeking review of their sentences. Permission to proceed *in forma pauperis* allows the petitioner to avoid filing and printing costs. Any criminal defendant who has had a court-appointed lawyer in a lower court proceeding is automatically entitled to proceed in this fashion.

In recent years, the Court has tended more and more to deny requests to file *in forma pauperis*. In *In re Sindram* (1991), for example, the Rehnquist Court chastised Michael Sindram for filing his petition *in forma pauperis* to require the Maryland courts to expedite his request to expunge a $35 speeding ticket from his record. Sindram was no stranger to the Supreme Court: During the previous three years, he had filed forty-two separate motions on various legal matters, twenty-four of them in the 1990 term. In denying Sindram's request to file as an indigent, the majority noted that

writ of *certiorari*: A formal document issued from the Supreme Court to a lower federal or state court that calls up a case.

***in forma pauperis*:** Literally, "in the form of a pauper"; a way for an indigent or poor person to appeal a case to the U.S. Supreme Court.

"[t]he goal of fairly dispensing justice . . . is compromised when the Court is forced to devote its limited resources to the processing of repetitious and frivolous requests." Along with the order denying the petition, the Court issued new rules to provide for denial of "frivolous" or "malicious" IFP motions.[35]

The Rule of Four.   Unlike other federal courts, the Supreme Court controls its own caseload through the *certiorari* process, deciding which cases it wants to hear, and rejecting most cases that come to it. All petitions for *certiorari* must meet two criteria:

1.   The case must come either from a U.S. Court of Appeals, a special three-judge district court, or a state court of last resort. Generally, this means that the case has already been decided by the state supreme court.

2.   The case must involve a federal question. This means that the case must present questions of interpretation of federal constitutional law or involve a federal statute or treaty. The reasons why the Court should accept the case for review and legal argument supporting that position are set out in the petition (also called a brief).

The Clerk of the Court's office transmits petitions for writs of *certiorari* first to the chief justice's office, where his clerks review the petitions, and then to the individual justices' offices. All the justices on the Rehnquist Court except Justice John Paul Stevens participate in what is called the "cert pool."[36] As part of the pool, they review their assigned fraction of petitions and share their notes with each other. Those cases that the justices deem noteworthy are then placed on what is called the "discuss list"— a list of cases to be discussed—prepared by the chief justice's clerks and circulated to the chambers of the justices. All others are dead listed and go no further unless a justice asks that the case be removed from the dead list and discussed at conference. Only about 30 percent of submitted petitions make it to the discuss list. During one of the justices' weekly conference meetings, the cases on the discuss list are reviewed. The chief justice speaks first, then the rest of the justices, according to seniority. The decision process ends when the justices vote, and by custom, *certiorari* is granted according to the **Rule of Four**—when at least four justices vote to hear a case.

Rule of Four: At least four justices of the Supreme Court must vote to consider a case before it can be heard.

How Does a Case Survive the Process?

It can be difficult to determine why the Court decides to hear a particular case. The Court does not offer reasons, and "the standards by which the justices decide to grant or deny review are highly personalized and necessarily discretionary," noted former Chief Justice Earl Warren. Moreover, he continued, "those standards cannot be captured in rules or guidelines that would be meaningful."[37] Political scientists have nonetheless attempted to determine the characteristics of the cases the Court accepts; not surprisingly, they are similar to those that help a case get on the discuss list. Among the cues are the following:

■   The federal government is the party asking for review.

■   The case involves conflict among the circuit courts.

■   The case presents a civil rights or civil liberties question.

■   The case involves ideological and/or policy preferences of the justices.

■   The case has significant social or political interest, as evidenced by the presence of interest group *amicus curiae* briefs.

The Solicitor General.　One of the most important cues for predicting whether the Court will hear a case is the position the **solicitor general** takes on it. The solicitor general, appointed by the president, is the fourth-ranking member of the Justice Department and is responsible for handling all appeals on behalf of the U.S. government to the Supreme Court. The solicitor's staff is like a small, specialized law firm within the Justice Department. But because this office has such a special relationship with the Supreme Court, even having a suite of offices within the Supreme Court building, the solicitor general is often referred to as the Court's "ninth and a half member."[38] Moreover, the solicitor general, on behalf of the U.S. government, appears as a party or as an *amicus curiae* in more than 50 percent of the cases heard by the Court each term.

This special relationship with the Court helps explain the overwhelming success the solicitor general's office enjoys before the Supreme Court. The Court generally accepts 70 to 80 percent of the cases where the U.S. government is the petitioning party, compared to about 5 percent of all others.[39] But because of this special relationship, the solicitor general often ends up playing two conflicting roles: representing in Court both the president's policy interests and the broader interests of the United States. At times, solicitors find these two roles difficult to reconcile. Former Solicitor General Rex E. Lee (1981–85), for example, noted that on more than one occasion he refused to make arguments in Court that had been advanced by the Reagan administration (a stand that ultimately forced him to resign his position). Said Lee, "I'm not the pamphleteer general; I'm the solicitor general. My audience is not 100 million people; my audience is nine people. . . . Credibility is the most important asset that any solicitor general has."[40]

Conflict Among the Circuits.　Conflict among the lower courts is apparently another reason why the justices take cases. When interpretations of constitutional or federal law are involved, the justices seem to want consistency throughout the federal court system.

Often these conflicts occur when important civil rights or civil liberties questions arise. Political scientist Lawrence Baum has commented, "Justices' evaluations of lower court decisions are based largely on their ideological position."[41] Thus it is not uncommon to see conservative justices voting to hear cases to overrule liberal lower court decisions or vice versa.

Interest Group Participation.　Another "quick" way for the justices to gauge the ideological ramifications of a particular case is by the amount of interest group participation. Richard C. Cortner has noted that "Cases do not arrive on the doorstep of the Supreme Court like orphans in the night."[42] Instead, most cases heard by the Supreme Court involve either the government or an interest group—either as the sponsoring party or as an *amicus curiae*. Liberal groups such as the ACLU, People for the American Way, the NAACP Legal Defense Fund, and conservative groups including the Washington Legal Foundation, Concerned Women for America, or Americans United for Life Legal Defense Fund routinely sponsor cases or file *amicus* briefs either urging the Court to hear a case or asking it to deny *certiorari*. Research by political scientists has found that "not only does [an *amicus*] brief in favor of *certiorari* significantly improve the chances of a case being accepted, but two, three and four briefs improve the chances even more."[43]

Clearly, it's the more the merrier, whether or not the briefs are filed for or against granting review.[44] Interest group participation may highlight lower court and ideological conflicts for the justices by alerting them to the amount of public interest in the issues presented in any particular case.

As Bill Clinton's first solicitor general of the United States, Drew Days III was responsible for handling litigation on behalf of the U.S. government before the Supreme Court. (Photo courtesy: David Burnett/Contact Press Images)

solicitor general:　The fourth-ranking member of the Justice Department; responsible for handling all appeals on behalf of the U.S. government to the Supreme Court.

Starting the Case

Once a case is accepted for review, a flurry of activity begins (see Figure 10.7). If a criminal defendant is proceeding *in forma pauperis*, the Court appoints an expert lawyer to prepare and argue the case. Unlike the situation in many state courts, where appointed lawyers are often novices, it is considered an honor to be asked to represent an indigent before the Supreme Court in spite of the fact that such representation is on a *pro bono*, or no fee, basis.

Whether they are being paid or not, lawyers on both sides of the case begin to prepare their written arguments for submission to the Court. In these briefs lawyers cite prior case law and make arguments as to why the Court should find in favor of their client.

amicus curiae: "Friend of the court"; a third party to a lawsuit who files a legal brief for the purpose of raising additional points of view in an attempt to influence a court's decision.

More often than not, these arguments are echoed or expanded in ***amicus curiae*** briefs filed by interested parties, especially interest groups. In the 1987 term, 80 percent of the cases decided by the Court had at least one *amicus curiae* brief.

Since the 1970s interest groups have increasingly used the *amicus* brief as a way to lobby the Court. Because litigation is so expensive, few individuals have the money (or time or interest) to pursue a perceived wrong all the way to the U.S. Supreme Court. All sorts of interest groups, then, find that joining ongoing cases through *amicus* briefs is a useful way of advancing their policy preferences. Major cases such as *Brown v. Board of Education of Topeka, Kansas* (1954), *Casey v. Planned Parenthood of Southeastern Pennsylvania* (1992), and *Harris v. Forklift Systems* (1993), which involved the degree of psychological damage a victim of sexual harassment must show, all attracted large numbers of *amicus* briefs as part of interest groups' efforts to lobby the judiciary and bring about desired political objectives[45] (see Highlight 10.3: *Amicus* Briefs in Support of *Harris*).

Interest groups also provide the Court with information not necessarily contained in the major-party briefs, help write briefs, and assist in practice moot-court sessions. In these sessions the lawyer who will argue the case before the nine justices goes through a complete rehearsal, with prominent lawyers and law professors playing the roles of the various justices.

Oral Arguments. Once a case is accepted by the Court for full review, and after briefs and *amicus* briefs are submitted on each side, oral argument takes place. The

FIGURE 10.7

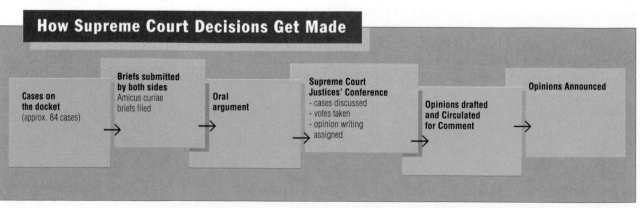

How Supreme Court Decisions Get Made

Cases on the docket (approx. 84 cases)

Briefs submitted by both sides Amicus curiae briefs filed

Oral argument

Supreme Court Justices' Conference
- cases discussed
- votes taken
- opinion writing assigned

Opinions drafted and Circulated for Comment

Opinions Announced

Highlight 10.3

Amicus Briefs in Support of Harris

Teresa Harris celebrates her victory after the Supreme Court ruled that her employer's conduct was illegal sexual harassment. (Photo courtesy: Fritz Hofmann/JB Pictures)

In *Harris v. Forklift Systems* (1993), the U.S. Supreme Court unanimously ruled that federal civil rights law created a "broad rule of workplace equality." In *Harris*, the Court found that Title VII of the Civil Rights Act was violated when Teresa Harris was subjected to "intimidation, ridicule, and insults" of a sexually harassing nature by her supervisor. The following groups or governments filed *amicus* briefs:

In support of *Harris*

1. United States
   Equal Employment Opportunity Commission

2. National Conference of Women's Bar Associations
   Women's Bar Association of District of Columbia

3. National Organization for Women Legal Defense and Education Fund
   American Jewish Committee
   American Medical Women Association
   Asian-American Legal Defense and Education Fund
   Association for Union Democracy

   Center for Women's Policy Studies
   Chicago Women in Trades
   Illinois Coalition Against Sexual Harassment
   National Organization for Women
   Northern Tradeswomen's Network
   Northern New England Tradeswomen Institute
   Puerto Rican Legal Defense and Education Fund
   Women's Law Project

4. NAACP Legal Defense and Education Fund
   National Conference of Jewish Women

5. Women's Legal Defense Fund
   National Women's Law Center
   AFL-CIO
   Ayuda, Inc.
   Bar Association of San Francisco
   California Women Lawyers

   Center for Women Policy Studies
   Coalition of Labor Union Women
   Committee for Justice for Women of North Carolina
   Federally Employed Women, Inc.
   Federation of Organizations for Professional Women
   Institute for Women's Policy Research
   Mexican American Women's National Association
   National Association of Female Executives
   National Association of Social Workers, Inc.
   National Center for Lesbian Rights
   National Council of Negro Women, Inc.
   National Association of Working Women
   9to5
   Older Women's League
   Trial Lawyers for Public Justice
   Wider Opportunities for Women

   Women Employed
   Women's Action Alliance
   Women's Bar Association of the District of Columbia
   Women's Law Center of Maryland
   YWCA of the U.S.A.

6. Employment Law Center
   California Women Lawyer's Committee
   Equal Rights Advocates

7. National Employment Lawyers Association

8. American Civil Liberties Union
   American Jewish Congress

9. Feminists for Free Expression

10. Southern States Police Benevolent Association
    North Carolina Police Benevolent Association

11. National Conference of Women's Bar Associations
    Women's Bar Association of the District of Columbia

In Support of *Forklift Systems*
   Equal Employment Advisory Council

For Neither Party
   American Psychological Association

Supreme Court's annual term begins the first Monday in October, as it has since the late 1800s, and runs through late June or early July. In the early 1800s, sessions of the Court lasted only a few weeks twice a year. Today, justices hear oral arguments from the beginning of the term until early April. Special cases, such as *U.S. v. Nixon* (1974), have been heard even later in the year.[46] During the term, "sittings," periods of about two weeks in which cases are heard, alternate with "recesses," also about two weeks long. Oral arguments are usually heard Monday through Wednesday during two-week sitting sessions.

Oral argument is generally limited to the immediate parties in the case, although it is not uncommon for the U.S. solicitor general to appear to argue orally as an *amicus curiae*. Oral argument at the Court is fraught with time-honored tradition and ceremony. At precisely 10:00 every morning when the Court is in session, the Court Marshal (dressed in a cutaway) emerges to intone "Oyez! Oyez! Oyez!" as the nine justices emerge from behind a reddish-purple velvet curtain to take their places on the raised and slightly angled bench. (From 1790 to 1972, the justices sat on a straight bench. Chief Justice Burger modified it so that justices at either end could see and hear better.) The chief justice sits in the middle with the justices to his right and left, alternating in seniority.

Almost all attorneys are allotted one-half hour to present their cases, and this allotment includes the time taken by questions from the bench. Justice John Marshall Harlan once noted that there was "no substitute for this method in getting at the heart of an issue and in finding out where the truth lies."[47] As the lawyer for the appellee approaches the mahogany lectern, a green light goes on, indicating that the attorney's time has begun. A white light flashes when five minutes remain. When a red light goes on, Court practice mandates that counsel stop immediately. One famous piece of Court lore told to all attorneys concerns a counsel who continued talking and reading from his prepared argument after the red light went on. When he looked up, he found an empty bench—the justices had quietly risen and departed while he continued to talk. On another occasion, Chief Justice Charles Evans Hughes stopped a leader of the New York bar in the middle of the word "if."

Although many Court watchers have tried to figure out how a particular justice will vote based on the questioning at oral argument, most find that the nature and number of questions asked does not help much in predicting the outcome of a case. Nevertheless, many believe that oral argument has several important functions. Oral argument is the only opportunity for even a small portion of the public (who may attend the hearings) and the press to observe the workings of the Court. It assures lawyers that the justices have heard their case, and it forces lawyers to focus on arguments believed important by the justices. It also provides the Court with additional information, especially concerning the Court's broader political role, an issue not usually addressed in written briefs. For example, the justices can ask how many people might be affected by its decision or where the Court (and country) would be heading if a case were decided in a particular way.

The Conference and the Vote.   The justices meet in closed conference on Fridays when the Court is hearing oral argument. Since the ascendancy of Chief Justice Roger B. Taney to the Court in 1836, the justices have begun each conference session with a round of handshaking. Once the door to the conference room closes, no others are allowed to enter. The justice with the least seniority acts as the doorkeeper for the other eight, communicating with those waiting outside to fill requests for documents, water, and so on.

Conferences highlight the importance and power of the chief justice, who presides over them and makes the initial presentation of each case. Each individual justice then discusses the case in order of his or her seniority on the Court, with the most senior justice speaking next. Most accounts of the decision-making process reveal that at this point some justices try to change the minds of others, but that most enter the conference room with a clear idea of how they feel. Although other Courts have followed different procedures, on the Rehnquist Court the justices generally vote at the same time they discuss the case. Initial conference votes are not final, allowing justices to change their minds before final votes are taken later.

Writing Opinions.   There are basically five kinds of opinions that can be written:

1. A *majority opinion* is written by one member of the Court, and as such reflects the views of at least a majority of the justices. This opinion usually sets out the legal reasoning justifying the decision, and this legal reasoning becomes a precedent for deciding future cases.

2. A *concurring opinion* is one written by a justice who agrees with the outcome of the case but not with the legal rationale for the decision.

3. A *plurality opinion* is one that attracts the support of three or four justices. Generally, this opinion becomes the controlling opinion of the Court. Usually one or more justices agrees with the outcome of the decision in a concurring opinion, but there is no solid majority for the legal reasoning behind the outcome. Plurality decisions do not have the precedential value of majority opinions.

4. A *dissenting opinion* is one that is written by one or more justices who disagree with the opinion of a majority or plurality of the Court.

5. *Per curiam opinion* is an unsigned opinions issued by the Court. Justices may dissent from *per curiam* opinions but do so fairly rarely.

The chief justice, if he is in the majority, has the job of assigning the writing of the opinion. This privilege enables him to wield tremendous power. (If he is in the minority, the assignment falls to the most senior justice in the majority.)

The justice assigned to write the majority opinion circulates drafts of the opinion to all members of the Court. The Court must provide legal reasons for its positions. The reasoning behind any decision is often as important as the outcome. Under our system of *stare decisis*, both are likely to be relied on as precedent later by lower courts confronted with cases involving similar issues. The justice who drafts the opinion can have an important impact on how any legal issues are framed. Informal caucusing and negotiation then often take place, as justices may "hold out" for word changes or other modifications as a condition of their continued support of the majority opinion. At the same time, dissenting opinions and/or concurring opinions also circulate through the various chambers. The justices are often assisted in their writing of opinions by their clerks, who also can serve as intermediaries between the justices as they talk among themselves.

A good example of how politics can be involved at the opinion-writing stage is evident in *Bowers* v. *Hardwick* (1986),[48] the Georgia consensual sodomy case discussed in chapters 5 and 6. Justices White and Burger voted for *certiorari* believing that the Constitution doesn't protect homosexual acts. The liberal Justices Marshall and Brennan thought they had enough votes to overturn the law, but when Brennan perceived he would lose, he withdrew his vote for *certiorari,* albeit too late. Once the case was argued, coalitions quickly shifted. According to papers kept by Justice Marshall, Justice Powell originally indicated at conference that he would vote with the majority to find the law unconstitutional. After drafts of the majority and minority opinions were circulated, however, he changed his mind, thus changing a five-to-four majority to strike down the law into a five-to-four majority to uphold it.[49]

This kind of communal work can result in poorly written opinions, as was the case with *U.S.* v. *Nixon* (1974).[50] Although the opinion involving President Nixon's refusal to turn over tape recordings of his conversations was issued under Chief Justice Burger's name, many believe that it was a combination of several justices' contributions and additions. Sensing the need for the Court to speak unanimously in such an important opinion—one that pitted two branches of government against each other—Justice Burger apparently made concessions to get support.[51] This process led to some very confused prose in some sections of the opinion.

Recently, tensions have grown on the Court concerning some issues, and dissents or concurring opinions have become quite pointed. The protocol of the Court has always been characterized by politeness, but this has not stopped some justices from openly ridiculing their colleagues from the bench. Justice Scalia, for example, publicly criticized Justice O'Connor's opinion in *Webster* v. *Reproductive Health Services* (1989), saying that her "assertion that a fundamental rule of judicial restraint requires [the Court] to avoid reconsidering *Roe* [v. *Wade*] cannot be taken seriously."[52] This kind of ridicule is unprecedented and perhaps just a reflection of how manners in politics are on the decline.

HOW THE JUSTICES VOTE

*J*ustices are human beings, and they do not make decisions in a vacuum. Principles of *stare decisis* dictate that the justices follow the law of previous cases in deciding cases at hand. But more factors are usually operating. A variety of legal and extra-legal factors have been found to affect Supreme Court decision-making.

Legal Factors

Judicial Philosophy and Original Intent.   One of the primary issues concerning judicial decision-making focuses on what is called the activism/restraint debate. Advocates of **judicial restraint** argue that courts should allow the decisions of other branches to stand, even when they offend a judge's own sense of principles.[53] Restraintists defend their position by asserting that the federal courts are composed of unelected judges, which makes the judicial branch the least democratic branch of government. Consequently, the courts should defer policy making to other branches of government as much as possible.

Restraintists refer to *Roe* v. *Wade* (1973), the case that liberalized abortion laws, as a classic example of **judicial activism** run amok. They maintain that the Court should have deferred policy making on this sensitive issue to the states or to the other branches of the federal government—the legislative and executive—because their officials are elected and therefore are more receptive to the majority's will.

Advocates of judicial activism contend that judges should use their power broadly to further justice, especially in the areas of equality and personal liberty. Activists argue that it is the courts' appropriate role to correct injustices committed by the other

judicial restraint: A philosophy of judicial decision-making that argues courts should allow the decisions of other branches of government to stand, even when they offend a judge's own sense of principles.

judicial activism: A philosophy of judicial decision-making that argues judges should use their power broadly to further justice, especially in the areas of equality and personal liberty.

branches of government. Explicit in this argument is the notion that courts need to protect oppressed minorities.[54]

Activists point to *Brown* v. *Board of Education of Topeka, Kansas* (1954) as an excellent example of the importance of judicial activism.[55] In *Brown,* the Supreme Court ruled that racial segregation in public schools violated the equal protection clause of the Fourteenth Amendment. Segregation was nonetheless practiced after passage of the Fourteenth Amendment. An activist would point out that if the Court had not reinterpreted its provisions of the amendment; many states probably would still have laws or policies mandating segregation in public schools.

The debate over judicial activism versus judicial restraint often focuses on how the Court should interpret the meaning of the Constitution. Advocates of judicial restraint generally agree that judges should be strict constructionists; that is, they should interpret the Constitution as it was written and intended by the Framers. They argue that in determining the constitutionality of a statute or policy, the Court should rely on the explicit meanings of the clauses in the document, which can be clarified by looking at the intent of the Framers.

Precedent. Most Supreme Court decisions are laced with numerous references to previous Court decisions. Some justices, however, believe that *stare decisis* and adherence to precedent is no longer as critical as it once was. Chief Justice Rehnquist, for example, has noted that while "*stare decisis* is a cornerstone of our legal system . . . it has less power in constitutional cases."[56] In contrast, Justices O'Connor, Kennedy, and Souter explained their reluctance to overrule *Roe* v. *Wade* (1973) in *Planned Parenthood of Southeastern Pennsylvania* v. *Casey* (1992): "to overrule under fire in the absence of the most compelling reason to reexamine a watershed decision would subject this Court's legitimacy beyond any serious question."[57]

Interestingly, a 1990 study of the American public's knowledge and perceptions of the Court indicated that only 44 percent believed that the Court decides cases primarily on the basis of facts and law. Nearly 50 percent believe that the Court makes decisions based on other factors, including political pressures (28 percent), political/personal beliefs (18 percent), and religious beliefs (1 percent). Although *theoretically* the Framers envisioned the Court to be above these pressures, the American public does not appear to be particularly upset about the role of politics and personal beliefs in the decision-making process. In fact, those polled want the Court to take a more active role in the areas of discrimination against women and minorities.

Extra-Legal Factors

Most political scientists who study what is called judicial behavior conclude that a variety of forces shape judicial decision-making. Of late, many have attempted to explain how judges vote by integrating a variety of models to offer a more complete picture of judicial decision-making.[58] Many of those models attempt to take into account justices' behavioral characteristics and attitudes as well as the fact patterns of the case.

Behavioral Characteristics. Some political scientists argue that social background differences, including childhood experiences, religious values, education, earlier political and legal careers, and political party loyalties are likely to influence how a judge evaluates the facts and legal issues presented in any given case. Justice Harry A. Blackmun's service at the Mayo Clinic is often pointed to as a reason why his opinion for the Court in *Roe* v. *Wade* was so soundly grounded in medical evidence. Similarly, Justice

The 1989 pro-choice rally in Washington, D.C., was part of an intense lobbying effort to influence the Court's decision in the *Webster* case. Justice Sandra Day O'Connor, viewed as a swing vote on the case, was a particular target of the lobbying. (Photo courtesy: Jodi Buren/Woodfin Camp & Associates)

Potter Stewart, who was generally considered a moderate on most civil liberties issues, usually took a more liberal position on cases dealing with freedom of the press. Why? It may be that Stewart's early job as a newspaper reporter made him more sensitive to these claims.

Ideology.   Critics of the social background approach argue that attitudes or ideologies can better explain the justices' voting patterns. Since the 1940s the two most prevailing ideologies in the United States have been conservative and liberal. On the Supreme Court, justices with "conservative" views generally vote against affirmative action, abortion rights, expanded rights for criminal defendants, and increased power for the national government. In contrast "liberals" tend to support the parties advancing these positions.

Over time, however, scholars have generally agreed that identifiable ideological voting blocs have occurred on the Court. During Franklin D. Roosevelt's first term, for example, five justices, a critical conservative bloc, routinely voted to strike down the constitutionality of New Deal legislation. Traditionally, such voting blocs or coalitions have centered on liberal/conservative splits on issues such as states' rights (conservatives supporting and liberals opposing), economic issues (conservatives being pro-business; liberals, pro-labor), and civil liberties and civil rights (conservatives being less supportive than liberals). On death-penalty cases, for example, Justices William Brennan, Jr. and Thurgood Marshall (sometimes joined by John Paul Stevens) consistently voted against the imposition of the death penalty.

The Attitudinal Model.   The attitudinal approach hypothesizes that there is a substantial link between judicial attitudes and decision-making.[59] Simply stated, the attitudinal model holds that Supreme Court justices decide cases in light of the facts of the cases according to their personal preferences toward issues of public policy. Among some of the factors used to derive attitudes are a justice's party identification,[60] the party of the appointing president,[61] and the liberal/conservative leanings of a justice. To date, the attitudinal model is generally characterized as being the best at explaining Supreme Court decision-making.[62]

Public Opinion.   Many political scientists also have examined the role of public opinion in Supreme Court decision-making.[63] Not only do the justices read legal briefs and hear oral arguments, they also read newspapers, watch television, and have some knowledge of public opinion—especially on controversial issues. In 1993 the Court's switchboard lit up like the national Christmas tree with calls about Baby Jessica, the two-year-old who was returned to her birth parents after they spent two years in legal wrangling with her custodial parents. Operators reported that some callers sobbed, some yelled, and others wanted to know how to impeach the chief justice. While actions like these probably have little impact on a particular justice's view of a particular case, they do make the Court aware of the intensity of public opinion on some issues. According to Chief Justice Rehnquist,

> Judges, so long as they are relatively normal human beings, can no more escape being influenced by public opinion in the long run than can people working at other jobs. And if a judge on coming to the bench were to decide to hermetically seal himself off from all manifestations of public opinion, he would accomplish very little; he would not be influenced by current public opinion, but instead would be influenced by the state of public opinion at the time he came to the bench.[64]

Political scientist Thomas R. Marshall has discovered substantial variation in the degree to which particular justices' decisions were congruent with public opinion.[65] Whether or not public opinion actually influences some justices, public opinion can act as a check on the power of the courts as well as an energizing factor. Activist periods on the Supreme Court have generally corresponded to periods of social or economic crisis. For example, the Marshall Court supported a strong national government, much to the chagrin of a series of pro-states' rights Democratic-Republican presidents in the early crisis-ridden years of the republic. Similarly, the Court capitulated to political pressures and public opinion when, after 1936, it reversed many of its earlier decisions that had blocked President Roosevelt's New Deal legislation.

The courts, especially the Supreme Court, also can be the direct target of public opinion. During the spring of 1989, when the case of *Webster* v. *Reproductive Health Services* was about to come before the Supreme Court, the Court was subjected to unprecedented lobbying as groups and individuals on both sides of the abortion issue marched and sent appeals to the Court. Earlier, in the fall of 1988, Justice Harry A. Blackmun, author of *Roe* v. *Wade*, had warned a law school audience in a public address that he feared that the decision was in jeopardy. This in itself was a highly unusual move; until recently, it was the practice of the justices never to comment on cases or the Court.

Speeches like Blackmun's put pro-choice advocates on guard, and many took advantage of the momentum that had built around their successful campaign against the nomination of Robert H. Bork. In 1989, their forces mounted one of the largest demonstrations in the history of the United States when more than 300,000 people marched from the Mall to the Capitol building, just across the street from the Supreme Court. In addition, full-page advertisements appeared in prominent newspapers, and supporters of *Roe* v. *Wade* were urged to contact members of the Court to voice their support. Justice Sandra Day O'Connor, at the time the Court's lone woman, was targeted by many who viewed her as the crucial swing justice on the issue. Mail at the Court, which usually averages about 1,000 pieces a day, rose to an astronomical 46,000 pieces when *Webster* reached the Court, virtually paralyzing normal lines of communication. Several justices spoke out against this kind of "extra-judicial" communication and voiced their belief in its ineffectiveness. In *Webster* v. *Reproductive Health Services* (1989) Justice Scalia lamented,

> We can now look forward to at least another Term with carts full of mail from the public, and streets full of demonstrators, urging us—their unelected and life tenured judges who have been awarded those extraordinary, undemocratic characteristics precisely in order that we might follow the law despite the popular will—to follow the popular will.

But the fact remains that the Court is very dependent on the public for its prestige as well as for compliance with its decisions. In times of war and other emergencies, for example, the Court frequently has decided cases in ways that commentators have attributed to the sway of public opinion and political exigencies. In *Korematsu* v. *The United States* (1944),[66] for example, the high Court upheld the obviously unconstitutional internment of Japanese-American citizens during World War II. Moreover, Chief Justice Rehnquist himself has suggested that the Court's restriction on presidential authority in *Youngstown Sheet & Tube Co.* v. *Sawyer* (1952),[67] which invalidated President Harry S Truman's seizure of the nation's steel mills, was largely attributable to Truman's unpopularity and that of the Korean War.[68] And, as Table 10.5 reveals, the public and the Court often are in agreement on many controversial issues.

TABLE 10.5

The Court *versus* the American Public

In recent years, the Court has agreed and disagreed with the public on various issues, such as:

ISSUE	COURT	PUBLIC
Should TV and other recording devices be permitted in the Supreme Court?	No	Yes (59%)
Should a parent be forced to reveal the whereabouts of a child even though it could violate Fifth Amendment rights?	Yes	Yes (50%) No (39%) Don't know (11%)
Should a family be allowed to decide to end life-support systems?	Yes	Yes (88%)
Before getting an abortion, whose consent should a teenager be required to gain?	One parent	Both parents (38%) One parent (37%) Neither parent (22%)
Is the death penalty constitutional?	Yes	Yes (72% favor)

Source: Table compiled from General Social Surveys and Gallup Poll data.

Public confidence in the Court, like other institutions of government, has ebbed and flowed. Public support for the Court was highest after the Court issued *U.S.* v. *Nixon* (1974), ultimately leading to Richard M. Nixon's resignation from office. At a time when Americans lost faith in the presidency, they could at least look to the Supreme Court to do the right thing. Of late, however, the Court and the judicial system as a whole have taken a beating in public confidence. In the aftermath of the O. J. Simpson trial, many white Americans faulted the judicial system. This dissatisfaction was reflected in low levels of confidence in the judicial system, although the Supreme Court itself continues to enjoy considerable popular support. Even the judicial system, often above the types of criticism leveled at big government, Congress, or the president, now, too, appears to be the target of some public frustration.

JUDICIAL POLICY MAKING AND IMPLEMENTATION

*A*ll judges, whether they like it or not, make policy. In 1996 when the U.S. Supreme Court ruled that Colorado could not prevent states and local governments from extending any constitutional protections to gay, lesbian, and bisexual citizens, the justices were making policy.[69] When the Court ruled that prayer at public school ceremonies was a violation of separation of church and state, the Court made policy. It is through interpreting statutes or the Constitution that federal courts, and the Supreme Court in particular, make policy in several ways. Judges can interpret a provision of a law to cover matters not previously understood to be covered by the law, or can "discover" new rights, such as that of privacy, from their reading of the Constitution. They can also affect lives, as was the case with Baby Jessica, or more extremely in death penalty cases.

This power of the courts to make policy presents difficult questions for democratic theory, as noted by Justice Scalia in *Webster,* because democratic theorists believe that the power to make law resides only in the people or their elected representatives. Yet court rulings, especially Supreme Court decisions, routinely affect policy far beyond the interests of the immediate parties.

One measure of the power of the courts is that more than one hundred federal laws have been declared unconstitutional. Although many of these laws have not been particularly significant, others have. For example, in *Immigration and Naturalization Service* v. *Chadha* (1983) (discussed in chapter 7), the Court found that legislative vetoes were unconstitutional.[70]

Another measure of the power of the Supreme Court is its ability to overrule itself. Although the Court generally abides by the informal rule of *stare decisis,* by one count it has overruled itself in more than 140 cases since 1810. *Brown* v. *Board of Education of Topeka, Kansas* (1954), for example, overruled *Plessy* v. *Ferguson* (1896), thereby reversing years of constitutional interpretation concluding that racial segregation was not a violation of the Constitution. Moreover, in the past few years, the Court has repeatedly reversed earlier decisions in the areas of criminal defendants' rights, affirmative action, and the establishment of religion, thus revealing its powerful role in determining national policy.

A measure of the growing power of the federal courts is the degree to which they now handle issues that, after *Marbury* v. *Madison* (1803), had been considered to be political questions more appropriately left to the other branches of government to decide. Prior to 1962, for example, the Court refused to hear cases questioning the size (and populations) of congressional districts, no matter how unequal they were.[71] The boundary of a legislative district was considered to be a political question. Then, in 1962, writing for the Court, Justice William Brennan, Jr. concluded that simply because a case involved a political issue it did not necessarily involve a political question. This opened up the floodgates to cases involving a variety of issues that the Court formerly had declined to address.[72]

Implementing Court Decisions

President Andrew Jackson, annoyed about a particular decision handed down by the Marshall Court, is alleged to have said, "John Marshall has made his decision; now let him enforce it." Jackson's statement raises a question: How do Supreme Court rulings translate into public policy? In fact, although judicial decisions carry legal and even moral authority, all courts must rely on other units of government to carry out their directives. If the president or Congress, for example, doesn't like a particular Supreme Court ruling, they can underfund programs needed to implement a decision or seek only lax enforcement. **Judicial implementation** refers to how and whether judicial decisions are translated into actual public policies affecting more than the immediate parties to the lawsuit.

judicial implementation:
Refers to how and whether judicial decisions are translated into actual public policies affecting more than the immediate parties to a lawsuit.

How well a decision is implemented often depends on how well crafted or popular it is. Hostile reaction in the South to *Brown* v. *Board of Education of Topeka, Kansas* (1954) and the absence of precise guidelines to implement the decision meant that the ruling went largely unenforced for years. The *Brown* experience also highlights how much the Supreme Court needs the support of both federal and state courts as well as other governmental agencies to carry out its judgments. For example, you may have graduated from high school since 1992, when the Supreme Court ruled that public middle school and high school graduations could not include a prayer. Yet your own commencement ceremony may have included one.

Students and government workers around the nation celebrate May 5, 1994, as National Prayer Day. In spite of Supreme Court decisions ordering a wall of separation between church and state, celebrations like this one at a Georgia public high school are held all over America each May in public buildings or on public grounds. (Photo courtesy: Dianne Laakso/*Atlanta Journal and Constitution*)

Charles Johnson and Bradley C. Canon suggest that the implementation of judicial decisions involves what they call an *implementing population* and a *consumer population*.[73] The implementing population consists of those people responsible for carrying out a decision. It varies, depending on the policy and issues in question, but can include lawyers, judges, public officials, police officers and police departments, hospital administrators, government agencies, and corporations. In the case of school prayer, the implementing population could include teachers, school administrators, or the school board. The consumer population consists of those people who might be directly affected by a decision.

For effective implementation of a judicial decision, the first requirement is that the members of the implementing population must act to show that they understand the original decision. For example, the Supreme Court ruled in *Reynolds* v. *Sims* (1964)[74] that every person should have an equally weighted vote in electing governmental representatives. This "one person, one vote" decision might seem simple enough at first glance, but in practice it can be very difficult to understand. The implementing population in this case consists chiefly of state legislatures and local governments, which determine voting districts for federal, state, and local offices (see chapter 7). If a state legislature draws districts in such a way that African-American voters are spread thinly across a number of separate constituencies, the chances are slim that any particular district will elect a representative who is especially sensitive to blacks' concerns. Does that violate "equal representation"? (In practice, through the early 1990s, courts and the Justice Department intervened in many cases to ensure that elected officials would include minority representation only ultimately to be overruled by the Supreme Court.)

The second requirement is that the implementing population must actually follow Court policy. Thus, when the Court ruled that men could not be denied admission to a state-sponsored nursing school, the implementing population—in this case, university administrators and the Board of Regents of the nursing school—had to enroll qualified male students.

Judicial decisions are most likely to be implemented smoothly if responsibility for implementation is concentrated in the hands of a few highly visible public officials, such as the president or a governor. By the same token, these officials can also thwart or impede judicial intentions. Recall from chapter 6, for example, the effect of Governor Orval Faubus's initial refusal to allow black children to attend all-white public schools in Little Rock, Arkansas.

The third requirement for implementation is that the consumer population must be aware of the rights that a decision grants or denies them. Teenagers seeking an abortion, for example, are consumers of the Supreme Court's decisions on abortion. They need to know that most states require them to inform their parents of their intention to have an abortion or to get parental permission to do so. Similarly, criminal defendants and their lawyers are consumers of Court decisions and need to know, for example, the implications of recent Court decisions for evidence presented at trial.

North—South

POLITICS AROUND THE WORLD

A prime example for arguments for "American exceptionalism" is the U.S. judiciary. The United States is one of the few countries in which the courts play a major role in the policy-making process because of their power of judicial review. Perhaps more importantly, the politics of judicial appointments aside, the United States is one of the few countries in which what the judicial system does is not largely determined by partisan politics—or worse. We can see the former by considering Canada; the latter, Mexico.

As in the United States, Canada has a nine-member Supreme Court. Its members are appointed by the Cabinet but do not require confirmation by either house of Parliament. Even more significant is the fact that the Court can do no more than issue advisory rulings on constitutional issues. Perhaps as a result, the Supreme Court and the judiciary as a whole have not been anywhere near as politically controversial as in the United States.

On paper, the Mexican legal system looks a lot more like the American system. The justices of its twenty-one member Supreme Court are named by the president, confirmed by the Senate, and then supposedly appointed for life. Like all other federal offices in Mexico, however, there is usually a complete turnover in the Court's membership with each new president. Not surprisingly, the federal courts have shied away from controversial and constitutional issues that might put the PRI's domination in question. Its decisions rarely set legal precedents. On the other hand, there are signs that the judiciary is becoming more important and will play a major role in enforcing the electoral reforms adopted in late 1996.

At the lower levels, there are reports of widespread corruption in the courts and of torture and arbitrary arrest by the police. Average citizens rarely feel they can turn to the judicial system to redress their grievances. Put simply, though Mexico's track record is not as bad as that of most other third-world countries, it could hardly be said to rely on the rule of law through a reasonably fair and impartial judicial system.

CHANGING THE JUDICIAL SYSTEM

Clearly, the American public regards the Supreme Court as a powerful policy maker. In a 1990 poll, most respondents said they believed that the Court was more powerful than the president (31 percent versus 21 percent), and that the Court was close to being as powerful as Congress (38 percent).

Considering how poorly informed the American public is about the Court, interest in its activities appears to be growing as more Americans come to understand the importance of the Court in shaping our social and economic agenda and as Court appointments continue to get extensive media coverage. Presidents, however, have always realized how important their judicial appointments, especially their Supreme Court appointments, were to their ability to achieve all or many of their policy objectives. After all, Franklin D. Roosevelt proposed his infamous court-packing plan because he wanted to add like-minded jurists to the Court to outweigh the votes of those opposed to federal governmental expansion and intervention into the economy. But, in spite of the fact that most presidents have tried to appoint jurists with particular political or ideological philosophies, they have often been wrong. Dwight D. Eisenhower is said to have bemoaned that his worst mistake was appointing Earl Warren Chief Justice of the United States. Eisenhower, a moderate/conservative, was appalled by the liberal opinions of the Warren Court concerning criminal defendants' rights, in particular. Who would have suspected that a former Republican state attorney general would lead the Court to expand the rights of criminals dramatically? Similarly, Justices O'Connor, Kennedy, and Souter, appointed by presidents Reagan (O'Connor) and Bush, have not been as conservative as some predicted. David Souter, in particular, has surprised many commentators with his moderate to liberal decisions in a variety of areas, including free speech, criminal rights, race and gender discrimination, and abortion. All three justices, moreover, worked together to make certain that *Roe* v. *Wade* was not overturned by the Court: This in spite of the fact that they were appointed by presidents who ran on the Republican Party platform that pledged the president to appoint only jurists who had strong pro-family and pro-life sentiments. Similarly, Justice Kennedy even wrote the Court's opinion in *Romer* v. *Evans* (1996), the first major case in which the justices handed gay rights advocates a victory.

This raises a question: Should judges and justices be ideological in the first instance? Is this what the Framers intended? During the Robert H. Bork and Clarence Thomas hearings, in particular, when the president was a conservative Republican and the Senate was controlled by Democrats, ideology was an issue of concern to many senators as they attempted to question Bork and Thomas on their views about controversial issues such as the death penalty, abortion, women's rights, and affirmative action. Should this be the case? Should jurists be less ideological? Should the president or even the Senate be concerned with anything other than the appointment of fair minded individuals? How could fairmindedness be determined, if at all?

Changing the System. In the wake of the Clarence Thomas hearings, much was said about the need to reform the judicial selection process. Criticism was directed in particular at Senate confirmation hearings, special interest groups, and ideological politics. As time has passed, however, little has been done in response to these concerns, and the Ruth Bader Ginsburg and Stephen Breyer hearings, which went like clockwork, seem to indicate that the Bork and Thomas hearings were anomalies.

Historically, in fact, there has been little inclination to tinker with the judicial system—even though the courts have grown in power—except when the Supreme Court has stepped on too many toes. Congress and the president have, from time to time, limited, or attempted to limit, the jurisdiction of the Court. When Democratic-Republicans were unable to get rid of Federalist judges by impeachment, they abolished the federal circuit courts. Following the Civil War, Radical Republicans cut the size of the Court and changed its appellate jurisdiction to prevent it from hearing a case involving the constitutionality of some Reconstruction legislation. And in 1936 President Franklin D. Roosevelt tried unsuccessfully to change the size of the Court so that he could pack it with supporters of his New Deal. Generally, however, presidents are content to wait until a vacancy occurs, and most presidents get to appoint at least one, and usually more, justices to the high Court.

More recently, proposals have been made to alter the Court's jurisdiction on matters such as abortion, but little has come of them. If the current Court continues its moderate/conservative pattern, it may someday find itself in conflict with a more liberal Democratic president and Congress. As revealed in Table 10.6, if the present members of the Court retire at the same average age as their recent predecessors, it would still take many years for the Court to be remade in a more liberal model, especially since the Clinton appointees, to date, have been considered moderates by most.

The question may more properly be: Are the courts too political? Should their independence be curbed? The courts and the judiciary occupy a peculiar place in our democratic system. Not elected by the people, federal judges serve for life, with no direct responsibility or accountability to those who can be affected so profoundly by their decisions. Yet suggestions such as the one made by Franklin D. Roosevelt to change the Supreme Court have not been met with much enthusiasm from Congress or the public.

TABLE 10.6

The Future Composition of the Supreme Court

JUSTICE	AGE IN 1996	PHILOSOPHY	PROJECTED YEAR OF RETIREMENT*
Stevens	76	Moderate	2001
Rehnquist	72	Conservative	2005
O'Connor	66	Conservative	2011
Scalia	60	Conservative	2017
Kennedy	60	Conservative	2017
Souter	57	Conservative	2020
Thomas	48	Conservative	2029
Ginsburg	64	Moderate/Liberal	2009
Breyer	58	Moderate	2019

*This is based on the age of the last six justices (Brennan, Burger, Marshall, Powell, White, and Blackmun) when they retired from 1986–1994—eighty-one years of age.

SUMMARY

The judiciary and the legal process—on both the national and state levels—are complex and play a far more important role in the setting of policy than the Framers ever envisioned. To explain the judicial process and its evolution, we have made the following points:

1. The Creation of the National Judiciary.

Many of the Framers viewed the judicial branch of government as little more than a minor check on the other two branches, ignoring Anti-Federalist concerns about an unelected judiciary and its potential for tyranny. The Judiciary Act of 1789 established the basic federal court system we have today. It was the Marshall Court (1801–35), however, that interpreted the Constitution to include the Court's major power, that of judicial review.

2. The American Legal System.

Ours is a dual judicial system consisting of the federal court system and the separate judicial systems of the fifty states. In each system there are two basic types of courts: trial courts and appellate courts. Each type deals with cases involving criminal and civil law. Original jurisdiction refers to a court's ability to hear a case as a trial court; appellate jurisdiction refers to a court's ability to review cases already decided by a trial court.

3. The Federal Court System.

The federal court system is made up of constitutional and legislative courts. Federal district courts, courts of appeals, and the Supreme Court are constitutional courts.

4. How Federal Court Judges Are Selected.

District court and court of appeals judges are nominated by the president and subject to Senate confirmation. Senators often play a key role in recommending district court appointees from their home state. Supreme Court justices are nominated by the president but must also win Senate confirmation. Presidents use different criteria for selection, but important factors include competence, standards, ideology, rewards, pursuit of political support, religion, race, and gender.

5. The Supreme Court Today.

Several factors go into the Court's decision to hear a case. Not only must the Court have jurisdiction, but at least four justices must vote to hear the case, and cases with certain characteristics are most likely to be heard. Once a case is set for review, briefs and *amicus curiae* briefs are filed and oral argument scheduled. The justices meet after oral argument to discuss the case, votes are taken, and opinions are written and circulated.

6. How the Justices Vote.

Several legal and extra legal factors affect how the Court arrives at its decision. Legal factors include judicial philosophy, the original intent of the Framers, and precedent. Extra-legal factors include public opinion and the behavioral characteristics and ideology of the justices.

7. Judicial Policy Making and Implementation.

The Supreme Court is an important participant in the policy-making process. The process of judicial interpretation gives the Court powers never envisioned by the Framers.

8. Changing the Judicial System.

Unlike the other two branches of government, the Supreme Court and the federal judiciary have not been the subjects of many reform efforts, and periodic calls for change have met with little support. Yet the question remains: Should jurists be political?

KEY TERMS

amicus curiae, p. 392

brief, p. 375

constitutional court, p. 370

in forma pauperis, p. 389

judicial activism, p. 396

judicial implementation, p. 401

judicial restraint, p. 396

judicial review, p. 365

Judiciary Act of 1789, p. 365

jurisdiction, p. 369

legislative courts, p. 371

Marbury v. *Madison*, p. 369

original jurisdiction, p. 369

precedent, p. 376

Rule of Four, p. 390

senatorial courtesy, p. 378

solicitor general, p. 391

stare decisis, p. 376

strict constructionist, p. 383

trial court, p. 369

writ of *certiorari*, p. 389

SUGGESTED READINGS

Abraham, Henry. *The Judicial Process,* 6th ed. New York: Oxford University Press, 1993.

Baum, Lawrence. *American Courts: Process and Policy,* 3rd ed. Boston: Houghton Mifflin, 1994.

————. *The Supreme Court,* 4th ed. Washington, D.C.: CQ Press, 1992.

Epstein, Lee, *et al. The Supreme Court Compendium: Data, Decisions, and Developments,* 2nd. ed.. Washington, D.C.: Congressional Quarterly Inc., 1996.

Hall, Kermit L., ed. *The Oxford Companion to the Supreme Court of the United States.* New York: Oxford University Press, 1992.

Marshall, Thomas R. *Public Opinion and the Supreme Court.* Boston: Unwin and Hyman, 1989.

O'Brien, David M. *Storm Center: The Supreme Court in American Politics,* 4th ed. New York: Norton, 1996.

Provine, Doris Marie. *Case Selection in the United States Supreme Court.* Chicago: University of Chicago Press, 1980.

Salokar, Rebecca Mae. *The Solicitor General: The Politics of Law.* Philadelphia: Temple University Press, 1992.

Wasby, Stephen. *The Supreme Court in the Federal Judicial System,* 4th ed. Chicago: Nelson-Hall, 1993.

Woodward, Bob, and Scott Armstrong. *The Brethren: Inside the Supreme Court.* New York: Simon and Schuster, 1979.

PUBLIC OPINION
AND POLITICAL
SOCIALIZATION

*T*he paradox of our time is that Americans are feeling bad about doing well," says national columnist Robert J. Samuelson.[1] According to Samuelson, since World War II, the personal lives of most Americans have gotten much better. As a group we are healthier, "work at less exhausting jobs," and live longer than our grandparents.[2] In spite of 1990s downsizing, overall job security actually has improved, and governmental programs offer some sort of a safety net for most of the poor, the disabled, and the elderly in a manner unlike other eras in our national history. Moreover, many forms of overt discrimination have disappeared. And, when surveyed by pollsters, most people say that they are pleased with their lives. But, as discussed in chapter 1, when the same people are asked about the nation and "whether it's moving in the right direction," they are not nearly so positive.

It's important to remember that pollsters have noted this concern about America's direction for the last twenty years. It is not a new phenomenon, just more pronounced and more widely reported by the media. Why this disenchantment has come about and what it means for democracy and the conduct of elected officials is now a target of more public opinion polling as well as the musings of numerous political pundits and pollsters.

Nearly 200 years ago, in 1787, John Jay wrote glowingly of the sameness of the American people. He and other writers of *The Federalist Papers* believed that Americans had more in common than not. Said John Jay in *Federalist No. 2*, we are "one united people—a people descended from the same ancestors, speaking the same language, professing the same religion, attached to the same principles of government, very similar in manners and customs." Many of those who could vote were of English heritage; almost all were Christian. Moreover, most believed that certain rights—such as freedom of speech, association, and religion—were unalienable rights. Jay also spoke of shared public opinion and of the need for a national government that reflected American ideals.

Today, however, Americans are a far more diverse lot. Election after election and public opinion poll after poll reveal that Americans are not only diverse, they are angry, afraid, and frustrated. Nonetheless, they appear to agree on many things. Most want less government, particularly at the national level. So did many citizens in 1787. Most want to leave a nation better for their children. So did the Framers. But the Framers did not have sophisticated public opinion polls to tell them this, nor did they have national news media to tell them the results of those polls. Today many people wonder what shapes public opinion: poll results or people's opinions? Do the polls drive public opinion, or does public opinion drive the polls?

The role of public opinion in the making of policy is just one question we explore in this chapter. In analyzing the role of public opinion in a democracy, the development of polling, and how politicians respond to public opinion, in this chapter we'll look at the following issues:

- First, we examine the question, *what is public opinion?* Here we offer a simple definition and then note the role of public opinion polls in determining public perception of political issues.

- Second, we describe *early efforts to influence and measure public opinion.* From *The Federalist Papers* to the Republicans' Contract with America and the Democrats' Families First, parties and public officials have tried to sway as well as gauge public opinion for political purposes.

- Third, we discuss *political socialization and other factors* that lead to the formation of opinions about political matters. We also examine the role of political ideology in public opinion formation.

- Fourth, we examine *how Americans form opinions about political issues.*

- Fifth, we analyze *how public opinion is measured* and note problems with various kinds of polling techniques.

- Sixth, we look at *how polling and public opinion affect politicians* as well as how politicians affect public opinion.

- Finally, we examine the *ramifications of policy based on faulty polling.* We also explore some reasons to consider *new kinds of polling practices* or changes in the way polling is conducted or utilized.

WHAT IS PUBLIC OPINION?

public opinion: What the public thinks about a particular issue or set of issues at any point in time.

public opinion poll: Interviews or surveys with a sample of citizens that are used to estimate public opinion of the entire population.

At first blush, **public opinion** seems to be a very straightforward term: It is what the public thinks about a particular issue or set of issues at a particular time. Since the 1930s, governmental decision makers have relied heavily on **public opinion polls**—interviews with a sample of citizens that are used to determine what the public is thinking. According to George Gallup, the founder of modern-day polling, polls have played a key role in defining issues of concern to the public, shaping administrative decisions, and helping "speed up the process of democracy" in the United States.[3] (See Roots of Government: George Gallup: The Founder of Modern Polling.)

According to Gallup, leaders must constantly take public opinion—no matter how short-lived—into account. Like the Jacksonians of a much earlier era, Gallup was distrustful of leaders who were not in tune with the "common man." According to Gallup,

> in a democracy we demand the views of the people be taken into account. This does not mean that leaders must follow the public's view slavishly; it does mean that they should have an available appraisal of public opinion and take some account of it in reaching their decision.[4]

Even though Gallup undoubtedly had a vested interest in fostering reliance on public opinion polls, his sentiments accurately reflect the feelings of many political thinkers concerning the role of public opinion and governance. Some, like Gallup, believe that the government should do what a majority of the public wants done. Others argue that the public as a whole doesn't have consistent opinions on day-to-day issues

Roots of Government

George Gallup: The Founder of Modern Polling

George Gallup earned a Ph.D. in journalism from the University of Iowa with a dissertation that examined methods of measuring the readership of newspapers. He first became interested in polling when his mother-in-law ran for public office in 1932. She was running against a popular incumbent, and most observers considered her candidacy a lost cause. Nevertheless, because of the Democratic landslide of 1932, she was swept into office on Franklin D. Roosevelt's coattails.

Gallup's interest in politics, fostered by his experience in his mother-in-law's campaign and his academic background in journalism and advertising, led him to take a job at a New York advertising agency. In 1935 he founded the American Institute of Public Opinion, headquartered at Princeton University in New Jersey. At the institute Gallup refined a number

(Photo courtesy: UPI/The Bettmann Archive)

of survey and sampling techniques to measure the public's attitudes on social, political, and economic issues. Weekly reports called the Gallup Polls were sent to more than forty subscribing newspapers.

Gallup attracted considerable national attention when he correctly predicted the outcome of the 1936 presidential election. Recognizing many of the flaws of *Literary Digest*'s poll, he relied on a sample of a few thousand people who represented the voting population in terms of important demographic variables,

such as age, gender, political affiliation, and region.

Through the late 1940s, the number of polling groups and increasingly sophisticated polling techniques grew by leaps and bounds as new businesses and politicians relied on the information they provided to market products and candidates. In 1948, however, the polling industry suffered a severe, although fleeting, setback when George Gallup and many other pollsters incorrectly predicted that Thomas E. Dewey would defeat President Harry S Truman (see Figure 11.1).

In spite of errors like these, pollsters have been quick to defend their craft. Gallup readily admitted the mistakes that affected his 1948 poll, including the early cutoff date of his sample, noting, "we are continually experimenting and we are continually learning."* He consistently argued that the judgment of the masses was basically good and often far better than that of their leaders.

*Benjamin Ginsberg, *The Captive Public* (New York: Basic Books, 1986).

but that subgroups within the public often hold strong views on some issues. These *pluralists* (see chapter 1) believe that the government must allow for the expression of these minority opinions and that democracy works best when these different voices are allowed to fight it out in the public arena.

But, as we will see later in this chapter, what the public or even subgroups think about various issues is difficult to know with certainty simply because public opinion can change so quickly. For example, two weeks before the United States bombed Iraq in January 1991, public opinion polls revealed that only 61 percent of the American public believed that the United States should engage in combat in Iraq. One week after the invasion, however, 86 percent reported that they approved of President Bush's handling of the situation.

EARLY EFFORTS TO INFLUENCE AND MEASURE PUBLIC OPINION

You can hardly read a newspaper or a news magazine or watch television without hearing the results of the latest public opinion poll on health care, crime, race, the president's performance, or even that of the First Lady. But long before modern polling, politicians tried to mold and win public opinion. *The Federalist Papers* were themselves one of the first major attempts to change public opinion—in this case, to gain public support for the newly drafted U.S. Constitution. Even prior to publication of *The Federalist Papers*, Thomas Paine's *Common Sense* and later his *Crisis* papers were widely distributed throughout the colonies in an effort to stimulate patriotic feelings and increase public support for the Revolutionary War.

From the very early days of the republic, political leaders recognized the importance of public opinion and used all the means at their disposal to manipulate it for political purposes. By the early 1800s, the term "public opinion" was frequently being used by the educated middle class. As more Americans became educated, they became more vocal about their opinions and were more likely to vote. A more educated, reading public led to increased demand for newspapers, which in turn provided more information about the process of government. And as the United States grew, there were more elections and more opportunities for citizens to express their political opinions through the ballot box. As a result of these trends, political leaders were more frequently forced to try to gauge public opinion in order to remain responsive to the wishes and desires of their constituents.

An example of the power of public opinion is the public's response to the 1851 through 1852 serialization of Harriet Beecher Stowe's *Uncle Tom's Cabin*. This novel was one of the most powerful propaganda statements ever issued about slavery. By the time the first shots of the Civil War were fired at Fort Sumter in 1861 more than 1 million copies of the book were in print. Even though Stowe's words alone could not have caused the public outrage over slavery that contributed to Northern support for the war, her book convinced the majority of the American people of the justness of the abolitionist cause and solidified public opinion in the North against slavery.

During World War I, some people argued that public opinion didn't matter at all. But President Woodrow Wilson (1913–21) argued that public opinion would temper the actions of international leaders. Therefore, only eight days after the start of the war,

During World War I, as part of "The world's greatest adventure in advertising," the Committee on Public Information created a vast gallery of posters designed to shore up public support for the war effort. (Photo courtesy: The Bettmann Archive)

Wilson created a Committee on Public Information. Run by a prominent journalist, the committee immediately undertook to unite U.S. public opinion behind the war effort. It used all of the tools available—pamphlets, posters, and speakers who exhorted the patrons of local movie houses during every intermission—in an effort to garner support and favorable opinion for the war. In the words of the committee's head, it was "the world's greatest adventure in advertising."[5]

In the wake of World War I, Walter Lippmann, a well-known journalist and author who was extensively involved in propaganda activities during the war, openly voiced his concerns about how easily public opinion could be manipulated and his reservations about the weight it should be given. In his seminal work, *Public Opinion* (1922), Lippmann wrote, "Since Public Opinion is supposed to be the prime mover in democracies, one might reasonably expect to find a vast literature [examining it]. One does not find it."[6] By the 1920s, although numerous efforts had been made to manipulate public opinion, scientific measurement of public opinion had yet to occur.

SPEED BUMP   **Dave Coverly**

GOOD GOD, NOT ANOTHER IDIOT WITH A STRAW POLL...

(Photo courtesy: Dave Covery/*Boston Herald*)

Early Efforts to Measure Public Opinion

Public opinion polling as we know it today did not begin to develop until the 1930s. Researchers in a variety of disciplines, including political science, heeded Lippmann's call to learn more about public opinion. Some tried to use scientific methods to measure political thought through the use of surveys or polls. As methods for gathering and interpreting data improved, survey data began to play an increasingly important role in all walks of life, from politics to retailing.

Early Election Forecasting. As early as 1824, one Pennsylvania newspaper tried to predict the winner of that year's presidential contest. Later, in 1883, the *Boston Globe* sent reporters to selected election precincts to poll voters as they exited voting booths, in an effort to predict the results of key contests. And in 1916, *Literary Digest*, a popular magazine, began mailing survey postcards to potential voters in an effort to predict election outcomes. *Literary Digest* drew its survey sample from "every telephone book in the United States, from the rosters of clubs and associations, from city directories, lists of registered voters [and] classified mail order and occupational data."[7] Using the data it received from the millions of postcard ballots sent out throughout the United States, *Literary Digest* correctly predicted every presidential election from 1920 to 1932.

Literary Digest used what were called **straw polls** to predict the popular vote in those four presidential elections. Its polling methods were widely hailed as "amazingly right" and "uncannily accurate."[8] In 1936, however, its luck ran out. *Literary Digest* predicted that Republican Alfred M. Landon would beat incumbent President Franklin D. Roosevelt by a margin of 57 percent to 43 percent of the popular vote. Roosevelt, however, won in a landslide election, receiving 62.5 percent of the popular vote and carrying all but two states.

straw poll: Unscientific survey used to gauge public opinion on a variety of issues and policies.

Polling Matures. Through the late 1940s, the number of polling groups and increasingly sophisticated polling techniques grew by leaps and bounds as new businesses and politicians relied on the information they provide to market products and candidates. In 1948, however, the polling industry suffered a severe, although fleeting, setback when Gallup and many other pollsters incorrectly predicted that Thomas E. Dewey would defeat President Harry S Truman.

Not only did advance polls in 1948 predict that Republican nominee Thomas E. Dewey would defeat Democratic incumbent Harry S Truman, but based on early and incomplete vote tallies, some newspapers' early editions even on the day *after* the election declared Dewey to have won. Here a triumphant Truman holds aloft the *Chicago Tribune.* (Photo courtesy: UPI/The Bettmann Archive)

What Went Wrong? *Literary Digest* reached out to as many potential respondents as possible, with no regard for modern sampling techniques that require that respondents be selected or sampled according to strict rules of cross-sectional representation. Respondents, in essence, were like "straws in the wind," hence the term "straw polls."

Literary Digest's sample had three fatal errors. First, its sample was drawn from telephone directories and lists of automobile owners. This technique oversampled the upper middle class and the wealthy, groups heavily Republican in political orientation. Moreover, in 1936, voting polarized along class lines. Thus the oversampling of wealthy Republicans was particularly problematic because it severely underestimated the Democratic vote.

Literary Digest's second problem was timing: Questionnaires were mailed in early September. Thus the changes in public sentiment that occurred as the election drew closer were not measured.

Its third error occurred because of a problem we now call self-selection: Only highly motivated individuals sent back the cards—only 22 percent of those surveyed responded. Those who respond to mail surveys are quite different from the general electorate; they often are wealthier and better educated and care more fervently about issues. *Literary Digest,* then, failed to observe one of the now well-known cardinal rules of survey sampling: "One cannot allow the respondents to select themselves into the sample."[9]

At least one pollster, however, correctly predicted the results of the 1936 election: George Gallup. Gallup had written his dissertation on how to measure the readership of newspapers, and then expanded his methods to study public opinion about politics. He was so confident about his methods that he gave all of his newspaper clients a money-back guarantee: If his poll predictions weren't closer to the actual election outcome than those of the highly acclaimed *Literary Digest,* he would refund them their money. The *Digest* predicted Alf Landon to win; Gallup predicted Roosevelt. Al-

FIGURE 11.1

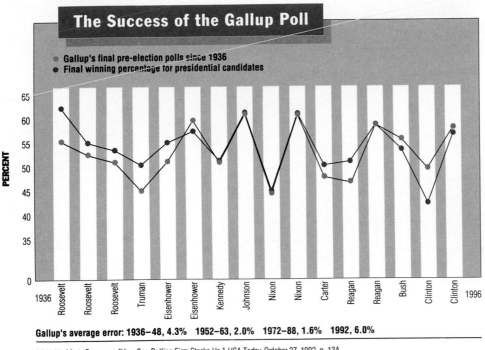

The Success of the Gallup Poll

● Gallup's final pre-election polls since 1936
● Final winning percentage for presidential candidates

Gallup's average error: 1936–48, 4.3% 1952–63, 2.0% 1972–88, 1.6% 1992, 6.0%

SOURCE: Marty Baumann, "How One Polling Firm Stacks Up," *USA Today*, October 27, 1992, p. 13A.
Copyright 1992, *USA Today*. Reprinted with permission.

though he underpredicted Roosevelt's victory by nearly 7 percent, the fact that he got the winner right was what everyone remembered, especially given *Literary Digest*'s dramatic miscalculation. And, as revealed in Figure 11.1, the Gallup Organization, now run by George Gallup's son, continues to be a successful predictor of elections.

The American Voter, Public Opinion, and Political Socialization

The American Voter was published in 1960.[10] This book "intellectually" "contributed the dominant model for thinking about mass attitudes and mass behavior in the social science research that followed."[11] Drawing on data from the 1952 and 1956 presidential elections, *The American Voter* showed how class coalitions, which were originally formed around social-welfare issues, led to party affiliations—the dominant force in presidential elections. This book also led directly to the "institutionalization of regular surveys of the American electorate, through a biennial series now recognized as the National Election Study."[12] As discussed in Highlight 11.1, the National Election Study has given political scientists a long-term view of the political beliefs and attitudes of the American public. Indeed, the NES drives the research of many political scientists as they try to understand what drives public opinion, voting, and the course of elections. Work by political scientists has told us much about political socialization and how and when, as well as why, we form opinions about politics, government, and other political matters.

Highlight 11.1

Doing Political Science: Social Science Surveys

Many of the tables and figures in this book are derived from data from two surveys frequently used by political scientists: the General Social Survey and the American National Election Studies.

The General Social Survey (GSS)

The GSS is produced at the National Opinion Research Center (NORC) of the University of Chicago, which has been conducting national surveys since the 1930s. These surveys are conducted through interviews based on questionnaires that cover a broad range of social topics, including political issues. Because NORC often uses the same questions in different surveys for years, the GSS provides investigators with useful indicators of public opinion as it changes. The data produced by researchers in Chicago are made available to users through the Roper Public Opinion Research Center. For each of its surveys, NORC usually interviews roughly 1,500 randomly selected English-speaking people over the age of eighteen who live in noninstitutionalized settings.

The American National Election Studies (NES)

The NES are conducted by social scientists at the Center for Political Studies of the Institute for Social Research at the University of Michigan. The Center's first major report was *The American Voter.*

NES surveys focus only on political attitudes and behavior of the electorate. Thus they include questions about how respondents voted, their party affiliation, and their opinion of the major political parties and candidates. These surveys also include questions about their interest in political matters, how they voted, and their political participation, including participation in nonelection-related activities, such as church attendance.

The surveys are conducted before and after midterm and presidential elections. A random sample of those eligible to vote on Election Day and living in the continental United States is used. Like the GSS, some of the same questions are used in each survey to compile long-term studies of the electorate to facilitate political scientists' understanding of how and why people vote and participate in politics.

POLITICAL SOCIALIZATION AND OTHER FACTORS THAT INFLUENCE OPINION FORMATION

political socialization: The process through which an individual acquires particular political orientations; the learning process by which people acquire their political beliefs and values.

*P*olitical scientists believe that many of our attitudes about issues are grounded in our political values. We learn these values through a process called **political socialization,** "the process through which an individual acquires his [or her] particular political orientations—his [or her] knowledge, feeling and evaluations regarding his [or her] political world."[13] Family, the mass media, schools, and peers are often important influences or agents of political socialization. For example, try to remember your earliest memory of the president of the United States. It may have been Ronald Reagan or George Bush (older students probably remember earlier presidents). What did you think of him? Of the Republican or Democratic Party? It's likely that your earliest feelings or attitudes were shaped by what your parents thought about that particular president and his party. Similar processes also apply to your early attitudes about the flag of the United States, or even the police.

Other factors, too, often influence how political opinions are formed or reinforced. These include political events; the social groups you belong to, including your church; demographic group, including your race, gender, and age; and even the region of the country in which you live.

The Family

The influence of the family can be traced to two factors: communication and receptivity. Children, especially during their preschool years, spend tremendous amounts of time with their parents; early on they learn their parents' political values, even though these concepts may be vague. One study, for example, found that the most important visible public figures for children under the age of ten were police officers and, to a much lesser extent, the president. Young children almost uniformly view both as "helpful." But by the age of ten or eleven, children become more selective in their perceptions of the president. By this age children raised in Democratic households are much more likely to be critical of a Republican president than are those raised in Republican households. In 1988, for example, 58 percent of children in Republican households identified themselves as Republicans, and many developed strong positive feelings toward Ronald Reagan, the Republican president. Support for and the popularity of Ronald Reagan translated into strong support for the Republican Party through the 1988 presidential election and also contributed to the growing conservative ideological self-identification of first-year college students depicted in Figure 11.2. Other forces, including the media, however, also affect political socialization.

Political values are shaped in childhood. (Photo courtesy: Nancy O'Connor Zeigler)

FIGURE 11.2

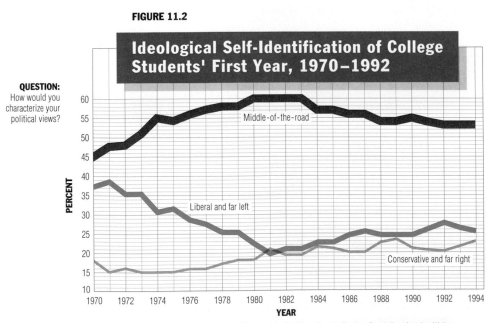

Ideological Self-Identification of College Students' First Year, 1970–1992

QUESTION: How would you characterize your political views?

Middle-of-the-road

Liberal and far left

Conservative and far right

SOURCE: E.L. Dey, A. W. Astin, and W. S. Korn, *The American Freshman: Twenty-five Year Trends* (Los Angeles: Higher Education Research Institute, University of California, Los Angeles, 1991); *The American Freshman: National Norms for Fall 1991* (Los Angeles: Higher Education Research Institute, University of California, Los Angeles, 1991); *Fall 1992* (1992). Adopted from Harold W. Stanley and Richard G. Niemi, *Vital Statistics on American Government*, 4E. (Washington, DC: CQ Press, 1994), p. 203. Reprinted by permission.

The Mass Media

The media today is taking on a growing role as a socialization agent. Adult Americans spend nearly thirty hours a week in front of their television sets; children spend even more.[14] Television has a tremendous impact on how people view politics, government, and politicians. TV talk shows and talk radio are an important source of information about politics for many, yet the information that people get from these sources is often skewed. One recent study, for example, found that 25 percent of all Americans learned about presidential campaigns from David Letterman and Jay Leno.[15] On those shows, emphasis was on Bob Dole's age and Bill Clinton's philandering and not on substance, as evidenced in Highlight 11.2. Bob Dole, in particular, took it hard as his age was the subject of repeated barbs by comedians who appeal to younger audiences.

Television can often act to turn out the vote or turn voters on to particular candidates. For example, MTV continued its successful "Rock the Vote" campaign in 1996 trying again to galvanize young people to participate and vote.

Only 22 percent of those under age thirty report that they watch nightly news; for 13 percent MTV was the major source of their information about politics.[16] MTV's election features are designed to spur those under twenty-five to vote and to increase their knowledge about issues and candidates. In 1992 Bill Clinton and his running mate, Al Gore, Jr., appeared on MTV to discuss issues and answer questions. The under-twenty-five vote went overwhelmingly for the more liberal candidate, Clinton, in contrast to the presidential elections in 1988 and 1984.

All of the major candidates in the 1996 election also attempted to use a new form of "media" to sway and inform voters: the Internet. Most had campaign home pages. It is unclear how many Americans currently get their information about politics online, but the explosion of Internet usage undoubtedly will someday play an important role in the transferal and acquisition of political information and opinion formation.

Highlight 11.2

Dave's Top Ten

Reasons Colin Powell Doesn't Want to Be Bob Dole's Running Mate"

10. His main responsibility would be cutting Dole's food.

9. Dole keeps asking him, "How are those wooden teeth working out, Gen. Washington?"

8. Suspects that what Dole is really after is one of his kidneys.

7. Has had dozens of conversations with Dole and not once did he understand a word the guy said.

6. Wants to devote himself to full-scale invasion of local "Hooters."

5. Dole cuts out of important meetings whenever "Golden Girls" reruns are on.

4. Wants to avoid the inevitable headline, "The General and the Geriatric."

3. It's hard to organize your schedule when every other hour is "naptime."

2. Feels uncomfortable when Dole tries to impress him by using terms like "Def Jam."

1. If he wanted to get his [rear] kicked, he'd be playing for the Detroit Tigers.

Source: The Atlanta Journal/Constitution (July 16, 1996): E4.

School and Peers

Researchers report mixed findings concerning the role of schools in the political socialization process. There is no question that, in elementary school, children are taught respect for their nation and its symbols. Most school days begin with the Pledge of Allegiance, and patriotism and respect for country are important, although subtle, components of most school curricula. The terms "flag" and the "United States" evoke very positive feelings from a majority of Americans. Support for these two icons serves the purpose of maintaining national allegiance and underlies the success of the U.S. political system in spite of relatively negative views about Congress, the courts, and the current government. In 1991, for example, few school children were taught to question U.S. involvement in the Persian Gulf. Instead, at almost every school in the nation, children were encouraged or even required to write servicemen and servicewomen stationed in the Gulf, involving these children with the war effort and implying school support for the war.

A child's peers—that is, children about the same age as a young person—also seem to have an important effect on the socialization process. Whereas parental influences are greatest during the tender years from birth to age five, a child's peer group becomes increasingly more important as the child gets older, especially as he or she get into middle school or high school.

High schools can also be important agents of political socialization. They continue the elementary school tradition of building good citizens and often reinforce textbook learning with trips to the state or national capital. They also offer courses on current U.S. affairs. Although the formal education of many people in the United States ends with high school, research shows that better-informed citizens vote more often as adults. Therefore, presentation of civic information is especially critical at the high school level.

At the college level, teaching style often changes. Many college courses and texts like this one are designed in part to provide you with the information necessary to think critically about issues of major political consequence. It is common in college for students to be called on to question the appropriateness of certain political actions or to discuss underlying reasons for certain political or policy decisions. Therefore most researchers believe that college has a liberalizing effect on students. Since the 1920s, studies have shown, students become more liberal each year they are in college. As we show in Figure 11.2, however, this trend, appeared to decline in the 1980s, as more and more students with conservative views entered colleges and universities during the Reagan era. The 1992 and 1996 victories of Bill Clinton and his equally youthful running mate, Al Gore, Jr., who went out of their way to woo the youth vote, probably contributed to the small bump in the ideological identification of first-year college students.

The Impact of Events

These is no doubt that parents—and, to a lesser degree, school and peers—play a role in a person's political socialization, but the role of key political events is also very important. You probably have some professors who remember what they were doing on the day that President John F. Kennedy was killed—November 22, 1963. This dramatic event is indelibly etched in the minds of virtually all people who were old enough to be aware of it. Similarly, most college students today remember where they were when the space shuttle *Challenger* exploded, or when they learned about the Oklahoma City bombing.

Throughout the United States, most school children start the day with a "Pledge to the Flag." From a very early age, children are taught respect for national symbols and ideals. (Photo courtesy: Charles Gupton/Stock Boston)

FIGURE 11.3

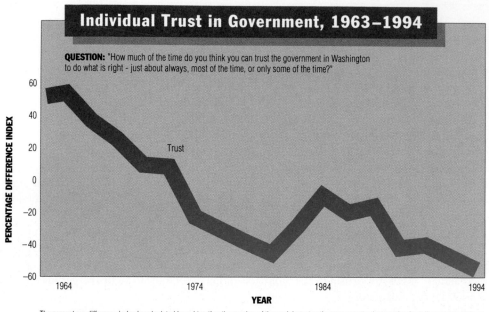

Individual Trust in Government, 1963–1994

QUESTION: "How much of the time do you think you can trust the government in Washington to do what is right - just about always, most of the time, or only some of the time?"

Trust

PERCENTAGE DIFFERENCE INDEX

YEAR

The percentage difference index is calculated by subtracting the number of those giving a trusting response to the question from the number of those giving a cynical response. A positive number in the index indicates an overall trust in government; a negative number indicates overall distrust.

SOURCE: Harold W. Stanley and Richard Niemi, *Vital Statistics on American Politics*, 4E. (Washington, DC: CQ Press, 1994), p. 169. Updated by the authors.

President Richard M. Nixon's fall from grace and forced resignation in 1973 also had a profound impact on the socialization process of all Americans. It made a particular impression on young people, who were forced to realize that their government was not always right or honest.

In fact, one problem in discussing political socialization is that many of the major studies on this topic were conducted in the aftermath of these and other crucial events, including the civil rights movement and the Vietnam War, all of which produced a marked increase in Americans' distrust of government. The findings reported in Figure 11.3 reveal the dramatic drop-off of trust in government that began in the mid-1960s and continued through the election of Ronald Reagan in 1980. In a study of Boston children conducted in the aftermath of the Watergate scandal, for example, one political scientist found that children's perception of the president went from that of a benevolent to a "malevolent" leader.[17] These findings are indicative of the low confidence most Americans had in government in the aftermath of Watergate and President Nixon's ultimate resignation from office to avoid impeachment. Similarly, while not having such a marked effect, the Whitewater investigation of the Clintons, Filegate and Travelgate, and the House Ethics Committee's probe of Speaker Newt Gingrich's book deals and GOPAC (see chapter 16) have not given Americans reason for increased trust in government.

Social Groups

Group effects, that is, certain characteristics that allow persons to be lumped into categories, also affect the development and continuity of political beliefs and opinions.

Among the most important of these groups are religion, education level, income, and race. More recently, researchers have learned that gender and age are becoming increasingly important determinants of public opinion, especially on certain issues. Region, too, while not a social group, per se, also appears to influence political beliefs and political socialization.

Religion.   Today religion plays a very important role in the life of Americans. Although only one in five citizens in 1776 belonged to a church or synagogue, today two-thirds of all Americans attend church. Moreover, almost all Americans (96 percent) believe in God and 72 percent believe in angels. Nearly half of all Americans attend church regularly, and 62 percent believe that religion "can answer all or most of today's problems."[18]

In 1996, 56 percent of Americans identified themselves as Protestant, 26 percent as Catholic, 36 percent describe themselves as born-again or evangelical Christians, 2 percent as Jewish, and 7 percent as other.[19] Only 9 percent claimed to have no religious affiliation.[20] Over the years, analysts have found continuing opinion differences among these groups, with Protestants being the most conservative on many issues and Jews the most liberal, as shown in Figure 11.4. Evangelical Christians, in particular, have strong conservative views and have mobilized to have their views and beliefs converted into public policy. As discussed in chapter 16, the Christian Coalition, made up largely of evangelical Christians, has a comprehensive legislative agenda it hopes to have enacted at all levels of government.

Shared religious attitudes tend to affect voting and stances on particular issues. Catholics tend to vote Democratic more than do Protestants, and they tend to vote for other Catholics. For example, in 1960 Catholics overwhelmingly cast their ballots for John F. Kennedy, who became the first Catholic president. Catholics as a group also favor aid to parochial schools, most Jews support aid to Israel, and many fundamen-

FIGURE 11.4

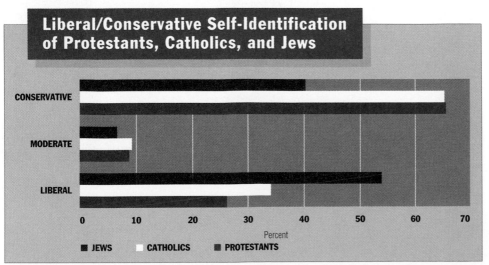

Liberal/Conservative Self-Identification of Protestants, Catholics, and Jews

SOURCE: Data compiled by authos from 1992 National Opinion Research General Election Study.

talist Protestants support organized prayer in public schools. Seventy-eight percent of regular church-attending evangelicals voted Republican in the 1994 elections.[21]

Race.   During the O. J. Simpson trial, public opinion poll after public opinion poll revealed in stark numbers the immense racial divide that continues to exist in the nation. Blacks distrust governmental institutions far more than do whites, and are much more likely to question police actions. Not surprisingly, then, while a majority of whites believed that Simpson was guilty, a majority of blacks believed that he was innocent.

Race is an exceptionally important factor in elections and in the study of public opinion. As highlighted by the O. J. Simpson example, the direction and intensity of African-American opinion on a variety of hot-button issues is often quite different from that of whites. As revealed in Figure 11.5, whites oppose affirmative action plans at significantly higher levels than do African Americans. Likewise, significant differences can be seen in other areas, including public assistance and welfare, food stamps, federal aid for cities, and support for the death penalty.

Hispanics, Asians/Pacific Islanders, and Native Americans are other identifiable ethnic minorities in the United States (see chapter 1, Figure 1.3) that often respond differently to issues than do whites. Generally, Hispanics and Native Americans hold similar opinions on many issues largely because many of them have low incomes and find themselves targets of discrimination. Within the Hispanic community, however, existing divisions often depend on national origin. Generally, Cuban Americans who clus-

FIGURE 11.5

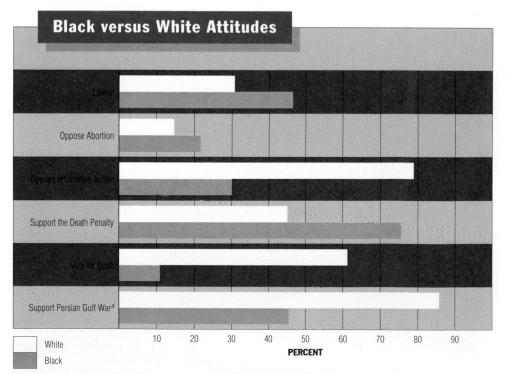

Black versus White Attitudes

Liberal

Oppose Abortion

Oppose Affirmative Action

Support the Death Penalty

Vote for Bush

Support Persian Gulf War[a]

10 20 30 40 50 60 70 80 90
PERCENT

White
Black

[a] One week after U.S. attack on Iraq

SOURCE: Compiled by authors from 1988 National Election Study and Sharen Shaw Johnson, "Vision of Short War Fading Fast," *USA Today* (January 21, 1991) p. 3A.

ter in Florida (and in the Miami–Dade County area in particular) are more likely to be conservative. They fled from communism and Fidel Castro in Cuba, and they generally vote Republican. In the 1976 presidential election, for example, only 40.2 percent of the Cuban Americans in the Miami–Dade area voted for Jimmy Carter.[22] In contrast, Chicanos (people of Mexican origin) voting in California, New Mexico, Arizona, Texas, and Colorado cast 83.1 percent of their votes for Carter that year.[23]

Gender.   From the time that the earliest public opinion polls were taken, women have been known to hold more negative views about war and military intervention than do men, and more strongly positive attitudes about issues touching on social welfare concerns, such as education, juvenile justice, capital punishment, and the environment. Many researchers have sought to explain this **gender gap.** Some suggest that women's more "nurturing" nature and their prominent role as mothers lead women to have more liberal attitudes on issues affecting the family or the safety of their children. Research by Pamela Johnson Conover and Virginia Sapiro, however, finds no support for a maternal explanation.[24]

gender gap: The tendency for women to vote for candidates of the Democratic Party.

Poll after poll continues to reveal that women hold very different opinions from men on a variety of issues, as shown in Table 11.1. Ironically, however, during the debate over the Equal Rights Amendment in the 1970s, men supported the amendment more than did women voters. Men also appear today to support a woman's right to have an abortion to a greater extent than do women.

These differences have often translated into substantial gaps in the way women and men vote. Women, for example, are more likely to be Democrats, and they often provide Democratic candidates with their margin of victory. This is one of the reasons that Republican presidential candidate Bob Dole asked Representative Susan Molanari (R–N.Y.) to be the keynote speaker at the Republican National Convention. The selection of Molanari, a pro-choice mother of an infant, was one way Dole tried to attract more women voters to the GOP.

TABLE 11.1

Gender Differences on Political Issues

FAVORED OR SUPPORTING	MALES	FEMALES
Increase Defense Spending	34	24
Aid to Foreign Military Groups	42	21
"Star Wars" (defense) spending	24	10
No return to a peacetime draft	48	61
Initial sending of troops to Gulf	72	53
Increase spending on food stamps	18	24
Contract with America	72	54
Approve of Bill Clinton's handling of the presidency	47	57
Favor affirmative action for women	52	69

Source: Data from Center for American Women and Politics, 1980; CNN/*USA Today* (December 28–30, 1994) and *The Public Perspective* (June/July 1995): 38 and (April/May 1996): 39.

Age.   As Americans live longer, senior citizens are becoming a potent political force. In states such as Florida, to which many Northern retirees have flocked seeking relief from cold winters and high taxes, the elderly have voted as a bloc to defeat school tax increases and to pass tax breaks for themselves. As a group senior citizens are much more likely to favor an increased governmental role in the area of medical insurance and to oppose any cuts in Social Security benefits.

In the future the "graying of America" will have major social and political consequences. As we discuss in chapter 13, the elderly under age seventy vote in much larger numbers than do their younger counterparts. Moreover, the fastest-growing age group in the United States is that of citizens over the age of sixty-five. Thus not only are there more people in this category, but they are more likely to be registered to vote, and often vote conservatively.

Age also seems to have a decided effect on one's view of the proper role of government, with older people continuing to be affected by having lived through the Depression and World War II. In *Young v. Old: Generational Combat in the 21st Century*, political scientist Susan A. MacManus predicts that as baby boomers age, the age gap in political beliefs about political issues, especially governmental programs, will increase.[25] Young people, for example, resist higher taxes to fund Medicare, while the elderly resist all efforts to limit it or Social Security.

Region.   Regional and sectional differences have been important factors in the development and maintenance of public opinion and political beliefs since colonial times. As the United States grew and developed into a major industrial nation, waves of immigrants with different religious traditions and customs entered the United States and often settled in areas they viewed as hospitable to their way of life. For example, thousands of Scandinavians settled in cold, snowy, rural Minnesota, and many Irish settled in the urban centers of the Northeast, as did many Italians and Jews. All brought with them unique views about many issues, as well as about the role of government. Many of these regional differences continue to affect public opinion today and sometimes result in conflict at the national level.

Recall, for example, that during the Constitutional Convention most Southerners staunchly advocated a weak national government. Nearly a hundred years later, the Civil War was fought in part because of basic differences in philosophy toward government (states' rights in the South versus national rights in the North). As we know from the results of modern political polling, the South has continued to lag behind the rest of the nation on support for civil rights, while continuing to favor return of power to the states at the expense of the national government, as revealed in Table 11.2.

The South is also much more religious than the rest of the nation, as well as more Protestant. Sixty-four percent of the South is Protestant (versus 39 percent for the rest of the nation), and 45 percent identify themselves as born-again Christians. Nearly half of all Southerners believe that "the United States is a Christian country, and the government should make laws to keep it that way."[26] It is not surprising, then, that the Christian Coalition has been very successful at mobilizing voters in the South.

Southerners also are much more supportive of a strong national defense. They accounted for 41 percent of the troops in the Persian Gulf in the early days of the war, even though they make up only 28 percent of the general population.

The West, too, now appears "different" from other sections of the nation. As discussed in chapter 3, some people have moved there to avoid city life; other residents have an antigovernment bias. And many who have sought refuge there are staunchly against any governmental action, especially on the national level.

TABLE 11.2

Does the South Differ?

Percentage giving "liberal" response among white Protestants living in different regions, 1988

ISSUE	EAST	MIDWEST	SOUTH	WEST
Economic and welfare issues:				
More government health care	48%	35%	37%	39%
Government job guarantees	19	19	22	21
Increase Social Security	56	50	59	53
Cut military spending	32	35	21	30
Civil rights and civil liberties issues:				
Aid to minorities	16	14	14	23
Homosexual rights	56	56	47	52
Women's equality	63	65	62	69
Right to abortion	65	49	45	60
Average percentage liberal, all issues	41	37	34	41

Source: Compiled by Daron Shaw. Reprinted with permission of the Center for Political Studies, University of Michigan.

Political Ideology and Public Opinion about Government

As discussed in chapter 1, an individual's coherent set of values and beliefs about the purpose and scope of government is called his or her **political ideology.** Americans' attachment to strong ideological positions has varied over time. In sharp contrast to spur-of-the-moment responses, these sets of values, which are often greatly affected by political socialization, can prompt citizens to favor a certain set of policy programs and adopt views about the proper role of government in the policy process.

Conservatives are generally likely to support smaller, less activist governments, limited social welfare programs, and limited government regulation of business. In contrast, liberals generally believe that the national government has an important role to play in a wide array of areas, including helping the poor and disadvantaged. Unlike most conservatives, they generally favor activist governments. Most Americans today, however, identify themselves as moderates.

Political scientists and politicians often talk in terms of conservative and liberal ideologies, and most Americans believe that they do hold a political ideology. When asked, most Americans (45 percent) respond that their political beliefs are "middle of the road" or moderate, although a substantial number call themselves conservatives (37 percent) (see chapter 1, Figure 1.5).

political ideology: An individual's coherent set of values and beliefs about the purpose and scope of government.

HOW WE FORM POLITICAL OPINIONS

*M*any of us hold opinions on a wide range of political issues, and our ideas can be traced to our social group and the different experiences each of us has had. Some individuals (called ideologues) think about politics and vote strictly on the basis of liberal or conservative ideology. Others use the party label. Most people, however, don't do either. In this section we explore how most people—those who are not ideologues—make up their minds on political issues. Chief among the factors that lead people to form political opinions are personal benefits, political knowledge, and cues from various leaders or opinion makers.

Personal Benefits

Most polls reveal that Americans are growing more and more "I" centered. This perspective often leads people to choose policies that best benefit them personally. You've probably heard the adage, "People vote with their pocketbooks." Taxpayers generally favor lower taxes; hence, the popularity of candidates pledging "No new taxes." Similarly, the elderly usually support Social Security increases, and Generation X, worried about the continued stability of the Social Security program, is not very supportive of federal retirement programs. Similarly, African Americans support strong civil rights laws and affirmative action programs, while most whites do not, as revealed in Figure 11.5.

Some government policies, however, don't really affect us individually. Legalized prostitution and the death penalty, for example, are often perceived as moral issues that few citizens experience. Individuals' attitudes on these issues are often based on underlying values they have acquired through the years.

When we are faced with policies that don't affect us personally and don't involve moral issues, we often have difficulty forming an opinion. Foreign policy is an area in which this phenomenon is especially true. Most Americans often know little of the world around them. Unless moral issues such as apartheid in South Africa or human-rights violations in China are involved, American public opinion is likely to be volatile in the wake of any new information.

Political Knowledge

Americans enjoy a relatively high literacy rate, and most Americans (34 percent) graduate from high school. Most Americans, moreover, have access to a range of higher education opportunities. In spite of that access to education, however, Americans' level of actual political knowledge is low. As illustrated in Table 11.3, Americans generally don't know much about politics. In 1996, for example, 94 percent couldn't identify the Chief Justice of the United States and nearly 50 percent didn't know that Newt Gingrich was the Speaker of the House. Moreover, only 33 percent of people surveyed could correctly identify their representative in Congress. Americans, alas, don't know much about foreign policy, and some would argue that many Americans are geographically illiterate. One Gallup study done in 1988, for example, found that 75 percent of all Americans were unable to locate the Persian Gulf on a map. Two-thirds couldn't find Vietnam. Americans age eighteen to twenty-four scored the lowest, with two-thirds not being able to point to France on an outline map.[27]

TABLE 11.3

American Political Knowledge

PERCENTAGE UNABLE TO IDENTIFY

Party with most members in Senate (1996)	38
Name of vice president (1996)	40
Name of the Speaker of the House (1996)	47
Both senators from their state (1996)	54
Chief Justice of United States (1996)	94

Source: Richard Morin, "Who's in Control: Many Don't Know or Care," *The Washington Post* (January 29, 1996): A1, A6.

In 1925 Walter Lippmann critiqued the American democratic experience and highlighted the large but limited role the population plays. Citizens, said Lippmann, cannot know everything about candidates and issues but they can, and often do, know enough to impose their views and values as to the general direction the nation should take.[28] This generalized information often stands in contrast and counterbalance to the views held by more knowledgeable political elites "inside the Beltway."

As early as 1966, V. O. Key argued in his book *The Responsible Electorate* that voters "are not fools." Since then, many political scientists have argued that generalizable knowledge is enough to make democracy work. Research, for example, shows citizens' perception "of the policy stands of parties and candidates were considerably more clear and accurate when the stands themselves were more distinct: in the highly ideological election of 1964, for example, as opposed to that of 1957, or in the primaries rather than the general election of 1968."[29] In elections with sharper contrasts between candidates, voters also seemed to pay more attention to issues when they cast their ballots, and to have more highly structured liberal-conservative belief systems.[30] In addition, the use of more sophisticated analytical methods involving perceived issue distances between candidates and voters seemed to reveal more issue voting in general than had previously been discovered.[31]

Cues from Leaders

Low levels of knowledge, however, can lead to rapid opinion shifts on issues. The ebb and flow of popular opinion can be affected dramatically (some might say "manipulated") by political leaders. Given the visibility of political leaders and their access to the media, it is easy to see the important role they play in influencing public opinion. Political leaders, members of the news media, and a host of other experts have regular opportunities to influence public opinion because of the lack of deep conviction with which most Americans hold many of their political beliefs.

The president, especially, is often in a position to mold public opinion through effective use of the "bully pulpit," as discussed in chapter 8. Political scientist John E. Mueller concludes, in fact, that there is a group of citizens—called *followers*—who are inclined to rally to the support of the president no matter what he does.[32]

Like President Ronald Reagan, Bill Clinton has been a master manipulator of the media and public opinion. He regular uses televised town meetings as a way to move public opinion. (Photo courtesy: Wally McNamee/Sygma)

According to Mueller, the president's strength, especially in the area of foreign affairs (where public information is lowest), derives from the "majesty" of his office and his singular position as head of state.[33] Recognizing this phenomenon, presidents often take to television in an effort to drum up support for their programs.[34] President Clinton, like Reagan before him, clearly realizes the importance of mobilizing public opinion. He frequently takes his case directly to the public, urging the people to support his programs and to convey that support to their elected officials. He has also used his vice president to mobilize public opinion in order to help him get his programs through Congress.

HOW WE MEASURE PUBLIC OPINION

*P*ublic officials at all levels use a variety of measures as indicators of public opinion to guide their policy decisions. These measures include election results; the number of telephone calls, faxes, or e-mail messages received pro and con on any particular issue; letters to the editor in hometown papers; and the size of demonstrations or marches. But the most commonly relied-on measure of public sentiment continues to be the public opinion survey, more popularly called a public opinion poll.

The polling process most often begins when someone says, "Let's find out about X and Y." Xs and Ys can be many things. Potential candidates for local office may want to know how many people have heard of them (the device used to find out is called a *name recognition survey*). Better-known candidates contemplating running for higher office might want to know how they might fare against an incumbent. Answers to questions including how to shape a candidate's campaign, how the public views the First Lady, how to market a new product, or how to market candidates can be partially acquired by knowing what the public wants at any given time. Polls can provide those answers. And news organizations routinely poll potential voters over the course of a campaign (or the duration of a war or presidential term, for example) to measure changes in public opinion and to measure the fluctuations in a candidate's popularity as Election Day nears. Polls can also be used to gauge how effective particular ads are or if a candidate is being well (or negatively) perceived by the public. Even incumbent presidents use polls. According to the Federal Election Commission, in 1993 alone, President Clinton spent $1,986,410 on polling. Remember, this is money for polls taken while in office . . . not for running for office.

Determining the Content and Phrasing the Questions

Once a candidate, politician, or news organization decides to use a poll to measure the public's attitudes, special care has to be taken in constructing the questions to be asked. For example, if your professor asked you, "Do you think my grading procedures are fair?" rather than asking, "In general, how fair do you think the grading is in your American Politics course?" you might give a slightly different answer. The wording of the first question tends to put you on the spot and personalize the grading style; the second question is more neutral. Even more obvious differences appear in the real world of polling, especially when interested groups want a poll to yield particular results. Responses to highly emotional issues such as abortion, busing, and affirmative action are often skewed depending on the wording of the question. As Highlight 11.3:

TABLE 11.4

Public Opinion on Abortion, 1962–94 (in percentages) Abortion Should Be Legal Under These Circumstances

YEAR	MOTHER'S HEALTH	RAPE	BIRTH DEFECT	LOW INCOME	SINGLE MOTHER	AS A FORM OF BIRTH CONTROL	ANY REASON
1965	70	56	55	21	17	15	—*
1973	91	81	82	52	47	46	—*
1983	87	80	76	42	38	38	33
1994	88	81	79	49	46	47	45

*Figures not available. Question: "Please tell me whether or not you think it should be possible for a pregnant woman to obtain a legal abortion [in the order asked in the survey] if there is a strong chance of serious defect in the baby? If she is married and does not want any more children? If the woman's own health is seriously endangered by the pregnancy? If the family has a very low income and cannot afford any more children? If she became pregnant as a result of rape? If she is not married and does not want to marry the man? If the woman wants it for any reason?"

Sources: 1965: National Opinion Research Center surveys; 1973–94: General Social Survey. Compiled in Harold W. Stanley and Richard G. Niemi, *Vital Statistics on American Politics*, 5th ed. (Washington, D.C.: CQ Press, 1995), 36.

Question the Numbers and Check the Wording suggests, answers to questions about all kinds of controversial issues appear to differ considerably depending on how the questions are worded. And, as revealed in Table 11.4, support for abortion can range from around 40 percent to 90 percent, depending on the question asked. (Respondents often react to emotional cues in the question, which tends to skew survey results.)

Selecting the Sample

Once the decision is made to take a poll, pollsters must determine the *universe,* or the entire group whose attitudes they wish to measure. This universe could be all Americans, all voters, all city residents, all women, or all Democrats. Although in a perfect world each individual would be asked to give an opinion, this kind of polling is simply not practical. Consequently, pollsters take a sample of the universe in which they are interested. One way to obtain this sample is by **random sampling.** This method of selection gives each potential voter or adult the same chance of being selected. In theory, this sounds good, but it is actually impossible to achieve because no one has lists of every person in any group. This is why the method of poll taking is extremely important in determining the validity and reliability of the results.

random sampling: A method of selection that gives each potential voter or adult the same chance of being selected.

Nonstratified Sampling. As discussed earlier, the *Literary Digest* polls suffered from an oversampling of voters whose names were drawn from telephone directories and car registrations; this group was hardly representative of the general electorate in the midst of the Depression. Thus the use of a nonstratified sample led to results that could not be used to predict accurately how the electorate would vote.

Interest groups often conduct even more unrepresentative polls when they ask their members to respond to "questionnaires" on a variety of issues. The tallies of these very biased polls are then sent to the press, members of Congress, and members of the executive branch to indicate "public" support of group goals.

Highlight 11.3

Question the Numbers and Check the Wording

Opinion polls are big news—especially during an election year. This summer and fall, the polling industry will be in overdrive, constantly gauging what Americans think and how they intend to vote. But even the most accurate polls can be very deceiving. In the past 60 years, polls have improved so much that we may be dazzled—and fooled—by their statistical precision.

The more we trust polls, the more likely they are to mislead us. Often, the fault is not in the pollsters but in ourselves: We're too eager to believe that the numbers add up to truth.

"Slight differences in question wording or in the placement of the questions in the interview can have profound consequences," says David Moore, vice president of the Gallup Organization. He points out that poll findings "are very much influenced by the polling process itself."

Consider, for instance, what researchers discovered in a 1985 national poll: Only 19 percent of the public agreed that the country wasn't spending enough money on "welfare." But when the question contained the phrase "assistance to the poor" instead of "welfare," affirmative responses jumped to 63 percent.

That 44 percent shift explains how people can make opposite—and equally vehement—claims about what "polls show." The truth is that, at best, polls offer us flat snapshots of a three-dimensional world.

At worst, when they're funded by partisans, polls may be purposely deceptive. In those cases, faulty polling can come back to haunt those who initially seemed to benefit from it.

In autumn 1994, Republican pollster Frank Luntz declared that each provision of the 10-point Contract with America had overwhelming support. Luntz failed to mention that he'd only surveyed responses to GOP slogans.

Last year, as details emerged about impacts of the Contract, public disapproval mounted—and congressional Republicans who took comfort in their pollster's propaganda were brought up short. Six months ago, when Knight-Ridder reporter Frank Greve exposed the polling sleight of hand, he noted that "the House GOP's legislative agenda isn't just losing popularity; it's probably shedding popularity that was overrated."

An editor at Congressional Quarterly, Philip Duncan, added: "The revelation that there are gaps in the Contract's appeal might have come sooner if the media had pressed Luntz during the 1994 campaign to document his claim of public support. But all too often, reporters simply pass along results of polls that were designed to influence voter sentiment, not merely measure it."

Regardless of their quality, polls that depict public opinion end up altering it. Poll data "influence perceptions, attitudes and decisions at every level of our society," Gallup executive David Moore writes in his recent book, *The Superpollsters.*

Some polls are skewed by intensive efforts to sway the electorate. For example, in times of crisis, many presidents have been able to orchestrate publicity that spikes the numbers—which are then cited as proof that the White House is in sync with the popular will.

While polling seems to offer choices, it also limits them. Author Herbert Schiller says that opinion-polling is commonly "a choice-restricting mechanism." Why? "Because ordinary polls reduce, and sometimes eliminate entirely, the . . . true spectrum of possible options." Schiller aptly describes poll responses as "guided" choices.

To make matters worse, the narrow range of options presented by pollsters is far from random. "Those who dominate governmental decision-making and private economic activity are the main supporters of the pollsters," Schiller observes. "The vital needs of these groups determine, intentionally or not, the parameters within which polls are formulated."

We become overly impressed with polls when we pay too much attention to the answers and not enough to the questions.

Source: Norman Solomon, "Question the Numbers," *The Atlanta Journal and Constitution* (May 17, 1995): A23.

```
                        NATIONAL STUDY

INTERVIEWER_____              STUDY #__5483____
TARRANCE & ASSOCIATES                     CODING_____
GREENBERG-LAKE                            COMPUTER_____
PERSONAL/CONFIDENTIAL                     FINANCE_____
                                          INTERVIEWING_____


Hello, I'm _____ of Tarrance & Associates, a national
research firm.  We're calling from our national telephone center.
We're talking to people in the nation today about public leaders
and issues facing us all.

A.   Are you registered to vote
     in your state and will you be
     able to vote in the election
     for President that will be
     held in 1992?


     _____
     IF "NO", ASK:  Is there someone
     else at home who is registered
     to vote?  (IF "YES", THEN ASK:
     MAY I SPEAK WITH HIM/HER?)
                          Yes (CONTINUE)

                          No  (THANK AND TERMINATE)
```

A typical polling instrument. (Photo courtesy: Stephen Savios/AP Wide World Photos)

Perhaps the most common form of unrepresentative sampling is the kind of straw poll used today by local television news programs. Many have nightly features asking viewers to call in their sentiments (with one phone number for pro and another for con). The results of these unscientific polls vary widely because those who feel very strongly about the issue often repeatedly call in their votes.

A more reliable nonprobability sample is a quota sample, in which pollsters draw their sample based on known statistics. Assume that a citywide survey has been commissioned. If the city is 30 percent African American, 15 percent Hispanic, and 55 percent white, interviewers will use those statistics to determine the proportion of particular groups to be questioned. These kinds of surveys are often conducted in local shopping malls. Perhaps you've wondered why the man or woman with the clipboard has let you pass by but has stopped the next shopper. Now you know it is likely that you did not match the profile of the subjects that the interviewer was instructed to locate.

Doonesbury BY GARRY TRUDEAU

(Photo courtesy: DOONSBURY, copyright 1989 G. B. Trueau. Reprinted with permission of Universal Press Syndicate. All rights reserved.)

Although this kind of sampling technique can produce relatively accurate results, the degree of accuracy falls short of those surveys based on probability samples. Moreover, these surveys generally oversample the visible population, such as shoppers, while neglecting the stay-at-homes who may be glued to the Home Shopping Network or CNN.

Stratified Sampling. Most national surveys and commercial polls use samples of from 1,000 to 1,500 individuals and use a variation of the random sampling method called **stratified sampling.** Simple random, nonstratified samples aren't very useful at predicting voting because they may undersample (or oversample) key populations that are not likely to vote.

stratified sampling: A variation of random sampling; census data are used to divide a country into four sampling regions. Sets of counties and standard metropolitan statistical areas are then randomly selected in proportion to the total national population.

To avoid these problems, reputable polling organizations use stratified sampling based on census data that provides the number of residences in an area and their location. Researchers divide the country into four sampling regions. They then randomly select a set of counties and standard metropolitan statistical areas in proportion to the total national population. Once certain primary sampling units are selected, they are often used for many years because it is cheaper for polling companies to train interviewers to work in a fixed area.

About twenty respondents from each primary sampling unit are selected to be interviewed. Generally four or five city blocks or areas are selected, and then four or five target families from each district are used. Large, sophisticated surveys like the National Election Study and General Social Survey, which produce the data commonly used by political scientists, attempt to sample from lists of persons living in each household. The key to the success of the stratified sampling method is not to let people volunteer to be interviewed—volunteers as a group often have different opinions from those who don't volunteer.

Stratified sampling (the most rigorous sampling technique) is generally not used by those who do surveys reported in *The New York Times* and *USA Today* or on network news programs. Instead, those organizations or pollsters working for them randomly survey every tenth, hundredth, or thousandth person or household. If those individuals are not at home, they go to the home or apartment next door.

How Are Respondents Contacted?

After selecting the methodology to conduct the poll, the next question is how to contact those to be surveyed. Television stations often ask people to call in, and some surveyors hit the streets. Telephone polls, however, are becoming the most frequently used mechanism by which to gauge the temper of the electorate.

Telephone Polls. The most common form of telephone polls are random-digit dialing surveys, in which a computer randomly selects telephone numbers to be dialed. Because it is estimated that as many as 95 percent of the American public have telephones in their homes, samples selected in this manner are likely to be fairly representative.

In spite of some problems (such as the fact that many people don't want to be bothered, especially at dinner time), most polls done for newspapers and news magazines are conducted this way. Most polls, in fact, contain language similar to that used by the Gallup Organization in reporting its survey results:

> The current results are based on telephone interviews with a randomly selected national sample of 1,008 adults, conducted _____ to _____ . For results based on a sample of this size, one can say with 95 percent confidence that the error attributable to sampling and other random effects could be plus or minus 3 percentage points. In addition to sampling error, question wording and practical

difficulties in conducting surveys can introduce error or bias into the findings of public opinion polls.[35] (See Politics Now: Polling, Public Opinion, and the Evolving Role of the First Lady.)

Politics Now

Polling, Public Opinion, and the Evolving Role of the First Lady

During the relatively predictable 1996 Republican Convention, there was one decided break with tradition. Elizabeth Hanford Dole, the wife of the nominee, addressed the convention. This, by itself, was unusual. But, what made Dole's appearance even more unusual was the manner in which she chose to address the convention and, of course, the nation. Eschewing the podium, she instead walked out on the floor of the convention hall in San Diego and spoke to public and those in the hall without notes for over a half hour. Dole is an effective and poised speaker. A graduate of Harvard Law School, she twice served in Republican presidential administrations as Secretary of Labor and then Transportation, and took a leave from her position as head of the American Red Cross to campaign for her husband.

Immediately after Dole spoke, the pollsters were out in full force. According to a *USA Today*/CNN poll, more than half of those polled—58%—gave her a favorable rating—a 7% increase from early August. Only 18% rated her unfavorably, while nearly 50% of those polled rated First Lady Hillary Rodham Clinton unfavorably.

Over the course of President Clinton's first term in office, Hillary Rodham Clinton was the object of unprecedented news coverage, much of it negative. It appeared that the American public was not in a mood to accept a First Lady in a highly visible policy-making role. In spite of efforts on the part of her handlers to stress her role as a mother and an advocate for the nation's children, Clinton continued to suffer in the polls. But, in the wake of Elizabeth Dole's performance, Hillary Clinton was nearly forced into a center stage role at the Democratic convention. And, her no-nonsense, more traditionally given speech appeared to go a long way to boost her image with the American public.

A poll taken the day after her speech showed that for the first time in a year, more than half of those polled had a favorable impression of the First Lady and those having an unfavorable view of her dropped to a thirty-two-month low. In fact, when those polled were asked who would be a better First Lady, Clinton and Dole were in a virtual dead heat—42% to 43%—with the poll having a margin of error of +/-4 points.[*]

While it wasn't until the 1980s that a First Lady actively campaigned for her husband, by 1996, in spite of a public that appeared ambivalent (at best) about a powerful First Lady, it now seems as if it is expected that a First Lady be a gifted public speaker and campaigner so long as she doesn't appear to be too involved in policy. And, just as the polls reflect tremendous volatility in attitudes toward Hillary Clinton in particular and expectations about First Ladies in general, the public attention paid to both women at the 1996 conventions probably means that the role of First Lady as campaigner has changed forever. Why do you think public expectations and opinions about the proper role of First Ladies are changing? Is it for the good or the bad?

[*]*CNN*/*USA Today*/Gallup Poll, August 29, 1996. (http://allpolitics.com/polls/national).

In-Person Polls.   Individual, in-person interviews are conducted by some groups, such as by the University of Michigan for the National Election Studies. Some analysts favor such in-person surveys, but others argue that the unintended influence of the questioner or pollster is an important source of errors. How the pollster dresses, relates to the person being interviewed, and even asks the questions can affect responses. (Some of these factors, such as tone of voice, can also affect the results of telephone surveys.)

New Kinds of Polls

As polling has become more and more sophisticated and networks, newspapers, and magazines compete with each other to report the most up-to-the-minute changes in public opinion on issues or political candidates, new types of polls have been suggested and put into use.

tracking poll: Continuous surveys that enables a campaign to chart its daily rise or fall.

Tracking Polls.   During the 1992 presidential elections, **tracking polls,** which were taken on a daily basis by some news organizations (see Figure 11.6), were introduced to allow candidates to monitor short-term campaign developments and the effects of their campaign strategy.

Tracking polls involve small samples and are conducted every twenty-four hours (usually of registered voters contacted at certain times of day). They are usually combined with some kind of a moving statistical average to boost the sample size and therefore the statistical reliability.[36] Even though such one-day surveys are fraught with reliability problems, many major news organizations continued their use in the 1996 campaign.

FIGURE 11.6

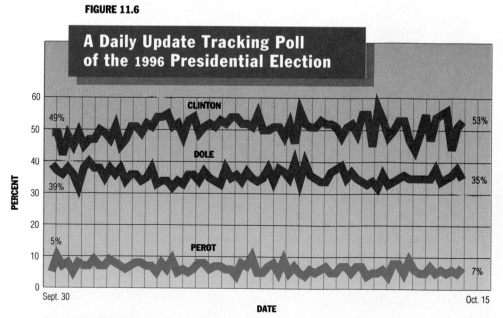

A Daily Update Tracking Poll of the 1996 Presidential Election

Copyright 1996, *USA Today.* Reprinted with permission.

Politics Now

Exit Polls

Exit polls supporters argue that by allowing television networks and other news outlets to quickly disseminate a wide array of electoral information only minutes after the polls have closed, exit polls serve a vital function. On the other hand, exit poll detractors contend that it is irresponsible for the media to report that one candidate or another has won or lost an electoral contest before any of the raw vote totals have been tabulated. While exit poll perceptions often match electoral reality, as the following article shows, this is not always the case.

Exit Polls Err In N.H. Race*

Wednesday, Nov. 6, 1996
© Associated Press

Manchester, N.H.—When the polls closed Tuesday evening, Sen. Bob Smith heard The Associated Press and television networks proclaim his Democratic opponent the winner. Smith told supporters it was "pretty rough" hearing he had lost, but he had a gut feeling the

projection was wrong. When the votes were counted, they proved him right.

"This race was won in the small towns where pollsters don't go," Smith said early today at his victory celebration. "I guess you could say I've been to hell and back in one night."

The wrong call was based on exit polls of voters by Voter News Service, a consortium of the AP, ABC, CBS, NBC, CNN and Fox.

Voter News Service interviewed 1,165 voters as they left 25 of the state's 300 precincts picked randomly in a process that was ordered to reflect state geography and past vote by party.

Exit polls are supposed to be more accurate that pre-election polls because they eliminate a major source of uncertainty—whether the people being questioned will actually vote.

Statistically, Tuesday's exit poll had a 95 percent chance of being no more than 3 percentage points either way from the final outcome of the election.

When the exit poll showed a 5-point spread, 52 percent for Swett to 47 percent to Smith and 1 percent for Libertarian Ken Blevens,

the AP and others declared Swett the winner.

The actual vote showed a 9-point swing. With 84 percent of the precincts reporting, Smith led by 4 percent—50 percent to 46 percent for Swett and 4 percent Blevens.

VNS said it was the only mistake in about 110 calls Tuesday, including the presidential race in each state.

"It was the largest error in any exit poll estimate I've ever seen since I've been doing this," said VNS' Murray Edelman, who has been calling races on exit polls since 1982 and has worked on polling in elections for more than a quarter-century.

Edelman said he did not yet know why the exit poll was so wrong.

Considering the many months—sometimes years—candidates spend trying to achieve electoral success, do you think the major television networks and other news outlets should continue their practice of predicting election outcomes based solely on information provided by exit polls?

*© The Associated Press, November 6, 1996.

Exit Polls. **Exit polls** are polls conducted at selected polling places on Election Day. Generally, large news organizations send pollsters to selected precincts to sample every tenth voter as he or she emerges from the polling place. The results of these polls are used to help the television networks predict the outcome of key races, often just a few minutes after the polls close in a particular state and generally before voters in other areas—sometimes in a later time zone—have cast their ballots. They also provide an independent assessment of why voters supported particular candidates "free from the spin that managers and candidates alike place on the 'meaning of an election'."[37]

In 1980 President Jimmy Carter's own polling and the results of network exit polls led him to concede defeat three hours before the polls closed on the West Coast. Many

exit poll: Poll conducted at selected polling places on Election Day.

Democratic Party officials and candidates criticized Carter and network predictions for harming their chances at victories, arguing that with the presidential election already "called," voters were unlikely to go to the polls. In the aftermath of that controversy, all networks agreed not to predict the results of presidential contests until all polling places were closed.

Exit polls have also been faulted because it appears that not all voters are willing to reply truthfully to pollsters' questions. In 1989, for example, when L. Douglas Wilder, an African American, ran for the Virginia governorship, the results of exit polls were way off. Surveys done before the race showed him winning by margins of 4 to 15 percent; a television exit poll showed him winning by 10 percent. Wilder won, but with a razor-thin margin of .0037 percent—6,582 votes out of a record 1.78 million cast. Clearly, pollsters had been lied to or misled by "some Democratic-leaning white Virginians who could not bring themselves to vote for a black candidate . . . and few voters are secure enough in their bigotry to confess such blatant bias.[38] It seems that many white voters were unwilling to say that they had not voted for Wilder, the African-American candidate; therefore they told pollsters that they had voted for Wilder, when they had not.

A similar phenomenon occurred during the Louisiana senatorial primary in 1990. Many whites who voted for David Duke, the former Ku Klux Klansman, apparently lied to pollsters, who underpredicted his support. Duke received a majority of the white vote, although ultimately he was soundly defeated in the general election.

Deliberative Polls. From January 18 to 21, 1996, a new experiment in polling and American democracy began in Austin, Texas. Six hundred Americans, selected by the National Opinion Research Center (NORC) through rigorous random sampling methods, came together for intensive briefings, discussions, and presentations about three large clusters of issues: foreign affairs, the status and needs of the American family, and the U.S. economy.

The **deliberative poll** is different from any others used by pollsters in the United States. "Ordinary polls model what the public is thinking, even though the public may not be thinking very much or paying much attention. A deliberative poll attempts to model what the public would think, had it a better opportunity to consider the question at issue."[39]

The idea of a deliberative poll, while novel, was quite simple. The logistics of bringing one off, however, were daunting. A random national sample of the electorate was transported from all over the United States to Austin, Texas. There they were administered one poll that included opinion and information questions. Then the attendees were bombarded with issue discussions and briefing papers in a carefully balanced manner. Vice President Al Gore, Jr., joined, but only one of the six invited Republican presidential candidates showed up.

The three days of talk and debate were broadcast on PBS for six hours. The deliberative poll thus marries "two technologies, polling and television, that have given us a superficial form of mass democracy, and harnesses them to a new and constructive purpose—giving voice to the people under conditions where the people can think,"[40] says the poll's creator, James S. Fishkin, a University of Texas political scientist.

The deliberative poll cost $4.5 million (more than any one news organization budgeted for its whole slate of preelection polls[41]) and was hailed by Fishkin, his colleagues, and those who attended as a great success.[42] But what was the overall import of the poll? Its organizers did not mean for the poll to be able to help describe and predict public opinion. Instead they viewed the poll as prescriptive in nature because a deliberative poll allows a microcosm of the country to think about issues and make recommendations to the country as a whole.

Former Virginia Governor L. Douglas Wilder's election in 1989 demonstrated some of the difficulties of polling. Despite advance surveys and exit polls that indicated a comfortable lead, Wilder's actual margin of victory was razor-thin. Apparently, voters, for fear of admitting racism, were unwilling to admit that they had voted against an African American. (Photo courtesy: UPI/Bettmann Archive)

deliberative poll: A new type of poll to bring a representative sample of people together to discuss and debate political issues in order to provide considered policy suggestions to lawmakers.

Did the National Issues Conference and the deliberative poll result in any changes in the opinion and perceptions of those who attended? Yes, as illustrated in Figure 11.7; but generally only on issues where new, correct information was key. For example, many (but not all) of those who thought foreign aid was the largest item in the federal budget changed their responses after the facts were discussed at the National Issues Conference.

FIGURE 11.7

Attitudes Before and After the Deliberative Poll

Selected before and after responses given by those attending the National Issues Conference.

		BEFORE THE CONFERENCE	AFTER THE CONFERENCE
Today, the average worker does not receive a fair day's pay for a fair day's work.	Strongly Agree	26.6%	40.4%
	Agree Somewhat	32.8	34.6
	Disagree Somewhat	29.6	18.9
	Disagree Strongly	6.7	4.2
	Don't Know	4.4	1.8
People like me don't have any say about what the government does.	Strongly Agree	17.9%	6.3%
	Agree Somewhat	26.3	24.5
	Disagree Somewhat	30.8	32
	Disagree Strongly	24.7	36.5
	Don't Know	.2	.7
Some say that the government in Washington should guarantee for low-income Americans a 'safety net' for welfare and health care. Others say that the government in Washington should just give the money to the states and let them decide how much help to give. Which is closer to your view?	Government in Washington should guarantee a 'safety net.'	37.7%	31.3%
	Money should go to the states to decide how much to give.	49.5	62.5
Do you agree or disagree with this statement?: "The United States should continue to engage in military cooperation with other nations, not to add trouble spots in the world."	Strongly Agree	20.8%	37.7%
	Agree Somewhat	50.8	44.1
	Disagree Somewhat	17.4	12.6
	Disagree Strongly	7.8	3.9
	Don't Know	3.2	1.8
Some people think that the biggest problem for the American family are economic problems. Others think that it is the breakdown of traditional family values. Which is closer to your view?	Economic Problems	35.5%	50.7%
	Breakdown of Family Values	57.6	47.7
	Don't Know	6.9	1.6

Source: Reported in Michelle Kay, "Fishkin: Poll Proves Value of Deliberation; Critics Say Experiences Like the Issues Convention are Too Impractical to Have a Wide Impact," *Austin American Statesman,* (January 26, 1996) A1.

The presumed prescriptive nature of the poll as well as the methodology employed to select participants and conclusions that could be drawn from any reported changes in their beliefs caused considerable disagreement in the polling community. Supporters say that the poll could help America "adapt democracy to the large nation state."[43] Others claim that if such a poll were broadcast before an election or a referendum, it could dramatically affect outcomes.[44] These claims may be overzealous and have been attacked by many other students of public opinion, who charge that the deliberative poll has even more defects than other, more commonly used polls, as discussed below. They charge that the sample size was too small to be representative, that attendees knew they were making history as they engaged in a citizenship experiment, thus making any inferences from their views to the general population ill advised, and that numerous problems existed in the survey instrument, making interpretation difficult. Still, the deliberative poll was an interesting, albeit expensive, experiment trying to prove the need for greater discussion of issues to facilitate informed citizen participation in politics.

Shortcomings of Polling.   In 1990 the networks consolidated their polling operations under the umbrella of Voter Research and Surveys (VRS), which was a major cost-saving measure for all involved. But the construction of a single questionnaire and one data set meant that problems could arise. In 1992 the VRS data significantly overpredicted the support for Republican candidate Patrick Buchanan in the New Hampshire primary, and showed President Bush to be in much more trouble than he was. Armed with these erroneous survey results, commentator after commentator (all relying on the same data) predicted a narrow victory for Bush—who actually went on to win by a healthy sixteen-point margin. Nevertheless, "(M)any Americans went to bed believing that the president had been badly damaged."[45] This kind of reporting based on inaccurate polls can skew the rest of a campaign, particularly in an era when campaigns are viewed as horse races and everyone wants to know who's winning and by how much. Thus polls and the way they are reported can affect election outcomes; they are a powerful tool that gives the media additional sway in the democratic process.

The accuracy of any poll depends on the quality of the sample that was drawn. Small samples, if properly drawn, can be very accurate if each unit in the universe has an equal opportunity to be sampled. If a pollster, for example, fails to sample certain populations, his or her results may reflect that shortcoming. Often, the opinions of the poor and homeless are underrepresented because insufficient attention is given to making certain that these groups are representatively sampled. And, in the case of tracking polls, if you choose to sample only on weekends or from 5 P.M. to 9 P.M., you may get more Republicans, who are less likely to have jobs that require them to work in the evening or on weekends. There comes a point in sampling, however, where increases in the size of the sample have little effect on a reduction of the **sampling error** (also called **margin of error**), the difference between the actual universe and the sample.

All polls contain errors. Standard samples of approximately 1,000 to 1,500 individuals provide fairly good estimates of actual behavior (in the case of voting, for example). Typically, the margin of error in a sample of 1,500 will be about 3 percent. If you ask 1,500 people "Do you like ice cream?" and 52 percent say "yes" and 48 percent say "no," the results are too close to tell whether more people like ice cream than not. Why? Because the margin of error implies that somewhere between 55 percent (52 + 3) and 49 percent (52 − 3) of the people like ice cream, while between 51 percent (48 + 3) and 45 percent (48 − 3) do not. The margin of error in a close election makes predictions very difficult.

Polls can be inaccurate when they limit responses. If you are asked, "How do you like this class?" and are given only like or dislike options, your full sentiments may not be tapped if you like the class very much or feel only so-so about it.

sampling error: A measure of the accuracy of a public opinion poll.

margin of error: A measure of the accuracy of a public opinion poll.

Public opinion polls may also be "off" when they attempt to gauge attitudes about issues that some or even many individuals don't care about or about which the public has little information. For example, few Americans probably care about the elimination of the electoral college. If a representative sample were polled, many would answer pro or con without having given much consideration to the question.

Most academic public opinion research organizations, such as the National Election Study, use some kind of filter question that first asks respondents whether or not they have thought about the question. These screening procedures generally allow surveyors to exclude as many as 20 percent of their respondents, especially on complex issues like the federal budget. Questions on more personal issues such as moral values, drugs, crime, race, and women's role in society get far fewer "no opinion" or "don't know" responses, as indicated in Table 11.5.

TABLE 11.5

Where the Public Stands on Key Issues

HOW MUCH GOVERNMENT?

Question: Would you say you favor smaller government with fewer services, or larger government with many services?

Larger: 23% Smaller: 68% Don't Know 9%

A NATION OF TREE HUGGERS?

Question: Are you in favor of protecting the environment even if that means some people will lose their jobs and the government will have to spend a great deal of money . . . or are you in favor of providing more jobs and expanding the economy even if that means some destruction of the environment?

Favor protecting the environment:	50%
Both about equally:	10
Favor expanding the economy:	34
Don't know:	6

GUNS OR BUTTER?

Question: Generally speaking, do you think the federal government should spend a great deal more money on national defense, or somewhat more, or somewhat less, or do you think the federal government should spend a great deal less money on national defense?

Great deal more:	8%
Somewhat more:	26
Somewhat less:	37
Great deal less:	21

WHO'S RESPONSIBLE?

Which statement comes closest to your view: "The government is responsible for the well-being of its citizens and it has an obligation to help people when they are in trouble," or "People are responsible for their own well-being and they have an obligation to take care of themselves when they are in trouble."

Government is responsible:	42%
People are responsible:	49%

Source: Survey conducted by the *Los Angeles Times*, October 27–30, 1995. Reported in "Where the Public Stands on 10 Key Issues," *The Public Perspective* (February/March 1996): 48–49.

Another shortcoming of polls concerns their inability to measure intensity of feeling about particular issues. Whereas a respondent might answer affirmatively to any question, it is likely that his or her feelings about issues such as abortion, the death penalty, or support for U.S. troops in the Gulf are much more intense than are his or her feelings about the electoral college.

The introduction of tracking polls into the 1992 election scenario brought more critics of political polling. According to one political scientist, their advent "played upon the worst tendencies of journalists to focus almost entirely upon who is ahead and by how much."[46] Moreover, the one-day polls were fraught with other problems. Sampling is conducted with limited or no callbacks and may be skewed because certain groups may not be at home at certain times. The CNN/Gallup poll, for example, used two different time periods—weekdays 5 P.M. to 9 P.M. and all day on the weekends. Thus midweek surveys produced candidate distributions that disproportionately favored Bush, while weekend surveys showed the reverse.

This problem was exacerbated by two shifts in the way data was collected. First, pollsters moved from surveying "registered" voters to surveying "likely" voters[47]; second, Gallup changed the way it allocated "undecided" voters. All of these methodologies created the impression that the race was closer than it was and gave a boost to Bush, the Republican candidate. Thus some argue that the danger of tracking polls needs to be highlighted and discussed before more emphasis is placed on them.

The deliberative poll has brought another set of criticisms to polling. Critics charge that the poll is elitist and that it created "an agenda and the setting for a discussion of [participants'] issues that meets *their* criteria for deliberation."[48] Opinion formation, moreover, in any election year, is "more of an evolution than an epiphany."[49] It is a rolling process as issues gel, candidates come and go, and new events occur that require public and candidate responses. Critics of deliberative polls argue that no issues are static and events—no matter what the setting—can't begin to mirror the actual deliberative process that goes on in the formation of a personal opinion about political issues or candidates.

HOW POLLING AND PUBLIC OPINION AFFECT POLITICIANS, POLITICS, AND POLICY

*I*n his first year in office, President Clinton revealed his understanding of the importance of public support. His major legislative victories—the budget bill, the North American Free Trade Agreement (NAFTA), and the Brady gun-control bill—were won with the support of very different groups of people. His efforts to mobilize public opinion included town hall meeting appearances and having his vice president, Al Gore, Jr., debate Ross Perot on *Larry King Live* in order to bring the case for NAFTA directly to the American public. He recognized that he needed to have as much public opinion on his side as possible to convince Congress to go along with his plan.

Much earlier, the authors of *The Federalist Papers* noted that "all government rests on public opinion," and, as a result, public opinion inevitably influences the action of politicians and public officials. The public's perception of crime as a problem, for example, was the driving force behind the comprehensive crime bill President Clinton submitted to Congress in 1994 and congressional passage of the Brady gun control bill

FIGURE 11.8

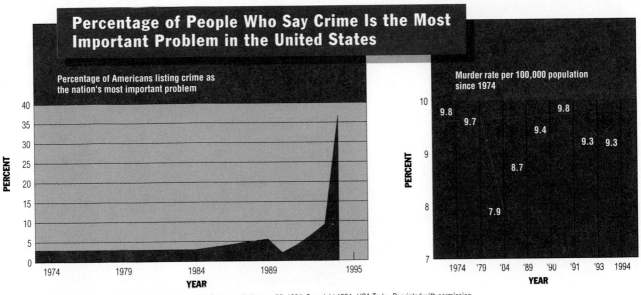

Percentage of People Who Say Crime Is the Most Important Problem in the United States

Percentage of Americans listing crime as the nation's most important problem

Murder rate per 100,000 population since 1974

SOURCE: From "Beseiged by Crime" by Judy Keen, *USA Today*, p. 1A, January 25, 1994. Copyright 1994, *USA Today*. Reprinted with permission.

in 1993. As Figure 11.8 shows, the public's concern with crime skyrocketed to an all-time high in 1994, and politicians at all levels were quick to convert that concern into a campaign issue. In 1996 during the presidential campaign, Bill Clinton even called for the addition of a constitutional amendment to protect crime victims' rights.

Politicians and government officials spend millions of dollars each year taking the "pulse" of the public. Even the federal government spends millions annually on polls and surveys designed to evaluate programs and to provide information for shaping policies. But, as political scientist Benjamin Ginsburg noted, "the data reported by opinion polls are actually the product of an interplay between opinion and the survey instrument." They interact with each other and, in essence, often change the "character of the views receiving public expression."[50] Polls can thus help transform public opinion.

We know that politicians rely on polls, but it's difficult to say to what degree. Several political scientists have attempted to study whether public policy is responsive to public opinion, with mixed results.[51] As we have seen, public opinion can fluctuate, making it difficult for a politician or policy maker to assess. Some critics of polls and of their use by politicians argue that polls hurt democracy and make leaders weaker. Ginsberg argues that public opinion polls weaken democracy.[52] He claims that these polls allow governments and politicians to say they have considered public opinion in spite of the fact that polls don't always measure the intensity of feeling on an issue or might overreflect the views of the responders who lack sufficient information to make educated choices. Ginsberg further argues that democracy is better served by politicians' reliance on telephone calls and letters—active signs of interest—than on the passive voice of public opinion. Some say that politicians are simply driven by the results of polls that do not reflect a serious debate of issues. In response to this argument, George Gallup retorted, "One might as well insist that a thermometer makes the weather."[53]

North—South

POLITICS AROUND THE WORLD

The billions of people around the world who watched the 1996 Olympic Games in Atlanta were treated to a remarkable display of American unity and patriotism—a display that many may have found excessively one-sided and commercial. What cannot be denied, though, is that almost everyone in the United States feels remarkably proud of its basic political arrangements, which political scientists refer to as its "regime."

None of that regime, of course, has been created out of thin air. It reflects strongly held beliefs reinforced through the process of political socialization, in which families, schools, the media, churches, peer groups, and other agents help shape the views of each new generation. In Mexico, Canada, and most other countries, political socialization is nowhere near as smooth or consensual, though the consequences for the system as a whole are much more pronounced in Mexico. That's the case for many reasons, most notably the fact that both countries have important subcultures.

There are relatively few differences in the ways people in the United States and English-speaking Canadians think. Canadians, for instance, are more likely to think that the state should play a major role in steering the economy or providing welfare. However, on balance, their views are quite similar. The same cannot be said of the 7.5 million people of French origin. As the ongoing support for Quebec separatism suggests, many have serious doubts about whether Canada should exist or not. Most are deeply resentful of the economic inequality and cultural oppression they have suffered at the hands of English-speaking Canadians for more than 200 years.

In Mexico, there is more widespread dissatisfaction with the regime, though it rarely is seen in public opinion polls. More in-depth anthropological research as well as speculative accounts have suggested that a substantial proportion of the Mexican population—perhaps as much as 10 percent—does not feel a part of mainstream society and political life and probably fed the discontent that has led to the recent revolts in Chiapas and other poor states. An even larger group of people supports the system, not so much because they like the PRI and its accomplishments, but because the party–state machine has been able to provide them with a sharply improved quality of life over the last three-quarters of a century. In recent years, however, the decline of that machine, the growth of independent media and other sources of information, the country's serious economic problems, and the increased support for opposition political parties and interest groups have contributed to widespread misgivings about and less frequent outbursts against the regime.

If we shift our attention to the issues of the day, the similarities among the three countries overshadow any of these differences. In particular, as in the United States, levels of trust or support for politicians and political parties of all stripes have declined precipitously. Thus a 1990 poll in all three countries showed that slightly more than a third of all Americans and Canadians, but only one in six Mexicans, expressed confidence in their government. In all three cases, those figures had dropped significantly since the same question had been asked nine years earlier, and have continued to decline even further in the last few years.

Polls can clearly distort the election process by creating what are called "bandwagon" and "underdog" effects. In a presidential campaign, an early victory in the Iowa caucuses or the New Hampshire primary, for example, can boost a candidate's standings in the polls as the rest of the nation begins to think of him or her in a more positive light. New supporters jump on the bandwagon. A strong showing in the polls, in turn, can generate more and larger donations, the lifeblood of any campaign. Political scientist Herbert Asher has noted that "bad poll results, as well as poor primary and caucus standings, may deter potential donors from supporting a failing campaign."[54]

CHANGING POLLING PRACTICES

*A*s discussed in chapter 1, most Americans—at least according to public opinion polls of almost any stripe—think that things are getting worse and that America isn't going in the right direction. Some say that these reports fuel the news media to report about more bad things—because good news, however heartwarming, doesn't make as "good" news as *bad* news, it is the murders, rapes, and political scandals that get reported.

At some point one must begin to question if public opinion based on misstatements, lack of political knowledge, and fear is really public opinion. And if polls that may not accurately reflect reality influence politicians, one must question whether such influence is good or bad for policy making and for the American public. Consider, for example, the issue of affirmative action. Poll after poll reveals that whites, especially white males, believe that African-American businesses get an enormous share of federal contracts and that African Americans take their jobs. Although statistics show this not to be the case, that is the way the situation is often portrayed in the media. As a result many whites think it is so and are therefore opposed to affirmative action. But are they opposed for philosophical reasons, or have they formed political opinions based on inaccuracies of fact? Should it be the job of opinion and policy makers to ferret out the reasons and take on the task of educating the public as to the facts—which, as we have seen earlier, are not a strong point for most Americans?

If one begins with the notion that leaders in a representative democracy must have some way of assessing public opinion, another question arises: Should elected officials make certain that polls really do reflect the views of the public? The deliberative poll, for example, received over $3 million in federal government support to measure public opinion. Not only did Professor Fishkin and his supporters conclude that they had an accurate assessment of the public's views on a variety of issues, they hypothesized that opinions can be changed if the public is actually educated about issues through listening to experts and discussing issues with each other. Could it be that another role of government, then, is to establish mechanisms whereby citizens can learn more about politics and be given opportunities to discuss the issues? Could Internet access be a first step in encouraging this process of opinion reformation?

SUMMARY

Public opinion is a subject constantly mentioned in the media, especially in presidential election years or when important policies (such as health care, balancing the budget, race, or crime) are under consideration. What public opinion is, where it comes from, how it's measured, and how it's used are aspects of a complex subject. To that end, this chapter has made the following points:

1.   What Is Public Opinion?

Public opinion is what the public thinks about an issue or a particular set of issues. Public opinion polls are used to estimate public opinion.

2.   Early Efforts to Influence and Measure Public Opinion.

Almost since the beginning of the United States, various attempts have been made to influence public opinion about particular issues or to sway elections. Modern-day polling did not begin until the 1930s, however. Over the years, polling to measure public opinion has become more and more sophisticated and more accurate because pollsters are better able to sample the public in their effort to determine their attitudes and positions on issues. Pollsters recognize that their sample must reflect the population whose ideas and beliefs they wish to measure.

3. Political Socialization and Other Factors that Influence Opinion Formation.

The first step in forming opinions occurs through a process called political socialization. The family, school, peers, the impact of events, the social group of which one is a member—including religion, race, gender, and age—as well as where one lives all affect how one views political events and issues, as do the major events themselves. Our political ideology—whether we are conservative, liberal, or moderate—also provides a lens through which we filter our political views, as does our level of personal benefit from and our political knowledge of issues and events. Even the views of other people affect our ultimate opinions of a variety of issues, including race relations, the death penalty, abortion, and federal taxes.

4. How We Form Political Opinions.

Myriad factors enter our minds as we form opinions about political matters. These include a calculation about the personal benefits involved, degree of personal political knowledge, and cues from leaders.

5. How We Measure Public Opinion.

Measuring public opinion can be difficult. The most frequently used measure is the public opinion poll. Determining the content, phrasing the questions, selecting the sample, and choosing the right kind of poll are critical to obtaining accurate and useable data.

6. How Polling and Public Opinion Affect Politicians, Politics, and Policy.

Knowledge of the public's views on issues is often used by politicians to tailor campaigns or to drive policy decisions.

7. Changing Polling Practices.

Good news doesn't sell papers, and members of the media often play up the bad about America. Faulty polls, too, can negatively affect public opinion and can have serious ramifications on the democratic system.

KEY TERMS

deliberative poll, p. 436
exit poll, p. 435
gender gap, p. 423
margin of error, p. 438
political ideology, p. 425
political socialization, p. 416
public opinion, p. 410

public opinion poll, p. 410
random sampling, p. 429
sampling error, p. 438
stratified sampling, p. 432
straw poll, p. 413
tracking poll, p. 434

SELECTED READINGS

Asher, Herbert. *Polling and the Public: What Every Citizen Should Know.* Washington, D.C.: CQ Press, 1988.

Brace, Paul, and Barbara Hinckley. *Follow the Leader: Opinion Polls and Modern Presidents.* New York: Basic Books, 1992.

Campbell, Angus, *et al. The American Voter.* New York: Wiley, 1960.

Carmines, Edward G., and James A. Stimson. *Issue Evolution.* Princeton, NJ: Princeton University Press, 1990.

Crespi, Irving. *Public Opinion, Polls, and Democracy.* Boulder, CO: Westview Press, 1989.

Ginsberg, Benjamin. *The Captive Public.* New York: Basic Books, 1986.

Graber, Doris. *Processing the News: How People Tame the Information Tide.* New York: Longman, 1984.

Herbst, Susan. *Numbered Voices: How Opinion Polling Has Shaped American Politics.* Chicago: University of Chicago Press, 1993.

Jennings, M. Kent, and Richard Niemi. *Generations and Politics: A Panel Study of Young Adults and Their Parents.* Princeton, NJ: Princeton University Press, 1981.

Key, V. O., Jr. *Public Opinion and American Democracy.* New York: Alfred E. Knopf, 1961.

MacManus, Susan A. *Young v. Old: Generational Combat in the 21st Century.* Boulder, CO: Westview Press, 1996.

Shafer, Bryon E., and William J. M. Claggett. *The Two Majorities: The Issue Context of Modern American Politics.* Baltimore: Johns Hopkins University Press, 1995.

Stimson, James A. *Public Opinion in America: Moods, Cycles and Swings.* Boulder, CO: Westview Press, 1991.

Yeric, Jerry L., and John R. Todd. *Public Opinion: The Visible Politics,* 3d ed. Itasca, IL: Peacock, 1994.

Zaller, John. *The Nature and Origins of Mass Opinions.* New York: The University Press, 1993.

(Photo courtesy: Dennis Brack/Black Star)

ducting elections, and providing social welfare services, had a major impact. Social services began to be seen as a right of citizenship rather than as a privilege extended in exchange for a person's support of a party. Also, as the flow of immigrants slowed dramatically in the 1920s, party organizations gradually withered in most places.

The **direct primary,** whereby party nominees were determined by the ballots of qualified voters rather than at party conventions, was widely adopted by the states in the first two decades of the twentieth century. The primary removed the power of nomination from party leaders and workers and gave it instead to a much broader and more independent electorate, thus loosening the tie between the party nominee and the party organization. **Civil service laws** also removed much of the patronage used by the parties to reward their followers. (Civil service laws require appointment on the basis of merit and competitive examinations, whereas **patronage**—-also called the **spoils system**—awards jobs on the basis of party loyalty.) These changes were encouraged by the Progressive movement (consisting of politically liberal reformers), which flourished in the first two decades of the twentieth century.

In the post-World War II era, extensive social changes led the movement away from strong parties. Broad-based education gave rise to **issue-oriented politics,** politics that focuses on specific issues, such as civil rights, tax cutting, environmentalism, or abortion, rather than on party labels. Issue politics tends to cut across party lines and encourages voters to **ticket-split,** that is, to vote for candidates of different parties for various offices in the same election. Another post-World War II social change that has affected the parties is the shift in the population. Millions of people have moved out of the cities, which are easily organizable because of population density, and into the sprawling suburbs, where a sense of privacy and detachment can deter the most energetic organizers.

Politically, many other trends have contributed to the parties' decline. Television, which has come to dominate U.S. politics, naturally emphasizes personalities rather than abstract concepts such as party labels. In addition, the modern parties have many rivals for the affections of their candidates, including **political consultants,** the hired guns who manage campaigns and design television advertisements. Both television and consultants have replaced the party as the intermediary between candidate and voter. It is little wonder that many candidates and office holders who have reached their posts without much help from their parties remain as free as possible of party ties.

The Parties Endure

The parties' decline can easily be exaggerated, however. Viewing parties in the broad sweep of U.S. history, it becomes clear that first, although political parties have evolved considerably and changed form from time to time, they usually have been reliable vehicles for mass participation in a representative democracy. In fact, the gradual but steady expansion of suffrage itself was orchestrated by the parties. As political scientist E. E. Schattschneider concluded, "In the search for new segments of the populace that might be exploited profitably, the parties have kept the movement to liberalize the franchise well ahead of the demand. . . .The enlargement of the practicing electorate has been one of the principal labors of the parties, a truly notable achievement for which the parties have never been properly credited."[7]

Second, the parties' journey through U.S. history has been characterized by the same ability to adapt to prevailing conditions that is often cited as the genius of the Constitution. Flexibility and pragmatism are characteristics of both and help ensure their survival and the success of the society they serve.

Political consultant James Carville addressing the New Jersey Democratic Convention, where state Democrats planned election strategy and selected delegates to the national convention. Seated at right is former Governor James Florio. (Photo courtesy: Mike Derer/AP Photo)

direct primary: The selection of party candidates through the ballots of qualified voters rather than at party nomination conventions.

civil service laws: These acts removed the staffing of the bureaucracy from political parties and created a professional bureaucracy filled through competition.

patronage: Jobs, grants, or other special favors that are given as rewards to friends and political allies for their support.

spoils system: The firing of public-office holders of a defeated political party and their replacement with loyalists of the newly elected party.

issue-oriented politics: Politics that focuses on specific issues rather than on party, candidate, or other loyalties.

ticket-split: To vote for candidates of different parties for various offices in the same election.

political consultant: Professional who manages campaigns and political advertisements for political candidates.

Highlight 12.2

The Death of a Party

In 1992 and 1994, voters in the United States changed parties, first ousting the Republicans from the White House and then evicting the Democrats from majority power in the Congress. But in some other countries where the two-party system is not as entrenched as it is here in America, the electorate has not merely rebuked but actually obliterated governing political parties. It happened in Canada in 1993, when the Progressive Conservatives, who had ruled for nine years, were reduced to a rump of two seats in Parliament by voters angry about economic problems and simply tired of the long-serving Conservative regime. Similarly, in Italy in March 1994, public disgust with widespread corruption felled the Christian Democrats. In power since 1948, they were nearly wiped out in Parliament. No major American party has faced such devastation since the Whigs in the late 1850s.

Third, despite massive changes in political conditions and frequent dramatic shifts in the electorate's mood, the two major parties have not only achieved remarkable longevity, but they also have almost consistently provided strong competition for each other and the voters at the national level. Of the twenty-nine presidential elections from 1884 to 1996, for instance, the Republicans won fifteen and the Democrats fourteen. Even when calamities have beset the parties—the Great Depression in the 1930s or the Watergate scandal of 1973–74 for the Republicans (see chapter 8), and the Civil War or left-wing McGovernism in 1972 for the Democrats—the two parties have proved tremendously resilient, sometimes bouncing back from landslide defeats to win the next election. (For the other possibility, see Highlight 12.2: The Death of a Party.) After losing the presidential election badly in 1988, for example, the Democrats managed to win the presidency in 1992 and 1996, demonstrating again that the only constant in politics is change.

Perhaps most of all, history teaches us that the development of parties in the United States (outlined in Figure 12.1) has been inevitable, as James Madison feared. Human nature alone guarantees conflict in any society; in a free state, the question is simply how to contain and channel conflict productively without infringing on individual liberties. The Founders' utopian hopes for the avoidance of partisan faction, Madison's chief concern, have given way to an appreciation of the parties' constructive contributions to conflict definition and resolution during the years of the American republic.

THE ROLES OF THE AMERICAN PARTIES

For 150 years the two-party system has served as the mechanism American society uses to organize and resolve social and political conflict. Although political parties are arguably less popular today than in previous times, it is important both to remember that political parties often are the chief agents of change in our political system and to discuss the vital services to society the parties provide and how difficult political life would be without them.

Mobilizing Support and Gathering Power

Party affiliation is enormously helpful to elected leaders. They can count on disproportionate support among their partisans in times of trouble and in close judgment calls. Therefore the parties thus aid office holders by giving them room to develop their policies and by mobilizing support for them. When the president addresses the nation and requests support for his policies, for example, his party's activists are usually the first to respond to the call, perhaps by flooding Congress with telegrams urging action on the president's agenda.

Because there are only two major parties, pragmatic citizens who are interested in politics or public policy are mainly attracted to one or the other standard, creating natural majorities or near-majorities for party office holders to command. The party creates a community of interest that bonds disparate groups over time into a **coalition.** This continuing mutual interest eliminates the necessity of creating a new coalition for every campaign or every issue. Imagine the constant chaos and mad scrambles for public support that would ensue without the continuity provided by the parties.

coalition: A group of interests or organizations that join forces for the purpose of electing public officials.

A Force for Stability

As mechanisms for organizing and containing political change, the parties are a potent force for stability. They represent continuity in the wake of changing issues and personalities, anchoring the electorate in the midst of the storm of new political policies and people. Because of its unyielding, practical desire to win elections (not just to contest them), each party in a sense acts to moderate public opinion. The party tames its own extreme elements by pulling them toward an ideological center in order to attract a majority of votes on Election Day.

Another aspect of the stability the parties provide is found in the nature of the coalitions they forge. There are inherent contradictions in these coalitions that, oddly enough, strengthen the nation even as they strain party unity. Franklin D. Roosevelt's Democratic New Deal coalition, for example, included many African Americans and most Southern whites, opposing elements nonetheless joined in common political purpose. This party union of the two groups, as limited a context as it may have been, provided a framework for acceptance of change and contributed to reconciliation of the races in the civil rights era. Nowhere can this reconciliation be more clearly seen than in the South, where most state Democratic parties remained predominant after the mid-1960s by building on the ingrained Democratic voting habits of both whites and blacks to create new, moderate, generally integrated societies.

Unity, Linkage, Accountability

Parties provide the glue that holds together the disparate elements of the fragmented U.S. governmental and political apparatus. The Framers designed a system that divides and subdivides power, making it possible to preserve individual liberty but difficult to coordinate and produce action in a timely fashion. Parties help compensate for this drawback by linking all the institutions of power one to another. Although rivalry between the executive and legislative branches of U.S. government is inevitable, the partisan affiliations of the leaders of each branch constitute a common basis for cooperation, as any president and his fellow party members in Congress usually demonstrate daily. Each time President Bill Clinton proposed a major new program (such as health care and crime control), for instance, Democratic members of the Congress were the first to speak up in favor of the program and to orchestrate efforts at its passage.

Even within each branch there is intended fragmentation, and the party once again helps narrow the differences between the House of Representatives and the Senate, or between the president and his chiefs in the executive bureaucracy. Similarly, the division of national, state, and local governments, while always an invitation to conflict, is made more workable and easily coordinated by the intersecting party relationships that exist among office holders at all levels. Party affiliation, in other words, is a basis for mediation and negotiation laterally among the branches and vertically among the layers.

The party's linkage function does not end there. Party identification and organization are natural connectors and vehicles for communication between the voter and the candidate, as well as between the voter and the office holder. The party connection is one means of increasing accountability in election campaigns and in government. Candidates on the campaign trail and elected party leaders in office are required from time to time to account for their performance at party-sponsored forums, nominating primaries, and conventions.

Political parties, too, can take some credit for unifying the nation by dampening sectionalism. Because parties must form national majorities in order to win the presidency, any single, isolated region is guaranteed minority status unless it establishes ties with other areas. The party label and philosophy build the bridge that enables regions to join forces; and in the process, a national interest, rather than a merely sectional one, is created and served.

In a platform turnaround reminiscent of the Republicans' 1992 Contract with America, in June of election year 1996 Democrats introduced the "Families First" plan. It called for eventually balancing the budget, reforming the welfare system, and improving education. (Photo courtesy: Joe Marquette/AP Photo)

The Electioneering Function

The election, proclaimed author H. G. Wells, is "democracy's ceremonial, its feast, its great function," and the political parties assist this ceremony in essential ways. First, the parties funnel eager, interested individuals into politics and government. Thousands of candidates are recruited each year by the two parties, as are many of the candidates' staff members—the people who manage the campaigns and go on to serve in key governmental positions once the election has been won.

This function is even more crucial in the British parliamentary system. In the postwar period, the only avenue to national power (that is, the prime minister's office or a choice seat on the Cabinet) has been through either the Conservative Party or the Labour Party. Ambitious politicians must work their way up through the party hierarchy and build a supporting coalition along the way.

Elections can have meaning in a democracy only if they are competitive, and in the United States they probably could not be competitive without the parties. Even in the South, traditionally the least politically competitive U.S. region, the parties today regularly produce reasonably vigorous contests at the state (and, increasingly, the local) level.

Party as a Voting and Issue Cue

A voter's party identification acts as an invaluable filter for information, a perceptual screen that affects how he or she digests political news. Therefore party affiliation provides a useful cue for voters, particularly for the least informed and least interested, who can use the party as a shortcut or substitute for interpreting issues and events they may not fully comprehend. But even better-educated and more involved voters find party identification helpful. After all, no one has the time to study every issue carefully or to become fully knowledgeable about every candidate seeking public office.

Policy Formulation and Promotion

U.S. Senator Huey Long (D–La.), one of the premier spokesmen for "the people" of this century, was usually able to capture the flavor of the average person's views about politics. Considering an independent bid for president before his assassination in 1935, Long liked to compare the Republican and Democratic parties to the two patent medicines offered by a traveling salesman. Asked the difference between them, the salesman explained that the "High Populorum" tonic was made from the bark of the tree taken from the top down, while "Low Populorum" tonic was made from bark stripped from the root up. The analogous moral, according to Long, was this: "The only difference I've found in Congress between the Republican and Democratic leadership is that one of 'em is skinning us from the ankle up and the other from the ear down!"[8]

Long would certainly have insisted that his fable applied to the **national party platform,** the most visible instrument by which parties formulate, convey, and promote public policy. Every four years, each party writes for the presidential nominating conventions a lengthy platform explaining its positions on key issues. Most citizens in our own era undoubtedly still believe that party platforms are relatively undifferentiated, a mixture of pabulum and pussyfooting. Yet political scientist Gerald M. Pomper's study of party platforms from 1944 through 1976 has demonstrated that each party's pledges were consistently and significantly different, a function in part of the varied groups in their coalitions.[9] Interestingly, about 69 percent of the specific platform positions were taken by one party but not the other. On abortion, for example, the Democrats are strongly for abortion rights while the Republicans are firmly against them in their most recent platforms.

national party platform: A statement of the general and specific philosophy and policy goals of a political party, usually promulgated at the national convention.

Senator Huey Long (D-La.) campaigned for the presidency in 1935 on a populist platform, arguing in fiery speeches that neither of the major parties' policies had the people's best interests at heart. (Photo courtesy: UPI/Bettmann Archive)

Granted, then, party platforms are quite distinctive. Does this elaborate party exercise in policy formulation mean anything? One could argue that the platform is valuable, if only as a clear presentation of a party's basic philosophy and as a forum for activist opinion and public education. But platforms have much more impact than that. About two-thirds of the promises in the victorious party's presidential platform have been completely or mostly implemented; even more astounding, one-half or more of the pledges of the losing party find their way into public policy (with the success rate depending on whether the party controls one, both, or neither house of Congress).[10] The party platform also has great influence on a new presidential administration's legislative program and on the president's State of the Union address. And while party affiliation is normally the single most important determinant of voting in Congress and in state legislatures,[11] the party-vote relationship is even stronger when party platform issues come up on the floor of Congress. Gerald M. Pomper concludes: "We should therefore take platforms seriously, because politicians appear to take them seriously."[12]

Besides mobilizing Americans on a permanent basis, then, the parties convert the cacophony of hundreds of identifiable social and economic groups into a two-part semi-harmony that is much more comprehensible, if not always on key and pleasing to the ears. The simplicity of two-party politics may be deceptive given the enormous variety in public policy choices, but a sensible system of representation in the American context might be impossible without it. And the people who would suffer most from its absence would not be the few who are individually or organizationally powerful; their voices would be heard under almost any system. As political scientist Walter Dean Burnham has pointed out, the losers would be the many individually powerless for whom the parties are the only effective devices yet created that can generate collective power on their behalf.[13]

ONE-PARTYISM AND THIRD-PARTYISM

The two-party system has not gone unchallenged. At the state level, two-party competition was severely limited or nonexistent in much of the country for most of this century.[14] Especially in the one-party Democratic states of the Deep South and the rock-ribbed Republican states of Maine, New Hampshire, and Vermont, the dominant party's primary nomination was often equivalent to election, and the only real contest was an unsatisfying intraparty one in which colorful personalities often dominated and a half-dozen major candidacies in each primary proved confusing to voters.[15] Even in most two-party states, many cities and counties had a massive majority of voters aligned with one or the other party and thus were effectively one-party in local elections. In Britain, one-partyism at the subnational level is a relatively common phenomenon; for example, certain regions like the Northeast have voted overwhelmingly for the Labour Party in general election after general election.

Historical, cultural, and sectional forces primarily accounted for the concentration of one party's supporters in certain areas. The Civil War's divisions, for instance, were mirrored for the better part of a century in the Democratic predisposition of the South and the Republican proclivities of the Yankee Northern states. Whatever the combination of factors producing **one-partyism**—a political system in which one party dominates and wins virtually all contests—the condition has certainly declined precipitously in the last quarter century.[16]

one-partyism: A political system in which one party dominates and wins virtually all contests.

The spread of two-party competition, while still uneven in some respects, is one of the most significant political trends of recent times, and virtually no one-party states are left. There are no purely Republican states any more, and the heavily Democratic contingent has been reduced to, at most, Louisiana, Arkansas, and Maryland. (Note, though, that in each of these states one or more Republicans have been elected to the governorship or U.S. Senate since 1970, and the Deep South states usually vote Republican in presidential contests, as well, unless a Southerner heads the Democratic ticket.)

Ironically, the growth of two-party competition has been spurred less by the developing strength of the main parties than by party weakness, as illustrated by the decline in partisan loyalty among the voters. In other words, citizens now are somewhat more inclined to cross party lines in order to support an appealing candidate regardless of party affiliation, thus making a victory for the minority party possible whether or not it has earned the victory through the party's own organizational hard work. It should also be noted that the elimination of pockets of one-party strength adds an element of instability to the system, since at one point, even in lean times of national electoral disaster, each party was assured of a regional base from which a comeback could be staged. Nonetheless, the increase in party competitiveness can be viewed positively, since it eliminates the effects of one-partyism and guarantees a comprehensible and credible partisan choice to a larger segment of the electorate than ever before.

Minor Parties: Third-partyism

Third-partyism has proved more durable than one-partyism, though its nature is sporadic and intermittent, and its effects on the political system are on the whole less weighty. Given all the controversy third parties generate, one could be excused for thinking that they were extraordinarily important on the American scene. But as Frank J. Sorauf has concluded, third parties in fact "have not assumed the importance that all the [academic] attention lavished on them suggests."[17] No minor party has ever come close to winning the presidency, and only eight minor parties have won so much as a single state's electoral college votes (see Table 12.1). Just five third parties (the farmer-backed Populists in 1892, Theodore Roosevelt's Bull Moose Party in 1912, the reform-minded Progressives in 1924, former Alabama Governor George Wallace's racially based American Independent Party in 1968, and Ross Perot's Independents in 1992) have garnered more than 10 percent of the popular vote for president. Theodore Roosevelt's 1912 effort was the most successful; the Bull Moose Party won 27 percent of the popular vote for president (although only 17 percent of the electoral college votes). Roosevelt's is also the only third party to run ahead of one of the two major parties (the Republicans). Roosevelt, incidentally, abandoned the Republican Party, under whose banner he had won the presidency in 1904, in order to form the Bull Moose Party, composed mainly of reformist Republicans.

Third parties find their roots in sectionalism (as did the South's states' rights Dixiecrats, who broke away from the Democrats in 1948); in economic protest (such as the agrarian revolt that fueled the Populists, an 1892 prairie-states party); in specific issues (such as the Prohibition Party's proposed ban on the sale of alcoholic beverages); in ideology (the Socialist, Communist, and Libertarian parties are examples); and in appealing, charismatic personalities (Theodore Roosevelt is perhaps the best case). Many of the minor parties have drawn strength from a combination of these sources. The American Independent Party enjoyed a measure of success because of a dynamic leader (George Wallace), a firm geographic base (the South), and an emotional issue (civil rights). In 1992 Ross Perot, the billionaire with a folksy Texas manner, was a charis-

third-partyism: The tendency of third parties to arise with some regularity in a nominally two-party system.

TABLE 12.1

Third-Party and Independent Presidential Candidates Receiving 5 Percent or More of Popular Vote

CANDIDATE (PARTY)	YEAR	PERCENTAGE OF POPULAR VOTE	ELECTORAL VOTES
Ross Perot (Reform Party)	1996	8.5	0
Ross Perot (Independent)	1992	18.9	0
John B. Anderson (Independent)	1980	6.6	0
George C. Wallace (American Independent)	1968	13.5	46
Robert M. LaFollette (Progressive)	1924	16.6	13
Theodore Roosevelt (Bull Moose)	1912	27.4	88
Eugene V. Debs (Socialist)	1912	6.0	0
James B. Weaver (Populist)	1892	8.5	22
John C. Brekinridge (Southern Democrat)	1860	18.1	72
John Bell (Constitutional Union)	1860	12.6	39
Millard Fillmore (Whig-American)	1856	21.5	8
Martin Van Buren (Free Soil)	1848	10.1	0
William Wirt (Anti-Masonic)	1832	7.8	7

Source: Congressional Quarterly Weekly Report (October 18, 1980): 3147 (as adapted), and official election returns for 1992, 1996.

matic leader whose campaign was fueled by the deficit issue (as well as by his personal fortune). And in 1996 Colin Powell's initial popularity stemmed from Americans' growing disillusion with politicians and the political system, a disillusion driven by the federal budget stalemate of 1995 and 1996.

Above all, third parties make electoral progress in direct proportion to the failure of the two major parties to incorporate new ideas or alienated groups or to nominate attractive candidates as their standard-bearers. Usually, though, these third parties are eventually co-opted by one of the two major parties, each of them eager to take the politically popular issue that gave rise to the third party and make it theirs in order to secure the allegiance of their supporters. For example, the Republicans of the 1970s absorbed many of the "states' rights" planks of George Wallace's 1968 presidential bid. Both parties have also more recently attempted to attract Perot voters by sponsoring reforms of the governmental process, such as limitations on the activities of Washington lobbyists.

Former Chairman of the Joint Chiefs of Staff Colin Powell at a booksigning, around the time his candidacy for president was being hotly debated. Some argued Powell, whether he ran as either a Republican or an Independent candidate, would have certain success. According to one commentator, "Powell's stature is rising like a balloon riding the hot air over Washington." The nation was "starving for leadership, and Powell oozes with leadership qualities." He subsequently announced that he would not run, alluding to the fact that such a race "requires a commitment and passion" to succeed. (Photo courtesy: Rick Falco/Black Star)

Why Third Parties Tend to Remain Minor

Third parties in the United States are akin to shooting stars that appear briefly and brilliantly but do not long remain visible in the political constellation. In fact, the United States is the only major Western nation that does not have at least one significant, enduring national third party. There are a number of explanations for this. Unlike many European countries that use **proportional representation** (awarding legislative seats in proportion to the number of votes received) and that guarantee parliamentary seats to any faction securing as little as 5 percent of the vote, the United States has a "single-member, plurality" electoral system that requires a party to get one more vote than any other party in a legislative district or in a state's presidential election in order to win. To paraphrase the legendary football coach Vince Lombardi, finishing first is not everything, it is the *only* thing in U.S. politics; placing second, even by a smidgen, doesn't count. This condition encourages the grouping of interests into as few parties as possible (the democratic minimum being two), though sometimes this strains partisan coalitions. For example, the religious right and the more moderate segments of the Republican party barely coexist. Nonetheless, we should not write off the possibility that an enduring third party will emerge.

Other institutional factors also undergird the two-party system:

- Most states have laws that require third parties to secure a place on the ballot by gathering large numbers of signatures, whereas the Democratic and Republican parties are often granted automatic access.

- Democrats and Republicans in the state legislatures may have little in common, but both want to make sure that the political pie is cut into only two sizable pieces, not three or more smaller slices.

proportional representation:
The practice of awarding legislative seats in proportion to the number of votes received.

■ The public funding of campaigns (financing from taxpayer dollars), where it exists, is much more generous for the two major parties. At the national level, for
instance, third-party presidential candidates receive money only after the general
election, if they have garnered more than 5 percent of the vote, and only in proportion to their total vote; the major-party candidates, by contrast, get large, full
general-election grants immediately upon their summer nominations. (This funding difference does not affect wealthy politicians like Perot.)

■ The news media gives relatively little coverage to minor parties compared with
that given to major-party nominees. The media's bias is legitimate—it only reflects political reality, and it would be absurd to expect them to offer equal time
to all comers. Still, this is a vicious cycle for minor-party candidates: A lack of
broad-based support produces slight coverage, which minimizes their chances of
attracting more adherents. Of course, once a third-party candidate such as Ross
Perot becomes prominent, the media flock to his appearances and clamor to
schedule him on their news shows.

dualist theory: The theory
claiming that there has always been
an underlying binary party nature to
U.S. politics.

Beyond the institutional explanations are historical, cultural, and social theories of
two-partyism in the United States. The **dualist theory,** frequently criticized as overly
simplistic, suggests that there has always been an underlying binary nature to U.S. politics. Whether it was the early conflict between Eastern financial interests and Western
frontiersmen, the sectional division of North and South, the more current urban-versus-
rural or urban-versus-suburban clashes, or even the natural tensions of democratic institutions (the government against the opposition, for instance), dualists believe that the
processes and interests of politics inevitably push the players into two great camps.

Other political scientists emphasize the basic social consensus existing in American life. Despite great diversity in our heritage, the vast majority of Americans accept
without serious question the fundamental structures of our system: The Constitution,
the governmental set-up, a lightly controlled free enterprise economy, for example. This
consensus, when allied with certain American cultural characteristics developed over
time (pragmatism, acceptance of the need for compromise, a lack of extreme and divisive social-class consciousness), produces the conditions necessary for relatively nonideological, centrist politics that can naturally support two moderate alternative parties
but has little need for more.

The passion for power and victory that drives both Democrats and Republicans
overrides ideology and prevents rigidity. Unless a kind of rigor mortis takes hold in the
future in one or both major parties—with, say, the capture of the party organization by
unyielding extremists of right or left—it is difficult to imagine any third party becoming a major, permanent force in U.S. politics (although Ross Perot's organization bears
watching). The corollary of this axiom, though, is that the major parties must be eter-
nally vigilant if they are to avoid ideologically inspired takeovers.

For the foreseeable future, however, third parties likely will continue to play useful supporting roles similar to their historically sanctioned ones: They can popularize
ideas that might not receive a hearing otherwise. They can serve as vehicles of popular
discontent with the major parties and thereby induce change in major-party behavior
and platforms, such as in 1992 when Ross Perot forced the two major parties to acknowledge and address the deficit issue. They may presage and assist party realignments in the future as they have sometimes done in the past. In a few states, third
parties will also continue to take a unique part in political life, as the Conservative and
Liberal Parties of New York State do. But in a two-party system that is supplemented
by generous means of expressing dissent and registering political opposition in other

ways (court challenges and interest group organizing, for example), third parties will probably continue to have a limited future in the United States.

THE BASIC STRUCTURE OF AMERICAN POLITICAL PARTIES

*W*hile the distinctions might not be as clear today as they were two or three decades ago, the two major parties remain fairly simply organized, with national, state, and local branches (Figure 12.2). The different levels of each party represent diverse interests in Washington, D.C., state capitols, and local governments throughout the nation.

FIGURE 12.2

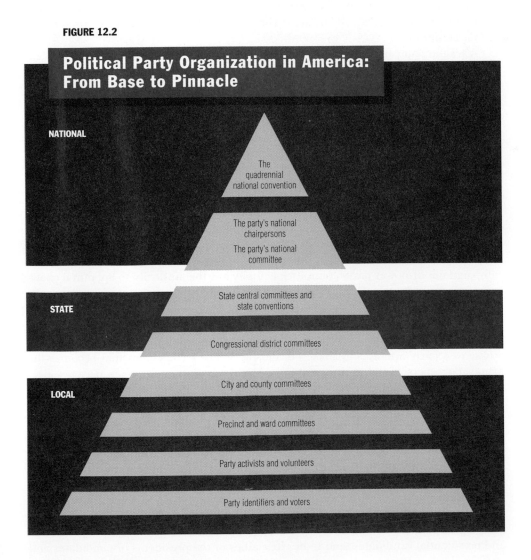

Political Party Organization in America: From Base to Pinnacle

NATIONAL

The quadrennial national convention

The party's national chairpersons
The party's national committee

STATE

State central committees and state conventions

Congressional district committees

LOCAL

City and county committees

Precinct and ward committees

Party activists and volunteers

Party identifiers and voters

Democratic National Committee Co-Chairman Donald W. Fowler delivers the keynote speech during the 1996 Democratic State Convention in Las Vegas, Nevada. (Photo courtesy: Jack Dempsey/AP Photo)

national convention: A party conclave (meeting) held in the presidential election year for the purposes of nominating a presidential and vice-presidential ticket and adopting a platform.

National Committees

The first national party committees were skeletal and formed some years after the creation of the presidential nominating conventions in the 1830s. Every four years, each party holds a **national convention** to nominate its presidential and vice-presidential candidates. First the Democrats in 1848 and then the Republicans in 1856 established national governing bodies (the Democratic National Committee, or DNC, and the Republican National Committee, or RNC) to make arrangements for the conventions and to coordinate the subsequent presidential campaigns. The DNC and RNC were each composed of one representative from each state; this was expanded to two in the 1920s after the post of state committeewoman was established. The states had complete control over the selection of their representatives to the national committees. In addition, to serve their interests, the congressional party caucuses in both houses organized their own national committees, loosely allied with the DNC and RNC. The National Republican Congressional Committee (NRCC) was started in 1866 when the Radical Republican congressional delegation was feuding with Abraham Lincoln's moderate successor, President Andrew Johnson, and wanted a counterweight to his control of the RNC. At the same time, House and Senate Democrats set up a similar committee.

After the popular election of U.S. senators was initiated in 1913 with the ratification of the Seventeenth Amendment to the Constitution, both parties organized separate Senate campaign committees. This three-part arrangement of national party committee, House party committee, and Senate party committee has persisted in both parties until the present day, and each party's three committees are located together in Washington, D.C.

Leadership

The key national party official is the chairperson of the DNC or RNC. Although the chair is formally elected by the national committee, he or she is usually selected by the sitting president or newly nominated presidential candidate, who is accorded the right to name the individual for at least the duration of his or her campaign. Only the post-campaign out-of-power party committee actually has the authority to appoint a chairperson independently. The committee-crowned chairpersons generally have the greatest impact on the party because they come to their posts at times of crisis when a leadership vacuum exists. (A defeated presidential candidate is technically the head of the national party until the next nominating convention, but the reality is naturally otherwise as a party attempts to shake off a losing image.) The chair often becomes the prime spokesperson and arbitrator for the party during the four years between elections. He or she is called on to damp down factionalism, negotiate candidate disputes, raise money, and prepare the machinery for the next presidential election. Balancing the interests of all potential White House contenders is a particularly difficult job, and strict neutrality is normally expected from the chair.

In recent times both parties have benefited from adept leadership while out of power. William Brock, RNC chairman during the Carter presidency, and Ron Brown, the first African American to chair the DNC (during the Bush term), both skillfully used their positions to strengthen their parties organizationally and to polish the party images. Brock and Brown frequently appeared on news shows to give the out-of-power party's viewpoint. By contrast, party chairpersons selected by incumbent presidents and presidential candidates tend to be close allies of the presidents or candidates and often subordinate the good of the party to the needs of the campaign or White House. During the Carter presidency, for example, DNC Chairman Kenneth Curtis and his successor John White were creatures of the White House; they acted as cheerleaders for their chief executive but did little to keep the Democratic Party competitive with the then-strengthening GOP organization.

Because of their command of presidential patronage and influence, a few national party chairpersons selected by presidents have become powerful and well known, such as Republican Mark Hanna during the McKinley presidency (1897–1901) and Democrat James Farley under President Franklin D. Roosevelt. Most presidentially appointed chairs, however, have been relatively obscure; the chance for a chairperson to make a difference and cut a memorable figure generally comes when there is no competition from a White House nominee or occupant. President Clinton originally named thirty-six-year-old national campaign manager David Wilhelm, a veteran of Chicago politics, to head the DNC. Wilhelm served until mid-1994, when he resigned to return to his native Chicago. Clinton then chose the team of Senator Christopher Dodd (D–Conn.) and South Carolina political activist Donald W. Fowler to head up the DNC. Dodd and Fowler's Republican counterpart is Haley Barbour, an ex-aide to Ronald Reagan; he was a Washington, D.C., lawyer and lobbyist at the time of his election by the RNC. Barbour was credited with reorganizing the GOP and contributing to its 1994 takeover of Congress. Nevertheless, he was criticized for the GOP's failure to substantially increase its numbers in Congress in 1996.

Senator Christopher Dodd (D-Ct.) took over as the general chair of the Democratic National Committee in early 1995. Along with his co-chair, Donald W. Fowler of South Carolina, Dodd's objective was to reinvigorate the party after its disastrous 1994 election losses. (Photo courtesy: Wide World Photos)

National Conventions

Much of any party chairperson's work involves planning the presidential nominating convention, or national convention, the most publicized and vital event on the party's calendar. Until 1984, gavel-to-gavel coverage was standard practice on all national television networks. Even after the recent cutbacks by some news organizations, a substantial block of time is still devoted to the conventions. (In 1996, for example, all the networks devoted at least a couple of prime-time hours per night to convention coverage.) Although the nomination of the presidential ticket naturally receives the lion's share of attention, the convention also fulfills its role as the ultimate governing body for the party itself. The rules adopted and the platform passed at the quadrennial conclave are durable guidelines that steer the party for years after the final gavel has been brought down.

Most of the recent party chairpersons, in cooperation with the incumbent president or likely nominee, have tried to orchestrate every minute of the conventions in order to project just the right image to voters. By and large, they have succeeded, though at the price of draining some spontaneity and excitement from the convention process.

States and Localities

Although national committee activities of all kinds attract most of the media attention, the party is structurally based not in Washington, but in the states and localities. Except for the campaign finance arena, virtually all governmental regulation of political parties is left to the states, for example, and most elected officials give their allegiance to the local party divisions they know best. Most important, the vast majority of party leadership positions are filled at subnational levels.

The pyramidal arrangement of party committees provides for a broad base of support. The smallest voting unit, the precinct, usually takes in a few adjacent neighbor-

Haley Barbour, Chairman of the Republican National Committee, addresses a rally celebrating the completion of the Contract with America. (Photo courtesy: John Harrington/Black Star)

hoods and is the fundamental building block of the party. Each of the more than 100,000 precincts in the United States potentially has a committee member to represent it in each party's councils. The precinct committee members are the key foot soldiers of any party, and their efforts are supplemented by party committees above them in the wards, cities, counties, towns, villages, and congressional districts.

The state governing body supervising this collection of local party organizations is usually called the state central (or executive) committee. It comprises representatives from all major geographic units, as determined by and selected under state law. Generally, state parties are free to act within the limits set by their state legislatures without interference from the national party, except in the selection and seating of presidential convention delegates. National Democrats have been particularly inclined to regulate this aspect of party life. With the decline of big-city political machines, few local parties have the clout to object to the national party's dictates.

Informal Groups

The formal structure of party organization is supplemented by numerous official, semi-official, and unaffiliated groups that combine and clash with the parties in countless ways. Both the DNC and RNC have affiliated organizations of state and local party women (The National Federation of Democratic Women and the National Federation of Republican Women). The youth divisions (the Young Democrats of America and the Young Republicans' National Federation) have a generous definition of "young," up to and including age thirty-five. The state governors in each party have their own party associations, too.

Just outside the party orbit are the supportive interest groups and associations that often provide money, labor, or other forms of assistance to the parties. Labor unions, progressive political action committees (PACs), teachers, African-American and liberal women's groups, and the Americans for Democratic Action are some of the Democratic Party's organizational groups. Business PACs, the Chamber of Commerce of the United States, fundamentalist Christian organizations, and some anti-abortion agencies work closely with the Republicans. Similar party-interest group pairings occur in Britain. Trade unions have aligned themselves with the Labour Party, providing the bulk of the party's contributions, and business has been closely allied with the Conservatives.

Each U.S. party also has several institutionalized sources of policy ideas. Though unconnected to the parties in any official sense, these so-called *think tanks* (institutional collections of policy-oriented researchers and academics) are quite influential. During the Reagan administration, for instance, the right-wing Heritage Foundation placed many dozens of its conservatives in important governmental positions, and its issue studies on subjects ranging from tax reform to South Africa carried considerable weight with policy makers. The more moderate and bipartisan American Enterprise Institute also supplied the Reagan team with people and ideas. On the Democratic side, liberal think tanks proliferated during the party's Reagan- and Bush-induced exile. More than a half-dozen policy institutes formed after 1980 in an attempt to nurse the Democrats back to political health. The Center for National Policy and the Progressive Policy Institute, to cite two, sponsored conferences and published papers on Democratic policy alternatives.

Finally, there are extra-party organizations that form for a wide variety of purposes, including "reforming" a party or moving it ideologically to the right or left. In New York City, for example, Democratic reform clubs were established in the late 1800s to fight the Tammany Hall machine, the city's dominant Democratic organization at the time. About seventy clubs still prosper by attracting well-educated activists committed to various liberal causes. More recently, both national parties have been favored (or bedeviled) by the formation of new extra-party outfits. The Democrats have been pushed by both halves of the ideological continuum. The Democratic Leadership Council (DLC) was launched in 1985 by moderate and conservative Democrats concerned about what they perceived as the leftward drift of their party and its image as the captive of liberal special-interest groups. It is composed of more than one hundred current and former Democratic office holders (such as Senator Sam Nunn of Georgia and House Minority Leader Richard Gephardt of Missouri). The DLC has not always been popular with the national party leadership, which has sometimes viewed it as a potential rival, but it nurtured and strongly backed Bill Clinton's candidacy in 1992 and 1996. Several DLC leaders were appointed to positions in the Clinton administration.

The DLC formed in part to counter a left-leaning force organizing from within the partisan ranks, Jesse Jackson's National Rainbow Coalition. The Coalition is partly a vehicle for Jackson's ambitions. Beyond that, its goals of mass membership, hundreds of state and local charter affiliates, and endorsements of independent candidates when Democratic nominees are found to be "unacceptable" present a challenge to the Democratic Party in the eyes of at least some party officials.

Republicans have their extraparty agents too. The most prominent is GOPAC, the political action committee associated with U.S. House Speaker for the 104th Congress Newt Gingrich. GOPAC helped dozens of Republican congressional candidates prior to the 1994 elections by training them and their staffs and providing money at critical points in their campaigns. GOPAC and Gingrich were credited with helping to produce the Republican landslide of 1994.

THE PARTY IN GOVERNMENT

*P*olitical parties are not restricted to their role as grassroots organizations of voters; they also have another major role inside government institutions. Parties are the organizing mechanisms for the branches and layers of American government.

The Congressional Party

In no segment of U.S. government is the party more visible or vital than in the Congress. In this century, the political parties have dramatically increased the sophistication and impact of their internal congressional organizations. Prior to the beginning of every session, each party in both houses of Congress gathers (or "caucuses") separately to select party leaders (House Speaker or minority leader, Senate majority and minority leaders, party whips, and so on) and to arrange for the appointment of members of each chamber's committees. In effect, then, the parties organize and operate the Congress. Their management systems have grown quite elaborate; the web of deputy and assistant whips for House Democrats now extends to about one-fourth of the party's entire membership. Although not invulnerable to pressure from the minority, the majority party in each house generally holds sway, even fixing the size of its majority on all committees—a proportion frequently in excess of the percentage of seats it holds in the house as a whole.

Discipline. Congressional party leaders have some substantial tools at their disposal to enforce a degree of discipline in their troops. Even though seniority usually determines most committee assignments, an occasional choice plum may be given to the loyal or withheld from the rebellious. For example, House Speaker for the 104th Congress Newt Gingrich rewarded his most loyal freshmen representatives with plum slots on major committees, such as Ways and Means, when he took the reins in January 1995. A member's bill can be lovingly caressed through the legislative process, or it can be summarily dismissed without so much as a hearing. Pork barrel—government projects yielding rich patronage benefits that sustain many a legislator's electoral survival—may be included or deleted during the appropriations process. Small favors and perquisites (such as the allocation of desirable office space or the scheduling of floor votes for the convenience of a member) can also be useful levers. Then, too, there are the campaign aids at the command of the leadership: money from party sources, endorsements, appearances in the district or at fund-raising events, and so on. On rare occasions the leaders and their allies in the party caucus may even impose sanctions of various sorts (such as the stripping of seniority rights or prized committee berths) in order to punish recalcitrant law makers.[18]

In spite of all these weapons in the leadership's arsenal, the congressional parties lack the cohesion that characterizes parliamentary legislatures. This is not surprising, since the costs of bolting the party are much less in the United States than in, say, Great Britain. A disloyal English member of Parliament might be replaced as a party candidate at the next election; in the United States, it is more likely that the independent-minded member of Congress would be electorally rewarded—hailed as a free spirit, an individual of the people who stood up to the party bosses. Moreover, defections from the ruling party in a parliamentary system bring a threat of the government's collapse along with early elections under possibly unfavorable conditions. Fixed election dates in the United States mean that the consequences of defection are much less dire. Also, a centralized, unicameral parliament (in which executive and legislative branches are effectively fused) permits relatively easy hierarchical control by party leaders.

There are other limits to coordinated, cohesive party action. For example, the separate executive branch, the bicameral power-sharing, and the extraordinary decentralization of Congress's work, all constitute institutional obstacles to effective party action. Finally, party discipline is hurt by the individualistic nature of U.S. politics: campaigns that are candidate-centered rather than party-oriented; diverse electoral constituencies to which members of Congress must understandably be responsive; the largely private system of election financing that indebts legislators to wealthy individuals and nonparty interest groups more than to their parties; and the importance to law makers of attracting the news media's attention—often more easily done by showmanship than by quiet, effective labor within the party system.

Despite all of the barriers to cohesive party action, events occasionally move a party in that direction. One such example occurred in 1994, when most Republican U.S. House candidates signed onto the so-called Contract with America, a party platform for Congressional campaigns similar in some respects to a formal presidential platform. The Contract included such popular items as tax relief, term limits for congressmen, and welfare reform, and it became the basis for the House of Representatives' legislative activity in early 1995. While not all of these items have yet been passed by the legislature and signed into law by the president, in debating and voting on the Contract both the Republicans and Democrats showed that cohesive party action can still be achieved.

The above are formidable barriers to the operation of responsible, potent legislative parties. Therefore it is impressive to discover that party labels have consistently been the most powerful predictor of congressional roll-call voting, and in the last few years even more votes have closely followed the partisan divide. While not invariably predictive, as in strong parliamentary systems, a member's party affiliation has proven to be the indicator of his or her votes more than 70 percent of the time in recent years; that is, the average representative or senator sides with his or her party on about 70 percent of the votes that divide a majority of Democrats from a majority of Republicans. In most recent years, more than half of the roll-call votes in the House and Senate also found majorities of Democrats and Republicans on opposite sides.

Until the 1980s there had been a substantial decline in party voting in Congress. In the past several years, however, party voting has increased noticeably, as reflected in the upward trend in party voting by both Democrats and Republicans in Figure 12.3. In 1993, for instance, both the average Democratic member and the average Republican member voted with his or her party (on votes dividing party majorities) about 88 percent of the time. President Clinton's economic programs in his first year in office clearly polarized the Congress, and the proportion of party voting jumped considerably from the already high (79 percent) level recorded in 1992. Partisanship in 1994 was less evident than in 1993, but still high, 83 percent among Democrats and 82 percent among Republicans. In 1995 partisans among Republicans took a major jump up; following their big election triumph, the GOP unity percentage was 91. Among Democrats it was 80 percent in 1995.

There are many reasons for the recent growth of congressional party unity and cohesion. Some are the result of long-term political factors. Both congressional parties, for instance, have gradually become more ideologically homogeneous and internally consistent. Southern Democrats today are more moderate and much closer philosophically to their Northern counterparts than the South's legislative barons of old ever were. Similarly, there are few liberal Republicans left in either chamber of Congress, and GOP House members from all regions of the country are—with a few exceptions—moderately to solidly conservative. At the same time, strong two-party competition has come to almost all areas of the nation. The electoral insecurity produced by vigorous competition seems to encourage party unity and cooperation in a legislature (perhaps as a kind of "circling the wagons" effect).[19]

The circumstances of contemporary politics are also producing greater party cohesion. There is renewed satisfaction on the Republican side of the House aisle with

FIGURE 12.3

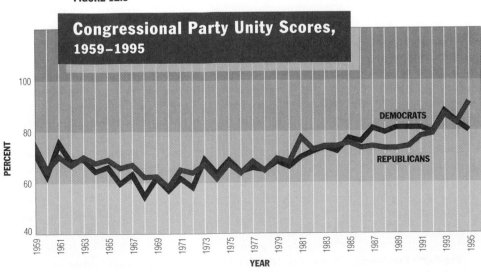

SOURCE: *Congressional Quarterly Almanacs* (Washington: Congressional Quarterly, Inc).

that party's return to majority status. The increased militancy of former Minority Whip and for the 104th Congress Speaker of the House Newt Gingrich of Georgia has raised the partisan hackles of many Democrats, polarizing the House a bit more along party lines. In fact, Gingrich's Contract with America generated very strong party voting in the House in early 1995; most floor votes found virtually all Republicans supporting the provisions of the Contract, with most Democrats voting in opposition. On the other side of the Capitol, the continuing, close partisan struggle since 1980 over control of the Senate has appeared to increase the party consciousness of both groups of senators.

The political party campaign committees have also played a role in the renewed cohesiveness observed within Congress. Each national party committee has been recruiting and training House and Senate candidates as never before, and devising common themes for all nominees in election seasons, work that may help to produce a consensual legislative agenda for each party. The carrot and stick of party money and campaign services, such as media advertising production and polling, are also being used to convert candidates into party team players. Clearly, the more important the party organization can be to a legislator's election and reelection, the more attention a legislator is likely to pay to his or her party.

The Presidential Party

Political parties may be more central to the operation of the legislative branch than the executive branch, but it is the presidential party that captures the public imagination and shapes the electorate's opinion of the two parties. In our very personalized politics, voters' perceptions of the incumbent president and the presidential candidates determine to a large extent how citizens perceive the parties.

A chief executive's successes are his party's successes; the president's failures are borne by the party as much as by the individual. The image projected by a losing presidential candidate is incorporated into the party's contemporary portrait, whether wanted or not. As the highest elected candidate of the national party, the president naturally assumes the role of party leader, as does the White House nominee of the other party (at least during the campaign).

The juggling of contradictory roles is not always easy for a president. Expected to bring the country together as ceremonial chief of state and also to forge a ruling consensus as head of government, the president must also be an effective commander of a sometimes divided party. Along with the inevitable headaches party leadership brings, though, are clear and compelling advantages that accompany it. Foremost among them is a party's ability to mobilize support among voters for a president's program. Also, the executive's legislative agenda might be derailed more quickly without the common tie of party label between the chief executive and many members of Congress; all presidents appeal for some congressional support on the basis of shared party affiliation, and they generally receive it depending on circumstances and their executive skill.

These party gifts to the president are reciprocated in many ways. In addition to compiling a record for the party and giving substance to its image, presidents appoint many activists to office, recruit candidates, raise money for the party treasury, campaign extensively for party nominees during election seasons, and occasionally provide some "coattail" help to fellow office seekers who are on the ballot in presidential election years.

Pro-Party Presidents.   Some presidents take their party responsibilities more seriously than others. In this century Democrats Woodrow Wilson and Franklin D. Roo-

sevelt were exceptionally party-oriented and dedicated to building their party electorally and governmentally. Republican Gerald R. Ford, during his brief tenure from
1974 to 1977, also achieved a reputation as a party builder. He was willing to undertake campaign and organizational chores for the GOP (especially in fund raising and
in barnstorming for nominees) that most other presidents minimized or shunned. Perhaps Ford's previous role as House minority leader made him more sensitive to the
needs of his fellow party office holders.

More recently, Ronald Reagan and George Bush exemplified the "pro-party" presidency. Ronald Reagan was one of the most party-oriented presidents of recent times.[20]
In 1983 and 1984, during his own reelection effort, Reagan made more than two dozen
campaign and fund-raising appearances for all branches of the party organization and
candidates at every level. He taped more than 300 television endorsements as well, including one for an obscure Honolulu city council contest. Reagan also showed a willingness to get involved in the nitty-gritty of candidate recruitment, frequently calling
strong potential candidates to urge them to run. Unlike Eisenhower, Reagan was willing to attempt a popularity transfer to his party and to campaign for Republicans
whether or not they were strongly loyal to him personally. Unlike Johnson, Reagan was
willing to put his prestige and policies to the test on the campaign trail. Unlike Nixon,
Reagan spent time and effort helping underdogs and long-shot candidates, not just
likely winners. Unlike Carter, Reagan signed more than seventy fund-raising appeals
for party committees and took a personal interest in the further strengthening of the
GOP's organizational capacity. George Bush, a former RNC chairman, emulated the
Reagan model during his own presidency.

However, neither Reagan nor Bush had long enough coattails to help elect their
party's nominees lower down on the ballot. Reagan's initial victory in 1980 was one factor in the election of a Republican Senate, but his landslide reelection in 1984 had, like
Nixon's in 1972, almost no impact on his party's congressional representation. And
Bush provided no coattails at all to the GOP in 1988. There is little question that the
coattail effect, the tendency of lesser-known or weaker candidates lower on the ballot
to profit in an election by the presence on the party's ticket of a more popular candidate, has diminished sharply compared with a generation ago.[21] Partly, the decreased
competitiveness of congressional elections has been produced by artful redistricting
and the growing value of incumbency.[22] But voters are also less willing to think and
cast ballots in purely partisan terms, a development that limits presidential leadership
and hurts party development. (We return to this subject in the next chapter.)

coattail effect: The tendency of lesser-known or weaker candidates lower on the ballot to profit in an election by the presence on the party's ticket of a more popular candidate.

Clinton.   Because Bill Clinton won with such a small plurality (43 percent) in
1992, he also produced little coattail for his party's candidates. Like Reagan and Bush,
though, he has campaigned vigorously for many Democrats across the country since
taking office. Unlike his predecessors, however, Clinton has enjoyed little success in
transferring popularity. Democrats lost both governor's races in 1993 (Virginia and
New Jersey) and a special Senate election in Texas since Clinton won the presidency.
Clinton vigorously stumped for New York Mayor David Dinkins as well, but even in
that heavily Democratic city, a Republican (Rudolph Giuliani) triumphed in November 1993. Then came the Republican deluge in 1994, when the GOP won fifty-two
House seats and nine Senate seats in an election widely regarded as a repudiation of
Clinton's presidency.

But before the ink was dry on the obituaries penned by journalists and political
pundits for Clinton and a Democratic party suddenly deemed out-of-touch and on the
verge of total collapse, Clinton and his Party rose from the ashes of the 1994 elections.
After outmaneuvering congressional Republicans during the costly government shut-

downs of late 1995 and early 1996, Clinton and congressional Democrats saw their popularity ratings climb. Meanwhile, the Republicans tried to regroup, a task made difficult by an acrimonious presidential primary season. By summer's end, Clinton's legislative and political maneuvering, along with a stable economy, produced the highest popularity ratings Clinton enjoyed during his first term as president. Two months later, Clinton was returned to the White House and Democrats significantly cut into the Republican Party's hold on the U.S. House of Representatives, proving again that we should not be too quick to write off any politician, let alone an entire political party.

Nonpartisan Presidents.   Most modern American chief executives have been cast in an entirely different mold. Dwight D. Eisenhower elevated "nonpartisanship" to a virtual art form; and while this may have preserved his personal popularity, it proved a disaster for his party. Despite a full two-term occupancy of the White House, the Republican Party remained mired in minority status among the electorate, and Eisenhower never really attempted to transfer his high ratings to the party. Lyndon B. Johnson kept the DNC busy with such trivial tasks as answering wedding invitations sent to the First Family. When many of the Democratic senators and representatives elected on his presidential coattails were endangered in the 1966 midterm election, LBJ canceled a major campaign trip on their behalf lest his policies get tied too closely to their possible defeats. Democrats lost forty-seven House seats, three Senate seats, and eight governorships in the 1966 debacle.

In 1972 Richard M. Nixon discouraged the GOP from nominating candidates against conservative Southern Democrats in order to improve his own electoral and congressional position, since the grateful unopposed legislators would presumably be less likely to cause Nixon trouble on the campaign trail or in Congress. Nixon also subordinated the party's agenda almost wholly to his own reelection. Shunting aside the Republican National Committee, Nixon formed the Committee to Re-Elect the President, which became known by the acronym CREEP. So removed were party leaders from the Committee's abuses (see the coverage on Watergate in chapter 8) that the Republican Party organization itself escaped blame during the Watergate investigations.

Jimmy Carter also showed little interest in his national party. Elected as an outsider in 1976, Carter and his top aides at first viewed the party as another extension of the Washington establishment they had pledged to ignore. Carter and his DNC chairmen failed to develop the Democratic Party organizationally and financially in order to keep it competitive during a critical period, while the Republicans were undergoing a dramatic revitalization stimulated by their desire to recover from the Watergate scandal. Later, during his unsuccessful 1980 reelection campaign, Carter was properly criticized for diverting DNC personnel and resources to his presidential needs, such as travel and Christmas cards, rather than permitting them to pursue essential partywide electoral tasks.

The Parties and the Judiciary

Many Americans view the judiciary as "above politics" and certainly as nonpartisan, and many judges are quick to agree. Yet not only do members of the judiciary sometimes follow the election returns and allow themselves to be influenced by popular opinion, but they are also products of their party identification and possess the same partisan perceptual screens as all other politically aware citizens.

Legislators are much more partisan than judges, but it is wrong to assume that judges reach decisions wholly independent of partisan values. First, judges are creatures of the political process, and their posts are considered patronage plums. Judges who are not elected are appointed by presidents or governors for their abilities but also as members of the executive's party and increasingly as representatives of a certain philosophy of or approach to government. In this century every president has appointed judges overwhelmingly from his own party; Jimmy Carter and Ronald Reagan, for instance, drew 95 percent or more of their judicial choices from their respective parties. Furthermore, Democratic executives are naturally inclined to select for the bench liberal individuals who may be friendly to the welfare state or critical of some business practices. Republican executives generally lean toward conservatives for judicial posts, hoping they will be tough on criminal defendants, anti-abortion, and restrained in the use of court power.

Research has long indicated that party affiliation is in fact a moderately good predictor of judicial decisions, at least in some areas.[23] In other words, party matters in the judiciary just as it does in the other two branches of government, although it certainly matters less on the bench than in the legislature and in the executive.

Many judges appointed to office have had long careers in politics as loyal party workers or legislators. Supreme Court Justice Sandra Day O'Connor, for example, was an active member of the National Republican Women's Club and is a former Republican state legislator. Some jurists are even more overtly political, since they are elected to office. In a majority of states at least some judicial positions are filled by election, and seventeen states hold outright partisan elections, with both parties nominating opposing candidates and running hard-hitting campaigns. In some rural counties across the United States, local judges are not merely partisanly elected figures; they are the key public officials, controlling many patronage jobs and the party machinery itself.

Clearly, in many places in the United States, judges by necessity and by tradition are not above politics but are in the thick of it. Although election of the judiciary is a questionable practice in light of its specially sanctioned role as impartial arbiter, partisan influence exerted both by jurists' party loyalties and by the appointment (or election) process is useful in retaining some degree of accountability in a branch often accused of being arrogant and aloof.

The Parties and State Governments

Most of the conclusions just discussed about the party's relationship to the legislature, the executive, and the judiciary apply to those branches on the state level as well. The national parties, after all, are organized around state units, and the basic structural arrangement of party and government is much the same in Washington and the state capitals. Remarkably, too, the major national parties are the dominant political forces in all fifty states. This has been true consistently; unlike Great Britain or Canada, the United States has no regional or state parties that displace one or both of the national parties in local contests. Occasionally in U.S. history a third party has proven locally potent, as did Minnesota's Farmer–Labor Party and Wisconsin's Progressives, both of which elected governors and state legislative majorities earlier in this century. But over time, no such party has survived,[24] and every state's two-party system mirrors national party dualism, at least as far as labels are concerned.

Parties and Governors.   There are some party-oriented differences at the state level, however. Governors in many states tend to possess even greater influence over their parties' organizations and legislators than do presidents. Many governors have many more patronage positions at their command than does a president, and these material rewards and incentives give governors added clout with activists and office holders. In addition, tradition in some states permits the governor to play a role in selecting the legislature's committee chairs and party floor leaders, and some state executives even attend and help direct the party legislative caucuses, activities no president would ever undertake. Moreover, forty-three governors possess a power denied the national executive until 1997, the line-item veto, which permits the governor to veto single items (such as individual pork barrel projects) in appropriations bills. Whereas many presidents prior to Clinton accepted objectionable measures as part of a bill too urgent or important to be vetoed, a governor could gain enormous leverage with legislators by means of the line-item veto. A Republican-sponsored measure in the 104th Congress gave the president this potent tool, beginning in January 1997.

Parties and State Legislatures.   Just as the party relationship between the executive and the legislature tends to be stronger at the state level than in Washington, so also is the party role in the legislature itself more high-profile and effective. Most state legislatures surpass the U.S. Congress in partisan unity and cohesion. Even though fewer than half of congressional roll calls in the post-World War II era have produced majorities of the two parties on opposite sides, a number of state legislatures (including Massachusetts, New York, Ohio, and Pennsylvania) have achieved party voting levels of 70 percent or better in some years. Not all states display party cohesion of this magnitude, of course. Nebraska has a nonpartisan legislature, elected without party labels on the ballot. In the South the lack of two-party competition has left essentially one-party legislatures split into factions, regional groupings, or personal cliques. As real interparty competition reaches the legislative level in Southern states, however, party cohesion in the legislatures is likely to increase.

One other party distinction is notable in many state legislatures. Compared with the Congress, state legislative leaders have much more authority and power; this is one reason party unity is higher in the state capitols.[25] The strict seniority system that usually controls committee assignments in Congress is less absolute in most states, and legislative leaders often have considerable discretion in appointing the committee chairs and members. The party caucuses, too, are usually more active and influential in state legislatures than in their Washington counterparts. In some legislatures, the caucuses meet weekly or even daily to work out strategy and count votes, and nearly one-fourth of the caucuses bind all the party members to support the group's decisions on key issues (such as appropriations measures, tax issues, and procedural questions).

Not just the leaders and caucuses but the party organizations as well have more influence over legislators at the state level. State legislators are much more dependent than their congressional counterparts on their state and local parties for election assistance. Whereas members of Congress have large government-provided staffs and lavish perquisites to assist (directly or indirectly) their reelection efforts, state legislative candidates need party workers and, increasingly, the party's financial support and technological resources at election time.

THE MODERN TRANSFORMATION OF PARTY ORGANIZATION

*P*olitical parties have moved from the labor-intensive, person-to-person operations of the first half of the century toward the utilization of modern high-technologies and communication strategies. Nevertheless, the capabilities of each party's organization vary widely.

Republican Strengths

Until 1992 the modern Republican Party thoroughly outclassed its Democratic rival in almost every category of campaign service and fund raising. There are a number of explanations for the disparity between the two major parties. From 1932 until 1980, the Republicans were almost perennially disappointed underdogs, especially in congressional contests; they therefore felt the need to give extra effort. The GOP had the willingness, and enough electoral frustrations, to experiment with new campaign technologies that might hold the key to elusive victories. Also, since Democrats held most of the congressional offices and thus had most of the benefits of incumbency and staff, Republican nominees were forced to rely more on their party to offset built-in Democratic advantages. The party staff, in other words, compensated for the Democratic congressional staff, and perhaps also for organized labor's divisions of election troops, which were usually at the beck and call of Democratic candidates. Then, too, one can argue that the business and middle-class base of the modern GOP has a natural managerial and entrepreneurial flair demonstrated by the party officers drawn from that talented pool.

Whatever the causes, the contemporary national Republican Party has organizational prowess unparalleled in American history. The Republicans have surpassed the Democrats in fund raising by large margins in recent election cycles—never by less than two to one and usually by a considerably higher ratio (see Figure 12.4). Democrats must struggle to raise enough money to meet the basic needs of most of their candidates, while, in the words of a past chairman of the Democratic Senatorial Campaign Committee, "The single biggest problem the Republicans have is how to legally spend the money they have."[26] Republican presidential candidate Bob Dole benefited from this large GOP war chest in the spring of 1996. After he had spent the maximum allowed by law in his successful presidential nomination bid, the Republican party opened its coffers to fund some of Dole's operation until the August GOP convention.

FIGURE 12.4

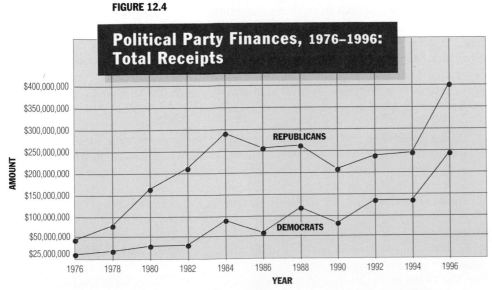

Political Party Finances, 1976–1996:
Total Receipts

Numbers represent total monies raised between Jan 2, 1996 and Oct 16, 1996. Includes total for national senatorial and congressional committees as well as all other reported national, state, and local spending.

SOURCE: Federal Election Commission.

Most of the Republican money is raised through highly successful mail solicitation. This procedure started in the early 1960s and accelerated in the mid-1970s, when postage and production costs were relatively low. From a base of just 24,000 names in 1975, for example, the national Republican Party has expanded its mailing list of proven donors to several million in the 1990s. Mailings produce about three-quarters of total revenue, and they do so with an average contribution of less than $35. In this fashion the GOP may have broadened its committed base, because contributing money usually strengthens the tie between a voter and any organization. Most of the rest of the GOP's funds come from donors of larger amounts who secure membership in various Republican contributor groups. For instance, the Republican National Committee designates any $10,000 annual giver an "Eagle."

The Republican cash is used to support a dazzling variety of party activities and campaign services. These include party staff, voter contact, polling, media advertising, and campaign staff training and research.

Party Staff.   Several hundred operatives are employed by the national GOP in election years, and even in the off years, many more than one hundred people hold full-time positions. There is great emphasis on field staff, that is, on staff members sent to and stationed in key districts and states who maintain close communication between local and national party offices.

Voter Contact.   The Republicans frequently conduct massive telephone canvassing operations to identify likely Republican voters and to get them to the polls on Election Day. In 1986, for instance, the GOP used paid callers in seventeen phone centers across the country to reach 10.5 million prospective voters in twenty-five states during the general election campaign. Nearly 5.5 million previously identified Republicans were called again just before Election Day. Many of them heard an automated message from the president that began: "This is Ronald Reagan and I want to remind you to go out and vote on Tuesday." In addition, 12 million pieces of "persuasive" (non-fund-raising) mail were sent to households in the last two weeks of the campaign.

Polling.   The national Republican committees have spent millions of dollars for national, state, and local public opinion surveys, and they have accumulated an enormous storehouse of data on American attitudes in general and on marginal districts in particular. Many of the surveys are provided to GOP nominees at a cut-rate cost. In important contests, the party will frequently commission tracking polls, continuous surveys that enable a campaign to chart its daily rise or fall. The information provided in such polls is invaluable in the tense concluding days of an election.

Media Advertising.   The national Republican Party operates a sophisticated in-house media division that specializes in the design and production of television advertisements for party nominees at all levels. About seventy to one hundred candidates are helped in an election cycle. They obtain expert and technically superior media commercials, and the party also offers its wares for a minimal fee, often including the actual buying of time, that is, the purchase of specific time slots on television shows for broadcasting the advertising spots. The candidates thus save the substantial commissions and fees usually charged by independent political consultants for the same services.

The GOP's party advertising is even more significant. Since 1978 the Republicans have aired spots designed to support not specific candidates, but the generic party label. Beginning with the 1980 election, the GOP has used institutional advertising to establish basic election themes. "Vote Republican, for a Change" spots attacked the Democratic Congress in 1980. In another spot House Speaker Thomas P. O'Neill was lampooned by an actor lookalike who ignored all warning signs and drove a car until it ran out of fuel. ("The Democrats are out of gas," announced the narrator as the "Speaker" futilely kicked the automobile's tire.)

In the 1982 midterm congressional elections, the defensive focus of a $15-million institutional campaign was "Give the guy [Reagan] a chance" and "Stay the course" with the president in the midst of a deep recession and high unemployment. For instance, a white-haired mailman was seen delivering Social Security checks fattened with a cost-of-living increase, reminding elderly voters that Reagan had kept his promise, and urging, "For gosh sake, let's give the guy a chance." The spot, like the earlier 1980 ads, was highly rated by viewers. Although some moderate Republican candidates resisted being tied to Reagan during one of the most unpopular periods of his presidency, pre- and postelection surveys suggested that the GOP-sponsored media campaign had been, on the whole, helpful to the party and to individual candidates. The Republican National Committee was also active throughout the Clinton administration, airing advertisements, for example, that poked fun at President Clinton's often-changed effort to craft a balanced budget within a fixed number of years.

Campaign Staff Training and Research. The party trains many of the political volunteers and paid operatives who manage the candidates' campaigns. Since 1976 the Republicans have held annually about a half-dozen week-long "Campaign Management Colleges" for staffers. In 1986 the party launched an ambitious million-dollar "Congressional Campaign Academy" that offers two-week, all-expenses-paid training courses for prospective campaign managers, finance directors, and press relations staff. Early in each election cycle, the national party staff also prepares voluminous research reports on Democratic opponents, analyzing their public statements, votes, and attendance records. The reports are made available to GOP candidates and their aides.

Despite its noted financial edge and service sophistication, all is not well in the Republican organization. Success has bred self-satisfaction and complacency, encouraged waste, and led the party to place too much reliance on money and technology, and not enough on the foundation of any party movement—people. As former U.S. Senator Paul Laxalt (R–Nev.), outgoing general chairman of the national Republican Party, was forced to admit in 1987: "We've got way too much money, we've got way too many political operatives, we've got far too few volunteers. . . . We are substituting contributions and high technology for volunteers in the field. I've gone the sophisticate route, I've gone the television route, and there is no substitute for the volunteer route."[27]

As Laxalt's comments imply, technology and money can probably add only two or three percentage points to a candidate's margin. The rest is determined by the nominee's quality and positions, the general electoral tide prevailing in any given year, and the energy of party troops in the field. Republicans were to learn this anew in 1992, when George Bush's large war chest could not stave off defeat. Similarly, many Democratic U.S. senators and representatives outspent their opponents by a wide margin in the 1994 elections, but they tasted defeat nonetheless. Similarly in 1996, Senate candidates in South Carolina and Virginia outspent their incumbent opponents and yet failed to win. Have the two major parties learned that while money helps, having more than your opponent(s) by no means guarantees electoral success, especially when running against incumbents? Only time and future elections will tell.

Democratic Party Gains

Parties, like people, change their habits slowly. The Democrats were reluctant to alter a formula that had been a winning combination for decades of New Deal dominance. The prevailing philosophy was, "Let a thousand flowers bloom"; candidates were encouraged to go their own way, to rely on organized labor and other interest groups allied with the Democrats, and to raise their own money, while the national party was kept subservient and weak.

The massive Democratic defeats suffered in 1980 forced a fundamental reevaluation of the party's structure and activities. Democrats, diverse by nature, came to an unaccustomed consensus that the party must change to survive, that it must dampen internal ideological disputes and begin to revitalize its organization. Thus was born the commitment to technological and fund-raising modernization, using the Republican Party's accomplishments as a model, that drives the Democratic Party today.

Comprehension of the task is the first step to realization of the goal, so even after more than a decade, Democrats still trail their competitors by virtually every significant measure of party activity. Yet the figures of party finances (receipts), graphed in Figure 12.4, can be read a different way. While the GOP has consistently maintained an enormous edge, the Democrats have considerably increased their total receipts, now raising many times more than just a few years ago. More importantly, Democrats are contributing much more to their candidates and have actually come close to the GOP's larger total recently (see Figure 12.5). Several national party chairs (Paul Kirk, Ron Brown, and David Wilhelm) have aggressively sought more funds from party supporters and friendly interest groups.

FIGURE 12.5

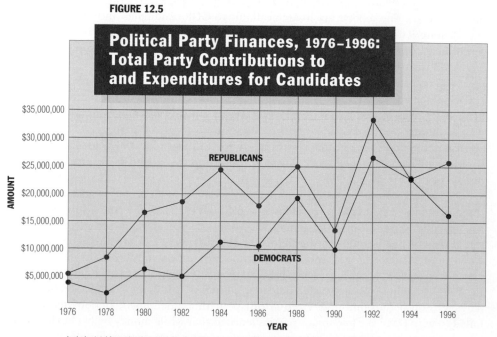

Political Party Finances, 1976–1996: Total Party Contributions to and Expenditures for Candidates

Includes total for national senatorial and congressional committees as well as all other reported national, state, and local spending; all presidential, Senate, and House candidates are included. Not included are "soft money" expenditures.

SOURCE: Federal Election Commission.

With the 1992 elections, the Democrats reaped the benefits of their substantially increased receipts, winning the presidency for the first time in sixteen years. The Clinton administration also redoubled Democratic Party efforts as the midterm elections of 1994 approached, and their exertions again made the Democrats more competitive with the Republicans. We witnessed a similar trend in 1996. The Democratic Party, buttressed especially by labor union contributions and independent expenditures, was again able to help make Democratic candidates more competitive with their Republican counterparts at all levels.

The decision in 1981 to begin a direct-mail program for the national party was a turning point. From a list of only 25,000 donors before the program began, the DNC's support base has grown to 500,000. The Democrats have imitated the Republicans not just in fund raising but also in the uses to which the money is put. For instance, in 1986 the party opened a $3-million media center that produces television and radio spots at rates much lower than those charged by independent political consultants. The Democratic Party is attempting to do more for its candidates and their campaign staffs, too, creating the Democratic National Training Institute in 1985. The Institute coordinates campaign schools for party workers from around the country. "Smart money" is a term used to describe campaign contributions that flow to the candidates and political party expected to win in an election year. With Bill Clinton leading every public opinion poll taken after mid-July during the 1992 campaign and almost every public opinion poll taken during the 1996 campaign, Democrats were flooded with smart money. As Figures 12.4 and 12.5 show, the Democratic Party dramatically increased both its receipts and expenditures in 1992 and then again in 1996. The Republicans did equally well, but the GOP's well-oiled fund-raising machinery has regularly produced massive war chests. For the Democrats, being financially well-off was a new and delightful experience.

Thus both party organizations have grown mightier in recent years, at the time when political parties have seemed to be in decline in some other ways. Most important, many voters appear to have less a sense of partisan identification and loyalty today than in generations past. Why is this so?

THE PARTY-IN-THE-ELECTORATE

A political party is much more than its organizational shell, however dazzling the technologies at its command, and its reach extends well beyond the relative handful of men and women who are the party-in-government. In any democracy, where power is derived directly from the people, the party's real importance and strength must come from the citizenry it attempts to mobilize. The **party-in-the-electorate**—the mass of potential voters who identify with the Democratic or Republican labels—is the most significant element of the political party, providing the foundation for the organizational and governmental parties. But in some crucial respects, it is the weakest of the components of the U.S. political party system. In recent decades fewer citizens have been willing to pledge their fealty to the major parties, and many of those who have declared their loyalties have done so with less intensity. Also, voters of each partisan stripe are increasingly casting ballots for some candidates of the opposing party, and partisan identification is a less reliable indicator of likely voting choices today than it once was. Notice, in Figure 12.6, the recent merging of party identification toward the political center.

party-in-the-electorate: The voters who consider themselves to be allied or associated with the party.

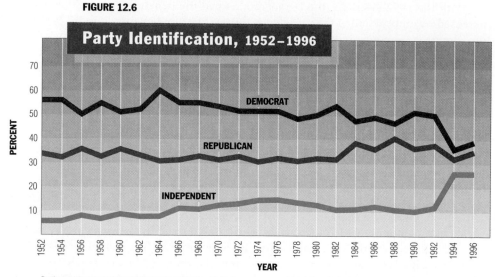

FIGURE 12.6

Party Identification, 1952–1996

Partisan totals do not add to 100% since "apolitical" and "other" responses were deleted. Sample size from poll to poll varied, from a low of 1,130 to a high of 2,850.

Pure Independents only. Independent "leaners" have been added to Democratic and Republican totals.

SOURCE: Center for Political Studies/Survey Research Center of the University of Michigan, made available through the Inter-University Consortium for Political and Social Research. Also, Leon D. Epstein, *Political Parties in the American Mold* (Madison: University of Wisconsin Press, 1986), Table 8.1, p. 257. Data for 1996 provided by election-day exit poll conducted by Voter Research and Surveys.

Party Identification

Most American voters identify with a party but do not belong to it. There is no universal enrolled party membership; there are no prescribed dues, no formal rules concerning an individual's activities, and no enforceable obligations to the party assumed by the voter. The party has no real control over or even an accurate accounting of its adherents, and the party's voters subscribe to few or none of the commonly accepted tenets of organizational membership, such as regular participation and some measure of responsibility for the group's welfare. Rather, **party identification** or affiliation is an informal and impressionistic exercise whereby a citizen acquires a party label and accepts its standard as a summary of his or her political views and preferences. To see which party you identify with, see Politics Now: Are You a Democrat, a Republican, or Neither?

However, just because the acquisition is informal does not mean that it is unimportant. The party label becomes a voter's central political reference symbol and perceptual screen, a prism or filter through which the world of politics and government flows and is interpreted. For many Americans, party identification is a significant aspect of their political personality and a way of defining and explaining themselves to others. The loyalty generated by the label can be as intense as any enjoyed by sports teams and alma maters; in a few areas of the country, "Democrat" and "Republican" are still fighting words.

On the whole, though, Americans regard their partisan affiliation with lesser degrees of enthusiasm, viewing it as a convenience rather than a necessity. The individual identifications are reinforced by the legal institutionalization of the major parties. Because of restrictive ballot laws, campaign finance rules, the powerful inertia of po-

party identification: A citizen's personal affinity for a political party, usually expressed by his or her tendency to vote for the candidates of that party.

Are You a Democrat, a Republican, or Neither?

Choosing a political party can be easy or quite difficult. The answer depends on you and your values.

Republicans in the 1980s and 1990s are generally identified as more conservative than Democrats and tend to be associated with free market economics, lower taxes, family values, hawkish foreign policy, and devolution of power from the federal government to the states.

Democrats of the last two decades, on the other hand, are associated with greater economic intervention, protection of minorities, a social safety net, including social security and medicare, government regulation, protection of the environment, a less aggressive foreign policy, and the cause of poor and working-class people.

Of course, the descriptions of the political parties above are generalizations of their views. Clearly, many people are concerned about a combination of issues that are associated with both of the political parties. The difficult question is: *How do you decide which party is generally more in line with your values?*

Try this exercise. Think about an issue or set of issues that is important to you. Ask yourself, are the positions taken by well-known politicians from the Republican and Democratic parties different? In what ways? If there are independent candidates, do their views differ greatly from those of major-party candidates?

Of course, the choice of a political party is not usually made on the basis of one issue but on the basis of *many* issues taken together. Parties are not made up of one type of person but many diverse groups of people combined. The people who make up the membership of these parties have compromised on some issues and emphasized others in their choice of party. The bottom line is that it is up to you to choose the combination of issues that concern you the most and the party you believe best represents your values.

Do you consider yourself a Democrat or a Republican? Does it matter? Perhaps you are one of the almost one-third of Americans who claim to be independents?

litical tradition, and many other factors, voters for all practical purposes are limited to a choice between a Democrat and a Republican in virtually all elections—a situation that naturally encourages the pragmatic choosing up of sides. The party registration process that exists in about half of the states, requiring a voter to state a party preference (or independent status) when registering to vote and thus restricting voter participation in primaries to party registrants, also is an incentive for voters to affiliate themselves with a party.[28]

Sources of Party Identification.   So from where do party loyalties come? Whatever the societal and governmental forces undergirding party identification, the explanations of partisan loyalty at the individual's level are understandably more personal. Not surprisingly, parents are the single greatest influence in establishing a person's first party identification. Politically active parents with the same party loyalty raise children who will be strong party identifiers, while parents without party affiliations or with mixed affiliations produce offspring more likely to be independents (see chapter 11).

Early socialization is hardly the last step in the acquisition and maintenance of a party identity; marriage and other aspects of adult life can change one's loyalty. So can charismatic political personalities, particularly at the national level (such as Franklin D. Roosevelt and Ronald Reagan), cataclysmic events (the Civil War and the Great Depression are the best examples), and maybe intense social issues (for instance, abortion). Interestingly, social class is not an especially strong indicator of likely partisan choice in the United States, at least in comparison with Western European democracies. Not only are Americans less inclined than Europeans to perceive class distinctions, preferring instead to see themselves and most other people as members of an exceedingly broad middle class, but other factors, including sectionalism and candidate-oriented politics, tend to blur class lines in voting.

Declining Loyalty

Over the past two decades, many political scientists as well as other observers, journalists, and party activists have become increasingly anxious about a perceived decline in partisan identification and loyalty. Many public opinion surveys have shown a significant growth in independents at the expense of the two major parties. The Center for Political Studies/Survey Research Center (CPS/SRC) of the University of Michigan, for instance, has charted the rise of self-described independents from a low of 19 percent in 1958 to a peak of 38 percent twenty years later. Before the 1950s (although the evidence for this research is more circumstantial because of the scarcity of reliable survey research data), there are indications that independents were fewer in number, and party loyalties considerably firmer.

Yet the recent decline of party identification can be exaggerated, and in some ways there has been remarkable stability in the voters' party choices. Over more than thirty years, during vast political, economic, and social upheavals that have changed the face of the nation, the Democratic Party has nearly consistently drawn the support of a small majority and the Republican Party has attracted a share of the electorate in the low to mid-30-percent range. Granted, there have been peaks and valleys for both parties. The Lyndon B. Johnson landslide of 1964 helped Democrats top the 60 percent mark, and the Reagan landslide of 1984 and the post-Persian Gulf war glow of 1991 sent Democratic stock below the majority midpoint. The Barry Goldwater debacle of 1964 and the Watergate disaster of 1974 left the Republicans with less than one-third of the populace; Reagan's reelection brought the GOP to the threshold of 40 percent. Some slight average erosion over time in Democratic Party strength is certainly apparent, as is a small Republican gain during the Reagan and Bush eras. Yet these sorts of gradations are more akin to rolling foothills than towering mountain ranges. The steady nature of modern partisanship goes beyond the fortunes of each party. Identification with the two parties in modern times has never dipped below 83 percent of the U.S. electorate (recorded during the disillusionment spawned by Watergate in 1974) and can usually be found in the mid-to-upper-80-percent range.

When pollsters ask for party identification information, they generally proceed in two stages. First, they inquire whether a respondent considers himself or herself a Democrat, Republican, or independent. Then the party identifiers are asked to categorize themselves as "strong" or "not very strong" supporters, while the independents are pushed to reveal their leanings with a question such as, "Which party do you normally support in elections, the Democrats or the Republicans?" It may be true that some independent respondents are thereby prodded to pick a party under the pressure of the interview situation, regardless of their true feelings. But research has demonstrated that independent "leaners" in fact vote very much like real partisans, in some elections more so than the "not very strong" party identifiers. There is reason to count the independent leaners as closet partisans, though voting behavior is not the equivalent of real partisan identification.

In fact, the reluctance of "leaners" to admit their real party identities is in itself worrisome because it reveals a change in attitudes about political parties and their role in our society. Being a socially acceptable, integrated, and contributing member of one's community once almost demanded partisan affiliation; it was a badge of good citizenship, signifying that one was a patriot. Today, the labels are avoided as an offense to a thinking person's individualism, and a vast majority of Americans insist that they vote for "the person, not the party."

The reasons for these anti-party attitudes are not hard to find. The growth of issue-oriented politics that cuts across party lines for voters who feel intensely about certain policy matters is partly the cause. So, too, is the emphasis on personality politics by the mass media (especially television) and political consultants. Underlying these causes, though, are two much more disturbing and destructive long-term phenomena: the perceived loss of party credibility and the decline of the party's tangible connections to the lives of everyday citizens. Although the underlying partisanship of the American people has not declined significantly since 1952, voter-admitted partisanship has dropped considerably. About three-quarters or more of the electorate volunteered a party choice without prodding from 1952 to 1964, but since 1970 an average of less than two-thirds has been willing to do so. Professed independents (including leaners) have increased from around one-fifth of the electorate in the 1950s to one-third or more in the 1970s and 1980s. Also cause for concern is the marginal decline in strong Democrats and strong Republicans. Strong partisans are a party's backbone, the source of its volunteer force, candidates, and dependable voters. Even a slight shrinkage in these ranks can be troublesome.

Group Affiliations.   Just as individuals vary in the strength of their partisan choice, so, too, do groups vary in the degree to which they identify with the Democratic Party or the Republican Party. There are enormous variations in party identification from one region or demographic group to another, particularly in geographic region, gender, race and ethnicity, age, social and economic factors, religion, marital status, and ideology.

Geographic Region.   While all other geographic regions in the United States are relatively closely contested between the parties, the South still exhibits some of the Democratic Party affinity cultivated in the last century and hardened in the fires of the Civil War. This is only still true in local elections, however, and even there, it is changing rapidly. In the 1994 election, for instance, Southerners elected Republicans to a majority of the U.S. House seats in the states of the old Confederacy, and dozens of sheriffs won under the GOP banner, too. In all regions, party strengths vary by locality, with central cities almost everywhere heavily Democratic, the swelling suburbs serving as the main source of GOP partisans, and the small town and rural areas split evenly between the two major parties.

Gender.   Women and men differ somewhat in their partisan choice, a phenomenon called the gender gap, which has yawned at least since 1980 (see Highlight 12.3). Women generally favor the Democratic Party by 5 percent to 10 percent, and men often give the GOP a similar edge. Besides abortion and women's rights issues, female concerns for peace and social compassion may provide much of the gap's distance. For instance, women are usually much less likely than men to favor American military action, and they are less inclined to support cuts in government funding of social welfare programs.

Race and Ethnicity.   African Americans are the most dramatically different population subgroup in party terms. The 80-percent-plus advantage they offer the Democrats dwarfs the edge given to either party by any other segments of the electorate, and their proportion of strong Democrats (about 40 percent) is three times that of whites. African Americans account almost entirely for the slight lead in party affiliation that Democrats normally enjoy over Republicans, since the GOP has recently been able to

The "Gender Gap"

Some political scientists argue that the difference in the way men and women vote first emerged in 1920, when newly enfranchised women registered overwhelmingly as Republicans. It was not until the 1980 presidential election, however, that a noticeable and possibly significant *gender gap* emerged. This time, the Democratic Party was the apparent beneficiary. While Ronald Reagan trounced incumbent Democratic President Jimmy Carter, he did so with the votes of only 46 percent of the women, compared to 54 percent of the men.

This gender gap continues to persist at all levels of elections. In 1990 exit polls conducted after seventy races revealed a gender gap in 61 percent of the races analyzed. In 1992, as in previous elections, more voters were women (54 percent) than men (46 percent). Again, more women—47 percent—voted for the Democrat (Clinton) than men—41 percent. Among working women the gap was even more pronounced—51 percent voted for Clinton, only 31 percent for Bush.

In 1996, the gender gap of 1994 had become a gender chasm. Women by anywhere between a 14 and 20 percent margin in polls taken during the summer leading up to the Democratic and Republican conventions favored President Clinton over his Republican challenger, Bob Dole. This difference was not offset by men who, prior to the conventions, tended to split their support evenly between the two candidates.

Hoping to bridge this gap, Republicans attempted to use their convention to woo women voters back into the fold. By moderating their message and their tone, Republicans did gain a brief post-convention boost in the polls, but following the Democratic convention, the pre-convention polling numbers returned. Two months later, the largest gender gap in the nation's history was recorded. While men split their vote evenly between the two candidates (Dole received 45 percent of the male vote and Clinton 44 percent), according to exit polls women supported Clinton by a 54 to 37 margin! One of the biggest challenges then facing Republicans is how to gain the support of women without alienating their male base. Time will tell how effectively they can perform this increasingly difficult balancing act.

---

attract a narrow plurality of whites to its standard. Perhaps as a reflection of the massive party chasm separating blacks and whites, the two races differ greatly on many policy issues, with blacks overwhelmingly on the liberal side and whites closer to the conservative pole. An exception, incidentally, is abortion, where religious beliefs may lead African Americans to the more conservative stance. The much smaller population group of Hispanics supplements this group as a Democratic stalwart; by more than three to one, Hispanics prefer the Democratic label. An exception is the Cuban–American population, whose anti-Fidel Castro tilt leads to Republicanism.

Age. Young people are once again becoming more Democratic. Polls in 1972 indicated that the group of eighteen- to twenty-four-year-olds, and particularly students, was the only age group to support Democratic presidential nominee George McGovern. But by the 1990s the eighteen-to-thirty-four-year-old age group was the most Republican of all. Much of this margin was derived from strong student affiliation with the Republicans. Perhaps because of the bad economy from 1990 to 1992, which limited job availability for college graduates, young people swung back to the Democrats in 1992. Bill Clinton ran strongly among eighteen- to twenty-four-year-olds, and they were among his best groups in the electorate.

Social and Economic Factors. Some traditional strengths and weaknesses persist for each party by occupation, income, and education. The GOP remains predominant among executives, professionals, and white-collar workers, whereas the Democrats lead substantially among blue-collar workers and the unemployed. Labor union members are also Democratic by two-and-a-half to one. The more conservative, retired population leans Republican. Women who do not work outside the home are less liberal and Democratic than those who do. Occupation, income, and education are closely related, of course, so many of the same partisan patterns can be detected in all three classifications. Democratic support usually drops steadily as one climbs the income scale. Similarly, as years of education increase, identification with the Republican Party climbs; in graduate school, however, the Democrats rally a bit and only narrowly trail GOP partisans.

Religion. The party preferences by religion are also traditional, but with modern twists. Protestants—especially Methodists, Presbyterians, and Episcopalians—favor the Republicans by a few percentage points, whereas Catholics and, even more so, Jews are predominantly Democratic in affiliation. Less polarization is apparent all around, though.[29] Democrats have made inroads among many Protestant denominations over the past three decades, and Republicans can now sometimes claim up to 25 percent of the Jewish population and nearly 40 percent of the Catholics. The "born again" Christians, who have received much attention in recent years, are somewhat less Republican than commonly believed. The GOP usually has just about a 10 percent edge among them, primarily because so many blacks classify themselves as members of this group.

Marital Status. Even marital status reveals something about partisan affiliation. People who are married, a traditionally more conservative group, and people who have never married, a segment weighted toward the premarriage young who currently lean toward the Republicans, are closely divided in party loyalty. But the widowed are Democratic in nature, probably because there are many more widows than widowers; in this, the gender gap is again expressing itself. The divorced and the separated, who may be experiencing economic hardship and appear to be more liberal than the married population, are a substantially Democratic group.

Ideology. Ideologically, there are few surprises. Lending credence to the belief that both parties are now relatively distinct philosophically, liberals are overwhelmingly Democratic and conservatives are staunchly Republican in most surveys and opinion studies.

As party identification has weakened, so, too, has the likelihood that voters will cast ballots predictably and regularly for their party's nominees. (Chapter 13 discusses this in some detail.) In the present day, as at the founding of the republic, Americans are simply not wedded to the idea or the reality of political parties. Said one Democratic pollster: "It took a lot of years for the trust and loyalty to dissipate, and it will take a lot of years to bring it back."[30] If this is true, then the dealigning patterns we have witnessed in recent times are likely to remain the norm in the foreseeable future.

The strong party system that prevails in Great Britain provides an illuminating contrast. A large majority of Britons strongly identifies with either the Conservative (Tory) or the Labour Party, and voters rarely switch allegiances on Election Day. Of course, the British parliamentary system is party-based, whereas U.S. politics is far more personality-oriented. In Britain, a voter essentially casts a ballot for a party rather than for a person who will serve as prime minister. The prime minister is elected by the parliament, not by the people directly; in the United States, many voters pick presidents more by their characters and personalities than on the basis of their party labels. The British parties also polarize the electorate because of the strong ideological cast of the Tories (free enterprise) and the Labour Party (socialist). While there are clear differences between a liberal Democratic Party and a conservative Republican Party, the American contrast is much less sharp than that of Great Britain. Nevertheless, observers of British politics point to recent developments that echo the U.S. experience. Within the past two decades, a general dealignment of the electorate has taken place, with stable party allegiances on the decline. Hardest hit has been the Labour Party, which has apparently lost its grip on traditional sources of support among the working class.

North—South

POLITICS AROUND THE WORLD

Even with the upsurge in "third party" candidates in recent years, people in the United States have a tendency to think that their loose, two-party system is somehow the norm. Nothing could be further from the truth.

As in most other industrialized democracies, four or more parties regularly win a significant share of the vote in Canada. For most of this century, there have been two dominant parties, the somewhat left-of-center Liberals (currently in office) and the slightly right-of-center Progressive Conservatives. Don't make too much of their differences, as one recent study showed that they have been closer together on most social and economic issues than the Republicans and Democrats in the United States since the end of World War II.

It's the other parties that make Canada so different from the United States. There is a social democratic alternative, the New Democratic Party, which routinely wins anywhere between 5 and 15 percent of the vote. Finally, Canada has had a series of other, often regionally based "anti-Ottawa" parties. Thus, in 1993, the Reform Party (largely in the rural plains and mountain provinces) and Bloc Québecois together won about a third of both the vote and the seats in the House of Commons. On the other hand, such regional parties have rarely done that well, and most have not lasted for more than a few elections. Still, one of the keys to the Canadian party system is that it is deeply divided along regional and linguistic lines more than the social and economic splits that matter most in the United States and much of Western Europe.

As should already be clear, the Mexican party system has little in common with ours. For most of its history, the Mexican republic has not had a competitive party system—another factor that has led to the doubts about Mexico's democracy. It was only in the late 1980s that the opposition began to mount a credible challenge to the

PRI's hegemony, or all-but-total control over Mexican political life.

Although the PRI started out as the party defending the egalitarian goals of the revolution, it no longer stands for much other than maintaining its hold on power. During the last three presidencies, the PRI has strongly supported market-oriented economic reforms (see North–South feature in chapter 18); but throughout its history it has changed its ideological position as social and economic circumstances warranted. There is therefore no reason to believe it will stick with its market-oriented views indefinitely.

Until the 1980s, the PRI kept winning without having to face serious opposition. Now, however, it has had to deal with two serious rivals—the revitalized PAN (National Action Party) on its right and the PRD (Party of the Democratic Revolution) on its left. In 1988 the two parties together almost certainly did well enough to deprive Salinas of a majority had the vote been counted honestly. Although current President Ernesto Zedillo probably did win an "honest majority" six years later, and the opposition is split between its left and right wings, most experts think it is only a matter of time until they or other opposition parties develop enough strength to finally force the PRI out of power.

Despite these differences, there are also two important common features to the three countries' party systems. First, they increasingly rely on the media and telegenic leaders rather than grassroots organizations in running their campaigns. Second, with the possible exception of new opposition forces like the Bloc Québecois or the PRD, all parties are losing support from activists and voters alike. In Canada, that led to the 1993 wipeout of the Conservatives at the national level, when they won only two seats. In Mexico, that dissatisfaction is most evident in the ongoing decline in support for the PRI and the interest groups associated with it.

CHANGING PARTISAN ALIGNMENTS

*W*hile the independent or third-party candidate is often talked about as a new phenomenon, most of the presidential elections since 1832 have included a third-party or independent candidate. Unfortunately for today's hopefuls, no route to the White House has proved more daunting than that of the independent candidate. No one has ever made it all the way; in fact, no one has ever even come close. Since 1831, only eight independent or third-party candidates have obtained more than 10 percent of the popular vote. Of the eight individuals who have broken the 10 percent plateau, the high-water mark was set by the former Republican president Theodore Roosevelt in 1912. Running as a representative of the Progressive "Bull Moose" Party, Roosevelt won 88 electoral votes and 27.4 percent of the popular vote. Twelve years later Robert LaFollette, also running as a Progressive, garnered 16.6 percent of the popular vote. But from 1924 to 1992, no independent or third-party candidate, save for George Wallace in 1968, was able to surpass the 10 percent mark. Furthermore, if you were to add every electoral vote that went for anyone other than a nominee of the Democratic or Republican party so far in the twentieth century, the total would still fall short of the 270 needed to win a single election!

But in 1992 a Texas billionaire spent $60 million of his own money and won almost one in five votes, an impressive showing for a third-party candidate. In 1996 several others considered following his lead. While many minor third-party candidates did emerge (for example, author Harry Brown for the Libertarian Party and economist Ralph Nader for the Green Party), Ross Perot was again the only major third-party or independent candidate to throw his hat into the electoral ring.

While some political pundits, focusing on the fact that a growing number of voters deem themselves "independents," have openly predicted the demise of Democratic and Republican dominance of the presidential selection process and the concurrent rise of a "third way," before we rush to support these opinions, we must remember that independent and third-party candidacies collide head-on with some forces of twentieth-century history:

- Voters tend to flirt with independent candidates early in the election process, but they routinely return to the two-party fold by late fall.

- In the twentieth century, only thirteen states have voted for a third-party candidate even once, and none have since 1968. Theodore Roosevelt proved to be the most successful, carrying six states; in 1980 John Anderson failed to carry any, as did Perot in 1992 and 1996.

- Independent or third-party candidates suffer from a "can't win" syndrome. Voters tell pollsters that they like the non-major party candidate but ultimately decide not to cast their vote on him if they suspect the candidate cannot win.

- Raising money and getting on the ballot in all fifty states poses a significant obstacle to third-party and independent candidates.

Over the course of our country's history, these hurdles have proved daunting to independent and third-party challengers. While many backers of the "third way" believed that retired General Colin Powell could have overcome these historical hurdles because of his moderate views and his ability to compete financially with any major party candidate, Powell declined to seek the presidency in 1996. Thus, for the time being, we might conclude that until a charismatic, moderate, well-heeled candidate who appeals to a wide array of voters emerges and steals the show from the usual stars, independent and third-party candidates are most likely doomed to failure. The hurdles of history await such a challenger.

SUMMARY

A political party is a group of office holders, candidates, activists, and voters who identify with a group label and seek to elect to public office individuals who run under that label. They encompass three separate components: (1) the governmental party comprises office holders and candidates who run under the party's banner; (2) the electoral party comprises the workers and activists who staff the party's formal organization; (3) the party-in-the-electorate refers to the voters who consider themselves to be allied or associated with the party. In this chapter we have made the following points:

1.   What Is a Political Party?

The goal of American political parties is to win office. This objective is in keeping with the practical nature of Americans and the country's longstanding aversion to most ideologically driven, "purist" politics.

2.   The Evolution of American Party Democracy.

The evolution of U.S. political parties has been remarkably smooth, and the stability of the Democratic and Republican groupings, despite name changes, is a wonder, considering all the social and political tumult in U.S. history.

3.   The Roles of the American Parties.

For 150 years, the two-party system has served as the mechanism American society uses to organize and resolve social and political conflict. The Democratic and Republican parties, through lengthy nominating processes, provide a sort of screening mechanism for those who aspire to the presidency, helping to weed out unqualified individuals, expose and test candidates' ideas on important policy questions, and ensure a measure of long-term continuity and accountability.

4.   One-Partyism and Third-Partyism.

The U.S. party system is uniquely a two-party system. While periods of one-partyism, third-partyism, or independent activism (such as the Perot phenomenon) can prevail, the greatest proportion of all federal, state, and local elections are contests between the Republican and Democratic parties only.

5.   The Basic Structure of American Political Parties.

While the distinctions might not be as clear today as they were two or three decades ago, the basic structure of the major parties remains simple and pyramidal. The state and local parties are more important than the national ones, though campaign technologies and fund raising concentrated in Washington are invigorating the national party committees.

6.   The Party in Government.

Political parties are not restricted to their role as grassroots organization of voters; they also have another major role *inside* government institutions. The party in government comprises the office holders and candidates who run under the party's banner.

7.   The Modern Transformation of Party Organization.

Political parties have moved from the labor-intensive, person-to-person operations of the first half of the century toward the utilization of modern high technologies and communication strategies. Nevertheless, the capabilities of the party organizations vary widely from place to place.

8. The Party-in-the-Electorate.

The party-in-the-electorate refers to the voters who consider themselves to be allied or associated with the party. This is the most significant element of the political party, providing the foundation for the organizational and governmental parties.

9. Changing Partisan Alignments.

While the independent or third-party candidate is often talked about as a new phenomenon, most of the presidential elections since 1832 have included a third-party or independent candidate. Unfortunately for 1996 presidential hopefuls, no route to the White House has proved more daunting than that of the independent candidate.

KEY TERMS

civil service laws, p. 455

coalition, p. 457

coattail effect, p. 473

direct primary, p. 455

dualist theory, p. 464

gender gap, p. 485

governmental party, p. 449

issue-oriented politics, p. 455

machine, p. 453

national convention, p. 466

national party platform, p.459

one-partyism, p. 460

organizational party, p. 449

party identification, p. 482

party-in-the-electorate, p. 481

patronage, p. 455

political consultant, p. 455

political party, p. 449

proportional representation, p. 463

spoils system, p. 455

third-partyism, p. 461

ticket-split, p. 455

tracking poll, p. 478

SELECTED READINGS

Broder, David S. *The Party's Over.* New York: Harper & Row, 1971.

Chambers, William Nisbet, and Walter Dean Burnham, eds. *The American Party Systems: Stages of Political Development,* 2d ed. New York: Oxford University Press, 1975.

Epstein, Leon. *Political Parties in the American Mold.* Madison: University of Wisconsin Press, 1986.

Fiorina, Morris P. *Divided Government.* Boston: Allyn and Bacon, 1996.

Kayden, Xandra, and Eddie Mahe. *The Party Goes On.* New York: Basic Books, 1985.

Key, V. O., Jr. *Politics, Parties, and Pressure Groups,* 5th ed. New York: Thomas Y. Crowell, 1964.

Maisel, L. Sandy, ed. *The Parties Respond.* 2nd ed. Boulder, CO: Westview Press, 1994.

Mayhew, David R. *Placing Parties in American Politics.* Princeton, NJ: Princeton University Press, 1986.

Polsby, Nelson W. *Consequences of Party Reform.* New York: Oxford University Press, 1983.

Pomper, Gerald M. *Passions and Interests: Political Party Concepts of American Democracy.* Lawrence, Kan.: University Press of Kansas, 1992.

Price, David E. *Bringing Back the Parties.* Washington, D.C.: CQ Press, 1984.

Riordan, William L., ed. *Plunkitt of Tammany Hall.* New York: Dutton, 1963.

Rohde, David W. *Parties and Leaders in the Postreform House.* Chicago: University of Chicago Press, 1991.

Sabato, Larry J. *The Party's Just Begun: Shaping Political Parties for America's Future.* Glenview, IL: Scott, Foresman/Little, Brown, 1988.

Schattschneider, E. E. *Party Government.* New York: Holt, Rinehart and Winston, 1942.

Shafer, Byron E. *Quiet Revolution: The Struggle for the Democratic Party and the Shaping of Post-Reform Politics.* New York: Russell Sage Foundation, 1983.

Sorauf, Frank J., and Paul Allen Beck. *Party Politics in America,* 7th ed. New York: Harper/Collins, 1995.

Sundquist, James L. *Dynamics of the Party System,* rev. ed. Washington, D.C.: The Brookings Institution, 1983.

Wattenberg, Martin P. *The Decline of American Political Parties, 1952–1992.* Cambridge, MA: Harvard University Press, 1994.

VOTING AND ELECTIONS

The 1996 Republican presidential nomination race was the quickest contest since the modern presidential selection process began in 1972. In 1996 seven of the ten most populous states scheduled their primaries before March 31. By the end of March 1996, nearly 70 percent of all Republican convention delegates had been chosen, compared to 36 percent selected by the end of March 1992. With so many delegate votes up for grabs so early in the process, a six-month campaign season was shortened to two months. What was once known as the marathon of American politics became a fifty-yard dash!

This radical transformation of the presidential nominating process is the result of what political scientists call *front-loading*, the scheduling of primaries and caucuses early in an election year to increase the overall influence of a particular state or region. New Hampshire, for example, is allocated only a few delegates, but has traditionally carried a great deal of weight in the nominating process. As the first primary, the New Hampshire race determines the presidential front-runners, a designation that, in turn, attracts more campaign contributions, endorsements, and media coverage for the lucky candidates. On the other hand, states whose primaries and caucuses come later in the nominating process usually have minimal influence. Voters in these states often feel disenfranchised since the party's nominee is selected before they vote. This was particularly true for California, historically the last state to hold its primary. This year California moved its primary to March instead of June in an effort to give the state more weight and influence.

While some supporters of a front-loaded primary season believe that the rapid-fire schedule of primaries and caucuses resulted in an improved, more representative nominating procedure in which Iowa and New Hampshire were forced to share the spotlight with other, more deserving states, other politicians and political pundits have questioned its wisdom. Under the old nominating system, there was a gradual building of momentum. A single primary victory ensured neither success nor failure, and the momentum could shift during the lengthy nominating procedure. This natural winnowing process provided candi-

In the latest electronic electoral development, the candidates' World Wide Web home pages provided ongoing coverage of the presidential campaign of 1996.

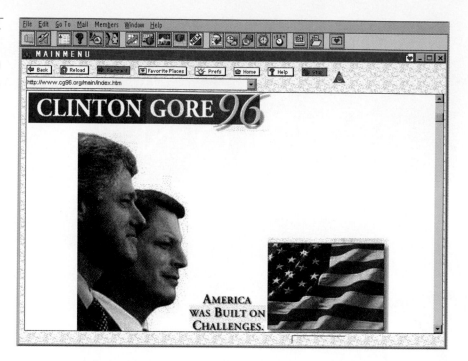

dates the opportunity to sell their views and voters the chance to digest them. Voters in states with later primaries thus had an opportunity to rethink and redirect the process, if they so chose.

The new system, however, heavily favors the front-runner. The continuous series of primaries provides little opportunity for long-shot candidates to sell their views or for a struggling campaign to jump-start itself after an early primary loss. A candidate may technically stay in the race, depending on his or her financial resources, but it is doubtful that the media or the public will focus attention on any candidate not deemed to be in the top tier. These possibilities lead many to conclude that by trying to upstage one another by moving up their primary dates, states seeking greater influence would actually accomplish the opposite of what they intended: They would give Iowa and New Hampshire an even more disproportionate role than before in choosing the nominee. Former presidential candidate Michael S. Dukakis said as much, characterizing this new front-loaded system as "madness." He explained, "There's something to be said for giving people a chance to look at the candidates over an extended period of time. This system puts more emphasis on [Iowa and New Hampshire, further relegating] the other states to irrelevance."[1]

Yet the experience of 1996 suggests the opposite. Even though Bob Dole barely won Iowa and lost New Hampshire, the front-loaded system enabled him to regroup quickly and bury his chief tormentors, Pat Buchanan and Steve Forbes.

Thus, with the 1996 election season, the presidential nomination process underwent a major transformation. But regardless of structural changes, elections still remain. For it is through free and competitive elections that the consent of the people is obtained and the government gains its democratic legitimacy.

Recall for a moment election day, November 5, 1996. A plurality of the voting electorate, simply by casting ballots peacefully across a continent-sized nation, reelected or replaced politicians at all levels of government—from the President of the United States, to members of the U.S. Congress, to state legislators. Other countries do not have the luxury of a peaceful transition of political power. We tend to take this process for granted, but in truth it is a marvel. Fortunately, most Americans, though not enough, understand why and how elections serve their interests. Elections take the pulse of average people and gauge their hopes and fears; the study of elections permits us to trace the course of the American revolution over 200 years of voting.

Today the United States of America is a democrat's paradise in many respects because it probably conducts more elections for more offices more frequently than any nation on earth. Moreover, in recent times the U.S. electorate (those citizens eligible to vote) has been the most universal in the country's history; no longer can one's race or sex or creed prevent participation at the ballot box. But challenges still remain. After all the blood spilled and energy expended to expand the suffrage (as the right to vote is called), only a little more than half the potentially eligible voters bother to go to the polls!

This chapter focuses on the purposes served by elections, the various kinds of elections held in the United States, and patterns of voting over time. We concentrate in particular on presidential and congressional contests, both of which have rich histories that tell us a great deal about the American people and their changing hopes and needs. We conclude by returning to contemporary presidential elections and addressing some topics of electoral reform.

- First, we examine *the purposes served by elections*, pointing out that they confer a legitimacy on regimes better than any other method of change.

- Second, we analyze *different kinds of elections*, including the many different types of elections held at the presidential and congressional levels.

- Third, we take a closer look at the elements of *presidential elections*, including primaries, conventions, and delegates.

- Fourth, we explore how *congressional elections*, although they share similarities with presidential elections, are really quite different.

- Fifth, we discuss *how voters behave* in certain distinct ways and exhibit unmistakable patterns each election cycle.

- Finally, we present arguments for *changing the electoral process* for the most powerful official in the world, the president of the United States.

THE PURPOSES SERVED BY ELECTIONS

Both the ballot and the bullet are methods of governmental change around the world, and surely the former is preferable to the latter. Although the United States has not escaped the bullet's awful effects, most change has come to this country through the election process. Regular free elections guarantee mass political action and enable citizens to influence the actions of their government. Election campaigns may often seem unruly, unending, harsh, and even vicious, but imagine the stark alternatives: violence and social disruption. Societies that cannot vote their leaders out of office are left with little choice other than to force them out by means of strikes, riots, or coups d'etat.

Popular election confers on a government the legitimacy that it can achieve no other way. Even many authoritarian and Communist systems around the globe recognize this. From time to time, they hold "referenda" to endorse their regimes or one-party elections, even though these so-called elections offer no real choice that would ratify their rule. The symbolism of elections as mechanisms to legitimize change, then, is important, but so is their practical value. After all, elections are the means to fill public offices and staff the government. The voters' choice of candidates and parties helps to organize government as well. Because candidates advocate certain policies, elections also involve a choice of platforms and point the society in certain directions on a wide range of issues, from abortion to civil rights to national defense to the environment.

electorate: Citizens eligible to vote.

Regular elections also ensure that government is accountable to the people it serves. At fixed intervals the **electorate,** citizens eligible to vote, is called on to judge those in power. If the judgment is favorable, and the incumbents are reelected, the office holders may continue their policies with renewed resolve. Should the incumbents be defeated and their challengers elected, however, a change in policies will likely result. Either way, the winners will claim a **mandate** (literally, a command) from the people to carry out their platform.

mandate: A command, indicated by an electorate's votes, for the elected officials to carry out their platforms.

Sometimes the claim of a mandate is suspect because voters are not so much endorsing one candidate and his or her beliefs as rejecting his or her opponent. Frequently, this occurs because the electorate is exercising **retrospective judgment;** that is, voters are rendering judgment on the performance of the party in power. This judgment makes sense because voters can evaluate the record of office holders much better than they can predict the future actions of the out-of-power challengers.

retrospective judgment: A voter's evaluation of the performance of the party in power.

At other times, voters might vote using **prospective judgment,** that is, they vote based on what a candidate pledges to do about an issue if elected. This forward looking approach to choosing candidates voters believe will best serve their interests requires that the electorate examine the views that the rival candidates have on the issues of the day and then cast a ballot for the person they believe will best handle these matters. Unfortunately, prospective voting requires lots of information about issues and candidates. Voters who cast a vote prospectively must be willing to spend a great deal of time seeking out information and learning about issues and how each candidate stands on them. Consider for a moment how voters retrospectively and prospectively judged recent presidential administrations in reaching their ballot decisions:

prospective judgment: A voter's evaluation of a candidate based on what he or she pledges to do about an issue if elected.

- *1968:* No one could know what Richard M. Nixon's promised "secret plan to end the Vietnam War" really was, but the electorate knew that President Lyndon B. Johnson had failed to resolve the conflict. Result: Voters retrospectively voted against the nominee of the party in power, Hubert H. Humphrey, and prospectively for Richard Nixon and his "secret plan."

- *1972:* The American people were satisfied with Nixon's stewardship of foreign affairs, especially his good relationship with the Soviet Union, the diplomatic opening of China, and the "Vietnamization" of the war. Thus they retrospectively judged his administration to have been a success and looked to the future, believing that he, rather than Democrat George McGovern, could best lead the country. The Watergate scandal (involving Nixon's coverup of his campaign committee's bugging of the Democrats' national headquarters) was only in its infancy, and the president was rewarded with a forty-nine-state sweep.

■ *1976:* This year retrospective judgments clearly prevailed over prospective considerations. Despite confusion about Jimmy Carter's real philosophy and intentions, the relatively unknown Georgia Democrat was elected president as voters held President Gerald R. Ford responsible for an economic recession and deplored his pardon of Richard M. Nixon for Watergate crimes.

■ *1980:* Burdened by difficult economic times and the Iranian hostage crisis (one year before Election Day, Iranian militants had seized fifty-three Americans, whom they held until January 20, 1981, Inauguration Day), Carter became a one-term president as the electorate rejected the Democrat's perceived weak leadership. At age sixty-nine, Ronald Reagan was not viewed as the ideal replacement by many voters, and neither did a majority agree with some of his conservative principles. But the retrospective judgment on Carter was so harsh and the prospective outlook of four more years under his stewardship so glum that an imperfect alternative was considered preferable to another term of the Democrat.

■ *1984:* A strong economic recovery from a midterm recession and an image of strength derived from a defense buildup and a successful military venture in Grenada combined to produce a satisfied electorate that retrospectively and prospectively decided to grant Ronald Reagan four more years. The result: A forty-nine-state landslide reelection for Reagan over Jimmy Carter's vice president, Walter Mondale.

■ *1988:* Continued satisfaction with Reagan, a product of strong economic expansion and superpower summitry, produced an electoral endorsement of Reagan's vice president, George Bush. Bush was seen as Reagan's understudy and natural successor; the Democratic nominee, Michael Dukakis, offered too few convincing reasons to alter the voters' considered retrospective judgment.

■ *1992:* A prolonged economic recession and weak growth in jobs plus Ross Perot's candidacy, which split the Republican base, denied a second term to George Bush, despite his many significant triumphs in foreign policy (the Persian Gulf War victory and arms control agreements, for example). In the end voters decided to vote retrospectively, gambling on a little-known governor, Bill Clinton, rather than order up more of the same by reelecting Bush.

■ *1996:* Similar to 1984, only with the party labels reversed, a healthy economy prompted Americans to retrospectively support President Bill Clinton in his quest for reelection. Voters also looked prospectively at the two candidates and again registered their support for President Clinton. Clinton then received relatively high marks by voters both for his stewardship during the first four years of his administration and his vision for the country's future.

Whether one agrees or disagrees with these election results, there is a rough justice at work here. When parties and presidents please the electorate, they are rewarded; when they preside over hard times, they are punished. A president is usually not responsible for all the good or bad developments that occur on his watch, but the voters nonetheless hold him accountable, not an unreasonable way for citizens to behave in a democracy.

On rare occasions, off-year congressional elections can produce mandates. In 1974 a tidal wave for Democrats produced a mandate to clean up politics after Watergate, while in 1994 Republicans enjoyed a similar wave and claimed a mandate for limiting government.

DIFFERENT KINDS OF ELECTIONS

 S o far we have referred mainly to presidential elections, but in the U.S. system, elections come in many varieties.

primary elections: Elections in which voters decide which of the candidates within a party will represent the party in the general election.

open primary: A primary in which party members, independents, and sometimes members of the other party are allowed to vote.

closed primary: A primary election in which only a party's registered voters are eligible to vote.

Primary Elections

In **primary elections,** voters decide which of the candidates within a party will represent the party's ticket in the general elections. The primaries themselves vary in kind. For example, **closed primaries** allow only a party's registered voters to cast a ballot, and **open primaries** allow independents and sometimes members of the other party to participate. (Figure 13.1 shows the states with open and closed primaries for presidential delegate selection.) Closed primaries are considered healthier for the party system ballot because they prevent members of one party from influencing the pri-

FIGURE 13.1

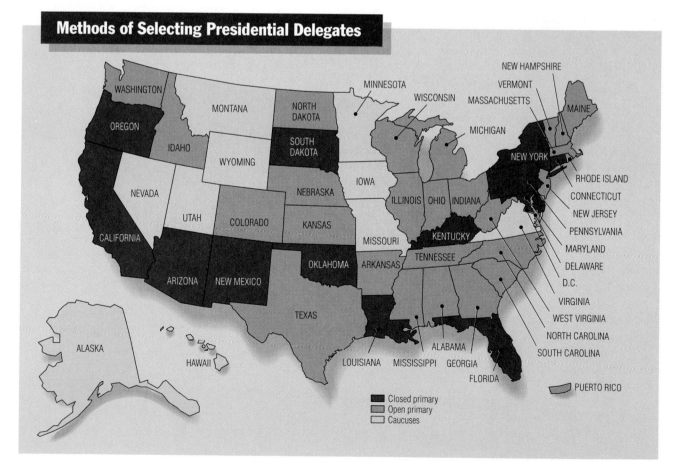

Methods of Selecting Presidential Delegates

- Closed primary
- Open primary
- Caucuses

maries of the opposition party. In the **blanket primary,** voters are permitted to vote in either party's primary (but not both) on an office-by-office basis. When none of the candidates in the initial primary secures a majority of the votes, there is a **runoff primary,** a contest between the two candidates with the greatest number of votes.

General Elections

Once the party candidates for various offices are chosen, general elections are held. In the **general election,** voters decide which candidates will actually fill the nation's elective public offices. These elections are held at many levels, including municipal, county, state, and national. While primaries are contests between the candidates within each party, general elections are contests between the candidates of opposing parties.

General elections come in many varieties because Americans perceive the various offices as substantially different from one another. In sizing up presidential candidates, voters look for leadership and character, and they base their judgments partly on foreign policy and defense issues that do not arise in state and local elections. Leadership qualities are vital for gubernatorial and mayoral candidates, as are the nuts-and-bolts issues (such as taxes, schools, and roads) that dominate the concerns of state and local governments. Citizens often choose their congressional representatives very differently than they select presidents. Knowing much less about the candidates, people will sometimes base a vote on simple name identification and visibility. This way of deciding one's vote obviously helps incumbents and therefore to some degree explains the high reelection rates of incumbent U.S. representatives: Since World War II, 92 percent of all U.S. House members seeking another term have won, and in several recent election years the proportion has been above 95 percent. In 1994 the percentage of those members reelected dipped a little, to 90 percent. But in 1996, it again approached recent election averages when fully 94 percent of the lawmakers who sought reelection won.

Initiative, Referendum, and Recall

Three other types of elections are the initiative, the referendum (plural, referenda), and the recall. Used in about twenty states, initiatives and referenda involve voting on issues (as opposed to voting for candidates). An **initiative** is a process that allows citizens to propose legislation and submit it to the state electorate for popular vote, as long as they have a certain number of signatures on petitions supporting the proposal. A **referendum** is a procedure whereby the state legislature submits proposed legislation to the state's voters for approval. Although both of these electoral devices provide for more direct democracy, they are not problem-free. In the 1990 elections, for instance, California had so many referenda and initiatives on its ballot that the state printed a lengthy two-volume guide in an attempt to explain them all to voters. Despite this, many Californians complained that it was virtually impossible for even a reasonably informed citizen to vote intelligently on so many issues.

The third type of election (or "de-election") found in many states is the **recall,** whereby an incumbent can be removed from office by popular vote. Recall elections are very rare, and sometimes they are thwarted by the official's resignation or impeachment prior to the vote. For example, Arizona Governor Evan Mecham was impeached and ousted in 1988 by the state legislature for mishandling campaign finances (among other offenses) just a few weeks before a recall election had been scheduled.

blanket primary: A primary in which voters may cast ballots in either party's primary (but not both) on an office-by-office basis.

runoff primary: A second primary election between the two candidates receiving the greatest number of votes in the first primary.

general election: Election in which voters decide which candidates will actually fill elective public offices.

initiative: A process that allows citizens to propose legislation and submit it to the state electorate for popular vote.

referendum: A procedure whereby the state legislature submits proposed legislation to the state's voters for approval.

recall: Removal of an incumbent from office by popular vote.

PRESIDENTIAL ELECTIONS

*V*ariety aside, no U.S. election can compare to the presidential contest. This spectacle, held every four years, brings together all the elements of politics and attracts the most ambitious and energetic politicians to the national stage. The election itself, though altered by a front-loaded primary season, remains a collection of fifty separate state elections within each party in which delegates to each party's national convention are allotted. The election of delegates is followed in midsummer by the parties' grand national conventions and then by a final set of fifty separate state elections all held on the Tuesday after the first Monday in November. This lengthy process exhausts candidates and voters alike, but it allows the diversity of the United States to be displayed in ways a shorter, more homogeneous presidential election process could not. Every state has its moment in the sun, every local and regional problem a chance to be aired, every candidate an opportunity to break away from the pack.

The state party organizations use a number of methods to elect national convention delegates:

1. *Winner-take-all:* Under this system the candidate who wins the most votes in a state secures all of that state's delegates. The Democrats moved away from this mode of delegate selection in 1976 and no longer permit its use because of the arguable unfairness to all candidates except the primary winner. Republicans do not prohibit winner-take-all contests, thus enabling a GOP candidate to amass a majority of delegates more quickly.

2. *Proportional representation:* Under this system, candidates who secure a threshold percentage of votes (usually around 15 percent) are awarded delegates in proportion to the number of popular votes won. This system is now strongly favored by the Democrats and is used in many states' Democratic primaries. Although proportional representation is probably the most fair way of allocating delegates to candidates, its downfall is that it renders majorities of delegates more difficult to accumulate and thus can lengthen the contest for the nomination.

3. *Proportional representation with bonus delegates; beauty contest with separate delegate selection; delegate selection with no beauty contest:* Used rarely, the first of these awards delegates to candidates in proportion to the popular vote won and then gives one bonus delegate to the winner of each district. The second serves as an indication of popular sentiment for the conventions to consider as they choose the actual delegates. Finally, under the "delegate selection with no beauty contest" system, the primary election chooses delegates to the national conventions who are not linked on the ballot to specific presidential contenders.

4. *The caucus:* The caucus is the oldest, most party-oriented method of choosing delegates to the national conventions. Traditionally, the caucus was a closed meeting of party members in each state that selected the party's choice for presidential candidate. In the late nineteenth and early twentieth centuries, however, these caucuses came to be viewed by many people as elitist and antidemocratic, and reformers succeeded in replacing them with direct primaries in most states. While there are still presidential nominating caucuses today, as in Iowa, they are now more open and attract a wider range of the party's membership.

Primaries Versus Caucuses

The mix of preconvention contests has changed over the years, with the most pronounced trend being the shift to primaries: Only seventeen states held presidential primaries in 1968, compared with thirty-eight in 1992 and forty-two in 1996. Figure 13.1 shows which states use primaries (open and closed) and which use caucuses to select presidential delegates.

The increase in the number of primaries is supported by some people who claim that this type of election is more democratic. The primaries are open not only to party activists, but also to anyone, wealthy or poor, urban or rural, Northern or Southern, who wants to vote. Theoretically, then, representatives of all these groups have a chance of winning the presidency. Related to this idea, advocates argue that presidential primaries are the most representative means by which to nominate presidential candidates. They are a barometer of a candidate's popularity with the party rank and file. Finally, the proponents of presidential primaries claim that they constitute a rigorous test for the candidates, a chance to display under pressure some of the skills needed to be a successful president.

Critics of presidential primaries, however, see the situation somewhat differently. First, they argue that although it may be true that primaries attract more participants than do caucuses, this quantity is more than matched by the quality of caucus participation. Compared with the unenlightening minutes spent at the primary polls, caucus attendees spend several hours learning about politics and the party, listening to speeches by candidates or their representatives, and taking cues from party leaders and elected officials. Moreover, voters may not know very much about any of the field of candidates in a primary, or they may be excessively swayed by popularity polls, television ads, and other media presentations, such as newspaper and magazine coverage.

Critics also argue that the scheduling of primaries unfairly affects their outcomes. For example, the earliest primary is in the small, atypical state of New Hampshire, which is heavily white and conservative, and it receives much more media coverage than it warrants simply because it is first. Such excessive coverage undoubtedly skews the picture for more populous states that hold their primaries later. The critics also argue that the qualities tested by the primary system are by no means a complete list of those a president needs to be successful. For instance, skill at playing the media game is by itself no guarantee of an effective presidency. Similarly, the exhausting schedule of the primaries may be a better test of a candidate's stamina than of his or her brain power.

The primary proponents have obviously had the better of the arguments so far, though the debate continues, as do efforts to experiment with the schedule of primaries. From time to time, proposals are made for **regional primaries.** Under this system, the nation would be divided into five or six geographic regions (such as the South or the Midwest). All the states in each region would hold their primary elections on the same day, with perhaps one regional election day per month from February through June of presidential election years. This change would certainly cut down on candidate wear and tear. Moreover, candidates would be inspired to focus more on regional issues. On the other hand, regional primaries would probably cost candidates at least as much as the state-by-state system, and the system might needlessly amplify the differences and create divisive rifts among the nation's regions.

Occasionally, a regional plan is adopted. In 1988, for instance, fourteen Southern and border South states joined together to hold simultaneous primaries on "Super Tuesday" (March 8) in order to maximize the South's impact on presidential politics. This was an attempt by conservative Democrats to influence the choice of the party

Republican primary candidate Pat Buchanan campaigning in Columbia, South Carolina, in March 1996. Never much of a threat to Dole's candidacy, Buchanan all but dropped out of the race in April, stating that he would instead try to influence the Republican Party on a variety of issues. (Photo courtesy: Rick Friedman/Black Star)

regional primary: A proposed system in which the country would be divided into five or six geographic areas and all states in each region would hold their presidential primary elections on the same day.

nominee. Their effort failed, however, since the two biggest winners of Super Tuesday were liberals Jesse Jackson (who won six Southern states) and Michael Dukakis, who carried the mega-states of Texas and Florida. This outcome occurred because, in general, the kinds of citizens who vote in Democratic primaries in the South are not greatly different from those who cast ballots in Northern Democratic primaries—most tend toward the liberal side of the ideological spectrum. This trend was repeated in 1996 with the construction of the so-called "Yankee Primary," with five of the six New England states holding their contests on March 5 (Massachusetts, Connecticut, Rhode Island, Vermont, and Maine) plus New York on March 7, and the continuation of a scaled-down Super Tuesday on March 12.

front-loading: The tendency of states to choose an early date on the primary calendar.

The primary schedule has also been altered, as we saw earlier in the chapter, by a process called **front-loading,** the tendency of states to choose an early date on the primary calendar. Seventy percent of all the delegates to both party conventions are now chosen before the end of March (see Table 13.1). This trend is hardly surprising, given the added press emphasis on the first contests and the voters' desire to cast their ballots before the competition is decided. The focus on early contests (such as the Iowa caucus and the New Hampshire primary), coupled with front-loading, can result in a party's being saddled with a nominee too quickly, before press scrutiny and voter reflection are given enough time to separate the wheat from the chaff.

THE PARTY CONVENTIONS

The seemingly endless nomination battle does have a conclusion: the national party convention held in the summer of presidential election years. The out-of-power party traditionally holds its convention first, in late July, followed by the party holding the White House in mid-August. Preempting some of prime-time television for four nights, these remarkable conclaves are difficult for the public to ignore; indeed, they are pivotal events in shaping the voters' perceptions of the candidates.

Yet the conventions once were much more: They were deliberative bodies that made actual decisions, where party leaders held sway and deals were sometimes cut in "smoke-filled rooms" to deliver nominations to little-known contenders called "dark horses" (see Roots of Government: Dark Horses versus Worn-out Horses). But this era predated the modern emphasis on reform, primaries, and proportional representation, all of which have combined to make conventions mere ratifying agencies for preselected nominees.

In the 1830s the national nominating convention replaced the congressional caucus (an organization of all the party's members of Congress) as the means for selecting the presidential ticket. The national convention consists of a delegation from each state. The delegation, whose size is determined by the national party, includes leaders from the state's various localities. Consequently, the nominee of the convention is, in effect, the choice of a congregation of state and local parties. Unlike the congressional caucus system, the convention is compatible with the federal separation of powers and provides for the broad participation of party members. In addition to selecting the party's presidential ticket, the convention drafts the party's platform (see chapter 12) and establishes party rules and procedures.

The first national convention was held in 1831 by the Anti-Masonic Party. In 1832 Andrew Jackson's nomination for reelection was ratified by the first Democratic National Convention. Just four years later, in 1836, Martin Van Buren became the first

TABLE 13.1

The 1996 Republican Presidential Nominating Season at a Glance

STATE	DATE	REPUBLICAN DELEGATE COUNT	TYPE OF DELEGATE SELECTION	METHOD OF ELECTING GOP DELEGATES
Alabama	June 4	40	Open Primary	WTA*
Alaska	Jan. 26–29	19	Closed Caucus	NFS*
Arizona	Feb. 27	39	Closed Primary	WTA
Arkansas	May 21	20	Open Primary	PR*
California	March 26	163	Closed Primary	WTA
Colorado	March 5	27	Open Primary	PR
Connecticut	March 5	27	Closed Primary	WTA
Delaware	Feb. 24	12	Closed Primary	WTA
Washington, D.C.	May 7	14	Closed Primary	WTA
Florida	March 12	98	Closed Primary	WTA
Georgia	March 5	42	Open Primary	WTA
Hawaii	Jan. 25–31	14	Closed Caucus	NFS
Idaho	May 28	23	Open Primary	PR
Illinois	March 19	69	Open Primary	DE*
Indiana	May 7	52	Open Primary	WTA
Iowa	Feb. 12	25	Open Caucus	NFS
Kansas	April 2	31	Open Primary	WTA
Kentucky	May 28	26	Closed Primary	PR
Louisiana	Feb. 6	28	Closed Primary	WTA
Maine	March 5	15	Open Primary	WTA
Maryland	March 5	32	Closed Primary	WTA
Massachusetts	March 5	37	Open Primary	WTA
Michigan	March 19	57	Open Primary	PR
Minnesota	March 5	33	Open Caucus	NFS
Mississippi	March 12	32	Open Primary	WTA
Missouri	March 9	36	Open Caucus	NFS
Montana	June 4	14	Open Caucus	NFS
Nebraska	May 14	24	Open Primary	DE
Nevada	March 26	14	Closed Caucus	NFS
New Hampshire	Feb. 20	16	Open Primary	PR
New Jersey	June 4	48	Open Primary	DE
New Mexico	June 4	18	Closed Primary	PR
New York	March 7	102	Closed Primary	DE
North Carolina	May 7	58	Open Primary	WTA
North Dakota	Feb. 27	18	Open Primary	PR
Ohio	March 19	67	Open Primary	WTA
Oklahoma	March 12	38	Closed Primary	WTA
Oregon	March 12	23	Closed Primary	PR
Pennsylvania	April 23	73	Closed Primary	DE

(Continued)

The 1996 Republican Presidential Nominating Season at a Glance, cont'd

STATE	DATE	REPUBLICAN DELEGATE COUNT	TYPE OF DELEGATE SELECTION	METHOD OF ELECTING GOP DELEGATES
Rhode Island	March 5	16	Open Primary	PR
South Carolina	March 2	37	Open Primary	WTA
South Dakota	Feb. 27	18	Closed Primary	PR
Tennessee	March 12	37	Open Primary	PR
Texas	March 12	123	Open Primary	PR
Utah	March 25	28	Open Caucus	NFS
Vermont	March 5	12	Open Primary	WTA
Virginia	April 13	53	Open Caucus	NFS
Washington	March 26	36	Open Primary	PR
West Virginia	May 14	18	Open Primary	DE
Wisconsin	March 19	36	Open Primary	WTA
Wyoming	March 23	20	Closed Caucus	NFS
Puerto Rico	March 3	14	Open Primary	WTA
U.S. Territories		12		
TOTAL		**1,984**		

DATE OF REPUBLICAN PRIMARY OR CAUCUS

January
25–31 Hawaii
26–29 Alaska

February
6 Louisiana
12 Iowa
20 New Hampshire
24 Delaware
27 Arizona
   North Dakota
   South Dakota

March
2 South Carolina
3 Puerto Rico

March, *continued*
5 Colorado
   Connecticut
   Georgia
   Maine
   Maryland
   Massachusetts
   Minnesota
   Rhode Island
   Vermont
7 New York
9 Missouri
12 Florida
   Mississippi
   Oklahoma
   Oregon

March, *continued*
12 Tennessee
   Texas
19 Illinois
   Michigan
   Ohio
   Wisconsin
23 Wyoming
25 Utah
26 California
   Washington

April
2 Kansas
13 Virginia
23 Pennsylvania

May
7 D.C.
   Indiana
   North Carolina
14 Nebraska
   West Virginia
21 Arkansas
28 Idaho
   Kentucky

June
4 Alabama
   Montana
   New Jersey
   New Mexico

*WTA: Winner-take-all; all delegates go to the statewide winner or are split between the statewide winner and each district winner.

NFS: No formal system; determined by participants in caucus process.

DE: Direct election of delegates.

PR: Proportional representation; delegates divided to reflect candidates' share of the vote.

Source: *Congressional Quarterly* 19 (August 1995): 2485.

The 1996 presidential candidates and their running mates. On the left, Vice President Al Gore, Jr., and President Bill Clinton. On the right, Republican presidential candidate Bob Dole and running mate Jack Kemp. (Photo courtesy: left, Dennis Brack/Black Star; right, Dave Zapotosky/AP Photo)

nonincumbent candidate nominated by a major party convention (the Democrats) to win the presidency.

From the 1830s to the mid-twentieth century, the national conventions remained primarily under the control of the important state and local party leaders, the so-called bosses or kingmakers, who would bargain within a splintered, decentralized party. During these years state delegations in the convention consisted mostly of *uncommitted delegates* (that is, delegates who had not pledged to support any particular candidate). These delegates were selected by party leaders, a process that enabled the leaders to broker agreements with prominent national candidates. Under this system a state party leader could exchange delegation support for valuable political plums—for instance, a Cabinet position or even the vice presidency—for an important state political figure.

Today the convention is fundamentally different. First, its importance as a party conclave, at which compromises on party leadership and policies can be worked out, has diminished. Second, although the convention still formally selects the presidential ticket, most nominations are settled well in advance. New preconvention political processes have lessened the role of the convention in three areas.

Delegate Selection. The selection of delegates to the conventions is no longer the function of party leaders but of primary elections and grassroots caucuses. Moreover, recent reforms, especially by the Democratic Party, have generally weakened any remaining control by local party leaders over delegates. A prime example of such reform is the Democrats' abolition of the **unit rule,** a traditional party practice under which the majority of a state delegation (say, twenty-six of fifty delegates) could force the minority to vote for its candidate. Another new Democratic Party rule decrees that a state's delegates be chosen in proportion to the votes cast in its primary or caucus (so that, for example, a candidate who receives 30 percent of the vote gains about 30 percent of the convention delegates). This change has had the effect of requiring delegates to in-

unit rule: A traditional party practice under which the majority of a state delegation can force the minority to vote for its candidate.

Roots of Government

Dark Horses Versus Worn-out Horses

The national party convention of the present day is a different animal from that of the past. No longer is it a deliberative forum for choosing the party presidential nominee; rather, the convention now merely ratifies the choices of the pre-convention state caucuses and primaries. A look at the Republican and Democratic Party conventions sixty years apart—in 1920 and 1980—illuminates one key contrast between the old-style and new-style conventions: the absence of dark horses—relatively unknown candidates who emerge at the convention and occasionally win a nomination as a compromise choice in order to break a deadlock.

The 1920 Republican convention featured a rift in the party. On one side was the party's old presidential faction, moderate and internationalist, with Abraham Lincoln and Theodore Roosevelt serving as its models. On the other side stood the more conservative wing of the party, with Senator Henry Cabot Lodge of Massachusetts at the helm and including most if not all of Capitol Hill's GOP leadership.

The "presidential" party during those days usually exerted more influence in presidential nominations than did the congressional party. But this changed in 1920 because Lodge's congressional party had garnered more power and influence during the latter part of Democratic President Woodrow Wilson's White House tenure (1913–21), when Wilson was seriously ill and his policies were under attack. Could the two wings of the party compromise on a presidential candidate for 1920? Any such compromise would undoubtedly be difficult to come by because most potential candidates were aligned firmly with one wing of the party or the other.

Senator Warren G. Harding of Ohio was one possible compromise candidate. A small-town politician and onetime editor of a staunchly Republican Ohio newspaper, Harding had a reputation in the Senate based primarily on his ability to win allies in all factions of the Republican Party. But Harding's chances appeared bleak at the outset of the convention, and after the first ballot, he was considerably behind a number of other Republican hopefuls. Yet, several frontrunners continued to deadlock in ballot after ballot, testing the patience of the delegates, who were baking in the hot Chicago summer.

The weather, combined with the seemingly unresolvable convention impasse, spurred a group of influential Senate leaders to meet at a nearby hotel room to attempt to hammer out a compromise—the classic gathering of party leaders behind the closed doors of a smoke-filled room. At the meeting, Harding's name continued to be floated. Although most of the party leaders questioned the Ohioan's convictions and leadership abilities, he did have some attractive qualities: He was handsome (it was said that Harding "looked like a president"), he hailed from a politically important state, and he could be expected to work with leaders of both party factions. The GOP kingmakers therefore decided to test the waters with Harding but agreed to reconvene later in the more likely event that the delegates rejected him. Harding soon went to work to ensure that no new meeting would be needed, however; he campaigned vigorously for his candidacy throughout the evening, roaming the halls and trying to convince any delegate he could find of his credibility as a candidate.

The deadlock at the convention continued for a few more ballots, but the frazzled delegates gradually realized that Harding perhaps was the only candidate with the potential to

dicate their presidential preference at each stage of the selection process. Consequently, the majority of state delegates now come to the convention already committed to a candidate. Again, this diminishes the discretionary role of the convention and the party leaders' capacity to bargain.

In sum, the many complex changes in the rules of delegate selection have contributed to the loss of decision-making powers by the convention. And even though many of these changes were initiated by the Democratic Party, the Republicans were carried along as many Democrat-controlled state legislatures enacted the reforms as secure a majority. This realization sent frontrunners scurrying around the convention to build a coalition to stop Harding. They failed, however, and dark-horse candidate Harding—on the tenth ballot—secured enough votes to win the nomination.

The Democrats also needed a candidate to unite the party in 1920, one who could emphasize Wilson's successes yet downplay his failures. After thirty-eight ballots at the Democratic National Convention, no majority candidate had yet emerged, instilling in Wilson a hope that the party might again turn to him as the nominee, despite his deteriorated physical condition. It was one thing for the Democrats to remain loyal to Wilson—which they did by endorsing his policies and paying him homage in the party platform—and another for the party to nominate him for a third term. A return to Wilson was ultimately unnecessary, as Ohio Governor James M. Cox finally secured the nomination on the forty-fourth ballot.

Conditions are very different today. Nominations are no longer decided in smoke-filled back rooms at the conventions; instead, the critical moments occur well beforehand in the highly visible primary-and-caucus obstacle course that creates not dark horses but worn-out horses by convention time.

In 1980, for example, many Democrats were dissatisfied with the Carter presidency. The situation was so dismal for the incumbent president that a strong nomination challenge came from a prominent fellow Democrat, Senator Edward M. Kennedy of Massachusetts. At first, the polls were encouraging for Kennedy—he enjoyed a two-to-one margin over Carter in the summer of 1979. But the Iran hostage crisis—the seizing by Iranian militants of more than fifty Americans from the U.S. embassy in Tehran—led to a sharp rise in public support for Carter, ultimately giving him a decisive margin over Kennedy in the vital early contests. Despite the initial strong challenge from Kennedy and the party's dissatisfaction with Carter's presidency, the incumbent's nomination was secured by April 1980, before the primaries had ended and four months before the Democratic convention opened. Even with a deep fissure in the Democratic Party, no dark-horse candidate emerged because most delegates arrived at the convention already bound by the rules of the party to either Carter or Kennedy.

No dark-horse candidate emerged in the Republican field in 1980, either. The most well-known of the Republicans was a former movie actor and California governor, Ronald Rea-

gan, sixty-nine years old and a conservative who appealed to the right wing of the party. Moderate U.S. Senate Minority Leader Howard Baker of Tennessee and Senator Robert Dole of Kansas were both in the running, as were former Texas Governor John Connally, Representative John Anderson of Illinois (who would later declare himself an independent candidate for president), and George Bush, a former member of Congress from Texas and U.S. ambassador to China. Though Bush won the Iowa precinct caucuses (the first major contest in 1980), Reagan won handily in the next big challenge, New Hampshire, securing almost twice Bush's vote. Like the Democratic nomination, the Republican contest was settled four months before the party convention, and only the brokering over Reagan's choice of a vice-presidential running mate was left to generate excitement at the convention.

The 1980 conventions are typical of those in the modern era, where presidential candidates secure victory by appealing directly to the people, not the party leaders. For better or worse, the deliberative conventions at which dark-horse candidates flourished, such as those of 1920, are probably consigned to the American political past.

state laws. There have been new rules to counteract some of these changes, however. For instance, since 1984 the number of delegate slots reserved for elected Democratic Party officials—called **superdelegates**—has been increased in the hope of adding stability to the Democratic convention. Before 1972 most delegates to a Democratic National Convention were not bound by primary results to support a particular candidate for president. This freedom to maneuver meant that conventions could be exciting and somewhat unpredictable gatherings, where last-minute events and deals could sway wavering delegates. Superdelegates are supposed to be party professionals concerned

superdelegate: Delegate slot to the Democratic Party's national convention that is reserved for an elected party official.

with winning the general election contest, not simply amateur ideologues concerned mainly with satisfying their policy appetites. All Democratic governors and 80 percent of the congressional Democrats, among others, are now included as voting delegates at the convention.

National Candidates and Issues.

The political perceptions and loyalties of voters are now influenced largely by national candidates and issues, a factor that has undoubtedly served to diminish the power of state and local party leaders at the convention. The national candidates have usurped the autonomy of state party leaders with their preconvention ability to garner delegate support. And issues, increasingly national in scope, are significantly more important to the new, issue-oriented party activists than to the party professionals, who, prior to the late 1960s, had a monopoly on the management of party affairs.

The News Media.

The mass media have helped to transform the national conventions into political extravaganzas for the television audience's consumption. They have also helped to preempt the convention, by keeping count of the delegates committed to the candidates; as a result, the delegates and even the candidates now have much more information about nomination politics well before the convention. From the strategies of candidates to the commitments of individual delegates, the media cover it all. Even the bargaining within key party committees, formerly done in secret, is now subject to some public scrutiny, thanks to open meetings. The business of the convention has been irrevocably shaped to accommodate television: Desirous of presenting a unified image to kick off a strong general election campaign, the parties assign important roles to attractive speakers, and most crucial party affairs are saved for prime-time viewing hours.

Extensive media coverage of the convention has its pros and cons. On the one hand, such exposure helps the party launch its presidential campaign with fanfare. On the other hand, it can expose rifts within a party, as happened in 1968 at the Democratic convention in Chicago. Dissension was obvious when "hawks," supporting the Vietnam war and President Lyndon B. Johnson, clashed with the antiwar "doves" both on the convention floor and in street demonstrations around the convention hall. Whatever the case, it is obvious that saturation media coverage of preelection events has led to the public's loss of anticipation and exhilaration about convention events.

Some reformers have spoken of replacing the conventions with national direct primaries, but it is unlikely that the parties would agree to this. Although its role in nominating the presidential ticket has often been reduced to formality, the convention is still a valuable political institution. After all, it is the only real arena where the national political parties can command a nearly universal audience while they celebrate past achievements and project their hopes for the future.

Who Are the Delegates?

In one sense, party conventions are microcosms of the United States: every state, most localities, and all races and creeds find some representation there. (For some historic "firsts" for women at conventions, see Highlight 13.1: Women as Delegates.) Yet delegates are an unusual and unrepresentative collection of people in many other ways. It is not just their exceptionally keen interest in politics that distinguishes delegates. These activists also are ideologically more pure and financially better off than most Americans.

In 1996, for example, both parties drew their delegates from an elite group that had income and educational levels far above the average American's. The distinctiveness of

Highlight 13.1

Women and the Conventions

Since 1980, Democratic Party rules have required that women comprise 50 percent of the delegates to its national convention. The Republican Party has no similar quotas. Neverthe-less, both parties have tried to increase the role of women at the convention. Some "firsts" for women at conventions include:

1876 First woman to address a national convention

1890 First woman delegates to con-ventions of both parties

1940 First woman to nominate a presidential candidate

1951 First woman asked to chair a national party

1972 First women keynote speaker

1984 First major party woman nominated for vice president (Democrat Geraldine Ferraro)

1996 Wives of both nominees make major addresses

Source: Center for the Study of American Women in Politics.

each party was also apparent. Democratic delegates tended to be younger and were more likely to be African American, female, divorced or single, and a member of a labor union. Republicans drew their delegates more heavily from people over forty-five years old, whites, married men, and Protestants. GOP conventioneers were also more likely to be elected or appointed officials and to have attended previous party conventions.

The contrast in the two parties' delegations is no accident; it reflects not only the differences in the party constituencies, but also conscious decisions made by party leaders. After the tumultuous 1968 Democratic National Convention (which, as noted, was torn by dissent over the Vietnam War), Democrats formed a commission to examine the condition of the party and to propose changes in its structure. As a direct consequence of the commission's work, the 1972 Democratic convention was the most broadly representative ever of women, African Americans, and young people, because the party required these groups to be included in state delegations in rough proportion to their numbers in the population of each state. (State delegations failing this test were not seated.) This new mandate was very controversial, and it has since been watered down considerably. Nonetheless, women and blacks are still more fully represented at Democratic conventions (as Table 13.2 shows) than at Republican conventions. GOP leaders have placed much less emphasis on proportional representation, and instead of procedural reforms, Republicans have concentrated on strengthening their state organizations and fund-raising efforts, a strategy that has clearly paid off at the polls in the elections of 1980, 1984, and 1988, which saw Republicans elected as president.

The delegates in each party also exemplify the philosophical gulf separating the two parties (see Table 13.3). Democratic delegates are well to the left of their own party's voters on most issues, and even further away from the opinions held by the nation's electorate as a whole. Republican delegates are a mirror image of their opponents—considerably to the right of GOP voters and even more so of the entire electorate. Although it is sometimes said that the two major parties do not present U.S. citizens with a "clear

TABLE 13.2

A Comparison of Delegates to the 1996 Presidential Nominating Conventions*

	DEMOCRATIC DELEGATES	REPUBLICAN DELEGATES	ALL VOTERS IN NOV. 1996 PRESIDENTIAL ELECTION
Ideology			
Liberal	36%	1%	21%
Moderate	47	19	46
Conservative	3	74	31
Age			
18–29	4%	2%	16%
30–39	12	14	21
40–59	60	52	38
60 and older	24	31	25
Race/Ethnicity			
White	67%	92%	81%
Black	21	2	11
Hispanic	6	2	4
Other	6	3	3
Labor Union			
Member	34%	2%	11%
Not a member	66	98	89
Sex			
Male	43%	61%	48%
Female	57	39	52

*Margin of sampling error is plus or minus 4.5 percentage points when figures do not include those who declined to answer the question; the margin of error is plus or minus 2 percentage points for all others. Other totals may not add up to 100 percent because of rounding.

Source: Figures in the first two columns are from a *Washington Post* telephone poll of 511 Republican delegates from July to August 1996, and 496 Democratic delegates from June to July. Figures in the last column are adapted from the Voter Research & Surveys (VRS) poll of 15,232 Americans as they exited from their voting booths on November 5, 1996. VRS is an association of ABC News, CNN, CBS News, and NBC News.

choice" of candidates, it is possible to argue the contrary. Our politics are perhaps too polarized, with the great majority of Americans, moderates and pragmatists overwhelmingly, left underrepresented by parties too fond of ideological purity.

The philosophical divergence is usually reflected in the party platforms, even in years such as 1996, when both parties attempted to water down their rhetoric and smooth over ideological differences (see Highlight 13.2: Selected Contrasts in the 1996 Party Platforms). (The Democrats did so in 1996; the Republicans have done so in earlier years, as in 1968.)

TABLE 13.3

Comparison of the Views of the Public with Those of Delegates to the 1996 Presidential Nominating Conventions*

Question: "I am going to read a few statements. After each, please tell me if you agree with the statement or disagree with it, or if, perhaps, you have no opinion about the statement." (Figures show percentage who agreed with the statement.)

	ALL VOTERS	DEMOCRATIC DELEGATES	DEMOCRATIC VOTERS	REPUBLICAN DELEGATES	REPUBLICAN VOTERS
A. A constitutional amendment to require a balanced federal budget.	82%	32%	77%	88%	87%
B. The death penalty for people convicted of murder.	76	48	67	88	88
C. Cut off public assistance payments a poor person can receive after a maximum of five years.	73	38	67	88	81
D. Ban the sale of most assault weapons.	73	93	78	47	67
E. Impose a five-year freeze on legal immigration.	59	15	57	29	65
F. Reduce spending on social programs.	55	20	44	84	71
G. Reduce spending on defense and the military.	44	65	47	11	29
H. Amend the U.S. Constitution to allow organized prayer in public schools.	66	19	66	50	73
I. Cancel affirmative action programs giving preference to women, blacks, and other minorities.	45	82	63	11	31
J. Bar illegal immigrants from public schools, hospitals, and other state-run social services.	48	16	36	65	61

*Margins of sampling error are plus or minus 5 percentage points for figures based on delegates (Republicans and Democrats) and 3 points for figures based on all voters.

Source: Figures are from a *Washington Post* telephone poll of Republican delegates August 11, 1996; Democratic delegates, August 25, 1996.

The Electoral College: How Presidents Are Elected

Given the enormous amount of energy, money, and time expended to nominate two major-party presidential contenders, it is difficult to believe that the general election could be more arduous than the nominating contests, but it usually is. The actual campaign for the presidency (and other offices) is described in chapter 14, but the object of the exercise is clear: winning a majority of the **electoral college.** This uniquely American institution consists of representatives of each state who cast the final ballots that actually elect a president.

The electoral college was the result of a compromise between Framers like Roger Sherman and Elbridge Gerry, who argued for selection of the president by the Con-

electoral college: Representatives of each state who cast the final ballots that actually elect a president.

Highlight 13.2

Selected Contrasts in the 1996 Party Platforms

DEMOCRATS	REPUBLICANS	DEMOCRATS	REPUBLICANS
State of the Economy		**Balanced Budget**	
"Today, America is moving forward. The economy is stronger, the deficit is lower, and the Government is smaller."	"We cannot go on like this. For millions of families, the American dream is fading."	Promise to balance the budget by 2002.	Support a constitutional amendment requiring a balanced budget.
Taxes		**Education**	
"America cannot afford to return to the era of something-for-nothing tax cuts." Support a "$500 tax cut for children" and additional reductions for college tuition payments, small businesses, and the self-employed. Allow money in individual retirement accounts to be used to buy a first home and to pay education and medical expenses.	Support a 15 percent reduction in tax rates, a $500-per-child tax credit, a 50 percent cut in the capital gains rate, expansion of I.R.A.'s, and lower taxes on Social Security benefits. These are "interim steps toward comprehensive tax reform." The Internal Revenue Service "must be dramatically downsized."	Support strengthening public schools.	Favor using federal money to help parents pay private school tuition.
		Homosexual Rights	
		Support efforts "to end discrimination against gay men and lesbians and further their full inclusion in the life of the nation."	"Reject the distortion" of civil rights laws that would "cover sexual preference."
		Trade	
Abortion		Insist that international trade agreements include standards to protect children, workers, and the environment.	Oppose using trade policy to pursue "social agenda items."
Support a woman's right to choose to have an abortion in all circumstances currently legal. "Respect the individual conscience of each American on this difficult issue."	Support a constitutional amendment that would outlaw abortion in all circumstances. No specific mention of tolerance for other views on abortion.	**Gun Control**	
		Support a waiting period for buying handguns and a ban on the sale of certain assault weapons.	"Defend the constitutional right to keep and bear arms" and favor mandatory penalties for crimes committed with guns.
Affirmative Action		**Arts and Broadcasting**	
"We should mend it, not end it."	"We will attain our nation's goal of equal rights without quotas or other forms of preferential treatment."	Favor public support of the arts and the Corporation for Public Broadcasting.	End federal financing for the arts and the Corporation for Public Broadcasting.
Immigration		**Environment**	
Permit the children of illegal immigrants to attend public schools; allow legal immigrants to receive welfare and other benefits; make it easier for eligible immigrants to become United States citizens.	Prohibit the children of illegal immigrants from attending public schools; restrict welfare to legal immigrants; support a constitutional amendment denying automatic citizenship to children born in the United States to illegal immigrants and legal immigrants who are in this country for a short time.	Emphasize government regulation to protect the environment.	Emphasize consideration of private property rights and economic development in conjunction with environmental protection.
		Star Wars	
		Oppose revival of the land-based missile defense system, known as Star Wars.	Favor development of the missile defense system.

Sources: 1996 Democratic and Republican Party Platforms.

gress, and those such as James Madison, James Wilson, and Gouverneur Morris, who favored selection by direct popular election. The electoral college compromise, while not a perfect solution, had practical benefits. Since there were no mass media in those days, it is unlikely that common citizens, even reasonably informed ones, would know much about a candidate from another state. This situation could have left voters with no choice but to vote for someone from their own state, thus making it improbable that any candidate would secure a national majority. On the other hand, the **electors** (members of the electoral college) would be men of character with a solid knowledge of national politics who were able to identify, agree on, and select prominent national statesmen. There are three essentials to understanding the Framers' design of the electoral college: (1) It was meant to work without political parties, (2) it was designed to cover both the nominating and electing phases of presidential selection, and (3) it was constructed to produce a nonpartisan president.

The machinery of the electoral college was somewhat complex. Each state designated electors (through appointment or popular vote) equal in number to the sum of its representation in the House and Senate. Figure 13.2 shows a map of the United

elector: Member of the electoral college chosen by methods determined in each state.

FIGURE 13.2

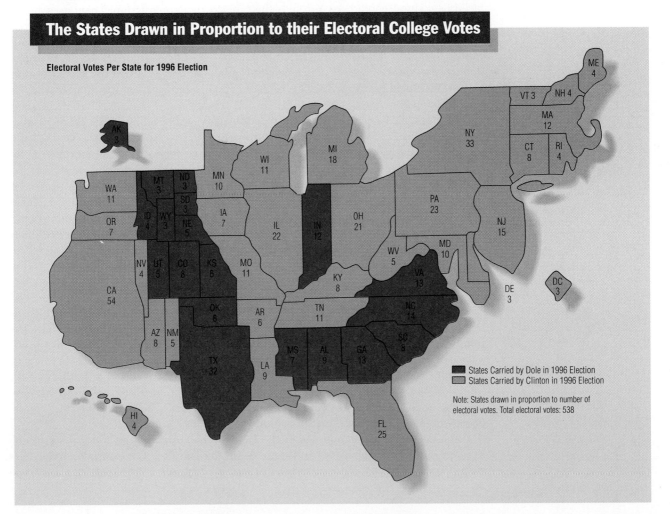

The States Drawn in Proportion to their Electoral College Votes

Electoral Votes Per State for 1996 Election

■ States Carried by Dole in 1996 Election
□ States Carried by Clinton in 1996 Election

Note: States drawn in proportion to number of electoral votes. Total electoral votes: 538

States drawn in proportion to their electoral college votes. The electors met in their respective states. Each elector had two votes for president, an attempt by the Founders to ensure that at least one candidate would secure a majority of electoral votes needed for victory. The candidate with the most votes, providing he received votes from a majority of the total number of electors, won the presidency; the candidate securing the second greatest number of votes won the vice presidency. If two candidates received the same number of votes and both had a majority of electors, the election was decided in the House of Representatives, with each state delegation acting as a unit and having one vote to cast. In the event that no candidate secured a majority, the election would also be decided in the House, with each state delegation having one vote to cast for any of the top five electoral vote-getters. In both of these scenarios, a majority of the total number of states was necessary to secure victory.

But the Framers' idea of nonpartisan presidential elections lasted barely a decade, ending for the most part after George Washington's two terms. In 1796 their arrangement for presidential selection produced a president and vice president with markedly different political philosophies, a circumstance much less likely in modern times.

The Election of 1800.   By the election of 1800, both of the two emerging national parties, the Federalists and the Democratic-Republicans, nominated presidential and vice-presidential candidates through their respective congressional caucuses before electors had even been chosen in the states. At the same time, the national parties were also gaining influence in the states, and this resulted in the selection of electors committed to their presidential and vice-presidential nominees. In other words, the once-deliberative electors lost their independent judgment and assumed the less important role of instructed party agents. This was, of course, a far cry from the nonpartisan system envisioned by the Founders.

The republic's fourth presidential election also revealed a flaw in the Framers' plan. In 1800, when Thomas Jefferson and Aaron Burr were, respectively, the Democratic-Republican Party's candidates for president and vice president, supporters of the Democratic-Republican Party controlled a majority of the electoral college. Accordingly, each Democratic-Republican elector in the states cast one of his two votes for Jefferson and the other one for Burr, a situation that resulted in a tie for the presidency between Jefferson and Burr, since there was no way under the constitutional arrangements for electors to earmark their votes separately for president and vice president. And even though most understood Jefferson to be the actual choice for president, the Constitution mandated that a tie be decided by the House of Representatives. And so it was, of course, and in Jefferson's favor, but only after much energy was expended to persuade lame-duck Federalists not to give Burr the presidency.

The Twelfth Amendment, ratified in 1804 and still the constitutional foundation for presidential elections, was an attempt to remedy the confusion between the selection of vice presidents and presidents that beset the election of 1800. The amendment provided for separate elections for each office, with each elector having only one vote to cast for each. In the event of a tie or when no candidate received a majority of the total number of electors, the election still went to the House of Representatives; now, however, each state delegation would have one vote to cast for one of the three candidates who had received the greatest number of electoral votes.

The electoral college modified by the Twelfth Amendment fared better than the college as originally designed, but it has not been problem-free. For example, in the 1824 election between John Quincy Adams and Andrew Jackson, neither presidential candidate secured a majority of electoral votes, once again throwing the election into the House. Despite the fact that Jackson had more electoral and popular votes than Adams, the House voted for the latter as president. On two other occasions in the nineteenth century, the presidential candidate with fewer popular votes than his opponent won the presidency. In the 1876 contest between Republican Rutherford B. Hayes and Democrat Samuel J. Tilden, no candidate received a majority of electoral votes; the House decided in Hayes's favor even though he had only one more (disputed) electoral vote and 250,000 fewer popular votes than Tilden. In the election of 1888, President Grover Cleveland secured about 100,000 more popular votes than did Benjamin Harrison, yet Harrison won a majority of the electoral college vote, and with it the presidency.

The Electoral College in the Twentieth Century.   Although generally more stable than the previous two centuries, the twentieth century has also witnessed a number of near crises pertaining to the electoral college. For instance, in the turbulent year of 1968, the possibility that the presidential election would be decided in the House increased considerably with the entrance into the race of third-party candidate George Wallace. And the election of 1976 was almost a repeat of those nineteenth-century contests in which the candidate with fewer popular votes won the presidency: Even though Democrat Jimmy Carter received about 1.7 million more popular votes than Republican Gerald Ford, a switch of some 8,000 popular votes in Ohio and Hawaii would have secured for Ford enough votes to win the electoral college, and hence the presidency. Had Ross Perot stayed in the 1992 presidential contest without his summer hiatus, it is possible that he could have thrown the election into the House of Representatives. His support had registered from 30 percent to 36 percent in the polls for much of the spring and early summer of 1992. When he reentered the race, some of that backing had evaporated, and he finished with 19 percent of the vote and carried no states. However, Perot drained a substantial number of Republican votes from George Bush, thus splitting the GOP base. This enabled Clinton to win many normally GOP-leaning states such as Georgia, Nevada, and Montana, although he carried them with well less than a majority of the votes.

(Left) Before the election of 1876, cartoonist Thomas Nast was quite confident that the Republican Party would easily trample Samuel Tilden and Thomas Hendricks, the Democratic nominees for president and vice president. (Right) After the election: Nast's elephant, battered and bandaged, moans with Pyrrhus, "Another such victory and I am undone." Hayes was elected by a margin of a single electoral vote. (Photos courtesy: The Bettmann Archive)

Patterns of Presidential Elections

The electoral college results reveal more over time than simply who won the presidency. They show which party and which region(s) are coming to dominance and how voters may be changing party allegiances in response to new issues and generational changes.

Party Realignments.   Usually such movements are gradual, but occasionally the political equivalent of a major earthquake swiftly and dramatically alters the landscape. During these rare events, called *party realignments,*[2] existing party affiliations are subject to upheaval: Many voters may change parties, and the youngest age group of voters may permanently adopt the label of the newly dominant party. Until recent times, at least, party realignments have been spaced about thirty-six years apart in the U.S. experience.

A major realignment is precipitated by one or more **critical elections,** which may polarize voters around new issues and personalities in reaction to crucial developments, such as a war or an economic depression. In Britain, for example, the first postwar election held in 1945 was critical, since it ushered the Labour Party into power for the first time and introduced to Britain a new interventionist agenda in the fields of economic and social welfare policies.

In the entire history of the United States, there have been six party alignments; three tumultuous eras in particular have produced significant critical elections (see Figure 13.3). First, during the period leading up to the Civil War, the Whig Party gradually dissolved and the Republican Party developed and won the presidency. Second, the populist radicalization of the Democratic Party in the 1890s enabled the Republicans to greatly strengthen their majority status and make lasting gains in voter attachments. Third, the Great Depression of the 1930s propelled the Democrats to power, causing large numbers of voters to repudiate the GOP and embrace the Democratic Party. In each of these cases, fundamental and enduring alterations in the party equation resulted.

The last confirmed major realignment, then, happened in the 1928–36 period, as Republican Herbert Hoover's presidency was held to one term because of voter anger about the Depression. In 1932 Democrat Franklin D. Roosevelt swept to power as the electorate decisively rejected Hoover and the Republicans. This dramatic vote of "no confidence" was followed by substantial changes in policy by the new president, who demonstrated in fact or at least in appearance that his policies were effective. The people responded to his success, accepted his vision of society, and ratified their choice of the new president's party in subsequent presidential and congressional elections.

Simultaneously, the former majority party (Republican) reluctantly but inevitably adjusted to its new minority role. So strong was the new partisan attachment for most voters that even when short-term issues and personalities that favored the Republican Party dislodged the Democrats from power, the basic distribution of party loyalties did not shift significantly. In 1952, 1956, 1968, and 1972, then, Republicans won the presidency, but the New Deal Democratic coalition was still visible in the voting patterns, and it survived to emerge again in future elections.

With the aid of timely circumstances, realignments are accomplished in two main ways.[3] Some voters are simply converted from one party to the other by the issues and candidates of the time. New voters may also be mobilized into action: Immigrants, young voters, and previous nonvoters may become motivated and then absorbed into

party realignment: A shifting of party coalition groupings in the electorate that remains in place for several elections.

critical election: An election that signals a party realignment through voter polarization around new issues.

FIGURE 13.3

Electoral College Results for Three Realigning Presidential Contests

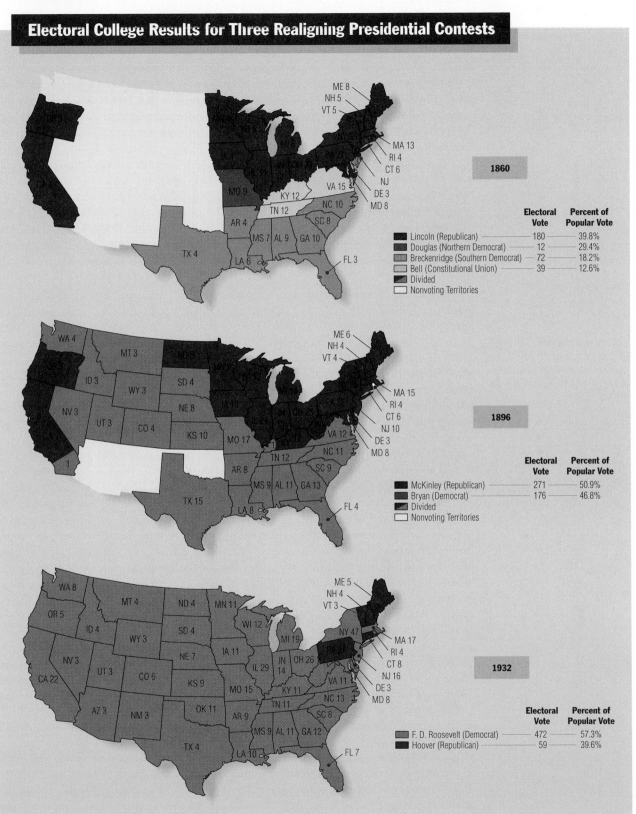

1860

	Electoral Vote	Percent of Popular Vote
Lincoln (Republican)	180	39.8%
Douglas (Northern Democrat)	12	29.4%
Breckenridge (Southern Democrat)	72	18.2%
Bell (Constitutional Union)	39	12.6%
Divided		
Nonvoting Territories		

1896

	Electoral Vote	Percent of Popular Vote
McKinley (Republican)	271	50.9%
Bryan (Democrat)	176	46.8%
Divided		
Nonvoting Territories		

1932

	Electoral Vote	Percent of Popular Vote
F. D. Roosevelt (Democrat)	472	57.3%
Hoover (Republican)	59	39.6%

a new governing majority. However vibrant and potent party coalitions may be at first, as they age, tensions increase and grievances accumulate. The majority's original reason for existing fades, and new generations neither remember the traumatic events that originally brought about the realignment nor possess the stalwart party identifications of their ancestors. New issues arise, producing conflicts that can be resolved only by a breakup of old alignments and a reshuffling of individual and group party loyalties. Viewed in historical perspective, party realignment has been a mechanism that ensures stability by controlling unavoidable change.

A critical realigning era is by no means the only occasion when changes in partisan affiliation are accommodated. In truth, every election produces realignment to some degree, since some individuals are undoubtedly pushed to change parties by events and by their reactions to the candidates. Recent research suggests that partisanship is much more responsive to current issues and personalities than had been believed earlier, and that major realignments are just extreme cases of the kind of changes in party loyalty registered every year.[4]

Secular Realignment.   Although the term *realignment* is usually applied only if momentous events such as war or depression produce enduring and substantial alterations in the party coalitions, political scientists have long recognized that a more gradual rearrangement of party coalitions could occur.[5] Called **secular realignment,** this piecemeal process depends not on convulsive shocks to the political system, but on slow, almost barely discernable demographic shifts—the shrinking of one party's base of support and the enlargement of the other's, for example—or simple generational replacement (that is, the dying off of the older generation and the maturing of the younger generation). A recent version of this theory, termed "rolling realignment,"[6] argues that in an era of weaker party attachments (such as we currently are experiencing), a dramatic, full-scale realignment may not be possible. Still, a critical mass of voters may be attracted for years to one party's banner in waves or streams, if that party's leadership and performance are consistently exemplary.

Some scholars and political observers also contend that the decline of party affiliation has in essence left the electorate dealigned and incapable of being realigned as long as party ties remain tenuous for so many voters. Voters shift with greater ease between the parties during dealignment, but little permanence or intensity exists in identifications made and held so lightly. If nothing else, the obsolescence of realignment theory may be indicated by the calendar; if major realignments occur roughly every thirty-six years, then we are long overdue. The last major realignment took place between 1928 and 1936, and so the next one might have been expected in the late 1960s and early 1970s.

As the trends toward ticket-splitting, partisan independency, and voter volatility suggest, there is little question that we have been moving through an unstable and somewhat "dealigned" period at least since the 1970s. The foremost political question today is whether dealignment will continue (and in what form) or whether a major realignment is in the offing. Each previous dealignment has been a precursor of realignment,[7] but realignment need not succeed dealignment, especially under modern conditions.

Clearly, major changes in the U.S. electorate have been occurring, but these changes may or may not constitute a major critical realignment of party balance. The Democrats are not the dominant party they once were, but the GOP has not obtained majority status, either. The struggle between the parties for dominance continues, and the outcome is as yet uncertain.

secular realignment: The gradual rearrangement of party coalitions, based more on demographic shifts than on shocks to the political system.

CONGRESSIONAL ELECTIONS

*M*any similar elements are present in different kinds of elections: Candidates, voters, issues, and television advertisements are constants. But there are distinctive aspects of each kind of election as well. Compared with presidential elections, congressional elections are a different animal.

First, most candidates for Congress labor in relative obscurity. While there are some celebrity nominees for Congress—television stars, sports heroes, even local TV news anchors—the vast majority of party nominees are little-known state legislators and local office holders. For them, just getting known, establishing name identification, is the biggest battle. No major-party presidential nominee need worry about this elementary stage because so much media attention is focused on the race for the White House. This is not so for most congressional contests; elections for spots in the House of Representatives receive remarkably little coverage in many states and communities.

The Incumbency Advantage

Under these circumstances the advantages of **incumbency** (that is, already being in office) are enhanced, and a kind of electoral inertia takes hold: Those people in office tend to remain in office. Every year the average member of the U.S. House of Representatives expends about $750,000 in taxpayer funds to run the office. Much of this money directly or indirectly promotes the legislator by means of mass mailings and *constituency services,* the term used to describe a wide array of assistance provided by a member of Congress to voters in need (for example, tracking a lost Social Security check, helping a veteran receive disputed benefits, or finding a summer internship for a college student). In addition to these institutional means of self-promotion, most incumbents are highly visible in their districts. They have easy access to local media, cut ribbons galore, attend important local funerals, and speak frequently at meetings and community events. Nearly a quarter of the people in an average congressional district claim to have met their representative, and about half recognize their legislator's name without prompting. This spending and visibility pay off: reelection rates for sitting House members range well above 90 percent in most election years.

Frequently, the reelection rate for senators is as high, but not always. In a "bad" year for House incumbents, "only" 88 percent will win (as in the Watergate year of 1974), but the senatorial reelection rate can drop much lower on occasion (to 60 percent in the 1980 Reagan landslide, for example). There is a good reason for this lower senatorial reelection rate. A Senate election is often a high-visibility contest; it receives much more publicity than a House race. So while House incumbents remain protected and insulated in part because few voters pay attention to their little-known challengers, a Senate-seat challenger can become well known more easily and thus be in a better position to defeat an incumbent.

Incidentally, the 1994 congressional elections are yet another example of the power of incumbency. The press focused on the Republican takeover of both houses of Congress, naturally enough, but another perspective is provided by the reelection rates for incumbents. More than 90 percent of the sitting representatives and senators who sought reelection won another term, despite electoral conditions that were termed a tidal wave.

incumbency: The condition of already holding elected office.

Redistricting, Scandals, and Coattails

For the relatively few incumbent members of Congress who do lose their reelection bids, three explanations are paramount: redistricting, scandals, and coattails. Every ten years, after the census, all congressional district lines are redrawn (in states with more than one congressperson) so that every legislator represents about the same number of citizens. Redistricting inevitably puts some incumbents in the same districts as other incumbents, and weakens the base of other congresspersons by adding territory favorable to the opposition party. In 1992 ten incumbents were paired together—five therefore lost—and about a dozen more incumbents were defeated in part because of unfavorable redistricting.

Scandals come in many varieties in this age of the investigative press. The old standby of financial impropriety (bribery and payoffs, for example) has been supplemented by other forms of career-ending incidents, such as personal improprieties (sexual escapades, for instance). The power of incumbency is so strong, however, that many legislators survive even serious scandal to win reelection. Congressman Barney Frank (D–Mass.), for instance, an acknowledged homosexual, hired a male prostitute who ran a prostitution service out of Frank's apartment in Washington. This situation became public knowledge in 1989. Though Frank claimed ignorance of the man's activities, he admitted having some of his parking tickets "fixed." Despite the sordid nature of this arrangement, most of Frank's constituents were satisfied with his representation of them and easily reelected him in 1990 and continued to reelect him.

The defeat of a congressional incumbent can also occur as a result of the presidential coattail effect. As Table 13.4 shows, successful presidential candidates usually

TABLE 13.4

Congressional Election Results, 1948–1996

GAIN (+) OR LOSS (–) FOR PRESIDENT'S PARTY

Presidential Election Years			Off-Year Elections		
President/Year	House	Senate	Year	House	Senate
Truman (D): 1948	+76	+9	1950	−29	−6
Eisenhower (R): 1952	+24	+2	1954	−18	−1
Eisenhower (R): 1956	−2	0	1948	−48	−13
Kennedy (D): 1960	−20	−2	1962	−4	+3
Johnson (D): 1964	+38	+2	1966	−47	−4
Nixon (R): 1968	+7	+5	1970	−12	+2
Nixon (R): 1972	+13	−2	Ford: 1974	−48	−5
Carter (D): 1976	+2	0	1978	−15	−3
Reagan (R): 1980	+33	+12	1982	−26	+1
Reagan (R): 1984	+15	−2	1986	−5	−8
Bush (R): 1988	−3	−1	1990	−9	−1
Clinton (D): 1992	−10	0	1994	−52	−9*
Clinton (D): 1996	+10	−2			

*Includes the switch from Democrat to Republican of Alabama U.S. Senator Richard Shelby.

carry into office congressional candidates of the same party in the year of their election. Notice the overall decline in the strength of the coattail effect in modern times, however, as party identification has weakened and the powers and perks of incumbency have grown. Whereas Harry S Truman's party gained seventy-six House seats and nine additional Senate seats in 1948, George Bush's party actually lost three House seats and one Senate berth in 1988, despite Bush's handsome 54 percent majority. The gains can be minimal even in presidential landslide reelection years, such as 1972 (Nixon) and 1984 (Reagan). Occasionally, though, when the issues are emotional and the voters' desire for change is strong enough, as in Reagan's original 1980 victory, the coattail effect can still be substantial.

Off-Year Elections

Elections in the middle of presidential terms, **off-year elections,** present a different threat to incumbents. This time it is the incumbents of the president's party who are most in jeopardy. Just as the presidential party usually gains seats in presidential election years, it usually loses seats in off years. The problems and tribulations of governing normally cost a president some popularity, alienate key groups, or cause the public to want to send the president a message of one sort or another. An economic downturn or a scandal can underline and expand this circumstance, as the Watergate scandal of 1974 and the recession of 1982 demonstrated.

What is most apparent from the off-year statistics of Table 13.3, however, is the frequent tendency of voters to punish the president's party much more severely in the sixth year of an eight-year presidency, a phenomenon associated with retrospective voting (1958, 1966, 1974).[8] After only two years, voters are still willing to "give the guy a chance"; but after six years, voters are often restless for change. (Interestingly, for the first time in this century, the United States in 1994 experienced a "sixth-year itch" in the second year of a presidency, such was the dissatisfaction with the Clinton Administration.) Finally, as the table shows, Senate elections are less inclined to follow these rules than are House elections. The idiosyncratic nature of Senate contests is due to both their intermittent scheduling (only one-third of the seats come up for election every two years) and the existence of well-funded, well-known candidates who can sometimes swim against whatever political tide is rising. Also worth remembering is that midterm elections in recent history have a much lower voter turnout than presidential elections. As Figure 13.4 shows, a midterm election may draw only 35 percent to 40 percent of adult Americans to the polls, while a presidential contest attracts between 50 percent and 55 percent. (1996 was obviously an exception, producing the lowest voter turnout in a presidential general election since 1924).

The 1994 Midterm Congressional Elections

As noted, the 1994 congressional elections were extraordinary, a massacre for the Democrats and a dream come true for the Republicans. Not since Harry Truman's loss in 1946 had a Democratic president lost both houses of Congress in a midterm election; but such was President Clinton's fate. For the first time since popular elections for the U.S. Senate began in the early 1900s, the entire freshman Senate class (that is, all newly elected Senators) was Republican. Moreover, every incumbent House member, senator, and governor who was defeated for reelection was a Democrat. Even the House Speaker, Thomas Foley (D–Wa.), fell in the onslaught. Republican George Nethercutt became the first person to unseat a House Speaker since 1862.

off-year election: Election that takes place in the middle of a presidential term.

FIGURE 13.4

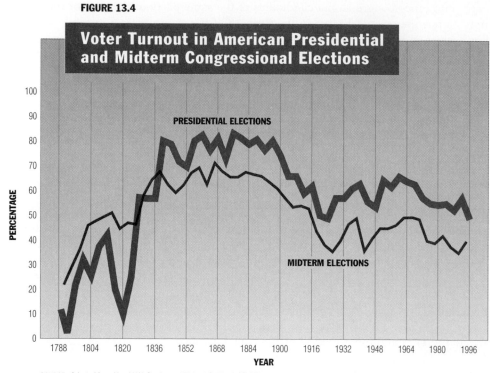

Voter Turnout in American Presidential and Midterm Congressional Elections

SOURCE: Adopted from Harold W. Stanley and Richard G. Niemi, *Vital Statistics on American Politics,* 3rd ed. (Washington: CQ Press, 1992), Figure 3-1, p. 85.

Republicans had just as much success at the state level. The GOP took control of nineteen houses in state legislatures, securing a majority of the legislative bodies. From just nineteen governors before the election, Republicans wound up with thirty governorships, including eight of the nine largest. (Only Florida, which reelected Democratic governor Lawton Chiles, resisted the trend.)

Where did the GOP margins at the polls come from? Men voted strongly Republican, overwhelming women's narrow preference for Democrats. Whites cast 58 percent of their ballots for the GOP, overwhelming the 88 percent of African Americans and 70 percent of Hispanics who voted Democratic. Americans who backed Ross Perot in 1992 also shifted heavily to the GOP column in 1994. And the once solidly Democratic South continued a decades-long trend toward the Republican party. For the first time since Reconstruction, the GOP captured a majority of all Southern U.S. House seats, Senate seats, and governorships.

All across the United States, but in the South in particular, voters seemed to be rejecting the Clinton presidency. Of the majority of Americans who disapproved of Clinton's performance as president, 82 percent cast ballots for GOP candidates for Congress, according to the networks' exit poll on Election Day. In 1996, however, Clinton won in several Southern states, including Florida, Louisiana, Tennessee, and his home state, Arkansas. Republicans won all but two contested Senate seats, however, and a majority of House members from the South were Republican.

The 1996 Congressional Elections

While the 1994 congressional elections were extraordinary, the 1996 congressional elections were immediately dubbed the "Status-Quo" election by political observers.

TABLE 13.5

Results of Some 1996 Key Races

STATE	CONTEST	WINNER	LOSER	SIGNIFICANCE
New Jersey	U.S. Senate	Rep. Robert G. Torricelli (D)	Rep. Dick Zimmer (R)	Torricelli secures seat vacated by retiring Sen. Bill Bradley (D) in what was called 1996's nastiest race.
Washington	Governor	Gary Locke (D)	Ellen Craswell (R)	Locke becomes the first Asian-American governor in the continental U.S.
North Carolina	U.S. Senate	Sen. Jesse Helms (R)	Harvey Gantt (D)	Former Charlotte, N.C. mayor fails to win 1996 rematch with Helms.
Massachusetts	U.S. Senate	Sen. John F. Kerry (D)	Gov. William F. Weld (R)	Incumbent Kerry holds off strong challenge from popular Republican governor.
New Hampshire	Governor	State Sen. Jeanne Shaheen (D)	Ovide Lamontagne (R)	Shaheen secures seat vacated by retiring Gov. Steve Merrill (R), becomes the Granite State's first female governor.
Virginia	U.S. Senate	Sen. John Warner (R)	Mark Warner (D)	Incumbent John fights off challenge of deep-pocketed Mark (no relation).
Minnesota	U.S. Senate	Sen. Paul Wellstone (D)	Rudy Boschwitz (R)	1990 political novice Wellstone wins rematch with former Sen. Boschwitz.
Kansas	U.S. Senate	Rep. Sam Brownback (R)	Jill Docking (D)	Brownback keeps Senate seat held by Bob Dole in the Republican camp.
Georgia	U.S. Senate	Max Cleland (D)	Guy Millner (R)	Triple amputee Cleland wins despite being outspent 4 to 1.
Georgia	U.S. House of Representatives	Rep. Cynthia McKinney (D)	John Mitnick (R)	Incumbent survives even though her district had been redrawn.
Louisiana	U.S. Senate	Mary Landrieu (D)	Woody Jenkins (R)	Daughter of legendary New Orleans mayor, Landrieu becomes first woman elected to the Senate in Louisiana.
South Dakota	U.S. Senate	Tim Johnson (D)	Incumbent Larry Pressler (R)	Only incumbent senator to lose seat.

Far less hostile than they were in 1992, when voters ousted Republicans from the White House for the first time since 1976, and in 1994, when those same voters booted the Democrats from Capitol Hill, this time the White House, Senate, and House all remained in the previous proprietors' hands.

The 1996 election results confirmed pre-election conventional wisdom. In the U.S. House of Representatives, Democrats were able to knock off a handful of vulnerable Republican freshmen in states like Illinois, New York, North Carolina, Maine, and New Jersey. Republicans offset some of these losses by taking nine seats from Democrats, most of which had been relinquished by retiring Democratic lawmakers. In the Senate, Republicans posted a net gain of two seats. New GOP senators from Colorado, Kansas, Wyoming, Alabama, Arkansas, and Nebraska guaranteed a more conservative shift on the Republican side. In fact, after the election many speculated that Republican Majority Leader Trent Lott's Senate would prove to be more conservative than the Newt Gingrich led House of Representatives.

In the end, post-election exit polls confirmed that Americans decided to hedge their bets, deciding to parcel out power to both parties by reelecting Clinton while giving Re-

Though some might not deem his celebrity an advantage in winning and keeping office, Representative Sonny Bono (R-Calif.) has come a long way since the days of his television series "The Sonny and Cher Show" of the mid-1960s. Says Bono, "I'm good at reading an audience." (Photos courtesy: left, AP/Wide World Photos; right, Mark Wilson/AP Photo)

publicans a dominant voice on Capitol Hill. Though Clinton won a larger percentage of the popular vote in 1996 than he did in 1992, fully half of Clinton's supporters said they had serious reservations about voting for him. In effect then, the electorate said it was not yet willing to entrust the transition to a new century exclusively to either party. Whether or not this trend will hold in 1998 will be the subject of much speculation.

VOTING BEHAVIOR

*W*hether they are casting ballots in congressional or presidential elections, voters behave in certain distinct ways and exhibit unmistakable patterns to political scientists who study them.

Participation

turnout: The proportion of the voting-age public that votes.

Turnout is the proportion of the voting-age public that votes. The first clear division is between citizens who turn out and those who do not. About 40 percent of the eligible adult population in the United States vote regularly, whereas 25 percent are occasional voters. Thirty-five percent rarely or never vote.

There are many differences, including socioeconomic and attitudinal, between voters and nonvoters. First, people who vote are usually more highly educated than nonvoters. Other things being equal, college graduates are much more likely to vote than those with less education. People with more education tend to learn more about politics, are less hindered by registration requirements, and are more self-confident about their ability to affect public life. Therefore one might argue that institutions of higher education provide citizens with opportunities to learn about and become interested in politics.

Income

There is also a relationship between income and voting. A considerably higher percentage of citizens with annual incomes over $40,000 vote than do citizens with incomes under $10,000. Income level is, to some degree, connected to education level, as wealthier people tend to have more opportunities for higher education and more education also may lead to higher income. Wealthy citizens are also more likely than poor ones to think that the "system" works for them and that their votes make a difference.

By contrast, lower-income citizens often feel alienated from politics, possibly believing that conditions will remain the same no matter for whom they vote. A factor that contributes to this feeling of alienation is that American political parties, unlike parties in many other countries which tend to associate themselves with specific social classes, do not attempt to link themselves intimately to one major class (such as the "working class"). Therefore, the feelings of alienation and apathy about politics prevalent among many lower-income Americans should not be unexpected.

Age

There is also a correlation between age and voter participation rates. The Twenty-Sixth Amendment, ratified in 1971, lowered the voting age to eighteen. While this amendment obviously increased the number of *eligible* voters, it did so by enfranchising the group that is least likely to vote. A much higher percentage of citizens age thirty and older vote than do citizens younger than thirty, although voter turnout decreases over the age of seventy, primarily because of physical infirmity, which makes it difficult to get to the polling location. Regrettably, less than half of eligible eighteen- to twenty-four-year-olds are even registered to vote. The most plausible reason for this is that younger people are more mobile; they have not put down roots in a community. Because voter registration is not automatic, people who relocate have to make an effort to register. Therefore the effect of adding this low-turnout group to the electorate has been to lower the overall turnout rate.

Race

Another voter difference is related to race: Whites vote more regularly than do blacks, though recently the proportions have been more nearly equal (64 percent of whites and 54 percent of blacks voted in 1992). This is due in part to the relative income and educational levels of the two racial groups. African Americans tend to be poorer and have less formal education than whites; and, as mentioned earlier, both of these factors affect voter turnout. Significantly, though, highly educated and wealthier African Americans are at least equally likely to vote, and sometimes more so, than whites of similar background.

Race also explains why the South has long had a lower turnout than the rest of the country (see Figure 13.5). In the wake of Reconstruction, the Southern states made it extremely difficult for African Americans to register to vote, and only a small percentage of the eligible African-American population was registered throughout the South. The Voting Rights Act of 1965 helped to change this situation, and gradually the South's voting participation has approached that of the rest of the nation, although the region still lags behind. (For more on voting rights, see Highlight 13.3.)

Interest in Politics

Although socioeconomic factors undoubtedly weigh heavily in voter participation rates, an interest in politics must also be included as an important factor. Many citizens who vote have grown up in families interested and active in politics, and they in

FIGURE 13.5

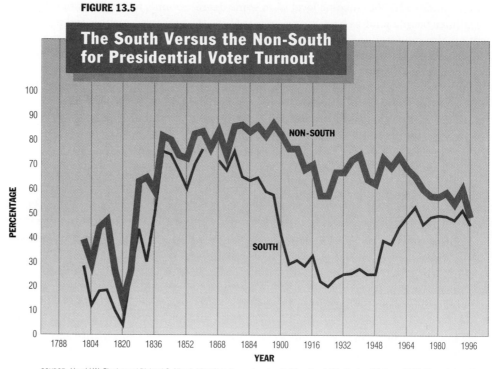

The South Versus the Non-South for Presidential Voter Turnout

SOURCE: Harold W. Stanley and Richard G. Niemi, *Vital Statistics on American Politics,* 4th ed. (Washington: CQ Press, 1993), Figure 3-2, p. 86.

turn stimulate their children to take an interest. Conversely, many nonvoters simply do not care about politics or the outcome of elections, never having been taught their importance at a younger age.

People who are highly interested in politics constitute only a small minority of the U.S. populace. For example, the most politically active Americans—party and issue-group activists—make up less than 5 percent of the country's 250 million people. And

Highlight 13.3

Voting Rights

Both the Civil Rights Act of 1964 and the Voting Rights Act of 1965 were intended to guarantee voting rights to African Americans nearly a century after passage of the Fifteenth Amendment.

Since 1965, African-American voters have used their strength at the ballot box to elect black officials at all levels of government. But while the results have been encouraging, the percentage of elected offices held by African Americans in the eleven Southern states covered by the Voting

Rights Act remains relatively small.

Today, the impact of these Acts tends to be felt most often in the courtroom. In each decade since their passage, both the Civil and Voting Rights Acts have either been invoked or challenged by individuals eager to prove

that their tenets have not been properly adhered to or the Acts are unconstitutional. The Civil Rights and Voting Rights Acts of the 1960s then remain a controversial symbol of our nation's tumultuous racial past.

those who contribute time or money to a party or a candidate during a campaign make up only about 10 percent of the total population. On the other hand, although these percentages appear low, they translate into millions of Americans who contribute more than just votes to the system.

Why Is Voter Turnout So Low?

There is no getting around the fact that the United States has one of the lowest voter participation rates of any nation in the industrialized world, and it has declined somewhat. Only 55 percent of the eligible electorate (that is, those age eighteen and over) voted in the 1992 general presidential election, compared with 62 percent in 1960. This downward trend continued in 1996, when an estimated 48.8 percent of eligible voters cast a ballot, producing the lowest general presidential election turnout since 1824. In contrast, turnout for British postwar elections has fluctuated between 72 percent and 84 percent. Table 13.6 lists several reasons for low voter turnout in the United States.

Difficulty of Registration. Interestingly, of those who are registered, the overwhelming majority vote. The real source of the participation problem in the United States seems to be that a relatively low percentage of the adult population is registered to vote. There are a number of reasons for the low U.S. registration rates. First, while nearly every other democratic country places the burden of registration on the government rather than on the individual, in the United States the registration process requires individual initiative—a daunting impediment in this age of political apathy. Thus the cost (in terms of time and effort) of registering to vote is higher in the United States than it is in other industrialized democracies. Second, many nations automatically register all of their citizens to vote. In the United States, however, citizens must jump the extra hurdle of remembering on their own to register. Indeed, it is no coincidence that voter participation rates dropped markedly after reformers pushed through strict voter registration laws in the early part of the twentieth century.

Difficulty of Absentee Voting. Stringent absentee ballot laws are another factor in the United States' low voter turnout. Many states, for instance, require citizens to apply in person for absentee ballots, a burdensome requirement given that one's inability to be present in his or her home state is often the reason for absentee balloting in the first place.

Number of Elections. Another explanation for low voter turnout in this country is the sheer number and frequency of elections, which few if any other democracies can

In 1992, MTV and Rock the Vote, a Santa Monica-based voter registration campaign, registered approximately 350,000 college students. In 1996, the campaign sported a red, white, and blue bus covered with quotes from President Harry S Truman to Snoop Doggy Dogg. "Choose or Lose" was also in evidence at the Republican National Convention in August. (Photo courtesy: Gillles Mingasson/Gamma-Liaison)

TABLE 13.6

Why People Don't Vote

1. Did not register	42%	7. Are new residents in area	4%
2. Do not like the candidates	17%	8. Are away from home	3%
3. No particular reason	10%	9. Cannot leave job	3%
4. Are sick or disabled	8%	10. Cannot get to polls	1%
5. Are not U.S. citizens	5%	11. Other	2%
6. Are not interested in politics	5%		

match. Yet an election cornucopia is the inevitable result of federalism and the separation of powers, which result in layers of often separate elections on the local, state, and national levels.

Voter Attitudes.   Although some of the reasons for low voter participation are due to the institutional factors we have just reviewed, voter attitudes play an equally important part. Some nations try to get around the effects of voter attitudes with compulsory voting laws (Australia and Belgium), or by taxing citizens who do not vote. Not surprisingly, voter turnout rates in Australia and Belgium are often greater than 95 percent.

As noted previously, alienation afflicts some voters, and others are just plain apathetic, possibly because of a lack of pressing issues in a particular year, satisfaction with the status quo, or uncompetitive (even uncontested) elections. Furthermore, many citizens may be turned off by the quality of campaigns in a time when petty issues and personal mudslinging are more prevalent than ever. Finally, perhaps turnout has declined due to rising levels of distrust of government. More and more people are telling pollsters that they lack confidence in political leaders. In the past some scholars argued that there is no correlation between distrust of political leaders and nonvoting. But as the levels of distrust rise, these preliminary conclusions might need to be revisited.

Weak Political Parties.   Political parties today are no longer as effective as they once were in mobilizing voters, ensuring that they are registered, and getting them to the polls. As we discussed in chapter 12, the parties once were grassroots organizations which forged strong party-group links with their supporters. Today these bonds have been stretched to the breaking point for many. Candidate-centered campaigns and the growth of expansive party bureaucracies have resulted in a somewhat more distant party with which most people do not identify very strongly.

How Can the United States Improve Voter Turnout?

Reformers have suggested many ideas to increase voter turnout in the United States. Always on the list is raising the political awareness of young citizens, a reform

A state registry of motor vehicles worker displays the form that makes it easy for those visiting the registry also to register to vote. (Photo courtesy: Dennis Brack/Black Star)

that inevitably must involve our nation's schools. No less important, and perhaps simpler to achieve, are the institutional reforms, though many of these reforms, if enacted, may result in only a marginal increase in turnout.

Easier Registration and Absentee Voting.   Registration laws vary by state; but in every state except North Dakota, registration is required in order to vote. Many observers believe that voter turnout could be increased if registering to vote were made simpler for citizens. The typical thirty-days-before-an-election registration deadline could be shortened to a week or ten days. After all, most people become more interested in voting as Election Day nears. Better yet, all U.S. citizens could be registered automatically at the age of eighteen. Absentee ballots could also be made easier to obtain by eliminating the in-person requirement.

In 1993 a major advance toward easier registration was achieved with the passage by Congress of the so-called motor-voter bill, which required states to permit individuals to register by mail, not just in person (see Politics Now: The Motor-Voter Law). The law, strongly backed by President Clinton, also allows citizens to register to vote when they visit any motor vehicles office, public assistance agency, or military recruitment division. Proponents of the law say it will result in the registration of the roughly 49 million Americans of voting age with driver's licenses or identification cards but who have failed to register to vote. Opponents claim the new law is yet another in a long line of intrusive and costly federal mandates that do not appropriate money to pay for the costs involved in implementing the programs. The motor-voter bill took effect in 1995, so it will be some time before we know how many people it will add to the registration rolls.

In an effort to improve voter turnout, Oregon allowed voters either to mail in their ballots or to deliver them to one of several dropoff locations. In 1996 this led to some delays in voting when over 20 percent of voters opted to mail their ballots. (Photo courtesy: Shane Young/AP Photo)

Politics Now

The Motor-Voter Law

The national Voter Registration Act, more commonly referred to as the "motor-voter" law, is so named because its main provision requires states to provide voter registration forms to citizens applying for or renewing their driver's licenses. It was passed by Congress in May 1993 after five long years of partisan battles in which Democrats generally favored it and Republicans opposed it. The legislation took effect on January 1, 1995, and also required states to provide registration through the mail and at certain agencies that provide public assistance.

Though we have yet to see the dramatic rise in the number or registered voters promised by defenders of the "motor-voter" law, supporters of the legislation estimate that an additional 50 million citizens will eventually be registered to vote as a result of the law. The opponents contend that the measure will increase the likelihood of voter fraud and will cost states too much to implement. Republicans also suspected the law was politically inspired to register more inner-city Democrats.

Initially, thirteen states (including California and Virginia) refused to comply with the law's provisions, citing financial burdens and states' rights. Some took their challenge to various courts, maintaining that the motor-voter law infringed on their Tenth Amendment right to govern their own affairs. The Amendment states that "The powers not delegated to the United States by the Constitution, nor prohibited by it to the States, are reserved to the States respectively, or to the people." These court challenges failed and now each of these states is slowly implementing the motor-voter law.

Where do you stand on this issue? Should voter registration procedures be eased, as the law provides? Or does this mandated registration infringe on state sovereignty?

Make Election Day a Holiday. Besides removing an obstacle to voting (the busy workday), making Election Day a holiday might focus more voter attention on the contests in the critical final hours.

Strengthen Parties. Reformers have long argued that strengthening the political parties would increase voter turnout, because parties have historically been the organizations in the United States best suited for and most successful at mobilizing citizens to vote. During the late 1800s and early 1900s, the country's "Golden Age" of powerful political parties, one of their primary activities was getting out the vote on Election Day. And even today, the parties' Election Day get-out-the-vote drives increase voter turnout by as many as several million in national contests.

Other Suggestions. Other ideas to increase voter turnout are less practical or feasible. For example, holding fewer elections might sound appealing, but it is difficult to see how this could be accomplished without diluting many of the central tenets of federalism and separation of powers that the Founders believed essential to the protection of liberty.

Does Low Voter Turnout Matter?

Some political observers have argued that nonvoting is not a critical problem. For example, some feel that the preferences of nonvoters are not much different from those who do vote. If this is true, the results would be about the same if everyone voted. Others contend that since legal and extralegal denial of the vote to previously disfranchised groups—African Americans, women, Hispanics, people over eighteen—have now been outlawed, nonvoting is voluntary. By choosing not to vote, these individuals are said to be indicating their acceptance of things as they are. Therefore we should not attempt to make it easier for these people, often characterized as apathetic and lazy, to vote. Finally, some even claim that low voter turnout is a positive benefit, based on the dubious supposition that less-educated people are more easily swayed. Thus low turnout supposedly increases the stability of the system and discourages demagogic, populist appeals.

We should not be too quick to accept these arguments, which have much in common with the early nineteenth-century view that the Nineteenth Amendment to the Constitution (which enfranchised women) need not be passed because husbands could protect the interests of their wives. First, the social makeup and attitudes of present-day nonvoters are significantly different from those of voters. Nonvoters tend to be low income, younger, blue collar, less educated, and more heavily minority. Even if their expressed preferences about politics do not look very distinctive, their objective circumstances as well as their need for government services differ from the majority of those who do vote. These people—those who require the most help from government—currently lack a fair share of electoral power. A political system that actively seeks to include and mobilize these people might well produce broader-based policies that differ from those we have today.

A New Voting Pattern: Ticket-Splitting

ticket-splitting: Voting simultaneously for candidates of both parties for different offices.

An important voting trend cannot be ignored among citizens who do cast their ballots. Citizens have been increasingly deserting their party affiliations in the polling booths. The practice of **ticket-splitting**, voting simultaneously for candidates of both parties for different offices, has soared dramatically.

The evidence of this development abounds. As already reviewed in this chapter, Republican presidential landslides in 1956, 1972, 1980, and 1984 were accompanied by the election of substantial Democratic majorities in the House of Representatives. Divided government, with the presidency held by one party and one or both houses of Congress held by the other party, has never been as frequent in U.S. history as it has been recently. From 1920 to 1944, about 15 percent of the congressional districts voted for presidential and House candidates of different parties. But from 1960 to 1996, at least 25 percent of the districts cast split tickets in any presidential year; and in 1984 nearly 50 percent of the districts did so. Similarly, at the statewide level, only 17 percent of the states electing governors in presidential years between 1880 and 1956 elected state and national executives from different parties. Yet from 1960 to 1992, almost 40 percent of states holding simultaneous presidential and gubernatorial elections recorded split results. (In 1992 and 1996, this proportion was somewhat lower, just 25 percent and 27 percent respectively.)

These percentages actually understate the degree of ticket-splitting by individual voters. The Gallup Poll has regularly asked its respondents, "For the various political offices, did you vote for all the candidates of one party, that is, a straight ticket, or did you vote for the candidates of different parties [ticket-splitting]?" Since 1968 the proportion of voters who have ticket-split in presidential years has consistently been around 60 percent of the total.[9] Other polls and researchers have found reduced straight-ticket balloting and significant ticket-splitting at all levels of elections, especially since 1952.

Not surprisingly, the intensity of party affiliation is a major determinant of a voter's propensity to split the ticket. Strong party identifiers are the most likely to cast a straight-party ballot; pure independents are the least likely. Somewhat greater proportions of ticket-splitters are found among high-income and better-educated citizens, but there is little difference in the distribution by gender or age. African Americans exhibit the highest straight-party rate of any population subgroup; about three-quarters of all black voters stay in the Democratic Party column from the top to the bottom of the ballot.

There are a number of explanations for the modern increase in ticket-splitting, many of them similar to the perceived causes of the dip in party identification levels (see chapter 12). The growth of issue-oriented politics, the mushrooming of single-interest groups, the greater emphasis on candidate-centered personality politics, and broader-based education are all often cited. A strong independent presidential candidacy such as Ross Perot's also helps to loosen party ties among many voters. So, too, does the marked gain in the value of incumbency. Thanks in part to the enormous fattening of congressional constituency services, incumbent U.S. representatives and senators have been able to attract a steadily increasing share of the other party's identifiers.[10] Therefore divided government, today's norm, should remain the norm until and unless strong partisan identification becomes prevalent.

CHANGING THE ELECTORAL PROCESS

*M*ost proposals for electoral reform center on the electoral college, starting with the faithless elector, that is, the elector who does not vote for the candidate to whom he or she is committed. In the twentieth century alone, electors have been faithless in seven elections: 1948, 1956, 1960, 1968, 1972, 1976, and 1988. In 1960 Alabama and Mississippi harkened back to the original design of the electoral college by electing a considerable number of "unpledged" electors, rather than supporting either Democrat John F. Kennedy or Republican Richard M. Nixon.

Electors in about half the states are required by law to cast a ballot for the presidential and vice-presidential candidates who win the most votes in the state. While some legal scholars have questioned the constitutionality of these laws, the Supreme Court has upheld them, though the laws are obviously difficult to enforce. Any law to remedy the problem of the faithless elector would therefore have to be in the form of a constitutional amendment, either mandating that electors vote for the candidate who wins a state's popular vote or removing altogether the office of elector and automatically awarding a state's electoral votes to the winner of its popular vote.

Other proposals for reforming the electoral college include getting rid of it altogether, that is, holding a direct national election. Such a change would have three major consequences: First, the popular vote would be the only determinant for winning the presidency. Second, the slight advantage given to states with small populations under the electoral college would be eliminated. Currently, each state (from lightly populated Wyoming and Vermont and populous Rhode Island to California) is given the same two additional electoral votes on top of the votes it receives to match the number of representatives it sends to the U.S. House of Representatives. Third, more minor-party candidates would run, since they would no longer be encumbered by the winner-take-all rules of the states and could accumulate votes nationally. In order to preclude a candidate with only a small plurality of the popular vote from winning the election, however, any reasonable plan for a direct national contest would have to stipulate that the winner must receive a certain percentage of the popular vote (perhaps 40 percent), with a runoff election necessary between the top two contenders if no one secures that proportion. A constitutional amendment proposing this reform was passed by a wide margin in the House of Representatives in 1969. However, in a vote ten years later, the Senate failed to come up with the two-thirds majority needed to send the proposal on to the states for ratification.

Another possible electoral reform, one which focuses on the nomination rather than the general election stage of presidential elections, is the idea of holding a series of regional primaries throughout the United States during the first week of each month beginning in February of a presidential election year. Under this system the country would be divided into five regions: the Southeast, Southwest, Far West, Midwest, and Northeast. In December of the year prior to the presidential election, a lottery would be held to determine the order in which the regions would hold their nomination races, with all regional contests held on the first of every month from February through June. The goals of this reform would be twofold: First, to end the current "permanent campaign" by preventing candidates from "camping out" in Iowa and New Hampshire for one to two years in the hopes of winning or doing better-than-expected in these small, unrepresentative states. Second, some rational order would be imposed on the electoral process, allowing candidates to focus on each region's concerns and people in turn.

The final suggestion for reform to be touched on here deals with campaign finance. Ross Perot in 1992 and Steve Forbes in 1996, one a billionaire and the other close to it, were able to bypass all campaign finance laws because they were able to bankroll their respective bids for the presidency independent of federal matching funds. Consequently, they were freed of both the spending and contribution limits, limits that still applied to the other presidential hopefuls. While neither was successful, the inherent problems posed by these sorts of candidates are clear. In response, some have argued that should a Ross Perot or Steve Forbes enter future presidential contests, then those candidates who rely on matching funds to finance their campaigns should be freed of the proscribed spending and contribution limits. This would allow all the candidates

North—South

POLITICS AROUND THE WORLD

To be considered democratic, a country has to choose its leaders through free and competitive elections. That seems simple enough. In practice, however, how a country conducts its elections and counts its votes can have a tremendous bearing on the way its democracy operates— or doesn't, as the case may be.

The most important reason why the way elections are run matters is that the United States, Canada, and Mexico use different electoral systems. People in the United States, for instance, vote in a number of federal, state, and local offices, no single one of which fully determines who governs.

In Canada and other parliamentary systems, there is no such uncertainty. Only the elections for the House of Commons really matter. And then, as noted in the North–South features in chapters 7 and 8, people cast only one vote that counts—for the members of Parliament from their own constituency, or riding.

Recent Canadian elections also show us one of the quirks of any system (including the United States for the House and Senate) that relies on "first past the post" contests in single member districts. In 1993 three parties—the Progressive Conservatives, the Reform Party, and the Bloc Québecois—all won between 13 and 19 percent of the vote. The same could not be said for the number of seats they won. Reform and the Bloc Québecois won fifty-two and fifty-four seats, respectively, while the Conservatives were reduced to only two MPs. That's the case because the Conservative vote is spread evenly around most of the country, so it rarely comes close to winning individual seats. Support for the other two parties is regionally concentrated, so they come in first in many districts in those areas but get next to no votes elsewhere.

The situation is quite different in Mexico, though it, too, uses an electoral system that has a significant impact on how the number of votes cast are turned into seats in Congress. The country is divided into 300 single-member districts in which elections are run much as they are in Canada or the United States. The other 200 seats are allocated through proportional representation, which gives each party seats in rough proportion to the share of the vote it has won. Thus the PAN won about 20 percent of the vote in 1994 and ended up with 101 of the total of 500 seats in the House of Representatives. The proportional side of the electoral system will become even more important when the reforms adopted in late 1996 take effect.

A far more important part of the electoral process in Mexico, though, is the frequent allegation that neither are its elections run nor its votes counted fairly. Stories of corruption in Mexican elections abound. Loyal PRI voters are said to follow one of the battle cries of early-twentieth-century American urban machines—"Vote early and often." People known to oppose the PRI go to vote, only to discover they are not on the list of registered voters. Ballot boxes in opposition areas somehow disappear. And, most worrisome of all, through what some Mexicans call *alchimia electoral,* there has been widespread fraud in the counting of votes.

We cannot know exactly how much corruption there is. However, most observers are convinced that President Salinas fell far short of the slim majority he officially won in the 1988 elections. The PRI probably also needs fraud of one form or another to hold onto many state governments and its congressional majority. The 1996 reforms are also designed to make future elections more honest, although most analysts are skeptical enough, given the PRI's track record, that they doubt that the PRI will ever allow itself to "lose" an election honestly.

to compete on a more level financial playing field. Whether this specific reform is adopted or not, we can certainly expect campaign financing as we now know it to be reworked in some fashion sooner or later.

These possible reform ideas should convince you that although individual elections may sometimes be predictable, the electoral system in the United States is anything but static. New generations, and party-changers in older generations, constantly remake the political landscape. At least every other presidential election brings a change of administration and a focus on new issues. Every other year at least a few fresh personalities and perspectives infuse the Congress, as newly elected U.S. senators and representatives claim mandates and seek to shake up the established order. Each election year the same tumult and transformation can be observed in the fifty states and in thousands of localities.

The welter of elections may seem like chaos, but from this chaos comes the order and often explosive productivity of a democratic society. For the source of all change in the United States, just as Hamilton and Madison predicted, is the individual citizen who goes to the polls and casts a ballot.

SUMMARY

The explosion of elections we have experienced in over 200 years of voting has generated much good and some harm. But all of it has been done, as Hamilton insisted, "on the solid basis of the consent of the people." In our efforts to explain the complex and multilayered U.S. electoral system, we covered these points in this chapter:

1. The Purposes Served by Elections.

Regular elections guarantee mass political action and governmental accountability. They also confer legitimacy on regimes better than any other method of change.

2. Different Kinds of Elections.

When it comes to elections, the United States has an embarrassment of riches. There are various types of primary elections in the country, as well as general elections, initiatives, referenda, and recall elections. In presidential elections, primaries are sometimes replaced by caucuses, in which party members choose a candidate in a closed meeting, but recent years have seen fewer caucuses and more primaries.

3. Presidential Elections.

Variety aside, no U.S. election can compare to the presidential contest. This spectacle, held every four years, brings together all the elements of politics and attracts the most ambitious and energetic politicians to the national stage.

4. The Party Conventions.

No longer closed affairs dominated by deals cut in "smoke-filled rooms," today's conventions are more open made-for-television events in which the party platform is drafted and adopted, and the presidential ticket is formally nominated.

5. Congressional Elections.

Many similar elements are present in different kinds of elections: Candidates, voters, issues, and television advertisements are constants. But there are distinctive aspects of each kind of election as well. Compared with presidential elections, congressional elections are a different animal.

6. Voting Behavior.

Whether they are casting ballots in congressional or presidential elections, voters behave in certain distinct ways and exhibit unmistakable patterns to political scientists who study them.

7. Changing the Electoral Process.

Most proposals for electoral reform center on the electoral college, a group chosen by the voters of each state to elect the president of the United States. Other possible reform ideas are regional primaries and campaign finance reform.

KEY TERMS

blanket primary, p. 499

closed primary, p. 498

critical election, p. 516

elector, p. 513

electoral college, p. 511

electorate, p. 496

front-loading, p. 502

general election, p. 499

incumbency, p. 519

initiative, p. 499

mandate, p. 496

off-year election, p. 521

open primary, p. 498

party realignment, p. 516

primary election, p. 498

prospective judgment, p. 496

recall, p. 499

referendum, p. 499

regional primary, p. 501

retrospective judgment, p. 496

runoff primary, p. 499

secular realignment, p. 518

superdelegate, p. 507

ticket-splitting, p. 530

turnout, p. 524

unit rule, p. 505

SELECTED READINGS

Bartels, Larry M. *Presidential Primaries and the Dynamics of Public Choice.* Princeton, NJ: Princeton University Press, 1988.

Berelson, Bernard R., Paul F. Lazarsfeld, and William N. McPhee. *Voting: A Study of Opinion Formation in a Presidential Campaign.* Chicago: University of Chicago Press, 1954.

Burnham, Walter Dean. *Critical Elections and the Mainsprings of American Politics.* New York: Norton, 1970.

Campbell, Angus, Philip E. Converse, Warren E. Miller, and Donald E. Stokes. *The American Voter.* New York: Wiley, 1960.

Carroll, Susan J., *Women as Candidates in American Politics.* Bloomington: Indiana University Press, 1994.

Ceaser, James W. *Upside Down and Inside Out: The 1992 Elections and American Politics.* Lanham, Md.: Rowman & Littlefield, 1993.

Conway, M. Margaret. *Political Participation in the United States,* 2d ed. Washington, D.C.: CQ Press, 1990.

Fiorina, Morris P. *Retrospective Voting in American National Elections.* New Haven, CT: Yale University Press, 1981.

Jacobson, Gary C. *The Politics of Congressional Elections,* 3rd ed. New York: Harper Collins, 1992.

———. *The Electoral Origins of Divided Government.* Boulder, CO: Westview Press, 1990.

Key, V. O., Jr., with the assistance of Milton C. Cummings. *The Responsible Electorate.* Cambridge, MA: Harvard University Press, 1966.

Nie, Norman H., Sidney Verba, and John R. Petrocik. *The Changing American Voter.* Cambridge, MA: Belknap Press of Harvard University, 1976.

Polsby, Nelson W., and Aaron Wildavsky. *Presidential Elections: Strategies and Structures of American Politics,* 7th ed. Chatham, NJ: Chatham House, 1996.

Sundquist, James L. *Dynamics of the Party System: Alignment and Realignment of Political Parties in the United States.* Washington, D.C.: Brookings Institution, 1983.

Teixeira, Ruy. *The Disappearing American Voter.* Washington, D.C.: Brookings Institution, 1992.

Verba, Sidney, Norman H. Nie, and Jae-on Kim. *Participation and Political Equality.* Cambridge, England: Cambridge University Press, 1978.

Verba, Sidney, Kay Lehman Schlozman and Henry E. Brady, *Voice and Equality: Civic Voluntarism in American Politics.* Cambridge: Harvard University Press, 1995.

Wayne, Stephen J. *The Road to the White House,* 6th ed. New York: St. Martin's Press, 1997.

(Photo courtesy: Vince Bucci/AP Photo)

THE CAMPAIGN PROCESS

*I*n February 1996 Republican presidential candidates Robert Dole, Patrick J. Buchanan, Lamar Alexander, Malcolm S. "Steve" Forbes, Phil Gramm, Alan Keyes, Bob Dornan, and Maury Taylor participated in the first major contest of the nomination season, the Iowa caucus. President Bill Clinton, unopposed for the Democratic nomination, was also on hand. Nine months later, after a long and arduous primary and general election campaign process, a president was elected.

While the Iowa caucus and the New Hampshire primary mark the "official" beginning of the presidential selection process, long before these events take place the nomination campaign—or "invisible primary"—begins. The invisible primary is the term applied to the period leading up to the presidential primary season. Sometimes this informal primary period begins before the presidential aspirants announce their candidacies. Sometimes the invisible primary for the *next* election starts before the general election that officially ends the current election season. (In 1992, prior to the New Hampshire primary, the press was already naming likely 1996 Republican candidates. Similarly, in April 1996 the press began speculating about the possible presidential candidacies of New Jersey Governor Christine Todd Whitman, New York Governor George Pataki, and California Governor Pete Wilson, Republicans all, in the year 2000.) During the invisible primary, presidential hopefuls attempt to stock their financial war chests and win straw polls, the goal being to attract favorable media coverage and enhance their standing with the electorate—as measured by various polling organizations.

Running for president has become terribly expensive. With the recent advent of a front-loaded nominating season (described in chapter 13), candidates need to spend more money in more states early if they hope to have any chance of winning their party's nomination. In 1996 not only did Iowa and New Hampshire hold early primary contests, they were joined by Texas, Florida, Illinois, Michigan, California, New York, Ohio, and Pennsylvania. By the end of February 1996, Republican presidential hopeful Bob Dole, with only eight primary states behind him, had already spent $30.4 million of the $37 million limit on spending during the primaries by candidates who receive federal financing. During that same period Steve Forbes, one of Dole's chief rivals, spent $32.6 million, most of which came from his personal wealth. These totals, when combined with the amounts spent by the other Republican candidates, made the 1996 primary season the most expensive in campaign history. Only by gearing up for the official campaign season many years in advance of the first contest are candidates able to raise the funds necessary to campaign in many states at once. Those who successfully stock their financial coffers during the invisible primary tend to benefit from favorable media coverage and front-runner status in the polls, thus increasing their chances of excelling in the first real contests.

Another feature of the invisible primary is the presidential straw poll. Straw polls are gatherings at which party activists get together to listen to speeches by their party's candidates and then vote for the straw poll "winner." Candidates, the media, potential donors, and the interested electorate look at the results of straw polls to gauge and report on the strength of the party's front-runner and size up the potential contenders. Favorable press coverage following a straw poll can help increase a candidate's poll standings and further his fund-raising efforts. On the other hand, negative media coverage can result in a decline in the polls, thus crippling a campaign and hindering fund-raising efforts. Candidates who do "well" or "better than expected" at important straw polls, like those held in Iowa or Florida, tend to benefit from favorable media coverage and increased financial contributions, both of which help their standings in the polls leading up to the nomination season.

Up to this point, we have focused on the election decision itself and have said little about the campaign conducted prior to the balloting. Many today denounce electioneering and politicians for their negative use of the airwaves and the perceived disproportionate influence of a few wealthy donors and a handful of well-endowed and well-organized political action committees and interest groups. Nonetheless, the basic purpose of modern electioneering remains intact: one person asking another for support, an approach unchanged since the dawn of democracy.

The art of campaigning involves the science of polls, the planning of sophisticated mass mailings, and the coordination of electronic telephone banks to reach voters. More importantly, it also involves the diplomatic skill of unifying disparate individuals and groups to achieve a fragile but election-winning majority. How candidates perform this exquisitely difficult task is the subject of this chapter, in which we discuss the following topics:

- First we'll look at *ambition and strategy.* Personal ambition leads most candidates to starting the race for election; campaign strategy (including financing) gets them out of the gate and keeps them running.

- Second, we explore *the structure of a campaign,* the process of seeking and winning votes in the run-up to an election, which consists of five separate components: the nomination campaign, the general election campaign, the personal campaign, the organizational campaign, and the broadcast media campaign.

- Third, we'll look at the question of *which we vote for: the candidate or the campaign.* Although campaign methods have clearly become very sophisticated, in most cases the candidate wins or loses the race according to his or her abilities, qualifications, communication skills, issues, and weaknesses.

- Fourth, we see how the modern candidate faces two major *modern campaign challenges:* raising the money needed to stay in the race and communicating through the media.

- Fifth, we discuss *the 1996 presidential campaign and election.* No liberal Democrats stepped forward to challenge a rejuvenated and popular President Clinton; the Republicans, despite protestations from party activists, nominated a moderate Washington insider—former Senate Majority Leader Bob Dole. Surprisingly, Dole's primary battle turned out to be a little more exciting than expected. But in the end he prevailed, securing the right to face Clinton in the general election for president.

- Finally, we look at *campaign finance laws,* exploring ways that these might be changed so that their effect can be strengthened.

AT THE STARTING BLOCK: AMBITION AND STRATEGY

Fortunately for U.S. democracy, a fair number of people find the often intangible rewards of public service to be sufficient inducement to enter the public arena. They are willing to put up with abuse from citizens, criticism from the press, invasion of their privacy, and frequently a drop in income in order to win the honor of office. Despite the common notion that "the office seeks the man or woman," it is personal ambition that leads most candidates to the starting gate.[1] The ambition is not always selfish. In addition to a desire for power, a candidate may wish to push an issue or cause dear to his or her heart.

Whatever their motivation, candidates quickly recognize the realities of running for office. The candidate's campaign must be geared to appeal to both rank-and-file vot-

"Next time, why don't you run? You're a well-known figure, people seem to like you, and you haven't had an original idea in years." (Reproduced by Special Permission of *Playboy* magazine. Copyright © 1992 by Playboy.)

ers and the leaders of various groups and voting blocs (such as business, labor, and key ethnic populations). The candidate must find issues that motivate voters and must take defensible stands on the controversies of the day. Unavoidably, the candidate must also raise large sums of money in order to compete, as we discuss later.

THE STRUCTURE OF A CAMPAIGN

A campaign for high office (such as the presidency, a governorship, or a U.S. Senate seat) is a highly complex effort akin to running a multimillion-dollar business, while campaigns for local offices are usually less complicated. But all campaigns, no matter what their size, have certain aspects in common. Indeed, each campaign really consists of several campaigns run simultaneously:

nomination campaign: That part of a political campaign aimed at winning a primary election.

general election campaign: That part of a political campaign following a primary election, aimed at winning a general election.

personal campaign: That part of a political campaign concerned with presenting the candidate's public image.

organizational campaign: That part of a political campaign involved in fund raising, literature distribution, and all other activities not directly involving the candidate.

media campaign: That part of a political campaign waged in the broadcast and print media.

1. The **nomination campaign.** The target is the party elite, the leaders and activists who choose nominees in primaries or conventions. Party leaders are concerned with electability, while party activists are often ideologically and issue oriented, so a candidate must appeal to both bases.

2. The **general election campaign.** A far-sighted candidate never forgets the ultimate goal: winning the general election. Therefore the candidate tries to avoid taking stands that, however pleasing to party activists in the primary, will alienate a majority of the larger general election constituency.

3. The **personal campaign.** This is the public part of the campaign. The candidate and his or her family and supporters make appearances, meet voters, hold press conferences, and give speeches.

4. The **organizational campaign.** Behind the scenes, another campaign is humming. Volunteers telephone voters and distribute literature, staffers organize events, and everyone raises money to support the operation.

5. The **media campaign.** On television and radio the candidate's advertisements (termed *paid media*) air frequently in an effort to convince the public that the candidate is the best person for the job. Meanwhile, campaigners attempt to influence the press coverage of the campaign by the print and electronic news reporters—the *free media*.

British election campaigns are very different from those in the United States. In the first place, candidate selection is controlled by local party organizations, not by any sort of primary system. Second, the national parties control key facets of the campaign. For example, they provide all the financing, which is regulated by national statute, and execute the campaign strategy. As a result, national party platforms—not candidate personalities—play a dominant role in British campaigns. Finally, the power of the prime minister to call elections at his or her discretion—literally at a moment's notice—produces campaigns of a mere four to five weeks in duration instead of the two-year (for a Senate seat) to four-year campaigns (for president) we endure in the United States.

In order to better comprehend the various campaigns, let's examine a few aspects of each, remembering that they must all mesh successfully for the candidate to win.

The Nomination Campaign

New candidates get their sea legs early on, as they adjust to the pressures of being in the spotlight day in and day out. This is the time for the candidates to learn that a single careless phrase could end the campaign or guarantee a defeat. This is also the time to seek the support of party leaders and interest groups and to test out themes, slogans, and strategies. The press and public take much less notice of shifts in strategy at this time than they will later in the general election campaign.

At this time there is a danger not widely recognized by candidates: Surrounded by friendly activists and ideological soulmates in the quest to win the party's nomination, a candidate can move too far to the right or the left and become too extreme for the November electorate. Conservative Barry Goldwater, the 1964 Republican nominee for president, and liberal George McGovern, the 1972 Democratic nominee for president, both fell victim to this phenomenon in seeking their party's nomination, and they were handily defeated in the general elections by Presidents Lyndon B. Johnson and Richard M. Nixon, respectively.

The General Election Campaign

Once the choice between the two major-party nominees is clear, both candidates can get to work. Most significant interest groups are courted for money and endorsements, although the results are mainly predictable: liberal, labor, and minority groups usually back Democrats, while conservative and business organizations support Republicans. The most active and intense groups are often coalesced around emotional issues such as abortion and gun control, and these organizations can produce a bumper crop of money and activists for favored candidates. Race and class divisions can often play an important role in general elections, although this tends not to be true in the United States.

Virtually all candidates adopt a brief theme, or slogan, to serve as a rallying cry in their quest for office. The first to do so was William Henry Harrison in 1840, with the slogan "Tippecanoe and Tyler, Too." Tippecanoe was a nickname given to Harrison, a reference to his participation in the battle of Tippecanoe, and Tyler was Harrison's vice-presidential candidate, John Tyler of Virginia. Some presidential campaign slogans have entered national lore, like Herbert Hoover's 1928 slogan "A chicken in every pot, a car in every garage." But most slogans can fit many candidates ("She thinks like us," "He's on our side," "She hears you," "You know where he stands"). Candidates try to avoid controversy in their selection of slogans, and some openly eschew ideology. (An ever-popular one of this genre: "Not left, not right—forward!") The clever candidate also attempts to find a slogan that cannot be lampooned easily. In 1964 Barry Goldwater's handlers may have regretted their choice of "In your heart you know he's right" when Lyndon B. Johnson's supporters quickly converted it into "In your guts you know he's nuts." (Democrats were trying to portray Goldwater as a warmonger after the Republican indicated a willingness to use nuclear weapons in Vietnam and elsewhere under some conditions.)

The Personal Campaign

In the effort to show voters that they are hard working, thoughtful, and worthy of the office they seek, candidates try to meet personally as many citizens as possible in

the course of a campaign. A candidate for high office may deliver up to a dozen speeches a day, and that is only part of the exhausting schedule most contenders maintain. The day may begin at 5 A.M. at the entrance gate to an auto plant with an hour or two of handshaking, followed by similar gladhanding at subway stops until 9 A.M. Strategy sessions with key advisers and preparation for upcoming presentations and forums may fill the rest of the morning. A luncheon talk, afternoon fund raisers, and a series of television and print interviews crowd the afternoon agenda. The light fare of cocktail parties is followed by a dinner speech, perhaps telephone or neighborhood canvassing of voters, and a civic-forum talk or two. More meetings with advisers and planning for the next day's events can easily take a candidate past midnight. Following only a few hours of sleep, the candidate starts all over again. After months of this grueling pace, the candidate may be functioning on automatic pilot and unable to think clearly.

Beyond the strains this fast-lane existence adds to a candidate's family life, the hectic schedule leaves little time for reflection and long-range planning. Is it any wonder that under these conditions many candidates commit gaffes and appear to have foot-in-mouth disease?

It's not all drudgery, however. The considerable rewards to be had on the campaign trail can balance the personal disadvantages. A candidate can affect the course of the government and community, and in so doing become admired and respected by peers. Meeting all kinds of people, solving problems, gaining exposure to every facet of life in one's constituency—these experiences help a public person live life fully and compensate for the hardships of campaigning.

The Organizational Campaign

If the candidate is the public face of the campaign, the organization behind the candidate is the private face. Depending on the level of the office sought, the organizational staff can consist of a handful of volunteers or hundreds of paid specialists supplementing and directing the work of thousands of volunteers. The most elaborate structure is found in presidential campaigns. Tens of thousands of volunteers distrib-

Media consultants arrange everything from paid advertising to daily photo opportunities, such as this "candid" Oval Office setting for President Clinton. (Photo courtesy: Reuters/Bettmann)

ute literature and visit neighborhoods. They are directed by paid staff that may number 300 or more, including a couple of dozen lawyers and accountants.

At the top of the organizational chart are the campaign manager and the key political consultants, the hired handlers who provide technologies, services, and strategies to the campaign. The best-known consultants for any campaign are usually the **media consultant,** who produces the candidate's television and radio advertisements; the **pollster,** who takes the public opinion surveys that guide the campaign; and the **direct mailer,** who supervises direct-mail fund raising. After the candidate, however, the most important person in the campaign is probably the finance chair, who is responsible for bringing in the large contributions that pay most of the salaries of the consultants and staff.

In addition to raising money, the most vital work of the candidate's organization is to get in touch with voters. Some of this is done in person by volunteers who walk the neighborhoods, going door to door to solicit votes. Some is accomplished by volunteers who use computerized telephone banks to call targeted voters with scripted messages. (See Politics Now: High-Tech Campaigning for a discussion of the types of technologies contemporary campaigns rely on.) Both contact methods are termed **voter canvass.** Most canvassing takes place in the month before the election, when voters are paying attention. Close to Election Day, the telephone banks begin the vital **get-out-the-vote (GOTV)** effort, reminding supporters to vote and arranging for their transportation to the polls if necessary.

The Media Campaign

What voters actually see and hear of the candidate is primarily determined by the **paid media** (such as television advertising) accompanying the campaign and the **free media** (newspaper and television coverage). The two kinds of media are fundamentally

media consultant: A professional who produces political candidates' television, radio, and print advertisements.

pollster: A professional who takes public opinion surveys that guide political campaigns.

direct mailer: A professional who supervises a political campaign's direct-mail fund-raising strategies.

voter canvass: The process by which a campaign gets in touch with individual voters: either by door-to-door solicitation or by telephone.

get-out-the-vote (GOTV): A push at the end of a political campaign to encourage supporters to go to the polls.

paid media: Political advertisements purchased for a candidate's campaign.

free media: Coverage of a candidate's campaign by the news media.

Politics Now

High-Tech Campaigning

The age of modern technology has brought many changes to the traditional campaign. Labor-intensive community activities have been replaced by carefully targeted mass-media messages. Candidates today are able to quickly reach more voters than at any time in our nation's history. Consequently, the well-organized party machine is no longer essential to winning an election. The results of this technology transformation are candidate-centered campaigns in which candidates build well-financed, finely tuned organizations centered around their personal aspirations.

At the heart of the move toward today's candidate-centered campaigns is an entire generation of technological improvements. While campaigns of the 1970s and early 1980s were dominated by radio and television, contemporary campaigns combine these "traditional" mediums with high-speed personal computers, copiers and printers, fax machines, video recorders, satellites, telecommunications, teleconferencing, the Internet, and the World Wide Web. As a result candidates and their organizations can better gather and disseminate information.

One outcome of these changes is the ability of candidates to employ "rapid-fire-response" techniques. Combining opinion polls with television spots or direct-mail pieces, candidates make use of all the technological advancements to better target their messages and effectively respond to their opponent's charges. In fact, within forty-eight hours of the airing of an opponent's ad, the candidate can conduct a public opinion poll and focus group, develop and test possible responses based on the information gathered, and release a reply.

In 1996 several presidential hopefuls attempted to make use of newer technologies like the World Wide Web and the Internet. Unlike the other technologies, these played an insignificant role in the outcome. A relatively small percentage of the population uses the Web for news information on a regular basis; and the Internet, while popular, is not yet a means for mass communication. But the other technologies are fast becoming staples of the modern campaign.

Currently, it appears that new technologies continue to serve mass-media, candidate-centered campaign strategies. Perhaps political parties will use these new technologies in the future to organize a massive voter base, one that supports the party as a whole rather than the candidate. If this occurs, do you think we might see a return to the more traditional, people-centered campaigning of America's past?

different: Paid advertising is completely under the control of the campaign, whereas the press is totally independent. Great care is taken in the design of the television advertising, which takes many approaches. (See Roots of Government: The Television Advertising Campaign of 1952 for information on the first national political ad campaign.) **Positive ads** stress the candidate's qualifications, family, and issue positions with no direct reference to the opponent. These are usually favored by the incumbent candidate. **Negative ads** attack the opponent's character and platform and (except for a brief, legally required identification at the ad's conclusion) may not even mention the candidate who is paying for their airing. In 1996 Steve Forbes made extensive use of nega-

positive ad: Advertising on behalf of a candidate that stresses the candidate's qualifications, family, and issue positions, without reference to the opponent.

negative ad: Advertising on behalf of a candidate that attacks the opponent's platform or character.

tive ads prior to the Iowa caucus and the New Hampshire primary, spending millions denouncing then front-runner Bob Dole. These attacks prompted Dole to tag Forbes "the king of negative advertising," before unleashing some negative ads of his own. These ads contributed to the generally held belief that the early stages of the 1996 Republican nomination battle was one of the most vicious ever witnessed. **Contrast ads** compare the records and proposals of the candidates, with a bias toward the sponsor. And whether the public likes them or not, all three kinds of ads can inject important (as well as trivial) issues into a campaign.

Occasionally, advertisements are relatively long (ranging from four-and-one-half-minute ads up to thirty-minute documentaries). Usually, however, the messages are short **spot ads,** sixty, thirty, or even ten seconds long.

While there is little question that negative advertisements have shown the greatest growth in the past two decades, they have been a part of American campaigns for some time. In 1796 Federalists portrayed Thomas Jefferson, the chief author of our Declaration of Independence, as an atheist and a coward. In 1800 Federalists again attacked Jefferson, spreading a rumor that Jefferson was dead! Clearly, although negative advertisements are more prevalent today, they are not solely the function of the modern media. Furthermore, their effects are well documented. While voters normally need a reason to vote for a candidate, they also frequently vote *against* the other candidate— and negative ads can provide the critical justification for such a vote.

Before the 1980s well-known incumbents usually ignored negative attacks from their challengers, believing that the proper stance was to be above the fray. But after some well-publicized defeats of incumbents in the early 1980s in which negative television advertising played a prominent role,[2] incumbents began attacking their challengers in earnest. The new rule of politics became "An attack unanswered is an attack agreed to." In a further attempt to stave off brickbats from challengers, incumbents even began anticipating the substance of their opponents' attacks and airing **inoculation advertising** early in the campaign to protect themselves in advance of the other side's spots. (Inoculation advertising attempts to counteract an anticipated attack from

contrast ad: Ad that compares the records and proposals of the candidates, with a bias toward the sponsor.

spot ad: Television advertising on behalf of a candidate that is broadcast in sixty-, thirty-, or ten-second duration.

inoculation advertising: Advertising that attempts to counteract an anticipated attack from the opposition before the attack is even launched.

The candidate's ability to relax and be just "one of the guys" is weighed in voters' minds right along with ads and sophisticated campaign strategies, leading one to wonder whether it is the campaign or the candidate we vote for. (Photo courtesy: Peter Turnley/Newsweek/Black Star)

The Television Advertising Campaign of 1952

Forty-four years—and a world of difference—separate the presidential campaigns of 1952 from that of 1996 when viewed through the camera lens of television advertising.

The initial, landmark year for political television was 1952. Television had become truly national, not just regional, and portions of the political parties' national conventions were telecast for the first time. With 45 percent of the nation's households owning television sets, the presidential campaign was forced to take notice. Republican presidential nominee Dwight D. Eisenhower's advisers were particularly intrigued with the device, seeing it as a way to counter Eisenhower's stumbling press-conference performances and to make him appear more knowledgeable.

Eisenhower's advertising campaign was a glimpse of the future. Two associates of the Ted Bates and Company advertising agency of New York designed the spots, targeted them to play in key swing areas of the country, and arranged a television and radio saturation blitz in the last three weeks of the campaign along with the Batten, Barton, Durstine, and Osborn (BBD&O) advertising agency, which actually bought the air time. The three primary themes of the commercials (corruption, high prices, and the Korean War) were chosen after consultation with pollster George Gallup. There was an extraordinarily large number of spots (forty-nine produced for television, twenty-nine for radio). Most spots were twenty seconds in length; the rest, sixty seconds. They played repeatedly in forty-nine selected counties in twelve non-Southern states as well as in a few

targeted Southern states. On the day before the election, in New York City alone, 130 Eisenhower television ads were shown at station breaks. The GOP's media strategy appeared to have been successful, and the Nielsen ratings showed that Eisenhower's telecasts consistently drew higher ratings than those of his Democratic opponent, Adlai Stevenson.

The commercials themselves were simplistic and technically very primitive in comparison with modern fare. Eisenhower had a peculiarly stilted way of speaking while reading cue cards, and his delivery was amateurish, albeit sincere and appealing. If nothing else, the GOP commercials from 1952 reveal that the issues in U.S. politics never seem to change. Eisenhower's slogan, "It's Time for a Change," is a perennial production, for example. One advertisement was a clever adaptation of the "March of Time" newsreel series that preceded the main features in U.S. movie theaters of the period, and various news clips of Eisenhower accompanied the audio.

Narrator: The man from Abilene. Out of the heartland of America, out of this small-frame house in Abilene, Kansas, came a man, Dwight D. Eisenhower. Through the crucial hours of historic D-Day, he brought us to the triumph and peace of VE-Day. Now, another crucial hour in our history. The big question . . .

Man's voice: General, if war comes, is this country really ready?

Eisenhower: It is not. The administration has spent many billions of dollars for national defense. Yet today we haven't enough tanks for the fighting men in Korea. It is time for a change.

Narrator: The nation, haunted by the stalemate in Korea, looks to Eisenhower. Eisenhower knows how to deal with the Russians. He has met

with Europe's leaders, has got them working with us. Elect the number-one man for the number-one job of our time. November fourth, vote for peace, vote for Eisenhower.

Yet this spot had an odd ring to it, perhaps because the approach ignored the intimate nature of television, which reaches its viewers in the home's cozy quarters as opposed to the blare of a newsreel in an auditorium. Some other Eisenhower commercials used an even less effective format wherein a film showed Eisenhower mechanically responding to off-camera questions.

By the best estimates, this first media blitz cost the Republicans close to $1.5 million. During that campaign, the Democrats spent only about $77,000 on television, and the new spots they produced played on New Deal themes and Republican responsibility for the Great Depression: "Sh-h-h-h. Don't mention it to a soul, don't spread it around . . . but the Republican party was in power back in 1932 . . . 13 million people were unemployed . . . bank doors shut in your face . . . ." The Democrats, who had wanted to run an ad blitz but could not raise the money to pay for it, turned instead to broadsides about the GOP's "soap campaign." Stevenson's supporters charged that the Republican ad managers conceived a multimillion-dollar production designed to sell a political party ticket to the American people in precisely the way they sell soap.

The poet Marya Mannes was moved to write "Sales Campaign" in reaction to the Eisenhower advertising effort. Her poem read, in part: "Phillip Morris, Lucky Strike, Alka Seltzer, I Like Ike." For better or worse, the pattern was set for future campaigns.

the opposition before the attack is even launched.) For example, a senator who fears a broadside about her voting record on Social Security issues might air advertisements featuring senior citizens praising her support of Social Security.

THE CANDIDATE OR THE CAMPAIGN: WHICH DO WE VOTE FOR?

*M*uch is said and written about about media and organizational techniques during the campaign, and they are often presented as political magic. Despite their sophistication, however, the technologies often fail the candidates and their campaigns. The political consultants who develop and master the technologies of polling, media, and other techniques frequently make serious mistakes in judgment. Despite popular lore and journalistic legend, few candidates are the creations of their clever consultants and dazzling campaign techniques. Partly, this is because politics always has been (and always will be) much more art than science, not subject to precise manipulation or formulaic computation. Of course, campaign techniques can enhance the candidate's strengths and downplay his or her weaknesses, and in that respect, technique certainly matters. In the end—in most cases—the candidate wins or loses the race according to his or her abilities, qualifications, communication skills, issues, and weaknesses. Although this simple truth is warmly reassuring, it has been remarkably overlooked by election analysts and reporters seemingly mesmerized by the exorbitant claims of consultants and the flashy computer lights of their technologies.[3]

The voter deserves much of the credit for whatever encouragement we can draw from this candidate-centered view of politics. Granted, citizens are often inattentive

(Photo courtesy: Toles/*The Buffalo News*)

to politics, almost forcing candidates to use empty slogans and glitz to attract their attention. But it is also true that most voters want to take the real measure of candidates, and they retain a healthy skepticism about the techniques of running for office. Political cartoonist Tom Toles suggested as much when he depicted the seven preparatory steps the modern candidate takes: (1) Set out to discover what voters want, (2) conduct extensive polling, (3) study demographic trends, (4) engage in sophisticated interpretation of in-depth voter interviews, (5) analyze results, (6) discover that what the voters want is a candidate who doesn't need to do steps one through five, and (7) pretend you didn't. The chastened politician then tells his assembled throng, "I follow my conscience."[4]

MODERN CAMPAIGN CHALLENGES

*T*he modern candidate faces two major challenges: communicating through the media and raising the money needed to stay in the race. We consider each challenge in turn.

The News Media

The news media present quite a challenge to candidates. Although politicians and their staffs cannot control the press, they nonetheless try to manipulate press coverage. They use three techniques to accomplish this aim. First, the staff often seeks to isolate the candidate from the press, thus reducing the chances that reporters will bait a candidate into saying something that might damage the candidate's cause. Naturally, the media are frustrated by such a tactic and insist on as many open press conferences as possible.

Second, the campaign stages media events—activities designed to include brief, clever quotes called *sound bites* and staged with appealing backdrops so that they are all but irresistible, especially to television news (see Highlight 14.1: Famous Sound Bites from Presidential Campaigns). In this fashion the candidate's staff can successfully fill the news hole reserved for campaign coverage on the evening news programs and in the morning papers.

Third, the handlers and consultants have perfected the technique termed *spin*—that is, they put the most favorable possible interpretation for their candidate on any circumstance occurring in the campaign, and they work the press to sell their point of view or at least to ensure that it is included in the reporters' stories. An example of spin can be seen in the early 1996 Republican presidential primaries. Those candidates who did not win the primary or caucus but placed better than expected were portrayed by their handlers as the real winners of the contest. Pat Buchanan, Steve Forbes, and Lamar Alexander all practiced this strategy. On the other hand Bob Dole, the winner of the Iowa caucus, failed in the expectations game by not winning the contest by more than 5 percentage points, the amount political pundits agreed on as the threshold for the Republican front-runner. This allowed Pat Buchanan, who finished second in the caucus, to claim victory and establish the momentum he needed to carry him to victory in the New Hampshire primary one week later. **Candidate debates,** especially the televised presidential variety, are also showcases for the consultants' spin patrol, and teams of staffers from each side swarm the press rooms to declare victory even before the candidates finish their closing statements.

candidate debates: Forums in which political candidates face each other to discuss their platforms, records, and character.

Highlight 14.1

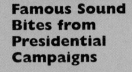

Famous Sound Bites from Presidential Campaigns

1996

"It's as easy as A-B-C, Alexander Beats Clinton."

—*Lamar Alexander (R), former Tennessee Governor and Secretary of Education, explaining to Republican primary and caucus voters why he should be the 1996 GOP presidential nominee.*

"I'm the most optimistic man in America."

—*Senator Robert Dole (R), speaking to Republican convention delegates during his acceptance speech.*

1992

"Message: I care"

—*George Bush (R), attempting to connect with New Hampshire's economically devastated voters.*

"Let's clean out the barn!"

—*Ross Perot (I)*

"Who am I? Why am I here?"

—*Retired Adm. James Stockdale, Ross Perot's 1992 vice presidential running mate, during a televised debate.*

1988

"Read my lips: no new taxes."

—*George Bush (R)*

"Stop lying about my record!"

—*Senator Robert Dole (R–Kans.), speaking to George Bush during their campaign for the Republican nomination.*

"I knew Jack Kennedy; he was a friend of mine. And, Senator, you're no Jack Kennedy."

—*Democratic vice-presidential nominee Lloyd Bentsen (D–Tex.), responding in an October debate to Republican nominee Dan Quayle's comparison of himself to John F. Kennedy.*

"Follow me around . . . [you'll] be very bored."

—*Gary Hart (D–Colo.) to a reporter shortly before his May 1987 weekend with model Donna Rice.*

1984

"Where's the beef?"

—*Walter Mondale to his Democratic rival Gary Hart, who claimed to have "new ideas."*

1980

"There you go again . . . ."

—*Ronald Reagan (R) to President Jimmy Carter (D), in response to some of Carter's charges against Reagan in a debate.*

"Are you better off today than you were four years ago?"

—*Reagan's oft-repeated question to the voters.*

Televised Debates. Candidate debates are media extravaganzas that are a hybrid of free and paid media. As with ads, much of the candidate dialogue (jokes included) is canned and prepackaged. Yet spontaneity cannot be completely eliminated, and gaffes, quips, and slips of the tongue can sometimes be revealing. President Gerald Ford's insistence during an October 1976 debate with Jimmy Carter that Poland was not under Soviet domination may have cost him a close election. Ronald Reagan's refrain, "Are you better off today than you were four years ago?" neatly summed up his case against Carter in 1980. Moreover, Reagan's easygoing performance reassured a skeptical public that wanted Carter out of the White House but was not certain it wanted Reagan in.

Senator John F. Kennedy's visually impressive showing in the first 1960 presidential debate dramatically reduced the edge that experience gave two-term Vice President Richard M. Nixon. Not only was Nixon ill at the time, but he also was poorly dressed and poorly made up for television. Interestingly, most of those who heard the debate on radio—and therefore could not see the contrast between the pale, anxious, sweating Nixon and the relaxed, tanned Kennedy—thought that Nixon had won.

The importance of debates can easily be overrated, however. A weak performance by Reagan in his first debate with Walter Mondale in 1984 had little lasting effect, in part because Reagan did better in the second debate. And most of the debates in 1960,

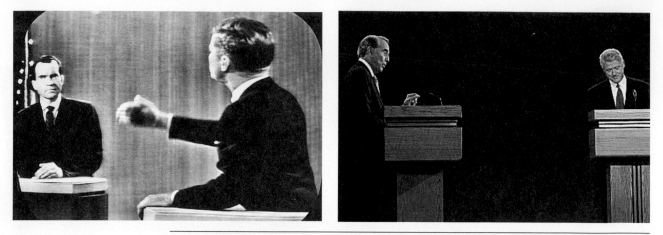

Presidential debates have come a long way—at least in terms of studio trappings—since the ill-at-ease Richard M. Nixon was visually bested by John F. Kennedy in the first 1960 televised debates. In the first of the 1996 debates, Robert Dole's rapid eye blinks were taken by many analysts as a sign of unease in the face of incumbent Clinton's comfortable position. (Photos courtesy: left, UPI/Corbis-Bettman; right, Wally McNamee/Folio)

1976, 1980, and 1988 were unmemorable and electorally inconsequential. Debates usually just firm up voters' predispositions and cannot change the fundamentals of an election (the state of the economy, scandal, and presidential popularity, for example). This is what appeared to happen in 1992, when none of the three presidential debates and one vice-presidential debate changed the underlying pro-Clinton trends in the election. Nonetheless, because debates are potentially educational and focus the public's mind on the upcoming election, they are useful. Since they have been held in every presidential campaign since 1976, debates are now likely to be an expected and standard part of the presidential election process. They are also an established feature of campaigns for governor, U.S. senator, and many other offices.

Can the Press Be "Handled"?   Whether in debates or elsewhere, efforts by candidates to manipulate the news media often fail because the press is wise to their tactics and determined to thwart them. Not even the candidates' paid media are sacrosanct anymore. Major newspapers throughout the country have taken to analyzing the accuracy of the television advertisements aired during the campaign—a welcome and useful addition to journalists' scrutiny of politicians.

Less welcome are some other news media practices in campaigns. Many studies have shown that the media are obsessed with the horse race aspect of politics—who's ahead, who's behind, who's gaining—to the detriment of the substance of the candidates' issues and ideas. Public opinion polls, especially tracking polls, many of them taken by the news outlets themselves, dominate coverage, especially on network television, where only a few minutes a night are devoted to politics. (Tracking polls were discussed in chapter 11.)

Related to the proliferation of polls is the media's expectations game in presidential primary contests. With polls as the objective backdrop, journalists set the margins by which contenders are expected to win or lose—so much so that even a clear victory of five percentage points can be judged a setback if the candidate had been projected to win by twelve or fifteen points. Finally, the news media often overemphasize trivial parts of the campaign, such as a politician's minor gaffe, and give too much attention to the private lives of candidates. This superficial coverage and the resources needed to generate it are displacing serious journalism on the issues. These subjects are taken up again in the next chapter, which deals with the news media.

Campaign Financing

To run all aspects of a campaign successfully requires a great deal of money. In 1992 alone, more than $675 million was raised and spent in U.S. House and Senate races.[5] This amount was an increase of 40 percent over the 1990 elections, mainly owing to greater competition because of a large number of open seats—one of the effects of redistricting. Because of a vacancy, there were also simultaneous elections in 1992 for two U.S. Senate seats in California, the largest and most expensive state for campaigns. On average, a House incumbent who was seriously challenged and received less than 55 percent of the vote spent nearly $750,000, while his or her opponent spent nearly $400,000. As humorist Will Rogers once remarked early in the twentieth century, "Politics has got so expensive that it takes lots of money even to get beat with."

All this political money is regulated by the federal government under the terms of the Federal Election Campaign Act of 1971, first passed in 1971 and substantially strengthened after Watergate in 1974 and again in 1976. (Still more amendments were passed in 1979.) Table 14.1 summarizes some of the important provisions of this law, which limits what individuals, interest groups, and political parties can give to candidates for president, U.S. senator, and U.S. representative. These limits on contributions

TABLE 14.1

Current Contribution Limits for Congressional Candidates (under the Federal Election Campaign Act)

CONTRIBUTIONS FROM	GIVEN TO CANDIDATE (PER ELECTION)[a]	GIVEN TO NATIONAL PARTY (PER CALENDAR YEAR)	TOTAL ALLOWABLE CONTRIBUTIONS (PER CALENDAR YEAR)
Individual	$1,000	$20,000	Limited to $25,000
Political action committee[b]	$5,000	$15,000	No limit
Any political party committee[c]	$5,000	No limit	No limit
All national and state party committees taken together	To House candidates: $30,000 plus "coordinated expenditures"[d] To Senate candidates: $27,500 plus "coordinated expenditures"[d]		

[a]Each of the following is considered a *separate* election: primary (or convention), run-off, general election.

[b]Multi-candidate PACs only. Multi-candidate committees have received contributions from at least fifty persons and have given to at least five federal candidates.

[c]Multi-candidate party committees only. Multi-candidate committees have received contributions from at least fifty persons and have given to at least five federal candidates.

[d]Coordinated expenditures are party-paid general election campaign expenditures made in consultation and coordination with the candidate.

are discussed in the passages that follow, but the goal of all limits is the same: to prevent any single group or individual from gaining too much influence over elected officials, who naturally feel indebted to campaign contributors.

Given the cash flow required by a campaign and the legal restrictions on political money, raising the funds necessary to run a modern campaign is a monumental task. Consequently, presidential and congressional campaigns have squads of fund raisers on staff. These professionals rely on several standard sources of campaign money.

Individual Contributions.   Individual contributions are donations from individual citizens. The maximum allowable contribution under federal law for congressional and presidential elections is $1,000 per election to each candidate, with primary and general elections considered separately. Individuals are also limited to a total of $25,000 in gifts to all candidates combined in each calendar year. Most candidates receive a majority of all funds directly from individuals, and most individual gifts are well below the maximum level.

Political Action Committee (PAC) Contributions.   Donations from **political action committees (PACs)** are those from interest groups (labor unions, corporations, trade associations, and ideological and issue groups). Under federal law these organizations are required to establish officially recognized fund-raising committees, called PACs, in order to participate in federal elections. (Some but not all states have similar requirements for state elections.) Approximately 4,000 PACs are registered with the Federal Election Commission—the governmental agency charged with administering the election laws. In 1994, all PACs together gave $179 million to Senate and House candidates. (By contrast, individual citizens donated nearly $336 million.) As of October 16, 1996, the last financial filing report before the election, PACs had contributed $160 million to Senate and House candidates, while individuals donated $335 million. On average, PAC contributions account for 33 percent of the war chests (campaign funds) of House candidates and 20 percent of the treasuries of Senate candidates. (Interest groups are treated in more detail in chapter 16.)

Political Party Contributions.   Candidates also receive donations from the national and state committees of the Democratic and Republican parties. As is mentioned in chapter 12, political parties can give substantial contributions to their congressional nominees. In 1994 both the Republicans and the Democrats funneled over $23 million to their standard-bearers. In competitive races the parties may provide 15 percent to 17 percent of their candidates' total war chests.

Candidates' Personal Contributions.   Candidates and their families may donate to the campaign. The Supreme Court ruled in 1976 in *Buckley* v. *Valeo* that no limit could be placed on the amount of money candidates can spend from their own families' resources, since such spending is considered a First Amendment right of free speech [424 U.S.1 (1976)]. For wealthy politicians such as U.S. Senators John D. Rockefeller IV (D–W. Va.) or Herbert H. Kohl (D–Wisc.), this allowance may mean personal spending in the millions. Most candidates, however, commit much less than $100,000 in family resources to their election bids. Ross Perot, who publicly committed to spend millions, was not the usual candidate. In 1994 House and Senate candidates loaned or contributed almost $82 million to their own campaigns. As of October 16, 1996, House and Senate candidate contributions to their own campaigns stood at $42.4 million, a decrease due mostly to 1996 senatorial candidates spending less of their own funds. Steve Forbes, though, did not follow the lead of the senatorial candidates. He spent more than $30 million of his own money on his bid for the Republican presidential nomination.

Public Funds. **Public funds** are donations from general tax revenues. Only presidential candidates (and a handful of state and local contenders) receive public funds. Under the terms of the Federal Election Campaign Act of 1971 (which first established public funding of presidential campaigns), a candidate for president can become eligible to receive public funds during the nominating contest by raising at least $5,000 in individual contributions of $250 or less in each of twenty states. Once the receipt of this money is certified, the candidate can apply for federal **matching funds,** whereby every dollar raised from individuals in amounts less than $251 is matched by the federal treasury on a dollar-for-dollar basis. This assumes there is enough money in the Presidential Election Campaign Fund to do so. The fund is accumulated by taxpayers who designate $3 of their taxes for this purpose each year when they send in their federal tax returns. (Only about 20 percent of taxpayers check off the appropriate box, even though participation does not increase their tax burden.)

For the general election, the two major-party presidential nominees are given a lump-sum payment in the summer before the election ($62 million each in 1996), from which all their general election campaign expenditures must come. A third-party candidate receives a smaller amount proportionate to his or her November vote total if that candidate gains a minimum of 5 percent of the vote. Note that in such a case the money goes to third-party campaigns only *after* the election is over; no money is given in advance of the general election. The only third-party candidate to qualify for general election funds before Ross Perot did so was John Anderson, the Independent candidate for president in 1980, who garnered 7 percent of the national vote. While Ross Perot chose not to take public funds for his campaign in 1992, a campaign which was largely self-financed, in 1996 Perot did accept public funding. He qualified for this funding by securing 19 percent of the popular vote in the 1992 presidential election.

Independent Expenditures. Individuals, groups, and PACs also spend money independent of any campaign or candidate. This spending is known as "soft money"—used to finance a party's general overhead and generic "get-out-the-vote" appeals. Unlike "hard money"—direct contributions to individual candidates—it is not under the direction or control of the campaign staff and is unlimited because First Amendment free speech is involved. Soft money, which the Federal Election Commission is virtually powerless to regulate because the funds are *supposedly* not used to influence federal elections, can be spent positively (advocating the election of a candidate) or negatively (urging the defeat of a targeted candidate) (see Figure 14.1).

Liberals, conservatives, environmentalists, supporters of Israel, and trade groups representing realtors, doctors, and car dealers are some organizations that have used this supplementary method of campaign spending over the years. In addition, untold millions are spent by labor, corporate, and community groups for grassroots organizing, voter registration, volunteer participation, and internal political communications with their members and employees. Depending on the sponsoring group, all of this activity has a political impact—favoring one candidate or party and hurting others—but that is not always obvious or well publicized. Also, unlike all the other forms of contributions discussed earlier, it is usually not necessary for these indirect gifts to be disclosed to the Federal Election Commission.

Some argue that the recent proliferation of soft money (as of October 16, 1996, the Republican and Democratic party committees had raised $121 million and $102 million respectively in soft money—a 166 percent increase for the Republicans and 232 percent increase for the Democrats in total soft money from 1992) is not to be lamented. They maintain that political parties deserve more fund-raising freedom, which would give these critical institutions a more substantial role in elections. But when individual contributors are able to donate as much money as they like via the soft money route,

Even though he dropped out of the race, Steve Forbes's (here shown on a bus tour through New Hampshire) and Ross Perot's participation in the campaign process raised questions about the role of personal funds. What if Microsoft's Bill Gates ran? With his multibillion-dollar fortune, he could buy up most commercial prime time spots for months. (Photo courtesy: Lisa Quinones/Black Star)

public funds: Donations from the general tax revenues to the campaigns of qualifying presidential candidates.

matching funds: Donations to presidential campaigns from the federal government that are determined by the amount of private funds a qualifying candidate raises.

FIGURE 14.1

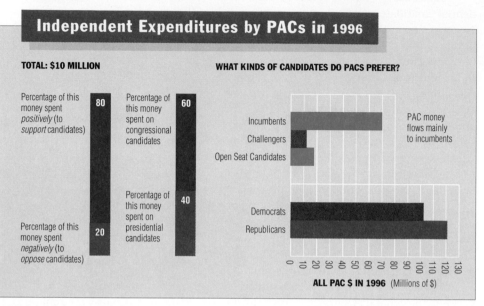

Independent Expenditures by PACs in 1996

TOTAL: $10 MILLION

Percentage of this money spent *positively* (to *support* candidates) — 80

Percentage of this money spent *negatively* (to *oppose* candidates) — 20

Percentage of this money spent on congressional candidates — 60

Percentage of this money spent on presidential candidates — 40

WHAT KINDS OF CANDIDATES DO PACS PREFER?

Incumbents
Challengers
Open Seat Candidates

PAC money flows mainly to incumbents

Democrats
Republicans

0 10 20 30 40 50 60 70 80 90 100 110 120 130

ALL PAC $ IN 1996 (Millions of $)

SOURCE: Federal Election Commission.

thus theoretically gaining a heightened level of access to politicians not enjoyed by the electorate as a whole—in May 1996 President Bill Clinton and the Democratic National Committee hosted a dinner where those invited to attend donated over $12 million to the Democratic party that evening alone—does this outweigh the supposed benefit to political parties?

Are PACs a Good or Bad Part of the Process?

Of all these forms of spending, probably the most controversial is that involving PAC money. Some PACs, due to the amount of money they are able to raise and their ability to get their supporters to the polls on Election Day, are more influential than others; but there are few poor, noninfluential PACs. Some observers claim that PACs are the embodiment of corrupt special interests that use campaign donations to buy the votes of legislators. Furthermore, they argue that the less affluent and minority members of our society do not enjoy equal access to these political organizations.

Most political scientists in the field of campaign finance have a quite different opinion, viewing PACs as a natural manifestation of interest group politics in a diverse democracy. Also, many political scientists point out that a person need not belong to a PAC to wield electoral and political influence. The Democrats' best-known external resources—and the ones that most pain Republicans—are the PACs associated with organized labor and minority groups as a whole. While organized labor has for decades provided Democrats with an army of volunteers and huge amounts of financial support, minorities have been the single most loyal Democratic voting bloc—in raw vote terms even more indispensable to the Democrats than labor.

Although a good number of PACs of all persuasions existed prior to the 1970s, it was during this decade—the decade of campaign reform—that the modern PAC era began. Spawned by the Watergate-inspired revisions of the campaign-finance laws,

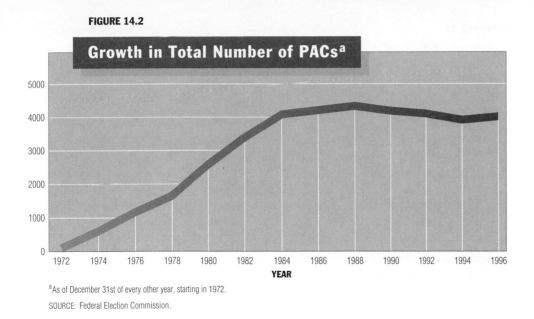

FIGURE 14.2

Growth in Total Number of PACs[a]

YEAR

[a] As of December 31st of every other year, starting in 1972.

SOURCE: Federal Election Commission.

PACs grew in number from 113 in 1972 to 4,100 by the early 1990s (see Figure 14.2), and their contributions to congressional candidates multiplied almost eighteenfold, from $8.5 million in 1971 and 1972 to $180.5 million in 1991 and 1992 (see Figure 14.3). The rapid rise of PACs has inevitably proved controversial, yet many of the charges made against political action committees are exaggerated and dubious.

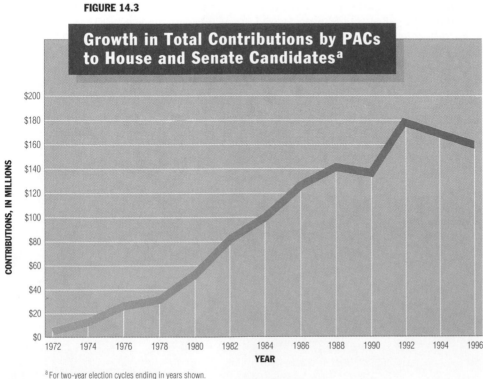

FIGURE 14.3

Growth in Total Contributions by PACs to House and Senate Candidates[a]

CONTRIBUTIONS, IN MILLIONS

YEAR

[a] For two-year election cycles ending in years shown.

SOURCE: Federal Election Commission.

Some people argue that PACs are newfangled inventions that have flooded the political system with money. Although the widespread use of the PAC structure is new, the fact remains that special-interest money of all types has always found its way into politics. Before the 1970s it did so in less traceable and much more disturbing and unsavory ways because little of the money given to candidates was regularly disclosed to public inspection. And although it is true that PACs contribute a massive sum to candidates in absolute terms, it is not clear that there is proportionately more interest group money in the system than before. The proportion of House and Senate campaign funds provided by PACs has certainly increased since the early 1970s; but individuals, most of whom are unaffiliated with PACs, together with the political parties, still supply more than 60 percent of all the money spent by or on behalf of House candidates, 75 percent of the campaign expenditures for Senate contenders, and 85 percent of the campaign expenditures for presidential candidates (see Figure 14.4). So while the importance of PAC spending has grown, PACs clearly remain secondary as a source of election funding and therefore pose no overwhelming threat to the system's legitimacy.

It can be argued that contemporary political action committees are another manifestation of what James Madison called "factions." Through the flourishing of competing interest groups or factions, said Madison in *Federalist No. 10*, liberty would be preserved. In any democracy, and particularly in one as pluralistic as that of the United States, it is essential that groups be relatively unrestricted in advocating their interests and positions (see Highlight 14.2, Women's PACs Continue to Make a Difference). Not only is unrestricted political activity by interest groups a mark of a free society, but also it provides a safety valve for the competitive pressures that build on all fronts in a democracy and also supplies a way to keep representatives responsive to legitimate needs.

The election outlays of PACs, like the total amount expended in a single election season, seem huge. But the cost of elections in the United States is less than or approximately the same as in some other nations, measured on a per-voter basis.[6] Moreover, the cost of all elections in the United States taken together is less than the amount many individual private corporations spend on advertising cereals, dog food, cars, and

FIGURE 14.4

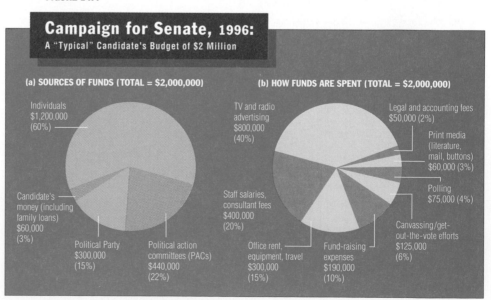

Campaign for Senate, 1996:
A "Typical" Candidate's Budget of $2 Million

(a) SOURCES OF FUNDS (TOTAL = $2,000,000)

Individuals $1,200,000 (60%)

Candidate's money (including family loans) $60,000 (3%)

Political Party $300,000 (15%)

Political action committees (PACs) $440,000 (22%)

(b) HOW FUNDS ARE SPENT (TOTAL = $2,000,000)

TV and radio advertising $800,000 (40%)

Staff salaries, consultant fees $400,000 (20%)

Office rent, equipment, travel $300,000 (15%)

Fund-raising expenses $190,000 (10%)

Legal and accounting fees $50,000 (2%)

Print media (literature, mail, buttons) $60,000 (3%)

Polling $75,000 (4%)

Canvassing/get-out-the-vote efforts $125,000 (6%)

Highlight 14.2

Women's PACs Continue to Make a Difference

Women's political action committees made a real difference in the 1990 and 1992 elections. In 1990, women's PACs contributed over $2.6 million to candidates and in 1992 nearly triple that.

EMILY's List, which stands for Early Money Is Like Yeast (it makes the dough rise), is the largest contributor to women's campaigns. Founded in 1985, its members contributed nearly $1.5 million to female candidates in 1990. Ann Richards, who ran a hotly contested race for the Texas governorship in 1990, credits EMILY's List with providing crucial funding at a key time. In 1992, EMILY's List provided $6.2 million to 55 pro-choice Democratic woman candidates, of whom 25 won. It spent more than that to support 38 candidates in the 1994 election cycle.

In 1996, it was again a major player in the state and congressional elections. A study released by the Federal Elections Commission in late September 1996, for example, reported that EMILY's List led all PACs raising $9.4 million; to that time no other PAC had raised more than $7 million. Similarly, the WISH LIST, which stands for Women in the House and Senate and backs Republican candidates, spent $325,000 through late September and the Susan B. Anthony List, a nonpartisan PAC, raised $250,000 for the twelve anti-abortion women candidates it backed for House election.

Sources: Center for the American Woman and Politics, *CAWP News & Notes* (Winter 1991): 10–11; *The Times-Picayune,* "EMILY's List Dough Helps Women Rise," (January 26, 1994): A1; and EMILY's List.

---

toothpaste. These days it is expensive to communicate, whether the message is political or commercial. The costs of television time, polling, consultants, and other items have soared over and above the inflation rate.

A SUMMARY OF CONTRIBUTIONS AND EXPENSES

Figure 14.4 gives an idea of where all the money comes from and goes to. A typical U.S. Senate campaign candidate in 1996 received most of his war chest (about 60 percent) from relatively small individual donations. PACs supplied about 22 percent, the political party committees 15 percent, and the candidates about 3 percent.

The single greatest outlay (40 percent of the total) was for television advertising; the next-largest item, staff and consultant salaries, was half television's cost (20 percent). The other 40 percent of the budget was spent on everything from polls to travel expenses. Keep in mind that in a large state with a dozen or more media markets (concentrated population centers with many television and radio stations), expenditures often balloon to $5 million, $10 million, and even more.

Some candidates have more difficulty than others in raising the necessary dollar amounts. Those in power—the incumbents—have the least trouble, although challengers who face incumbents weakened by scandal can also find the task of financing the campaign relatively easy. The size of a challenger's war chest is really the key variable. There is a point of diminishing returns for incumbent spending, since most office holders are already well known to the voters. But the challenger's name and platform are likely to be obscure. If the challenger can raise and spend enough to get his or her basic message across, there is a reasonable chance that the election will be at least moderately competitive. As is more common, though, if the challenger is starved for funds, the contest will probably turn into a romp for the well-heeled incumbent.

BRINGING IT TOGETHER: THE 1996 PRESIDENTIAL CAMPAIGN AND ELECTION

Roughly a year before the November 1996 presidential election, it looked to be a somewhat uneventful affair. No liberal Democrats stepped forward to challenge a rejuvenated and popular President Clinton, who had rebounded from his 1994 midterm congressional electoral defeats. Republicans, despite vehement protestations from party activists, seemed poised to nominate a moderate Washington insider—Senate Majority Leader Bob Dole. Although Dole's primary battle turned out to be a little more exciting than expected, in the end he prevailed, securing the right to face Clinton in the general election for president.

As it turned out, Dole was no match for a rejuvenated and popular President Clinton. Buoyed mainly by a healthy economy (unemployment and interest rates were down, economic productivity and growth were up), voters revived the time honored tradition of voting their pocketbooks, returning Clinton to the Oval Office for four more years.

The Party Nomination Battle

President Clinton's hopes for an uncontested renomination were realized when Democrats decided to coalesce around their embattled party leader. Afraid that an intraparty squabble would open the door for Republicans both to build upon their congressional advantage and secure the presidency, Democratic liberals and moderates alike decided early on to pledge their support to the sitting president. They hoped for a repeat of 1948, when Democrats, after losing control of Congress in 1946, rallied behind Democratic President Harry Truman, returning him to the White House for another term and recapturing Congress from a Republican congressional majority that was regularly criticized during that period for flirting with extremism in domestic legislation.

Republicans, on the other hand, sponsored an unusual free-for-all for the presidential nomination in 1996 that was reminiscent of many former Democratic nomination battles. The leading announced candidate from the beginning was Senator Robert Dole of Kansas. Despite some weak straw poll showings in the latter months of 1995 against the more conservative GOP candidates, Dole, buttressed by strong financial support and the endorsement of virtually every GOP stalwart, seemingly had the nomination wrapped up. But after conservative television commentator Patrick J. Buchanan single-handedly ended Phil Gramm's candidacy in Louisiana and came within 5 percentage points of winning the Iowa caucus, other Republican candidates—most notably the multi-millionaire publisher of *Forbes* magazine, Malcolm S. "Steve" Forbes, and the former Secretary of Education and Governor of Tennessee, Lamar Alexander—began to press Dole as well. A week later at the New Hampshire primary, Buchanan bested Dole, with Alexander and Forbes close behind. But after some lackluster performances by Buchanan, Forbes, and Alexander in South Carolina and the "Yankee" primary (Forbes did win the Delaware and Arizona contests, but these victories were not unexpected), the well-financed Dole campaign began to generate unstoppable momentum. By mid-March Dole had managed to outlast all his rivals, becoming the presumptive Republican presidential nominee.

Republicans, like Democrats in 1992, seemed more resigned than enthusiastic as they looked to a Dole candidacy. Dole trailed Clinton in the polls by anywhere between 10 and 20 percentage points (some polls had him in the 30s in a two-way race and some even had him in the 20s in a three-way contest with Texas billionaire and 1992 independent presidential candidate Ross Perot). But on May 16 Dole, in a stunning move, relinquished the Senate seat he had held for twenty-seven years to campaign for the presidency in earnest. Stating that his campaign was "about telling the truth, it's about doing what is right, it's about electing a president who's not attracted to the glories of the office but rather to its difficulties," Dole placed his future in the hands of the American electorate with but two possible destinations: the White House or back to Kansas.

The Third Force: Ross Perot

Though many names surfaced, most notably Colin Powell, the former Chairman of the Joint Chiefs of Staff, Ross Perot in 1996 remained the only major third-party challenger for the presidency. (Other independent or third-party candidates did join the 1996 presidential race, for example, author Harry Brown of the Libertarian Party and Ralph Nader of the Green Party, but none of them were able to generate the levels of support necessary to offer a realistic threat to either Clinton or Dole.)

Perot again made use of his favorite medium—the television—and his favorite forum—*Larry King Live*—to announce his intention to run for president "if the voters want me to." His announcement followed on the heels of the news that former Colorado Governor and Democrat Richard Lamm would be seeking the nomination of Ross Perot's Reform Party. Though he had previously remained coy regarding whether or not he would join the 1996 presidential race, Richard Lamm's entry seemed to ignite Perot's interest.

In the weeks that followed, Perot and Lamm did make some joint appearances, though they never were on stage at the same time. Both tended to focus their discussions more on the failures of the country's two major parties to deal with the pressing issues of the day rather than on what they would do to bring about true deficit reduction as well as tax and campaign finance reform.

In the end, Perot's hold on the Reform Party proved too strong for Lamm to overcome. After an accounting firm had tabulated the votes (though over 1 million ballots were mailed out to Reform Party members, only about 50,000 were filled out and mailed back, a 5% return), Perot had secured the support of two-thirds of those Reform Party members who chose to participate in the mail-in election.

Three weeks later, Perot announced that his running mate would be economist Pat Choate, a Perot confidant and adviser during the 1992 presidential election effort, and the man regarded by many as the chief architect of Perot's thoughts concerning taxes, the economy, the budget, and deficit reduction. Though virtually unknown outside of economic and political circles, it was thought that Choate would prove to be a more capable running mate than Perot's 1992 choice, political novice Admiral James Stockdale. (Who can forget the image of Stockdale during the 1992 vice presidential debate beginning his opening remarks with the comment "Who am I? Why am I here?") Intelligent and relatively comfortable in front of the television camera as well as behind a microphone (Choate had been hosting his own radio talk show before accepting Perot's offer), many felt that had Choate been allowed to participate in the vice presidential debate, the event would have been a more interesting affair.

While the impact of Perot and Choate on the 1996 presidential election did not approach Perot's 19 percent of the popular vote showing in 1992, their presence did help to insure that difficult domestic policy issues such as deficit reduction, and tax and campaign finance reform, would be addressed. The true value of third-party and independent candidates has tended to be not so much their effect on the actual outcome of the election as it has been their ability to force the two major political parties to address issues they might otherwise chose to ignore. When looked at in this perspective, one can understand why many an attentive voter and well-informed citizen, though they might intend to vote Republican or Democratic, welcome presidential campaigns which include these party crashers.

The Party Conventions

Republicans and Democrats, as well as the fledgling Reform Party, each held conventions in the month of August.

The Reform Party kicked off convention month, meeting in Long Beach, California August 11. After announcing one week earlier that Ross Perot had defeated Richard Lamm for the party's nomination, this convention like those of the two major parties was more of an infomercial which touted the accomplishments of Perot and the correctness of his vision for America than anything else. Shorter in duration than its four-day counterparts, and covered extensively only by CNN and C-SPAN, the Reform Party convention did not even contain the drama reserved for most conventions featuring a challenge to the present administration—the party's vice presidential selection and the introduction of that selection to the country. (Perot had not yet settled on a nominee and was also unsure about the reception he would receive from his top choices.) By the close of the weekend, the Reform Party had attempted to make its case to the American people. In a pattern that would be repeated during the Republican and Democratic conventions, few were listening.

The very next day, Republicans kicked off their convention in San Diego, California, gathering to officially nominate Robert Dole. While many felt that the convention itself contained little real news, as Republicans attempted to put on their own spin on the proceedings without any interference from what they view as an unsympathetic and sometimes hostile liberal-leaning media, the days leading up to the convention were just the opposite. First, Dole announced that his economic agenda would include a 15 percent across the board income tax cut as well as a 50 percent reduction in the capital gains tax. This announcement, one which championed supply-side economics (supply-side economics is based upon the belief that lower tax levels result in increased revenue and capital which in turn spurs economic growth) over Dole's deficit reduction instincts, was followed by his announcement that supply-side champion Jack Kemp, a former professional football player, congressman, and Secretary of Housing and Urban Development, would be his running mate. This move surprised many, some of whom recalled a widely reported "joke" attributed to Dole earlier in his career: "Did you hear the good news? A bus load of supply-siders just went over a cliff. Did you hear the bad news? Jack Kemp wasn't on it."

The uniting of Dole, a self-described deficit hawk who throughout his career placed deficit and spending reductions ahead of tax cuts and was always wary of supply-side economic theories, with Kemp, a man 13 years his junior whose view on the economy as well as immigration and affirmative action could not have been more different from Dole's before he joined the Republican presidential ticket, showed once again that politics can make strange bedfellows.

While Dole was introducing Jack Kemp to the country, behind the scenes, moderate and conservative Republicans vied for control of the party platform. While moderate Republicans demanded that language which included toleration for the views of those Republicans who did not support the passage of a constitutional amendment banning abortion be added to the platform, conservative Republicans demanded that any language that hinted at tolerance on this issue be stricken from the platform. In the end, the two sides struck a compromise which temporarily satisfied the opponents and helped to avoid a fight over the issue on the convention floor, an outcome which all Republicans hoped to avoid.

The convention itself contained a number of highlights. On the opening night, Republicans led off with former Presidents Gerald R. Ford and George Bush. They were followed by a stirring video tribute to former President Ronald Reagan which brought many in the convention hall to tears. Afterward, Nancy Reagan appeared on stage and offered an emotional speech on behalf of her ailing husband. She was followed by the night's keynote speaker, retired General Colin Powell. Making the case for a "big tent" party, one that was big enough to include social conservatives and those whose views were more moderate, Powell gave a rousing speech, offering us a glimpse of a possible future Powell candidacy. Bob Dole's wife, Elizabeth Dole, made her first significant campaign appearance at the convention. Moving from the podium to the convention floor during her address, Elizabeth Dole discussed her husband's accomplishments in a manner that endeared her to the convention delegates as well as the viewing audience. After her unexpectedly stunning performance, many openly wondered how the Democratic Party and Hillary Clinton would respond.

On the convention's final night, Bob Dole gave what many considered to be his best speech of the campaign. Offering himself up as a bridge to America's future as well as its past, Dole went on the offensive, attacking President Clinton and many of his "liberal" supporters, most notably the teacher's union, touting his economic agenda, and promising to renew and reinvigorate efforts to crack down on crime and drug use. By convention's end, some polls showed that Dole had received anywhere between a 10 and 20 percent post-convention "bounce" in the polls, narrowing his gap with Bill Clinton considerably. For all the criticism then heaped on the Republican convention by journalists and some political pundits who felt the GOP had offered up a carefully crafted political spectacle, one devoid of real news that generated dismal television ratings, Republicans claimed they had accomplished their major goals—erase memories of the contentious 1992 convention in Houston, paint a picture of a unified Republican party, and rally support for the Dole/Kemp ticket.

Two weeks later, Democrats gathered in Chicago, home of the infamous 1968 Democratic convention in which Vietnam war protesters and Chicago police repeatedly clashed in the city parks and streets. Unlike the Republican convention, the days leading up to the Democratic gathering contained few significant developments. But, while the Democrats might have seemed like a unified party, beneath the surface, fissures in the foundation could be detected. A week earlier, President Clinton signed a bill which ended the federal guarantee of welfare, transferring all responsibility for managing welfare to the states. This move, though popular with the majority of Americans, angered many Democrats, especially Democratic delegates who tend to be more liberal than both Democrats and the country as a whole. This convention though, like the Republican gathering, was designed to showcase unity, not division. The welfare debate then was not highlighted by convention organizers.

Similar to the Republican gathering, the Democratic convention contained some highlights. Former Ronald Reagan Chief of Staff James Brady and his wife Sarah Brady appeared on-stage to thank President Clinton for championing the passage of the Brady Bill, a bill that called for a waiting period before an individual could purchase a gun which Republicans found difficult to support in the past due to their close affiliation with the National Rifle Association. Seeing Jim Brady, who has been confined to a

Despite dropping out of the presidential race in April, Pat Buchanan remained a presence at the Republican National Convention. Here, Buchanan and his wife, Shelley, work their way through a crowd of reporters and delegates at the convention. (Photo courtesy: Ron Edmonds/AP Photo)

wheelchair and undergone untold amounts of physical and speech therapy since he was shot during an assassination attempt on President Reagan, both address the convention hall and do so standing was an emotional moment. Vice President Gore also gave a moving speech, discussing his sister's fight against lung cancer—a fight she eventually lost—in an effort to crystallize the Democrat's opposition to tobacco use by teenagers. Democrats did also decide to feature Hillary Clinton, a decision which became a necessity after Elizabeth Dole's performance at the Republican convention. Mrs. Clinton deftly responded to her conservative critics while all the while touting the achievements of the first four years of her husband's administration. In the end, Hillary Clinton's convention performance, though not as well received as Elizabeth Dole's, was praised rather than panned, an outcome that relieved many Democratic operatives who had pre-convention jitters because of the First Lady's somewhat negative pre-convention poll ratings. Finally, President Clinton closed the convention with a speech that outlined his accomplishments during his first four years as president and sketched out his agenda for the next four years, an agenda which promised "more of the same." Marred only by the untimely resignation of Dick Morris, President Clinton's chief political adviser, this convention like the Republican one before it received criticism for being more a staged event than real news. But in spite of this criticism and continued low viewer ratings, much like the Republicans before them Democrats achieved their overriding goals, painting a picture of a unified Democratic party that had put their differences aside and embraced the opportunity to champion the Clinton/Gore ticket.

One measure of the Democrat's success can be seen in the public opinion polling. Polls the next day showed that Clinton's post-convention bounce had placed him again anywhere from 10 to 20 percentage points ahead of Dole, and that both Clinton and Dole held substantial leads over Ross Perot. Overall, while all three conventions were a success as judged by their organizers, the dramatic bounce we have sometimes seen occur after previous conventions, where one candidate trailing badly in the polls makes a sudden and sustained jump following their convention, failed to occur in 1996. By month's end, each of the three major presidential candidates saw poll ratings similar to those they enjoyed before the first convention was held. Whether or not this is a trend we will continue to see as these affairs become more tightly organized and orchestrated remains to be seen.

The Debates

After weeks of discussion, the Commission on Presidential Debates, a bipartisan panel of five Republicans and five Democrats, brokered a deal with Republican presidential candidate Bob Dole and Democrat Bill Clinton, agreeing on a debate schedule that included two presidential debates along with one vice presidential debate. The format of the first presidential debate, held in Hartford, Connecticut on October 6, was a traditional one, 90 minutes in length and moderated by a single individual—Jim Lehrer, the host of public television's evening news program. The second debate, held in San Diego, California, made use of the popular "town-hall" style first used at the presidential level in the 1992 presidential contest, with those in attendance asking questions of the candidates.

The big early news was the debate commission's decision to bar Reform Party presidential candidate Ross Perot and vice presidential candidate Pat Choate from the debates. In addition to several objective guidelines, such as whether or not Perot or Choate were on enough ballots in enough states to win, the debate commission examined whether or not Perot and Choate stood a "realistic chance" of winning.

The debate commission's decision to exclude Perot and Choate was quickly followed by a lawsuit. Demanding that the Federal Election Commission (FEC) or the debate commission halt the scheduled debates unless he and his running mate were allowed to participate, Perot alleged that the debate commission violated recent FEC regulations, first by including President Clinton and Republican Bob Dole solely because of their major party affiliation and, second, by then using subjective standards for admitting any other debaters. Two days before the first presidential debate, a panel of federal appeals court judges turned Perot down, citing the fact that Perot needed to take his arguments through the months-long FEC complaint process instead of jumping straight to court.

Going into the first presidential debate, the stakes were high and the goals of each of the two major-party candidates clear. Republican challenger Dole hoped to use the debates to kick off a campaign turnaround. Trailing President Clinton by roughly 15 percent in most polls, Dole wanted to reintroduce himself to voters and demonstrate that despite his age, he is upbeat, vigorous, and sharp. Aiming simply to avoid substantive blunders and nonverbal gaffes (in 1992, a camera caught then President George Bush glancing down at his watch, giving many viewers the impression he thought he had better places to be), Clinton's goal was much simpler—to do no harm to his own successful campaign.

During the generally civil first presidential debate, both Bob Dole and Bill Clinton took steps towards accomplishing their debate goals. While Dole took great care to draw a picture of a nation lacking in leadership and establish himself as a man to lead the country into the 21st century, Clinton's oft-repeated reply echoed his basic theme—"It is not midnight in America, Senator. We are better off than we were four years ago." Offering contrasting views of the 21st century, the basic difference that emerged from the debate was Clinton's contention that government should provide people with the tools necessary to make the most out of their own lives and Dole's response that in most cases, it is better to reduce the reach and cost of the federal government and trust the people to make their own way.

Post-debate polls gave Clinton the edge, although almost two-thirds of the respondents contacted within the first half-hour after the debate for a CNN/Newsweek poll replied that Bob Dole had won the expectations game, doing better than they expected prior to the debate. Two polls, one by ABC news and the other by Newsweek, conducted immediately after the debate had Clinton winning the contest by a 50 to 28 percent margin and a 55 to 38 percent margin, respectively. But it should be remembered that debates usually reinforce rather than change opinions, and that was mainly what happened on October 6. Among those who supported Clinton before the debate, 82 percent thought he won it, and 95 percent still supported him after it. Among viewers who supported Bob Dole before the debate, 63 percent thought he won it, and 94 percent still supported him after it.

Vice President Al Gore and Republican vice presidential candidate Jack Kemp squared off October 9th in St. Petersburg, Florida. Focusing on the familiar issues that differentiated their top-of-the-ticket running mates just three days earlier, both Gore and Kemp cast the election as a referendum on the country's direction. Gore, characterizing Dole's 15 percent across the board tax cut proposal as a risky tax scheme, argued that the Republicans' plan would "blow a hole" in the deficit, sending the nation's economy over "Niagara Falls" in a barrel. Kemp shot back that "the only hole it would blow is a hole in the plans of this administration to tinker with the tax code." While a post-debate poll conducted by ABC News showed that sampled voters preferred Gore's performance to Kemp's by a 50 to 27 percent margin (with 21 percent calling it a tie), the big story was how few voters watched the debate. As with the August 1996 conventions, when television ratings hit an all-time low, viewership for this debate as well as the first presidential debate was down over 20 percent from four years ago.

In the final presidential debate, an audience of 113 San Diego citizens who had been selected by the Gallup Organization (a well-known national polling organization) because they had supposedly not yet made up their minds about whom they intended to vote for in November posed questions to President Clinton and Senator Dole. Still trailing Clinton in the polls by a double-digit margin, Dole turned his attention to more personal issues, raising doubts both about the personal and public character of Clinton and his administration. An extremely comfortable Clinton—Clinton has always been at his best in settings like the one in San Diego—responded to none of the accusations, instead displaying an easygoing attitude in a setting that allowed him to sympathize with voters one minute and display a mastery of policy the next. Having made use of the town meeting format since his days as governor of Arkansas, Clinton realized early on in his political career that audience members want to be part of a civil enterprise more than a pro wrestling match. His instincts proved correct this night. In an ABC News post-debate poll, while 14 percent of viewers called the contest a tie, 55 percent thought Clinton won, while 28 percent viewed Bob Dole as the winner. Again though, in a pattern similar to the first presidential debate, 97 percent of those people surveyed who supported either Clinton or Dole prior to the debate still supported them after it, proving once again how little the 1996 presidential debates did to change the attitudes of a largely disinterested electorate.

The Fall Campaign and General Election Results

As the campaign developed in the months following the August conventions, all of the pre-election public opinion polls showed President Clinton well in front of his GOP challenger. Without question, he again ran a superb campaign. His strategy, targeted television advertising, use of the media, and energetic stumping proved to be largely on target. Fielding a strong Democratic campaign team that included many familiar faces from 1992, Clinton was again able to successfully project a moderate, centrist image that appealed to a wide range of voters. Keeping his message focused on the relatively strong economy, Clinton secured the support of many so-called "Reagan Democrats"—registered Democrats who had voted for Republican candidates in the 1980s. Clinton also appealed directly and effectively to young voters, senior citizens, minorities, and women, securing the strong support of each of these voting groups.

Dole's campaign, in contrast, was slow to organize and even slower to focus on consistent themes. Finding his voice only late in the campaign, the Dole campaign hopped, skipped, and jumped from one topic to another before finally settling on trust and character issues just a few weeks prior to election day. Reminding many of the inept campaign efforts of former President Bush in 1992 and Michael S. Dukakis in 1988, even Republicans were quick to criticize their presidential nominee.

Although the differences between the two campaigns was certainly a factor in the outcome of the election, as we have seen, it is also true that any election involving an incumbent president is essentially a referendum on his incumbency. In 1980, Ronald Reagan hit on this point when he asked voters to consider whether they were better off today than they were four years ago. The electorate decided it was not and voted accordingly.

To illustrate this point, in 1992 a number of reasons beyond George Bush's lackluster campaign drove voters to Bill Clinton, the most important of which was the state of the U.S. economy. The most basic of all forces in presidential elections, the economy suffered a serious recession in 1990–91 and began to recover only fitfully and painfully in the months leading up to the 1992 election. In many ways relating to their pocket-

President Bill Clinton confers with campaign strategists during the 1996 presidential campaign. (Photo courtesy: Jim Colburn/ Photoreporters, Inc.)

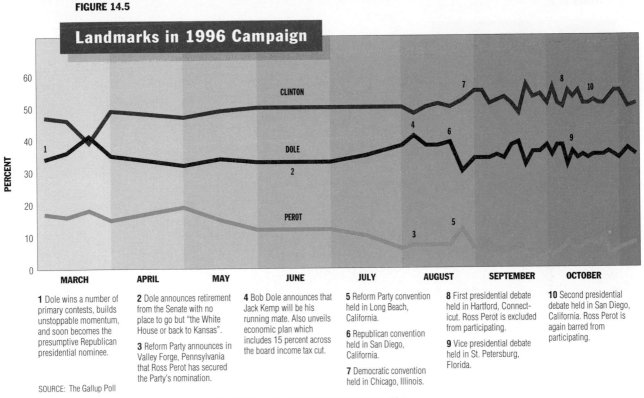

FIGURE 14.5

Landmarks in 1996 Campaign

CLINTON

DOLE

PEROT

PERCENT

60
50
40
30
20
10
0

MARCH   APRIL   MAY   JUNE   JULY   AUGUST   SEPTEMBER   OCTOBER

1 Dole wins a number of primary contests, builds unstoppable momentum, and soon becomes the presumptive Republican presidential nominee.

2 Dole announces retirement from the Senate with no place to go but "the White House or back to Kansas".

3 Reform Party announces in Valley Forge, Pennsylvania that Ross Perot has secured the Party's nomination.

4 Bob Dole announces that Jack Kemp will be his running mate. Also unveils economic plan which includes 15 percent across the board income tax cut.

5 Reform Party convention held in Long Beach, California.

6 Republican convention held in San Diego, California.

7 Democratic convention held in Chicago, Illinois.

8 First presidential debate held in Hartford, Connecticut. Ross Perot is excluded from participating.

9 Vice presidential debate held in St. Petersburg, Florida.

10 Second presidential debate held in San Diego, California. Ross Perot is again barred from participating.

SOURCE: The Gallup Poll

Percentages indicate percentage of registered voters sampled by the Gallup poll who said they would vote for the candidates.

books, voters simply did not believe they were better off in 1992 than four years earlier, which predisposed them to change the status quo. By contrast, in 1996 Clinton was fortunate enough to have presided over four years of relatively stable economic growth. This general optimism about the economy spilled over into a general sense of well-being. Over half of those voters surveyed said the country was on the right track. This represented a reversed scenario from 1992, when only 39 percent said the country was on the right track while 56 percent said it was on the wrong track. As the election approached its conclusion, voters looked back to 1992 and concluded that in fact they were better off than four years earlier.

Election Results

Capping a remarkable comeback just two years after voters soundly rejected his policies and threw the Democrats out of power in Congress, Clinton became the first Democrat since Franklin D. Roosevelt to win reelection. Clinton stitched together a victory by winning the vast majority of the black and Hispanic vote and splitting the white vote with Dole. Clinton also defeated Dole in all age categories (18–29; 30–44; 45–59; 60+)—from Generation Xers to seniors, with his biggest margin among young voters (53 to 35 percent). Clinton's grand prize, however, was the women's vote: He beat Dole 54 to 37 percent among women. Among white women, the 1996 gender chasm narrowed somewhat—49 to 42 percent. Having split the male vote with Dole (44 percent for Clinton, 45 percent for Dole), Clinton's edge among women proved to be the difference in the 1996 election.

Voter turnout was down in 1996. Just an estimated 48.8% of those Americans eligible to vote did so. These numbers represent a sharp decline from 1992, when about

TABLE 14.2

1996 Election Results

STATE	CLINTON	DOLE	PEROT	STATE	CLINTON	DOLE	PEROT
Alabama	43%	51%	6%	Montana	41%	44%	14%
Alaska	33	51	11	Nebraska	35	53	11
Arizona	47	44	8	Nevada	44	43	9
Arkansas	54	37	8	New Hampshire	50	40	10
California	51	38	7	New Jersey	53	36	9
Colorado	44	46	7	New Mexico	49	41	6
Connecticut	52	35	10	New York	59	31	8
Delaware	52	37	11	North Carolina	44	49	7
District of Columbia	85	9	2	North Dakota	40	47	12
Florida	48	42	9	Ohio	47	41	11
Georgia	46	47	6	Oklahoma	40	48	11
Hawaii	57	32	8	Oregon	47	37	11
Idaho	34	52	13	Pennsylvania	49	40	10
Illinois	54	37	8	Rhode Island	60	27	11
Indiana	42	47	10	South Carolina	44	50	6
Iowa	50	40	9	South Dakota	43	46	10
Kansas	36	54	9	Tennessee	48	46	6
Kentucky	46	45	9	Texas	44	49	7
Louisiana	52	40	7	Utah	33	54	10
Maine	52	31	14	Vermont	54	31	12
Maryland	54	38	7	Virginia	45	47	7
Massachusetts	62	28	9	Washington	51	36	9
Michigan	52	38	9	West Virginia	51	37	11
Minnesota	51	35	12	Wisconsin	49	39	10
Mississippi	44	49	6	Wyoming	37	50	12
Missouri	48	41	10				

SOURCE: *The Associated Press*, Wednesday, November 6, 1996.

55 percent of Americans aged eighteen and over turned up at the polling places. In fact, voter turnout in 1996 was the lowest since 1924.

Clinton's Electoral College victory (379 for Clinton, 159 for Dole, and 0 for Perot) was much broader than his popular vote plurality (49 percent for Clinton, 41 percent for Dole, and 9 percent for Perot) (See Table 14.2). He was thus again to be a "minority president"—elected by less than half of the popular vote*—but one whose win was nonetheless impressive.

The Democrats won states in every region of the country. As in 1992, they swept the Northeast, again winning even reliably Republican New Hampshire. Except for Indiana, the Midwest was solidly Democratic, as was the Pacific Coast.

Bob Dole achieved a respectable showing only in the South, the Plains states, and the Rocky Mountains. But even in the South, which had long been solidly Republican, Florida went to Bill Clinton, as did Kentucky, Louisiana, as well as Clinton's Arkansas and Gore's Tennessee.

*Fifteen of our forty-two chief executives were elected with less than a majority. The most recent prior to Clinton's 1996 and 1992 elections was Richard Nixon, who garnered 43 percent of the popular vote in 1968's three-way race.

By the standards of recent history, Clinton's Electoral College majority (an improvement from his 370 Electoral College votes in 1992) was the most impressive and diverse for a Democrat since Lyndon Johnson's landslide election in 1964. Dole fared worse than Bush, who in 1992 won 168 Electoral College votes, but did better than former President Jimmy Carter, who in his 1980 reelection bid captured just forty-nine Electoral College votes, the post-World War II record for the most decisive defeat of an incumbent.

CHANGING CAMPAIGN FINANCE LAWS

*I*n response to growing concerns about the amounts of money spent on federal elections, both Republicans and Democrats have sponsored major campaign finance reform bills in Congress. But changing the rules of the game can alter the results of elections. Not surprisingly, Democratic proposals tend to favor Democratic candidates while Republican proposals tend to favor Republican candidates. For many years now, as a consequence, Congress has created more smoke than fire on campaign reform.

Prior to the 1994 congressional elections, Democrats supported setting a limit on the amount of money congressional candidates could spend in an effort to win office. (For the House a candidate would have been limited to $600,000; the Senate limit would have depended on each state's population, with a more heavily populated state having a higher limit.) Republicans, long the congressional minority, were adamantly against these spending caps. They argued that the limits mainly hurt challengers who are not as well known as incumbents and who need to spend more money to increase their name identification. For example, from 1978 to 1988, only seven of the thirty-two winning Senate challengers remained within the spending limits proposed by the Democrats. The Democrats responded that without limits on total campaign spending, personally wealthy candidates, like Steve Forbes, have an advantage over less affluent candidates. This advantage results from the present federal contribution limits and the Supreme Court decision in *Buckley* v. *Valeo*, which ruled that limits on a candidate's spending of personal funds violates his Constitutional right to free speech. In the spring of 1992, the proposed legislation was passed by the Democratic legislative majority only to be vetoed by then Republican President George Bush.

In the four years since President Bush's veto, Democratic President Bill Clinton and Republican lawmakers have championed campaign finance reform only to later renege on their pledges. Prior to the 1992 presidential election, then candidate Bill Clinton pledged to support and sign strong campaign finance reform legislation. Once in office, this promise fell by the wayside. In 1994 Democratic legislators were swept out of office and replaced with Republicans, who had also campaigned on the promise of change. Yet, conspicuously absent from the Republican Contract with America was campaign finance reform. In June 1995 President Clinton and Republican Speaker of the House of Representatives Newt Gingrich, in a joint appearance, were asked by an audience member whether they would support the formation of a commission to reform the campaign finance system. Both men said yes—shaking hands in mutual agreement for the cameras. Predictably, since that handshake, neither Speaker Gingrich nor President Clinton has seriously addressed the need for campaign finance reform. The impasse continues!

Of course, both parties' positions on this issue are rooted in self-interest. The Republicans are usually more successful than are Democrats at raising money, and the

Democrats want to limit that advantage. Moreover, the cost to either party of conceding too much on this issue is the possibility of relinquishing control of Congress. This makes campaign spending an issue that does not easily lend itself to compromise.

While most discussions of campaign finance reform focus on spending and contribution limits, many experts inside and outside of Congress argue that there are other ideas concerning campaign finance that would create a more wholesome system without resorting to limits. One idea is to limit the influence of political action committees (PACs). Critics charge that PACs reduce political competition by giving overwhelmingly to incumbents—usually about two-thirds to three-quarters of their war chests—while at the same time they corrupt the system by indebting legislators to the special interests that form PACs. Supporters argue that PACs better represent the "little guys" in American politics by allowing them to pool their funds and have a greater impact on campaigns and elections. Abolishing PACs altogether, however, is probably unconstitutional, since doing so would violate the First Amendment's guarantee of free political association. Restricting their contribution limits too greatly would only divert their money into other forms of political spending that are not easily revealed (such as funneling cash to state and local parties in states that do not require full campaign finance disclosure). As reformers through the years have discovered, it is nearly impossible to dam the flow of political money in a free and open democratic system in which participation is encouraged.

A better way to control PACs and special-interest groups is to increase the influence and level of spending by political parties. This would limit PACs indirectly by augmenting the power of a rival source of campaign funds. As is discussed in chapter 12, parties can be strengthened in many ways, especially by loosening or eliminating current restrictions on what citizens may give to a party or what a party may donate to its candidates. In addition, parties ought to receive some free broadcast time on all television and radio stations. This air time could then be allocated to the most needy nominees—incumbents who are in trouble, as well as promising challengers. Since candidates spend a major portion of their campaign funds for media advertising time—up to 60 percent in some Senate races—such a reform could conceivably help to cut the burgeoning costs of campaigns. And it would aid challengers and less wealthy candidates in particular, balancing some of the advantages of incumbency. Of course, this reform also has First Amendment problems because, along with the "free" air time, candidates would likely be required to agree on total television advertising time. The United States, incidentally, is the only major democratic country that does not provide some free media time to parties or candidates.

There is one other possible workable solution to the campaign finance ills, one that takes advantage of both current realities and the remarkable self-regulating tendencies of a free-market democracy. Consider the American stock market. Most government oversight simply makes sure that publicly traded companies accurately disclose vital information about their finances. The philosophy is that buyers, given the information they need, are intelligent enough to look out for themselves. There will be winners and losers, of course, both among companies and the consumers of their securities, but it is not the government's role to guarantee anyone's success. The notion that people are smart enough—and indeed have the duty—to think and choose for themselves also underlies our basic democratic arrangement. There is no reason why the same principle cannot be successfully applied to a free market for campaign finance. In this scenario disclosure laws would be broadened and strengthened, and penalties for failure to disclose would be ratcheted up, while rules on other aspects—such as sources of funds and sizes of contributions—could be greatly loosened or even abandoned altogether.

Call it *deregulation plus*. Let a well-informed marketplace, rather than a committee of federal bureaucrats, be the judge of whether someone has accepted too much money

North—South

POLITICS AROUND THE WORLD

Campaigning is probably the area in which the United States, Mexico, and Canada are most alike, or at least becoming so. Over the last thirty or forty years, the explosion in the use of television has dramatically altered the way campaigns are run (see also North–South feature in chapter 15). In part because it is expensive, networks devote only a limited amount of time to news, and only certain types of people and themes come across well in the medium. We have seen a shift everywhere toward telegenic candidates, spin doctors, and sound bites, because whatever goes on television has to be presented in a few minutes of air time at most and has to be visually appealing. Canada and Mexico have not gone as far in these directions as the United States, but they are certainly moving that way.

In Canada, both the nature of the parliamentary system and some specific laws governing the electoral process have slowed "progress" along these lines. Remember, the real contests in Canada take place in the individual ridings among candidates representing highly disciplined political parties. While that makes campaigns from one district to another more uniform than in the United States, where congressional and senatorial candidates shy away from their parties more often than not, there is somewhat less emphasis on the candidates for prime minister than one finds in U.S. presidential elections. Similarly, money matters somewhat less because there is a brief, three-week formal campaign period, the government reimburses parties and candidates for many of their expenses, and there is far less television advertising (none on the state-owned Canadian Broadcasting Corporation, CBC).

In Mexico, television probably matters less than in either of the other two countries, both because of the expense involved and because of the PRI's hold over the main stations. As a result, the parties have to rely more on their grassroots organizations and "old-style," locally based campaigns. The PRI in particular still draws heavily on the personalized local cliques, or *camarillas*. These are really support groups for local politicians, and are part of larger such bodies linked all the way up the party's hierarchy and which are also used to recruit candidates and appointed officials at all levels of government. Nonetheless, the 1994 presidential campaign did see something with which readers north of the border should be familiar—the first nationally televised presidential debate.

---

from a particular interest group or spent too much to win an election. Reformers who object to money in politics would lose little under such a scheme, since the current system has already utterly failed to inhibit special-interest influence. On the other hand, reform advocates might gain substantially by bringing all financial activity out into the open where the public can see for itself the truth about how campaigns are conducted.

Campaign finance reform is a favorite Washington topic; but for all the good (and bad) ideas that are proposed, little legislation is ever passed. Many incumbents prefer not to alter the system that—whatever its faults—elected them. Democrats and Republicans are also at loggerheads over the partisan effects of various reforms. The American people also remain skeptical of political parties, and little popular support can be found for strengthening them. The last set of campaign finance reforms passed in the wake of Watergate, and it may take more scandal to generate enough momentum to pass a successor package of reforms in the Congress.

As the analysis of the 1996 election suggests, the campaign process in the United States is far from perfect. Campaigns seem to stretch out interminably. Moreover, trivialities rather than the important issues of the day often determine the success or failure of campaigns, voters cast many ballots for the lesser of two evils, and some contenders for lower office never raise enough money to get a fair hearing. But those who follow campaigns would also do well to remember the wise words of one of this century's greatest political scientists, V. O. Key, Jr. Key's central observation was simple but powerful: "Voters are not fools." Not every citizen devotes enough time to politics, and many people are woefully uninformed at times. But virtually all voters know their basic interests and cast their ballots accordingly. They are not always right in their judgments, yet over time there is a rough justice to election results. Parties and office holders who produce a measure of prosperity and happiness for the electorate are usually rewarded, and those who do not keep the home folks satisfied may be forced to find another line of work (see chapter 13).

SUMMARY

With this chapter we switched our focus from the election decision itself and turned our attention to the actual campaign process. What we have seen is that while modern campaigning makes use of dazzling new technologies and a variety of strategies to attract voters, campaigns still tend to rise and fall on the strength of the individual candidate. In this chapter we have stressed the following observations:

1. At the Starting Block: Ambition and Strategy.

Campaigns, the process of seeking and winning votes in the run-up to an election, consist of five separate components: the nomination campaign or "invisible primary," in which party leaders and activists are courted to ensure that the candidate is nominated in primaries or conventions; the general election campaign, in which the goal is to appeal to the nation as a whole; the personal campaign, in which the candidate and his or her family make appearances, meet voters, hold press conferences, and give speeches; the organizational campaign, in which volunteers telephone voters, distribute literature, organize events, and raise money; and the broadcast media campaign waged on television and on the radio.

2. The Structure of a Campaign.

Campaign staffs combine volunteers, a manager to oversee them, and key political consultants—including media consultants, a pollster, and a direct mailer. In recent years media consultants have assumed greater and greater importance, partly because the cost of advertising has skyrocketed, so that campaign media budgets consume the lion's share of available resources.

3. The Candidate or the Campaign: Which Do We Vote For?

Despite the dazzle of technology and the celebrity of well-known consultants, the candidate remains the most important component of any campaign. The candidate's strengths, weaknesses, and talents are central to the success or failure of the campaign.

4. Modern Campaign Challenges.

Candidates tell their story directly in paid broadcast media advertising. They are much less successful in managing and directing their press coverage.

5. A Summary of Contributions and Expenses.

Receiving the majority of their financial war chest from individuals, and spending most of these funds for television advertising, today's senatorial candidates struggle to keep pace with the rising costs associated with campaigning for a seat in the U.S. Senate.

6. Bringing It Together: The 1996 Presidential Campaign and Election.

Campaigns receive money from several sources. Individual contributions are currently limited to $1,000 per candidate per election; political action committees, which represent interest groups, are limited to $5,000. In addition, candidates can receive large supplements from their party, and they can spend as much of their own money as they like.

7. Changing Campaign Finance Laws.

Campaign finance is regularly a reform issue because candidates who outspend their opponents tend to win, and raising money is easier for some candidates than for others. Incumbents enjoy a fund-raising edge as well as advantages related to name recognition and some of the perks of office, such as mailing privileges.

KEY TERMS

candidate debate, p. 550

contrast ad, p. 547

direct mailer, p. 545

free media, p. 545

general election campaign, p. 542

get-out-the-vote (GOTV), p. 545

inoculation advertising, p. 547

matching funds, p. 555

media campaign, p. 542

media consultant, p. 545

negative ad, p. 546

nomination campaign, p. 542

organizational campaign, p. 542

paid media, p. 545

personal campaign, p. 542

political action committee (PAC), p. 554

pollster, p. 545

positive ad, p. 546

public funds, p. 555

spot ad, p. 547

voter canvass, p. 545

SELECTED READINGS

Abramson, Paul R., John H. Aldrich, and David W. Rohde. *Change and Continuity in the 1992 Elections*. Washington, D.C.: CQ Press, 1995.

Ansolabehere, Stephen and Shanto Iyengar. *Going Negative: How Attack Ads Shrink and Polarize the Electorate*. New York: Free Press, 1995.

Fenno, Richard F. *Senators on the Campaign Trail: The Politics of Representation*. Norman: University of Oklahoma Press, 1996.

Goldenberg, Edie, and Michael W. Traugott. *Campaigning for Congress*. Washington, D.C.: CQ Press, 1984.

Greive, R. R. Bob. *The Blood, Sweat, and Tears of Political Victory—and Defeat*. Lanham, Md.: University Press of America, 1996.

Herrnson, Paul S. *Congressional Elections: Campaigning at Home and in Washington*. Washington, D.C.: CQ Press, 1995.

Hertzke, Allen D. *Echoes of Discontent: Jesse Jackson, Pat Robertson, and the Resurgence of Populism*. Washington, D.C.: CQ Press, 1993.

Holbrook, Thomas M. *Do Campaigns Matter?* Thousand Oaks, CA: Sage Publications, 1996.

Jackson, Brooks. *Honest Graft: Big Money and the American Political Process*. Washington, D.C.: Farragut, 1990.

Kern, Montague. *30-Second Politics: Political Advertising in the Eighties*. New York: Praeger, 1989.

Nelson, Michael, ed. *The Elections of 1996*. Washington, D.C.: CQ Press, 1997.

Orren, Gary R., and Nelson W. Polsby, eds. *Media and Momentum: The New Hampshire Primary and Nomination Politics*. Chatham, NJ: Chatham House, 1987.

Patterson, Thomas E. *The Mass Media Election*. New York: Praeger, 1980.

Pika, Josepha A. and Richard A. Watson, *The Presidential Contest*, 5th ed. Washington, D.C.: CQ Press, 1995.

Pomper, Gerald M., ed. *The Election of 1992: Reports and Interpretations*. Chatham, NJ: Chatham House, 1993.

Sabato, Larry J., and Glenn R. Simpson. *Dirty Little Secrets: The Persistence of Corruption in American Politics*. New York: Times Books, 1996.

Sabato, Larry J., ed. *Campaigns and Elections: A Reader in Modern American Politics*. Glenview, IL: Scott, Foresman, 1989.

——. *PAC Power: Inside the World of Political Action Committees*. New York: Norton, 1985.

——. *Paying for Elections: The Campaign Finance Thicket*. New York: Priority Press for the Twentieth Century Fund, 1989.

——. *The Rise of Political Consultants: New Ways of Winning Elections*. New York: Basic Books, 1981.

Salmore, Barbara G., and Stephen Salmore. *Candidates, Parties, and Campaigns*, 2d ed. Washington, D.C.: CQ Press, 1989.

Sorauf, Frank J. *Inside Campaign Finance*. New Haven: Yale University Press, 1992.

Troy, Gil. *See How They Ran: The Changing Role of the Presidential Candidate*. Cambridge: Harvard University Press, 1996.

(Photo courtesy: Stephan Savoia/AP Photo)

THE NEWS MEDIA

*T*he old argument that the networks and other media elites have a liberal bias is so blatantly true that it's hardly worth discussing anymore." So claimed a senior network news correspondent outraged over a colleague's news segment on the flat tax proposal advocated by Republican presidential candidate Malcolm "Steve" Forbes, Jr., during the 1996 presidential campaign. In the disputed segment, aired on the *CBS Evening News,* the correspondent referred to Forbes' "Number One Wackiest Flat Tax Promise," and the segment ended with the reporter commenting, "The fact is the flat tax is one giant, untested theory. One economist suggested, before we put it in, we should test it out someplace—like Albania." The segment clearly seemed to some viewers to go beyond merely relaying the facts. The controversy over the news segment reopened a debate over whether network correspondents editorialize during the news segments by providing too much commentary and pushing their own views.

The CBS news story capped a dramatic reversal of Forbes's fortune with the media. Two weeks before the 1996 Iowa caucus, Forbes, buoyed by early self-financed advertisements, emerged in the polls as the dark-horse rival to early front-runner Bob Dole. After months of dominance in the polls by Dole, making the Republican nomination seem a foregone conclusion, the media seized the chance to turn the campaign into a heated contest. In typical "horse-race" journalism, the media identified Forbes as the chief contender to Dole and lavished positive media attention on Forbes. Whether due to the media attention or not, Forbes's rating in the polls climbed higher, closing the gap between him and Dole.

But as the Iowa caucus neared, the media seemed to turn against Forbes. Major newspapers and newsmagazines came out strongly against the Forbes flat tax. The unflattering media coverage was exacerbated by Forbes's own overreliance on highly negative ads (which polls revealed turned off voters) in both Iowa and New Hampshire. The CBS news story, which appeared shortly after the Iowa caucus, was but one part of a media barrage against the flat tax. Forbes eventually placed a distant fourth in both Iowa and New Hampshire and, after poor showings in other primaries, left the race in March 1996.

Many claim that such reversals of fortune are the nature of the game and that the media should focus attention on chief rivals to the front-runners in order to better inform voters. This attention inevitably brings scrutiny of the is-

573

sues, and some issues may not hold under closer inspection. Defenders of the media assert that it is the media's legitimate role to bring these facts to light. Undoubtedly, this is a proper function of the media, but at issue *is* whether the media is fairly exploring issues of the candidates or interjecting their own positions on the issues. Are assertions that the flat tax is suitable only for Albania dispassionate analysis of the facts designed to better inform voters? Or is it editorial commentary telling us what we should think about it? While liberals and conservatives alike claim media bias, both agree that the media often engage in more commentary than information. In the end even top CBS officials seemed to recognize that they had gone too far, admitting that the controversial segment on Forbes's flat tax was flawed and should have stuck to the facts.

The media have the potential to exert enormous influence over Americans. Not only does the press tell us what is important by setting the agenda for what we will watch and read, but they can also influence what we think about issues through the content of the news stories. The simple words of the Constitution's First Amendment, "Congress shall make no law . . . abridging the freedom of the speech, or of the press" have shaped the American republic as much as or more than any others in the Constitution and its amendments. With the Constitution's sanction, as interpreted by the Supreme Court over two centuries, a vigorous and highly competitive press has emerged. This freedom has been crucial in facilitating the political discourse and education necessary for the maintenance of democracy. But does this freedom also entail responsibility on the part of the press? Has the press, over the years, met its obligation to provide objective, issue-based coverage of our politicians and political events, or does the media tend to focus on the trivial and sensational, ignoring the important issues and contributing to voter frustration with their government and their politicians? How this freedom evolved, the ways in which it is manifested, and whether press freedom is used responsibly are subjects we examine further in this chapter.

The chapter reviews the historical development of the press in the United States, and then explores the contemporary media scene. Does the press go too far in their coverage of public figures and issues, and are they biased in their reporting? Does the press really influence public opinion, and does the press allow itself to be manipulated by skilled politicians? We also explore the ways in which the government controls the organization and operation of the press, attempting to promote a balance between freedom and responsibility on the one hand, and competitiveness and consumer choice on the other. In discussing the changing role and impact of the media, we will address the following:

- First, we discuss *the evolution of the press*, from the founding of the country up to modern times.

- Second, we examine the *current structure and role of the media*.

- Third, we discuss the *contemporary trends in media attention* toward investigative journalism during the Watergate era and, more recently, toward character issues and intrusive examination of the private lives of public figures.

- Fourth, we investigate *the media's influence on the public*, and whether public opinion is significantly swayed by media coverage.

- Fifth, we observe *the ways politicians use the media* and attempt to influence press coverage for their own ends.

- Sixth, we explain how *the government regulates the electronic media,* and identify the motivations for and evolution of such control.

- Finally, we look at *change in the news media*—in particular, the phenomenal growth of cable television during the past two decades and how this growth has changed the face of broadcast journalism.

THE AMERICAN PRESS OF YESTERYEAR

*J*ournalism—the process and profession of collecting and disseminating the news (that is, new information about subjects of public interest)—has been with us in some form since the dawn of civilization (see Highlight 15.1: Landmarks of the American Media for a history of the media in the United States).[1] Yet its practice has often been remarkably uncivilized, and it was much more so at the beginning of the American republic than it is today.

The first newspapers were published in the American colonies in 1690. The number of newspapers grew throughout the 1700s, as colonists began to realize the value of a press free from government oversight and censorship. Thus it was not surprising that one of the most important demands made by Anti-Federalists (see chapter 2) during our country's constitutional debate was that an amendment guaranteeing the freedom of the press be included in the final version of the Constitution.

Highlight 15.1

Landmarks of the American Media

1690 First newspaper published

1789 First party newspapers circulated

1833 First penny press

1890 Yellow journalism spreads

1900 Muckraking in fashion

1928 First radio broadcast of an election

1948 First election results to be covered by television

1952 First presidential campaign advertisements aired on television

1960 First televised presidential campaign debates

1979 The Cable Satellite Public Affairs Network (C-SPAN) is founded, providing live round-the-clock coverage of politics and government.

1980 Cable News Network (CNN) is founded by media mogul Ted Turner, making national and international events available instantaneously around the globe.

1992 Talk-show television circumvents the news, allowing candidates to go around journalists to reach the voting public directly.

1996 Official candidate home pages containing among other things candidate profiles, issue positions, campaign strategy and slogans, and e-mail addresses appear on the World Wide Web.

North—South

POLITICS AROUND THE WORLD

From what we have seen in the last few chapters, it should be clear that the mass media, especially television, play a vital role in any country and will continue to do so even more in the future as access continues to expand. Not surprisingly, there are some important differences between the media in the United States and its two neighbors.

Overall, the American media are more decentralized and national than in the other two countries. That is to say, people in the United States still get most of their information from newspapers and radio and television stations that are locally owned or controlled. Similarly, despite the spread of cable and satellite TV and, to a lesser degree, the Internet, very few Americans are exposed to news and other information presented to them by foreigners.

Canada occupies an intermediate position between the United States and more centralized countries such as France or Great Britain, which are dominated by national print and audiovisual media. The CBC (Canadian Broadcasting Corporation) is a national organization, but as in the United States, local, especially non-CBC, stations develop much of their own programming, including their news. Although state-owned, the CBC has a strong tradition of independence from government interference in the content of its news. As in the United States, there is no national "newspaper of record," although the *Toronto Globe and Mail* comes close, much like the *New York Times* and *Washington Post*. Most Canadians, however, read a local newspaper (if they read one at all), and almost all of the 100 or so titles are owned by only two companies. It should also be pointed out that there is a separate media network for French-speaking Canada, although some television shows appear in both languages.

Far more important than any of this, however, is the fact that, unlike people in the United States, Canadians get much of their news from foreign (mostly American) sources. Since most Canadians live within seventy-five miles of the U.S. border, they were able to watch American television and listen to American radio long before the cable/satellite explosion. Now, virtually everyone has access to CNN (not to mention Fox, ESPN, and the Home Shopping Network), and many seem to rely heavily on U.S. (and to a lesser extent British and French) networks for news as well as entertainment.

The situation in Mexico is quite different. The problem isn't access to the media; virtually everyone can watch television or listen to its hundreds of AM (there is no FM) radio stations. Instead, the concern is with the lack of a free press. There is next to no opposition in Mexican newspapers, which are beholden to the PRI government for access to everything from news to newsprint. The government exerts similar leverage over the mostly privately owned television networks, some of which are carried on American cable systems. The Mexican media are by no means as controlled as those in the old Communist countries were, but it is very difficult for people to gain independent perspectives on events from them, and there is little evidence that sources such as CNN International's Spanish service have yet made much of a difference.

During his presidency, George Washington escaped most press scrutiny but detested journalists nonetheless; his battle tactics in the Revolutionary War had been much criticized in print, and an early draft of his "Farewell Address to the Nation" at the end of his presidency (1796) contained a condemnation of the press that has often been described as savage.[2] Thomas Jefferson was treated especially harshly by elements of the early U.S. press. For example, one Richmond newspaper editor, angered by Jefferson's refusal to appoint him as postmaster, concocted a falsehood that survives to this day: that Jefferson kept a slave as his concubine and had several children by her.[3] One can understand why Jefferson, normally a defender of a free press, commented that "even the least informed of the people have learned that nothing in a newspaper is to be believed."

Jefferson probably did not intend that statement literally, since he himself was instrumental in establishing the *National Gazette,* the newspaper of his political faction and viewpoint. The *Gazette* was created to compete with a similar paper (called the *Gazette of the United States*) founded earlier by Alexander Hamilton and his anti-Jefferson Federalists. The era of party newspapers extended from Washington's tenure through Andrew Jackson's presidency. The editor of Jackson's party paper, *The Globe,* was included in the president's influential "kitchen cabinet" (a group of informal advisers), and all of Jackson's appointees with annual salaries greater than $1,000 were required to buy a subscription. (Incidentally, from George Washington through James Buchanan, who left office in 1861, all government printing contracts were awarded to the newspaper associated with the incumbent administration).

A Less Partisan Press

The partisan press eventually gave way to the penny press. In 1833 Benjamin Day founded the *New York Sun,* which cost a penny at the newsstand. Because it was not tied to one party, it was politically more independent than the party papers. The *Sun* was the forerunner of the modern press built on mass circulation and commercial advertising to produce profit. By 1861 the penny press had so supplanted partisan papers that President Abraham Lincoln (who succeeded Buchanan) announced that his administration would have no favored or sponsored newspaper.

"Uncle Sam's Next Campaign—the War Against the Yellow Press." In this 1898 cartoon in the wake of the Spanish-American War, yellow journalism is attacked for its threats, insults, filth, grime, blood, death, slander, gore, and blackmail, all of which are "lies." The cartoonist suggests that, after winning the foreign war, the government ought to attack its own yellow journalists at home. (Photo courtesy: Stock Montage, Inc.)

The press thus became markedly less partisan but not necessarily more respectable. Mass-circulation dailies sought wide readership, and readers were clearly attracted by the sensational and the scandalous. The sordid side of politics became the entertainment of the times. One of the best-known examples occurred in the presidential campaign of 1884, when the *Buffalo Evening Telegraph* headlined "A Terrible Tale" about Grover Cleveland, the Democratic nominee.[4] In 1871, while sheriff of Buffalo, the bachelor Cleveland had allegedly fathered a child. Even though the woman in question had been seeing other men, Cleveland willingly accepted responsibility since all the other men were married, and he had dutifully paid child support for years. Fortunately for Cleveland, another newspaper, the *Democratic Sentinel,* broke a story that helped to offset this scandal: Republican presidential nominee James G. Blaine and his wife had had their first child just three months after their wedding. There is a lesson for politicians in this double-edged morality tale. Cleveland acknowledged his responsibility forthrightly and took his lumps, whereas Blaine told a fabulously elaborate, completely unbelievable story about having had two marriage ceremonies six months apart. Cleveland won the election (although other factors also played a role in his victory).

In the late 1800s and early 1900s, the era of the intrusive press was in full flower. First yellow journalism and then muckraking were in fashion. Pioneered by prominent publishers such as William Randolph Hearst and Joseph Pulitzer, **yellow journalism**[5] featured pictures, comics, and color designed to capture a share of the burgeoning immigrant population market. These newspapers also oversimplified and sensationalized many news developments. The front-page editorial crusade became common, the motto for which frequently seemed to be, "Damn the truth, full speed ahead."

After the turn of the century, the muckrakers—so named by President Theodore Roosevelt after a special rake designed to collect manure[6]—took charge of a number of newspapers and nationally circulated magazines. **Muckraking** journalists such as Upton Sinclair and David Graham Phillips searched out and exposed real and apparent misconduct by government, business, and politicians in order to stimulate reform.[7] There was no shortage of corruption to reveal, of course, and much good came from these efforts. But an unfortunate side effect of the emphasis on crusades and investigations was the frequent publication of gossip and rumor without sufficient proof.

The modern press corps may also be guilty of this offense, but it has achieved great progress on another front. Throughout the nineteenth century, payoffs to the press were not uncommon. Andrew Jackson, for instance, gave one in ten of his early appointments to loyal reporters;[8] and during the 1872 presidential campaign, the Republicans slipped cash to about 300 newsmen.[9] Wealthy industrialists also sometimes purchased editorial peace or investigative cease-fire for tens of thousands of dollars. Examples of such press corruption are exceedingly rare today, and not even the most extreme of the modern media's critics believe otherwise.

As the news business grew, its focus gradually shifted from passionate opinion to corporate profit. Newspapers, hoping to maximize profit, were more careful to avoid alienating the advertisers and readers who produced their revenues, and the result was less harsh, more objective reporting. Meanwhile, media barons became pillars of the establishment; for the most part, they were no longer the antiestablishment insurgents of yore.

Technological advances had a major impact on this transformation in journalism. High-speed presses and more cheaply produced paper made mass-circulation dailies possible. The telegraph and then the telephone made news gathering easier and much faster, and nothing could compare to the invention of radio and television. When radio became widely available in the 1920s, millions of Americans could hear national politi-

yellow journalism: A form of newspaper publishing in vogue in the late nineteenth century that featured pictures, comics, color, and sensationalized, oversimplified news coverage.

muckraking: A form of newspaper publishing, in vogue in the early twentieth century, concerned with reforming government and business conduct.

cians instead of merely reading about them. With television—first introduced in the late 1940s, and nearly a universal fixture in U.S. homes by the mid-1950s—citizens could see and hear candidates and presidents. The removal of newspapers and magazines as the foremost conduits between politicians and voters had profound effects on the electoral process, as we discuss shortly.

THE CONTEMPORARY MEDIA SCENE

he editors of the first partisan newspapers could scarcely have imagined what their profession would become more than two centuries later. The number and diversity of media outlets existing in the 1990s are stunning: The **print press**—many thousands of daily and weekly newspapers, periodicals, magazines, newsletters, and journals; and the **electronic media**—radio and television stations and networks, and computerized information services. In some ways the news business is more competitive now than at any time in history; yet, paradoxically, the news media have expanded in some ways and contracted in others, dramatically changing the ways in which they cover politics.

The growth of the political press corps is obvious to anyone familiar with government or campaigns. Since 1983, for example, the number of print (newspaper and magazine) reporters accredited at the U.S. Capitol has jumped from 2,300 to more than

print press: The traditional form of mass media, comprising newspapers, magazines, and journals.

electronic media: The newest form of broadcast media, including television, radio, and cable.

In March 1996, at the Radio and Television Correspondents Association annual gala in Washington, D.C., radio "shock jock" Don Imus stretched the limits of propriety in roasting President Bill Clinton in what became an unprecedented and unanticipated media event. (Photo courtesy: J. Scott Applewhite/AP Photo)

4,100; the gain for broadcast (television and radio) journalists was equally impressive and proportionately larger, from about 1,000 in 1983 to more than 2,400 by 1990.[10] On the campaign trail, a similar phenomenon has been occurring. In the 1960s a presidential candidate in the primaries would attract a press entourage of at most a couple of dozen reporters, but in the 1990s a hundred or more print and broadcast journalists can be seen tagging along with a front-runner. Consequently, a politician's every public utterance is reported and intensively scrutinized and interpreted in the media.

Although there are more journalists, they are not necessarily attracting a larger audience, at least on the print side. Daily newspaper circulation has been stagnant for twenty years at 62 million to 63 million papers per day (see Figure 15.1). On a per-household basis, circulation has actually fallen 44 percent from 1976 to 1996.[11] Barely half of the adult population reads a newspaper every day. Among young people age eighteen to twenty-nine, only one-third are daily readers—a decline of 50 percent in two decades.

Along with the relative decline of readership has come a drop in the overall level of competition. In 1880, 61 percent of U.S. cities had at least two competing dailies, but by 1990 a mere 2 percent of cities did so. Not surprisingly, the number of dailies has declined significantly, from a peak of 2,600 in 1909 to 1,611 today.[12] Most of the remaining dailies are owned by large media conglomerates called chains. In 1940, 83 percent of all daily newspapers were independently owned, but by 1990 just 24 percent remained independent of a chain (such as Gannett, Hearst, Knight-Ridder, and Newhouse). Chain ownership usually reduces the diversity of editorial opinions and can result in the homogenization of the news.

FIGURE 15.1

Circulation of Daily Newspapers, 1850–1993 (Selected Years)

YEAR	NUMBER OF DAILY NEWSPAPERS	CIRCULATION (IN THOUSANDS)	CIRCULATION AS A PERCENTAGE OF POPULATION
1850	254	758	2.3%
1890	1,610	8,387	13.3%
1909	2,600	24,212	26.2%
1919	2,441	33,029	31.0%
1927	2,091	41,368	35.7%
1937	2,065	43,345	34.1%
1947	1,854	53,287	37.0%
1958	1,778	58,713	33.6%
1970	1,748	62,100	30.3%
1991	1,586	60,687	23.9%
1993	1,556	59,812	

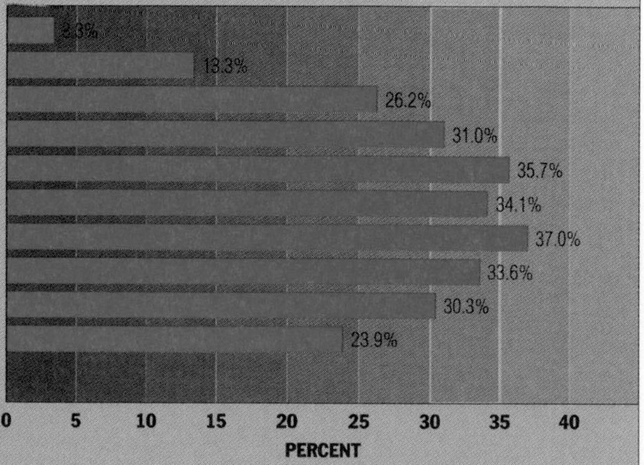

PERCENT: 0 5 10 15 20 25 30 35 40

SOURCE: Adapted from Harold W. Stanley and Richard G. Niemi, *Vital Statistics on American Politics*, 4th ed. (Washington: CQ Press, 1994), Table 2–3, pp. 56–57. Reprinted by permission.

FIGURE 15.2

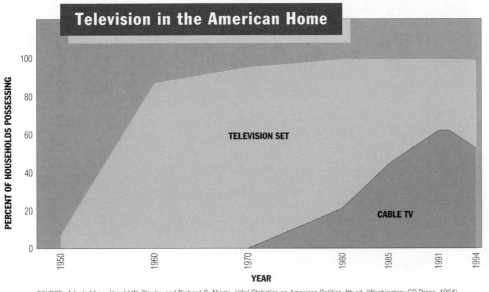

Television in the American Home

SOURCE: Adapted from Harold W. Stanley and Richard G. Niemi, *Vital Statistics on American Politics*, 4th ed. (Washington: CQ Press, 1994), Table 2–1, p 53. Reprinted by permission.

Part of the cause of the newspapers' declining audience has been the increased numbers of television sets and cable subscribers (see Figure 15.2) and the increased popularity of television as a news source. At the dawn of the 1960s, a substantial majority of Americans reported that they got most of their news from newspapers; but by the latter half of the 1980s, television was the people's choice by an almost two-to-one margin.[13] Moreover, by a margin of 55 percent to 21 percent, Americans now say that they are inclined to believe television over newspapers when conflicting reports about the same story arise. Of course, most individuals still rely on both print *and* broadcast sources,[14] but there can be little question that television news is increasingly important. Despite its many drawbacks (such as simplicity, brevity, and entertainment orientation), television news is "news that matters."[15] Although not totally eclipsing newspapers, television frequently overshadows them, even though it often takes its agenda and lead stories from the headlines produced by print reporters (especially those working for the print elite—papers such as the *New York Times*, the *Washington Post*, and the *Wall Street Journal*; wire services such as the Associated Press and United Press International; and journals such as *Time, Newsweek,* and *U.S. News & World Report*). Regrettably, busy people today appear to have less time to review the printed word, and consequently they rely more on television's brief headline summaries to stay in touch.

The television news industry differs from its print counterpart in a variety of ways. The number of outlets has been increasing, not declining, as with newspapers. The three major networks now receive broadcast competition from Cable News Network (CNN), *Headline News*, Cable Satellite Public Affairs Network (C-SPAN), and PBS's *NewsHour/Jim Lehrer*. Although the audiences of all the alternate shows are relatively small compared with those of the network news shows, they are growing while the networks' audience shares contract. The potential for cable expansion is still large, too; fewer than half of all U.S. households are currently wired for cable. Adding to television's diversity, the national television news corps is often outnumbered on the cam-

Politics Now

Media Mergers

The last ten years have seen radical changes in the structure of the communications industry. As the 1995 Disney/ABC, Westinghouse/CBS, and Time–Warner/Turner Broadcasting mergers illustrate, mega-corporations are fast becoming the rule rather than the exception in the world of communications.

These multimillion-dollar mergers are a new phase in the life of the communications industry. Until the 1960s newspapers were under family ownership and television stations were locally owned. The 1960s generated the first tide of mergers within the communications industry. Unlike the mergers of today—where a broadcasting company may own many television stations, newspapers, magazines, and cable operations—early mergers consisted mostly of newspaper chains buying other newspapers and broadcasting operations purchasing other radio or TV stations.

The contemporary shift from the limited mergers of yesterday to the conglomerate mergers of today is the result of changes in the economic outlook of these companies. First, when one company merges with another, the increased competition forces other companies to follow suit. Thus you might think of the wave of mergers that swept the communications industry in 1995 as a chain reaction: Each new merger provided the impetus for the next one. Secondly, the communications industry is one of the fastest growing in the United States. Couple this growth with the recent passage by Congress of telecommunications deregulation legislation—a bill that helps lift virtually all restrictions on the number of radio and television stations that a single company can own—and you have the recipe for money-making mergers!

Despite the rush of excitement surrounding the "year of the merger," voices of caution persist. Within the communications community and in Congress, too, there are some doubts about the practical consequences of these mergers. In short, jobs are always at stake when companies merge. A merger that might look good for the economic future of the company is not necessarily good for the hundreds or thousands of employees who face the possibility of having their position with the new multimedia conglomerate terminated.

Those outside of the media industry also express fear about the consequences of these mergers, remarking that the ability of journalists to report the news in an unbiased manner can be undermined by unsupervised corporate control. For example, if a corporation is lobbying Congress to gain the passage of favorable legislation, that corporation might encourage the journalism arm of its conglomerate to produce stories that support their position (or at least, to refrain from criticizing its plans).

The mass buying of local television stations, cable companies, phone companies, newspapers, and magazines also causes some to fear the end of diversity in news reporting. While it is clear that recent deregulation will offer the opportunity for more of these types of mergers in the future, we must be sure that the level of diversity and multiplicity of voices that a thriving democracy requires is not sacrificed in the rush to merge. These mergers might be good for the bottom line. But with only a few mega-corporations controlling the vast majority of communication outlets, will different voices still be heard?

paign trail by local television reporters. Satellite technology has provided any of the 1,300 local stations willing to invest in the hardware an opportunity to beam back reports from the field. On a daily basis, local news is watched by more people (67 percent of adults) than is network news (49 percent), so increased local attention to politics has some real significance. But see Politics Now: Media Mergers, for some concerns about the future of objective journalistic standards.

The decline of the major networks' audience shares and the local stations' decreasing reliance on the major networks for news—coupled with stringent belt tightening ordered by the networks' corporate managers—resulted in severe news staff cutbacks at NBC, CBS, and ABC during the 1980s. These economy measures have affected the quality of broadcast journalism. Many senior correspondents bemoan the loss of desk assistants and junior reporters, who did much of the legwork necessary to get less superficial, more in-depth pieces on the air. As a consequence, stories requiring extensive research are often discarded in favor of simplistic, eye-catching, "sexy" items that increasingly seem to dominate campaign and government coverage.

Media That Matter

Every newspaper, radio station, and television station is influential in its own area, but only a handful of media outlets are influential in a national sense. The United States has no nationwide daily newspapers to match the influence of Great Britain's *The Times, Guardian,* and *Daily Telegraph,* all of which are avidly read in virtually every corner of the United Kingdom. The national orientation of the British print media can be traced to the smaller size of the country and also to London's role as both the national capital and the largest cultural metropolis. The vastness of the United States and the existence of many large cities, such as New York, Los Angeles, and Chicago, effectively preclude a nationally united print medium in this country.

However, national distribution of *The New York Times,* the *Wall Street Journal, USA Today,* and the *Christian Science Monitor* does exist, and other newspapers, such as the *Washington Post* and the *Los Angeles Times,* have substantial influence from coast to coast. These six newspapers also have a pronounced effect on what the four national **networks** (ABC, CBS, NBC, and CNN) broadcast on their evening news programs—or, in the case of CNN, air on cable around the clock. A major story that breaks in one of these papers is nearly guaranteed to be featured on one or more of the network news shows. These news shows are carried by hundreds of local stations—called **affiliates**—that are associated with the national networks and may choose to carry their programming. A **wire service,** such as the Associated Press (AP) (established in 1848), also nationalizes the news. Most newspapers subscribe to the service, which not only produces its own news stories but also puts on the wire major stories produced by other media outlets.

The national newspapers, wire services, and broadcast networks are supplemented by a number of national news magazines, whose subscribers number in the millions. *Time, Newsweek,* and *U.S. News & World Report* bring the week's news into focus and headline one event or trend for special treatment. Other news magazines stress commentary from an ideological viewpoint, including *The Nation* (left-wing), *The New Republic* (moderate–liberal), and *The National Review* (conservative). These last three publications have much smaller circulations, but because their readerships are composed of activists and opinion leaders, they have disproportionate influence.

network: An association of broadcast stations (radio or television) that share programming through a financial arrangement.

affiliates: Local television stations that carry the programming of a national network.

wire service: An electronic delivery of news gathered by the news services' correspondents and sent to all member news media organizations.

HOW THE MEDIA COVER POLITICIANS AND GOVERNMENT

*M*uch of the media's attention is focused on our politicians and the day-to-day operations of our government. In this section we will discuss how the press covers the three constitutionally created branches of government (Congress, the president, and the courts), and show how the tenor of this coverage has changed since the Watergate scandal of the early 1970s.

Covering the Presidency

The three branches of the U.S. government—the executive, the legislative, and the judicial—are roughly equal in power and authority, but in the world of media coverage, the president is first among equals. All television cables lead to the White House, and a president can address the nation on all networks almost at will. On television, Congress and the courts appear to be divided and confused institutions—different segments contradicting others—whereas the commander-in-chief is in clear focus as chief of state and head of government. The situation is scarcely different in other democracies. In Great Britain, all media eyes are on No. 10 Downing Street, the office and residence of the prime minister.

Since Franklin D. Roosevelt's time, chief executives have used the presidential press conference to shape public opinion and explain their actions (see Figure 15.3). The pres-

FIGURE 15.3

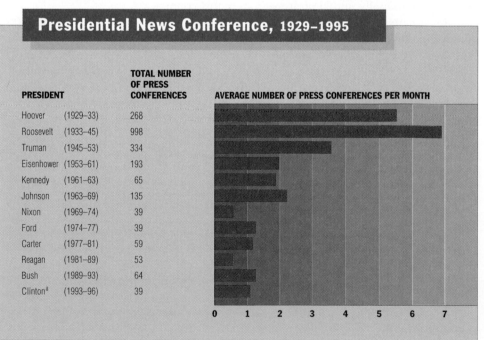

Presidential News Conference, 1929–1995

PRESIDENT		TOTAL NUMBER OF PRESS CONFERENCES	AVERAGE NUMBER OF PRESS CONFERENCES PER MONTH
Hoover	(1929–33)	268	
Roosevelt	(1933–45)	998	
Truman	(1945–53)	334	
Eisenhower	(1953–61)	193	
Kennedy	(1961–63)	65	
Johnson	(1963–69)	135	
Nixon	(1969–74)	39	
Ford	(1974–77)	39	
Carter	(1977–81)	59	
Reagan	(1981–89)	53	
Bush	(1989–93)	64	
Clinton[a]	(1993–96)	39	

[a]As of May 15, 1995.

SOURCE: Adapted from Harold W. Stanley and Richard G. Niemi, *Vital Statistics on American Politics*, 4th ed. (Washington: CQ Press, 1994), Table 2 4, pp. 59. Reprinted by permission

Highlight 15.2

The White House Press Corps

Perhaps the most visible part of the national press corps is the group of correspondents who work at the White House. Every network, many large television stations, and virtually all big-city daily newspapers have at least one representative who works in the White House to cover the president and his chief advisers. Other media outlets representing foreign countries are also given access to the White House and are included in the presidential press corps.

White House reporters are usually restricted to the press room, where the president makes announcements and holds informal question-and-answer sessions. Although presidential appearances in the press room rarely occur more than once or twice a week, the president's news secretary appears daily to brief reporters on the chief executive's current schedule and activities. Frequently the press secretary also makes announcements on behalf of the president (perhaps the chief executive's comments on just-released economic statistics, for example).

Formal presidential news conferences, often held in the East Room of the White House, are an elaborate production, especially if held during prime-time hours. All the networks carry them live and in full, and correspondents jockey to attract the president's attention. The best-known reporters are nearly guaranteed to be selected to ask a question, and these are prime opportunities for them and for the news organizations they represent. Over the years, many of the networks' most prominent professionals have served on the White House beat, including CBS's Dan Rather and Lesley Stahl, NBC's Tom Brokaw, and ABC's Sam Donaldson.

It is not always easy for the president to have reporters literally underfoot. But the instantaneous access to the American people they give the president is essential to his work, and the scrutiny of the chief executive they offer the American people is vital to the voters as well.

---

ence of the press in the White House (see Highlight 15.2: The White House Press Corps) enables a president to appear even on very short notice and to televise live, interrupting regular programming. The White House's press-briefing room is a familiar sight on the evening news, not just because presidents use it so often, but also because the presidential press secretary has almost daily question-and-answer sessions there.

The press secretary's post has existed only since Herbert Hoover's administration (1929–1933), and the individual holding it is the president's main conduit of information to the press. For this vital position, a number of presidents have chosen close aides who were very familiar with their thinking. For example, John F. Kennedy had Pierre Salinger (now an ABC News foreign correspondent), Lyndon B. Johnson had Bill Moyers (who now hosts many PBS documentaries), and Jimmy Carter chose his longtime Georgia associate Jody Powell. Probably the most famous recent presidential press secretary is James Brady, who was wounded and disabled in the March 1981 assassination attempt on President Ronald Reagan.

Covering Congress

Press coverage of Congress is very different from media coverage of the president. The size of the institution alone (535 members) and its decentralized nature (bicameralism, the committee system, and so on) make it difficult for the media to survey. Nevertheless, the congressional press corps has more than 3,000 members.[16] Most news organizations solve the size and decentralization problems by concentrating coverage on three groups of individuals. First, the leaders of both parties in both houses receive the lion's share of attention because only they can speak for a majority of their party's members. Usually the majority and minority leaders in each house and the Speaker of the House are the preferred spokespersons, but the whips also receive a substantial share of air time and column inches. Second, key committee chairs command center stage when subjects in their domain are newsworthy. Heads of the most prominent committees (such as Ways and Means or Armed Services) are guaranteed frequent coverage, but even the chairs and members of minor committees or subcommittees can achieve fame when the time and issue are right. Third, local newspapers and broadcast stations will normally devote some resources to covering their local senators and representatives, even when these legislators are junior and relatively lacking in influence. Most office holders, in turn, are mainly concerned with meeting the needs of their local media contingents, since these reporters are the ones who directly and regularly reach the voters in their home constituencies.

One other kind of congressional news coverage is worth noting: investigative-committee hearings. Occasionally, a sensational scandal leads to televised congressional committee hearings that transfix and electrify the nation. In the early 1950s, Senator Joseph R. McCarthy (R–Wis.) held a series of hearings to expose and root out what he claimed were Communists in the State Department and other U.S. government agencies, as well as Hollywood's film industry. The senator's style of investigation, which involved many wild charges made without proof and the smearing and labeling of some innocent opponents as Communists, gave rise to the term *McCarthyism*.

The Watergate hearings of 1973 and 1974—which stemmed from White House efforts to eavesdrop on officials of the Democratic National Committee and then to cover up presidential involvement in the scheme—made heroes out of two committee chairs, Senator Sam Ervin (D–N.C.) and U.S. Representative Peter Rodino (D–N.J.). They uncovered many facts behind the Watergate scandal and then pursued the impeachment of President Richard M. Nixon. (Nixon resigned in August 1974, before the full House could vote on his impeachment.)

In 1987 the Iran–Contra hearings—set up to investigate a complicated Reagan administration scheme in which arms were sold to Iran and the profits were then diverted to the Nicaraguan anti-Communist Contras—also created a popular hero. This time, however, the hero was not the committee chair but a witness, Lieutenant Colonel Oliver North, a White House aide deeply involved in the plot. North's boyish appeal and patriotic demeanor projected well on television, on which all the hearings were carried live (as were the McCarthy and Watergate hearings). North capitalized on his fame and in 1994 launched an unsuccessful campaign for a U.S. Senate seat from Virginia. In October 1991, the nation viewed another televised committee spectacle when Supreme Court nominee Clarence Thomas was accused of sexual harassment (see Highlight 15.3: The Clarence Thomas Hearings). More recently, throughout the latter months of 1995 and 1996, Whitewater hearings led by Senator Alfonse D'Amato (R–N.Y.) questioned the actions of President Clinton and Hillary Rodham Clinton in a failed investment venture while Clinton was Governor of Arkansas.

Coverage of Congress has been greatly expanded through use of the cable industry channel C-SPAN, the Cable Satellite Public Affairs Network, founded in 1979. C-SPAN1 and C-SPAN2 provide gavel-to-gavel coverage of House and Senate sessions as well as many committee hearings. For the first time, Americans can watch their representatives in action (or inaction, as the case may be), and do so twenty-four hours a day.

During the Senate Whitewater hearings, Paul Sarbanes (D-Md.) and Alfonse D'Amato (R-N.Y.) listen to testimony on the actions of President Bill Clinton and First Lady Hillary Rodham Clinton. (Photo courtesy: Dennis Brack/Black Star)

Covering the Courts

The branch of government that is the most different, in press coverage as in many other respects, is the judicial branch. Cloaked in secrecy—because judicial deliberations and decision-making are conducted in private—the courts receive scant coverage under most circumstances. However, a volatile or controversial issue, such as abortion, can change the usual type of coverage, especially when the Supreme Court is rendering the decision. Each network and major newspaper has one or more Supreme Court reporters, people who are usually well schooled in the law and whose instant analysis of court opinions interprets the decisions for the millions of people without legal training. Gradually, the admission of cameras into state and local courtrooms across the United States is offering people a more in-depth look at the operation of the judicial system. As yet, though, the Supreme Court does not permit televised proceedings.

Even more than the Court's decisions, presidential appointments to the high Court are the focus of intense media attention. As the judiciary has assumed a more important role in modern times, the men and women considered for the post are being subjected to withering scrutiny of their records and even of their private lives. For example, the media's disclosure that Douglas Ginsberg had smoked marijuana extensively as an adult forced President Reagan to withdraw his Supreme Court nomination in 1987.

Watergate and the Era of Investigative Journalism

The Watergate scandal of the Nixon administration had the most profound impact of any modern event on the manner and substance of the press's conduct. In many respects Watergate began a chain reaction that today allows for intense scrutiny of pub-

Highlight 15.3

The Clarence Thomas Hearings

As with Watergate and the Iran–Contra scandal, Clarence Thomas's nomination to the Supreme Court in 1991 gave rise to a television extravaganza that mesmerized the American people. The U.S. Senate Judiciary Committee hearings on allegations of sexual harassment that were lodged against Thomas drew a large audience for three full days in early October 1991.

A few months earlier, President George Bush had nominated Thomas, a black conservative, to succeed retiring Justice Thurgood Marshall, a pillar of the civil rights movement. Thomas appeared to be heading for an easy Senate confirmation when National Public Radio's correspondent Nina Totenberg reported the harassment charges just days before Thomas's scheduled confirmation vote. The all-male Senate Judiciary Committee had earlier disregarded the charges, in part because the chief accuser, University of Oklahoma Law School Professor Anita Hill, was reluctant to come forward publicly. But after the information was leaked to National Public Radio and other news outlets, the Sen-

ate was forced to postpone its confirmation vote and hold an additional Judiciary Committee hearing to investigate the allegations, which dated back to Thomas's chairmanship of the Equal Employment Opportunity Commission (EEOC) during the Reagan administration. (Hill had also been an EEOC employee and one of Thomas's subordinates.)

The hearings became a national obsession—a real-life soap opera made for television. Hill's graphic accusations of Thomas's advances and vivid sexual allusions shocked many Americans, who were equally riveted by Thomas's angry denial of the charges and denouncement of the Judiciary Committee inquiry as "a high-tech lynching." Convincing and sincere character witnesses

for both sides were produced, leaving most viewers puzzled about the truth. In the absence of hard evidence, a substantial majority of people (as measured by public opinion polls) eventually sided with Thomas, and he managed to win confirmation in the full Senate by a vote of fifty-two to forty-eight—the narrowest affirmative vote for a Supreme Court justice in this century.

The most damaging political consequences of the hearings were visited on the senators themselves. Both sides agreed that the Senate handled the matter poorly—first, by not treating Hill's accusations seriously, then by conducting a public spectacle. The Watergate hearings made heroes of many of the participating legislators (such as U.S. Senator Sam

Ervin [D–N.C.], the folksy chairman of the Senate Watergate panel). But the Thomas hearings only diminished the reputations of most senators who had the misfortune to be in the spotlight. Democrats not known to have a spotless private life, such as Senator Edward M. Kennedy (D–Mass.), were derided for hypocrisy, while Republicans such as Arlen Specter (R–Pa.) and Alan Simpson (R–Wyo.) were criticized for their often harsh questioning of Anita Hill.

The contrast between the Watergate and Thomas hearings demonstrates that intense media coverage is a double-edged sword: When the television cameras are trained on elected officials, these officials can easily emerge as national heroes—or as national objects of scorn.

The intense media attention focused on the Senate Judiciary Committee's confirmation hearings of Judge Clarence Thomas created a three-way spectacle: the senators, the testifiers (pictured at right is Thomas), and the media themselves. (Photo courtesy: Reuters/The Bettmann Archive)

llc officials' private lives. Moreover, coupled with the civil rights movement and the Vietnam War, Watergate shifted the orientation of journalism away from mere description (providing an account of happenings) and toward prescription—helping to set the campaign's (and society's) agenda by focusing attention on the candidates' shortcomings as well as on certain social problems.

A new breed and a new generation of reporters were attracted to journalism, particularly to its investigative role. As a group they were idealistic, although aggressively mistrustful of authority, and they shared a contempt for "politics as usual." The Vietnam and Watergate generation dominates journalism today. They and their younger colleagues hold sway over most newsrooms, with two-thirds of all reporters now under the age of thirty-six and an ever-increasing number of editors and executives who had their start in journalism in the Watergate era.[17]

A volatile mix of guilt and fear is at work in the post-Watergate press. The guilt stems from regret that experienced Washington reporters failed to detect the telltale signs of the Watergate scandal early on; that even after the story broke, most journalists underplayed the unfolding disaster until forced to take it more seriously by the two young *Post* reporters; that over the years journalism's leading lights had become too close to the politicians they were supposed to check and therefore for too long failed to tell the public about dangerous excesses in the government. The press's ongoing fear is deep-seated and complements the guilt. Every political journalist is apprehensive about missing the next big story, of being left on the platform when the next scandal train leaves Union Station.

The Post-Watergate Era

In the post-Watergate era, the sizable financial and personnel investments many major news organizations have made in investigative units almost guarantee that greater attention will be given to scandals and that probably more of them—some real and some manufactured—will be uncovered.

The Character Issue in Media Coverage of Politicians.   Another clear consequence of Watergate has been the increasing emphasis by the press on the character of candidates. The issue of character has always been present in U.S. politics—George Washington was not made the nation's first president for his policy positions—but rarely if ever has character been such an issue as it has in elections from 1976 onward. (See Roots of Government: The Character Issue from Grover Cleveland to Bill Clinton.) Jimmy Carter's 1976 presidential campaign was characterized by moral posturing in the wake of Watergate. Edward M. Kennedy's 1980 presidential candidacy was destroyed in part by lingering character questions. The 1988 race witnessed an explosion of character concerns so forceful that several candidates (including Gary Hart) were badly scarred by it. And the 1992 contest for the White House became a tawdry debate about the alleged mistresses of Bill Clinton and George Bush. (The evidence in both of the 1992 cases was less than convincing, but that did not stop the media.)

The character issue may in part have been an outgrowth of the "new journalism" popularized by author Tom Wolfe in the 1970s.[18] Contending that conventional journalism was sterile and stripped of color, Wolfe and others argued for a reporting style that expanded the definition of news and, novel-like, highlighted all the personal details of the newsmaker. Then, too, reporters had witnessed the success of such books as Theodore H. White's *The Making of the President* series and Joe McGinniss's *The Selling of the President 1968*, which offered revealing, behind-the-scenes vignettes of the

Roots of Government

The Character Issue from Grover Cleveland to Bill Clinton

(Photo courtesy: AP/Wide World Photo)

The character issue—which focuses press attention on the private-life activities and personalities of candidates—has been with us throughout U.S. history, as this text's reference to President Grover Cleveland's out-of-wedlock child suggests. Yet the intensity and the reach of the character issue have grown over the centuries, and particularly in recent years, as Democratic presidential candidate Gary Hart discovered to his chagrin in 1987. The press corps had long heard stories about Hart's alleged extramarital affairs, but no usable evidence had come to light. The situation changed dramatically in May 1987, shortly after Hart declared his candidacy for a second run at the White House.

The *Miami Herald* received an anonymous tip that Hart would be meeting an attractive model for a weekend tryst in Washington, D.C. This tip closely followed Hart's public insistence that the womanizing rumors about him were false and that his once-rocky marriage was again on firm ground. Hart had said to one reporter, E. J. Dionne of *The New York Times*, "Follow me around . . . [You'll] be very bored."

Bored the *Miami Herald* was not when it decided to stake out Hart's Washington townhouse. The paper's reporters apparently observed Hart and Donna Rice, the model, inhabiting the townhouse, although the journalists' surveillance was not continuous and both house entrances were not always covered. Despite the flaws in the investigation, the circumstances were suspicious enough to generate a major scandal that dominated Hart's campaign.

When other indiscretions surfaced in an overwhelming media maelstrom, Hart withdrew from the race on May 8, 1987, with a bitter blast at the "intrusive" press that had brought him down. He briefly reentered the presidential contest in December, but by then Hart was a spent force and received only a handful of votes in the early 1988 primaries.

Probably no event from the 1988 presidential campaign has proved to be as memorable as the undoing of Gary Hart. The Hart episode also marked a milestone for the news media. They had helped eliminate the Democratic Party's front-runner before a single ballot had been cast in the primaries, and they had done it by aggressively investigating the private life of the unlucky candidate.

Four years later Bill Clinton learned from Gary Hart's mistakes. Before formally announcing his presidential candidacy, he admitted unspecified extramarital indiscretions, but—with the support of his spouse, Hillary Rodham Clinton—Clinton stressed that his marriage had weathered its storms. When lounge singer Gennifer Flowers claimed a past relationship with Clinton in January 1992, the candidate was able to point to his previous revelation (while denying Flowers's specific charge). With a well-timed visit to CBS's *60 Minutes* right after the Super Bowl, the Clintons were able to demonstrate marital solidarity at a moment of crisis. And the mainstream press itself was embarrassed to follow the lead of a supermarket tabloid, *The Star*, which had first carried—and hyped—Flowers's allegations.

With a strong organization behind him, Clinton managed a second-place finish in the New Hampshire primary and dubbed himself "the comeback kid." Clinton earned the title, overcoming an obstacle that had unhorsed front-runner Hart earlier. Unfortunately for Clinton, various allegations about his involvement with women continued to be made during his presidency, but none threatened seriously to cut short his term—just as Flowers failed to derail his candidacy.

previous election's candidates.[19] Why not give readers and viewers this information before the election? the press reasoned. There was encouragement from academic quarters as well. "Look to character first" when evaluating and choosing among presidential candidates, wrote Duke University political science professor James David Barber in a widely circulated 1972 volume, *The Presidential Character* (see chapter 8).[20]

Whatever the precise historical origins of the character trend in reporting, it is undergirded by certain assumptions. First, the press sees that it has mainly replaced the political parties as the screening committee that winnows the field of candidates and filters out the weaker or more unlucky contenders. (This fact may be another reason to support the strengthening of the political parties. Politicians are in a much better position than the press to provide professional peer review of colleagues who are seeking the presidency.) Second, many journalists believe it necessary to tell people about any of a candidate's foibles that might affect his or her public performance. The press's third supposition is that it is giving the public what it wants and expects, more or less. Perhaps television has conditioned voters to think about the private lives of the rich and famous. The rules of television prominence now seem to apply to all celebrities equally, whether they reside in Hollywood or Washington. And, perhaps more important, scandal sells papers and attracts television viewers.

Loosening of the Libel Law.   Another factor permits the modern press to undertake character investigations. In the old days, a reporter would think twice about filing a story critical of a politician's character, and the editors probably would have killed the story had the reporter been foolish enough to do so. The reason? Fear of a libel suit. (Recall from chapter 5 that libel is published defamation of character that unjustly injures a person's reputation.) The first question editors would ask about even an ambiguous or suggestive phrase about a public official was, "If we're sued, can you prove beyond a doubt what you've written?"

Such inhibitions were ostensibly lifted in 1964, when the Supreme Court ruled in *New York Times Co. v. Sullivan*[21] that simply publishing a defamatory falsehood is not enough to justify a libel judgment. Henceforth a public official would have to prove "actual malice," a requirement extended three years later to all public figures, such as Hollywood stars and prominent athletes.[22] The Supreme Court declared that the First Amendment requires elected officials and candidates to prove that the publisher either believed the challenged statement was false or at least entertained serious doubts about its truth and acted recklessly in publishing it in the face of those doubts. The actual malice rule has made it very difficult for public figures to win libel cases.

New York Times Co. v. Sullivan: Supreme Court decision ruling that simply publishing a defamatory falsehood is not enough to justify a libel judgment.

Despite *Sullivan,* the threat of libel litigation (and its deterrent effect on the press) persists for at least two reasons. First, the *Sullivan* protections do little to reduce the expense of defending defamation claims. The monetary costs have increased enormously, as have the required commitments of reporters' and editors' time and energy. Small news organizations without the financial resources of a national network or the *New York Times* are sometimes reluctant to publish material that might invite a lawsuit because the litigation costs could threaten their existence. The second reason for the continuing libel threat is a cultural phenomenon of heightened sensitivity to the harm that words can do to an individual's emotional tranquility. As a result, politicians are often more inclined to sue their press adversaries, even when success is unlikely.

But high costs and the politicians' propensity to sue cut both ways. The overall number of libel suits filed in recent years has dropped because plaintiffs also incur hefty legal expenses, and—perhaps more important—they have despaired of winning. Some news outlets have added another disincentive by filing countersuits charging their antagonists with bringing frivolous or nuisance actions against them.

In practice, then, the loosening of libel law has provided journalists with a safer harbor from liability in their reporting on elected officials and candidates. Whether it has truly diminished press self-censorship, especially for financially less well-endowed media outlets, is a more difficult question to answer. However, at least for the wealthy newspapers and networks, the libel laws are no longer as severe a restraint on the press as they once were.

The Question of Bias. Whenever the media break an unfavorable story about a politician, the politician usually counters with a cry of "biased reporting"—a claim that the press has told an untruth, has told only part of the truth, or has reported facts out of the complete context of the event. Who is right? Are the news media biased? The answer is simple and unavoidable: Of course they are. Journalists are fallible human beings who inevitably have values, preferences, and attitudes galore—some conscious, others subconscious, but all reflected at one time or another in the subjects selected for coverage or the slant of that coverage. Given that the press is biased, it is important to know in what ways it is biased and when and how the biases are shown.

Truth be told, most journalists lean to the left. First of all, those in the relatively small group of professional journalists (not many more than 100,000, compared with more than 4 million teachers in the United States) are drawn heavily from the ranks of highly educated social and political liberals, as a number of studies, some conducted by the media themselves, have shown.[23] Journalists are substantially Democratic in party affiliation and voting habits, progressive and antiestablishment in political orientation, and well to the left of the general public on most economic, foreign policy, and social issues (such as abortion, affirmative action, gay rights, and gun control). Second, dozens of the most influential reporters and executives entered (or reentered) journalism after stints of partisan involvement in campaigns or government, and a substantial majority worked for Democrats.[24]

Third, this liberal press bias does indeed show up frequently on screen and in print. A study of reporting on the abortion issue, for example, revealed a clear slant to the pro side on network television news, matching in many ways the reporters' own abortion-rights views.[25]

Other Sources of Bias. From left to right, all of these criticisms have some validity in different times and circumstances, in one media forum or another. But these critiques ignore some non-ideological factors probably more essential to an understanding of press bias. Owing to competition and the reward structure of journalism, the deepest bias most political journalists have is the desire to get to the bottom of a good campaign story—which is usually negative news about a candidate. The fear of missing a good story, more than bias, leads all media outlets to the same developing headlines and encourages them to adopt the same slant.

A related nonideological bias is the effort to create a horse race where none exists. Newspeople, whose lives revolve around the current political scene, naturally want to add spice and drama, minimize their boredom, and increase their audience. Other human, not just partisan, biases are also at work. Whether the press likes or dislikes a candidate personally is often vital. Former Governor Bruce Babbitt and U.S. Representative Morris K. Udall, both wisecracking, straight-talking Arizona Democrats, were press favorites in their presidential bids (in 1988 and 1976, respectively), and both enjoyed favorable coverage. Richard M. Nixon, Jimmy Carter, and Gary Hart—all aloof politicians—were disliked by many reporters who covered them, and they suffered from a harsh and critical press. More recently, House Speaker for the 104th Congress Newt Gingrich has been the favorite target of the press. Repeatedly, the stories news-

Conservative talk show host Rush Limbaugh became the symbol for the talk-radio phenomenon of the 1990s. In addition to his daily three-hour radio broadcast, Limbaugh also had a nightly syndicated television show. (Photo courtesy: Jacques Chenet/Gamma-Liaison)

paper editors decide to print about Speaker Gingrich cast him in a negative light. This treatment has contributed to his seemingly ever-increasing negative popularity ratings.

Finally, in their quest to avoid bias, reporters frequently seize on nonideological offenses such as gaffes, ethical violations, and campaign finance problems. These objective items are intrinsically free of partisan taint and can be pursued without guilt.

For all the emphasis here on bias, it is undeniably true that the modern U.S. news media are much fairer than their predecessors ever were. News blackouts of the editors' enemies, under which all positive information about the targeted politicians was banned from print, were once shockingly common but are now exceedingly rare and universally condemned. No longer do organized groups of reporters take out advertisements to support or oppose candidates or send telegrams to the president and members of Congress advocating certain public policies or events, which occurred as recently as the 1970s.

In sum, then, press bias of all kinds—partisan, agenda-setting, and nonideological—can and does influence the day-to-day coverage of politicians. But bias is not the be-all and end-all that critics on both the right and left often insist it is. Press tilt has a marginal to moderate effect, and it is but one piece in the media's news mosaic.

THE MEDIA'S INFLUENCE ON THE PUBLIC

$\mathcal{S}$ome bias in media coverage clearly exists, as we have just discussed. But how does this bias affect the public that reads or views or listens to biased reporting?

In most cases the press has surprisingly little effect. To put it bluntly, people tend to see what they want to see; that is, human beings will focus on parts of a report that reinforce their own attitudes and ignore parts that challenge their core beliefs. Most of us also selectively tune out and ignore reports that contradict our preferences in politics and other fields. Therefore a committed Democrat will remember certain portions of a televised news program about a current campaign—primarily the parts that reinforce his or her own choice—and an equally committed Republican will recall very different sections of the report or remember the material in a way that supports the GOP position. In other words, most voters are not empty vessels into which the media can pour their own beliefs. This fact dramatically limits the ability of news organizations to sway public opinion.

And yet the news media do have some influence (called **media effects**) on public opinion. Let's examine how this is so.

First, reporting can sway people who are uncommitted and have no strong opinion in the first place. On the other hand, this sort of politically unmotivated individual is probably unlikely to vote in a given election, and therefore the media influence is of no particular consequence.

Second, the press has a much greater impact on topics far removed from the lives and experiences of its readers and viewers. News reports can probably shape public opinion about events in foreign countries fairly easily. Yet what the media say about rising prices, neighborhood crime, or child rearing may have relatively little effect because most citizens have personal experience of and well-formed ideas about these subjects.

Third, news organizations can help tell us what to think about, even if they cannot determine what we think. As mentioned earlier, the press often sets the agenda for gov-

media effects: The influence of news sources on public opinion.

ernment or a campaign by focusing on certain issues or concerns. For example, in the week following the *Exxon Valdez*'s massive oil spill off the Alaska coast in 1989, every national network devoted extensive coverage to the accident. And sure enough, concern about the environment quickly began to top the list of national problems considered most pressing by the public, as measured by opinion polls. Without the dramatic pictures and lavish media attention that accompanied the spill, it is doubtful that the environment would have risen so quickly to the forefront of the country's political agenda. Thus, perhaps not so much in *how* they cover an event, but in *what* they choose to cover, the media make their effect felt. By deciding to focus on one event while ignoring another, the media can determine to a large extent the country's agenda, an awe-inspiring power.

HOW POLITICIANS USE THE MEDIA

*T*he Clinton administration set the pace for shrewd political use of the television media. President Clinton, First Lady Hillary Rodham Clinton, and Vice President Albert Gore, Jr., all appeared on CNN's *Larry King Live*. Clinton appeared on MTV to speak directly to young voters, and Gore was a featured guest on David Letterman's late-night CBS show. Journalists, individually and in groups, are wined and dined at numerous White House receptions and intimate gatherings.

Our emphasis so far has been mainly on the ways and means of press coverage of politicians. But, as suggested by the Clinton example, the other side of the story is every

Left: President Franklin D. Roosevelt during a fireside chat in 1941. Roosevelt's skillful use of radio boosted his popularity throughout his tenure in the White House. Right: Today, President Bill Clinton (shown with Bryant Gumbel on the *Today* show) typifies the proactive stance many politicians take toward controlling their media coverage. (Photos courtesy: left, The Bettmann Archive; right, Reuters/The Bettman Archive)

bit as interesting: how politicians use the media to achieve their own ends. In chapter 14 we discuss media events (press conferences at picturesque locations, for example) that are staged to attract coverage. Other manipulations of the press can be more subtle, however. Frequently, elected officials pass along tips to reporters, seeking to curry favor or produce stories favorable to their interests. (Reporters and editors usually decide whether to publish a tip based on its newsworthiness rather than on the motivations of their sources.)

On other occasions, candidates and their aides will go on background to give trusted newspersons juicy morsels of negative information about rivals. **On background**—meaning that none of the news can be attributed to the source—is one of several journalistic devices used to solicit and elicit information that might otherwise never come to light. **Deep background** is another such device; whereas background talks can be attributed to unnamed senior officials, deep background news must be completely unsourced, with the reporter giving the reader no hint about the origin of the information. An even more drastic form of obtaining information is the **off-the-record** discussion, in which nothing the official says may be printed. (If a reporter can obtain the same information elsewhere, however, he or she is free to publish it.) By contrast, in an **on-the-record** session, such as a formal press conference, every word an official utters can be printed—and used against that official. It is no wonder that office holders often prefer the nonpublishable alternatives!

Clearly, these rules are necessary for reporters to do their basic job—informing the public. But ironically, the same rules keep the press from fully informing their readers and viewers. Every public official knows that journalists are pledged to protect the confidentiality of their sources, and therefore the rules can sometimes be used to an official's own benefit—-by, say, giving reporters derogatory information to print about a rival without having to be identified as the source. However regrettable the manipulation, it is an unavoidable part of the process.

on background: A term for when sources are not included in a news story.

deep background: Information gathered for news stories that must be completely unsourced.

off the record: Term applied to information gathered for a news story that cannot be used at all.

on the record: Term applied to information gathered for a news story that can be used and cited.

GOVERNMENT REGULATION OF THE ELECTRONIC MEDIA

*N*ot only do politicians manipulate the media, but the U.S. government also regulates the electronic component of the media. Unlike radio or television, the print media are exempt from most forms of government regulation, although even print media must not violate community standards for obscenity, for instance. There are two reasons for this unequal treatment. First, the airwaves used by the electronic media are considered public property; they are leased by the federal government to private broadcasters. Second, those airwaves are in limited supply, and without some regulation, the nation's many radio and television stations would interfere with one another's frequency signals. It was not, in fact, the federal government but rather private broadcasters, frustrated by the numerous instances in which signal jamming occurred, that initiated the call for government regulation in the early days of the electronic media. Newspapers, of course, are not subject to these technical considerations.

The first government regulation of the electronic media came in 1927, when Congress enacted the Federal Radio Act, which established the Federal Radio Commission (FRC) and declared the airwaves to be public property. In addition, the act required that all broadcasters be licensed by the FRC. In 1934 the Federal Communications Commission (FCC) replaced the FRC as the electronic media regulatory body. The FCC is composed of five members, of whom not more than three can be from the same political party. These members are selected by the president for five-year terms on an overlapping basis. Because the FCC is shielded from direct, daily control by the president or Congress—although both have influence over the FCC commissioners—it is an independent regulatory agency (see chapter 9). In addition to regulating public and commercial radio and television, the FCC oversees telephone, telegraph, satellite, and foreign communications in the United States.

In 1996 Congress passed the sweeping Telecommunications Act, deregulating whole segments of the electronic media. The goal of the legislation is to break down the barriers required by federal and state laws and by the legal settlement that broke up the AT&T/Bell monopoly in 1984 to separate local phone service, long-distance service, and cable television service. It is hoped that such deregulation and increased competition will create cheaper and better programming options for consumers and increase the global competitiveness of U.S. telecommunications firms. Under the new law, consumers might soon receive phone service from their cable provider, television programming from their local phone company, or local phone service from their long-distance phone provider. Besides more flexible service options, the legislation is expected to spur the development of new products and services such as unlimited movie selections, interactive television, and advanced computer networking that would permit more people to work from their homes.

The core of the new legislation is the federal preemption of state and local laws that grant monopolies to local telephone carriers. The seven "baby Bells," the regional phone companies that have been allowed to monopolize local telephone service since the 1984 breakup of AT&T, would be required to allow competitors to use their local networks. In return for opening their local networks to competition, the regional Bells would be allowed to enter the long-distance service market, from which they have been barred since the AT&T breakup.

There are also significant changes in the regulations for private ownership of broadcast stations. First, there is no longer a cap on how many FM and AM stations a single company can own. In the 1950s, under the 7-7-7 rule, companies were limited to seven each of television, AM, and FM stations that they could own throughout the nation. By the 1990s, however, this limit had been progressively raised to twelve television stations and twenty each of FM and AM stations. Despite eliminating the cap, there will still be limits on how many stations any one firm can own in each market. The FCC will examine on a case-by-case basis whether an owner should be allowed to have two television stations in the same local market, which is currently prohibited.

The legislation has provoked criticism by civil libertarian groups that objected to provisions designed to curb "cyberpornography." The act would ban the dissemination of "indecent" material on the Internet and online services. Indecency is a very broad legal standard that includes use of profanity. While it has been applied to broadcasting in a limited way, it has not been used in recent years as a standard for written material. The act also requires all large-screen televisions to include built-in "v-chips" that permit parents to block objectionable material they do not wish their family to view.

Content Regulation

content regulation: Governmental attempts to regulate the electronic media.

The government also subjects the electronic media to substantial **content regulation** that, again, does not apply to the print media. Charged with ensuring that the airwaves "serve the public interest, convenience, and necessity," the FCC has attempted to promote equity in broadcasting. For example, the **equal time rule** requires that broadcast stations sell campaign air time equally to all candidates if they choose to sell it to any, which they are under no obligation to do. An exception to this rule is a political debate: Stations may exclude from this event less well-known and minor-party candidates.

Another noteworthy FCC regulation is the **right-of-rebuttal rule,** which requires that a person who is attacked on a radio or television station be offered the opportunity to respond. This rule was sanctioned judicially in the 1969 Supreme Court case *Red Lion Broadcasting Company* v. *FCC*, in which the Court ruled that Fred Cook, the author of a book on U.S. Senator Barry Goldwater (R–Ariz.) (the 1964 Republican nominee for president), must be afforded the chance to answer an attack on him aired by a Pennsylvania radio station.

Perhaps the most controversial FCC regulation was the **fairness doctrine.** Implemented in 1949 and in effect until 1985, the fairness doctrine required broadcasters to be "fair" in their coverage of news events—that is, they had to cover the events adequately and present contrasting views on important public issues. Many broadcasters disliked this rule, however, claiming that fairness is simply too difficult to define and that the rule abridged their First Amendment freedoms. They also argued that it ultimately forced broadcasters to decrease coverage of controversial issues out of fear of a deluge of requests for air time from interest groups involved in each matter.

In a hotly debated 1985 decision, the FCC, without congressional consent, abolished the fairness doctrine, arguing that the growth of the electronic media in the United States during the preceding forty years had created enough diversity among the stations to render unnecessary the ordering of diversity within them. In 1986 a federal circuit court of appeals vindicated the FCC decision, holding that the FCC did not need congressional approval to abolish the rule. Seeking to counter the FCC's decision, Congress attempted to write the fairness doctrine into law, which, if successful, would have forced the FCC to implement it. Although both the House and the Senate passed the bill, President Reagan temporarily ended the controversy by vetoing it, citing his First Amendment concerns about government regulation of the news media.

The abolition of the fairness doctrine has by no means ended debate over its merit, however. Proponents, still trying to reinstate the doctrine, argue that its elimination results in a reduction of quality programming on public issues. In their view deregulation means more advertisements, soap operas, and situation comedies wasting air time and leaving less room for public discourse on important matters. Opponents of the fairness doctrine, on the other hand, continue to call for decreased regulation, arguing that the electronic media should be as free as the print media—especially because the electronic media are now probably more competitive than are the print media.

Censorship

The media in the United States, while not free of government regulation, enjoy considerably more liberty than do their counterparts in Great Britain. One of the world's oldest democracies, Great Britain nonetheless owns that nation's main electronic medium, the British Broadcasting Company (BBC). And the BBC, along with the privately owned media, is subjected to unusually strict regulation on the publication of governmental secrets. For example, the sweeping Official Secrets Acts of 1911 makes it a criminal offense for a Briton to publish any facts, material, or news collected in that person's capacity as a public minister or civil servant. The act was invoked most recently when the British government banned the publication of *Spy Catcher,* a 1987

equal time rule: The rule that requires broadcast stations to sell campaign air time equally to all candidates if they choose to sell it to any.

right-of-rebuttal rule: A Federal Communications Commission regulation that people attacked on a radio or television broadcast be offered the opportunity to respond.

fairness doctrine: Rule in effect from 1949 to 1985 requiring broadcasters to cover events adequately and to present contrasting views on important public issues.

novel written by Peter Wright, a former British intelligence officer, who undoubtedly collected much of the book's information while on the job.

In the United States, only government officials can be prosecuted for divulging classified information; no such law applies to journalists. Nor can the government, except under extremely rare and confined circumstances, impose prior restraints on the press—that is, the government cannot censor the press. This principle was clearly established in *New York Times* v. *United States* (1971).[26] In this case the Supreme Court ruled that the government could not prevent publication by the *New York Times* of the Pentagon Papers, classified government documents about the Vietnam War that had been stolen, photocopied, and sent to the *Times* and the *Washington Post* by Daniel Ellsberg, an antiwar activist. "Only a free and unrestrained press can effectively expose deception in the government," Justice Hugo Black wrote in a concurring opinion for the Court. "To find that the President has 'inherent power' to halt the publication of news by resort to the courts would wipe out the First Amendment."

To assist the media in determining what is and is not publishable, Great Britain provides a system called D-notice, which allows journalists to submit questionable material to a review committee before its publication. But D-notice has not quelled argument over media freedom in the United Kingdom. Indeed, the debate came to the fore during the 1982 Falkland Islands war between Great Britain and Argentina, when it centered on questions of how much information the public had a right to know and whether the media should remain neutral in covering a war in which the nation is involved. Once again, however, the British government prevailed in arguing for continued strict control of the media, declaring, "There can be sound military reasons for withholding the whole truth from the public domain, [or] for using the media to put out 'misinformation.' "[27]

Similar questions and arguments arose in the United States during the 1991 Persian Gulf war. Reporters were upset that the military was not forthcoming about events on and off the battlefield, while some Pentagon officials and many persons in the general public accused the press of telling the enemy too much in their dispatches. Unlike the case in Great Britain, however, the U.S. government had little recourse but to attempt to isolate offending reporters by keeping them away from the battlefield. Even this maneuver was highly controversial and very unpopular with news correspondents because it directly interfered with their job of reporting the news. (See Highlight 15.4: Miles Apart for a recent account of the relationship between the media and the military in light of Navy Admiral Jeremy M. Boorda's suicide, a suicide reportedly triggered by a media inquiry into his military record.)

Such arguments are an inevitable part of the landscape in a free society. Whatever their specific quarrels with the press, most Americans would probably prefer that the media tell them too much rather than not enough. Totalitarian societies have a tame journalism, after all, so press excesses may be the price of unbridled freedom. Without question, a free press is of incalculable value to a nation, as the recent revolution in the former Soviet Union (now the Commonwealth of Independent States) has shown. The 1991 coup against then Soviet President Mikhail Gorbachev failed in part because the coup leaders could not smother the public's continued desire for freedom, stoked by the relatively uncensored television and print journalism that existed in the final years of Gorbachev's rule.

In the United States, freedom is secured mainly by the Constitution's basic guarantees and institutions. But freedom is also ensured by the thousands of independently owned and operated newspapers, magazines, and broadcast stations. The cacophony of media voices may often be off-key and harsh, but its very lack of orchestration enables us all to continue to sing the sweet song of freedom.

Highlight 15.4

Miles Apart*

Was Adm. Jeremy M. Boorda another victim of a Washington media obsession with tearing down the reputations of the high and mighty? Are today's media instinctively anti-military?

Those questions have been raised in the wake of Boorda's suicide. They come particularly, and understandably, from the military. They deserve a lot of thought, and some answers, from the media.

Adm. Boorda's suicide was above all a personal tragedy for his family, his friends, and his service. They should have our sympathy and condolences.

And we are unlikely ever to know exactly what triggered this act of self-annihilation. But the press inquiry into Boorda's medals plays a large role in his final notes and must be addressed.

A cruel irony of this tragedy is that Boorda was liked and respected by the reporters I know who dealt with him as commander of NATO forces in the Bosnia theater. I mentioned this to him last month after he had spent four hours dealing in straightforward, cheerful fashion with ques-

tions raised during a meeting of foreign affairs experts. I understood why he got along well with my colleagues. He brushed the compliment aside, and I did not dwell on it. I wish I had.

Not that it would have changed things. The Greek chorus was already singing in this Washington tragedy. But I wish I had reflected more then on the special relationship that reporters develop with soldiers and sailors in the field, and why it does not carry over into military-press relations back in the free-fire zone that Washington has become.

That field relationship is built on a trust (sometimes betrayed by those on each side) and a camaraderie inspired by mutual danger or obstacles. Military officers frequently seem to ignore the fact that war correspondents do not make their judgments about battles, strategy, and command leadership in a vacuum or because of orders from headquarters. The good ones take their cues from the military people they know and cover.

The first generation of Vietnam correspondents questioned not the war but the way it was being fought. Their impressions

were shaped by the majors and captains who wanted the South Vietnamese to win the war and were infuriated that they could not. Later, younger and less experienced American reporters learned much of their cynicism about the war and the commanders who planned it from the younger and less experienced GIs who did the searching, destroying, and dying.

Traveling with and covering a dozen regular and guerrilla armies in Africa and the Middle East no doubt colored my belief that soldiers and reporters had more in common than in conflict, especially in battlefield situations where false or faulty information can get you killed. I have always been impressed with the candor of the military in the field, and Boorda was impressive to have kept that direct, truth-telling manner in Washington.

There is nothing here to replace the connective tissue of shared danger. In this city, the military deals with the press through a bureaucracy dedicated to and shaped by image and politics. Even in the field, that is increasingly true: In the Gulf War, reporters arrived with their own

store of cynicism that seems to have become standard issue for many since Vietnam and Watergate. And the Pentagon took advantage of that desert war to constrain, manipulate, and punish a press it (unfairly) blames for defeat in Vietnam.

The Boorda tragedy underscores the same point: The chasm between the institutions of military life and of journalism has become enormous, and continues to grow. The journalists whose inquiries seem to have lit the fuse in this case did nothing irresponsible, unethical, or even out of the ordinary. That is what is chilling: They were simply doing their jobs, as those jobs are understood today.

Journalism has become a much more competitive, bottom-line driven profession, with television playing a disproportionate role in shaping its values. The demands of that kind of journalism, and the now all-professional military, mean that few people entering journalism today have any personal exposure to the military. The military has decreasing confidence that it will be understood or treated fairly by the press and by society at large.

(Continued)

Highlight 15.4, cont'd

The media are not inherently anti-military. But the conclusion cannot be escaped that increasingly journalists are indifferent to the military and its values. Politicians who attack government indiscriminately also help undermine the national cohesion needed by the military.

It is time for all the players in this self-reinforcing cycle of chasm-building to pause, look at the results their behavior and words produce, and ask if it is really what they want.

*Source: Jim Hoaglund, *Washington Post* (May 23, 1996): A21. Reprinted with permission.

CHANGING AMERICAN NEWS MEDIA

The phenomenal growth of cable television during the past two decades has given new competition to the three major commercial television networks (ABC, CBS, and NBC). With half of all U.S. households now wired for cable television, the networks' share of the national television audience has declined steadily. Today fewer than six in every ten viewers are watching the three networks during many prime-time hours, compared with the networks' near-monopoly twenty years ago.

Some aspects of cable television's recent growth have been undesirable, at least in the eyes of critics. A case in point is the trend toward cross ownership—the possession of commercial and cable stations by the same people and corporations. As cable has become more popular and therefore more threatening to the commercial networks, these networks have been buying some cable franchises; other media giants, such as Time Warner Communications and Times–Mirror, have done the same. The concentration of commercial and cable television ownership in relatively few hands can be troubling, not least because this arrangement can reduce the diversity of programming that was originally cable's great promise.

So far, though, any fair observer would conclude that cable television has greatly increased consumer choice and made available many new options for the U.S. public. The large number of cable channels and information services suggests as much. In March 1988, for instance, 77 percent of all homes that subscribed to cable had access to thirty or more channels, and 90 percent had access to twenty or more channels.

One vital difference between cable and commercial television is the emergence of interactive systems—cable systems that allow interaction between the sender and the consumer. These interactive systems permit viewers to respond instantly to televised polls by using hand-held devices, for example. Potentially, such an arrangement could lead to televised town meetings on issues of general interest. (Both Ross Perot and Bill Clinton talked about holding electronic "town halls" in the future.) Of course, such developments must be viewed with caution as well as enthusiasm: Instant polls are unscientific and imprecise, since participants are not randomly selected, and those who respond to such public affairs programming constitute only a minute and usually unrepresentative proportion of the population.

The rise of cable television is also having a significant effect on political campaigns. For example, cable systems carry a large number of debates by local candidates. Although debates for state and national offices are televised frequently by the commercial stations, campaigns for local offices have often been neglected, largely because they are of interest to only a relatively small audience. Cable channels are so numerous that access for local candidates is much less of a problem. Cable channels also permit candidates to target paid political advertisements at small, select audiences. Such narrow casting to targeted groups—as opposed to broadcasting to a large, diversified audience—enables candidates to tailor a message to Hispanics watching a Spanish-language channel, sports fans who watch ESPN, or younger voters who watch MTV, for example.

In general, then, cable means more choice in media and less influence for the commercial networks. These changes can prove to be beneficial, a frequent result of diversity and decentralization, or cable could turn out to be just more wasted fluff in programming that is distinct only because it is packaged a bit differently. Consumers of television—all of us who make up the audience—will help to determine cable television's quality.[28]

The U.S. press is constantly evolving, including in its relationship with the public. Television talk shows, such as CNN's *Larry King Live*, came to prominence in 1992 in part because both the voters and the candidates wanted to communicate directly, without the news media's filter. Yet there will always be a prominent role for a vigorous press to play. As we have reviewed, only the media have the credibility and the resources to inform the public about the government and elected officials. At the same time, the press can do its job better, and journalists must constantly strive to minimize bias and reduce the investigative and competitive excesses that have cost them some respect in recent years.

SUMMARY

The simple words of the Constitution's First Amendment, that "Congress shall make no law . . . abridging the freedom of speech, or of the press," have shaped the American republic as much as or more than any others in the Constitution and its amendments. With the Constitution's sanction, as interpreted by the Supreme Court over two centuries, a vigorous and highly competitive press has emerged. In this chapter we examined the following topics:

1. **The American Press of Yesteryear.**

Journalism—the process and profession of collecting and disseminating the news—was introduced in America in 1690 with the publication of the nation's first newspaper. Until the mid- to late-1800s, when independent papers first appeared, newspapers were partisan; that is, they openly supported a particular party. In the twentieth century, first radio in the late 1920s and then television in the late 1940s revolutionized the transmission of political information, leading to more candidate-centered, entrepreneurial politics in the age of television.

2. **The Contemporary Media Scene.**

The modern media consist of print press (many thousands of daily and weekly newspapers, magazines, newsletters, and journals) and electronic media (television and radio stations and networks as well as computerized information services). In the United States the media are relatively uncontrolled and free to express many views, although that has not always been the case here and remains a problem in other countries.

3. How The Media Cover Politicians and Government.

The media have shifted focus in recent years, first toward investigative journalism in the Watergate era and then toward character issues. While there are useful aspects of both kinds of coverage, excesses have occurred, especially unnecessary invasions of privacy and the publication and broadcast of unsubstantiated rumor.

4. The Media's Influence on the Public.

Studies have shown that by framing issues for debate and discussion, the media have clear and recognizable effects on voters. For example, people who are relatively uninformed about a topic can be more easily swayed by press coverage about that topic. However, in most cases the press has surprisingly little effect on people's views.

5. How Politicians Use the Media.

Politicians constantly try to manipulate and influence press coverage. One method many officials use is passing along tips (information) on an off-the-record basis in the hopes of currying favor or producing stories favorable to their interests. However regrettable the manipulation might be at times, it is an unavoidable part of the political process.

6. Government Regulation of the Electronic Media.

The press is a business—big business, in the case of the networks and large newspapers—and as such it is regulated to some extent by the government. The government has gradually loosened its restrictions on the media. Officially, the Federal Communications Commission (FCC) licenses and regulates broadcasting stations, although in practice it has been quite willing to grant and renew licenses, and recently it has reduced its regulation of licensees. Additionally, cable transmission was first allowed on a widespread basis in the late 1970s, from whence it has grown into a large supplier of information. Finally, content regulations have loosened, with the courts using a narrow interpretation of libel. All of these trends toward deregulation were accelerated by the enactment in February 1996 of a telecommunications bill designed to further deregulate the communications landscape.

7. Changing American News Media.

The rise in the number and type of media outlets means more choice in media and less influence for the major commercial networks (ABC, CBS, and NBC). These changes might prove beneficial, providing consumers with more unbiased, objective reporting, or they could turn out to be just more wasted fluff in programming that is distinct only because it is packaged differently than before.

KEY TERMS

affiliates, p. 583
content regulation, p. 596
deep background, p. 595

electronic media, p. 579
equal time rule, p. 597
fairness doctrine, p. 597

SELECTED READINGS

Arterton, F. Christopher. *Media Politics: The News Strategies of Presidential Campaigns.* Lexington, MA: Lexington Books, 1984.

Berkman, Ronald, and Laura W. Kitch. *Politics in the Media Age.* New York: McGraw-Hill, 1986.

Broder, David S. *Behind the Front Page.* New York: Simon & Schuster, 1987.

Cook, Timothy E. *Making Laws and Making News: Media Strategies in the U.S. House of Representatives.* Washington, D.C.: The Brookings Institution, 1989.

Crouse, Timothy. *The Boys on the Bus.* New York: Ballantine, 1973.

Entman, Robert M. *Democracy Without Citizens: Media and the Decay of American Politics.* New York: Oxford University Press, 1989.

Garment, Suzanne. *Scandal.* New York: Random House, 1991.

Graber, Doris A. *Mass Media and American Politics,* 5th ed. Washington, D.C.: CQ Press, 1996.

———. *Media Power in Politics,* 3rd ed. Washington, D.C.: CQ Press 1992.

Grossman, Michael Baruch, and Martha Joynt Kumar. *Portraying the President: The White House and the News Media.* Baltimore: Johns Hopkins University Press, 1981.

Hamilton, John Maxwell. *Hold the Press: The Inside Story on Newspapers.* Baton Rouge: Louisiana State University Press, 1996.

Iyengar, Shanto, and Donald R. Kinder. *News That Matters.* Chicago: University of Chicago Press, 1987.

Kerbel, Matthew Robert. *Remote and Controlled: Media Politics in a Cynical Age.* Boulder, CO: Westview Press, 1995.

Lichter, S. Robert, Stanley Rothman, and Linda S. Lichter. *The Media Elite.* Bethesda, MD: Adler & Adler, 1986.

Linsky, Martin. *Impact: How the Press Affects Federal Policymaking.* New York: Norton, 1986.

Patterson, Thomas E. *Out of Order.* New York: Vintage, 1993.

Press, Charles, and Kenneth VerBurg. *American Politicians and Journalists.* Glenview, IL: Scott, Foresman, 1988.

Ranney, Austin. *Channels of Power: The Impact of Television on American Politics.* New York: Basic Books, 1983.

Sabato, Larry J. *Feeding Frenzy: How Attack Journalism Has Transformed American Politics,* updated ed. New York: Macmillan/The Free Press, 1993.

Stephens, Mitchell. *A History of News: From the Drum to the Satellite.* New York: Viking, 1989.

West, Darrell M. *Air Wars: Television Advertising in Election Campaigns, 1952–1992.* Washington, D.C.: CQ Press, 1993.

(Photo courtesy: © 1995 *The Washington Post*)

INTEREST GROUPS

*I*n 1994 Linda Liotta was a former PTA president and an artist who worked alone in her spacious house in Potomac, Maryland. Privately, she worried that something was deeply awry in America. Then she entered the electronic universe of fax networks and discovered that she was not alone at all.

Today Liotta's art studio is one of thousands of outposts of a new grassroots political movement, a union of technology and fear whose potency has begun to alarm established politicians. It has no name, no headquarters, and no official leaders. But it does have members—millions, according to groups monitoring it—linked by fax machines and united by a radical distrust of government borne of wide-ranging grievances about American society.

Increasingly, these individuals are making common cause out of what appears to be little common ground, building mushrooming computer networks of angry taxpayers, property rights groups, states' rights groups, gun owners, home schoolers, right-to-lifers, John Birchers, and Christian patriots. While it echoes the militia movement—charting conspiracies from Waco to the United Nations—the new movement is far more mainstream and middle class.

"This is not a top-down movement," said Chip Berlet of Political Research Associates in Cambridge, Massachusetts. "People have set up horizontally connected low-level networks from the bottom up." One example of their power is the defeat of the so-called Conference of the States. Championed by the nation's governors and legislative leaders, and blessed by House Speaker for the 104th Congress Newt Gingrich, it was billed as a high-level forum for reasserting states' rights. But Liotta and her compatriots feared it was a plot to rewrite the Constitution, weaken states, and maybe even install global government.

They faxed alerts to thousands of sympathizers, who faxed them to thousands more, enlisting radio talk show hosts in dozens of states, until one state capitol building after another bulged with opponents. By summer 1995 the governors threw in the towel, abandoned their more ambitious plans, and instead held a federalism summit.

The movement, whose members often call themselves "patriots," appears to be growing rapidly. A national fax network founded by Detroit-area sales representative Karen Mazzarella to fight President Clinton's 1993 tax package began during the health care debate and mushroomed to 100,000 people while fighting the Conference of the States.

The fax networkers are closely allied with talk radio. Liotta has been a guest on a Baltimore show hosted by Alan Keyes, a former GOP presidential hopeful. Mazzarella, whose network is called Speak Out America, has been on the *Mike Reagan Show* hosted by the former president's son in Pasadena, California. She phoned nightly bulletins to Reagan during the Conference of the States fight, and he told listeners to call or write, state by state. "Every time he gave out our number, we got one hundred calls a day," she said.

The movement also coalesced to help vote Democrats out of power in November 1994, to oppose the General Agreement on Tariffs and Trade (they called GATT a step toward global government), and to fight the Clinton administration's new antiterrorism legislative package as a breach of constitutional protections against unreasonable searches. The movement isn't easy to pigeonhole politically. While in many ways it is ultraconservative, its members have allied with the labor movement on global trade and now side with the American Civil Liberties Union on antiterrorism bills. Though many movement sympathizers supported the GOP in 1994 and 1996, they show no sign of making a permanent home there.

Some of Liotta's research has travelled widely on fax networks, for example, she found a letter from a Justice Department lawyer in the task force archives explaining how to "avoid the Tenth Amendment limitation" on federal power over the states. The letter said the government instead could put conditions on federal funds or move to preempt state authority, as in the Clean Air Act.

"When you send someone a fax, you don't know where it will end up exactly," Liotta said. "They'll send it to someone and that person will send it to someone else and all of a sudden you get a call from somebody all the way across the country and you don't even know who that person is. People put it on the Internet, on talk radio. You could be reaching millions.

"I would wake up in the morning and find the floor literally carpeted with faxes about the Conference of the States," said Liotta, who was working the fax network herself, calling talk radio hosts, and lobbying her legislature. Today, Liotta is working mostly on antiterrorism, but she remains watchful of the governors and the unfolding stories of Whitewater, Waco, and Oklahoma City. Standing in her doorway in Potomac, Maryland after a long conversation with a reporter, she said again that it was laughable that anyone would characterize her and her compatriots as part of the militia movement. "The militia is very small and extreme," she said. "It's middle America where it's happening."[1]

The face of interest group politics is changing as quickly as technology will allow it. Conventional, formal participation in interest groups is declining, as revealed in Figure 16.1, which presents membership trends for a range of interest group types. This should come as no surprise, given today's political climate, in which voter turnout, newspaper reading, trust in institutions, and group memberships have all plummeted. At the same time, however, people are reporting more *individual* acts—many of them, like Linda Liotta's, designed to pressure policy makers at all levels of government (see Table 16.1).

Interest groups often fill voids left by the traditional political parties and give Americans another opportunity to take their claims directly to the government. Interest groups give the unrepresented or underrepresented an opportunity to have their voices heard, thereby making the government and its policy-making process more representative of diverse populations and perspectives. Organized efforts, whether in the form of concerted fax action or influence from formalized groups, continue to exert major influence on elected officials and policy makers at all levels of government. To explore this phenomenon, in this chapter we'll look at the following issues:

FIGURE 16.1

Membership Trends in Interest Groups:
1974–1994 (by Type of Group [education controled])

Y-axis label: Exp (B) for "year" in logistic regression, education controlled

Y-axis values: 1.01, 1.01, 1.00, 1.00, 0.99, 0.99, 0.98, 0.98, 0.97

X-axis categories: Nationality, Other, Hobby/garden, Service, Farm, Sports, Veterans, Professional, Youth, Sorority/fraternity, Literary/art/study, School-service, Political, Church-related, Labor unions, Fraternal, ALL GROUPS

SOURCE: Robert D. Putnam, "Tuning In, Tuning Out: The Strange Disappearance of Social Capital in America," *PS: Political Science & Politics* XXVIII (Dec. 1995), p. 665.

- First, we examine *what interest groups are.*
- Second, we categorize the *types of interest groups* active today.
- Third, we explore the *historical roots of interest groups* in America.
- Fourth, we discuss the various *strategies and tactics used by organized interests.*
- Fifth, we analyze *what factors contribute to interest group success.*
- Finally, we discuss the *changing nature of our interest group society* and recent congressional efforts to reform the lobbying system.

WHAT ARE INTEREST GROUPS?

*I*nterest groups go by a variety of names: special interests, pressure groups, organized interests, political groups, lobby groups, and public interest groups are among the common ones. These various terms have produced a diverse collection of operational definitions:

- "Any association of individuals, whether formally organized or not, that attempts to influence public policy."[2]
- "An organization which seeks or claims to represent people or organizations which share one or more common interests or ideals."[3]
- "Any group that, on the basis of one or more shared attitudes, makes certain claims upon other groups in society for the establishment, maintenance, or enhancement of forms of behavior that are implied by the shared attitudes."[4]

TABLE 16.1

Reported Acts Designed to Influence Policy Makers (in percentages)

POLITICAL ACTIVITY	AGE GROUP				
	18–34	35–44	45–54	55–64	65+
Direct Contacting					
Written a letter to any elected official	21.1	32.6	41.2	28.3	33.8
Called or sent a letter to your Congress member	23.5	42.9	48.0	50.1	53.9
Called or sent a letter to the White House	6.9	14.4	21.9	22.3	21.3
Indirect Contacting					
Written a letter to the editor of a newspaper	11.0	16.0	16.6	12.9	12.7
Called in to a television station or cable company to complain about a program	11.3	9.9	9.5	14.4	7.6
Called in or sent a response to a question or issue put up for discussion by a newspaper or TV station	13.4	17.1	20.3	12.9	7.3
Tried to call in to a talk show to discuss views on a public or political issue	7.9	14.7	5.9	7.8	7.6
Dialed an 800 or 900 number to register an opinion on some issue of public concern	14.2	20.6	13.8	15.3	10.1
Participated in a poll sent by a group one belongs to	22.3	33.5	38.9	31.2	19.8
Joining/Attending					
Joined an organization in support of a particular cause	19.9	24.9	27.1	20.1	15.2
Attended a city or town meeting in one's community	21.7	27.5	33.4	39.8	38.6
Attended a public hearing	27.7	34.3	43.9	40.6	35.6
Participated in a "town meeting" or public affairs discussion group	17.7	28.1	30.6	32.8	24.5
Contributing					
Contributed money to a PAC	8.9	17.5	16.3	18.0	17.0
Contributed money to a candidate running for public office	10.7	21.4	26.9	23.1	26.9

Note: Respondents were asked: "People express their opinions about politics and current events in a number of ways besides voting. I'm going to read a list of some of these ways. Please just tell me if you have or have not ever done each. Have you ever [X]?"

Source: Susan A. MacManus, *Young* v. *Old: Generational Combat in the 21st Century* (Boulder, CO: Westview Press, 1996).

Some definitions stress what a group does. This definition is offered by political scientist Robert H. Salisbury:

■ "An interest group is an organized association which engages in activity relative to governmental decisions."[5]

And distinguished political scientist V. O. Key, Jr. tried to differentiate political parties from interest groups by arguing that

■ "[Interest groups] promote their interests by attempting to influence government rather than by nominating candidates and seeking responsibility for the management of government."[6]

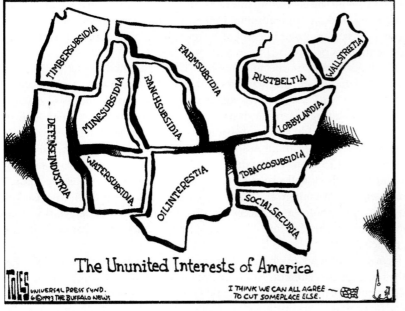

The Ununited Interests of America

I THINK WE CAN ALL AGREE — TO CUT SOMEPLACE ELSE.

Originally, most political scientists used the term "pressure group" because it best described what these groups did. Today most political scientists use the terms *interest group* or *organized interest.*[7] In this book we use **interest group** as a generic term to describe the numerous organized groups that try to influence government policy. Thus interest groups can be what we normally think of as organized interests as well as state and local governments, political action committees, and individual businesses and corporations. We also consider less formal groups, such as the fax brigade described at the beginning of this chapter, as interest groups. Although these groups are more nebulous in form than interest groups traditionally studied by political scientists, they, too, engage in concerted action to influence government policy.

interest group: An organized group that tries to influence public policy.

TYPES OF INTEREST GROUPS

*I*nterest groups generally can be characterized by the kinds of interests they represent or the number of issues in which they are involved. We'll look at economic, public interest, multi-issue, and single-issue interest groups.

Economic Interest Groups

Most groups have some sort of "economic" agenda, even if it only involves acquiring enough money in donations to pay the telephone bill or send out the next mailing. **Economic interest groups** are, however, a special type of interest group: Their pri-

economic interest group: A group with the primary purpose of promoting the financial interests of its members.

mary purpose is to promote the economic interests of their members. Historically, business groups (including trade and professional groups), labor organizations (unions), and organizations representing the interests of farmers have been considered the "big three" of economic interest groups.

As revealed in Figure 16.2, union membership has plummeted as the nation has changed from a land of manufacturing workers and farmers to a nation of white-collar professionals and service workers. As a consequence, unions and agricultural organizations no longer have the large memberships or the political clout they once held in governmental circles. Today trade and professional associations such as the Chamber of Commerce or the American Medical Association (AMA) are usually more powerful and find few doors closed to them in Washington. Businesses and corporations, too, can be powerful individually or collectively as organized interests. Most large corporations, for example, employ Washington, D.C.-based lobbyists to keep them apprised of legislation that may affect them or to lobby for the consideration of legislation that could help them. Corporations also hire D.C.-based lobbyists to lobby bureaucrats for government contracts.

State and local governments often act as organized interests when they lobby for benefits from the national government. Not only are there strong lobbying groups, such as the National League of Cities and the National Governors' Association; most states also retain lobbyists to make certain that they will get their share (if not more) of the federal budget designated to go back to the states in a variety of forms including block grants, and so on. (See chapter 3 for a discussion of the intergovernmental lobby.)

Groups that mobilize to protect particular economic interests generally are the most fully and effectively organized of all the types of interest groups.[8] They exist to make profits and to obtain economic benefits for their members. To achieve these goals, however, they often find that they must resort to political means rather than trust the operation of economic markets to produce outcomes favorable for their members.

FIGURE 16.2

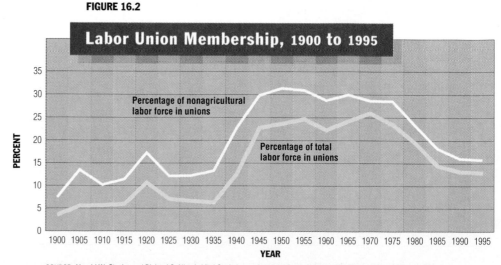

SOURCE: Harold W. Stanley and Richard G. Niemi, *Vital Statistics on American Politics*, 4th ed. (Washington D.C.: CQ Press, 1994), Table 6–11, p. 190. Additional data from authors.

Public Interest Groups

Political scientist Jeffrey M. Berry defines **public interest groups** as organizations "that seek a collective good, the achievement of which will not selectively and materially benefit the membership or activists of the organization."[9] Unlike economic interest groups, public interest groups do not tend to be particularly motivated by the desire to achieve goals that would benefit their members. As Berry notes, the public interest has many faces. In the past, for example, many Progressive era groups were created in the late 1800s and early 1900s to solve the varied problems of new immigrants and the poor. Today civil and constitutional rights groups, environmental groups, good government groups such as Common Cause, peace groups, church groups, and groups that speak out for those who cannot (such as children, the mentally ill, or animals) are examples of public interest groups. The American Civil Liberties Union (ACLU) (see Highlight 5.1: The American Civil Liberties Union), for example, is a public interest organization that fights against, among other things, government entanglement with religion. When ACLU lawyers argue that the government should not allow nativity scenes to be erected on public lands, group members realize no financial gain. Similarly, its members derive no direct economic benefits when the ACLU challenges the constitutionality of New York State's practice of awarding college scholarships to students based on their SAT scores. (The ACLU successfully argued that the SATs discriminate against women.)[10] The Christian Coalition is another example of a public interest group. Like the ACLU, its agenda is broad in scope but generally at the other end of the ideological spectrum.

public interest group: An organization that seeks a collective good that will not selectively and materially benefit the members of the group.

Multi-Issue *Versus* Single-Issue Groups

Many of the economic and public interest groups just discussed are multi-issue groups; that is, they are concerned with more than just a single issue. For example, the AFL–CIO, the umbrella organization for seventy-eight labor unions in the United

The AFL-CIO, the largest and among the oldest labor unions in the nation, rallied its membesr to campaign against NAFTA. It lost with the passage of NAFTA in late 1993. (Photo courtesy: Reuters/The Bettmann Archive)

States, was formed to represent the interests of organized labor. It is also concerned with health care, Social Security, and civil rights, among other issues. In 1993 it lobbied hard against passage of the North American Free Trade Agreement (NAFTA), arguing that jobs of union workers would be lost to Mexico. Similarly, although the NAACP is interested primarily in race relations, it is also involved in other areas, including education, the criminal justice system, housing, and welfare rights—all areas of potential concern to its members.

Single-issue groups differ from multi-issue groups in both the range and the intensity of their interests. Concentration on one area generally leads to greater zeal in a group's lobbying efforts. Probably the most visible single-issue groups today are those organized on either side of the abortion and gun control debates. Anti-abortion groups like Operation Rescue and pro-choice groups like the National Abortion and Reproductive Rights Action League (NARAL) are good examples of single-issue groups, as are the National Rifle Association (NRA) and Handgun Control, Inc. Today people single-mindedly pursue all kinds of interests. Drug- or AIDS-awareness groups, environmental groups, and antinuclear power groups, for example, can be classified as single-issue groups. Table 16.2 categorizes a number of prominent interest groups by their issue concentration.

THE ROOTS AND FORMATION OF AMERICAN INTEREST GROUPS

Political scientists have long debated how and why interest groups arise, their nature, and their role in a democratic society. Do they contribute to the betterment of society, or are they an evil best controlled by government? From his days in the Virginia Assembly, James Madison knew that factions occurred in all political systems and that the struggle for influence and power among such groups was inevitable in the political process. This knowledge led him and the other Framers to tailor a governmental system of multiple pressure points to check and balance these factions, or what today we call interest groups, in the natural course of the political process. As we discuss in chapter 2, Madison and many of the other Framers were intent on creating a government of many levels—local, state, and national—with the national government consisting of three branches. It was their belief that this division of power would prohibit any one individual or group of individuals from becoming too influential. They also believed that decentralizing power would neutralize the effect of special interests, who would not be able to spread their efforts throughout so many different levels of government. Thus the "mischief of faction" could be lessened. But, farsighted as they were, the Framers could not have envisioned the vast sums of money or technology that would be available to some interest groups.

Ironically, however, *The Federalist Papers* were a key component of one of the most skillful and successful examples of interest group activity in the history of this nation. If "the Federalists [themselves an interest group] had not been as shrewd in manipulation as they were sound in theory, their arguments could not have prevailed."[11]

Today, Robert H. Salisbury argues that groups are formed when resources—be they clean air, women's rights, or rights of the unborn, for example—are inadequate or scarce.[12] Jack L. Walker contends that without what he terms **patrons** (those who often finance a group) few organizations could begin.[13] And David B. Truman, one of the first

patron: Individual who finances an interest group.

TABLE 16.2

Profiles of Selected Interest Groups

NAME (FOUNDED)	SINGLE- OR MULTI-ISSUE	1993 BUDGET (MILLIONS)	MEMBERS	PAC
Economic Groups				
AFL–CIO	M	62	14.1 million	AFL–CIO PAC
American Medical Association (AMA)	M	205	300,000	AMA PAC
Association of Trial Lawyers of America	M	19	60,000	Association of Trial Lawyers of America PAC
National Association of Manufacturers (NAM) (1895)	M	16	12,500	no
Tobacco Institute	S	38	13 (cigarette companies)	no
U.S. Chamber of Commerce (1912)	M	70	180,000 companies	National Chamber Alliance for Politics
Public Interest Groups				
American Association of Retired Persons (AARP) (1958)	M	305	33,000,000	no
Amnesty International U.S.A. (1961)	S	22.3	386,000	no
Handgun Control, Inc. (1974)	S	8	360,000	Handgun Control Voter Education Fund
League of United Latin American Citizens (LULAC) (1929)	M	N/A	110,000	no
National Abortion and Reproductive Rights Action League (NARAL) (1969)	S	9.3	450,000	NARAL PAC
National Association for the Advancement of Colored People (NAACP) (1909)	M	16	500,000	no
National Gay and Lesbian Task Force (1973)	S	1.4	17,000	no
National Rifle Association (NRA) (1871)	S	86.9 (1990)	2,650,000	Political Victory Fund
National Right to Life Committee (1973)	S	13.5	400,000	National Right to Life PAC
Environmental Groups				
Environmental Defense Fund (EDF) (1967)	S	16	150,000	no
Greenpeace USA (1971)	S	35 (1990)	1,690,500 (1996)	no
Sierra Club (1892)	S	39	550,000 (1996)	Sierra Club Political Committee
Good Government Groups				
Common Cause (1970)	S	11.3	270,000	no
Public Citizen, Inc. (1971)	M	6.2	100,000	no

Source: Public Interest Profiles, 1993–1994 (Washington, D.C.: Congressional Quarterly, 1993); "Profiles of Interest Groups," Health Line (October 13, 1993); "Legal Times: Profiles of Interest Groups Part II," Health Line (October 14, 1993): NEXIS.

political scientists to study interest groups, posed what he termed **disturbance theory** to explain why interest groups form.[14] He hypothesizes that groups form in part to counteract the activities of other groups or of organized special interests. According to Truman, the government's role is to provide a forum in which the competing demands

disturbance theory: The theory offered by political scientist David B. Truman that posits that interest groups form in part to counteract the efforts of other groups.

of groups and the majority of the U.S. population can be heard and balanced. He argues that the government's role in managing competing groups is to balance their conflicting demands. Nevertheless, when examining the evolution and growth of interest groups in the United States, we are not always looking at clashes of one group against another, but of one group against the majority of the American public.

As with the many different definitions of interest groups, a variety of sound reasons have been offered to explain why interest groups form. Generally, however, interest groups tend to arise in response to changes. These can be political or economic changes, changes in the population, technological changes, or even changes in society itself. During the 1770s, for example, many groups (such as the Sons of Liberty) arose to fight for political and economic independence from Great Britain. After the Civil War, trade unions flourished, and the Grange was founded to help farmers. Business associations proliferated in the 1880s and 1890s, and other groups were created in the early 1900s in reaction to big business and other social and economic forces.

After the Depression, the New Deal, and the country's entry into World War II, many groups fell into disarray or ceased to exist. The National American Woman Suffrage Association, for example, dissolved after the Nineteenth Amendment was ratified in 1920. Other groups remained active, but with less vitality. Many business, labor, and professional groups, however, continued to flourish. According to a study conducted by Kay Lehman Schlozman and John T. Tierney, nearly 70 percent of today's Washington, D.C.-based political organizations established their offices after 1960.[15] Nearly half opened their offices after 1970. Not surprisingly, given the social and economic thrust of President Lyndon B. Johnson's "Great Society" programs, most of the new groups were formed to take advantage of the money and opportunities those programs offered.

From 1960 to 1996, the number of interest group representatives registered (as required by law) in Washington increased from fewer than 500 to 14,000. The federal government had clearly become the primary target of policy change, and it was natural for interest groups (businesses, states, and local governments) to concentrate their resources in the nation's capital as they hired D.C.-based lobbyists and law firms.

Public Interest Groups

During the 1960s and 1970s, the Progressive spirit of the late 1800s found renewed vigor in the rise of public interest groups. Generally, these groups devoted themselves to representing the interests of African Americans, women, the elderly, the poor, and consumers, or to working on behalf of the environment. Many of their leaders and members had been active in the civil rights and anti-Vietnam War movement efforts of the 1960s. Other groups, like the ACLU and NAACP, which had survived for nearly a century, gained renewed vigor. Many of them had as their patron the liberal Ford Foundation, which helped to bankroll numerous groups, including the Women's Rights Project of the ACLU, the Mexican American Legal Defense and Education Fund, the Puerto Rican Legal Defense and Education Fund, and the Native American Rights Fund.[16] Another group that came to prominence in this era was the American Association of Retired Persons (AARP). The elderly are the fastest growing group in the United States, and AARP is the largest single interest group in the country, with 33 million members in 1996 (see Politics Now: The Downside of Being on the Wrong Side).

The successes of the civil rights and antiwar movements left many Americans feeling cynical about a government that they believed failed to respond to the will of the majority. They also believed that, if citizens banded together, they could make a difference. Thus two major new public interest groups—Common Cause and Ralph Nader's Public Citizen, Inc.—were founded. Common Cause, a "good government" group similar to some of the early Progressive movement's good government groups, has effectively challenged aspects of the congressional seniority system, successfully urged the passage of sweeping campaign financing reforms, and played a major role in the enactment of legislation authorizing federal financing of presidential campaigns. It continues to lobby for accountability in government and for more efficient and responsive governmental structures and practices.

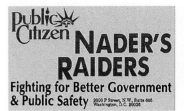

Perhaps more well known than Common Cause is the collection of groups headed by Ralph Nader under the name Public Citizen, Inc. In 1965 Nader, a young lawyer, was thrust into the limelight with the publication of his book *Unsafe at Any Speed*. In it he charged that the Corvair, a General Motors (GM) car, was unsafe to drive; he produced voluminous evidence of how the car could flip over at average speeds on curved roads. In 1966 he testified about auto safety before Congress and then learned that General Motors had spied on him in an effort to discredit his work. The $250,000 that GM subsequently paid to Nader in an out-of-court settlement allowed him to establish the Center for the Study of Responsive Law in 1969. The Center analyzed the activities of regulatory agencies and concluded that few of them enforced antitrust regulations or cracked down on deceptive advertising practices. Nader then turned again to lobbying

Politics Now

The Downside of Being on the Wrong Side

As the Republicans took control of Congress in 1995, business groups gained new access at the same time other groups fell from grace.

Many groups give to candidates on both sides of the aisle to hedge their bets. But some are considered so "liberal" or so "conservative" that they draw the ire of their ideological foes almost immediately. Such has been the case with the American Association of Retired Persons (AARP). In June 1995, for example, Sen. Alan Simpson

(R–Wyo.) opened investigative hearings into AARP to focus attention on the "propriety" of AARP's activities—which included profitable business interests and its tax-exempt status. AARP, with 33 million members, lobbies on behalf of older Americans while it "collects millions of dollars in federal grants—$86 million in 1994 alone."* Simpson and other Republicans, angered by AARP's support of health care reform and lobbying against Medicare cuts, wanted to investigate to determine if AARP should retain its tax-exempt status, a loss of which would be a stunning blow to the group.

Upset by these partisan attacks, House Minority Whip David Bonior

(D–Mich.) suggested that the Senate investigate several conservative groups, including the National Rifle Association and Accuracy in Media (which was trying to raise money through ads charging that the liberal media failed to adequately cover White House aide Vincent Foster's suicide. While any laws passed concerning a group's tax-exempt status would apply to all groups, it's not pleasant for any group to be called to the Hill to testify before Congress. Is this a way for Congress to exercise control of groups not in tune with its politics? How could this kind of scrutiny be beneficial to a group?

*Andrew Mollisar, "Senators Want Other Nonprofits Probed," *The Atlanta Constitution* (June 14, 1994): A8

Pat Robertson on "The 700 Club" television show. (Photo coutesy: Colburn/Photoreporters)

Congress, which led him to create Public Citizen, Inc., which would act as an umbrella organization for what was to be called the "Nader Network" of groups. In 1996 Nader was the unsuccessful Green Party candidate for president.

Conservative Backlash: Religious and Ideological Groups. The growth and successes that various public interest groups and the civil rights and women's rights movements had in the 1960s and 1970s (see chapter 5) ultimately led to a conservative backlash. Conservatives became very concerned about the successes liberal groups had in shaping and defining the public agenda, and religious and ideological conservatives became a potent force in U.S. politics. The largest new religious group was the Reverend Jerry Falwell's Moral Majority, founded in 1978. At one time the conservative Moral Majority had an extensive television ministry, and in its peak year, 1984, raised $11 million for political lobbying. It was widely credited with assisting Ronald Reagan's 1980 presidential victory as well as the defeats of several liberal Democratic senators that same year. Falwell claimed to have sent from 3 million to 4 million newly registered voters to the polls.[17] In June 1989 Falwell announced that he was terminating the Moral Majority after the group suffered from a series of financial and sexual scandals involving television evangelists. Televangelist Jimmy Swaggert, for example, was found cavorting with women in a seedy motel, and Jim Bakker was found guilty of defrauding his followers of millions of dollars and was consequently sentenced to prison.

In 1990 televangelist Pat Robertson, host of the popular television program *The 700 Club*, formed a new group, the Christian Coalition, to fill the void left by the demise of the Moral Majority. Since then, it has grown in power and influence by leaps and bounds. In 1994, for example, it took credit for the Republican Party's incredible successes. Its exit polling showed that religious conservatives accounted for one-third of all votes cast in 1994 and provided the margin of victory for all Republicans, who won with 53 percent of the vote or less.[18] Said Kate Michelman, president of NARAL, "Led by Christian Coalition, the radical right organized furiously," contributing to an election catastrophe for abortion rights supporters.[19] The Coalition's Contract with the American Family, which it claims is "a bold plan . . . to strengthen the family and restore common-sense values," includes calls for local control of education, school choice plans, passage of constitutional amendments to allow prayer in schools and to ban abortion, elimination of the marriage penalty in the tax code, restriction of pornography, and privatizing the arts.[20] As Figure 16.3 shows, the typical member of the Christian Coalition is a married white woman over sixty-five years of age, with an income between $15,000 and $55,000, and a high school diploma.

Since the Republican "revolution" of November 1994, different interest groups, in particular conservative and business groups, now have greater access to the levers of power. The partisan battles stemming from the Republican 104th Congress and a Democratic president have affected interest groups in some interesting ways, as revealed in Politics Now: The Downside of Being on the Wrong Side.

Business Groups. Conservative public interest groups were not the only ones organized in the 1970s to advance conservative views. Many business people, dissatisfied with the work of the National Association of Manufacturers or the Chamber of Commerce, decided to start new, more politically oriented organizations to advance their political and financial interests in Washington, D.C. The Business Roundtable, for example, was created in 1972 (largely made up of the chief executive officers of major businesses). The Roundtable, say some, is "a fraternity of powerful and prestigious business leaders that tells 'business's side of the story' to legislators, bureaucrats, White

House personnel, and other interested public officials."[21] It urges its members to engage in direct lobbying to influence the course of policy formation.

Unlike public interest groups, organizations like the Chamber of Commerce and the Business Roundtable, as well as **trade associations** (groups that represent specific industries), enjoy many of the benefits other businesses do as lobbyists: They already have extensive organization, expertise, large numbers, a strong financial base, and a longstanding relationship with key actors in government. Such natural advantages have led to a huge number of business groups. One observer describes their proliferation this way:

> If you want to understand government, don't begin by reading the Constitution. It conveys precious little of today's statecraft. Instead, read selected portions of the Washington Telephone Directory, such as pages 354–58, which contain listings for all of the organizations with titles beginning with the word "National." . . . There are, of course, the big ones, like the National Association of Manufacturers, and the National Association of Broadcasters. But the pages teem with others, National Cigar Leaf Tobacco Association, National Association of Mirror Manufacturers, National Association of Miscellaneous Ornamental and Architectural Product Contractors, National Association of Margarine Manufacturers.[22]

Many of these national groups devote tremendous resources to fighting government regulation. Quite often, they find themselves on the opposite side of organized labor on any issue.

Organized Labor.   Labor became a stronger force in U.S. politics when the American Federation of Labor merged with the Congress of Industrial Organizations in 1955. Concentrating its efforts largely on the national level, the new AFL–CIO immediately turned its energies to pressuring the government to protect concessions won from employers at the bargaining table and to other issues of concern to its members, including minimum wage laws, the environment, civil rights, medical insurance, and health care.

But the once-fabled political clout of organized labor has been on the wane. By the late 1970s, it was clear that even during a Democratic administration (Carter's), organized labor lacked the impact it had during earlier decades. During the Reagan administration, organized labor's influence fell to an all-time modern-day low. In spite of the tremendous resources behind the AFL–CIO and other unions, membership has dropped and continues to do so, as was revealed in Figure 16.2. In 1970 over 25 percent of workers were unionized; in 1996 only 15 percent were. Recognizing that labor is an endangered species, in 1996 the AFL launched an ambitious, unprecedented campaign to return the Congress to Democratic hands (see Highlight 16.1: Politics and the AFL–CIO).

Professional Associations.   In contrast to the labor union situation, the membership and political influence of professional societies continues to expand. In the early 1960s, the American Medical Association (AMA) spent millions of dollars in an unsuccessful effort to fight Medicare. Once some sort of medical assistance for the elderly was inevitable, the AMA turned its efforts toward the drafting and implementing of new legislation and regulations, an effort that produced considerable financial rewards for physicians. More recently, it lobbied effectively against the wide-ranging changes in the health care system proposed by the Clinton administration and played an important role in shaping the eventual compromise health care reform bill passed in 1996.

trade association: A group that represents specific industries.

FIGURE 16.3

Profile of the Christian Coalition

SEX

Female	55.5%
Male	45.5

AGE

18–24	0.9%
25–34	5.7
35–44	15.9
45–54	19.5
55–64	17.9
65–74	20.4
75 and over	15.8
No response	3.9

MARITAL STATUS

Single (never married)	6.9%
Single (previously married)	15.9
Married	76.2
No response	1.0

INCOME

Under $15,000	8.3%
$15,000–$34,999	25.8
$35,000–$54,999	24.8
$55,000–$74,999	12.8
More than $75,000	10.8
No response	17.4

EDUCATION

Some high school	9.1%
Completed high school	24.5
Vocational school	31.3
College graduate	20.6
Post graduate	11.9
No response	2.6

SOURCE: Based on a telephone poll conducted by the Luntz Research Companies of 1,000 members of the Christian Coalition. The Coalition has 1.7 million members. Numbers may not add to 100 percent because of rounding. *The New York Times*, September 8, 1995, D18.

Highlight 16.1

Politics and the AFL–CIO

In 1996 the newly elected president of the AFL–CIO, John J. Sweeney, launched a campaign to "take back the Congress and take back our country." The AFL spent $35 million for broadcast ads and field organizing in the name of political education. The campaign initially focused on seventy-five House members, many of them Republican freshmen in districts with high proportions of union members. Targeted TV and radio ads, for example, were run in districts of members who voted against the minimum wage increase that was later signed into law by President Clinton. Other ads were designed to inform viewers about Republican efforts to change longstanding labor laws.

This $35 million was above what labor unions gave to candidates through their voluntary contributions to their own PACs. In 1994 labor unions spent over $42 million, with 95 percent going to Democrats. Final figures for 1996 are not available at this writing, but by all indications, the AFL–CIO spent even more in the 1996 elections. While these efforts were resoundingly criticized by Republicans, AFL-CIO say that the campaign was not about the "election or defeat of specific members of Congress."* Rather, they said, their spending was a matter of survival for the organization and the labor movement. Given the outcome of the 1996 elections, how successful do you think its efforts were?

*Juliana Gruenwald and Robert Marshall Wells, "At Odds with Some Workers, AFL–CIO Takes Aim at GOP," *CQ Weekly Report* (April 12, 1996): 3.

WHAT DO INTEREST GROUPS DO?

As illustrated by the discussion of groups above, "In Washington, money talks, and it is foolish for anyone to pretend it is irrelevant to this debate," as the director of the Center for Public Integrity, a nonprofit research center financed by foundations, corporations, and unions, underscored in discussing the wide range of expensive policy-oriented activities engaged in by many interest groups.[23] For example, more than $100 million was spent in campaign contributions, television ads, and expense-paid trips for lawmakers as interests on both sides of the health-care reform issue reacted to reform initiatives by President Clinton soon after he took office in 1993. Twenty-five million dollars alone went to campaign contributions, and $8.2 million went to members of five health-related committees.

All in all, 650 health-related organizations made campaign contributions. Forty bought air time to air their views on the health-care debate. The AMA sponsored fifty-five trips—largely to California and Florida—where lawmakers addressed groups, golfed, and sunned. Moreover, at least eighty ex-lawmakers and former White House officials went to work for well-heeled health-related interests.[24] Hiring lobbyists to sway policy thus "remains the bedrock of the Washington landscape."[25]

Not all interest groups are political, but they may become politically active when their members feel that a government policy threatens or affects group goals. Interest groups also enhance political participation by motivating like-minded individuals to work toward a common goal. Legislators are often much more likely to listen to or be concerned about the interests of a group as opposed to the interests of any one individual. The congressional testimony of Kathie Lee Gifford, for example, brought considerable attention to the problem of unsafe working conditions for garment workers. But it is likely to take sustained pressure from one or more interest groups before there is greater enforcement of existing laws and passage of new ones to combat sweat shops.

Just as members of Congress are assumed to represent the interests of their constituents in Washington, D.C., interest groups are assumed to represent the interests of their members to policy makers at all levels of government. In the 1950s, for example, the National Association for the Advancement of Colored People (NAACP) was able to articulate and present the interests of African Americans to national decision makers even though as a group they had little or no electoral clout, especially in the South. Without the efforts of the civil rights groups discussed in chapter 6, it is unlikely that either the courts or Congress would have acted as quickly to make discrimination illegal. All sorts of individuals—from railroad workers to women to physical therapists to campers to homosexuals to mushroom growers—have found that banding together with others who have similar interests can advance their collective interests. Hiring a lobbyist to advocate those interests in Washington, D.C. or a state capital also increases the likelihood that issues of concern to them will be addressed and acted on favorably.

There is also a downside to interest groups. Because groups make claims on society, they can increase the cost of public policies. The elderly can push for more costly health care and Social Security programs, people with disabilities for improved access to public buildings, industry for tax loopholes, and veterans for improved benefits. Many Americans believe that interest groups exist simply to advance their own selfish interests, with little regard for the rights of other groups or, more important, of people not represented by any organized group.

Whether good or bad, interest groups play an important role in U.S. politics. In addition to enhancing the democratic process by providing increased representation and participation, they increase public awareness about important issues, help frame the public agenda, and often monitor programs to guarantee effective implementation. Most often they accomplish these things through some sort of lobbying or informational campaign.

Lobbying

Most interest groups put lobbying at the top of their agendas. **Lobbying** is the process by which interest groups attempt to assert their influence on the policy process. The term **lobbyist** refers to any representative of a group that attempts to influence a policy maker by one or more of the tactics illustrated in Table 16.3. It is important to note that not only do large, organized interests have their own lobbyists, but other groups, including colleges, trade associations, cities, states, and even foreign nations, also hire lobbying firms (some law firms have lobbying specialists) to represent them in the halls of Congress or to get through the bureaucratic maze.

Most politically active groups use lobbying to make their interests heard and understood by those who are in a position to influence or cause change in governmental policies. (See Roots of Government: Lobbying: Yesterday and Today.) Depending on the type of group and on the role it is looking to play, lobbying can take many forms. You probably have never thought of the Boy Scouts or Girl Scouts of America as "political." Yet, when Congress began debating the passage of legislation dealing with discrimination in private clubs, representatives of both organizations testified in an attempt to

lobbying: The activities of groups and organizations that seek to influence legislation and persuade political leaders to support a group's position.

lobbyist: Interest group representative who seeks to influence legislation that will benefit his or her organization through political persuasion.

persuade Congress to allow each one to remain a single-sex organization. Similarly, you probably don't often think of garden clubs as political. Yet, when issues of highway beautification come before a legislature, representatives from numerous garden clubs are likely to be there to lobby for, or to advance, their interests.

As Table 16.3 indicates, there are at least twenty-seven ways to lobby. Lobbying allows interest groups to try to convince key governmental decision makers and the public of the correctness of their positions. Almost all interest groups lobby by testifying at hearings and contacting legislators. Other groups also provide information that de-

TABLE 16.3

Lobbying Techniques of Interest Groups

LOBBYING TECHNIQUE USED	PERCENTAGE USING
Testifying at hearings	99%
Contacting government officials directly to present your point of view	98
Engaging in informal contact with officials—at conventions, over lunch, etc.	95
Presenting research results or technical information	92
Sending letters to members of your organization to inform them about your activities	92
Entering into coalitions with other organizations	90
Attempting to shape the implementation of policies	89
Talking with people from the press and the media	86
Consulting with government officials to plan legislative strategy	85
Helping to draft legislation	85
Inspiring letter-writing or telegram campaigns	84
Shaping the government's agenda by raising new issues and calling attention to previously ignored problems	84
Mounting grassroots lobbying efforts	80
Having influential constituents contact their member of Congress	80
Helping to draft regulations, rules, or guidelines	78
Serving on advisory commissions and boards	76
Alerting members of Congress to the effects of a bill on their districts	75
Filing suit or otherwise engaging in litigation	72
Making financial contributions to electoral campaigns	58
Doing favors for officials who need assistance	56
Attempting to influence appointments to public office	53
Publicizing candidates' voting records	44
Engaging in fund raising for your organization	44
Running advertisements in the media about your position on issues	31
Contributing work or personnel to electoral campaigns	24
Making public endorsements of candidates for office	22
Engaging in protests or demonstrations	20

Source: Adapted from Kay Lehman Schlozman and John T. Tierney, "More of the Same: Washington Pressure Group Activity in a Decade of Change," *Journal of Politics* 45 (1988): 351–75.

cision makers might not have the time, opportunity, or interest to gather on their own. Of course, information these groups provide is designed to present the group's position in a favorable light, although a good lobbyist for an interest group will also note the downside to proposed legislation. Interest groups also file lawsuits to lobby the courts, and some even engage in protests or demonstrations as a form of "lobbying" public opinion or decision makers.

Lobbying Congress. Members of Congress are the targets of a wide variety of lobbying activities: congressional testimony on behalf of a group, individual letters from interested constituents, campaign contributions, trips, speaking fees, or the outright payment of money for votes. Of course, the last item is illegal, but there are numerous documented instances of money changing hands for votes.

Lobbying Congress is a skill that many people have developed over the years. In 1869, for example, women meeting in Washington, D.C. for the second annual meeting of the National Woman Suffrage Association marched to Capitol Hill to hear one of their members (unsuccessfully) ask Congress to pass legislation to enfranchise women under the terms of the Fourteenth Amendment.

Practices such as these floor speeches are no longer permitted. Some interest groups do, however, still try mass marches to Congress. For example, after the Supreme Court ruled in 1976 that discrimination against a pregnant woman was not prohibited by the Civil Rights Act of 1964, hordes of lobbyists from various women's rights groups descended on Congress at one time. In response, Congress quickly enacted the Pregnancy Discrimination Act of 1978.

Today lobbyists try to develop close relationships with senators and representatives in an effort to enhance their access to the policy-making process, as the Packwood diaries (discussed in Roots of Government: Lobbying: Yesterday and Today) indicate. A symbiotic relationship between members, interest group representatives, and affected bureaucratic agencies often develops. In these iron triangles, representatives and their staff members, who face an exhausting workload and legislation they know little about, frequently look to lobbyists for information. "Information is the currency on Capitol Hill, not dollars," said one lobbyist.[26] According to one aide:

> My boss demands a speech and a statement for the Congressional Record for every bill we introduce or co-sponsor—and we have a lot of bills. I just can't do it all myself. The better lobbyists, when they have a proposal they are pushing, bring it to me along with a couple of speeches, a *Record* insert, and a fact sheet.[27]

Not surprisingly, lobbyists work most closely with representatives who share their interests. A lobbyist from the National Rifle Association (NRA), for example, would be unlikely to try to influence a liberal representative who was on record as strongly in favor of gun control. It is much more effective for a group like the NRA to provide useful information for its supporters and to those who are undecided. Good lobbyists can also encourage members to file amendments to bills favorable to their interests. They can also urge their supporters in Congress to make speeches (often written by the group) and to pressure their colleagues in the chamber.

A lobbyist's effectiveness depends largely on his or her reputation for fair play and provision of accurate information. No member of Congress wants to look uninformed. As one member noted:

> It doesn't take very long to figure out which lobbyists are straightforward, and which ones are trying to snow you. The good ones will give you the weak points as well as the strong points of their case. If anyone ever gives me false or misleading information, that's it—I'll never see him again.[28]

Roots of Government

Lobbying: Yesterday and Today

The exact origin of the term *lobbying* is disputed. In mid-seventeenth century England, there was a room located near the floor of the House of Commons where members of Parliament would congregate and could be approached by their constituents and others who wanted to plead a particular cause. Similarly, in the United States, people often waited outside the chambers of the House and Senate to speak to members of Congress as they emerged. Because they waited in the lobbies to argue their cases, by the nineteenth century they were commonly referred to as "lobbyists." Another piece of folklore explains that when Ulysses S. Grant was president, he would frequently walk from the White House to the Willard Hotel on Pennsylvania Avenue just to relax in its comfortable and attractive lobby. Interest group representatives and those seeking favors from Grant would crowd into that lobby and try to press their claims. Soon they were nicknamed "lobbyists."

Lobbying reached an infamous peak in the late 1800s, when railroads and other big businesses openly bribed state and federal legislators to obtain favorable legislation. Congress finally got around to regulating some aspects of lobbying in 1946 with the Regulation of Lobbying Act, which required paid lobbyists to register with the House and Senate and to file quarterly financial reports, including an account of all contributions and expenditures as well as the names and

FEMALE LOBBYISTS.

(Photo courtesy: The Bettmann Archive)

addresses of those to whom they gave $500 or more. Organizations also were required to submit financial reports, although they did not have to register officially. The purpose of the act was to publicize the activities of lobbyists and remove some of the uncertainty surrounding the influence of lobbying on legislation. In 1954, however, a lower court ruled the act unconstitutional. Although the Supreme Court reversed the decision, the Court's narrow interpretation undermined the effectiveness of the act. The Court ruled that the act was applicable only to persons or organizations who solicited, collected, or received money for the principal purpose of influencing legislation by directly lobbying members of Congress. Consequently, many lobbyists did not register at all. The National Association of Manufacturers, for example, was formed in 1895, but did not register as a lobbying group until 1975.

Of the organizations that do register, more than 90 percent do not file complete financial reports.

Today lobbying in Congress has many faces. Consider, for instance, this example. The budget package sent to President Clinton in 1994 would have reduced federal aid to a variety of farmers, including those who grow wheat, corn, cotton, rice, sugar, and peanuts, and nearly all other farm products. But, largely on account of the unswerving stance of Representative Gerald B. Solomon (R–N.Y.), all of the provisions involving the dairy industry were removed from the legislation and milk supplies would retain their federal subsidies.

To recognize and reward Solomon's achievements on their behalf, lobbyists for dairy farmers held a breakfast in his honor. The breakfast, says *The New York Times,* "is an example of how the American system of campaign finance often puts politicians,

(Continued)

even those who, like Mr. Solomon, have sterling reputations for integrity, in the position of seeming to take payoffs when they raise money.[*] In an invitation extended by the head of the National Milk Producers Federation, lobbyists were invited "To show your appreciation to Mr. Solomon, please join us . . . for an enjoyable breakfast with your colleagues . . . PACs throughout the industry are asked to contribute $1000. Mr. Solomon would prefer that the checks be made to his leadership fund, 'Leadership for America Committee.' If your PAC is unable to comply with this request, please make your PAC check to 'Solomon for Congress.' "[**] The letter was dated the same day that Republicans, at Solomon's insistence, removed all the dairy provisions from the bill,

These activities probably seem questionable to you. But they are not illegal under current laws. Senator Bob Packwood's (R-Ore.) infamous diaries, however, provide a startling picture of a lawmaker's votes for sale, not all that different from earlier times. Packwood's diaries clearly reveal how a lawmaker "can come to rely on lobbyists, influence peddlers, and fundraisers for friendship, counsel, and political cash."[***] When Packwood, for example, feared he couldn't make his alimony payments, he told his diary he'd "hit up" lobbyists and businesses for whom he had done favors and ask them to hire his ex-wife. One lobbyist offered $37,500 for some part-time work, saying, "If you're a chairman of the Finance Committee I can probably double that." The senator noted one $1,269 dinner for ten, all paid for by a Japanese corporation. When he was offered $3,000 from a timber and paper company, he scoffed at the small amount but wrote, "I'm glad to have anything I can get."

One of Packwood's closest friends, Ronald Crawford, was a lobbyist who made it known to companies and trade associations that if they wanted access to Packwood, they'd have to hire him. His client list included Shell Oil, the American Iron and Steel Institute, the National Cable Association, and General Motors, all companies or interest with huge stakes at risk depending on congressional legislation. Packwood supported laws to deregulate the campaign industry and later blocked bills opposed by cable companies. His campaign even hired Crawford as a $5,000-a-month consultant. Was Packwood a legislator for sale? What do you think?

Citizen outrage at stories like Packwood's and even Solomon's are at the heart of many citizens' distrust of government. And it's probably no wonder that as much as some good government groups press for reform of the political system, those who profit from it remain opposed to any major change.

[*]David E. Rosenbaum, "Defying Odds, New Yorker Saves Milk Subsidies,": *The New York Times* (December 6, 1995): A1.

[**]Rosenbaum, "Defying Odds."

[***]Stephan Engleberg, "Packwood Diaries: A Rare Look at Washington's Tangled Web," *The New York Times* (September 10, 1995): A1.

Because lobbying plays such an important role in Congress, many effective lobbyists often are former members of that body, former staff aides, former White House officials or Cabinet officers, or Washington insiders. This type of lobbyist frequently drops in to visit members of Congress or their staff members and often takes them to lunch, golf, or parties. Although much of that activity may be ethically questionable, most is not illegal. (See Highlight 16.2: Ethics in Government Act). There are well-publicized exceptions, however. Michael K. Deaver, once a top aide to President Ronald Reagan, was convicted of perjury in connection with a grand jury investigation of his use of his former government contacts to help clients in his public relations firm.

Highlight 16.2

Ethics in Government Act

In 1978, in the wake of Watergate, Congress passed the Ethics in Government Act. Its key provisions dealt with financial disclosure and employment after government service:

Financial disclosure: The president, vice president, and top-ranking executive employees must file annual public financial disclosure reports that list:

- The source and amount of all earned income; all income from stocks, bonds, and property; any investments or large debts; and the source of a spouse's income, if any.

- Any position or offices held in any business, labor, or nonprofit organizations.

Employment after government services: Former executive branch employees may not:

- Represent anyone before any agency for two years after leaving government service on matters that came within the former employees' sphere of responsibility (even if they were not personally involved in the matter).

- Represent anyone on *any* matter before their former agency for one year after leaving it, even if the former employees had no connection with the matter while in the government.

Sources: National Journal (November 19, 1977): 1796–1803; and *Congressional Quarterly Weekly Report* (October 28, 1978): 3121–27.

Attempts to Reform Congressional Lobbying. In 1946, in an effort to limit the power of lobbyists, Congress passed the Federal Regulation of Lobbying Act, which required anyone hired to lobby any member of Congress to register and file quarterly financial reports. Few lobbyists actually file these reports. Through 1995, in fact, the Justice Department did not even opt to try to enforce the provisions of the act, believing its vagueness makes it virtually unenforceable. For years, numerous good government groups argued that lobbying laws should be strengthened to avoid situations like those described in the Packwood diaries. Civil liberties groups such as the American

★ HOW a bill becomes law in Congress ★

Congressman, here's your bill.

Here's your law.

Special Interest

Mike Luckovich Atlanta Constitution ©

Highlight 16.3

New Rules, New Definitions

In 1995 nearly 6,000 people were registered as Washington, D.C., lobbyists. Many inside the Beltway are expecting that number to be three to ten times larger by the end of 1996. The new rules require lobbyists to:

- register with the Clerk of the House and the Secretary of the Senate
- report their clients and issues and the agency or house they lobbied
- estimate the amount they are paid by each client

The new act also included new definitions. Lobbyists are now defined as persons who:

- spend at least 20 percent of their time lobbying members, their staffs, or executive branch officials
- are compensated for more than one lobbying contact in six months
- lobby on behalf of foreign interests. Lawyers are no longer exempt from the new definition.

What do you think these new rules will accomplish? Will they have any impact on the legal profession, whose members now include a growing number of Washington, D.C., lobbyists? Will changing the rules make more Americans less cynical about the lobbying process?

Civil Liberties Union (ACLU), however, argue that registration provisions violate the First Amendment's guarantee of freedom of speech and the right of citizens to petition the government.

But public opinion polls continued to reveal that many Americans believed that the votes of numerous members of Congress were often available to the highest bidder. After nearly fifty years of inaction, in late 1995 Congress passed the first effort to regulate lobbying since the 1946 act. The new act, the 1995 Lobbying Disclosure Act, was passed overwhelmingly in both houses of Congress. As revealed in Highlight 16.3: New Rules, New Definitions, the new rules employ a strict definition of lobbyist, which should trigger far greater reporting of lobbyist activities. The reporting of clients and issues should make it easier for those kinds of activities to be monitored by watchdog groups or the media.

Lobbying the Executive Branch.   As the scope of the federal government has expanded, lobbying the executive branch has increased in importance and frequency. Groups often target one or more levels of the executive branch because there are so many potential access points—the president and White House staff, and the numerous levels of the executive branch bureaucracy. Groups try to work closely with the administration in an effort to influence policy decisions at their formulation and implementation stages. And, like the situation with congressional lobbying, the effectiveness of a group often lies in its ability to provide decision makers with important information and a sense of where the public stands on the issue.

Historically, group representatives have met with presidents or their staff members to urge policy directions. In 1992 representatives of the auto industry even accompanied President Bush to lobby the Japanese for more favorable trade regulations. Most presidents also specifically set up staff positions "explicitly to serve as brokerages or clearinghouses to provide greater access to presidential attention for professional, demographic, or specialized organizations."[29] Political scientist Thomas Cronin has suggested that "presidents have appointed either an aide or an office for every American dilemma."[30] Many of these offices, such as those dealing with consumer affairs, the environment, and minority affairs, are routinely the target of organized interests. And, at various times, even more interest-oriented special liaison offices have been created to deal with women, Jews, African Americans, and bankers, among others.

Lobbying Regulatory Agencies.   An especially strong link exists between interest groups and regulatory agencies (see chapter 8). While these agencies are ostensibly independent of Congress and the president, interest groups often have clout there. Because of the highly technical aspects of much regulatory work, many groups employ Washington attorneys to deal directly with the agencies. So great is interest group influence in the decision-making process of these agencies that many people charge that the agencies have been captured by the interest groups.

Program Monitoring.   Groups often monitor how the laws or policies they advocated are implemented. Thus interest groups often find it useful, once a law is passed or a regulation written that affects them, to monitor how that law or regulation is implemented. The National Organization for Women (NOW), for example, created the Project on Educational Equity Review (PEER) to monitor the enforcement of Title IX, the purpose of which is to ban sex discrimination in schools receiving federal funding. Its newsletter, *PEER Perspective*, provides detailed analyses of Title IX legislative and administrative activity. Moreover, PEER staffers are in regular contact with government officials to discuss enforcement and to lobby against regulations that would hinder the enforcement of Title IX.

Lobbying the Courts.   The courts, too, have proved a useful target for interest groups.[31] Although you might think that the courts decide cases that affect only the parties involved or that they should be immune from political pressures, interest groups have for years recognized the value of lobbying the courts, especially the Supreme Court, and many political scientists view it as a form of political participation.[32] As shown in Table 16.3, 72 percent of the Washington-based groups surveyed participated in litigation as a lobbying tool. Richard C. Cortner has noted that "Cases do not arrive on the doorstep of the Supreme Court like orphans in the night."[33] Most major cases noted in this book have either been sponsored by an interest group or one or both of the parties in the case have been supported by an *amicus curiae* (friend of the court) brief.

Generally, interest group lobbying of the courts can take two forms: direct sponsorship and *amicus curiae* briefs. When cases come to the Supreme Court that raise issues a particular organization is interested in but not actually sponsoring, often the organization will file an *amicus* brief—either alone or with other like-minded groups—to inform the justices of their policy preference, generally offered in the guise of legal arguments (see Highlight 10.3: *Amicus* Briefs in Support of Harris). Over the years, as the number of both liberal and conservative groups viewing litigation as a useful tactic has increased, so has the number of briefs submitted to the Court.

In addition to litigating, interest groups try to influence who is nominated to the federal courts. They also have played an important role of late in Senate confirmation hearings, as discussed in chapter 10. In 1991, for example, 112 groups testified or filed prepared statements for or against the nomination of Clarence Thomas to the U.S. Supreme Court. Several of the most well known are listed in Table 16.4. Thomas's nomination was unusual in that it attracted so much opposition, including that of the NAACP. In contrast, the subsequent nominations of Justices Ginsburg and Breyer attracted the attention of far fewer interest groups.

TABLE 16.4

Interest Groups Taking Sides on the Nomination of Clarence Thomas to the U.S. Supreme Court

FOR THOMAS	AGAINST THOMAS
U.S. Chamber of Commerce	NAACP
Coalition for Self-Reliance	AFL–CIO
Coalitions for America	National Organization for Women
American Conservative Union	National Abortion Rights Action League
Concerned Women for America	United Church of Christ
Eagle Forum	League of United Latin American Citizens
Family Research Council	Congressional Black Caucus
The Council of 100	National Women's Political Caucus
Simon Wiesenthal Center	National Education Association
Women For Judge Thomas[*]	Americans for Democratic Action
	Women's Legal Defense Fund
	People for the American Way
	Service Employees International Union
	Alliance for Justice

[*]Group created expressly to support Thomas.

Source: "The Opposition Mounts," *USA Today* (August 8, 1991): A–1.

Grassroots Lobbying.   As the term implies, *grassroots lobbying* is a form of pressure group activity that attempts to involve those people at the bottom level of the political system. Although it often involves door-to-door informational or petition drives—a tried and true method of lobbying—the term also can be used to encompass the kind of fax and Internet lobbying of lawmakers described at the beginning of this chapter. As early as the 1840s, women (who could not vote) used petition campaigns to persuade state legislators to enact Married Women's Property Acts that gave women control of their earnings and a greater legal say in the custody of their children. Petitioning has come a long way since then. In 1996 the Fund for a Feminist Majority held a weekend symposium to teach women how to use the Internet to petition lawmakers.

Today interest groups regularly try to stir up their members to inspire grassroots activity, hoping that lawmakers will respond to those pressures and the attendant publicity. For example, when Congress was debating the so-called Brady Bill (to limit the sale of handguns) in the early 1990s, groups on both sides of the debate used mass mailings and print ads to educate the public. In essence, the goal of many organizations is to persuade ordinary voters to serve as their advocates. In the world of lobbying, there are few things more useful than a list of committed supporters. Radio talk show hosts like Rush Limbaugh also try to stir up their listeners by urging them to contact their representatives in Washington, D.C. Those undefined masses, however, are not an interest group; but as they join together on the Internet or via faxes, they may be mobilized into one or more groups.

Interest groups' use of electronic technologies to reach and recruit thousands of Americans at the grassroots level quickly has caused "Congress to govern more by fear and an intense desire for simple, easy answers,"[34] said Representative Steve Gunderson (R–Wis.) before he left office. Today the simple grassroots campaigns of just a few years ago (fill-in-the-blank postcards and forms torn out of the newspaper) have grown much more sophisticated and become much more effective. Many interest groups and trade groups have installed banks of computerized fax machines to send faxes automatically around the country overnight, instructing each member to ask his or her employees, customers, or other people to write, call, or fax their members of Congress. Other interest groups now run carefully targeted and costly television advertisements pitching one side of an argument. Their opponents must generally respond or lose. Many of these advertisements end with a toll-free phone number that viewers can call if they find the pitch convincing. New telemarketing companies answer these calls and transfer the callers directly to the offices of the appropriate members of Congress.[35]

Protest Activities.   Most groups have few members so devoted as to put everything on the line for their cause. Some will risk jail or even death, but it is much more usual for a group's members to opt for more conventional forms of lobbying or to influence policy through the electoral process. When these forms of pressure group activities are unsuccessful or appear to be too slow to achieve results, however, some groups (or individuals within groups) resort to more forceful legal and illegal measures to attract attention to their cause. During the civil rights movement, as discussed in chapter 6, the Reverend Martin Luther King, Jr,. and his followers frequently resorted to nonviolent marches to draw attention to the plight of African Americans in the South. These forms of organized group activity were legal. Proper parade permits were obtained, and government officials notified. The protesters who tried to stop the freedom marchers, however, were engaging in illegal protest activity, another form of activity sometimes resorted to by interest groups.

Since the Revolutionary War, violent, illegal protest has been one tactic of organized interests. The Boston Tea Party, for example, involved breaking all sorts of laws, although no one was hurt physically. Other forms of protest, such as Shays's Rebellion, ended in tragedy for some participants.

Groups on both ends of the political spectrum historically have resorted to violence. Abolitionists, antinuclear power activists, antiwar activists, animal-rights advocates, and other groups on the "left" have broken laws, damaged property, and even injured or killed innocent bystanders. On the "right," groups such as Lambs of Christ (an anti-abortion group) and the Ku Klux Klan (KKK) have broken the laws and even hurt or killed people in the furtherance of their objectives. From the early 1900s until the 1960s, African Americans were routinely lynched by KKK members. Today some radical anti-abortion groups regularly block the entrances to abortion clinics; others active in the anti-abortion movement have taken credit for clinic bombings.

Election Activities

In addition to trying to achieve their goals through the conventional and unconventional forms of lobbying and protest activity, many interest groups also become involved more directly in the electoral process.

Endorsements.   Many groups claim to be nonpartisan, that is, nonpolitical. Usually they try to have friends in both political parties to whom they can look for assistance and access. Some organizations, however, routinely endorse candidates for public office, pledging money, group support, and often even campaign volunteers. For example, at one time candidates in the Northeast fought for labor union endorsement, recognizing that their support would bring money, volunteers, and votes. In 1996, however, presidential candidate Bob Dole openly attacked teachers' unions in a speech as he accepted his party's nomination for president. EMILY's List, a women's group (EMILY stands for "Early Money Is Like Yeast—it makes the dough rise"), not only endorses candidates, but contributes heavily to races. It is not unusual, moreover, for conservation or environmental groups to endorse candidates that they view as friends.

More recently, the Christian Coalition, which claims to be nonpartisan, has come under attack for its involvement in partisan elections. The Coalition uses score cards to evaluate candidates, and some claim that it has played a key role in some Republican candidates' races. It does not, however, formally endorse candidates.

Endorsements from some groups may be used by a candidate's opponent to attack a candidate. While labor union endorsements can add money to a candidate's campaign coffers, for example, they risk being labeled a "tool of the labor unions" by their opponents.

Rating the Candidates or Office Holders.   Many liberal and conservative ideological groups rate candidates to help their members (and the general public) evaluate the voting records of members of Congress. The American Conservative Union (conservative) and the Americans for Democratic Action (liberal)—two groups at ideological polar extremes—routinely rate candidates and members of Congress based on their votes on key issues of importance to the group, as illustrated in Table 16.5. So do groups including the ACLU, the Christian Coalition, and the League of Conservation Voters. These scores help voters to know more about their representatives' votes on issues that concern them.

Some groups target certain individuals and campaign against them to show their clout and to scare other elected officials into paying more attention to them. Beginning in 1970, for example, Environmental Action (EA) labeled twelve members of the House of Representatives "the dirty dozen" because of their votes against bills that the group believed were necessary to protect the environment. Over the years, EA's regular designation of more than thirty members of Congress with a similar label has been widely publicized by the media and through direct-mail campaigns to voters interested in the environment. Through 1995 only seven members to earn EA's anti-environmental nickname have been able to survive their dubious distinction in their bid to be reelected.

In 1994 the National Rifle Association similarly successfully targeted several members of the House who voted for the Brady Bill and even unseated Representative Jack Brooks (D–Tex.), the veteran chair of the subcommittee in charge of the bill that restricted the sale of guns.

Creating Political Parties.   Another interest group strategy is to form a political party to publicize a cause and even possibly win a few public offices. In 1848 the Free Soil Party was formed to publicize the crusade against slavery; twenty years later the Prohibition Party was formed to try to ban the sale of alcoholic beverages. Similarly, in the early 1970s, the National Right-to-Life Party was formed to publicize the antiabortion position, and it even ran its own candidate for president in 1976.

In 1995 Ross Perot turned his group, United We Stand, into the Reform Party to highlight the group's goals, including government reform (in particular, passage of new campaign finance laws) and fiscal responsibility. Similarly, consumer advocate Ralph Nader was the 1996 nominee of the new Green Party, created to bring attention to en-

TABLE 16.5

Interest Group Ratings of Selected Members of Congress*

MEMBER	ACU	ACLU	ADA	AFL–CIO	CC	CoC	CFA	LCV
Senate								
Jesse Helms (R–N.C.)	100	16	0	14	100	89	8	0
Kay Bailey Hutchinson (R–Tex.)	96	33	10	0	78	100	17	9
Carol Moseley-Braun (D–Ill.)	4	76	85	75	8	35	83	77
Edward M. Kennedy (D–Mass.)	0	79	90	88	0	18	75	92
House								
Bill Paxon (R–N.Y.)	100	13	0	0	100	92	10	17
Susan Molinari (R–N.Y.)	71	43	20	44	64	92	30	17
Vic Fazio (D–Cal.)	14	87	75	78	7	42	90	61
Cynthia McKinney (D–Ga.)	0	87	100	100	0	33	100	100

Key

ACU = American Conservative Union

ACLU = American Civil Liberties Union

ADA = Americans for Democratic Action

AFL–CIO = American Federation of Labor–Congress of Industrial Organizations

CC = Christian Coalition

CoC = Chamber of Commerce

CFA = Consumer Federation of America

LCV = League of Conservation Voters

*Members are rated on a scale from 1 to 100, with 1 being the lowest and 100 being the highest support of a particular group's policies.

vironmental issues. Groups often see forming political parties as ways to draw attention to their legislative goals and to drive one of the major parties to give their demands more serious attention.

The effectiveness of an interest group in the election arena has often been overrated by members of the news media. In general, it is very difficult to assess the effect of a particular group's impact on any one election because of the number of other factors present in any election or campaign. However, the one area in which interest groups do seem able to affect the outcome of elections directly is through a relatively new device called the political action committee.

Interest Groups and Political Action Committees.   Throughout most of history, powerful interests and individuals have often used their money to "buy" politicians or their votes. Even if outright bribery was not involved, huge corporate or other interest group donations certainly made some politicians look as if they were in the "pocket" of certain special interests. Congressional passage of the Federal Election Campaign Act began to change most of that. The 1971 act required candidates to disclose all campaign contributions and limited the amount of money that they could spend on media advertising.

In 1974, in the wake of the Watergate scandal (see chapter 8), amendments to the act made it more far-reaching by sharply limiting the amount of money any interest group could give to a candidate for federal office. However, the act also made it legal for corporations, labor unions, and interest groups to form what were termed **political action committees,** often referred to as **PACs,** which could make contributions to candidates for national elections. (See chapter 14 for more on this subject.)

Technically, a PAC is a political arm of a business, labor, trade, professional, or other interest group legally authorized to raise funds on a voluntary basis from employees or members in order to contribute to a political candidate or party. These monies have changed the face of U.S. elections. Unlike some contributions to interest groups, however, contributions to PACs are not tax deductible, and PACs generally don't have members who call legislators; instead, PACs have contributors who write checks specifically for the purpose of campaign donations. PAC money plays a significant role in the campaigns of many congressional incumbents, often averaging over half a House candidate's total campaign spending. PACs generally contribute to those who have helped them before and who serve on committees or subcommittees that routinely consider legislation of concern to that group. For example, the landmark telecommunications bill began to be seriously debated in Congress in 1995. Over fifty political action committees representing companies in the telecommunications and broadcasting industries then contributed over $1.7 million to House and Senate candidates in the first half of the year, when talks about the bill had yet to begin. And the major players in the debate got the most money. Larry Pressler (R–S.D.), the chair of the Senate Commerce Committee, charged with overseeing the bill, received almost $100,000 from telecommunications PACs.

The number of PACs is increasing rapidly. In 1975 there were 608; by 1995 nearly 4,000 PACs were registered with the Federal Elections Commission. Roughly 3,000 PACs contributed in the 1994 congressional elections, spending nearly $180 million in that election accounting cycle, with most going to incumbents (see Figure 16.4).[36] Corporate PACs lead the way in terms of contributions, as also indicated in Table 16.6.

political action committee (PAC): A federally registered fund-raising committee that represents an interest group in the political process through campaign donations.

FIGURE 16.4

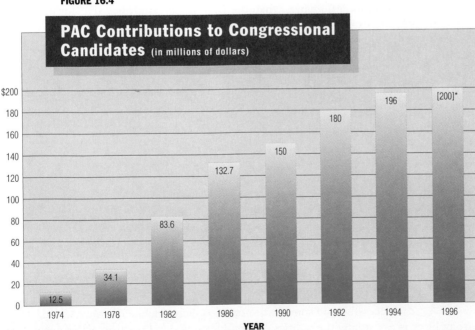

PAC Contributions to Congressional Candidates (in millions of dollars)

* Projected figure

SOURCE: Congressional Research Service and Federal Election Commission.

TABLE 16.6

Doling out PAC Dollars

ELECTION CYCLE	CORPORATE	LABOR	TRADE MEMBERSHIP/ HEALTH	NON-CONNECTED	OTHER CONNECTED	TOTAL
1977–1978	$15.2	$18.6	$23.8	$17.4	$2.4	$77.4
1979–1980	31.4	25.1	32.0	38.6	4.0	131.2
1981–1982	43.3	34.8	41.9	64.3	5.8	190.2
1983–1984	59.2	47.5	54.0	97.4	8.7	266.8
1985–1986	79.3	57.9	73.3	118.4	11.1	340.0
1987–1988	89.9	74.1	83.7	104.9	11.7	364.2
1989–1990	101.1	84.6	88.1	71.4	12.5	357.6
1991–1992	112.2	94.3	97.4	76.1	14.1	394.1
1993–1994	116.9	88.2	94.1	74.6	13.7	387.4

Note: Figures are in current dollars. Detail may not add to totals because of rounding.

Sources: 1977–1978: Norman J. Ornstein *et al.*, eds., *Vital Statistics on Congress*, 1987–1988 (Washington, D.C.: Congressional Quarterly, 1987), 105; 1979–1994: Federal Election Commission, "PAC Activity in 1994 Elections Remains at 1992 Levels," press release, March 31, 1995, 12.

Source: Harold W. Stanley and Richard G. Niemi, *Vital Statistics on American Politics*, 5th ed. (Washington, D.C.: CQ Press, 1995), 164.

The 1994 election of large numbers of Republicans to Congress brought about a pronounced change in PAC giving. When the Democrats controlled the House and the Senate in 1993, for example, PAC contributions were divided fairly evenly between the parties. This pattern was reversed dramatically after the Republican takeover. In the first half of 1995, PAC contributions to GOP members were $1,267,122, while Democrats received only $473,289.[37]

One of the biggest increases in PAC contributions has come from women's groups, which experienced a 314 percent increase in giving from 1990 to 1992 alone. Especially important was EMILY's List; this group was the largest single contributor to Democratic women congressional candidates in 1992, 1994, and 1996. Its early successes even spawned a Republican counterpart—WISH (Women in the Senate and House). (See Highlight 14.2: Women's PACs Continue to Make a Difference.)

WHAT MAKES AN INTEREST GROUP SUCCESSFUL?

Throughout our nation's history, a range of interests in society have organized to pressure the government for policy change. Some have been successful, and some have not. E. E. Schattschneider once wrote, "Pressure politics is essentially the politics of small groups. . . . Pressure tactics are not remarkably successful in mobilizing general interests."[38] He was correct; historically, corporate interests often prevail over the concerns of public interest groups, such as environmentalists.

To understand why some groups don't fare better, it's important to distinguish between an actual and a potential group and to understand that most groups attract only members who agree with them on most (if not all) issues. Theoretically, all women could be members of a women's rights group, all campers members of a conservation group, or all gun owners members of the National Rifle Association. Potential groups include all people who might be group members because they share a common trait or interest.[39] An actual group consists of only those people who actually join, and it is almost always smaller than the potential group. No group can ever attract all potential members; no one group is so monolithic that it could appeal to all people in the potential group. All farmers won't want to belong to the Grange, and all anti-abortion activists don't want to join Operation Rescue.

Groups vary tremendously in their ability to enroll potential members, as revealed in Table 16.7. Economist Mancur Olson, Jr. notes that all groups, whether economic or noneconomic, provide some **collective good**—that is, something of value, such as money, a tax write-off, a good feeling, or a better environment—that can't be withheld from a non-group member.[40] If one union member at a factory gets a raise, for example, all other workers at that factory will, too. Therefore those who don't join or work for the benefit of the group still reap the rewards of the group's activity. This phenomenon is called the **free rider** problem. Consequently, Olson asserts, potential members are unlikely to join a group because they realize that they will receive many of the benefits the group achieves regardless of their participation. Not only is it irrational for free riders to join any group, but the bigger the group, the greater the free rider problem. Small groups like the AMA or the American Political Science Association have an

Demonstration on "Fur Free Friday" by members of PETA (People for the Ethical Treatment of Animals). (Photo courtesy: Gabe Kirchheimer/Black Star)

collective good: Something of value that cannot be withheld from a noninterest group member, for example, a tax write-off, a good feeling.

free rider: A problem that occurs when those who don't join or work for the benefit of the group still reap the rewards of the group's activity.

TABLE 16.7

Potential *versus* Actual Interest Groups

The goal of most groups is to mobilize all potential members. Often that task is impossible. As Mancur Olson, Jr. points out, the larger the group, the more difficult it is to mobilize. To illustrate the potential versus actual membership phenomenon, here are several examples of groups and their potential memberships.

POPULATION	GROUP	NUMBER OF POTENTIAL MEMBERS	NUMBER OF ACTUAL MEMBERS
Governors	National Governor's Association	55	55 (includes territories)
Political Science Faculty	American Political Science Association	17,000	8,250
Doctors	American Medical Association (AMA)	548,000	288,000
Women	National Organization for Women (NOW)	127,000,000	250,000
African Americans	National Association for the Advancement of Colored People (NAACP)	30,600,00	500,000

organizational advantage because, in a small group, any individual's share of the collective good may be great enough to make it rational to join.

Patrons, be they large foundations such as the Ford Foundation or individuals such as Jane Fonda, who pledged $500,000 from the Turner Foundation to the Georgia Campaign for Adolescent Pregnancy Prevention in 1995, often eliminate the free rider problem for public interest groups. They make the "costs" of joining minimal because they contribute much of the group's necessary support.[41]

The Role of Leaders

Interest group theorists frequently acknowledge the key role that leaders play in the formation, viability, and success of interest groups. The role of an interest group leader is similar to that of an entrepreneur in the business world. As in the marketing of a new product, an interest group leader must have something attractive to offer to persuade members to join. Potential members of the group must be convinced that the benefits of joining outweigh the costs. Union members, for example, must be persuaded that the cost of their union dues will be offset by the union's winning higher wages for them.

Frances Willard was the prime mover behind the Women's Christian Temperance Union (WCTU); Marian Wright Edelman was behind the Children's Defense Fund in 1968; and Pat Robertson and Ralph Reed are the prime movers of the Christian Coalition today. Most successful groups, especially public interest groups, are led by charismatic individuals who devote most of their energies to "the cause." Moreover, leaders often differ from the rank and file of the group in that they are usually more future oriented, better educated, and affluent.[42]

Funding

Funding is crucial to all interest groups. Governments, foundations, and wealthy individuals can serve as patrons providing crucial start-up funds for groups, especially public interest groups.

Groups also rely heavily on membership contributions, dues, and other fund-raising activities.[43] During the 1980s conservative groups, for example, relied on the direct-mail skills of marketing wizard Richard Viguerie to raise monies for a variety of conservative causes. In the early 1990s, pro choice groups appealed to supporters by requesting funds to campaign for legislation in anticipation of the Supreme Court's reversal of *Roe* v. *Wade* (see Highlight 16.4: How Events Can Affect Interest Groups). When the Supreme Court did not overrule *Roe* in 1992, and Ruth Bader Ginsburg was appointed to the Supreme Court, contributions to pro-choice groups such as NARAL and Planned Parenthood dropped precipitously.

Similarly, after the murders of Nicole Brown and Ronald Goldman, money to shelters for abused and battered women rose around the country. And every time O. J. Simpson made an appearance at a public event after his acquittal for their murders, donations to shelters went up.

Alexis de Tocqueville, a French aristocrat and philosopher, toured the United States extensively during 1831 and 1832. A keen observer of American politics, he was very much impressed by the tendency of Americans to join groups in order to participate in the policy-making process. "Whenever at the head of some new undertaking you see government in France, or a man of rank in England, in the United States you will be

Highlight 16.4

How Events Can Affect Interest Groups

In the wake of the Clarence Thomas hearings in 1991, liberal women's interest groups attempted to capitalize on women's anger through a variety of well-written pleas for funds to prevent any other women from being treated as Anita Hill was treated by the then all-male Senate Judiciary Committee. The results:

ORGANIZATION	RESULTS
EMILY's List	$300,000 raised in a direct-mail solicitation sent out two weeks after the hearings
Fund for the Feminist Majority	30% increase in direct-mail contributions
National Organization for Women (NOW)	Direct-mail contributions up 25%–30%; threefold increase in paid memberships
National Women's Political Caucus	$85,000 raised from one newspaper ad
Women's Campaign Fund	50% increase in direct-mail contributions

Source: Jill Abramson, "Women's Anger About Hill–Thomas Hearings Has Brought Cash into Female Political Causes," *Wall Street Journal* (January 6, 1992): A–16. Reprinted by permission of the *Wall Street Journal* © copyright 1992 Dow Jones & Company, Inc. All rights reserved worldwide.

sure to find an association,"[44] wrote de Tocqueville. He was especially impressed by the ability of groups to influence the formal institutions of government, noting:

> It is true that they [representatives of these associations] have not the right, like the others, of making the laws, but they have the power of attacking those which are in force and of drawing up beforehand those which ought to be enacted.[45]

The United States is still a nation of joiners, although as noted in Figure 16.1, fewer younger people are getting involved. As a college student, think of the number of interest groups or voluntary associations to which you belong. It's likely that you belong to some kind of organized religion; to a political party; or to a college, or university social, civic, athletic, or academic group, at a bare minimum. You may also belong to a more general special interest group, such as Greenpeace, the National Rifle Association, the National Right-to-Life Committee, or Amnesty International.

Organizations are usually composed of three kinds of members. At the top are a relatively small number of leaders who devote most of their energies to the single group. The second tier of members is generally involved psychologically as well as organizationally. They are the workers of the group—they attend meetings, pay dues, and chair committees to see that things get done. In the bottom tier are the rank and file, members who don't actively participate. They pay their dues and call themselves group members, but they do little more. Most group members fall into this last category.

North—South

POLITICS AROUND THE WORLD

The collapse of communism and the emergence of new and fragile democratic regimes around the world has drawn our attention back to interest groups and the role of "civil society." Although it is clear that a society with any degree of political freedom develops interest groups, what they do and how effective they are in an individual country is often quite different from what we are used to in the United States, because of the kinds of institutional and attitudinal differences discussed so far.

If you were to make a list of interest groups in Canada, it would not look very different from those covered in this chapter in the United States. There are nationally organized business associations and trade unions as well as smaller groups representing the interests of local groups. There will be others representing the "new social movements" of the last thirty years or so, including religious and ethnic minorities, women, gays, the Christian right, and so on.

The key difference lies in what those interest groups try to do. Given the importance of national rather than subnational government, most concentrate their efforts in Ottawa, though there are plenty of examples (such as gays trying to keep the police from raiding bathhouses in Toronto) of groups concentrating their efforts locally. They do not, however, concentrate on lobbying the House of Commons once a bill is proposed as much as their counterparts do with Congress in the United States. Instead, they concentrate their efforts on influencing the civil service and majority party before a bill is actually drafted, since those are the most important decision-making points in a parliamentary system (see North–South features in chapters 7 and 8). Most also operate in each province be-

cause much social and economic policy is determined at that level. There, too, most of their lobbying effort is directed at the cabinet and bureaucracy, as they, not the legislature, are the most important de facto decision makers.

You would also be able to put together the same kind of list for Mexico. But once you scratched the surface, you would discover that the differences are even more striking. In the United States or Canada, interest groups tend to be voluntary associations that, in the jargon of comparative politics, articulate the interests of their members, independent of and often against the wishes of those in power. By contrast, Mexican interest groups have historically been "corporatist," or created by the PRI-led government for its own purposes and integrated into ongoing decision-making processes. If we can think of interest groups in the United States or Canada as being "bottom up" in origin and orientation, those in Mexico have been "bottom down" and served to bolster the government and its interests. For instance, the Confederation of Mexican Labor (CTM) has rarely sought to influence public policies to benefit its members, as a "normal" trade union does in Europe or North America, rather it has sought to incorporate the working class into the PRI system and thereby strengthen its hold on power.

In the last twenty to thirty years, more autonomous interest groups have emerged, including feminist and environmental movements and organizations representing the poor. But, as the Chiapas revolt and other instances of political violence in the 1990s suggest, the absence of regularized channels of access "within the system" has convinced many people in those movements that they have no option but to take to the streets and even take up arms to get their point across.

Political scientist E. E. Schattschneider has noted that the interest group system in the United States has a decidedly "upper-class bias," and he concluded that 90 percent of the population does not participate in an interest group, or what he called the pressure group, system.[46] Since the 1960s, survey data have revealed that group membership is drawn primarily from people with higher income and education levels. Individuals who are wealthier can afford to belong to more organizations because they have more money and, often, more leisure time. Money and education are also associated with greater confidence that one's actions will bring results, a further incentive to devote time to organizing or supporting interest groups. As discussed in chapter 11, these elites are often more involved in politics and hold stronger opinions on many political issues.

People who do belong to groups often belong to more than one. Overlapping memberships can often affect the cohesiveness of a group. Imagine, for example, that you are an officer in the college Young Republicans. If you call a meeting, people may not attend because they have academic, athletic, or social obligations. Divided loyalties and multiple group memberships can often affect the success of a group, especially if any one group has too many members who simply fall into the dues-paying category.

Getting Ideas on the Public Agenda

Most of the groups we discuss in this chapter have been the "successful" ones—the ones that were lucky enough to have committed leaders, adequate financing or patrons, and ideas that appealed to enough people to make those ideas viable in the political process. A successful group usually can use its resources to put its ideas on the government's policy agenda. As groups mobilize to push their policy goals, they often bring into the public forum issues that might not have otherwise surfaced at that time. The Humane Society, for example, has been in existence since the turn of the century; but it was not until more aggressive groups such as People for the Ethical Treatment of Animals (PETA) made the public aware of the widespread testing of many products on animals that public pressure effectively forced many manufacturers to alter their testing programs. In many sections of the country, for example, wearing fur coats is no longer socially acceptable. PETA effectively used celebrities, demonstrations, and illegal activities to bring its position to the public.

For many groups, simply getting their issues on the public agenda equals success. Government responses may not be forthcoming, but their activities can mean that the public is made sufficiently aware of a certain practice or policy to work for changes to be made (or, at the very least, to make the changes themselves).

CHANGING THE INTEREST GROUP SOCIETY

Although the United States has always been a nation of joiners, numerous commentators have recently noted that fewer Americans are engaging in face-to-face kinds of organizational activity. From bowling leagues to the PTA, membership has declined—many Americans believe they have less time for group activity because they see themselves forced to work harder all of the time. They will, however, write a check to an organization that works for principles in which they believe. Successes of groups such as EMILY'S List, which exists largely as a conduit for checks to support the campaigns of Democratic female candidates, underscore the willingness of many who believe in causes to belong to groups that don't require time commitments. Still, it is largely older Americans who engage in checkbook advocacy, and it really is unknown yet whether younger Americans, who are not joining groups at the rate of their parents and grandparents, will eventually become comfortable with contributing to causes or candidates.

As more and more political groups, including PACs, are formed or are transformed into checkbook or multimedia advocacy, interesting questions arise concerning the role of groups in a democracy. What kind of voice will there be for the poor or minorities that the political system was envisioned to protect? People who can write checks for $25 or $100 or who have access to computers and online services often have quite different perspectives on issues than do those who are technologically challenged—whether through income or education. Similarly, as also suggested in Table 16.1, the young, those age eighteen to thirty-four, are much more likely to feel comfortable with using technology to contact their representatives—a trend that also has important implications for the future of our interest group society.

Many citizens are also turned off by government and politics and are disgusted by the apparent role that many PACs and special interests play in the political process. There is pressure being placed on legislators to change campaign finance laws to minimize the influence of special interests, but there has not been enough support for these measures in Congress to see them enacted to bring about meaningful change.

SUMMARY

Interest groups lie at the heart of the American social and political system. National groups first emerged in the 1830s. Since that time the type, nature, sophistication, and tactics of groups have changed dramatically. To that end we have made the following points:

1. What Are Interest Groups?

Those who study interest groups have offered a variety of definitions to explain what they are. Most definitions revolve around notions of "associations or groups of individuals" who "share" some sort of "common" "interest" or "attitude" and who try to "influence" or "engage in activity" to affect "governmental policies" or the people in "government."

2. Types of Interest Groups.

In general, interest groups represent economic or social interests of the public and are single- or multi-issue.

3. The Roots of American Interest Groups.

Interest groups, national in scope, did not begin to emerge until around the 1830s. Beginning in the 1960s, hundreds of new interest groups were formed; many of them were Washington, D.C.-based in order to better advance their interests in the nation's capital. This time, however, a new, more effective breed of conservative groups arose to counter their claims before legislatures, as well as in the courts. Professional associations, too, became an active presence in Washington, D.C.

4. What Do Interest Groups Do?

Interest groups often fill voids left by the major political parties and give Americans opportunities to make claims, as a group, on government. The most common activity of interest groups is lobbying, which takes many forms. Groups routinely pressure members of Congress and their staffs, the president and the bureaucracy, and the courts; they use a variety of techniques to educate and stimulate the public also to pressure key governmental decision makers. Interest groups also attempt to influence the outcome of elections; some even run their own candidates for office. Others rate elected officials to inform their members how particular legislators stand on issues of importance to them. Political action committees (PACs), a way for some groups to contribute money to candidates for office, are another method of gaining support from elected officials and ensuring that their "friends" stay in office. Reaction to public criticism of this influence led Congress to pass the first major lobbying reforms in 50 years.

5. What Makes an Interest Group Successful?

Just as groups are diverse, so are the ways in which they become successful and measure their success. Strong leaders or patrons are critical to the success of most interest groups, as are adequate resources, whether in the form of a dedicated membership or a reliable source of funds. Leaders and funds allow groups to engage in a variety of lobbying activities and, once they get the programs or laws they seek, to monitor their implementation.

6. Changing the Interest Group Society.

We are at a defining point in our interest group society. Fewer people are joining groups; but, at the same time, some interest groups and political action committees play increasingly important roles in politics, much to the chagrin of many voters.

KEY TERMS

collective good, p. 633
disturbance theory, p. 614
economic interest group, p. 609
free rider, p. 633
interest group, p. 609
lobbying, p. 619

lobbyist, p. 619
patron, p. 613
political action committee (PAC), p. 631
public interest group, p. 611
trade associations, p. 617

SELECTED READINGS

Berry, Jeffrey M. *The Interest Group Society,* 2d ed. Glenview, IL: Scott, Foresman/Little, Brown, 1989.

——. *Lobbying for the People: The Political Behavior of Public Interest Groups.* Princeton, NJ: Princeton University Press, 1977.

Cigler, Allan J., and Burdett A. Loomis, eds. *Interest Group Politics,* 4th ed. Washington, D.C.: CQ Press, 1994.

McGlen, Nancy E., and Karen O'Connor. *Women, Politics and American Society.* Englewood Cliffs, NJ: Prentice Hall, 1995.

Olson, Mancur, Jr. *The Logic of Collective Action: Public Good and the Theory of*

Groups. Cambridge, MA: Harvard University Press, 1965.

Sabato, Larry J. *PAC Power: Inside the World of Political Action Committees.* New York: Norton, 1984.

Schlozman, Kay Lehman, and John T. Tierney. *Organized Interests and American Democracy.* New York: Harper & Row, 1986.

Truman, David B. *The Governmental Process: Political Interests and Public Opinion.* New York: Knopf, 1951.

Wolpe, Bruce C. and Bertram J. Levine. *Lobbying Congress: How the System Works,* 2nd ed. Washington, D.C.: CQ Press, 1996.

The Policy-Making Process

Social Welfare Policies

Income Security

Medical Care

Public Education

Changing American Social Policy

SOCIAL WELFARE POLICY

The watchword of Bill Clinton's 1992 presidential campaign was "It's the economy, stupid!" The Democratic challenger roundly criticized the incumbent for failing to create more jobs and for allowing the economy to stagnate. The press contributed to Republican woes with pictures of a president out of touch with average voters by reporting that George Bush was fascinated to see prices scanned from bar codes on a rare trip to a grocery store.[1] In contrast, Clinton empathized with voters: "I feel your pain."

As America rushes toward a new century, the state of the economy joins crime and family values as the holy trinity of campaign issues. The stakes are high for taming an economy in which job insecurity has become a hallmark. The party that devises a long-term solution to today's economic uncertainty may reap rewards similar to the twenty-year control of the presidency and even longer dominance of Congress that Franklin D. Roosevelt won for his party by getting the country through the Great Depression.

Fueling widespread concern are stories, reported with monotonous regularity, that first one industry and then another is downsizing or merging and laying off thousands of workers. Against this backdrop, voters reward the "out" party as it chastises the government and promises to do better.

Both Democrats and Republicans have discovered that promises are easy but performance is elusive. In 1992 voters worried about the economy went massively to the Democrats and ended twelve years of Republican control of the presidency.[2] Two years later, when the new administration had not delivered on promises to "end welfare as we know it" or to develop a more comprehensive health-care plan, Newt Gingrich—with his Contract for America—was the Pied Piper for voters still worried about making ends meet. Support from white males in this group, coupled with a disproportionate drop-off among women who voted in 1992 but not in 1994, contributed to the Republican sweep up and down the ticket.[3] Continued displeasure with the failure of either party to convert campaign slogans into economic security showed up in early 1996 when 60 percent of the voters said they blamed both parties for the problems facing them.

Some of America's poorest live in single-parent households, the bulk of which are headed by a woman. These women, who too often had their first child early, have limited educations, few skills, and discouraging job prospects. Many struggle along on welfare, but their sisters who work two low-paying jobs also have problems keeping up with rising costs. The vulnerability of these mothers who sustain their families in a frail nest knitted together from food stamps, WIC vouchers (WIC, which stands for Women, Infants and Children, provides nutrition for expectant mothers and their young children), Medicaid, income tax credits, and housing programs. Republican proposals to limit the scope of these programs, the length of eligibility, or their funding contribute to the gender gap which reached a record 16 percent in the 1996 presidential election. The rising frustration among women, especially when their voting rates equal or even exceed those of their husbands and lovers, can offset angry white males' preference for Republicans.

Adding to the frustration of many working Americans has been the sharp contrast between their treadmill existence, in which harder work does not get them ahead of the economic curve, and the record profits recorded by large corporations and skyrocketing salaries and bonuses for corporate leaders. Executives who give pink slips to thousands of workers are rewarded by higher stock prices and bigger salaries.

During the spring of 1996, in recognition of the potency of the issue of fair treatment for those on the bottom rung of the wage ladder, both parties embraced the idea of raising the minimum wage. Boosting the minimum wage to above $5 per hour is largely symbolic, however. Neither angry white males nor blue-collar women will be satisfied with that level of pay. The frustrations of these groups will continue as long as health care is expensive or unavailable, good-paying jobs are scarce, and the safety net is threatened because tax money is wasted on the "undeserving."

Social welfare policy is a term that designates a broad and varied range of government programs designed to provide people with protection against want and deprivation, to improve their health and physical well-being, to provide educational and employment training opportunities, and otherwise to enable them to lead more satisfactory, meaningful, and productive lives. In a nutshell, social welfare policies are intended to enhance the quality of life. They are meant to benefit all segments of society, but especially the less fortunate members, who often find it more difficult to provide for themselves and their families. More specifically, social welfare policies focus on such matters as public education, income security, medical care, sanitation and disease prevention, public housing, employment training, children's protective services, and improvements in human nutrition.

The issue of who is deserving and what they deserve is at the heart of the debate over social welfare programs. Over time, the focus of social welfare programs has expanded from providing minimal assistance to the destitute to helping the working poor attain a degree of security, to help them provide for their health, nutritional, income security, employment, and education needs.

In a more optimistic time, when political leaders expected the economic pie to continue expanding, the scope and generosity of social welfare programs grew. In the 1960s, for example, new programs provided food stamps and health care to meet two critical needs of the disadvantaged. The level of benefits for older programs like Social Security grew to keep pace with the cost of living.

Many Americans and their elected officials worry about the size of the federal budget deficit. Both Democrats and Republicans are loathe to increase taxes, and the parties vie with one another in devising plans for cutting taxes. Republicans have led the way in proposing ways in which to cut social welfare spending as a step toward budget balancing. Democrats, sensing public dissatisfaction with endless streams of money going to programs that seem unable to get people off welfare and into jobs, have increasingly joined critics. At present, welfare is under attack from both sides, and the full extent of reforms is uncertain. For the minority of Americans who depend on these programs, and the even greater numbers who want them to be available if needed, tinkering with their design is unnerving.

Social welfare policy is clearly changing in the United States—almost daily. In order to enable you to follow its progress in a more informed manner, in this chapter we explore the following issues:

■ First, we consider the nature of the *policy-making process* itself, presenting a model that provides a manageable way of dissecting the policy-making process and examining its components.

■ Second, we focus on three key areas of *social welfare policy*.

■ Third, we examine *income security* programs to relieve economic dependency and poverty.

■ Fourth, we evaluate *medical care* programs.

■ Fifth, we devote substantial attention to the national government's involvement in *public education*.

■ Finally, we keep track of the *changing social welfare policy*.

THE POLICY-MAKING PROCESS

Public policy is a purposive course of action followed by government in dealing with some problem or matter of concern.[4] Public policies are thus governmental policies, based on law; they are authoritative and binding on people. Individuals, groups, and even government agencies that do not comply with policies can be penalized through fines, loss of benefits, or even jail terms. As the phrase "course of action" implies, policies develop or unfold over time. They involve more than a legislative decision to enact a law or a presidential decision to issue an executive order. Also important is how the law or executive order is carried out. Whether a policy is vigorously enforced, enforced only in some instances, or not enforced at all helps determine its meaning and impact.

public policy: A purposive course of action followed by government in dealing with some problem or matter of concern.

Political scientists and other social scientists have developed many theories and models of the formation of public policies. Some theories, such as elite theory and pluralist theory, focus on who dominates or controls the making of policy. As discussed in chapter 1, elite theorists contend that policy reflects the interests of a small, well-to-do segment of society. Pluralists, in contrast, argue that policy is the product of interaction and struggle among many groups and powerholders in society. Needless to say, these are markedly divergent theories that have provoked continuing intellectual conflict.

Who dominates or controls the formation of public policy is an important question, but we do not wrestle with it here. Rather, we present a widely used model (see Figure 17.1) of the policy-making process that views it as a sequence of stages or func-

644

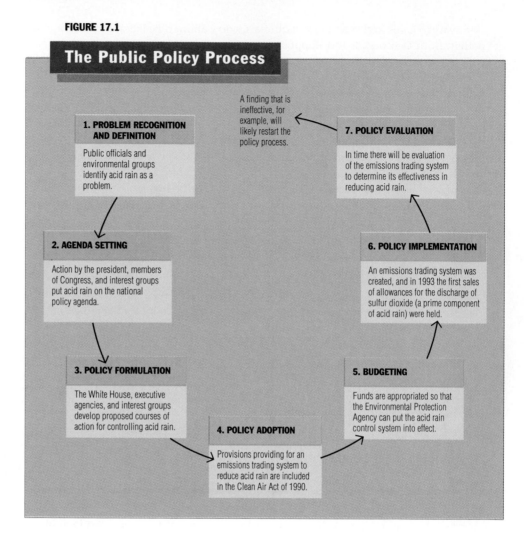

FIGURE 17.1

The Public Policy Process

1. PROBLEM RECOGNITION AND DEFINITION

Public officials and environmental groups identify acid rain as a problem.

2. AGENDA SETTING

Action by the president, members of Congress, and interest groups put acid rain on the national policy agenda.

3. POLICY FORMULATION

The White House, executive agencies, and interest groups develop proposed courses of action for controlling acid rain.

4. POLICY ADOPTION

Provisions providing for an emissions trading system to reduce acid rain are included in the Clean Air Act of 1990.

5. BUDGETING

Funds are appropriated so that the Environmental Protection Agency can put the acid rain control system into effect.

6. POLICY IMPLEMENTATION

An emissions trading system was created, and in 1993 the first sales of allowances for the discharge of sulfur dioxide (a prime component of acid rain) were held.

7. POLICY EVALUATION

In time there will be evaluation of the emissions trading system to determine its effectiveness in reducing acid rain.

A finding that is ineffective, for example, will likely restart the policy process.

tional activities. Public policies do not just happen; rather, they are typically the products of such a predictable pattern of events. Models for analyzing the policy-making process do not always explain *why* public policies take the specific forms that they do, however. That depends on the political struggles over particular policies. Nor do models necessarily tell us *who* dominates or controls the formation of public policy. This model can be applied and used to analyze any of the issues discussed earlier in this volume.

Despite the limitations of models, however, policy making frequently does follow the sequence of stages in the model. Sometimes some of the stages may merge, such as the policy formulation and adoption stages. Another instance of stages merging occurs when administrative agencies like the Occupational Safety and Health Administration (OSHA) are making policy through rule-making at the same time that they are implementing it. Finally, we need to recognize that what happens at one stage of the policy-making process affects action at later stages, and sometimes such action is done deliberately in anticipation of these effects. Thus particular provisions may be included in a law either to help or hinder its implementation, depending on the interests of the provisions' proponents.

(1) A *problem* that disturbs or distresses people gives rise to demands for relief, often through governmental action. Individual or group efforts are then made to get the problem (2) placed on a governmental *agenda*. If successful, this step is followed by (3) the *formulation* of alternatives for dealing with the problem. (4) *Policy adoption* involves the formal enactment or approval of an alternative. (5) *Budgeting* provides financial resources to carry out the approved alternative, which can now truly be called a "policy." (6) *Policy implementation*, the actual administration or application of the policy to its targets, may then be followed by (7) *policy evaluation* to determine the policy's actual accomplishments, consequences, or shortcomings. Evaluation may restart the policy process by identifying a new problem and touching off an attempt to modify or terminate the policy. With this overview in mind, let's now look in more detail at the various stages of the policy process or cycle.

Problem Recognition and Definition

A problem involves some condition or situation that causes distress or dissatisfaction or generates needs for which some kind of relief or corrective action is sought—often from the government (national, state, or local). At any given time, there are many conditions that disturb or distress people—polluted air, unsafe workplaces, earthquakes and hurricanes, too much or too little rain, the rising cost of medical care, the poor academic performance of high school students, too many handguns, too few "dedicated" public officials, or no prayers in the public schools, for example. All disturbing conditions do not automatically become problems; some of them may be accepted as trivial, appropriate, inevitable, or beyond the control of government.

"Rescue of Children from a Drunken Mother"—an artist's depiction of an early crusader for the Society for the Prevention of Cruelty to Children. (Photo courtesy: Corbis-Bettmann)

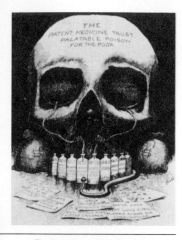

The formation and implementation of social welfare policy is both highly visible and contentious. It is visible because, as this cartoon penned before the Pure Food and Drug Act of 1906 illustrates, it is often meant to have a direct effect on the public good. It is contentious because other interests, often economic ones, come into opposition. This conflict falls along the lines political theorists characterize as pluralist versus elitist. (Photo courtesy: Colliers)

For a condition to become a problem, there must be some criterion—a standard or value—that leads people to believe that the condition does not have to be accepted or acquiesced to and, further, that it is something with which government can deal effectively and appropriately. Earthquakes, for example, are unlikely to become a policy problem because there is nothing that government can do about them directly. The consequences of earthquakes, the human distress and property destruction that they bring, are another matter. Their relief can be a focus of government action, as it was in the instance of the January 1994 Los Angeles earthquake, for which Congress appropriated several billion dollars for recovery activities. Conditions that at one time are accepted as appropriate and beyond government responsibility may at a later time be perceived as problems because of changes in public attitudes. Child abuse is illustrative (see Roots of Government: Child Abuse as a Public Policy Problem).

Usually there is not a single agreed-on definition of a problem. Indeed, political struggle often occurs over defining the problem because how the problem is defined

Roots of Government

Child Abuse as a Public Policy Problem

Until the 1870s, reports Barbara J. Nelson,[*] the maltreatment of children was of minimal concern to society. The disciplining of children, even when harsh, was usually viewed as a parental prerogative, except perhaps in instances of extreme brutality. Newspaper accounts of a gruesome instance of child beating in New York City in 1874 put the matter on the public agenda. In fact, some of the first efforts to protect children occurred under laws barring cruelty to animals! In the late 1800s, many large cities created units of the Society for the Prevention of Cruelty to Children modeled after the SPCA. In time, however, the problem receded from public view, although some protective activity for children continued.

Child abuse was rediscovered as a problem in the 1960s, a time of social activism and concern about people's rights. According to Professor Nelson, an article entitled "The Battered Child Syndrome," written by a physician and published in a leading medical journal, was the catalyst. Newspapers and popular magazines picked up the issue, and child abuse was again viewed as an urgent public problem.[**] Between 1963 and 1967, all fifty state legislatures enacted laws requiring the reporting of child abuse. In 1974 Congress manifested its concern by passing the Child Abuse Prevention and Treatment Act, which requires the states to have child protection agencies. Since that time the problem of child abuse has continued to concern policy makers. In 1993 President Clinton signed the National Child Abuse Protection Act. This act establishes a national database to track child abusers in an effort to prevent their employment in child-care centers.

[*]Barbara J. Nelson, *Making an Issue of Child Abuse* (Chicago: University of Chicago Press, 1984), 1–17.

[**]Henry Kempe, *et al.*, "The Battered Child Syndrome," *The Journal of The American Medical Association* 181 (July 7, 1962): 17–24.

In 1993 President Clinton signed the National Child Protection Act. The Act, which establishes a national database to track child abusers, is the latest of several pieces of legislation passed over many years, as the problem of child abuse has waxed and waned on the public agenda. (Photo courtesy: Jeffrey Markowitz/Sygma)

helps determine what sort of action is appropriate. If access to transportation for people with disabilities is defined as a transportation problem, then an acceptable solution is to provide the people with transportation by adapting the regular transportation system or by establishing other means of transport, such as a special van service. If access to transportation is defined as a civil rights problem, however, then people with disabilities are entitled to equal access to the regular transportation system. Solving a problem once defined as a civil right might require extensive and expensive alterations to make *all* public transport accessible to people with disabilities. After some wavering between these definitions in the 1980s, the national government appeared to be moving toward the transportation view of the problem. But congressional passage of the Americans with Disabilities Act forced a civil rights perspective on local governments by mandating that they make transportation accessible to the elderly and to all people with disabilities.

Problems differ not only in terms of how they are defined, but also in terms of their tractability, that is, in terms of how easy they are to ameliorate or resolve. For instance, problems that affect large numbers of people or require widespread behavioral changes are more difficult to resolve. The Voting Rights Act of 1965, intended to ensure equal voting rights for African Americans, was easier to implement than was policy requiring desegregation of public schools. Only a small number of voting registrars were directly affected in the first instance; vast numbers of school officials, students, and parents were affected by school desegregation. Tangible problems, such as low incomes or potholes in streets, often are more amenable to solutions than are more intangible problems, such as racism or sexism.

One additional point needs to be made. Public policies themselves are frequently viewed as problems or the causes of problems. Thus, for some people, gun control legislation is a solution to the handgun problem. To the National Rifle Association (NRA), however, any law that restricts gun ownership is a problem because of the NRA's view that such laws inappropriately restrict an individual's right to keep and bear arms. To conservatives overly generous welfare programs are a problem; whereas for many liberals laws restricting the right to abortion falls into the problem category.

Agenda Setting

Once a problem is recognized and defined, it must be brought to the attention of public officials and it must secure a place on an agenda.

agenda: A set of problems to which policy makers believe they should be attentive.

systemic agenda: All public issues that are viewed as requiring governmental attention; a discussion agenda.

governmental (institutional) agenda: The changing list of issues to which governments believe they should address themselves.

Defining Agendas.   An **agenda** is a set of problems to which policy makers believe they should be attentive. Professors Roger W. Cobb and Charles D. Elder have identified two basic agenda types: the systemic agenda and the governmental or institutional agenda.[5] The **systemic agenda** is essentially a discussion agenda; it comprises "all issues that are commonly perceived by the members of the political community as meriting public attention and as involving matters within the legitimate jurisdiction" of governments.[6] Every political community—national, state, and local—has a systemic agenda.

A **governmental** or **institutional agenda** includes only problems to which legislators or other public officials feel obliged to devote active and serious attention. Not all the problems that attract the attention of officials are likely to have been widely discussed by the general public, or even the "attentive" public—those who follow certain issues closely. Acid rain was a widely discussed public problem in the 1980s that was addressed by the Clean Air Act of 1990, but there was little public awareness of the Pollution Prevention Act, also adopted in 1990. This act set priorities for pollution control programs in an attempt to improve their effectiveness.

Problems or issues (an issue emerges when disagreement exists over what should be done about a problem) may move onto an institutional agenda, whether from the systemic agenda or elsewhere, in several ways. The congressional agenda is the focus of the discussion here.

Getting on the Congressional Agenda.   As discussed in chapter 8, the president is an important agenda-setter for Congress. In his State of the Union address, his budget, and special messages, the president presents Congress with a legislative program for its consideration. Much of Congress's time is spent deliberating presidential recommendations, although by no means does Congress always respond as the president might wish. Congress can be balky even when the president and congressional majorities come from the same party, as Bill Clinton discovered in his first year in the White House on such issues as homosexuals in the armed forces and tax increases. Clinton's problems multiplied in 1995 when Republicans with a markedly different agenda took control of both the House and the Senate. As Republicans, led by Speaker Newt Gingrich (R–Ga.), clashed with the president over key issues involving the size of the budget, annual deficits, and the very scope of federal responsibilities, government literally came to a halt when Congress and the president could not agree on a budget.

agenda setting: The constant process of forming the list of issues to be addressed by government.

Interest groups are major actors and initiators in the **agenda-setting** process. Interest groups and their lobbyists frequently ask Congress to legislate on problems of special concern to them. Environmentalists, for instance, call for government action on such issues as global warming, the protection of wetlands, and the reduction of air pollution. Business groups may seek protection against foreign competitors, restrictions on product liability lawsuits, or government financial bailouts.

Problems may secure agenda status because of some crisis, natural disaster, or other extraordinary event. Coal mine explosions in the past put mining safety on the congressional agenda. When seven-year-old Jessica Dubroff's dream of becoming the youngest person to pilot a plane across the United States crashed in a Wyoming neighborhood, there were widespread calls for regulations on the age at which a person could take the controls of an aircraft. Some four years earlier, the massive oil spill in Prince

William Sound in Alaska, caused when the supertanker *Exxon Valdez* ran aground, focused attention on ocean oil spills and led to enactment of the Oil Pollution Act of 1990. Such events trigger the interest of policy makers and the public.

Some problems and issues draw the attention of the news media and consequently gain agenda status, more salience, or both. Poignant television coverage was instrumental in putting hunger and starvation in Somalia in the early 1990s on both congressional and presidential agendas. The news media probably are more important in developing and sustaining interest in problems than in initially identifying them.

Individual private citizens, members of Congress, and other officials, acting as policy entrepreneurs, may push issues onto the congressional agenda. In the 1960s Ralph Nader's book *Unsafe at Any Speed* and Rachel Carson's *Silent Spring* brought motor vehicle safety and the misuse of pesticides, respectively, to the attention of Congress and many citizens. Representative Leonor Sullivan (D–Mo.) worked for a decade to secure the adoption in 1964 of a permanent food stamp program to help the needy. Senator Edmund Muskie (D–Maine) for many years was a leader in securing and shaping governmental action to protect the environment, as has been Vice President Al Gore, Jr. His book, *Earth in the Balance*, written while he was a U.S. senator, was a wake-up call to many people about possible environmental disaster.

Finally, political changes may contribute to agenda setting. The landslide election of Democratic President Lyndon B. Johnson in 1964, along with strong, favorable Democratic majorities in Congress, made possible the enactment of a flood of Great Society legislation intended to mitigate social welfare problems such as poverty and

The wreckage of the airplane in which Jessica Dubroff, her father, Lloyd, and instructor Joe Reid were killed, being loaded onto a trailer at the crash scene in Cheyenne, Wyoming. Some agenda setters hold that the seven-year-old would still be alive if federal regulations on pilot age had been stricter. (Photo courtesy: Ed Andrieski/AP Photo)

inadequate medical care for the elderly and needy and to provide education for disadvantaged children. Similarly, the 1980 election of conservative Republican Ronald Reagan, who in his inaugural address asserted that "Government is not the solution; government is the problem," brought issues concerning the size and activities of government onto national policy agendas. His administration, however, had only limited success in cutting back the size of the government.[7]

The 1994 GOP congressional victory is potentially even more significant than the agenda changes ushered in by the Johnson and Reagan victories. Newt Gingrich seized the speaker's gavel intending to launch the most radically different domestic policy proposals since President Franklin D. Roosevelt's New Deal ushered in the welfare state. Gingrich's plans for reducing the rate of growth of federal funds allocated for welfare and health care and giving greater responsibility to the states often cause Congress and the president to be at loggerheads.

As illustrated by the Clinton–Gingrich jousting, it is useful to think of agenda setting as a competitive process. Congress, for instance, does not have the time or resources to take on all the problems and issues it is called on to handle. Whether because of their influence, skill in developing political support, or presentation of more attractive issues, some players are more successful than others in steering items onto the agenda. Chance plays a small role in agenda setting, except in cases of accidents or natural disasters.

Policy Formulation

policy formulation: The crafting of appropriate and acceptable proposed courses of action to ameliorate or resolve public problems.

Policy formulation involves the crafting of appropriate and acceptable proposed courses of action to ameliorate or resolve public problems. It has both political and technical components. The political aspect of policy formulation encompasses determining generally what should be done to reduce acid rain, for example—whether standard setting and enforcement or emissions testing should be used. The technical facet involves correctly stating in specific language what one wants to authorize or accomplish, so as to adequately guide those who must implement policy and to prevent distortion of legislative intent. Political scientist Charles O. Jones suggests that formulation may take different forms:[8]

1. *Routine formulation* is "a repetitive and essentially changeless process of reformulating similar proposals within an issue area that is well established on the government agenda." For instance, the formulation of policy on agricultural price and income supports had not changed much in recent years until coming under attack from conservatives in 1995 and 1996.

2. In *analogous formulation* a new problem is handled by drawing on the experience of developing proposals for similar problems in the past. What has been done in the past to cope with the activities of terrorists? What has been done in other states to deal with child abuse or divorce law reform?

3. *Creative formulation* involves attempts to develop new or unprecedented proposals that represent a departure from existing practices and that will better resolve a problem. The people seeking to reform the welfare system, for example, have sought to develop innovative proposals that will provide care for the needy while preserving the incentive to work. This is a daunting task.

Policy formulation may be undertaken by various players in the policy process—the president and his aides, agency officials, specially appointed task forces and commissions, interest groups, private research organizations (or "think tanks"), and legislators and their staffs. The Bush administration's version of the Clean Air Act of 1990 was drafted by White House aides working with officials in the Environmental Protection Agency. In Congress, professional aides played a major role in drafting the detailed provisions of the law. Several competing alternatives may be formulated for a problem, such as was the case with welfare reform in 1996 (discussed later in this chapter).

The people engaged in formulation are usually looking down the road toward policy adoption. Particular provisions may be included or excluded from a proposal in an attempt to enhance its likelihood of adoption. To the extent that formulators think in this strategic manner, the formulation and adoption stages of the policy process often become muddled. Political feasibility is always on the mind of the wise policy formulators; they are more interested in getting action on a problem than in creating political issues.

Policy Adoption

Policy adoption involves the approval of a policy proposal by the people with requisite authority, such as a legislature or chief executive. This approval gives the policy legal force. Because most public policies in the United States are based on legislation, policy adoption frequently requires the building of majority coalitions necessary to secure the enactment of legislation.

In chapter 7 we discuss how power is diffused in Congress and how the legislative process comprises a number of roadblocks or obstacles—House subcommittee, House Committee, House Rules Committee, and so on—that a bill must successfully navigate before it becomes law. A majority is needed to clear a bill through each of these obstacles; hence, not one majority but a series of majorities are needed for congressional policy adoption. To secure the needed votes, a bill may be watered down or modified at each of these decision points. Or, the bill may fail to win a majority at one of them and die, at least for the time being.

Much negotiation, bargaining, and compromise are entailed in the adoption of major legislation, such as the Tax Reform Act of 1986 or the Brady Bill. In some instances years or even decades may be needed to secure the enactment of legislation on a controversial matter. Federal aid to public education was considered by Congress off and on over several decades before finally winning approval in 1965. At other times, the approval process may move quickly. The Flag Protection Act, for example, was passed quickly by Congress after the Supreme Court ruled that a Texas statute banning flag burning was constitutional.[9] The Supreme Court, however, quickly found that the new federal law was also an unconstitutional violation of the First Amendment.[10]

The tortuous nature of congressional policy adoption has some important consequences. First, substantial periods of time may be required in order to pass complex legislation. Second, the legislation passed is often incremental, making only limited or marginal changes in existing policy. Third, legislation is frequently written in general or ambiguous language, as in the Clean Air Act. Necessary to reduce conflict over a law's adoption, such language may both provide considerable discretion to the people who implement the law and also leave them in doubt as to its intended purposes.

Not all policy adoption necessitates formation of majority coalitions. Presidential decision-making on foreign affairs, military actions, and other matters is often unilateral. Although the president has many aides and advisers and is bombarded with information and advice, the final decision rests with him. Ultimately, too, it is the president who decides whether to veto a bill passed by Congress. President Clinton's decision not to intervene militarily in 1995 in Bosnia, for example, was ultimately his

policy adoption: The approval of a policy proposal by the people with the requisite authority, such as a legislature.

responsibility. Congress grudgingly acceded to the president's decision to help NATO enforce peace in the tattered remnants of Yugoslavia after he announced his intention to commit 20,000 American troops. It should be noted that the president is much more likely to get his way with Congress on foreign than domestic policy issues. The Republican Congress let the president send troops even as a budget impasse was closing down parts of the federal government.

Budgeting

Most policies require money in order to be carried out; some policies, such as those involving income security (discussed later in this chapter), essentially involve the transfer of money from taxpayers to the government and back to individual beneficiaries. Funding for most policies and agencies is provided through the budgetary process (discussed in chapter 18). Whether a policy is well funded or poorly funded has a significant effect on its scope, impact, and effectiveness.

A policy can be nullified by an absence of funding or refusal to fund, which was the fate of the Noise Control Act. In 1981 the Reagan administration decided not to seek funds for the Office of Noise Abatement and Control, the unit within EPA that enforced the act. Because Congress followed the president's lead, this decision ended implementation of noise control policy.

Other policies or programs often suffer from inadequate funding. Thus the Occupational Safety and Health Administration (OSHA) can afford to inspect only a small fraction of the workplaces within its jurisdiction annually. Similarly, the Department of Housing and Urban Development has funds sufficient to provide rent subsidies only to approximately 20 percent of the eligible low-income families. When failure to adopt a budget in late 1995 caused a number of agencies to shut down operations (see Politics Now: Budget Deadlock), many functions, including most environmental enforcement, had to be suspended.

The budgetary process also gives the president and the Congress an opportunity to review the government's many policies and programs, to inquire into their administration, to appraise their value and effectiveness, and to exercise some influence on their conduct. Not all of the government's hundreds of programs are fully examined every year. But, over a period of several years, most programs come under scrutiny. Some agencies, moreover, may come under sharp attack and experience cutbacks and restraints. In recent years, for example, conservatives in Congress have used the budget as a venue for attacking the activities of the National Endowment for the Arts (NEA). Charging that some of the projects funded by the Endowment are obscene or pornographic, they have sought to reduce funding for the NEA. Their actions have apparently made NEA officials more cautious in the funding of art projects.

In a given year, most agencies experience only limited or marginal changes in their funding. Still, budgeting is a vital part of the policy process that helps determine the impact and effectiveness of public policies. Having the potential to curb funding can be a powerful tool for congressional committee chairs.

Policy Implementation

policy implementation: The process of carrying out public policy through governmental agencies and the courts.

Policy implementation refers to how public policies are carried out. Most public policies are implemented primarily by administrative agencies (see chapter 9). Some, however, are enforced in other ways. Product liability and product dating are two examples. Product liability laws are usually enforced by lawsuits initiated in the courts

Politics Now

Budget Deadlock

In 1995 Congress and President Clinton played a game of chicken. Congress attached substantive elements to appropriations bills that the president found objectionable. Since the president does not have a line-item veto, he must accept or reject legislation as Congress sends it to him; he cannot approve portions while rejecting other parts, as most governors can. The Constitution authorizes Congress to enact a budget, but all laws must be signed by the president or enacted over his veto. When a strong-willed chief executive runs into an ideologically driven legislature, the collision can bring the government to a stop. That is precisely what happened late in 1995. Shutting down the government because no budget had been passed had occurred before but never for as long.

Congressional Republicans operated from two assumptions. First, they interpreted their victory in 1994 as indicative of widespread support for their agenda of balancing the budget in seven years by cutting welfare and eliminating whole departments. Second, they expected President Clinton to back down and sign the appropriations bills and to agree to a balanced budget plan. Expecting Clinton to bargain seemed reasonable in light of the president's professed interest in balancing the budget and the frequency with which he had changed his mind on other issues.

Republicans, led by their House contingent, sought to pressure the president by painting him as the opponent of a balanced budget.

President Clinton counterattacked by adopting the role of protector of popular social welfare programs such as Medicare, Medicaid, environmental protection, and aid to education. He vetoed congressional appropriations bills and refused to agree to a plan to achieve a balanced budget by 2002.

Press reports of federal employees unable to buy Christmas presents for their children, of businesses with government contracts teetering on the brink of bankruptcy, and the worries of beneficiaries of federal payments placed mounting pressures on Congress to reopen government. Finally, the public relations disaster forced Republicans to sue for peace on the president's terms. Moderates in the Senate led the way to a reconciliation with the president. When the House leadership saw the weakening resolve of some of its members, they came to the bargaining table. In early January they agreed to temporary legislation that ended the twenty-one-day layoffs for nonessential federal workers.

What strategy might have been better for Republicans than closing down the government? Did President Clinton win this struggle because his ideas were better or because he had better spin doctors?

---

by injured consumers or their survivors. In contrast, state product-dating laws are implemented more by voluntary compliance when grocers take out-of-date products off their shelves or by consumers when they choose not to buy food products after the use dates stamped on them. The courts also get involved in implementation when they are called on to interpret the meaning of legislation, review the legality of agency rules and actions, and determine whether the administration of institutions such as prisons and mental hospitals conforms to legal and constitutional standards.

Administrative agencies may be authorized to use a number of techniques to implement the public policies within their jurisdictions. These techniques can be categorized as authority, incentive, capacity, and hortatory techniques, depending on the behavioral assumptions on which they are based.[11]

Authoritative techniques for policy implementation rest on the notion that people's actions must be directed or restrained by government in order to prevent or eliminate activities or products that are unsafe, unfair, evil, or immoral. Thus people who drive while intoxicated can, by law, have their driver's licenses revoked. On the federal level, consumer products must meet certain safety regulations and radio stations can have their broadcasting licenses revoked if they broadcast obscenities.

Many governmental agencies have authority to issue rules and set standards to regulate such matters as meat and food processing, the discharge of pollutants into the environment, the healthfulness and safety of workplaces, and the safe operation of commercial airplanes. Compliance with these standards is determined by inspection and monitoring, and penalties may be imposed on people or companies that violate the rules and standards set forth in a particular policy. For example, under Title IX, the federal government can terminate funds to colleges or universities that discriminate against female students. This pattern of action is sometimes stigmatized as "command and control regulation" by its detractors, although in practice it often involves much education, bargaining, and persuasion in addition to the exercise of authority. In the case of Title IX, for instance, the Department of Education will try to negotiate with a school to bring it into compliance before funding is terminated.

Incentive techniques for policy implementation are based on the assumption that people are utility maximizers who act in their own best interest and must be provided with payoffs or financial inducements to get them to comply with public policies. Tax deductions may be given to encourage charitable giving, or grants awarded to companies for the installation of pollution control equipment. Subsidies are given to farmers to make their production (or nonproduction) of wheat, cotton, and other commodities more profitable. Conversely, sanctions such as high taxes may be adopted to discourage the purchase and use of such products as tobacco or liquor, and pollution fees may be levied to reduce the discharge of pollutants by making this action more costly to businesses.

Capacity techniques provide people with information, education, training, or resources that will enable them to undertake desired activities. The assumption underlying the provision of these techniques is that people have the incentive or desire to do what is right but lack the capacity to act accordingly. Job training may enable able-bodied people to find employment, and accurate information on interest rates will enable people to protect themselves against interest-rate gouging. Financial assistance can help the needy acquire better housing and warmer winter coats and perhaps lead more comfortable lives.

Hortatory techniques encourage people to comply with policy by appealing to people's "better instincts" in an effort to get them to act in desired ways. In this instance the policy implementers assume that people decide how to act on the basis of their personal values and beliefs on matters such as right and wrong, equality, and justice. In the mid-1960s and late 1970s, the Johnson and Carter administrations, respectively, instituted voluntary (that is, there were no "punishments" for noncompliance) wage and price control programs to control inflation. Presidential appeals were made to individuals, labor unions, and businesses to avoid inflation-causing behavior. Hortatory techniques also include the use of highway signs that tell us "Don't Be a Litterbug" and "Don't Mess with Texas" to discourage littering. And slogans such as "Only You Can Prevent Forest Fires" are meant to encourage compliance with fire and safety regulations in national parks and forests.

The capacity of agencies to administer public policies effectively depends partly on whether the agencies are authorized to use appropriate implementation techniques. Many other factors also come into play, including the clarity and consistency of the policies' statutory mandates, adequacy of funding, political support, and the will and skill of agency personnel. There is no easy formula that will guarantee successful policy implementation; in practice, many policies only partially achieve their goals.

Policy Evaluation

Practitioners of **policy evaluation** are concerned with determining what a policy is actually accomplishing. They may also try to determine whether a policy is being fairly or efficiently administered. In the case of welfare programs, for instance, uncovering evidence of "waste, fraud, or abuse" in their administration has often been of more interest to official evaluators than whether the programs are meeting the needs of the poor.

policy evaluation: The process of determining whether a course of action is achieving its intended goals.

Policy makers frequently make judgments on the effectiveness and necessity of particular policies and programs. These evaluations are often based mostly on anecdotal and fragmentary evidence rather than on solid facts and thorough analyses. Sometimes a program has been adjudged to be a good program simply because it is politically popular. In recent decades, however, policy evaluation has often taken a more rigorous, systematic, and objective form. Carefully designed studies or inquiries by social scientists and qualified investigators are undertaken to measure the societal impact of programs and to determine whether these programs are achieving their specified goals or objectives. The national executive departments and agencies often contain officials and units with responsibility for policy evaluation; so do state governments.

Policy evaluation may be conducted by a variety of players: congressional committees, through investigations and other oversight activities; presidential commissions; administrative agencies themselves; university researchers; private research organizations, such as the Brookings Institution and the American Enterprise Institute; and the General Accounting Office (GAO). The GAO, for example, originally created in 1921, is an important evaluator of public policies. Every year the GAO undertakes hundreds of studies of government agencies and programs either at the request of members of Congress or on its own initiative. The titles of three of its 1993 evaluations convey a notion of its work: *Pesticides: Pesticide Reregistration May Not Be Completed Until 2006; Energy Conservation: Appliance Standards and Labeling Programs Can Be Improved;* and *Federal Research: Super Collider Is Over Budget and Behind Schedule.* Subsequent congressional and agency actions may be guided by these studies.

Evaluation research and studies can stimulate attempts to modify or terminate policies and thus restart the policy process. Legislators and administrators may formulate and advocate amendments designed to correct problems or shortcomings in a policy. In 1988, for example, legislation was adopted to correct weaknesses in the enforcement of the Fair Housing Act of 1968, which banned discrimination in the sale or rental of most housing. Or, some people may decide that the best alternative is simply to eliminate the policy. On occasion, policies are terminated; for example, by the Airline Deregulation Act of 1978, Congress eliminated the Civil Aeronautics Board and its program of economic regulation of commercial airlines. This action was taken on the assumption that competition in the marketplace would better protect the interests of airline users. On December 31, 1995, the Interstate Commerce Commission expired after more than a century of regulating railroads and other modes of transportation. The demise of programs is rare, however; more often, a troubled program is modified or allowed to limp along because it is doing something that some people strongly want done, even if the program is not doing it well.

SOCIAL WELFARE POLICIES

social welfare policy: Governmental program designed to improve or enhance individuals' quality of life.

The remainder of this chapter focuses on three areas of **social welfare policy**—income security, health care, and public education—governmental programs designed to enhance or improve quality of life. Each area encompasses many complex policies and programs. While all levels of government (national, state, and local) are involved with the development and implementation of social welfare policies, we highlight the national government's role. The discussion in each of the three areas illustrates the expansion of national action as a consequence of dissatisfaction with what the state and local governments were doing. More recently, the tide has turned and President Clinton along with Republican leaders have devised plans to give states greater control over public welfare and health-care programs.

Most income security programs in the United States are largely a product of the twentieth century, although their origins can be traced far into the nation's past. As U.S. society became more urban and industrial, self-sufficiency declined and people became more interdependent and reliant on a vast system of production, distribution, and exchange. The Great Depression of the 1930s revealed both that hard work alone would not provide economic security for everyone and that the state governments and private charities lacked adequate resources to alleviate economic want and distress. Beginning with the Social Security Act of 1935, a variety of national programs aimed at providing economic security have emerged. We survey some of them in the section on income security policies.

Federal concern with national health is much more recent. The federal health program was a result of the Sheppard Towner Maternity Act of 1923, which provided money to the states to fund prenatal programs for pregnant women. Over the years, the national government's role in health care has grown tremendously. In 1965 the Medicaid program sought to bring health care to the nation's poor. The federal government is extensively involved not only in the provision of health care, through Medicaid and the U.S. Public Health Service, but also in the improvement of the health of all Americans. The Center for Disease Control and Prevention (CDC), in particular, works to prevent disease.

Public health policies, for example, have been highly effective in reducing the incidence of infectious disease such as measles, infantile paralysis (poliomyelitis), and smallpox. A separate federal agency, the National Cancer Institute, has funded efforts to isolate causes of that killer and, in recent years, debate has surrounded the issue of whether Washington is doing enough to combat AIDS. Most Americans accept and support extensive government spending on medical research. Congress, in fact, often appropriates more money for medical research than the president recommends.

Public education was almost the exclusive province of the state and local governments until well into the twentieth century. Even though some commentators and critics argue that education was one area the Framers intended to be reserved to the states by the Tenth Amendment, the national government has been involved in education since passage of the Northwest Ordinance in 1785. Moreover, constitutional justification for the national government's action on public education rests on a broad view of

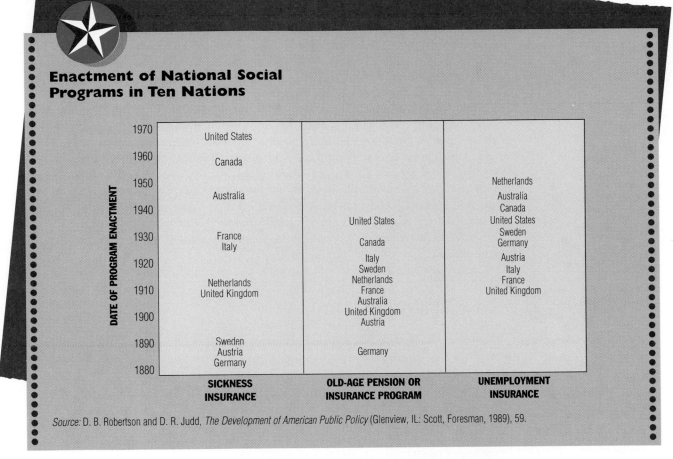

Enactment of National Social Programs in Ten Nations

Source: D. B. Robertson and D. R. Judd, *The Development of American Public Policy* (Glenview, IL: Scott, Foresman, 1989), 59.

its delegated powers, such as taxing and spending for the general welfare. National financial aid for the public schools has been an agenda item from time to time during the twentieth century and has now become a permanent aspect of public school funding. This topic draws much of our attention here.

Beginning with the GI Bill, which paid for college for many World War II veterans, the federal government has helped students secure the funds needed to continue their educations beyond high school. Some programs, such as Pell Grants, have been targeted to students from poorer families. Loan guarantee programs have been available to students from a wider range of economic backgrounds. Loan guarantees are attractive because the federal government pays the interest on the loans as long as the recipient remains in school. The average student who takes advantage of this program owes $6,000, but there are indications that borrowing is increasing.[12]

Student loans have not been immune from the budget cutters. Both the Clinton administration in the 103rd Congress and Republicans in the 104th explored ways to reduce costs. Democrats urged having the government make the loans directly to students, replacing banks and private lenders. Republicans, eager to privatize as many functions as possible, objected to reducing the role of private lenders. The GOP also suggested allowing students to avoid interest payment while in school but requiring that they cover these costs on graduation. Members of both parties have been troubled by the high default rates of students who attend some proprietary vocational schools.

There have been demands that tighter standards be developed to protect both students who may feel that they are not getting much training and the government that must pay off the loans for students who do not.

To receive AFDC, teenage mothers must remain in school and live with an adult. Welfare benefits will no longer be available to help these young mothers establish separate households.

Presidential advisers divided sharply over whether he should sign the legislation. President Clinton acknowledged that the bill was tougher than he would have preferred. It did, however, include some provisions that softened the blow. While states could tighten up the eligibility standards for welfare, they must continue to provide Medicaid for a year to families excluded from the program as a result of the new standards. Another provision promised to increase funding for child care facilities serving the poor.

The welfare reform bill passed by an overwhelming margin once the president agreed to support it. Enactment allowed both the president and the Republican Congress to claim credit for reforming a policy area widely perceived by the public to be wasteful and ineffective. The results of this major overhaul of the system, however, are yet to be felt.

INCOME SECURITY

*I*ncome security programs protect people against loss of income because of retirement, disability, unemployment, or death or absence of the family breadwinner. Although cases of total deprivation are now rare, many people are unable to provide a minimally decent standard of living for themselves and their families. They are poor in a relative if not an absolute sense. In 1995 an urban family of four earning $15,150 or less per year was officially below the poverty line. Millions of family units do not fare that well.

Income security programs fall into two general categories. *Social insurance* programs are non-means-based programs that provide cash assistance to qualified beneficiaries. **Means-tested programs** require that people must have incomes below specified levels to be eligible for benefits (see Table 17.1). Benefits of means-tested programs may come either as cash or in-kind benefits, such as food stamps.

In his book *Losing Ground*, policy analyst Charles Murray argues that, rather than helping the poor get on their feet, welfare programs encourage dependency.[13] He calls for the abolition of such programs. Even many who find Murray's prescription too harsh believe that the poor should do more to help themselves. Liberals, on the other hand, generally support income security programs; they believe that dependency and want result more from social causes than from personal shortcomings, such as laziness. But even liberals sometimes question the effectiveness of some income security programs and call for reforms that will help the poor become less dependent.

means-tested program: Income security program intended to assist those whose incomes fall below a designated level.

Roots of Income Security Programs

Until well into the twentieth century, programs to assist the needy were mostly the responsibility of state and local governments and private charitable organizations. When assistance was available, and often it was not, it came grudgingly and in small amounts.

Social welfare efforts by the national government were limited to groups for which it had particular responsibility or political obligation, namely veterans, Native Ameri-

TABLE 17.1

Recipients of Social Insurance Programs, 1990

PROGRAM	NUMBER OF RECIPIENTS (MILLIONS)	PERCENTAGE OF U.S. POPULATION
Non-means-tested		
Social Security (OASDI)*	42.2	16.4
Medicare (hospital insurance)	35.9	13.9
Veterans programs	2.7	1.0
Railroad programs	0.8	0.3
State unemployment insurance	2.6	1.0
Means-tested		
Medicaid	33.4	13.0
Supplementary Security Income (SSI)	6.1	2.4
Aid to Families with Dependent Children (AFDC)	13.8	5.4
Food stamps	27.0	10.5
General assistance	1.2	0.5

Note: "Means-tested" refers to the requirement of demonstration of financial need based on income and assets. People may receive benefits from more than one program. For example, in 1985, 16 percent of U.S. households received one or more means-tested benefits; in addition to the programs listed above, these include free or reduced-price school lunches and publicly owned or subsidized housing.

*OASDI beneficiaries as of December 31. Medicare enrollees as of July 1. Veterans' programs beneficiaries as of December 31. Railroad programs beneficiaries as of December 31 (except for unemployment). State unemployment insurance is the average weekly number in December. Medicaid is the number of recipients during the year. SSI is the number of recipients in December. AFDC is the average number of monthly recipients. Food stamp number is the average during the year. General assistance is the average monthly number.

Source: Social Security Bulletin, Annual Statistical Supplement, 1994 (Washington, D.C.: U.S. Government Printing Office, 1994), 13–15.

cans, and merchant seamen. Interestingly, in the late decades of the nineteenth century and in the early twentieth century, the national government provided pensions for most of the veterans who had fought for the North during the Civil War (a substantial portion of the elderly white male population at the time).[14]

The Great Depression of the 1930s completely overwhelmed existing sources of assistance for the needy. In 1934 twenty-eight states had laws authorizing old-age assistance programs, but often these had closed down because of the lack of funding. Only ten states had fully functioning programs, and these typically paid pensions of less than $10 monthly—with Indiana paying $4.50 a month, a princely sum compared to the 69 cents doled out monthly in North Dakota.[15]

Limited assistance had been made available by the national government to the needy during the Hoover administration (1929–33), which was in accord with the individualistic philosophy of President Herbert Hoover. The response of Franklin D. Roosevelt's New Deal (begun in 1933) took a very different tack. Initially, programs for direct cash assistance and work relief, such as the Works Progress Administration (WPA), were created to help the needy. Although frequently derided as a "make work"

The Great Depression, beginning in late 1929 and continuing throughout the 1930s, dramatically pointed out to average Americans the need for a broad social safety net, and gave rise to a host of income, health, and finance legislation. (Photo courtesy: UPI/The Bettmann Archive)

program that paid people for such activities as leaf raking, the WPA helped many people weather the Great Depression.

The Roosevelt administration also designed permanent programs that would address the problems of income insecurity and economic dependency. Roosevelt appointed the Committee on Economic Security to investigate the economic situation and make policy recommendations. Most of its proposals were subsequently endorsed by the president and enacted into law by Congress in 1935 as the **Social Security Act.**

The Social Security Act transformed public social welfare policy. The national government became the major contributor on a permanent and extensive basis in the income security area. Three major programs were put in place by the act: old age insurance (what we now call Social Security); public assistance for the needy, aged, blind, and families with dependent children (later, people with disabilities were added); and unemployment insurance (or compensation). Even though the programs instituted as part of the Social Security Act have been modified and other income security programs have been added, these three programs form the foundation of today's income security policies.

Social Security Act: A 1935 law that established old age insurance (Social Security), assistance for the needy, children, and others; and unemployment insurance.

Social Insurance

Social insurance programs operate in a manner somewhat similar to private automobile or life insurance. Contributions are made by or on behalf of the prospective beneficiaries, their employers, or both. When a person becomes eligible for benefits, the monies are paid as a matter of right, regardless of how much wealth or unearned income (for example, from dividends and interest payments) the recipient has. (For Social Security, a limit is imposed on earned income. There is no means test.)

Old Age, Survivors, and Disability Insurance. This program began as old age insurance, providing benefits only to retired workers. Its coverage was extended to survivors of covered workers in 1939 and to the permanently disabled in 1956. This is the program customarily called Social Security. It is not, as many people believe, a pension program that collects contributions from workers, invests them, and then returns them with interest to beneficiaries. Instead the current generation of workers pays taxes to provide benefits for the previous generation. Presently, a payroll tax of 7.65 percent on the first $61,200 of wages or salaries is paid by the employee and another 7.65 percent is paid by the employer into the Social Security trust fund. Nearly all employees and most of the self-employed (who pay a 15.3 percent tax) are now covered by Social Security. People earning less money pay a greater share of their income into the Social Security program than do workers earning more.

People are eligible to receive retirement benefits at age sixty-five. Individuals who opt to retire earlier, at age sixty-two, receive a reduced benefit. In the early 1990s, the average retired worker received about $700 a month. The maximum benefit in 1994 for a retired worker was $1,147 per month. An additional 50 percent was paid if the worker had a spouse. Social Security is the primary source of income for many retirees and keeps them from living in poverty. However, eligible people are entitled to Social Security benefits regardless of how much *unearned* income (for example, dividends and interest payments) they also receive. Until they reach the age of seventy, there is a limit of $11,280 on the annual *earned* income they can receive without a reduction in their benefits. A dollar of benefits is lost for every three dollars by which one exceeds that limit. The Republicans' Contract with America sought to raise the threshold for reducing payments to retirees to $30,000 by 2002. After age seventy there are no restrictions on outside earnings.

Expenditures for Social Security have greatly increased during the last couple of decades because the number of beneficiaries is growing, they are living longer, and benefit levels are rising. More than 40 million people, including some 3 million workers with disabilities, currently receive benefits. Social Security is by far the national government's largest entitlement program (see Figure 17.2).

In the early 1980s, because of unstable economic conditions and a major increase in benefits, Social Security was in severe economic trouble. Benefits paid out were exceeding revenues, and the program's reserve fund was emptying, leading to fears that

BY TOLES FOR THE BUFFALO NEWS

FIGURE 17.2

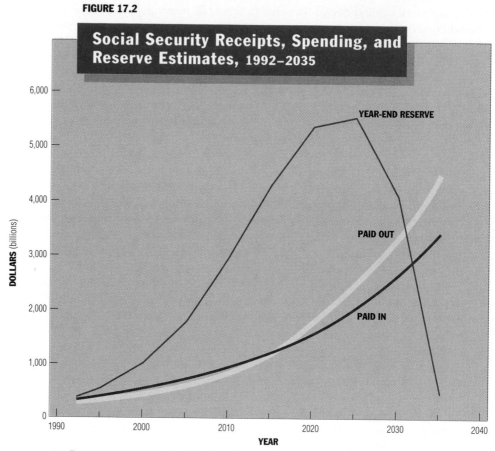

Social Security Receipts, Spending, and Reserve Estimates, 1992–2035

NOTE: The combined OASI and DI Trust Funds (Social Security) are estimated to become exhausted during 2035 under alternative II projections. For details see source.

SOURCE: U.S. Congress, House, House Committee on Ways and Means, "1992 Report of The Board of Trustees of the Federal Old-Age and Survivors Insurance and Disability Insurance Trust Funds," 102d Cong., 2d sess., April 2, 1992, p. 182.

the programs would go broke. To solve this problem Democrats in Congress favored increasing Social Security taxes, while Republicans called for reduced benefits. Neither alternative drew much public support.

To lessen the political conflict surrounding the issue, President Ronald Reagan created the bipartisan National Commission on Social Security Reform. However, the commission was unable to reach agreement on a rescue plan. Consequently, in January 1983, a small group of White House officials, members of Congress, and private experts began negotiating a solution. After a few days of hard bargaining, they reached agreement on a bailout plan. Major components of the plan included higher Social Security taxes, reduced cost-of-living adjustments (COLAs) for retirement benefits, extension of Social Security coverage to all nonprofit organization employees and new federal workers, and taxation of the Social Security benefits of upper-income retirees. It was thought that this package would ensure the solvency of Social Security well into the twenty-first century.

The proposal was enacted into law in 1983 with minimal changes by Congress. As it turned out, the Social Security solvency program has worked much better than expected in the short run. Annual revenues have greatly exceeded benefit payments, thus swelling the size of the Social Security Trust Fund. In 1993 the fund had a $46.8 billion surplus. Despite this success it is expected to be insolvent by 2030 because the ratio of workers to retirees will decline as baby boomers hit retirement age (see Figure 17.2).[16] In anticipation of this problem, several members of Congress have called for a round of new reforms, including the removal of the Social Security Administration from the Department of Health and Human Services to make it an independent agency.

Unemployment Insurance.   Financed by a payroll tax paid by employers, the unemployment insurance program pays benefits to covered workers who are unemployed through no fault of their own; for example, by being laid off during a recession. The Social Security Act provided that if a state set up a comparable program and levied a payroll tax for its support, most of the federal tax would be forgiven (not collected). The states were thus accorded a choice: either they could set up and administer an acceptable unemployment program, or they could let the national government handle the matter. Within a short time, all states had their own programs.

Unemployment insurance covers employers of four or more people, but not part-time or occasional workers. Benefits are paid to unemployed workers who have neither been fired nor quit their jobs and who are willing and able to accept suitable employment. State unemployment programs differ considerably in levels of benefits, length of benefit payment, and eligibility for benefits. Average weekly benefit payments, for example, range from $226 in Massachusetts and $225 in New Jersey to $123 in Mississippi and $118 in Louisiana. The most generous programs exist in the northern industrial states, where labor unions are more powerful and influence the nature of these programs. Nationwide, only about half of the people counted as unemployed at any given time will be receiving benefits. (Figure 17.3 illustrates the variation among the states in unemployment rates.)

In recent years, during periods of economic slowdown, Congress has provided emergency unemployment benefits for long-term unemployed workers who have exhausted regular state-paid benefits. These emergency benefits are paid entirely by the national government and have extended the payment period from twenty to seven weeks, depending on the level of unemployment in each state.[17]

Means-Tested Programs

Means-tested income security programs are intended to help the needy, that is, individuals or families whose incomes fall below specified levels, such as a percentage of the official poverty line. Included in this category are the Supplementary Security Income (SSI), Aid to Families with Dependent Children (AFDC), and Food Stamp programs (see Table 17.1).

Supplementary Security Income.   This program began under the Social Security Act as a categorical grant-in-aid program to help the needy aged or blind. Financed jointly by the national and state governments from general revenues, the states played a major role in determining standards of eligibility and benefit levels. In 1950 Congress extended coverage to needy people who were permanently and totally disabled.

With the support of the Nixon administration, Congress reconfigured these programs into the Supplementary Security Income (SSI) programs in 1974. Primary funding for SSI is provided by the national government, which prescribes uniform benefit levels throughout the nation. To be eligible, beneficiaries can own only a limited amount of possessions. In 1995, monthly payments were about $350. The states may

FIGURE 17.3

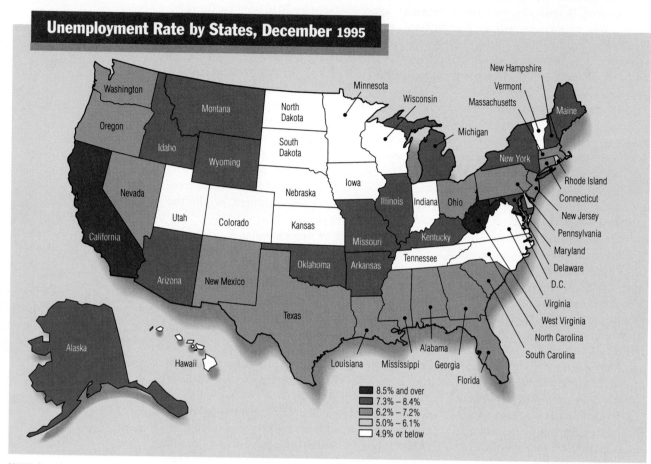

Unemployment Rate by States, December 1995

Legend:
- 8.5% and over
- 7.3% – 8.4%
- 6.2% – 7.2%
- 5.0% – 6.1%
- 4.9% or below

SOURCE: Annual Report of the Council of Economic Advisers, 1996, p. 77.

choose to supplement the federal benefits, and forty-eight states do. For years this program generated little controversy, as the modest benefits go to people who obviously cannot provide for themselves. In 1995, however, the Republican Congress sought to deny funds to legal immigrants and to people impoverished as a result of their own alcoholism or drug addiction.

Aid to Families with Dependent Children (AFDC). In the early 1930s, nearly all states operating under the Social Security Act offered cash assistance to mothers (mostly widows) with dependent children. In 1950 Aid to Families with Dependent Children (AFDC) was broadened to include not only dependent children but also mothers themselves or other adults with whom dependent children were living.

Initially, AFDC was small because there were few unmarried mothers in 1935. The AFDC rolls have expanded greatly since 1960 because of the increasing numbers of children born to unwed mothers, the growing divorce rate, and the migration of poor people to cities, where they are more likely to apply for and be provided benefits. Now, most families covered by AFDC are headed by single mothers.

Because of its clientele, the AFDC program is the focus of much controversy and is frequently stigmatized as "welfare." Critics who point to the rising number of recipients claim that it encourages promiscuity and out-of-wedlock births and promotes dependency, which results in a permanent class of welfare families. There is, however, little hard evidence to document these claims fully. Much effort has been expended by public officials to restrict the availability of aid, to ferret out fraud and abuse, and to hold down AFDC cost.

The cash benefits paid to AFDC families are often modest if not stingy. Nationally, in 1994 the average monthly AFDC family benefit was $377. Since this program is jointly funded by states and the national government, for the lower forty-eight states, maximum monthly family payments ranged from $703 in New York and $680 in Connecticut to $120 in Mississippi and $164 in Alabama. AFDC recipients are also eligible for Medicaid and food stamps. The total cost of serving 13.6 million people is $22 billion.

In 1988, with strong support from the National Governor's Association and the American Public Welfare Association, Congress passed legislation to reform AFDC. Titled the Family and Child Support Act, the law seeks to move people off welfare and into productive jobs. Each state must operate a Job Opportunities and Basic Skills (JOBS) program to provide education, training, and job experience for members of welfare families. Most adult welfare recipients are to be enrolled, with the states providing child care and other services necessary to permit participation. Funding for JOBS is shared by the national and state governments.

States are also required by the Family and Child Support Act to participate in the AFDC–UP, program, which provides benefits for two-parent families in which the principal wage-earner is unemployed. A workfare provision included at the insistence of the Reagan administration requires one parent in a UP family to spend at least sixteen hours weekly in a work activity. Other provisions of the act call for stronger enforcement of court orders for child support payments and greater efforts to establish paternity for children born out of wedlock.

The Family and Child Support Act has been called the most significant reform of the welfare system in half a century. Because its provisions were phased in, it was not fully implemented until the early 1990s.[18] By early 1992, however, some 500,000 persons were participating in the act's education and training programs, a number that exceeded the required level of participation.[19] On the other hand, some states have difficulty providing welfare recipients with sufficient job and training opportunities.[20]

During the 1992 campaign, President Clinton pledged to "end welfare as we know it," and the Republican majority in the 104th Congress also moved to tackle the welfare problem. Sharply restricting access to AFDC was part of the Contract with America. To carry out this platform plank, congressional leaders sought to allow states greater latitude in providing welfare, thereby opening the way to end the entitlement status conferred by AFDC. Enactment of initial GOP proposals would have given states block grants and authority to determine eligibility standards although, with a few exceptions, recipients would not be able to collect payments for more than five years. Most teenage mothers would no longer be eligible for benefits and some bills would prohibit increasing assistance to families that had additional children while on welfare rolls. Copying from the welfare reforms advocated by Clinton, most adults on welfare would have to enroll in a job-training program within two years or find a job.

Reformers justify limiting the length of time that benefits can be collected as necessary to break the cycle of dependency from one generation to the next. They argue that by capping the benefits per family, they force welfare recipients to live in a world like that faced by workers who get no pay raise when they bring another child into the world. Phil Gramm (R-Tex.), as a candidate for his party's presidential nomination, spoke against the status quo, "a system that subsidizes illegitimacy, which gives cash bonuses to people who have more and more children on welfare."[21]

Opponents warned that the victims of tougher standards will be blameless infants who face bleak futures even under the current program. Senator Edward M. Kennedy (D–Ma.) chided the GOP majority claiming that "The Senate is on the brink of committing legislative child abuse."[22] Critics pointed out that proposed payments were so frugal that no rational mother would have children as a strategy to increase AFDC benefits. President Clinton, who found the Republican reforms too lacking in protections for the needy, vetoed the effort.

Then, in August 1996, President Clinton agreed to legislation that sweeps away the New Deal covenant that guaranteed assistance to the poor. To secure the president's approval, Republicans backed away from turning the food stamp program into a block grant to the states and agreed to retain national standards for participating in the program. The nutrition program was changed, however, to exclude legal immigrants, the unemployed who do not have children at home, and convicted drug felons. Non-citizens will also be cut off from the Supplemental Security Income program.

The welfare reform bill passed by an overwhelming margin once the president agreed to support it. Enactment allowed both the president and the Republican Congress to claim credit for reforming a policy area widely perceived by the public to be wasteful and ineffective. And, by agreeing to this legislation, the president took away a campaign issue from GOP nominee Bob Dole, who had hoped to castigate his Democratic opponent for failing to deliver on his 1992 pledge.

Presidential advisers divided sharply over whether the president should sign the legislation. President Clinton acknowledged that the bill was tougher than he would have preferred. It did, however, include some provisions that softened the blow. While states could tighten up the eligibility standards for welfare, they must continue to provide Medicaid for a year to families excluded from the program as a result of the new standards. Another provision promised to increase funding for child care facilities serving the poor.

The changes that Republicans predict will save $55 billion over six years limit receipt of welfare to five years over the course of an individual's life. States can, if they wish, invoke an exception for as many as 20 percent of the families who get benefits. Able-bodied heads of families who get welfare will have to find a job within two years or see assistance cut off. Exceptions from the work requirement are made for the mothers of young children if care for the children is unavailable. If a job cannot be found in the private sector, heads of households will be expected to do community service. States that do not find jobs for welfare recipients will lose some of their funding.

To receive AFDC, teenage mothers must remain in school and live with an adult. Welfare benefits will no longer be available to help these young mothers establish separate households.

Earned Income Tax Credit Program (EITC). Designed to help the working poor, this program was created in 1975 at the insistence of Senator Russell Long (D–La.). It helps the working poor by subsidizing their wages, and it also provides an incentive for people to go to work. Drawing extensive support from both Democrats and Republicans in Congress, the Earned Income Tax Credit is frequently described as being "pro-work and pro-family."

Currently, the EITC provides working-poor families with two or more children a $4 tax credit for every $10 of the first $8,425 that they earn. The maximum EITC is

$3,370. When a family's income reaches $11,000, the credit will begin to be reduced and will be totally eliminated at an income level of $25,296 for a family with two children, or $23,755 when a family has one child. In 1995 a childless worker could get up to $306, while the maximum tax credit for families with children is $2,528. It is expected that in 1996 around 19 million families will qualify for the tax credit, at a total cost of $25 billion. The EITC program is administered by the Internal Revenue Service through the income tax system.

Food Stamp Program. The initial food stamp program (1939–43) was primarily an effort to expand domestic markets for farm commodities. Attempts to reestablish the program during the Eisenhower administration failed, but in 1961 a $381,000 pilot program began under the Kennedy administration. It was made permanent in 1964 and extended nationwide in 1974. Although strongly opposed by the Republicans in Congress, Democrats put together a majority coalition when urban members agreed to support a wheat and cotton price support program wanted by rural and Southern Democrats in return for their support of food stamps.

Initially, food stamp recipients had to pay cash for them, but this practice ceased in 1977. Benefiting poor and low-income families, the program has helped to combat hunger and reduce malnutrition. Food stamps went to more than 27.5 million beneficiaries in 1995 at a cost of $28 billion. The average participant received $69 worth of stamps per month. In 1995 families of four earning less than $1,642 per month qualified for food stamps.

Growth in the size of the food stamp program (in 1974 the cost of 12.9 million beneficiaries ran $2.8 billion) made this a target for Republican budget cutters. While 1995 House and Senate efforts differed on specifics, both sought to save more than $30 billion in projected food stamps costs over the seven years leading up to an anticipated balanced budget in 2002. Whether costs are reined in by capping appropriations, reducing benefits, or slowing cost-of-living increases, it appears likely that Republican-led efforts will reduce the meals on many poor families' tables.

The national government operates several other food programs for the needy. These programs include a special nutritional program for women, infants, and children (WIC); a school breakfast and lunch program; and an emergency food assistance program.

General Assistance. Some states and local governments, especially in the Northeast and Midwest, administer general assistance programs that assist poor people who are ineligible for AFDC or SSI. Persons who are physically able but not working may receive assistance, for instance. General assistance programs receive no support from the national government. Budgetary pressures have caused several states to cut back on their programs in recent years.

The Effectiveness of Income Security Programs

Many of the income security programs, including Social Security, Social Security Insurance, and food stamps, are **entitlement programs.** That is, Congress sets eligibility criteria—such as age, income level, or unemployment—and those who meet the criteria are legally "entitled" to receive benefits. Moreover, unlike such programs as public housing, military construction, and space exploration, spending for entitlement programs is mandatory. Year after year, funds *must* be provided for them unless the laws creating the programs are changed. This feature of entitlement programs has made it

entitlement program: Income security program to which all those meeting eligibility criteria are entitled.

quite difficult to control spending for them—which helps explain why Republicans in the 104th Congress sought to limit entitlements as a step toward budget balancing.

Although poverty and economic dependency have not been eliminated by income security programs, such programs have improved the lives of large numbers of people. Millions of elderly people in the United States would be living below the poverty line were it not for Social Security. Income security programs are basically alleviative rather than curative or remedial in their consequences. Poverty and economic dependency will not be eradicated so long as the conditions that give rise to them persist. And there will probably always be people who are unable to provide adequately for themselves, whether because of old age, mental or physical disability, adverse economic conditions, or youth. A panoply of income security programs is a characteristic of all democratic industrial societies.

MEDICAL CARE

Governments in the United States have long been active in the health field. Local governments began to establish public health departments in the first half of the nineteenth century, and were followed by state health departments in the second half. Knowledge of the bacteriological causes of diseases and human ailments discovered in the late nineteenth and early twentieth centuries led to significant advances in improving public health. Public sanitation and clean water programs, pasteurization of milk, immunization programs, and other activities reduced greatly the incidence of infectious and communicable diseases. The increase in life expectancy at birth in the United States from forty-seven years in 1900 to seventy-five years in 1990 is mostly due to public health programs.

Beginning in 1798 with the establishment of the National Marine Service (NMS) for "the relief of sick and disabled seamen," which was the forerunner of the Public Health Service, the national government has provided health care for some segments of the population. Currently, many millions of people receive medical care through the medical branches of the armed forces, the hospitals and medical programs of the Department of Veterans Affairs, and the Indian Health Service. Billions of dollars are expended for the construction and operation of facilities and for the salaries of the doctors and other medical personnel making the government's medical business truly a big business.

Most medical research currently is financed by the national government, primarily through the National Institutes of Health (NIH). The National Cancer Institute, the National Heart, Lung, and Blood Institute, the National Institute of Allergy and Infectious Diseases, and the other NIH institutes and centers expend more than $10 billion annually on biomedical research. The research is conducted both by NIH scientists and by scientists at universities, medical schools, and other research centers receiving NIH research grants.

In recent years national government spending for AIDS research has expanded greatly, exceeding $1.5 billion in recent years. In the early 1980s, however, many public officials were disinclined to do much about AIDS, regarding it as a condition afflicting a narrow segment of the population. In part, at least, the decision to hold back on funding AIDS research reflected moralistic, antihomosexual sentiments.[23] Research scientists and advocates for the gay community, however, convinced policy makers that

TABLE 17.2

Government Expenditures as a Percentage of Total Health Expenditures, 1991, by Country

United States	43.9%	Germany (West)	75.0%	New Zealand	83.6%
Australia	62.9%	Greece	82.2%	Norway	98.4%
Austria	68.8%	Iceland	88.2%	Portugal	72.4%
Belgium	83.4%	Ireland	82.2%	Spain	79.9%
Canada	74.7%	Italy	81.1%	Sweden	92.5%
Denmark	85.2%	Japan	70.8%	Switzerland	67.5%
Finland	79.0%	Luxembourg	92.8%	Turkey	27.3%
France	78.8%	Netherlands	74.7%	United Kingdom	89.6%

Source: Statistical Abstract of the United States 1993 (Washington, D.C.: U.S. Government Printing Office, 1993), 849.

AIDS constituted a dire public health problem and that a major governmental response was required. Some critics now assert that too large a share (around one-sixth) of medical research dollars is being channeled into AIDS research, while others still believe that not enough is being done.

A different situation exists in government programs that assist individuals in paying the costs of their own medical care. In helping people defray their medical costs, the United States continues to provide less assistance than other western industrial democracies, as shown in Table 17.2; all of them have long had some sort of national health insurance program.

The Roots of National Health Insurance

The Committee on Economic Security considered national health insurance when it was planning Social Security legislation. Because of the strong opposition of the American Medical Association (AMA), which was the dominant force in American medicine, health insurance was omitted for fear that its inclusion would jeopardize adoption of the other Social Security programs. Health insurance remained on the policy back burner for several years.

In late 1945 President Harry S Truman put the issue on the national policy agenda by calling for the enactment of compulsory national health insurance. Truman's advocacy touched off a titanic political struggle. The initial public reaction to compulsory health insurance was favorable: Of those who had heard of the proposal, 58 percent expressed approval in public opinion polls.[24] Support for the proposal came from many liberal and labor groups. In opposition were the AMA, drug manufacturers, private insurance companies, and conservatives—some of the same groups that oppose health care reform today. The AMA and its allies succeeded in stigmatizing compulsory health insurance as "socialized medicine," and by 1950 it was a dead issue.

Liberal political leaders did not lose interest in national health insurance. In 1958 a bill introduced in Congress covered only the hospital costs of elderly people receiv-

Passage of a universal health care bill was the first priority of the Clinton administration. But hope for massive reform died in the 103rd Congress when Democrats and Republicans were unable to agree on coverage and cost issues. (Photo courtesy: Reuters/The Bettmann Archive)

ing Social Security. The AMA again weighed in against this proposal; but by focusing on the aged, the proponents of health insurance changed the terms of the struggle. Strong support developed for providing medical assistance to the elderly, and in 1960 Congress passed legislation benefiting the needy aged. This provision, however, did not satisfy liberals and other supporters of a broader program. The issue was resolved by the 1964 elections, which produced sufficient votes in Congress to enact medical care legislation.

The Johnson administration proposed Medicare, which would provide hospital benefits for all aged people covered by Social Security. The Republicans countered with a plan for subsidized voluntary insurance that would cover major medical risks and physicians' services. The AMA sponsored a similar proposal. Representative Wilbur Mills (D–Ark.), chair of the House Ways and Means Committee (which had jurisdiction over the legislation), took hold of the policy process at this point. Wanting to put his own stamp on the legislation, he proposed combining the administration and Republican proposals and also adding an expanded program for the poor. This expanded proposal was enacted into law as Medicare and Medicaid.

Medicare: The federal program established in the Johnson administration that provides medical care to elderly Social Security recipients.

Medicare. **Medicare,** which covers persons receiving Social Security benefits, is administered by the Health Care Financing Administration in the Department of Health and Human Services. Medicare coverage has two components, Parts A and B. Benefits under Part A come to all Americans automatically at age sixty-five, when they qualify for Social Security. It covers hospitalization, some skilled nursing care, and home health services. Individuals have to pay about $700 in medical bills before they are eligible for Part A benefits. Medicare is financed by a payroll tax of 1.45 percent paid each by both employees and employers on the total amount of one's wages or salary.

Part B, which is optional, covers payment for physicians' services, outpatient and diagnostic services, X-rays, and some other items not covered by Part A. Excluded from coverage are prescription drugs, eyeglasses, hearing aids, and dentures. This portion of the Medicare program is financed partly by monthly payments from beneficiaries and partly by general tax revenues. Almost all of the eligible people have opted for Part B coverage, which in 1995 cost $46.10 a month.

Medicare has become a costly program because people live longer, the elderly need more hospital and physicians' services, and medical care costs are rising rapidly. Attempts to limit or cap expenditures for the program have had only marginal effects. One attempt occurred in 1983, when Congress authorized use of the diagnosis related group (DRG) system, which pays a prescribed amount to a hospital for a given medical procedure or operation, regardless of the actual cost to the hospital. Previously, Medicare had compensated hospitals for "all reasonable costs." Hospitals responded by reducing the length of patient stays and otherwise economizing on medical care costs. They have also shifted the unreimbursed costs of Medicare patients that result from the application of the DRG system to privately insured patients, which increases the share of total medical costs paid by private insurance companies. Figure 17.4 shows the various sources of payment for all medical costs in the United States.

In 1989 the Congress turned its attention to the costs of physicians' services for Medicare patients. The Physician Payment Review Commission, which advises Congress on Medicare's physician reimbursement policies, recommended that payments to physicians be determined on the basis of the work involved in a given treatment plus geographical factors (whether service is provided in a large city or rural area, for instance) and other considerations.[25] Enacted into law by Congress, these physician-cost-control practices were being placed into effect in the mid-1990s.

FIGURE 17.4

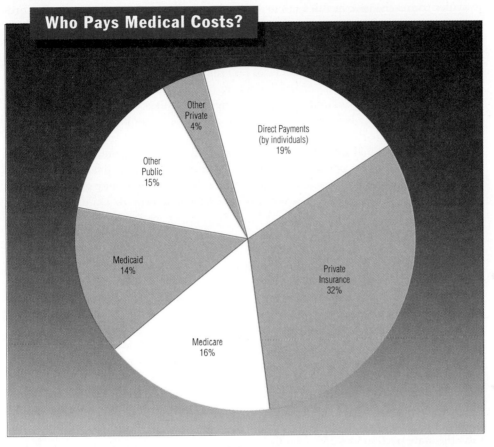

Who Pays Medical Costs?

Other Private 4%

Direct Payments (by individuals) 19%

Other Public 15%

Private Insurance 32%

Medicaid 14%

Medicare 16%

* Other public includes public health, medical research, veterans care, and other programs.

SOURCE: *Statistical Abstract of the United States,* 1993 (Washington D.C.: Government Printing Office, 1993), 108.

Medicare does not cover long-term or catastrophic health care costs. Congress sought to remedy this situation in 1988 when, with the support of the Reagan administration, it passed the Catastrophic Health Care Act. This act provided elderly people with expanded hospital and physicians' benefits and limited nursing home and prescription drug coverage. These expenses were to be financed by a small monthly fee levied on all Medicare recipients and also by a tax paid by the more well-to-do among Medicare recipients. President Reagan had insisted that the elderly themselves had to pay for the program.

Many better-off elderly people quickly mobilized to protest the new law. Outraged elderly constituents bombarded members of Congress with letters, petitions, and telephone calls and accosted legislators at town meetings. Overwhelmed by this stampede of opposition from the wealthier elderly, Congress rushed to repeal the Catastrophic Health Care Act in 1989. Although many of the wealthier elderly had private health insurance providing protection for themselves similar to that in the act, the poorer elderly were left with no protection.[26] Many people did not view this action as one of Congress's finer moments.

Medicaid: An expansion of Medicare, this program subsidizes medical care for the poor.

Medicaid.   Enacted into law at the same time as Medicare, the **Medicaid** program provides comprehensive health care, including hospitalization, physicians service, prescription drugs, and long-term nursing home care (unlike Medicare) to all who qualify as needy under AFDC and SSI.

In 1986 Congress extended Medicaid coverage for pregnant women and children under age six in families with incomes of less than 133 percent of the official poverty level. The states were also accorded the option of extending coverage to all pregnant women and to all children under one year of age in families with incomes below 185 percent of the poverty level. By 1993 twenty-nine of the states had chosen to provide this coverage.

The Congressional Budget Office expected that Medicaid would serve 38.4 million people in 1996 at a cost of $156 billion. Most of the benefits paid out under the program went to elderly people, with about one-third of the money going for nursing homes. Approximately one-seventh of the benefits went to children receiving AFDC.

Jointly financed by the national and state governments, the national government pays 50 to 79 percent of Medicaid costs on the basis of a formula based on average per capita income, which awards more financial support to poor than to wealthy states. Each state is responsible for the administration of its own program and sets specific standards of eligibility and benefit levels within the boundaries set by national guidelines. Nearly all needy people are covered by Medicaid in some states; in others only one-third or so of the needy are protected. Some states also award coverage to the "medically indigent," that is, to people who do not qualify for welfare but for whom large medical expenses would constitute a severe financial burden. Because of the options available to states, the actual share of the Medicaid budget paid by a state varies widely. In 1994 Mississippi paid 21 percent of all Medicaid costs, while in California the state share was 48 percent.[27] Texas shouldered 36 percent of Medicaid expenses, Florida and New York handled almost half the cost in their states, and in Massachusetts the state portion was 55 percent.

While the share paid for by the states varies, the portion of state budgets going to Medicaid is similar—ever upward. From 1987 to 1994, the percentage of state budgets going to feed the insatiable Medicaid appetite almost doubled to 19.4 percent.[28] Obviously, growth at that rate will drive other worthy projects out of state budgets and therefore cannot be sustained for long.

The Cost of Health Care

The costs of Medicare and Medicaid, which vastly exceed early estimates, have been major contributors to the ballooning costs of health care and the budget deficit. In 1994 national expenditures for Medicare were $159 billion and for Medicaid, $82 billion, as indicated in Table 17.3. The states collectively spent another $60 billion on Medicaid. If changes are not enacted, costs of these two programs will rise sharply over the next decade (see Figure 17.5).

Total health care expenditures in the United States have also soared in recent decades, growing from $27.1 billion in 1960 to $250.1 billion in 1980 to $884.2 billion in 1993.[29] A survey of business found that average health care benefits per employee stood at $3,821 in 1995.[30] Health care costs now comprise about 14 percent of the gross domestic product. The government's health spending for Medicare, Medicaid, medical research, and other purposes amounted to 40 percent of total health spending.

TABLE 17.3

Entitlements and Projections

THE BIGGEST ENTITLEMENTS IN 1994 (IN BILLIONS)		PROJECTIONS FOR 2000 (IN BILLIONS)	
1. Social Security	$321	1. Social Security	$436
2. Medicare	163	2. Medicare	247
3. Medicaid	89	3. Medicaid	136
4. Federal civilian retirement	37	4. Federal civilian retirement	49
5. Veterans' benefits and services	37	5. Supplemental Security Income	43
6. Unemployment compensation	29	6. Veterans' benefits and services	40
7. Food stamps	28	7. Food stamps	34
8. Military retirement	27	8. Military retirement	33
9. Supplemental Security Income	27	9. Unemployment compensation	27
10. Farm price supports	16	10. Earned Income Tax Credit	26

Source: Budget for Fiscal Year, 1995 (Washington, D.C.: U.S. Government Printing Office, 1995), 75–78.

FIGURE 17.5

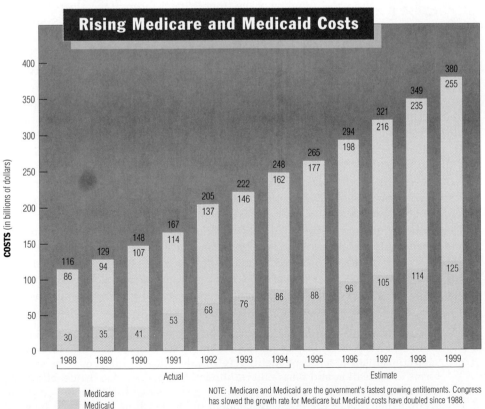

Rising Medicare and Medicaid Costs

COSTS (in billions of dollars)

Year	Medicare	Medicaid
1988	86	30
1989	94	35
1990	107	41
1991	114	53
1992	137	68
1993	146	76
1994	162	86
1995	177	88
1996	198	96
1997	216	105
1998	235	114
1999	255	125

(Totals shown atop bars: 116, 129, 148, 167, 205, 222, 248, 265, 294, 321, 349, 380)

Actual: 1988–1994   Estimate: 1995–1999

Medicare
Medicaid
(Federal share only)

NOTE: Medicare and Medicaid are the government's fastest growing entitlements. Congress has slowed the growth rate for Medicare but Medicaid costs have doubled since 1988.

SOURCE: *United States Budget for Fiscal Year 1996* (Washington D.C.: U.S. Government Printing Office, 1995), 242.

A number of factors have contributed to the high and rising costs of health care. First, more people are living longer and are requiring costly and extensive care in their declining years. Second, the range and sophistication of diagnostic practices and therapeutic treatments, which are often quite expensive, have increased. Third, the expansion of private health insurance, along with Medicare and Medicaid, has reduced the direct costs of health care to most people and increased the demand for services. More people, in short, can afford needed care. They may also be less aware of the costs of care. Fourth, the costs of health care have also increased because of its higher quality and because labor costs have outpaced productivity in the provision of hospital care.[31] Fifth, U.S. medicine focuses less on preventing illnesses and more on curing them, which is more costly.

Public opinion polls indicate that the major cause of Americans' dissatisfaction with the health care system is its cost. While most people indicate that they are satisfied with the quality of health care services provided by physicians and hospitals, a substantial majority express dissatisfaction over the costs of health care.[32] There is, as a consequence, a strong belief in the need to improve the nation's health care system.

PUBLIC EDUCATION

Historically, state and local governments funded public education. From the founding of the United States through the nineteenth century, local governments bore most of the responsibility. State government involvement has grown during the twentieth century and at present it is the largest source of public school funding. State education departments control curricula, textbook selection, graduation requirements, eligibility for extracurricular activity, and teacher and administrator certification. Nonetheless, local school districts, governed by appointed or elected boards, continue to control many daily operations of the public schools. The school districts are responsible, for example, for constructing and maintaining school buildings, hiring teachers, transporting students, operating school lunch programs, and designing educational programs. The balance between state and local funding responsibilities varies widely from state to state. In Hawaii, for example, local school systems bear little of the financial burden, while in New Hampshire localities pay the lion's share. Generally, the state shoulders more of the responsibility in the South, while the local school board has a greater voice in the Northeast.

The primary mission of American public schools once was to educate students, to provide them with reading, writing, and cognitive skills so that they could live more satisfactory and productive lives and become better citizens. This is still the primary mission of public schools, but they have also had many additional tasks loaded on them as parents and society increasingly view schools as a place to learn values and norms. As political scientist Thomas R. Dye portrays the situation:

> Today, schools are expected to do many things: resolve racial conflict and build an integrated society; inspire patriotism and good citizenship; provide values, aspirations, and a sense of identity to disadvantaged children; offer various forms of recreation and mass entertainment (football games, bands, choruses, majorettes, and the like); teach children to get along with others and adjust to group living; reduce the highway accident toll by teaching students to be good drivers; fight disease and ill health through physical education, health training, and even medical treatment; eliminate unemployment and poverty by teaching

job skills; end malnutrition and hunger though school lunch and milk programs; produce scientists and other technicians to continue America's progress in science and technology; fight drug abuse and educate children about sex; and act as custodians for teenagers who have no interest in education but who are not permitted to work or roam the streets unsupervised.[33]

If there is some hyperbole in Dye's statement, most of it still rings true. Much is expected of the public schools, perhaps more than they can fairly be expected to deliver.

Many political issues are generated by the tasks that Dye lists, but we lack space here to examine them. Rather, we focus on another matter of fundamental importance—financing the public schools—especially as this involves federal financial aid to the public schools, a contentious political issue for many years.

In 1992, national, state, and local governments in the United States spent nearly $250 billion on public (elementary and secondary) education (see Figure 17.6). Of this amount, 46.8 percent came from the state governments, 46.1 percent from local school districts, and 7.1 percent from the national government, with the remainder coming from private sources. There is much variation among states, and among school districts within states, on educational expenditures, as measured by spending on a per-student basis. Some states spend two or three times as much as other states according to this measure.

Although federal dollars are the smallest share of public school funding, these dollars are still vital to school systems that are usually financially strapped and sometimes in dire need of additional revenue.

FIGURE 17.6

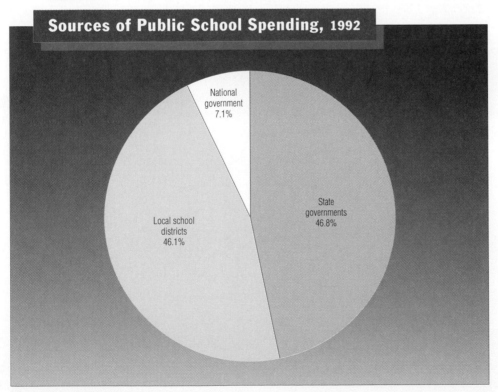

Sources of Public School Spending, 1992

National government
7.1%

State governments
46.8%

Local school districts
46.1%

SOURCE: *Statistical Abstract of the United States*, 1995 (Washington D.C.: Government Printing Office, 1995), 168.

Federal Aid to Education

The national government's participation in public education began with the Northwest Ordinance of 1787, which set aside one section of land in each township in the Northwest Territory (now the states of Ohio, Michigan, Indiana, Illinois, and Wisconsin) to support education.

In the two decades following World War II, the school-age population doubled. Classroom shortages became so severe that many urban schools operated on two shifts. At the same time technological knowledge was expanding rapidly, further challenging the adequacy of public education. Many people came to view federal financial assistance (more simply, federal aid) as a necessary part of the solution to the inadequacies of public education. Consequently, federal aid to education has been an item on the national policy agenda almost continually from the early 1950s.

In 1988 President George Bush and the nation's governors agreed to a program called Goals 2000 to improve the nation's schools. In 1994 Congress enacted the Goals 2000: Educate America Act to help all children achieve higher educational standards. For the first time, national standards were established (see Highlight 17.2: What High School Graduates Should Know). Compliance with these standards by the states is voluntary.

National legislation also sometimes imposes requirements on the public schools that are mandatory but not fully funded by the national government. An example is education for children with disabilities. Several million school-age children currently have disabilities that can range from mild physical disability to severe mental retardation. In the past many of the more handicapped children were excluded from the regular public school systems; some were enrolled in special state institutions, such as schools for the "deaf and dumb," as they were once called.

Highlight 17.2

What High School Graduates Should Know

According to Goals 2000, some of the items high school graduates must know are:

Arts

- Know dances and dancers prior to the 20th century
- Identify historical sources of American musical theater
- Identify famous musicians

Math

- Know how to use a calculator
- Interpret tables, charts, graphs

Civics and Government

- Identify the Bill of Rights, Magna Carta, Declaration of Independence
- Explain the difference between a citizen and an alien
- Know the function of the U.N., NATO, Amnesty International

Geography

- Know how to use an atlas, a map, a globe
- Explain how war, famine, and disease play significant roles in human migration

Science

- Know what matter is
- Understand reproduction and heredity
- Define a cell

English

- Write clearly
- Know how to use a thesaurus

History

- Develop a position as to whether the Civil War was avoidable

Source: "The Multitudinous Rs," *Time* (April 4, 1994): 14.

Beginning in the 1960s, the education of children with learning disabilities moved from the state to the national policy agenda. In 1975 Congress passed what is now called the Individuals with Disabilities Education Act to mandate that the states educate children with disabilities.[34] This law stated that every such child is entitled to a "free appropriate public education" provided through the regular public school system, which, for children with severe disabilities, can be a costly task. Because national funding covers only about one-fifth of the costs of educating children with disabilities, the states and local school districts bear the major costs of this unfunded federal mandate.

Inequality in Spending Among School Districts

The revenues raised by most local school districts come almost entirely from property taxes. Because of substantial differences among districts in the value of the taxable property within their boundaries, some communities are able to generate much more revenue than others, even with lower tax rates. This variation is then reflected in spending disparities among schools when measured on a per-pupil basis. Within a given state some districts may spend more than twice as much per pupil as others. Many parents, educators, and public officials believe that such unequal spending results in significant disparities in the quality of the education that students receive.

A challenge to inequality in education spending that arose out of the Texas public school system was decided in 1973 by the U.S. Supreme Court.[35] The five-justice majority ruled that the right to an education was not of such fundamental character that differences in per-pupil spending among districts violated the Fourteenth Amendment's equal protection clause. Although concerned about the inequalities in school funding, the Court held that this was a problem for the state governments to resolve.

Most conflicts concerning the quality of education that a state must provide have been solved through state administrative procedures. In some situations, however, disputes have ended up in the U.S. Supreme Court. In 1993, for example, the Court ruled that a school district must provide a sign language interpreter for a deaf child attending a Roman Catholic school.[36] In 1994, however, the U.S. Supreme Court ruled that a New York school district had gone too far to accommodate religious needs. The creation of a new school district to educate the special-needs children of the Satmar Hasidim, a strict Jewish sect, was found to violate the First Amendment's establishment clause.[37]

Since the early 1970s, school finance has been a priority item on the policy agendas in many states. In some states inequality in expenditures among districts has been held to violate the state constitution. In New Jersey, for instance, the state court practically forced the legislature to adopt an income tax to finance the schools.[38] School finance has been a volatile and vexing issue in many other states. Most people want good schools; paying for good schools, particularly if this requires raising taxes, stirs up much opposition in a time when "no new taxes" is a mantra with wide popular appeal.

CHANGING AMERICAN SOCIAL POLICY

*C*hange, actual and potential, continues to swirl around American social policy. Since the national government became a major player in developing social policy during the New Deal, we have tinkered, experimented, and considered an array of programs. Ideas, including some which have called for a far more intrusive central government, have been debated but rejected. For example, European democracies adopted health-care programs decades ago far more comprehensive than anything ever instituted on this side of the Atlantic.

A cataclysmic electoral change in 1932 that ushered in twenty uninterrupted years of Democratic control of the White House and rarely broken dominance in both chambers of Congress for generations heralded the onset of Social Security, AFDC, and SSI. The infusion of a new generation of Democrats in the wake of the assassination of President John F. Kennedy gave rise to federal aid to education, food stamps, Medicare, and Medicaid.

Reforming health care has featured a remarkable change of roles from 1994 to 1995. After a campaign that featured pledges to make affordable health care available to all Americans, President Clinton and Hillary Rodham Clinton led reform efforts during the 103rd Congress. The 1,300-page Clinton plan contained the thoughts of a talented and diverse set of advisers drawn from inside and outside government. The goals seemed incompatible to some, however, as the plan boasted that no American would be denied needed care, but at the same time, the plan promised to restrain costs. Americans have an incurable infatuation with proposals to provide more benefits at less cost.

The Clinton plan would provide health care to most people through state-run or nonprofit purchasing cooperatives called "health alliances." Businesses objected to the proposal, which called for employers to pay 80 percent of health-care costs. The most visible attack in turning the tide against the proposal came from the Health Insurance Association of America, which ran a series of television ads in which Harry and Louise worried about the President's initiative, especially the possibility that people would have less latitude in selecting their physician.

Having been rebuffed by Congress in 1994, the president stayed on the sidelines during much of 1995 as Republicans fashioned a reform. When the first Republican-run Congress in forty years took office in 1995, it had a leader with a plan. House Speaker Newt Gingrich (R–Ga.) immediately set about pursuing his response to the public malaise that had turned a Republican out of the White House in 1992 and a Democratic majority out of Congress two years later. Gingrich believed that the American public was using the clumsy tool provided by the ballot to enforce discipline. He interpreted the electoral returns as indicating that Americans wanted a balanced budget, more control over their own destinies, and a leaner and meaner federal government. While Republicans and a number of Democrats saw in their horoscopes a sign of change, some, particularly in the Senate, wanted to move more slowly than the eager class of seventy-three freshman Republicans in the House. Consequently, the House in the 104th Congress often pushed through reforms by a party line vote only to see them stalled or modified on the other side of the Capitol. The 1996 elections, although returning congressional Republicans to power, were not a resounding affirmation of the conservative revolution. The re-election of Bill Clinton, in fact, is likely to derail the more dramatic changes offered by Speaker Gingrich, although both sides agree that policy modifications are essential.

Unless Americans are willing to pay substantially higher taxes—and there is nothing to indicate a greater desire to share wealth with Uncle Sam—it will be impossible to sustain the current level of social services far into the future. Social Security is secure for a generation, but will be bankrupted as baby boomers demand benefits from a shrinking pool of people paying into the program. The current entitlement to Medicaid is sucking up growing shares of state budgets, which pits health care for the poor against public schools and needs for more prisons prompted by hard-nosed politicians who promise to put criminals away sooner and for longer terms.

The imminence of social program bankruptcy became more ominous when Medicare trustees announced that this fund would be operating in the red a year earlier than had been anticipated. Current predictions show Medicare with a surplus until the onset of the new century. From that point on, as growing numbers of retirees turn to the fund to cover health-care costs, deficits will escalate and are projected to exceed $400 billion in 2005. Annual deficits of that magnitude dwarf the estimated savings promised by either Democrats or Republicans. While partisans bickered over the GOP plan that boasted savings of $168 billion versus the Democratic effort to trim $124 billion, the system edged closer to collapse.

While Social Security has icon status, with politicians frightened to even suggest taking away benefits from current recipients, AFDC has never enjoyed widespread support. The general belt tightening urged by Gingrich, Ross Perot, and, at times, Bill Clinton has made means-tested programs especially vulnerable.

Change in political control of Congress has not changed the dire predictions for the future of Medicare. Even with massive numbers of new dollars pouring into Medicare, some projections show Part A going broke early in the next century. In light of these hard realities, both President Clinton and Republican leaders agree that the rate of increase in the health-care budget must be restrained, but disagree over how vigorously to step on the brakes.

Under the congressional as well as the presidential scenario, funding for Medicare will increase, but more slowly than the 10 percent annually that had been expected. The president wants to see funding for Medicare grow by about 7 percent, while the Republican proposal would slow that to 5 percent.

President Clinton and the GOP also disagree on charges for Part B insurance. Seniors who had been paying 31.25 percent of the cost saw their share drop to 25 percent in 1996, a level the president would like to maintain for seven years. Republicans want to restore the 31.25 percent rate as a step toward eliminating the budget deficit. The projected difference in premiums under the Clinton and the congressional plan in 2002 is about $12 per month per person. Republicans propose an "affluence test" to make those who are better off pay a larger share of the cost, with the wealthiest paying the full cost of their insurance.

Republican congressional leaders predict that their changes would save $270 billion over seven years. The president says that he would save $124 billion and provide more extensive care to the less affluent elderly.

One proposal for saving money, which is always popular with lawmakers, would reduce payments made to health-care providers. As a result of previous cuts in reimbursement, the average hospital was already losing ten cents for every dollar of service provided to a Medicare patient.[39] Making Medicare a "capped entitlement" would mean that everyone who is eligible would receive benefits but with limited funding available to providers.

Another component of the GOP initiative encourages Medicare recipients to join health maintenance organizations (HMOs). Currently, only one in ten Medicare participants belongs to an HMO, but the Republican plan calls for 40 percent to 50 percent to sign up. Realizing that ability to choose one's own physician is a major concern for many patients, Republicans vow that entering an HMO would be voluntary, leading doubters to question the likelihood of the massive rise in membership that cost-cutters envision. HMO proponents hope that additional benefits, such as free eyeglasses and prescription drugs and less paperwork, will be an inducement to join. Republicans want to expand the availability of HMOs while holding down costs by making it easier for hospitals and physicians to create networks to deliver health care.

Republican strategy would allow Medicare recipients to buy cheaper insurance with the federal dollars sent to them and then invest the remainder in a medical sav-

North—South

POLITICS AROUND THE WORLD

The 1990s have marked a major turning point in social welfare policy in the United States. Hopes for a system of universal health-care coverage were dashed during the first two years of the Clinton administration. The traditional system of benefits paid to the poor was scrapped in favor of a much harsher set of state-administered block grants by the end of the second.

The Canadian government, like its counterparts in Western Europe, has traditionally provided more extensive (and popular) social service programs, which have not undergone anything like the attack from the "new right" we have seen in the United States. Canada, for instance, has long provided "free" health care (actually paid for, of course, through taxes) to everyone. Canadians simply go to the doctor for treatment, and no money changes hands, as the doctor and other health-care providers are paid by the state. Through an elaborate system of grants and tax credits, the cost of raising children is subsidized, especially for poor families. Similar grants and tax credits exist to equalize incomes between the richest and poorest regions. Finally, to pick an example undoubtedly of interest to readers of this book, federal and provincial grants have kept tuition and fees at Canadian universities far below those in the United States.

While there are some problems with Canadian health care (for example, giving people speedy access to expensive procedures), most people seem quite happy with a system that was among the first to be rejected by the Clinton health-care task force in 1993. Although there has been somewhat of a conservative backlash against these programs, which has fueled the support of the English-speaking "anti-Ottawa" parties, most politicians and voters still think they are worth maintaining, despite their expense and the rather high taxes they require.

Mexico does not offer anywhere near as much, even though it is far poorer than either the United States or Canada. GNP per capita is about one-eighth that of the United States. Unemployment is officially about 15 percent, but the real rate is much higher. Infant mortality is four to five times as common as in the United States. Millions of people do not have electricity or safe drinking water in their homes.

To begin with, Mexico does less for its poor because it cannot do more. It is one of the tragedies of the world today that the poorest countries, which need the most extensive social services, lack the resources to develop them beyond the most rudimentary levels. In Mexico's case, the existing programs are hampered by the same problem that has cropped up in every chapter so far—the PRI's domination of political life. The party has manipulated most such programs literally to buy support at future elections and, even worse, to line the pockets of its activists. Although some effort has been made to clean up those efforts, it is currently under pressure to improve or shut down the new PRONASOL program established in the 1990s supposedly to ease the transition to a market economy for those who, for instance, lost their jobs in companies that were privatized.

ings account that could be tapped later for emergencies. President Clinton opposes medical savings plans, worrying that they would undermine Medicare.

Republicans and President Clinton also disagree over how sharply to restrict the growth in Medicaid, with Republicans hoping to save $163 billion by 2002 while the administration's target is one-third that amount. Republicans in Congress have been especially attentive to GOP governors who have called for turning the program over to the states. The governors believe that if given blocks of federal funds and allowed to set standards for eligibility and reimbursement, they could operate the program far more efficiently than Washington has. President Clinton insists on retaining federal guidelines to ensure coverage of the poor, with special attention given to pregnant women, children, and the disabled. The strings attached cause the governors to balk since they fear they may be left holding the financial bag with insufficient control over who can get money out of the bag. Of special concern is the cost of long-term nursing home care since Medicaid pays 80 percent of this tab.[40]

As mentioned earlier, one idea for trimming Medicare costs is to key the premium for Part B to the recipient's income. This is part of a broader move to convert what have been social insurance programs available to all contributors as a matter of right into means-tested welfare programs. Some have questioned why Social Security, which is funded by contributions from current workers, should tax young families struggling to make ends meet to send monthly checks to wealthy retirees.

Advocates of the social insurance concept, while acknowledging that some money goes to those who could get by without it, worry that applying needs tests will undercut support for Social Security and Medicare. The broad base of beneficiaries has kept these programs from being stigmatized as welfare. If they come to be seen as welfare, the public may balk at increasing benefits and focus more on setting tough eligibility standards.

Such an orientation would be another step toward reducing government costs and a reversal of the trend that characterized much of the history of the Social Security program where politicians competed to see who could offer the most generous benefit increases. Involved in proposed changes to the system is the potential for generational conflict. Retirees feel that the government owes them for a lifetime of labor and contributions to Social Security. Young workers, many of whom doubt that they will enjoy a quality of life equal to that of their parents, not only resent the loss of income needed to raise families and buy homes, they doubt that they will ever draw any benefits from the social policy trust funds now projected to go bust during the next century.

Today's political leaders face the challenge of honoring commitments made long past to elder citizens while trying to get control of annual budget deficits. The stands taken by candidates and the relative importance of these conflicting goals to voters may structure electoral decisions for years to come. The results of the 1994 election, if reinforced, may prove to be as significant in shaping social welfare policy for the first part of the twenty-first century as the 1932 election was for the last two-thirds of this century.

SUMMARY

This chapter examined the policy-making process and social welfare policies. To that end, we made the following points:

1. The Policy-Making Process.

The policy-making process can be viewed as a sequence of functional activities beginning with the identification and definition of public problems. Once identified, problems must get on the governmental agenda. Other stages of the process include policy formulation, policy adoption, budgeting for policies, policy implementation, and the evaluation of policy.

2. Social Welfare Policies.

Governments at all levels are involved in the policy process. The social welfare policies highlighted here are education, income security, and national health.

3. Income Security.

Income security programs to relieve economic dependency and poverty were mostly handled by state and local governments, albeit in minimal fashion, through the nineteenth century. With the adoption of the Social Security Act in 1935 the national government moved to become the dominant player in the economic security policy area. Most income security programs generally take two forms: non-means-based programs and means-tested programs, which means that all people who meet eligibility criteria are automatically entitled to receive benefits.

4. Medical Care.

Governments in the United States have a long history of involvement in the health of Americans. Most state and local governments have health departments, and the U.S. government has several public health and medical research divisions. Since Harry S Truman's presidency, there has been a push for national health insurance. Medicare and Medicaid are the two most prominent national programs. As the cost of health care has risen, however, new demands have been made to restrain the rate of growth in costs.

5. Public Education.

Public education was the province of state and local governments through the nineteenth century. In the twentieth century the national government has become more deeply involved. Through a variety of federal laws, Congress has attempted to improve educational standards, especially for disadvantaged students and also for people with disabilities. Today the national government provides a modest but vital share of the financing for public schools.

6. Changing American Social Policy.

Since the election of Bill Clinton in 1992, reform of the public welfare and health-care systems have been major policy issues on the public agenda. Republicans and the president agree that costs must be cut but disagree over how much to cut.

KEY TERMS

agenda, p. 648

agenda setting, p. 648

entitlement program, p. 667

governmental (institutional) agenda, p. 648

Medicaid, p. 672

Medicare, p. 670

means-tested program, p. 658

policy adoption, p. 651

policy evaluation, p. 655

policy formulation, p. 650

policy implementation, p. 652

public policy, p. 643

social welfare policy, p. 656

systemic agenda, p. 648

SELECTED READINGS

Chubb, John, and Terry Moe. *Politics, Markets and America's Schools.* Washington, D.C.: Brookings Institution, 1990.

Coleman, James S. *Public and Private High Schools: The Impact of Community.* New York: Basic Books, 1987.

Derthick, Martha. *Agency Under Stress: The Social Security Administration in American Government.* Washington, D.C.: Brookings Institution, 1990.

Gutmann, Amy. *Democratic Education.* Princeton, NJ: Princeton University Press, 1987.

Katz, Michael B. *In the Shadow of the Poorhouse.* New York: Basic Books, 1986.

Lindbloom, Charles E., and Edward J. Woodhouse. *The Policy-Making Process,* 3d ed. Englewood Cliffs, NJ: Prentice Hall, 1993.

Marmor, Theodore R. *The Politics of Medicare.* Chicago: Aldine, 1973.

Norris, Donald F., and Lyke Thompson, eds. *The Politics of Welfare Reform.* Thousand Oaks, CA: Sage, 1995.

Ripley, Randall B., and Grace A. Franklin. *Congress, the Bureaucracy, and Public Policy,* 5th ed. Pacific Grove, CA: Brooks/Cole, 1991.

Shilts, Randy. *And the Band Played On.* New York: St. Martin's Press, 1987.

Smith, David G. *Paying for Medicare: The Politics of Reform.* Chicago: Aldine, 1992.

Starr, Paul. *The Social Transformation of American Medicine.* New York: Basic Books, 1982.

Van Horn, Carl E., Donald C. Baumer, and William T. Gormley, Jr. *Politics and Public Policy,* 2d ed. Washington, D.C.: CQ Press, 1992.

Wilsford, David. *Doctors and the State: The Politics of Health Care in France and in the United States.* Durham, NC: Duke University Press, 1991.

Wirt, Frederick, and Michael Kirst. *Schools in Conflict: The Politics of Education.* Berkeley, CA: McCutchan, 1982.

Roots of Government Intervention in the Economy

Stabilizing the Economy

The Economics of Regulating Environmental Pollution

Changing American Economic Policy

ECONOMIC POLICY

The Republican congressional majority came to power in 1995 intent on reducing the size and scope of the federal bureaucracy. They saw a smaller bureaucracy as offering the dual advantages of expanding the range of individual actions and lowering taxes by cutting the cost of government. A number of new Republicans, particularly those from the West and South, thought that environmental protection was a policy-making area in which federal officials had overstepped their authority.

These Republicans were particularly concerned with what they perceived to be the tradeoffs involved in federal policy. They believed that the Environmental Protection Agency (EPA), the federal agency entrusted with enforcing many environmental laws, was willing to sacrifice jobs for the environment. The complaint that the EPA was overly zealous in protecting trivial concerns was not new. Construction of a major dam in Tennessee had been delayed for years as a result of the Endangered Species Act's protection of a small fish, the snail darter. More recently, the Oregon timber industry attributed its decline to the EPA's concern about the habitat of spotted owls.

Federal legislation limiting private land usage has been particularly galling to conservatives. In addition to banning activities that threaten the habitats of rare plants and animals, another law restricts the development of wetlands. Individuals and businesses complain that they are being denied the right to develop their property simply because it is their misfortune that some obscure plant or animal lives on the land. Those denied the right to drain, log, or develop their land see the prohibition as a violation of the constitutional guarantee that private property is not to be taken for public use without just compensation. Republicans in the 104th Congress pushed for legislation that would pay landowners when the Endangered Species Act or wetlands protection measures substantially reduced the value of the property. They argue that if the public is going to benefit from maintaining the land in its natural state, it should pay for that privilege. Although this legislation became bogged down, Congress did restrict the scope of the Endangered Species legislation by prohibiting the inclusion of new species on the list.

Some aspects of the Superfund Act, which was designed to clean up hazardous chemical dumps, have troubled GOP reformers—particularly the provision that requires businesses to pay for cleaning up sites even if no law was broken when the wastes were deposited on the site. Reformers claim that it is unfair to force a private entity to pay for actions that were legal when they were taken. Environmentalists counter that if businesses do not bear the financial burden, then the clean-up cost will be passed on to the taxpayers—and they are even more innocent of wrongdoing than was the entity that deposited the wastes.

Republican efforts to scale back environmental standards proved difficult to push through Congress. Democratic-led opposition stiffened as it became apparent that while voters favored less federal regulation as a concept, they did not want to see federal protections of the environment decimated. In recent years survey research has found that most Americans feel that the government is doing too little—not too much—to protect the environment.[1] And even as Republicans were winning control of Congress, most Americans said they thought environmental protection should take precedence over economic growth. Vice President Al Gore, Jr. (who wrote a well-received book on environmental protection while still a senator) and President Clinton have sought to paint the GOP as being extremists ready to sacrifice the environmental future for short-term private profits.

Despite recent pulling back from economic policies such as those supporting environmental protection (a topic we will discuss later in this chapter), the government and the economy in the United States have always been closely intertwined and a subject for debate. The U.S. economic system would be unable to survive and thrive in the absence of government activities such as environmental protection, the definition and protection of property rights, the maintenance of law and order, the enforcement of contracts, the provision of a common monetary system, the granting of corporate charters, the issuance of patents and copyrights, and the adoption of legislation to handle bankruptcy. This core of government activities, many of which are the responsibility of the state governments, provide the foundation for the U.S. capitalist (or free enterprise) economy. Many other governmental policies intended to influence and control economic activity have always been a part of the political landscape. In the twentieth century, such policies have become much more numerous and important.

In this chapter we deal somewhat selectively with public economic policies. In total, the chapter highlights the growth and impact of government intervention in the economy.

■ First, we take a historical look at some of the major developments in *government intervention in the economy*—the kinds of interventions feared by Anti-Federalists.

■ Second, we examine the government's role in *stabilizing the economy,* sometimes called "macroeconomic regulation."

■ Third, we look at *regulation to control environmental pollution,* an important area of microeconomic regulation.

■ Fourth, we look ahead at *ongoing proposals for balancing the federal budget.*

ROOTS OF GOVERNMENT INTERVENTION IN THE ECONOMY

*D*uring our nation's first century, most economic regulation was undertaken by states. The national government defined its role narrowly, although it did collect tariffs, fund public improvements, and regulate interstate commerce. Only with the perception that problems had outpaced the ability of states to provide adequate controls did Congress become active in setting national standards.

The Nineteenth Century

Although the U.S. economic system is a mixed free enterprise system, characterized by the private ownership of property, private enterprise, and marketplace competition, governments in the United States have always been deeply involved in the economy. The national government has long played an important role in fostering economic development through its tax, tariff, public lands disposal, and public works policies, and also through the creation of a national bank (see chapter 3). For much of the nineteenth century, however, national regulatory programs were few and were restricted to such topics as steamboat inspection and the regulation of trade with the Native American tribes.

The state governments, in comparison, were quite active in both promoting and regulating private economic activity. They constructed such public works as the Erie Canal, built roads, and subsidized railroads to encourage trade within and among the states; they also carried on many licensing, inspection, and regulatory programs.

The experience of Pennsylvania is a case in point. Pennsylvania regulated such matters as creditor–debtor relations, labor relations, liquor traffic, and banks and insurance company activities. Inspection programs to guarantee the quality of products covered "such articles as flour, fish, beef, pork, hogslard, flaxseed, butter, biscuits, harness and leather, tobacco, shingles, potash and pearlash, staves, heading and lumber, ground black-oak bark, pickled fish, spirituous liquors, and gunpowder." Licenses were required for "innkeepers, peddlers, retailers of foreign goods, liquor merchants, brokers of various kinds, wharfage pilots, and auctioneers."[2] On the whole, the state governments were capable of dealing adequately with the small-scale and mostly agrarian economy of early nineteenth-century America.

Following the Civil War, however, the United States entered a period of rapid economic growth. The rise of industrial capitalism brought about extensive industrialization and the creation of large-scale manufacturing enterprises. Many people began working in factories for wages and crowded into large cities. New problems resulted

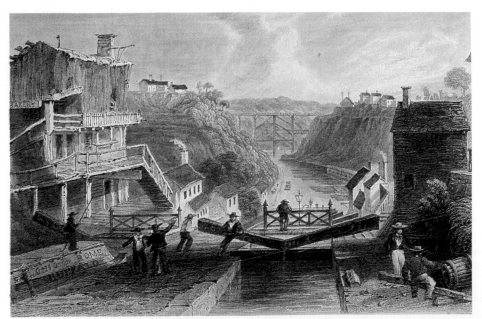

Public works projects such as the building of the Erie Canal spurred settlement and building throughout New York State. (Photo courtesy: The Bettmann Archive)

business cycles: Fluctuation between expansion and recession which is a part of modern capitalist economies.

from industrialization—industrial accidents and disease, labor–management conflict, unemployment, and the emergence of huge businesses that could exploit workers and consumers. Another problem was the loss of income by people because of business cycles, which became more severe in the new industrial society. **Business cycles** involve fluctuations between growth and recession, or periods of "boom and bust," and seem an inherent part of modern capitalist economies. During recessions many people lose their jobs, and a low or even negative growth rate afflicts the economy.

Many people, disturbed by the problems resulting from industrialization, turned to government for help. Because the states, with their limited jurisdictions, appeared inadequate to cope with industrial problems, the national government was called on to control these new forces. Businesses and conservatives, who had welcomed national action to aid economic development in the early decades of the nineteenth century, now proclaimed their faith in *laissez-faire*. Based on Adam Smith's *The Wealth of Nations* (published in 1776), the doctrine of **laissez-faire** holds that governmental regulation of the economy is wrong and that the role of government should be limited to the maintenance of order and justice, the conduct of foreign affairs, and the provision of necessary public works such as roads or lighthouses, which are not profitable for private persons to provide. Beyond that, individuals should be left free to pursue their self-interest. In so doing, Smith held, people would be guided by an "unseen hand" to promote the public welfare; that is, to provide consumers with a sufficient quantity of goods at reasonable prices. Competition and the laws of supply and demand would control their behavior and ensure that self-interest did not get out of hand.

laissez-faire: A French term literally meaning "to allow to do, to leave alone." It is a hands-off governmental policy that is based on the belief that governmental regulation of the economy is wrong.

Although opposed to regulation of their activities, businesses did not shun other forms of governmental intervention in the economy. They strongly supported tariffs that provided protection from foreign competitors. Other favored policies included the giveaway of public lands, subsidies for railroad construction, and the use of armed force to put down strikes. Essentially, what businesses and their supporters wanted, and what they thought of as *laissez-faire,* was an economic system and a set of governmental policies that would be congenial to the amassing of business profits.[3]

In time, because of pressures from small businesses, reformers in the cities, and the Grangers (see chapter 16) and other powerful agrarian protest groups in the Midwest, the national government was impelled to action. In 1887, following nearly two decades of agitation, Congress adopted the Interstate Commerce Act to regulate the railroads. The act, to be enforced by the new Interstate Commerce Commission (ICC), required that railroad rates should be "just and reasonable."[4] The act also prohibited such practices as pooling (rate agreements), rate discrimination, and charging more for a short haul than for a long haul of goods.

Three years later Congress dealt with the problem of "trusts," the name given to large-scale, monopolistic business that dominated many areas of production, including oil, sugar, whiskey, salt, cordage, and meatpacking. The Sherman Antitrust Act of 1890 is simple in its terms. Section 1 prohibits all restraints of trade, and section 2 prohibits all monopolization or attempts to monopolize. (Restraint of trade includes price-fixing, bid-rigging, and market allocation agreements; monopolization involves domination of a market by one company or a few companies.) The act was to be enforced by the Antitrust Division of the Department of Justice, which was empowered to sue violators in the federal courts. The Interstate Commerce Act and the Sherman Antitrust Act comprise the nineteenth- and early twentieth-century response of the national government to the new industrialization.

Agriculture was the largest sector of the economy throughout the nineteenth century. But as it shifted from subsistence farming to production for the market, farmers became more dependent on a vast system of distribution and exchange for their livelihoods. As this change occurred, and notwithstanding their storied individualism, farmers turned successfully to the national government for aid to improve their economic situation. The year 1862 was notably good for agriculture: It saw the establishment of the Department of Agriculture, which gained Cabinet status in 1889; the adoption of the Homestead Act, which gave 160 acres of public land in the West free to people willing to live on the land and improve it; and passage of the Morrill Land Grant Act, which subsidized the establishment of state colleges ("land grant schools") that offered instruction in the "agricultural and mechanical arts" (see chapter 3). Further intervention occurred in 1887, when the Hatch Act funded agriculture experiment stations in the various states to do basic and applied research. Other legislation provided regulatory programs to deal with such farm problems as pesticides, commodity standards, plant and insect pests, and the rail shipment of livestock. The expansion of farm programs continued in the early decades of the twentieth century. By the beginning of World War I, the Department of Agriculture had became a major regulatory agency.

The Progressive Era (1901–17)

The Progressive movement drew much of its support from the middle class and sought to reform the political, economic, and social systems of U.S. society. Economically, there was a desire to bring corporate power fully under the control of government and make it more responsive to democratic ends. Presidents Theodore Roosevelt's and Woodrow Wilson's progressive administrations strengthened regulatory programs to control railroads, business, and banking, and to protect consumers. Several laws intended to make railroad regulation more effective were passed. Notable among these laws was the Hepburn Act (1906), which gave the Interstate Commerce Commission authority to set maximum reasonable rates for railroads. Strongly opposed by most of the railroads, the Hepburn Act helped make the ICC a more effective regulator.

Consumer protection legislation came in the form of the Pure Food and Drug Act and the Meat Inspection Act, both enacted in 1906. These statutes mark the beginning of consumer protection as a major task of the national government. The Meat Inspection Act was passed partly in response to publication of Upton Sinclair's novel *The Jungle*, which graphically portrayed the unsavory and unsanitary conditions in the Chicago meatpacking plants. The food and drug law prohibited the adulteration and mislabeling of foods and drugs, which were common practices at this time.

In 1913 Congress passed the Federal Reserve Act. The act created the Federal Reserve System to regulate the national banking system and to provide for flexibility in the money supply in order to better meet commercial needs and to combat financial panics.

Passage of the Federal Trade Commission (FTC) Act and Clayton Act of 1914 strengthened antitrust policy. The FTC Act created the Federal Trade Commission and authorized it to prevent "unfair methods of competition." The commission also shared jurisdiction with the Department of Justice to enforce the Clayton Act, which prohibited a number of unfair business practices, such as price discrimination, exclusive dealing contracts, and corporate mergers that lessened competition. These statutes sought to prevent businessmen from forming monopolies or trusts.

Throughout the nineteenth century, the revenue needs of the national government were adequately met by protective tariffs and a few excise taxes, such as those on alcoholic beverages. Indeed, in the late decades of the nineteenth century, the government was sometimes hard pressed to spend all of the funds generated by protective tariffs. Generous government pensions for Northern veterans of the Civil War and ample spending on internal infrastructure improvements helped absorb the available revenues.

Here, a political cartoonist depicts how the U.S. government is perceived by some as being built by and of various trusts. (Photo courtesy: The Bettmann Archive)

As the national government's functions expanded in the early twentieth century, however, the government began to experience shortages of revenue. New sources of revenues became necessary, and the attention of public officials focused on the income tax as a way to raise money. In 1895, however, the Supreme Court had held that the income tax was a direct tax, which, according to the U.S. Constitution, had to be allocated among the states in proportion to their population.[5] This ruling made the income tax a political and administrative impossibility. Consequently, the Sixteenth Amendment to the Constitution, adopted in 1913, reversed that decision. The Sixteenth Amendment authorized the national government "to lay and collect taxes on incomes, from whatever source derived" without being apportioned among the states. Personal and corporate income taxes have since become the national government's major sources of general revenues. They have also been a source of political controversy.

The Great Depression and the New Deal

The outbreak of World War I brought the Progressive era to an end. During the 1920s, under the conservative aegis of the administrations of Warren G. Harding, Calvin Coolidge, and Herbert Hoover, the expansion of national intervention in the economy was slowed almost to a halt.[6] Only a few new regulatory programs were adopted; the Railway Labor Act and the Packers and Stockyards Act stand out among the programs. The economy grew at a rapid pace, and many Americans thought that the resulting prosperity would last forever.

But "forever" came to an end on Thursday, October 27, 1929, when the stock market collapsed and the catastrophic worldwide economic decline known as the Great Depression set in. The initial response of the Hoover administration was to declare that the economy was fundamentally sound, a claim that few believed. Investors, businesspeople, and others lost confidence in the economy. Prices dropped, production declined, and unemployment rose. In the winter of 1932 to 1933, an estimated quarter of the labor force was unemployed. Many other people worked only part-time or at jobs below their skill levels. The economic distress produced by the Great Depression, which lasted for a decade, was unparalleled before or since that time.

There had been numerous financial panics and recessions before 1929, but none on the scale of the Great Depression had ever occurred. Although the Depression was worldwide in scope, the United States was especially hard hit. All sectors of the economy suffered—business, finance, labor, agriculture, and manufacturing. No economic group or social class was spared, although some fared better than others. Fully industrialized, the United States could no longer rely on subsistence agriculture as a refuge in times of economic decline.

Many intellectuals, economic experts, and disgruntled citizens viewed the Depression as a massive institutional failure of the capitalist system. Whatever its shortcomings, such as substantial inequality in the distribution of wealth and income and the exploitation of some workers and farmers, no one had seriously questioned capitalism's productive capabilities. When economic declines had occurred, it was accurately assumed that they would be short. Moreover, before the Depression, few people thought there was much that the government could do to prevent recessions or to stabilize the economy. These assumptions were now called into question.

Calling for a "New Deal" for the American people, Franklin D. Roosevelt overwhelmed Herbert Hoover and the Republican Party in the 1932 presidential election. Although Roosevelt's campaign speeches and declarations were often general and ambiguous, it was clear that he favored strong government action to relieve economic distress and to reform the capitalist economic system, while preserving its basic features through the processes of democratic government.

The Depression and the New Deal marked a major turning point in U.S. history in general and in U.S. economic history in particular. During the 1930s the *laissez-faire* state was replaced with the **interventionist state,** in which the government plays an active and extensive role in guiding and regulating the private economy. Until the 1930s, the national government's role in the economy was consistent with a broad interpretation of *laissez-faire* doctrine in that the government mostly provided a framework of rules within which the economy was left alone to operate. After the 1930s, however, that was no longer true. The New Deal established the national government as a *major* regulator of private businesses, as a provider of social security (see chapter 17), and as ultimately responsible for maintaining a stable economy (see Highlight 18.1: The WPA).

Although the New Deal was not (and is not) without critics, most people today accept the notion that these areas of responsibility are properly within the scope of national governmental power. Specifically, *how* matters of Social Security and economic stability should be handled rather than *whether* they should be the province of the national government has been the basis for political conflict. Recently, however, Republicans have led a growing chorus of critics who argue that federal intervention is part of the problem and not the solution. These critics would replace Social Security with private retirement plans and allow the market a freer hand.

The New Deal brought about a number of reforms in almost every area, including finance, agriculture, labor, industry, and consumer protection.

Financial Reforms.   The first actions of the New Deal were directed at reviving and reforming the nation's financial system (see Roots of Government: Regulation of Financial Markets and the Fed). Because of bad investments and poor management, many banks failed in the early 1930s. To restore confidence in the banks, the day after he was inaugurated, Roosevelt declared a bank holiday, closing all of the nation's banks. Then, on the basis of emergency legislation passed by Congress, only financially sound banks were permitted to reopen. Many unsound banks were closed for good and their depositors paid off.

The major New Deal banking laws were the Glass–Steagall Act (1933) and the Banking Act (1935). The Glass–Steagall Act required the separation of commercial and investment banking and set up the Federal Deposit Insurance Corporation (FDIC) to insure bank deposits, originally for $5,000 per account. Although it had long been opposed by conservatives, bank deposit insurance has now become an accepted feature of the U.S. banking system. The Banking Act reorganized the Federal Reserve System, removed the Secretary of the Treasury as an ex-officio member, and formally established the Open Market Committee (discussed later in this chapter).

Legislation was also passed to control other abuses in the stock markets. The Securities Act (1933) required that prospective investors be given full and accurate information about the stocks or securities being offered to them. And the Securities Exchange Act (1934) created the Securities and Exchange Commission (SEC), an independent regulatory commission. The SEC was authorized to regulate the stock exchanges, to enforce the Securities Act, and to reduce the number of stocks bought on margin (that is, with borrowed money).

Agriculture.   The economic condition of U.S. agriculture, which had been weak even during the prosperous 1920s, became much worse with the Depression. The Agriculture

interventionist state: Replaced the *laissez-faire* state as the government took an active role in guiding and regulating the private economy.

Highlight 18.1

The WPA

The largest and most famous of the New Deal's job-creation programs was the WPA—the Works Progress Administration. Enacted in the midst of the Great Depression, the programs purpose was not simply to provide jobs for the unemployed—it was also intended to build public works, and this it did on a massive scale. Variety and magnitude of what the WPA accomplished is staggering. From 1935 to 1941, more than 600,000 miles of roads and streets were built or repaired, enough to encircle the world twenty-four times! Bridges were constructed or rebuilt, 116,000 of them; and nearly 600 airplane landing fields were constructed. More than 100,000 public libraries, schools, and other public buildings were erected. If only the *new* buildings were distributed evenly among

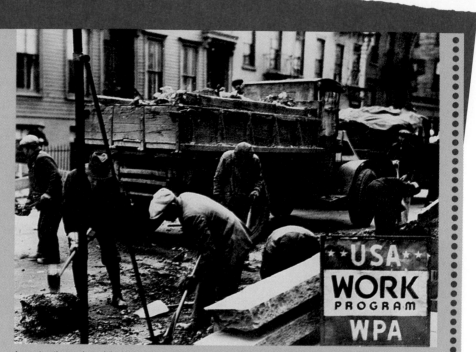

A construction project of the Works Progress Administration (WPA). This New Deal government program was created to provide jobs building roads, bridges, parks, and other public facilities. (Photo courtesy: The Bettmann Archive)

the 3,000 counties in the United States, each county would have had about ten. WPA projects included draining swamps and repairing library books; teaching illiterate adults and serving school lunches; building stadiums and painting murals; and plant-

ing trees and harvesting oysters. The projects ranged from modest ones costing a few hundred dollars to the building of major municipal airports and bridges, each of which cost tens of millions of dollars.

The WPA was not free of controversy and criti-

cism. Some people objected in principle to the government's provision of jobs to so many people, and others complained that too much of the money was wasted on "make work" and used by politicians to reward their friends.

Source: Donald S. Howard, *The WPA and Federal Relief Policy* (New York: Russell Sage Foundation, 1943).

Adjustment Act (AAA) of 1933 sought to boost farm income by restricting agriculture production in order to bring it into better balance with demand. Farmers who reduced their crop production in line with the program were eligible to receive cash payments and other benefits. In 1936, however, the Supreme Court held the AAA unconstitutional on the grounds that the national government lacked authority to regulate farming through any of its powers set out in Article I, section 8.[7] Congress quickly replaced the AAA with the Soil Conservation and Domestic Allotment Act, which paid farmers for taking land out of crop production and devoting it to soil conservation purposes. The crops taken out of production generally were those whose prices the AAA had been designed to increase. This ploy did not work very well to increase farm income.

In 1938 Congress adopted the second Agricultural Adjustment Act. The second AAA provided for subsidies to farmers raising crops such as corn, cotton, and wheat who grew no more than their allotted acreage. If two-thirds of the growers of a commodity voting in a referendum approved, then the allotments became mandatory, and farmers exceeding them were penalized. Direct payments and commodity loans were also available to participating farmers. In 1941 the Supreme Court upheld the constitutionality of the second AAA as an appropriate exercise of Congress's power to regulate interstate commerce.[8] The act, the foundation of the agricultural price support programs, has come under increasing attack from conservatives who claim that the program promotes inefficiency. Republicans, who took control of Congress in 1995, sought to phase out crop supports as part of the effort to curb federal spending.

Labor. Organized labor had long been handicapped in its relationships with management by unfriendly public officials and hostile public policies. The fortunes of labor unions, which were strong supporters of the New Deal, improved significantly in 1935 when Congress passed the National Labor Relations Act. Better known as the Wagner Act after its sponsor, Senator Robert Wagner (D–N.Y.), this statute guaranteed workers' right to organize and bargain collectively through unions of their own choosing. A series of "unfair labor practices," such as discriminating against employees because of their union activities, was prohibited. The National Labor Relations Board (NLRB) was created to carry out the act and to conduct elections to determine which union, if any, employees wanted to represent them. Unions prospered under the protection provided by the Wagner Act.

The last major piece of New Deal economic legislation was the Fair Labor Standards Act (FLSA) of 1938. Intended to protect the interests of low-paid workers, the law set twenty-five cents an hour and forty-four hours per week as initial minimum standards. Within a few years, wages were to rise to forty cents per hour and hours to decline to forty per week. Not all employees were covered by the FLSA, however; farm workers, domestic workers, and fishermen, for example, were exempted. The act also banned child labor.

In 1996 Congress approved a two-step increase in the minimum wage. It was raised from $4.25 an hour, where it had been for the last five years, to $4.75. In September 1997, it will be raised to $5.15. Controversy continues over whether minimum wage legislation creates employment by pricing some workers out of the labor market. Some economists argue that these workers, especially unskilled young people just entering the job market, would have jobs if they could be paid a lower wage. Figure 18.1 shows the growth of the minimum wage since its creation.

Industry Regulations. Several industries were the subjects of new or expanded regulatory programs. The Federal Communications Commission (FCC), created in 1934 to replace the old Federal Radio Commission, was given extensive jurisdiction over the radio, telephone, and telegraph industries. The Civil Aeronautics Board (CAB) was put in place in 1938 to regulate the commercial aviation industry. And the Motor Carrier Act of 1935 put the trucking industry under the jurisdiction of the Interstate Commerce Commission (ICC). Regulation of industries such as trucking and commercial aviation, like railroad regulation, extended to such matters as entry into the business, routes of service, and rates. To a substantial extent, government regulation, as a protector of the public interest, replaced competition in these industries. Supporters of these programs frequently spoke of a need to prevent destructive or excessive competition, as could

FIGURE 18.1

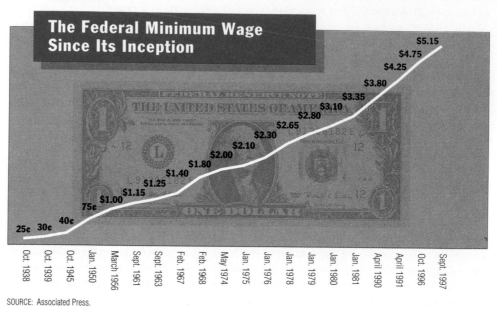

The Federal Minimum Wage Since Its Inception

SOURCE: Associated Press.

occur among large numbers of trucking companies. Critics warned that limiting competition resulted in users having to pay more for the services.

Consumer Protection.   Even though consumers as a group were poorly organized in the 1930s, a few laws were passed to help protect their interests. The Wheeler–Lea Act (1938) expanded the jurisdiction of the Federal Trade Commission (FTC) to include deceptive practices and false and misleading advertising. The act gave the FTC a clear mandate to engage in consumer protection.

The Pure Food, Drug, and Cosmetic Act (1938) represented an effort to plug some of the loopholes and remedy the shortcomings of the Pure Food and Drug Act of 1906. Cosmetic and therapeutic devices were added to foods and drugs as matters subject to government regulation. All traffic in foods that were injurious to health was banned. Also, factories producing foods, drugs, and cosmetics were brought under inspection by the Food and Drug Administration (FDA). Drugs and cosmetics had to bear informative labels relating to their use. Moreover, the marketing of any drug was prohibited until it had been tested and found safe when properly used. Most responsibility for enforcing the 1938 law was given to the Food and Drug Administration, which today is part of the Department of Health and Human Services.

Just as World War I brought down the curtain on the Progressive era, the war clouds gathering in Western Europe in the late 1930s diverted Americans' attention from domestic reform to international affairs and brought an end to the New Deal era. Many of the New Deal programs, however, became permanent parts of our public policy landscape. Moreover, the New Deal established the legitimacy and viability of national governmental intervention in the economy. Passive government was replaced with activist government, and the government in Washington became the people's primary source of solutions for economic problems.

The Post-World War II Era

In the two decades following the end of World War II, many areas of economic policy were fairly well settled and produced few major policy struggles. Transportation, finance and banking, agriculture, and consumer protection, for example, experienced little change. There were, however, some important policy developments in other areas. Here, we look at two of the most significant developments: the Employment Act and the Taft–Hartley Act.

The Employment Act.   As World War II neared its conclusion, policy planners and public officials began to worry that the conversion from a wartime to a peacetime economy would bring with it a new depression, as had happened after World War I. Officials in the administration of President Harry S Truman and liberal and labor groups wanted to commit the national government to the use of **fiscal policy** (the government's taxing and spending policies) to create conditions providing full employment.[9] They backed a bill introduced in Congress by Senator James Murray (D–Mont.) to guarantee a "right to employment" to anyone willing and able to work. To accomplish this goal, Murray proposed that the president submit a "National Production and Employment Budget" to estimate the size of the labor force, the total national production needed to provide jobs for all, and the total investment required to provide that level of production. If the anticipated level of private investment was insufficient to achieve this level of production, then the national government would provide the additional investment and spending needed to reach the goal of full employment.

The Murray proposal ran into strong opposition from a conservative coalition of Republicans and Southern Democrats, egged on by many business groups. They feared that this bill would result in excessive government spending and control of the economy. Conservatives stressed the capacity of the private economy to provide jobs. What finally emerged from Congress as the Employment Act of 1946 was a substantially weakened version of the Murray bill. The declaration of policy in section 2 of the Employment Act states that "It is the continuing policy and responsibility of the federal government to use all practicable means consistent with its needs and obligations . . . to promote maximum employment, production and purchasing power."

Some policy machinery was established to carry out this policy. A Council of Economic Advisers (CEA), consisting of three professional economists and a small support staff, was created to advise the president on economic issues. The CEA later became quite influential in the Kennedy, Johnson, and Carter administrations. The president was directed to present an annual economic report to Congress. In this report the president analyzed current economic conditions and recommended a program for meeting the act's goals. Within Congress the Employment Act set up a Joint Economic Committee composed of ten senators and ten representatives to consider the president's economic report and to advise the two houses on its content and recommendations. The Committee also holds hearings and commissions studies on economic policy. In all, the Joint Economic Committee has helped increase the "economic literacy" of Congress.

It is incorrect to dismiss the Employment Act as merely symbolic and without real impact. Its enactment reflected a high level of agreement among the members of Congress and provided a general direction for public policy makers. As economist Herbert Stein states, "It helped put an end to futile, tiresome, and meaningless debate between extremists and cleared the way for practical work to evolve a program" for stabilizing the economy and putting more people to work.[10] Since 1946 the national government has performed the role of overall manager of the economy.

fiscal policy: The deliberate use of the national government's taxing and spending policies to influence the overall economy and maintain economic stability.

The Taft–Hartley Act.   Business and conservative groups, which had stoutly opposed the Wagner Act in 1935, continued to be highly critical of it. When the Republican Party gained control of Congress following the 1946 elections, it got the opportunity to do something about its dissatisfaction with the Wagner Act and labor union power. Major strikes in the automobile, steel, meatpacking, railroad, and other industries in the months following the end of World War II had created negative public feelings toward unions. If organized labor and the Truman administration had been able to agree on moderate labor reform proposals, they might have been able to fend off the drastic changes in labor law contained in the Taft–Hartley act. They were not, however, and the conservative coalition favoring the act was strong enough to enact it into law in 1947 over Democratic President Harry S Truman's veto.

Essentially, the Taft–Hartley Act sought to increase the power of management in collective bargaining by imposing a variety of restraints on labor unions while also strengthening management prerogatives. The act prohibited as unfair a number of union activities, such as featherbedding (requiring that extra employees be assigned to a job), jurisdictional strikes, and coercing employees to join a union. Unions were directed to file detailed reports on their finances and procedures with the Department of Labor. Employees of the national government were absolutely barred from striking. A procedure involving an eighty-day injunction against striking was authorized to help settle strikes that affected the "national health or safety." The closed shop arrangement, under which an employer agreed to hire only union members, was prohibited. A union shop, under which workers had to join the union (or at least pay union dues) within a designated time to retain their jobs, was permitted, except in states that had "right-to-work" laws. These laws, which now exist in about twenty states, provide that union membership or nonmembership cannot be a condition of employment. The result is an open shop. Labor union officials often called the Taft–Hartley Act a "slave labor" law.

Now, decades later, when labor unions have declined in membership and lost some of their political and economic strength (see Figure 16.2), it is difficult to imagine the bitterness and intensity of the conflict that for years swirled around the Taft–Hartley Act. It injected government much more deeply into labor–management relations than did the Wagner Act. Conservatives who feared that the Full Employment Act would result in too much government control of the economy shed that concern when the control of labor unions was at stake. Sooner or later, everyone finds government programs of which he or she approves; this is one major reason for the growth and persistence of big government.

The Social Regulation Era

economic regulation: Governmental regulation of business practices, industry rates, routes, or areas serviced by particular industries.

social regulation: Governmental regulation of the quality and safety of products as well as the conditions under which goods and services are produced.

Economists and political scientists frequently distinguish between economic regulation and social regulation. **Economic regulation** focuses on such matters as control of entry into a business, prices or rates of charge, and service routes or areas. Regulation is usually tailored to the conditions of particular industries, such as railroads or stock exchanges. "Simply put, economic regulation places government in the driver's seat with respect to the economic direction and performance of the regulated industry."[11] In contrast, **social regulation** is concerned with such areas as the quality and safety of products and the conditions under which goods are produced and services rendered. Put another way, social regulation strives to protect and enhance the quality of life. Regulation of product safety by the Consumer Product Safety Commission is an example of social regulation. Professor Michael Reagan helps make the distinction between the two kinds of regulation: "Social regulation can generally be differentiated from economic regulation by the former's concern with harm to our physical (and sometimes moral and aesthetic) well-being, rather than harm to our wallets."[12]

Most of the regulatory programs established through the 1950s fell into the category of economic regulation. From the mid-1960s to the mid-1970s, however, a huge wave of social regulatory legislation emanated from the national government on such topics as consumer protection, health and safety, and environmental protection. Congress enacted this legislation under its commerce clause authority.

Several major new regulatory agencies were set up to implement these new social regulations. These agencies include the Consumer Product Safety Commission, the Occupational Safety and Health Administration (OSHA), the Environmental Protection Agency (EPA), the Office of Surface Mining Reclamation and Enforcement, the Mining Enforcement and Safety Administration, and the National Transportation Safety Administration (see chapter 9). Most of these agencies have jurisdictions that cut across industry lines, in contrast to the industry-focused agencies born during the New Deal.

The social regulatory statutes took various forms. Some had specific targets and goals, such as the Egg Product Inspection Act and the Lead-Based Paint Poison Prevention Act. Others were quite lengthy and detailed, loaded with specific standards, deadlines, and instructions for the administering agency. Illustrative are the Clean Air Act of 1970 and Employee Retirement Income Security Act (intended to protect workers' pensions provided by private employers). Other statutes conferred broad substantive discretion on the implementing agency. Thus the Occupational Safety and Health Act guarantees workers a safe and healthful workplace, but it contains no health and safety standards with which workplaces must comply. These standards are set through rule-making proceedings conducted by the Occupational Safety and Health Administration, which also has responsibility for their enforcement (see chapter 9).

As a consequence of this flood of social regulation, many industries that previously had had limited dealings with government now found government regulation to be of major importance in the conduct of their operations. A good example is the automobile industry, which previously had been lightly touched by antitrust, labor relations, and other general statutes. By the early 1970s, however, the quality of its products was heavily regulated by EPA motor vehicle emissions standards and federally mandated safety standards. The automobile companies found this experience both galling and expensive. The chemical industry found itself in much the same situation.

Four factors contributed to the surge of social regulation.[13] First, the late 1960s and early 1970s were a time of social activism; the consumer and environmental movements were at the peak of their influence. Public interest groups such as the Consumers Union, Common Cause, the Environmental Defense Fund, the Sierra Club, and Ralph Nader's numerous organizations were effective voices for consumer, environmental, and other programs (see chapter 16). Strong support also came from organized labor.

Second, the public had become much more aware of the dangers to health, safety, and the environment associated with various modern products. Unsafe products had always existed, but their numbers had been multiplied by modern technology. Products widely viewed as unsafe included the chemical DDT, cigarettes, leaded gasoline, poisonous household cleaners, the Chevrolet Corvair, spray cans, phosphates, vinyl chloride, lead-based paint, cyclamates, and some forms of intrauterine birth control devices such as the Dalkon Shield. Furthermore, add to this list the large quantities of toxic substances spewed into the air, dumped in streams and lakes, and buried in the ground. There was, noted one observer, "a level of public consciousness about environmental, consumer, and occupational hazards that appears to be of a different order of magnitude from public outrage over such issues during both the Progressive era and the New Deal."[14]

The Lead-Based Paint Poison Prevention Act has led to redoubled efforts to test dwellings for lead paint, as this contractor is doing by taking samples. (Photo courtesy: Stephen Agricola/The Image Works)

Third, members of Congress, aided and abetted by their professional staffs, saw the advocacy of social regulation as a way to gain visibility and national prominence and thus to enhance their election prospects. Some members became policy entrepreneurs. Senator Edmund Muskie (D–Me.), for example, took the lead on environmental issues, and Senator Warren Magnuson (D–Wash.) successfully pushed for a number of consumer protection laws.

Fourth, the presidents in office during most of this period—Lyndon B. Johnson and Richard M. Nixon, one a liberal, the other a pragmatic conservative—each gave support to the social regulation movement. For them, too, it was good politics to be in favor of health, safety, and environmental legislation. Also, in most instances, the direct costs to the government of this legislation were minimal.

Deregulation

Even before the wave of social regulation began to wane, deregulation emerged as an attractive political issue. Although this situation may seem paradoxical, there is a fairly simple explanation for what happened. The focus of the deregulation movement was on the economic regulatory programs for such industries as railroads, motor carriers, and commercial air transportation; most social regulatory programs continued to enjoy strong public support and were left largely alone by the deregulation movement.

Beginning in the 1950s and 1960s, economists, political scientists, and journalists began to point out defects in some of the economic regulatory programs.[15] They contended that regulation sometimes produced monopoly profits, discrimination in services, and inefficiency in the operation of regulated industries. Moreover, regulation often made it difficult for industries to compete on the basis of prices and also for new competitors to enter the market. For instance, no new major commercial airline was permitted to enter the industry after the Civil Aeronautics Board (CAB) began to regulate the industry in 1938. Consequently, consumers paid higher prices for airfares and had fewer choices than they would in a more competitive market. Regulated firms like the commercial airlines, on the other hand, were comfortable with the higher profits and less competitive rigors of their regulated markets. Critics contended that regulatory commissions like the CAB and the Interstate Commerce Commission were more responsive to the interests of the regulated firms than to the public interest.

For some time nothing changed in the regulatory arena, despite these criticisms. In the mid-1970s, however, President Gerald R. Ford decided to make deregulation a focal point of his administration. He saw regulation as one cause of the inflation that was then besetting the economy. Also, as a conservative Republican, he found deregulation consistent with his beliefs in less government and a free market. About this time Senator Edward M. Kennedy (D–Mass.) became chair of a subcommittee of the Senate Judiciary Committee. Wanting to use his new position and acting on the advice of his staff, he decided to hold hearings on airline deregulation. The combined actions of Ford and Kennedy put deregulation on the national policy agenda and got the deregulatory movement underway. Democrats and Republicans, liberals and conservatives, all found deregulation to be an appealing political issue.

Some of the many economists who favored deregulation were appointed to the regulatory commissions. Once on the commissions, they used the discretionary authority available to them to reduce the impact of regulation. This was done, for example, by economist Alfred Kahn, who was appointed chair of the CAB. Commission action of this sort both pressured and made it easier for Congress to act on deregulation. Economists also mustered a substantial body of empirical research showing that efficiency gains would flow from deregulation and, further, that deregulation would not have disruptive effects on the economy, as some opponents argued. Competition was depicted as a beneficent and effective regulator of the economy.[16]

Only one deregulation act was passed during the Ford administration. However, deregulation picked up momentum after Jimmy Carter became president in 1977. He made deregulation a high priority for his administration. Legislation that deregulated aspects of commercial airlines, railroads, motor carriers, and financial institutions was enacted during his term. Two additional deregulation laws were adopted in the early years of the first Reagan administration.

Deregulation usually involved a reduction in the entry, rate, and other controls imposed on an industry. The exception was the Airline Deregulation Act, which completely eliminated economic regulation of commercial airlines over several years. Although many new passenger carriers flocked into the industry when barriers to entry were first removed, they were unable to compete successfully with the existing major airlines. All of these new entrants have now disappeared. Indeed, so have some of the major airlines that were operating at the time of deregulation. Consequently there are now fewer major carriers than under the regulatory regime, although new airlines such as Valujet try to compete by offering low fares. Competition has lowered some passenger rates, but the extent to which passengers have benefited from deregulation is in dispute because many routes have been abandoned and airline safety has been called into question in the wake of tragic crashes like ValuJet Flight 592 in the Everglades.

The deregulation of the savings and loan business, coupled with the failure of the Reagan administration adequately to enforce the remaining controls on savings and loans, led in time to a costly instance of deregulatory failure. Previously restricted to financing individual homes, deregulation took the lid off of what savings and loans could invest in. As a consequence of poor management, bad commercial investments, and corruption, hundreds of savings and loans, especially in Southwestern states, went bankrupt, sometimes to the tune of hundreds of millions of dollars or more.[17] After years of delay, during which the problem got worse, the Bush administration and Congress finally took action. The Financial Institutions Reform, Recovery, and Enforcement Act (1989) revamped the regulatory system for savings and loans, provided for the liquidation of insolvent associations, and bailed out their depositors. Expectations are that the total direct cost to taxpayers of the bailout will be $150 billion to $200 billion. With interest, the cost may increase to $500 billion.[18] Much of the cost of the bailout could have been avoided by more timely and effective action. What is surprising is that the public has accepted this financial debacle with minimal complaint or criticism.

In some policy areas, the pendulum has now completed its deregulatory swing. The broad consensus that made possible "pro-competitive" or economic deregulation does not exist for the field of social regulation. Strong support continues for regulation to protect consumers, workers, and the environment. In some areas in which deregulation occurred, there have been calls to "reregulate." This has occurred in the airline industry because of concern about its domination by a small number of companies. While congressional Republicans, in response to public outrage, have backed away from some of their ideas for weakening environmental regulations, they continue to call for less government involvement in a number of other areas. They have been particularly critical of affirmative action requirements designed to earmark a share of government contracts and public jobs for minorities.

In the following sections of this chapter, we take a detailed look at two areas of government regulation of economic activity, both of which are of much interest to most

Americans. The first is macroeconomic regulation to influence the overall performance of the economy. The second is regulation to control environmental pollution.

STABILIZING THE ECONOMY

*U*ntil the early 1930s the prevailing view in the United States was that the country's economy was controlled by natural economic laws that could be disrupted but not improved on by the government. Fluctuations in the economy were accepted with a sense of inevitability. At a Conference on Unemployment sponsored by the national government in 1921, President Warren G. Harding stated the position of the government in his opening remarks: "There has been vast unemployment before and there will be again. There will be depression and inflation just as the tides ebb and flow. I would have little enthusiasm for any proposed remedy that seeks palliation or tonic from the Public Treasury."[19] At the time it was thought that the best things the government could do if a depression struck would be to increase taxes, cut spending, and balance the budget, or the situation might be made worse by a lack of public confidence in the government's financial condition. This was the tack taken by Herbert Hoover and, for a time, by Franklin D. Roosevelt during the early years of the Great Depression.

The policy change represented by the Employment Act of 1946, which committed the government to maintaining "maximum employment, production, and purchasing power," stemmed from a confluence of several factors.[20] First, the massive scale and persistence of the Great Depression refuted the notion that depressions were self-correcting. Second, new techniques of economic measurement and analysis enabled people to better understand the operation of the economy.

Third, the ideas of English economist John Maynard Keynes had gained acceptance and influence. In his *General Theory of Employment, Interests, and Money* (1936), Keynes argued that deficit spending by a government could supplement the total or aggregate demand for goods and services. Government spending would offset a decline in private spending and thus help maintain high levels of spending, production, and employment. During the New Deal, the national government engaged in limited deficit spending, which was sometimes referred to as "pump-priming," but it was not sufficient to bring economic recovery. Fourth, World War II brought with it a tremendous increase in government spending and large budget deficits. The economy expanded, production rose, and unemployment fell below 2 percent. The interaction of these factors contributed to the national government's assuming responsibility for maintaining economic stability.

economic stability: A situation in which there is economic growth, rising national income, high employment, and steadiness in the general level of prices.

inflation: A rise in the general price levels of an economy.

recession: A short-term decline in the economy that occurs as investment sags, production falls off, and unemployment increases.

Economic stability is often defined as a situation in which there is economic growth, a rising national income, high employment, and a steadiness in the general level of prices. Conversely, economic instability may involve inflation or recession. **Inflation** occurs when there is too much demand for the available supply of goods and services, with the consequence that general price levels rise as buyers compete for the available supply. Prices may also rise if large corporations and unions have sufficient economic power to push prices and wages above competitive levels. A **recession** involves a decline in the economy. Investment sags, production falls off, and unemployment increases.

The primary means available to government to maintain economic stability or, if one prefers, to combat instability are monetary and fiscal policy. Our attention now turns to a discussion of these concepts.

Monetary Policy

Monetary policy, which is a form of macroeconomic regulation, involves regulating a nation's money supply and interest rates. A modern industrial economy operates on the basis of money, which is the medium through which nearly all income and all buying and selling transactions take place. When money is mentioned, most of think of currency and coins, items we can feel, count, and carry in our pockets. But currency and coins are only a small portion of the nation's money supply. The term *money* also includes bank deposits and other financial assets. The Federal Reserve Board has three definitions of **money** based on this broader conception. *M1* (the first definition) includes currency, checking accounts, travelers checks, NOW accounts, and other checkable deposits. *M2* includes all of M1 plus savings and small time deposits and money market account balances. *M3* includes M2 plus large time deposits and institutional money market fund balances. The M2 definition is of the most concern to the Federal Reserve Board.

The Federal Reserve Board has responsibility for the formation and implementation of monetary policy because of its ability to control the credit-creating and lending activities of the nation's banks. When individuals and corporations deposit their money in financial institutions such as commercial banks (which accept deposits and make loans) and savings and loan associations (S&Ls), these deposits serve as the basis for loans to borrowers. In effect, the loaning of money creates new deposits or financial liabilities—new money that did not previously exist. But, we are getting ahead of our story. First, we'll look at the Federal Reserve System and its authority.

The Federal Reserve System.   Created in 1913 to adjust the money supply to the needs of agriculture, commerce, and industry, the Federal Reserve System is comprised of the Federal Reserve Board (FRB) (formally, the Board of Governors of the Federal Reserve System; informally, "the Fed"), the Federal Open Market Committee, and the twelve Federal Reserve Banks in regions throughout the country (see Figure 18.2). The Fed represents a mixture of private interests and governmental authority.

The seven members of the Federal Reserve Board, who direct the system, are appointed by the president for fourteen-year, overlapping terms with the approval of the Senate. A member can be removed from office by the president for stated causes, but this has never occurred. One board member is designated by the president to serve as chair for a four-year term, which runs from the midpoint of one presidential term to the midpoint of the next to ensure economic stability during a change of administrations. Formally, the FRB has much independence from the executive branch, ostensibly so that monetary policy will not be influenced by political considerations. Defenders of the FRB's independent position assert that monetary policy is too important, complex, and technical to be under the day-to-day control of elected public officials, who might be inclined to make monetary decisions to advance their own short-term political interests (such as being reelected).

At the base of the Federal Reserve System are the twelve Federal Reserve Banks. These are "bankers' banks"; they are formally owned by the Federal Reserve System member banks in each region, and they do not do business with the public. A majority of the board of directors of each Federal Reserve Bank is elected by the commercial member banks in its region. The president of a Federal Reserve Bank is selected by its board of directors, not by the president of the United States.

The middle of the Federal Reserve System is occupied by the Federal Open Market Committee (FOMC). This committee consists of twelve members—all seven FRB members, plus five presidents from the Federal Reserve Banks. The representatives from the reserve banks rotate among the twelve regions, except for the New York Fed-

monetary policy: A form of government regulation in which the nation's money supply and interest rates are controlled.

money: A system of exchange for goods and services that includes currency, coins, and bank deposits.

Alan Greenspan, chairman of the Federal Reserve, testifying before Congress. Because of the enormous power of the "Fed," public statements by its leader are always closely attended to. Often, when the chairman testifies to Congress, his statements are examined closely for signals of future changes in monetary policy, and hundreds of private investors react accordingly. (Photo courtesy: UPI/Bettmann Newsphotos)

FIGURE 18.2

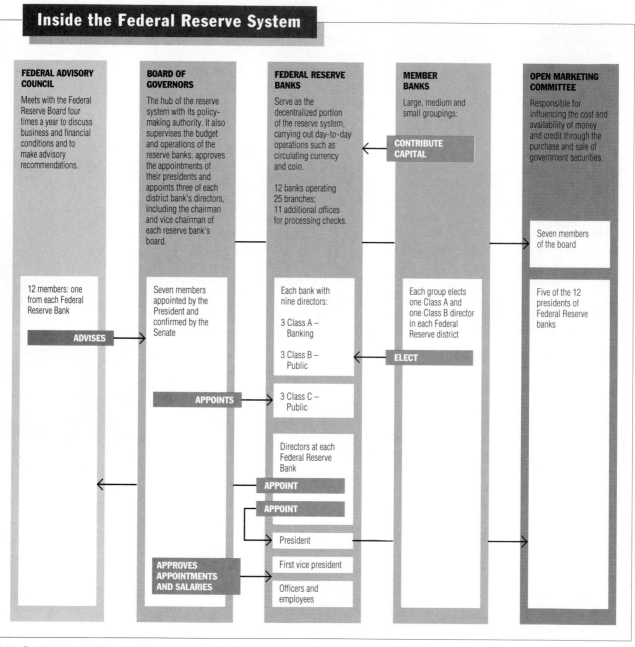

Inside the Federal Reserve System

FEDERAL ADVISORY COUNCIL

Meets with the Federal Reserve Board four times a year to discuss business and financial conditions and to make advisory recommendations.

12 members: one from each Federal Reserve Bank

ADVISES

BOARD OF GOVERNORS

The hub of the reserve system with its policy-making authority. It also supervises the budget and operations of the reserve banks, approves the appointments of their presidents and appoints three of each district bank's directors, including the chairman and vice chairman of each reserve bank's board.

Seven members appointed by the President and confirmed by the Senate

APPOINTS

APPROVES APPOINTMENTS AND SALARIES

FEDERAL RESERVE BANKS

Serve as the decentralized portion of the reserve system, carrying out day-to-day operations such as circulating currency and coin.

12 banks operating 25 branches; 11 additional offices for processing checks.

Each bank with nine directors:

3 Class A – Banking

3 Class B – Public

3 Class C – Public

Directors at each Federal Reserve Bank

APPOINT

APPOINT

President

First vice president

Officers and employees

MEMBER BANKS

Large, medium and small groupings:

CONTRIBUTE CAPITAL

Each group elects one Class A and one Class B director in each Federal Reserve district

ELECT

OPEN MARKETING COMMITTEE

Responsible for influencing the cost and availability of money and credit through the purchase and sale of government securities.

Seven members of the board

Five of the 12 presidents of Federal Reserve banks

SOURCE: From Martin Mayer, "Well Fed—or not? The Federal Reserve faces a new era while raising rates and trying to keep independence, *The Dallas Morning News,* May 22, 1994. Copyright © May 22, 1994.

eral Reserve Bank. Because of its importance in the financial world, the New York Federal Reserve Bank is always represented on the FOMC.

The primary monetary policy tools are the setting of reserve requirements for member banks, control of the discount, and open market operations. Formally, authority to use these tools is allocated to the FRB, the Federal Reserve Bank boards of

Roots of Government

Regulation of Financial Markets and the Fed

Throughout the eighteenth and nineteenth centuries, the U.S. economy was plagued periodically by financial panics. Downturns in the business cycles were accompanied by runs on banks, widespread defaults on loans, bankruptcies of large enterprises, and sharp declines in stock prices. Panics, often preceded by speculative booms in real estate or securities, usually resulted when a spectacular failure caused a sudden, drastic reappraisal of business prospects. From 1790 to 1907, there were twenty-one panics, or about one every six years. In 1914 Congress passed the Federal Reserve Act to regulate the currency and credit operations of banks in the United States, which had been manipulating financial markets. The law was designed to improve cooperation among the nation's banks and to decentralize financial control. As illustrated in Figure 18.2 on page 702, it divided the United States into twelve districts with a Federal Reserve Bank in each.

In spite of these precautions, the stock market crash in October 1929 set off a succession of banking panics, with more than 9,000 bank failures between 1930 and 1933. The Federal Reserve Banks had no authority to prevent these disasters, to keep them from spreading, or to ease their effects.

Thus in 1933, Congress passed the Banking Act of 1933. It changed some of the ways in which Federal Reserve Banks worked and created the Federal Deposit Insurance Corporation. The objective of the act was to stabilize banking in the United States.

Today, the Federal Reserve System is empowered to create money to meet the seasonal needs of business and to counteract panic. In addition, the Federal Reserve imposed controls over bank reserves, accounting procedures, and management, produced a uniform currency, cleared checks and collections, and handled government finance. The Federal Reserve injects money into the financial system by purchasing government bonds. So when "the Fed" decides that the economy needs more money, it prints new money and promptly spends some (on bonds).

The Federal Reserve plays a critical role in stabilizing the financial system. For instance, without the Fed in operation, the 1987 stock market crash could have had a more devastating impact than it did. When the stock market crashed, the Federal Reserve immediately flooded the financial markets with money in order to prevent further panic.

For all of its power and importance, the Federal Reserve System is a mysterious entity to most Americans. One observer has likened it to a religious institution, a characterization that, at first, seems bizarre, but that on closer examination reveals a bit of truth about the Fed. Housed in a dignified marble "temple" on Constitu-

tion Avenue in Washington, D.C., the "high priests" of monetary policy direct the economy in ways that are hidden from, and incomprehensible to, the average citizen. Their deliberations take place in secret. Their debates are conducted in the technical language of economics. Their powers to create money and to make it disappear inspire awe and fear. Such powers cannot be entrusted to ordinary "mortals" but must be exercised only by "priests" undefiled by "political considerations."

The Fed's mystique has not been lost on the Fed itself, which has often portrayed itself as the master of an arcane science. A former officer of the Fed described the induction of economists into the fraternity of the Fed staff as "taking the veil," similar to nuns entering a convent. One member of Congress described the senior economists at the Fed as "the monks." Richard Syron, a vice president of the Boston Fed, compared the institution to the Catholic church:

> The System is just like the Church. That's probably why I feel so comfortable with it. It's got a pope, the chairman; and a college of cardinals, the governors and bank presidents; and a curia, the senior staff. The equivalent of the laity is the commercial banks . . . . We even have different orders of religious thought like Jesuits and Franciscans and Dominicans only we call them pragmatists and monetarists and neoKeynesians.

Source: Quotation and paraphrasing from William Greider, *Secrets of the Temple: How the Federal Reserve Runs the Country* (New York: Simon & Schuster, 1987), chapter 2.

directors, and the FOMC, respectively. In actuality, however, all three are dominated by the FRB, which, in recent decades, has been under the sway of its chair. Arthur Burns and Paul Volcker (past chairs) and Alan Greenspan, the current chair, have been influential and respected policymakers. Much attention is given by public officials and the financial community to the utterances of the Fed's chair for clues to the future course of monetary policy.

reserve requirement: Governmental requirements that a portion of member banks' deposits must be retained to back loans made.

Reserve requirements designate the portion of the banks' deposits that must be retained as backing for their loans. Raising the reserve requirement limits the capacity of banks to make new loans; lowering it enables them to expand their loans. Hypothetically, if the reserve requirement is 10 percent of deposits, banks can make more loans on a given amount of deposits than they can if the requirement is raised to 15 percent. When the FRB wants to increase the money supply in circulation, it can lower the reserve requirements; to reduce the money supply, it can raise the reserve requirement.

discount rate: The rate of interest at which member banks can borrow money from their regional Federal Reserve Bank.

The **discount rate** is the rate of interest at which member banks can borrow money from their regional Federal Reserve Bank when they need additional reserves to support their loans. Raising the discount rate should discourage borrowing by banks to make loans and, in turn, will make loans more costly to people who want to borrow money. Conversely, lowering the discount rate should expand the money supply and encourage borrowing both by member banks and by people who want money to expand business and for other purposes. The assumption here is that what people do will be directly affected by whether interest rates are raised or lowered.

open market operations: The buying and selling of government securities by the Federal Reserve Bank in the securities market.

Open market operations involve the buying and selling of government securities by the FRB in the market, that is, wherever government securities are bought and sold. Government securities are interest-bearing bonds that are regularly bought and sold by investors in their quest for profits. When the FRB buys securities in the market, it ultimately pays for them by creating deposits for the sellers in the federal reserve banks. These deposits serve as additional reserves for commercial banks and enable them to expand their loans to borrowers. On the other hand, when the FRB sells government securities in the market, the buyers' payments for them are deducted from commercial banks, reserve accounts, reducing these reserves and thus the capacity of banks to lend money to their customers. As a rule of thumb, when the FRB buys securities, it expands the money supply; when the FRB sells securities, it restricts, or "tightens," the money supply. Open market operations are the tools the FRB uses most frequently because of their flexibility and direct impact.

Moral suasion refers to the capacity of the FRB to influence the actions of banks and other members of the financial community by suggestion, exhortation, and informal agreement. Because of its commanding position as a monetary policy maker, much attention and respect are given by the media, economists, and market observers to verbal signals about economic trends and conditions emitted by the FRB and its chair.

How the FRB uses these policy tools depends in part on how it perceives the state of the economy. (Ironically, we know more about the condition of the economy six months ago than about its current state because of lags in the availability of needed data.) If inflation appears to be the problem, then the Fed would likely restrict or tighten the money supply. The Fed could raise the reserve requirement and the discount rate and could sell government securities in the market. If a recession with rising unemployment appears to threaten the economy, then the FRB would probably act to loosen or expand the money supply in order to stimulate the economy. The Fed could lower the reserve and discount rates and could buy government securities in the market. In the early 1990s the Fed continually lowered interest rates to counteract a recession. Then, in early 1994, as the economy gained momentum, the FRB began to worry about inflation and acted several times to nudge up interest rates, somewhat to the consternation of Clinton administration officials.[21] In late 1995, in the wake of hints of an economic slowdown, interest rates dropped a few ticks. Such short-term actions are often characterized as "leaning against the wind."[22]

The President and the FRB.   Although the public generally holds the president responsible for maintaining a healthy economy, he does not really possess adequate constitutional or legal authority to meet this obligation. Responsibility for fiscal policy is shared with Congress, and the FRB is authorized by Congress to make monetary policy. In the area of monetary policy, presidential power is truly "the power to persuade." There are many informal contacts between the White House and the FRB, however, such as during periodic luncheon meetings, at which monetary policy is discussed. More formal meetings also take place. A group called the Quadriad, which consists of the secretary of the treasury, the director of the Office of Management and Budget, the chair of the Council of Economic Advisers, and the chair of the Federal Reserve Board, has met with varying frequency with the president since the time of the Kennedy administration. These meetings allow the president to express his views on monetary policy to the FRB. In turn, the FRB chair can convey some of his views on the economy to the administration. In all, there is quite a bit of contact and cooperation between the White House and the FRB. The result of this activity is that the monetary policy made by the FRB is customarily acceptable to the president, even if it is not precisely what he would prefer.[23]

Fiscal Policy

Fiscal policy involves the deliberate use of the national government's taxing and spending policies to influence the overall operation of the economy and maintain economic stability. Fiscal policy is formulated by the president and Congress and is conducted through the federal budget process. The powerful instruments of fiscal policy are budget surpluses and deficits. These are achieved by manipulating the overall or "aggregate" levels of revenue and expenditures.

According to standard fiscal policy theory, at some level of total or aggregate spending, the economy will operate at a full employment level. Total spending is the sum of consumer spending, private investment spending, and government spending. If consumer and business spending does not create demand sufficient to cause the economy to operate at full employment, then the government should make up the shortfall by increasing spending in excess of revenues. This was essentially what Keynes recommended that the national government should do during the Great Depression. If inflation is the problem confronting policy makers, then government can reduce demand for goods and services by reducing its expenditures and running a budget surplus.[24]

Discretionary fiscal policy involves deliberate decisions by the president and Congress to run budget surpluses or deficits. This can be done by increasing or decreasing spending while holding taxes constant; by increasing or cutting taxes while holding spending stable; or by some combination of changes in taxing and expenditure.

The first significant application of fiscal policy theory occurred in 1964. When John F. Kennedy, an activist president committed to getting the country "moving again," took office in 1961, he brought Keynesian economists to Washington as his economic advisers. These advisers believed that government action was needed to stimulate the economy in order to achieve full employment, and they were able to convince President Kennedy of this. The need, as they saw it, was for a budget deficit to add to aggregate demand. The problem was, however, that budget deficits were strongly opposed by many conservatives as bad public policy and perhaps even as immoral. Thinking strategically, President Kennedy's advisers decided that many conservatives and members of the business community would find deficits more palatable, or less objectionable, if they were achieved by cutting taxes rather than by increasing government spending. (Businesses had been complaining about high taxes.) Furthermore, a tax cut would increase private sector spending on goods and services. Higher government spending, on the other hand, would mean more spending on public goods and services and bigger government.

The result was the adoption of the Revenue Act of 1964, which reduced personal and corporate income tax rates. This variant of fiscal policy, which was more acceptable to the business community, has been labeled "commercial Keynesianism." The tax-cut stimulus contributed to the expansion of the economy through the remainder of the 1960s and reduced the unemployment rate to less than 4 percent, its lowest peacetime rate and what many people then considered to be full employment.[25]

In 1968 Congress enacted a tax increase at the urging of the Johnson administration in order to restrain inflation, which was stimulated by increased spending for Great Society programs and the Vietnam War. The tax increase contributed to a balanced budget in fiscal year 1969, the last year in which the national budget has been balanced. Tax changes were also used during the 1970s to stabilize the economy. Since the early 1980s, however, the government has incurred large annual budget deficits. These deficits can be viewed either as "neutralizing" fiscal policy, because they have politically foreclosed most major alterations in taxing and spending rates, or as a source of continuing stimulation to the economy.[26] Consequently, much of the burden of economic stabilization has been placed on FRB and monetary policy.

What we have discussed thus far is discretionary fiscal policy, so called because public officials must make overt decisions concerning its use. There are also some automatic stabilizers that have been built into the economy, whether intentionally or unintentionally, that operate without decisions by policy makers. These automatic stabilizers "act as buffers when the economy weakens by automatically reducing taxes and increasing government spending."[27] When the economy declines, for example, mandatory spending for such programs as unemployment insurance, food stamps, and Medicaid increases because eligibility for benefits depends on people's income or employment status. The tax system also acts as an automatic stabilizer. When the economy slows down and personal income and corporate profits decline, tax payments fall and help reduce the decline in after-tax incomes that would otherwise occur.[28] Conversely, when the economy revives, taxes begin to take a bigger bite out of incomes and thus help hold down spending. Although the automatic stabilizers are helpful in mitigating economic fluctuations, they are by themselves inadequate to stabilize the economy.

The Budgetary Process

The Budget and Accounting Act of 1921 gave the president authority to prepare an annual budget and submit it to Congress for approval. A staff agency now called the Office of Management and Budget (OMB) was created to assist the president and handle the details of budget preparation (see also chapter 8). The budget runs for a single fiscal year, now beginning on October 1 of one calendar year and running through September 30 of the following calendar year. The fiscal year takes its name from the calendar year in which it ends; thus the time period from October 1, 1997, through September 30, 1998, is designated fiscal year (FY) 1998. An overview of where the federal government gets its money and how the money is spent is presented in Figure 18.3.

FIGURE 18.3

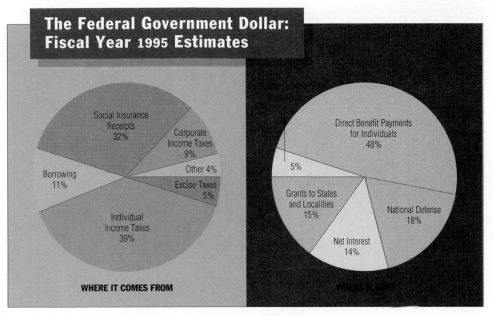

The Federal Government Dollar: Fiscal Year 1995 Estimates

WHERE IT COMES FROM

Social Insurance Receipts 32%
Corporate Income Taxes 9%
Other 4%
Excise Taxes 5%
Borrowing 11%
Individual Income Taxes 39%

WHERE IT GOES

Direct Benefit Payments for Individuals 48%
5%
Grants to States and Localities 15%
National Defense 18%
Net Interest 14%

SOURCE: *Budget of the United States Government, Fiscal Year 1995*, (Washington D.C.: Government Printing Office, 1994), 12.

The president sends his budget to Congress in January or February of each year. Work on the budget within the executive branch will have begun nine or ten months earlier, however (see Highlight 18.2: The Federal Budget Process). Acting in accordance with presidential decision on the general structure of the budget, the OMB provides the various departments and agencies with instructions and guidance on presidential priorities to help them in preparing their budget requests. The departments and agencies then proceed to develop their detailed funding requests. Each agency believes in the value and necessity of its set of programs and seeks to expand or at least maintain its budget. The OMB's role, on the other hand, is to put together a budget that reflects the president's preferences and priorities. Consequently, agency budget requests are frequently modified and revised downward by the OMB. Agencies that are aggrieved by OMB reductions may try to appeal these decisions to the president. If this happens, the president usually agrees with the OMB. During the early years of the Reagan administration, this traditional "bottom-up" process of preparing the budget, in which the agencies' requests shape the budget, was replaced by a "top-down" process. In "top-down" budgeting, directives from the president and the OMB dominate the budgetary process.[29]

Article I of the Constitution provides that "no money shall be drawn from the Treasury, but in consequence of appropriations made by law." Congress and its legislative committees (such as the committees on Resources, Education and Educational Opportunities, and National Security) may authorize that money be spent on programs, but it is Congress *and* the appropriations committees in each chamber that actually provide the funding needed to carry out these programs. The appropriations committees often deny some, and once in a while all, of the funding authorized by the legislative committees. Consequently, the legislative committees sometimes have resorted to

The Federal
Budget Process

First Monday in February	Congress receives the president's budget.
February 15	Congressional Budget Office (CBO) reports to the Budget Committees on fiscal policy and budget priorities, including an analysis of the president's budget.
February 25	Congressional committees submit views and estimates on spending to the Budget Committee.
April 1	Budget committees report concurrent resolution on the budget, which sets a total for budget outlays, an estimate of expenditures for major budget categories, and the recommended level of revenues. This resolution acts as an agenda for the remainder of the budgetary process.
April 15	Congress completes action on concurrent resolution on the budget.
May 15	Annual appropriations bills may be considered in the House.
June 10	House Appropriations Committee completes action on regular appropriations bills.
June 15	Congress completes action on reconciliation legislation, bringing budget totals into conformity with established ceilings.
June 30	House completes action on all appropriations bills.
October 1	The new fiscal year begins.

Source: Adapted from Howard E. Shuman, *Politics and the Budget,* 3d ed. (Englewood Cliffs, NJ: Prentice Hall, 1992), 67.

backdoor spending—authorizing agencies to borrow money from the Treasury or creating entitlement programs that make funding mandatory in order to circumvent the appropriations committees.[30]

Conflicts often develop between Congress and the president over both the details of the budget and its overall dimensions, such as the size of the deficit, the balance between military and domestic spending, or international agreements affecting domestic economics (see Politics Now: Standoff over NAFTA). Throughout the 1980s there was conflict between the Democrats in Congress, who favored more domestic spending and less military spending, and President Ronald Reagan and his administration, whose spending preferences leaned in the opposite direction. In 1993 the Clinton administration touched off a titanic partisan political struggle in Congress with its budget deficit-reduction plan involving a combination of spending cuts and tax increases. Drawing almost unanimous opposition from the Republicans in Congress and also from some conservative Democrats, the Clinton proposal was passed by Vice President Albert Gore, Jr.'s tie-breaking vote in the Senate and by a margin of two votes in the House.[31] The Clinton administration, moreover, had to make many deals with members of Congress in order to secure the votes needed to adopt its budget proposal.

Standoff over NAFTA

Almost from the moment of his inauguration in 1993, President Bill Clinton has clashed with congressional Republicans. After the GOP secured majorities in both chambers in the 1994 election, the conflict intensified. Foreign trade stands out as one of the few economic policy areas to evoke agreement between the president and Republicans in Congress. In November 1993 the North American Free Trade Agreement (NAFTA) was approved in the House by a margin of eighteen votes. Supporting the president in his efforts to reduce our trade barriers with Canada and Mexico were 132 of 175 Republicans. Democrats who represented districts outside the South rejected this measure by a vote of 124 to 49.

Republicans and most Southern Democrats supported this measure, which they hoped would open up new opportunities for American business. Northern Democrats and many labor organizations balked, fearing that American jobs would be lost to less well-paid workers south of the border.

In the 1996 presidential primaries, former conservative television commentator Pat Buchanan latched on to the trade issue in an effort to broaden the Republican base and derail Bob Dole's presidential nomination. By claiming that NAFTA was exporting jobs, Buchanan appealed to some blue-collar workers who have traditionally been Democratic Party stalwarts.

While neither his criticism of NAFTA nor of other issues was sufficient to win the nomination, trade was an issue that brought votes to Buchanan at least in the critical early primaries. In South Carolina, which opened the way to the South's presidential primaries, almost 60 percent of those who ranked foreign trade as the most important issue supported Buchanan. The problem was that fewer than one in ten voters judged the issue to be that significant. Among voters who thought that greater foreign trade costs Americans jobs, Buchanan beat Dole 46 to 35 percent. However, Dole bested Buchanan 51 to 19 percent among the even greater number of South Carolina voters who believed that trade creates more jobs. Exit polls revealed similar splits in Georgia.

The issue of expanded trade does not affect all workers equally. Even within a single state, some workers benefit and others may see their jobs disappear. In South Carolina the location of the BMW automobile assembly plant between Greenville and Spartanburg brought well-paying jobs not just to assembly line workers but to those employed by suppliers who located in the area and also created opportunities for those who would sell goods and services to a growing population. While automobile assembly was moving from Germany to the Palmetto State, the much older textile industry was playing a diminished role, as producers found that they could manufacture clothing much less expensively abroad. How has your community been affected by NAFTA?

The 1993 congressional–presidential struggle was a love fest compared to the 1995–1996 stalemate. Under the leadership of Speaker Newt Gingrich, the first Republican congressional majority in generations devised a plan to balance the budget in seven years. While President Clinton also professed a desire to eliminate annual deficits, he and Congress clashed over strategies and over what standard to apply to decide if the budget was likely to balance. Republicans favored sharper cuts in the rate at which Medicare, Medicaid, and various welfare and education programs would grow. Some of the savings from these cuts would be used to fund a tax cut. As negotiations struggled along, the president came to embrace most of the primary goals of the GOP. The Clinton administration, however, preferred less drastic cuts in the rate at which Medicare and other programs grew and also a less generous tax cut.

Since no one proposed that a balanced budget be achieved immediately, all sides relied on projections for the amounts to be raised in taxes and to be spent through the year 2002. President Clinton and his congressional allies preferred to use the more optimistic projections of his OMB, while Republicans relied on the more conservative estimates developed by the Congressional Budget Office.

President Clinton vetoed appropriations bills for FY 1996 designed to start the government down the road toward a Republican-style balanced budget. Despite widespread consensus among many partisanly neutral economists that something had to be done to curb federal health-care expenditures—and the sooner the better—President Clinton found that in late 1995 his public approval ratings rose as he flayed Congress for imperiling health care for the elderly. When a president who had never achieved broad-based popularity, and who was worried about reelection, confronted a congressional majority that believed that it had been sent to Washington to balance the budget, it was little wonder that agreement proved to be elusive. Both president and Congress believed that they were doing not just what was popular, but what was morally correct.

As with other legislation, appropriations bills passed by Congress need the president's approval to become law. Conventional wisdom once held that appropriations bills were "veto proof" because they provided the funds necessary to keep the government in operation. However, Presidents Richard M. Nixon and Gerald R. Ford both vetoed appropriations bills that they called "budget-busting" and inflationary because more funds were appropriated for some programs than the presidents wanted. These bills were later enacted into law after appropriations were reduced in an effort to meet presidential preferences. In 1995 and 1996, Bill Clinton vetoed appropriations bills that he believed cut social programs too severely.

The struggle between president and Congress ultimately closed parts of the government for extended periods in late 1995 and early 1996. When public opinion polls showed that Americans resented the shutdown and blamed Republicans, Congress relented and funded government programs for the rest of fiscal year 1996 at levels acceptable to President Clinton. As detailed in the previous chapter, a major restructuring of welfare programs was enacted in the summer of 1996.

The use of the budget as a part of fiscal policy to counteract fluctuations in the economy is handicapped by the fact that planning begins roughly a year and a half before the beginning of the fiscal year in which it is to take effect. Once a budget is adopted, it takes time to implement its provisions. Add to this the difficulty of predicting the future state of the economy and one discovers that the budget—which embodies changes in taxing and spending rates—is a rather blunt instrument for manipulating the economy.

For many years the budgetary process was a fragmented and disjointed operation. Appropriations and revenue decisions were considered separately by different committees. For purposes of congressional consideration and enactment, the president's budget was (and still is) divided into thirteen appropriations bills, each of which was handled by a different subcommittee of the House Appropriations Committee, where the most intensive examinations were accorded to budget requests. Each of the bills was also considered separately in the Senate Appropriations Committee. One by one the thirteen appropriations bills were eventually enacted into law. This disjointed process created two problems. First, it was difficult to establish spending priorities between domestic and military programs or among the many domestic programs. Second, the determination of total revenues and expenditures and, consequently, the size of the budget surplus or deficit was accidental, something that simply happened rather than being planned.

To provide itself with more control over the budget process, Congress initiated and enacted the Budget and Impoundment Control Act of 1974. The act establishes a budget process that includes setting overall levels of revenues and expenditures, the size of the budget surplus or deficit, and priorities among different "functional" areas (for example, national defense, transportation, agriculture, foreign aid, and health). New budget committees were established in the House and Senate to perform these tasks. The Congressional Budget Office (CBO), a professional staff of technical experts, was created to assist the budget committees and to provide members of Congress with their own source of budgetary information so they would be more independent of OMB.

The budget committees hold hearings on the president's proposed budget, soliciting advice from the OMB and CBO, executive agencies, and other members of Congress. The committees then formulate a concurrent budget resolution that set targets for overall levels of revenues and spending, and ceilings for each functional area in the budget. The budget resolution is supposed to be completed by April 15, although this deadline is often missed. Once the concurrent budget resolution is adopted (it does not require the president's approval), the House and Senate appropriations committees and their subcommittees are expected to act within its limits when making their decisions on the details of appropriations requests by various agencies. In most years reconciliation legislation is necessary to ensure that the revenue and spending targets in the budget resolution are actually met. The reconciliation process requires the taxation and legislative committees to propose changes in existing tax laws and entitlement programs, such as Medicare and food stamps. Typically, these changes involve cutting spending, although increasing taxes is an alternative. The budget committees then consolidate these proposed changes into a single reconciliation bill, which must be passed by both houses. Unlike the budget resolution, which is an internal congressional matter, the reconciliation bill requires presidential approval. Reconciliation legislation makes permanent changes in the laws involving the affected policies and programs. For instance, taxes may be increased or the benefits available under an entitlement program may be lowered.[32] Overall growth in both entitlements and discretionary spending are shown in Figure 18.4.

Legislative action on all appropriations bills is supposed to be completed by October 1, the start of the fiscal year. It is rare, however, for all appropriations bills to emerge from Congress by this date. For programs still unfunded at the start of the fiscal year, Congress can pass a continuing resolution, which authorizes agencies to continue operating on the basis of last year's appropriation until their new budget is approved. This procedure can cause some uncertainty in agency operations and when, as in 1995, president and Congress cannot agree, some programs may actually be shut down until terms for a continuing resolution can be worked out.

The budget process put into place in 1974 was intended to make the national budgetary process more rational, comprehensive, and coherent. To some extent it has done that. It has also compelled members of Congress to consider the overall dimensions of the budget and to directly confront the deficit. It has not, however, prompted Congress to balance the budget.

FIGURE 18.4

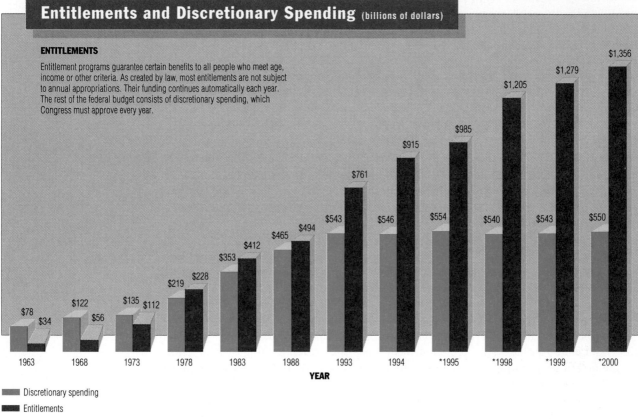

Entitlements and Discretionary Spending (billions of dollars)

ENTITLEMENTS

Entitlement programs guarantee certain benefits to all people who meet age, income or other criteria. As created by law, most entitlements are not subject to annual appropriations. Their funding continues automatically each year. The rest of the federal budget consists of discretionary spending, which Congress must approve every year.

Discretionary spending
Entitlements

*Projections

SOURCE: *United States Budget for Fiscal Year 1995*, (Washington D.C.: Government Printing Office, 1995), 173.

The Deficit and the Debt

Large annual budget deficits and a rapidly growing national debt (which is the cumulation of the annual budget deficits) have characterized government finance since the early 1980s. Several factors have contributed to this situation: a severe recession in the early 1980s; the large tax cut enacted in 1981; sharply increased spending for national defense during the 1980s; and continuously expanding spending on such entitlement programs as Social Security, Medicare, and Medicaid.[33] National budget deficits, which rarely exceeded $60 billion before 1980 and usually were much less than that, averaged $150 billion during the decade of the 1980s (see Table 18.1). These dollar figures have increased in part because of inflation. One way to control for inflation when comparing budget deficits is to view the deficits as a percentage of **gross domestic product (GDP).** (GDP is the total market value of all goods and services produced in the United States during a year.) During the 1960s the budget deficit typically was less than 1 percent of GDP, compared with between 3 percent and 5 percent of GDP during the 1980s. This comparison also reveals a major increase in absolute budget deficit levels.

gross domestic product (GDP): The total market value of all goods and services produced in a country during a year.

TABLE 18.1

National Government Finances, Selected Years, 1940–2000 (billions of current dollars)

YEAR	RECEIPTS	OUTLAYS	SURPLUS OR DEFICIT
1940	6.5	9.5	−2.9
1945	45.2	92.7	−47.6
1950	39.4	42.6	−3.1
1955	65.5	68.4	−3.0
1960	92.5	92.2	0.3
1965	116.8	118.2	−1.4
1970	192.8	195.6	−2.8
1975	279.1	332.3	−53.2
1980	517.1	590.9	−72.7
1985	734.1	946.4	−212.3
1988	909.0	1064.1	−155.2
1989	990.7	1143.2	−152.5
1990	1031.3	1252.7	−221.4
1991	1054.3	1323.8	−269.5
1992	1090.5	1380.9	−290.4
1993	1153.5	1408.2	−254.7
1994	1257.7	1460.9	−203.1
1995	1346.4	1538.9	−192.5
1996*	1415.5	1612.1	−196.7
1997*	1471.6	1684.7	−213.1
1998*	1548.8	1745.2	−196.4
1999*	1624.7	1822.2	−197.4
2000*	1710.9	1905.3	−194.4

*Estimates

Source: *United States Budget for Fiscal Year 1995* (Washington, D.C.: U.S. Government Printing Office, 1995), 14.

The national debt tripled during the 1980s. Standing at $909 billion in 1980, it soared beyond $2.87 trillion in 1989. (In 1996 the national debt was nearly $5 trillion.) Measured against GDP, the national debt increased from 34 to 55 percent of GDP during the 1980s (see Figure 18.5). Interest payments on the national debt now account for about 15 percent of the national budget. It may make the reader feel better to know that, while the national debt has grown, so has the value of the national government's assets—including land, buildings, military installations, and equipment. According to one calculation, the government's assets approximately equaled its liabilities in 1960; by 1980 assets exceeded liabilities by $279 billion.[34] But a massive selloff of assets is highly unlikely.

FIGURE 18.5

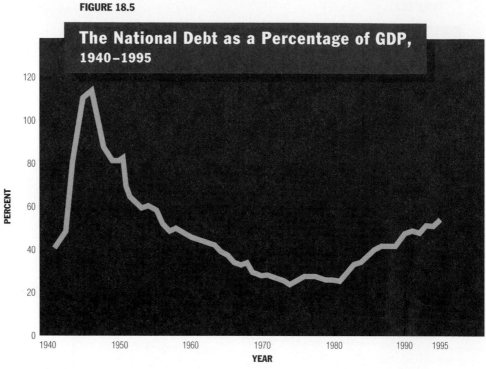

The National Debt as a Percentage of GDP, 1940–1995

NOTE: Figures reflect debt held by the public and do not include debt held by federal government accounts.

SOURCE: 1940–1992: Office of Management and Budget, *Budget Baselines, Historical Data, and Alternatives for the Future* (Washington D.C.: U.S. Government Printing Office, 1993), 1346. 1993–1998: Office of Management and Budget, *Budget of the U.S. Government Fiscal Year 1994* (Washington D.C.: U.S. Government Printing Office, 1993), 32., Statistical Abstracts of the United States (Washington D.C.: U.S. Government Printing Office, 1995), 333.

Strong partisan conflict and policy differences between the Democrats in Congress and the president during the Reagan administration over the size and composition of the budget made reduction of the budget deficit impossible through conventional budgetary procedures. The alarming size of the deficits and public concern over them pushed Congress into taking extraordinary action in 1985. Called "a bad idea whose time had come," the Balanced Budget and Emergency Deficit Reduction Act created a procedure for automatic deficit reduction. This act is better known as the Gramm–Rudman–Hollings Act after its three Senate sponsors—Phil Gramm (R–Tex.), Warren Rudman (R–N.H.), and Ernest Hollings (D–S.C.). There were three basic components to the act:

1. Budget deficit goals of $171.9 billion and $144 billion were set for 1986 and 1987. After that, the deficit goal would be lowered annually by $36 million decrements until it reached zero in 1991.

2. Several programs were exempted from automatic budget cuts, including Social Security, Medicaid, veterans' benefits, food stamps, Aid to Families with Dependent Children, child nutrition, and interest on the national debt.

3. If at the beginning of a fiscal year the deficit target was not met, then, by a process called sequestration (Congress seems to like these clumsy terms), automatic, across-the-board budget cuts, divided equally between nonexempt domestic and military programs, would be levied, sufficient to meet the deficit target.

Senators (left to right) Warren B. Rudman (R-N.H.), Phil Gramm (R-Tex.), and Ernest F. Hollings (D-S.C.), who cosponsored a 1985 law that attempted to control spiraling deficits. The budget process has proven very difficult to control, however, and their original statute was revised and superseded by the budget agreement of 1990. (Photo courtesy: UPI/Bettmann Archive)

In 1987 Congress and the Reagan administration were confronted with the need to reduce the deficit by $45 billion in order to meet the Gramm–Rudman–Hollings Act target. Most members of Congress found this disagreeable, as did the Reagan administration because of the required military spending cuts that would be required. Consequently, the act was amended to revise the budget deficit targets and make them easier to meet. The zero target date then became 1993, a year that, in reality, saw a deficit of $254.7 billion.

The Gramm–Rudman–Hollings Act did not accomplish much deficit reduction, although arguably budget deficits might have been larger had the act not been in effect. In this sense the act may have imposed some restraint. It was, however, possible for Congress to avoid the requirements of the act. Deficit targets set by Congress can be altered by Congress, as they were in 1987.

The Gramm–Rudman–Hollings Act was extensively revised and extended by the Budget Enforcement Act of 1990, which was negotiated by Bush administration officials and congressional leaders. As amended in 1993, the Budget Enforcement Act (BEA) runs through fiscal year 1998.[35] It seeks to lower deficits by imposing controls on spending. The BEA distinguishes between discretionary spending, which is controlled through annual appropriations, and direct spending, which is also called mandatory spending. Approximately two-thirds of national spending falls into the direct or mandatory category, with monies going mostly for entitlement programs and interest on the national debt.

Most likely, however, the BEA, or any similar effort, will not eliminate the budget deficit. Such approaches essentially involve an attempt to contrive a procedural solution for a substantive problem. The deficit exists because people in the United States like receiving the benefits and services of government programs more than they like paying taxes to finance them. Government officials reflect this ambivalence in their behavior. There is no easy, painless way to balance the budget, although the alternatives can be quickly stated: increase taxes, cut spending, or use a combination of the two. All the decision makers have to determine is which taxes to raise or which spending programs to cut. The difficulties in doing that account for the existing budget situation and continue to handicap the quest for a solution.

North—South

POLITICS AROUND THE WORLD

In these last two chapters, you will see one more way in which the United States is different from its neighbors and every other country—its international influence. Mexico and Canada are sovereign states that make their own policies. However, increasingly what they can do is shaped not by what happens in their legislatures or corporate boardrooms but what occurs outside their borders. At the top of any list of those outside influences are the actions of both the U.S. government and U.S.-based companies. There is no conscious attempt by Americans to take control of these two or other countries, but the evolution of the international economic and political (see the next chapter) systems has reinforced its de facto influence, along with that of the other rich and powerful states.

The Canadian economy has long been deeply under American influence. To be sure, it has its own industrial corporations, banks, and mines. However, for at least fifty years, it has been highly dependent on American capital and companies at home and on American markets for its exports. It has not been purely a one-way street. Subsidized Canadian fish and timber have undercut markets for domestic goods in New England. And successive Canadian governments have done far more to shape the domestic economy than their counterparts below the border, including, for example, aiding development in poorer parts of the country.

In recent years, however, Conservative and Liberal Party governments alike have reduced the federal government's role in steering the economy. Most notably, federal spending was cut by 20 percent between 1994 and 1996,

the federal workforce has been cut by 300,000, and all the signs are that the Canadian budget will be balanced by 1998. Although there are many domestic reasons why that has occurred, the most important force has been the need to make the economy more competitive now that Canada has entered into the North American Free Trade Agreement (NAFTA) with the United States, Mexico, and the broader World Trade Organization.

Economic shifts have been even more pronounced in Mexico. Until the early 1980s, Mexican governments pursued a policy known as *import substitution*, in which it used a combination of policies, including restrictions on foreign investment, state ownership and control of key industries, and economic planning, to help develop its own manufacturing industries. For a while those policies worked. However, by the late 1970s, the country found itself facing economic problems that could not be met—most notably its debt to foreign governments and banks, which at times topped $100 billion. As a result, the last three presidents have had little choice but to follow structural adjustment policies more in line with what those northern creditors want, including the privatization of industry, deregulation of the economy as a whole, and more openness to outside investment.

Outside (and not just American) influence is likely to grow as the provisions of two major international agreements take effect, establishing the World Trade Organization and NAFTA. These agreements will limit the ability of all countries, including the United States and Canada, to shape their own economic destinies. But they will hit relatively small and economically vulnerable countries like Mexico far harder.

THE ECONOMICS OF REGULATING ENVIRONMENTAL POLLUTION

A large number and variety of the national government's economic policies entail some sort of direct control of or restriction on private economic activity. These economic regulatory policies are variously intended to prevent or mitigate actions and conditions regarded as unfair, undesirable, unhealthy, and/or immoral. Collectively, they comprise an extensive framework of rules governing the conduct of private (and occasionally public) economic activity. Here, we focus on one important segment of this web of regulatory policies—regulation of environmental activity to protect the public health and the national environment.

Until the late 1960s, the national government was only minimally involved in the control of environmental pollution. The national government had long been concerned with the conservation of natural resources and the management of public lands—national forests, national parks, and grazing lands in the Western states. However, air and water pollution were seen as matters for the state and local governments to handle, if they so chose. But few states opted to do this—indeed, many states did little or nothing to control pollution in the pre-World War II decades of the twentieth century. Pollution was not perceived as a problem, partly because the environment had considerable capacity to absorb wastes without great harm to people. Also, the volume of pollution was lower than it would become in later years.

Population growth, increased urbanization, industrialization, and the extensive production and use of chemicals after World War II changed this situation. In the course of the 1960s, the problem of environmental pollution became a prominent item on the national political agenda. Because of strong public concern about environmental pollution it continues to have that status.

Pollution involves the discharge into the environment of harmful and noxious substances—chemicals, human and animal waste, and other contaminants—that prevent or interfere with desired human uses of the air, water, and soil. Chemicals discharged into streams, for example, make them unsafe as sources of drinking water or for recreational purposes. (The fish often don't fare too well, either.) Because this definition of pollution hinges on *human* use (which is not limited to consumption of environmental resources), it implies that desirable levels of environmental quality will depend on preferred uses. Thus the quality of water that should be maintained in a given river depends on whether it is to be used as a source of drinking water or for fishing and swimming, transportation, or waste disposal. Much cleaner water is required for the river if it is used as a source of drinking water than primarily as a medium of transportation. The levels of water quality required for particular uses can be scientifically determined (although in practice scientists often disagree); whether a particular level of quality *should* be sought is a political issue over which various prospective users of our hypothetical river disagree.

Pollution interferes with human uses of the environment in various ways. Pollution may make the air unsafe to breathe, especially for people with respiratory ailments, or water unsafe to drink. Bodies of water may become unsafe or uninhabitable for fish populations for human consumption. Lake Erie, for example, became nearly a "dead" body of water in the 1970s because of industrial pollution. Damage to forest, crops, and property may occur from pollution. Natural curiosities may be damaged, and scenic vistas may be obscured. In the 1980s air pollution often made it impossible to see across the Grand Canyon. Because Americans seem health conscious, the effects of pollution on human health often attract the greatest attention from policy makers.

Environmental Policy Making

Pollution control is the responsibility of government operating through the policy process. The market, which works through competition and the price system, is unable to deal satisfactorily with the problem of pollution. As economists tell us, pollution is an *externality,* or a *social cost* of industrial activity. This is so because, in the nature of things, air and water are "free" or public goods. Industries can dispose of wastes (pollutants) at low or no cost by emitting them into the air or dumping them into nearby bodies of water.

Consequently, the costs of waste disposal are borne by the people adversely affected by the wastes, for example, by people who breathe the air or use the water. Because the costs of waste disposal do not need to be considered in determining the prices of products, industries can sell—and consumers can buy—products at lower prices. A business has no incentive to clean up its pollutants because this action would drive up its expenses and thus the prices it charges. Moreover, if a business did clean up its pollutants, this would put it at an economic disadvantage with competitors who chose not to withstand the costs of pollution reduction. Consequently, in the absence of government action, control of pollution is unlikely to occur.

The organized groups supporting environmental protection have greatly increased in number, membership size, technical skill, and political sophistication since the early 1970s. Such well-known groups as the Wilderness Society, the Sierra Club, the National Wildlife Federation, the Environmental Defense Fund, and the Natural Resources Defense Council constitute the core of the environmental movement. They are flanked on the left by more radical groups, such as Earth First! and Greenpeace, who take direct action to protect the environment.[36] On the right, the Nature Conservancy works through the marketplace, buying land valuable for natural resource protection and thus removing it from business use. These and other environmental groups have been major forces pushing Congress to enact new environmental legislation and to strengthen existing laws. During the years of the Reagan administration, which was skeptical toward environmental and pollution control programs, environmental groups thrived.

Environmental groups have also benefited from strong public opinion in support of pollution control. Conflicts over pollution control legislation typically become a struggle between liberal environmental groups and their supporters (organized labor usually takes a pro-pollution-control stance) and business groups and conservatives favoring fewer or less costly pollution controls. Pollution controls are often quite costly and, on the basis of the principle that "the polluter pays," most of the financial and other costs of complying with them fall initially on the business community. Thus Bush administration officials estimated that the costs of complying with the Clean Air Act of 1990 would run more than $20 billion annually.[37] Pollution controls, by increasing the costs of doing business, may also discourage economic growth and job creation, or so it is frequently argued. Environmental groups want the strongest legislation possible. Business and economic development groups usually do not oppose all controls; rather, they favor controls that will be less stringent, intrusive, and costly to business. This is a politically more viable policy position than total opposition. As one would expect, resulting legislation usually reflects compromise between the environmental and business perspectives. An exception was the Clean Air Act of 1970, which called for a 90 percent reduction in automobile emissions and strong controls on industrial pollution. Driven by exceptionally strong public support for environmental protection, which was highlighted by the first Earth Day (April 22, 1970), this legislation became stronger as it moved through Congress.[38]

Since 1970 Congress has enacted a large volume of pollution control legislation intended to help clean up the nation's air and water and to regulate the disposal of hazardous and toxic wastes. A brief summary of the major laws is presented here.[39]

■ *Clean Air Act.* This statute directs the Environmental Protection Agency to set standards for motor vehicle emissions, ambient air quality, hazardous air pollutants, and new sources of pollution; to prevent significant deterioration of air quality in clean air areas; to reduce stratospheric ozone depletion; and to control acid rain through an emissions trading system.

■ *Clean Water Act.* This law creates a federal grant program to help finance sewage treatment plant construction, authorizes technological standards to reduce water pollution, and establishes programs to control non-point source pollution, such as runoff from parking lots and livestock feedlots.

■ *Safe Drinking Water Act.* This act provides for drinking water standards to protect public health, the regulation of underground waste injection, and control of water contaminants.

■ *Toxic Substances Control Act.* This act authorizes testing of chemicals and regulation of their use in order to protect health and the environment.

■ *Resource Conservation and Recovery Act.* This statute provides a cradle-to-grave system of regulation for hazardous substances and waste, as well as a control program for underground storage tanks, such as those at gasoline stations.

■ *Comprehensive Environmental Response, Compensation, and Liability Act.* Commonly referred to as Superfund, this statute creates a fund from taxes levied on polluters to pay the costs of cleaning up abandoned hazardous waste sites.

■ *Federal Insecticide, Fungicide, and Rodenticide Act.* This statute calls for EPA registration and regulation of the use of pesticides.

■ *National Environmental Policy Act.* This act requires agencies taking actions that will have a major impact on the environment to prepare environmental impact statements (EISs), which are subject to review by the EPA.

■ *Pollution Prevention Act.* This act stipulates that the prevention of pollution shall be an EPA priority and authorizes actions for reducing the sources of pollution.

Responsibility for the implementation of these laws rests primarily with the Environmental Protection Agency, to which we now turn.

The Environmental Protection Agency

The Environmental Protection Agency (EPA) was created in 1970 by Congress at the urging of President Richard M. Nixon. A number of environmental programs previously located in five executive departments were vested in the EPA, which is an independent agency (that is, the agency is located outside of the executive departments) that reports directly to the president. The EPA administrator is appointed by the president, with the approval of the Senate. Efforts to make the EPA an executive department, which would enhance its clout both within the government and in its dealings with other countries, are unlikely to succeed in the current climate where Republicans, eager to make government smaller, seek to eliminate some existing departments.

The EPA is the nation's largest regulatory agency. In 1996 it had approximately 18,000 employees located in Washington and in ten regional offices throughout the country. Its annual budget for operations was around $2.6 billion dollars. Although this may seem like a lot of money and employees, it really is not—given the extensive research, rule-making, and implementation duties assigned to the EPA under the statutes listed above, plus many other lesser statutes, such as some relating to ocean dumping of medical and other wastes. In fact, the EPA's budget has not grown proportionately as the duties assigned to it have multiplied in recent years. Consequently, it lacks the resources necessary to enforce adequately all of the legislation over which it has jurisdiction.

The activities of the EPA can be conveniently grouped under the headings of research, rule-making, and enforcement. The agency has to perform much research on the effects of various pollutants on human health and the natural environment in order to provide an evidentiary basis for its rule-making. The expectation is that EPA rules will be supported by substantial evidence; hunches and fragments of evidence will not do. Rules are necessary to convert the goals and requirements of pollution control legislation into standards and specifications that can be implemented. For example, the Clean Air Act directs the EPA to set ambient air standards (ambient air is air that circulates around us) for such pollutants as carbon dioxide, ozone, and lead that will provide an "adequate margin of safety" to protect public health. The standards, stated in terms of parts per million, are enforced against potential polluters.

State pollution control agencies, with the cooperation and supervision of EPA regional offices, do much of the actual enforcement work. Pollution control enforcement is thus basically a two-step process. The EPA must induce state agencies to act in appropriate ways, and the state agencies must then secure compliance from the companies and individuals to whom the pollution standards apply. There is often considerable slippage in both steps of the process.

There have been three major eras in the political life of the EPA.[40] The first era, which extended through the 1970s, was characterized by growth in the EPA's budget, increase in the number of employees, expansion of its legislative authority, and substantial efforts to gain compliance with pollution control standards, both through legal enforcement and voluntary compliance. The second era began with the inception of the Reagan administration in 1981 and lasted through 1983. Opposed to strong pollution control programs, the Reagan administration appointed people to top-level EPA positions who were hostile or indifferent to its goals. Substantial cuts were made in the agency's budget and personnel, and it became demoralized.

The third era began in late 1983 and continues to the present. The EPA's budget and personnel levels have been restored. Enforcement activity has been strengthened, but it features "explicit efforts to balance environmental protection against its economic costs." The Republican majority in the 104th Congress mistrusted the EPA, which like other regulators, was often thought to be overly zealous in enforcement. Republican enthusiasm for weakening environmental standards abated in the face of polls showing that most Americans want to protect the environment.

Two environmental problems of concern in recent years are the disposal of hazardous and toxic wastes and the control of acid rain. An examination of each problem can highlight both the difficulties and politics of protecting the environment.

Hazardous and Toxic Wastes. Hazardous substances are toxic, corrosive, ignitable, or chemically reactive materials that present threats to human beings or the environment. Toxic substances, which are a smaller category, produce "detrimental effects in living organisms."[41] Most chemical substances are not considered harmful either to people or to the environment, but more than a few are. People are most concerned about carcinogenic substances. The increase in the production and use of chemicals in the twentieth century has contributed importantly to a higher standard of living in the United States, but not without social costs. Safe disposal of waste chemicals is a major problem. Whether emitted into the air, injected into the ground, dumped into bodies of water, or incinerated, chemicals still pose risks to human health and to the environment; many people find these risks intolerable.

National policy to control hazardous wastes takes three approaches. The Toxic Substances Control Act (1976) takes the preventive approach. The act is designed to regulate the manufacture and distribution of toxic substances in order to identify hazardous chemicals and keep them out of the environment. The EPA is authorized to suspend production of a chemical permanently when it has "a reasonable basis to conclude that the chemical will present an unreasonable risk of injury to the health of the environment."

The Resource Conservation and Recovery Act (1976) is focused on ensuring the safe disposal of hazardous wastes currently being produced. The EPA is directed to develop criteria for environmentally safe hazardous-waste disposal sites and for identifying hazardous wastes. The EPA is also authorized to create a "manifest system" (receipts) that would permit tracking hazardous wastes from their points of origin to their final, safe disposal. This "cradle-to-grave" regulation was intended to eliminate "midnight dumping" and other unsafe forms of waste disposal. In 1984 amendments to the act provided for the elimination of leaking underground storage tanks, such as might be found at gasoline stations. If their enforcement programs meet national standards, state agencies can implement these regulations.

In 1980 Congress enacted the Comprehensive Environmental Response, Compensation, and Liability Act, commonly referred to as Superfund, to provide for the cleanup of abandoned hazardous waste sites, of which there are tens of thousands in the United States. One such site was Love Canal, near Niagara Falls in upstate New York. In the 1940s and 1950s, the Hooker Chemical Company used the dry canal bed as a disposal site for hazardous chemical wastes. The canal was then covered with a layer of earth and later donated as a site for a public school and homes. In the 1970s chemicals began to ooze to the surface, and noxious fumes entered people's homes. Adults and children suffered from a variety of medical ailments. These occurrences led to a major controversy and to the eventual evacuation of people from the area. In time the site was cleaned up at a cost of more than $300 million. In the 1980s people began moving back into the area.

The Love Canal disaster contributed to Congress's hurried enactment of the Superfund legislation in late 1980. The EPA was directed to compile a National Priority List (NPL) of hazardous waste sites urgently in need of cleanup. If the responsible parties could not be located or failed to clean up a site, the EPA would do so. A Hazardous Substance Response Fund, financed mostly by a tax on oil, chemical, and other industries, was set up to pay the costs of cleaning up hazardous waste sites. Subsequent amendments have increased the size of the Superfund to more than $15 billion.

Superfund cleanups have been slow and tedious because of problems in determining financial liability for cleaning up waste sites (which often entails much litigation), in deciding how clean each site must be, and in designing and carrying out remedial work. By early 1994, out of the 1,345 sites placed on the NPL, only 56 had been fully cleaned up; another 168 sites were nearly cleaned up.[42] Given the complexity of this task, the EPA's record is better than the numbers indicate because on only a few of the NPL sites has no action been taken.

Acid Rain. Acid rain is a by-product of the consumption of fossil fuels, especially high-sulfur coal.[43] Acid rain (or acid deposition, which is the more descriptive term) occurs when sulfur and nitrogen oxides combine with water vapor in the atmosphere and later fall to earth as rain, snow, mist, or as particulate matter. The acidity of the precipitation can harm both fish and plant populations. Fish, for instance, cannot live in highly acidic lakes.

Acid rain did not become a major environmental issue until the early 1980s. It was not recognized as a problem in 1970, when the Clean Air Act was adopted. Indeed, tall smokestacks (200 to 800 feet in height) built at coal-burning electric utility plants in the Midwest and elsewhere contributed to the problem. These smokestacks spewed sulfur and nitrogen oxides higher into the atmosphere, which improved the quality of ambient air in their vicinity and helped localities comply with air quality standards under the Clean Air Act. These smokestacks also increased the likelihood that these pollutants would fall to earth somewhere downwind.[44] The sulfur and nitrogen oxides emitted by electric utility plants, particularly in the Midwest, fall to earth as acid rain in the Northeastern states and in Eastern Canada.

The Reagan administration delayed taking regulatory action on acid rain on the grounds that more research was needed to better understand its causes and consequences. Electric utility companies, high-sulfur coal producers, and other businesses endorsed this point of view. As research findings accumulated, however, it became increasingly clear that action on the acid rain problem was necessary. Action of some kind became a near certainty in early 1989, when President George Bush, who said he wanted to be the "environmental president," called for major amendments to the Clean Air Act, including action on acid rain.

The Clean Air Act Amendments of 1990 provided for a major reduction in the emission of sulfur dioxide, the prime component of acid raid, by electric utility plants. As part of the strategy to control acid rain, the act authorized an emissions trading system. Each of the 110 electric utility plants named in the act, most of which are located in the Midwest, was allocated a specified number of "allowables." Effective in 1995 an allowable authorizes a utility plant to discharge legally one ton of sulfur dioxide. In the year 2000, more stringent limitations on sulfur dioxide emissions will be phased in. If a company reduces its emissions below its specified level by burning low-sulfur coal, installing smokestack scrubbers, or using other pollution control methods, it can "bank" its excess allowables or sell them to other utility companies. A company that exceeds its specified limit and does not buy allowables to cover its excess emissions is subject to heavy fines. The Chicago Board of Trade, a large commodity exchange, has been authorized by the EPA to establish a market for the purchase and sale of sulfur dioxide allowables.

Economists have argued that the use of economic incentives, as in an emissions trading system, would be more effective in controlling pollution than is the traditional standard setting and enforcement pattern of regulation.[45] The argument runs economic incentives will provide companies with positive motivation—the pursuit of their self-interest—to reduce the discharge of pollutants. Whether the emissions trading system for acid rain reduction will be successful remains to be seen. If it is, its success will encourage wider use of economic incentives as a regulatory device, whether to control pollution or for other purposes.

The 104th Congress and Environmental Protection

Two objectives of the Republican-controlled 104th Congress clashed with environmentalists' policy goals. Republican efforts to cut the budget and to eliminate federal regulations posed threats to the enforcement powers of the EPA and the operation of the Superfund. The belief that environmental protection was under attack provoked spirited Democratic opposition that won over greater numbers of Republican legislators as 1995 wore on.

A Democratic-led bipartisan coalition turned aside Republican efforts to amend the appropriations bill to prohibit the EPA from issuing new regulations on discharges such as arsenic levels in water. Nor was Congress able to agree on a budget proposal that would have cut EPA funds by a fifth. Efforts to revamp the Superfund also stalled, although revenues for the Superfund fell victim to the squabble between President Clinton and Congress. A consequence of the president's budget veto was that the tax used to fund the cleanup of hazardous dump sites expired at the end of 1995.

Early in 1996, Speaker Newt Gingrich (R–Ga.) expressed concern that his party had mishandled environmental policy in 1995. As the head of the Atlanta zoo observed, "We don't trust Democrats with a checkbook. We don't trust the Republicans with the environment."[46] Realizing that this view might be widespread, Gingrich and moderate fellow partisans feared that if Democrats painted the GOP as a party ready to rape the environment, a number of Republicans narrowly elected in 1994 might be turned out when seeking second terms. An anti-environmental label was pinned on the GOP when GOP House Whip Tom Delay (R–Tex.) referred to the EPA as "the Gestapo." Survey data indicating that at least 60 percent of the public supports strict controls to regulate what goes into the nation's air and water suggested the wisdom of Gingrich's plans to chart a moderate course.[47] Thus, in the policy area of the environment, as in many others, the ideals on which Republicans ran in 1994 clash with reality once they set out to implement their ideals.

CHANGING AMERICAN ECONOMIC POLICY

*I*n the area of economic policy, the national budget deficit has been the nation's primary problem, drawing the most attention from reformers in recent years. Although budget deficits have long been a nagging concern, their huge size since the early 1980s has stimulated intensified efforts to cope with them. Public opinion polls reveal that a substantial majority of people in the United States favor a balanced national budget.

A recently adopted reform gives the president a line-item veto on appropriations legislation. President Ronald Reagan sometimes stated that if Congress would give him the line-item veto, which would allow him to veto specific portions of a bill without rejecting the bill in its entirety, he would balance the budget. Four-fifths of the state governors do possess line-item veto authority. This power makes it difficult for state legislators to slip favored projects or programs past the governor by tucking them into general appropriations bills.

A frequently debated proposal that has not been adopted is an amendment to the U.S. Constitution requiring that each year's budget be balanced. The proposal was part of the Contract with America. Believed to hold out the prospect for reducing the deficit, these reforms received high priority treatment from Republicans in the 104th Congress.[48]

The balanced budget proposal, designed as an amendment to the Constitution, called on the president to draw up an annual budget in which expenditures did not exceed revenues and stipulated that the consent of two-thirds of the members of both houses would be necessary before Congress could adopt a budget that contained a deficit. During wartime, a deficit could be approved with a simple majority in each chamber. The constitutional amendment proposed in early 1995 also provided that bills to increase taxes would need the support of 60 percent of the representatives and senators. This last provision proved to be a sticking point in the House and was dropped from the proposed amendment to secure enough Democratic votes to obtain the support of two-thirds of the membership, as required for constitutional amendments.

The Senate failed to follow suit. On March 2, 1995, the proposed amendment came up one vote short as Oregon's Mark Hatfield, the only Republican to oppose the proposal, voted nay.

Some of the enthusiasm for amending the Constitution evident in early 1995 has waned. During congressional debate, Democrats warned that holding expenditures to the level of revenues would endanger popular programs such as Medicare and aid to education. Moreover, having a constitutional requirement that budgets be balanced would not alleviate pressures to pursue programs to bring money into individual member's districts. If Congress gave in and approved pork barrel legislation for highways, river and harbor improvements, and research grants to universities, and these resulted in a deficit, would the president veto the proposals? If the president joined Congress in approving more expenditures than taxes, the courts would be called in to determine how to implement the balanced budget amendment. Some people thought that the courts should not be placed in that position.

Passage of the line-item veto was less ambitious than the balanced budget amendment, since giving the president the ability to wield the veto as a stiletto rather than as a meat axe will not guarantee the elimination of deficits. The line-item veto allows the president to remove from appropriations or revenue bills specific projects or exceptions. Financially unsound but politically popular projects can be culled from legislation without having to kill an entire bill. Thus, questionable local projects—such as a park dedicated to steam engines in the district of a powerful Pennsylvania representative, or weapons systems no longer wanted by the Department of Defense—can be cut out by the president even if they survived a favor-trading Congress. Appropriations bills, sometimes referred to as Christmas tree bills because they include funding for projects in so many congressional districts, have rarely been vetoed by a president because it can usually be rationalized that the legislation does more good than harm. Now that the president has the line-item veto, legislation loaded up with pork-barrel projects may get closer scrutiny.

The interest in the line-item veto as a vehicle of reining in the budget and a balanced budget amendment are but the latest in a continuing search for structural changes that will enable the federal government to do what Congress already has the power to do. If a majority in Congress were committed to ending deficit financing, all it has to do is to cut spending, raise taxes, or some combination of the two actions. Both alternatives are painful. No one wants to pay higher taxes; and what some view as wasteful pork barrel projects, others see as worthy investments. The choices are not easy, but there are no other ways to bring revenues and expenditures into balance.

SUMMARY

The nature and role of the government in the economy, especially the national government, have changed significantly since colonists first came to America in the 1600s. In analyzing these developments, this chapter has made the following points:

1. Roots of Government Intervention in the Economy.

Efforts by the national government to regulate the economy began with antimonopoly legislation. Under President Franklin D. Roosevelt, the interventionist state replaced the *laissez-faire* state. After World War II, many areas of economic policy were well settled. Full employment, employee–employer relations, and social regulation became new concerns of government. Even before social regulation began to ebb, economic deregulation, which involves the reduction in the entry, rate, and other controls, emerged as an attractive political issue.

2. Stabilizing the Economy.

The national government continues to shape monetary policy by regulating the nation's money supply and interest rates. Monetary policy is controlled by the Federal Reserve Board. Fiscal policy, which involves the deliberate use of the national government's taxing and spending policies, is another tool of the national government and involves the president and Congress setting the national budget. Although the budget is initially suggested by the president, Congress has asserted itself in the process. Despite efforts to control the national budget, annual deficits have led to a growing national debt and thus to calls for major budgetary reform.

3. The Economics of Regulating Environmental Pollution.

The environment is one area in which the national government has used its economic regulatory powers to alter business practices. Conflicts over environmental regulation frequently pit the business community against environmental groups. The Environmental Protection Agency (EPA), which was created as an independent agency, is the nation's largest regulatory agency.

4. Changing American Economic Policy.

The huge national debt has led many people to suggest reforms in economic policy. Chief among these have been calls for a line-item veto and a constitutional amendment to require a balanced budget.

KEY TERMS

business cycle, p. 688

discount rate, p. 704

economic regulation, p. 696

economic stability, p. 700

fiscal policy, p. 695

gross domestic product, p. 712

inflation, p. 700

interventionist state, p. 691

laissez-faire, p. 688

monetary policy, p. 701

money, p. 701

open market operations, p. 704

recession, p. 700

reserve requirement, p. 704

social regulation, p. 696

SELECTED READING

Bailey, Stephen. *Congress Makes a Law: The Story Behind the Employment Act of 1946.* New York: Columbia University Press, 1950.

Bryner, Gary C. *Blue Skies, Green Politics: The Clean Air Act of 1990.* Washington, D.C.: CQ Press, 1993.

Conlan, Timothy J., Margaret T. Wrightson, and David R. Beam. *Taxing Choices: The Politics of Tax Reform.* Washington, D.C.: CQ Press, 1990.

Derthick, Martha, and Paul J. Quirk. *The Politics of Deregulation.* Washington, D.C.: Brookings Institution, 1985.

Eisner, Marc Allen. *Regulatory Politics in Transition.* Baltimore: Johns Hopkins University Press, 1993.

Harr, Johnathan. *A Civil Action.* New York: Random House, 1995.

Hughes, Jonathan R. T. *The Governmental Habit,* 2d ed. Princeton, NJ: Princeton University Press, 1991.

Kettl, Donald F. *Deficit Politics: Public Budgeting in Its Institutional and Historical Context.* New York: Macmillan, 1992.

Pfiffner, James P., ed. *The President and Economic Policy.* Philadelphia: Institute for the Study of Human Issues, 1986.

Regens, James L., and Robert W. Rycroft. *The Acid Rain Controversy.* Pittsburgh: University of Pittsburgh Press, 1988.

Rosenbaum, Walter A. *Environmental Politics and Policy,* 2d ed. Washington, D.C.: CQ Press, 1991.

Switzer, Jacqueline Vaughn. *Environmental Politics: Domestic and Global Dimension.* New York: St. Martin's, 1994.

Wilson, James Q., ed. *The Politics of Regulation.* New York: Basic Books, 1980.

Woolley, John T. *Monetary Politics: The Federal Reserve and the Politics of Monetary Policy.* London: Cambridge University Press, 1984.

Young, James Harvey. *Pure Food: Securing the Federal Food and Drugs Act of 1906.* Princeton, NJ: Princeton University Press, 1990.

(Photo courtesy: Robert E. Daemmrich/Tony Stone Images)

DEFEAT NAFTA

DON'T LET CORPORATE AMERICA TAKE U.S. JOBS TO MEXICO

FOREIGN AND MILITARY POLICY

On April 12, 1996, Jim Hill, a Ford assembly plant manager in Atlanta, was surrounded by an unusual mixture of labor and management leaders from the U.S. auto industry, bipartisan Congressional delegations, and President Clinton and senior administration officials. Hill explained his team's goal: "the day when our Taurus is in Japan's top ten."[1] Since October 1995 Hill's 2,800 person team had been building a new version of the Taurus with the steering wheel on the right-hand side of the car, designed specifically to appeal to Japanese consumers. Parked outside the White House were seventeen right-hand steering autos—including the Ford Taurus, the GM Cavalier, the Chrysler Neon—which many speakers that day saw as a major step in redressing the imbalance in U.S.–Japanese trade over the next two years. As Jim Hill saw it, these cars meant "more exports, more sales, more job opportunities, and greater job security" for auto workers and others associated with the U.S. auto industry. Jim Hill closed by thanking the administration for its efforts to bring new trade opportunities for his team, and calling President Clinton a "car guy."

The event celebrated the results of the first six months of the U.S.–Japan Auto and Auto Parts Agreement, which included a one-third increase in the export of autos and auto parts to Japan. An increased emphasis on foreign economic policy characterized the early years of the first Clinton administration, especially in its relations with Asian countries. A priority in overall administration economic strategy was to open more foreign markets to U.S. products as a means of creating and sustaining high-paying jobs for U.S. workers. The principal method for achieving this objective was engaging in more negotiations with other governments to ensure better access for U.S. goods and services. More so than prior administrations, U.S. negotiators were likely to threaten to close U.S. markets to foreign goods to achieve agreements tied to numerical increases in exports and market shares. Many in Congress share this view that the United States needs a new strategy that emphasizes economic goals in light of the end of the Cold War. Opening hearings in November 1995 on how the United States could stay competitive in world markets, Representative Toby Roth (R–Wisc.) set the tone: "In today's world—and tomorrow's—our national security depends more on our economic strength than our military might."[2]

If economic strength is more important than military might after the Cold War, then the main rivals for the United States may not be military or ideological, as they were in the Cold War, but commercial and economic, including Japan and the European Union. In the 1996 primary campaign, an early casualty was Senator Richard Lugar (R–Ind.), who often focused on nonproliferation and military security issues. Candidates such as Steve Forbes and Pat Buchanan, who emphasized economic issues, got much interest. Similarly, economic issues dominated the 1994 "Contract with America"; and the 1992 Clinton campaign (with the theme, "It's the economy, stupid"). By 1996 more than half the House members had been elected since the end of the Cold War, when the threat of global war and nuclear annihilation had diminished.

In this chapter we expand on these themes as we look at the following issues:

- First, we review the concept of *grand strategy* in foreign policy, and what kind of priorities governments adopt.

- Second, we examine *the roots of modern U.S. foreign and military policy* by seeing how policy evolved as America slowly became a world power.

- Third, we focus on *the expanding global role of the United States* by studying U.S. policies during the Cold War.

- Fourth, we discuss *the machinery of modern foreign policy* by examining the role of various departments and agencies in shaping policy and the key role of the president.

- Fifth, we explore the *challenges to the president's power* by seeing how Congress, the press, the public, and the bureaucracy place limits on the president.

- Finally, we look at the development of *a new grand strategy* for foreign policy into the twenty-first century as the old issues of the Cold War are replaced by new foreign and military issues, including proliferation of nuclear weapons, promoting the spread of democracy, and preserving a healthy global environment.

Not everyone holds the belief that economic concerns should outweigh military security issues in U.S. foreign policy (see Politics Now: China as Partner, China as Rival). Despite the enormous economic costs involved, for example, Senator John McCain (R–Ariz.) and former Senator Larry Pressler (R–S.D.) have called for harsher economic sanctions against the People's Republic of China (PRC) for the export of Chinese nuclear and missile technology to Iran and Pakistan. Many have pointed to human rights abuses and threats against Taiwan as further reasons to take action against the PRC. Regional security, if not global peace, seems threatened by conflicts old and new: ethnic, political, racial, and religious violence, as in Bosnia, Chechnya, Kashmir, Mexico, Northern Ireland, Rwanda, and Sri Lanka; territorial disputes between countries, as in the South China Sea and dozens of other places; the development of nuclear, chemical, or biological arsenals in Iran, Iraq, Libya, North Korea, and more than thirty other states; and the use of weapons of mass destruction by nongovernment groups such as Aum Shinrikyo in Japan.

Even if one accepts that economic concerns are of primary importance to U.S. national security, it's not clear what policies should be adopted. Patrick Buchanan's "America First" theme, for example, stresses protecting the United States by erecting barriers to foreign trade and immigration. This parallels arguments made by Democrats like Dick Gephardt (D–Mo.), U.S. labor unions like the United Auto Workers, and disgruntled independents like Ross Perot. Most of the 1994 freshman class of Republi-

Politics Now

China as Partner, China as Rival

The economic and political relationships between the United States and the People's Republic of China (PRC) are complex. The PRC began to move toward a more market-oriented economy in 1978. Since then, it has doubled its gross domestic product (GDP) roughly every eight years and the economy shows few signs of slowing. In 1995 U.S. companies invested nearly $5.5 billion in the PRC. It is the fifth largest trading partner of the United States. Thousands of students from the PRC attend universities and colleges in the United States, while country music CDs, Nike shoes, and Coca-Cola products fill Chinese urban markets.

Nonetheless, the PRC remains sharply at odds with the United States on many issues. The PRC received the worst possible score for support for political rights and civil liberties in Freedom House's 1996 global survey. Chinese companies, perhaps with government support, have sold dangerous nuclear, chemical, and missile technologies to Pakistan, Iran, and other rogue nations. In March 1996 the PRC held military exercises and used missiles near Taiwan. The PRC meant to dissuade the people of the Republic of China (Taiwan) from voting for Lee Teng-hui in Taiwan's

first free presidential election (Lee won by a large margin anyway). Widespread pirating of Western CDs and name brand clothing, and other violations of standard commercial and financial practices (and a $34 billion trade surplus), have kept the United States from supporting Chinese integration into various world economic institutions, such as the World Trade Organization.

Refusing to grant China permanent most-favored-nation trade status would hurt the PRC relatively more than the United States. For example, about one-third of all Chinese exports go to the United States, while only 2 percent of U.S. exports go to the PRC. Still, many U.S. companies would lose huge sales to foreign competitors because of U.S. sanctions. Imposing sanctions on the PRC on every issue from human rights to trade also risks increasing a dangerous sense of isolation and alienation from the world community among Chinese leaders. Well into the next century, the U.S. government will grapple with finding appropriate policies for a country that may be neither a full partner nor a committed rival.

As China and other countries such as Brazil, India, Indonesia, or Turkey, emerge as great powers in the next century, how should the United States respond? Should the United States try to contain the military strength of these countries? Should we ally with them? Can we ignore them?

can House members viewed the North American Free Trade Agreement (NAFTA) or the $20 billion loan package to Mexico as threats to U.S. sovereignty or the U.S. economy. The new World Trade Organization, which manages multilateral negotiations to reduce barriers to trade and settle trade disputes between nations, has drawn particular wrath from those who favor isolationist or unilateralist strategies. In contrast, from President Clinton to Speaker Newt Gingrich, many Democrats and Republicans see free trade policies and free trade agreements as essential to U.S. economic growth.

The arguments over the relative importance of economics and military security or what kind of foreign economic policy is appropriate for the United States are not new.

For hundreds of years, governments have struggled with how to pursue both power and plenty.[3] From 1500 to 1800, mercantilism dominated the beliefs and actions of most policy makers around the world. Mercantilists advocated policies to limit imports to achieve a trade surplus (more exports than imports). Similarly, modern critics of U.S. trade policy point to the sustained and large overall U.S. trade deficit (where imports exceeded exports by $111 billion in 1995), and the trade deficit with Japan in particular ($59 billion in 1995) as a sign that the United States needs to place more restrictions on imports, or at least get more access for our exports through government trade negotiations.

A revolution of ideas began with the publication of Adam Smith's attack on mercantilism, *The Wealth of Nations*, in 1776. Smith demonstrated how barriers to international trade hurt rather than helped a nation's economy (Smith made exceptions for trade barriers that protected the military might of a nation or temporarily helped avoid economic injury to a large number of workers). These ideas of free trade, much like the notions of political liberty that drove Americans to contest British rule, became the basis for classical and modern trade theory on which many, if not most, countries base their trade policies. Most U.S. free trade advocates point out that U.S. exporters are now highly competitive, unlike a few years ago, and that the high trade deficit is a function of the U.S. economy growing much more rapidly than most of our major trading partners, particularly Japan and Germany in recent years. Even so, U.S. exports grew over 14 percent in 1995, reaching a record value of $575 billion. Free trade advocates argue that adopting protectionist policies would merely invite other countries to raise barriers on U.S. exports. Exports support the jobs of more than 11 million U.S. workers, along with nearly one-third of all the new U.S. jobs created in 1995. From this perspective, Joseph Gorman, CEO of TRW, argues that "protectionism now would be little short of insane."[4]

GRAND STRATEGY

grand strategy: The choices a government makes to balance and apply its economic, military, diplomatic, and other national resources to preserve their people and territory.

During the Cold War, the United States focused almost exclusively on balancing the military threat posed by the Soviet Union. With the end of the Cold War, the Soviet military threat is no longer a plausible rationale for public policy. For the first time in more than four decades, Americans are engaging in a wide-ranging debate about grand strategy. **Grand strategy** refers to the choices a government makes to balance and apply their economic, military, diplomatic, and other national resources to preserve its people and territory.[5] Grand strategy need not be planned, public, or explicit, but it often is in the United States. It is also often controversial, as when the Department of Defense considered a new proposal for its defense policy guidance early in the first Clinton administration. The draft plan called on the United States to deter "potential competitors from even aspiring to a larger regional or global role," including current allies like Japan or members of the European Union.[6] When the plan was leaked to the press, the harsh public response helped the Pentagon drop the goal of seeking and preserving U.S. global dominance. Instead, the United States has sought to work with Japan and the European Union to shoulder more responsibility and burden for regional peace and security. The choices associated with grand strategy, about NAFTA and NATO, about foreign investment in the United States and military intervention in Bosnia, about all aspects of foreign and military policy, help define who we are, both to ourselves and to the rest of the world.

In their own form of grand strategy, John Jay and other Federalists argued that the United States could avoid being a battleground in European power struggles only if it were united. The Federalist views on the importance of national unity derive from the emergence of the **nation–state,** where, ideally, all of the people would share the same nationality and govern themselves. This form of political organization is based on the idea that one government should have sole authority over a well-defined territory. Though often associated with ethnicity and other common characteristics, nationality does not depend solely on shared racial, ethnic, religious, or linguistic ties, particularly in countries like the United States. Instead, nationality stems from a shared belief that a people have a common identity and destiny and, often, a common historical experience. By appealing to this sense of common nationality or nationalism, governments can support large military forces and sustain other costs to defend their interests. These national interests include preserving the nation's territorial boundaries, maintaining a relatively sovereign (independent) form of government, and promoting economic prosperity.

Nation–states range in size and resources from micro-states, such as Grenada, Monaco, and Tuvalu, to superpowers like the United States and the former Soviet Union. Though nation–states are still the most powerful type of political organization in international relations, the Framers of the Constitution could not have foreseen that other kinds of political organizations would become increasingly important in world affairs. Not until 1815, for example, did countries create the first **international governmental organization** (IGO) (an organization formed by three or more countries, with regular meetings and a permanent staff). Now hundreds of IGOs, from the Association of Southeast Asian Nations (ASEAN) to the United Nations (UN), play key roles in world politics.[7] Similarly, few international nongovernmental organizations (INGOs) existed in 1787. Now tens of thousands of IGOs, from Amnesty International to Greenpeace to the International Olympic Committee, influence many aspects of our daily lives as well as world affairs. In addition, the twentieth century witnessed an unprece-

nation–state: Ideally, a country where almost all of the people of one nationality govern themselves. This form of political organization is based on the idea that one government should have sole authority over a well-defined territory.

international governmental organization (IGO): An organization formed by three or more countries, with regular meetings and a permanent staff.

Parade of flags at the closing ceremony of the 1996 Summer Olympic Games in Atlanta. The International Olympic Committee (IOC) is a powerful international nongovernmental organization of which most of us are aware. (Photo courtesy: Thomas Kienzle/AP Photo)

The caldron fire burned brightly in Atlanta, Georgia as a symbol of the Olympics, sponsored by an INGO. (Photo courtesy: Meghan O'Connor McDonogh)

dented growth in transnational economic organizations, such as multinational corporations, which some suggest will transcend nation–states in importance.[8]

International power—that is, the power of any one organization relative to another—depends on the issue involved. Japan, for example, has more power in international trade and aid issues than in military security issues. International power also varies over time. Even though the collapse of the Soviet Union increased the relative military power of the United States in the 1990s, many scholars argue that the overall power of the United States has been in decline since the early 1970s, similar to the rise and fall of other great powers over the last four centuries. As noted historian Paul Kennedy contends, the United States

> cannot avoid confronting the two great tests which challenge the longevity of every major power that occupies the "number one" position in world affairs: whether . . . it can preserve a reasonable balance between the nation's perceived defense requirements and the means it possesses to maintain those commitments; and whether . . . it can preserve the technological and economic bases of its power from relative erosion in the face of ever-shifting patterns of global production.[9]

These challenges emerge in every era, but are most difficult when key political, social, technological, or economic changes have taken place either at home or abroad. Japan and Germany, for example, have had lengthy debates in the 1990s about whether their militaries should participate in U.N. peacekeeping operations, given their troubled histories of military aggression. Until the late 1980s and the emergence of the North American Free Trade Agreement (NAFTA), most Mexican governments had tried to restrict U.S. trade and investment in the Mexican economy. While Mexico relied on the military strength of its northern neighbor to deter any external military threat, formal ties with the U.S. military were limited. Until recently, for example, no U.S. secretary of defense had ever even gone to Mexico to meet with the head of the Mexican defense forces. Each nation, weak or strong, large or small, new or old, must answer these challenges.

THE ROOTS OF U.S. FOREIGN AND MILITARY POLICY

*I*n its early years, the United States was a weak country on the margins of international affairs. Historically, weak states often depend on more powerful countries for security. The Atlantic Ocean and other physical barriers to the projection of European power in the Americas and abundant natural and human resources meant that the United States had another option: It could choose not to be involved in European affairs. To understand the origins of U.S. foreign and military policy, we must examine both the pre-constitutional era and the Constitution itself.

The Pre-Constitutional Era

John Adams, under the direction of the Continental Congress, developed a *Plan of Treaties* in 1776 that outlined many of the primary themes of early U.S. foreign policy.[10] Adams called for greater freedom of trade between nations without political or mili-

North—South

POLITICS AROUND THE WORLD

For every government, the defense of its people and terri-tory is a top priority. Thus, in introductory international relations courses, students learn that in a world without a state akin to a national government, policy makers have to ensure their own country's survival and its people's secu-rity. As with everything else, that does not mean that all such sovereign states are equally able to do so.

The interests and concerns of the United States have long dwarfed those of its two neighbors. During the Cold War, from 1945 until the collapse of the Soviet Union, most of the world's countries "had" to line up with one su-perpower or the other, and Mexico and Canada certainly were no exceptions. Although there have been no such clear imperatives since the end of the Cold War, neither Canada nor Mexico normally defies U.S. wishes, at least on questions that matter a great deal to Washington.

That influence is actually a little harder to see for Canada, because most Canadians—politicians and average citizens alike—agree with the broad outlines of U.S. for-eign policy. Canada is also a significant power in its own right, deserving its status as a member of the G-7, the in-formal group bringing together the leaders of the seven most powerful capitalist and democratic countries.

Nonetheless, Canadian and American foreign policies are virtually identical. Although there have been some oc-casions (such as the Canadian acceptance of U.S. draft re-sisters during the Vietnam War) when Canadian and American foreign policies have been somewhat at odds, this is not usually the case. During the Cold War, the fact that the United States and Canada share such a long bor-der and that a Soviet attack on the United States would also undoubtedly involve at least an invasion of Canadian airspace, it had little choice but to support most U.S. ini-tiatives. It has continued to do so ever since, most notably

in supporting the war against Iraq in 1991. Thus Canadian troops have been integrated into the unified NATO com-mand, and Canada has long been a loyal U.S. ally in the Organization of American States (OAS).

During the Cold War, Mexico did carve out what might look like a somewhat more autonomous foreign policy. For example, in the 1980s it opposed U.S. development of new nuclear weapons, aid to the Contras in Nicaragua, and at-tempts to isolate the Communist regime in Cuba. Mexicans are also quick to criticize the fact that U.S. troops have re-peatedly entered Mexican territory uninvited, most recently during World War I.

What's more important to note is the influence the United States exercises in two policy areas that matter a great deal to the Mexicans. First, the United States has in-sisted that the Mexican government give its agents the right to operate on Mexican land and in U.S. airspace in the "war against drugs," even though drugs are not much of a problem in Mexico itself. Second, and even more im-portantly, the United States has established what amounts to a militarized border and adopted other policies that harm the Mexican economy to stop the flow of illegal im-migrants, especially into Canada. It has thus passed the Immigration and Naturalization Reform Act of 1986 and other legislation that directly affects Mexico without seri-ously taking Mexican needs and desires into account.

Finally, we should note that Mexico has a relatively large army with more than 110,000 professional soldiers. The army is large in part for historical reasons; it was a major force in the revolution of the 1910s and provided many of the early PRI leaders. It remains large today not to protect Mexico from any foreign threat, as it really doesn't face any. Instead, its main role is to protect the government from real, imagined, and potential domestic enemies, thus reinforcing many people's doubts about whether or not Mexico should be considered a democracy.

tary ties. This echoed the views of Thomas Paine, who argued in *Common Sense* that independence was the only way to avoid entanglements.

The struggle for independence made foreign aid and military assistance an un-avoidable requirement. The French gave substantial military and economic assistance to the newborn United States only because France was locked in a conflict with the British for global power at that time. With the Franco–American Treaty of 1778, the

United States joined in a military alliance with France. The United States sought similar alliances with other European powers, but this proved to be its only military alliance with a European power until the twentieth century.

The Constitution

The Framers generally agreed that the republic's foreign policy was important but limited—its tasks were to keep the United States out of European affairs and to keep European countries out of U.S. affairs. The institutional framework for foreign and defense policy is laid out in the Constitution. Making and implementing foreign policy is a power clearly given to the federal government rather than to the states, although the states had an important function in creating state militia.

Scholars agree that the Framers intended to divide responsibility between Congress and the president in foreign affairs. Although the office of the president combines the powers of head of state (with the authority to appoint and receive ambassadors, sign treaties, and otherwise represent the United States in dealings with other countries) and head of government (with the responsibility for overseeing the daily affairs of making and executing public policy), the power of the president was not to be comparable to the greater power of the monarchs of the time. The Framers gave Congress the power to fund the army and navy and declare war; while as commander-in-chief—that is, having constitutional power over all combined U.S. armed forces—the president leads the nation's military forces. Congress got the power to regulate commerce with foreign nations; the president got authority to negotiate and sign the treaties that govern such commerce (although for such treaties to become valid, two-thirds of the Senate is constitutionally required to ratify them). The president appoints ambassadors and other key foreign and military officials; the Senate grants advice and consent on these appointments.

Additionally, many powers not enumerated in the Constitution generally are accorded to the national government. In the wake of the U.S. victory in the Spanish American war, for example, the United States acquired colonies in the Philippines and elsewhere in 1898. This went against the anticolonial principles of many Americans, and many claimed the United States government had no right to acquire territory. In a series of U.S. Supreme Court cases, collectively called the Insular cases, the Justices affirmed the right of the national government to take new territories and to create new forms of government for those territories.[11] In many other instances, through the doctrines of implied and inherent powers, the president and Congress have often gone beyond the powers specifically outlined in the Constitution.

The Early History of U.S. Military and Foreign Policy

The pre-Constitutional desire for a limited foreign and defense policy carried over to the new republic. When the first Congress of the new United States eventually met in 1789, it authorized an army, but only at a maximum strength of 840. Most of the nation's military strength was decentralized in the form of state militia. Similarly, the Tariff Act of 1789 imposed low duties on imports (the Constitution bars taxes on exports), helping to keep trade relatively free from government interference.

The first important treaty entered into by the new United States regularized relations with Great Britain. The treaty, generally referred to as the *Jay's Treaty* after its chief negotiator, John Jay, helped settle disputes between Great Britain and the United States over the boundaries of the new nation, debts incurred during the war, and commerce between the two nations. Bitterness in the aftermath of the Revolutionary War led some members of Congress to oppose the treaty.

In 1796 George Washington, in his last public statement as president, discussed the dangers of divisive party politics and warned strongly against foreign entanglements. In his Farewell Address (written with Alexander Hamilton), Washington suggested that it be "our true policy to steer clear of permanent alliances with any portion of the foreign world." Washington believed that U.S. democracy and economic prosperity, two key national interests, depended not on complete isolation, but on keeping free of European politics.

From 1804 Great Britain began to adopt rules of the sea that worsened Anglo–American relations, especially the right to search any ship for deserting sailors. After one incident in June 1807, mobs gathered and demanded that President Jefferson seek war on Great Britain. Instead, Jefferson tried peaceful measures, negotiating the return of three of four sailors and arranging compensation (the fourth had been hanged). The British would not, however, renounce their right to search ships for deserting sailors. In December 1807 the United States passed the Embargo Act, stopping U.S. ships from leaving the country for any port in another country without approval by the federal government. Jefferson and Secretary of State James Madison believed that the European powers relied so much on U.S. shipping and raw materials that the Embargo Act would force the Europeans to change their policies and respect the rights of Americans at sea.

The Embargo Act proved very costly. Not only did European policies fail to change, but U.S. exports also fell by 80 percent, harming economic interests in virtually every region except those bordering Canada (since overland trade was not prohibited). With as many as 100,000 people out of work and inflation climbing in the depression created by the Embargo Act, dissatisfaction with the act allowed the Federalist Party to make noticeable gains in the election of 1808. In April 1809 an exchange of diplomatic notes between U.S. Secretary of State Robert Smith and David Erskine, the British minister in Washington, settled some of the disputes temporarily. The Erskine agreement, as this was called, became the first important executive agreement, a government-to-government accord entered into by the United States and binding only on the current administration.

Continued deterioration of Anglo–American relations led Great Britain and the United States to fight each other in the War of 1812. While peace talks began even before the first battles, the war ended only when the British decided to concentrate on defeating Napoleon. The British agreed to abide by the borders, treaty obligations, and other conditions in existence before the war, signing the Treaty of Ghent in December 1814 (the Battle of New Orleans was fought after the signing of the peace treaty). With the defeat of Napoleon in the summer of 1815, the British ceased the practice of impressment, and Anglo–American tensions eased. Great Britain and the United States also experimented with a new form of diplomacy by committing themselves to a process to settle future disputes by consultation and binding arbitration rather than military conflict.

For U.S. industries, however, global peace meant increased competition at home and abroad. Both before and immediately after the War of 1812, the U.S. government relied on the two key commercial principles in the Treaty Plan of 1776 in trade negotiations with other countries: *reciprocity* and *unconditional most-favored-nation (MFN)* status. Reciprocity meant a policy of national treatment, where U.S. traders would receive the same treatment as a national of another country. In practice, unconditional MFN status meant that U.S. exports would face the lowest **tariffs** (taxes on imports) offered to any other country. These principles were in line with the free trade and low tariffs advocated by Adam Smith's *The Wealth of Nations*.

tariffs: Taxes on imports, used to raise government revenue and to protect domestic industry.

As early as 1791, Alexander Hamilton, in the *Report on Manufactures,* had urged Congress to take action to protect some domestic industries from foreign competition. In 1816 the United States took the crucial step of adopting protectionist tariffs instead of simply using tariffs to raise money for the federal government. By this time Henry Clay urged an "American system" of trade protection, which came into full force in 1824. Overall, Congress and the president proved very receptive to demands for economic protection; and high tariffs—usually from 20 percent to 30 percent of the value of the import, but with some individual tariffs as high as 100 percent—became the norm for the next 120 years.[12] High tariffs, however, discouraged U.S. exports, since other countries kept their tariffs on U.S. goods high in retaliation for most of this period. For most of the years before the Civil War, the United States imported more than it exported, and the volume of trade declined steadily through 1830. Although trade increased after 1830, international trade grew at a rate slower than that of trade within the United States.

The Monroe Doctrine

The limited capacity of the U.S. government to provide military or foreign economic assistance helps explain its response to the revolutions in the 1820s that helped most Latin American countries gain their independence. President James Monroe threatened action if European powers attempted to recolonize the region and if the Russians extended their presence on the western coast of North America. In an annual message to Congress in December 1823, Monroe declared that it would be dangerous to American peace and safety for European states to attempt to extend their system to the Western hemisphere. This approach to hemispheric relations became known as the **Monroe Doctrine.**

Although tough sounding, the Monroe Doctrine was more preference than policy. Great Britain also aimed to keep other European powers out of the Western hemisphere to preserve British commercial interests. The difference between British and U.S. policy was that the incomparable British navy could enforce Britain's policy. In fact, the British expanded their limited colonial presence in Latin America several times after 1823 without U.S. policy makers invoking the doctrine.

Monroe Doctrine: President James Monroe's 1823 pledge that the United States would oppose attempts by European states to extend their political control over the Western Hemisphere.

The United States as an Emerging Power

At this time U.S. foreign policy dealt mainly with events in the Western hemisphere or with trade policy. Military activity was mainly within or on the borders of the United States, for example hostile relations with Canada during and following the War of 1812, hostile relations with Spain over Florida, war with Mexico in 1846, war with the seceding confederate states between 1861 and 1865, and wars in the South and West with Chief Tecumseh's confederacy and other Native American nations (Creeks, Seminoles, Sioux, Comanches, Apaches) that resisted expansion into their territory. During the Civil War (1861–65), the Confederacy even tried to bring the European powers into the war. The lack of a substantial confederate victory on Northern soil, the growing industrial and military might of the Union forces, and antislavery sentiment in Great Britain and elsewhere all thwarted Southern efforts to involve the Europeans in the conflict.

Eventually, the country stretched from one ocean to another. In particular, the defeat of Mexico in 1848 brought California under U.S. control. Some called this **manifest destiny,** a divinely mandated obligation to expand across North America to

manifest destiny: A popular theory during the U.S. expansion westward that it was a divinely mandated obligation to expand across North America to the Pacific Ocean.

the Pacific Ocean and "overspread the continent allotted by Providence for the free development of our yearly multiplying millions."[13] The Pacific did not stop the westward expansion of the United States. Soon after the British forced the Chinese to open their markets to British goods, U.S. officials negotiated a commercial treaty with China and sought to keep any single European power from restricting U.S. trade with China. In 1852 and 1854, Commodore Matthew C. Perry took the East India Squadron of the U.S. navy into Japanese waters and opened Japan to Western interests.

For the last half of the century, Americans reached no consensus on the appropriate role for the United States in global affairs. Both major political parties were generally against acquiring colonies but were divided on such issues as free trade and military intervention, and no one party regularly controlled all branches of government during the period. The United States did take Midway, the Hawaiian islands, and the Samoan islands to protect its interests in the Pacific, but these actions heightened the debate about how to use U.S. power.

President Theodore Roosevelt supported building the Panama Canal to strengthen the U.S. naval presence in the world. (Photo courtesy: The Bettmann Archive)

The belief in manifest destiny did not prepare the U.S. public for the revolution in the Philippines against U.S. rule in 1899. The United States sent nearly 200,000 troops to the islands over the next three years. When the fighting ceased in 1902, tens of thousands of Filipinos had died, along with 5,000 Americans. The atrocities committed on both sides dampened U.S. enthusiasm for foreign adventures. Nonetheless, the Spanish–American War propelled the United States from a regional to a world power (see Figure 19.1). A war hero with an expansionist vision of the U.S. global role, Theodore Roosevelt, became president. As president, Roosevelt supported the construction of the Panama Canal to make it easier for the U.S. Navy to operate in two oceans. He also received the newly created Nobel Peace Prize for his efforts to end the Russo–Japanese War of 1904–05 and the Franco–German crisis over Morocco in 1905.

Foreign Trade and Aid Policy at the Turn of the Century

Debate between Democrats and Republicans grew as the high tariff rates occasionally created surpluses in government revenue (and few wanted the government to have too much money), and as the European countries began to adopt lower tariffs and other free trade policies. The Democrats and Republicans made the tariff a major election issue throughout the 1880s, but the Republican victory in 1888 ensured the continuation of high tariffs. The 57 percent average rate of the Dingley Tariff Act of 1897 raised tariffs to a new high. They would remain high until Democratic electoral victories in 1912.[14]

From the Civil War on, the United States became increasingly self-sufficient. Self-sufficiency, coupled with high tariffs, reduced the relative demand for imported goods. At the same time, U.S. agriculture became more mechanized and U.S. industry more productive as many European states, particularly England, had greatly reduced their tariffs. This meant that U.S. goods became relatively cheaper to other countries and thus much more competitive on the world market. After 1895 the United States exported more than it imported for all but a few of the next seventy-five years.

The late nineteenth century witnessed the rise of thousands of extremely wealthy business tycoons, some through ruthless means. A few, such as John D. Rockefeller and Andrew Carnegie, believed their fortunes brought responsibility as well as power, and they created charitable foundations to aid society, mainly in the United States but also overseas. Though the U.S. government provided no aid, these tycoons helped found new private institutions to assist the international community, such as the Carnegie Endowment for International Peace and the World Peace Foundation.

FIGURE 19.1

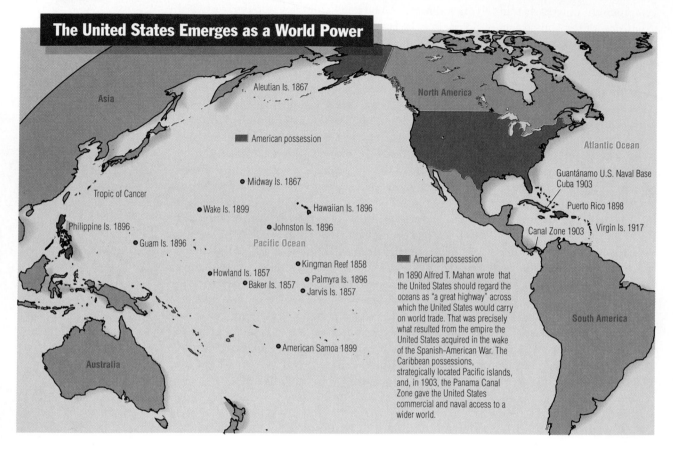

The United States Emerges as a World Power

Asia

Aleutian Is. 1867

North America

■ American possession

Midway Is. 1867

Atlantic Ocean

Guantánamo U.S. Naval Base
Cuba 1903

Tropic of Cancer

Wake Is. 1899   Hawaiian Is. 1896

Puerto Rico 1898

Philippine Is. 1896   Johnston Is. 1896

Guam Is. 1896

Pacific Ocean

Canal Zone 1903   Virgin Is. 1917

Kingman Reef 1858

Howland Is. 1857   Palmyra Is. 1896
Baker Is. 1857   Jarvis Is. 1857

■ American possession

In 1890 Alfred T. Mahan wrote that
the United States should regard the
oceans as "a great highway" across
which the United States would carry
on world trade. That was precisely
what resulted from the empire the
United States acquired in the wake
of the Spanish-American War. The
Caribbean possessions,
strategically located Pacific islands,
and, in 1903, the Panama Canal
Zone gave the United States
commercial and naval access to a
wider world.

South America

Australia

American Samoa 1899

World War I

When World War I broke out in Europe in 1914, it was politically expedient for a nation of immigrants to stay out of the war because choosing sides would inevitably anger one group or another. President Woodrow Wilson ran for a second term in 1916 on the slogan "He kept us out of war," yet world events pressed the United States to enter the conflict. Especially disturbing was the German policy of "unrestricted" submarine warfare, which meant that U.S. ships carrying cargo to Great Britain would be sunk even though the United States had declared itself neutral.

Talking of a "war to end all wars," Wilson took the United States into its first great European conflict. Troops and aid from the United States began to arrive just when the human and material resources of its main allies, Britain and France, were nearly exhausted. Almost 5 million Americans served in the armed forces during the war. The newly created Food Administration, under Herbert Hoover (who had run a successful campaign to provide relief to Belgium early in the war), dramatically increased food production to supply the United States and its allies. The United States also provided the allies with $11 billion in loans during and shortly after the war. Even though it had entered the war late, the United States, by intervening militarily and economically, helped make possible the defeat of the German and Austro-Hungarian empires.

Wilson put great faith in an international organization that would be formed after the war to keep the peace. He was instrumental in writing the document that set up the **League of Nations**—the first IGO dedicated to preserving global peace. Wilson was so absorbed in foreign policy, however, that he neglected to build support for the League at home. He was a Democratic president facing a Senate controlled by Republicans, and he had not courted them by devices such as including a senator among the U.S. delegates to the Versailles Peace Conference. Many senators found membership in the new world body incompatible with the principles of U.S. independence. The Senate refused to give the necessary two-thirds vote to approve the ratification of the treaty.

League of Nations: Created in the peace treaty that ended World War I, it was the first IGO dedicated to preserving global peace; superseded by the United Nations.

The United States returned to a policy of high tariffs and a limited role in the international economy soon after the war. The destruction of Europe during the war benefited the U.S. economy. As a source of credit and goods, the United States became the leading country of the world, and new technologies and cheap energy sustained this boom. In the 1920s a Republican-controlled Congress began raising tariffs to protect U.S. industry, especially manufacturers that had prospered during the war from reduced European competition. In 1930, in response to demands by U.S. industry for protection from foreign competition, Congress passed a very high tariff, called the Smoot–Hawley Tariff Act after its congressional sponsors. As many people had predicted, other countries responded by raising their tariffs and world trade declined rapidly. By 1932, the middle of the Great Depression, trade was at only about one-third of its former level.[15]

Many Americans thought that U.S. national interests were best served by keeping out of foreign political or economic affairs (**isolationism**) and by acting alone (unilateralism), often without consulting friendly governments. The Great Depression began to change this view. Not only did it create a better understanding of the links between the U.S. and foreign economies, but leaders later attributed the rise of Adolf Hitler and other rulers bent on world domination to the economic turmoil of the times. Without the power of the United States to support it, a weak League of Nations also meant that the world community had little chance of preserving the peace.

isolationism: Grand strategy designed to keep a nation out of foreign political or economic affairs; dominated U.S. foreign policy until World War II.

The desire to stay out of European affairs persisted throughout the 1930s in many quarters in the United States, particularly Congress. There, American isolationists passed a series of Neutrality Acts to keep President Franklin D. Roosevelt, other officials, or private citizens from involving the country in foreign conflicts. Through its immigration policy, the United States also prevented many refugees fleeing from persecution in Europe and Asia from entering the country, although many scientists fleeing European oppression did arrive in the 1930s and later played an important role in developing U.S. military and nuclear power.

THE UNITED STATES BECOMES A WORLD LEADER

*T*he world found itself at war again in 1939. By not acting sooner to deter foreign aggression and foster global prosperity, the United States found that its grand strategy of isolationism, unilateralism, and strict neutrality failed to keep it out of a major war. The influence of American isolationists crumbled in December 1941, when the Japanese attacked U.S. territory by bombing Pearl Harbor in Hawaii and Germany declared war on the United States.

President Franklin D. Roosevelt quickly mobilized the U.S. economy for war. Increased spending for war materials helped boost U.S. industry out of its slow recovery from the Great Depression. Through its Lend–Lease program, by which Congress gave the president the authority to lend or lease any equipment to any country whose defense he believed necessary to the defense of the United States, the country provided its allies with the weapons, equipment, and supplies necessary to wage war against the Axis powers (Germany, Italy, and Japan).

Even before the end of World War II, the United States and fifty-one of its allies created a new international governmental organization, the **United Nations.** Its purpose was to guarantee the security of member nations when attacked and to promote economic, physical, and social well-being around the world. This guarantee depended on the cooperation of the five great powers that worked together to defeat the Axis powers—China, France, Great Britain, the Soviet Union, and the United States; these nations held the only permanent seats on the new United Nations Security Council. The search for peace became even more important with the development of a weapon of immense destructive power, the atomic bomb, which the United States had dropped on Hiroshima and Nagasaki in August 1945 to help end the war with Japan.

As the war ended, the allies also created new international economic organizations to encourage trade, which many people believed would lead to both greater prosperity and peace. To stabilize exchange rates among various currencies, the allies established the **International Monetary Fund (IMF),** which fixed the price of currencies in terms of the United States dollar and the price of gold. To provide funds for large-scale projects in an effort to help heal the war-torn economies of Europe and Japan, the allies started the International Bank for Reconstruction and Development, better known as the **World Bank.** Finally, to lower trade barriers, the allies hoped to create an International Trade Organization, but fears that the organization would threaten control over the national economy led the U.S. Congress to reject these efforts until the creation of the World Trade Organization in 1995. Instead, the allies began work on the **General Agreement on Tariffs and Trade (GATT),** a set of agreements that brought about a substantial reduction in tariff levels. This included lowering U.S. tariffs, which permitted greater access to the large U.S. market.

U.S. participation in these institutions indicated a shift in grand strategy toward **multilateralism,** that is, a belief that foreign policy actions should be taken in cooperation with other states after extensive consultation. To many, sustaining economic recovery seemed as important as any military measures in preserving U.S. national security. At the end of the war, moreover, the United States accounted for about half of the world's total economic product and world trade. With promises of peace and cooperation in the air, the U.S. Army's size dropped from more than eight million at the close of World War II to less than one million by 1947. The United States, however, still had nuclear weapons and the most technologically advanced land, sea, and air forces.

The Origins of the Cold War

Cooperation between the United States and the Soviet Union, critical to peace after the war, quickly eroded. The leader of the Soviet Union, Joseph Stalin, seemed willing to do anything to make the countries of Central Europe communist. In the eastern Mediterranean, particularly Greece and Turkey, the British had maintained a sphere of influence (an area dominated although not directly controlled by a country) before World War II. A crisis erupted when the British, weakened financially by the war, no longer believed they could counter Communist aggression in the region. They asked the United States to assume support for these countries. In a flurry of activity, the State Department, in a period of fifteen weeks in early 1947, devised a set of policies that turned the United States into a global power.

United Nations: IGO created shortly before the end of World War II to guarantee the security of member nations when attacked, and to promote economic, physical, and social well-being around the world.

International Monetary Fund (IMF): An IGO created shortly before the end of World War II designed to stabilize international financial relations through a system of fixed exchange rates.

World Bank: Originally designed to provide loans for large economic projects in Western Europe's efforts to recover from the devastation of World War II; now the major multilateral lender for development projects in poor countries.

General Agreements on Tariffs and Trade (GATT): Devised shortly after World War II as an interim measure until a World Trade Organization could be created, multilateral trade negotiations conducted under the GATT helped lower tariff and other trade barriers substantially.

multilateralism: The foreign policy practice that actions should be taken in cooperation with other states after extensive consultation.

During much of the Cold War, both the United States and the Soviet Union carried on testing of nuclear weapons. The rapid expansion of nuclear arsenals resulted in a stalemate position known as Mutually Assured Destruction (MAD), whereby a first strike by either superpower would result in a devastating counterstrike. (Photo courtesy: Naval Photographic Center, Washington, D.C.)

The Republican chair of the Senate Foreign Relations Committee, Arthur Vandenberg of Michigan, was sympathetic to this policy shift but remembered how Republicans—Vandenberg himself among them—had resisted President Roosevelt's attempts to end isolationism before World War II. Senator Vandenberg and others counseled President Harry S Truman to "scare hell out of the country" in order to win support for global policies. Truman did, in a 1947 speech to both houses of Congress that laid out the policy known as the **Truman Doctrine,** a policy of containment of Soviet expansion. In a key passage, Truman stated, "It must be the policy of the United States to support free peoples who are resisting attempted subjugation by armed minorities or by outside pressures."[16] The speech helped create an ideological consensus that cut across all parties and justified participation in world events—the consensus of anti-communism. It also created the belief that national security was something Americans needed to worry about even when the world was at peace and even when there was no apparent direct military threats to the United States.

Truman Doctrine: President Truman's 1947 strategy to provide U.S. military and economic assistance to Greece and Turkey to contain Soviet expansion.

The Marshall Plan, NATO, and Containment

Truman got Congress to approve the European Recovery Program, often called the **Marshall Plan** (Secretary of State George C. Marshall proposed the idea in a Harvard commencement speech). In a break with tradition, the Marshall Plan provided a massive transfer of aid from the United States mainly to Western Europe. In its first year alone, 1948–49, the Marshall Plan sent the West Europeans more than $6 billion. At that time that amounted to 10 percent of the entire federal budget, 4.1 percent of the gross domestic product, and 2.8 percent of the gross national product, comparable to more than $100 billion today. The plan succeeded in rebuilding the basis for strong economies in Western Europe, which, in turn, prevented Communist parties from winning control of governments in the region.

Marshall Plan: The European Recovery Program, named after Secretary of State George C. Marshall, which provided a massive transfer of aid from the United States to Western Europe in the years after World War II.

For the first time, the United States joined a political and military alliance in peacetime. The North Atlantic Treaty, signed in 1949, provided that a military attack against any of the signatories (Belgium, Canada, Denmark, France, Great Britain, Iceland, Italy, Luxembourg, the Netherlands, Norway, Portugal, and the United States) would be considered an attack against all of them. The following year treaty members created the **North Atlantic Treaty Organization (NATO),** a regional defense alliance, to implement the treaty (see Figure 19.2). Even though the United States was not at war and was not directly threatened by any hostile state, hundreds of thousands of U.S. troops were moved to Europe. Though many crises occurred in Europe after the creation of NATO, the organization deterred large-scale war in Europe until the collapse of the former Yugoslavia in the 1990s.

Across the globe, Truman soon confronted a new crisis in Asia. After World War II, Korea had been partitioned into two zones, the one in the North occupied by Soviet troops, the one in the South by U.S. troops. Disagreements between the United States and the Soviet Union prevented reunification and led instead to the creation of separate states. Then in June 1950, North Korea invaded South Korea. The United States was taken by surprise, but after brief consideration Truman decided to commit U.S. forces, through United Nations auspices, to help South Korea resist. The United States was able to get support for its action from the United Nations only because the Sovi-

North Atlantic Treaty Organization (NATO): A political and military regional defense alliance created in 1950 to implement the North Atlantic Treaty of 1949; the first peace-time military alliance made by the United States.

FIGURE 19.2

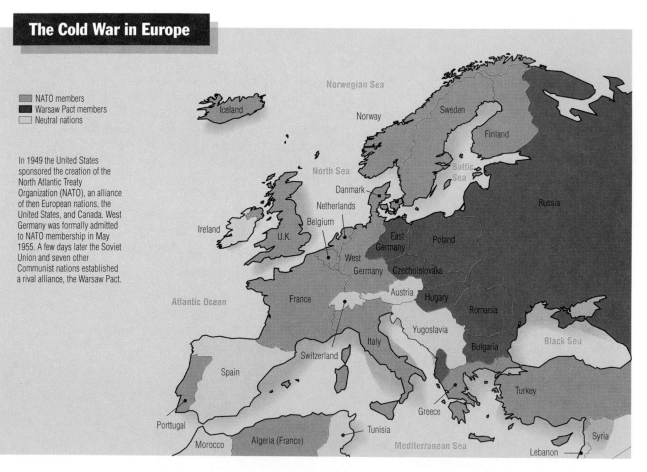

The Cold War in Europe

In 1949 the United States sponsored the creation of the North Atlantic Treaty Organization (NATO), an alliance of then European nations, the United States, and Canada. West Germany was formally admitted to NATO membership in May 1955. A few days later the Soviet Union and seven other Communist nations established a rival alliance, the Warsaw Pact.

ets were not attending Security Council meetings in protest (Security Council resolutions require unanimous approval of all permanent members present). U.S. troops did not stop the North Koreans in the first weeks, but the tide of the war reversed after a dramatic amphibious landing staged by the U.S. commander General Douglas MacArthur at the port city of Inchon. The tide of war reversed again when Chinese troops intervened in force on North Korea's behalf in November 1950. After months of indecisive fighting, the warring parties agreed to a truce, dividing the peninsula nearly in half by a demilitarized zone for the next five decades.

The Marshall Plan, NATO, and U.S. actions in Korea are examples of the grand strategy of **containment.** Based on the observations of a U.S. diplomat, George Kennan, the United States sought to contain Soviet communism. Kennan argued that if the allies could stop the spread of communism, the nature of the Soviet leadership and its political system would collapse. In practice this meant surrounding the Soviet Union with U.S. or allied military forces in an effort to deter the Red Army, and deny or delay Soviet access to many Western goods and technologies through restrictions on trade and investment. This strategy was criticized by the left as too hostile (because the military deployments would provoke the Soviets) and by the right as too soft (because the United States did not roll back communism in Eastern Europe and China). Much of the strategy was clarified in a complete review of U.S. foreign and defense policy conducted by the president's National Security Council. NSC Study number 68 (NSC-68), completed in 1950, maintained that the security of the United States was linked closely with the security of the Western, democratic world. With some modifications, the grand strategy of containment became the framework of U.S. foreign and military policy until the 1990s.

> **containment:** A strategy to oppose any further expansion of Soviet power, particularly in Western Europe and East Asia, by surrounding the Soviet Union with U.S. or Allied military forces.

The Cold War Era

In retrospect, containment did limit Communist expansion in Europe until the Soviet Union collapsed, as Kennan theorized. More important, containment did not lead to another world war. The political and military stability provided by the policy of containment and the economic stability promoted by international economic institutions, such as the IMF, the World Bank, and the GATT, allowed the Western allies (particularly the NATO members and Japan) to focus on economic development. The rapid recovery of Western Europe resulted in a spectacular round of global economic prosperity. Between 1950 and 1973, world trade grew at unprecedented rates in every year but one. Private U.S. investment overseas, mainly in Western Europe, and foreign investment in the United States increased dramatically after 1950. Finally, the gross national product (GNP) of the United States in constant dollar terms expanded in all but seven years between 1948 and 1990.

The grand strategy of containment raised the importance of the military in the United States. In 1940, the last year before the United States entered World War II, federal expenditures on defense were equal to 17.5 percent of the total federal budget and only 1.7 percent of the U.S. gross domestic product (GDP). In contrast, between 1947 and 1987, U.S. defense expenditures averaged 39.9 percent of the budget and 7.7 percent of GDP. Also, in contrast to efforts to curb arms sales before World War II, after the war the United States became the major supplier of arms to the rest of the Western world. As President Eisenhower noted in his last public address, the United States now had a vast "military–industrial complex" that made the military and defense industries a dominant factor in U.S. politics, with the "potential for the disastrous rise of misplaced power."

After the Soviet Union exploded its own atomic bomb in 1949, both sides began to build nuclear arsenals. Although the United States maintained a significant advantage in the early years, both sides eventually had enough nuclear weapons to absorb an attack by the other and launch a devastating nuclear strike in retaliation. This situation, known as **mutually assured destruction (MAD),** deterred each side from attacking the other.[17] As the dangers of nuclear war became clearer after the Cuban Missile Crisis (the United States–Soviet Union confrontation in 1962 over attempts to install Soviet ballistic missiles in Cuba), both sides began efforts to agree on limits to the size of their own nuclear forces through negotiations and treaties, culminating in the Strategic Arms Reduction Treaties (START I and START II), where the United States and Russia promised to cut their nuclear forces by more than half (and Ukraine and Belarus agreed to return the nuclear weapons on their territory to Russia).[18]

Containment was less clear on defining the appropriate role for the United States in wars of "national liberation," such as Vietnam.[19] With little information on the nature of the Vietnam conflict, such as the relative independence of the Vietnamese Communist movement from Soviet or Chinese control or the history of U.S. involvement in the region, Congress and the public were easily deceived on the extent and consequences of U.S. involvement by more than one administration. Perhaps the worst instance was the degree to which the Johnson administration misled Congress in order to pass the Gulf of Tonkin Resolution, which originally authorized a massive commitment of U.S. forces to support a series of anti-Communist—though not democratic—governments in South Vietnam.

U.S. forces left South Vietnam in 1973, but the 57,000 dead and 300,000 other casualties, the unpopularity of the war at home (see Figure 19.3), and the failure to build a truly democratic government in Vietnam created a much longer legacy. In the 1960s many U.S. political leaders believed that appeasing Hitler rather than confronting him years earlier helped cause World War II. Just as this idea framed the debate about U.S. intervention in Vietnam, many current leaders see Vietnam as a lesson on the limits of U.S. military power today. In the days following the death of several U.S. soldiers in Somalia in 1993, for example, many members of Congress echoed the sentiment of Representative Jim Ramstad (R–Minn.), who warned, "The president better get his foreign policy act together before Somalia becomes another Vietnam."[20] In addition to its impact on political leaders, the Vietnam experience had a significant impact on public opinion. In the late 1940s through the 1960s, about a fourth of all Americans thought that the United States should stay out of world affairs. Since the early 1970s, however, this view has been shared by about a third of all Americans.[21]

Containment also said little about an appropriate foreign economic policy for the United States once Europe and Japan recovered from World War II. Though originally seeking a policy of "trade, not aid," President Eisenhower began to assist countries in Asia and elsewhere in response to an expansion of Soviet assistance programs. Encouraged by U.S. success in rebuilding Europe in the early 1950s, President John F. Kennedy saw U.S. foreign aid and assistance programs and international economic institutions as means of transforming poor countries in Africa, Asia, and Latin America into prosperous, anti-Communist nations. The United States, together with other wealthy countries, however, did not offer programs as large as the Marshall Plan for problems that turned out to be much more difficult to solve.

Foreign assistance programs today take many forms, including low-interest loans, free food or weapons, and outright grants-in-aid. Often, direct aid to another country is tied to that country's promises to purchase goods from the donor. One reason for the success of multilateral lending institutions, such as the International Development Agency of the World Bank, is the demand for aid without such strings attached.

FIGURE 19.3

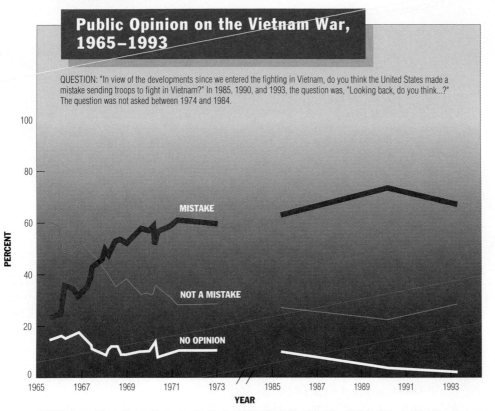

Public Opinion on the Vietnam War, 1965–1993

QUESTION: "In view of the developments since we entered the fighting in Vietnam, do you think the United States made a mistake sending troops to fight in Vietnam?" In 1985, 1990, and 1993, the question was, "Looking back, do you think...?" The question was not asked between 1974 and 1984.

MISTAKE

NOT A MISTAKE

NO OPINION

PERCENT

YEAR

SOURCES: Gallup polls cited in John Mueller, *War, Presidents and Public Opinion* (New York: Wiley, 1973), 54–55 (reprinted in 1985 by University Press of America, Lanham, MD); *The Gallup Poll, 1972–1975*, vol. 1 (Wilmington, Del: Scholarly Resources, 1977), 87; *The Gallup Poll Monthly*, January 1993, 37.
"Foreign and Military Policy," p. 356 in: Harold Stanley and Richard Niemi, eds. *Vital Statistics on American Politics*, 4th ed. 1994 Congressional Quarterly, Inc. Reprinted by permission.

Most U.S. assistance loans and grants are made by the U.S. Agency for International Development. Although for most of the last four decades the United States has made the largest foreign aid contributions (in dollar amounts) of any country, the total aid is typically around one-half of one percent of the federal budget, much less than that given by many other rich countries. Despite this fact, since 1973 most polls indicate that 70 percent or more of Americans believe that the United States spends too much on foreign aid, though younger Americans are slightly less critical of these policies.[22] For the 1996 fiscal year, Congress appropriated $12.1 billion, $1.4 billion less than the previous year, and $1.9 billion less than requested for foreign aid by the Clinton administration. The Chair of the Senate Foreign Relations Committee, Jesse Helms (R–N.C.), even battled to eliminate the Agency for International Development, among other foreign policy institutions, altogether.

Of the roughly $78 billion distributed by the U.S. Agency for International Development or its predecessors between 1962 and 1989, much went to governments threatened by Communist forces, as in El Salvador, Korea, Pakistan, the Philippines, South Vietnam, and Turkey. The two countries receiving the most aid were Israel and Egypt, because of their roles in the Middle East conflict. Diplomatic and military policies, however, are not the only determinant of U.S. aid. Substantial sums of money and sup-

Highlight 19.1

The Third World

In 1952 Alfred Sauvy, a French sociologist, coined the term *tiers monde*, or Third World, to describe the countries that were neither aligned with the United States (the First or Free World) or the Soviet Union (the Second or Com- munist World). The term is patterned after the phrase *Third Estate* used to de- scribe the less powerful commoners of France when it was ruled by a king and the Catholic clergy. Al- though widely used in the United States in the 1960s to refer to most Asian, African, and Arab countries, the term is now in disre- pute. By grouping so many countries together, many policy makers and analysts underestimated crucial so- cial, economic, and political variations in the Third World. In the last two decades, oil- and export- induced economic growth made some Third World countries much richer than others, causing some to suggest that there was now a Fourth World comprising the poorest of the poor countries. Coupled with the collapse of Soviet commu- nism, the phrase *Third World* seems to have little meaning for international relations in the 1990s.

Source: William Safire, *Safire's New Political Dictionary* (New York: Random House, 1993), 795.

plies have gone for humanitarian and economic development purposes to countries in the Third World (see Highlight 19.1).

Aid policies are often controversial. Many in Congress, particularly the new Re- publicans elected in 1994, wanted to restrict access to U.S. aid by family planning agen- cies that provide abortions overseas. Providing a wide range of services, not just abortions, these private agencies play a central role in population control worldwide, so many opposed this effort to restrict funds. Similarly, the United States owes more in unfulfilled contributions to the United Nations than any other country. For many years congressional critics of the United Nations have argued that the U.S. share of U.N. costs is too high, and that many U.N. operations are managed inefficiently, so Con- gress has limited appropriations for U.N. activities.

By the 1970s global economic conditions, however, changed dramatically from the years immediately after World War II, affecting the relative influence of the United States in determining global economic activities. Japan and some of the countries of the European Community (now known as the **European Union,** or **EU,** an economic and political association consisting mainly of the allies of the United States in Western Europe) greatly improved their economic strength and technological ability. Their products and companies challenged those of the United States in the global market- place. By the 1990s, Japan's program of Official Development Assistance (ODA) made Japan, not the United States, the world leader in foreign aid contributions.

In the early 1970s, the global economy suffered its first major depression in three decades. Many people in the United States began to complain that nontariff barriers to trade used by other governments were hurting U.S. exports, while the U.S. market was relatively open. As a result, support for U.S. free trade policies began to decline. The U.S. trade deficit, particularly with Japan and Germany, increased steadily. Some won- dered if Japan would eventually overtake the United States as the world's largest and richest economy. By the 1990s the economies of many Asian states, including Malaysia,

European Union (EU): The union that joins most of the coun- tries of Western Europe in their ef- forts to develop common economic, social, and foreign policies; succes- sor to the European Communities.

Singapore, South Korea, and Taiwan, were also growing much more rapidly than the U.S. economy. Instead of Japan, whose economic bubble burst in the early 1990s, the People's Republic of China may have the largest, if not the richest, economy in the world in the next century. In most cases these governments used a strategy of export-led economic growth to achieve prosperity, usually based on trade with the United States.

One key element of postwar economic recovery was the stability of the U.S. dollar, with the values of most currencies fixed to the value of gold and the dollar (called the fixed exchange-rate system). Through the International Monetary Fund (IMF), the dollar had become the global currency, with large deposits of U.S. dollars overseas. This meant that the U.S. government lost some capacity to influence inflation and interest rates through its control over its own money supply. In 1971 President Richard M. Nixon abandoned fixed exchange rates. This led to the current system where the value of the U.S. dollar and other major currencies depends on what people are willing to pay for them (called a floating exchange-rate system). When the value of the dollar increases, it helps attract foreign investment to the United States but often worsens the U.S. trade deficit considerably as the price of U.S. goods increases in the local currency of the other countries.

Finally, many Third World countries now viewed the United States and other rich, industrialized countries as economic adversaries and called for the creation of a new world economic order. In 1960 some of these countries joined together in a cartel known as the Organization of Petroleum Exporting Countries (OPEC). They gained influence in the global economy by raising the price of oil during much of the 1970s. Although the success of OPEC proved to be an exception compared with other efforts by Third World countries to control the supply or price of raw commodities, it symbolized Third World dissatisfaction with the global economy.[23]

The United States and the other key industrial powers have tried to coordinate their trade, investment, and monetary policies more closely since the 1970s. The leaders of seven countries—Canada, France, Germany, Great Britain, Italy, Japan, and the United States—now hold annual summits to discuss political and economic issues of mutual concern. Recently, Russian leaders have become involved in these Group of Seven (G-7) discussions. Substantial disagreements exist within the G-7, and many people fear that the world is dividing into three competing economic blocs—East Asia, Europe, and North America. Taken together, these problems have diminished support in the United States for a grand strategy that includes freer trade and open economic policies.

THE MACHINERY OF MODERN FOREIGN POLICY MAKING

*I*n *Federalist No. 8* John Jay noted that "it is the nature of war to increase the executive at the expense of the legislative authority." As the likelihood of international conflict became clearer in the 1930s, Congress granted the president broad authority to act in foreign affairs and specifically to allow the president to prohibit arms shipments to participants in foreign wars. In *United States v. Curtiss-Wright Export Corporation* (1936), the U.S. Supreme Court upheld the right of the Congress to grant this authority.[24] While referring to an isolationist strategy, in this ruling the U.S. Supreme Court recognized the primary importance of the president in foreign policy and affirmed that the national government did not share power over foreign relations with the states. This marked the first time that the Supreme Court formally recognized the concept of inherent powers of the national government in foreign affairs.

Both World War II and the Cold War helped secure the central role of the president in the U.S. foreign policy-making process. Congress supported a larger role for the United States in global military affairs with the **National Security Acts of 1947 and 1949.** These acts consolidated the army, the navy, and the new air force into one department under civilian leadership, now known as the Department of Defense. The legislation also set up two new organizations: (1) the Central Intelligence Agency (CIA), which would collect and analyze the information deemed necessary to meet national security threats, and (2) the National Security Council (NSC), made up of the president, the vice president, the secretaries of state and defense, the chair of the Joint Chiefs of Staff, and the director of Central Intelligence. The NSC, along with the newly created post of assistant to the president for National Security Affairs (the national security adviser), would advise the president on foreign and military affairs.

The National Security Council, the National Economic Council, and the Central Intelligence Agency.   The modern policy-making process differs sharply from the process the United States followed in the past. The president now commands a vast military–industrial complex supported by a large foreign policy and intelligence network. The NSC, set up to institutionalize the system by which the U.S. government had conducted World War II, began to coordinate a wide range of foreign policy issues, such as dealing with the fall of the Shah of Iran or negotiating a new canal treaty with Panama. In addition to collecting intelligence information in the Cold War against the Soviet Union, the CIA ran covert (secret) operations to alter political outcomes in many countries.[25] At times, these secret operations undermined broader U.S. objectives by supporting assassinations, corruption, and other scandalous activities. In the 1970s Congress intensely criticized the CIA and mandated changes in procedures to provide more oversight over its covert actions. In the early 1990s, the end of the Cold War, the penetration of the CIA by foreign spy agencies, and other scandals again raised congressional interest in reforming the CIA. Consequently, Congress formed a special commission to consider how to reform the CIA in 1995.

In most critical military and foreign policy matters, direction is provided by the president with advice from the members of the NSC, the national security adviser, and the NSC staff, with input from other executive departments and agencies as the president desires. For foreign economic policy, President Bill Clinton created a National Economic Council (NEC) with a role parallel to the NSC's influence on security policy. The inner core of the NEC includes a presidential adviser who chairs the council; the secretaries of labor, treasury, and commerce; the director of the Office of Management and Budget; the U.S. trade representative; and the head of the Council of Economic Advisers. The NSC and the NEC work together, and even share staff on a number of issues, including trade. They also work with the Domestic Policy Council on some noneconomic issues.

Each president has an individual management style, and the precise pattern of foreign policy making differs for each administration as a result.[26] President Eisenhower, for example, wanted very formal lines of authority and divisions of responsibility. Presidents Clinton and Kennedy preferred a collegial management style, relying on *ad hoc* working groups. President Nixon changed from a collegial style to a more formal NSC over time. These styles affect the roles of the national security adviser in each administration.

The State and Defense Departments.   In addition to providing information and advice through the NSC, these two departments have primary responsibility for implementing foreign and military policy. In 1994 its 191 diplomatic and ninety consular posts overseas helped the State Department gather information on political, economic, social, and military conditions overseas, represent the United States in international negotiations, and provide standard services such as assisting U.S. citizens or processing visa applications. In addition to foreign service officers and other members of the State Department, many other departments and agencies may have personnel stationed overseas. Typically, an ambassador, the personal representative of the president to the head of government of another country (or a group of countries or an international organization), serves as the leader of all U.S. officials stationed in that country, even if they are not members of the State Department. From their main offices in the Foggy Bottom section of Washington, most of the few thousand State Department officials are responsible for either specific issues or specific countries.

The Defense Department, with its far-flung system of bases and military units, provides the forces to conduct military operations abroad. The United States maintains its largest military presence in Western Europe and East Asia and the Pacific. In Western Europe the U.S. military serves as part of the NATO forces. After the end of the Cold War, the United States had cut its number of troops in Europe from about 350,000 to 166,000 in 1993. Still, U.S. forces in Europe made key contributions during the Gulf War and as part of the Implementation Force (IFOR) in Bosnia. In East Asia and the Pacific, the United States maintains about 100,000 personnel, mainly in South Korea and Japan. Clinton administration officials considered reducing this further in light of the end of the Cold War, but rejected this approach when many countries in the region expressed the need for a U.S. military presence to preserve regional stability and peace.

The United States also maintains one of the world's most potent nuclear forces. In recent years the United States and the states of the former Soviet Union have started to eliminate many of their nuclear warheads and the missiles and bombers to deliver them. Nonetheless, the limits reached through START I and START II still mean that the United States and Russia each have far more nuclear weapons than any other country. If fully implemented by 2003, START II, which the Senate ratified in January 1996, still would

U.S. troops in Tuzla, Bosnia, as part of the Implementation Force charged with keeping the peace in a war-torn foreign nation. (Photo courtesy: Klaus Resinger/Black Star)

allow each side to have as many as 3,500 nuclear warheads on strategic vehicles (missiles and bombers). To put this in perspective, estimates suggest the next largest nuclear arsenal is France's 525 warheads (which it is reducing) and China's 435 warheads.

Civilian control over the armed forces has been one of the most sacred foundations for preserving the U.S. Constitution. Under the Secretary of Defense and other appointed civilian officials, the Defense Department directs U.S. forces from its main offices in the Pentagon, across the Potomac from the District of Columbia. With thousands of officials overseeing its massive operations, the Defense Department is among the most influential federal bureaucracies. While defense spending has declined with the end of the Cold War, it still accounted for nearly one-fifth of the federal government budgets during the mid-1990s.

The presence of tens of thousands of U.S. military personnel overseas causes some tension with the host nations, and not just from the noise made by low-flying planes or the damage of tanks to local fields. Members of Congress often questioned the costs of maintaining troops in Europe, even at the height of the Cold War. The United States removed most of its forces from the Philippines in recent years as disputes over the cost of maintaining the forces increased. Isolated instances of outrageous conduct by military personnel can damage relations as well. Three U.S. servicemen in Okinawa, for example, were convicted of raping a twelve-year-old Japanese girl. The furor raised by Japanese citizens caused both governments to promise to reduce U.S. military operations and presence on the island.

Presidential Primacy in Foreign Affairs

Compared with domestic policy, Congress and interest groups generally have a relatively smaller role in making foreign and military policy than does the president. Their role in foreign economic and military funding policies is somewhat larger, but not as large as their role in purely domestic policies. This occurs because the nature of foreign and military policy differs from the nature of domestic policy in ways that reinforce the power of the president.

Alexander Hamilton, in *Federalist No. 75*, recognized that foreign policy was different from domestic policy because it required:

1. Accurate and comprehensive knowledge of foreign politics
2. A steady and systematic adherence to the same views
3. A nice and uniform sensibility to national character
4. Decision, secrecy, and despatch [sic]

On each point, the office of the president has an advantage over Congress. Perhaps the most important source of power is the president's greater access to and control over information (see Roots of Government: Communication Technology and Foreign Policy). In domestic politics, many people, including those in the Congress, the media, and interest groups, often have important information that bears on policy decisions. When dealing with foreign affairs, however, the president has exclusive sources of information—diplomats working for the State Department, military attachés working for the Defense Department, agents controlled by the CIA, and technical means (such as satellites) controlled by the CIA and the National Security Agency (the NSA, which is in charge of electronic intelligence gathering). Private citizens, companies, interest groups, even Congress cannot balance the president's information with their own on issues such as the number of Soviet missiles in Cuba or the extent of Iraq's nuclear weapons program. Even the main source of information available to the president's critics, the news media, is dominated by the president (see chapter 15).

Roots of Government

Communication Technology and Foreign Policy

Traditionally the slowness of communications and the vast oceans separating the United States from the rest of the world permitted a slow and orderly reaction to world events. The war between the British and the United States that began in 1812 illustrates how slowly news traveled.

A traditional American banjo tune known as "The 8th of January" celebrates the 1815 date of the Battle of New Orleans, when General Andrew Jackson held off the British, suffering 350 casualties to the British's 2,450. But officially the War of 1812 had already been ended by a treaty signed in Belgium on December 24, 1814. The British ratified the treaty and then Americans and Britons boarded a ship in London on January 2, 1815, to bring the treaty and the British ratification to the United States. Because of bad weather, the ship did not arrive in New York until February 11. News did not reach the nation's capital until February 15.

By contrast, when U.S. aircraft and cruise missiles began their opening strike against Iraq on January 17, 1991, the event was covered live on U.S. television. Several cable network reporters in a hotel room were able to broadcast the battle of Baghdad as it happened. It became the first prime-time war. Later, television recorded Iraqi Scud missiles landing in Israel, a practice criticized as providing important targeting information to the Iraqis. During the war in the Persian Gulf, cable subscriptions increased dramatically, and cable audiences increased 350 percent in February 1993.

Since then, many world leaders have come to rely on cable television news as a source of information for current events. Television crews bring starvation in Somalia, shelling in Bosnia, the Russian elections, and terrorism in Saudi Arabia into our homes and into the White House.

The president's authority is enhanced by the aura of secret information available to him: diplomatic cables, CIA reports, NSA intercepts. Sometimes, to win points in debates against rivals, the president will declassify secret information. Virtually any other citizen could be prosecuted for revealing classified material, but the president may do so freely. In the 1980 election campaign, for example, President Jimmy Carter, under attack from Republican opponents for neglecting U.S. defenses, authorized his secretary of defense to reveal that the United States had been developing a plane that would be invisible to radar, which became the B-2 Stealth bomber.

CHALLENGES TO PRESIDENTIAL POWER IN FOREIGN AND MILITARY POLICY

The president is powerful but not omnipotent in the field of foreign policy. International factors place limits on the power of the president. The foreign and military policy of the United States is often criticized as simply a reaction to the policies of other countries. In addition, all presidents face domestic constraints on their power from Congress, the bureaucracy, the media, and the public as well.

Congress

The most consistent restraint on presidential power in foreign affairs comes from Congress.[27] The Constitution gives a lesser role to Congress in foreign affairs than in domestic affairs, but much of the modern-day power of the president comes from broad authority granted to the executive through legislation, not through the Constitution. Congress also exercises its oversight powers on the foreign policy and military activities of the president and the executive branch. In this sense Congress has more power in holding the administration accountable for its foreign policy than legislatures in parliamentary systems, where members of the parliamentary majority also serve as government ministers. The British Parliament, for example, required a court inquiry and an independent investigation (the Scott Report) to find out that the administration misled it about approval of British exports of weapons-related goods to Iraqi military programs in the 1980s, whereas Congress (and the courts) were active in uncovering the extent of U.S. involvement in Iraqi military programs.

Congressional Leadership.   Normally the president proposes a foreign policy and Congress accepts, modifies, or rejects it. Congress also has the power to develop and implement policy. When the Soviet Union launched Sputnik, the first artificial Earth satellite, in 1957, President Dwight D. Eisenhower did not treat it as a serious threat to U.S. security. Other prominent Americans, however, were worried. With no proposal of action from the president, under the guidance of Senate Majority Leader Lyndon B. Johnson, the Preparedness Subcommittee of the Senate Armed Services Committee

Presidential power in matters of foreign policy, while broader than that of the legislative branch, is not absolute. President Clinton seeks public support for his foreign policy initiatives, just as he does for his domestic policies. (Photo courtesy: Joey Ivansco/Atlanta Constitution)

held hearings on the threat posed by Soviet space potential. Determining that there was indeed a threat, Congress set up the National Aeronautics and Space Administration (NASA) to run a U.S. space program and the National Defense Education Act to provide funding for science and foreign language education. Although technically civilian programs, these were seen at the time as very much a part of U.S. defense policy.

Congressional Oversight.   Congressional oversight is a relatively new check on the president's power to set foreign and military policy. During and after World War II, weapons became more and more complex, and Congress was willing to defer to presidential recommendations and military advice on what weapons the country needed. But in 1969 Congress for the first time challenged a president on a major defense expenditure. President Richard M. Nixon proposed a nationwide system of radar and interceptor missiles to defend against incoming missiles, known at the time as Anti-Ballistic Missiles (ABMs). The Senate, relying on expert testimony by Defense Department officials who had actually tried to develop such systems and believed they would not work, came within a single vote of turning down Nixon's request. Since 1969 the U.S. public has become accustomed to congressional scrutiny of weapon development and deployment.

Treaties and Executive Agreements.   The Constitution gives the Senate explicit power to approve treaties. Even though the Senate has rejected treaties outright only sixteen times in U.S. history, the power is effective because presidents try to avoid direct defeats or filibusters. Until the Senate reached a compromise in the spring of 1996, Senator Helms, chair of the Senate Foreign Relations Committee, kept the Senate from considering ratification of the Chemical Weapons Convention. He unsuccessfully tried to compel the Clinton administration to eliminate the Agency for International Development and the Arms Control and Disarmament Agency or to merge them into the State Department (eventually, the Senate and the administration left ratification to the 105th Congress).

As noted in chapter 8, presidents can avoid the treaty process altogether by using executive agreements and have done so more and more frequently since World War II, as illustrated in Table 19.1. Senate ratification is not required for an executive agreement; and, prior to the Case Act of 1972, the president did not even have to inform Congress of the texts of these accords. Normally, presidents use executive agreements for routine business matters, such as purchasing and running embassies. But sometimes executive agreements have important policy implications. Several executive agreements that established U.S. military bases overseas in such countries as Spain and the Philippines, for example, had the effect of allying the United States with these countries.

Appointments.   As head of state and government, the president appoints ambassadors and other persons involved in the formation and implementation of foreign and defense policy. The Constitution gives the Senate the right to provide advice and consent on these posts. As in the domestic arena, important political appointees for foreign and defense policy frequently have close connections to Congress. A key link in President Ronald Reagan's foreign policy was the appointment of Richard Perle as assistant secretary of defense. A proponent of a strong anti-Soviet policy, Perle worked for many years as a staff adviser to conservative Senator Henry "Scoop" Jackson (D–Wash.), and his knowledge of Congress, the issue area, and President Reagan's policy aims made Perle a powerful figure.

Senators can put a hold on the confirmation process of some foreign policy positions to express concern about an issue as well as about the appointee (see chapter

TABLE 19.1

Treaties and Executive Agreements Concluded by the United States, 1789–1994

YEARS	NUMBER OF TREATIES	NUMBER OF EXECUTIVE AGREEMENTS
1789–1839	60	27
1839–1889	215	238
1889–1929	382	763
1930–1932	49	41
1933–1944 (F. Roosevelt)	131	369
1945–1952 (Truman)	132	1,324
1953–1960 (Eisenhower)	89	1,834
1961–1963 (Kennedy)	36	813
1964–1968 (L. Johnson)	67	1,083
1969–1974 (Nixon)	93	1,317
1975–1976 (Ford)	26	666
1977–1980 (Carter)	79	1,476
1981–1988 (Reagan)	125	2,840
1989–1992 (Bush)	67	1,371
1993–1994 (Clinton)	17	256

Note: Number of treaties includes those concluded during the indicated span of years. Some of these treaties did not receive the consent of the U.S. Senate. Varying definitions of what comprises an executive agreement and their entry-into-force date make the above numbers approximate.

Sources: 1789–1980: *Congressional Quarterly's Guide to Congress,* 291; 1981–1982: Office of the Assistant Legal Adviser for Treaty Affairs, U.S. Department of State; 1993–1994: Harold Stanley and Richard Niemi, eds., *Vital Statistics on American Politics,* 4th ed. (Washington, D.C.: Congressional Quarterly, Inc., 1994), 280. Reprinted by permission. Clinton data provided by Treaties Office, Department of State.

7). Senator Jesse Helms (R–N.C.) used the hold privilege in 1994 to delay the appointment of political scientist Robert Pastor as ambassador to Panama. Helms distrusted Pastor's role in the Carter administration policy toward Nicaragua's formerly Marxist government.

Appropriations.   Congress has a critical role in shaping defense policy through its power to appropriate funds, especially defense spending. In 1996, for example, the House passed a defense spending measure of $265 billion, about $7 billion more than requested by the Clinton administration. Much of the additional funding was for more weapons, including $493 million for more B-2 Stealth bombers. Similarly, Congress cut about $110 million out of the F-22 advanced fighter program in 1995.

Congress can also try to control foreign policy through its power to appropriate funds. The power to go to war is shared between the executive and legislative branches of government, but the power to appropriate funds belongs to the legislature alone. Congress has been cautious about applying this power. In 1996 the House voted to cut off funding for the deployment of 20,000 U.S. troops as part of the 60,000-strong NATO Implementation Force in Bosnia. As failure to contribute these troops would scuttle the Dayton peace plan before it got started, the Senate rejected the cut off. Instead, the Senate agreed to support efforts to fulfill U.S. obligations, but did not use the word "approve" in its resolution.

In 1982 Congress used its appropriation power to limit U.S. involvement in Nicaragua. In 1979 an insurrection led by guerrillas named after an earlier Nicaraguan hero, Augusto Sandino, helped the Sandinistas to come to power. Because the Sandinistas received aid from Cuba and the Soviet Union, those opposing them—known as counterrevolutionaries, or Contras—found that the Reagan administration was willing to aid them. Many people in the United States opposed funding the Contras, and after much debate, Congress decided to cut appropriations. The Contras continued to receive supplies of weapons, however. In 1986 it was revealed that the supplies had been paid for with funds solicited from foreign states and from private individuals and with proceeds from arms deals with the Khomeini regime in Iran in which members of the Reagan administration participated.

The War Powers Act. Nicaragua was not the first instance when the executive branch supported military action against the will of Congress. With the Gulf of Tonkin Resolution in 1964, Congress had given broad authority to President Lyndon B. Johnson to conduct military operations in Vietnam. As support for the war dwindled, members of Congress became frustrated with their failure to influence policy on Vietnam. In 1973 Congress tried to prevent future interventions overseas without congressional approval by passing the War Powers Act (see Highlight 19.2: The War Powers Act). Under

Highlight 19.2

The War Powers Act

Key provisions of the law:

- The president must consult Congress "in every possible instance" before committing military forces to imminent or probable combat overseas and must report any such mission to Congress within forty-eight hours.
- Military forces must be brought home within sixty days unless Congress either declares war, otherwise approves of the mission, or extends the withdrawal deadline.

Proposals made in 1988 and 1993 by Senator Sam Nunn (D–Ga.):

- Set up a "permanent consultative body" of House and Senate leaders and key committee chairs to meet regularly with the president on foreign policy issues.
- Once military forces are committed overseas, Congress can force their withdrawal only by passing specific legislation. Congress can also pass legislation approving of the mission.
- Spending of federal funds contrary to congressional legislation, such as an order to withdraw troops, would be prohibited.

the act the president can deploy troops to hostile situations overseas only for a sixty-day period in peacetime (which could be extended for an extra thirty days to permit withdrawal) unless Congress explicitly gives its approval for a longer period. Under the act, the president could respond to an emergency, such as rescue of endangered Americans abroad, but not engage in a prolonged struggle without congressional approval.

The War Powers Act has been an issue in the struggle for control of foreign policy between the president and Congress ever since. When first passed, it was vetoed by President Richard M. Nixon. Congress overrode the veto in March 1973, but Nixon called the act unconstitutional and said he was not bound by it. No issue arose to test the competing claims before Nixon was forced to resign in 1974, but such issues did arise under his successors.

The first serious test of the War Powers Act came under President Ronald Reagan. In 1982 Reagan ordered Marines into Lebanon as part of a peacekeeping mission. Because the troops were not in combat, Congress did not object. But after a year, the Marines came under increasing fire from various factions in Lebanon's civil war. Although Marines were being killed, Congress was slow to invoke the War Powers Act. In the midst of a drawn-out debate over U.S. involvement in Lebanon, a Lebanese terrorist drove an explosive-filled truck into the Marine barracks in Beirut, killing 241 servicemen. Shortly thereafter, all Marines were withdrawn on the president's initiative. In this and subsequent actions, presidents have usually complied with parts of the War Powers Act, especially the requirements for notifying key members of Congress.

When Iraq invaded Kuwait on August 2, 1990, President George Bush had to build domestic support for the U.S. response. Congressional attempts to restrain the president could be circumvented in the short run, but a lengthy war would require substantial funds. Iraq was a more formidable opponent than either Panama or Nicaragua had been, and the United States would require several months of preparation before any serious military campaign could be undertaken. During the preparatory period, Congress tried to force the issue, with the Senate holding hearings on the war.

Bush was reluctant to ask for a resolution of support until he was certain it would pass, and Congress was reluctant to act until asked. But as the January 15, 1991, deadline for Iraq to leave Kuwait—agreed to by the United Nations—approached, members of Congress took the initiative in pressing for a debate. As the date of debate neared, the Bush administration began to focus discussion on Iraqi efforts to obtain nuclear, chemical, and biological weapons (and the missiles to deliver them) as well as on the aggression in Kuwait and the atrocious human rights record of the Hussein regime.

Congress avoided a direct declaration of war by debating instead a resolution authorizing the use of U.S. armed forces to carry out a U.N. resolution (which had itself only suggested that armed force could be used but had not called for it). Congress side-stepped the issue of war powers by stating that the resolution was "consistent with" (as opposed to "pursuant to") the War Powers Act, which did not mean the president accepted the act.

After several days of serious debate, legislators voted for the resolution by a substantial margin (250 to 183) in the House and a narrow margin (52 to 47) in the Senate. Members of Congress closed ranks once the vote was taken: The Democrats who had opposed the resolution declared that they too would support the president. Some Middle East experts suggested that Saddam Hussein, the ruler of Iraq, had misread the U.S. constitutional process and assumed the debate meant that he faced a divided and therefore irresolute opponent. In fact, building the necessary political coalitions to gain congressional and public support strengthens U.S. commitment to specific policies once they are adopted.

The Bureaucracy

Another major check on the foreign policy and military powers of the president comes from inside the executive branch. While not as powerful as bureaucrats in Japan, where the career officers in the Ministry of International Trade and Industry (MITI), the Ministry of Foreign Affairs, and other government agencies determine most foreign policies no matter who is prime minister, the U.S. federal bureaucracy wields power since it implements presidential decisions and Congressional mandates. Without full support of career bureaucrats, who usually have expert knowledge of the issues and procedures, policy decisions and actions can be ignored or delayed, and information can be leaked to Congress or the media to raise issues on the political agenda or to embarrass the president. Since many bureaucrats have strong ties to Congress or interest groups such as the defense industries, their loyalties may be divided.

Information.   The president has access to a broader range of information than any other public official or private individual in the United States, but rarely is this information received in the form of raw data. Even presidents who are "policy wonks" (people who immerse themselves in the numerous details of policy), such as Jimmy Carter and Bill Clinton, cannot filter the huge amount of information that comes in every day. By the time the president gets information from the CIA, the State Department, and other sources, it has usually gone through a few levels of bureaucratic screening. During the early years of the Cold War, for example, air force intelligence sources consistently argued that the Soviet Union had more long-range bombers than the CIA estimated. Not surprisingly, the more Soviet long-range bombers there were, the more funding air force officials could demand to meet the increased Soviet threat.

Implementation.   Once the president makes a foreign or military policy decision, the bureaucracy must act. As with many large organizations, however, federal bureaucracies can develop a culture of values that make implementation of presidential orders difficult. Decisions to integrate blacks and women into the U.S. military were resisted by many career military personnel, and incidents of racial and gender discrimination persisted long after the original orders. Female officers, for example, were assaulted or harassed by male Navy and Marine pilots at the 1991 Tailhook Association meeting in Las Vegas. As a result of subsequent investigations, the Navy undertook a program to more fully address these issues. More recently, President Bill Clinton's interest in ending discrimination against homosexuals in the military was opposed by so many career military personnel (as well as many members of Congress and the public) that he compromised to develop a "don't ask, don't tell" policy regarding sexual orientation.

The News Media

Along with Congress and the bureaucracy, the press provides some check on presidential power in foreign and military affairs. In some countries most news media are government owned and operated, limiting the capacity to hold a government accountable for its actions. Government control of the media in the former Soviet Union and a policy of secrecy regarding airline crashes and other disasters that might damage the image of the Communist government, for example, meant that news of the Chernobyl nuclear reactor accident was hidden from the public and neighboring countries for some time, further endangering lives and property. As Soviet leader Gorbachev relaxed restrictions on the press with the policy of *glasnost* to make the Communist Party and government more accountable, media coverage of government excesses contributed to the sharp drop in public legitimacy of Communist rule.

Investigation.   During World War II and the early Cold War years, the U.S. press tended to support the president. As a rule, editors assumed that government statements were true and printed them as unquestioned fact. In the mid-1960s, however, the press's role as a prop for foreign policy began to change.

As U.S. involvement in Vietnam grew, the press increasingly challenged statements issued by government officials. The daily military briefing in Vietnam became known among the media as "the Five O'Clock Follies" for its lack of candor. The press examined in great detail the differences between what administrations claimed and the reality of the battlefield. Beginning with the live coverage of parts of the Foreign Relations Committee hearings on the Vietnam War in February 1966, dissent became a regular feature of television coverage as well. From 1966 on, about 20 percent of all Vietnam coverage (on CBS television, for which data are available) concerned various forms of domestic controversy.[28]

In the years since, the news media have not been uniformly hostile to the president. During the Persian Gulf War in 1991, some critics suggested that the press too willingly accepted the government's version of events. The glowing initial reports of the success of the Patriot antimissile missiles in downing Iraqi SCUD missiles proved highly inaccurate upon investigation after the war.

The fact that the media discussed their own shortcomings suggests that the country will not return to the innocent days of the past. The mass media were very critical of the Clinton administration's foreign policy regarding Bosnia, Haiti, Somalia, and Cuba. President Clinton's first secretary of defense, Les Aspin, resigned partly as a result of the criticism. President Clinton complained that the press ignored the administration's foreign policy successes with the former Soviet Union on proliferation, with the European Union with the General Agreements on Tariffs and Trade, and in the Middle East. In his whirlwind visit to Europe in January 1994, for example, much of the press coverage of the tour was on presidential reaction to a domestic question, the Whitewater real estate deal, instead of on the substantive issues of the trip, including defining a new role for NATO, clarifying the fate of nuclear weapons and foreign aid to the former Soviet Union, and improving the prospects for Syrian–Israeli peace talks.

Agenda Setting.   The media can put issues on the foreign policy agenda. The problem of famine in the 1980s in East Africa, especially in Ethiopia, was well known to aid agencies such as CARE and OXFAM, and to government officials. It did not become a major issue in U.S. politics until television crews broadcast stories on the subject, complete with pictures of the dead and dying, into American living rooms. Countless reports about atrocities in Bosnia raised calls for action by the president, although long, brutal civil wars in many other parts of the world, such as the Sudan, remain virtually unknown to most of the U.S. public. Such complex issues as increasing international trade or reducing Third World debt that take time to explain and offer little opportunity for startling footage receive less attention than do stories about war and disaster, even though their ultimate impact may be much more significant to the average citizen.

The Public

The division of U.S. public opinion on general dimensions of foreign policy also constrains the president. Many scholars argue that public opinion has two dimensions, militarism/nonmilitarism and isolationism/internationalism, creating four basic opinion groups.[29] Others argue that a third dimension, unilateralism/multilateralism (essentially the difference between acting alone and acting in concert with other countries), is also important. Although the public is not equally divided among different opinion groups, U.S. foreign policies usually have to appeal across these dimensions to two or more groups in order to achieve widespread popular support. At the same time, the existence of these various dimensions means that almost every U.S. foreign policy will have a core group of opponents who are likely to try to limit the impact of the policy.

A crisis in foreign policy generally leads to a rise in a president's popularity, although the increase is often temporary, as noted in chapter 8. Support for leaders in other democracies follows this pattern too. The Falkland Islands war in 1982 between Great Britain and Argentina greatly increased the popularity of Prime Minister Margaret Thatcher, whose popularity had slipped because of a slumping domestic economy. The British victory in the Falklands provided her with a theme that she used to gain a victory in the general election the following year. But British prime ministers can (within limits) call for elections when they think they will win. President George Bush, by contrast, could not take advantage of his exceptionally high popularity in the wake of the Persian Gulf War to win reelection. Instead, he had to wait until his constitutionally ordained four-year cycle was completed, by which time the country was in a recession that contributed to Bush's defeat.

Elections. Harry S Truman completed President Franklin D. Roosevelt's unexpired term and then won election in 1948 in his own right. He was eligible to run again in 1952, but his popularity was very low. The issue that made Truman so unpopular was one of foreign and military policy, the Korean War. Truman committed the United States to fight on behalf of South Korea in 1950, but the war stalemated by 1952, with about 250,000 U.S. troops committed to combat on the Korean peninsula and deaths approaching what would be their final total of 34,000. Popular dissatisfaction with the no-win war was very high. Sensing sure defeat, Truman withdrew from the race. The voters chose as president a popular military leader and hero from World War II, General Dwight D. Eisenhower, who helped bring an end to the fighting by agreeing to a truce with North Korea in 1953.

Similarly, in 1968 Lyndon B. Johnson decided not to run for a second term, in large part because of the unpopularity of his policy of escalating the war in Vietnam. A surprisingly strong showing for peace candidate Senator Eugene McCarthy (D–Minn.) in the New Hampshire primary suggested to Johnson that although he would probably win his party's nomination, he might not win the election.

Electoral control on the president's power is exercised in only the crudest of ways and only at set intervals—every fourth year when an election is held. Even then, the voters can approve or disapprove of an existing policy, but they can send no clear message for an alternative policy. In 1952 Eisenhower was elected on a vague promise to end the war in Korea. With such a promise, he was as free to end the war by introducing nuclear weapons (which he did not) as he was by negotiating a truce (which he did). In a similar vein, Richard M. Nixon succeeded Lyndon B. Johnson without having made clear what he would do to end the war in Vietnam other than to say "I have a plan" to end the war.

Public Opinion. As revealed in Figure 19.4, the U.S. public is much more interested in what goes on at home. Since the 1960s Americans have considered domestic problems to be much more important than foreign ones. Yet even when it is not an election year, or Congress is not exerting pressure, or foreign policy is not the subject of media

FIGURE 19.4

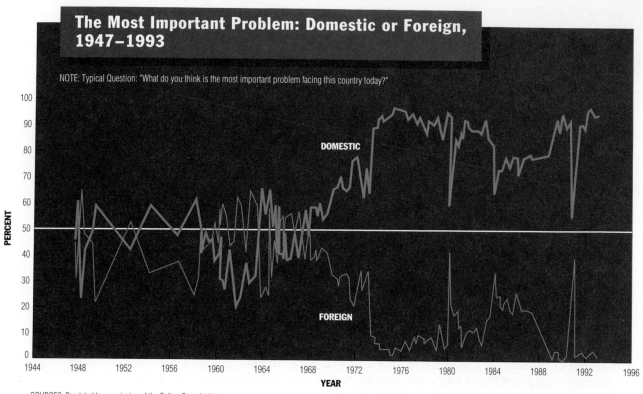

The Most Important Problem: Domestic or Foreign, 1947–1993

NOTE: Typical Question: "What do you think is the most important problem facing this country today?"

SOURCES: Reprinted by permission of the Gallup Organization.
"Foreign and Military Policy," 356 in: *Vital Statistics on American Politics*, 4th ed. Harold Stanley and Richard Niemi, eds. 1994 Congressional Quarterly, Inc. Reprinted by permission.

attention, public opinion is likely to be on the president's mind when examining foreign policy.

President Ronald Reagan's standing in the Gallup public opinion polls in the later years of his administration was higher than that of any of his recent colleagues. Yet Reagan and his advisers found themselves restrained by their perceptions of what the public would tolerate. Shortly after taking office, Reagan emphasized the need to help the right-wing Central American government of El Salvador fight leftist insurgents. The White House saw El Salvador as an issue that would generate even more support for Reagan, playing as it did on themes of anticommunism and national security. Yet to the White House's surprise, Reagan's standing in the public opinion polls began to go down. The president's advisers determined that their problem was that the conflict in El Salvador was being portrayed as another Vietnam. Advisers quickly stopped mentioning El Salvador. Reagan's ratings in the polls went back up. As other presidents had learned, the president could influence what went on the public's agenda but not the opinions the public would form.

Public Action. Foreign and military policies do not consist only of government action. Without the public taking action that supports these policies, they are not likely to be effective. Widespread resistance to the draft during the Vietnam War made it much more difficult to reach the personnel levels desired by the military and helped move the U.S. military toward an all-volunteer force. In the 1990s the Bush and Clinton administrations tried to increase U.S. private investment in Russia with little impact because many Americans are simply reluctant to invest there, given Russia's highly uncertain political and economic environment.

Direct action by the public can often lead to a change in foreign policy. Two planes carrying members of the anti-Castro group Brothers to the Rescue were shot down by the Cuban military in February 1996. The group began by helping families with relatives in Cuba, a problem that was magnified by the most recent exodus of Cuban refugees to the United States. By 1996 changes in Clinton administration policy (and in Cuba) made contact with relatives easier for family members, and U.S.–Cuban relations appeared to be warming. Many saw these changes as helping Castro stay in power, and called for harsher restrictions. These found a congressional voice in the Helms–Burton bill, which President Clinton opposed on many grounds. With the downing of the two planes, however, President Clinton agreed to support the Helms–Burton legislation as a substantive means of condemning the acts of the Cuban government.

State and local governments do play some role in foreign and military policy. Border states make compacts with local governments in Canada and Mexico on a variety of issues, particularly in the area of transportation. State and local governments court overseas investors by offering tax breaks and other incentives. State governments promote home-grown products in the global market, most maintaining at least one office in Europe or Asia. Local activists join or work with international nongovernmental organizations that may oppose the president on issues ranging from the environment (Greenpeace, for example) or sports (such as the International Olympic Committee). Even in military affairs, the president faces potential opposition from state and local government officials. In the 1980s some state governors argued that their national guard units could not be used overseas without their approval, in order to keep the units from being used to support Reagan administration initiatives in Central America.

The authority of the president in foreign and military policy is constrained by Congress, the federal bureaucracy, the media, and citizens expressing their will. Yet each of these restraints on presidential authority is imperfect. In part this imperfection comes from certain advantages bestowed on the president by the Constitution. One restraint is that the president combines the roles of head of government and head of state. Unlike the British system, where the monarch serves as head of state and the prime minister serves as head of government, the United States Constitution puts both of these functions in the hands of the president. This union has the effect of making the president not just a political actor but also the symbol of the nation. Another advantage is that the president (along with a hand-picked vice president) is the only official elected by the nation as a whole. It is not surprising, then, that Congress, the media, and the American people look to the president as a national leader. One senator summarized the prevailing view after a foreign policy vote: "In foreign policy initiatives, there should be a presumption in favor of supporting the President of the United States."[30]

CHANGING FOREIGN AND MILITARY POLICY

The anti-Communist consensus that dominated U.S. grand strategy for four decades from World War II to the late 1980s had some desirable results even for people who did not always share in its approach. Without that consensus, for example, it is unlikely the Congress would ever have appropriated money for foreign aid in the quantities that it did. The large burden of the Marshall Plan was justified primarily in the name of strengthening Europe against communism. With the fading of the threat that provoked the consensus, old programs need new justification. Some people still advocate providing foreign aid for humanitarian reasons. But they must prevail against many others who want to use the money for domestic purposes—sheltering the homeless, rescuing savings institutions, or just reducing the deficit.

Only at rare times in history, such as at the end of World War II, does one country have sufficient power to shape the world largely to its own desires. The last few years of the 1990s, however, may be the best chance for many decades to use the relative power of the United States to define a new vision of the world.[31] Some suggest, with the end of the Cold War, the United States once again attained a pinnacle of power and could and should take unilateral action to achieve its ends. Others believe that the demise of Soviet communism meant the "end of history," with no serious political and economic differences remaining between the major powers. This would mean that any crisis would be settled by collaboration, probably through the United Nations.

Both of these views appear to offer false hope. While leadership demands unilateral action at times, the United States (or any other country) has little hope of forging effective policy toward peace in Bosnia, trade restrictions on China, the use of products that destroy the ozone layer, or almost any other international issue, without widespread multilateral support. Similarly, the ideological clash with communism was never the only cause of international conflicts. Nationalism, economic self-interest, calls for governments based on the most narrow-minded versions of Islamic or Asian values, and many other ideas or identities will cause conflicts in the next century.

The Lack of Consensus

In the absence of a consensus on the grand strategy of the United States, foreign policy issues have become partisan issues, provoking debates between Republicans and Democrats, liberals and conservatives. Some partisanship in foreign policy has always been present, of course, but there has been a perceptible increase as the Cold War has waned. Although controversial and costly, the objective of anticommunism gave U.S. foreign policy a consistent direction for more than forty years. Without anticommunism as a guide, debate on the direction of U.S. foreign policy has become more partisan.

In June 1989, for example, television audiences around the world watched in horror as the Chinese government used tanks to crush prodemocracy demonstrators in Tienanmen Square. Some members of Congress indicated their outrage at the Chinese government by calling for Chinese students already in the United States on student visas to be able to extend their stays. President George Bush, who was the U.S. envoy to China during the Ford administration, thought this action would anger the Chinese government. The resulting debate in Congress, the votes in Congress to allow the students to stay, the veto by the president, and finally the failed attempt to override the veto went almost completely along party lines.

Without the guidance of the anti-Communist consensus, debates on the procedure of U.S. foreign and military policy making increased as well. Presidents have dispatched U.S. forces on more than 200 occasions when combat was very likely or did occur, including the situations in Korea, Vietnam, and, more recently, Somalia. When these deployments became unpopular, Congress tried to stop them, using legislative devices such as the War Powers Act or bill amendments that curtail specific foreign policy activities. Presidents at the time called these efforts an unconstitutional meddling in their authority.

President Jimmy Carter tried to build a new grand strategy based on support for human rights, much as the United States had formed a domestic consensus in support of civil rights. Proponents argued that this would align U.S. policy against both Communists, such as the Soviets, and non-Communist dictators, such as the Shah of Iran. Opponents argued that U.S. policy should not be based on ideal principles and that the battle against communism sometimes required helping nondemocratic leaders. President Ronald Reagan tried to rebuild the anti-Communist consensus by identifying the Soviet Union as an "evil empire" and supporting less-than-democratic forces in struggles against Communists in Angola, Nicaragua, and elsewhere.

The invasion of Kuwait in 1990 spurred President Bush to call for a "new world order." In a speech to the United Nations, Bush suggested that the United States and the other major powers could create a global order in which they would share responsibility for preserving freedom, justice, the rule of law, and protection of the rights of the weak, in which the United Nations would play an important institutional role through its peacekeeping activities.[32] While noble sentiments in the effort to defeat Iraq, this approach proved less effective in settling problems in Somalia and Bosnia, and seemed to have little to do with the troubles in the international economy.

Challenges for the United States in the Next Century

Despite the apparent success of the Persian Gulf War, the United States faces many challenges that require a coherent grand strategy. Poverty, food shortages, and economic collapse in many parts of the world are so severe that they may threaten U.S. security. Similarly, civil wars and political oppression in one country often disrupt life in other countries through the spread of terrorism or the influx of refugees. Rising economic tensions among the United States, the European Union, Japan, and the other emerging industrial nations of the Pacific Rim, however, suggest that economic policy issues, more than global or regional war, will dominate the agenda of international politics into the next century.

Public opinion polls suggest that the most important long-range foreign policy objectives should be, in order, protecting American jobs, the nonproliferation of weapons of mass destruction, securing adequate energy supplies, improving the global environment, and reducing the trade deficit.[33] Much lower on the list is protecting human rights in other countries, strengthening the United Nations, helping U.S. businesses overseas, improving Third World living standards, promoting democracy abroad, and protecting weaker nations. Public opinion on many foreign policy issues varies considerably over time, such as protecting U.S. foreign imports. In contrast foreign policy is often fairly stable. On trade issues, for example, all recent U.S. presidents have declared their support for free trade. In finalizing the Uruguay Round trade talks in 1993, President Bill Clinton concluded negotiations begun under President Ronald Reagan with the other members of the GATT to decrease tariffs generally and liberalize nontariff barriers to trade in agriculture and the service industries, among others. These nearly global negotiations also led to the creation of the **World Trade Organization (WTO),** which replaced the GATT institutions on January 1, 1995, to oversee and promote freer trade and settle trade disputes.

Though the Clinton administration has emphasized that international trade helps create jobs in the United States, the promised benefits of free trade, especially in the short term, contend with the real economic costs of trade. As foreign imports put pres-

World Trade Organization: The IGO created in 1995 that manages multilateral negotiations to reduce barriers to trade and settle trade disputes between nations.

sure on U.S. business, Congress slowly began recapturing trade policy from the president. A major milestone was the 1988 Omnibus Trade and Competitiveness Act, which limited presidential discretion in making trade policy. It imposed mandatory requirements for retaliation under Section 301 of the act, for example, against countries that maintained substantial barriers to trade and whose exports greatly exceeded their imports from the United States. Through the mandatory provisions of Section 301, Congress attempted to gain more control over U.S. trade policy. Because Congress responds readily to economic interests (such as automobile producers), the president develops a coherent national policy on trade only with difficulty.[34] The debate on the passage of the **North American Free Trade Agreement (NAFTA)** has brought the role of economic interest groups more clearly into focus. More recently, the Clinton administration failed in its efforts to interest Congress in considering a Free Trade Agreement with Chile, which many saw as the next step in extending free trade throughout the hemisphere.

> **North American Free Trade Agreement (NAFTA):** A treaty that promotes the free movement of goods and services between Canada, Mexico, and the United States.

To address these concerns, President Clinton has been more willing to threaten to use economic sanctions, as in the trade negotiations between then U.S. Trade Representative Mickey Kantor and then Japanese Minister of International Trade and Industry Ryutaro Hashimoto (who later became Prime Minister of Japan in part because of his views that Japan should get tougher in its negotiations with the United States) over autos and auto parts. The administration also sought to increase U.S. exports to $1.2 trillion by the year 2000 by easing restrictions on trade and providing more incentives and assistance to promote U.S. trade. The administration, for example, adopted the "Big Emerging Markets (BEMs)" strategy, where the United States would help U.S. companies expand their exports to Argentina, Brazil, Mexico, the countries in ASEAN (the Association of Southeast Asian Nations), the Chinese economic zone (the People's Republic of China, Taiwan, and Hong Kong), India, South Korea, Poland, Turkey, and South Africa.

Many found the emphasis on economic relations overplayed in the first years of the first Clinton administration, particularly in Asia. In part, this came from the desire to see military spending fit into a coherent post-Cold War foreign policy strategy. With the decline of the Soviet military threats, many expected a "peace dividend" in the shape of major cuts in defense spending. When faced with an impending cut in the military budget, presidents look to the impact on key electoral states and members of Congress look at the effect on their districts—and just about every congressional district benefits from defense spending. Even members of Congress conspicuous for their vocal opposition to the vague concept of military spending fight to retain military bases that provide jobs for their constituents. In 1994, for example, President Clinton and then chair of the House Armed Services Committee Ron Dellums (D–Ca.) looked for ways to soften the impact of base closings and defense cutbacks on California companies and communities by consolidating, extending or transferring base operations.

More important are choices about the scope of the threat facing the United States. In 1993 then Secretary of Defense Les Aspin identified four major threats to U.S. national security, in a unique **bottom-up review** of the mission and needs of the Defense Department:

> **bottom-up review:** Post-Cold War review of U.S. defense forces and policies.

1. The proliferation of weapons of mass destruction, such as nuclear bombs, and the means to deliver those weapons.
2. Regional conflicts in the Middle East, Korea, and elsewhere.
3. The emergence of anti-democratic forces in Russia.
4. The erosion of U.S. economic strength.[35]

A critical decision in the bottom-up review was that the United States needed sufficient military forces to conduct Desert Shield/Desert Storm-type operations against two "rogue nations" at the same time. Currently, the United States sees Iraq, Iran, Libya,

North Korea, and possibly Syria as rogue nations, while Defense Department scenarios picture a number of other states, such as China or India, as prospective problem states. In calling for forces to fight two conflicts like the Gulf War at about the same time, the United States requires most of the advanced conventional forces it used to face the old Soviet threat. In addition, proposed withdrawals of U.S. military forces from Asia and the Pacific were met with considerable alarm in the region. Many countries feared a smaller U.S. military presence would promote an arms race and military adventures by other states in the region, so the Clinton administration promised to maintain current levels of its forces in the region. Together, this means that the "peace dividend" is peace, not a huge decline in the U.S. defense budget.

Wholly new international issues that challenge U.S. policy makers have emerged in foreign affairs. The dramatic international impact of the Russian nuclear accident at Chernobyl, and the discovery of a large hole in the ozone layer of the earth's atmosphere that appears to be related to the use of chlorofluorocarbons (CFCs) and other gases, are two incidents in a growing understanding of the importance of international environmental threats to the security of the United States. In a provocative 1989 article, Jessica Tuchman Matthews argued for a broader definition of national security "to include resource, environmental, and demographic issues."[36] To some extent, United States participation in the 1992 United Nations Conference on Environment and Development, signing the 1993 Convention on Biological Diversity, bilateral aid for sustaining tropical forests, and other policies indicate that these issues are becoming part of a new definition of U.S. national security. Critics suggest, however, that in some instances environmental activists are trying to use the legitimacy associated with national security to advance their cause when in fact many environmental issues pose no real threat to U.S. security. Nonetheless, the threat of global climate modification and the loss of the ozone layer appear to pose direct threats to U.S. security, while other environmental problems, such as ocean pollution, overpopulation, and the loss of biodiversity are indirect but real threats to national security.

Even the use of cyberspace, the seemingly borderless world of the Internet and modern telecommunications systems, raises new national security concerns. The Department of Defense is already exploring measures (and countermeasures) to combat computer viruses and other electronic or physical threats to the information network that are crucial economic and military systems. The export of common encryption programs, for example, threatens the government's capability to gather intelligence on terrorists, international criminal organizations, and rogue states.

Building a New Grand Strategy

The end of the Cold War, as was the end of World War II, is an opportunity for the United States to define its role in the world. Congress is likely to take more responsibility in foreign affairs. In 1988 and again in 1993, Senator Sam Nunn (D–Ga.) attempted to rewrite the War Powers Act and to restructure U.S. security institutions. Said Catherine Kelleher, a National Security Council staff member under President Jimmy Carter and now a senior fellow at the Brookings Institution, "Until you dismantle a lot of that, the Congress is just never going to get it. . . . We built the national security state, this whole apparatus, around the threat of the Cold War, surrounding and almost ennobling the president to make all of these tough decisions that were going to have to be taken because the missile threat was twenty-four minutes away."[37]

With the immense powers of the office, however, the president is primarily responsible for defining the grand strategy of the United States and building a political

engagement: A policy that says the United States will take the lead in international political and economic affairs, largely through constructive dialogue, but also by securing regional and global peace.

enlargement: A policy that says the United States will promote democracy, open markets, and other Western political, economic, and social values around the world.

coalition to support the appropriate policies. In February 1995 the Clinton administration outlined its grand strategy for the post-Cold War era in its report *A National Security Strategy of Engagement and Enlargement.* The primary national security objectives of the United States are enhancing military security, promoting prosperity at home, and promoting democracy. The report argues that U.S. grand strategy to achieve these objectives should be based on two principles, engagement and enlargement. **Engagement** means that the United States will not retreat into isolationism but will continue to take the lead in international political and economic affairs. The United States would address new threats posed by rogue nations, develop means to counter the proliferation of weapons of mass destruction, combat terrorism, stifle drug trafficking, and protect the environment to permit sustainable economic prosperity. **Enlargement** means that the United States will promote democracy, open markets, and other Western political, economic, and social values around the world.

In practical terms engagement and enlargement meant creating the Partnership for Peace, designed to more closely attune the formerly Communist states of Eastern Europe and the former Soviet Union to NATO and the West. It meant engaging in a constructive dialogue with North Korea to get them to freeze their nuclear weapons program in return for economic and political incentives designed to reduce their isolation from the world community. It also meant that other than assistance to Israel, Egypt, and the post-Communist countries, most foreign aid to support specific countries would be cut. Instead, aid would be used to promote democracy, resist terrorism, and combat the proliferation of weapons of mass destruction (nuclear, chemical, and biological) and their delivery systems. Foreign aid programs would also emphasize population control and raising the status of women, closely coordinated between the U.S. Agency for International Development and the aid recipients.

Promoting access to foreign markets for U.S. goods and services is an integral part of the strategy. From this perspective, enlarging the global market by supporting the World Trade Organization, the Asia-Pacific Economic Cooperation Forum, NAFTA, the Summit of the Americas, and other multilateral economic activities and institutions is essential to United States national security. Enlarging global markets provides jobs and help U.S. companies, especially the high-technology companies that are essential to U.S. military strength, stay competitive.

The idea (supported by current research) that countries that are market democracies do not fight wars with one another has become an important rationale in U.S. grand strategy.[38] By promoting market democracy abroad, particularly in Russia, the United States, in theory, will reduce the number of potential military threats it might face in the next century. At the same time, promoting economic reforms that move countries away from government-run economies to economies run by market forces would increase access for U.S. goods.

Will engagement and enlargement be the basis for a new consensus on the appropriate role of and grand strategy for the United States? Under the leadership of a strong president who understands the nation's capabilities, the United States can meet these challenges proactively with a coherent foreign policy. Although now only the United States appears to have the military and economic power to influence almost any issue in virtually any place in the world, U.S. power remains limited. Into the next century, Russia, China, the European Union, and Japan are likely to remain great powers, for either military or economic reasons or both. Some other pivotal countries, such as the oil-rich states of the Middle East or the increasingly industrialized countries in Asia and Latin America, are likely to increase their influence on global affairs. Finally, rogue nations, such as North Korea and Iraq, with their interest in weapons of mass destruction, may challenge any emerging world order not to their liking. Unlike the bipolar conflict between the United States and the Soviet Union, the multipolar world of the 1990s creates new opportunities for cooperation and conflict.

The grand strategy of containment helped give shape and purpose to the Cold War world order. Unless the president and Congress develop a new framework to guide U.S. actions in the post-Cold War era, not only will U.S. foreign and military policy in the late 1990s drift from one problem to another, but the U.S. government also will influence the shape of the next world order only by accident, not design. For two decades, the United States has been divided on involvement in the global arena. The end of the Cold War will bring new military and economic challenges for U.S. policy makers trying to mold a sophisticated and prevention-oriented grand strategy.

SUMMARY

Foreign and military policies differ in significant ways from other components of U.S. government. Their history has not been one of continuous development. To demonstrate that development, this chapter has made the following points:

1. Grand Strategy.

Every government tries to develop a grand strategy that enhances its prospects for power and plenty. Federalists and the Framers believed that a strong national government was the key to assuring a strong nation. To this end, after winning a war of national liberation, with crucial support from France, Americans withdrew behind their two-ocean moat.

2. The Roots of U.S. Foreign and Military Policy.

For more than a century, foreign and military policy played—with occasional exceptions—only a minor part in American life. George Washington's warnings against foreign entanglements were heeded. As U.S. economic interests grew, it became more difficult for the United States to stay out of wars without risking its sovereignty and security. Despite prolonged attempts to regain its relative isolation after intervening in World War I, the United States was unable to avoid participating in World War II.

3. The United States Becomes a World Leader.

During World War II and the years of the Cold War, foreign and military policy began to dominate the political agenda. Defense spending went from a small fraction of the federal budget to one of its biggest components, even during peacetime. Global affairs went from a peripheral issue of concern only to specialists to the focus of presidential attention and public debate.

4. The Machinery of Modern Foreign Policy Making.

The complex balances found in many other parts of the U.S. system are absent in the machinery of foreign and military policies. One branch of government, the executive (and one individual in that branch, the president), predominates. The predominance of the president has given rise to criticism of an imperial presidency, but debate about both the content and the process of foreign and military policy has been inhibited by fears of endangering national security.

5. Challenges to Presidential Power in Foreign and Military Policy.

The countervailing forces in the Congress, the bureaucracy, the news media, and the public play an important role in limiting the power of the president. Other components of U.S. government, such as the judicial branch and the state and local levels, play almost no role at all.

6. Changing Foreign and Military Policy.

With the ending of the Cold War and the disintegration of the Soviet Union, the sense of military threat has diminished. The nation can expect a more robust debate on both on grand strategy, including the content and decision-making process in foreign and military policy. As foreign affairs increasingly concern economic issues, the country can expect the president's authority to diminish, both because the Constitution allocates appropriation powers to Congress and because economic issues affect the pocketbooks of citizens in immediate and tangible ways.

KEY TERMS

bottom-up review, p. 764

containment, p. 743

engagement, p. 766

enlargement, p. 766

European Union (EU) p. 746

General Agreement on Tariffs and Trade (GATT), p. 740

grand strategy, p. 730

international governmental organization (IGO), p. 731

International Monetary Fund (IMF), p. 740

isolationism, p. 739

League of Nations, p. 739

manifest destiny, p. 736

Marshall Plan, p. 741

Monroe Doctrine, p. 736

multilateralism, p. 740

mutually assured destruction (MAD), p. 744

nation–state, p. 731

National Security Acts of 1947 and 1949, p. 748

North American Free Trade Agreement (NAFTA), p. 764

North Atlantic Treaty Organization (NATO), p. 742

tariffs, p. 735

Truman Doctrine, p. 741

United Nations, p. 740

War Powers Act, p. 755

World Bank, p. 740

World Trade Organization, p. 763

SUGGESTED READINGS

Allison, Graham T. *Essence of Decision: Explaining the Cuban Missile Crisis.* Boston: Little, Brown, 1971.

Ambrose, Stephen. *Rise to Globalism,* 6th ed. New York: Penguin, 1991.

Barnet, Richard J. *The Rockets' Red Glare. When America Goes to War: The Presidents and the People.* New York: Simon and Schuster, 1990.

Bundy, McGeorge. *Danger and Survival: Choices about the Bomb in the First Fifty Years.* New York: Random House, 1988.

Eckes, Alfred E., Jr. *Opening America's Market: U.S. Foreign Trade Policy Since 1776.* Chapel Hill: University of North Carolina Press, 1995.

Halberstam, David. *The Best and the Brightest.* New York: Random House, 1972.

Hallin, Daniel. *The "Uncensored War."* Berkeley: University of California Press, 1989.

Karnes, Margaret P., and Karen A. Mingst. *The United States and Multilateral Institutions.* New York: Routledge, 1992.

Kennan, George. *American Diplomacy 1900–1950.* Chicago: University of Chicago Press, 1951.

Kissinger, Henry. *Diplomacy.* New York: Simon & Schuster, 1994.

Klare, Michael. *Rogue States and Nuclear Outlaws: America's Search for a New Foreign Policy.* New York: Hill and Wang, 1995.

McGlen, Nancy E., and Meredith Reid Sarkees. *Women in Foreign Policy.* New York: Routledge, 1993.

Mueller, John E. *War, Presidents and Public Opinion.* New York: Wiley, 1973.

Perret, Geoffrey. *A Country Made by War.* New York: Random House, 1989.

Rosecrance, Richard, and Arthur A. Stein, eds. *The Domestic Bases of Grand Strategy.* Ithaca: Cornell University Press, 1993.

Schlesinger, Arthur. *The Imperial Presidency.* Boston: Houghton Mifflin, 1989.

Woodward, Bob. *The Commanders.* New York: Simon & Schuster, 1991.

THE DECLARATION OF INDEPENDENCE

In Congress, July 4, 1776

The Unanimous Declaration of the Thirteen United States of America

*W*hen in the Course of human events it becomes necessary for one people to dissolve the political bands which have connected them with another, and to assume, among the powers of the earth, the separate and equal station to which the Laws of Nature and of Nature's God entitle them, a decent respect to the opinions of mankind requires that they should declare the causes which impel them to the separation.

We hold these truths to be self-evident, that all men are created equal, that they are endowed by their Creator with certain unalienable Rights, that among these are Life, Liberty and the pursuit of Happiness. That to secure these rights, Governments are instituted among Men, deriving their just powers from the consent of the governed. That whenever any Form of Government becomes destructive of these ends, it is the Right of the People to alter or to abolish it, and to institute new Government, laying its foundation on such principles and organizing its powers in such form, as to them shall seem most likely to effect their Safety and Happiness. Prudence, indeed, will dictate that Governments long established should not be changed for light and transient causes; and accordingly all experience hath shewn that mankind are more disposed to suffer, while evils are sufferable, than to right themselves by abolishing the forms to which they are accustomed. But when a long train of abuses and usurpations, pursuing invariably the same Object evinces a design to reduce them under absolute Despotism, it is their right, it is their duty, to throw off such Government, and to pro-vide new Guards for their future security.—Such has been the patient sufferance of these Colonies; and such is now the necessity which constrains them to alter their former Systems of Government. The history of the present King of Great Britain is a history of repeated injuries and usurpations, all having in direct object the establishment of an absolute Tyranny over these States. To prove this, let Facts be submitted to a candid world.

He has refused his Assent to Laws, the most wholesome and necessary for the public good.

He has forbidden his Governors to pass Laws of immediate and pressing importance, unless suspended in their operation till his Assent should be obtained; and when so suspended, he has utterly neglected to attend to them.

He has refused to pass other Laws for the accommodation of large districts of people, unless those people would relinquish the right of Representation in the Legislature, a right inestimable to them and formidable to tyrants only.

He has called together legislative bodies at places unusual, uncomfortable, and distant from the depository of their Public Records, for the sole purpose of fatiguing them into compliance with his measures.

He has dissolved Representative Houses repeatedly, for opposing with manly firmness his invasions on the rights of the people.

He has refused for a long time, after such dissolutions, to cause others to be elected; whereby the Legislative Powers, incapable of Annihilation, have returned to the People at large for their exercise, the State remaining in the mean time exposed to all the dangers of invasion from without, and convulsions within.

He has endeavored to prevent the population of these States; for that purpose obstructing the Laws of Naturalization of Foreigners; refusing to pass others to encourage their migration hither, and raising the conditions of new Appropriations of Lands.

He has obstructed the Administration of Justice, by refusing his Assent to Laws for establishing Judiciary powers.

He has made Judges dependent on his Will alone, for the tenure of their offices, and the amount and payment of their salaries.

He has erected a multitude of New Offices, and sent hither swarms of Officers to harass our people, and eat out their substance.

He has kept among us, in times of peace, Standing Armies without the Consent of our legislatures.

He has affected to render the Military independent of and superior to the Civil power.

He has combined with others to subject us to a jurisdiction foreign to our constitution, and unacknowledged by our laws, giving his Assent to their Acts of pretended Legislation:

For quartering large bodies of armed troops among us:

For protecting them, by a mock Trial, from punishment for any Murders which they should commit on the Inhabitants of these States:

For cutting off our Trade with all parts of the world:

For imposing Taxes on us without our Consent:

For depriving us in many cases, of the benefits of Trial by Jury:

For transporting us beyond Seas to be tried for pretended offences:

For abolishing the free System of English Laws in a neighboring Province, establishing therein an Arbitrary government, and enlarging its Boundaries so as to render it at once an example and fit instrument for introducing the same absolute rule into these Colonies:

For taking away our Charters, abolishing our most valuable Laws, and altering fundamentally the Forms of our Governments:

For suspending our own Legislatures, and declaring themselves invested with power to legislate for us in all cases whatsoever.

He has abdicated Government here, by declaring us out of his Protection and waging War against us.

He has plundered our seas, ravaged our Coasts, burnt out towns, and destroyed the lives of our people.

He is at this time transporting large Armies of foreign Mercenaries to compleat the works of death, desolation and tyranny, already begun with circumstances of Cruelty and perfidy scarcely paralleled in the most barbarous ages, and totally unworthy the Head of a civilized nation.

He has constrained our fellow Citizens taken Captive on the high Seas to bear Arms against their Country, to become the executioners of their friends and Brethren, or to fall themselves by their Hands.

He has excited domestic insurrections amongst us, and has endeavored to bring on the inhabitants of our frontiers, the merciless Indian Savages, whose known rule of warfare, is an undistinguished destruction of all ages, sexes and conditions.

In every stage of these Oppressions We have Petitioned for Redress in the most humble terms: Our repeated Petitions have been answered only by repeated injury: A Prince, whose character is thus marked by every act which may define a Tyrant, is unfit to be the ruler of a free people.

Nor have We been wanting in attention to our British brethren. We have warned them from time to time of attempts by their legislature to extend an unwarrantable jurisdiction over us. We have reminded them of the circumstances of our emigration and settlement here. We have appealed to their native justice and magnanimity; and we have conjured them by the ties of our common kindred to disavow these usurpations, which would inevitably interrupt our connections and correspondence. They too have been deaf to the voice of justice and consanguinity. We must, therefore, acquiesce in the necessity, which denounces our Separation, and hold them, as we hold the rest of mankind, Enemies in War, in Peace Friends.

We, therefore, the Representatives of the United States of America, in General Congress, Assembled, appealing to the Supreme Judge of the world for the rectitude of our intentions, do, in the Name, and by Authority of the good People of these Colonies, solemnly publish and declare, That these United Colonies are, and of Right ought to be Free and Independent States; that they are Absolved from all Allegiance to the British Crown, and that all political connection between them and the State of Great Britain, is and ought to be totally dissolved: and that as Free and Independent States, they have full power to levy War, conclude Peace, contract Alliances, establish Commerce, and to do all other Acts and Things which Independent States may of right do. And for the support of this Declaration, with a firm reliance on the protection of divine Providence, we mutually pledge to each other our Lives, our Fortunes and our sacred Honor.

JOHN HANCOCK

NEW HAMPSHIRE
Josiah Bartlett,
Wm. Whipple,
Matthew Thornton.

MASSACHUSETTS BAY
Saml. Adams,
John Adams,
Robt. Treat Paine,
Elbridge Gerry.

RHODE ISLAND
Step. Hopkins,
William Ellery.

CONNECTICUT
Roger Sherman,
Samuel Huntington,
Wm. Williams,
Oliver Wolcott.

NEW YORK
Wm. Floyd,
Phil. Livingston,
Frans. Lewis,
Lewis Morris

NEW JERSEY
Richd. Stockton,
In. Witherspoon,
Fras. Hopkinson,
John Hart,
Abra. Clark.

PENNSYLVANIA
Robt. Morris,
Benjamin Rush,
Benjamin Franklin,
John Morton,
Geo. Clymer,
Jas. Smith,
Geo. Taylor,
James Wilson,
Geo. Ross.

DELAWARE
Caesar Rodney,
Geo. Read,
Tho. M'kean.

MARYLAND
Samuel Chase,
Wm. Paca,
Thos. Stone,
Charles Caroll of Caroll-ton.

VIRGINIA
George Wythe,
Richard Henry Lee,
Th. Jefferson,
Benjamin Harrison,
Thos. Nelson, jr.,
Francis Lightfoot Lee,
Carter Braxton.

NORTH CAROLINA
Wm. Hooper,
Joseph Hewes,
John Penn.

SOUTH CAROLINA
Edward Rutledge,
Thos. Heyward, Junr.,
Thomas Lynch, jnr.,
Arthur Middleton.

GEORGIA
Button Guinnett,
Lyman Hall,
Geo. Walton.

THE CONSTITUTION OF THE UNITED STATES OF AMERICA

*W*e the People of the United States, in Order to form a more perfect Union, establish Justice, insure domestic Tranquility, provide for the common defence, promote the general Welfare, and secure the Blessings of Liberty to ourselves and our Posterity, do ordain and establish this Constitution for the United States of America.

ARTICLE I

SECTION 1. All legislative Powers herein granted shall be vested in a Congress of the United States, which shall consist of a Senate and House of Representatives.

SECTION 2. The House of Representatives shall be composed of Members chosen every second Year by the People of the several States, and the Electors in each State shall have the Qualifications requisite for Electors of the most numerous Branch of the State Legislature.

No person shall be a Representative who shall not have attained to the Age of twenty five Years, and been seven Years a Citizen of the United States, and who shall not, when elected, be an Inhabitant of that State in which he shall be chosen.

Representatives and direct Taxes shall be apportioned among the several States which may be included within this Union, according to their respective Numbers which shall be determined by adding to the whole Number of free Persons, including those bound to Service for a Term of Years, and excluding Indians not taxed, three fifths of all other Persons. The actual Enumeration shall be made within three Years after the first Meeting of the Congress of the United States, and within every subsequent Term ten Years, in such Manner as they shall by Law direct. The Number of Representatives shall not exceed one for every thirty Thousand, but each State shall have at Least one Representative; and until such enumeration shall be made, the State of New Hampshire shall be entitled to chuse three, Massachusetts eight, Rhode-Island and Providence Plantations one, Connecticut five, New-York six, New Jersey four, Pennsylvania eight, Delaware one, Maryland six, Virginia ten, North Carolina five, South Carolina five, and Georgia three.

When vacancies happen in the Representation from any State, the Executive Authority thereof shall issue Writs of Election to fill such Vacancies.

The House of Representatives shall chuse their speaker and other Officers; and shall have the sole Power of Impeachment.

SECTION 3. The Senate of the United States shall be composed of two Senators from each State chosen by the Legislature thereof, for six Years; and each Senator shall have one Vote.

Immediately after they shall be assembled in Consequence of the first Election, they shall be divided as equally as may be into three Classes. The Seats of the Senators of the first Class shall be vacated at the Expiration of the second year, of the second Class at the Expiration of the fourth Year, and of the third Class at the Expiration of the sixth Year, so that one third may be chosen every second Year and if Vacancies happen by Resignation, or otherwise, during the Recess of the Legislature of any State, the Executive thereof may make temporary Appointments until the next Meeting of the Legislature, which shall then fill such Vacancies.

No Person shall be a Senator who shall not have attained to the Age of thirty Years, and been nine Years a Citizen of the United States, and who shall not, when elected, be an Inhabitant of that State for which he shall be chosen.

The Vice President of the United States shall be President of the Senate, but shall have no Vote, unless they be equally divided.

The Senate shall chuse their other Officers, and also a President pro tempore, in the Absence of the Vice President, or when he shall exercise the Office of President of the United States.

The Senate shall have the sole Power to try all Impeachments. When sitting for that Purpose, they shall be on Oath or Affirmation. When the President of the United States is tried, the Chief Justice shall preside: And no Person shall be convicted without the Concurrence of two thirds of the Members present.

Judgment in Cases of Impeachment shall not extend further than to removal from Office, and disqualification to hold and enjoy any Office of honor, Trust or Profit under the United States; but the Party convicted shall nevertheless be liable and subject to Indictment, Trial, Judgment and Punishment, according to Law.

SECTION 4. The Times, Places and Manner of holding Elections for Senators and Representatives, shall be prescribed in each State by the Legislature thereof; but the Congress may at any time by law make or alter such Regulations, except as to the Places of chusing Senators.

The Congress shall assemble at least once in every Year, and such Meeting shall be on the first Monday in December, unless they shall by Law appoint a different Day.

SECTION 5. Each House shall be the Judge of the Elections, Returns and Qualifications of its own Members, and a Majority of each shall constitute a Quorum to do Business; but a smaller Number may adjourn from day to day, and may be authorized to compel the Attendance of absent Members, in such Manner, and under such Penalties as each House may provide.

Each House may determine the Rules of its Proceedings, punish its Members for disorderly Behaviour, and with the Concurrence of two thirds, expel a Member.

Each House shall keep a journal of its Proceedings, and from time to time publish the same, excepting such Parts as may in their judgment require Secrecy; and the Yeas and Nays of the Members of either House on any question shall, at the Desire of one fifth of those present, be entered on the Journal.

Neither House, during the Session of Congress, shall, without the Consent of the other, adjourn for more than three days, nor to any other Place than that in which the two Houses shall be sitting.

SECTION 6. The Senators and Representatives shall receive a Compensation for their Services, to be ascertained by Law, and paid out of the Treasury of the United States. They shall in all Cases, except Treason, Felony and Breach of the Peace, be privileged from Arrest during their Attendance at the Session of their respective Houses, and in going to and returning from the same; and for any Speech or Debate in either House, they shall not be questioned in any other Place.

No Senator or Representative shall, during the Time for which he was elected, be appointed to any civil Office under the Authority of the United States, which shall have been created, or the Emoluments whereof shall have been increased during such time; and no Person holding any Office under the United States, shall be a Member of either House during his Continuance in Office.

SECTION 7. All Bills for raising Revenue shall originate in the House of Representatives; but the Senate may propose or concur with Amendments as on other Bills.

Every Bill which shall have passed the House of Representatives and the Senate, shall, before it become a Law, be presented to the President of the United States; If he approves he shall sign it, but if not he shall return it, with his Objections to that House in which it shall have originated, who shall enter the Objections at large on their journal, and proceed to reconsider it. If after such Reconsideration two thirds of that House shall agree to pass the Bill, it shall be sent, together with the Objections, to the other House, by which it shall likewise be reconsidered, and if approved by two thirds of that House, it shall become a Law. But in all such Cases the Votes of both Houses shall be determined by Yeas and Nays, and the Names of the Persons voting for and against the Bill shall be entered on the Journal of each House respectively. If any Bill shall not be returned by the President within ten Days (Sundays excepted) after it shall have been presented to him, the Same shall be a Law, in like Manner as if he had signed it, unless the Congress by their Adjournment prevent its Return, in which Case it shall not be a Law.

Every Order, Resolution, or Vote to which the Concurrence of the Senate and House of Representatives may be necessary (except on a question of Adjournment) shall be presented to the President of the United States; and before the Same shall take Effect, shall be approved by him, or being disapproved by him, shall be repassed by two thirds of the Senate and House of Representatives, according to the Rules and Limitations prescribed in the Case of a Bill.

SECTION 8. The Congress shall have Power To lay and collect Taxes, Duties, Imposts and Excises, to pay the Debts and provide for the common Defence and general Welfare of the United States; but all Duties, Imposts and Excises shall be uniform throughout the United States;

To borrow Money on the credit of the United States;

To regulate Commerce with foreign Nations, and among the several States, and with the Indian Tribes;

To establish a uniform Rule of Naturalization, and uniform Laws on the subject of Bankruptcies throughout the United States;

To coin Money, regulate the Value thereof, and of foreign Coin, and fix the Standard of Weights and Measures;

To provide for the Punishment of counterfeiting the Securities and current Coin of the United States;

To establish Post Offices and post Roads;

To promote the Progress of Science and useful Arts, by securing for limited Times to Authors and Inventors the exclusive Right to their respective Writings and Discoveries;

To constitute Tribunals inferior to the supreme Court;

To define and punish Piracies and Felonies committed on the high Seas, and Offences against the Law of Nations;

To declare War, grant Letters of Marque and Reprisal, and make Rules concerning Captures on Land and Water;

To raise and support Armies, but no Appropriation of Money to that Use shall be for a longer Term than two Years;

To provide and maintain a Navy;

To make Rules for the Government and Regulation of the land and naval Forces;

To provide for calling forth the Militia to execute the Laws of the Union, suppress Insurrections and repel Invasions;

To provide for organizing, arming, and disciplining, the Militia, and for governing such Part of them as may be employed in the Service of the United States, reserving to the States respectively, the Appointment of the Officers, and the Authority of training the Militia according to the discipline prescribed by Congress;

To exercise exclusive Legislation in all Cases whatsoever, over such District (not exceeding ten Miles square) as may, by Cession of particular States, and the Acceptance of Congress, become the Seat of the Government of the United States, and to exercise like Authority over all Places purchased by the Consent of the Legislature of the State in which the Same shall be for the Erection of Forts, Magazines, Arsenals, dock-Yards, and other needful Buildings;—And

To make all Laws which shall be necessary and proper for carrying into Execution the foregoing Powers, and all other Powers vested by this Constitution in the Government of the United States, or in any Department or Officer thereof.

SECTION 9. The Migration or Importation of such Persons as any of the States now existing shall think proper to admit, shall not be prohibited by the Congress prior to the Year one thousand eight hundred and eight, but a Tax or duty may be imposed on such Importation, not exceeding ten dollars for each Person.

The Privilege of the Writ of Habeas Corpus shall not be suspended, unless when in Cases of Rebellion or Invasion the public Safety may require it.

No Bill of Attainder or ex post facto Law shall be passed.

No Capitation, or other direct, Tax shall be laid, unless in Proportion to the Census or Enumeration herein before directed to be taken.

No Tax or Duty shall be laid on Articles exported from any State.

No Preference shall be given by any Regulation of Commerce or Revenue to the Ports of one State over those of another; nor shall Vessels bound to, or from, one State, be obliged to enter, clear, or pay Duties in another.

No Money shall be drawn from the Treasury, but in Consequence of Appropriations made by Law; and a regular Statement and Account of the Receipts and Expenditures of all public Money shall be published from time to time.

No Title of Nobility shall be granted by the United States: And no Person holding any Office of Profit or Trust under them, shall, without the Consent of the Congress, accept of any present, Emolument, Office, or Title, of any kind whatever, from any King, Prince, or foreign State.

SECTION 10. No state shall enter into any Treaty, Alliance, or Confederation; grant Letters of Marque and Reprisal; coin Money; emit Bills of Credit; make any Thing but gold and silver Coin a Tender in Payment of Debts; pass any Bill of Attainder, ex post facto Law, or Law impairing the Obligation of Contracts, or grant any Title of Nobility.

No State shall, without the Consent of the Congress, lay any Imposts or Duties on Imports or Exports, except what may be absolutely necessary for executing its inspection Laws: and the net Produce of all Duties and Imposts, laid by any State on Imports or Exports, shall be for the Use of the Treasury of the United States, and all such Laws shall be subject to the Revision and Controul of the Congress.

No State shall, without the Consent of Congress, lay any Duty of Tonnage, keep Troops, or Ships of War in time of Peace, enter into any Agreement or Compact with another State, or with a foreign Power, or engage in War, unless actually invaded, or in such imminent Danger as will not admit of delay.

ARTICLE II

SECTION 1. The executive Power shall be vested in a President of the United States of America. He shall hold his Office during the Term of four Years, and, together with the Vice President, chosen for the same Term, be elected as follows.

Each State shall appoint, in such Manner as the Legislature thereof may direct, a Number of Electors, equal to the whole Number of Senators and Representatives to which the State may be entitled in the Congress; but no Senator or Representative, or Person holding an Office of Trust of Profit under the United States, shall be appointed an Elector.

The Electors shall meet in their respective States, and vote by Ballot for two Persons, of whom one at least shall not be an Inhabitant of the same State with themselves. And they shall make a List of all the Persons voted for, and, of the Number of Votes for each; which List they shall sign and certify, and transmit sealed to the Seat of the Government of the United States, directed to the President of the Senate. The President of the Senate shall, in the Presence of the Senate and House of Representatives, open all the Certificates, and the Votes shall then be counted. The Person having the greatest Number of Votes shall be the President, if such Number be a Majority of the whole Number of Electors appointed; and if there be more than one who have such Majority, and have an equal Number of Votes, then the House of Representatives shall immediately chuse by Ballot one of them for President; and if no Person have a Majority, then from the five highest on the List the said House shall in like Manner chuse the President. But in chusing the President, the Votes shall be taken by States, the Representation from each State having one Vote; A quorum for this Purpose shall consist of a Member or Members from two thirds of the States, and a Majority of all the States shall be necessary to a Choice. In every Case, after the Choice of the President, the Person having the greatest Number of Votes of the Electors shall be the Vice President. But if there should remain two or more who have equal Votes, the Senate shall chuse from them by Ballot the Vice President.

The Congress may determine the Time of chusing the Electors, and the Day on which they shall give their Votes; which Day shall be the same throughout the United States.

No Person except a natural born Citizen, or a Citizen of the United States, at the time of the Adoption of this Constitution, shall be eligible to the Office of President; neither shall any Person be eligible to that Office who shall not have attained to the Age of thirty five Years, and been fourteen Years a Resident within the United States.

In Case of the Removal of the President from Office, or of his Death, Resignation, or Inability to discharge the Powers and Duties of the said Office, the Same shall devolve on the Vice President, and the Congress may by Law provide for the Case of Removal, Death, Resignation or Inability, both of the President and Vice President, declaring what Officer shall then act as President, and such Officer shall act accordingly, until the Disability be removed, or a President shall be elected.

The President shall, at stated Times, receive for his Services, a Compensation, which shall neither be encreased nor diminished during the Period for which he shall have been elected, and he shall not receive within that Period any other Emolument from the United States, or any of them.

Before he enter on the Execution of his Office, he shall take the following Oath or Affirmation—"I do solemnly swear (or affirm) that I will faithfully execute the Office of President of the United States, and will to the best of my Ability, preserve, protect and defend the Constitution of the United States."

SECTION 2. The President shall be Commander in Chief of the Army, and Navy of the United States, and of the Militia of the several States, when called into the actual Service of the United States; he may require the Opinion, in writing, of the principal Officer in each of the executive Departments, upon any Subject relating to the Duties of their respective Offices, and he shall have Power to grant Reprieves and Pardons for Offences against the United States, except in Cases of Impeachment.

He shall have Power, by and with the Advice and Consent of the Senate, to make Treaties, provided two thirds of the Senators present concur; and he shall nominate, and by and with the Advice and Consent of the Senate, shall appoint Ambassadors, other public Ministers and Consuls, Judges of the supreme Court, and all other Officers of the United States, whose Appointments are not herein otherwise provided for, and which shall be established by Law: but the Congress may by Law vest the Appointment of such inferior Officers, as they think proper, in the President alone, in the Courts of Law, or in the Heads of Departments.

The President shall have Power to fill up all Vacancies that may happen during the Recess of the Senate, by granting Commissions which shall expire at the end of their next Session.

SECTION 3. He shall from time to time give to the Congress Information of the State of the Union, and recommend to their Consideration such Measures as he shall judge necessary and expedient; he may, on extraordinary Occasions, convene both Houses, or either of them, and in Case of Disagreement between them, with Respect to the Time of Adjournment, he may adjourn them to such Time as he shall think proper; he shall receive Ambassadors and other public Ministers; he shall take Care that the Laws be faithfully executed, and shall Commission all the Officers of the United States.

SECTION 4. The President, Vice President and all civil Officers of the United States, shall be removed from Office on Impeachment for, and Conviction of, Treason, Bribery, or other high Crimes and Misdemeanors.

ARTICLE III

SECTION 1. The judicial Power of the United States, shall be vested in one supreme Court, and in such inferior Courts as the Congress may from time to time ordain and establish. The Judges, both of the supreme and inferior Courts, shall hold their Offices during good Behaviour, and shall, at stated Times, receive for their Services, a Compensation, which shall not be diminished during their Continuance in Office.

SECTION 2. The judicial Power shall extend to all Cases, in Law and Equity, arising under this Constitution, the Laws of the United States, and Treaties made, or which shall be made, under their Authority;—to all Cases affecting Ambassadors, other public Ministers and Consuls;—to all Cases of admiralty and maritime Jurisdiction;—to Controversies to which the United States shall be a Party;—to Controversies between two or more States;—between a State and Citizens of another State;—between Citizens of different States,—between Citizens of the same State claiming Lands under Grants of different States,—and between a State, or the Citizens thereof, and foreign States, Citizens of Subjects.

In all Cases affecting Ambassadors, other public Ministers and Consuls, and those in which a State shall be Party, the supreme Court shall have original Jurisdiction. In all the other Cases before mentioned, the supreme Court shall have appellate Jurisdiction, both as to Law and Fact, with such Exceptions, and under such Regulations as the Congress shall make.

The Trial of all Crimes, except in Cases of Impeachment, shall be by Jury; and such Trial shall be held in the State where the said Crimes shall have been committed; but when not committed within any State, the Trial shall be at such Place or Places as the Congress may by Law have directed.

SECTION 3. Treason against the United States, shall consist only in levying War against them, or in adhering to their Enemies, giving them Aid and Comfort. No Person shall be convicted of Treason unless on the Testimony of two Witnesses to the same overt Act, or on Confession in open Court.

The Congress shall have Power to declare the Punishment of Treason, but no Attainder of Treason shall work Corruption of Blood, or Forfeiture except during the Life of the Person attainted.

ARTICLE IV

SECTION 1. Full Faith and Credit shall be given in each State to the public Acts, Records, and judicial Proceedings of every other State. And the Congress may by general Laws prescribe the Manner in which such Acts, Records and Proceedings shall be proved, and the Effect thereof.

SECTION 2. The Citizens of each State shall be entitled to all Privileges and Immunities of Citizens in the several States.

A Person charged in any State with Treason, Felony, or other Crime, who shall flee from Justice, and be found in another State, shall on Demand of the executive Authority of the State from which he fled, be delivered up, to be removed to the State having Jurisdiction of the Crime.

No Person held to Service or Labour in one State under the Laws thereof, escaping into another, shall, in Consequence of any Law or Regulation therein, be discharged from such Service or Labour, but shall be delivered up on Claim of the Party to whom such Service or Labour may be due.

SECTION 3. New States may be admitted by the Congress into this Union; but no new State shall be formed or erected within the Jurisdiction of any other State; nor any State be formed by the Junction of two or more States, or Parts of States, without the Consent of the Legislatures of the States concerned as well as of the Congress.

The Congress shall have Power to dispose of and make all needful Rules and Regulations respecting the Territory or other Property belonging to the United States; and nothing in this Constitution shall be so construed as to Prejudice any Claims of the United States, or of any particular State.

SECTION 4. The United States shall guarantee to every State in this Union a Republican Form of Government, and shall protect each of them against Invasion, and on Application of the Legislature, or of the Executive (when the Legislature cannot be convened) against domestic Violence.

ARTICLE V

The Congress, whenever two thirds of both Houses shall deem it necessary, shall propose Amendments to this Constitution, or, on the Application of the Legislatures of two thirds of the several States, shall call a Convention for proposing Amendments, which, in either Case, shall be valid to all Intents and Purposes, as Part of this Constitution, when ratified by the Legislatures of three fourths of the several States, or by Conventions in three fourths thereof, as the one or the other Mode of Ratification may be proposed by the Congress; Provided that no Amendment which may be made prior to the Year One thousand eight hundred and eight shall in any Manner affect the first and fourth Clauses in the Ninth Section of the first Article; and that no State, without its Consent, shall be deprived of its equal Suffrage in the Senate.

ARTICLE VI

All Debts contracted and Engagements entered into, before the Adoption of this Constitution, shall be as valid against the United States under this Constitution, as under the Confederation.

This Constitution, and the laws of the United States which shall be made in Pursuance thereof; and all Treaties made, or which shall be made, under the Authority of the United States, shall be the supreme Law of the Land; and the Judges in every State shall be bound thereby, any Thing in the Constitution or Laws of any State to the Contrary notwithstanding.

The Senators and Representatives before mentioned, and the Members of the several State Legislatures, and all executive and judicial Officers, both of the United States and of the several States, shall be bound by Oath or Affirmation, to support this Constitution; but no religious Test shall ever be required as a

Qualification to any Office or public Trust under the United States.

ARTICLE VII

The Ratification of the Conventions of nine States, shall be sufficient for the Establishment of this Constitution between the States so ratifying the Same.

Done in Convention by the Unanimous Consent of the States present the Seventeenth Day of September in the Year of our Lord one thousand seven hundred and Eighty seven and of the Independence of the United States of America the Twelfth. IN WITNESS whereof we have hereunto subscribed our Names,

Go. WASHINGTON
Presid't. and deputy from Virginia

Attest
WILLIAM JACKSON
Secretary

DELAWARE
Geo. Read
Gunning Bedford jun
John Dickinson
Richard Basset
Jaco. Broom

MASSACHUSETTS
Nathaniel Gorham
Rufus King

CONNECTICUT
Wm. Saml. Johnson
Roger Sherman

NEW YORK
Alexander Hamilton

NEW JERSEY
Wh. Livingston
David Brearley
Wm. Paterson
Jona. Dayton

PENNSYLVANIA
B. Franklin
Thomas Mifflin
Robt. Morris
Geo. Clymer
Thos. FitzSimons
Jared Ingersoll
James Wilson
Gouv. Morris

NEW HAMPSHIRE
John Langdon
Nicholas Gilman

MARYLAND
James McHenry
Dan of St. Thos. Jenifer
Danl. Carroll

VIRGINIA
John Blair
James Madison, Jr.

NORTH CAROLINA
Wm. Blount
Richd. Dobbs Spaight
Hu. Williamson

SOUTH CAROLINA
J. Rutledge
Charles Cotesworth Pinckney
Charles Pinckney
Pierce Butler

GEORGIA
William Few
Abr. Baldwin

Articles in addition to, and amendment of the Constitution of the United States of America, proposed by Congress and ratified by the Legislatures of the several states, pursuant to the Fifth Article of the original Constitution.

(The first ten amendments were passed by Congress on September 25, 1789, and were ratified on December 15, 1791.)

Amendment I

Congress shall make no law respecting an establishment of religion, or prohibiting the free exercise thereof; or abridging the freedom of speech, or of the press; or the right of the people peaceably to assemble, and to petition the Government for a redress of grievances.

Amendment II

A well regulated Militia, being necessary to the security of a free State, the right of the people to keep and bear Arms, shall not be infringed.

Amendment III

No Soldier shall, in time of peace be quartered in any house, without the consent of the Owner, nor in time of war, but in a manner to be prescribed by law.

Amendment IV

The right of the people to be secure in their persons, houses, papers, and effects, against unreasonable searches and seizures, shall not be violated, and no warrants shall issue, but upon probable cause, supported by Oath or affirmation, and particularly describing the place to be searched, and the persons or things to be seized.

Amendment V

No person shall be held to answer for a capital, or otherwise infamous crime, unless on a presentment or indictment of a Grand Jury, except in cases arising in the land or naval forces, or in the Militia, when in actual service in time of War or public danger; nor shall any person be subject for the same offence to be twice put in jeopardy of life or limb; nor shall be compelled in any criminal case to be a witness against himself, nor be deprived of life, liberty, or property, without due process of law; nor shall private property be taken for public use, without just compensation.

Amendment VI

In all criminal prosecutions, the accused shall enjoy the right to a speedy and public trial, by an impartial jury of the State and district wherein the crime shall have been committed, which district shall have been previously ascertained by law, and to be informed of the nature and cause of the accusation; to be confronted with the witnesses against him; to have compulsory process for obtaining witnesses in his favor, and to have the assistance of counsel for his defence.

Amendment VII

In Suits at common law, where the value in controversy shall exceed twenty dollars, the right of trial by jury shall be preserved, and no fact tried by a jury, shall be otherwise re-examined in any Court of the United States, than according to the rules of the common law.

Amendment VIII

Excessive bail shall not be required, nor excessive fines imposed, nor cruel and unusual punishments inflicted.

Amendment IX

The enumeration in the Constitution, of certain rights, shall not be construed to deny or disparage others retained by the people.

Amendment X

The powers not delegated to the United States by the Constitution, nor prohibited by it to the States, are reserved to the States respectively, or to the people.

Amendment XI   *(Ratified on February 7, 1795)*

The Judicial power of the United States shall not be construed to extend to any suit in law or equity, commenced or prosecuted against one of the United States by Citizens of another State, or by Citizens or Subjects of any Foreign State.

Amendment XII   *(Ratified on June 15, 1804)*

The Electors shall meet in their respective states, and vote by ballot for President and Vice-President, one of whom, at least, shall not be an inhabitant of the same state with themselves; they shall name in their ballots the person voted for as President, and in distinct ballots the person voted for as Vice-President, and they shall make distinct lists of all persons voted for as President, and of all persons voted for as Vice-President, and of the number of votes for each, which lists they shall sign and certify, and transmit sealed to the seat of the government of the United States, directed to the President of the Senate;—The President of the Senate shall, in the presence of the Senate and House of Representatives, open all the certificates and the votes shall then be counted;—The person having the greatest number of votes for President, shall be the President, if such number be a majority of the whole number of Electors appointed; and if no person have such majority; then from the persons having the highest numbers not exceeding three on the list of those voted for as President, the House of Representatives shall choose immediately, by ballot, the President. But in choosing the President, the votes shall be taken by states, the representation from each state having one vote; a quorum for this purpose shall consist of a member or members from two-thirds of the states, and a majority of all the states shall be necessary to a choice. And if the House of Representatives shall not choose a President whenever the right of choice shall devolve upon them, before the fourth day of March next following, then the Vice-President shall act as President, as in the case of the death or other constitutional disability of the President.—The person having the greatest number of votes as Vice-President, shall be the Vice-President, if such number be a majority of the whole number of Electors appointed, and if no person have a majority, then from the two highest numbers on the list, the Senate shall choose the Vice-President; a quorum for the purpose shall consist of two-thirds of the whole number of Senators, and a majority of the whole number shall be necessary to a choice. But no person constitutionally ineligible to the office of President shall be eligible to that of Vice-President of the United States.

Amendment XIII   *(Ratified on December 6, 1865)*

SECTION 1. Neither slavery nor involuntary servitude, except as a punishment for crime whereof the party shall have been duly convicted, shall exist within the United States, or any place subject to their jurisdiction.

SECTION 2. Congress shall have power to enforce this article by appropriate legislation.

Amendment XIV   *(Ratified on July 9, 1868)*

SECTION 1. All persons born or naturalized in the United States, and subject to the jurisdiction thereof, are citizens of the United States and of the State wherein they reside. No State shall make or enforce any law which shall abridge the privileges or immunities of citizens of the United States; nor shall any State deprive any person of life, liberty, or property, without due process of law; nor deny to any person within its jurisdiction the equal protection of the laws.

SECTION 2. Representatives shall be apportioned among the several States according to their respective numbers, counting the whole number of persons in each State, excluding Indians not taxed. But when the right to vote at any election for the choice of electors for President and Vice President of the United States, Representatives in Congress, the Executive and Judicial officers of a State, or the members of the Legislature thereof, is denied to any of the male inhabitants of such State, being twenty-one years of age, and citizens of the United States, or in any way abridged, except for participation in rebellion, or other crime, the basis of representation therein shall be reduced in the proportion which the number of such male citizens shall bear to the whole number of male citizens twenty-one years of age in such State.

SECTION 3. No person shall be a Senator or Representative in Congress, or elector of President and Vice President, or hold any office, civil or military, under the United States, or under any State, who, having previously taken an oath, as a member of Congress, or as an officer of the United States, or as a member of any State legislature, or as an executive or judicial officer of any State, to support the Constitution of the United States, shall have engaged in insurrection or rebellion against the same, or given aid or comfort to the enemies thereof. But Congress may by a vote of two-thirds of each House, remove such diability.

SECTION 4. The validity of the public debt of the United States, authorized by law, including debts incurred for payment of pensions and bounties for services in suppressing insurrection or rebellion, shall not be questioned. But neither the United States nor any State shall assume or pay any debt or obligation incurred in aid of insurrection or rebellion against the United States, or any claim for the loss or emancipation of any slave, but all such debts, obligations and claims shall be held illegal and void.

SECTION 5. The Congress shall have power to enforce, by appropriate legislation, the provisions of this article.

Amendment XV   *(Ratified on February 3, 1870)*

SECTION 1. The right of citizens of the United States to vote shall not be denied or abridged by the United States or by any State on account of race, color, or previous condition of servitude.

SECTION 2. The Congress shall have power to enforce this article by appropriate legislation.

Amendment XVI   *(Ratified on February 3, 1913)*

The Congress shall have power to lay and collect taxes on incomes, from whatever source derived, without apportionment among the several States, and without regard to any census or enumeration.

Amendment XVII   *(Ratified on April 8, 1913)*

The Senate of the United States shall be composed of two Senators from each State, elected by the people thereof, for six years; and each Senator shall have one vote. The electors in each State shall have the qualifications requisite for electors of the most numerous branch of the State legislatures.

When vacancies happen in the representation of any State in the Senate, the executive authority of such State shall issue writs of election to fill such vacancies: Provided, That the legislature of any State may empower the executive thereof to make temporary appointments until the people fill the vacancies by election as the legislature may direct.

This amendment shall not be so construed as to affect the election or term of any Senator chosen before it becomes valid as part of the Constitution.

Amendment XVIII   *(Ratified on January 16, 1919)*

SECTION 1. After one year from the ratification of this article the manufacture, sale, or transportation of intoxicating liquors within, the importation thereof into, or the exportation thereof from the United States and all territory subject to the jurisdiction thereof for beverage purposes is hereby prohibited.

SECTION 2. The Congress and the several States shall have concurrent power to enforce this article by appropriate legislation.

SECTION 3. This article shall be inoperative unless it shall have been ratified as an amendment to the Constitution by the legislatures of the several States, as provided in the Constitution, within seven years from the date of the submission hereof to the States by the Congress.

Amendment XIX   *(Ratified on August 18, 1920)*

The right of citizens of the United States to vote shall not be denied or abridged by the United States or by any State on account of sex.

Congress shall have power to enforce this article by appropriate legislation.

Amendment XX   *(Ratified on February 6, 1933)*

SECTION 1. The terms of the President and Vice President shall end at noon on the 20th day of January, and the terms of Senators and Representatives at noon on the 3d day of January, of the years in which such terms would have ended if this article had not been ratified; and the terms of their successors shall then begin.

SECTION 2. The Congress shall assemble at least once in every year, and such meeting shall begin at noon on the 3d day of January, unless they shall by law appoint a different day.

SECTION 3. If, at the time fixed for the beginning of the term of the President, the President elect shall have died, the Vice President elect shall become President. If a President shall not have been chosen before the time fixed for the beginning of his term, or if the President elect shall have failed to qualify, then the Vice President elect shall act as President until a President shall have qualified; and the Congress may by law provide for the case wherein neither a President elect nor a Vice President elect shall have qualified, declaring who shall then act as President, or the manner in which one who is to act shall be selected, and such person shall act accordingly until a President or Vice President shall have qualified.

SECTION 4. The Congress may by law provide for the case of the death of any of the persons from whom the House of Representatives may choose a President whenever the rights of choice shall have devolved upon them, and for the case of the death of any of the persons from whom the Senate may choose a Vice President whenever the right of choice shall have devolved upon them.

SECTION 5. Sections 1 and 2 shall take effect on the 15th day of October following the ratification of this article.

SECTION 6. This article shall be inoperative unless it shall have been ratified as an amendment to the Con-

stitution by the legislatures of three-fourths of the several States within seven years from the date of its submission.

Amendment XXI   *(Ratified on December 5, 1933)*

SECTION 1. The eighteenth article of amendment to the Constitution of the United States is hereby repealed.

SECTION 2. The transportation or importation into any State, Territory, or possession of the United States for delivery or use therein of intoxicating liquors, in violation of the laws thereof, is hereby prohibited.

SECTION 3. This article shall be inoperative unless it shall have been ratified as an amendment to the Constitution by conventions in the several States, as provided in the Constitution, within seven years from the date of the submission hereof to the States by the Congress.

Amendment XXII   *(Ratified on February 27, 1951)*

No person shall be elected to the office of the President more than twice, and no person who has held the office of President, or acted as President, for more than two years of a term to which some other person was elected President shall be elected to the office of the President more than once. But this Article shall not apply to any person holding the office of President when this Article was proposed by the Congress, and shall not prevent any person who may be holding the office of President, or acting as President, during the term within which this Article becomes operative from holding the office of President or acting as President during the remainder of such term.

Amendment XXIII   *(Ratified on March 29, 1961)*

SECTION 1. The District constituting the seat of Government of the United States shall appoint in such manner as the Congress may direct:

A number of electors of President and Vice President equal to the whole number of Senators and Representatives in Congress to which the District would be entitled if it were a State, but in no event more than the least populous State; they shall be in addition to those appointed by the States, but they shall be considered, for the purposes of the election of President and Vice President, to be electors appointed by a State; and they shall meet in the District and perform such duties as provided by the twelfth article of amendment.

SECTION 2. The Congress shall have power to enforce this article by appropriate legislation.

Amendment XXIV   *(Ratified on January 23, 1964)*

SECTION 1. The right of citizens of the United States to vote in any primary or other election for President or Vice President, for electors for President or Vice President, or for Senator or Representative in Congress, shall not be denied or abridged by the United States or any State by reason of failure to pay any poll tax or other tax.

SECTION 2. The Congress shall have power to enforce this article by appropriate legislation.

Amendment XXV   *(Ratified on February 10, 1967)*

SECTION 1. In case of the removal of the President from office or of his death or resignation, the Vice President shall become President.

SECTION 2. Whenever there is a vacancy in the office of the Vice President, the President shall nominate a Vice President who shall take office upon confirmation by a majority vote of both Houses of Congress.

SECTION 3. Whenever the President transmits to the President pro tempore of the Senate and the Speaker of the House of Representatives his written declaration that he is unable to discharge the powers and duties of his office, and until he transmits to them a written declaration to the contrary, such powers and duties shall be discharged by the Vice President as Acting President.

SECTION 4. Whenever the Vice President and a majority of either the principal officers of the executive departments or of such other body as Congress may by law provide, transmit to the President pro tempore of the Senate and the Speaker of the House of Representatives their written declaration that the President is unable to discharge the powers and duties of his office, the Vice President shall immediately assume the powers and duties of the office as Acting President.

Thereafter, when the President transmits to the President pro tempore of the Senate and the Speaker of the House of Representatives his written declaration that no inability exists, he shall resume the powers and duties of his office unless the Vice President and a majority of either the principal officers of the executive department or of such other body as Congress may by law provide, transmit within four days to the President pro tempore of the Senate and the Speaker of the House of Representatives their written declaration that the President is unable to discharge the powers and duties of his office. Thereupon Congress shall decide the issue, assembling within forty-eight hours for that purpose if not in session. If the Congress, within twenty-one days after receipt of the latter written declaration, or, if Congress is not in session, within twenty-one days after Congress is required to assemble, determines by two-thirds vote of both Houses that the President is unable to discharge the powers and duties of his office, the Vice President shall continue to discharge the same as Acting President; otherwise, the President shall resume the powers and duties of his office.

Amendment XXVI   *(Ratified on July 1, 1971)*

SECTION 1. The right of citizens of the United States, who are eighteen years of age or older, to vote shall not be denied or abridged by the United States or by any State on account of age.

SECTION 2. The Congress shall have power to enforce this article by appropriate legislation.

Amendment XXVII   *(Ratified on May 7, 1992)*

No law varying the compensation for the services of Senators and Representatives shall take effect until an election of Representatives shall have intervened.

THE FEDERALIST NO. 10

November 22, 1787

James Madison

TO THE PEOPLE OF THE STATE OF NEW YORK.

Among the numerous advantages promised by a well constructed Union, none deserves to be more accurately developed than its tendency to break and control the violence of faction. The friend of popular governments, never finds himself so much alarmed for their character and fate, as when he contemplates their propensity to this dangerous vice. He will not fail therefore to set a due value on any plan which, without violating the principles to which he is attached, provides a proper cure for it. The instability, injustice and confusion introduced into the public councils, have in truth been the mortal diseases under which popular governments have every where perished; as they continue to be the favorite and fruitful topics from which the adversaries to liberty derive their most specious declamations. The valuable improvements made by the American Constitutions on the popular models, both ancient and modern, cannot certainly be too much admired; but it would be an unwarrantable partiality, to contend that they have as effectually obviated the danger on this side as was wished and expected. Complaints are every where heard from our most considerate and virtuous citizens, equally the friends of public and private faith, and of public and personal liberty; that our governments are too unstable; that the public good is disregarded in the conflicts of rival parties; and that measures are too often decided, not according to the rules of justice, and the rights of the minor party; but by the superior force of an interested and overbearing majority. However anxiously we may wish that these complaints had no foundation, the evidence of known facts will not permit us to deny that they are in some degree true. It will be found indeed, on a candid review of our situation, that some of the distresses under which we labor, have been erroneously charged on the operation of our governments; but it will be found, at the same time, that other causes will not alone account for many of our heaviest misfortunes; and particularly, for that prevailing and increasing distrust of public engagements, and alarm for private rights, which are echoed from one end of the continent to the other. These must be chiefly, if not wholly, effects of the unsteadiness and injustice, with which a factious spirit has tainted our public administrations.

By a faction I understand a number of citizens, whether amounting to a majority or minority of the whole, who are united and actuated by some common impulse of passion, or of interest, adverse to the rights of other citizens, or to the permanent and aggregate interests of the community.

There are two methods of curing the mischiefs of faction: the one, by removing its causes; the other, by controlling its effects.

There are again two methods of removing the causes of faction: the one by destroying the liberty which is essential to its existence; the other, by giving to every citizen the same opinions, the same passions, and the same interests.

It could never be more truly said than of the first remedy, that it is worse than the disease. Liberty is to faction, what air is to fire, an aliment without which it instantly expires. But it could not be a less folly to abolish liberty, which is essential to political life, because it nourishes faction, than it would be to wish the annihilation of air, which is essential to animal life, because it imparts to fire its destructive agency.

The second expedient is as impracticable, as the first would be unwise. As long as the reason of man continues fallible, and he is at liberty to exercise it, different opinions will be formed. As long as the connection subsists between his reason and his self-love, his opinions and his passions will have a reciprocal influence on each other; and the former will be objects to which the latter will attach themselves. The diversity in the faculties of men from which the rights of property originate, is not less an insuperable obstacle to a uniformity of interests. The protection of these faculties is the first object of Government. From the protection of different and unequal faculties of acquiring property, the possession of different degrees and kinds of property immediately results: and from the influence of these on the sentiments and views of the respective proprietors, ensues a division of the society into different interests and parties.

The latent causes of faction are thus sown in the nature of man; and we see them every where brought into different degrees of activity, according to the different circumstances of civil society. A zeal for different opinions concerning religion, concerning Government and many other points, as well of speculation as of practice; an attachment to different leaders ambitiously contending for pre-eminence and power; or to persons of other descriptions whose fortunes have been interesting to the human passions, have in turn divided mankind into parties, inflamed them with mutual animosity, and rendered them much more disposed to vex and oppress each other, than to cooperate for their common good. So strong is this propensity of mankind to fall into mutual animosities, that where no substantial occasion presents itself, the most frivolous and fanciful distinctions have been sufficient to kindle their unfriendly passions, and excite their most violent conflicts. But the most common and durable source of factions, has been the various and unequal distribution of property. Those who hold, and those who are without property, have ever formed distinct interests in society. Those who are creditors, and those who are debtors, fall under a like discrimination. A landed interest, a manufacturing interest, a mercantile interest, a monied interest, with many lesser interests, grow up of necessity in civilized nations, and divide them into different classes, actuated by different sentiments and views. The regulation of these various and interfering interests forms the principal task of modern Legislation, and involves the spirit of party and faction in the necessary and ordinary operations of Government.

No man is allowed to be a judge in his own cause; because his interest would certainly bias his judgment, and, not improbably, corrupt his integrity. With equal, nay with greater reason, a body of men, are unfit to be both judges and parties, at the same time; yet, what are many of the most important acts of legislation, but so many judicial determinations, not indeed concerning the rights of single persons, but concerning the rights of large bodies of citizens, and what are the different classes of legislators, but advocates and parties to the causes which they determine? Is a law proposed concerning private debts? It is a question to which the creditors are parties on one side, and the debtors on the other. Justice ought to hold the balance between them. Yet the parties are and must be themselves the judges; and the most numerous party, or, in other words, the most powerful faction must be expected to prevail. Shall domestic manufactures be encouraged, and in what degree, by restrictions on foreign manufactures? are questions which would be differently decided by the landed and the manufacturing classes; and probably by neither, with a sole regard to justice and the public good. The apportionment of taxes on the various descriptions of property, is an act which seems to require the most exact impartiality; yet, there is perhaps no legislative act in which greater opportunity and temptation are given to a predominant party, to trample on the rules of justice. Every shilling with which they over-burden the inferior number, is a shilling saved to their own pockets.

It is in vain to say, that enlightened statesmen will be able to adjust these clashing interests, and render them all subservient to the public good. Enlightened statesmen will not always be at the helm: Nor, in many cases, can such an adjustment be made at all, without taking into view indirect and remote considerations, which will rarely prevail over the immediate interest which one party may find in disregarding the rights of another, or the good of the whole.

The inference to which we are brought, is, that the *causes* of faction cannot be removed; and that relief is only to be sought in the means of controlling its *effects*.

If a faction consists of less than a majority, relief is supplied by the republican principle, which enables the majority to defeat its sinister views by regular vote: It may clog the administration, it may convulse the society; but it will be unable to execute and mask its violence under the forms of the Constitution. When a majority is included in a faction, the form of popular government on the other hand enables it to sacrifice to its ruling passion or interest, both the public good and the rights of other citizens. To secure the public good, and private rights, against the danger of such a faction, and at the same time to preserve the spirit and the form of popular government, is then the great object to which our enquiries are directed: Let me add that it is the great desideratum, by which alone this form of government can be rescued from the opprobrium under which it has so long labored, and be recommended to the esteem and adoption of mankind.

By what means is this object attainable? Evidently by one of two only. Either the existence of the same passion or interest in a majority at the same time, must be prevented; or the majority, having such co-existent passion or interest, must be rendered, by their number and local situation, unable to concert and carry into effect schemes of oppression. If the impulse and the opportunity be suffered to coincide, we well know that neither moral nor religious motives can be relied on as an adequate control. They are not found to be such on the injustice and violence of individuals, and lose their efficacy in proportion to the number combined together; that is, in proportion as their efficacy becomes needful.

From this view of the subject, it may be concluded, that a pure Democracy, by which I mean, a Society, consisting of a small number of citizens, who assemble and administer the Government in person, can admit of no cure for the mischiefs of faction. A common passion or interest will, in almost every case, be felt by a majority of the whole; a communication and concert results from the form of Government itself; and there is nothing to check the inducements to sacrifice the weaker party, or an obnoxious individual. Hence it is, that such Democracies have ever been spectacles of turbulence and contention; have ever been found incompatible with personal security, or the rights of property; and have in general been as short in their lives, as they have been violent in their deaths. Theoretic politicians, who have patronized this species of Government, have erroneously supposed, that by reducing mankind to a perfect equality in their political rights, they would, at the same time, be perfectly equalized and assimilated in their possessions, their opinions, and their passions.

A republic, by which I mean a government in which the scheme of representation takes place, opens a different prospect, and promises the cure for which we are seeking. Let us examine the points in which it varies from pure democracy, and we shall comprehend both the nature of the cure and the efficacy which it must derive from the union.

The two great points of difference, between a democracy and a republic, are, first, the delegation of the government, in the latter, to a small number of citizens, elected by the rest; secondly, the greater number of citizens, and greater sphere of country, over which the latter may be extended.

The effect of the first difference is, on the one hand, to refine and enlarge the public views, by passing them through the medium of a chosen body of citizens, whose wisdom may best discern the true interest of their country, and whose patriotism and love of justice, will be least likely to sacrifice it to temporary or partial considerations. Under such a regulation, it may well happen, that the public voice, pronounced by the representatives of the people, will be more consonant to the public good, than if pronounced by the people themselves, convened for the purpose. On the other hand the effect may be inverted. Men of factious tempers, of local prejudices, or of sinister designs, may by intrigue, by corruption, or by other means, first obtain the suffrages, and then betray the interest of the people. The question resulting is, whether small or extensive republics are most favorable to the election of proper guardians of the public weal, and it is clearly decided in favor of the latter by two obvious considerations.

In the first place, it is to be remarked that, however small the republic may be, the representatives must be raised to a certain number, in order to guard against the cabals of a few; and that however large it may be, they must be limited to a certain number, in order to guard against the confusion of a multitude. Hence, the number of representatives in the two cases not being in proportion to that of the constituents, and being proportionally greatest in the small republic, it follows, that if the proportion of fit characters be not less in the large than in the small republic, the former will present a greater option, and consequently a greater probability of a fit choice.

In the next place, as each Representative will be chosen by a greater number of citizens in the large than in the small Republic, it will be more difficult for unworthy candidates to practise with success the vicious arts, by which elections are too often carried; and the suffrages of the people being more free, will be more likely to center on men who possess the most attractive merit, and the most diffusive and established characters.

It must be confessed, that in this, as in most other cases, there is a mean, on both sides of which inconveniences will be found to lie. By enlarging too much the number of electors, you render the representatives too little acquainted with all their local circumstances and lesser interests; as by reducing it too much, you render him unduly attached to these, and too little fit to comprehend and pursue great and national objects. The Federal Constitution forms a happy combination in this respect; the great and aggregate interests being referred to the national, the local and particular, to the state legislatures.

The other point of difference is, the greater number of citizens and extent of territory which may be brought within the compass of Republican, than of Democratic Government; and it is this circumstance principally which renders factious combinations less to be dreaded in the former, than in the latter. The smaller the society, the fewer probably will be the distinct parties and interests composing it; the fewer the distinct parties and interests, the more frequently will a majority be found of the same party; and the smaller the number of individuals composing a majority, and the smaller the compass within which they are placed, the more easily will they concert and execute their plans of oppression. Extend the sphere, and you take in a greater variety of parties and interests; you make it less probable that a majority of the whole will have a common motive to invade the rights of other citizens; or if such a common motive exists, it will be more difficult for all who feel it to discover their own strength, and to act in unison with each other. Besides other impediments, it may be remarked, that where there is a consciousness of unjust or dishonorable purposes, communication is always checked by distrust, in proportion to the number whose concurrence is necessary.

Hence it clearly appears, that the same advantage, which a Republic has over a Democracy, in controlling the effects of faction, is enjoyed by a large over a small Republic—is enjoyed by the Union over the States composing it. Does this advantage consist in the substitution of Representatives, whose enlightened views and virtuous sentiments render them superior to local prejudices, and to schemes of injustice? It will not be denied, that the Representation of the Union will be most likely to possess these requisite endowments. Does it consist in the greater security afforded by a greater variety of parties, against the event of any one party being able to outnumber and oppress the rest? In an equal degree does the increased variety of parties, comprised within the Union, increase this security? Does it, in fine, consist in the greater obstacles opposed to the concert and accomplishment of the secret wishes of an unjust and interested majority? Here, again, the extent of the Union gives it the most palpable advantage.

The influence of factious leaders may kindle a flame within their particular States, but will be unable to spread a general conflagration through the other States: a religious sect, may degenerate into a political faction in a part of the Confederacy but the variety of sects dispersed over the entire face of it, must secure the national Councils against any danger from that source: a rage for paper money, for an abolition of debts, for an equal division of property, or for any other improper or wicked project, will be less apt to pervade the whole body of the Union, than a particular member of it; in the same proportion as such a malady is more likely to taint a particular county or district, than an entire State.

In the extent and proper structure of the Union, therefore, we behold a Republican remedy for the diseases most incident to Republican Government. And according to the degree of pleasure and pride, we feel in being Republicans, ought to be our zeal in cherishing the spirit, and supporting the character of Federalists.

Publius

THE FEDERALIST NO. 51

February 6, 1788

James Madison

TO THE PEOPLE OF THE STATE OF NEW YORK.

To what expedient then shall we finally resort for maintaining in practice the necessary partition of power among the several departments, as laid down in the constitution? The only answer that can be given is, that as all these exterior provisions are found to be inadequate, the defect must be supplied, by so contriving the interior structure of the government, as that its several constituent parts may, by their mutual relations, be the means of keeping each other in their proper places. Without presuming to undertake a full development of this important idea, I will hazard a few general observations, which may perhaps place it in a clearer light, and enable us to form a more correct judgment of the principles and structure of the government planned by the convention.

In order to lay a due foundation for that separate and distinct exercise of the different powers of government, which to a certain extent, is admitted on all hands to be essential to the preservation of liberty, it is evident that each department should have a will of its own; and consequently should be so constituted, that the members of each should have as little agency as possible in the appointment of the members of the others. Were this principle rigorously adhered to, it would require that all the appointments for the supreme executive, legislative, and judiciary magistracies, should be drawn from the same fountain of authority, the people, through channels, having no communication whatever with one another. Perhaps such a plan of constructing the several departments would be less difficult in practice than it may in contemplation appear. Some difficulties however, and some additional expense, would attend the execution of it. Some deviations therefore from the principle must be admitted. In the constitution of the judiciary department in particular, it might be inexpedient to insist rigorously on the principle; first, because peculiar qualifications being essential in the members, the primary consideration ought to be to select that mode of choice, which best secures these qualifications; secondly, because the permanent tenure by which the appointments are held in that department, must soon destroy all sense of dependence on the authority conferring them.

It is equally evident that the members of each department should be as little dependent as possible on those of the others, for the emoluments annexed to their offices. Were the executive magistrate, or the judges, not independent of the legislature in this particular, their independence in every other would be merely nominal.

But the great security against a gradual concentration of the several powers in the same department, consists in giving to those who administer each department, the necessary constitutional means, and personal motives, to resist encroachments of the others. The provision for defense must in this, as in all other cases, be made commensurate to the danger of attack. Ambition must be made to counteract ambition. The interest of the man must be connected with the constitutional right of the place. It may be a reflection on human nature, that such devices should be necessary to control the abuses of government. But what is government itself but the greatest of all reflections on human nature? If men were angels, no government would be necessary. If angels were to govern men, neither external nor internal controls on government would be necessary. In framing a government which is to be administered by men over men, the great difficulty lies in this: You must first enable the government to control the governed; and in the next place, oblige it to control itself. A dependence on the people is no doubt the primary control on the government; but experience has taught mankind the necessity of auxiliary precautions.

This policy of supplying by opposite and rival interests, the defect of better motives, might be traced through the whole system of human affairs, private as well as public. We see it particularly displayed in all the subordinate distributions of power; where the constant aim is to divide and arrange the several offices in such a manner as that each may be a check on the other; that the private interest of every individual, may be a sentinel over the public rights. These inventions of prudence cannot be less requisite in the distribution of the supreme powers of the state.

But it is not possible to give to each department an equal power of self defense. In republican government the legislative authority, necessarily, predominates. The remedy for this inconveniency is, to divide the legislature into different branches; and to render them by different modes of election, and different principles of action, as little connected with each other, as the nature of their common functions, and their common dependence on the society, will admit. It may even be necessary to guard against dangerous encroachments by still further precautions. As the weight of the legislative authority requires that it should be thus divided, the weakness of the executive may require, on the other hand, that it should be fortified. An absolute negative, on the legislature, appears at first view to be the natural defense with which the executive magistrate should be armed. But perhaps it would be neither altogether safe, nor alone sufficient. On ordinary occasions, it might not be exerted with the requisite firmness; and on extraordinary occasions, it might be prefidiously abused. May not this defect of an absolute negative be supplied, by some qualified connection between this weaker department, and the weaker branch of the stronger department, by which the latter may be led to support the constitutional rights of the former, without being too much detached from the rights of its own department?

If the principles on which these observations are founded be just, as I persuade myself they are, and they be applied as a criterion, to the several state constitutions, and to the federal constitution, it will be found, that if the latter does not perfectly correspond with them, the former are infinitely less able to bear such a test.

There are moreover two considerations particularly applicable to the federal system of America, which place that system in a very interesting point of view.

First. In a single republic, all the power surrendered by the people, is submitted to the administration of a single government; and usurpations are guarded against by a division of the government into distinct and separate departments. In the compound republic of America, the power surrendered by the people, is first divided between two distinct governments, and then the portion allotted to each, subdivided among distinct and separate departments. Hence a double security arises to the rights of the people. The different governments will control each other; at the same time that each will be controlled by itself.

Second. It is of great importance in a republic, not only to guard the society against the oppression of its rulers; but to guard one part of the society against the injustice of the other part. Different interests necessarily exist in different classes of citizens. If a majority be united by a common interest, the rights of the minority will be insecure. There are but two methods of providing against this evil: The one by creating a will in the community independent of the majority, that is, of the society itself, the other by comprehending in the society so many separate descriptions of citizens, as will render an unjust combination of a majority of the whole, very improbable, if not impracticable. The first method prevails in all governments possessing an hereditary or self appointed authority. This at best is but a precarious security; because a power independent of the society may as well espouse the unjust views of the major, as the rightful interests, of the minor party, and may possibly be turned against both parties. The second method will be exemplified in the federal republic of the United States. While all authority in it will be derived from and dependent on the society, the society itself will be broken into so many parts, interests and classes of citizens, that the rights of individuals or of the minority, will be in little danger from interested combinations of the majority. In a free government, the security for civil rights must be the same as for religious rights. It consists in the one case in the multiplicity of interests, and in the other, in the multiplicity of sects. The degree of security in both cases will depend on the number of interests and sects; and this may be presumed to depend on the extent of country and number of people comprehended under the same government. This view of the subject must particularly recommend a proper federal system to all the sincere and considerate friends of republican government: Since it shows that in exact proportion as the territory of the union may be formed into more circumscribed confederacies or states, oppressive combinations of a majority will be facilitated, the best security under the republican form, for the rights of every class of citizens, will be diminished; and consequently, the stability and independence of some member of the government, the only other security, must be proportionally increased. Justice is the end of government. It is the end of civil society. It ever has been, and ever will be pursued, until it be obtained, or until liberty be lost in the pursuit. In a society under the forms of which the stronger faction can readily unite and oppress the weaker, anarchy may as truly be said to reign, as in a state of nature where the weaker individual is not secured against the violence of the stronger: And as in the latter state even the stronger individuals are prompted by the uncertainty of their condition, to submit to a government which may protect the weak as well as themselves: So in the former state, will the more powerful factions or parties be gradually induced by a like motive, to wish for a government which will protect all parties, the weaker as well as the more powerful. It can be little doubted, that if the state of Rhode Island was separated from the confederacy, and left to itself, the insecurity of rights under the popular form of government within such narrow limits, would be displayed by such reiterated oppressions of factious majorities, that some power altogether independent of the people would soon be called for by the voice of the very factions whose misrule had proved the necessity of it. In the extended republic of the United States, and among the great variety of interests, parties and sects which it embraces, a coalition of a majority of the whole society could seldom take place on any other principles than those of justice and the general good; and there being thus less danger to a minor from the will of the major party, there must be less pretext also, to provide for the security of the former, by introducing into the government a will not dependent on the latter; or in other words, a will independent of the society itself. It is no less certain than it is important, notwithstanding the contrary opinions which have been entertained, that the larger the society, provided it lie within a practicable sphere, the more duly capable it will be of self government. And happily for the *republican cause,* the practicable sphere may be carried to a very great extent, by a judicious modification and mixture of the *federal principle.*

PUBLIUS

PRESIDENTS, CONGRESSES, AND CHIEF JUSTICES: 1789-1996

TERM	PRESIDENT AND VICE PRESIDENT	PARTY OF PRESIDENT	CONGRESS	MAJORITY PARTY		CHIEF JUSTICE OF THE UNITED STATES
				HOUSE	SENATE	
1789–1797	**George Washington** John Adams	None	1st 2d 3d 4th	(N/A) (N/A) (N/A) (N/A)	(N/A) (N/A) (N/A) (N/A)	John Jay (1789–1795) John Rutledge (1795) Oliver Ellsworth (1796–1800)
1797–1801	**John Adams** Thomas Jefferson	Federalist	5th 6th	(N/A) Fed	(N/A) Fed	Oliver Ellsworth (1796–1800) John Marshall (1801–1835)
1801–1809	**Thomas Jefferson** Aaron Burr (1801–1805) George Clinton (1805–1809)	Democratic-Republican	7th 8th 9th 10th	Dem-Rep Dem-Rep Dem-Rep Dem-Rep	Dem-Rep Dem-Rep Dem-Rep Dem-Rep	John Marshall (1801–1835)
1809–1817	**James Madison** George Clinton (1809–1812)[a] Elbridge Gerry (1813–1814)[a]	Democratic-Republican	11th 12th 13th 14th	Dem-Rep Dem-Rep Dem-Rep Dem-Rep	Dem-Rep Dem-Rep Dem-Rep Dem-Rep	John Marshall (1801–1835)
1817–1825	**James Monroe** Daniel D. Tompkins	Democratic-Republican	15th 16th 17th 18th	Dem-Rep Dem-Rep Dem-Rep Dem-Rep	Dem-Rep Dem-Rep Dem-Rep Dem-Rep	John Marshall (1801–1835)
1825–1829	**John Quincy Adams** John C. Calhoun	National-Republican	19th 20th	Nat'l Rep Dem	Nat'l Rep Dem	John Marshall (1801–1835)
1829–1837	**Andrew Jackson** John C. Calhoun (1829–1832)[b] Martin Van Buren (1833–1837)	Democrat	21st 22d 23d 24th	Dem Dem Dem Dem	Dem Dem Dem Dem	John Marshall (1801–1835) Roger B. Taney (1836–1864)

TERM	PRESIDENT AND VICE PRESIDENT	PARTY OF PRESIDENT	CONGRESS	MAJORITY PARTY		CHIEF JUSTICE OF THE UNITED STATES
				HOUSE	SENATE	
1837–1841	**Martin Van Buren**	Democrat	25th	Dem	Dem	Roger B. Taney (1836–1864)
	Richard M. Johnson		26th	Dem	Dem	
1841	**William H. Harrison**[a]	Whig				Roger B. Taney (1836–1864)
	John Tyler (1841)					
1841–1845	**John Tyler**	Whig	27th	Whig	Whig	Roger B. Taney (1836–1864)
	(VP vacant)		28th	Dem	Whig	
1845–1849	**James K. Polk**	Democrat	29th	Dem	Dem	Roger B. Taney (1836–1864)
	George M. Dallas		30th	Whig	Dem	
1849–1850	**Zachary Taylor**[a]	Whig	31st	Dem	Dem	Roger B. Taney (1836–1864)
	Millard Fillmore					
1850–1853	**Millard Fillmore**	Whig	32d	Dem	Dem	Roger B. Taney (1836–1864)
	(VP vacant)					
1853–1857	**Franklin Pierce**	Democrat	33d	Dem	Dem	Roger B. Taney (1836–1864)
	William R.D. King (1853)[a]		34th	Rep	Dem	
1857–1861	**James Buchanan**	Democrat	35th	Dem	Dem	Roger B. Taney (1836–1864)
	John C. Breckinridge		36th	Rep	Dem	
1861–1865	**Abraham Lincoln**[a]	Republican	37th	Rep	Rep	Roger B. Taney (1836–1864)
	Hannibal Hamlin (1861–1865)		38th	Rep	Rep	Salmon P. Chase (1864–1873)
	Andrew Johnson (1865)		38th	Rep	Rep	
1865–1869	**Andrew Johnson**	Republican	39th	Union	Union	Salmon P. Chase (1864–1873)
	(VP vacant)		40th	Rep	Rep	
1869–1877	**Ulysses S. Grant**	Republican	41st	Rep	Rep	Salmon P. Chase (1864–1873)
	Schuyler Colfax (1869–1873)		42d	Rep	Rep	Morrison R. Waite (1874–1888)
	Henry Wilson (1873–1875)[a]		43d	Rep	Rep	
			44th	Dem	Rep	
1877–1881	**Rutherford B. Hayes**	Republican	45th	Dem	Rep	Morrison R. Waite (1874–1888)
	William A. Wheeler		46th	Dem	Dem	
1881	**James A. Garfield**[a]	Republican	47th	Rep	Rep	Morrison R. Waite (1874–1888)
	Chester A. Arthur					
1881–1885	**Chester A. Arthur**	Republican	48th	Dem	Rep	Morrison R. Waite (1874–1888)
	(VP vacant)					
1885–1889	**Grover Cleveland**	Democrat	49th	Dem	Rep	Morrison R. Waite (1874–1888)
	Thomas A. Hendricks (1885)[a]		50th	Dem	Rep	Melville W. Fuller (1888–1910)
1889–1893	**Benjamin Harrison**	Republican	51st	Rep	Rep	Melville W. Fuller (1888–1910)
	Levi P. Morton		52d	Dem	Rep	

TERM	PRESIDENT AND VICE PRESIDENT	PARTY OF PRESIDENT	CONGRESS	MAJORITY PARTY		CHIEF JUSTICE OF THE UNITED STATES
				HOUSE	SENATE	
1893–1897	**Grover Cleveland**	Democrat	53d	Dem	Dem	Melville W. Fuller (1888–1910)
	Adlai E. Stevenson		54th	Rep	Rep	
1897–1901	**William McKinley**[a]	Republican	55th	Rep	Rep	Melville W. Fuller (1888–1910)
	Garret A. Hobart (1897–1899)[a]		56th	Rep	Rep	
	Theodore Roosevelt (1901)					
1901–1909	**Theodore Roosevelt**	Republican	57th	Rep	Rep	Melville W. Fuller (1888–1910)
	(VP vacant, 1901–1905)		58th	Rep	Rep	
	Charles W. Fairbanks (1905–1909)		59th	Rep	Rep	
			60th	Rep	Rep	
1909–1913	**William Howard Taft**	Republican	61st	Rep	Rep	Melville W. Fuller (1888–1910)
	James S. Sherman (1909–1912)[a]		62d	Dem	Rep	Edward D. White (1910–1921)
1913–1921	**Woodrow Wilson**	Democrat	63d	Dem	Dem	Edward D. White (1910–1921)
	Thomas R. Marshall		64th	Dem	Dem	
			65th	Dem	Dem	
			66th	Rep	Rep	
1921–1923	**Warren G. Harding**[a]	Republican	67th	Rep	Rep	William Howard Taft (1921–1930)
	Calvin Coolidge					
1923–1929	**Calvin Coolidge**	Republican	68th	Rep	Rep	William Howard Taft (1921–1930)
	(VP vacant, 1923–1925)		69th	Rep	Rep	
	Charles G. Dawes (1925–1929)		70th	Rep	Rep	
1929–1933	**Herbert Hoover**	Republican	71st	Rep	Rep	William Howard Taft (1921–1930)
	Charles Curtis		72d	Dem	Rep	Charles Evans Hughes (1930–1941)
1933–1945	**Franklin D. Roosevelt**[a]	Democrat	73d	Dem	Dem	Charles Evans Hughes (1930–1941)
	John N. Garner (1933–1941)		74th	Dem	Dem	Harlan F. Stone (1941–1946)
	Henry A. Wallace (1941–1945)		75th	Dem	Dem	
	Harry S Truman (1945)		76th	Dem	Dem	
			77th	Dem	Dem	
			78th	Dem	Dem	
1945–1953	**Harry S Truman**	Democrat	79th	Dem	Dem	Harlan F. Stone (1941–1946)
	(VP vacant, 1945–1949)		80th	Rep	Rep	Frederick M. Vinson (1946–1953)
	Alben W. Barkley (1949–1953)		81st	Dem	Dem	
			82d	Dem	Dem	
1953–1961	**Dwight D. Eisenhower**	Republican	83d	Rep	Rep	Frederick M. Vinson (1945–1953)
	Richard M. Nixon		84th	Dem	Dem	Earl Warren (1953–1969)
			85th	Dem	Dem	
			86th	Dem	Dem	
1961–1963	**John F. Kennedy**[a]	Democrat	87th	Dem	Dem	Earl Warren (1953–1969)
	Lyndon B. Johnson (1961–1963)					

TERM	PRESIDENT AND VICE PRESIDENT	PARTY OF PRESIDENT	CONGRESS	MAJORITY PARTY		CHIEF JUSTICE OF THE UNITED STATES
				HOUSE	SENATE	
1963–1969	**Lyndon B. Johnson**	Democrat	88th	Dem	Dem	Earl Warren (1953–1969)
	(VP vacant, 1963–1965)		89th	Dem	Dem	
	Hubert H. Humphrey (1965–1969)		90th	Dem	Dem	
1969–1974	**Richard M. Nixon**[c]	Republican	91st	Dem	Dem	Earl Warren (1953–1969)
	Spiro T. Agnew (1969–1973)[b]		92d	Dem	Dem	Warren E. Burger (1969–1986)
	Gerald R. Ford (1973–1974)[d]					
1974–1977	**Gerald R. Ford**	Republican	93d	Dem	Dem	Warren E. Burger (1969–1986)
	Nelson A. Rockefeller[d]		94th	Dem	Dem	
1977–1981	**Jimmy Carter**	Democrat	95th	Dem	Dem	Warren E. Burger (1969–1986)
	Walter Mondale		96th	Dem	Dem	
1981–1989	**Ronald Reagan**	Republican	97th	Dem	Rep	Warren E. Burger (1969–1986)
	George Bush		98th	Dem	Rep	William H. Rehnquist (1986–)
			99th	Dem	Rep	
			100th	Dem	Dem	
1989–1993	**George Bush**	Republican	101st	Dem	Dem	William H. Rehnquist (1986–)
	J. Danforth Quayle		102d	Dem	Dem	
1993–2001	**William J. Clinton**	Democrat	103d	Dem	Dem	William H. Rehnquist (1986–)
	Albert Gore Jr.		104th	Rep	Rep	
			105th	Rep	Rep	

[a]Died in office.
[b]Resigned from the vice presidency.
[c]Resigned from the presidency.
[d]Appointed vice president.

GLOSSARY

administrative adjudication: A quasi-judicial process in which a bureaucratic agency settles disputes between two parties in a manner similar to the way courts resolve disputes.

administrative discretion: The ability of bureaucrats to make choices concerning the best way to implement congressional intentions.

advisory referendum: A process in which voters cast nonbinding ballots on an issue or proposal.

affiliates: Local television stations that carry the programming of a national network.

affirmative action: A policy or program designed to redress prior discrimination.

agenda setting: The constant process of forming the list of issues to be addressed by government.

agenda: A set of problems to which policy makers believe they should be attentive.

amicus curiae: "Friend of the court"; a third party to a lawsuit who files a legal brief for the purpose of raising additional points of view in an attempt to influence a court's decision.

Anti-Federalists: Those who favored strong state governments and a weak national government; opposed the ratification of the U.S. Constitution.

appellate court: Courts that generally review only findings of law made by lower courts.

apportionment: The determination and assignment of representation in a legislature based on population.

aristocracy: A system of government in which control is based on rule of the highest.

Articles of Confederation: The compact among the thirteen original states that was the basis of their government. Written in 1776, the Articles were not ratified by all the states until 1781.

articles of impeachment: The specific charges brought against a president or a federal judge by the House of Representatives.

at-large election: Election in which candidates for office must compete throughout the jurisdiction as a whole.

bicameral legislature: A legislature divided into two houses; the U.S. Congress and every U.S. state legislature are bicameral (except Nebraska, which is unicameral).

bill of attainder: A law declaring an act illegal without a judicial trial.

Bill of Rights: The first ten amendments to the U.S. Constitution guaranteeing specific rights and liberties.

bill: A proposed law.

Black Codes: Laws denying most legal rights to newly freed slaves; passed by Southern states following the Civil War.

blanket primary: A primary in which voters may cast ballots in either party's primary (but not both) on an office-by-office basis.

block grant: Broad grant with few strings given to states by the federal government for specified activities, such as secondary education or health services.

bottom-up review: Post-Cold War review of U.S. defense forces and policies.

Brown v. Board of Education of Topeka, Kansas: U.S. Supreme Court decision holding that school segregation is inherently unconstitutional because it violates the Fourteenth Amendment's guarantee of equal protection; marked the end of legal segregation in the United States.

brief: A document containing the collected legal written arguments in a case filed with a court by a party prior to a hearing or trial.

bureaucracy: A set of complex hierarchical departments, agencies, commissions, and their staffs that exist to help the president carry out his constitutionally mandated charge to enforce the laws of the nation.

business cycles: Fluctuation between expansion and recession which is a part of modern capitalist economies.

Cabinet: The formal body of presidential advisers who head the fourteen departments. Presidents often add others to this body of formal advisers.

candidate debates: Forums in which political candidates face each other to discuss their platforms, records, and character.

capitalism: The economic system that favors private control of business and minimal governmental regulation of private industry.

casework: The process of solving constituents' problems dealing with the bureaucracy.

categorical grant: Grant for which Congress appropriates funds for a specific purpose.

charter: A document that, like a constitution, specifies the basic policies, procedures, and institutions of a municipality.

checks and balances: A governmental structure that gives each of the three branches of government some degree of oversight and control over the actions of the others.

Civil Rights Cases: Name attached to five cases brought under the Civil Rights Act of 1875. In 1883 the Supreme Court decided that discrimination in a variety of public accommodations, including theaters, hotels, and railroads, could not be prohibited by the act because it was private and not state discrimination.

city council: The legislature in a city government.

civil liberties: The personal rights and freedoms that the federal government cannot abridge by law, constitution, or judicial interpretation.

Civil Rights Act of 1964: Legislation passed by Congress to outlaw segregation in public facilities and racial discrimination in employment, education, and voting; created the Equal Employment Opportunity Commission.

civil rights: Refers to the positive acts governments take to protect individuals against arbitrary or discriminatory treatment by governments or individuals based on categories such as race, sex, national origin, age, or sexual orientation.

civil service laws: These acts removed the staffing of the bureaucracy from political parties and created a professional bureaucracy filled through competition.

civil service system: The system created by civil service laws by which many appointments to the federal bureaucracy are made.

clear and present danger test: Used by the Supreme Court to draw the line between protected and unprotected speech; the Court looks to see if there is an imminent danger that illegal action would occur in response to the contested speech.

clientele agency: Executive department directed by law to foster and promote the interests of a specific segment or group in the U.S. population (such as the Department of Education).

closed primary: A primary election in which only a party's registered voters are eligible to vote.

797

coalition: A group of interests or organizations that join forces for the purpose of electing public officials.

coattail effect: The tendency of lesser-known or weaker candidates lower on the ballot to profit in an election by the presence on the party's ticket of a more popular candidate.

collective good: Something of value that cannot be withheld from a noninterest group member, for example, a tax write-off, a good feeling.

commission: Form of local government in which several officials are elected to top positions which have both legislative and executive responsibilities.

Committees of Correspondence: Organizations in each of the American colonies created to keep colonists abreast of developments with the British; served as powerful molders of public opinion against the British.

common law: Traditions of society that are for the most part unwritten but based on the aggregation of rulings and interpretations of judges beginning in thirteenth-century England.

concurrent powers: Powers shared by the national and state governments.

confederation: Type of government in which the national government derives its powers from the states; a league of independent states.

conference committee: Joint committee created to iron out differences between Senate and House versions of a specific piece of legislation.

congressionalist: A view of the president's role in the law-making process that holds Article II's provision that the president should ensure "faithful execution of the laws" should be read as an injunction against substituting presidential authority for legislative intent.

conservative: One thought to believe that a government is best that governs least and that big government can only infringe on individual, personal, and economic rights.

constitutional court: Federal courts specifically created by the U.S. Constitution or by Congress pursuant to its authority in Article III.

containment: A strategy to oppose any further expansion of Soviet power, particularly in Western Europe and East Asia, by surrounding the Soviet Union with U.S. or Allied military forces.

content regulation: Governmental attempts to regulate the electronic media.

contrast ad: Ad that compares the records and proposals of the candidates, with a bias toward the sponsor.

cooperative federalism: A term used to characterize the relationship between the national and state governments that began with the New Deal.

county: A geographic district created within a state with a government that has general responsibilities for land, welfare, environment, and, where appropriate, rural service policies.

critical election: An election that signals a party realignment through voter polarization around new issues.

de facto discrimination: Racial discrimination that results from practice (such as housing patterns or other social factors) rather than the law.

de jure discrimination: Racial segregation that is a direct result of law or official policy.

Declaration of Independence: Document drafted by Thomas Jefferson in 1776 that proclaimed the right of the American colonies to separate from Great Britain.

deep background: Information gathered for news stories that must be completely unsourced.

delegate: Role played by elected representatives who vote the way their constituents would want them to, regardless of their own opinions.

deliberative poll: A new type of poll to bring a representative sample of people together to discuss and debate political issues in order to provide considered policy suggestions to lawmakers.

democracy: A system of government that gives power to the people, whether directly or through their elected representatives.

department: A major administrative unit with responsibility for a broad area of government operations. Departmental status usually indicates a permanent national interest in that particular governmental function, such as Defense, Health, or Agriculture.

direct (popular) referendum: A process in which voters can veto a bill recently passed in the legislature by placing the issue on a ballot and expressing disapproval.

direct democracy: A system of government in which members of the polity meet to discuss all policy decisions and then agree to abide by majority rule.

direct incitement test: The advocacy of illegal action is protected by the First Amendment unless imminent action is intended and likely to occur.

direct initiative: A process in which voters can place a proposal on a ballot and enact it into law without involving the legislature or the governor.

direct mailer: A professional who supervises a political campaign's direct-mail fund-raising strategies.

direct primary: The selection of party candidates through the ballots of qualified voters rather than at party nomination conventions.

discharge petition: Petition that gives a majority of the House of Representatives the authority to bring an issue to the floor in the fact of committee inaction.

discount rate: The rate of interest at which member banks can borrow money from their regional Federal Reserve Bank.

district-based election: Election in which candidates run for an office that represents only the voters of a specific district within the jurisdiction.

disturbance theory: The theory offered by political scientist David B. Truman that posits that interest groups form in part to counteract the efforts of other groups.

dual federalism: The belief that having separate and equally powerful levels of government is the best arrangement.

dualist theory: The theory claiming that there has always been an underlying binary party nature to U.S. politics.

due process clause: Clause contained in the Fifth and Fourteenth Amendments. Over the years, it has been construed to guarantee to individuals a variety of rights ranging from economic liberty to criminal procedural rights to protection from arbitrary governmental action.

due process rights: Procedural guarantees provided by the Fourth, Fifth, Sixth, and Eighth Amendments for those accused of crimes.

economic interest group: A group with the primary purpose of promoting the financial interests of its members.

economic regulation: Governmental regulation of business practices, industry rates, routes, or areas serviced by particular industries.

economic stability: A situation in which there is economic growth, rising national income, high employment, and steadiness in the general level of prices.

elastic clause: A name given to the "necessary and proper clause" found in the final paragraph of Article I, section 8, of the U.S. Constitution. It gives Congress the authority to pass all laws "necessary and proper" to carry out the enumerated powers specified in the Constitution.

elector: Member of the electoral college chosen by methods determined in each state.

electoral college: Representatives of each state who cast the final ballots that actually elect a president.

electorate: Citizens eligible to vote.

electronic media: The newest form of broadcast media, including television, radio, and cable.

engagement: A policy that says the United States will take the lead in international political and economic affairs, largely through constructive dialogue, but also by securing regional and global peace.

enlargement: A policy that says the United States will promote democracy, open markets, and other Western political, economic, and social values around the world.

entitlement program: Income security program to which all those meeting eligibility criteria are entitled.

enumerated powers: Seventeen specific powers granted to Congress under Article I, section 8, of the U.S. Constitution; these powers include taxation, coinage of money, regulation of commerce, and the authority to provide for a national defense.

Equal Employment Opportunity Commission: Federal agency created to enforce the Civil Rights Act of 1964, which forbids discrimination on the basis of race, creed, national origin, religion, or sex in hiring, promotion, or firing.

equal protection clause: Section of the Fourteenth Amendment that guarantees that all citizens receive "equal protection of the laws"; has been used to bar discrimination against blacks and women.

equal time rule: The rule that requires broadcast stations to sell campaign air time equally to all candidates if they choose to sell it to any.

establishment clause: The first clause in the First Amendment. It prohibits the national government from establishing a national religion.

European Union (EU): The union that joins most of the countries of Western Europe in their efforts to develop common economic, social, and foreign policies; successor to the European Communities.

ex post facto law: Law passed after the fact, thereby making previously legal activity illegal and subject to current penalty; prohibited by the U.S. Constitution.

exclusionary rule: Judicially created rule that prohibits police from using illegally seized evidence at trial.

executive agreement: secret and highly sensitive arrangements with foreign nations entered into by the president that do not require the "advise and consent" of the Senate.

Executive Office of the President (EOP): Establishment created in 1939 to help the president oversee the bureaucracy.

executive order: Presidential directive to an agency that provides the basis for carrying out laws or for establishing new policies.

exit poll: Poll conducted at selected polling places on Election Day.

fairness doctrine: Rule in effect from 1949 to 1985 requiring broadcasters to cover events adequately and to present contrasting views on important public issues.

Federal Employees Political Activities Act: 1993 liberalization of Hatch Act. Federal employees are now allowed to run for office in nonpartisan elections and to contribute money to campaigns in partisan elections.

federal system: Plan of government created in the U.S. Constitution in which power is divided between the national government and the state governments and in which independent states are bound together under one national government.

federalism: The philosophy that describes the governmental system created by the Framers; see also federal system.

Federalists: Those who favored a stronger national government and supported the proposed U.S. Constitution; later became the first U.S. political party.

Fifteenth Amendment: One of the three Civil War amendments; specifically enfranchises blacks.

filibuster: A formal way of halting action on a bill by means of long speeches or unlimited debate in the Senate.

First Continental Congress: Meeting held in Philadelphia from September 5 to October 26, 1774, in which fifty-six delegates (from every colony except Georgia) adopted a resolution that opposed the Coercive Acts.

fiscal policy: The deliberate use of the national government's taxing and spending policies to influence the overall economy and maintain economic stability.

Fourteenth Amendment: One of the three Civil War amendments; guarantees equal protection and due process of laws to all U.S. citizens.

franchise: The right to vote.

free exercise clause: The second clause of the First Amendment. It prohibits the U.S. government from interfering with a citizen's right to practice his or her religion.

free market economy: The economic system in which the "invisible hand" of the market regulates prices, wages, product mix, and so on.

free media: Coverage of a candidate's campaign by the news media.

free rider: A problem that occurs when those who don't join or work for the benefit of the group still reap the rewards of the group's activity.

front-loading: The tendency of states to choose an early date on the primary calendar.

gender gap: The tendency for women to vote for candidates of the Democratic Party.

General Agreements on Tariffs and Trade (GATT): Devised shortly after World War II as an interim measure until a World Trade Organization could be created, multilateral trade negotiations conducted under the GATT helped lower tariff and other trade barriers substantially.

general election campaign: That part of a political campaign following a primary election, aimed at winning a general election.

general election: Election in which voters decide which candidates will actually fill elective public offices.

gerrymandering: The legislative process through which the majority party in each statehouse tries to assure that the maximum number of representatives from its political party can be elected to Congress through the redrawing of legislative districts.

get-out-the-vote (GOTV): A push at the end of a political campaign to encourage supporters to go to the polls.

government corporation: Business set up and created by Congress that performs functions that could be provided by private businesses (such as the U.S. Postal Service).

governmental (institutional) agenda: The changing list of issues to which governments believe they should address themselves.

governmental party: The office holders and candidates who run under a political party's banner.

governor: Chief elected executive in state government.

grand strategy: The choices a government makes to balance and apply its economic, military, diplomatic, and other national resources to preserve their people and territory.

grandfather clause: Statute that allowed only those whose grandfathers had voted before Reconstruction to vote unless they passed a wealth or literacy test.

Great Compromise: A decision made during the Philadelphia Convention to give each state the same number of representatives in the Senate regardless of size; representation in the House was determined by population.

gross domestic product (GDP): The total market value of all goods and services produced in a country during a year.

Hatch Act: Laws enacted in 1939 to prohibit civil servants from taking activist roles in partisan campaigns. This act prohibited federal employees from making political contributions, working for a particular party, or campaigning for a particular candidate.

hold: A tactic by which a senator asks to be informed before a particular bill is brought to the floor.

Immigration and Naturalization Service v. Chadha: Legislative veto ruled unconstitutional.

impeachment: The power delegated to the House of Representatives in the Constitution to charge the president, vice president, or other "civil officers," including federal judges, with "Treason, Bribery, or other high Crimes and Misdemeanors."

implementation: The process by which a law or policy is put into operation by the bureaucracy.

implied power: A power derived from an enumerated power and the necessary and proper clause. These powers are not stated specifically but are considered to be reasonably implied through the exercise of delegated powers.

in forma pauperis: Literally, "in the form of a pauper"; a way for an indigent or poor person to appeal a case to the U.S. Supreme Court.

incorporation doctrine: Principle in which the Supreme Court has held that most, but not all, of the specific guarantees in the Bill of Rights limit state and local governments by making those guarantees applicable to the states through the due process clause of the Fourteenth Amendment.

incumbency factor: The fact that being in office helps a person stay in office because of a variety of benefits which go with the position.

independent agency: Governmental unit that closely resembles Cabinet departments, these have narrower areas of responsibility (such as the Central Intelligence Agency), and are not part of any Cabinet departments.

independent regulatory commission: An agency created by Congress that is generally concerned with a specific aspect of the economy.

indirect (representative) democracy: A system of government that gives citizens the opportunity to vote for representatives who will work on their behalf.

indirect initiative: A process in which the legislature places a proposal on a ballot and allows voters to enact it into law, without involving the governor or further action by the legislature.

inflation: A rise in the general price levels of an economy.

inherent powers: Powers of the president that can be derived or inferred from specific powers in the Constitution.

initiative: A process that allows citizens to propose legislation and submit it to the state electorate for popular vote.

inoculation advertising: Advertising that attempts to counteract an anticipated attack from the opposition before the attack is even launched.

interest group: An organized group that tries to influence public policy.

intergovernmental lobby: The pressure group or groups that are created when state and local governments hire lobbyists to lobby the national government.

international governmental organization (IGO): An organization formed by three or more countries, with regular meetings and a permanent staff.

International Monetary Fund (IMF): An IGO created shortly before the end of World War II designed to stabilize international financial relations through a system of fixed exchange rates.

interventionist state: Replaced the *laissez-faire* state as the government took an active role in guiding and regulating the private economy.

iron triangle: The relatively stable relationship and pattern of interaction that occur among an agency, interest groups, and congressional committees or subcommittees.

isolationism: Grand strategy designed to keep a nation out of foreign political or economic affairs; dominated U.S. foreign policy until World War II.

issue network: A term used to describe the loose and informal set of relationships that exist among a large number of actors who work in broad policy areas.

issue-oriented politics: Politics that focuses on specific issues rather than on party, candidate, or other loyalties.

Jim Crow laws: Laws enacted by Southern states that discriminated against blacks by creating "whites only" schools, theaters, hotels, and other public accommodations.

judicial activism: A philosophy of judicial decision-making that argues judges should use their power broadly to further justice, especially in the areas of equality and personal liberty.

judicial implementation: Refers to how and whether judicial decisions are translated into actual public policies affecting more than the immediate parties to a lawsuit.

judicial restraint: A philosophy of judicial decision-making that argues courts should allow the decisions of other branches of government to stand, even

when they offend a judge's own sense of principles.

judicial review: The authority of a court to review the acts of the legislature, the executive, or states to determine their constitutionality; enunciated by Chief Justice John Marshall in *Marbury* v. *Madison* (1803).

Judiciary Act of 1789: Established the basic three-tiered structure of the federal court system.

jurisdiction: Authority vested in a particular court to hear and decide the issues in any particular case.

laissez-faire: A French term literally meaning "to allow to do, to leave alone." It is a hands-off governmental policy that is based on the belief that governmental regulation of the economy is wrong.

Lemon test: The Court test devised to measure the constitutionality of state laws that appear to further a religion.

League of Nations: Created in the peace treaty that ended World War I, it was the first IGO dedicated to preserving global peace; superseded by the United Nations.

legislative courts: Courts established by Congress for specialized purposes, such as the Court of Military Appeals.

legislative veto: A procedure by which one or both houses of Congress can disallow an act of the president or executive agency by a simple majority vote; ruled unconstitutional by the Supreme Court.

libel: False statements or statements tending to call someone's reputation into disrepute.

liberal: One considered to favor extensive governmental involvement in the economy and the provision of social services and to take an activist role in protecting the rights of women, the elderly, minorities, and the environment.

line-item veto: The power to veto specific provisions of a bill without vetoing the bill in its entirety.

lobbying: The activities of groups and organizations that seek to influence legislation and persuade political leaders to support a group's position.

lobbyist: Interest group representative who seeks to influence legislation that will benefit his or her organization through political persuasion.

Louisiana Purchase: The 1803 land purchase authorized by Thomas Jefferson, which expanded the size of the United States dramatically and expanded the concept of inherent powers.

Marbury* v. *Madison: Court first asserted the power of judicial review in finding that the congressional statute extending the Court's original jurisdiction was unconstitutional.

machine: A party organization that recruits its members with tangible incentives and is characterized by a high degree of control over member activity.

majority leader: The elected leader of the party controlling the most seats in the U.S. House of Representatives or the Senate; is second in authority to the Speaker of the House and in the Senate is regarded as its most powerful member.

majority party: The political party in each house of Congress with the most members.

majority rule: The central premise of direct democracy in which only policies that collectively garner the support of a majority of voters will be made into law.

manager: A professional executive hired by a city council or county board to manage daily operations and to recommend policy changes.

mandate: A command, indicated by an electorate's votes, for the elected officials to carry out their platforms.

mandate: National law that directs states or local governments to comply with federal rules or regulations (such as clean air or water standards) under threat of civil or criminal penalties or as a condition of receipt of any federal grants.

manifest destiny: A popular theory during the U.S. expansion westward that it was a divinely mandated obligation to expand across North America to the Pacific Ocean.

margin of error: A measure of the accuracy of a public opinion poll.

Marshall Plan: The European Recovery Program, named after Secretary of State George C. Marshall, which provided a massive transfer of aid from the United States to Western Europe in the years after World War II.

matching funds: Donations to presidential campaigns from the federal government that are determined by the amount of private funds a qualifying candidate raises.

mayor: Chief elected executive of a city.

means-tested program: Income security program intended to assist those whose incomes fall below a designated level.

media campaign: That part of a political campaign waged in the broadcast and print media.

media consultant: A professional who produces political candidates' television, radio, and print advertisements.

media effects: The influence of news sources on public opinion.

Medicaid: An expansion of Medicare, this program subsidizes medical care for the poor.

Medicare: The federal program established in the Johnson administration that provides medical care to elderly Social Security recipients.

mercantile system: A system that binds trade and its administration to the national government.

merit system: The system by which federal civil service jobs are classified into grades or levels to which appointments are made on the basis of performance on competitive examinations.

Miranda **rights:** Statements that must be made by the police informing a suspect of his or her constitutional rights protected by the Fifth Amendment, including the right to an attorney provided by the court if the suspect cannot afford one.

Miranda **v.** *Arizona:* The Fifth Amendment requires that individuals arrested for a crime must be advised of their right to remain silent and to have counsel present.

minority leader: The elected leader of the party with the second highest number of elected representatives in either the House or the Senate.

minority party: Party with the second most members in either house of Congress.

monarchy: A form of government in which power is vested in hereditary kings and queens.

monetary policy: A form of government regulation in which the nation's money supply and interest rates are controlled.

money: A system of exchange for goods and services that includes currency, coins, and bank deposits.

Monroe Doctrine: President James Monroe's 1823 pledge that the United States would oppose attempts by European states to extend their political control over the Western Hemisphere.

muckraking: A form of newspaper publishing, in vogue in the early twentieth century, concerned with reforming government and business conduct.

multilateralism: The foreign policy practice that actions should be taken in cooperation with other states after extensive consultation.

municipality: A government with general responsibilities that is created in response to the emergence of relatively densely populated areas.

mutually assured destruction (MAD): The situation where one nation could absorb a nuclear strike by another and have sufficient nuclear forces to launch a devastating retaliatory strike; seen as a means of deterring nuclear war.

nation–state: Ideally, a country where almost all of the people of one nationality govern themselves. This form of political organization is based on the idea that one government should have sole authority over a well-defined territory.

national convention: A party conclave (meeting) held in the presidential election year for the purposes of nominating a presidential and vice-presidential ticket and adopting a platform.

national party platform: A statement of the general and specific philosophy and policy goals of a political party, usually promulgated at the national convention.

National Security Acts of 1947 and 1949: The acts that unified the armed services and created the modern U.S. security establishment, including the National Security Council and the Central Intelligence Agency.

natural law: A doctrine that society should be governed by certain ethical principles that are part of nature and, as such, can be understood by reason.

New York Times Co. **v.** *Sullivan:* Supreme Court decision ruling that simply publishing a defamatory falsehood is not enough to justify a libel judgment. "Actual malice" must be proved to support a finding of libel against a public figure.

necessary and proper clause: A name given to the clause found in the final paragraph of Article I, section 8 of the U.S. Constitution giving Congress the authority to pass all laws "necessary and proper" to carry out the enumerated powers specified in the Constitution; the "elastic" clause.

negative ad: Advertising on behalf of a candidate that attacks the opponent's platform or character.

network: An association of broadcast stations (radio or television) that share programming through a financial arrangement.

New Deal: The name given to the program of "Relief, Recovery, Reform" begun by President Franklin D. Roosevelt, in 1933 designed to bring the United States out of the Great Depression.

New Jersey Plan: A framework for the Constitution proposed by a group of small states; its key points were a one-house legislature with one vote for each state, a multiperson "executive," the establishment of the acts of Congress as the "supreme law" of the land, and a supreme judiciary with limited power.

nomination campaign: That part of a political campaign aimed at winning a primary election.

nonpartisan election: A contest in which candidates run without formal identification or association with a political party.

North American Free Trade Agreement (NAFTA): A treaty that promotes the free movement of goods and services between Canada, Mexico, and the United States.

North Atlantic Treaty Organization (NATO): A political and military regional defense alliance created in 1950 to implement the North Atlantic Treaty of 1949; the first peace-time military alliance made by the United States.

nullification doctrine: The claimed right of a state to nullify, or reject, a federal law.

off the record: Term applied to information gathered for a news story that cannot be used at all.

off-year election: Election that takes place in the middle of a presidential term.

oligarchy: A form of government in which the right to participate is always conditioned on the possession of wealth, social status, military position, or achievement.

on background: A term for when sources are not included in a news story.

on the record: Term applied to information gathered for a news story that can be used and cited.

one-partyism: A political system in which one party dominates and wins virtually all contests.

open market operations: The buying and selling of government securities by the Federal Reserve Bank in the securities market.

open primary: A primary in which party members, independents, and sometimes members of the other party are allowed to vote.

organizational campaign: That part of a political campaign involved in fund raising, literature distribution, and all other activities not directly involving the candidate.

organizational party: The workers and activists who staff the party's formal organization.

original jurisdiction: The jurisdiction of courts that hear a case first, usually in trial. Courts determine the facts of a case under their original jurisdiction.

oversight: Congressional review of the activities of an agency, department, or office.

package or general veto: The authority of a chief executive to void an entire bill that has been passed by the legislature. This veto applies to all bills, whether or not they have taxing or spending components, and the legislature may override this veto, usually with a two-thirds majority of each chamber.

paid media: Political advertisements purchased for a candidate's campaign.

pardon: The restoration of all rights and privileges of citizenship to a specific individual charged or convicted of a crime.

party caucus: A formal gathering of all party members.

party identification: A citizen's personal affinity for a political party, usually expressed by his or her tendency to vote for the candidates of that party.

party realignment: A shifting of party coalition groupings in the electorate that remains in place for several elections.

party-in-the-electorate: The voters who consider themselves to be allied or associated with the party.

patron: Individual who finances an interest group.

patronage: Jobs, grants, or other special favors that are given as rewards to friends and political allies for their support.

Pendleton Act: Reform measure that created the Civil Service Commission to administer a partial merit system. It classified the federal service by grades to which appointments were made based on the results of a competitive examination. It made it illegal for political appointees to be required to contribute to a particular political party.

personal campaign: That part of a political campaign concerned with presenting the candidate's public image.

personal liberty: A key characteristic of U.S. democracy. Initially meaning freedom from governmental interference, today it includes demands for freedom to engage in a variety of practices free from governmental discrimination.

Plessy v. Ferguson: *Plessy* challenged a Louisiana statute requiring that railroads provide separate accommodations for blacks and whites. The Court found that separate but equal accommodations did not violate the equal protection clause of the Fourteenth Amendment.

pocket veto: If Congress adjourns during the ten days the president has to consider a bill passed by both houses of Congress, without the president's signature, the bill is considered vetoed.

policy adoption: The approval of a policy proposal by the people with the requisite authority, such as a legislature.

policy evaluation: The process of determining whether a course of action is achieving its intended goals.

policy formulation: The crafting of appropriate and acceptable proposed courses of action to ameliorate or resolve public problems.

policy implementation: The process of carrying out public policy through governmental agencies and the courts.

political action committee (PAC): A federally registered fund-raising committee that represents an interest group in the political process through campaign donations.

political consultant: Professional who manages campaigns and political advertisements for political candidates.

political ideology: An individual's coherent set of values and beliefs about the purpose and scope of government.

political party: A group of office holders, candidates, activists, and voters who identify with a group label and seek to elect to public office individuals who run under that label.

political socialization: The process through which an individual acquires particular political orientations; the learning process by which people acquire their political beliefs and values.

politico: Role played by elected representatives who act as a trustee or as a delegate, depending on the issue.

politics: The process by which policy decisions are made.

pollster: A professional who takes public opinion surveys that guide political campaigns.

popular consent: The idea that governments must draw their powers from the consent of the governed.

popular sovereignty: The right of the majority to govern themselves.

pork barrel: Legislation that allows representatives to "bring home the bacon" to their districts in the form of public works programs, military bases, or other programs designed to benefit their districts directly.

positive ad: Advertising on behalf of a candidate that stresses the candidate's qualifications, family, and issue positions, without reference to the opponent.

precedent: Prior judicial decision that serves as a rule for settling subsequent cases of a similar nature.

preemption: A concept derived from the Constitution's supremacy clause that allows the national government to override or preempt state or local actions in certain areas.

presidentialist: One who believes that Article II's grant of executive power is a broad grant of authority and power allowing a president wide discretionary powers.

primary elections: Elections in which voters decide which of the candidates within a party will represent the party in the general election.

print press: The traditional form of mass media, comprising newspapers, magazines, and journals.

prior restraint: Judicial doctrine stating that the government cannot prohibit speech or publication before the fact.

privacy: The right to be let alone; a judicially created doctrine encompassing an individual's decision to use birth control or secure an abortion.

proportional representation: The practice of awarding legislative seats in proportion to the number of votes received.

prospective judgment: A voter's evaluation of a candidate based on what he or she pledges to do about an issue if elected.

public funds: Donations from the general tax revenues to the campaigns of qualifying presidential candidates.

public interest group: An organization that seeks a collective good that will not selectively and materially benefit the members of the group.

public opinion poll: Interviews or surveys with a sample of citizens that are used to estimate public opinion of the entire population.

public opinion: What the public thinks about a particular issue or set of issues at any point in time.

public policy: A purposive course of action followed by government in dealing with some problem or matter of concern.

random sampling: A method of selection that gives each potential voter or adult the same chance of being selected for a poll.

recall: Removal of an incumbent from office by popular vote.

recession: A short-term decline in the economy that occurs as investment sags, production falls off, and unemployment increases.

redistricting: The redrawing of congressional districts to reflect increases or decreases in seats allotted to the states, as well as population shifts within a state.

referendum: A procedure whereby the state legislature submits proposed legislation to the state's voters for approval.

regional primary: A proposed system in which the country would be divided into five or six geographic areas and all states in each region would hold their presidential primary elections on the same day.

regulation: Rule that governs the operation of a particular government program and has the force of law.

republic: A government rooted in the consent of the governed; a representative or indirect democracy.

reserve (or police) powers: Powers reserved to the states by the Tenth Amendment that lie at the foundation of a state's right to legislate for the public health and welfare of its citizens.

reserve requirement: Governmental requirements that a portion of member banks' deposits must be retained to back loans made.

retrospective judgment: A voter's evaluation of the performance of the party in power.

revenue sharing: Method of redistributing federal monies back to the states with "no strings attached"; favored by President Richard M. Nixon.

right-of-rebuttal rule: A Federal Communications Commission regulation that people attacked on a radio or television broadcast be offered the opportunity to respond.

Roe v. Wade: The Supreme Court found that a woman's right to an abortion was protected by the right to privacy that could be implied from specific guarantees found in the Bill of Rights and the Fourteenth Amendment.

rule making: A quasi-legislative administrative process that has the characteristics of a legislative act.

Rule of Four: At least four justices of the Supreme Court must vote to consider a case before it can be heard.

runoff primary: A second primary election between the two candidates receiving the greatest number of votes in the first primary.

sampling error: A measure of the accuracy of a public opinion poll.

Second Continental Congress: Meeting that convened in Philadelphia on May 10, 1775, at which it was decided that an army should be raised and George Washington of Virginia was named commander-in-chief.

secular realignment: The gradual rearrangement of party coalitions, based more on demographic shifts than on shocks to the political system.

selective incorporation: A judicial doctrine whereby most but not all of the protections found in the Bill of Rights are made applicable to the states via the Fourteenth Amendment.

senatorial courtesy: A practice by which senators can have near veto power over appointments to the federal judiciary if the opening is in a district in their state.

separation of powers: A way of dividing power among three branches of government in which members of the House of Representatives, members of the Senate, the president, and the federal courts are selected by and responsible to different constituencies.

Shays's Rebellion: A 1786 rebellion in which an army of 1,500 disgruntled and angry farmers led by Daniel Shays marched to Springfield, Massachusetts, and forcibly restrained the state court from foreclosing on their farms.

slander: Untrue spoken statements that defame the character of a person.

social contract theory: The belief that people are free and equal by God-given right and that this in turn requires that all people give their consent to be governed; espoused by John Locke and influential in the writing of the Declaration of Independence.

social regulation: Governmental regulation of the quality and safety of products as well as the conditions under which goods and services are produced.

Social Security Act: A 1935 law that established old age insurance (Social Security), assistance for the needy, children, and others; and unemployment insurance.

social welfare policy: Governmental program designed to improve or enhance individuals' quality of life.

solicitor general: The fourth-ranking member of the Justice Department; responsible for handling all appeals on behalf of the U.S. government to the Supreme Court.

Speaker of the House: The only officer of the House of Representatives specifically mentioned in the Constitution; elected at the beginning of each new Congress by the entire House; traditionally a member of the majority party.

special district: A local government that is responsible for a particular function, such as K–12 education, water, sewerage, or parks.

spoils system: The firing of public-office holders of a defeated political party and their replacement with loyalists of the newly elected party.

spot ad: Television advertising on behalf of a candidate that is broadcast in sixty-, thirty-, or ten-second duration.

stare decisis: In court rulings, a reliance on past decisions or precedents to formulate decisions in new cases.

Stamp Act Congress: Meeting of representatives of nine of the thirteen colonies held in New York City in 1765, during which representatives drafted a document to send to the king listing how their rights had been violated.

standing committee: Committee to which proposed bills are referred.

stewardship theory: The theory that holds that Article II confers on the president the power *and* the duty to take whatever actions are deemed necessary in the national interest, unless prohibited by the Constitution or by law.

stratified sampling: A variation of random sampling; census data are used to divide a country into four sampling regions. Sets of counties and standard metropolitan statistical areas are then randomly selected in proportion to the total national population.

straw poll: Unscientific survey used to gauge public opinion on a variety of issues and policies.

strict constructionist: An approach to constitutional interpretation that emphasizes the Framers' initial intentions.

strict scrutiny: A heightened standard of review used by the Supreme Court to determine the constitutional validity of a challenged practice.

suffrage movement: Term used to refer to the drive for votes for women that took place in the United States from 1890 to 1920.

superdelegate: Delegate slot to the Democratic Party's national convention that is reserved for an elected party official.

supremacy clause: Portion of Article IV of the U.S. Constitution that mandates that national law is supreme to (that is, supersedes) all other laws passed by the states or by any other subdivision of government.

suspect classification: Category or class, such as race, that triggers the highest standard of scrutiny from the Supreme Court.

symbolic speech: Symbols, signs, and other methods of expression generally also considered to be protected by the First Amendment.

systemic agenda: All public issues that are viewed as requiring governmental attention; a discussion agenda.

Taftian theory: The theory that holds that the president is limited by the specific grants of executive power found in the Constitution.

tariffs: Taxes on imports, used to raise government revenue and to protect domestic industry.

term limit: Legislation designating that state or federal elected legislators can serve only a specified number of years.

The Federalist Papers: A series of eighty-five political papers written by John Jay, Alexander Hamilton, and James Madison in support of ratification of the U.S. Constitution.

third-partyism: The tendency of third parties to arise with some regularity in a nominally two-party system.

Thirteenth Amendment: One of the three Civil War amendments; specifically bans slavery in the United States.

Three-Fifths Compromise: Agreement reached at the Constitutional Convention stipulating that each slave was to be counted as three-fifths of a person for purposes of determining population for representation in the U.S. House of Representatives.

ticket-split: To vote for candidates of different parties for various offices in the same election.

ticket-splitting: Voting simultaneously for candidates of both parties for different offices.

tracking poll: Continuous surveys that enables a campaign to chart its daily rise or fall.

trade association: A group that represents specific industries.

trial court: Court of original jurisdiction where cases begin.

Truman Doctrine: President Truman's 1947 strategy to provide U.S. military and economic assistance to Greece and Turkey to contain Soviet expansion.

trustee: Role played by elected representatives who listen to constituents' opinions and then use their best judgment to make final decisions.

turnout: The proportion of the voting-age public that votes.

United States* v. *Nixon: There is no constitutional absolute executive privilege that would allow a president to refuse to comply with a court order to produce information needed in a criminal trial.

unit rule: A traditional party practice under which the majority of a state delegation can force the minority to vote for its candidate.

United Nations: IGO created shortly before the end of World War II to guarantee the security of member nations when attacked, and to promote economic, physical, and social well-being around the world.

veto power: The formal, constitutional authority of the president to reject bills passed by both houses of Congress thus preventing their becoming law without further congressional action.

Virginia Plan: The first general plan for the Constitution, proposed by James Madison. Its key points were a bicameral legislature, an executive chosen by the legislature, and a judiciary also named by the legislature.

voter canvass: The process by which a campaign gets in touch with individual voters: either by door-to-door solicitation or by telephone.

War Powers Act: Law requiring presidents to obtain congressional approval before introducing U.S. troops into a combat situation; passed in 1973 over President Nixon's veto.

Watergate: Term used to describe the events and scandal resulting from a break-in at the Democratic National Committee headquarters in 1972 and the subsequent coverup of White House involvement.

whip: One of several representatives who keep close contact with all members and take "nose counts" on key votes, prepare summaries of bills, and in general act as communications links within the party.

wire service: An electronic delivery of news gathered by the news services' correspondents and sent to all member news media organizations.

World Bank: Originally designed to provide loans for large economic projects in Western Europe's efforts to recover from the devastation of World War II; now the major multilateral lender for development projects in poor countries.

World Trade Organization: The IGO created in 1995 that manages multilateral negotiations to reduce barriers to trade and settle trade disputes between nations.

writ of *certiorari:* A formal document issued from the Supreme Court to a lower federal or state court that calls up a case.

yellow journalism: A form of newspaper publishing in vogue in the late nineteenth century that featured pictures, comics, color, and sensationalized, over-simplified news coverage.

NOTES

Chapter 1 Notes

1. See "How Fares the American Dream?" *The Public Perspective* (June/July 1995): 57.
2. "How Fares the American Dream?"
3. The English and Scots often signed covenants with their churches in a pledge to defend and further their religion. In the Bible, covenants were solemn promises made to humanity by God. In the colonial context, then, covenants were formal agreements sworn to a new government to abide by its terms.
4. The term *men* is used here because only males were considered fit to vote.
5. Jack C. Plano and Milton Greenberg, *The American Political Dictionary*, 6th ed. (New York: Holt, Rinehart and Winston, 1982).
6. Frank Michelman, "The Republican Civic Tradition," 97 *Yale Law Journal* (1988): 1503.
7. Susan A. MacManus, *Young v. Old: Generational Combat in the 21st Century* (Boulder, CO: Westview Press, 1996), 3.
8. MacManus, *Young v. Old*, 4.
9. "Californians Vote Against Illegal Aliens," *Agence France Presse* (November 9, 1994).
10. James Davison Hunter, *Culture Wars: The Struggle to Define America* (New York: Basic Books, 1991), 42.
11. Hunter, *Culture Wars*, 42.
12. Plano and Greenberg, *The American Political Dictionary*, 10.
13. William Safire, *Safire's New Political Dictionary* (New York: Random House, 1993), 144–45.
14. Safire, *Safire's New Political Dictionary*.
15. Philip E. Converse, "The Nature of Belief Systems in Mass Publics," in David E. Apter, ed., *Ideology and Discontent* (New York: Free Press, 1964), 206–21.
16. Colin Powell with Joseph E. Persico, *My American Journey* (New York: Random House, 1995).
17. Joe Klein, "Stalking the Radical Middle," *Newsweek* (September 25, 1995): 32–34.
18. Klein, "Stalking the Radical Middle."
19. Gene Stephens, "We Are Facing a Global Crime Wave," *USA Today Magazine* (July 1995): 26; Ben J. Wattenberg, *Values Matter Most* (New York: Free Press, 1995); and Hunter, *Culture Wars*, chapter 8.
20. *Business Week* (March 11, 1996): 50.
21. *The Public Perspective* (April/May 1995): 26.
22. *The Public Perspective* (April/May 1995): 26.
23. James W. Brosnan, "Term-Limits Bill Dies in Senate as GOP Jockeys for High Ground," *The Commercial Appeal* (April 24, 1996): 6A.

Chapter 2 Notes

1. Quoted in Holly Adelson, "Ruling Pressures Congress to Address Term Limits," *Congressional Quarterly Weekly Report* (May 27, 1995): 1479.
2. Adelson, "Ruling Pressures Congress to Address Term Limits."
3. Newt Gingrich, Dick Armey, and the House Republicans, *Contract with America* (New York: Times Books, 1994), 157.
4. 872 U.S. 2703 (1994).
5. Jennifer Babson, "Supporters to Fight On," *Congressional Quarterly Weekly Report* (May 27, 1995): 1481.
6. Steven S. Smith quoted in Babson, "Supporters Vow to Fight On."
7. Idelson, "Ruling Pressures Congress to Address Term Limits."
8. For an account of the early development of the colonies, see D. W. Meining, *The Shaping of America*, vol. 1: *Atlantic America, 1492–1800* (New Haven, CT: Yale University Press, 1986).
9. For an excellent chronology of the events leading up to the writing of the Declaration of Independence and the colonists' break with Great Britain, see Calvin D. Lonton, ed., *The Bicentennial Almanac* (Nashville, TN: Thomas Nelson, 1975).
10. See Gary Wills, *Inventing America: Jefferson's Declaration of Independence* (New York: Random House, 1978). Wills argues that the Declaration was signed solely to secure foreign aid for the ongoing war effort.
11. See Gordon Wood, *The Creation of the American Republic, 1776–1787* (Chapel Hill: University of North Carolina Press, 1969).
12. For more about the Articles of Confederation, see Merrill Jensen, *The Articles of Confederation* (Madison: University of Wisconsin Press, 1940).
13. Quoted in Selma R. Williams, *Fifty-Five Fathers: The Story of the Constitutional Convention* (New York: Dodd, Mead, 1970), 10.
14. Quoted in Doris Faber and Harold Faber, *We the People* (New York: Charles Scribner's Sons, 1987), 25.
15. Faber and Faber, *We the People*, 31.
16. For more on the political nature of compromise at the convention, see Calvin C. Jillson, *Constitution Making: Conflict and Consensus in the Federal Constitution of 1787* (New York: Agathon, 1988).
17. This kind of assumption about slaves was never specifically spelled out in the Constitution. In fact, slavery is nowhere specifically mentioned in that document. Although many of the Framers were morally opposed to slavery, they recognized that if the convention attempted to abolish or seriously restrict it in the short term, the Southern states would walk away from the new union (as they eventually did, resulting in the Civil War).
18. Quoted in Richard N. Current, T. Harry Williams, Frank Freidel, and Alan Brinkley, *American History: A Survey*, 6th ed. (New York: McGraw Hill, 1983), 168.
19. Bernard Bailyn, *The Ideological Origins of the American Revolution* (Cambridge, MA: Harvard University Press, 1967).
20. Richard E. Neustadt, *Presidential Power: The Politics of Leadership from FDR to Carter* (New York: Macmillan, 1980), 26.
21. See E. P. Panagopoulos, *Essays on the History and Meaning of Checks and Balances* (Lanham, MD: University Press of America, 1985).
22. Quoted in Faber and Faber, *We the People*, 51–52.
23. Federal Republicans favored a republican or representative form of government (do not confuse this term with the modern Republican Party, which came into being in 1854; see chapter 12). Ultimately, the word *federal* came to mean the form of government embodied in the new Constitution, just as *confederation* meant the "league of states" under the Articles, and later came to mean the "Confederacy" of 1861–65.

24. Numerous editions of *The Federalist Papers* exist. One of the commonly used is Clinton Rossiter, ed., *The Federalist* (New York: New American Library, 1961).

25. See Ralph Ketcham, ed., *The Anti-Federalist Papers and the Constitutional Debates* (New York: New American Library, 1986).

26. See Alan P. Grimes, *Democracy and the Amendments to the Constitution* (Lexington, MA: Lexington Books, 1978).

27. David E. Kyvig, *Repealing National Prohibition* (Chicago: University of Chicago Press, 1978).

28. See Jane J. Mansbridge, *Why We Lost the ERA* (Chicago: University of Chicago Press, 1986).

29. Eleanor Flexner, *Century of Struggle: The Woman's Rights Movement in the United States* (New York: Atheneum, 1974).

30. Speech by Attorney General Edwin Meese III before the American Bar Association, July 9, 1985, Washington, D.C.

31. Speech by William J. Brennan, Jr., at Georgetown University, Text and Teaching Symposium, October 10, 1985, Washington, D.C.

Chapter 3 Notes

1. Jim Woolf, "Who Owns Utah? 'Land' Lords Square Off in Wilderness Fight," *The Salt Lake Tribune* (April 7, 1996): A1.

2. Daniel J. Elazar, *American Federalism: A View From the States* (New York: Harper & Row, 1984).

3. Michael Satchell, "The West's Last Range War," *U.S. News & World Report* (September 18, 1995): 53–58.

4. Satchell, "The West's Last Range War," 53–58.

5. John H. Cushman, Jr., "Bradley Leads Filibuster on Public-Lands Measure," *The New York Times* (March 26, 1996): B10.

6. "How Much Government—Devolution," *The Public Perspective* (April/May 1995): 26.

7. In *City of Burbank* v. *Lockheed*, 411 U.S. 624 (1973), the U.S. Supreme Court ruled that the city could not impose curfews on plane takeoff or landing times. The Court said that one uniform *national* standard was critical for safety and the national interest.

8. *Missouri* v. *Holland*, 252 U.S. 416 (1920).

9. *McCulloch* v. *Maryland*, 4 Wheat. 316 (1819).

10. *Puerto Rico* v. *Branstad*, 483 U.S. 219 (1987)

11. *McCulloch* v. *Maryland*, 4 Wheat. 316 (1819).

12. *Gibbons* v. *Ogden*, 22 U.S. 1 (1824).

13. 16 Wall. 36 (1873).

14. *Lane County* v. *Oregon*, 74 U.S. 71 (1869).

15. 163 U.S. 537 (1896).

16. *Panhandle Oil Co.* v. *Knox*, 277 U.S. 71 (1928).

17. *Indian Motorcycle Co.* v. *United States*, 238 U.S. 570 (1931).

18. *Pensacola Telegraph* v. *Western Union*, 96 U.S. 1 (1877).

19. *U.S.* v. *E.C. Knight*, 156 U.S. 1 (1895).

20. *NLRB* v. *Jones and Laughlin Steel Co.*, 301 U.S. 1 (1937).

21. *United States* v. *Darby*, 312 U.S. 1 (1937).

22. *Wickard* v. *Filburn*, 317 U.S. 111 (1942).

23. Morton Grodzins, "Centralization and Decentralization in the American Federal System," in Robert A. Goldwin, ed. *A Nation of States* (Chicago: Rand McNally, 1963), 3–4.

24. Alice M. Rivlin, *Reviving the American Dream* (Washington, D.C.: Brookings Institution, 1992), 92.

25. Rivlin, *Reviving the American Dream*, 98.

26. Advisory Commission on Intergovernmental Relations, *The Federal Role in the Federal System: The Dynamics of Growth* (Washington, D.C.: 1980), 120–1.

27. Aaron Wildavsky, "Birthday Cake Federalism," in Robert E. Hawkins, ed., *American Federalism: A New Partnership for the Republic* (New Brunswick, NJ: Transaction Press, 1982), 182.

28. Samuel H. Beer, "The Modernization of American Federalism," *Publius* 3 (Fall 1973): 74–79.

29. Edward I. Koch, "The Mandate Millstone," *The Public Interest* 61 (Fall 1980): 43.

30. Richard P. Nathan, *et al.*, *Reagan and the States* (Princeton, NJ: Princeton University Press, 1987), 4.

31. Quoted in David E. Anderson, "Conservative Think Tanks Go Local," *UPI* (June 10, 1991).

32. John Kincaid, "From Cooperation to Coercion in American Federalism: Housing, Fragmentation, and Preemption, 1789–1992," *Journal of Law and Politics* 9 (Winter 1993): 333–430.

33. This discussion of preemption relies heavily on Joseph F. Zimmerman, *Contemporary American Federalism: The Growth of National Power* (New York: Praeger, 1992), 55–81.

34. Timothy J. Conlan and David R. Beam, "Federal Mandates: The Record of Reform and Future Prospects," *Intergovernmental Perspectives* (Fall 1992): 9.

35. Conlan and Beam, "Federal Mandates."

36. William Claiborne, "States Demand an Explanation: Federal Lawmakers Summoned to Justify Unfunded Mandates," *The Washington Post* (July 5, 1993): A17.

37. When senators were directly elected by state legislators, senators were much more responsive to state legislators than they are today. In fact, these summonses have no legal force. But it is unlikely they can be ignored without a high political cost.

38. "Devolutionary Thinking Is Now Part of a Larger Critique of Modern Governmental Experience," *The Public Perspective* (April/May 1995): 28.

39. *Harper* v. *Virginia Board of Elections*, 383 U.S. 663 (1966).

40. 115 S.Ct. 1842 (1995).

41. Wilfred M. McClay, "A More Perfect Union? Toward a New Federalism," *Commentary* (September 1995): 28.

42. 469 U.S. 528 (1985).

43. McClay, "A More Perfect Union?"

44. *U.S.* v. *Lopez*, 115 U.S. 1624 (1995).

45. Marianne Arneberg, "Cuomo Assails Judicial Hodgepodge," *Newsday* (August 15, 1990): 15.

46. 492 U.S. 490 (1989).

47. 112 S.Ct. 931 (1992).

48. Maralee Schwartz, "Louisiana Lawmakers Override Abortion Bill Veto," *The Washington Post* (June 19, 1991): A4.

49. David B. Walker, *The Rebirth of Federalism* (Chatham, NJ: Chatham House, 1994).

50. David S. Broder, "The Right Time for a Test of Ideas," *The Washington Post* (February 1, 1995): A19.

Chapter 4 Notes

1. This vignette, although fictional, is based on a case involving the Prune Yard Shopping Center, the California courts, and the U.S. Supreme Court. See *Robins* v. *Prune Yard Shopping Center*, 23 Cal. 3d 899, 592 P.2 341 (1979).

2. Raymond Wolfinger, "Reputation and Reality in the Study of Community Power," *American Sociological Review* 25 (October 1960): 636–44; Nelson Polsby, *Community Power and Political Theory* (New Haven: Yale University Press, 1963); and Robert E. Agger, Daniel Goldrich, and Bert Swanson, *The Rulers and the Ruled: Political Power and Impotence in American Communities* (New York: Wiley, 1964).

3. Laura R. Woliver, *From Outrage to Action: The Politics of Grass-Roots Dissent* (Urbana: University of Illinois Press, 1993); Matthew A. Crenson, *Neighborhood Politics* (Cambridge: Harvard University Press, 1983).

4. Albert L. Sturm, "The Development of American State Constitutions," *Publius* 12 (Winter 1982): 62–68.
5. Albert L. Kohlmeier, *The Old Northwest as the Keystone of the Arch of the American Federal Union* (Bloomington, IN: Principia Press, 1938); *Pathways to the Old Northwest* (Indianapolis: Indiana Historical Society, 1988).
6. Theodore Clarke Smith, *Parties and Slavery* (New York: Harper and Brothers, 1906); Arthur Charles Cole, *The Irrepressible Conflict, 1850–1865* (New York: Macmillan, 1934).
7. George E. Mowry, *The Progressive Era, 1900–20* (Washington, D.C.: American Historical Association, 1972).
8. Janice C. May, "Constitutional Amendment and Revision Revisited," *Publius* 12 (Winter 1982): 153–79.
9. Charles Wiggins, "Executive Vetos and Legislative Overrides in the American States," *Journal of Politics* 54 (November 1980): 42. Also, Glenn Abney and Thomas Lauth, "The Line-Item Veto in the States," *Public Administration Review* 45 (January/February 1985): 66–79.
10. F. Ted Hebert, Jeffrey L. Brudney, and Deil S. Wright, "Gubernatorial Influence and State Bureaucracy," *American Politics Quarterly* 11 (April 1983); Glenn Abney and Thomas Lauth, "The Governor as Chief Administrator," *Public Administration Quarterly* 3 (January/February 1983): 40–49.
11. Thad L. Beyle and Robert Dalton, "Appointment Power: Does It Belong to the Governor?" *State Government* 54 (Winter 1981): 6.
12. Leon W. Blevins, *Texas Government in National Perspective* (Englewood Cliffs, NJ: Prentice Hall, 1987), 169.
13. James L. Garnett, *Reorganizing State Government: The Executive Branch* (Boulder: Westview, 1980), 8 and 9; Diane Kincaid Blair, "The Gubernatorial Appointment Power: Too Much of a Good Thing?" *State Government* 55, (Summer 1982): 88–91.
14. Timothy O'Rourke, *The Impact of Reapportionment* (New Brunswick, NJ: Transaction Books, 1980).
15. *Reynolds* v. *Sims*, 377 U.S. 533 (1964).
16. Gerald Benjamin and Michael J. Malbin, eds., *Limiting Legislative Terms* (Washington, D.C.: Congressional Quarterly Press, 1992).
17. Alan Rosenthal, *Governors and Legislatures* (Washington, D.C.: Congressional Quarterly Press, 1990); Malcolm E. Jewell and Marcia Lynn Whicker, *Legislative Leadership in the American States* (Ann Arbor: University of Michigan Press, 1994).
18. Gary T. Clarke and Charles R. Grezlak, "Legislative Staffs Show Improvement," *National Civic Review* 65 (June 1976): 292.
19. Diana Gordon, "Citizen Legislators—Alive and Well," *State Legislatures* 20 (January 1994): 24–27.
20. Earl M. Maltz, "Federalism and State Court Activism," *Intergovernmental Perspective* (Spring 1987): 23–26.
21. Bradley Cannon, "The Impact of Formal Selection Processes on Characteristics of Judges—Reconsidered," *Law and Society Review* (May 1972): 570–93.
22. Thomas E. Cronin, *Direct Democracy* (Cambridge: Harvard University Press, 1989); David B. Magleby, *Direct Legislation* (Baltimore: Johns Hopkins University Press, 1984).
23. Alexis de Tocqueville, *Democracy in America*, ed. Phillips Bradley (New York: Knopf, 1945), 40.
24. *City of Clinton* v. *Cedar Rapids and Missouri River Railroad Co.* (24 Iowa 455, 1868).
25. Steven P. Erie, *Rainbow's End: Irish-Americans and the Dilemmas of Urban Machine Politics, 1840–1985* (Berkeley: University of California Press, 1988); Alfred Steinberg, *The Bosses* (New York: New American Library, 1972); Seymour Mandelbaum, *Boss Tweed's New York* (New York: Wiley, 1955); Milton Rakove, *Don't Make No Waves—Don't Back No Losers: An Insider's Analysis of the*

Daley Machine (Bloomington: Indiana University Press, 1975).
26. Samuel P. Hays, "The Politics of Reform in Municipal Government in the Progressive Era," *Pacific Northwest Quarterly* 55 (October 1964): 157–66.
27. U.S. Bureau of the Census, *Government Finances in 1993–94* (Washington, D.C.: Government Printing Office, 1994), 12–19.

Chapter 5 Notes

1. This paragraph draws heavily on William Claiborne, "Suit to Test Police Interrogations," *The Washington Post* (December 20, 1995): A3.
2. Claiborne, "Suit to Test Police Interrogations."
3. Claiborne, "Suit to Test Police Interrogations."
4. 384 U.S. 436 (1966).
5. Claiborne, "Suit to Test Police Interrogations."
6. The absence of a bill of rights led Mason to refuse to sign the proposed Constitution, noting that he "would sooner chop off his right hand than put it to the constitution as it now stands." (Quoted in Eric Black, *Our Constitution: The Myth That Binds Us* [Boulder, CO: Westview Press, 1988], 75.)
7. Quoted in Jack N. Rakove, "Madison Won Passage of the Bill of Rights But Remained a Skeptic," *Public Affairs Report* (March 1991): 6.
8. 7 Pet. 243 (1833).
9. *Allgeyer* v. *Louisiana*, 165 U.S. 578 (1897).
10. *Gitlow* v. *New York*, 268 U.S. 652 (1925).
11. 283 U.S. 697 (1931). For more about *Near*, see Fred W. Friendly, *Minnesota Rag* (New York: Random House, 1981).
12. *Palko* v. *Connecticut*, 302 U.S. 319 (1937).
13. Continental Congress to the People of Great Britain, October 21, 1774, in Philip Kurland and Ralph Lerner, eds., *The Founders' Constitution*, vol. 5 (Chicago: University of Chicago Press, 1987), 61.
14. *Reynolds* v. *U.S.*, 98 U.S. 145 (1879).
15. *Cantwell* v. *Connecticut*, 310 U.S. 296 (1940).
16. *Zobrest* v. *Catalina Foothills School District*, 506 U.S. 813 (1992).
17. 370 U.S. 421 (1962).
18. *Lee* v. *Weisman*, 505 U.S. 577 (1992).
19. 403 U.S. 602 (1971).
20. 403 U.S. 602 (1971).
21. *Stone* v. *Graham*, 449 U.S. 39 (1980).
22. *Widmar* v. *Vincent*, 454 U.S. 263 (1981).
23. *Board of Education* v. *Mergens*, 496 U.S. 226 (1990).
24. *Lamb's Chapel* v. *Center Moriches Union Free School District*, 508 U.S. 384 (1993).
25. *Rosenberger* v. *University of Virginia*, 115 S. Ct. 2510 (1995).
26. *Rosenberger* v. *University of Virginia*, 115 S. Ct. 2510 (1995).
27. *Sherbert* v. *Verner*, 374 U.S. 398 (1963).
28. *Employment Division, Dept. of Human Resources of Oregon* v. *Smith*, 494 U.S. 872 (1990).
29. *Church of the Lukumi Babalu Aye* v. *Hialeah*, 508 U.S. 525 (1993).
30. *Cruz* v. *Beto*, 405 U.S. 319 (1972).
31. *O'Lone* v. *Shabazz*, 482 U.S. 342 (1987).
32. See, for example, the opinion in *Boissonneault* v. *Flint City Council*, 392 Mich. 685 (1974).
33. *Ex parte McCardle*, 74 U.S. 506 (1869).
34. David M. O'Brien, *Constitutional Law and Politics*, vol. 2 (New York: Norton, 1991), 345.
35. See Frederick Siebert, *The Rights and Privileges of the Press* (New York: D. Appleton-Century, 1934), 886, 931–40.
36. *Schenck* v. *United States*, 249 U.S. 47 (1919).

37. *Frohwerk* v. *United States*, 249 U.S. 204 (1919).
38. 250 U.S. 616 (1919).
39. 395 U.S. 444 (1969).
40. *Abrams* v. *United States*, 250 U.S. 616 (1919).
41. 283 U.S. 359 (1931).
42. 393 U.S. 503 (1969).
43. *Texas* v. *Johnson*, 491 U.S. 397 (1989).
44. *U.S.* v. *Eichman*, 496 U.S. 310 (1990).
45. 403 U.S. 713 (1971).
46. *Nebraska Press Association* v. *Stuart*, 427 U.S. 539 (1976).
47. "Penn Students Drop Racism Charge," *Facts on File, World News Digest* (June 10, 1993): 427, A1.
48. 376 U.S. 254 (1964).
49. 315 U.S. 568 (1942).
50. *Regina* V. *Hicklin*, L. R. 2 Q. B. 360 (1868).
51. 354 U.S. 476 (1957).
52. 413 U.S. 15 (1973).
53. *Jenkins* v. *Georgia*, 418 U.S. 153 (1974).
54. *Jacobellis* v. *Ohio*, 378 U.S. 184 (1964).
55. *Barnes* v. *Glen Theater*, 501 U.S. 560 (1991).
56. *Furman* v. *Georgia*, 408 U.S. 238 (1972).
57. *Gregg* v. *Georgia*, 428 U.S. 153 (1976).
58. *Stein* v. *N.Y.*, 346 U.S. 156 (1953).
59. *Wilson* v. *Arkansas*, 115 S. Ct. 1914 (1995).
60. *U.S.* v. *Sokolov*, 490 U.S. 1 (1989).
61. *U.S.* v. *Matlock*, 415 U.S. 164 (1974).
62. *Johnson* v. *United States*, 333 U.S. 10 (1948).
63. *Winston* v. *Lee*, 470 U.S. 753 (1985).
64. *South Dakota* v. *Neville*, 459 U.S. 553 (1983).
65. *Michigan* v. *Tyler*, 436 U.S. 499 (1978).
66. *Hester* v. *U.S.*, 265 U.S. 57 (1924).
67. *Carroll* v. *U.S.*, 267 U.S. 132 (1925).
68. *California* v. *Acevedo*, 500 U.S. 565 (1991).
69. *Skinner* v. *Railway Labor Executives' Association*, 489 U.S. 602 (1989).
70. *Vernonia School District* v. *Acton*, 115 S. Ct. 2386 (1995).
71. *Counselman* v. *Hitchcock*, 142 U.S. 547 (1892).
72. *Brown* v. *Mississippi*, 297 U.S. 278 (1936).
73. *Lynumn* v. *Illinois*, 372 U.S. 528 (1963).
74. *Rhode Island* v. *Innis*, 446 U.S. 291 (1980).
75. *Arizona* v. *Fulminante*, 500 U.S. 938 (1991).
76. 232 U.S. 383 (1914).
77. *Stone* v. *Powell*, 428 U.S. 465 (1976).
78. *Johnson* v. *Zerbst*, 304 U.S. 458 (1932).
79. *Powell* v. *Alabama*, 287 U.S. 45 (1932).
80. 372 U.S. 335 (1963).
81. *Argersinger* v. *Hamlin*, 407 U.S. 25 (1972).
82. *Scott* v. *Illinois*, 440 U.S. 367 (1979).
83. *Strauder* v. *West Virginia*, 100 U.S. 303 (1880).
84. *Taylor* v. *Louisiana*, 419 U.S. 522 (1975).
85. Peremptory challenges are discretionary challenges. A lawyer representing an abortion clinic protester, for example, could use peremptory challenges to rid the jury of pro-choice advocates. "For cause" challenges, by contrast, are based on legal reasoning and not on an educated guess about the best persons to serve on the jury. In a capital case, for example, persons morally opposed to the death penalty could be removed "for cause."
86. *Batson* v. *Kentucky*, 476 U.S. 79 (1986).
87. 114 S. Ct. 1419 (1994).
88. *Hallinger* v. *Davis*, 146 U.S. 314 (1892).
89. *O'Neil* v. *Vermont*, 144 U.S. 323 (1892).
90. See Michael Meltsner, *Cruel and Unusual: The Supreme Court and Capital Punishment* (New York: Random House, 1973).
91. 408 U.S. 238 (1972).
92. *Gregg* v. *Georgia*, 428 U.S. 153 (1976).
93. 481 U.S. 279 (1987).
94. 501 U.S. 1224 (1991).

95. *Olmstead* v. *United States*, 277 U.S. 438 (1928).
96. 381 U.S. 481 (1965).
97. *Poe* v. *Ullman*, 367 U.S. 497 (1961).
98. *Eisenstadt* v. *Baird*, 410 U.S. 113 (1972).
99. 410 U.S. 113 (1973).
100. *Beal* v. *Doe*, 432 U.S. 438 (1977) and *Harris* v. *McRae*, 448 U.S. 297 (1980).
101. 492 U.S. 490 (1989).
102. 502 U.S. 1056 (1992).
103. *Barnes* v. *Moore*, 506 U.S. 1013 (1992).
104. *Bray* v. *Alexandria Women's Health Clinic*, 506 U.S. 263 (1993).
105. *Rust* v. *Sullivan*, 500 U.S. 173 (1991).
106. The National Abortion and Reproductive Rights Action League, "Congressional Votes on Reproductive Choice, 1977–1995," February 1996.
107. "House Sends Partial Birth Abortion Bill To Clinton," *Politics USA* (March 28, 1996): 1 (www).
108. *Board of Education of City of Oklahoma City* v. *National Gay Task Force*, 470 U.S. 903 (1985).
109. 478 U.S. 186 (1986).
110. Reported in O'Brien, *Constitutional Law and Politics*, 1223.
111. *Romer* v. *Evans*, 116 S. Ct. 1620 (1996).
112. 110 S. Ct. 2841 (1990).
113. *In re Quinlan*, 70 N.J. 10 (1976).
114. *National Organization for Women* v. *Scheidler*, 114 S. Ct. 798 (1994).
115. Ralph Reed, *Contract with the American Family* (Nashville, TN: Moorings, 1995), xi.

Chapter 6 Notes

1. Julia Malone and Chris Roush, "Restaurant Chain Goes to Battle," *Atlanta Constitution* (November 16, 1995), F3.
2. Malone and Roush, "Restaurant Chain Goes to Battle."
3. Catherine Drinker Bowen, *Miracle at Philadelphia: The Story of the Constitutional Convention May to September 1787* (Boston: Little, Brown, 1986), 201.
4. 83 U.S. (16 Wall.) 36 (1873).
5. 83 U.S. (16 Wall.) 130 (1873).
6. 88 U.S. (21 Wall.) 162 (1875). See also Karen O'Connor, *Women's Organizations' Use of the Courts* (Lexington, MA: Lexington Books, 1980).
7. 109 U.S. 3 (1883).
8. 163 U.S. 537 (1896).
9. 170 U.S. 213 (1898).
10. 175 U.S. 528 (1899).
11. Juan Williams, *Eyes on the Prize: America's Civil Rights Years, 1954–1965* (New York: Penguin, 1987), 10.
12. 208 U.S. 412 (1908).
13. *Missouri ex rel. Gaines* v. *Canada*, 305 U.S. 337 (1938).
14. Richard Kluger, *Simple Justice* (New York: Vintage, 1975), 268.
15. *Sweatt* v. *Painter*, 339 U.S. 629; *McLaurin* v. *Oklahoma*, 339 U.S. 637 (1950).
16. 347 U.S. 483 (1954).
17. But see Gerald Rosenberg, *Hollow Hope: Can Courts Bring About Social Change* (Chicago: University of Chicago Press, 1991).
18. Quoted in Joan Williams, *Eyes on the Prize: America's Civil Rights Years, 1954–1965* (New York: Penguin, 1987), 10.
19. 349 U.S. 294 (1955).
20. Quoted in Williams, *Eyes on the Prize*, 37.
21. *Cooper* v. *Aaron*, 358 U.S. 1 (1958).
22. *Heart of Atlanta Motel* v. *United States*, 379 U.S. 241 (1964).
23. 402 U.S. 1 (1971).
24. *Missouri* v. *Jenkins*, 115 S. Ct. 2038 (1995).
25. *Griggs* v. *Duke Power Co.*, 401 U.S. 424 (1971).

26. Jo Freeman, *The Politics of Women's Liberation* (New York: David McKay, 1975), 57.
27. 368 U.S. 57 (1961).
28. Betty Friedan, *The Feminine Mystique* (New York: Dell, 1963).
29. 323 U.S. 214 (1944). This is the only case involving race-based distinctions applying the strict scrutiny standard where the Court has upheld the restrictive law.
30. 404 U.S. 71 (1971).
31. 429 U.S. 190 (1976).
32. *Rostker* v. *Goldberg*, 453 U.S. 57 (1981).
33. Joyce Gelb and Marian Lief Palley, *Women and Public Policies* (Princeton: Princeton University Press, 1982).
34. Rennard Strickland, "Native Americans," in Kermit Hall, ed., *The Oxford Companion to the Supreme Court of the United States* (New York: Oxford University Press, 1992), 557.
35. Dee Brown, *Bury My Heart at Wounded Knee* (New York: Holt, Rinehart & Winston, 1971).
36. Strickland, "Native Americans," 579.
37. Hugh Dellios, "Rites by Law: Indians Seek Sacred Lands," *Chicago Tribune* (July 4, 1993): C1.
38. John R. Hermann, "American Indians in Court: The Burger and Rehnquist Years, 1969–1992 Terms," Ph.D. dissertation, Emory University, 1995.
39. F. Chris Garcia, *Latinos and the Political System* (Notre Dame, IN: University of Notre Dame Press, 1988), 1.
40. *White* v. *Register,* 412 U.S. 755 (1973).
41. *San Antonio Independent School District* v. *Rodriguez,* 411 U.S. 1 (1973).
42. 478 U.S. 186 (1986).
43. *Romer* v. *Evans,* 116 S. Ct. 1620 (1996).
44. Julie Stacey, "Poll: Less Concern about Racial Issues," *USA Today* (February 11, 1994): 8A.
45. 438 U.S. 186 (1986).
46. *Johnson* v. *Santa Clara County,* 480 U.S. 616 (1987).
47. Ruth Marcus, "Hill Coalition Aims to Counter Court in Job Bias," *Washington Post* (February 8, 1990): A10.
48. *Adarand Constructors Inc.* v. *Pena,* 115 S. Ct. 2097 (1995).
49. Cert. denied, *Texas* v. *Hopwood,* 116 S. Ct. 2581 (1996). See also Terrance Stutz, "UT Minority Enrollment Tested By Suit: Fate of Affirmative Action in Education is at Issue," *Dallas Morning News* (October 14, 1995): 1A.
50. John Kincaid, "The New Judicial Federalism," *Spectrum: The Journal of State Governments* (1992).

Chapter 7 Notes

1. Richard E. Cohen, "The Transformers," *National Journal* 27 (March 4, 1995): 528.
2. Humphrey Taylor, "Louis Harris Poll: Confidence in Leaders Down," Gannett New Service, March 6, 1994, NEXIS.
3. 369 U.S. 186 (1962).
4. *Wesberry* v. *Sanders,* 376 U.S. 1 (1964).
5. *Thornburg* v. *Gingles,* 478 U.S. 30 (1986). The act was amended in 1982.
6. *Shaw* v. *Reno,* 113 S. Ct. 2816 (1993).
7. *Miller* v. *Johnson,* 115 S. Ct. 2475 (1995).
8. *Bush* v. *Vera,* 116 U.S. 1941 (1996); *Shaw* v. *Hunt,* 116 U.S. 1894 (1996).
9. Charles S. Bullock, III, "House Careerists: Changing Patterns of Longevity and Attrition," *American Political Science Review* 66 (December 1972): 1295–1300.
10. Quoted in Hedrick Smith, *The Power Game* (New York: Ballentine Books, 1989), 97.
11. Don Terry, "Illinois Seat is Battleground in War for Senate," *The New York Times* (March 19, 1996): A16.
12. Richard F. Fenno, Jr., *Home Style* (Boston: Little, Brown, 1978), 32.

13. Hedrick Smith, *The Power Game* (New York: Ballentine Books, 1989), 108.
14. Marjorie Randon Hershey, "Congressional Elections," in Gerald M. Pomper, *et al., The Election of 1992: Reports and Interpretations* (Chatham, NJ: Chatham House, 1993), 159.
15. Alan I. Abramowitz, "Incumbency, Congressional Spending, and the Decline of Competition in House Elections," *Journal of Politics* 53 (February 1991): 34–56.
16. *U.S. Term Limits, Inc.* v. *Thornton,* 115 U.S. 1842 (1995).
17. Andrew C. Revkin, "Back to Her Roots," *The New York Times* (October 10, 1995): B1.
18. Revkin, "Back to Her Roots."
19. Warren E. Miller and Donald Stokes, " Constituency Influence in Congress," *American Political Science Review* 57 (March 1963): 45–57.
20. Sue Thomas, *How Women Legislate* (New York: Oxford University Press, 1994).
21. Center for the American Woman and Politics, *Voices, Views, Votes: The Impact of Women in the 103rd Congress* (New Brunswick, NJ: Eagleton Institute of Politics, Rutgers, 1995), 15.
22. Center for The American Woman and Politics, *Voices, Views, Votes,* 15.
23. "Lawmakers: Redskins' Name is a Slur," *Star Tribune* (November 6, 1993): 7C.
24. Adam Clymer, "Daughter of Slavery Hushes Senate," *The New York Times* (July 23, 1993): B6.
25. Clymer, "Daughter of Slavery Hushes Senate."
26. Barbara Hinckley, *Stability and Change in Congress,* 3d ed. (New York: Harper & Row, 1983), 166.
27. Jackie Koszcuk, "Gingrich Puts More Power into Speaker's Hands," *CQ Weekly Report* (October 7, 1995): w.w.w., 3049–53.
28. Koszcuk, "Gingrich Puts More Power into Speaker's Hands."
29. Kevin Phillips, "Congress Fizzles Out," *St. Louis Dispatch* (February 25, 1996): 3B.
30. Richard Wolfe, "Gingrich Ready to Pick Up Where He Left Off," *USA Today* (March 24, 1996): 4A.
31. Lydia Saad and Frank Newport, "Public Divided Over Accomplishments of Gingrich and Congress," *The Gallup Organization April 1995 Newsletter Archive* (April 8, 1995): 1.
32. Clifford Krauss, "Whips' Honeyed Touch: The Recipe for Success," *The New York Times* (August 7, 1993).
33. Barbara Sinclair, "The Struggle Over Representation and Lawmaking in Congress: Leadership Reforms in the 1990s," in James A. Thurber and Roger H. Davidson, eds., *Remaking Congress: Change and Stability in the 1990s* (Washington, D.C.: CQ Press, 1995), 105.
34. Quoted in Donald R. Matthews, *U.S. Senators and Their Worlds* (Chapel Hill, NC: University of North Carolina Press, 1960), 97–98.
35. Matthews, *U.S. Senators and Their World,* 97–98.
36. "A Short History of the Democratic Caucus," 1. Homepage; HillSource, House Republican Conference, "Our Mission," 1
37. Woodrow Wilson, *Congressional Government: A Study in American Government* (New York: Meridian Books, 1956, originally published in 1885), 79.
38. Roger H. Davidson, "Congressional Committees in the New Reform Era: From Combat to the Contract," in Thurber and Davidson, *Remaking Congress,* 28.
39. Quoted in Steven Smith and Christopher J. Deering, *Committees in Congress,* 2d ed. (Washington, D.C.: CQ Press, 1990), 126.
40. Kenneth A. Shepsle, *The Giant Jigsaw Puzzle: Democratic Committee Assignments in the Modern House* (Chicago: University of Chicago Press, 1978).

41. Reported in Roger H. Davidson an Walter J. Oleszek, *Congress and Its Members*, 3d ed. (Washington, D.C.: CQ Press, 1990), and *Woman's Almanac* (New York: Newspaper Enterprises Association, 1977), 200.

42. Roger H. Davidson, "Building a Republican Regime on Capitol Hill," *Extension of Remarks* (December 1995): 2.

43. Barbara Sinclair, *The Transformation of the U.S. Senate* (Baltimore: Johns Hopkins University Press, 1989).

44. Thomas E. Mann and Norman J. Ornstein, *Renewing Congress: A Second Report* (Washington, D.C.: American Enterprise Institute and the Brookings Institution, June. 1993).

45. Quoted in "Senate 'Holds' System Developing as Sophisticated Tactic for Leverage, Delay," *Daily Reports for Executives* 165 (August 26, 1991): C-1.

46. James A. Thurber, "If the Game Is Too Hard, Change the Rules: Congressional Budget Reform in the 1990s," in Thurber and Davidson, *Remaking Congress*, 140.

47. CBS News Poll data in *National Journal* 27 (December 9, 1995): 3060.

48. Gallup Poll data in *National Journal* 27 (December 9, 1995): 3060.

49. Data in *National Journal* 26 (December 17, 1994): 2996.

50. As late as March 1995, 54 percent of Americans believed that the 104th Congress would be more productive than most. *National Journal* 27 (March 25, 1995): 770.

51. NBC Poll data in *National Journal* 27 (March 4, 1995): 572.

52. Aage R. Clausen, *How Congressmen Decide: A Policy Focus* (New York: St. Martin's Press, 1973); John Kingdon, *Congressmen's Voting Decisions*, 3d ed. (Ann Arbor: University of Michigan, 1989).

53. Kingdon, *Congressmen's Voting Decisions*.

54. Kingdon, *Congressmen's Voting Decisions*.

55. Richard F. Fenno, Jr., *Home Style: House Members in Their Districts* (Boston: Little, Brown, 1978).

56. Howard Fineman, *et al.*, "Whew!" *Newsweek* (August 16, 1993): 19.

57. Clausen, *How Congressmen Decide*.

58. David W. Brady, Joseph Cooper, and Patricia Hurley, "The Decline of Party in the U.S. House of Representatives, 1887–1968," *Legislative Studies Quarterly* 4 (August 1979): 381–407.

59. Barbara Sinclair, *Congressional Realignment, 1925–1978*. (Austin: University of Texas Press, 1982).

60. Stephen Labaton, "Defying Polls, Gingrich Raises Big Money," *The New York Times* (April 12, 1996): 1A.

61. Labaton, "Defying Polls."

62. Lynn Marek, "Schroeder Hails Women's Gains," *The Plain Dealer* (December 28, 1993): 1C.

63. Jonathan D. Salant, "LSOs are No Longer Separate, the Work's Almost Equal," *Congressional Quarterly* 53 (May 27, 1995): 1483.

64. A. B. Stoddard, "Caucuses Lose Influence after LSOs Abolished," *The Hill* (February 14, 1996), 2.

65. James Sterling Young, *The Washington Community, 1800–1820* (New York: Columbia University Press, 1966), 98–105.

66. William J. Eaton, "Battling Caucuses—Congressional Cheer-Leaders Rally Round Their Caucuses," *Los Angeles Times* (July 31, 1990): A5.

67. Ann Reilly Dowd, "How To Get Things Done in Washington," *Fortune* (August 9, 1993): 60.

68. Lloyd Grove, "White House Declares War on Upstart Senator," *Atlanta Constitution* (April 6, 1993), A15.

69. Grove, "White House Declares War on Upstart Senator."

70. Arthur Schlesinger, *The Imperial Presidency* (New York: Houghton Mifflin, 1973).

71. Joel D. Aberbach, *Keeping a Watchful Eye: The Politics of Congressional Oversight* (Washington, D.C.: The Brookings Institution, 1990).

72. 462 U.S. 919 (1983).

73. Roger H. Davidson, *The Postreform Congress*, 7.

Chapter 8 Notes

1. Quoted in "Dear Abby," *Atlanta Journal and Constitution* (March 13, 1996): D11.

2. Richard E. Neustadt, *Presidential Power: The Politics of Power from FDR to Carter* (New York: Wiley, 1980).

3. Edward S. Corwin, *The President: Office and Powers, 1787–1957*, 4th ed. (New York: New York University Press, 1957), 5.

4. F. N. Thorpe, ed., *American Charters, Constitutions, Etc.* (Washington, D.C., 1909), VIII, 3816–17.

5. Quoted in Corwin, *The President*, 11.

6. Winston Solberg, *The Federal Convention and the Formation of the Union of the American States* (Indianapolis: Bobbs-Merrill, 1958), 235.

7. Alfred Steinberg, *The First Ten: The Founding Presidents and Their Administrations* (New York: Doubleday, 1967), 59.

8. "Is the Vice Presidency Necessary?" *Atlantic* 233 (May 1974): 37.

9. Benjamin I. Page and Mark P. Petracca, *The American Presidency* (New York: McGraw-Hill, 1983), 262.

10. Page and Petracca, *The American Presidency*, 268.

11. Quoted in Solberg, *The Federal Convention*, 91.

12. "Address Before a Joint Session of the Congress of the Union, January 28, 1992," *Weekly Compilation of Presidential Documents* 28 (February 3, 1992): 175.

13. *Public Papers of the Presidents* (1963), 889.

14. Quoted in Richard E. Neustadt, *Presidential Power*, 9.

15. Quoted in Paul F. Boller, Jr., *Presidential Anecdotes* (New York: Penguin Books, 1981), 78.

16. Abraham Lincoln, "Special Session Message," July 4, 1861, in Edward Keynes and David Adamany, eds., *Borzoi Reader in American Politics*, (New York: Knopf, 1973), 539.

17. Quoted in Page and Petracca, *The American Presidency*, 57.

18. Merlin Gustafson, "The President's Mail," *Presidential Studies Quarterly* 8 (1978): 36.

19. Franklin D. Roosevelt, Press Conference, July 23, 1937.

20. See, generally, Richard Pious, *The American Presidency*, 213, 254, 255.

21. Lyndon B. Johnson, *The Vantage Point* (New York: Holt, Rinehart and Winston, 1971), 448.

22. Morris Fiorina, *Divided Government* (New York: Macmillan, 1992).

23. Quoted in Thomas E. Cronin, *The State of the Presidency*, 2d ed. (Boston: Little, Brown, 1980), 169.

24. *Congressional Quarterly Weekly Report* (December 1, 1990): 4034.

25. Thomas Cronin, *The State of the Presidency* (Boston: Little, Brown, 1975).

26. Paul C. Light, *The President's Agenda: Domestic Policy Choice from Kennedy to Carter* (Baltimore: Johns Hopkins University Press, 1983).

27. George Reedy, *The Twilight of the Presidency* (New York: New American Library), 38–9.

28. Samuel Kernell, *New Strategies of Presidential Leadership*, 2nd ed. (Washington, D.C.: CQ Press, 1993), 3.

29. Reedy, *Twilight of the Presidency*, p. 33.

30. Neustadt, *Presidential Power*. 1–10.

31. Michael R. Kagay, "History Suggests Bush's Popularity Will Ebb," *The New York Times* (May 22, 1991): A-10.

Chapter 9 Notes

1. Dirk Johnson, "Shutdown Causes Anger and Confusion for Many," *The New York Times* (November 15, 1995): B9.

2. Clyde Haberman, "The Nation: Showing Up in a Shutdown," *The New York Times* (November 19, 1995): D6.
3. The word *bureau* originally referred to the cloth covering of desks and writing tables used by seventeenth-century French government officials. In the eighteenth century, the word was coupled with the suffix *-cracy*, signifying rule of government (as in aristocracy, democracy, and theocracy). In Britain the bureaucracy is commonly referred to as the civil service or Whitehall, the name of the building in London that houses many government ministries.
4. Harold D. Lasswell, *Politics: Who Gets What, When and How* (New York: McGraw-Hill, 1938).
5. H. H. Gerth and C. Wright Mills, *From Max Weber* (New York: Oxford University Press, 1958).
6. Quoted in Robert C. Caldwell, *James A. Garfield* (Hamden, CT: Archon Books, 1965).
7. *NLRB* v. *Jones & Laughlin Steel Corp.*, 301 U.S. 1 (1937).
8. *U.S.* v. *Darby Lumber Co.* 312 U.S. 100 (1941); and *Wickwood* v. *Filburn*, 317 U.S. 111 (1942).
9. "Federal News: Hatch Act," *Inc., Government Employee Relations Report* (October 11, 1993): 1317.
10. David Osborne and Ted Gaebler, *Reinventing Government* (Reading, MA: Addison-Wesley, 1992), 20–21.
11. Osborne and Gaebler, *Reinventing Government*, 20–21.
12. On the difficulty of counting the exact number of government agencies, see David Nachmias and David H. Rosenbloom, *Bureaucratic Government: U.S.A.* (New York: St. Martin's Press, 1980).
13. The classic work on regulatory commissions is Marver Bernstein, *Regulating Business by Independent Commission* (Princeton, NJ: Princeton University Press, 1955).
14. *Humphrey's Executor* v. *U.S.*, 295 U.S. 602 (1935).
15. For more on iron triangles, see Randall Ripley and Grace Franklin, *Congress, Bureaucracy and Public Policy*, 4th ed. (Homewood, IL: Dorsey Press, 1984).
16. "Issue Networks and the Executive Establishment," in Anthony King, ed., *The New American Political System* (Washington, D.C.: American Enterprise Institute, 1978), 87–124.
17. Martin Shapiro, "The Presidency and the Federal Courts," in Arnold Meltsner, ed., *Politics and the Oval Office* (San Francisco: Institute for Contemporary Studies, 1981), chapter 8.
18. Michael Lipsky, *Street-Level Bureaucracy: Dilemmas of the Individual in Public Services* (New York: Russell Sage Foundation, 1980).
19. Lipsky, *Street-Level Bureaucracy*.
20. Cornelius M. Kerwin, *Rulemaking: How Government Agencies Write Law and Make Policy* (Washington, D.C.: CQ Press, 1994), xv.
21. Jack C. Plano and Milton Greenberg, *The American Political Dictionary*, 6th ed. (New York: Holt, Rinehart and Winston, 1982), 236.
22. Arthur Schlesinger, Jr., *A Thousand Days* (Greenwich, CT: Fawcett Books, 1967), 377.
23. Irene Murphy, *Public Policy on the Status of Women* (Lexington, MA: Lexington Books, 1974).
24. Matthew McCubbins and Thomas Schwartz, "Congressional Oversight Overlooked: Police Patrols versus Fire Alarms," *American Journal of Political Science* 28 (1987): 165–79.
25. According to Greek legend, Damocles was a courtier and constant flatterer of Dionysus, King of Syracuse. Damocles coveted the happiness and glory of kings until Dionysus gave a banquet in his honor. Damocles enjoyed the banquet immensely until he looked up and saw a sword over his head, hung by a single thread. The sword was meant to teach him of the constant danger faced by the kings he so envied.
26. Kerwin, *Rulemaking*, 225.
27. Barbara Hinkson Craig, *The Legislative Veto: Congressional Control of Regulation* (Boulder, CO: Westview Press, 1983).
28. Craig, *The Legislative Veto*, 27.
29. 462 U.S. 919 (1983).
30. Rosemary O'Leary, *Environmental Change: Federal Courts and the EPA* (Philadelphia: Temple University Press, 1993).
31. Thomas V. DiBacco, "Veep Gore Reinventing Government—Again!" *USA Today* (September 9, 1993): 13A.
32. John Erlichman, "Government Reform: Will Al Gore's Package of Changes Succeed Where Others Failed? Washington's 'Iron Triangles,'" *Atlanta Journal and Constitution* (September 16, 1993): A15.
33. Al Gore, *Creating a Government that Works Better and Costs Less: Report of the National Performance Review* (Washington, D.C.: U.S. Government Printing Office, 1993).
34. See Joyce Gelb and Marian Lief Palley, *Women and Public Policies* (Princeton, NJ: Princeton University Press, 1982), chapter 5.

Chapter 10 Notes

1. Timothy M. Phelps, "Incomplete Course in Justice for Two New Jersey Teachers," *Newsday* (June 18, 1995): 6.
2. *U.S.* v. *Board of Education of Township of Piscataway*, 832 F. Supp. 836 (1993).
3. Bernard Schwartz, *The Law in America* (New York: American Heritage, 1974), 48.
4. Julius Goebel, Jr., *History of the Supreme Court of the United States*, vol. 1: *Antecedents and Beginnings to 1801* (New York: Macmillan, 1971), 206.
5. 1 (Wheat.) 14 U.S. 304 (1816).
6. Quoted in Goebel, *History of the Supreme Court of the United States*, 280.
7. Schwartz, *The Law in America*, 11.
8. 2 Dall. 419 (1793).
9. 3 Dall. 171 (1796).
10. 5 U.S. 137 (1803).
11. David W. Neubauer, *Judicial Process: Law, Courts and Politics* (Pacific Grove, CA: Brooks/Cole, 1991), 57.
12. Cases involving citizens from different states can be filed in state or federal court.
13. John R. Vile and Mario Perez-Reilly, "The U.S. Constitution and Judicial Qualifications: A Curious Omission," *Judicature* (December/January 1991): 198–202.
14. Quoted in Nina Totenberg, "Will Judges Be Chosen Rationally?" *Judicature* (August/September 1976): 93.
15. Elliot E. Slotnick, "Federal Appellate Judge Selection During the Carter Administration: Recruitment Changes and Unanswered Questions," *Justice System Journal* 6 (Fall 1981): 293–304.
16. Sheldon Goldman, "Judicial Selection Under Clinton: A Midterm Evaluation," *Judicature* 78 (May–June 1995): 278. This paragraph relies heavily on this article.
17. U.S. Courts Administrative Office, Bruce Ragsdale.
18. Tony Mauro, "Are Clinton Judges Too Liberal?" *USA Today* (May 7, 1996): 1A.
19. Quoted in Judge Irving R. Kaufman, "Charting a Judicial Pedigree," *The New York Times* (January 24, 1981): 23.
20. Quoted in Lawrence Baum, *The Supreme Court*, 3d. ed. (Washington. D.C.: CQ Press, 1989), 108.
21. See Barbara A. Perry, *A Representative Supreme Court? The Impact of Race, Religion and Gender on Appointments* (New York: Greenwood Press, 1991).
22. Clarence Thomas was raised a Catholic, but attended an Episcopalian church at the time of his appointment having been barred from Catholic sacraments because of his remarriage.
23. Saundra Torry, "ABA's Judicial Panel Is a Favorite Bipartisan Target," *The Washington Post* (April 29, 1996): F7.

24. Torry, "ABA's Judicial Panel."
25. M. A. Stapleton, "Judicial Selection Process Survives Flaws," *Chicago Daily Law Bulletin* (February 7, 1996): 1.
26. See Bruce Allen Murphy, *The Brandeis/Frankfurter Connection* (New York: Oxford University Press, 1982).
27. Phil Rosenthal, "Why Not Wapner?" *The San Diego Union-Tribune* (March 25, 1993): F-5.
28. Marcia Coyle, "How Americans View High Court," *The National Law Journal* (February 26, 1990): 1.
29. John Brigham, *The Cult of the Court* (Philadelphia: Temple University Press, 1987).
30. Stephen L. Wasby, *The Supreme Court in the Federal Judicial System*, 4th ed. (Chicago: Nelson-Hall, 1988), 194.
31. Wasby, *The Supreme Court*, 194.
32. Wasby, *The Supreme Court*, 199. Much of this change occurred as the result of an increase in state criminal cases, of which nearly 100 percent concerned constitutional questions.
33. Neubauer, *Judicial Process*, 370.
34. William P. McLauchan, "The Business of the United States Supreme Court, 1971–1983: An Analysis of Supply and Demand," paper presented at the 1986 annual meeting of the Midwest Political Science Association.
35. 111 S. Ct. 596 (1991).
36. Justice Stevens chooses not to join this pool. According to one former clerk, "He wanted an independent review," but Stevens himself examines only about 20 percent of the petitions, leaving the rest to his clerks. Tony Mauro, "Ginsburg Plunges into the Cert Pool," *Legal Times* (September 6, 1993): 8.
37. "Retired Chief Justice Warren Attacks . . . Freund Study Group's Composition and Proposal," *American Bar Association Journal* 59 (July 1973): 728.
38. Kathleen Werdegar, "The Solicitor General and Administrative Due Process," *George Washington Law Review* (1967–1968): 482.
39. Rebecca Mae Salokar, *The Solicitor General: The Politics of Law* (Philadelphia: Temple University Press, 1992), 3.
40. Quoted in Elder Witt, *A Different Justice: Reagan and the Supreme Court* (Washington, D.C.: CQ Press, 1986), 133.
41. Lawrence Baum, *The Supreme Court*, 4th ed. (Washington, D.C.: CQ Press, 1992), 106.
42. Richard C. Cortner, *The Supreme Court and Civil Liberties* (Palo Alto, CA: Mayfield, 1975), vi.
43. Gregory A. Caldeira and John R. Wright, "*Amicus Curiae* before the Supreme Court: Who Participates, When and How Much?" *Journal of Politics* 52 (August 1990): 803.
44. See also John R. Hermann, "American Indians in Court: The Burger and Rehnquist Years," Ph.D. dissertation, Emory University, 1996.
45. 114 S. Ct. 367 (1993).
46. 418 U.S. 683 (1974).
47. Quoted in Wasby, *The Supreme Court*, 229.
48. 478 U. S. 186 (1986).
49. "Justices' Files Show Struggle Over Georgia Sodomy Case," *Atlanta Journal and Constitution* (May 25, 1993): A9. The Marshall papers also reveal politics at the *certiorari* stage.
50. 418 U.S. 683 (1974).
51. Bob Woodward and Scott Armstrong, *The Brethren* (New York: Simon and Schuster, 1979), 65, 288–347.
52. 492 U. S. 490 (1989).
53. Stanley C. Brubaker, "Reconsidering Dworkin's Case for Judicial Activism," *Journal of Politics* 46 (1984): 504.
54. Donald L. Horowitz, *The Courts and Social Policy* (Washington, D.C.: Brookings Institution, 1977), 538.
55. 347 U.S. 483 (1954).
56. *Webster* v. *Reproductive Health Services*, 492 U.S. at 518 (1989).
57. 112 S. Ct. 2791 (1992).
58. See, for example, Tracy E. George and Lee Epstein, "On the Nature of Supreme Court Decision Making," *Ameri-can Political Science Review* 86 (1992): 323–37, and Melinda Gann Hall and Paul Brace, "Justices' Responses to Case Facts: An Interactive Model," *American Politics Quarterly* (April 1996): 237–261.
59. Jeffrey A. Segal and Harold Spaeth, *The Supreme Court and the Attitudinal Model*. Cambridge: Cambridge University Press, 1993.
60. Gerard Gryski, Eleanor C. Main, and William Dixon, "Models of State High Court Decision Making in Sex Discrimination Cases," *Journal of Politics* 48 (1986): 143–55; and C. Neal Tate and Roger Handberg, "Time Binding and Theory Building in Personal Attribute Models of Supreme Court Voting Behavior, 1916–1988," *American Political Science Review* 35 (1991): 460–80.
61. Donald R. Songer and Sue Davis, "The Impact of Party and Region on Voting Decisions in the U.S. Courts of Appeals, 1955–86," *Western Political Quarterly* 43: 830–44.
62. Hall and Brace, "Justices' Response to Case Facts."
63. Thomas R. Marshall, "Public Opinion, Representation and the Modern Supreme Court." *American Politics Quarterly* 16 (1988): 296–316.
64. William H. Rehnquist, "Constitutional Law and Public Opinion," paper presented at Suffolk University School of Law, Boston, April 10, 1986, 40–41.
65. Thomas R. Marshall, *Public Opinion and the Supreme Court* (Boston: Unwin and Hyman, 1989).
66. 323 U.S. 214 (1944).
67. 343 U.S. 579 (1952).
68. 343 U.S. 579 (1952). The Supreme Court ruled that President Truman's seizure and operation of U.S. steel mills in the face of a strike threat were unconstitutional, because the Constitution implied no such broad executive power. See Alan Westin, *Anatomy of a Constitutional Law Case* (New York: Macmillan, 1958) and Maeva Marcus, *Truman and the Steel Seizure Case* (New York: Columbia, 1977).
69. *Romer* v. *Evans*, 116 S. Ct. 1620 (1996).
70. 462 U.S. 919 (1983).
71. See *Colegrove* v. *Green*, 328 U.S. 549 (1946), for example.
72. *Baker* v. *Carr*, 369 U.S. 186 (1962).
73. Charles Johnson and Bradley C. Canon, *Judicial Policies' Implementation and Impact* (Washington, D.C.: CQ Press, 1984), chapter 1.
74. 377 U.S. 533 (1964).

Chapter 11 Notes

1. Robert J. Samuelson, *The Good Life and its Discontents: The American Dream in the Age of Entitlement, 1945–1995* (New York: Times Books, 1995), 1.
2. Samuelson, *The Good Life*, 1.
3. Allan M. Winkler, "Public Opinion," in Jack Greene, ed., *The Encyclopedia of American Political History* (New York: Charles Scribner's Sons, 1988), 1038.
4. *Public Opinion Quarterly* 29 (Winter 1965–66): 547.
5. Winkler, "Public Opinion," 1035.
6. Winkler, "Public Opinion," 1035.
7. *Literary Digest* 122 (August, 22 1936): 3.
8. *Literary Digest* 125 (November, 14 1936): 1.
9. Robert S. Erikson, Norman Luttbeg, and Kent Tedin, *American Public Opinion: Its Origin, Content and Impact* (New York: Wiley, 1980), 28.
10. Angus Campbell, Philip Converse, Warren Miller, and Donald Stokes, *The American Voter* (New York: Wiley, 1960).
11. Byron E. Shafer and William J. M. Claggett, *The Two Majorities: The Issue Context of Modern American Politics* (Baltimore: The Johns Hopkins University Press, 1995), 12.
12. Shafer and Claggett, *The Two Majorities*, 13.

13. Richard Dawson, *et al. Political Socialization,* 2d ed. (Boston: Little, Brown, 1977), 33.
14. Statistical Abstract of the United States, p. 1011.
15. Sandor M. Polster, "Bad News for Much TV News," *Bangor Daily News* (May 18, 1996), NEXIS.
16. Polster, "Bad News for Much TV News."
17. F. Christopher Arterton, "The Impact of Watergate on Children's Attitudes Toward Political Authority," *Political Science Quarterly* 89 (June 1974): 273.
18. "Basic Religious Beliefs," *The Public Perspective* (October/November 1995): 4–5.
19. "Basic Religious Beliefs."
20. Statistical Abstract of the United States, 930.
21. Lyman A. Kellstedt, *et al.,* "Has Godot Finally Arrived? Religion and Realignment," *The Public Perspective* (June/July 1995): 19.
22. Alejandro Portest and Rafael Mozo, "The Political Adaptation Process of Cubans and Other Ethnic Minorities in the United States: A Preliminary Analysis," in F. Chris Garcia, ed., *Latinos and the Political System* (Notre Dame, IN: University of Notre Dame Press, 1988), 161.
23. John A. Garcia and Carlos H. Arce, "Political Orientations and Behaviors of Chicanos: Trying to Make Sense Out of Attitudes and Participation," in Garcia, *Latinos and the Political System,* 125–151.
24. Pamela Johnson Conover and Virginia Sapiro, "Gender, Feminist Consciousness and War," *American Journal of Political Science* 37 (November 1993): 1079–99.
25. Susan A. MacManus, *Young v. Old: Generational Combat in the 21st Century* (Boulder, CO: Westview Press, 1996).
26. Richard Morin, "Southern Exposure," *The Washington Post* (July 14, 1996): A18.
27. "Geography: A Lost Generation," *Nation* (August 8, 1988): 19.
28. Everett Carl Ladd, "Fiskin's 'Deliberative Poll' Is Flawed Science and Dubious Democracy," *The Public Perspective* (December/January 1996): 41.
29. Gerald M. Pomper, *The Performance of American Government,* (New York: Free Press, 1972); Benjamin I. Page, *Choices and Echoes in Presidential Elections* (Chicago: University of Chicago Press, 1978).
30. Norman H. Nie, Sidney Verba, and John R. Petrocik, *The Changing American Voter* (Cambridge, MA: Harvard University Press, 1976).
31. Ladd, "Fiskin's 'Deliberative Poll,'" 42.
32. John E. Mueller, *War, Presidents and Public Opinion* (New York: Wiley, 1973), 69.
33. Mueller, *War, Presidents and Public Opinion,* 69.
34. Roderick P. Hart, *The Sound of Leadership: Presidential Communication in the Modern Age* (Chicago: University of Chicago Press, 1987).
35. David W. Moore, "Public Opposes Gay Marriages," The Gallup Organization, April 4, 1996.
36. Michael W. Traugott, "The Polls in 1992: Views of Two Critics: A Good General Showing, But Much Work Needs to Be Done," *The Public Perspective* 4 (November/December 1992): 14–16.
37. Michael W. Traugott, "The Polls in 1992: It Was the Best of Times, It Was the Worst of Times," *The Public Perspective* (December/January 1992): 14.
38. Walter Shapiro, "Breakthrough in Virginia," *Time* (November 20, 1989): 54.
39. James S. Fishkin, *The Voice of the People: Public Opinion and Democracy* (New Haven, CT: Yale University Press, 1995), 161.
40. James S. Fishkin, "Bringing Deliberation to Democracy," *The Public Perspective* (December/January 1996): 1.
41. Warren J. Mitofsky, "It's Not Deliberative and It's Not a Poll," *The Public Perspective* (December/January 1996):6.
42. Fishkin, "Bringing Deliberation to Democracy," 1.
43. Fishkin, *The Voice of the People,* 162.
44. Mitofsky, "Deliberative Poll," 3.
45. Traugott, "The Polls in 1992."
46. Traugott, "The Polls in 1992."
47. Michael W. Traugott and Clyde Tucker, "Strategies for Predicting Whether a Citizen Will Vote and Estimation of Electoral Outcomes," *Public Opinion Quarterly* (Spring 1984): 330–43.
48. Mitofsky, "It's Not Deliberative," 4.
49. Mitofsky, "It's Not Deliberative."
50. Benjamin Ginsberg, "How Polls Transform Public Opinion," in Michael Margolis and Gary A. Mauser, eds., *Manipulating Public Opinion* (Pacific Grove, CA: Brooks/Cole, 1989), 273.
51. See, for example, Benjamin Page and Robert Shapiro, "Effects of Public Opinion on Policy," *American Political Science Review* 57 (March 1983): 175–90.
52. Benjamin Ginsberg, *The Captive Public* (New York: Basic Books, 1986), chapter 4.
53. Quoted in Pace, "George Gallup Is Dead at 82," A-1.
54. Herbert Asher, *Polling and the Public: What Every Citizen Should Know* (Washington, D.C.: CQ Press, 1988), 109.

Chapter 12 Notes

1. E. E. Schattschneider, *Party Government* (New York: Holt, Rinehart and Winston, 1942), 1. This book stands as one of the most eloquent arguments for a strong political party system ever penned.
2. For more information on this topic, see Larry J. Sabato, *The Party's Just Begun: Shaping Political Parties for America's Future* (Glenview, IL: Scott, Foresman/Little, Brown, 1988).
3. The National Republican (one forerunner of the Whig Party) and the Anti-Masonic parties each had held more limited conventions in 1831.
4. By contrast, Great Britain did not develop truly national, broad-based parties until the 1870s.
5. Voter turnout in presidential elections from 1876 to 1900 ranged from 75 percent to 82 percent of the potential (male) electorate, compared with 50 percent to 55 percent in contemporary elections. See *Historical Statistics of the United States: Colonial Times to 1970,* part 2, series Y–27–28 (Washington, D.C.: Government Printing Office, 1975), based on unpublished data prepared by Walter Dean Burnham.
6. Frank J. Sorauf, *Party Politics in America,* 5th ed. (Boston: Little, Brown, 1984), 22.
7. Schattschneider, *Party Government,* 48.
8. As quoted in Ken Bode, "Hero or Demagogue?" *The New Republic* 195 (March 3, 1986): 28.
9. Gerald M. Pomper with Susan Lederman, *Elections in America,* 2d ed. (New York: Longman, 1980), 145–50, 167–73.
10. See David E. Price, *Bringing Back the Parties* (Washington, D.C.: CQ Press, 1984), 284–88.
11. See, for example, Sarah McCally Morehouse, "Legislatures and Political Parties," *State Government* 59 (1976): 23.
12. Pomper with Lederman, *Elections in America,* 150.
13. Walter Dean Burnham, *Critical Elections and the Mainsprings of American Politics* (New York: Norton, 1970), 132–33.
14. See V. O. Key, Jr., *American State Politics: An Introduction* (New York: Knopf, 1956).
15. See V. O. Key, Jr., *Southern Politics in State and Nation* (New York: Knopf, 1949).
16. See Bibby, *et al.,* "Parties in State Politics," in Virginia Gray, Herbert Jacob, and Kenneth Vines, eds., *Politics in the American States,* 4th ed. (Boston: Little, Brown, 1983), Table 3.3, 66; also see Larry J. Sabato, *Goodbye to Good-Time Charlie: The American Governorship Transformed,* 2d ed. (Washington, D.C.: CQ Press, 1983), 116–38.

17. Sorauf, *Party Politics in America,* 51.
18. Such cases are few, but a deterrent nonetheless. Several U.S. senators were expelled from the Republican Caucus in 1925 for having supported the Progressive candidate for president the previous year. In 1965 two Southern House Democrats lost all their committee seniority because of their 1964 endorsement of GOP presidential nominee Barry Goldwater, as did another Southerner in 1968 for backing George Wallace's third-party candidacy. In early 1983 the House Democratic Caucus removed Texas Representative Phil Gramm from his Budget Committee seat because of his "disloyalty" in working more closely with Republican committee members than with his own party leaders. (Gramm resigned his seat in Congress, changed parties, and was reelected as a Republican. He then used the controversy to propel himself into the U.S. Senate in 1984.)
19. Joseph A. Schlesinger, "The New American Political Party," *American Political Science Review* 79 (1985): 1168.
20. Rhodes Cook, "Reagan Nurtures His Adopted Party to Strength," *Congressional Quarterly Weekly* 43 (September 28, 1985): 1927–30.
21. George C. Edwards III, *Presidential Influence in Congress* (New York: Freeman, 1980); and Herbert M. Kritzer and Robert B. Eubank, "Presidential Coattails Revisited: Partisanship and Incumbency Effects," *American Journal of Political Science* 23 (1979): 615–26.
22. Lyn Ragsdale, "The Fiction of Congressional Elections as Presidential Events," *American Politics Quarterly* 8 (1980): 375–98; and Thomas E. Mann and Raymond E. Wolfinger, "Candidates and Parties in Congressional Elections," *American Political Science Review* 74 (1980): 617–32.
23. See S. Sidney Ulmer, "The Political Party Variable on the Michigan Supreme Court," *Journal of Public Law* 11 (1962): 352–62; Stuart Nagel, "Political Party Affiliation and Judges' Decisions," *American Political Science Review* 55 (1961): 843–50; David W. Adamany, "The Party Variable in Judges' Voting: Conceptual Notes and a Case Study," *American Political Science Review* 63 (1969): 57–73; Sheldon Goldman, "Voting Behavior on the United States Courts of Appeals, 1961–1964," *American Political Science Review* 60 (1966): 374–83; and Robert A. Carp and C. K. Rowland, *Policymaking and Politics in the Federal District Courts* (Knoxville: University of Tennessee Press, 1983).
24. The Farmer–Labor Party did survive in a sense; having endured a series of defeats, it merged in 1944 with the Democrats, and Democratic candidates still officially bear the standard of the Democratic–Farmer–Labor (DFL) Party. At about the same time, also having suffered severe electoral reversals, the Progressives stopped nominating candidates in Wisconsin. The party's members either returned to the Republican Party, from which it had split early in the century, or became Democrats.
25. Morehouse, "Legislatures and Political Parties," 19–24.
26. Senator George J. Mitchell (D–Me.), as quoted in *The Washington Post* (February 9, 1986): A14.
27. As quoted in a speech to the RNC by the Associated Press, January 24, 1987, and in *The Washington Post* (January 24, 1987): A3.
28. See Steven E. Finkel and Howard A. Scarrow, "Party Identification and Party Enrollment: The Difference and the Consequence," *Journal of Politics* 47 (May 1985): 620–42.
29. The presidential election of 1960 may be an extreme case, but John F. Kennedy's massive support among Catholics and Nixon's less substantial but still impressive backing by Protestants demonstrates the polarization that religion could once produce. See Philip E. Converse, "Religion and Politics: The 1960 Election," in Angus

Campbell *et al., Elections and the Political Order* (New York: Wiley, 1966), 96–124.
30. Richard Benedetto, "Fed-Up Voters in Search of a Better Candidate," *USA Today* (August 11, 1995): A4.

Chapter 13 Notes

1. Richard L. Berke, "First, the Winner, Now, the Voting," *The New York Times* (March 10, 1996) 4:1.
2. On the subject of party realignment, see Walter Dean Burnham, *Critical Elections and the Mainsprings of American Politics* (New York: Norton, 1970); Kristi Andersen, *The Creation of a Democratic Majority* (Chicago: University of Chicago Press, 1979); and John R. Petrocik, "Realignment: New Party Coalitions and the Nationalization of the South," *Journal of Politics* 49 (May 1987): 347–75.
3. Barbara Farah and Helmut Norpoth, "Trends in Partisan Realignment, 1976–1986: A Decade of Waiting," paper prepared for delivery at the annual meeting of the American Political Science Association, Washington, D.C., August 27–31, 1986.
4. Morris P. Fiorina, *Retrospective Voting in American National Elections* (New Haven, CT: Yale University Press, 1981); and Charles H. Franklin and John E. Jackson, "The Dynamics of Party Identification," *American Political Science Review* 77 (1983): 957–73.
5. See, for example, V. O. Key, Jr., "A Theory of Critical Elections," *Journal of Politics* 17 (February 1955): 3–18.
6. The less dynamic term *creeping realignment* is also sometimes used by scholars and journalists.
7. See Paul Allen Beck, "The Dealignment Era in America," in Russell J. Dalton, et al., *Electoral Change in Advanced Industrial Democracies: Realignment or Dealignment?* (Princeton, NJ: Princeton University Press, 1984), 264. See also Philip M. Williams, "Party Realignment in the United States and Britain," *British Journal of Political Science* 15 (January 1985): 97–115.
8. The Kennedy–Johnson years (1961–69) and the Nixon–Ford years (1969–77) are each considered an eight-year unit for our purposes here.
9. Cited in Everett Carl Ladd, Jr., "On Mandates, Realignments, and the 1984 Presidential Election," *Political Science Quarterly* 100 (Spring 1985): 23.
10. Thomas E. Mann and Raymond E. Wolfinger, "Candidates and Parties in Congressional Elections," *American Political Science Review* 74 (September 1980): 617–32; Albert D. Cover, "One Good Term Deserves Another: The Advantage of Incumbency in Congressional Elections," *American Journal of Political Science* 21 (August 1977): 535; and Gary C. Jacobson, *The Politics of Congressional Elections,* 2d ed. (Boston: Little, Brown, 1987), 86.

Chapter 14 Notes

1. See Alan Ehrenhalt, *The United States of Ambition* (New York: Random House, 1990).
2. Five liberal Democratic U.S. senators, including George McGovern of South Dakota, were defeated in this way in 1980, for example.
3. See Larry J. Sabato, ed., *Campaigns and Elections: A Reader in Modern American Politics* (Glenview, IL: Scott, Foresman, 1989), 3–4.
4. From a 1987 cartoon by Tom Toles, copyrighted by the *Buffalo News.*
5. Data provided by the Federal Election Commission.
6. See Howard Penniman, "U.S. Elections: Really a Bargain?" *Public Opinion* (June/July 1984): 51.

Chapter 15 Notes

1. See Mitchell Stephens, *A History of News: From the Drum to the Satellite* (New York: Viking, 1989).

2. Charles Press and Kenneth VerBurg, *American Politicians and Journalists* (Glenview, IL: Scott, Foresman, 1988), 8–10.

3. See Merrill D. Peterson, *Thomas Jefferson and the New Nation* (New York: Oxford University Press, 1970), 185–87.

4. For a delightful rendition of this episode, see Shelley Ross, *Fall from Grace* (New York: Ballantine, 1988), chapter 12.

5. The name strictly derived from printing the comic strip "Yellow Kid" in color.

6. Doris A. Graber, *Mass Media and American Politics*, 3d ed. (Washington, D.C.: CQ Press, 1989), 12.

7. See Thomas C. Leonard, *The Power of the Press: The Birth of American Political Reporting* (New York: Oxford University Press, 1986), chapter 7.

8. Richard L. Rubin, *Press, Party, and Presidency* (New York: Norton, 1981), 38–39.

9. Stephen Bates, *If No News, Send Rumors* (New York: St. Martin's Press, 1989), 185.

10. Barbara Matusow, "Washington's Journalism Establishment," *The Washingtonian* 23 (February 1989): 94–101, 265–70.

11. See Eleanor Randolph, "Extra! Extra! Who Cares?" *The Washington Post* (April 1, 1990): C1, 4.

12. Sunday newspapers are exceptions to the trend. More than 100 new Sunday papers were created in the 1980s, and Sunday circulation as a whole has increased 25 percent since 1970.

13. Harold W. Stanley and Richard G. Niemi, *Vital Statistics on American Politics* (Washington, D.C.: CQ Press, 1988), Table 2–8, 58.

14. See Evans Witt, "Here, There, and Everywhere: Where Americans Get Their News," *Public Opinion* 6 (August/September 1983): 45–48; June O. Yum and Kathleen E. Kendall, "Sources of Political Information in a Presidential Primary Campaign," *Journalism Quarterly* 65 (Spring 1988): 148–51, 177.

15. This was the fundamental conclusion of Shanto Iyengar and Donald R. Kinder, *News That Matters* (Chicago: University of Chicago Press, 1987).

16. Harold W. Stanley and Richard G. Niemi, *Vital Statistics on American Politics*, 4th ed. (Washington, D.C.: CQ Press, 1994), 28.

17. American Society of Newspaper Editors, *The Changing Face of the Newsroom* (Washington: ASNE, May 1989), 29.

18. See Tom Wolfe, *The New Journalism* (New York: Harper & Row, 1973), especially 9–32.

19. The first and best in White's series was *The Making of the President 1960* (New York: Atheneum, 1961). See also Joe McGinniss, *The Selling of the President 1968* (New York: Trident, 1969).

20. See James David Barber, *The Presidential Character* (Englewood Cliffs, NJ: Prentice Hall, 1972), 445.

21. 376 U.S. 254 (1964). See also Steven Pressman, "Libel Law: Finding the Right Balance," *Editorial Research Reports* 2 (August 18, 1989): 462–71.

22. *Curtis Publishing Co.* v. *Butts*, 388 U.S. 130 (1967); *Associated Press* v. *Walker*, 388 U.S. 130 (1967).

23. American Society of Newspaper Editors, "The Changing Face," 33; William Schneider and I. A. Lewis, "Views on the News," *Public Opinion* 8 (August/September 1985): 6–11, 58–59; and S. Robert Lichter, Stanley Rothman, and Linda S. Lichter, *The Media Elite* (Bethesda, MD: Adler & Adler, 1986).

24. See Dom Bonafede, "Crossing Over," *National Journal* 21 (January 14, 1989): 102; Richard Harwood, "Tainted Journalists," *The Washington Post* (December 4, 1988): L6; Charles Trueheart, "Trading Places: The Insiders Debate," *The Washington Post* (January 4, 1989): D1, 19;

and Kirk Victor, "Slanted Views," *National Journal* 20 (June 4, 1988): 1512.

25. "*Roe* v. *Webster*," *Media Monitor* 3 (October 1989): 1–6. See also David Shaw, "Abortion and the Media" (four-part series), *Los Angeles Times* (July 1, 1990): A1, 50–51; (July 2, 1990): A1, 20; (July 3, 1990): A1, 22–23; (July 4, 1990): A1, 28–29.

26. 403 U.S. 713 (1971).

27. House of Commons, Defense Committee, *The Handling of the Press and Public Information During the Falklands Conflict* (London: Her Majesty's Stationery Office, 1982), x.

28. For further reading, see Jeffrey B. Abramson, F. Christopher Arterton, and Gary R. Orren, *The Electronic Commonwealth: The Impact of Media Technologies on Democratic Politics* (New York: Basic Books, 1988).

Chapter 16 Notes

1. This vignette draws heavily from Dale Russakoff, "NO-NAME Movement Fed by Fax Expands: Political Networks Combine Technology Fear," *The Washington Post* (August 20, 1995): A1.

2. Clive Thomas and Ronald Hrebenar, "Changing Patterns of Interest Group Activity: A Regional Perspective," in Mark Petracca, ed., *The Politics of Interests* (Boulder, CO: Westview Press, 1992), 4.

3. Graham Wilson, *Interest Groups in the United States* (New York: Oxford University Press, 1981), 4.

4. David B. Truman, *The Governmental Process: Political Interests and Public Opinion* (New York: Knopf, 1951), 33.

5. Robert H. Salisbury, "Interest Groups," in Fred I. Greenstein and Nelson W. Polsby, eds., *Handbook of Political Science*, vol. 4 (Reading, MA: Addison-Wesley, 1975), 175.

6. V. O. Key, Jr., *Politics, Parties and Pressure Groups* (New York: T. J. Crowell, 1942), 23.

7. Mark P. Petracca, "The Rediscovery of Interest Group Politics," in Petracca, ed., *The Politics of Interests*, 5.

8. Robert H. Salisbury, "An Exchange Theory of Interest Groups," *Midwest Journal of Political Science* 13 (1969): 1–32.

9. Jeffrey M. Berry, *Lobbying for the People: The Political Behavior of Public Interest Groups* (Princeton, NJ: Princeton University Press, 1977), 7.

10. "Will Ruling on S.A.T. Affect College Admissions?" *The New York Times* (February 8, 1989): B10.

11. Samuel Eliot Morrison and Henry Steel Commager, *The Growth of the American Republic* (New York: Oxford University Press, 1930), 163.

12. Salisbury, "An Exchange Theory of Interest Groups," 1–32.

13. Jack L. Walker, "The Origins and Maintenance of Interest Groups in America," *American Political Science Review* 77 (June 1983): 390–406.

14. Truman, *The Governmental Process*, chapter 16.

15. Kay Lehman Schlozman and John T. Tierney, *Organized Interests and American Democracy* (New York: Harper & Row, 1986).

16. Walker, "The Origins and Maintenance of Interest Groups in America."

17. Peter Steinfels, "Moral Majority to Dissolve; Says Mission Accomplished," *The New York Times* (June 12, 1989): A14.

18. Steve Goldstein, "The Christian Right Grows in Power," *The Atlanta Journal* (November 11, 1994): A8.

19. Goldstein, "The Christian Right Grows in Power."

20. Ralph Reed, *Contract with the American Family* (Nashville, TN: Moorings, 1995).

21. David Mahood, *Interest Groups Participation in America: A New Intensity* (Englewood Cliffs, NJ: Prentice Hall, 1990), 23.

22. Quoted in Ronald J. Hrebenar and Ruth K. Scott, *Interest Group Politics in America*, 2d ed. (Englewood Cliffs, NJ: Prentice Hall, 1990), 263.

23. Brenda Rios, "Big Blitz from TV to the Hill: A $100 Million Whirlwind of Spin Control," *The Atlanta Journal* (July 22, 1994): A4.

24. Rios, "Big Blitz."

25. Rios, "Big Blitz."

26. Michael Wines, "For New Lobbyists, It's What They Know," *The New York Times* (November 3, 1993): B14

27. Quoted in Schlozman and Tierney, *Organized Interests*, 85.

28. Quoted in Norman J. Ornstein and Shirley Elder, *Interest Groups, Lobbying and Policy Making* (Washington, D.C.: CQ Press, 1978), 77.

29. Thomas Cronin, *The State of the Presidency* (Boston: Little, Brown, 1975), 123.

30. Cronin, *The State of the Presidency.*

31. Some political scientists speak of "iron rectangles," reflecting the growing importance of a fourth party, the courts, in the lobbying process.

32. Clement E. Vose, "Litigation as a Form of Pressure Group Activity," *The Annals* 319 (September 1958): 20–31.

33. Richard C. Cortner, "Strategies and Tactics of Litigation in Constitutional Cases," *Journal of Public Law* 17 (1968): 287.

34. Joel Brinkley, "Cultivating the Grass Roots to Reap Legislative Benefits," *The New York Times* (November 1, 1993): Al.

35. Brinkley, "Cultivating the Grass Roots."

36. Federal Elections Commissions Reports.

37. Stephen Wildstrom, "Reach Out and Touch Some Pol," *Business Week* (March 4, 1996): 4.

38. E. E. Schattschneider, *The Semi-Sovereign People* (New York: Holt, Rinehart and Winston, 1960), 35.

39. Truman, *The Governmental Process*, 511.

40. Mancur Olson, Jr., *The Logic of Collective Action: Public Goods and the Theory of Groups* (Cambridge, MA: Harvard University Press, 1965).

41. Walker, "The Origins and Maintenance of Interest Groups," 390–406.

42. Jeffrey M. Berry, *The Interest Group Society* (Boston: Little, Brown, 1989).

43. Salisbury, "An Exchange Theory of Interest Groups"; Allan J. Cigler and Anthony J. Nownes, "Public Interest Entrepreneurs and Group Patrons," in Allan J. Cigler and Burdett A. Loomis, eds., *Interest Group Politics*, 4th ed. (Washington, D.C.: CQ Press, 1995), 77–100.

44. Alexis de Tocqueville, *Democracy in America*, vol. 1, trans. Phillips Bradley (New York: Knopf, Vintage Books, 1945; orig. published in 1835), 191.

45. de Tocqueville, *Democracy in America*, 191.

46. Schattschneider, *The Semi-Sovereign People*, 35.

Chapter 17 Notes

1. Mary Matalin denies the accuracy of this story. Mary Matalin and James Carville, *All's Fair: Love, War, and Running for President* (New York: Random House, 1994), 129–30.

2. This section draws on figures in *U.S. News and World Report* (January 22, 1996).

3. Mary Beth Cahill, "What Do Angry Women Want?" *The New York Times* (May 10, 1996): A15.

4. James E. Anderson, *Public Policymaking: An Introduction*, 2d ed. (Boston: Houghton Mifflin, 1994), 5. This discussion draws on Anderson's study.

5. Roger W. Cobb and Charles D. Elder, *Participation in American Politics: The Dynamics of Agenda-Building*, 2d ed. (Baltimore: Johns Hopkins University Press, 1983), chapter 5.

6. Cobb and Elder, *Participation in American Politics*, 85.

7. Charles O. Jones, ed., *The Reagan Legacy: Promise and Performance* (Chatham, NJ: Chatham House, 1988). The essays in this volume examine several aspects of the Reagan administration.

8. Charles O. Jones, *An Introduction to the Study of Public Policy*, 3d ed. (Monterey, CA: Brooks/Cole, 1984), 87–89.

9. *Texas v. Johnson*, 492 U.S. 397 (1989).

10. *U.S. v. Eichman*, 496 U.S. 310 (1990).

11. This discussion draws on Anne Schneider and Helen Ingram, "Behavioral Assumptions of Policy Tools," *Journal of Politics*, 52 (May 1990): 510–29.

12. Alisa J. Rubin, "Parties Square Off Over Student Loans," *Congressional Quarterly Weekly Report* 35 (May 20, 1995): 1401.

13. Charles Murray, *Losing Ground: American Social Policy, 1950–1980* (New York: Basic Books, 1984).

14. Theda Skocpol, *Protecting Soldiers and Mothers: The Political Origins of Social Policy in the United States* (Cambridge, MA: Harvard University Press, 1992), chapter 2.

15. Merle Fainsod, Lincoln Gordon, and Joseph C. Palamountain, Jr., *Government and the American Economy*, 3d ed. (New York: Norton, 1959), 776.

16. *Bondweek* (April 25, 1994), NEXIS.

17. *Congressional Quarterly Weekly Report* 51 (November 27, 1993): 3276.

18. *BNA Daily Labor Report* (March 16, 1994).

19. *Congressional Quarterly Weekly Report* 50 (March 28, 1992): 809–10.

20. *New York Times* (May 5, 1993): C23.

21. Jeffrey L. Katz, "Uneasy Compromise Reached on Welfare Overhaul," *Congressional Quarterly Weekly Report* 53 (September 16, 1995): 2807.

22. Jeffrey L. Katz, "Senate Overhaul Plan Provides Road Map for Compromise," *Congressional Quarterly Weekly Report* 53 (September 23, 1995): 2911.

23. See Randy Shilts, *And the Band Played On* (New York: St. Martin's Press, 1987).

24. Paul Starr, *The Social Transformation of American Medicine* (New York: Basic Books, 1982), 282.

25. *Congressional Quarterly Weekly Report* 47 (February 25, 1989): 588–89.

26. David Wilsford, *Doctors and the State: The Politics of Health Care in France and the United States* (Durham, NC: Duke University Press, 1991), 189–93.

27. Colette Fraley, "Governors Looking for the Key to Open Way for Medicaid," *Congressional Quarterly Weekly Report* 53 (December 16, 1995): 3814.

28. Colette Fraley, "Republicans Are Standing Firm on Giving Medicaid to States," *Congressional Quarterly Weekly Report* 53 (September 23, 1995): 2901.

29. *Statistical Abstract of the United States, 1993* (Washington, D.C.: U.S. Government Printing Office, 1993), 92; and *The New York Times* (January 5, 1993): 1.

30. Andy Miller, "Health Benefits Cost Employees Just 2.1% More in '95 Survey Says," *Atlanta Journal* (January 30, 1996): D3.

31. Henry J. Aaron, *Serious and Unstable Condition: Financing America's Health Care* (Washington, D.C.: Brookings Institution, 1991), chapter 2.

32. Marilyn Werber Serafina, "Medicrunch," *National Journal* 27 (July 29, 1995): 1937.

33. Thomas R. Dye, *Politics in States and Communities*, 7th ed. (Englewood Cliffs, NJ: Prentice Hall, 1991), 411.

34. Erwin L. Levine and Elizabeth M. Wexler, *PL94–142: An Act of Congress* (New York: Macmillan, 1981).

35. *San Antonio Independent School District* v. *Rodriguez*, 411 U.S. 1 (1973).

36. *Zobrest* v. *Catalina Foothills School District*, 113 S. Ct. 2462 (1993).

37. *Board of Education of Kiriass Joel Village School District* v. *Grumet*, 114 S. Ct. 2481 (1994).

38. John J. Harrigan, *Policy and Politics in States and Communities*, 3d ed. (Glenview IL: Scott, Foresman, 1988), 300–1.
39. Colette Fraley, "Clinton Plan Does Little to End Major Medicaid Disputes," *Congressional Quarterly Weekly Report* 53 (December 9, 1995): 3744.
40. Lawrence R. Jacobs, Robert Y. Shapiro, and Eli C. Schulman, "Medical Care in the United States: An Update," *Public Opinion Quarterly* 57 (Fall 1993): 394–427. This article contains data from a large number of opinion polls.

Chapter 18 Notes

1. See the poll results in Bob Benenson, "GOP Sets the 104th Congress on New Regulatory Course," *Congressional Quarterly Weekly Report* 53 (June 17, 1995): 1697.
2. Louis Hartz, *Economic Policy and Democratic Thought: Pennsylvania 1776–1860* (Cambridge, MA: Harvard University Press, 1948).
3. Howard R. Smith, *Government and Business* (New York: Ronald Press, 1958), 99.
4. After 108 years of operation, the ICC expired at the end of 1995 as part of the effort by congressional Republicans to reduce federal regulations and allow market forces more freedom in which to operate.
5. *Pollock* v. *Farmers' Loan and Trust Co.* 158 U.S. 429 (1895).
6. This discussion of the New Deal draws on Louis M. Hacker and Helene S. Zahler, *The United States in the 20th Century* (New York: Appleton-Century-Crofts, 1952); and William E. Leuchtenburg, *Franklin D. Roosevelt and the New Deal* (New York: Harper & Row, 1963).
7. *U.S.* v. *Butler*, 297 U.S. 1 (1936).
8. *Wickard* v. *Filburn*, 317 U.S. 111 (1942).
9. Stephen A. Bailey, *Congress Makes a Law: The Story Behind the Employment Act of 1946* (New York: Columbia University Press, 1951).
10. Herbert Stein, *The Fiscal Revolution in America* (Chicago: University of Chicago Press, 1969), 204.
11. Larry N. Gerston, Cynthia Fraleigh, and Robert Schwab, *The Deregulated Society* (Pacific Grove, CA: Brooks/Cole, 1988), 27.
12. Michael Reagan, *Regulation: The Politics of Policy* (Boston: Little, Brown, 1987), 86.
13. Gerston, Fraleigh, and Schwab, *The Deregulated Society*, 32–34.
14. David Vogel, "The 'New' Social Regulation in Historical and Comparative Perspective," in Thomas K. McCraw, ed., *Regulation in Perspective* (Cambridge, MA: Harvard University Press, 1981), 160.
15. A leading study is Martha Derthick and Paul J. Quirk, *The Politics of Deregulation* (Washington, D.C.: Brookings Institution, 1985).
16. Derthick and Quirk, *The Politics of Deregulation*, chapters 1, 2; Dorothy Robyn, *Braking the Special Interests: Trucking Deregulation and the Politics of Policy Reform* (Chicago: University of Chicago Press, 1987), chapter 4.
17. Martin Mayer, *The Greatest-Ever Bank Robbery: The Collapse of the Savings and Loan Industry* (New York: Scribner's, 1990).
18. L. William Seidman, *Full Faith and Credit: The Great S&L Debacle and Other Washington Sagas* (New York: Times Books, 1993). Seidman was in charge of the Resolution Trust Corporation during the early years of the S&L bailout.
19. Quoted in Robert A. Gordon, *Economic Instability and Growth: The American Record* (New York: Harper & Row, 1974), 22.
20. The following discussion draws on James E. Anderson, David W. Brady, Charles S. Bullock III, and Joseph Stew-

art Jr., *Public Policy and Politics in America*, 2d ed. (Monterey, CA: Brooks/Cole, 1984), chapter 2.
21. *Time* (March 7, 1994): 42.
22. William Greider, *Secrets of the Temple: How the Federal Reserve Runs the Country* (New York: Simon & Schuster, 1987), chapter 10.
23. This is the conclusion reached by John T. Woolley, *Monetary Politics: The Federal Reserve and the Politics of Monetary Policy* (New York: Cambridge University Press, 1984).
24. Anderson, *et al.*, *Public Policy and Politics in America*, 38–40.
25. James D. Savage, *Balanced Budgets and American Politics* (Ithaca, NY: Cornell University Press, 1988), 176–79.
26. Herbert Stein, *Presidential Economics: The Making of Economic Policy from Roosevelt to Reagan and Beyond* (New York: Simon & Schuster, 1984), 290–91.
27. *Annual Report of the Council of Economic Advisers, 1993* (Washington, D.C.: Government Printing Office, 1993), 108.
28. *Annual Report of the Council of Economic Advisers, 1993*, 109.
29. This discussion of budgeting draws on James E. Anderson, *Public Policymaking: An Introduction*, 2d ed. (Boston: Houghton Mifflin, 1994), chapter 5.
30. Donald F. Kettl, *Deficit Politics: Public Budgeting in Its Institutional and Historical Context* (New York: Macmillan, 1992), 140–1.
31. *Congressional Quarterly Weekly Report* (August 7, 1993): 2122–29.
32. John Cranford, *Budgeting for America*, 2d ed. (Washington, D.C.: CQ Press, 1989), 197–98.
33. Paul E. Peterson, "The New Politics of Deficits," in John E. Chubb and Paul E. Peterson, eds., *The New Direction in American Politics* (Washington, D.C.: The Brookings Institution, 1985), chapter 13.
34. Robert Eisner and Paul J. Peiper, "A New View of the Federal Debt and Budget Deficits," *American Economic Review* 74 (March 1994): 23.
35. This discussion is based on *Budget of the United States, Fiscal Year 1995: Analytical Perspectives* (Washington, D.C.: Government Printing Office, 1994), 423–24.
36. Rick Scarce, *Eco-Warriors: Understanding the Radical Environmental Movement* (Chicago: Noble Press, 1990).
37. Richard E. Cohen, *Washington at Work: Back Rooms and Clean Air* (New York: Macmillan, 1992).
38. Charles O. Jones, *Clean Air: The Policies and Politics of Pollution Control* (Pittsburgh: University of Pittsburgh Press, 1975).
39. This listing relies partly on Walter A. Rosenbaum, "The Clenched Fist and the Open Hand: Into the 1990s at EPA," in Norman J. Vig and Michael E. Kraft, eds., *Environmental Policy in the 1990s*, 2d ed. (Washington D.C.: CQ Press, 1994), 126–27.
40. Kent E. Portney, *Controversial Issues in Environmental Policy: Science vs. Economics vs. Politics* (Newbury Park, CA: Sage Publications, 1992), 47–49. The quotation is on 49.
41. Walter A. Rosenbaum, *Environmental Politics and Policy*, 2d ed. (Washington, D.C.: CQ Press, 1991), 214.
42. *Congressional Quarterly Weekly Report* (February 5, 1994): 239–40.
43. Gary C. Bryner, *Blue Skies, Green Politics: The Clean Air Act of 1990* (Washington, D.C.: CQ Press, 1993), 68.
44. James L. Regens and Robert W. Rycroft, *The Acid Rain Controversy* (Pittsburgh: University of Pittsburgh Press, 1988), 45–47.
45. See Charles L. Schultze, *The Public Use of Private Interest* (Washington, D.C.: The Brookings Institution, 1977).
46. Allan Freedman, "Republicans Concede Missteps in Effort to Rewrite Rules," *Congressional Quarterly* 53 (December 2, 1995): 3646.

47. See, for example, Margaret Kriz, "The Green Card," *National Journal* 27 (September 16, 1995): 2265.
48. A readable discussion of the congressional activities surrounding efforts to adopt the balanced budget amendment and the line-item veto during the early days of the 104th Congress is provided in James G. Gimpel, *Filling Out the Contract: The First 100 Days* (Needham Heights, MA: Allyn and Bacon, 1996).

Chapter 19 Notes

1. "Clinton Delivers First Report Card on Japan's Progress Toward Opening Its Markets to Autos and Auto Parts," FDCH Political Transcripts, April 12, 1996. Lexis/Nexis.
2. Federal News Service, "Hearing of the International Economic Policy and Trade Subcommittee of the House International Relations Committee," November 9, 1995. Lexis/Nexis.
3. Jacob Viner, "Power *vs.* Plenty as Objectives of Foreign Policy in the Seventeenth and Eighteenth Centuries," *World Politics* 1 (1948): 1–29.
4. Ben Belton and Bill Montague, "Gains Boost Economy: U.S. Trade Scenario Better Than 10 Years Ago," *USA Today* (February 29, 1996): 1B
5. Richard Rosecrance and Arthur A. Stein, "Beyond Realism: The Study of Grand Strategy," in Richard Rosecrance and Arthur A. Stein, eds., *The Domestic Bases of Grand Strategy* (Ithaca: Cornell University Press, 1993), 1–21.
6. Barton Gellman, "Keeping the U.S. First: Pentagon Would Preclude a Rival Superpower," *The Washington Post* (March 11, 1992): A1.
7. Harold K. Jacobson, William M. Reisinger, and Todd Mathers, "National Engagements in Governmental Organizations," *American Political Science Review*, 80 (March 1986): 141–59.
8. Raymond Vernon, *Sovereignty at Bay* (New York: Basic Books, 1971).
9. Paul Kennedy, *The Rise and Fall of the Great Powers: Economic Change and Military Conflict from 1500 to 2000* (New York: Vintage Books, 1989), 514.
10. Howard Jones, *The Course of American Democracy*, vol. 2, 2d ed. (Chicago: Dorsey Press, 1988), 6–8.
11. See, for example, *DeLima* v. *Bidwell*, 182 U.S. 1 (1901) and *Dooley* v. *United States*, 182 U.S. 222 (1901).
12. Alfred E. Eckes, Jr., *Opening America's Market: U.S. Foreign Trade Policy Since 1776* (Chapel Hill: University of North Carolina Press, 1995).
13. John L. O'Sullivan, writing in 1845, quoted in Julius W. Pratt, "The Ideology of American Expansion," in Avery Craven, ed., *Essays in Honor of William E. Dodd* (Chicago: University of Chicago Press, 1935), 343–44.
14. John A. C. Conybeare, "Voting for Protection: An Electoral Model of Tariff Policy," *International Organization* 45 (Winter 1991): 57–81.
15. Charles P. Kindleberger, *The World in Depression, 1929–1939* (Berkeley: University of California Press, 1986).
16. Henry Steel Commager, *Documents of American History*, 7th ed. (New York: Appleton-Century-Crofts, 1963), 525.
17. Richard Smoke, *National Security and the Nuclear Dilemma* (Reading, MA: Addison-Wesley, 1984).
18. See "START Supplement," *Arms Control Today* 21 (November 1991) and "START II Supplement," *Arms Control Today* 23 (January/February 1993).
19. Stanley Karnow, *Vietnam, A History: The First Complete Account of Vietnam at War* (New York: Viking Press, 1983).
20. "U.S. Boosts Forces in Somalia," *Star Tribune* (October 5, 1993): 1A.
21. William O. Chittick, Keith R. Billingsley, and Rick Travis, "A Three-Dimensional Model of American Foreign Policy Beliefs," *International Studies Quarterly* 39 (September 1995): 313–31.
22. Susan A. MacManus, *Young v. Old: Generational Combat in the 21st Century* (Boulder, CO: Westview, 1996), 216.
23. Stephen D. Krasner, *Structural Conflict: The Third World Against Global Liberalism* (Berkeley: University of California Press, 1985).
24. 299 U.S. 304 (1936).
25. Loch K. Johnson, *America's Secret Power: The CIA in a Democratic Society* (New York: Oxford University Press, 1989).
26. Alexander L. George, *Presidential Decisionmaking in Foreign Policy: The Effective Use of Information and Advice* (Boulder, CO: Westview, 1980).
27. James M. Lindsay, "Congress, Foreign Policy, and the New Institutionalism," *International Studies Quarterly* 38 (June 1994): 281–304.
28. Daniel Hallin, *The "Uncensored War"* (Berkeley: University of California Press, 1989), 192.
29. Eugene R. Wittkopf, "On the Foreign Policy Beliefs of the American People: A Critique and Some Evidence," *International Studies Quarterly*, 30 (December 1986): 425–55.
30. Steven V. Roberts, "Senate, 52–48, Supports Reagan on AWACs Sale to Saudis," *The New York Times* (October 29, 1981): A4
31. Charles Krauthammer, "The Unipolar Movement," *Foreign Affairs* 70 (Winter, 1990–91): 23–33.
32. *Congressional Quarterly Almanac* (1990): 731.
33. MacManus, *Young v. Old*, 236.
34. See, for example, E. E. Schattschneider, *Politics, Pressures, and the Tariff* (New York: Prentice, 1935) or Robert Pastor, *Congress and the Politics of U.S. Foreign Economic Policy* (Berkeley: University of California Press, 1980).
35. Frank Oliveri, "DoD Mulls 1997 Bottom-Up Review," *Defense News* (September 11, 1995).
36. Jessica Tuchman Matthews, "Redefining Security," *Foreign Affairs* 68 (Spring 1989): 162–77.
37. Mike Christensen, "Nunn Aims to Give Congress More Clout in Post-Soviet World," *Atlanta Journal and Constitution* (October 30, 1993).
38. Bruce Russett, *Grasping the Democratic Peace: Principles for a Post-Cold War World* (Princeton, NJ: Princeton University Press, 1993).

INDEX